The Guinness Book of Records 1994

Editor

Peter Matthews

Founding Editor

Norris D. McWhirter

Copyright

British Library Cataloguing in Publication Data
Guinness book of records.-40th edition
1. Records of achievement-Collections-Serials
031'.02

ISBN 0-85112-772-X.
'Guinness' is a registered trade mark of Guinness Publishing Ltd.
Printed and bound by Cox & Wyman Ltd., Reading

Contents

Introduction

Welcome to the 40th Edition of *The Guinness Book of Records*. As ever our small editorial team has completely re-illustrated the book and thoroughly revised the text. If you compare this edition with that of a decade ago you will find tremendous changes — not only in the records themselves, but also in the categories included and in their presentation.

We are continually looking for new items to include. Many existing categories are permanent, but others we like to change to provide fresh information for our readers. Of course such a policy does mean, from time to time, that we have to disappoint long-time record holders whose records we 'rest'.

For logistic reasons, we tend to concentrate on categories that are the subject of widespread, and preferably international, competitiveness. Ours is not the book in which to find details of weird one-off stunts, but rather records that are measurable and comparable.

We would like to help people achieve their record breaking ambitions. If you wish to attempt a potential new record category for *The Guinness Book of Records*, then contact us and submit a brief proposal at least two months in advance of your attempt. This gives us a chance to comment on the possibilities of including your activity. We receive hundreds of letters every week, so please give us the time to give your enquiry the attention it deserves.

To encourage submissions we have listed a number of possible new or replacement categories that we have been considering for inclusion and some areas where we would be keen for further information:

Oldest human beings — are you, your parent or even your grandparent over 105? If so, we would like to hear from you.

Tallest people — somewhere in the world there may be a man or woman who is taller than our current candidates.

The most fluent linguist — who speaks or uses the most languages?

New environmental records — We suggest a challenge for the most trees planted by a team in, say, a week. Also, how about building the largest pyramid from re-cycled cans in a set period of time?

Longest golf ball carry — from drive to pitching on a level surface.

Step climbing — the most step-ups in a set period of time.

The largest ice-cream cone

Honey production records

Peter Matthews

Peter Matthews, Editor

GUINNESS PUBLISHING LTD, 33 LONDON ROAD, ENFIELD, MIDDLESEX, EN2 6DJ, ENGLAND

The story of the Guinness Book

The Guinness Book of Records was first produced to assist in resolving arguments that might take place on matters of fact.

The genesis of the idea came in 1951 when the then managing director of Guinness, Sir Hugh Beaver (1890–1967), was out shooting on the North Slob, by the River Slaney in County Wexford in the south-east of Ireland. Some golden plover were missed by the party, and later he discovered that reference books in the library of his host at Castlebridge House could not confirm whether that bird was Europe's fastest game bird.

Sir Hugh's experience led him to the view that there must be numerous such questions debated nightly in the 81 400 pubs in Britain and in Ireland in which Guinness was on sale. On 12 September 1954 Norris and Ross McWhirter, then running a fact finding agency in London, were invited to the Guinness Brewery at Park Royal in north-west London to discuss the proposition that a collection of records should be published, and they so impressed the Guinness Board that they were immediately commissioned to follow it through.

An office was set up at 107 Fleet Street and intense work began. Less than a year later the inaugural edition, containing 198 pages, was produced, with the first copy bound on 27 August 1955. Well before Christmas the Guinness Book was No. 1 on the best-sellers list, and every edition since has been similarly represented.

The first US edition was published in New York in 1956, followed by editions in French (1962) and German (1963). In 1967 there were first editions in Danish, Japanese, Norwegian and Spanish, while the following year editions were published in Finnish, Italian and Swedish. In the 1970s there followed Czech, Dutch, Hebrew, Icelandic, Portuguese and Serb; in the 1980s translations into Arabic, Chinese, Greek, Hindi, Hungarian, Indonesian, Malay, Slovene and Turkish followed. Most recently, in the 1990s, editions have been published in Bulgarian, Korean, Macedonian, Malayalam, Polish, Romanian and Russian.

Our hope remains that, as for the first edition, so this new edition can assist in resolving inquiries on facts, and may turn the heat of argument into the light of knowledge.

Earth &Space

- The Universe
- The Earth
- Structure and Dimensions
- Natural Phenomena
- Weather
- Gems, Jewels and Precious Stones

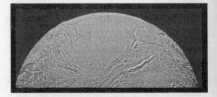

The Universe

Large structures in the Universe Our own Milky Way galaxy is only one of ten billion galaxies. It is part of the so-called 'Local Group', which is being gravitationally attracted towards the centre of the 'Local Supercluster', which is dominated by the Virgo Cluster of galaxies. However, this is being drawn towards the even more massive Hydra-Centaurus Supercluster and both are being drawn towards a vast concentration of galaxies known as the 'Great Attractor'. The absolute motion of our galaxy in space is 600 km/sec *370 miles/sec* with respect to the cosmological frame.

In November 1989 Margaret Geller and John Huchra (USA) announced the discovery of a 'Great Wall' in space, a concentration of galaxies in the form of a 'crumpled membrane' with a minimum extent of 280×800 million light years ($2·6×10^{21}$ km × $7·5×10^{21}$ km *1·6 × 10²¹ miles × 4·7×10²¹ miles*) and a depth of up to 20 million light years ($1·5×10^{20}$ km *9·6×10¹⁹ miles*).

Based on the effect of line of sight on the spectra of distant quasars, Josef Hoell and Wolfgang Priester (Germany) suggested in July 1991 that the large scale structure of the Universe consists of 'bubbles' each up to 100 million light years ($9·4×10^{20}$ km *5·8 ×10²⁰ miles*) in diameter with galaxies being formed on the 'surfaces' of the 'bubbles' and with the interiors being virtually devoid of matter.

Galaxies The largest is the central galaxy of the Abell 2029 galaxy cluster, 1070 million light years ($1·01 × 10^{22}$ km *6·3 × 10²¹ miles*) distant in Virgo. Its discovery was announced in July 1990 by Juan M. Uson, Stephen P. Boughn and Jeffrey R. Kuhn (USA). It has a major diameter of 5600000 light years ($5·3×10^{19}$ km *3·3×10¹⁹ miles*), which is eighty times the diameter of our own Galaxy, and has a light output equivalent to 2 trillion ($2×10^{12}$) Suns.

The brightest galaxy (or galaxy in the process of forming) is IRAS F10214+4724, which was detected as a faint source by IRAS (Infra Red Astronomy Satellite) in 1983 but was shown in February 1991 to have a far-infrared luminosity $3×10^{14}$ times greater than that of the Sun. It has a red shift of 2·286, equivalent to a distance of 11600 million light years ($1·10 × 10^{23}$ km *6·8×10²² miles*), but the remotest galaxy is the radio source 4C41.17, determined by K. Chambers, G. Miley and W. Van Bruegel in January 1990 to have a red shift of 3·800, equivalent to a distance of 12800 million light years ($1·21×10^{23}$ km *7·5×10²² miles*).

Age of the Universe For the age of the Universe a consensus value of 14±3 aeons or gigayears (an aeon or gigayear being 1000 million years) is obtained from various cosmological techniques. The equivalent value of the Hubble constant—named after Edwin Hubble (1889–1953) who first measured galactic distances in the 1920s—is 70±15 km/s/Mpc. In order to explain their observations of the large scale structure of the Universe, Hoell and Priester (⇔ above) have made the bold suggestion that the Universe must be at

Age of the Universe

It was announced on 23 Apr 1992 that the COBE (Cosmic Background Explorer) satellite, launched by NASA on 18 Nov 1989, had detected minute fluctuations from the cosmic microwave background temperature of −270·414°C *−454·745°F*. This has been interpreted as evidence for the initial formation of galaxies within the Universe only a million years after the Big Bang. (⬦ also *Age of the Universe* opposite)

Longest star name

Torcularis Septentrionalis is the name applied to the star omicron Piscium in the constellation Pisces.

---

least twice as old as currently considered and that the cosmological constant must be non-zero.

Remotest object The interpretation of the red shifts of quasars in terms of distance is limited by a lack of knowledge of the Universal constants. The record red shift is 4·897 for the quasar PC1247+3406 as determined by Donald P. Schneider, Maarten Schmidt and James E. Gunn and announced in May 1991, following spectroscopic and photometric observations made in February and April of the same year using the Hale Telescope at Palomar Observatory, California, USA. If it is assumed that there is an 'observable horizon', where the speed of recession is equal to the speed of light, i.e. at 14 000 million light years or $1·32 \times 10^{23}$ km *8·23 × 10^{22} miles*, then a simple interpretation would place this quasar at 94·4 per cent of this value or 13 200 million light years ($1·25 \times 10^{23}$ km *7·8 × 10^{22} miles*).

Farthest visible object The remotest heavenly body visible with the naked eye is the Great Galaxy in Andromeda (mag. 3·47), known as Messier 31. It was first noted from Germany by Simon Marius (1570–1624). It is a rotating nebula in spiral form at a distance from the Earth of about 2 309 000 light years,

or $2·18 \times 10^{19}$ km *1·36 × 10^{19} miles*, and our Galaxy is moving towards it. Under good conditions for observations, Messier 33, the Spiral in Triangulum (mag. 5·79), can be glimpsed by the naked eye at a distance of 2 509 000 light years.

Quasars An occultation of 3C 273, observed from Australia on 5 Aug 1962, enabled the existence of quasi-stellar radio sources ('quasars' or QSOs) to be announced by Maarten Schmidt (⬦ above).

Quasars have immensely high luminosity for bodies so distant and of such small diameter. The discovery of the most luminous object in the sky, the quasar HS 1946+7658, which is at least $1·5 \times 10^{15}$ times more luminous than the Sun, was announced in July 1991 following the Hamburg Survey of northern quasars. This quasar has a red shift of 3·02 and is therefore at a distance of 12 400 million light years ($1·17 \times 10^{23}$ km *7·3 × 10^{22} miles*).

The first double quasar (0957+561) among over 4300 known quasars was announced in May 1980.

The most violent outburst observed in a quasar was recorded on 13 Nov 1989 by a joint US-Japanese team who noted that the energy output of the quasar PKS 0558−504 (which is about 2000 million light years distant) increased by two thirds in three minutes, equivalent to all the energy released by the Sun in 340 000 years.

Stars

The first direct measurement of the distance of a star was made in 1838 when Friedrich W. Bessel (1784–1846) of the Königsberg Observatory, Germany used the parallax method to measure the distance of 61 Cygni to be about six light years (modern value 11·08 light years).

Nearest Excepting the special case of our own Sun, the nearest star is the very faint Proxima Centauri, discovered in 1915, which is 4·225 light years ($4·00 \times 10^{13}$ km *2·48 × 10^{13} miles*) away.

The nearest 'star' visible to the naked eye is the southern hemisphere binary Alpha Centauri, or Rigel Kentaurus (4·35 light years distant), with an apparent

Largest scale model

The largest scale model of the solar system was developed by the Lakeview Museum of Arts and Sciences in Peoria, Illinois, USA and first displayed in April 1992. The Sun, with a diameter of 11 m *36 ft*, was painted on the exterior of the museum's planetarium, and the planets (spheres ranging in diameter from 2·5 cm *1 in* in the case of Pluto up to 1·1 m *3 ft 9 in* for Jupiter) were situated in appropriate locations in accordance with their distance from the Sun. This meant that the Earth was 1·2 km *¾ mile* away, with Pluto being in the town of Kewanee, some 64 km *40 miles* from the museum.

A smaller model of the solar system was created by Lars Broman and inaugurated by the Futures' Museum, Borlänge, Sweden on 29 Nov 1986. Its Sun had a diameter of 1·5 m *5 ft* and the planets ranged from 3·5 mm *⅛ in* to 140 mm *5½ in* in diameter, with the closest to the Sun being 60 m *200 ft* away and the furthest 6 km *3¾ miles* away. Unlike the American model it also included the nearest star to the Sun, Proxima Centauri, which was sited to scale in the Museum of Victoria, Melbourne, Australia.

magnitude of −0·29. By AD 29 700 this binary will reach a minimum distance from the Earth of 2·84 light years and should then be the second brightest 'star', with an apparent magnitude of −1·20.

Largest The largest star is the M-class supergiant Betelgeux (Alpha Orionis—the top left star of Orion) which is 310 light years distant. It has a diameter of 700 million km *400 million miles*, which is about 500 times greater than that of the Sun. It is surrounded by a dust 'shell' and also by an outer tenuous gas halo up to 8·5×10¹¹ km *5·3×10¹¹ miles* in diameter.

Heaviest The heaviest star is the variable Eta Carinae, 9100 light years

distant in the Carinae Nebula, with a mass 200 times greater than our own Sun.

Most luminous If all the stars could be viewed at the same distance, Eta Carinae would also be the most luminous star, with a total luminosity 6 500 000 times that of the Sun. However, the *visually* brightest star is the hypergiant Cygnus OB2 No. 12, which is 5900 light years distant. It has an absolute visual magnitude of −9·9 and is therefore visually 810 000 times brighter than the Sun. This brightness may be matched by the supergiant IV b 59 in the nearby galaxy Messier 101. During 1843 the absolute luminosity and absolute visual brightness of Eta Carinae temporarily increased to values 60 and 70 million times the corresponding values for the Sun.

Smallest The smallest star appears to be the white dwarf L362−81 with an estimated diameter of 5600 km *3500 miles* or only 0·004 that of the Sun.

Lightest A mass 0·014 that of the Sun is estimated for RG 0058.8−2807, which was discovered by I. Neill Reid and Gerard Gilmore using the UK Schmidt telescope (announced in April 1983).

Dimmest RG 0058.8−2807 is also the faintest star detected, with a total luminosity only 0·0021 that of the Sun and an absolute visual magnitude of 20·2, so that the visual brightness is less than one millionth that of the Sun.

Brightest (As seen from earth) Sirius A (Alpha Canis Majoris), also known as the Dog Star, is the brightest star of the 5776 stars visible to the naked eye. It has an apparent magnitude of −1·46 but because of the relative motions of this star and the Sun this should rise to a maximum value of −1·67 by around AD 61 000. Sirius is 8·64 light years distant and has a luminosity 26 times greater than that of the Sun. It has a diameter of 2·33 million km *1·45 million miles* and a mass 2·14 times that of the Sun. The faint white dwarf companion Sirius B has a diameter of only 10 000 km *6000 miles*, which is less than that of the Earth, but its mass is slightly greater than that of the Sun. Sirius is in the constellation Canis Major and is visible in the winter months of the northern hemisphere, being due south at midnight on the last day of the year.

Youngest The youngest stars appear to be two protostars known collectively as IRAS−4 buried deep in dust clouds in the nebula NGC1333, which is 1100 light years (1.04×10^{16} km 6.5×10^{15} *miles*) distant. Announced in May 1991 by a combined British, German and American team, these protostars will not blaze forth as fully fledged stars for at least another 100 000 years.

Oldest The oldest stars in the Galaxy have been detected in the halo, high above the disc of the Milky Way, by a group led by Timothy Beers (USA) who discovered 70 such stars by January 1991 but eventually expect to detect 500. These stars are characterized by having the lowest abundances of heavy elements whereas later generation stars (such as our own Sun) have higher heavy element abundances because of a build-up of such elements in galaxies from the successive explosions of supernova stars.

Pulsars The earliest observation of a pulsating radio source or 'pulsar', CP 1919 (now PSR 1919+21), by Dr Jocelyn Burnell (*née* Bell, b. 1943) was announced from the Mullard Radio Astronomy Observatory, Cambs on 24 Feb 1968. It had been detected on 28 Nov 1967.

For pulsars whose spin rates have been accurately measured, the fastest spinning is PSR 1937+214, which was discovered by a group led by Donald C. Backer in November 1982. It is in the minor constellation Vulpecula (the Little Fox), 16000 light years (1.51×10^{17} km 9.4×10^{16} *miles*) distant, and has a pulse period of $1.557\,806\,4850$ millisec, which is equivalent to a spin rate of $641.928\,2560$ revolutions per sec. However, the pulsar which has the slowest spin down rate, and is therefore the most accurate stellar clock, is PSR 1855+09 (discovered in December 1985) at only 2.1×10^{-20} sec per sec.

Brightest and latest supernova The brightest ever seen by historic man is believed to be SN 1006, noted in April 1006 near Beta Lupi, which flared for two years and attained a magnitude of −9 to −10. The remnant is believed to be the radio source G327·6+14·5, nearly 3000 light years distant. Others have occurred in 1054, 1604, 1885, and most recently on 23 Feb 1987, when Ian Shelton sighted that designated −69°202 in the Large Magellanic Cloud 170 000 light years distant. This supernova was visible to the naked eye when at its brightest in May 1987.

Black Holes The concept of superdense bodies was first adumbrated by the Marquis de LaPlace (1749−1827). This term for a star that has undergone complete gravitational collapse was first used by Prof. John Archibald Wheeler at an Institute for Space Studies meeting in New York City, USA on 29 Dec 1967.

The first tentative identification of a black hole was announced in December 1972 in the binary-star X-ray source Cygnus X−1.

The best black hole candidate is the central star of the binary (or triple) star system V404 which is 5000 light years (4.7×10^{16} km 2.9×10^{16} *miles*) distant in the constellation Cygnus and which first showed a possible black hole signature

A supernova is an exploding star whose luminosity suddenly increases greatly on eruption. Supernovæ occur very infrequently, and the nearest and brightest in modern times was in 1987 in a galaxy known as the Large Magellanic Cloud. The resulting effect was visible with the naked eye—on average this will happen only four times in a thousand years.
(Photo: Science Photo Library)

Zodiac

The term 'Zodiac' comes from the Greek 'zodiakos' — of living things — originally formalized by the Greek astronomer Hipparchus in 150 BC, who divided the sky extending 8 degrees either side of the ecliptic (the path of the Sun in the sky) into twelve equal zones of 30 degrees each. With the redefinition of constellation boundaries in 1928, the zodiacal constellations are no longer of equal size, with the largest being Virgo of area 1294·428 square degrees and the smallest Capricornus (Capricorn) of area 413·947 square degrees. Taurus is the zodiacal constellation with the most bright stars, with 125 down to magnitude 6, whilst Aries, Capricornus and Libra have only 50 each.

as the transient X-ray source GS 2023+338, discovered by the Ginga satellite in May 1989. In September 1991 J. Casares, P.A. Charles and T. Naylor firmly established the mass as being greater than six times that of the Sun (and more likely eight to fifteen times) and for the first time obtained a black hole candidate mass unequivocally above the maximum value of five solar masses for a neutron star.

For a black hole weighing ten times the mass of our Sun, light cannot escape (i.e. the point at which the black hole becomes 'black') if it is within 29·5 km *18·3 miles* of the centre (the Schwarzschild or gravitational radius, named after the German astronomer Karl Schwarzschild).

Evidence continues to accumulate to suggest that galaxies are powered by super massive black holes at their centres. In the case of our own Galaxy there is increasing evidence of a two million solar mass black hole in the region of the radio point source Sagittarius A*.

Constellations The largest of the 88 constellations is Hydra (the Sea Serpent), which covers 1302·844 deg² or 3·16 per cent of the whole sky and contains at least 68 stars visible to the naked eye (to 5·5 mag). The constellation Centaurus (Centaur), ranking ninth in area, however, embraces at least 94 such stars.

The smallest constellation is Crux Australis (Southern Cross), with an area of only 0·16 per cent of the whole sky, viz. 68·477 deg² compared with the 41 252·96 deg² of the whole sky.

The Sun

Distance extremes The true distance of the Earth from the Sun is 1·00000102 astronomical units or 149 598 020 km *92 955 900 miles*. Our orbit being elliptical, the distance of the Sun varies between a minimum (perihelion) of 147 097 800 km *91 402 300 miles* and a maximum (aphelion) of 152 098 200 km *94 509 400 miles*. Based on an orbital circumference of 939 886 400 km *584 018 400 miles* and an orbital period (sidereal year) of 365·256 366 days, the average orbital velocity is 107 210 km/h *66 620 mph*, but this varies between a minimum of 105 450 km/h *65 520 mph* at aphelion and a maximum of 109 030 km/h *67 750 mph* at perihelion.

Temperature and dimensions The Sun has a stellar classification of a *yellow dwarf* type G2, although its mass at 1·9889×10²⁷ tonnes is 332 946·04 times that of the Earth and represents over 99 per cent of the total mass of the Solar System. The solar diameter at 1 392 140 km *865 040 miles* leads to a density of 1·408 times that of water or a quarter that of the Earth.

The Sun has a central temperature of about 15 400 000 K and a core pressure of 25·4 PPa *1650 million tons/in²*. It uses up about 4 million tonnes of hydrogen per sec, equal to an energy output of 3·85×10²⁶ watts, although it will have taken 10 000 million years to exhaust its energy supply (about 5000 million years from the present). The luminous intensity of the Sun is 2·7×10²⁷ candela, which is equal to a luminance of 4·5×10⁸ candela/m² *290 000 candela/ in²*. (⊙ also Sunspots)

Sunspots To be visible to the *protected* naked eye, a sunspot must cover about one two-thousandth part of the Sun's disc and thus have an area of about 1300 million km² *500 million miles²*. The largest sunspot ever noted was in the Sun's southern hemisphere on 8 Apr 1947. Its area was about 18 000 million km² *7000 million miles²*, with an extreme longitude of 300 000 km *187 000 miles* and an extreme latitude of 145 000 km *90 000 miles*. Sunspots appear darker because they are more than 1500°C *2700°F* cooler than the rest of the Sun's surface temperature of 5507°C *9945°F*.

In October 1957 a smoothed sunspot count showed 263, the highest recorded index since records started in 1755 (cf. the previous record of 239 in May 1778). In 1943 one sunspot lasted for 200 days, from June to December.

Planets

Largest The nine major planets (including the Earth) are bodies within the Solar System and revolve round the Sun in definite orbits.

Jupiter, with an equatorial diameter of 142 984 km *88 846 miles* and a polar diameter of 133 708 km *83 082 miles*, is the largest of the nine major planets, with a mass 317·828 times, and a volume 1323·3 times, that of the Earth. It also has the shortest period of rotation, resulting in a Jovian day of only 9 hr 50 min 30·003 sec in the equatorial zone.

Smallest and coldest Pluto was first recorded by Clyde William Tombaugh (b. 4 Feb 1906) at Lowell Observatory, Flagstaff, Arizona, USA on 18 Feb 1930 from photographs taken on 23 and 29 January. His find was announced on 13 March. The planet has a diameter of 2302 km *1430 miles* and a mass 0·0023 that of the Earth.

The discovery of Pluto's moon Charon was announced on 22 Jun 1978 from the

---

Jupiter is the largest of the nine major planets. This photograph, taken from a distance of 28·4 million km *17·6 million miles* by the *Voyager 1* spacecraft, also shows two of its satellites—volcanic Io, which can be seen towards the right of the planet's disc, and billiard-ball smooth Europa, at the far right of the picture.

(Photo: Science Photo Library)

US Naval Observatory, Flagstaff, Arizona. It has a diameter of 1186 km *737 miles* and a mass about one eleventh of that of Pluto. The lowest observed surface temperature of any natural body in the Solar System is −235°C *−391°F* for Neptune's moon Triton, but the discovery in 1992 of solid nitrogen, methane and carbon monoxide on Pluto's surface indicates that its surface temperature must be very similar to that of Triton.

Outermost The outermost planet is Pluto, with the Pluto–Charon system orbiting at a mean distance from the Sun of 5 913 514 000 km *3 674 488 000 miles* in a period of 248·54 years. Because of their large orbital eccentricity they are closer to the Sun than Neptune between 23 Jan 1979 and 15 Mar 1999. However, Pluto–Charon lost their status as the outermost bodies in the Solar System with the annoucement on 14 Sep 1992 of the discovery of a 200 km *124 mile* diameter asteroid or comet by David Jewitt (UK) of the University of Hawaii and Jane Luu (USA) of the University of California, Berkeley, California from observations between 30 August and 1 September. Given the temporary designation 1992 QB$_1$, the object orbits at a mean distance of 6640 million km *4126 million miles* in a period of 295·72 years.

Fastest Mercury, which orbits the Sun at an average distance of 57 909 200 km *35 983 100 miles*, has a period of revolution of 87·9686 days, so giving the highest average speed in orbit of 172 248 km/h *107 030 mph*.

Hottest For Venus a surface temperature of 462°C *864°F* has been estimated from measurements made from the Soviet *Venera* and American *Pioneer* surface probes.

Nearest The fellow planet closest to the Earth is Venus, which is, at times, only 41 360 000 km *25 700 000 miles* inside the Earth's orbit, compared with Mars' closest approach of 55 680 000 km *34 600 000 miles* outside the Earth's orbit. Mars, known since 1965 to be cratered, has temperatures ranging from 29°C *85°F* to −123°C *−190°F*.

Surface features By far the highest and most spectacular surface feature on any planet is the volcano Olympus Mons (formerly Nix Olympica) in the Tharsis region of Mars. It has a diameter of 500–600 km *310–370 miles* and a height of 26 ± 3 km *75 450–95 150 ft* above the surrounding plain.

Brightest and faintest Viewed from the Earth, by far the brightest of the five planets visible to the naked eye is Venus, with a maximum magnitude of −4·4. Uranus, the first to be discovered by telescope when it was sighted by Sir William Herschel from his garden at 19 New King St, Bath on 13 Mar 1781, is only marginally visible, with a magnitude 5·5. The faintest planet is Pluto, with a magnitude of 15·0.

Densest and least dense Earth is the densest planet, with an average density of 5·515 times that of water, while Saturn has an average density only about one-eighth of this value or 0·685 times that of water.

Conjunctions The most dramatic recorded conjunction (coming together) of the other seven principal members of the Solar System (Sun, Moon, Mercury, Venus, Mars, Jupiter and Saturn) occurred on 5 Feb 1962, when 16° covered all seven during an eclipse in the Pacific area. It is possible that the seven-fold conjunction of September 1186 spanned only 12°. The next notable conjunction will take place on 5 May 2000.

Satellites

Largest and smallest The largest and heaviest satellite is Ganymede (Jupiter III), which is 2·017 times heavier than the Earth's Moon and has a diameter of 5268 km *3273 miles*. Of satellites whose diameters have been measured the smallest is Deimos, the outermost moon of Mars. Although irregularly shaped it has an average diameter of 12·5 km *7·8 miles*.

Distance extremes The distance of satellites from their parent planets varies from the 9377 km *5827 miles* of Phobos from the centre of Mars, to 23 700 000 km *14 700 000 miles* for Jupiter's outer satellite Sinope (Jupiter IX).

Most recent The most recently discovered satellite, announced on 16 Jul

1990 by Mark R. Showalter (USA), is the Saturnian satellite Pan (Saturn XVIII) which was found on eleven *Voyager 2* photographs taken during the close approach in August 1981. It has a diameter of only about 20 km *12 miles* and orbits within the 320 km *200 mile* Encke gap in the A ring.

Asteroids

Number and distance extremes There are estimated to be about 45 000 asteroids but the orbits of only just over 5700 have been accurately computed. Whilst most orbit between Mars and Jupiter, average distances from the Sun vary between 116 300 000 km *72 200 000 miles* (just outside of Venus' orbit) for the Aten asteroid 1954XA (discovered 5 Dec 1954 but currently lost) and for objects which appear to be of an asteroidal nature 3061 million km *1902 million miles* (just outside of Uranus' orbit) for 5145 Pholus, discovered on 9 Jan 1992. (➪ Planets, outermost)

Because of their large orbital eccentricities the closest approach to the

The Solar System has a total of 61 satellites or moons.
Saturn has 18
Jupiter 16
Uranus 15
Neptune 8
Mars 2
Earth 1
Pluto 1
Mercury 0
Venus 0

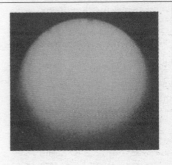

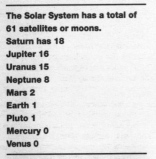

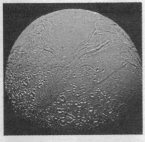

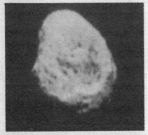

Satellites can come in various sizes, and even different shapes. Three of Saturn's record 18 moons are shown here. The largest of these is Titan (above), which is larger than both Mercury and Pluto, and is the only satellite with an extensive atmosphere.
Enceladus (above left) reflects back all of the light which it receives, making it the most reflective body in the Solar System.
Hyperion (left) is potato-shaped and is the only satellite not to have a fixed rotation period. It is possibly the remnant of a larger impact with a comet.

(Photos: NASA/Image Select)

Eclipses

Although normally the maximum possible duration of an eclipse of the Sun is 7 min 31 sec, durations can be 'extended' when observers are airborne. The totality of the Sun was extended to 74 min for observers aboard a Concorde which took off from Toulouse, France and stayed in the Moon's shadow from 10:51 to 12:05 GMT on 30 Jun 1973 over the Atlantic before landing in Chad.

Sun is by the Apollo asteroid 3200 Phaethon (discovered 11 Oct 1983) to within 20 890 000 km *12 980 000 miles* at perihelion, whilst the farthest distance is achieved by 5145 Pholus (⇔ above), which reaches to 4823 million km *2997 million miles* from the Sun at aphelion (beyond the orbit of Neptune). The closest known approach to the Earth by an asteroid was to within 170 000 km *105 600 miles* on 18 Jan 1991 by 1991BA (the day after its discovery).

Largest and smallest The largest asteroid is 1 Ceres (the first discovered, by G. Piazzi at Palermo, Sicily on 1 Jan 1801) with an equatorial diameter of 959 km *596 miles* and a polar diameter of 907 km *563 miles*. The smallest asteroid is 1991BA (⇔ above) with a diameter of 9m *30 ft*.

The only asteroid visible to the naked eye is 4 Vesta (discovered 29 Mar 1807), which is 520 km *323 miles* in diameter and has a maximum apparent magnitude as viewed from the Earth of 5·0.

The Moon

The Earth's closest neighbour in space and its only natural satellite is the Moon, which has an average diameter of 3475·1 km *2159·3 miles* and a mass of $7·348 \times 10^{19}$ tonnes, or 0·0123 Earth masses, so that its density is 3·344 times that of water.

The Moon orbits at a mean distance of 384 399·1 km *238 854·5 miles* centre-to-centre. In the present century the closest approach (smallest perigee) was 356 375 km *221 441 miles* centre-to-centre on 4 Jan 1912 and the farthest distance

(largest apogee) was 406 711 km *252 718 miles* on 2 Mar 1984. The orbital period (sidereal month) is 27·321 661 days, giving an average orbital velocity of 3683 km/h *2289 mph*.

Craters Only 59 per cent of the Moon's surface is directly visible from the Earth because it is in 'captured rotation', i.e. the period of rotation is equal to the period of orbit. The largest wholly visible crater is the walled plain Bailly, towards the Moon's South Pole, which is 295 km *183 miles* across, with walls rising to 4250 m *14 000 ft*. The Orientale Basin, partly on the averted side, measures more than 960 km *600 miles* in diameter.

The deepest crater is the Newton Crater, with a floor estimated to be between 7000–8850 m *23 000–29 000 ft* below its rim and 4250 m *14 000 ft* below the level of the plain outside. The brightest (most reflective) directly visible spot on the Moon is *Aristarchus*.

Highest mountains In the absence of a sea level, lunar altitudes are measured relative to an adopted reference sphere of radius 1738·000 km *1079·943 miles*. Thus the greatest elevation attained on this basis by any of the US astronauts has been 7830 m *25 688 ft* on the Descartes Highlands by Capt. John Watts Young (USN) and Major Charles M. Duke, Jr on 27 Apr 1972.

Temperature extremes When the Sun is overhead the temperature on the lunar equator reaches 117°C *243°F* (17 deg C *31 deg F* above the boiling point of water). By sunset the temperature is 14°C *58°F*, but after nightfall it sinks to −163°C *−261°F*.

Eclipses

Earliest recorded Although computer programmes can predict eclipses way back into history, there now appears to be no real evidence for ancient descriptions of eclipses prior to the partial eclipse observed in Ninevah in Assyria on 15 Jun 763 BC. The first definite evidence for a total eclipse stems from Chu-fu in China, observed on 17 Jul 709 BC.

The first decription of a solar eclipse in Britain is that of 15 Feb 538, described in the Anglo-Saxon Chronicles with the Sun being two-thirds eclipsed in London. No centre of path of totality for a solar eclipse crossed London for the 837 years from 2 Nov 878 to 3 May 1715. On 14 Jun 2151 an eclipse will be 99 per cent total in London but total for a path stretching from Dover, Kent to Belfast. The next total eclipse in London will not occur until 5 May 2600. The most recent occasion when a line of totality of a solar eclipse crossed Great Britain was on 29 Jun 1927 but totality lasted only for 40 seconds and most of the track over north Wales and northern England was covered by cloud. The next instance of such an eclipse will clip the coast of Cornwall at St. Just at 10:10 a.m. on 11 Aug 1999 with totality lasting 2 min 2 sec.

Longest duration The maximum *possible* duration of an eclipse of the Sun is 7 min 31 sec. The longest of recent date was on 20 Jun 1955 (7 min 8 sec), west of the Philippines, although it was clouded out along most of its track. An eclipse of 7 min 29 sec should occur in the mid-Atlantic Ocean on 16 Jul 2186.

The longest possible eclipse in the British Isles is 5 min 30 sec. In recent times that of 3 May 1715 was 4 min 4 sec but that of 22 Jul 2381, which will be observed in the Borders area, will be 5 min 10 sec.

The longest totality of any lunar eclipse is 104 minutes and has occurred many times.

Most and least frequent The highest number of eclipses possible in a year is seven, as in 1935, when there were five solar and two lunar eclipses. In 1982 there were four solar and three lunar eclipses. The lowest possible number in a year is two, both of which must be solar, as in 1944 and 1969.

The only recent example of three total solar eclipses occurring at a single location was at a point 44° N, 67° E in Kazakhstan, east of the Aral Sea. These took place on 21 Sep 1941, 9 Jul 1945 and 25 Feb 1952.

Aurorae

Most frequent Polar lights, known since 1560 as Aurora Borealis or Northern Lights in the northern hemisphere, and since 1773 as Aurora Australis in the southern, are caused by electrical solar discharges in the upper atmosphere and occur most frequently in high latitudes. Aurorae are visible at some time on *every* clear dark night in the polar areas within 20 degrees of the magnetic poles. The extreme height of aurorae has been measured at 1000 km *620 miles*, while the lowest may descend to 72 km *45 miles*.

Reliable figures exist only from 1952, since when the record high and low number of nights of auroral displays in Shetland (geomagnetic Lat. 63°) has been 203 (1957) and 58 (1965).

Lowest latitudes Extreme cases of displays in very low latitudes were recorded at Cuzco, Peru (2 Aug 1744), Honolulu, Hawaii (1 Sep 1859), and possibly Singapore (25 Sep 1909).

Noctilucent clouds These remain sunlit long after sunset owing to their great altitude, and are thought to consist of ice crystals or meteoric dust. Regular observations (at heights of *c.* 85 km *52 miles*) in Western Europe date only from 1964; since that year the record high and low number of nights on which these phenomena have been observed have been 43 (1979) and 15 (1970).

Comets

Earliest recorded Records date from the 7th century BC. The speeds of the estimated 2 million comets vary from 1150 km/h *700 mph* in the outer solar system to 2000000 km/h *1250000 mph* when near the Sun.

The successive appearances of Halley's Comet have been traced back to 467 BC. The first prediction of its return by Edmund Halley (1656–1742) proved true on Christmas Day 1758, 16 years after his death. On 13–14 Mar 1986, the

---

Comets—closest approach

On 1 Jul 1770, Lexell's Comet, travelling at 138600 km/h *86100 mph* (relative to the Sun), came to within 1200000 km *745000 miles* of the Earth. However, more recently the Earth is believed to have passed through the tail of Halley's Comet on 19 May 1910.

European satellite *Giotto* (launched 2 Jul 1985) penetrated to within 540 km *335 miles* of the nucleus of Halley's Comet. It was established that the core was 15 km *9 miles* in length and velvet black in colour.

Largest The tail of the brilliant Great Comet of 1843 trailed for 330 000 000 km *205 000 000 miles*. The bow shock wave of Holmes Comet of 1892 once measured 2 400 000 km *1 500 000 miles* in diameter.

Brightest The brightest comets are held to be either the Cruls Comet of 1862 or the Ikeya-Seki Comet of 1965.

Shortest period Of all the recorded periodic comets (which are members of the Solar System), the one which returns most frequently is the increasingly faint Encke's Comet, first identified in 1786. Its period of 1206 days (3·3 years) is the shortest established. Only 8 of its 63 returns have been missed by astronomers—most recently in 1944.

The most frequently observed comets are Schwassmann-Wachmann I, Kopff and Oterma, which can all be observed every year between Mars and Jupiter.

Longest period The longest period determined for a comet is 958 years, in the case of Comet 1894 Gale.

Meteoroids

Meteoroids are of cometary or asteroidal origin. A meteor is the light phenomenon caused by the entry of a meteoroid into the Earth's atmosphere.

Meteorites

Meteorites When a *meteoroid* (consisting of broken fragments of cometary or asteroidal origin and ranging in size from fine dust to bodies several kilometres in diameter) penetrates to the Earth's surface, the remnant, which could be either aerolite (stony) or siderite (metallic), is described as a *meteorite*. Such events occur about 150 times per year over the whole land surface of the Earth.

Oldest A revision by T. Kirsten in 1981 of the age estimates of meteorites which have remained essentially undisturbed after their formation suggests that the oldest which has been accurately dated

Meteorites

The most anxious time of day for meteorophobes should be 3 p.m. In historic times, the only recorded person injured by a meteorite was Mrs Ann Hodges of Sylacauga, Alabama, USA. On 30 Nov 1954 a 4 kg *9 lb* stone, some 18 cm *7 in* in length, crashed through the roof of her home, hitting Mrs Hodges on the arm and bruising her hip. The physician who examined her, Dr Moody D. Jacobs, declared her fit but she was subsequently hospitalized as a result of the attendant publicity.

Meteor 'shower'

The greatest shower on record occurred on the night of 16–17 Nov 1966, when the Leonid meteors (which recur every 33¼ years) were visible between western North America and eastern Russia (then USSR). It was calculated that meteors passed over Arizona, USA at a rate of 2300 per min for a period of 20 min from 5 a.m. on 17 Nov 1966.

is the Křahenberg meteorite at 4600 ± 20 million years, which is just within the initial period of Solar System formation. It was reported in August 1978 that dust grains in the Murchison meteorite which fell in Australia in September 1969 may be older than the Solar System.

Largest There was a mysterious explosion of 10–15 megatons (high explosive equivalent) in Lat. 60°55′N, Long. 101°57′E, in the basin of the Podkamennaya Tunguska River, 64 km *40 miles* north of Vanavar, in Siberia, Russia at 00hr 17min 11sec UT on 30 Jun 1908 resulting in the devastation of an area of 3900 km² *1500 miles²* with the shock wave being felt up to 1000 km *625 miles* away. The cause was variously attributed to a meteorite (1927), a comet (1930), a nuclear explosion (1961), anti-matter (1965), a small black hole (1973) and an exploding flying saucer (1976).

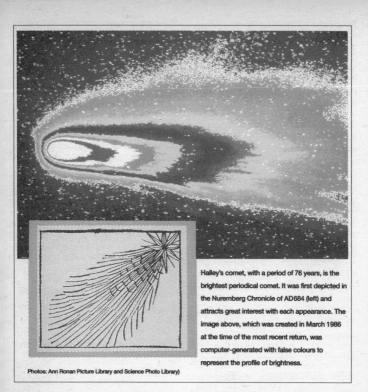

Halley's comet, with a period of 76 years, is the brightest periodical comet. It was first depicted in the Nuremberg Chronicle of AD684 (left) and attracts great interest with each appearance. The image above, which was created in March 1986 at the time of the most recent return, was computer-generated with false colours to represent the profile of brightness.

Photos: Ann Ronan Picture Library and Science Photo Library)

Although the meteorite theory was initially rejected, a new assessment in 1992 suggests that the explosion can be accounted for by the energy released following the total disintegration at an altitude of 10km *33000ft* of a 30m *98ft* diameter common type stony asteroid travelling at hypersonic velocity at an incoming angle of 45 degrees. A similar event may have occurred over the Isle of Axholm, Humberside a few thousand years before.

The largest known meteorite was found in 1920 at Hoba West, near Grootfontein in Namibia and is a block 2·7m *9ft* long by 2·4m *8ft* broad, estimated to weigh 59 tonnes. The largest meteorite exhibited by any museum is the 'Tent' meteorite, weighing 30883kg *68085lb*, found in 1897 near Cape York, on the west coast of Greenland, by the expedition of Commander (later Rear-Admiral) Robert Edwin Peary (1856–1920). It was known to the Inuits as the Abnighito and is now exhibited in the Hayden Planetarium in New York City, USA. The largest piece of stony meteorite recovered is a piece weighing 1770kg *3902lb*, part of a 4tonne shower which struck Jilin (formerly Kirin), China on 8 Mar 1976.

The heaviest of the 23 meteorites known to have fallen on the British Isles since 1623 was one weighing at least 46kg *102lb* (the largest known fragment being 7·88kg *17lb 6oz*), which fell at 4:12p.m. on 24 Dec 1965 at Barwell, Leics. Scotland's largest recorded meteorite fell in Strathmore, Tayside on 3 Dec 1917. It weighed 10·09kg *22¼ lb* and was the largest of four totalling 13·324kg *29lb 6oz*. The largest recorded meteorite to fall in Ireland was the Limerick Stone of 29·5kg *65lb*, part of a shower weighing more

19

than 48 kg *106 lb* which fell near Adare, Co. Limerick on 10 Sep 1813. Debris from the Bovedy Fall in Northern Ireland in 1969 spread over 80 km *50 miles*. The larger of the two recorded meteorites to land in Wales weighed 794 g *28 oz* of which a piece weighing 723 g *25½ oz* went through the roof of the Prince Llewellyn Hotel in Beddgelert, Gwynedd shortly before 3:15 a.m. on 21 Sep 1949.

Lunar Twelve known meteorites are believed to be of lunar origin as distinguished by characteristic element and isotopic ratios. The first eleven were found in Antarctica but the most recently discovered, which is only 3 cm *1 in* in diameter and weighs 19 g *0·67 oz*, was found at Calcalong Creek on the Nullarbor Plain to the north of the Great Australian Bight by D.H. Hill, W.V. Boynton and R.A. Haag (USA) with the discovery being announced in January 1991. The name 'Calcalong' is a corruption of the Aboriginal word meaning 'seven sisters went up to the sky, chased by the Moon'.

Craters It has been estimated that some 2000 asteroid Earth collisions have occurred in the last 600 million years. One hundred and two collision sites or astroblemes have been identified. A crater 240 km *150 miles* in diameter and 800 m *½ mile* deep was attributed to a meteorite in 1962 in Wilkes Land, Antarctica. Such a crater could have been caused by a meteorite weighing 13 billion tonnes striking at 70 800 km/h *44 000 mph*.

Soviet scientists reported in December 1970 an astrobleme with a diameter of 95 km *60 miles* and a maximum depth of 400 m *1300 ft* in the basin of the River Popigai. There is a crater-like formation or astrobleme 442 km *275 miles* in

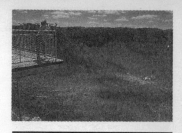

The world's largest crater known to have been formed by a meteorite— the Coon Butte or Barringer Crater in the USA.

(Photo: Spectrum Colour Library)

diameter on the eastern shore of the Hudson Bay, Canada, where the Nastapoka Islands are just off the coast. The largest and best-preserved crater which was definitely formed by a meteorite is the Coon Butte or Barringer Crater, discovered in 1891, near Winslow, Arizona, USA. It is 1265 m *4150 ft* in diameter and now about 175 m *575 ft* deep, with a parapet rising 40–48 m *130–155 ft* above the surrounding plain. It has been estimated that an iron-nickel mass of some 2 million tonnes and a diameter of 61–79 m *200–260 ft* gouged this crater in *c.* 25 000 BC.

Tektites These are characteristic pieces of natural glass which are formed from molten rock that has been flung at high velocity through the air following the impact of a large meteorite. The largest tektite of which details have been published weighed 3·2 kg *7·0 lb* and was found in 1932 at Muong Nong, Saravane Province, Laos. It is now in the Louvre Museum, Paris. Eight SNC meteorites (named after their find sites at Shergotty in India, Nakla in Egypt and Chassigny in France), are believed to have emanated from Mars.

The Earth

The Earth is approximately 4540 million years old. It is not a true sphere, but flattened at the poles and hence an oblate spheroid. The equatorial diameter (12 756·2726 km *7926·3803 miles*) is 42·7694 km *26·5757 miles* larger than the polar diameter of 12 713·5032 km *7899·8046 miles*. The Earth has a pear-shaped asymmetry with the north pole radius being 45 m *148 ft* longer than the south pole radius. There is also a slight ellipticity of the equator with its major diameter at 14·95°W being 139 m *456 ft* longer than its minor axis. The greatest departures from the reference ellipsoid are a protuberance of 73 m *240 ft* in the area of Papua New Guinea and a depression of 105 m *344 ft* south of Sri Lanka, in the Indian Ocean.

The greatest circumference of the Earth, at the equator, is 40 075·012 km *24 901·458 miles*, compared with 40 007·858 km *24 859·731 miles* for the meridian. The surface area is estimated at 510 065 500 km² *196 937 400 miles²* and the volume at 1 083 207 000 000 km³ *259 875 300 000 miles³*.

The mass of the Earth, which was first assessed by Dr Nevil Maskelyne (1732–1811) in Perthshire in 1774, is 5·974×10²¹ tonnes and the density is 5·515 times that of water. The Earth picks up cosmic dust but estimates vary widely, with 30 000 tonnes a year being the upper estimate. The true rotation period of the Earth, i.e. the mean sidereal day increased by 0·0084 sec to amount for precession, is 23 hr 56 min 4·0989 sec mean solar time.

Modern theory is that the Earth exists in three distinct layers, with the outermost being the very thin crust, which has an average depth of 24 km *15 miles*, but this can vary between 80 km *50 miles* under mountain ranges and can be as thin as 3 km *2 miles* under oceanic fracture zones. The crust overlays the 2865 km *1789 mile* thick mantle, the outermost layer of which is the strong rigid layer known as the lithosphere, which is up to 100 km *62 miles* thick under oceans and up to 200 km *124 miles* thick under continents. Below the lithosphere is the 320 km *199 mile* thick weaker layer called the asthenosphere, where average temperatures of 1300°C *2370°F* approach the melting point of rocks and it is probably in this area that magma (molten or semi-molten rock) is formed.

A major seismic discontinuity at a depth of 670 km *416 miles* separates the upper and lower mantles. At the centre is the iron-rich core of radius 3482 km *2164 miles*, and this consists of an outer liquid core of thickness 2260 km *1404 miles* and a solid inner core of radius 1222 km *759 miles*. If the iron-rich theory of the core is correct, iron would be the most abundant element in the Earth at 34 per cent. At the centre of the core the estimated density is 13·09 g/cm³, the temperature 4530°C *8186°F* and the pressure 364 GPa or 23 600 tons f/in².

Structure and Dimensions

Oceans

The area of the Earth covered by oceans and seas (the hydrosphere) is estimated to be 362 033 000 km² *139 782 000 miles²* or 70·98 per cent of the total surface. The mean depth of the hydrosphere is 3729 m *12 234 ft* and the volume 1 349 930 000 000 km³ *323 870 000 miles³*, which compares with 35 000 000 km³ *8 400 000 miles³* of fresh water. The total weight of the water is 1·41×10¹⁸ tonnes, or 0·024 per cent of the Earth's weight.

Largest The largest ocean in the world is the Pacific. Excluding adjacent seas, it represents 45·9 per cent of the world's oceans and covers 166 241 000 km² *64 185 600 miles²* in area. The average depth is 4188 m *13 740 ft*. The shortest navigable trans-Pacific distance between Guayaquil, Ecuador and Bangkok, Thailand is 17 550 km *10 905 miles*.

Deepest The deepest part of the ocean was first pinpointed in 1951 by HM Survey Ship *Challenger* in the Marianas

---

Deepest ocean

A metal object, for example a kilogram ball of steel, dropped into water above the Marianas Trench (⇨ Oceans Deepest) would take nearly 64 min to fall to the sea bed, where hydrostatic pressure is over 1250 bars *18 000 lb/in²*.

Trench in the Pacific Ocean. On 23 Jan 1960 the US Navy bathyscaphe *Trieste* descended to the bottom at 10916m *35813ft*. A more recent visit produced a figure of 10924m ± 10m *35839ft ± 33ft*, from data obtained by the survey vessel *Takuyo* of the Hydrographic Department, Japan Maritime Safety Agency in 1984, using a narrow multi-beam echo sounder.

The deepest point in the territorial waters of the UK is an area 6 cables (*1100m*) off the island of Raasay, near Skye, in the Inner Sound at Lat. 57°30'33"N, Long. 5°57'27"W, which is 316m *1037ft* deep.

Largest sea The largest of the world's seas is the South China Sea, with an area of 2974600km² *1148500miles²*.

Largest bay The largest bay in the world measured by shoreline length is Hudson Bay, northern Canada, with a shoreline of 12268km *7623miles* and an area of 1233000km² *476000miles²*. The area of the Bay of Bengal, in the Indian Ocean, is larger, at 2172000km² *839000miles²*.

Great Britain Great Britain's largest bay is Cardigan Bay, which has a shoreline 225km *140miles* long and measures 116km *72miles* across from the Lleyn Peninsula, Gwynedd to St David's Head, Dyfed.

Largest gulf The largest gulf in the world is the Gulf of Mexico, with an area of 1544000km² *596000miles²* and a shoreline of 5000km *3100miles* from Cape Sable, Florida, USA, to Cabo Catoche, Mexico.

Longest fjord The world's longest fjord is the Nordvest Fjord arm of the Scoresby Sund in eastern Greenland, which extends inland 313km *195miles* from the sea. The longest Norwegian fjord is the Sognefjord, which extends 204km *127miles* inland from the island of Sognoeksen to the head of the Lusterfjord arm at Skjolden. Its width ranges from 2·4km *1½ miles* at its narrowest up to 5·1km *3¼ miles* at its widest. It has a deepest point of 1296m *4252ft*. The longest Danish fjord is Lim-fjorden (160km *100miles*).

Longest sea loch Loch Fyne, Scotland, extends 60·5km *37·6miles* inland into Strathclyde.

Highest seamount The highest known submarine mountain, or seamount, is one discovered in 1953 near the Tonga Trench, between Samoa and New Zealand. It rises 8700m *28500ft* from the sea bed, with its summit 365m *1200ft* below the surface.

Most southerly The most southerly part of the oceans is located at 85°34' S, 154° W, at the snout of the Robert Scott Glacier, 490km *305miles* from the South Pole.

Sea temperature The temperature of the water at the surface of the sea varies greatly. It is as low as −2°C *28°F* in the White Sea and as high as 36°C *96°F* in the shallow areas of the Persian Gulf in summer. The highest temperature recorded in the ocean is 404°C *759°F*, for a hot spring measured by an American research submarine some 480km *300miles* off the American west coast, in an expedition under the direction of Prof. Jack Diamond of Oregon State University, USA in 1985. Remote probes measured the temper-ature of the spring, which was only kept from vaporising by the weight of water above it.

Clearest The Weddell Sea, 71°S, 15°W off Antarctica, has the clearest water of any sea. A 'Secchi' disc was visible to a depth of 80m *262ft* on 13 Oct 1986, as measured by Dutch researchers at the German Alfred-Wegener Institute. Such clarity corresponds to what is attainable in distilled water.

Straits

Longest The longest straits in the world are the Tatarskiy Proliv or Tartar Straits between Sakhalin Island and the Russian mainland, running from the Sea of Japan to Sakhalinsky Zaliv—800km *500miles*, thus marginally longer than the Malacca Straits, between Malaysia and Sumatra.

Broadest The broadest *named* straits in the world are the Davis Straits between Greenland and Baffin Island, Canada, with a minimum width of 338km *210miles*. The Drake Passage between the Diego Ramirez Islands,

Chile and the South Shetland Islands is 1140 km *710 miles* across.

Narrowest The narrowest navigable straits are those between the Aegean island of Euboea and the mainland of Greece. The gap is only 40 m *45 yd* wide at Khalkis.

The Seil Sound, Inner Hebrides, Scotland narrows to a point only 6 m *20 ft* wide where the Clachan bridge joins the island of Seil to the mainland, and has thus been said to span the Atlantic.

Waves

Highest The highest officially recorded sea wave was calculated at 34 m *112 ft* from trough to crest; it was measured by Lt Frederic Margraff, USN from the USS *Ramapo* proceeding from Manila, Philippines to San Diego, California, USA on the night of 6–7 Feb 1933, during a 126 km/h *68 knot* hurricane. The highest instrumentally measured wave was one 26 m *86 ft* high, recorded by the British ship *Weather Reporter*, in the North Atlantic on 30 Dec 1972 in Lat. 59°N, Long. 19°W.

It has been calculated on the statistics of the Stationary Random Theory that one wave in more than 300 000 may exceed the average by a factor of four. On 9 Jul 1958 a landslip caused a 160 km/h *100 mph* wave to wash 524 m *1720 ft* high along the fjord-like Lituya Bay in Alaska, USA.

Highest seismic The highest *tsunami* (often wrongly called a tidal wave) was one with an estimated height of 360 m *1180 ft*, which struck the northern Shetland Isles *c.*4950 BC at 180 km/h *110 mph*. It was generated by a massive undersea landslip from the Storegga area of the South Norwegian Sea involving 1800 km³ *430 miles³* of mud and rock. The highest known in modern times appeared off Ishigaki Island, Ryukyu Chain on 24 Apr 1771. It tossed a 750-tonne block of coral more than 2·5 km *1·3 miles*. Tsunami (a Japanese word: *nami*, a wave; *tsu*, overflowing) have been observed to travel at 790 km/h *490 mph*.

Currents

Greatest The greatest current in the oceans is the Antarctic Circumpolar Current or West Wind Drift Current. On the basis of four measurements taken in 1982 in the Drake Passage, between South America and Antarctica, it was found to be flowing at a rate of 130 000 000 m³ *4·3 billion ft³* per sec. Results from computer modelling in 1990 estimate a higher figure of 195 000 000 m³ *6·9 billion ft³* per sec. Its width ranges from 300 – 2000 km *185 – 1240 miles* and it has a proven surface flow rate of 0·75 km/h *¹⁄₁₀ of a knot*.

Strongest The world's strongest currents are the Nakwakto Rapids, Slingsby Channel, British Columbia, Canada (Lat. 51°05′N, Long. 127°30′W), where the flow rate may reach 30 km/h *16 knots*.

Great Britain The fastest current in British territorial waters is 19·8 km/h *10·7 knots* in the Pentland Firth between the Orkney Islands and Highland.

Tides

Extreme tides are due to lunar and solar gravitational forces affected by their perigee, perihelion and syzygies. Barometric and wind effects can superimpose an added 'surge' element. Coastal and sea-floor configurations can accentuate these forces. The normal interval between tides is 12 hr 25 min.

Greatest The greatest tides occur in the Bay of Fundy, which divides the peninsula of Nova Scotia, Canada from the United States' north-easternmost state of Maine and the Canadian province of New Brunswick. Burncoat Head in the Minas Basin, Nova Scotia, has the greatest mean spring range, with 14·5 m *47 ft 6 in*. A range of 16·6 m *54 ft 6 in* was recorded at springs in Leaf Basin, in Ungava Bay, Quebec, Canada in 1953. Tahiti, in the mid-Pacific Ocean, experiences virtually no tide.

Great Britain The place with the greatest mean spring range in Great Britain is Beachley, on the Severn, with a range of 12·40 m *40 ft 8½ in*, compared with the British Isles' average of 4·6 m *15 ft*. Prior to 1933, tides as high as 8·80 m *28 ft 11 in* above and 6·80 m *22 ft*

23

3½ in below datum (total range 15·60 m *51 ft 2½ in*) were recorded at Avonmouth, though an extreme range of 15·90 m *52 ft 2½ in* for Beachley was officially accepted. In 1883 a freak tide of greater range was reported from Chepstow, Gwent.

Icebergs

Largest and tallest The largest iceberg on record was an antarctic tabular iceberg of over 31 000 km² *12 000 miles²*, 335 km *208 miles* long and 97 km *60 miles* wide (and thus larger than Belgium), sighted 240 km *150 miles* west of Scott Island, in the South Pacific Ocean, by the USS *Glacier* on 12 Nov 1956. The 60 m *200 ft* thick arctic ice island T.1 (360 km² *140 miles²*), discovered in 1946, was tracked for 17 years. The tallest iceberg measured was one of 167 m *550 ft* reported off western Greenland by the US icebreaker *East Wind* in 1958.

Most southerly arctic The most southerly arctic iceberg was sighted in the Atlantic by a USN weather patrol in Lat. 28° 44′ N, Long. 48° 42′ W, in April 1935. The southernmost iceberg reported in British home waters was sighted 96 km *60 miles* from Smith's Knoll, on the Dogger Bank, in the North Sea.

Most northerly antarctic The most northerly antarctic iceberg was a remnant sighted in the Atlantic by the ship *Dochra* in Lat. 26° 30′ S, Long. 25° 40′ W, on 30 Apr 1894.

Land

There is strong evidence that about 300 million years ago the Earth's land surface comprised a single primeval continent of 1·5 × 10⁸ km² *60 million miles²*, now termed Pangaea, and even prior to its existence it is possible that there had been other super-continents. Pangaea is believed to have split about 190 million years ago, during the Jurassic Period, into two super-continents. These are termed Laurasia (Eurasia, Greenland and North America) and Gondwana (Africa, Arabia, India, South America, Oceania and Antarctica). The South Pole is thought to have been in the area of the Sahara as recently as the Ordovician Period of *c.* 450 million years ago.

Remotest spot from land
The world's most distant point from land is a spot in the South Pacific, 48° 30′ S, 125° 30′ W, which is 2670 km *1660 miles* from the nearest points of land, namely Pitcairn Island, Ducie Island and Cape Dart, Antarctica. Centred on this spot is a circle of water with an area of 22 421 500 km² *8 657 000 miles²*—more than 5 000 000 km² *2 000 000 miles²* larger than Russia, the world's largest country.

Consequently the Sahara, now one of the hottest areas of the world, was at the time the coldest.

Rocks

The age of the Earth is generally considered to be within the range of 4540 ± 40 million years, based on the lead isotope systematics. However, no rocks of this great age have yet been found on the Earth, since geological processes have presumably destroyed them.

Oldest The greatest reported age for any scientifically dated rock is 3962 million years in the case of Acasta Gneisses found in May 1984. The rocks were discovered approximately 320 km *200 miles* north of Yellowknife, Northwest Territories, Canada by Dr Samuel Bowring as part of an ongoing Canadian geology survey mapping project. When the samples were analysed in June 1989, Dr Bowring and scientists from the Australian National University in Canberra established their age, using a machine called SHRIMP (Sensitive Highmass Resolution Ion MicroProbe).

Older minerals which are not rocks have also been identified. Some zircon crystals discovered by Bob Pidgeon and Simon Wilde in the Jack Hills, 700 km *430 miles* north of Perth, Western Australia in August 1984 were found to be 4276 million years old, again using SHRIMP. These are the oldest fragments of the Earth's crust discovered so far.

Great Britain The oldest rocks in Great Britain are the original volcanic products from which were formed the gneiss and

Dr Samuel Bowring with some of the samples of the oldest rocks.

(Photo: Washington University/Joe Angeles)

granulite rocks of the Scourian complex in the north-west Highlands and the Western Isles which were crystallized 2800 million years ago.

Largest The largest exposed monolith in the world is Ayers Rock, which rises 348 m *1143 ft* above the surrounding desert plain in Northern Territory, Australia. It is 2·5 km *1·5 miles* long and 1·6 km *1 mile* wide. The nearest major town is Alice Springs, which is 400 km *250 miles* to the north-east. It was estimated in 1940 that La Gran Piedra, a volcanic plug located in the Sierra Maestra, Cuba, weighs 61 355 tonnes.

Largest Of the Earth's surface 41·25 per cent, or 210 400 000 km² *81 200 000 miles²*, is covered by continental masses, of which only 148 021 000 km² *57 151 000 miles²* (about two-thirds, or 29·02 per cent of the Earth's surface), is land above water, with a mean height of 756 m *2480 ft* above sea level. The Eurasian land mass is the largest, with an area (including islands) of 53 698 000 km² *20 733 000 miles²*. The Afro-Eurasian land mass, separated artificially only by the Suez Canal, covers an area of 84 702 000 km² *32 704 000 miles²* or 57·2 per cent of the Earth's land mass.

Smallest The smallest continent is the Australian mainland, with an area of 7 618 493 km² *2 941 526 miles²*, which, together with Tasmania, New Zealand, Papua New Guinea and the Pacific Islands, is sometimes described as Oceania.

Peninsula The world's largest peninsula is Arabia, with an area of about 3 250 000 km² *1 250 000 miles²*.

Islands

Largest Discounting Australia, which is usually regarded as a continental land mass, the largest island in the world is Greenland, with an area of about 2 175 000 km² *840 000 miles²*. There is evidence that Greenland is in fact several islands overlaid by an ice cap without which it would have an area of 1 680 000 km² *650 000 miles²*. The largest sand island in the world is Fraser Island, Queensland, Australia with a sand dune 120 km *75 miles* long.

Greenland is normally classified as the largest island in the world. Its main physical feature is its huge ice sheet, which occupies some 85 per cent of the total area. The average depth of the ice is 1500 m *5000 ft* and the maximum about 3000 m *10 000 ft*. This shot shows a typical landscape in the west of the island.

(Photo: Robert Estall Photographs)

Great Britain The mainland of Great Britain is the eighth largest island in the world, with an area of 229 979 km² *88 795 miles²*. It stretches 971 km *603½ miles* from Dunnet Head in the north to Lizard Point in the south and 463 km *287½ miles* across from Porthaflod, Dyfed to Lowestoft, Suffolk. The island of Ireland (84 418 km² *32 594 miles²*) is the twentieth largest in the world.

Freshwater The largest island surrounded mostly by fresh water (48 000 km² *18 500 miles²*) is the Ilha de Marajó, in the mouth of the River Amazon, Brazil. The world's largest inland island (i.e. land surrounded by rivers) is Ilha do Bananal, Brazil (20 000 km² *7700 miles²*). The largest island in a lake is Manitoulin Island (2766 km² *1068 miles²*) in the Canadian section of Lake Huron.

Great Britain The largest lake island in Great Britain is Inchmurrin, in Loch Lomond, Strathclyde/Central with an area of 115 ha *284 acres*.

Remotest The remotest island in the world is Bouvet Island (Bouvetøya), discovered in the South Atlantic by J.B.C. Bouvet de Lozier on 1 Jan 1739, and first landed on by Capt. George Norris on 16 Dec 1825. Its position is 54° 26′ S, 3° 24′ E. This uninhabited Norwegian dependency is about 1700 km *1050 miles* from the nearest land— the uninhabited Queen Maud Land coast of eastern Antarctica.

The remotest inhabited island in the world is Tristan da Cunha, discovered in the South Atlantic by Tristão da Cunha, a Portuguese admiral, in March 1506. It has an area of 98 km² *38 miles²*. The first permanent inhabitant was Thomas Currie, who landed in 1810. The island was annexed by the UK on 14 Aug 1816. After evacuation in 1961 (due to volcanic activity), 198 islanders returned in November 1963. The nearest inhabited land to the group is the island of St Helena, 2435 km *1315 nautical miles* to the north-east. The nearest continent, Africa, is 2740 km *1700 miles* away.

The remotest of the British islets is Rockall, 307 km *191 miles* west of St Kilda, Western Isles. In June 1986 it was found by an RAF Nimrod to be 1509 m

26

Land remotest from the sea

The point of land remotest from the sea is at Lat. 46° 16·8′ N, Long. 86° 40·2′ E in the Dzungarian Basin, which is in the Sinkiang Uighur Autonomous Region (Xinjiang Uygur Zizhiqu), China's most north-westerly province. It is at a straight-line distance of 2648 km *1645 miles* from the nearest open sea— Baydaratskaya Guba to the north (Arctic Ocean), Feni Point to the south (Indian Ocean) and Bohai Wan to the east (Yellow Sea).

The point furthest from the sea in Great Britain is near Meriden, W Mids, which is 117 km *72½ miles* equidistant from the Severn bridge, the Dee and Mersey estuaries and the Welland estuary in the Wash. The equivalent point in Scotland is in the Forest of Atholl, north-west Tayside, 65 km *40½ miles* equidistant from the head of Loch Leven, Inverness Firth and the Firth of Tay. The geographical centre of the island of Great Britain is at national grid reference SD 676424, in a field near the hamlet of Chadswell, by the River Hodder, 7 km *4·3 miles* west of Clitheroe, Lancs.

4950 ft to the south-east of its hitherto charted location. This rock, measuring 21 m *70 ft* high and 25 m *83 ft* across, was not formally annexed until 18 Sep 1955. It was 'occupied' by Tom McClean for 38 days 22 hr 52 min from 25 May to 4 Jul 1985.

The remotest British island which has ever been inhabited is North Rona, which is 71 km *44 miles* from the next nearest land at Cape Wrath and the Butt of Lewis. It was evacuated *c.* 1844. Currently the most remote inhabited British island is Fair Isle, 38·5 km *24 miles* to the south-west of Sumburgh Head, Shetland. It has a population of some 80 people.

Greatest archipelago The world's greatest archipelago is the crescent of more than 13 000 islands, 5600 km *3500 miles* long, which forms Indonesia.

Highest rock pinnacle The world's highest rock pinnacle is Ball's Pyramid near Lord Howe Island in the Pacific, which is 561 m *1843 ft* high, but has a base axis of only 200 m *220 yd*. It was first scaled in 1965.

Northernmost land On 26 Jul 1978 Uffe Petersen of the Danish Geodetic Institute observed the islet of Odaaq Ø, 30 m *100 ft* across, 1·36 km *1478 yd* north of Kaffeklubben Ø off Pearyland, Greenland in Lat. 83° 40′ 32·5″ N, Long. 30° 40′ 10·1″ W. It is 706·4 km *438·9 miles* from the North Pole.

Southernmost land The South Pole, unlike the North Pole, is on land. The Amundsen–Scott South Polar station was built there at an altitude of 2855 m *9370 ft* in 1957. The station is drifting bodily with the ice cap 8–9 m *27–30 ft* per annum in the direction 43° W and was replaced by a new structure in 1975.

Newest The world's newest island is Pulau Batu Hairan ('Surprise Rock Island'), some 65 km *40 miles* to the north-east of Kudat, in Sabah, Malaysia. It was first sighted by three local fishermen on 14 Apr 1988. A week later it had doubled in height and now has an area of 0·77 ha *1·9 acres* and a maximum height of 3·1 m *10 ft*.

Largest atoll The largest atoll in the world is Kwajalein in the Marshall Islands, in the central Pacific Ocean. Its slender coral reef 283 km *176 miles* long encloses a lagoon of 2850 km² *1100 miles²*. The atoll with the largest land area is Christmas Atoll, in the Line Islands in the central Pacific Ocean. It has an area of 649 km² *251 miles²*, of which 321 km² *124 miles²* is land. There are four settlements on the island, the principal one, London, being only 4 km *2½ miles* away from another one, Paris.

Longest reef The Great Barrier Reef off Queensland, north-eastern Australia is 2027 km *1260 miles* in length. It is not actually a single reef, but consists of thousands of separate reefs. Between 1959 and 1971, and again between 1979 and 1991, corals on large areas of the central section of the reef — approximately between Cooktown and Proserpine — were devastated by the crown-of-thorns starfish (*Acanthaster planci*).

Depressions

Deepest The deepest depression so far discovered is the bedrock of the Bentley sub-glacial trench, Antarctica at 2538 m *8326 ft* below sea level. The greatest submarine depression is an area of the north-west Pacific floor which has an average depth of 4600 m *15 000 ft*. The deepest exposed depression on land is the shore surrounding the Dead Sea, now 400 m *1310 ft* below sea level. The deepest point on the bed of this saltiest of all lakes is 728 m *2388 ft* below sea level. The rate of fall in the lake surface since 1948 has been 350 mm *13¾ in* per annum. The deepest part of the bed of Lake Baikal in Russia is 1181 m *3875 ft* below sea level.

Great Britain The lowest-lying area in Great Britain is in the Holme Fen area of the Great Ouse, in Cambridgeshire, at 2·7 m *9 ft* below sea level. The deepest depression in England is the bed of part of Lake Windermere, 28·6 m *94 ft* below sea level, and in Scotland the bed of Loch Morar, Inverness, 300·8 m *987 ft* below sea level.

Largest The largest exposed depression in the world is the Caspian Sea basin in Azerbaijan, Russia, Kazakhstan, Turkmenistan and Iran. It is more than 518 000 km² *200 000 miles²*, of which 371 800 km² *143 550 miles²* is lake area. The preponderant land area of the depression is the Prikaspiyskaya Nizmennost, lying around the northern third of the lake and stretching inland for a distance of up to 450 km *280 miles*.

Caves

Longest The most extensive cave system in the world is that under the Mammoth Cave National Park, Kentucky, USA, first entered in 1799. Explorations by many groups of cavers have revealed the interconnected cave passages beneath the Flint, Mammoth Cave and Toohey Ridges to make a system with a total mapped length which is now 560 km *348 miles*.

Deepest Caves by Countries

Depth m	ft	Location	
1602	5256	Réseau Jean Bernard	France
1508	4947	Shakta Pantjukhina	Georgia
1485	4872	Lamprechtsofen	Austria
1441	4728	Sistema del Trave	Spain
1415	4642	Boj Bulok	Uzbekistan
1386	4547	Cueva Cheve	Mexico
1210	3970	Abisso Olivifer	Italy
1198	3930	Veliko Fbrego	Slovenia
1190	3904	Cukurpinar Dudeni	Turkey
1159	3802	Anou Ifflis	Algeria
1020	3346	Siebenhengste System	Switzerland
308	1010	Ogof Ffynnon Ddu	Wales
214	702	Giant's Hole System	England
181	594	Poll na Gceim	Republic of Ireland

Great Britain The longest cave system in Great Britain is the Ease Gill system, W Yorks which now has 70 km *44 miles* of explored passage.

Largest The world's largest cave chamber is the Sarawak Chamber, Lubang Nasib Bagus, in the Gunung Mulu National Park, Sarawak, discovered and surveyed by the 1980 British–Malaysian Mulu Expedition. Its length is 700 m *2300 ft*, its average width is 300 m *980 ft* and it is nowhere less than 70 m *230 ft* high. It is large enough to span the West End of London, reaching from Trafalgar Square to beyond Piccadilly Circus and Leicester Square.

Underwater cave The longest explored underwater cave is the Nohoch Na Chich cave system in Quintana Roo, Mexico, with 21 363 m *70 087 ft* of mapped passages. Exploration of the system, which began in November 1987, has been carried out by the CEDAM Cave Diving Team under the leadership of Mike Madden.

The longest dive into a single flooded cave passage is one of 4055 m *13 300 ft* into the Doux de Coly, Dordogne, France by Olivier Issler (Switzerland) on 4 Apr 1991.

Greatest descent The world depth record was set by the Groupe Vulcain in

the Gouffre Jean Bernard, France at 1602 m *5256 ft* in 1989. However, this cave, explored via multiple entrances, has never been entirely descended, so the 'sporting' record for the greatest descent into a cave is recognized as 1508 m *4947 ft* in the Shakta Pantjukhina in the Caucasus Mountains of Georgia by a team of Ukrainian cavers in 1988.

Longest stalactite The longest known stalactite in the world is a wall-supported column extending 59 m *195 ft* from roof to floor in the Cueva de Nerja, near Málaga, in Spain. The longest free-hanging stalactite in the world is believed to be one of 6·2 m *20 ft 4 in*, in the Poll an Ionain cave in Co. Clare, Republic of Ireland.

Tallest stalagmite The tallest known stalagmite in the world is in the Krásnohorská cave, near Rožňava, Slovakia, which is generally accepted as being about 32 m *105 ft* tall. The tallest cave column is considered to be the Flying Dragon Pillar, 39 m *128 ft* high, in Daji Dong, Guizhou, China.

Mountains

Highest An eastern Himalayan peak known as Peak XV on the Tibet–Nepal border was discovered to be the world's highest mountain in 1856 by the Survey Department of the Government of India,

from theodolite readings taken in 1849 and 1850. Its height was calculated to be 8840m *29002ft*. It was named Mt Everest after Col. Sir George Everest (1790–1866), formerly Surveyor-General of India, who pronounced his name 'Eve-rest'.

The status of Everest (Eve-rest) as the world's highest mountain was challenged in 1987 by K2 (formerly Godwin Austen), in the disputed Kashmiri Northern Areas of Pakistan. The satellite transit surveyor of the US K2 Expedition yielded altitudes of between 8858 and 8908m *29064 and 29228ft*. However, Chinese authorities subsequently reaffirmed their own heights of 8848·2m *29029ft 3in* for Everest and 8611m *28250ft* for K2, and the Research Council in Rome, Italy announced on 23 Oct 1987 that new satellite measurements restored Everest to primacy at 8863m *29078ft*, with K2 down to 8607m *28238ft*. These are the latest accepted figures. (For details of ascents of Everest ⬦ Mountaineering)

The mountain whose summit is farthest from the Earth's centre is the Andean peak of Chimborazo (6267m *20561ft*), 158km *98miles* south of the equator in Ecuador, South America. Its summit is

It is now more than forty years since Mount Everest, the world's highest mountain, was first climbed, on 29 May 1953. In May 1993 Sir Edmund Hillary spoke about being the first man to reach the top of Everest—just before his valued fellow-mountaineer Sherpa Tenzing. Sir Edmund said 'I had no feeling of extreme pleasure or excitement but more a sense of quiet satisfaction and even a bit of surprise. I reached out to shake hands with Tenzing in the Anglo-Saxon fashion but that was not enough for him. He threw his arms round my shoulders and we gave each other a hearty hug.'

(Photo: Bruce Herrod)

2150m *7057ft* further from the Earth's centre than the summit of Mt Everest.

The highest mountain on the equator is Volcán Cayambe (5790m *18996ft*), Ecuador, at Long. 77° 58′ W. If a mountaineer were on the summit he or

Highest mountain

The most recent survey of the height of Mt Everest (<> p. 28–9) has produced a different result from those calculated previously. The height announced on 20 Apr 1993 following measurements using the most advanced technology was given as 8846·1 m *29 022 ft 8 in*, although this may be revised further as the analysis of the findings is still continuing. The research was carried out by a team of Italian and Chinese scientists.

---

she would be moving at 1671 km/h *1038 mph* relative to the Earth's centre, due to the Earth's rotation.

The highest insular mountain in the world is Puncak Jaya (formerly Puncak Sukarno, formerly Carstensz Pyramide) in Irian Jaya, Indonesia. A survey by the Australian Universities' Expedition in 1973 yielded a height of 4884 m *16 023 ft*. Ngga Pulu (also in Irian Jaya), which is now 4861 m *15 950 ft*, was in 1936 possibly *c.* 4910 m *16 110 ft* before the melting of its snow cap.

The highest mountain in the UK is Ben Nevis (1343·4 m *4407 ft 6 in* above 1992 sea level excluding the 3·65 m *12 ft* cairn), 6·85 km *4¼ miles* south-east of Fort William, Argyll, Highland. It was climbed before 1720, but though acclaimed the highest in 1790, was not officially recognized to be higher than Ben Macdhui (1310 m *4300 ft*) until 1870. In 1834 Ben Macdhui and Ben Nevis (Gaelic, *Beinn Nibheis*) (first reference, 1778) were respectively quoted as 4570 ft *1393 m* and 4370 ft *1332 m*. The highest mountain in England is Scafell Pike (978 m *3210 ft*) in Cumbria, in Wales the highest is Snowdon (*Yr Wyddfa*) (1085 m *3560 ft*) in Gwynedd and in Northern Ireland it is Slieve Donard, Co. Down (852 m *2796 ft*). The highest in the Republic of Ireland is Carrantuohill (1041 m *3414 ft*) in Co. Kerry.

There is some evidence that, before being ground down by the ice cap, mountains in the Loch Bà area of the Isle of Mull, Strathclyde were 4600 m *15 000 ft* above sea level. There are 577 peaks and tops over 915 m *3000 ft* in the whole British Isles and 165 peaks and 136 tops in Scotland higher than England's highest point, Scafell Pike. The Scottish peaks and tops are known as Munros, after Sir Hugh Munro (1856–1919). The highest mountain off the mainland is Sgùrr Alasdair (1008 m *3309 ft*) on Skye, named after Alexander (Gaelic, *Alasdair*) Nicolson, who made the first ascent in 1873.

Unclimbed The highest unclimbed mountain is Kankar Pünsum (7541 m *24741 ft*), on the Bhutan/Tibet border. It is the 67th named mountain peak in order of height. The highest unclimbed summit is Lhotse Middle (8414 m *27605 ft*), one of the peaks of Lhotse, in the Khumbu district of the Nepal Himalaya. It is the tenth highest individually recognized summit in the world, Lhotse being the fourth highest mountain.

Tallest The world's tallest mountain measured from its submarine base (6000 m *3280 fathoms*) in the Hawaiian Trough to its peak is Mauna Kea (White Mountain) on the island of Hawaii, with a combined height of 10 205 m *33 480 ft*, of which 4205 m *13 796 ft* are above sea level.

Greatest ranges The greatest of all mountain ranges is the submarine Mid-Ocean Ridge, extending 65 000 km *40 000 miles* from the Arctic Ocean to the Atlantic Ocean, around Africa, Asia and Australia, and under the Pacific Ocean to the west coast of North America. It has a greatest height of 4200 m *13 800 ft* above the base ocean depth.

The world's greatest land mountain range is the Himalaya-Karakoram, which contains 96 of the world's 109 peaks of over 24 000 ft *7315 m*. Himalaya derives from the Sanskrit *him*, snow; *alaya*, home. The longest range is the Andes of South America, which is approximately 7600 km *4700 miles* in length.

Longest lines of sight Vatnajökull (2118 m *6952 ft*), Iceland has been seen by refracted light from the Faeroe Islands 550 km *340 miles* away. In Alaska, Mt McKinley (6193 m *20 320 ft*) has been sighted from Mt Sanford (4949m *16 237ft*)—a distance of 370km *230 miles*. McKinley, so named in 1896, was called Denali (Great One) in the Athabascan language of North American Indians and is the highest mountain in the United States.

Greatest plateau The most extensive high plateau in the world is the Tibetan Plateau in Central Asia. The average altitude is 4900m *16 000ft* and the area is 200 000 km² *77000 miles²*.

Sheerest wall Mt Rakaposhi (7788m *25 550ft*) rises 5·99 vertical kilometres *3·72 miles* from the Hunza Valley, Pakistan in 10 horizontal kilometres *6·2 miles* with an overall gradient of 31°.

The 975m *3200ft* wide north-west face of Half Dome, Yosemite, California, USA is 670 m *2200 ft* high but nowhere departs more than 7° from the vertical. It was first climbed (Class VI) in 1957 by Royal Robbins, Jerry Gallwas and Mike Sherrick.

Highest halites Along the northern shores of the Gulf of Mexico for 1160km *725 miles* there exist 330 subterranean 'mountains' of salt, some of which rise more than 18 300 m *60 000 ft* from bedrock and appear as the low salt domes first discovered in 1862.

Waterfalls

Highest The highest waterfall (as opposed to vaporized 'Bridal Veil') in the world is the Salto Angel in Venezuela, on a branch of the River Carrao, an upper tributary of the Caroní, with a total drop of 979m *3212ft*—the longest single drop being 807 m *2648 ft*. The 'Angel Falls' were named after the American pilot Jimmy Angel (died 8 Dec 1956), who recorded them in his log book on 14 Nov 1933. The falls, known by the Indians as Churun-Meru, had been reported by Ernesto Sánchez la Cruz in 1910.

The highest waterfall in the UK is Eas a'Chùal Aluinn, from Glas Bheinn (774m *2541ft*), Sutherland, with a drop of 200m *660ft*. The greatest single drop is one of 67 m *220ft* in the case of the Falls of Glomach, near Dornie, Highland. In England there is no clear-cut tallest waterfall. Cautley Spout, in Howgill Falls, Cumbria, with very broken cascades down a deep gully, has a total drop of 180m *591ft*. Scale Force, near Buttermere, Cumbria, has the longest unbroken drop, of 45 m *148 ft*. The underground cascade in the Gaping Gill Cave, Ingleborough, N Yorks descends an unbroken 111m *365ft*. The highest Welsh waterfall is the Pistyll-y-Llyn on the Powys–Dyfed border, which exceeds 90m *300ft* in descent. The highest falls in Ireland are the Powerscourt Falls (106m *350ft*), on the River Dargle, Co. Wicklow.

Greatest On the basis of the average annual flow, the greatest waterfall in the world is the Boyoma (formerly Stanley) Falls in Zaïre with 17000m³/sec *600000 cusec*. The flow of the Guaíra (Salto das Sete Quedas) on the Alto Paraná River between Brazil and Paraguay did on occasions in the past attain a rate of 50 000 m³/sec *1750 000 cusec*. However, the completion of the Itaipú dam in 1982 ended this claim to fame. It has been calculated that a waterfall 26 times greater than the Guaíra and perhaps 800 m *2620ft* high was formed, when some 5·5 million years ago the Mediterranean basins began to be filled from the Atlantic through the Straits of Gibraltar.

Widest The widest waterfall in the world is the Khône Falls (15–21 m *50–70ft* high) in Laos, with a width of 10·8 km *6·7 miles* and a flood flow of 42500m³/sec *1500000 cusec*.

Rivers

Longest The two longest rivers in the world are the Nile (*Bahr el-Nil*), flowing into the Mediterranean, and the Amazon (*Amazonas*), flowing into the South Atlantic. Which is the longer is more a matter of definition than simple measurement.

Not until 1971 was the true source of the Amazon discovered, by Loren McIntyre (USA) in the snow-covered Andes of southern Peru. The Amazon begins with snowbound lakes and brooks—the actual source has been named Laguna McIntyre—which converge to form the Apurimac. This joins other streams to become the Ene, the Tambo and then the Ucayali. From the confluence of the Ucayali and the Marañón the river is called the Amazon for the final 3700km

31

Subterranean river

In August 1958 a crypto-river, tracked by radio isotopes, was discovered flowing under the Nile with six times its mean annual flow, or 500 000 million m³ *20 trillion ft³.*

Submarine river

In 1952 a submarine river 300 km *190 miles* wide, known as the Cromwell current, was discovered flowing eastward below the surface of the Pacific for 6500 km *4000 miles* along the equator. In places it flows at depths of up to 400 m *1300 ft.* Its volume is 1000 · times that of the Mississippi.

────────

2300 miles as it flows through Brazil into the Atlantic Ocean. The Amazon has several mouths which widen towards the sea, so that the exact point where the river ends is uncertain. If the Pará estuary (the most distant mouth) is counted, its length is approximately 6750 km *4195 miles.*

The length of the Nile watercourse, as surveyed by M. Devroey (Belgium) before the loss of a few miles of meanders due to the formation of Lake Nasser, behind the Aswan High Dam, was 6670 km *4145 miles.* This course is unitary from a hydrological standpoint and runs from the source in Burundi of the Luvironza branch of the Kagera feeder of the Victoria Nyanza via the White Nile (*Bahr el-Jebel*) to the delta in the Mediterranean.

The longest river in Great Britain is the Severn, which empties into the Bristol Channel and is 354 km *220 miles* long. Its basin extends over 11 419 km² *4409 miles².* It rises in north-western Powys, Wales, and flows through Shropshire, Hereford and Worcester, Gloucestershire and Avon. With 17 tributaries, it has more than any other British river.

The longest river wholly in England is the Thames, which is 346 km *215 miles* long to The Nore. Its highest and remotest source is at Seven Springs, Gloucs (213 m

c. *700 ft*), source of the River Churn, a tributary which enters the Thames at Cricklade. The traditional source of the Thames proper is Trewsbury Mead, Coates, near Cirencester, Gloucs. The basin measures 12 934 km² *4994 miles².* The Yorkshire Ouse's 11 tributaries aggregate 1012 km *629 miles.*

The longest river wholly in Wales is the Usk, with a freshwater length of 110·2 km *68·5 miles.* Including the tidal limit, the length increases to 137·2 km *85·3 miles.* It rises on the border of Dyfed and Powys and flows out via Gwent into the Severn Estuary.

The longest river in Scotland is the Tay, with Dundee, Tayside on the shore of the estuary. It is 188 km *117 miles* long from the source of its remotest head-stream, the River Tummel, Tayside and has the greatest volume of any river in Great Britain, with a flow of up to 1400 m³/sec *49 000 cusec.* Of Scottish rivers the Tweed and the Clyde have most tributaries, with 11 each.

The longest river in Ireland is the Shannon, which is longer than any river in Great Britain. It rises 79 m *258 ft* above sea level, in Co. Cavan, and flows through a series of loughs to Limerick. It is 386 km *240 miles* long, including the 90 km *56 mile* long estuary to Loop Head. The basin area is 15 695 km² *6060 miles².*

Shortest As with the longest river, two rivers could also be considered to be the shortest river with a name. The Roe River, near Great Falls, Montana, USA, has two forks fed by a large fresh water spring. These relatively constant forks measure 61 m *201 ft* (East Fork Roe River) and 17·7 m *58 ft* (North Fork Roe River) respectively. The Roe River flows into the larger Missouri River. The D River, located at Lincoln City, Oregon, USA, connects Devil's Lake to the Pacific Ocean. Its length is officially quoted as 37 ± 1·5 m *120 ± 5 ft.*

Largest basin The largest river basin in the world is that drained by the Ama-on, which covers about 7 045 000 km² *2 720 000 miles².* It has countless tributaries and sub-tributaries, including the Madeira, which at 3380 km *2100 miles* is the longest tributary in the world, being surpassed by only 17 other rivers.

Longest estuary The world's longest estuary is that of the Ob', in the north of Russia, at 885 km *550 miles*. It is up to 80 km *50 miles* wide, and is also the widest river which freezes solid.

Largest delta The world's largest delta is that created by the Ganges (Ganga) and Brahmaputra in Bangladesh and West Bengal, India. It covers an area of 75 000 km² *30 000 miles²*.

Greatest flow The greatest flow of any river in the world is that of the Amazon, which discharges an average of 120 000 m³/sec *4 200 000 cusec* into the Atlantic Ocean, increasing to more than 200 000 m³/sec *7 000 000 cusec* in full flood. The lower 1450 km *900 miles* of the Amazon average 17 m *55 ft* in depth, but the river reaches a depth of 90 m *300 ft* in some places. The flow of the Amazon is 60 times greater than that of the Nile.

Largest swamp The world's largest tract of swamp is the Gran Pantanal of Mato Grosso state in Brazil. It is about 109 000 km² *42 000 miles²* in area.

River Bores

The bore (abrupt rise of tidal water) on the Qiantong Jiang (Hangzhou He) in eastern China is the most remarkable of the 60 in the world. At spring tides the wave attains a height of up to 7·5 m *25 ft* and a speed of 24–27 km/h *13–15 knots*. It is heard advancing at a range of 22 km *14 miles*. The annual downstream flood wave on the Mekong, in south-east Asia, sometimes reaches a height of 14 m *46 ft*. The greatest volume of any tidal bore is that of the Furo do Guajarú, a shallow channel which splits Ilha Caviana in the mouth of the Amazon.

The most notable of the eight river bores in the UK is that on the Severn, which attained a measured height of 2·8 m *9 ft 3 in* on 15 Oct 1966 downstream of Stonebench, and a speed of 20 km/h *13 mph*. It travels from Framilode towards Gloucester.

Lakes and Inland Seas

Largest The largest inland sea or lake in the world is the Caspian Sea (in

Lake in a lake
The largest lake in a lake is Manitou Lake (106·42 km² *41·09 miles²*) on the world's largest lake island, Manitoulin Island (2766 km² *1068 miles²*), in the Canadian part of Lake Huron. The lake itself contains a number of islands.

Underground lake
The world's largest underground lake is believed to be that in the Drachenhauchloch cave near Grootfontein, Namibia, discovered in 1986. When surveyed in April 1991 the surface area was found to be 2·61 ha *6·45 acres*. The surface of the lake is some 66 m *217 ft* underground, and its depth 84 m *276 ft*.

Azerbaijan, Russia, Kazakhstan, Turkmenistan and Iran). It is 1225 km *760 miles* long and its area is 371 800 km² *143 550 miles²*. Of the total area, some 143 200 km² *55 280 miles²* (38·5 per cent) are in Iran, where it is called the Darya-ye-Khazar. Its maximum depth is 1025 m *3360 ft* and the surface is 28·5 m *93 ft* below sea level. Its estimated volume is 89 600 km³ *21 500 miles³* of saline water. Its surface has varied between 32 m *105 ft* (11th century) and 22 m *72 ft* (early 19th century) below sea level. (⟺ also Depressions)

Deepest The deepest lake in the world is Lake Baikal in the southern part of eastern Siberia, Russia. It is 620 km *385 miles* long and between 32–74 km *20–46 miles* wide. In 1974 the lake's Olkhon Crevice was measured by the Hydrographic Service of the Soviet Pacific Navy and found to be 1637 m *5371 ft* deep, of which 1181 m *3875 ft* is below sea level. (⟺ also Depressions)

The deepest lake in Great Britain is the 16·57 km *10·30 mile* long Loch Morar, in Inverness. Its surface is 9 m *30 ft* above sea level and its extreme depth 310 m *1017 ft*. England's deepest lake is Wast Water (78 m *258 ft*), in Cumbria. The lake with the greatest mean depth is Loch Ness, with 130 m *427 ft*.

Highest   The highest navigable lake in the world is Lake Titicaca (maximum depth 370 m *1214 ft*, with an area of about 8290 km² *3200 miles²*) in South America (4790 km² *1850 miles²* in Peru and 3495 km² *1350 miles²* in Bolivia). It is 160 km *100 miles* long and is 3811 m *12 506 ft* above sea level. There are higher lakes in the Himalayas, but most are glacial and of a temporary nature only. A survey of the area carried out in 1984 showed a lake at a height of 5414 m *17 762 ft*, named Panch Pokhri, which was 1·6 km *1 mile* long.

The highest lake in the UK is the 0·76 ha *1·9 acre* Lochan Buidhe at 1100 m *3600 ft* above sea level in the Cairngorms, Scotland. England's highest is Broad Crag Tarn (837 m *2746 ft* above sea level) on Scafell Pike, Cumbria and the highest named freshwater lake in Wales is The Frogs Pool, a tarn near the summit of Carnedd Llywelyn, Gwynedd, at 830 m *2723 ft*.

Freshwater   The freshwater lake with the greatest surface area is Lake Superior, one of the Great Lakes of North America. The total area is 82 350 km² *31 800 miles²*, of which 53 600 km² *20 700 miles²* are in Minnesota, Wisconsin and Michigan, USA and 27 750 km² *11 100 miles²* in Ontario, Canada. It is 180 m *600 ft* above sea level. The freshwater lake with the greatest volume is Lake Baikal in Siberia, Russia, with an estimated volume of 23 000 km³ *5500 miles³*.

The largest lake in the UK is Lough Neagh (14·6 m *48 ft* above sea level) in Northern Ireland. It is 29 km *18 miles* long and 17·7 km *11 miles* wide, and has an area of 381·73 km² *147·39 miles²*. Its extreme depth is 31 m *102 ft*.

Freshwater loch   The largest lake in Great Britain, and the largest inland loch in Scotland, is Loch Lomond, which is situated in the Strathclyde and Central regions at a height of 7 m *23 ft* above sea level. It is 36·44 km *22·64 miles* long and has a surface area of 70·04 km² *27·45 miles²*. Its greatest depth is 190 m *623 ft*. The lake or loch with the greatest volume is, however, Loch Ness, with 7 443 000 000 m³ *262 845 000 000 ft³*. The longest lake or loch is Loch Ness, which measures 38·99 km *24·23 miles*, although

the three arms of the Y-shaped Loch Awe, Strathclyde aggregate 40·99 km *25·47 miles*. The largest lake in England is Windermere, in Cumbria. It is 17 km *10½ miles* long, has a surface area of 14·74 km² *5·69 miles²* and a greatest depth of 66·75 m *219 ft*, in the northern half. The largest *natural* lake in Wales is Llyn Tegid, with an area of 4·38 km² *1·69 miles²*, although the largest lake in Wales is that formed by the reservoir at Lake Vyrnwy, where the total surface area is 453·25 ha *1120 acres*.

Freshwater loughs   The largest lough in the Republic of Ireland is Lough Corrib in Mayo and Galway. It measures 43·5 km *27 miles* in length and is 11·25 km *7 miles* across at its widest point, with a total surface area of 168 km² *65 miles²*.

Largest lagoon   Lagoa dos Patos in southernmost Brazil is 280 km *174 miles* long and extends over 9850 km² *3803 miles²*.

Other Features

Desert   Nearly an eighth of the world's land surface is arid, with a rainfall of less than 25 cm *10 in* per annum. The Sahara in North Africa is the largest desert in the world. At its greatest length it is 5150 km *3200 miles* from east to west. From north to south it is between 1280 and 2250 km *800 and 1400 miles*. The area covered by the desert is about 9 269 000 km² *3 579 000 million miles²*. The land level varies from 132 m *436 ft* below sea level

Largest mirage

The largest mirage on record was that sighted in the Arctic at 83°N 103°W by Donald B. MacMillan in 1913. This type of mirage, known as the Fata Morgana, appeared as the same 'hills, valleys, snow-capped peaks extending through at least 120 degrees of the horizon' that Peary had mis-identified as Crocker Land six years earlier. On 17 Jul 1939 a mirage of Snaefells Jokull (1437 m *4715 ft*) on Iceland was seen from the sea at a distance of 540–560 km *335–350 miles*.

in the Qattâra Depression, Egypt to the mountain Emi Koussi (3415 m *11 204 ft*) in Chad. The daytime temperature in the western Sahara may vary by more than 45 deg C or *80 deg F*. Desert surfaces have been known to heat up to 82°C *180°F*.

Sand dunes The world's highest measured sand dunes are those in the Saharan sand sea of Isaouane-N-Tifernine of east central Algeria in Lat. 26° 42' N, Long. 6° 43' E. They have a wavelength of 5 km *3 miles* and attain a height of 465 m *1525 ft*.

Largest gorge The largest land gorge in the world is the Grand Canyon on the Colorado River in north-central Arizona, USA. It extends from Marble Gorge to the Grand Wash Cliffs, over a distance of 446 km *277 miles*. It averages 16 km *10 miles* in width and 1·6 km *1 mile* in depth. The submarine Labrador Basin canyon is 3440 km *c. 2150 miles* long.

Deepest canyon A canyon or gorge is generally regarded as a valley with steep rock walls and a considerable depth in relation to its width. The Grand Canyon (⬦ above) has the characteristic vertical sections of wall, but is much wider than its depth. The Vicos Gorge in the Pindus mountains of north-west Greece is 900 m *2950 ft* deep and only 1100 m *3600 ft* between its rims. Gorges in many countries have a higher depth/width ratio, but none is as deep.

The often cited Colca canyon in Peru has the cross-profile of a valley, but is neither as deep nor as steep-sided as the Kali Gandaki valley (⬦ below). The deepest submarine canyon yet discovered is one 40 km *25 miles* south of Esperance, Western Australia which is 1800 m *6000 ft* deep and 32 km *20 miles* wide.

Deepest valley The Kali Gandaki valley lies 4400 m *14 436 ft* deep between the Dhaulagiri and Annapurna ranges of the Nepal Himalayas. The closest bastions of these ranges are Tukuche Peak (6920 m *22 703 ft*) and Nilgiri North Peak (7061 m *23 166 ft*), just 18·2 km *11·3 miles* apart, with the Gandaki River in between, at an elevation of 2580 m *8464 ft*.

Cliffs The highest sea cliffs yet pinpointed anywhere in the world are those on the north coast of east Moloka'i, Hawaii near Umilehi Point, which descend 1010 m *3300 ft* to the sea at an average gradient of more than 55°.

The highest cliffs in north-west Europe are those on the north coast of Achill Island, in Co. Mayo, Republic of Ireland, which rise 668 m *2192 ft* sheer above the sea at Croaghan. The highest cliffs in the UK are the 400 m *1300 ft* Conachair cliffs on St Kilda, Western Isles (425 m *1397 ft*). The highest sheer sea cliffs on the mainland of Great Britain are at Clo Mor, 5 km *3 miles* south-east of Cape Wrath, Sutherland which drop 281 m *921 ft*. England's highest cliff (gradient more than 45°) is Great Hangman Hill, near Combe Martin, in north Devon, which descends from 318 m *1043 ft* to the sea in 300 m *984 ft*, the last 213 m *700 ft* of which is at an angle of 65°.

Natural arches The longest natural arch in the world is the Landscape Arch in the Arches National Park, 40 km *25 miles* north of Moab in Utah, USA. This natural sandstone arch spans 88 m *291 ft* and is set about 30 m *100 ft* above the canyon floor. In one place erosion has narrowed its section to 1·8 m *6 ft*. Larger, however, is the Rainbow Bridge, Utah, USA, discovered on 14 Aug 1909, which although only 82·3 m *270 ft* long, is more than 6·7 m *22 ft* wide.

Longest glaciers It is estimated that 13 600 000 km² *5 250 000 miles²*, or 9·7 per cent of the Earth's land surface, is permanently covered by glacier ice. The Antarctic ice sheet accounts for 86 per cent of this and the Greenland ice sheet 11 per cent. The world's longest glacier is the Lambert Glacier, discovered by an Australian aircraft crew in Australian Antarctic Territory in 1956–7. Draining about a fifth of the East Antarctic ice sheet, it is up to 64 km *40 miles* wide and, with its seaward extension (the Amery Ice Shelf) it measures at least 700 km *440 miles* in length. The longest Himalayan glacier is the Siachen in the Karakoram range (at 75·5 km *47 miles* in length), although the Hispar and Biafo glaciers combine to form a continuous stream of ice 122 km *76 miles* long. The fastest-moving major glacier is the Jakobshavn Isbrae in Greenland, flowing at an average of 19 m *62 ft* per day.

Thickest ice The greatest recorded thickness of ice is 4·78 km *2·97 miles*

World's Strongest Earthquakes

Progressive list of instrumentally recorded earthquakes

Kanamori Scale Magnitudes M_W	Richter Scale Magnitude M_s	Location	Date
8·8	8·6	Ecuador	1906 Jan 31
9·0	8¼	Kamchatka, Russia (then USSR)	1952 Nov 4
9·1	7¾	Andreanof Islands, Aleutian Islands, USA	1957 Mar 9
9·5	8·3	Chile	1960 May 22

$\log E = 1 \cdot 5M + 4 \cdot 8$ (joules)

measured by radio echo soundings from a US Antarctic research aircraft at 69° 9′ 38″ S, 135° 20′ 25″ E, 400 km *250 miles* from the coast in Wilkes Land on 4 Jan 1975.

Deepest permafrost The deepest recorded permafrost is more than 1370m *4500ft*, reported from the upper reaches of the Viluy River, Siberia, Russia in February 1982.

Natural Phenomena

Avalanches

Greatest The greatest natural avalanches, though rarely observed, occur in the Himalayas but no estimates of their volume have been published. It was estimated that 3 500 000 m³ *120 000 000 ft³* of snow fell in an avalanche in the Italian Alps in 1885. The 400 km/h *250 mph* avalanche triggered by the Mount St Helens eruption in Washington State, USA on 18 May 1980 was estimated to measure 2800 million m³ *96 000 million ft³* (⇨ Accidents and Disasters).

Earthquakes

(Seismologists record all dates with the year *first*, based not on local time but on Universal Time/Greenwich Mean Time).

Greatest It is estimated that each year there are some 500 000 detectable seismic or micro-seismic disturbances, of which 100 000 can be felt and 1000 cause damage. The deepest recorded hypocentres are of 720km *447 miles* in Indonesia in 1933, 1934 and 1943.

The scale most commonly used to measure the size of earthquakes is Richter's magnitude scale (1954). It is named after the American seismologist Dr Charles Richter (1900–85) and the most commonly used form is M_s, based on amplitudes of surface waves, usually at a period of 20 sec. The largest reported magnitudes on this scale are about 8·9, but the scale does not properly represent the size of the very largest earthquakes (those having an M_s of more than about 8), for which it is better to use the concept of seismic moment, M_o devised by K. Aki in 1966. Moment can be used to derive a 'moment magnitude', M_w, first used by Hiroo Kanamori in 1977. The largest recorded earthquake on the M_w scale is the Chilean shock of 1960 May 22, which had $M_w = 9.5$, but measured only 8.3 on the M_s scale. For the largest events, such as the Chilean 1960 earthquake, the energy released is more than 10^{19} joules.

Worst death toll The greatest estimate for a death toll is the 830000 fatalities in a prolonged earthquake (*dizhen*) in the Shaanxi, Shanxi and Henan provinces of China, of 1556 Feb 2 (new style) (Jan 23 old style). The highest death toll in modern times has been in the Tangshan earthquake (Mag. $M_s = 7.9$) in eastern China on 27 Jul 1976 (local time was 3a.m. July 28). The first figure published on 4 Jan 1977 revealed 655237 killed, later adjusted to 750000. On 22 Nov 1979 the New China News Agency inexplicably reduced the death toll to 242000. The figure of 1100000 sometimes attributed to the eastern Mediterranean earthquake of 1202 May 20 is a gross exaggeration since it includes those dying in a famine the following year. A more plausible death toll is *c.* 30000.

Material damage The greatest physical devastation was in the earthquake on the Kanto plain, Japan, of 1923 Sep 1 (Mag. $M_s = 8.2$, epicentre in Lat. 35°15'N, Long. 139°30'E); in Sagami Bay the sea bottom in one area sank 400 m *1310 ft*. The official total of persons killed and missing in this *Shinsai* or great 'quake and the resultant fires was 142807. In Tokyo and Yokohama 575000 dwellings were destroyed. The cost of the damage was estimated at £1 billion.

Great Britain and Ireland The East Anglian or Colchester earthquake of 1884 Apr 22 (9:18a.m.) (epicentre Lat. 51°49'N, Long. 0°54'E) caused damage estimated at more than £12000 to 1250 buildings. Langenhoe Church was wrecked. Windows and doors were rattled over an area of 137250 km² *53000 miles²* and the shock was felt in Exeter, Devon and Ostend, Belgium. It is estimated to be Mag. 4.4 on the Richter scale.

The highest instrumentally measured Magnitude is 5.5 for the Dogger Bank event of 1931 Jun 7. The highest measured on land was 4.8 for the North Wales earthquake of 1984 Jul 19. The strongest Scottish tremor occurred at Inverness at 10:45p.m. on 1816 Aug 13, and was felt over an area of 130000 km² *50000 miles²*.

The strongest Welsh tremor occurred in Swansea at 9:45a.m. on 1906 Jun 27 (epicentre Lat. 51°38'N, Long. 4°W). It was felt over an area of 97900 km² *37800 miles²*.

No earthquake with its epicentre in Ireland has yet been instrumentally measured, though the effects of the North Wales shock (⬦ above) dislocated traffic lights in Dublin.

Tallest The Waimangu (Maori 'black water') geyser, in New Zealand, erupted to a height in excess of 460 m *1500 ft* in 1903, when it was erupting every 30–36 hours, but has not been active since late 1904. Currently the world's tallest active

Worst British earthquake

The total of the undisputed death toll for Great Britain is two—an apprentice, Thomas Grey, struck by falling masonry from Christ's Hospital Church, near Newgate, London at 6 p.m. on 6 Apr 1580, and another young person, Mabel Everet, who died of injuries four days later. The shock was centred in the Straits of Dover.

Tallest geyser

Four people were killed in August 1903 during one of Waimangu's violent eruptions (⬦ 'Geysers' above). They were standing 27 m *90 ft* away, but their bodies were found up to 800 m *½ mile* away. One was jammed between two rocks, one in a hole in the ground, one suspended in a tree and the fourth on flat ground.

37

Violent
Volcanoes

When Mount Pinatubo in the Philippines erupted in 1991, the whole world saw the destruction which an erupting volcano can cause. The total volume of matter discharged was some 9 km³ (2 miles³), but this was not even the greatest eruption this century. Novarupta, in Alaska, holds this honour, yet pales into insignificance compared to past eruptions, as the chart shows.

Lava flows records

Longest ever
Pomona, Washington State, USA; 500 km *300 miles* long, 15 million years ago.

Largest in historic times
Laki, Iceland; 65 km *40 miles*, 1783.

Most continuous eruption
Kilauea, Hawaii; Continuous lava outpouring since 1983 at 5 m³ *7 yd³* per second. Still erupting.

Most rapid flow
Nyiragongo, Zaïre (breach of crater lake); 60–70 km/h *35–45 mph*, 1977.

Artwork: Peter Harper

(Photo: Gamma/Flanchenault)

In terms of lives lost, the most devastating volcanic eruption was that of Tambora, on the Indonesian island of Sumbawa in April 1815. Some 92 000 people lost their lives either directly, or as a result of the tsunamis — tidal waves — and the famine which followed. The eruption had far-reaching consequences, with an unusually cold summer in Europe and North America in 1816.

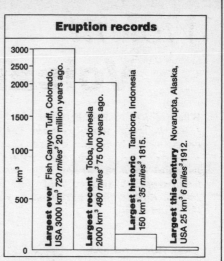

Eruption records

(km³ scale: 0, 500, 1000, 1500, 2000, 2500, 3000)

Largest ever Fish Canyon Tuff, Colorado, USA 3000 km³ *720 miles³* 20 million years ago.

Largest recent Toba, Indonesia 2000 km³ *480 miles³* 75 000 years ago.

Largest historic Tambora, Indonesia 150 km³ *35 miles³* 1815.

Largest this century Novarupta, Alaska, USA 25 km³ *6 miles³* 1912.

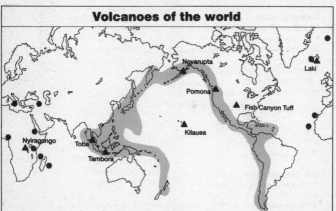

Volcanoes of the world

(Map labels: Novarupta, Laki, Pomona, Fish Canyon Tuff, Kilauea, Nyiragongo, Toba, Tambora)

The name volcano derives from the now dormant Vulcano Island (from the god of fire Vulcanus) in the Mediterranean. The total number of volcanoes in the world which might be described as active (believed to have erupted in the past 10 000 years) is 1343, of which many are submarine. The greatest active concentration is in the so-called *Ring of Fire* (shown in shaded area on the map), which runs down the west coast of the Americas from Alaska to Chile and in a similar fashion down the east coast of Asia from Russia to New Zealand. It contains around 75 per cent of the world's active volcanoes. Volcanic activity has also occurred in various other parts of the world, and some of the most notable of these are shown as circles. Antarctica, although not shown on the map, also has volcanoes, including two which were only discovered in the 1980s.

geyser is Steamboat Geyser in Yellowstone National Park, Wyoming, USA. During the 1980s it erupted at intervals ranging from 19 days to more than four years, although there were occasions in the 1960s when it erupted as frequently as every 4–10 days. The maximum height ranges from 60–115 m *195–380 ft*. The greatest measured water discharge was an estimated 28 000–38 000 hl *616 000–836 000 gal* by the Giant Geyser, also in Yellowstone National Park. However, this estimate, made in the 1950s, was only a rough calculation.

Volcanoes

Greatest explosion The greatest explosion in historic times (possibly since Santoriní in the Aegean Sea, 95 km *60 miles* north of Crete, in 1628 BC) occurred at *c.* 10 a.m. (local time), or 3.00 a.m. GMT, on 27 Aug 1883, with an eruption of Krakatoa, an island (then 47 km² *18 miles²*) in the Sunda Strait, between Sumatra and Java, in Indonesia. One hundred and sixty-three villages were wiped out, and 36 380 people killed by the wave it caused. Pumice was thrown 55 km *34 miles* high and dust fell 5330 km *3313 miles* away 10 days later. The explosion was recorded four hours later on the island of Rodrigues, 4776 km *2968 miles* away, as 'the roar of heavy guns', and was heard over one thirteenth of the surface of the globe. This explosion, estimated to have had about 26 times the power of the greatest H-bomb test (by the USSR), was still only a third of the Santoriní cataclysm.

Greatest eruption The total volume of matter discharged in the eruption of Tambora, a volcano on the Indonesian island of Sumbawa, from 5–10 Apr 1815, was 150–180 km³ *36–43 miles³*. This compares with a probable 60–65 km³ *14–16 miles³* ejected by Santoriní (⇨ above) and 20 km³ *5 miles³* ejected by Krakatoa (⇨ above). The energy of the Tambora eruption, which lowered the height of the island by 1250 m *4100 ft* from 4100 m *13 450 ft* to 2850 m *9350 ft*, was 8.4×10^{19} joules. A crater 8 km *5 miles* in diameter was formed. More than 90 000 were killed or died as a result of the subsequent famine.

The ejecta in the Taupo eruption in New Zealand *c.* AD 130 has been estimated at 30 000 million tonnes of pumice moving at one time at 700 km/h *400 mph*. It flattened 16 000 km² *6200 miles²* (over 26 times the devastated area of Mount St Helens, which erupted in Washington State, USA on 18 May 1980). Less than 20 per cent of the 14×10^9 tonnes of pumice carried up into the air in this most violent of all documented volcanic events fell within 200 km *125 miles* of the vent.

Longest lava flow The longest lava flow in historic times is a mixture of *pahoehoe* ropey lava (twisted cord-like solidifications) and *aa* blocky lava, resulting from the eruption of Laki in 1783 in south-east Iceland, which flowed 65–70 km *40½–43½ miles*. The largest known prehistoric flow is the Roza basalt flow in North America *c.* 15 million years ago, which had an unsurpassed length (300 km *190 miles*), area (40 000 km² *15 400 miles²*) and volume (1250 km³ *300 miles³*).

Largest active Mauna Loa, on Hawaii, has the shape of a broad gentle dome 120 km *75 miles* long and 50 km *31 miles* wide (above sea level), with lava flows which occupy more than 5125 km² *1980 miles²* of the island. It has a total volume of 42 500 km³ *10 200 miles³*, of which 84·2 per cent is below sea level. Its caldera, Mokuaweoweo, measures 10·5 km² *4 miles²* and is 150–180 m *500–600 ft* deep. Mauna Loa rises 4170 m *13 680 ft* and has averaged one eruption every 4½ years since 1843, although none since 1984.

Highest active The highest volcano regarded as active is Ojos del Salado (which has fumaroles), at a height of 6887 m *22 595 ft*, on the frontier between Chile and Argentina.

Northernmost and southernmost The northernmost volcano is Beeren Berg (2276 m *7470 ft*) on the island of Jan Mayen (71°05′N) in the Greenland Sea. It erupted on 20 Sep 1970 and the island's 39 inhabitants (all male) had to be evacuated. It was possibly discovered by Henry Hudson the English navigator and explorer (died 1611) in 1607 or 1608, but was definitely visited by Jan Jacobsz Mayen (Netherlands) in 1614. It was annexed by Norway on 8 May 1929.

The Ostenso seamount (1775 m *5825 ft*), 556 km *346 miles* from the North Pole in Lat. 85° 10′ N, Long. 133° W, was volcanic. The most southerly known active volcano is Mt Erebus (3794 m *12 447 ft*), on Ross Island (77° 35′ S) in Antarctica. It was discovered on 28 Jan 1841 by the expedition of Capt. (later Rear-Admiral Sir) James Clark Ross, RN (1800–62), and first climbed at 10 a.m. on 10 Mar 1908 by a British party of five, led by Prof. (later Lt-Col. Sir) Tannatt William Edgeworth David (1858–1934).

Largest crater The world's largest caldera (Spanish *caldaria*, boiling pot) or volcano crater is that of Toba, north-central Sumatra, Indonesia, covering 1775 km² *685 miles²*.

Weather

The meteorological records given below necessarily relate largely to the last 150–170 years, since data before that time are both sparse and often unreliable. Reliable registering thermometers were introduced as recently as *c.* 1820. The longest continuous observations have been maintained at the Radcliffe Observatory, Oxford since 1815, though discontinuous records have enabled the Chinese to assert that 903 BC was a very bad winter.

Palaeo-entomological evidence is that there was a southern European climate in England *c.* 90 000 BC, while in *c.* 6000 BC the mean summer temperature reached 19° C *67° F*, or 3 deg C *6 deg F* higher than the present. It is believed that 1·2 million years ago the world's air temperature averaged 35° C *95° F*. The earliest authentic recording of British weather relates to the period 26 Aug–17 Sep 55 BC. The earliest reliably known hot summer was in AD 664 during our driest-ever century and the earliest known severe winter was that of AD 763–4. In 1683–4 there was frost in London from November to April. Frosts were recorded during August in the period 1668–89.

Most equable temperature The location with the most equable recorded temperature over a short period is Garapan, on Saipan in the Mariana Islands, Pacific Ocean. During the nine years from 1927–35, inclusive, the lowest temperature recorded was 19·6° C *67·3° F* on 30 Jan 1934 and the highest was 31·4° C *88·5° F* on 9 Sep 1931, giving an extreme range of 11·8 deg C *21·2 deg F*. Between 1911 and 1990 the Brazilian off-shore island of Fernando de Noronha had a minimum temperature of 17·7° C *63·9° F* on 27 Feb 1980 and a maximum of 32·2° C *90·0° F* on 3 Mar 1968, 25 Dec 1972 and 17 Apr 1973, giving an extreme range of 14·5 deg C *26·1 deg F*.

Greatest temperature ranges The greatest recorded temperature ranges in the world are around the Siberian 'cold pole' in the east of Russia. Temperatures in Verkhoyansk (67° 33′ N, 133° 23′ E) have ranged 105 deg C *188 deg F*, from −68° C *−90° F* to 37° C *98° F*. The greatest temperature variation recorded in a day is 56 deg C *100 deg F* (a fall from 7° C *44° F* to −49° C *−56° F*) at Browning, Montana, USA on 23–24 Jan 1916.

The British record is 29 deg C *52·2 deg F* (−7° C *19·4° F* to 22° C *71·6° F*) at Tummel Bridge, Tayside on 9 May 1978.

Highest shade temperature The highest ever recorded shade temperature is 58° C *136° F* at Al'Azīzīyah, Libya (alt. 111 m *367 ft*) on 13 Sep 1922.

Longest-lasting rainbow
A rainbow lasting over three hours was reported from the coastal border of Gwynedd and Clwyd, north Wales on 14 Aug 1979.

Falsest St Swithin's Days
The legend that the weather on St Swithin's Day, celebrated on 15 July (old and new style) since AD 912, determines the rainfall for the next 40 days is one which has long persisted. There was a brilliant 13½ hr of sunshine in London on 15 Jul 1924, but 30 of the next 40 days were wet. On 15 Jul 1913 there was a downpour lasting 15 hr, yet it rained on only nine of the subsequent 40 days in London.

Death Valley in south-east California, USA can make a justifiable claim to be the hottest place, having experienced temperatures of over 120°F *49°C* on 43 consecutive days in 1917. It is 225km *140 miles* long and 8km *5 miles* wide at its narrowest point. The name dates from the mid 19th century, when a group of migrants endured great suffering whilst crossing it. One of the series of mountains adjoining it is called Funeral Mountain.

(Photo: Spectrum Colour Library/ G.R. Richardson)

The highest in Britain is 37·1°C *98·8°F* at Cheltenham (Glos) on 3 Aug 1990. The 38°C *100°F* which was once reported from Tonbridge (Kent) was a non-standard exposure and is estimated to be equivalent to 36–37°C *97–98°F*.

Hottest place On an annual mean basis, with readings taken over a six-year period from 1960 to 1966, the temperature at Dallol, in Ethiopia, was 34°C *94°F*. In Death Valley, California, USA, maximum temperatures of over 120°F *49°C* were recorded on 43 consecutive days, between 6 Jul and 17 Aug 1917. At Marble Bar, Western Australia (maximum 121°F *49°C*), 162 consecutive days with maximum temperatures of over 100°F *38°C* were recorded between 30 Oct 1923 and 8 Apr 1924. At Wyndham, also in Western Australia, the temperature reached 90°F *32°C* or more on 333 days in 1946.

In Britain, annual mean temperatures of 11·5°C *52·7°F* were recorded both at Penzance, in Cornwall, and the Isles of Scilly in the period 1931 to 1960.

42

Record temperature change

FORECASTERS GOT IT WRONG

An incredible weather record was set yesterday, when the town of Spearfish, in South Dakota, USA had one of the strangest mornings imaginable.

At 7.30, after a freezing night, and with the temperature rising, it was still – 4°F (–20°C), but by 7.32 it was a comparatively mild 45° F (7°C). This represents an astounding rise of 49 degrees F (27 degrees C) in two minutes, or more than 1 degree F every 2½ seconds (1 degree C every 4½ seconds). Never before has such a freakish rise been recorded.

The weather forecasters may sometimes get criticized for inaccurate predictions, but not even the people of Spearfish could really blame them this time!

Driest place

The annual mean rainfall on the Pacific coast of Chile between Arica and Antofagasta is less than 0·1mm *0·004in*.

In Britain, the lowest annual mean rainfall on record is at Lee Wick Farm, St Osyth, Essex, with 513mm *20·2in*, based on the period 1964 to 1982. The lowest rainfall recorded in a single year was 236mm *9·3in* at one station in Margate, Kent in 1921.

Longest drought Desierto de Atacama, in Chile, experiences virtually no rain, although several times a century a squall may strike a small area of it.

Britain's longest drought lasted 73 days, from 4 Mar to 15 May 1893, at Mile End, Greater London.

Most sunshine The annual average at Yuma, Arizona, USA is 90 per cent (over 4000 hr). St Petersburg, Florida, USA recorded 768 consecutive sunny days from 9 Feb 1967 to 17 Mar 1969.

The best in Britain was 78·3 per cent of the maximum possible in one month

Lightning, most times struck

The only man in the world to be struck by lightning seven times is ex-park ranger Roy C. Sullivan (US), the human lightning conductor of Virginia, USA. His attraction for lightning began in 1942 (lost big toe nail), and was resumed in July 1969 (lost eyebrows), in July 1970 (left shoulder seared), on 16 Apr 1972 (hair set on fire), on 7 Aug 1973 (new hair re-fired and legs seared), on 5 Jun 1976 (ankle injured), and he was sent to Waynesboro Hospital with chest and stomach burns on 25 Jun 1977 after being struck while fishing. In September 1983 he died by his own hand, reportedly rejected in love.

(382 hours out of 488) at Pendennis Castle, Cornwall in June 1925.

Least sunshine At the South Pole there is nil sunshine for 182 days every year and at the North Pole the same applies for 176 days.

From 18 November to 8 February each winter the south-eastern end of the village of Lochranza, Isle of Arran, Strathclyde is in shadow of mountains, and for the whole of December 1890, a figure of nil was registered at Westminster, London.

Best and worst British summers According to Prof. Gordon Manley's survey over the period 1728–1978 the best (i.e. driest and hottest) British summer was that of 1976 and the worst (i.e. wettest and coldest) that of 1879. Temperatures of more than 32°C *90°F* were recorded on 13 consecutive days (25 Jun–7 Jul 1976) within Great Britain, peaking at 35·9°C *96·6°F* in Cheltenham on 3 July. In 1983 there were 40 days with temperatures above 80°F *27°C* in Britain between 3 July–31 August, including 17 consecutively (3–19 July). London experienced its hottest month (July) since records began in 1840.

Lowest screen temperature A record low of −89·2°C *−128·6°F* was registered at Vostok, Antarctica (alt. 3419 m *11 220 ft*)

on 21 Jul 1983. The coldest permanently inhabited place is the Siberian village of Oymyakon (pop. 4000), 63° 16′ N, 143° 15′ E (700 m *2300 ft*), in Russia where the temperature reached −68°C *−90°F* in 1933, and an unofficial −72°C *−98°F* has been published more recently.

Britain's lowest was −27°C *−17°F* on 11 Feb 1895 and again on 10 Jan 1982, both times at Braemar, Grampian. The −31°C *−23°F* at Blackadder, Borders, on 4 Dec 1879, and the −29°C *−20°F* at Grantown-on-Spey on 24 Feb 1955, were not standard exposures. The lowest official temperature in England is −26°C *−15°F* at Newport, Shrops on 10 Jan 1982. The lowest maximum temperature for a day was −19·1°C *−2·4°F* at Braemar, again on 10 Jan 1982.

Coldest place Polus Nedostupnosti, Antarctica at 78°S, 96°E, is the coldest place in the world, with an extrapolated annual mean of −58°C *−72 °F*. The coldest measured mean is −57°C *−70°F*, at Plateau Station, Antarctica.

For Britain, the coldest mean temperature is 6·3°C *434°F*, at Braemar, Grampian, based on readings taken between 1952 and 1981.

Longest freeze The longest recorded unremitting freeze in the British Isles was one of 40 days at the Great Dun Fell radio station, Appleby, Cumbria, from 23 Jan to 3 Mar 1986. Less rigorous early data include a frost from 5 Dec 1607 to 14 Feb 1608 and a 91-day frost on Dartmoor, Devon in 1854–5. No temperature lower than 1°C *34°F* has ever been recorded on Bishop Rock, Isles of Scilly.

Wettest place By average annual rainfall, the wettest place in the world is Mawsynram, in Meghalaya State, India, with 11 873 mm *467½ in* per annum.

Styhead Tarn (487 m *1600 ft*), in Cumbria, with 4391 mm *173 in*, is Britain's wettest place.

Most rainy days Mt Wai-'ale-'ale (1569 m *5148 ft*), Kauai, Hawaii has up to 350 rainy days per annum.

The place in the British Isles which has had the most rainy days in a calendar year is Ballynahinch, in Co. Galway, Republic of Ireland, with 309 in 1923.

Most intense rainfall Difficulties attend rainfall readings for very short periods, but the figure of 38·1mm *1½ in* in one min at Barst, Guadeloupe on 26 Nov 1970 is regarded as the most intense recorded in modern times.

The cloudburst of 'near 2ft *600mm* in less than a quarter of half an hour' at Oxford on the afternoon of 31 May (old style) 1682 is regarded as unacademically recorded. The most intense rainfall in Britain recorded to modern standards has been 51mm *2in* in 12min at Wisbech, Cambs on 27 Jun 1970.

Greatest rainfall A record 1870mm *73·62in* of rain fell in 24 hours in Cilaos (alt. 1200m *3940ft*), La Réunion, Indian Ocean on 15 and 16 Mar 1952. This is equal to 7554 tonnes of rain per acre. For a calendar month the record is 9300mm *366 in* at Cherrapunji, Meghalaya, India in July 1861, and the 12-month record was also set at Cherrapunji, with 26 461mm *1041¾in* between 1 Aug 1860 and 31 Jul 1861.

In Great Britain, the 24-hour record is 279mm *11in* at Martinstown, Dorset on 18 and 19 Jul 1955. At Llyn Llydau, Snowdon, Gwynedd 1436mm *56½ in* fell in October 1909, and over a 12-month period, 6527mm *257in* fell at Sprinkling Tarn, Cumbria, in 1954.

Greatest flood Scientists reported the discovery of the largest fresh water flood in history in January 1993. It occurred *c.* 18 000 years ago when an ancient ice dammed-lake in the Altay Mountains of Siberia, Russia broke, allowing the water to pour out. The lake was estimated to be 120 km *75 miles* long and 760 m *2500ft* deep. The main flow of water was reported to be 490m *1600ft* deep and travelling at 160km/h *100mph*.

Windiest place The Commonwealth Bay, George V Coast, Antarctica, where gales reach 320km/h *200mph*, is the world's windiest place.

In Britain, an average reading of 33·1km/h *20·6 mph* was registered at Fair Isle in the period 1974–8.

Highest surface wind-speed A surface wind-speed of 371km/h *231mph*

was recorded at Mt Washington (1916m *6288ft*), New Hampshire, USA on 12 Apr 1934. The highest speed at a low altitude was registered on 8 Mar 1972 at the USAF base at Thule (44m *145ft*), in Greenland, when a peak speed of 333km/h *207mph* was recorded. The highest speed measured to date in a tornado is 450km/h *280mph* at Wichita Falls, Texas, USA on 2 Apr 1958.

The record high surface wind-speed for Britain is 150 knots (278km/h *172mph*), on Cairn Gorm Summit (1245m *4084ft*), on 20 Mar 1986. A figure of 285·2km/h *177·2mph*, at RAF Saxa Vord, Unst, in the Shetlands on 16 Feb 1962, was not recorded with standard equipment. British tornadoes may reach 290km/h *180 mph*. There were storms of great severity on 15 Jan 1362, 26 Nov 1703 and 16 Oct 1987.

Tornadoes (⇨ also Accidents and Disasters) Britain's strongest tornado was at Southsea, Portsmouth, Hants on 14 Dec 1810 (Force 8 on the Meaden-TORRO scale). The Newmarket tornado (Force 6) of 3 Jan 1978 caused property damage estimated at up to £1 000 000. On 23 Nov 1981, 58 tornadoes were reported in one day from Anglesey to eastern England.

Highest waterspout The highest waterspout of which there is a reliable record was one observed on 16 May 1898 off Eden, New South Wales, Australia. A theodolite reading from the shore gave its height as 1528m *5014ft*. It was about 3m *10ft* in diameter.

The Spithead waterspout off Ryde, Isle of Wight on 21 Aug 1878 was measured by sextant to be 1600m or *'about a mile'* in height. A more realistic estimate of a waterspout was one which developed off Yarmouth, Isle of Wight on 6 Aug 1987. It was some 760m *2500ft* in height.

Greatest snowfall Over a 12-month period from 19 Feb 1971 to 18 Feb 1972, 31 102mm *1224½ in* of snow fell at Paradise, Mt Rainier, in Washington State, USA. The record for a single snowstorm is 4800mm *189in* at Mt Shasta Ski Bowl, California, USA from 13–19 Feb 1959 and for a 24–hr period it is 1930mm *76 in* at Silver Lake, Colorado, USA on 14–15 Apr 1921. The greatest depth of snow on the ground was 1146 cm *37 ft 7 in* at Tamarac, California, USA in March 1911.

Britain's 12-month record is the 1524 mm *60 in* which fell in Upper Teesdale and also in the Denbighshire Hills, Clwyd, in 1947. London's earliest recorded snow was on 25 Sep 1885, and the latest on 2 Jun 1975. Less reliable reports suggest snow on 12 Sep 1658 (old style) and on 12 Jun 1791.

Most recent white Christmas and Frost Fair London has experienced eight 'white' or snowing Christmas Days since 1900. These have been 1906, 1917 (slight), 1923 (slight), 1927, 1938, 1956 (slight), 1970 and 1981. These were more frequent in the 19th century and even more so before the change of the calendar which by removing 3–13 September brought forward all dates subsequent to 2 Sep 1752 by 11 days. The last of the nine recorded Frost Fairs held on the Thames since 1564/5 was from December 1813 to 26 Jan 1814.

Heaviest hailstones The heaviest hailstones on record, weighing up to 1 kg *2¼ lb*, are reported to have killed 92 people in the Gopalganj district of Bangladesh on 14 Apr 1986.

The heaviest hailstones in Britain fell on 5 Sep 1958 at Horsham, W Sussex, and weighed 142 g *5 oz*. Much heavier ones are sometimes reported, but usually these are coalesced rather than single stones.

Cloud extremes The highest standard cloud form is cirrus, averaging 8200 m *27 000 ft* and higher, but the rare nacreous or mother-of-pearl formation may reach nearly 24 500 m *80 000 ft* (⇔ also Noctilucent clouds). Cirrus cloud is composed almost entirely of ice crystals at temperatures of −40°C *−40°F* or below. The lowest is stratus, below 460 m *1500 ft*. The cloud form with the greatest vertical range is cumulonimbus, which has been observed to reach a height of nearly 20 000 m *68 000 ft* in the tropics.

Upper atmosphere The lowest temperature ever recorded in the atmosphere is −143°C *−225°F* at an altitude of about 80–95 km *50–60 miles*, during noctilucent cloud research above Kronogård, Sweden from 27 Jul to 7 Aug 1963.

A jet stream moving at 656 km/h *408 mph* at 47 000 m *154 200 ft* (47 km *29·2 miles*) was recorded by Skua rocket above South Uist, Outer Hebrides on 13 Dec 1967.

Thunder-days In Tororo, Uganda an average of 251 days of thunder per annum was recorded for the 10-year period 1967–76. Between Lat. 35°N and 35°S there are some 3200 thunderstorms every 12 night-time hours, some of which can be heard at a range of 29 km *18 miles*.

The record number of thunder-days recorded in a specific place in a calendar year in Britain is 38, twice. The first time was in 1912, at Stonyhurst, in Lancashire, and the second was in 1967, at Huddersfield, in W Yorks.

Lightning The visible length of lightning strokes varies greatly. In mountainous regions, when clouds are very low, the flash may be less than 90 m *300 ft* long. In flat country with very high clouds, a cloud-to-earth flash may measure 6 km *4 miles*, though in the most extreme cases such flashes have been measured at 32 km *20 miles*. The intensely bright central core of the lightning channel is extremely narrow. Some authorities suggest that its diameter is as little as 1·25 cm *½ in*. This core is surrounded by a 'corona envelope' (glow discharge), which may measure 3–6 m *10–20 ft* in diameter.

The speed of a discharge varies from 160–1600 km/sec *100–1000 miles/sec* for the downward leader track, and reaches up to 140 000 km/sec *87 000 miles/sec* (nearly half the speed of light) for the powerful return stroke. Every few million strokes there is a giant discharge, in which the cloud-to-earth and return strokes flash from and to the top of the thunder clouds. In these 'positive giants' energy of up to 3 billion joules (3×10^{16} ergs) has been recorded. The temperature reaches about 30 000°C, which is higher than that of the surface of the Sun.

Longest sea-level fogs Sea-level fogs—with visibility less than 900 m *1000 yd*—persist for weeks on the Grand Banks, Newfoundland, Canada, with the average being more than 120 days per year.

The duration record for Britain is 4 days 18 hours, twice, in both cases in London. The first time was from 26 Nov to 1 Dec

1948 and the second from 5 to 9 Dec 1952. Lower visibilities occur at higher altitudes. Ben Nevis is reputedly in cloud 300 days per year.

Barometric pressure The highest barometric pressure ever recorded was 1083·8 mb *32 in* at Agata, Siberia, Russia (alt. 262 m *862 ft*) on 31 Dec 1968.

The highest in Britain was 1054·7 mb *31·15 in*, in Aberdeen on 31 Jan 1902. The lowest sea-level pressure was 870 mb *25·69 in* in Typhoon Tip, 480 km *300 miles* west of Guam, Pacific Ocean, in Lat. 16° 44′ N, Long. 137° 46′ E, on 12 Oct 1979. Britain's lowest was 925·5 mb *27·33 in*, at Ochtertyre, near Crieff, Tayside on 26 Jan 1884.

Humidity and discomfort Human comfort or discomfort depends not merely on temperature but on the combination of temperature, humidity, radiation and wind-speed. The United States Weather Bureau uses a Temperature-Humidity Index, which equals two-fifths of the sum of the dry and wet bulb thermometer readings plus 15. A THI of 98·2 has been twice recorded in Death Valley, California—on 27 Jul 1966 (119°F and 31 per cent) and on 12 Aug 1970 (117°F and 37 per cent).

Gems, Jewels and Precious Stones

Largest 3106 carats. This was found on 26 Jan 1905 at the Premier Diamond Mine, near Pretoria, South Africa. It was named *The Cullinan* after Thomas Cullinan (knighted 1910) who was chairman of the syndicate that discovered the diamond pipe three years earlier. It was cut into 106 polished diamonds and produced the largest cut fine quality colourless diamond which weighs 530·2 carats. Several large pieces of low quality diamonds have been found including a carbonado of 3167 carats discovered in Brazil in 1905, but these stones are of very poor quality. Currently the largest known single piece of rough diamond still in existence weighs 1462 carats and is retained by De Beers Central Selling Organisation in London for exhibition purposes.

Largest natural intense fancy blue 45·52 carats, known as the *Hope Diamond* after a London banker Henry Thomas Hope. The diamond has a long and complex history and is now on display in the Smithsonian Institute, Washington, D.C., USA.

Smallest brilliant cut 0·000102 carats, polished by D. Drukker & Zn NV of Amsterdam, Netherlands in 1985. The stone was polished with all 57 facets and has a diameter of 0·22 mm *0·009 in*.

Rarest colour Blood red. The largest is a 5·05 carat flawless stone found in Lichtenburg, South Africa in 1927; it is now owned by a private collector of fancy coloured diamonds.

Highest priced $12 760 000 for an 11-sided pear-shaped mixed cut diamond of 101·84 carats. The stone is now known as the *Mouwad Splendour*, and was bought at Sotheby's, Geneva, Switzerland on 14 Nov 1990.

The highest price known to be paid for a rough diamond was £5·8 million ($10 million) for a 255·10 carat stone from Guinea, by the William Goldberg Diamond Corporation in partnership with the Chow Tai Fook Jewellery Co. Ltd of Hong Kong, in March 1989. *Many polished diamond sales are considered private transactions and the prices paid are not disclosed.*

Largest cut diamond

The Unnamed Brown weighs 545·67 carats. It was fashioned from a 755·50 carat rough into a fire rose cushion cut and acted as the forerunner to the Centenary Diamond, the world's largest flawless top colour modern fancy cut diamond at 273·85 carats. Both stones were found at the Premier Diamond Mine and were designed by master cutter Gabi Tolkowsky. The stones are owned by De Beers Consolidated Mines Ltd.

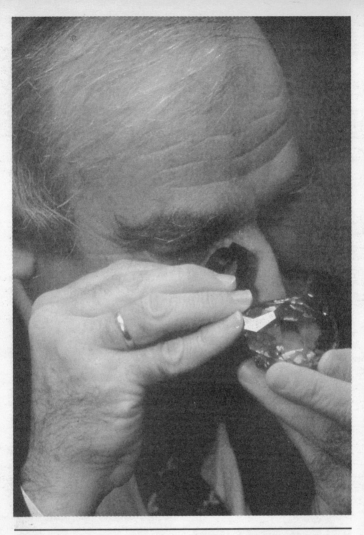

Gabi Tolkowsky examines the largest cut diamond — see details on p. 47.

(Photo: De Beers)

The record per carat is $926 315·79, for a 0·95 carat fancy purplish red stone sold at Christie's, New York, USA on 28 Apr 1987.

Largest star 6465 carats. The *Eminent Star* ruby, believed to be of Indian origin, is owned by Eminent Gems Inc. of New York, USA. It is an oval cabochon with a six ray star, and measures 109 × 90·5 × 58 mm *4¼ × 3⅝ × 2¼ in.*

Largest 8500 carats. In July 1985 jeweller James Kazanjian of Beverly Hills, California, USA displayed a 14cm *5½ in* tall red corundum carved in the form of the Liberty Bell.

Highest priced $4 620 000. A ruby and diamond ring made by Chaumet in Paris, France, weighing 32·08 carats was sold at Sotheby's, New York, USA on 26 Oct 1989. The record per carat is $227300 for a ruby ring with a stone weighing 15·97 carats, which was sold at Sotheby's, New York, USA on 18 Oct 1988.

Emerald

Largest cut 86 136 carats. A natural beryl was found in Carnaiba, Brazil in August 1974. It was carved by Richard Chan in Hong Kong and valued at £718000 in 1982.

Largest single crystal 7025 carats. The largest single emerald crystal of gem quality was found in 1969 at the Cruces Mine, near Gachala, Colombia, and is owned by a private mining concern. Larger Brazilian and Russian stones do exist, but they are of low quality.

Highest priced $3 080 000 (Single lot of emeralds). An emerald and diamond necklace made by Cartier, London in 1937 (a total of 12 stones weighing 108·74 carats) was sold at Sotheby's, New York, USA on 26 Oct 1989. The highest price for a single emerald is $2 126 646, for a 19·77 carat emerald and diamond ring made by Cartier in 1958, which was sold at Sotheby's, Geneva, Switzerland on 2 Apr 1987. This also represented the record price per carat for an emerald, at $107 569.

Sapphire

Largest carved 2302 carats. Found at Anakie, Queensland, Australia in *c.* 1935, this corundum was carved into a 1318 carat head of Abraham Lincoln and is now in the custody of the Kazanjian Foundation of Los Angeles, California, USA.

Largest star 9719·50 carats. A stone, cut in London in November 1989, has been named *The Lone Star* and is owned by Harold Roper.

Highest priced $2 791 723. A step-cut stone of 62·02 carats was sold as a sapphire and diamond ring at Sotheby's, St Moritz, Switzerland on 20 Feb 1988.

Crystal Ball

Largest 48·62 kg *106·75 lb.* The world's largest flawless rock crystal ball is 33 cm *13 in* in diameter, and was cut in China from Burmese rough material. It is now in the Smithsonian Institution in Washington, DC, USA.

Opal

Largest 26350 carats. The largest single piece of gem quality white opal was found in July 1989 at the Jupiter Field at Coober Pedy in South Australia. It has been named *Jupiter-Five* and is in private ownership.

Largest polished opal 3749 carats. The largest free-form cabochon cut precious opal is named *Galaxy*, and measures 139·7 × 101·6 × 41·1 mm *5½ × 4 × 1⅝ in.* It was excavated in Brazil in 1976.

Largest black opal 1520 carats. A stone found on 4 Feb 1972 at Lightning Ridge, New South Wales, Australia produced this finished gem, called the *Empress of Glengarry.* It measures 121 × 80 × 15 mm *4¾ × 3⅛ × ⅝ in,* and is owned by Peter Gray.

Largest rough black opal 2020 carats. The largest gem quality uncut black opal was also found at Lightning Ridge, on 3 Nov 1986. After cleaning it measures 100 × 66 × 63 mm *4 × 2⅝ × 2½ in.* It has been named *Halley's Comet* and is owned by a team of opal miners known as The Lunatic Hill Syndicate.

Pearl

Largest 6·37kg *14lb 1oz.* The *Pearl of Lao-tze* (also known as the *Pearl of Allah*) was found at Palawan, Philippines on 7 May 1934 in the shell of a giant clam. The property of Wilburn Dowell Cobb until his death, this molluscan concretion, 24 cm *9½ in* long by 14 cm *5½ in* diameter, was bought at auction on 15 May 1980 in San Francisco, California, USA by Peter Hoffman and Victor Barbish for $200 000. An appraisal by the San Francisco Gem Laboratory in May 1984 suggested a value of $40–42 million.

Largest abalone pearl 469·13 carats. A baroque abalone pearl measuring 7 × 5 × 2·8cm *2¾ × 2 × 1⅛ in* was found at Salt Point State Park, California, USA in May 1990. It is owned by Wesley Rankin and is called the *Big Pink*. It has been valued at US$4·7 million.

Largest cultured pearl 138·25 carats. A 40 mm *1½ in* round cultured pearl weighing 27·65g *1 oz* was found near Samui Island, off Thailand, in January 1988. The stone is owned by the Mikimoto Pearl Island Company, Japan.

Highest priced $864 280. *La Régente*, an egg-shaped pearl weighing 15·13g *302·68 grains* and formerly part of the French Crown Jewels, was sold at Christie's, Geneva, Switzerland on 12 May 1988.

Topaz

Largest 22 892·5 carats. The rectangular, cushion-cut *American Golden Topaz*, with 172 facets and 149·2mm *5⅞ in* in overall width, has been on display at the Smithsonian Institution, Washington, DC, USA since 4 May 1988.

Jade

Largest 577 tonnes. A single lens of nephrite jade was found in the Yukon Territory of Canada by Max Rosequist in July 1992. It is owned by Yukon Jade Ltd.

Amber

Largest 15·25 kg *33 lb 10 oz*. The 'Burma Amber' is located in the Natural History Museum, London. Amber is a fossil resin derived from extinct coniferous trees, and often contains trapped insects.

Gold

Largest nugget 214·32 kg *7560 oz*. The *Holtermann Nugget*, found on 19 Oct 1872 in the Beyers & Holtermann Star of Hope mine, Hill End, New South Wales, Australia, contained some 99·8 kg *220 lb* of gold in a 285·7 kg *630 lb* slab of slate.

Largest pure nugget 69·92kg *2248 troyoz*. The *Welcome Stranger*, found at Moliagul, Victoria, Australia in 1869, yielded 69·92kg *2248 troyoz* of pure gold from 70·92kg *2280¼ oz*.

Platinum

Largest 9635 g *340 oz*. The largest platinum nugget ever found was discovered in the Ural Mountains in Russia in 1843, but was melted down shortly after its discovery.

Largest existing 7860 g *277 oz*. The largest surviving platinum nugget is known as the *Ural Giant* and is currently in the custody of the Diamond Foundation in the Kremlin, Moscow, Russia.

Living World

- **General Records**
- **Animal Kingdom**
- **Species on the Brink**
- **Extinct Animals**
- **Plant Kingdom**
- **Protista, Fungi, Procaryota**
- **Parks, Zoos, Oceanaria, Aquaria**

Animal Kingdom

Unless otherwise stated, all measurements refer to adult specimens.

General Records

Noisiest The low-frequency pulses made by blue whales when communicating with each other have been measured at up to 188 decibels, making them the loudest sounds emitted by any living source. They have been detected 850 km *530 miles* away.

The world's noisiest land animals are the howling monkeys (*Alouatta*) of Central and South America. The males have an enlarged bony structure at the top of the windpipe which enables the sound to reverberate, and their fearsome screams have been described as a cross between the bark of a dog and the bray of an ass increased a thousandfold. Once in full voice they can be heard clearly up to 16 km *10 miles* away.

Most fertile It has been calculated that a single cabbage aphid (*Brevicoryne brassicae*) can give rise in a year to a mass of descendants weighing 822 million tonnes, or more than three times the total weight of the world's human population. Fortunately the mortality rate is tremendous.

Strongest In proportion to their size, the strongest animals are the larger beetles of the family Scarabaeidae, which are found mainly in the tropics. In tests carried out on a rhinoceros beetle of the family Dynastinae, it was found that it could support 850 times its own weight on its back (cf. 25 per cent of its bodyweight for an elephant).

Strongest bite Experiments carried out with a Snodgrass gnathodynamometer

---

Sponges, which are made up of a mass of cells and fibres, can not only restore damaged or lost parts, but adults can also undergo complete regeneration from fragments or even individual cells. This fingerlike *Latrunculia corticata* of the Red Sea is just one of about 5000 known species.

(Photo: Planet Earth Pictures/ Warren Williams)

(shark-bite meter) at the Lerner Marine Laboratory in Bimini, Bahamas revealed that a 2m *6 ft 6¾ in* long dusky shark (*Carcharhinus obscurus*) could exert a force of 60kg *132 lb* between its jaws. This is equivalent to a pressure of 3 tonnes/cm² or *19·6 tons/in²* at the tips of the teeth.

Suspended animation In 1846 two specimens of the desert snail *Eremina desertorum* were presented to the British Museum (Natural History) as dead exhibits. They were glued to a small tablet and placed on display. Four years later, in March 1850, the Museum staff, suspecting that one of the snails was still alive, removed it from the tablet and placed it in tepid water. The snail moved and later began to feed. This hardy little creature lived for a further two years before it fell into a torpor and died.

Regeneration The sponge (*Porifera*) has the most remarkable powers of regeneration of lost parts of any animal, as it can regrow its entire body from a tiny fragment of itself. If a sponge is squeezed through a fine-meshed silk gauze, the separate fragments can reform into a full-size sponge.

Most dangerous The world's most dangerous animals (excluding Man) are the malarial parasites of the genus *Plasmodium* carried by mosquitoes of the genus *Anopheles*, which, if we exclude wars and accidents, have probably been responsible directly or indirectly for 50 per cent of all human deaths since the Stone Age. Even today, despite major campaigns to eradicate malaria, at least 200 million people are afflicted by the disease each year, and more than one million babies and children die annually from it in Africa alone.

Oldest land animals

Animals moved from the sea to the land 414 million years ago, according to discoveries made in 1990 near Ludlow, Shrops. The first land animals include two kinds of centipede and a tiny spider found among plant debris, suggesting that life moved on to land much earlier than previously thought.

Most poisonous The most active known poison is the batrachotoxin derived from the skin secretions of the golden poison-dart frog (*Phyllobates terribilis*), which was not discovered until 1973 in western Colombia. Its skin secretions are at least 20 times more toxic than those of any other known poison-dart frog (human handlers have to wear thick gloves), and an average specimen contains enough poison (1900 micrograms) to kill nearly 1500 people. Rather surprisingly, this species is preyed upon by the frog-eating snake (*Leimadophis epinephelus*), which is obviously immune to its poison.

Largest colonies The black-tailed prairie dog (*Cynomys ludovicianus*), a rodent of the family Sciuridae found in the western USA and northern Mexico, builds the largest colonies. One single 'town' found in 1901 contained about 400 million individuals and was estimated to cover 61 440 km² *24 000 miles²*.

Greatest concentration The greatest concentration of animals ever recorded was a huge swarm of Rocky Mountain locusts (*Melanoplus spretus*) which passed over Nebraska, USA on 15–25 Aug 1875. According to one local scientist who watched their movements for five days, these locusts covered an area of 514 374 km² *198 600 miles²* as they flew over the state. If he overestimated the size by 50 per cent (most locusts do not fly at night), the swarm still covered 257 187 km² *99 300 miles²*, which is some 13 000 km² *5000 miles²* greater than the area of the United Kingdom. It has been calculated that this swarm of locusts contained at least 12·5 trillion ($12·5 \times 10^{12}$) insects, weighing 25 million tonnes. For reasons unexplained this pest mysteriously disappeared in 1902 and has not been seen since.

Most prodigious eater The larva of the polyphemus moth (*Antheraea polyphemus*) of North America consumes an amount equal to 86 000 times its own birthweight in the first 56 days of its life. In human terms, this would be equivalent to a 3·17 kg *7 lb* baby taking in 273 tonnes of nourishment.

Greatest weight loss During a 7-month lactation period, a 120-tonne female blue whale (*Balaenoptera mus-*

culus) can lose up to 25 per cent of her bodyweight nursing her calf.

Most valuable The most valuable animals in cash terms are thoroughbred racehorses. The most paid for a yearling is $13·1 million on 23 Jul 1985 at Keeneland, Kentucky, USA by Robert Sangster and partners for *Seattle Dancer*. (⇨ Horse Racing)

Size difference Although many differences exist in the animal world between the male and female of any species, the most striking difference in size can be seen in the marine worm *Bonellia viridis*. The females of this species are 10–100 cm *4–40 in* long compared with just 1–3 mm *0·04–0·12 in* for the male, thus also making the females millions of times heavier than the males.

Slowest growth The slowest growth rate in the Animal Kingdom is that of the deep-sea clam *Tindaria callistisormis*, which takes about 100 years to reach a length of 8 mm *⅓ in*. It is found in the North Atlantic.

Largest eye The Atlantic giant squid has the largest eye of any animal—living or extinct. It has been estimated that the eyes of the heaviest squid, found at Thimble Tickle Bay, Newfoundland, Canada, measured 400 mm *15¾ in* in diameter—almost the width of this open book. (⇨ Molluscs)

Mammals

Mammalia

Largest The world's heaviest and longest mammal, and also the largest animal ever recorded, is the blue or sulphur-bottom whale (*Balaenoptera musculus*), also called Sibbald's rorqual. Newborn calves are 6·5–8·6 m *21 ft 3½ in–28½ ft* long and weigh up to 3 tonnes. The barely visible ovum of the blue-whale calf weighing a fraction of a milligram grows to a weight of *c.* 26 tonnes in 22¾ months, made up of 10¾ months' gestation and the first 12 months of life. This is equivalent to an increase of 3×10^{10}. (⇨ General records)

Despite being protected by law since 1967 and the implementation of a global ban on commercial whaling, the population of the blue whale has declined to tens of thousands from peak estimates of about 220 000 at the turn of the century.

Heaviest A female weighing 190 tonnes and measuring 27·6 m *90 ft 6 in* in length was caught in the Southern Ocean on 20 Mar 1947.

Longest The longest specimen ever recorded was a female measuring 33·58 m *110 ft 2½ in* landed in 1909 at Grytviken, South Georgia in the South Atlantic.

British Isles A blue whale stranded on Lewis, Western Isles *c.* 1870 was credited with a length of 32 m *105 ft*, but the carcass was cut up by the local people before this measurement could be verified and was probably exaggerated or taken along the curve of the body instead of in a straight line from the tip of the snout to the notch in the flukes (the lobes of the tail). In December 1851 the carcass of a blue whale measuring 28·87 m *94 ft 9 in* in length (girth 13·7 m *42 ft*) was brought into Bantry harbour, Co. Cork, Republic of Ireland.

Deepest dive In 1970 US scientists, by triangulating the location clicks of sperm whales (*Physeter catodon*), calculated that the *maximum* depth reached by this species was 2500 m *8202 ft*. However, on 25 Aug 1969 a bull sperm whale was killed 160 km *100 miles* south of Durban, South Africa after it had surfaced from a dive lasting 1 hr 52 min, and inside its stomach were two small sharks which had been swallowed about an hour earlier. These were later identified as of the *Scymnodon* species, a type of dogfish found only on the sea floor. The water there exceeds a depth of 3193 m *9876 ft* for a radius of 48–64 km *30–40 miles*, which suggests that the sperm whale sometimes descends to over 3000 m *9840 ft* when seeking food and is limited by pressure of time rather than by pressure of pressure.

Largest on land The largest living land animal is the African bush elephant (*Loxodonta africana*). The average bull stands 3·2 m *10 ft 6 in* at the shoulder and weighs 5·7 tonnes. The largest specimen ever recorded was a bull shot in Mucusso, Angola on 7 Nov 1974. Lying on its side this elephant measured 4·16 m

Largest litter

The greatest number of young born to a *wild* mammal at a single birth is 31 (30 of which survived) in the case of the tail-less tenrec (*Tenrec ecaudatus*), found in Madagascar and the Comoro Islands. The normal litter size is 12–15, although females can suckle up to 24.

Sleepiest

Some armadillos (Dasypodidae), opossums (Didelphidae) and sloths (Bradypodidae) spend up to 80 per cent of their lives sleeping or dozing, while it is claimed that Dall's porpoise (*Phocoenoides dalli*) never sleeps at all. (◇ also Fastest marine)

13 ft 8 in in a projected line from the highest point of the shoulder to the base of the forefoot, indicating a standing height of about 3·96 m 13 ft. Other measurements included an overall length of 10·67 m 35 ft (tip of extended trunk to tip of extended tail) and a forefoot circumference of 1·8 m 5 ft 11 in. Its weight was computed as 12·24 tonnes.

Tallest The tallest elephants are those of the endangered desert species from Damaraland, Namibia (reduced to 84 individuals in August 1981) because they have proportionately longer legs than other elephants. The tallest recorded example was a bull shot near Sesfontein, Damaraland on 4 Apr 1978 after it had allegedly killed 11 people and caused widespread crop damage. Lying on its side, this mountain of flesh measured 4·42 m 14½ ft in a projected line from the shoulder to the base of the forefoot, indicating a standing height of about 4·21 m 13 ft 10 in. Other measurements included an overall length of 10·38 m 34 ft 1 in, and a forefoot circumference of 1·57 m 5 ft 2 in. This particular animal weighed an estimated 8 tonnes.

UK Red deer (*Cervus elaphus*) stags are normally about 1·11 m 3 ft 8 in tall at the shoulder and weigh 104–113 kg 230–250 lb. The heaviest ever recorded was a stag killed at Glenfiddich,

Grampian in 1831, which weighed 238 kg 525 lb. The heaviest park red deer on record was a stag weighing 215 kg 476 lb (1·37 m 4 ft 6 in tall at the shoulder), killed at Woburn, Beds in 1836.

The so-called wild pony (*Equus caballus*) may weigh up to 320 kg 700 lb, but there are no truly feral populations living today.

Largest marine The largest toothed mammal ever recorded is the sperm whale or cachalot (*Physeter catodon*). In the summer of 1950 a record-sized bull measuring 20·7 m 67 ft 11 in was captured off the Kurile Islands in the Pacific, but much larger bulls were reported in the early days of whaling. The 5 m 16 ft 4¾ in long lower jaw of a sperm whale exhibited in the British Museum (Natural History) belonged to a bull measuring nearly 25·6 m 84 ft, and similar lengths have been reported for other outsized individuals killed.

British Isles A bull sperm whale measuring 19 m 61 ft 5 in was washed ashore at Birchington, Kent on 18 Oct 1914. Another huge bull stranded at Derryloughan, Co. Galway, Republic of Ireland on 2 Jan 1952 reportedly measured 19·8 m 65 ft, but the carcass was so badly decomposed that there must have been some length extension.

Tallest on land The tallest living animal is the giraffe (*Giraffa camelopardalis*), which is now found only in the dry savannah and semi-desert areas of Africa south of the Sahara. The tallest specimen ever recorded was a Masai bull (*G. c. tippelskirch* named 'George', received at Chester Zoo on 8 Jan 1959 from Kenya. His 'horns' *almost* grazed the roof of the 6·09 m 20 ft high Giraffe House when he was nine years old. 'George' died on 22 Jul 1969. Less credible heights of up to 7 m 23 ft (measured between pegs) have been claimed for bulls shot in the field.

Smallest on land Kitti's hog-nosed bat (*Craseonycteristhonglongyai*), also called the bumblebee bat, has a wing span of about 160 mm 6·3 in and weighs 1·75–2 g 0·06–0·07 oz. It is confined to about 21 limestone caves on the Kwae Noi River, Kanchanaburi, Thailand. (◇ Bats)

This killer whale at Sea World, California, USA would be more at home swimming at speeds of up to 55·5 km/h 34·5 mph in the open sea.

(Photo: Planet Earth Pictures/James D. Watt)

The smallest land mammal in terms of length is Savi's white-toothed pygmy shrew, also called the Etruscan shrew (*Suncus etruscus*), which has a head and body length of 36–52mm *1·32–2·04in*, a tail length of 24–29mm *0·94–1·14in* and weighs 1·5–2·5g *0·05–0·09oz*. It is found along the Mediterranean coast and southwards to Cape Province, South Africa. (⇨ Insectivores)

UK The European pygmy shrew (*Sorex minutus*) has a head and body length of 43–64mm *1·69–2·5in*, a tail length of 31–46mm *1·22–1·81in* and weighs 2·4–6·1g *0·084–0·213oz*.

Smallest marine In terms of weight, the smallest totally marine mammal is probably Commerson's dolphin (*Cephalorhynchus commersonii*), also known as Le Jacobite, which is found off the tip of South America. The weights of a group of six specimens ranged from 23 kg *51lb* to 35kg *77lb*. The sea otter (*Enhydra lutris*) of the north Pacific is of comparable size (25–38·5kg *55–81lb*), but this species sometimes comes ashore during storms.

Fastest marine On 12 Oct 1958 a bull killer whale (*Orcinus orca*) measuring an estimated 6·1–7·6 m *20–25 ft* in length was timed at 55·5km/h *34·5mph* in the east Pacific. Similar speeds have also been reported for Dall's porpoise (*Phocoenoides dalli*) in short bursts. (⇨ also Sleepiest)

Fastest on land Over a short distance (i.e. up to 550m *600yd*) the cheetah or hunting leopard (*Acinonyx jubatus*) of the open plains of east Africa, Iran, Turkmenistan and Afghanistan has a probable maximum speedof 96–101 km/h *60–63mph* on level ground.

The fastest land animal over a sustained distance (914m *1000yd* or more) is the pronghorn antelope (*Antilocapra americana*) of the western United States. Specimens have been observed to travel at 56km/h *35mph* for 6km *4 miles*, at 67km/h *42mph* for 1·6km *1 mile* and 88·5km/h *55mph* for 0·8km *½ mile*.

UK On 19 Oct 1970 a frightened runaway red deer (*Cervus elaphus*) charging through a street in Stalybridge, Greater Manchester registered 67·5km/h *42mph* on a police radar speed trap. Over a sustained distance the roe deer (*Capreolus capreolus*) can cruise at 40–48km/h *25–30mph* for more than 32km *20miles*, with occasional bursts of up to 64km/h *40mph*.

Slowest The ai or three-toed sloth (*Bradypus tridactylus*) of tropical South America has an average ground speed of 1·8–2·4m *6–8ft* per minute (0·1–0·16km/h *0·07–0·1mph*), but in the trees it can 'accelerate' to 4·6m *15ft* per minute (0·27km/h *0·17mph*).

Oldest No other mammal can match the extreme proven 120 years attained by Man (*Homo sapiens*) (⇨ Human Being), but the Asiatic elephant (*Elephas maximus*) probably comes closest. Sri Lanka's bull elephant 'Rajah', who led the annual Perahera procession through Kandi carrying the Sacred Tooth of the Buddha from 1931, died on 16 Jul 1988 allegedly aged 81 years. The greatest verified age is 78 years for a cow named 'Modoc', who died at Santa Clara, California, USA on 17 Jul 1975. She was imported from Germany in 1898 at the age of two.

Highest living The yak (*Bos grunniens*) of Tibet and the Sichuanese Alps, China occasionally climbs to altitudes of 6100m *20000ft* when foraging.

Largest herds The largest herds on record were those of the springbok (*Antidorcas marsupialis*) during migration across the plains of the western parts of southern Africa in the 19th century. In 1849 John (later Sir John) Fraser observed a *trekbokken* that took three days to pass through the settlement of Beaufort West, Cape Province. Another herd seen moving near Nels Poortje, Cape Province in 1888 was estimated to contain 100 million head, although 10 million is probably a more realistic figure. Another herd estimated to be 24 km *15 miles* wide and more than 160 km *100 miles* long was reported from Karree Kloof, Orange River, South Africa in July 1896.

Longest gestation period The Asiatic elephant (*Elephas maximus*) has an average gestation period of 609 days (over 20 months) and a maximum of 760 days—more than two and a half times that of humans.

Shortest gestation period The gestation periods of the American opossum (*Didelphis marsupialis*), also called the Virginian opossum, the rare water opossum or yapok (*Chironectes minimus*) of central and northern South America and the eastern native cat (*Dasyurus viverrinus*) of Australia are all normally 12–13 days but can be as short as eight days.

Youngest breeder The streaked tenrec (*Hemicentetes semispinosus*) of Madagascar is weaned after only five days, and females can breed 3–4 weeks after their birth.

Carnivores

Largest on land The average male Kodiak bear (*Ursus arctos middendorffi*) of Kodiak Island and the adjacent

---

Litigon
The male litigon (a hybrid of an Indian lion and a tigon—itself the offspring of a tiger and a lioness)—named 'Cubanacan' at Alipore Zoological Gardens, Calcutta, India was believed to weigh at least 363 kg *800 lb*. This unique animal stood 1·32 m *52 in* at the shoulder (cf. 1·11 m *44 in* for the lion 'Simba') and measured a record 3·5 m *11½ ft* in total length. Its death was reported on 12 Apr 1991.

Afognak and Shuyak islands in the Gulf of Alaska, USA has a nose-to-tail length of 2·4 m *8 ft*, with the tail measuring about 10 cm *4 in*. They are 1·32 m *52 in* at the shoulder and weigh 476–533 kg *1050–1175 lb*. In 1894 a weight of 751 kg *1656 lb* was recorded for a male shot at English Bay, Kodiak Island, whose *stretched* skin measured 4·11 m *13½ ft* from nose to tail. This weight was exceeded by a 'cage-fat' male weighing 757 kg *1670 lb* at the time of its death on 22 Sep 1955 in the Cheyenne Mountain Zoological Park, Colorado Springs, Colorado, USA.

Heaviest In 1981 an unconfirmed weight of over 907 kg *2000 lb* was reported for a peninsula giant bear (*Ursus a. gyas*) from Alaska on exhibition at the Space Farms Zoological Park at Beemerville, New Jersey, USA.

Weights exceeding 907 kg *2000 lb* have also been reported for the polar bear (*Ursus maritimus*), but the average male weighs 386–408 kg *850–900 lb* and measures 2·4 m *8 ft* from nose to tail. In 1960 a polar bear allegedly weighing 1002 kg *2210 lb* was shot at the polar entrance to Kotzebue Sound, Alaska, USA. This 3·38 m *11 ft 1¼ in* tall mounted specimen the was put on display at the Seattle World Fair in April 1962.

UK The largest land carnivore found in Britain is the badger (*Meles meles*). The average boar (sows are slightly smaller) is 90 cm *3 ft* long (including a 10 cm *4 in* tail) and weighs 12·3 kg *27 lb* in the early spring and 14·5 kg *32 lb* at the end of the summer when it is in 'grease'. In December 1952 a boar weighing 27·2 kg *60 lb* was killed near Rotherham, S Yorks.

Smallest The smallest member of the order Carnivora is the least weasel (*Mustela rixosa*), also called the dwarf weasel, which is circumpolar in distribution. The smallest of the four recognized races is *Mustela r. pygmaea*, which has an overall length of 177–207 mm *6·96–8·14 in* and weighs 35–70 g *1¼–2½ oz*. It is native to Siberia, Russia.

Largest feline The largest member of the cat family (Felidae) is the protected long-furred Siberian tiger (*Panthera tigris altaica*), also called the Amur or Manchurian tiger. Males average 3·15 m

Highest detectable pitch

Because of their ultrasonic echolocation, bats have the most acute hearing of any terrestrial animal. Vampire bats (family Desmodontidae) and fruit bats (Pteropodidae) can hear frequencies as high as 120–210 kHz, compared with 20 kHz for the human limit and 280 kHz for the common dolphin (*Delphinus delphis*).

---

10 ft 4 in in length from the nose to the tip of the extended tail, stand 99–107 cm *39–42 in* at the shoulder and weigh about 265 kg *585 lb*. In 1950 a male weighing 384 kg *846½ lb* was shot in the Sikhote Alin Mountains, Maritime Territory, Russia. This weight was exceeded by an Indian tiger (*Panthera t. tigris*) shot in northern Uttar Pradesh in November 1967 which measured 3·22 m *10 ft 7 in* between pegs (3·37 m *11 ft 1 in* over the curves) and weighed 389 kg *857 lb* (cf. 2·82 m *9 ft 3 in* and 190 kg *420 lb* for an average male). It is now on display at the Smithsonian Institution, Washington, DC, USA.

Captive The largest tiger ever held in captivity, and the heaviest 'big cat' on

Largest colonies

The largest concentration of bats found living anywhere in the world today is that of the Mexican free-tailed bat (*Tadarida brasiliensis*) in Bracken Cave, San Antonio, Texas, USA, where up to 20 million animals assemble after migration.

UK A bat colony in Greywell Canal Tunnel, Hants contains about 2000 individuals made up of six different species.

Deepest

The little brown bat (Myotis lucifugus) has been recorded at a depth of 1160 m *3805 ft* in a zinc mine in New York, USA. The mine serves as winter quarters for 1000 members of this species, which normally roosts at a depth of 200 m *650 ft*.

---

record, is a nine-year-old male Siberian named 'Jaipur', owned by animal trainer Joan Byron-Marasek of Clarksburg, New Jersey, USA. This tiger measured 3·32 m *10 ft 11 in* in total length and weighed 423 kg *932 lb* in October 1986.

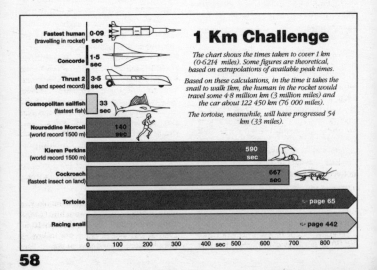

1 Km Challenge

The chart shows the times taken to cover 1 km (0·6214 miles). Some figures are theoretical, based on extrapolations of available peak times.

Based on these calculations, in the time it takes the snail to walk 1 km, the human in the rocket would travel some 4·8 million km (3 million miles) and the car about 122 450 km (76 000 miles).

The tortoise, meanwhile, will have progressed 54 km (33 miles).

Fastest human (travelling in rocket)	0·09 sec
Concorde	1·5 sec
Thrust 2 (land speed record)	3·5 sec
Cosmopolitan sailfish (fastest fish)	33 sec
Noureddine Morceli (world record 1500 m)	140 sec
Kieren Perkins (world record 1500 m)	590 sec
Cockroach (fastest insect on land)	667 sec
Tortoise	⇦ page 65
Racing snail	⇦ page 442

0   100   200   300   400   sec   500   600   700   800

Lions The average African lion (*Panthera leo*) measures 2·7m *9ft* overall, stands 91–97cm *36–38in* at the shoulder and weighs 181–185kg *400–410lb*. The heaviest wild specimen on record weighed 313kg *690lb* and was shot near Hectorspruit, Transvaal, South Africa in 1936.

UK In July 1970 a weight of 375kg *826lb* and a shoulder height of 1·11m *44in* was reported for a black-maned lion named 'Simba' (b. Dublin Zoo, 1959) at Colchester Zoo, Essex. He died on 16 Jan 1973 at the now defunct Knaresborough Zoo, N Yorks.

Smallest feline The smallest member of the cat family is the rusty-spotted cat (*Felis rubiginosa*) of southern India and Sri Lanka. Average males are 64–71cm *25–28in* long overall (the tail measures 23–25cm *9–10in*) and weigh about 1·35kg *3lb*.

Primates

Largest The male eastern lowland gorilla (*Gorilla gorilla graueri*) of eastern Zaïre and south-western Uganda is 175cm *5ft 9in* tall and weighs 165kg *360lb*. The mountain gorilla (*G. g. beringei*) of the volcanic mountain ranges of western Rwanda, south-western Uganda and eastern Zaïre is of comparable size, i.e. 173cm *5ft 8in* tall and 155kg *343lb*, and most of the exceptionally large gorillas taken in the field have been of this race.

Tallest The greatest height (top of crest to heel) recorded for a gorilla in the wild is 1·88m *6ft 2in* for a mountain bull shot in the eastern Congo (Zaïre) *c.* 1920. The tallest gorilla ever kept in captivity is reportedly an eastern lowland male named 'Colossus' (b. 1966), who is currently on display at a zoo in Gulf Breeze, Florida, USA. He allegedly stands 1·88m *6ft 2in* tall and weighs 260·8kg *575lb*, but these figures have not yet been confirmed.

Heaviest The heaviest gorilla ever kept in captivity was a male of the mountain race named 'N'gagi', who died in San Diego Zoo, California, USA on 12 Jan 1944 at the age of 18. He weighed 310kg *683lb* at his heaviest in 1943. He was

1·72m *5ft 7¾in* tall and boasted a record chest measurement of 198cm *78in*.

UK Britain's largest captive gorilla is probably 'Djoum' (b. 1969) of Howletts Zoo, Kent, whose weight is stable at 213kg *470lb*. Another male example of the western lowland gorilla (*Gorilla g. gorilla*) named 'Bukhama' (b. 1960) at Dudley Zoo, W Mids was reportedly 227kg *500lb* in 1969, but has not been weighed since.

Monkey The only species of monkey reliably credited with weights of over 45kg *100lb* is the mandrill (*Mandrillus sphinx*) of equatorial west Africa. The highest recorded weight is 54kg *119lb* for a captive male, but an unconfirmed weight of 59kg *130lb* has been reported. (Females are about half the size of males.)

Smallest The rare pen-tailed tree shrew (*Ptilocercus lowii*) of Malaysia has a total length of 230–330mm *9–13in* (head and body 100–140mm *4–5½in*; tail 130–190mm *5–7½in*) and weighs 35–50g *1·23–1·76oz*.

The pygmy marmoset (*Cebuella pygmaea*) of the Upper Amazon Basin and the lesser mouse-lemur (*Microcebus murinus*) of Madagascar are of comparable length to the shrew but heavier, weighing 50–75g *1·8–2·6oz* and 45–80g *1·6–2·8oz* respectively. The pygmy marmoset is also the smallest monkey.

Oldest The greatest age recorded for a non-human primate is 59 years 5 months for a chimpanzee (*Pan troglodytes*) named 'Gamma', who died at the Yerkes Primate Research Center in Atlanta, Georgia, USA on 19 Feb 1992. 'Gamma' was born at the Florida branch of the Yerkes Center in September 1932. A similar age was reached by a male orang-utan (*Pongo pygmaeus*) named 'Guas', who died in Philadelphia Zoological Garden, Pennsylvania, USA on 9 Feb 1977. He was at least 13 years old on his arrival at the zoo on 1 May 1931.

Monkey The world's oldest monkey, a male white-throated capuchin (*Cebus capucinus*) called 'Bobo', died on 10 Jul 1988 at the age of 53 years following complications related to a stroke.

(Seals, sea-lions, walruses)

Largest The largest of the 34 known species of pinniped is the southern elephant seal (*Mirounga leonina*) of the sub-Antarctic islands. Bulls average 5 m *16½ ft* in length from the tip of the inflated snout to the tips of the outstretched tail flippers, have a maximum girth of 3·7 m *12 ft* and weigh about 2268 kg *5000 lb*. The largest accurately measured specimen was a bull which probably weighed at least 4 tonnes and measured 6·5 m *21 ft 4 in* after flensing (stripping of the blubber or skin). Its original length was about 6·85 m *22½ ft*. It was killed in the south Atlantic at Possession Bay, South Georgia on 28 Feb 1913.

Live The largest recorded live specimen is a bull nicknamed 'Stalin' from South Georgia at 2662 kg *5869 lb* and 5·10 m *16 ½ ft* long, recorded by members of the British Antarctic Survey on 14 Oct 1989.

British Isles The largest pinniped found in British waters is the grey seal (*Halichoerus grypus*), also called the Atlantic seal. The heaviest example was a male weighing 310 kg *683½ lb* and measuring 2·45 m *8 ft* from the nose to the tip of the flippers recorded from a breeding group on Farne Islands, Northumberland.

Smallest The smallest pinnipeds are the ringed seal (*Phoca hispida*) of the Arctic, the closely related Baikal seal (*P. sibirica*) of Lake Baikal and the Caspian seal (*P. caspica*) of the Caspian Sea. Males are up to 1·67 m *5½ ft* long and can weigh up to 127 kg *280 lb*.

British Isles The average male common seal (*Phoca vitulina*) is 1·5–2·0 m *5–6½ ft* long and weighs up to 150 kg *330 lb*.

Oldest A female grey seal (*Halichoerus grypus*) shot at Shunni Wick, Shetland on 23 Apr 1969 was believed to be 'at least 46 years old' based on a count of dentine rings. The captive record is an estimated 41 years (1901–42) for a bull grey seal named 'Jacob' at Skansen Zoo, Stockholm, Sweden.

Most abundant The total population of the crabeater seal (*Lobodon carcinopha-gus*) of Antarctica was estimated in 1977 to be nearly 15 million.

Fastest The highest swimming speed recorded for a pinniped is a short spurt of 40 km/h *25 mph* by a Californian sea-lion (*Zalophus californianus*). The fastest pinniped on land is the crabeater seal (*Lobodon carcinophagus*), which has been timed at 19 km/h *12 mph*.

Deepest dive In May 1988 scientists from the University of California at Santa Cruz, USA tested the diving abilities of the northern elephant seal (*Mirounga angustirostris*) off Ano Nuevo Point, California. One female reached a record depth of 1257 m *4135 ft*, and another remained submerged for 48 minutes. Similar experiments carried out by Australian scientists on southern elephant seals (*M. leonina*) in the Southern Ocean recorded a dive of 1134 m *3720 ft*, with other dives lasting nearly two hours also observed. It was discovered that the seals regularly swam down to about 820 m *2500 ft* and when they re-surfaced apparently had no 'oxygen debt'.

Largest The only flying mammals are bats (order Chiroptera), of which there are about 950 species. The largest in terms of wing span is the Bismarck flying fox (*Pteropus neohibernicus*) of the Bismarck Archipelago and New Guinea. A specimen in the American Museum of Natural History has a wing spread of 165 cm *5 ft 5 in*, but some unmeasured bats can probably reach 183 cm *6 ft*.

UK The very rare, large mouse-eared bat (*Myotis myotis*) has a wing span of 355–450 mm *14–17¾ in* and weighs up to 45 g *1·6 oz* in the case of females.

Smallest The smallest bat in the world is Kitti's hog-nosed bat at 160 mm *6·3 in* and 1·75–2 g *0·062–0·071 oz*. (⇨ Smallest land mammal)

UK The smallest bat native to Britain is the pipistrelle (*Pipistrellus pipistrellus*), which has a wing span of 190–250 mm *7·5–10 in* and weighs 3–8 g *0·1–0·3 oz*.

Fastest Because of great practical difficulties, little information on bat speeds has been published. The greatest velocity attributed to a bat is 51 km/h *32 mph* in the case of a Mexican free-tailed bat (*Tadarida brasiliensis*), but this may have been wind-assisted. In one American experiment using an artificial mine tunnel and 17 different kinds of bat, only four managed to exceed 20.8 km/h *13 mph* in level flight.

Oldest The greatest age reliably reported for a bat is 32 years for a banded female little brown bat (*Myotis lucifugus*) in the United States in 1987.

Rodents

Largest The capybara (*Hydrochoerus hydrochaeris*), also called the carpincho or water hog, of tropical South America, has a head and body length of 1.0–1.4 m *3¼–4½ ft* and can weigh up to 113 kg *250 lb* (cage-fat specimen).

UK Britain's largest rodent was the coypu (*Myocastor coypus*), males of which were 76–91 cm *30–36 in* long (including a short tail) and weighed up to 13 kg *28 lb* in the wild (18 kg *40 lb* in captivity). Also known as the nutria, it was introduced from Argentina by East Anglian fur-breeders in 1929. Subsequent escapes led to the implementation of a Ministry of Agriculture campaign of extermination to combat the population explosion. The last coypu was killed in December 1989 and later sightings (the latest on 24 May 1993) are believed to be cases of mistaken identity.

Smallest The northern pygmy mouse (*Baiomys taylori*) of Mexico and Arizona and Texas, USA is up to 109 mm *4.3 in* in total length and weighs 7–8 g *0.24–0.28 oz*.

UK The Old World harvest mouse (*Micromys minutus*) is up to 135 mm *5.3 in* in total length and weighs 7–10 g *0.24–0.35 oz*.

Oldest The greatest reliable age reported for a rodent is 27 years 3 months for a Sumatran crested porcupine (*Hystrix brachyura*) which died in the National Zoological Park, Washington, DC, USA on 12 Jan 1965.

Fastest breeder The female meadow vole (*Microtus agrestis*), found in Britain, can reproduce from the age of 25 days and can have up to 17 litters of 6–8 young in a year.

Largest The moon rat (*Echinosorex gymnurus*), also known as Raffles' gymnure, has a head and body length of 265–445 mm *10½–17½ in*, a tail measuring 200–210 mm *7.9–8.3 in* and weighs up to 1400 g *3.1 lb*. It is found in Myanmar (Burma), Thailand, Malaysia, Sumatra and Borneo.

Heaviest The European hedgehog (*Erinaceus europaeus*) is much shorter overall (196–298 mm *7.7–11.7 in*), but well-fed examples have been known to weigh as much as 1.9 kg *4.2 lb*.

Smallest The smallest insectivore is Savi's white-toothed pygmy shrew (*Suncus etruscus*) at up to 81 mm *3.2 in* in total length and 2.2 g *0.09 oz* in weight. (<> Smallest land mammal)

Oldest The greatest reliable age recorded for an insectivore is over 16 years for a lesser hedgehog-tenrec (*Echinops telfairi*), born in Amsterdam Zoo, Netherlands in 1966 and later sent to Jersey Zoo, Channel Islands. It died on 27 Nov 1982.

Antelopes

Largest The rare giant eland (*Taurotragus derbianus*) of western and central Africa can attain a height of 1.8 m *6 ft* at the shoulder and weigh over 907 kg *2000 lb*. The common eland (*Taurotragus oryx*) of eastern and southern Africa can reach similar heights (1.78 m *5 ft 10 in*) but is not quite so massive, although there is one record of a 1.65 m *5 ft 5 in* bull shot in Malawi *c.* 1937 which weighed 943 kg *2078 lb*.

Smallest The royal antelope (*Neotragus pygmaeus*) of western Africa stands just 25–31 cm *10–12 in* tall at the shoulder and weighs 3–3.6 kg *7–8 lb*, which is the size of an average large brown hare (*Lepus europaeus*).

Lightest Salt's dik-dik (*Madoqua saltina*) of north-eastern Ethiopia and Somalia weighs only 2.2–2.7 kg *5–6 lb*, but stands about 35.5 cm *14 in* at the withers.

Oldest The greatest reliable age recorded for an antelope is 25 years 4 months for an addax (*Addax nasomaculatus*) which died in Brookfield Zoo, Chicago, Illinois, USA on 15 Oct 1960.

Largest The largest deer is the Alaskan moose (*Alces alces gigas*), bulls of which average 1·83 m *6 ft* at the shoulder and weigh about 500 kg *1100 lb*. A bull standing 2·34 m *7 ft 8 in* between pegs and weighing an estimated 816 kg *1800 lb* was shot in the Yukon Territory of Canada in September 1897. Unconfirmed measurements of up to 2·59 m *8 ft 6 in* at the shoulder and estimated weights of up to 1180 kg *2600 lb* have been claimed.

UK The largest British deer is the red deer, which is usually about 1·11 m *3 ft 8 in* tall and weighs 113 kg *250 lb*. (⇨ Largest land mammal)

Smallest The smallest true deer (family Cervidae) is the northern pudu (*Pudu mephistopheles*), which is 33–35 cm *13–14 in* tall at the shoulder and weighs 7·2–8·1 kg *16–18 lb*. It is found in Ecuador and Colombia.

The smallest ruminant is the lesser Malay chevrotain (*Tragulus javanicus*) of south-east Asia, Sumatra and Borneo, standing 20–25 cm *8–10 in* at the shoulder and weighing 2·7–3·2 kg *6–7 lb*.

Oldest The world's oldest recorded deer is a red deer (*Cervus elaphus scoticus*) named 'Bambi' (b. 8 Jun 1963), owned by the Fraser family of Kiltarlity, Beauly, Highland.

Largest The male red kangaroo (*Megaleia rufa* or *Macropus rufus*) of central, southern and eastern Australia stands up to 213 cm *7 ft* tall, measures up to 245 cm *8 ft ½ in* in total length and weighs up to 85 kg *187 lb*.

Smallest The smallest known marsupial is the rare long-tailed planigale (*Planigale ingrami*), a flat-skulled mouse of north-eastern and north-western Australia. Males have a head and body length of 55–63 mm *2·16–2·48 in*, a tail length of 57–60 mm *2·24–2·36 in* and weigh 3·9–4·5 g *0·13–0·19 oz*.

Fastest The highest speed recorded for a marsupial is 64 km/h *40 mph* for a mature female eastern grey kangaroo (*Macropus giganteus* or *M. canguru*). The highest sustained speed is 56 km/h *35 mph* recorded for a large male red kangaroo which died from its exertions after being paced for 1·6 km *1 mile*.

A red kangaroo in the Sturt National Park, New South Wales, Australia. Males can reach an overall length of 2·45 m *8 ft ½ in* and can also sustain a speed of 56 km/h *35 mph*.

(Photo: Planet Earth Pictures/ Ford Kristo)

Longest hibernation

The barrow ground squirrel (*Spermophilus parryi barrowensis*) of Point Barrow, Alaska, USA hibernates for nine months of the year. During the remaining three months it feeds, breeds and collects food for storage in its burrow.

Oldest marsupial

The greatest reliable age recorded for a marsupial is 26 years 22 days for a common wombat (*Vombatus ursinus*) which died in London Zoo on 20 Apr 1906.

Highest jump A captive eastern grey kangaroo once cleared a 2·44m *8ft* fence when a car backfired, and there is also a record of a hunted red kangaroo clearing a stack of timber 3·1m *10ft* high.

Longest jump During a chase in New South Wales, Australia in January 1951, a female red kangaroo made a series of jumps, including one of 12·8m *42ft*. There is also an unconfirmed report of an eastern grey kangaroo jumping nearly 13·5m *44ft 8½in* on the flat.

Tusks

Longest The longest recorded tusks (excluding prehistoric examples) are a pair from an elephant taken from Zaïre and kept in the New York Zoological Society in Bronx Park, New York City, USA. The right tusk measures 3·49m *11ft 5½in* along the outside curve, the left 3·35m *11ft* and their combined weight is 133kg *293lb*. A single tusk of 3·5m *11ft 6in* has also been reported.

Heaviest A pair of elephant tusks in the British Museum (Natural History) from a bull shot in Kenya in 1897 originally weighed 109kg *240lb* (length 3·11m *10ft 2½in*) and 102kg *225lb* (length 3·18m *10ft 5½in*), giving a total weight of 211kg *465lb*, but their combined weight today is 200kg *440½lb*. A single elephant tusk collected in Benin and exhibited at the Paris Exposition in 1900 weighed 117kg *258lb*.

Horns

Longest The longest horns grown by any living animal are those of the water buffalo (*Bubalus arnee=B. bubalis*) of India. One bull shot in 1955 had horns measuring 4·24m *13ft 11in* from tip to tip along the outside curve across the forehead. The longest single horn on record measured 2·06m *6ft 9¼in* along the outside curve and belonged to a specimen of domestic ankole cattle (*Bos taurus*) from near Lake Ngami, Botswana.

A record spread of 3·2m *10ft 6in* was recorded for a Texas longhorn steer on exhibition at the Heritage Museum, Big Springs, Texas, USA.

Antlers

Largest The record antler spread or 'rack' is 1·99m *6ft 6½in* (skull and antlers weighed 41kg *91lb*) for a set taken from a moose killed near the Stewart River, Yukon, Canada in October 1897 and now on display in the Field Museum, Chicago, Illinois, USA.

Horses and Ponies

(⇔ Agriculture for record prices)

Earliest domestication Evidence from the Ukraine indicates that horses may have been ridden by at least 4000 BC. (⇔ Agriculture)

Largest The tallest and heaviest documented horse was the shire gelding 'Sampson' (later renamed 'Mammoth'), bred by Thomas Cleaver of Toddington Mills, Beds. This horse (foaled 1846) measured 21·2½ hands (2·19m *7ft 2½in*) in 1850 and was later said to have weighed 1524kg *3360lb*.

'Boringdon Black King' (foaled 1984), a shire gelding born and bred at the National Shire Horse Centre in Plymouth, Devon, stands 19·2 hands (1·98m *6½ft*), making him the world's tallest living horse.

Thoroughbred The tallest recorded non-draught horse was a Canadian thoroughbred gelding named 'Tritonis', owned by Christopher Ewing of Southfield, Michigan, USA. This show jumper, which died in September 1990 at the age of seven, stood 19·2 hands

Caged Pet Longevity

Animal/Species	Name, Owner, etc.	YR	Mth
BIRD *Parrot*	Prudle captured 1958, I. Frost, East Sussex	35	—
Budgerigar	Charlie April 1948–20 Jun 1977, J. Dinsey, Stonebridge, London	29	2
RABBIT *Wild*	Flopsy caught 6 Aug 1964, died 29 Jun 1983, L.B. Walker Longford, Tasmania, Australia	18	10¾
GUINEA PIG	Snowball died 14 Feb 1979, M. A. Wall, Bingham, Notts	14	10½
GERBIL *Mongolian*	Sahara May 1973–4 Oct 1981, Aaron Milstone, Lathrup Village, Michigan, USA	8	4½
MOUSE *House*	Fritzy 11 Sep 1977–24 April 1985, Bridget Beard West House School, Edgbaston, Birmingham, W Mids	7	7
RAT *Common*	Rodney January 1983–25 May 1990, Rodney Mitchell Tulsa, Oklahoma, USA	7	4

(1·98 m *6½ ft*) and weighed 950 kg *2100 lb*.

Smallest The smallest breed of horse is the Falabella of Argentina, developed by Julio Falabella of Recco de Roca over a period of 70 years by inbreeding and crossing a small group of undersized horses originally discovered in the southern part of the country. Most specimens stand less than 76 cm *30 in* and average 36–45 kg *80–100 lb* in weight. The smallest example bred by Falabella before his death in 1981 was a mare which was 38 cm *15 in* tall and weighed 11·9 kg *26¼ lb*.

The smallest recorded horse was the stallion 'Little Pumpkin' (foaled 15 Apr 1973), which stood 35·5 cm *14 in* and weighed 9 kg *20 lb* on 30 Nov 1975. It was owned by J.C. Williams Jr of Della Terra Mini Horse Farm, Inman, South Carolina, USA.

Oldest The greatest age reliably recorded for a horse is 62 years for 'Old Billy' (foaled 1760), believed to be a cross between a Cleveland and eastern blood, bred by Edward Robinson of Wild Grave Farm, Woolston, Lancs. 'Old Billy' later worked along the local canals until 1819 and died on 27 Nov 1822.

Thoroughbred The oldest recorded thoroughbred racehorse was the 42-year-old chestnut gelding 'Tango Duke' (foaled 1935), owned by Carmen J. Koper of Barongarook, Victoria, Australia. The horse died on 25 Jan 1978.

Pony The greatest age reliably recorded for a pony is 54 years for a stallion (*fl.*1919) owned by a farmer in central France.

UK A moorland pony called 'Joey', owned by June and Rosie Osborne of the Glebe Equestrian Centre, Wickham Bishop, Essex, died in May 1988 at the age of 44.

Mules The largest mules on record are 'Apollo' (foaled 1977) and 'Anak' (foaled 1976), owned by Herbert L. Mueller of Chicago, Illinois, USA. 'Apollo' stands 19·1 hands (1·96 m *6 ft 5 in*) tall and weighs 998 kg *2200 lb*, with 'Anak' at 18·3 hands (1·91 m *6 ft 3 in*) and 952·2 kg *2100 lb*. Both are the hybrid offspring of Belgian mares and mammoth jacks.

Dogs

Largest The heaviest breeds of domestic dog (*Canis familiaris*) are the Old English mastiff and the St Bernard, with males of both species regularly weighing 77–91 kg *170–200 lb*. The heaviest (and longest) dog ever recorded is 'Aicama Zorba of La-Susa' (whelped 26 Sep 1981), an Old English mastiff owned by Chris Eraclides of London. 'Zorba' stands 94 cm *37 in* at the shoulder and weighed a peak 155·58 kg *343 lb* in November 1989. Other statistics include a chest girth of 149 cm *58¾ in*, a length of 2·53 m *8 ft 3½ in* and a neck measurement of 95·25 cm *37½ in*.

Tallest The great Dane and the Irish wolfhound can exceed 99 cm *39 in* at the shoulder, and the tallest dog ever recorded was 'Shamgret Danzas' (whelped 1975), a great Dane owned by Wendy and Keith Comley of Milton Keynes, Bucks. This dog stood 105·4cm *41½in* tall (106·6cm *42in* with hackles raised) and weighed up to 108kg *238lb*. He died on 16 Oct 1984.

Smallest Mature *miniature* versions of the Yorkshire terrier, the Chihuahua and the toy poodle have been known to weigh less than 453g *16oz*. The smallest dog on record was a matchbox-sized Yorkshire terrier owned by Arthur Marples of Blackburn, Lancs, a former editor of *Our Dogs*. This tiny atom, which died in 1945 aged nearly two, stood 6·3cm *2½in* at the shoulder and measured 9·5cm *3¾in* from the tip of its nose to the root of its tail. It weighed just 113g *4oz*.

The smallest living dog is 'Summerann Thumberlina', a Yorkshire terrier measuring 14cm *5½in* at the shoulder, 20·3cm *8in* long and weighing 567g *20oz*. Born on 5 Jan 1992, she is owned by Maureen Howes of Stourport-on-Severn, Hereford & Worcester.

Oldest Most dogs live for 8–15 years, and authentic records of dogs living over 20 years are rare and generally involve the smaller breeds. The greatest reliable age recorded for a dog is 29 years 5 months for an Australian cattle-dog named 'Bluey', owned by Les Hall of Rochester, Victoria, Australia. 'Bluey' was obtained as a puppy in 1910 and worked among cattle and sheep for nearly 20 years before being put to sleep on 14 Nov 1939.

UK A Welsh collie named 'Taffy', owned by Evelyn Brown of Forge Farm, West Bromwich, W Mids, lived for 27 years and 313 days. He was whelped on 2 Apr 1952 and died on 9 Feb 1980.

Sled dog trails *Oldest* The oldest established sled dog trail is the 1688 km *1049 mile* Iditarod Trail from Anchorage to Nome, Alaska, USA, which has existed since 1910 and has been the course of an annual race since 1967. The fastest time was set by Jeff King of Alaska in 1993 with 10 days 15 hr 38 min 15 sec. Rick

8000 sec

Guide dog

The longest period of *active service* reported for a guide dog is 14 years 8 months (August 1972–March 1987) in the case of a Labrador-retriever bitch named 'Cindy-Cleo' (whelped 20 Jan 1971), owned by Aron Barr of Tel Aviv, Israel. The dog died on 10 Apr 1987.

Ratting

During the period 1820–24 a 11·8kg *26 lb* 'bull and terrier' dog named 'Billy' dispatched 4000 rats in 17hr, a remarkable feat considering that he was blind in one eye. His most notable feat was the killing of 100 rats in 5min 30sec at the Cockpit in Tufton Street, Westminster, London on 23 Apr 1825. He died on 23 Feb 1829 at the age of 13.

James Searle's famous 'bull and terrier' bitch 'Jenny Lind' was another outstanding ratter. On 12 Jul 1853 she was backed to kill 500 rats in under 3hr at The Beehive in Old Crosshall Street, Liverpool, and completed the job in 1hr 36min.

Swenson (US) has won the race a record five times (1977–79, 1981–82 and 1991).

Longest The longest race is the 2000km *1243 miles* Berengia Trail from Esso to Markovo, Russia, which started as a 250km *155 miles* route in April 1990. Now established as an annual event, the 1991 race was won by Pavel Lazarev in 10days 18hr 17min 56sec.

Most prolific The greatest ever sire was the champion greyhound *Low Pressure*, nicknamed 'Timmy' (whelped September 1957), owned by Bruna Amhurst of Regent's Park, London. From December 1961 until his death on 27 Nov 1969 he fathered 2414 registered puppies, with at least 600 others unregistered.

Most valuable The largest legacy devoted to a dog was £15 million bequeathed by Ella Wendel of New York,

Largest show

The centenary of the annual Crufts show, held outside London for the first time at the National Exhibition Centre, Birmingham, Mids on 9–12 Jan 1991, attracted a record 22 993 entries.

Tracking

In 1925 a Dobermann pinscher named 'Sauer', trained by Detective-Sergeant Herbert Kruger, tracked a stock-thief 160 km *100 miles* across the Great Karroo, South Africa by scent alone.

USA to her standard poodle 'Toby' in 1931.

Highest jump The canine high jump record for a leap and scramble over a smooth wooden wall (without ribs or other aids) is 3·58 m *11 ft 9 in* achieved by a German shepherd dog named 'Volse' at a demonstration in Avignon, France in November 1989. The dog is owned by Philippe Clément of Aix-en-Provence.

'Duke', a three-year-old German shepherd dog handled by Corporal Graham Urry of RAF Newton, Notts, scaled a ribbed wall with regulation shallow slats to a height of 3·58 m *11 ft 9 in* on the BBC *Record Breakers* programme on 11 Nov 1986.

Longest jump A greyhound named 'Bang' jumped 9·14 m *30 ft* while hare coursing at Brecon Lodge, Glos in 1849. He cleared a 1·4 m *4 ft 6 in* gate and landed on a road, damaging his pastern bone.

Top show dogs The greatest number of Challenge Certificates won by a dog is 78 by the chow chow *Ch. U'Kwong King Solomon* (whelped 21 Jun 1968). Owned and bred by Joan Egerton of Bramhall, Cheshire, 'Solly' won his first CC at the Cheshire Agricultural Society Championship Show on 4 Jun 1969, and his 78th CC was awarded at the City of Birmingham Championship Show on 4 Sep 1976. He died on 3 Apr 1978.

The greatest number of 'Best-in-Show' awards won by any dog in all-breed

shows is 203 by the Scottish terrier bitch *Ch. Braeburn's Close Encounter* (whelped 22 Oct 1978) by 10 Mar 1985. She is owned by Sonnie Novick of Plantation Acres, Florida, USA.

Drug sniffing 'Snag', a US customs labrador retriever trained and partnered by Jeff Weitzmann, initiated the discovery of a 3·9-tonne haul of cocaine hidden in a tanker in San Diego, California in October 1990. Adopted as a stray in 1988 and trained at the US Customs Detector Dog Academy, to date 'Snag' has made 118 drug seizures worth a canine record $810 million (£580 million).

The greatest number of seizures by dogs is 969 (worth $182 million) in 1988 alone by 'Rocky' and 'Barco', a pair of malinoises patrolling the Rio Grande Valley ('Cocaine Alley') along the Texas border, where the pair were so proficient that Mexican drug smugglers put a $30 000 price on their heads. The dogs hold the rank of honorary Sergeant Major and always wear their stripes on duty.

UK In October 1988 a German shepherd owned by the Essex Police sniffed out 2 tonnes of cannabis worth £6 million when sent into a remote cottage on the outskirts of Harlow, Essex.

Cats

Largest The largest of the 330 breeds of domestic cat is the ragdoll, with males weighing 6·8–9 kg *15–20 lb*. In the majority of domestic cats (*Felis catus*) the average weight of the male (tom) is 3·9 kg *8·6 lb*, compared with 3·2 kg *7·2 lb* for the female or queen. Neuters and spays are generally heavier.

In Feb 1988 an unconfirmed weight of 21·7 kg *48 lb* was reported for a cat named 'Edward Bear', owned by Jackie Fleming of Sydney, New South Wales, Australia.

The heaviest reliably recorded domestic cat was a neutered male tabby named 'Himmy', which weighed 21·3 kg *46 lb 15¼ oz* (neck 38·1 cm *15 in*, waist 83·8 cm *33 in* and length 96·5 cm *38 in*) at the time of his death from respiratory failure on 12 Mar 1986 at the age of 10 years 4 months. 'Himmy' was owned by Thomas Vyse of Redlynch, Cairns, Queensland, Australia.

Largest Pet Litters

Animal/Breed	No.	Owner	Date
CAT *Burmese/Siamese*	19[1]	V. Gane, Church Westcote, Kingham, Oxon	7 Aug 1970
DOG *American foxhound*	23	W. Ely, Ambler, Pennsylvania, USA	19 Jun 1944
St Bernard	23[2]	R. and A. Rodden, Lebanon, Missouri, USA	6–7 Feb 1975
Great Dane	23[3]	M. Harris, Little Hall, Essex	June 1987
FERRET *Domestic*	15	J. Cliff, Denstone, Uttoxeter, Staffs	1981
GERBIL *Mongolian*	14[4]	S. Kirkman, Bulwell, Notts	May 1983
GUINEA PIG	12	Laboratory specimen	1972
HAMSTER *Golden*	26[5]	L. and S. Miller, Baton Rouge, Louisiana, USA	28 Feb 1974
MOUSE *House*	34[6]	M. Ogilvie, Blackpool, Lancs	12 Feb 1982
RABBIT *New Zealand white*	24	J. Filek, Cape Breton, Nova Scotia, Canada	1978

[1] Four stillborn. [2] Fourteen survived. [3] Sixteen survived. [4] Litter of 15 recorded in 1960s by George Meares, geneticist-owner of gerbil-breeding farm in St Petersburg, Florida, USA using special food formula. [5] Eighteen killed by mother. [6] Thirty-three survived.

UK An 11-year-old male tabby called 'Poppa', owned by Gwladys Cooper of Newport, Gwent, weighed 20·19 kg *44½ lb* in November 1984. It died on 25 Jun 1985.

Smallest The smallest breed of domestic cat is the Singapura or drain cat of Singapore. Males average 2·7 kg *6 lb* in weight and females 1·8 kg *4 lb*.

'Tinker Toy', a male blue point Himalayan-Persian cat owned by Katrina and Scott Forbes of Taylorville, Illinois, USA, is just 7 cm *2¾ in* tall and 19 cm *7½ in* long.

Best climber

On 6 Sep 1950 a four-month-old kitten belonging to Josephine Aufdenblatten of Geneva, Switzerland followed a group of climbers to the top of the 4478 m *14691 ft* Matterhorn in the Alps.

Mousing champion

A female tortoiseshell cat named 'Towser' (b. 21 Apr 1963), owned by Glenturret Distillery Ltd near Crieff, Tayside, notched up an estimated lifetime score of 28899. She averaged three mice per day until her death on 20 Mar 1987.

Oldest Cats generally live longer than dogs and the average life expectancy of un-doctored, well-fed males raised under household conditions and receiving good medical attention is 13–15 years (15–17 years for intact females), but neutered males and females live on average one to two years longer.

A tabby named 'Puss' owned by Mrs T. Holway of Clayhidon, Devon reportedly celebrated his 36th birthday on 28 Nov 1939 and died the next day, but conclusive evidence is lacking. The oldest reliably recorded cat was the female tabby 'Ma', which was put to sleep on 5 Nov 1957 at the age of 34. She was owned by Alice St George Moore of Drews-teignton, Devon.

Most prolific A tabby named 'Dusty' (b. 1935) of Bonham, Texas, USA produced 420 kittens during her breeding life. She gave birth to her last litter (a single kitten) on 12 Jun 1952.

In May 1987 'Kitty', owned by George Johnstone of Croxton, Staffs, produced two kittens at the age of 30 years, making her the oldest feline mother on record. She died in June 1989, just short of her 32nd birthday, having given birth to a known total of 218 kittens.

Rabbits and Hares

Largest The largest breed of domestic rabbit (*Oryctolagus cuniculus*) is the Flemish giant, averaging 7–8·5 kg *15 lb 7 oz–18 lb 12 oz*, but with weights of up to 11·3 kg *25 lb* also reliably reported for this breed. Its average toe-to-toe length when fully stretched is 91 cm *36 in*. In April 1980 a five-month-old French lop doe weighing 12 kg *26 lb 7 oz* was exhibited at the Reus Fair in north-east Spain.

The heaviest recorded wild rabbit (average weight 1·6 kg *3½ lb*) weighed 3·74 kg *8 lb 4 oz* and was killed on 20 Nov 1982.

Smallest Both the Netherland dwarf and the Polish have a weight range of 0·9–1·13 kg *2–2½ lb*, but in 1975 Jacques Bouloc of Coulommière, France announced a new hybrid of these weighing 396 g *14 oz*.

Most prolific The most prolific domestic breeds are the New Zealand white and the Californian. Does produce 5–6 litters a year, each containing 8–12 kittens during their breeding life, compared with five litters and 3–7 young for the wild rabbit.

Longest ears The longest ears are found in the lop family (four strains), and in particular the English lop. The ears of a typical example measure about 61 cm *24 in* from tip to tip (taken across the skull), and 14 cm *5½ in* in width. In 1901 Capt. Youden exhibited a specimen in England which had ears measuring 77·4 cm *30½ in*, but it is not known whether this length had been attained naturally or if weights had been used to stretch the ears, as the veins inside were badly varicosed.

'Sweet Majestic Star', a champion black English lop owned and bred by Therese and Cheryl Seward of Exeter, Devon, had naturally-developed ears measuring 72·4 cm *28½ in* long and 18·4 cm *7¼ in* wide. He died on 6 Oct 1992. The ears of his grandson 'Sweet Regal Magic' are also this length.

Largest hare In November 1956 a brown hare weighing 6·83 kg *15 lb 1 oz* was shot near Welford, Northants. The average weight is 3·62 kg *8 lb*.

Birds

Aves

Largest The largest living bird is the North African ostrich (*Struthio c. camelus*), found in reduced numbers south of

68

the Atlas Mountains from Upper Senegal and Niger across to the Sudan and central Ethiopia. Male examples (hens are smaller) of this flightless (ratite) sub-species have been recorded up to 2·74 m *9 ft* tall and weighing 156·5 kg *345 lb*. The heaviest sub-species is *Struthio c. australis* which can weigh 150 kg *330 lb*, although there is an unsubstantiated record of 160 kg *353 lb*.

Largest flying The world's heaviest flying (carinate) birds are the Kori bustard or paauw (*Ardeotis kori*) of north-east and southern Africa and the great bustard (*Otis tarda*) of Europe and Asia. Weights of 19 kg *42 lb* have been reported for the former, and there is an unconfirmed record of 21 kg *46 lb 4 oz* for a male great bustard shot in Manchuria which was too heavy to fly. The heaviest reliably recorded great bustard weighed 18 kg *39 lb 11 oz*.

The mute swan (*Cygnus olor*), which is resident in Britain, can reach 18 kg *40 lb* on very rare occasions, and there is a record from Poland of a cob (male) weighing 22·5 kg *49 lb 10 oz* which had temporarily lost the power of flight.

Bird of prey The heaviest bird of prey is the Andean condor (*Vultur gryphus*), males of which average 9–11 kg *20–25 lb*. A weight of 14·1 kg *31 lb* has been claimed for a male California condor (*Gymnogyps californianus*) now preserved in the California Academy of Sciences at Los Angeles, USA, but this species is generally much smaller than the Andean condor and rarely exceeds 10·4 kg *23 lb*.

Largest wing span The wandering albatross (*Diomedea exulans*) of the southern oceans has the largest wing span of any living bird, with male wings averaging 3·15 m *10 ft 4 in* at full stretch. The largest recorded specimen was a very old male with a wing span of 3·63 m *11 ft 11 in*, caught by members of the Antarctic research ship USNS *Eltanin* in the Tasman Sea on 18 Sep 1965. Unconfirmed measurements of up to 4·22 m *13 ft 10 in* have also been claimed for this species.

The only other bird reliably credited with a wing span exceeding 3·35 m *11 ft* is the vulture-like marabou stork (*Leptoptilus crumeniferus*) of tropical Africa.

Smallest The world's smallest bird is the bee hummingbird (*Mellisuga helenae*) of Cuba and the Isle of Pines. Males measure 57mm *2¼ in* in total length, half of which is taken up by the bill and tail, and weigh 1·6g *0·056 oz* (females are slightly larger). (<> Smallest nest)

The smallest regularly breeding British bird is the goldcrest or golden crested wren (*Regulus regulus*), which is 90mm *3½ in* long and weighs 3·8–4·5g *0·13–0·16 oz*, half the weight of the common wren (*Troglodytes troglodytes*).

Bird of prey The smallest bird of prey is the 35g *1·23 oz*, 140–152mm *5½–6 in* long, white-fronted falconet (*Microhierax latifrons*) of north-western Borneo.

Longest bills The bill of the Australian pelican (*Pelicanus conspicillatus*) is 34–47cm *13–18½ in* long. The longest beak in relation to overall body length is that of the sword-billed hummingbird (*Ensifera ensifera*) of the Andes from Venezuela to Bolivia. It measures 10·2cm *4 in* making it longer than the bird's body excluding the tail.

Shortest bills The shortest bills in relation to body length are those of the smaller swifts (Apodidae) and in particular the glossy swiftlet (*Collocalia esculenta*), whose bill is almost non-existent.

Most abundant The red-billed quelea (*Quelea quelea*), a seed-eating weaver of the drier parts of Africa south of the Sahara, has an estimated adult breeding population of 1·5 billion, and at least 1 billion of these 'feathered locusts' are slaughtered annually without having any impact on the population. One huge roost in the Sudan contained 32 million birds.

UK Of the estimated 126–150 wild bird species found in Britain, the commonest is now the blackbird (*Turdus merula*), with a breeding population of 5 million pairs. It is followed by the robin (*Erithicius rubecula*) and the blue tit (*Parus caeruleus*) with 4 million pairs each, the house sparrow (*Passer domesticus*) with 3 million pairs and the song thrush (*Turdus philamelos*) with 2·5 million pairs. Between 1964–74 the population of the wren (*Troglodytes troglodytes*) increased tenfold after a series of mild winters, and at the end of this period there were an estimated 10 million pairs. This species, however, is severely affected by cold weather, and the harsh winter of 1978–79 alone reduced the wren population by 40 per cent.

Fastest flying The fastest living creature is the peregrine falcon (*Falco peregrinus*) when stooping from great heights during territorial displays. In one series of German experiments, a velocity of 270km/h *168 mph* was recorded at a 30° angle of stoop, rising to a maximum of 350km/h *217 mph* at an angle of 45°. The brown-throated spine-tail swift *Hirundapus giganteus* of Asia is also capable of 250–300km/h *155–186 mph*.

The fastest fliers in level flight are found among the ducks and geese (Anatidae). Some powerful species such as the red-breasted merganser (*Mergus serrator*), the eider (*Somateria mollissima*), the canvasback (*Aythya valisineria*) and the spur-winged goose (*Plectropterus gambiensis*) can probably exceed 104km/h *65 mph*.

The bill of the Australian pelican can be up to 47 cm *18½ in* long, making it very useful for fishing and for reaching those awkward areas.

(Photo: Planet Earth Pictures/Pete Atkinson)

Most talkative bird

A number of birds are renowned for their talking ability (i.e. the reproduction of words) but the African grey parrot (*Psittacus erythacus*) excels in this ability. A female named 'Prudle', formerly owned by Lyn Logue (died January 1988) and now in the care of Iris Frost of East Sussex, won the 'Best talking parrot-like bird' title at the National Cage and Aviary Bird Show in London each December for 12 consecutive years (1965–76). 'Prudle', who has a vocabulary of nearly 800 words, was taken from a nest at Jinja, Uganda in 1958. She retired undefeated. (⇔ Pet longevity)

Poisonous bird

The only poisonous bird found so far is the unsavoury-sounding pitohui of the *Pitohui* genus from New Guinea, identified in 1992. The skin, feathers and internal organs of this striking orange and black bird contain a homobatrachotoxin like that secreted by poison-dart frogs, which have similar warning colours. (⇔ General records)

UK Britain's fastest game bird is the red grouse (*Lagopus l. scoticus*) which, in still air, has recorded speeds of up to 93–100km/h *58–63mph* over very short distances. Air speeds of 112km/h *70mph* have been claimed for the golden plover (*Pluvialis apricaria*) when flushed, but it is very doubtful whether this bird could exceed 80–88km/h *50–55mph*—even in an emergency.

Fastest wing-beat The wing-beat of the horned sungem (*Heliactin cornuta*) of tropical South America is 90 beats/sec.

Slowest flying Probably at least 50 per cent of the world's flying birds cannot exceed 64km/h *40mph* in level flight. The slowest-flying birds are the American woodcock (*Scolopax minor*) and the Eurasian woodcock (*S. rusti-*

cola), which have been timed at 8km/h *5mph* without stalling.

Oldest An unconfirmed age of about 82 years was reported for a male Siberian white crane (*Crus leucogeranus*) named 'Wolf' at the International Crane Foundation, Baraboo, Wisconsin, USA. Said to have been hatched at a zoo in Switzerland in about 1905, 'Wolf' died in late 1988 after breaking his bill while repelling a visitor near his pen.

The greatest irrefutable age reported for any bird is over 80 years for a male sulphur-crested cockatoo (*Cacatua galerita*) named 'Cocky', who died at London Zoo in 1982. He was presented to the zoo in 1925, and had been with his previous owner since 1902 when he was already fully mature.

Domestic Excluding the ostrich, which has been known to live up to 68 years, the longest-lived domesticated bird is the goose (*Anser a. domesticus*), which has a normal life-span of about 25 years. On 16 Dec 1976 a gander named 'George', owned by Florence Hull of Thornton, Lancs, died aged 49 years 8 months. He was hatched in April 1927.

Brooding A female royal albatross (*Diomedea epomophora*) named 'Grandma' ('Blue White'), the oldest ringed seabird on record, laid an egg in November 1988 at the age of 60. She was first banded as a breeding adult in 1937 (such birds do not start breeding until they are 9 years old). She has raised 10 chicks of her own and fostered 3 others with her mate 'Green White Green', who is 47.

Longest flights The greatest distance covered by a ringed bird is 22530km *14000miles* by an Arctic tern (*Sterna paradisea*), banded as a nestling on 5 Jul 1955 in the Kandalaksha Sanctuary on the White Sea coast of Russia and captured alive by a fisherman 13km *8miles* south of Fremantle, Western Australia on 16 May 1956. The bird had flown south via the Atlantic Ocean and then circled Africa before crossing the Indian Ocean. It did not survive to make the return journey. There is also a report of an Arctic tern flying from Greenland to Australasia, but further details are lacking.

In 1990 six foraging wandering albatross (*Diomedea exulans*) were tracked across the Indian Ocean by satellite via radio transmitters fitted by Pierre Jouventin and Henri Weimerskirch of the National Centre for Scientific Research at Beauvoir, France. Results showed that the birds covered 3600–15 000 km *2240–9320 miles* in a single feeding trip and that they easily maintained a speed of 56 km/h *35 mph* over a distance of more than 800 km *500 miles*, with the males going to sea for up to 33 days while their partners remained ashore to incubate the eggs.

Most airborne The most aerial of all birds is the sooty tern (*Sterna fuscata*), which, after leaving the nesting grounds, remains aloft continuously from 3–10 years whilst maturing before returning to land to breed as an adult.

The most aerial land bird is the common swift (*Apus apus*), which remains airborne for 2–3 years, during which time it sleeps, drinks, eats and even mates on the wing.

Fastest swimmer The gentoo penguin (*Pygoscelis papua*) has a maximum burst of speed of about 27 km/h *17 mph*.

Deepest dive In 1969 a depth of 265 m *870 ft* was recorded for a small group of 10 emperor penguins (*Aptenodytes forsteri*) at Cape Crozier, Antarctica by a team of US scientists. One bird remained submerged for 18 minutes.

Keenest vision Birds of prey (Falconiformes) have the keenest eyesight in the avian world, and large species with eyes similar in size to ours have at least twice our visual acuity. It has also been calculated that a large bird of prey can detect a target object at a distance 3–8 times greater than that achieved by humans, and therefore a peregrine falcon (*Falco peregrinus*) can spot a pigeon, for example, at a range of over 8 km *5 miles* under ideal conditions.

Experiments carried out at the University of Birmingham, W Mids in 1977 revealed that the eyes of the tawny owl (*Strix aluco*) are 2½ times more sensitive than the human eye. It was also discovered that this nocturnal bird sees perfectly adequately in daylight and that

Cuckoos

It is unlikely that the cuckoo (*Culculus canorus*) has ever been *heard and seen* in Britain earlier than 2 March, on which date one was observed under acceptable conditions by William Haynes of Trinder Road, Wantage, Oxon in 1972. Because of unseasonably mild temperatures, a great spotted cuckoo, which should have been in Africa, was reported on Lundy, off the north coast of Devon on the weekend of 24–25 Feb 1990. The two latest dates are 16 Dec 1912 at Anstey's Cove, Torquay, Devon and 26 Dec 1897 or 1898 in Cheshire.

Vision

The woodcock (family Scolopacidae) has eyes set so far back on its head that it has a 360° field of vision, enabling it to see all round and even over the top of its head.

its visual acuity is only slightly inferior to that of humans.

Highest g force American experiments have shown that the beak of the red-headed woodpecker (*Melanerpes erythrocephalus*) hits the bark of a tree with an impact velocity of 20·9 km/h *13 mph*, subjecting the brain to a deceleration of about 10 *g* when the head snaps back.

Longest feathers The longest feathers grown by any bird are those of the Phoenix fowl or onagadori (a strain of red junglefowl *Gallus gallus*), which has been bred in south-western Japan since the mid-17th century. In 1972 a tail covert measuring 10·6 m *34 ft 9½ in* was reported for a rooster owned by Masasha Kubota of Kochi, Shikoku, Japan.

Among flying birds the tail feathers of the male crested pheasant (*Rheinhartia ocellata*) of south-east Asia regularly reach 173 cm *5 ft 8 in* in length and 13 cm *5 in* in width, and the central tail feathers of Reeves' pheasant (*Syrmaticus reevesi*) of

Migration

Migratory patterns vary considerably throughout the animal world and the diagram illustrates a small selection of diverse habits, showing aspects such as distances travelled and numbers of animals involved for different species. Further details can be found in the relevant sections of this chapter.

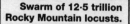

Swarm of 12·5 trillion Rocky Mountain locusts.

Polar bear

Polar bear *(above)*
Despite their great bulk, polar bears can cover distances of 1600 km *975 miles* walking across the ice from Alaska, USA via the Bering Strait to set up winter dens in Russia.

The grey whale holds the mammalian distance record of 9660 km *6000 miles*.

Monarch butterfly travelling from Canada to Mexico.

Tagging butterflies *(right)*
The photographs show a tagged monarch butterfly and an example of an actual alar tag used to monitor the movement of the insects. Distances travelled are then calculated from the known release and recapture sites.

REPORT
NO. TO
ZOOLOGY
UNIVERSITY
TORONTO
CANADA

28009

The all-time distance record is 22 530 km *14 000 miles* by the Arctic tern.

Golden oriole

A herd of springbok covering 3480 km² *1500 miles.²*

Golden oriole *(top right)* Every year over 140 species of bird follow one of Europe's most important migratory routes from the Basque region of the Pyrenees to North Africa and beyond. Unfortunately, because of this predictability, as many as 900 million birds — 15 per cent of the 6 billion-strong migrating flocks — are killed each year by hunters. The golden oriole (*Oriolus oriolus*) is among the top ten species endangered through this practice.

Green turtle

Green turtle *(above)* Reptiles only migrate during the reproduction cycle and the green turtle (*Chelonia mydas*), in particular, swims vast distances (also showing amazing navigational skills) to lay its eggs on the specific beach of its own spawning. Distances of 2300 km *1400 miles* have been recorded for green turtles swimming between Ascension Island and the South American coast.

Fastest bird

The fastest bird on land is the ostrich which, despite its bulk, can run at a speed of up to 65 km/h *40 mph* when necessary.

Highest flying birds

Most migrating birds fly at relatively low altitudes (i.e. below 90 m *300 ft*), with only a few dozen species flying higher than 900 m *3000 ft*.

The highest confirmed altitude recorded for a bird is 11 277 m *37 000 ft* for a Ruppell's vulture (*Gyps rueppellii*), which collided with a commercial aircraft over Abidjan, Ivory Coast on 29 Nov 1973. The impact damaged one of the aircraft's engines, causing it to shut down, but the plane landed safely without further incident. Sufficient feather remains of the bird were recovered to allow the US Museum of Natural History to make a positive identification of this high-flier, which is rarely seen above 6000 m *20 000 ft*.

On 9 Dec 1967 about 30 whooper swans (*Cygnus cygnus*) were recorded at an altitude of just over 8230 m *27 000 ft* flying in from Iceland to winter at Loch Foyle bordering Northern Ireland and the Republic of Ireland. They were spotted by an airline pilot over the Outer Hebrides, and the height was also confirmed on radar by air traffic control.

central and northern China have reached 2·43 m *8 ft* in exceptional cases.

Most and least feathers In a series of feather counts on various species of bird a whistling swan (*Cygnus columbianus*) was found to have 25 216 feathers, 20 177 of which were on the head and neck. In contrast, the ruby-throated hummingbird (*Archilochus colubris*) has only 940.

Largest egg The egg of an ostrich (*Struthio camelus*) normally measures 15–20 cm *6–8 in* long, 10–15 cm *4–6 in* in diameter and weighs 1·65–1·78 kg *3·6–3·9 lb* (around the volume of two dozen hens' eggs). The egg requires about 40 min for boiling and the shell, although only 1·5 mm *0·06 in* thick, can support the weight of a 127 kg *20 st* person. The largest egg on record weighed 2·3 kg *5·1 lb* and was laid on 28 Jun 1988 by a 2-year-old northern/southern hybrid (*Struthio c. camelus×S. c. australis*) at the Kibbutz Ha'on collective farm, Israel.

UK The largest egg laid by any bird on the British list is that of the mute swan (*Cygnus olor*) at 109–124 mm *4·3–4·9 in* long, 71–78·5 mm *2·8–3·1 in* in diameter and weighing 340–370 g *12–13 oz*.

Smallest egg Eggs emitted from the oviduct before maturity, known as 'sports', are not considered to be of significance. The smallest egg laid by any bird is that of the vervain hummingbird (*Mellisuga minima*) of Jamaica. Two specimens measuring less than 10 mm *0·39 in* in length weighed 0·365 g *0·0128 oz* and 0·375 g *0·0132 oz*. (⇔ Smallest nest)

UK The smallest egg laid by a bird on the British list is that of the goldcrest (*Regulus regulus*), which measures 12·2–14·5 mm *0·48–0·57 in* in length, 9·4–9·9 mm *0·37–0·39 in* in diameter and weighs 0·6 g *0·021 oz*.

Longest incubation The longest normal incubation period is 75–82 days for the wandering albatross (*Diomedea exulans*). There is an isolated case of an egg of the mallee fowl (*Leipoa ocellata*) of Australia taking 90 days to hatch, compared with its normal 62 days.

Shortest incubation The shortest incubation period is 10 days in the case of the great spotted woodpecker (*Dendrocopus major*) and the black-billed cuckoo (*Coccyzus erythropthalmus*).

The idlest of cock birds include hummingbirds (family Trochilidae), the eider duck (*Somateria mollissima*) and the golden pheasant (*Chrysolophus pictus*), whose breeding partners are responsible for 100 per cent of incubation duties. In contrast, the female common kiwi (*Apteryx australis*) leaves the male in charge for 75–80 days.

Tallest bird

The tallest of the flying birds are cranes, tall waders of the family Gruidae, some of which can stand almost 2 m *6 ft 6 in* high.

Largest nest A nest measuring 2·9 m *9½ ft* wide and 6 m *20 ft* deep was built by a pair of bald eagles (*Haliaeetus leucocephalus*), and possibly their successors, near St Petersburg, Florida, USA. It was examined in 1963 and was estimated to weigh more than 2 tonnes. The golden eagle (*Aquila chrysaetos*) also constructs huge nests, and one 4·57 m *15 ft* deep was reported from Scotland in 1954. It had been used for 45 years. The incubation mounds built by the mallee fowl (*Leipoa ocellata*) of Australia are much larger, measuring up to 4·57 m *15 ft* in height and 10·6 m *35 ft* across, and it has been calculated that a nest site may involve the mounding of 229 m³ *8100 ft³* of material weighing 300 tonnes.

Smallest nest The smallest nests are built by hummingbirds (Trochilidae). That of the vervain hummingbird (*Mellisuga minima*) is about half the size of a walnut, while the deeper one of the bee hummingbird (*M. helenae*) is thimble-sized. (⊳ Smallest bird, Smallest egg)

UK The smallest nest built by a British bird is that of the goldcrest (*Regulus regulus*), with a diameter of about 8–9 cm *3–3½ in*.

Bird-spotters The world's leading bird-spotter or 'twitcher' is Phoebe Snetsinger of Webster Groves, Missouri, USA, who has logged 7212 of the 9672 known species since 1965, representing over 74 per cent of the available total. (The exact number of species at any given time can vary because of changes to classifications.)

UK The British life list record is 485 by Ron Johns (b. 1941) of Slough, Bucks, who started spotting in 1952. The British year list record is 359 by Lee Evans (b. 1960) of Luton, Beds, established in 1990 after travelling over 123 916 km *77 000 miles*, compared with his average yearly total of 96 000 km *60 000 miles*.

The greatest number of species spotted in a 24-hour period is 342 by Kenyans Terry Stevenson, John Fanshawe and Andy Roberts on day two of the Birdwatch Kenya '86 event held on 29–30 November. The 48-hour record is held by Don Turner and David Pearson of Kenya, who spotted 494 species at the same event.

Peter Kaestner of Washington, DC, USA was the first person to see at least one species of each of the world's 159 bird families. He saw his final family on 1 Oct 1986. Since then Dr Ira Abramson of Miami, Florida, USA, Dr Martin Edwards of Kingston, Ontario, Canada and Harvey Gilston of Lausanne, Switzerland (last family seen in December 1988) have also matched this achievement.

Reptiles
Reptilia

Crocodilians

Largest The largest reptile in the world is the estuarine or saltwater crocodile (*Crocodylus porosus*) of south-east Asia, the Malay Archipelago, Indonesia, northern Australia, Papua New Guinea, Vietnam and the Philippines. Males average 4·2–4·8 m *14–16 ft* in length and weigh about 408–520 kg *900–1150 lb*.

The Bhitarkanika Wildlife Sanctuary in Orissa State, India houses four protected estuarine crocodiles measuring more than 6 m *19 ft 8 in* in length, the largest being over 7 m *23 ft* long.

Captive The largest crocodile ever held in captivity is an estuarine/Siamese hybrid named 'Yai' (b. 10 Jun 1972) at the Samutprakarn Crocodile Farm and Zoo, Thailand. He is 6 m *19 ft 8 in* long and weighs 1115 kg *2465 lb*.

Smallest Osborn's dwarf crocodile (*Osteolaemus osborni*), found in the upper region of the Congo River, west Africa, rarely exceeds 1·2 m *3 ft 11 in* in length.

Oldest The greatest authenticated age for a crocodilian is 66 years for a female American alligator (*Alligator mississippiensis*) which arrived at Adelaide Zoo, South Australia on 5 Jun 1914 as a two-year-old, and died there on 26 Sep 1978.

Lizards

Largest The largest lizard is the Komodo monitor or ora (*Varanus komodoensis*), a dragonlike reptile found on the Indonesian islands of Komodo, Rintja, Padar and Flores. Males average 225cm *7ft 5in* in length and weigh about 59kg *130lb*. Lengths up to 9·15m *30ft* have been claimed for this species, but the largest accurately measured specimen was a male presented to an American zoologist in 1928 by the Sultan of Bima. In 1937 it was put on display in St Louis Zoological Gardens, Missouri, USA for a short period, by which time it was 3·10m *10ft 2in* in long and weighed 166kg *365lb*.

Longest The slender Salvadori monitor (*Varanus salvadori*) of Papua New Guinea has been reliably measured at up to 4·75m *15ft 7in* in length, but nearly 70 per cent of its total length is taken up by the tail.

Smallest *Sphaerodactylus parthenopion*, a tiny gecko indigenous to the island of Virgin Gorda, one of the British Virgin Islands, is believed to be the world's smallest lizard. It is known only from 15 specimens, including some pregnant females found between 10 and 16 Aug 1964. The three largest females measured 18mm *0·70in* from snout to vent, with a tail of approximately the same length.

It is possible that another type of gecko, *Sphaerodactylus elasmorhynchus*, may be even smaller. The only known specimen was an apparently mature female with a snout–vent measurement of 17mm *0·67in* and a tail of the same length. This specimen was found on 15 Mar 1966 among the roots of a tree in the western part of the Massif de la Hotte in Haiti.

Fastest The highest speed measured for any reptile on land is 29km/h *18mph* for a six-lined race runner (*Cnemidophorus sexlineatus*) near McCormick, South Carolina, USA in 1941.

Chelonians

Largest The largest living chelonian is the widely distributed leatherback turtle

(*Dermochelys coriacea*), which averages 1·83–2·13m *6–7ft* from the tip of the beak to the end of the tail (carapace 1·52–1·67m *5–5½ft*), about 2·13m *7ft* across the front flippers and weighs up to 450kg *1000lb*.

The largest leatherback turtle ever recorded was a male found dead on the beach at Harlech, Gwynedd on 23 Sep 1988. It measured 2·91m *9ft 5½in* in total length over the carapace (nose to tail), 2·77m *9ft* across the front flippers and weighed 961·1kg *2120lb*. Although most museums refuse to exhibit large turtles because they can drip oil for up to 50 years, this specimen was put on display at the National Museum of Wales, Cardiff on 16 Feb 1990.

Tortoise The largest living tortoise is the Aldabra giant tortoise (*Geochelone gigantea*) of the Indian Ocean islands of Aldabra, Mauritius and the Seychelles (introduced 1874). A male called 'Esmerelda', a long-time resident on Bird Island, Seychelles, weighed 304kg *670lb* in November 1992.

Smallest The smallest marine turtle in the world is the Atlantic ridley (*Lepidochelys kempii*), which has a shell length of 50–70cm *19·7–27·6in* and a maximum weight of 36kg *80lb*.

Oldest The greatest authentic age recorded for a chelonian is over 152 years for a male Marion's tortoise (*Testudo sumeirii*) brought from the Seychelles to Mauritius in 1766 by the Chevalier de Fresne, who presented it to the Port Louis army garrison. This specimen, which went blind in 1908, was accidentally killed in 1918. The greatest proven age of a continuously observed tortoise is more than 116 years for a Mediterranean spur-thighed tortoise (*Testudo graeca*).

Fastest The highest speed claimed for any reptile in water is 35km/h *22mph* by a frightened Pacific leatherback turtle.

Deepest dive In May 1987 it was reported by Dr Scott Eckert that a leatherback turtle (*Dermochelys coriacea*) fitted with a pressure-sensitive recording device had reached a depth of 1200m *3973ft* off the Virgin Islands in the West Indies.

Egg-laying

Female reptiles usually lay eggs, but some species give birth to live young. Among the egg-layers, some turtles may lay up to 200 at a time, compared with 20–70 by crocodiles and only two by geckos.

Oldest lizard

The greatest age recorded for a lizard is over 54 years for a male slow worm (*Anguis fragilis*) kept in the Zoological Museum, Copenhagen, Denmark from 1892 until 1946.

Fastest tortoise

The National Tortoise Championship record is 5·48m *18ft* up a 1:12 gradient in 43·7sec (0·45km/h *0·28mph*) by 'Charlie' at Tickhill, S Yorks on 2 Jul 1977.

Longest fangs

The longest fangs of any snake are those of the highly venomous gaboon viper (*Bitis gabonica*) of tropical Africa. In a specimen of 1·83m *6ft* length they measured 50mm *1·96in*.

On 12 Feb 1963 a gaboon viper under severe stress sank its fangs into its own back at Philadelphia Zoo, Pennsylvania, USA and died from traumatic injury to a vital organ. It did not, as was widely reported, succumb to its own venom.

Snakes, General

Longest The reticulated python (*Python reticulatus*) of south-east Asia, Indonesia and the Philippines regularly exceeds 6·25m *20ft 6in*, and the record length is 10m *32ft 9½in* for a specimen shot in Celebes, Indonesia in 1912.

Captive The longest (and heaviest) snake ever held in captivity was a female reticulated python named 'Colossus' who was 8·68m *28ft 6in* long and weighed 145kg *320lb* at her heavi-

77

est. She died in Highland Park Zoo, Pennsylvania, USA on 15 Apr 1963.

UK The longest of the three species of snake native to Britian is the grass snake (*Natrix natrix*), also known as the common European water snake, found throughout southern England, parts of Wales and in Dumfries and Galloway, Scotland. It can reach nearly 1·8m *6ft* in length, but usually averages less than 1m *3ft 3in*.

In September 1816 a 2·13m *7ft* long female was allegedly killed at Trebun, Anglesey, Gwynedd and 'left for public curiosity at Llangefni', but further details are lacking. The longest accurately measured specimen was a 1·78m *5ft 10in* long female killed in South Wales in 1887. (⇨ Fastest snake)

Shortest The world's shortest snake is the very rare thread snake (*Leptotyphlops bilineata*), known only from Martinique, Barbados and St Lucia. The longest examples measured 108mm *4¼in*.

UK The smallest native British snake is the smooth snake (*Coronella austriaca*), which has an average length of up to 50cm *2in*.

Heaviest The most massive snake is the anaconda (*Eunectes murinus*) of tropical South America and Trinidad. A female shot in Brazil *c.* 1960 was not weighed, but as it was 8·45m *27ft 9in* long with a girth of 111cm *44in*, it must have weighed nearly 227kg *500lb*. The average length is 5·5–6·1m *18–20ft*.

Venomous Snakes

Longest The longest venomous snake is the king cobra (*Ophiophagus hannah*), also called the hamadryad, which averages 3·65–4·57m *12–15ft* in length and is found in south-east Asia and the Philippines. A 5·54m *18ft 2in* specimen captured alive near Fort Dickson in the state of Negri Sembilan, Malaya in April 1937 later grew to 5·71m *18ft 9in* in London Zoo. It was destroyed at the outbreak of war in 1939.

UK The only, and thus the longest, venomous snake found in Britain is the adder or viper (*Vipera berus*), the longest recorded specimen of which was a female measuring 110·5cm *43½in*

Uncoil this reticulated python and it could be over 6·25m *20½ft* long.
(Photo: Planet Earth Pictures/Ken Lucas)

killed at Paradise Farm, Pontrilas, Hereford & Worcester in August 1977. (⇨ Most venomous)

Shortest The namaqua dwarf adder (*Bitis schneideri*) of Namibia, has an average length of 200mm *8in*.

Heaviest The heaviest venomous snake is probably the eastern diamondback rattlesnake (*Crotalus adamanteus*) of the south-eastern United States, which averages 5·5–6·8kg *12–15lb* (1·52–1·83m *5–6ft* in length). The heaviest on record weighed 15kg *34lb* and was 2·36m *7ft 9in* long.

The West African gaboon viper (*Bitis gabonica*) of the tropical rain forests is probably bulkier than the eastern diamond, but its average length is only 1·22–1·52m *4–5ft*. A 1·83m *6ft* long female weighed 11·34kg *25lb* and another female measuring 1·74m *5ft 8½in* weighed 8·2kg *18lb* with an empty stomach.

Most venomous All sea snakes are venomous, but the species *Hydrophis belcheri* has a myotoxic venom a hundred times as toxic as that of the Australian taipan (*Oxyuranus scutellatus*), whose bite can kill a man in minutes. The snake abounds round Ashmore Reef in the Timor Sea, off north-west Australia.

The most venomous land snake is the 2m *6ft 6¾in* long smooth-scaled snake (*Parademansia microlepidotus*) of the Diamantina River and Cooper's Creek drainage basins in Channel County, Queensland and western New South Wales, Australia, whose venom is nine times as toxic as that of the tiger snake (*Notechis scutatus*) of South Australia and Tasmania. One specimen yielded 110 mg *0·00385 oz* of venom after milking—enough to kill 125 000 mice—but so far no human fatalities have been reported.

More people die of snakebites in Sri Lanka than any comparable area in the world. An average of 800 people are killed annually on the island by snakes, with over 95 per cent of the fatalities caused by the common krait (*Bungarus caeruleus*), the Sri Lankan cobra (*Naja n. naja*) and Russell's viper (*Vipera russelli pulchella*).

The saw-scaled or carpet viper (*Echis carinatus*), which ranges from West Africa to India, bites and kills more people in the world than any other species.

UK The only venomous snake in Britain is the adder, or viper, (*Vipera berus*), whose bite has caused ten human deaths since 1890, including six children. The most recent recorded death was on 1 Jul 1975 when a 5-year-old was bitten at Callander, Perthshire and died 44 hours later. (⇨ Longest venomous)

Oldest The greatest reliable age recorded for a snake is 40 years 3 months 14 days for a male common boa (*Boa constrictor constrictor*) named 'Popeye', who died at Philadelphia Zoo, Pennsylvania, USA on 15 Apr 1977.

Fastest The fastest land snake in the world is the slender black mamba (*Dendroaspis polylepis*) of the eastern part of tropical Africa. Top speeds of 16–19 km/h *10–12 mph* may be possible in short bursts over level ground, and it is said to chase people aggressively.

UK The grass snake (*Natrix natrix*) has a maximum speed of 6·8 km/h *4·2 mph*. (⇨ Longest snake)

Amphibians

Amphibia

Largest The largest amphibian is the Chinese giant salamander (*Andrias davidianus*) of north-eastern, central and southern China. It averages 114 cm *3 ft 9 in* in length and weighs 25–30 kg

55–66 lb. One specimen collected in Hunan province was 1·8 m *5 ft 11 in* long and weighed 65 kg *143 lb*.

UK The largest British amphibian is the common toad (*Bufo bufo*), found throughout England, Scotland and Wales. A huge female collected from Marlpit Pond, Boxley, Kent measured 99 mm *3·9 in* from snout to vent and weighed 118 g *4·2 oz*.

Smallest The smallest known amphibian is the tiny Cuban frog (*Sminthillus limbatus*), which is less than 12 mm *½ in* long.

UK The smallest amphibian found in Britain is the palmate newt (*Triturus helveticus*), which is 75–92 mm *3–3½ in* long and weighs up to 2·39 g *0·083 oz*.

The female natterjack or running toad (*Bufo calamita*) has a maximum snout-to-vent length of only 80 mm *3·14 in*, but it is bulkier than the palmate newt.

Oldest The greatest authenticated age for an amphibian is 55 years for a Japanese giant salamander (*Andrias japonicus*) which died in Amsterdam Zoo, Netherlands in 1881.

Highest and lowest The greatest altitude at which an amphibian has been

---

Longest amphibian gestation

The viviparous (giving birth to live young) Alpine black salamander (*Salamandra atra*) has a gestation period of up to 38 months at altitudes above 1400 m *4600 ft* in the Swiss Alps, but this drops to 24–26 months at lower altitudes.

Longest jump

Competition frog jumps are invariably the aggregate of three consecutive leaps.

The greatest distance covered by a frog in a triple jump is 10·3 m *33 ft 5½ in* by a South African sharp-nosed frog (*Ptychadena oxyrhynchus*) named 'Santjie' at a frog Derby held at Lurula Natal Spa, Paulpietersburg, Natal, South Africa on 21 May 1977.

found is 8000m *26246ft* for a common toad collected in the Himalayas. This species has also been found at a depth of 340m *1115ft* in a coal mine.

Frogs

Largest The largest known frog is the rare African giant frog or goliath frog (*Conrana goliath*) of Cameroon and Equatorial Guinea. A specimen captured in April 1989 on the Sanaga River, Cameroon by Andy Koffman of Seattle, Washington, USA had a snout-to-vent length of 36·83cm *14½ in* (87·63cm *34½ in* overall with legs extended) and weighed 3·66kg *8lb 1oz* on 30 Oct 1989.

UK The largest frog found in Britain is the *introduced* marsh frog (*Rana r. ridibunda*). Females have been measured up to 133mm *5¼ in* long from snout to vent, with weights of 95g *3oz*.

The largest captive frog in Britain was a male African bull frog (*Pyxicephalus adspersus*) named 'Colossus' (1978–92), owned by Steve Crabtree of Southsea, Hants. It had a snout-to-vent length of 22·2cm *8¾ in*, a girth of 45·7cm *18in* and weighed 1·89kg *4lb 3oz*.

Smallest The world's smallest frog is *Sminthillus limbatus* of Cuba. (⇔ Smallest amphibians)

Toads

Largest The largest known toad is the marine toad (*Bufo marinus*) found in tropical South America and Queensland, Australia (introduced). An average specimen weighs 450g *1lb* and the largest ever recorded was a male named 'Prinsen' (The Prince), owned by Håkan Forsberg of Åkers Styckebruk, Sweden. It weighed 2·65kg *5lb 13½oz* and measured 38cm *15in* from snout to vent (53·9cm *21⅓in* when extended) in March 1991.

UK The largest toad and heaviest amphibian found in Britain is the common toad (*Bufo bufo*). (⇔ Largest amphibians)

Smallest The world's smallest toad is the sub-species *Bufo taitanus beiranus*, originally of Mozambique, the largest specimen of which measured 24mm *1in* in length.

Fishes

Agnatha, Gnathostomata

(⇔ also Angling)

General Records

Largest The world's largest fish is the rare plankton-feeding whale shark (*Rhincodon typus*), which is found in the warmer areas of the Atlantic, Pacific and Indian Oceans. The largest scientifically recorded example was 12·65m *41½ft* long, measured 7m *23ft* round the thickest part of the body and weighed an estimated 15tonnes. It was captured off Baba Island, near Karachi, Pakistan on 11 Nov 1949.

British Isles The largest fish recorded in British waters was a basking shark (*Cetorhinus maximus*) measuring 11·12m *36ft 6in* and weighing an estimated 8tonnes, found washed ashore at Brighton, E Sussex in 1806.

Bony The longest of the bony or 'true' fishes (Pisces) is the oarfish (*Regalecus glesne*), also called the 'King of the Herrings', found world-wide. In *c.* 1885 a specimen 7·6m *25ft* long and weighing 272kg *600lb* was caught off Pemaquid Point, Maine, USA, but unconfirmed claims of 15·2m *50ft* have been made.

Heaviest The heaviest bony fish in the world is the ocean sunfish (*Mola mola*), which is found in all tropical, sub-tropical and temperate waters, including those around the British Isles. On 18 Sep 1908 a specimen accidentally injured off Bird Island near Sydney, New South Wales, Australia weighed 2235kg *4927lb* and measured 4·26m *14ft* between the anal and dorsal fins.

British Isles The largest bony fish recorded from British waters was an ocean sunfish weighing 363kg *800lb* stranded near Montrose, Tayside on 14 Dec 1960.

Carnivorous The largest carnivorous fish (excluding plankton-eaters) is the comparatively rare great white shark (*Carcharodon carcharias*), also called the 'man-eater'. Average females (males are smaller) are 4·3–4·6m *14–15ft* long and weigh 520–770kg *1150–1700lb*. The largest example accurately measured was 6·2m *20ft 4in* long and weighed

The much-maligned great white shark, whose only enemy is Man, can reach lengths of 6·2 m *20 ft 4 in* and weights of 2268 kg *5000 lb* if allowed to.

(Photo: Planet Earth Pictures/Marty Snyderman)

2268 kg *5000 lb*. It was harpooned and landed in the harbour of San Miguel, Azores in June 1978. (◇ Angling)

Smallest The shortest recorded marine fish — and the shortest known vertebrate — is the dwarf goby (*Trimmatom nanus*) of the Chagos Archipelago in the Indian Ocean. Average lengths recorded for a series of specimens collected by the 1978–79 Joint Services Chagos Research Expedition of the British Armed Forces were 8·6 mm *0·34 in* for males and 8·9 mm *0·35 in* for females.

Most abundant fish

The most abundant species of fish is probably the 76mm *3in* long deep-sea bristlemouth (*Cyclothone elongata*), which has a world-wide distribution. It would take about 500 of them to weigh 0·45kg *1lb*.

Oldest goldfish

Goldfish (*Carassius auratus*) have been reported to live for over 50 years in China.

A goldfish named 'Fred', owned by A.R. Wilson of Worthing, W Sussex, died on 1 Aug 1980 aged 41 years.

Most ferocious

The razor-toothed piranhas of the genera *Serrasalmus*, *Pygocentrus* and *Pygopristis* are the most ferocious freshwater fish in the world. They live in the sluggish waters of the large rivers of South America, and will attack any creature, regardless of size, if it is injured or making a commotion in the water. On 19 Sep 1981 more than 300 people were reportedly killed and eaten when an overloaded passenger-cargo boat capsized and sank as it was docking at the Brazilian port of Obidos. According to one official, only 178 of the estimated number of people aboard the boat survived.

British Isles Guillet's goby (*Lebetus guilleti*), recorded from the English Channel, the west coast of Ireland and the Irish Sea, does not exceed 24mm *0·94in*.

Lightest The lightest of all vertebrates and the smallest catch possible is the dwarf goby (*Schindleria praematurus*), which weighs only 2mg (equivalent to 14184 to the ounce) and is 12–19mm ½–¾in long. It is found in Samoa.

Shark The spined pygmy shark (*Squaliolus laticaudus*) of the western Pacific matures at 150mm *6in* in length.

Fastest The maximum swimming speed of a fish is dependent on its length and

temperature. The cosmopolitan sailfish (*Istiophorus platypterus*) is considered to be the fastest species of fish over short distances, although practical difficulties make measurements extremely difficult to secure. In a series of speed trials carried out at the Long Key Fishing Camp, Florida, USA, one sailfish took out 91m *300ft* of line in 3 sec, which is equivalent to a velocity of 109km/h *68mph* (cf. 96km/h *60mph* for the cheetah).

Oldest Aquaria originated too recently to establish with certainty which species of fish can be regarded as the longest-lived. Indications are, however, that it may be the lake sturgeon (*Acipenser fulvescens*) of North America. In one study of the growth rings (annuli) of 966 specimens caught in the Lake Winnebago region, Wisconsin, USA between 1951 and 1954 the oldest sturgeon was found to be a male (length 2·01m *6ft 7in*), which gave a reading of 82 years and was still growing.

In 1948 the death was reported of an 88-year-old female European eel (*Anguilla anguilla*) named 'Putte' in the aquarium at Hälsingborg Museum, Sweden. She was allegedly born in 1860 in the Sargasso Sea, North Atlantic, and was caught in a river as a 3-year-old elver.

In July 1974 a growth-ring count of 228 years was reported for a female koi fish (a form of fancy carp), named 'Hanako', living in a pond in Higashi Shirakawa, Gifu Prefecture, Japan, but the greatest authoritatively accepted age for this species is 'more than 50 years'.

The perch-like marine fish *Notothenia neglecta* of the Antarctic Ocean, whose blood contains a natural anti-freeze, is reported to live up to 150 years, but this claim has not yet been verified.

Shortest-lived The shortest-lived fishes are probably certain species of the sub-order Cyprinodontei (Killifish), found in Africa and South America, which normally live for about eight months.

Deepest Brotulids of the genus *Bassogigas* are generally regarded as the deepest-living vertebrates. The greatest depth from which a fish has been recovered is 8300m *27230ft* in the Puerto Rico Trench (8366m *27488ft*) in the Atlantic by Dr Gilbert L. Voss of the US research vessel *John Elliott*, who captured a 16·5 cm *6½ in* long *Bassogigas profundissimus* in April 1970. It was only the fifth such brotulid ever caught.

Dr Jacques Piccard and Lt Don Walsh of the US Navy reported seeing a sole-like fish about 33 cm *1ft* long (tentatively identified as *Chascanopsetta lugubris*) from the bathyscaphe *Trieste* at a depth of 35 820 ft *10 917 m* in the Challenger Deep (Marianas Trench) in the western Pacific on 24 Jan 1960, but this sighting has, however, been questioned by some authorities.

Most eggs The ocean sunfish (*Mola mola*) produces up to 30 million eggs, each measuring about 1·3 mm *0·05 in* in diameter, at a single spawning.

Fewest eggs The mouth-brooding cichlid *Tropheus moorii* of Lake Tanganyika, east Africa produces seven eggs or fewer during normal reproduction.

Most valuable The world's most valuable fish is the Russian sturgeon (*Huso huso*). One 1227 kg *2706 lb* female caught in the Tikhaya Sosna River in 1924 yielded 245 kg *541 lb* of best-quality caviar, which would be worth £189 350 on today's market.

The 76 cm *30 in* long ginrin showa koi, which won supreme championship in nationwide Japanese koi shows in 1976, 1977, 1979 and 1980, was sold two years later for 17 million yen (about £50 000). In March 1986 this ornamental carp was acquired by Derry Evans, owner of the Kent Koi Centre near Sevenoaks, Kent for an undisclosed sum, but the 15-year-old fish died five months later. It has since been stuffed and mounted to preserve its beauty.

Most venomous The most venomous fish in the world are the stonefish (Synanceidae) of the tropical waters of the Indo-Pacific, and in particular *Synanceja horrida*, which has the largest venom glands of any known fish. Direct contact with the spines of its fins, which contain a strong neurotoxic poison, often proves fatal.

Most electric The most powerful electric fish is the electric eel (*Electrophorus electricus*) from the rivers of Brazil, Colombia, Venezuela and Peru. An aver-age-sized specimen can discharge 400 volts at 1 amp, but measurements up to 650 volts have been recorded.

Marine

Largest The largest marine fish is the whale shark (*Rhincodon typus*), which can reach 9 m *30 ft* in length. (⇔ General records)

Smallest The shortest recorded marine fish in the world is the dwarf goby (*Trimmatom nanus*) of the Chagos Archipelago in the Indian Ocean, with average lengths of 8·6–8·9 mm *0·34– 0·35 in*. (⇔ General records)

Freshwater

Largest The largest fish which spends its whole life in fresh or brackish water is the rare pla beuk (*Pangasianodon gigas*), found only in the Mekong River and its major tributaries in China, Laos, Cambodia and Thailand. The largest specimen, captured in the River Ban Mee Noi, Thailand, was reportedly 3 m *9 ft 10¼ in* long and weighed 242 kg *533½ lb*. This was exceeded by the European catfish or wels (*Silurus glanis*) in earlier times (in the 19th century lengths of 4·6 m *15 ft* and weights of 336 kg *720 lb* were reported for Russian specimens), but today anything over 1·83 m *6 ft* and 90 kg *200 lb* is considered large.

The arapaima or pirarucu (*Arapaima glanis*), found in the Amazon and other South American rivers and often claimed to be the largest freshwater fish, averages 2 m *6½ ft* and 68 kg *150 lb*. The largest authentically recorded specimen was 2·48 m *8 ft 1½ in* long and weighed 147 kg *325 lb*. It was caught in the Rio Negro, Brazil in 1836.

British Isles The largest fish ever caught in a British river was a common sturgeon (*Acipenser sturio*) weighing 230 kg *507½ lb* and measuring 2·74 m *9 ft*, which was accidentally netted in the Severn at Lydney, Glos on 1 Jun 1937. Larger specimens have been taken at sea—notably one weighing 317 kg *700 lb* and 3·18 m *10 ft 5 in* in length netted by the trawler *Ben Urie* off Orkney and landed on 18 Oct 1956.

Smallest The shortest and lightest freshwater fish is the dwarf pygmy goby

(*Pandaka pygmaea*), a colourless and nearly transparent species found in the streams and lakes of Luzon in the Philippines. Males are only 7·5–9·9 mm *0·28–0·38 in* long and weigh 4–5 mg *0·00014–0·00018 oz*.

The world's smallest commercial fish is the now endangered sinarapan (*Mistichthys luzonensis*), a goby found only in Lake Buhi, Luzon, Philippines. Males are 10–13 mm *0·39–0·51 in* long, and a dried 454 g *1 lb* fish cake would contain about 70 000 of them.

Starfish

Asteroidea

Largest The largest of the 1600 known species of starfish in terms of arm-span is the very fragile brisingid *Midgardia xandaros*. A specimen collected by the Texas A&M University research vessel *Alaminos* in the Gulf of Mexico in 1968 measured 1·38 m *4½ ft* from tip to tip, but its disc was only 26 mm *1·02 in* in diameter. Its dry weight was 70 g *2·46 oz*.

Heaviest The heaviest species of starfish is the five-armed *Thromidia catalai* of the western Pacific. One specimen collected off Ilot Amédée, New Caledonia on 14 Sep 1969 and later moved to Nouméa Aquarium weighed an estimated 6 kg *13 lb 4 oz* (total arm-span 630 mm *24·8 in*).

British Isles The largest starfish found in British waters is the spiny starfish (*Marthasterias glacialis*). In January 1979 Jonathon MacNeil from the Isle of Barra, Western Isles found a specimen on the beach which originally spanned 76 cm *30 in*.

Smallest The smallest known starfish is the asterinid sea star *Patiriella parvivipara*, discovered by Wolfgang Zeidler on the west coast of the Eyre peninsula, South Australia in 1975. It has a maximum radius of only 4·7 mm *0·18 in* and a diameter of less than 9 mm *0·35 in*.

Deepest The greatest depth from which a starfish has been recovered is 7584 m *24 881 ft* for a specimen of *Porcellanaster ivanovi* collected by the Soviet research ship *Vityaz* in the Marianas Trench, west Pacific *c.* 1962.

Crustaceans

Crustacea

(*Crabs, lobsters, shrimps, prawns, crayfish, barnacles, water fleas, fish lice, woodlice, sandhoppers, krill etc*)

Largest marine The largest of all crustaceans (although not the heaviest) is the taka-ashi-gani or giant spider crab (*Macrocheira kaempferi*), also called the stilt crab, found in deep waters off south-eastern Japan. It usually has a body measuring 250×300 mm *10×12 in* and a claw-span of 2·4–2·7 m *8–9 ft*, but unconfirmed measurements of up to 5·8 m *19 ft* have been reported. A specimen with a claw-span of 3·7 m *12 ft 1½ in* weighed 18·6 kg *41 lb*.

Heaviest The heaviest crustacean, and the largest species of lobster, is the American or North Atlantic lobster (*Homarus americanus*). On 11 Feb 1977 a specimen weighing 20·14 kg *44 lb 6 oz* and measuring 1·06 m *3 ft 6 in* from the end of the tail-fan to the tip of the largest claw was caught off Nova Scotia, Canada and later sold to a New York restaurant owner.

Europe The largest crustacean found in British waters is the common or European lobster (*Homarus vulgaris*), which averages 900–1360 g *2–3 lb*. The heaviest on record weighed 10 kg *22 lb* and was caught off the west coast of Floroe, Norway by an amateur fisherman in March 1988. In June 1931 another European lobster weighing 5·80 kg *20½ lb* and measuring 1·26 m *4 ft 1½ in* in total length was caught at Fowey, Cornwall. Its crushing claw weighed 1188 g *2 lb 10 oz* after the meat had been removed.

Most destructive starfish

The crown-of-thorns (*Acanthaster planci*) of the Indo-Pacific region and the Red Sea has 12–19 arms and can measure up to 60 cm *24 in* in diameter. Feeding on coral polyps, it can consume 300–400 cm² *46½–62 in²* of coral in one day and has been responsible for the destruction of large parts of the Great Barrier Reef. (<> Coral and Longest reef)

Largest concentration

The largest single concentration of crust-aceans ever recorded was a swarm of krill (*Euphausia superba*), estimated to weigh 10 million tonnes, which was tracked by US scientists off Antarctica in March 1981.

Largest freshwater The largest fresh-water crustacean is the crayfish or crawfish (*Astacopsis gouldi*), found in the streams of Tasmania, Australia. It has been measured up to 61cm *2ft* in length and may weigh as much as 4kg *9lb*. In 1934 an unconfirmed weight of 6·35kg *14lb* (total length 73·6cm *29in*) was reported for one caught at Bridport.

Smallest Water fleas of the genus *Alonella*, found in British waters, may be less than 0·25mm *0·01in* long.

Oldest Very large specimens of the American lobster (*Homarus americanus*) may be up to 50 years old.

Deepest The greatest depth from which a crustacean has been recovered is 10 500 m *34450ft* for *live* amphipods from the Challenger Deep (Marianas Trench) in the western Pacific by the US research vessel *Thomas Washington* in November 1980.

Highest Amphipods and isopods have also been collected in the Ecuadorean Andes at a height of 4053m *13300ft*.

Arachnids
Arachnida

Spiders (Araneae)

Largest The world's largest known spider is the goliath bird-eating spider (*Theraphosa leblondi*) of the coastal rainforests of Surinam, Guyana and French Guiana, but isolated specimens have also been reported from Venezuela and Brazil. A male collected by members of the Pablo San Martin Expedition at Rio Cavro, Venezuela in April 1965 had a record leg-span of 280mm *11·02in*.

UK Of the 617 known species of British spider covering an estimated population of over 500 billion, the cardinal spider (*Tegenaria gigantea*) of southern England has the greatest average leg-span. In October 1985 Lyndsay Jarrett of Marston Meysey, Wilts collected a female in her home with a leg-span of 139mm *5½in*.

The well-known 'daddy longlegs' spider (*Pholcus phalangioides*) rarely exceeds 114mm *4½in* in leg-span, but one speci-men collected in England measured 15·2cm *6in* across.

Heaviest Female bird-eating spiders are more heavily built than males and in February 1985 Charles J. Seiderman of New York City, USA captured a female example near Paramarido, Surinam which weighed a record peak of 122·2g *4·3oz* before its death from moulting problems in January 1986. Other mea-surements included a maximum leg-span of 267mm *10½in*, a total body length of 102mm *4in* and 25mm *1in* long fangs.

UK The heaviest spider found in Britain is the orb weaver (*Araneus quadratus*). On 10 Sep 1979 a female example weighing 2·25g *0·08oz* was collected at Lavington, W Sussex by J. R. Parker.

Smallest The smallest known spider is *Patu marplesi* (family Symphyto-gnathidae) of Western Samoa. The type specimen (male) found in moss at about 600 m *2000ft* in Madolelei, Upolu in January 1965 measured 0·43 mm *0·017in* overall—about the size of a full-stop on this page.

UK The extremely rare money spider *Glyphesis cottonae* is found only in a swamp near Beaulieu Road Station, Hants and on Thursley Common, Surrey. Both sexes have a body length of 1mm *0·04in*.

Fastest arachnids

The long-legged sun spiders (solpugids) of the order Solifugae (formerly Solpugida), found in the semi-desert regions of Africa and the Middle East, feed on geckos and other lizards and can reach speeds of over 16km/h *10mph*.

This orange-kneed tarantula *Aphonopelma emiliae* from Mexico is one example of the primitive Mygalomorphae spiders which can live for up to 28 years. Although harmless to humans and often kept as pets, they can inflict a nasty bite when provoked.

(Photo: Planet Earth Pictures/Mary Clay)

Oldest The longest-lived of all spiders are the primitive *Mygalomorphae* (tarantulas and allied species). One female therasophid collected in Mexico in 1935 lived for an estimated 26–28 years.

UK The longest-lived British spider is probably the purse web spider (*Atypus affinis*), one specimen of which was kept in a greenhouse for nine years.

Largest webs Aerial webs spun by the tropical orb weavers of the genus *Nephila* have been measured up to 573cm *18ft 9¾ in* in circumference.

Smallest webs The smallest webs are spun by spiders such as *Glyphesis cottonae* and cover about 4·8cm² *¾in²*. (⇔ Smallest spider)

Most venomous The world's most venomous spiders are the Brazilian wandering spiders of the genus *Phoneutria*, and

particularly *Phoneutria fera*, which has the most active neurotoxic venom of any living spider. These large and highly aggressive creatures often enter human dwellings and hide in clothing or shoes. When disturbed they bite furiously several times, and hundreds of accidents involving these species are reported annually. Fortunately, however, an effective antivenin is available, and when deaths do occur they are usually of children under the age of seven.

Scorpions (Scorpiones)

Largest The largest of the 800 or so species of scorpion is the tropical 'emperor' *Pandinus imperator* found in Guinea, males of which can have a body length of 18cm *7in* or more.

Smallest The world's smallest scorpion is *Microbothus pusillus*, which measures about 13mm *½in* in total length and is found on the Red Sea coast.

Most venomous The most venomous scorpion in the world is the Palestine yellow scorpion (*Leiurus quinquestriatus*), which ranges from the eastern part of North Africa through the Middle East to the Red Sea. Fortunately, the amount of venom it delivers is very small (0·255mg *0·000009oz*) and adult lives are seldom endangered, but it has been responsible for a number of fatalities among children under the age of five.

Insects

Insecta

It is estimated that there may be as many as 30 million species of insect—more than all other phyla and classes put together—but thousands are known only from a single or type specimen.

Heaviest The heaviest insects are the Goliath beetles (family Scarabaeidae) of Equatorial Africa. The largest are *Goliathus regius*, *G. goliathus* (=*G. giganteus*) and *G. druryi* and in measurements of one series of males (females are smaller) the lengths from the tips of the small frontal horns to the end of the abdomen were up to 110mm *4·33in*, with weights of 70–100g *2½–3½oz*.

The elephant beetles (*Megasoma*) of Central America and the West Indies attain the greatest dimensions in terms of volume, but they lack the massive build-up of heavy chiton forming the thorax and anterior sternum of the goliaths, thus making them lighter.

UK The heaviest insect found in Britain is the stag beetle (*Lucanus cervus*) which is widely distributed over southern England. The largest specimen on record was a male which was 87·4mm *3·04in* long (body plus mandibles) and probably weighed over 6g *0·21oz* when alive. It was collected at Sheerness, Kent in 1871 and is now in the British Museum (Natural History), London.

Longest The longest insects in the world are stick-insects (walking sticks), especially of the African species *Palophus*,

Largest grasshopper

The largest grasshopper seen in Britain, and possibly in the world, is an unidentified species from the border of Malaysia and Thailand measuring 25·4cm *10in* in length and capable of leaping 4·6m *15ft*.

which can reach lengths of 400mm *15¾in* in the case of *Palophus leopoldi*.

Smallest The smallest recorded insects are the 'feather-winged' beetles of the family Ptiliidae (=Trichopterygidae) and the battledore-wing fairy flies (parasitic wasps) of the family Mymaridae, which are smaller than some species of protozoa (single-celled animals).

Lightest The male bloodsucking banded louse (*Enderleinellus zonatus*) and the parasitic wasp *Caraphractus cinctus* may each weigh as little as 0·005mg, or 5670000 to an oz. Eggs of the latter each weigh 0·0002mg (141750000 to an oz).

Fastest flying Acceptable modern experiments have established that the highest maintainable airspeed of any insect, including the deer bot-fly, hawk moths (Sphingidae), horse flies (*Tabanus bovinus*) and some tropical butterflies (Hesperiidae), is 39km/h *24mph*, rising to a maximum of 58km/h *36mph* for the Australian dragonfly *Austrophlebia costalis* for short bursts. Experiments have also proved that the widely publicised claim by an American scientist in 1926 that the deer bot-fly (*Cephenemyia pratti*) could attain a speed of 1316km/h *818mph* (sic) at an altitude of 3657m *12000ft* was wildly exaggerated. If true, the fly would have to develop the equivalent of 1·1 kW *1·5 hp* and consume 1½ times its own weight in food per second to acquire the energy needed and, even if this were possible, it would still be torn open by the air pressure and incinerated by the friction.

Fastest moving The fastest insects on land are certain large tropical cockroaches and the record is 5·4 km/h *3·36 mph*, or 50 body lengths per second, registered by *Periplaneta americana* at the University of California at Berkeley, USA in 1991.

A tasty meal is one way to slow down the American cockroach, the sprint champion of the insect world which has clocked record speeds of 5·4 km/h 3·36 mph.

(Photo: Planet Earth Pictures/John Lythgoe)

Highest g force The click beetle (*Athous haemorrhoidalis*) averages 400 *g* when 'jack-knifing' into the air to escape predators. One example measuring 12 mm *½ in* in length and weighing 40 mg *0·00014 oz* which jumped to a height of 30 cm *11¾ in* was calculated to have endured a peak brain deceleration of 2300 *g* by the end of the movement.

Oldest The longest-lived insects are the splendour beetles (Buprestidae). On 27 May 1983 a specimen of *Buprestis aurulenta* appeared from the staircase timber in the home of Mr W. Euston of Prittlewell, Southend-on-Sea, Essex after 47 years as a larva.

Fastest wing-beat The fastest wing-beat of any insect under natural conditions is 62760 per min by a tiny midge of the genus *Forcipomyia*. In experiments with truncated wings at a temperature of 37°C *98·6°F* the rate increased to 133080 beats/min. The muscular contraction–expansion cycle in 0·00045 sec further represents the fastest muscle movement ever measured.

Slowest wing-beat The slowest wing beat of any insect is 300 per min by the

88

Largest termite mound
In 1968 W. Page photographed a specimen south of Horgesia, Somalia estimated to be 8·7 m *28½ ft* tall.

Ants
The most dangerous ant in the world is the bulldog ant (*Myrmecia pyriformis*) of mainland Australia and Tasmania. It has been responsible for at least three reported human fatalities since 1936, the last occurring in November 1988.

Mantle of bees
Jed Shaner was covered by a mantle of an estimated 343000 bees weighing 36·3 kg *80 lb* at Staunton, Virginia, USA on 29 Jun 1991.

Loudest insect
At 7400 pulses/min the tymbal organs of the male cicada (family Cicadidae) produce a noise (officially described by the US Department of Agriculture as 'Tsh-ee-EEEE-e-ou') detectable more than 400 m *¼ mile* away. The only British species is the very rare mountain cicada (*Cicadetta montana*), which is confined to the New Forest area in Hampshire.

Largest cockroach
The world's largest cockroach is *Megaloblatta longipennis* of Colombia. A preserved female in the collection of Akira Yokokura of Yamagata, Japan measures 97 mm *3·81 in* in length and 45 mm *1·77 in* across.

swallowtail butterfly (*Papilio machaon*). The average is 460–636 per min.

Dragonflies (Odonata)

Largest. The species *Megaloprepus caeruleata* of Central and South America has been measured up to 120mm *4·72in* across the wings and 191mm *7·52in* in body length.

UK The largest British species is *Anax imperator*, with a wing span of up to 106mm *4·17in*.

Smallest The world's smallest dragonfly is *Agriocnemis naia* of Myanmar (Burma). A specimen in the British Museum (Natural History) had a wing spread of 17·6mm *0·69in* and a body length of 18mm *0·71in*.

UK The smallest British species is *Lestes dryas*, which has a body length of 20–25mm *0·8–1in*.

Fleas (Siphonaptera)

Largest Siphonapterologists recognize 1830 varieties, of which the largest known is *Hystrichopsylla schefferi*, which was described from a single specimen taken from the nest of a mountain beaver (*Aplodontia rufa*) at Puyallup, Washington, USA in 1913. Females are up to 8mm *0·3in* long.

UK The largest of the 61 species found in Britain is the mole and vole flea (*Hystrichopsylla talpae*), females of which have been measured up to 6mm *0·23in*.

Longest jump The champion jumper among fleas is the common flea (*Pulex irritans*). In one American experiment carried out in 1910 a specimen allowed to leap at will performed a long jump of 330mm *13 in* and a high jump of 197mm *7¾in*. In jumping 130 times its own height a flea subjects itself to a force of 200g.

Butterflies and Moths (Lepidoptera)

Largest The largest known butterfly is the protected Queen Alexandra's birdwing (*Ornithoptera alexandrae*) which is restricted to the Popondetta Plain in Papua New Guinea. Females may have a wing span exceeding 280mm *11in* and weigh over 25g *0·9oz*. (⇔ Species on the Brink)

The largest moth in the world (although not the heaviest) is the Hercules moth (*Cosdinoscera hercules*) of tropical Australia and New Guinea. A wing area of up to 263cm² *41in²* and a wing

spread of 280mm *11 in* have been recorded. In 1948 an unconfirmed measurement of 360mm *14in* was reported for a female captured in Innisfail, Queensland, Australia.

A wing span of up to 308mm *12⅕in* has been measured on a rare female owlet moth (*Thysania agrippina*) of Brazil, taken in 1934.

UK The largest butterfly found in Britain is the monarch butterfly (*Danaus plexippus*), also called the milkweed or black-veined brown butterfly, a rare vagrant which breeds in the southern United States and Central America. It has a wing span of up to 127mm *5in* and weighs about 1g *0·04oz*. (⇔ Migration)

The largest *native* butterfly is the swallowtail (*Papilio machaon britannicus*), females of which have a wing span up to 100mm *3·93in*. This species is now confined to the Norfolk Broads.

The largest (but not the heaviest) of the 21000 species of insect found in Britain is the very rare death's head hawkmoth (*Acherontia atropos*). One female found dead in a garden at Tiverton, Devon in 1931 had a wing span of 145mm *5¾in* and weighed nearly 3g *0·10oz*.

On 9 Jun 1988 a giant moth with a wing span of 150mm *6 in* was found by workmen at a plant hire firm in Wolleston, Northants. It was later identified as a great peacock silk moth (*Saturnia pyri*) which had probably escaped from a butterfly house.

Smallest The smallest of the 140000 known species of Lepidoptera is *Stigmella ridiculosa*, which has a wing span of 2mm *0·079in* with a similar body length and is found in the Canary Islands.

UK The moth *Johansonnia acetosae* has a wing span of 3mm *0·12in* and a corresponding body length.

Most acute sense of smell The most acute sense of smell exhibited in nature is that of the male emperor moth (*Eudia pavonia*), which, according to German experiments in 1961, can detect the sex attractant of the virgin female at the almost unbelievable range of 11 km *6·8miles* upwind. This scent has been identified as one of the higher alcohols

$(C_{16}H_{29}OH)$, of which the female carries less than 0·0001 mg.

Migration A tagged female monarch butterfly (*Danaus plexippus*) released by Donald Davis at Presqu'ile Provincial Park near Brighton, Ontario, Canada on 6 Sep 1986 was recaptured 3432 km *2133 miles* away, on a mountain near Angangueo, Mexico, on 15 Jan 1987. This distance was obtained by measuring a line from the release site to the recapture site, but the actual distance travelled could be up to double this figure. (⇔ Largest butterfly)

Largest butterfly farm The Stratford-upon-Avon Butterfly Farm, Warks can accommodate 2000 exotic butterflies in authentic rainforest conditions. The total capacity of all flight areas at the farm, which opened on 15 Jul 1985, is over 4000 m³ *141 259 ft³*. The complex also comprises insect and plant houses and educational facilities.

Centipedes

Chilopoda

Longest The longest known species of centipede is a large variant of the widely distributed *Scolopendra morsitans* found on the Andaman Islands in the Bay of Bengal. Specimens measuring 330 mm *13 in* long and 38 mm *1½ in* wide have been recorded.

UK The native British species *Henia vesuviana* is over 70 mm *2¾ in* long and individuals found in north-east London in 1989 by Dr Steve Hopkin of the University of Reading, Berks measured 80 mm *3⅗ in*.

Shortest The shortest recorded centipede is an unidentified species which measures only 5 mm *0·19 in*.

UK The smallest British species is *Lithobius dubosequi*, which is up to 9·5 mm *0·37 in* long.

Most legs *Himantarum gabrielis* has 171–177 pairs of legs and is found in southern Europe.

Fastest The fastest centipede is probably *Scrutigera coleoptrata* of southern Europe, which can travel at 1·8 km/h *1·1 mph*.

Millipedes

Diplopoda

Longest Both *Graphidostreptus gigas* of Africa and *Scaphistostreptus seychellarum* of the Seychelles have been measured up to 280 mm *11 in* in length and 20 mm *0·8 in* in diameter.

UK Cylindroiulus londinensis can be up to 50 mm *1·96 in* long.

Shortest The world's shortest millipede is the British species *Polyxenus lagurus*, which is 2·1–4·0 mm *0·08–0·15 in* long.

Most legs The greatest number of legs reported for a millipede is 375 pairs (750 legs) for *Illacme plenipes* of California, USA.

Segmented Worms

Annelida

Longest The longest known species of earthworm is *Microchaetus rappi* (=*M. microchaetus*) of South Africa. In *c.* 1937 a giant measuring 6·7 m *22 ft* in length when naturally extended and 20 mm *0·8 in* in diameter was collected in the Transvaal.

UK The longest segmented worm found in Britain is the marine king ragworm (*Nereis virens*). On 19 Oct 1975 a specimen measuring 111·7 cm *44 in* when fully extended was collected by James Sawyer in Hauxley Bay, Northumberland. The longest earthworm found in Britain is *Lumbricus terrestris*. Its normal

Worm charming
At the first World Worm Charming Championship held at Willaston, near Nantwich, Cheshire on 5 Jul 1980 a local farmer's son, Tom Shufflebotham (b. 1960), charmed a record 511 worms out of the ground (a 3 m² *9·84 ft²* plot) in the allotted time of 30 min. Garden forks or other implements are vibrated in the soil by competitors to coax up the worms, but water is banned.

Most venomous cephalopod

The two closely related species of blue-ringed octopus *Hapalochlaena masculosa* and *H. lunulata*, found around the coasts of Australia, carry a neurotoxic venom so potent that scientists at the Commonwealth Serum Laboratories in Melbourne, Victoria consider one bite sufficient to paralyse (or sometimes kill) seven people. The venom acts so quickly that an antivenin could only rarely, if ever, be used in time to save life. These molluscs have a radial spread of just 100–150 mm *4–6 in*.

range is 90–300 mm *3½–12 in* but this species has been reliably measured up to 350 mm *13¾ in* when naturally extended. Measurements of up to 508 mm *20 in* have been claimed, but in each case the body was probably first macerated or mistaken for the intestinal tract of some small buried mammal.

Shortest *Chaetogaster annandalei* measures less than 0·5 mm *0·02 in* in length.

Molluscs
Mollusca

Cephalopods

Largest invertebrate The Atlantic giant squid (*Architeuthis dux*) is the world's largest known invertebrate. The heaviest ever recorded was a 2 tonne monster which ran aground in Thimble Tickle Bay, Newfoundland, Canada on 2 Nov 1878. Its body was 6·1 m *20 ft* long and one tentacle measured 10·6 m *35 ft*. (⬦ General records, Largest eye)

British Isles The largest squid ever recorded in British waters was an example of *Architeuthis monachus* which measured 7·3 m *24 ft* in total length, found at Whalefirth Voe, Shetland on 2 Oct 1959.

Longest The longest mollusc ever recorded was another giant squid *Architeuthis longimanus* measuring 17·4 m *57 ft* which was washed up on Lyall Bay, Cook Strait, New Zealand in

October 1887. Its two long slender tentacles each measured 15·01 m *49 ft 3 in*.

Largest octopus The largest known octopus is the Pacific giant (*Octopus dofleini*), which ranges from California to Alaska, USA and off eastern Asia south to Japan. It is not known exactly how large these creatures can grow but the average male weighs about 23 kg *51 lb* and has an arm span of about 2·5 m *8 ft*. The largest recorded specimen, found off western Canada in 1957, had an estimated arm span of 9·6 m *31½ ft* and weighed about 272 kg *600 lb*.

British Isles The largest octopus found in British waters is the common octopus (*Octopus vulgaris*), which may span 2·13 m *7 ft* and weigh more than 4·5 kg *10 lb*.

Smallest The smallest cephalopod is the squid *Idiosepius* which rarely reaches 25·4 mm *1 in* in length.

Oldest The longest-lived mollusc is the ocean quahog (*Arctica islandica*), a thick-shelled clam found in the mid-Atlantic. A specimen with 220 annual growth rings was collected in 1982.

Most tentacles Most cephalopods have eight or 10 tentacles but some types of *Nautilus* use up to 94 suckerless tentacles for catching prey on the ocean floor.

Bivalves

Largest The largest of all existing bivalve shells is that of the marine giant clam *Tridacna gigas*, found on the Indo-Pacific coral reefs. One specimen measuring 115 cm *45⅓ in* in length and weighing 333 kg *734 lb* was collected off Ishigaki Island, Okinawa, Japan in 1956 but was not scientifically examined until August 1984. It probably weighed just over 340 kg *750 lb* when alive (the soft parts weigh up to 9·1 kg *20 lb*).

Longest Another giant clam collected at Tapanoeli (Tapanula), Sumatra, Indonesia before 1817 and now preserved at Arno's Vale is 137 cm *54 in* long and weighs 230 kg *507 lb*.

British Isles It was reported on 14 Aug 1991 that a Pacific oyster weighing 12·25 kg *27 lb* and measuring 508 mm *20 in* long and 254 mm *10 in* wide had been found in the Fleet at Weymouth, Dorset.

No-one knows exactly how large the giant Pacific octopus can grow, but the largest recorded example found so far had an estimated arm-span of 9·6m 31½ft and weighed some 272kg 600lb.

(Photo: Planet Earth Pictures/ Ken Lucas)

Smallest The smallest bivalve shell is the coinshell *Neolepton sykesi*, which is known only from a few examples collected off Guernsey, Channel Islands and western Ireland. It has an average diameter of 1·2mm *0·047in*.

Most venomous There are some 400–500 species of cone shell (*Conus*), all of which can deliver a poisonous neurotoxin. The geographer cone (*Conus geographus*) and the court cone (*C. aulicus*), marine molluscs found from Polynesia to east Africa, are considered to be the most deadly. The venom is injected by a unique fleshy, harpoon-like proboscis and symptoms include impaired vision, dizziness, nausea, paralysis and death. Of the 25 people known to have been stung by these creatures, five have died, giving a mortality rate exceeding that for common cobras and rattlesnakes.

Gastropods

Largest The largest known gastropod is the trumpet or baler conch (*Syrinx aru-*

anus) of Australia. One specimen collected off Western Australia in 1979 and now owned by Don Pisor of San Diego, California had a shell 77·2cm *30·4in* long with a maximum girth of 101cm *39¾in*. It weighed nearly 18kg *40lb* when alive.

The largest known land gastropod is the African giant snail *Achatina achatina*, the largest recorded specimen of which measured 39·3cm *15½in* from snout to tail when fully extended (shell length 27·3cm *10¾in*) in December 1978 and weighed exactly 900g *2lb*. Named 'Gee Geronimo', this snail was owned by Christopher Hudson (1955–79) of Hove, E Sussex and was collected in Sierra Leone in June 1976.

UK The largest land snail found in Britain is the Roman or edible snail (*Helix pomatia*), with a body length of up to 10cm *4in* when fully extended and a shell length of 5cm *2in*. It weighs up to 85g *3oz*.

Smallest The smallest known shell-bearing species is probably the gastropod *Ammonicera rota*, found in British waters. It measures 0·5mm *0·02in* in diameter. A gastropod shell of the species *Bittium* measuring 0·39mm *0·015in* long and 0·31mm *0·012in* wide was found off the Nansha Islands by Zheng Genhai of Shanghai, China.

Oyster opening

The record for opening oysters is 100 in 2min 20·07sec, by Mike Racz in Invercargill, New Zealand on 16 Jul 1990.

Winkling

Sheila Bance picked 50 shells (with a straight pin) in 1min 30·55sec at the European Food and Drink Fair at Rochester, Kent on 7 May 1993.

Snail racing

On 20 Feb 1990 a garden snail named 'Verne' completed a 31cm *12·2in* course at West Middle School in Plymouth, Michigan, USA in a record 2min 13sec at 0·233cm/sec.

The British record was set on 20–21 Jul 1991 when a garden snail named 'Streaker' reportedly completed the 33cm *13in* course at the World Snail Racing Championships in Congham, Norfolk in 2min 22sec. Life on a gastropod breeding farm awaited the winner.

Fastest The world's fastest gastropods are probably banana slugs of the species *Ariolimax*. The fastest recorded speed was 0·734cm/sec over 91cm *36in* (a time of 2min 4sec) set by a specimen of *A. columbianus* in a slug race at Northwest Trek, Washington, USA in July 1983.

Snail The fastest land snails are probably the carnivorous (and cannibalistic) species such as *Euglandina rosea* which out-pace other snails in their hunt for prey. The snail-racing equivalent of a four-minute mile is 61cm *24in* in 3min, or a 5½ day mile, by the common garden snail (*Helix aspersa*).

Ribbon Worms

Nemertina

Longest The longest of the 550 recorded species of ribbon worm, also called nemertines (or nemerteans), is the boot-lace worm (*Lineus longissimus*), found in the shallow waters of the North Sea. A specimen washed ashore at St Andrews, Fife in 1864 after a severe storm was over 55m *180ft* long.

Jellyfish and Corals

Cnidaria

Largest jellyfish The Arctic giant (*Cyanea capillata arctica*) of the north-western Atlantic is the world's largest jellyfish. One washed up in Massachusetts Bay, USA had a bell diameter of 2·28m *7ft 6in* and tentacles stretching 36·5m *120ft*.

British Isles The largest cnidarian found in British waters is the rare lion's mane jellyfish (*Cyanea capillata*), also known as the common sea blubber. One specimen measured at St Andrew's Marine Laboratory, Fife had a bell diameter of 91cm *35·8in* and tentacles stretching over 13·7m *45ft*.

Most venomous The beautiful but deadly Australian sea wasp (*Chironex fleckeri*) is the most venomous cnidarian in the world. Its cardiotoxic venom has caused the deaths of 66 people off the coast of Queensland since 1880, with victims dying within 1–3 minutes if medical aid is not available. One effective defence, however, is women's hosiery, outsize versions of which are now worn by Queensland lifesavers at surfing tournaments.

Coral The world's greatest stony coral structure is the Great Barrier Reef off Queensland, north-east Australia. It stretches for 2027km *1260 miles* and covers 207 000km² *80 000 miles²*. (⇨ Most destructive starfish)

The world's largest reported example of discrete coral is a stony colony of *Galaxea fascicularis* found in Sakiyama Bay off Iriomote Island, Japan on 7 Aug 1982 by Dr Shohei Shirai of the Institute for Development of Pacific Natural Resources. It had a long axis measurement of 7·8m *23ft 9in*, a height of 4m *13ft 1½in* and a maximum circumference of 19·5m *59ft 5in*.

Largest structure

The largest structure ever built by living creatures is the 2027 km *1260 mile* long Great Barrier Reef, off Queensland, Australia, covering 207 000 km² *80 000 miles²*. It consists of countless millions of dead and living stony corals (order Madreporaria or Scleractinia). Over 350 species of coral are currently found there, and its accretion is estimated to have taken 600 million years.

Sponges
Porifera

Largest The largest known sponge is the barrel-shaped loggerhead sponge (*Spheciospongia vesparium*), measuring up to 105 cm *3 ft 6 in* in height and 91 cm *3 ft* in diameter. It if found in the West Indies and the waters off Florida, USA. Neptune's cup or goblet (*Poterion patera*) from Indonesia grows to 120 cm *4 ft* in height but is less bulky than the loggerhead.

Heaviest In 1909 a wool sponge (*Hippospongia canaliculatta*) measuring 183 cm *6 ft* in circumference was collected off the Bahamas. It initially weighed 36–41 kg *80–90 lb* but this fell to 5·44 kg *12 lb* after it had been dried and relieved of all excrescences. It is now preserved in the US National Museum, Washington, DC, USA.

Smallest The widely distributed *Leucosolenia blanca* is just 3 mm *0·11 in* tall when fully grown.

Deepest Sponges have been recovered from depths of 5637 m *18 500 ft.*

Species on the Brink

A number of mammals are known only from a single or type specimen.

General The Javan rhinoceros (*Rhinoceros sondaicus*) is considered to be the world's rarest large mammal. This solitary, single-horned species is up to 1·7 m *5½ ft* tall at the shoulder and weighs 1400 kg *3086 lb*. Once widely distributed, its population has declined to just 50–70 wild specimens, mainly as result of illegal hunting of its horns for use in traditional Oriental medicines and the destruction of its habitats. There are none held in captivity.

The red wolf (*Canis rufus*) of the southeast United States became extinct in the wild in the early 1970s, but a successful captive breeding programme by the US Fish and Wildlife Service has resulted in the release of two breeding pairs in North Carolina in 1988.

Felines The Iriomote cat (*Felis iriomotensis*), which is confined to the small (292 km² *113 miles²*) Japanese-owned island from which it takes its name, was only discovered in 1967, since when its population has fallen to about 80. This nocturnal animal, the size of an average domestic cat, is protected by Japanese law and has been declared a national monument.

The general population of the tiger in the wild, estimated at about 100 000 in 1900, has fallen to some 7000 and three of the eight subspecies, namely the Bali (*Panthera tigris balica*), Caspian (*P. t. sondaica*) and Javan (*P. t. virgata*) tigers, are already extinct.

Primates The greater bamboo broad-nosed gentle lemur (*Hapalemur simus*) of Madagascar reportedly became extinct in the early 1970s, but in 1986 a group of 60–80 individuals was discovered near Ranomafana in the south-eastern part of the island by an expedition from Duke University, Durham, North Carolina, USA.

The golden-rumped tamarin (*Léontopithecus chrysopygus*), which is now restricted to two areas of forest in the state of São Paulo, Brazil, is also on the verge of extinction, with only 75–100 surviving in 1986.

Bats At least three species of bat are known only from the type specimen. They are: the small-toothed fruit bat (*Neopteryx frosti*) from Tamalanti, Celebes in 1938–39; *Paracoelops megalotis* from Vinh, Vietnam (1945); and

Latidens salimalii from the High Wavy Mountains, India (1948).

UK The rarest of the 15 British species is the large mouse-eared bat (*Myotis myotis*) of southern England, the population of which is down from 48 to a single male which has lived in Sussex for 15 years forlornly waiting for a mate. The last known female was killed by the felling of a tree in Sussex in 1977.

Rodents The rarest rodents in the world are Garrido's hutia (*Capromys garridoi*) of the Canarreos Archipelago, Cuba and the little earth hutia (*C. sanfelipensis*) from Juan Garcia Cay, an islet off southern Cuba. The latter species has not been recorded since its discovery in 1970.

Antelopes The Arabian oryx (*Oryx leucoryx*) has been saved from the brink of extinction by a captive breeding programme at San Diego Zoo, California, USA and strict protective measures in the wild, resulting in its successful reintroduction into the deserts of Oman and Jordan, where the population has reached at least 150.

Deer Fea's muntjac (*Muntiacus feae*) was known only from two specimens collected on the borders of southern Myanmar (Burma) and western Thailand. In December 1977 a female was received at Dusit Zoo, Bangkok, followed by two females in 1981 and three males and three females from Xizang, Tibet between February 1982 and April 1983.

Marsupials The thylacine, also known as the Tasmanian wolf or tiger (*Thylacinus cynocephalus*) and feared extinct since the last captive specimen died in Beaumaris Zoo, Hobart, Tasmania on 7 Sep 1936, was possibly identified in July 1982 when a wildlife ranger claimed he saw one of these predatory marsupials in the spotlight of his parked car. Since then, however, there have been no more positive sightings.

Marine Mammals

Cetaceans Longman's beaked whale (*Indopacetus pacificus*) is known only from two skulls, one discovered on a beach near MacKay, Queensland, Australia in 1922, and the second near Mogadishu, Somalia in 1955.

Of the eight subspecies of tiger, the Bali, Javan and Caspian varieties, shown here as drawings (top to bottom), are already extinct. Also pictured is the Mediterranean monk seal, which now numbers only a few hundred and is under constant threat from pollution and hunters.
(Photos: WWF Photolibrary/Helmut Diller/ J. Trotignon)

95

New and recent discoveries

Following the discovery in 1990 of the previously unknown black-faced lion tamarin in Brazil, another new primate species, the Rio Maués marmoset (*Callithrix mauesi*) was reported in 1992 from the same country. Brazil is already home to over 25 per cent (some 68 species) of the world's known species of primate and this was the third new discovery in as many years. Although first seen in 1985, the Maués marmoset was not recognized as a new species for seven years.

Troglodiplura lowryi, a species of blind, underground spider similar to trap-door spiders and thought to be extinct, was reported to be living in a cave under the Nullarbor Plain, South Australia in 1991. This is one of only three known species of blind and subterranean spider.

The joy of discovering a new species of bird was short-lived when four new bishop birds of the genus *Euplectes* were found in Dar es Salaam, Tanzania in 1992. Caged in preparation for probable export as pets to Europe or the United States, two of the birds were already dead, and the others died shortly afterwards.

Sightings of the vaquita or Gulf porpoise (*Phocoena sinus*) in the Gulf of California in 1986 (the first since 1980) suggest an estimated population of just 30, making this probably the rarest cetacean.

The Baiji, or Yangzi River, dolphin (*Lipotes vexillifer*) is probably the most endangered of all the cetaceans (whales, dolphins and porpoises), with a population estimated at about 300 and falling due to competition for fish supplies with China's human population (dolphins are often caught up in fishing gear) and the reduction of overall food supplies because of environmental degradation.

Pinnipeds The last reliable sighting of the Caribbean or West Indian monk seal (*Monachus tropicalis*) was on Serranilla Bank off the Yucatan Peninsula, Mexico in 1952 and this species is almost certainly extinct. Monk seals were once common throughout the Pacific, the Caribbean and the Mediterranean. The first pinnipeds recorded by Aristotle (384–322BC), monk seals were the first to be spotted by Christopher Columbus (1451–1506) in the New World.

Europe The population of the once common Mediterranean monk seal (*M. monachus*) is believed to have fallen to less than 300, mainly because of overhunting and pollution.

Birds

General The number of threatened bird species world-wide has risen in the past 10 years from 290 to 1029 as a result of human activity, according to a survey published in October 1988. Many species are now extinct in the wild but may be surviving in captivity, usually as a result of breeding programmes. Because of the practical difficulties in assessing bird populations in the wild, it is virtually impossible to establish the identity of the world's rarest living bird. The most probable contender, however, is Spix's macaw (*Cyanopsitta spixii*) of Brazil, the world's most endangered parrot, which had been reduced to a single specimen in the wild at July 1990. There are only 15 left in captivity around the world.

The kakapo (*Strigops habrotilus*), a flightless parrot from New Zealand, is also in imminent danger of extinction from hunting and predation by introduced alien species, despite several attempts to relocate it to increasingly inaccessible islands. In 1990 there were 43 known survivors but, as the kakapo breeds somewhat sporadically (only once in 4 or 5 years), it may go the way of the dodo, the only bird with which it apparently shares any features.

British Isles According to the British Ornithologists' Union, there are over 50 species of birds which have been recorded only once in the British Isles—most of them since the end of the Second World War.

Reptiles

Crocodilians The total wild population of the protected Chinese alligator (*Alligator sinensis*) of the lower Yangzi River in the Anhui, Zhejiang and Jiangsu provinces of China is currently estimated at no more than a few hundred. Although captive breeding programmes are proving successful, the alligator cannot be reintroduced into the wild because of the destruction of its habitats and its extinction outside capivity is expected before the end of the century, if not sooner.

Chelonians The world's rarest chelonian is the protected short-necked swamp tortoise (*Pseudemydura umbrina*), which is confined to Ellen Brook and Twin reserves near Perth, Western Australia. The total wild population is now only 20–25, with another 22 held at Perth Zoo.

Snakes The world's rarest snake is now considered to be the St Lucia racer or couresse (*Liophis ornatus*), found only on Maria Island, off St Lucia, West Indies. Estimates by Dr David Corke of the Polytechnic of East London put its population at under 100 in 1989, with no specimens held in captivity.

The Round Island boa (*Bolyeria multicarinata*) is only known from two specimens collected in the past 40 years and probably became extinct in 1980.

UK The rarest of Britain's three indigenous species of snake is the smooth snake (*Coronella austriaca*) of southern England, with a total wild population of about 2000.

Amphibians

General Only five specimens of the painted frog (*Discoglossus nigriventer*) of Lake Huleh, Israel have been reported since 1940.

UK Although cases exist where 'pet' amphibia are released into gardens and establish breeding colonies, it is illegal to introduce non-native animals into the country. Britain's rarest native amphibian is the natterjack toad (*Bufo calamita*), which is restricted to sand-dunes and heathlands with temporary pools where it breeds. Its population is further threatened by the disappearance of most of the inland colonies.

Fishes

Marine A coelacanth, a large, deepwater fish formerly known only from fossilized remains dating from 400–65 million years old, was landed at East London, South Africa on 22 Dec 1938 and only later identified as such and named *Latimeria chalumnae*. It has been claimed to be the 'missing link' between man and fish. Since this discovery, living coelacanths have been observed in their natural habitat 200 m *656 ft* below the waters off the Comoros in the Indian Ocean in the late 1980s.

Freshwater In January 1992 it was reported that almost a quarter of Britain's native species of freshwater fish were close to extinction or seriously endangered, partly because of overfishing and pollution. Among the most endangered are the burbot (*Lota lota*), the sturgeon (*Acipenser fulvescens*) and the Arctic char (*Salvelinus alpinus*).

Arachnids

Spiders The most elusive of all spiders are the rare trapdoor spiders of the genus *Liphistius*, found in south-east Asia.

UK Britain's rarest spider is the fen or great raft spider (*Dolomedes plantarius*), whose single colony of a few individuals was reported in 1991 to have been saved from extinction by a private water pipe supplied by Suffolk Water Company.

Insects

General The current status of the St Helena giant earwig (*Labidura herculeana*) is unknown and, as the last reliable sighting was in 1967, this insect may be close to extinction. It is the largest of the order Dermaptera, with a maximum recorded total length (body and tail pincers) of 78 mm *3 in*. Its decline is a result of the accidental introduction of rats to its habitat and predation by the fearsome giant centipede, which can attack the nocturnal earwigs deep in their protective burrows.

Butterflies and moths The rarest butterfly is considered to be the Queen Alexandra's birdwing (*Ornithoptera* *alexandrae*), which is found with its only source of nutrition, the vine *Aristolochia dielsiana*, in Papua New Guinea. Its population is extremely difficult to estimate as it flies very high and is seldom seen. Its caterpillars are also somewhat elusive 40m *131ft* above the ground in the vine leaves, and only three were sighted in 1990 during surveys of an area covering 90–130 ha *220–320acres*. (▷ Largest butterfly)

Another species of birdwing, *Ornithoptera* (=*Troides*) *allottei* of Bougainville, Solomon Islands, is known from less than a dozen specimens, but this is a natural hybrid of *Ornithoptera victoriae* and *Ornithoptera urvillianus* and not a true species.

UK Britain's rarest resident butterfly (59 species) is the large copper (*Lycaena dispar*) which became extinct in 1851 but was re-introduced in 1927 to Wood Walton Fen, Cambs, where it still survives. Already rarer than the large blue (*Maculinea arion*), declared extinct in 1979 but 150 adults of which were recorded in 1988 following a breeding programme and re-release, its population is steadily declining due to drying out of the fen and it is in danger of becoming extinct again in the near future.

Although the chequered skipper (*Carterocephalus palaemon*) became extinct from England in 1975, it is relatively common in parts of Scotland.

Plants

General Plants thought to be extinct are rediscovered each year and there are thus many plants of which specimens are known from only a single locality.

The last surviving specimen (a female) of the cycad *Encephalartos woodii*, a palm-like tropical plant of a group known to have existed for between 65 and 225 million years, is held at the Royal Botanic Gardens at Kew, Surrey. It is possible that this plant is a hybrid of the specimen *Encephalartos altensteinii*, also at Kew. (▷ Oldest pot plant)

Pennantia baylisiana, a tree found in 1945 on Three Kings Island, off New Zealand, also only exists as a female and cannot produce fertilized fruit.

In May 1983 it was reported that there was a sole surviving specimen of the lady's slipper orchid (*Cypripedium calceolus*) in Britain.

Rothschild's slipper orchid (*Paphiopedilum rothschildianum*) was discovered in 1888 and thought to be extinct until its rediscovery in 1959. The spectacular beauty of this plant has, naturally, contributed greatly to its imminent extinction at the hands of illegal collectors and traders, although its highly specific ecological requirements are also a major factor. Seeds were gathered in 1982 and its only chance for survival in the wild is propagation and re-release in new and highly secret locations.

Trees The palm tree genus *Hyophorbe* contains only five species and is endemic to the Mascarene Islands. All five species are considered endangered, but especially the Mauritius palm (*H. amaricaulis*), whose once abundant population has been reduced to a single specimen, probably planted deliberately, at the Curepipe Botanic Garden, Mauritius. Attempts at propagation have so far proved unsuccessful and this species faces certain extinction.

Extinct Animals

Dinosaurs

(▷ also Other reptiles)

Part of the reptile order, dinosaurs are undoubtedly the best known group of extinct animals. The first dinosaur to be described scientifically was *Megalosaurus bucklandi* ('great fossil lizard') in 1824. Remains of this bipedal flesh-eater were found by workmen before 1818 in a slate quarry near Woodstock, Oxon and later placed in the University Museum at Oxford. The first fossil bone of *Megalosaurus* was actually illustrated in 1677, but its true nature was not realized until much later. It was not until 1842 that the name Dinosauria ('terrible lizards') was given to the newly-discovered giants.

Disappearance No wholly satisfactory theory has been offered for the dinosaurs' sudden extinction 65 million years ago. Evidence from the Hell Creek Formation of Montana, USA suggests that dinosaurs dwindled in importance over a period of 5–10 million years and were replaced progressively by mammals, possibly because of long-term climatic changes.

Another theory is their sudden elimination by the impact of an asteroid, which would have had a diameter of some 9 km *5·6 miles*, or by a shower of comets causing clouds of dust to block out the sun. This theory is supported strongly by the discovery of significant levels of the element iridium, a good indicator of extraterrestrial impact, at numerous locations around the world. In 1991 the possible impact crater was found in the Yucatán region of Central America, called the Chicxulub Crater. It dates to 65 million years ago and is associated with iridium, melt glasses and evidence of tsunamis (giant sea waves) around the proto-Caribbean.

A further hypothesis is that there was a period of severe volcanic activity, which would also result in darkness caused by dust, and acid rain and iridium.

Earliest The most primitive dinosaur is *Eoraptor lunensis* ('dawn stealer'), named in 1993 from a skeleton found in the foothills of the Andes in Argentina in rocks dated as 230 million years old. This dinosaur was 1m *39 in* long and is classified as a theropod, a member of the group of meat-eating dinosaurs. It is the most primitive of the group since it lacks the dual-hinged jaw present in all other members. (⬦ Feature)

Another dinosaur from the same area and rocks is *Herrerasaurus*, a carnivore known best from an almost complete skeleton discovered in 1989. *Herrerasaurus* was about 2–2·5m *6½–8 ft* in length and weighed over 100 kg *220 lb*. Although of the same age as *Eoraptor*, it had the dual-hinged jaw.

Other dinosaurs of a similar age from the Late Triassic are known from incomplete remains found in Brazil, Morocco, India and Scotland.

Largest The largest ever land animals were sauropod dinosaurs, a group of long-necked, long-tailed, four-legged plant-eaters that lumbered around most

Earliest ancestor

It was reported on 10 Jun 1992 that mankind's oldest ancestor may have been an eel-like fish that lived 515 million years ago, which is over 40 million years earlier than previous estimates. The claim, made by scientists at Birmingham and Durham Universities, was based on studies of fossilized teeth from vertebrates known as conodonts found in Middle Ordovician and Late Cambrian deposits dating from 475–515 million years ago. The first complete fossilized conodont was discovered near Edinburgh, Lothian in 1983.

Most brainless

Stegosaurus ('plated lizard'), which roamed across Colorado, Oklahoma, Utah and Wyoming, USA about 150 million years ago, measured up to 9m *30 ft* in total length but had a walnut-sized brain weighing only 70g *2½ oz*. This represented 0·004 of 1 per cent of its computed bodyweight of 1·75 tonnes (cf. 0·074 of 1 per cent for an elephant and 1·88 per cent for a human).

of the world during the Jurassic and Cretaceous periods 208–65 million years ago. However, it is difficult to determine precisely which of these sauropod dinosaurs was the largest (longest, tallest or heaviest). This is because many of the supposed giants are based only on incomplete fossil remains, and also because many discoverers have tended to exaggerate the sizes of their dinosaur finds. Estimating dinosaur lengths and heights is relatively straightforward when there is a complete skeleton. Sauropods are divided into five main groups: cetiosaurids, brachiosaurids, diplodocids, camarasaurids, and titanosaurids. The world's biggest dinosaur has been identified at different times as a brachiosaurid, a diplodocid or a titanosaurid.

Tallest The tallest and largest dinosaur species known from a complete skeleton is *Brachiosaurus brancai* ('arm lizard') from the Tendaguru site in Tanzania, dated as Late Jurassic (150 million years ago). The site was excavated by German expeditions during the period 1909–11 and the bones prepared and assembled at the Humboldt Museum für Naturkunde in Berlin. A complete skeleton was constructed from the remains of several individuals and put on display in 1937. It measures 22·2 m *72 ft 9½ in* in overall length (height at shoulder 6 m *19 ft 8 in*) and has a raised head height of 14 m *46 ft*. The dinosaur was likely to have weighed 30–40 tonnes. However, larger sizes are suggested by an isolated fibula from another *Brachiosaurus* in the same museum.

Heaviest The main contenders for the heaviest dinosaur are probably the titanosaurid *Antarctosaurus giganteus* ('Antarctic lizard') from Argentina and India, at 40–80 tonnes; the brachiosaurid *Brachiosaurus altithorax* (45–55 tonnes); the diplodocids *Seismosaurus halli* ('earthquake lizard') and *Supersaurus vivianae* (both over 50 tonnes).

Such weights do not necessarily represent the ultimate limit for a land vertebrate, and theoretical calculations suggest that some dinosaurs approached the maximum body weight possible for a terrestrial animal, namely 120 tonnes. At weights greater than this, such massive legs would have been needed that the dinosaur could not have moved.

UK Britain's heaviest known dinosaur was the diplodocid *Cetiosaurus oxoniensis* ('whale lizard'), from southern England about 170 million years ago at about 45 tonnes based on estimates on part of a femur found in Clifton Regnes, Olney, Bucks.

Longest Based on the evidence of footprints, the brachiosaurid *Breviparopus* attained a length of 48 m *157 ft*, which would make it the longest vertebrate on record. However, a diplodocid from New Mexico, USA named *Seismosaurus halli* was estimated in 1991 to be 39–52 m *128–170 ft* long based on comparisons of individual bones.

Complete The longest dinosaur known from a complete skeleton is the

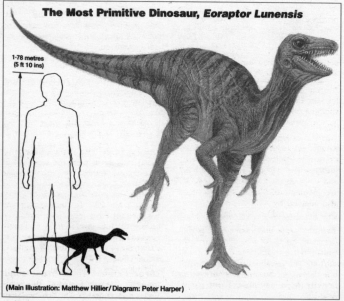

The Most Primitive Dinosaur, *Eoraptor Lunensis*

1·78 metres
(5 ft 10 ins)

(Main Illustration: Matthew Hillier / Diagram: Peter Harper)

diplodocid *Diplodocus carnegii* ('double beam'), assembled at the Carnegie Museum in Pittsburgh, Pennsylvania, USA from remains found in Wyoming in 1899. *Diplodocus* was 26·6 m *87½ ft* long, with much of that length made up by an extremely long whip-like tail, and probably weighed 5·8–18·5 tonnes, the higher estimates being the most likely. The mounted skeleton was so spectacular that casts were requested by other museums, and copies may be seen in London, La Plata, Washington, Frankfurt and Paris.

UK On the evidence of a haemal arch (the bone running beneath the vertebrae of the tail) found on the Isle of Wight, Hants, the brachiosaur *Pelorosaurus* ('monstrous lizard') may have reached 24 m *80 ft* in length. A more complete brachiosaurid was found on the island in 1993 and the jumbled bones, including much of the hips, ribs, shoulders and arms, indicated a 12 m *40 ft* long animal.

Largest predatory dinosaur The largest flesh-eating dinosaur recorded so far is *Tyrannosaurus rex* ('king tyrant lizard'), which, 70 million years ago, reigned over parts of the USA and the provinces of Alberta and Saskatchewan, Canada. The largest and heaviest example, as suggested by a discovery in South Dakota, USA in 1991, was 5·9 m *19½ ft* tall, had a total length of 11·1 m *36½ ft* and weighed an estimated 6–7·4 tonnes.

A composite skeleton of a slightly smaller specimen of this nightmarish beast can be seen in the American Museum of Natural History, New York, USA.

Longest Specimens of the allosaur *Epanterias amplexus* from Masonville, Colorado, USA suggest that this theropod reached a length of 15·24 m *50 ft* and a weight of 4 tonnes, but remains are incomplete. Similar lengths were also attained by *Spinosaurus aegyptiacus* ('thorn lizard') of Niger and Egypt.

Tallest *Dynamosaurus imperiosus* ('dynamic lizard') of Shandong province, China had a bipedal length of 6·1 m *20 ft* and an overall length of 14 m *46 ft*, but these tyrannosaurids were not as heavily built as those from North America.

Smallest The chicken-sized dinosaur *Compsognathus* ('pretty jaw') of southern Germany and south-east France, and an undescribed plant-eating fabrosaurid from Colorado, USA measured 75 cm *29½ in* from the snout to the tip of the tail and weighed about 6·8 kg *15 lb*.

Longest trackway In 1983 a series of four *Apatosaurus* (= *Brontosaurus*) trackways which ran parallel for over 215 m *705 ft* were recorded from 145-million-year-old Morrison strata in south-east Colorado, USA.

Fastest Trackways can be used to estimate dinosaur speeds, and one from the Late Morrison of Texas, USA discovered in 1981 indicated that a carnivorous dinosaur had been moving at 40 km/h *25 mph*. Some ornithomimids were even faster, and the large-brained, 100 kg *220 lb Dromiceiomimus* ('emu mimic lizard') of the Late Cretaceous of Alberta, Canada could probably outsprint an ostrich, which has a top speed of 65 km/h *40 mph*.

Largest footprints In 1932 the gigantic footprints of a large bipedal hadrosaurid ('duckbill') measuring 1·36 m *53½ in* in length and 81 cm *32 in* wide were discovered in Salt Lake City, Utah, USA, and other reports from Colorado and Utah refer to footprints 95–100 cm *37–40 in* wide. Footprints attributed to the largest brachiosaurids also range up to 100 cm *40 in* wide for the hind feet.

Longest neck The sauropod *Mamenchisaurus* ('mamenchi lizard') of the Late Jurassic of Sichuan, China had the longest neck of any animal that has ever lived. It measured 11 m *36 ft*—half the total length of the dinosaur.

Largest skull The skulls of the long-frilled ceratopsids were the largest of all known land animals and culminated in the long-frilled *Torosaurus sp.* ('piercing lizard'). This herbivore, which measured about 7·6 m *25 ft* in total length and weighed up to 8 tonnes, had a skull measuring up to 3 m *9 ft 10 in* in length (including fringe) and weighing up to 2 tonnes. It ranged from Montana to Texas, USA.

Largest claws The therizinosaurids ('scythe lizards') from the Late Cretaceous period of the Nemegt Basin,

Mongolia had the largest claws of any known animal. In the case of *Therizinosaurus cheloniformis* they measured up to 91 cm *36 in* along the outer curve (cf. 20·3 cm *8 in* for *Tyrannosaurus rex*). It has been suggested that these talons were designed for grasping and tearing apart large victims, but this creature had a feeble skull partially or entirely lacking teeth and probably lived on termites.

UK In January 1983 a claw-bone measuring 30 cm *11·8 in* in length was found by amateur fossil collector William Walker near Dorking, Surrey. The claw was later identified as possibly belonging to a spinosaur measuring more than 9 m *29 ft 6 in* overall (estimated weight 2 tonnes), with a bipedal height of 3–4 m *9–13 ft*. It was also distinguished from other theropods by having 128 teeth instead of the usual 64. This enigma, said to be the most important dinosaur fossil found in Europe this century, was subsequently named *Baryonyx walkeri* ('heavy claw').

Largest eggs The largest known dinosaur eggs are those of *Hypselosaurus priscus* ('high ridge lizard'), a 12 m *40 ft* long titanosaurid which lived about 80 million years ago. Examples found in the Durance valley near Aix-en-Provence, France in October 1961 would have had, uncrushed, a length of some 300 mm *12 in* and a diameter of 255 mm *10 in* (capacity 3·3 litres *5·8 pt*).

Other Reptiles

(⇔ also Dinosaurs)

Earliest The oldest reptile fossil, nicknamed 'Lizzie the Lizard', was found on a site in Scotland by palaeontologist Stan Wood in March 1988. The 20 cm *8 in* long reptile is estimated to be about 340 million years old, 40 million years older than previously discovered reptiles. 'Lizzie' was officially named *Westlothiana lizziae* in 1991.

Largest predator The largest ever land predator may have been an alligator found on the banks of the Amazon in rocks dated as 8 million years old. Estimates from a skull 1·5 m *5 ft* long (complete with 10 cm *4 in* long teeth) indicate a length of 12 m *40 ft* and a weight of about 18 tonnes, making it

larger than the fearsome *Tyrannosaurus rex*. It was subsequently identified as a giant example of *Purussaurus brasiliensis*, a species named in 1892 on the basis of smaller specimens.

Longest Other fossil crocodiles suggest that the longest predator was probably the euschian *Deinosuchus riograndensis* ('terrible crocodile') from the lakes and swamps of what is now Texas, USA about 75 million years ago. Fragmentary remains discovered in Big Bend National Park, Texas indicate a hypothetical length of 16 m *52 ft 6 in*.

Largest chelonians The largest prehistoric chelonian was *Stupendemys geographicus*, a pelomedusid turtle which lived about 5 million years ago. Fossil remains found by Harvard University palaeontologists in northern Venezuela in 1972 indicate that this turtle had a carapace (shell) measuring 218–230 cm *7 ft 2 in–7 ft 6½ in* in midline length, measured 3 m *9 ft 10 in* in overall length and had a computed weight of 2040 kg *4500 lb*.

Tortoise The largest prehistoric tortoise was probably *Geochelone* (= *Colossochelys*) *atlas*, which lived in what is now northern India, Myanmar (Burma), Java, the Celebes and Timor, about 2 million years ago. In 1923 the fossil remains of a specimen with a carapace 180 cm *5 ft 11 in* long (223 cm *7 ft 4 in* over the curve) and 89 cm *2 ft 11 in* high were discovered near Chandigarh in the Siwalik Hills, India. This animal had a total length of 2·44 m *8 ft* and is computed to have weighed 850 kg *2100 lb*.

Longest snake The longest prehistoric snake was the python-like *Gigantophis garstini*, which inhabited what is now Egypt about 38 million years ago. Parts of a spinal column and a small piece of jaw discovered at Fayum in the Western Desert indicate a probable length of some 11 m *37 ft*.

Largest marine reptile *Kronosaurus queenslandicus*, a short-necked pliosaur from the Early Cretaceous period (135 million years ago) of Australia, was up to 15 m *50 ft* long and had a 3 m *10 ft* long skull containing 80 massive teeth.

UK Britain's largest marine reptile was *Stretosaurus macromerus*, a short-necked pliosaur from the Kimmeridge Clay of Stretham, Cambs and Oxfordshire. A mandible found at Cumnor, Oxon and now in the University Museum, Oxford has a restored length of over 3 m *9 ft 10 in* and must have belonged to a reptile measuring at least 14 m *46 ft* in total length.

Largest flying creature The largest ever flying creature was the pterosaur *Quetzalcoatlus northropi* ('feathered serpent'). About 70 million years ago it soared over what is now Texas, Wyoming and New Jersey, USA, Alberta, Canada and Senegal and Jordan. Partial remains discovered in Big Bend National Park, Texas, USA in 1971 indicate that this reptile must have had a wing span of 11–12 m *36–39 ft* and weighed about 86–113 kg *190–250 lb*.

UK *Ornithodesmus latidens*, from the Wealden Shales of Atherfield, Isle of Wight about 120 million years ago, had a wing span of c. 5 m *16 ft 4¼ in*.

Mammals

Earliest In 1991 a partial skull of a mammal named *Adelobasileus cromptoni* was reported from 225 million year-old rocks in New Mexico, USA. The first true mammals, as represented by odd teeth, appeared about 220 million years ago during the Late Triassic. Modern mammals (therians) arose in the Mid-Cretaceous period, and the earliest representatives of modern orders, such as *Purgatorius*, the first primate, by the end of the Cretaceous period, 65 million years ago. This creature was similar in appearance to modern tree shrews of the order Scandentia.

Largest The largest land mammal ever recorded was *Indricotherium* (=*Baluchitherium* or *Paraceratherium*), a long-necked, hornless rhinocerotid which roamed across western Asia and Europe about 35 million years ago and first known from bones discovered in the Bugti Hills of Baluchistan, Pakistan in 1907–8. A restoration in the American Museum of Natural History, New York City, USA measures 5.41 m *17 ft 9 in* to the top of the shoulder hump and 11.27 m *37 ft* in total length. The most likely maximum weight of this browser

was revised in 1993 to 15–20 tonnes from earlier estimates of 34 tonnes.

Antlers The prehistoric giant deer (*Megaloceros giganteus*), found in northern Europe and northern Asia as recently as 8000 BC, had the longest horns of any known animal. One specimen recovered from an Irish bog had greatly palmated antlers measuring 4.3 m *14 ft* across, which corresponds to a shoulder height of 1.83 m *6 ft* and a weight of 500 kg *1100 lb*.

Primates The largest known primate was *Gigantopithecus* of the Middle Pleistocene of what is now northern Vietnam and southern China. Males are estimated to have stood 2.74 m *9 ft* tall and weighed about 272 kg *600 lb*. The only remains discovered so far are three partial lower jaws and more than 1000 teeth. It is risky, however, to correlate tooth size and jaw depth of primates

Mammoths The largest prehistoric elephant was the Steppe mammoth (*Mammuthus* (*Parelephas*) *trogontherii*), which, one million years ago, roamed what is now central Europe. A fragmentary skeleton found in Mosbach, Germany indicates a shoulder height of 4.5 m *14 ft 9 in*.

Tusks The longest tusks of any prehistoric animal were those of the straight-tusked elephant (*Palaeoloxodon antiquus germanicus*), which lived in northern Germany c. 300000 years ago. The average length for tusks of bulls was 5 m *16 ft 5 in*. A single tusk of a woolly mammoth (*Mammuthus primigenius*) preserved in the Franzens Museum at Brno, Slovakia measures 5.02 m *16 ft 5½ in* along the outside curve.

Heaviest The heaviest single fossil tusk on record weighed 150 kg *330 lb* (maximum circumference of 89 cm *35 in*) and is now preserved in the Museo Civico di Storia Naturale, Milan, Italy. The tusk, which is in two pieces, is 3.58 m *11 ft 9 in* long.

with their height and bodyweight, and *Gigantopithecus* may have had a disproportionately large head, jaws and teeth in relation to body size.

Largest marine mammal The serpentine *Basilosaurus* (*Zeuglodon*) *cetoides*, which swam in the seas which covered modern-day Arkansas and Alabama, USA 50 million years ago, measured up to 21 m *70 ft* in length.

Birds

Earliest The earliest fossil bird is known from two partial skeletons found in Texas, USA in rocks dating from 220 million years ago. Named *Protoavis texensis* in 1991, this pheasant-sized creature has caused much controversy by pushing the age of birds back 45 million years from the previous record, that of the more familiar *Archeopteryx lithographica* from Germany.

Largest The largest prehistoric bird was the flightless *Dromornis stirtoni*, a huge emu-like creature which lived in central Australia 11 million years ago. Fossil leg bones found near Alice Springs in 1974 indicate that the bird must have stood *c.* 3 m *10 ft* tall and weighed about 500 kg *1100 lb*.

The giant moa *Dinornis maximus* of New Zealand may have been even taller, attaining a height of 3·6 m *12 ft*, though 2·5 m *8 ft* is the maximum accepted by most experts. It weighed about 227 kg *500 lb*.

Flying bird The largest known flying bird was the giant teratorn (*Argentavis magnificens*), which lived in Argentina about 6 million years ago. Fossil remains discovered at a site 160 km *100 miles* west of Buenos Aires, Argentina in 1979 indicate that this gigantic vulture had a wing span of over 6 m *19 ft 8 in* (possibly up to 7·6 m *25 ft*) and weighed 100–120 kg *220–265 lb*.

Largest amphibian The largest amphibian on record was the gharial-like *Prionosuchus plummeri*, which lived 270 million years ago. Fragmented remains were discovered in northern Brazil in 1972. In 1991 the total body length was estimated at 9 m *30 ft* based on a 1·6 m *5 ft 3 in* long skull.

Largest fish No prehistoric fish larger than living species has yet been discovered. Modern estimates suggest that the great shark *Carcharodon megalodon* which abounded in Miocene seas some 15 million years ago did not exceed 13·1 m *43 ft* in length, far less than the 24 m *80 ft* claimed in early, erroneous estimates based on ratios from fossil teeth.

Oldest insect A shrimp-like creature found in 1991 in rocks dated as 420 million years old is the world's oldest known insect. Found in Western Australia, this euthycarcinoid was a large (13 cm *5 in* long) freshwater predator.

Largest insect The largest prehistoric insect was the dragonfly *Meganeura monyi*, which lived about 300 million years ago. Fossil remains (impressions of wings) discovered at Commentry, France indicate a wing span of up to 70 cm *27½ in*.

UK Britain's largest insect was the dragonfly *Pupus diluculum* (family Meganeuridae), which is known only from a wing impression found on a lump of coal in Bolsover colliery, Derbys in July 1978. It had an estimated wing span of 50–60 cm *20–24 in* and lived about 300 million years ago, making it the oldest flying creature so far recorded.

Plant Kingdom

Plantea

General Records

Oldest 'King Clone', the oldest known clone of the creosote plant (*Larrea tridentata*), of California, USA, was estimated in February 1980 by Prof. Frank C. Vasek to be 11 700 years old. It is possible that crustose lichens in excess of 500 mm *20 in* in diameter may be as old, and in 1981 it was estimated that Antarctic lichens larger than 100 mm *4 in* in diameter are at least 10 000 years old.

Most massive The most massive organism was reported in December 1992 to be a network of quaking aspen trees (*Populus tremuloides*) growing in the Wasatch Mountains, Utah, USA from a single root system, covering 43 ha *106 acres* and weighing an estimated

6000 tonnes. The clonal system is genetically uniform and acts as a single organism, with all the component trees, part of the willow family, changing colour or shedding leaves in unison. This particular network was first described in 1975.

Northernmost The yellow poppy (*Papaver radicatum*) and the Arctic willow (*Salix arctica*) survive, the latter in an extremely stunted form, on the most northerly land at Lat. 83°N.

Southernmost Lichens resembling *Rhinodina frigida* have been found in Moraine Canyon at Lat. 86°09′S, Long. 157°30′W in 1971 and in the Horlick Mountain area of Antarctica at Lat. 86°09′S, Long. 131°14′W in 1965.

The southernmost recorded flowering plant was the Antarctic hair grass (*Deschampsia antarctica*) found in Lat. 68°21′S on Refuge Island, Antarctica on 11 Mar 1981.

Highest The greatest certain altitude at which any flowering plants have been found is 6400 m *21000 ft* on Mt Kamet (7756 m *25447 ft*) in the Himalayas by N.D. Jayal in 1955. They were *Ermania himalayensis* and *Ranunculus lobatus*.

Deepest The greatest depth at which plant life has been found is 269 m *884 ft* for algae found by Mark and Diane Littler off San Salvadore Island, Bahamas in October 1984. These maroon-coloured plants survived although 99·9995 per cent of sunlight was filtered out.

Roots The greatest reported depth to which roots have penetrated is a calculated 120 m *400 ft* for a wild fig tree at Echo Caves, near Ohrigstad, Transvaal, South Africa. A single winter rye plant (*Secale cereale*) has been shown to produce 622·8 km *387 miles* of roots in 0·051 m³ *1·83 ft³* of earth.

UK An elm tree root at least 110 m *360 ft* long was reported from Auchencraig, Largs, Strathclyde in about 1950.

Fastest growing Some species of the 45 genera of bamboo have been found to grow at a rate of up to 91 cm *3 ft* per day (0·00003 km/h *0·00002 mph*) (⇔ Grasses)

Earliest flower A flower believed to be 120 million years old was identified in 1989 by Drs Leo Hickey and David Taylor of Yale University, Connecticut, USA from a fossil discovered near Melbourne, Victoria, Australia. The flowering angiosperm, which resembles a modern black pepper plant, had two leaves and one flower and is known as the Koonwarra plant.

Largest The largest of all blooms are those of the parasitic stinking corpse lily (*Rafflesia arnoldii*), which can grow to 91 cm *3 ft* wide, 1·9 cm *¾ in* thick and weigh up to 7 kg *15 lb*. The plants attach themselves to cissus vines in the jungles of south-east Asia and, true to name, have an extremely offensive scent.

UK The largest bloom of any native British plant is that of the wild white water lily (*Nymphaea alba*), at 15 cm *6 in* across.

Inflorescence The largest known inflorescence (as distinct from bloom) is that of *Puya raimondii*, which is a rare Bolivian monocarpic member of the Bromeliaceae family. Its erect panicle (diameter 2·4 m *8 ft*) emerges to a height of 10·7 m *35 ft* and each of these bears up to 8000 white blooms. (⇔ Slowest flowering plant)

The flower-spike of an agave measured in Berkeley, California, USA in 1974 was found to be 15·8 m *52 ft* long.

Blossoming plant The giant Chinese wisteria (*Wisteria sinensis*) at Sierra Madre, California, USA was planted in 1892 and now has branches 152 m *500 ft* long. It covers nearly 0·4 ha *1 acre*, weighs 22 tonnes and has an estimated 1·5 million blossoms during its blossoming period of five weeks, when up to 30000 people pay admission to visit it.

Smallest flowering and fruiting The floating, flowering aquatic duckweed (*Wolffia angusta*) of Australia, described in 1980, is only 0·6 mm *0·024 in* long and 0·33 mm *0·013 in* wide. It weighs about 0·00015 g *5·2×10⁻⁶ oz* and its fruit, which resembles a minuscule fig, weighs 0·00007 g *2·4×10⁻⁶ oz*.

UK The smallest land plant regularly flowering in Britain is the chaffweed

The 91 cm *3ft* wide, 7 kg *15lb* stinking corpse lily has only been seen in flower by a few people brave enough to approach it.

(Photo: WWF Photolibrary/Alain Compost)

(*Cetunculus minimus*), a single seed of which weighs 0·00003g *1×10⁻⁷oz*.

Fastest growing It was reported from Tresco Abbey, Isles of Scilly in July 1978 that a *Hesperoyucca whipplei* of the Liliaceae family had grown 3·65m *12ft* in 14 days, a rate of about 254mm *10in* per day.

Slowest flowering The slowest flowering plant is the rare *Puya raimondii*, the largest of all herbs, discovered at 3960m *13000ft* in Bolivia in 1870. The panicle emerges after about 80–150 years of the plant's life. It then dies. One planted near sea level at the University of California's Botanical Garden, Berkeley, USA in 1958 grew to 7·6m *25ft* and bloomed as early as August 1986 after only 28 years. (⇔ Largest blooms)

Orchids *Tallest* The tallest of all orchids is *Grammatophyllum speciosum*

from Malaysia, specimens of which have been recorded up to 7·6m *25ft* tall.

A height of 15m *49ft* has been recorded for *Galeola foliata*, a saprophyte of the vanilla family. It grows in the decaying rain forests of Queensland, Australia, but is not free-standing.

Largest flower The largest orchid flower is that of *Paphiopedilum sanderianum*, whose petals are reported to grow up to 90cm *3ft* long in the wild. It was discovered in 1886 in the Malay Archipelago. A plant of this variety grown in Somerset in 1991 had three flowers averaging 61cm *2 ft* from the top of the dorsal sepal to the bottom of the ribbon petals, giving a record stretched length of 122cm *4ft*.

Most flowers The first flowering in Britain of *Grammatophyllum wallisii* from Mindanao, Philippines at Burnham Nurseries, Kingsteignton, Devon in 1982 produced 557 flowers.

Smallest The smallest orchid is the Central American *Platystele jungermannoides*, whose flowers are just 1 mm *0·04in* in diameter.

Largest cactus The largest of all cacti is the saguaro (*Cereus giganteus* or *Carnegiea gigantea*), found in Arizona

Flowers

All plants should, where possible, be entered in official international, national or local garden and/or horticultural contests.

WORLD RECORDS

Type	Size		Grower	Location	Year
ASPIDISTRA	1·42m	4ft 8in	C. Evans	Kiora, New South Wales, Australia	1989
CACTUS	10·7m	35ft 1in	A. Kashi	Mysore, India	1992
CHRYSANTHEMUM	2·5m	8ft 2½in	F. Santini	Indre-et-Loire, France	1988
DAHLIA	7·8m	25ft 7in	R. Blythe	Nannup, Western Australia	1990
PETUNIA	4·16m	13ft 8in	B. Lawrence	Windham, New York, USA	1985
PHILODENDRON	339·55m	1114ft	F. Francis	University of Massachusetts, USA	1984
SUNFLOWER[1]	7·76m tall	25ft 5½ in	M. Heijms	Oirschot, Netherlands	1986

UK NATIONAL RECORDS

Type	Size		Grower	Location	Year
AMARYLLIS	1·32m	4ft 4in	Rev. and Mrs Miles	West Malling, Kent	1993
ASPIDISTRA	1·27m	4ft 2in	G. James	Staveley, Chesterfield, Derbys	1979
DAFFODIL	1·55m	5ft 1in	M. Lowe	Chessell, Isle of Wight	1979
DAHLIA	3·3m	10ft 10in	R. Lond	Diss, Norfolk	1989
GLADIOLUS	2·55m	8ft 4½in	A. Breed	Melrose, Borders	1981
LUPIN	1·9m	6ft 3in	K. Barnes	Guildford, Surrey	1988
PETUNIA	2·53m	8ft 4in	G. Warner	Dunfermline, Fife	1978
PHILODENDRON	11·7m	38½ft	B. Lavery	Llanharry, Mid Glam	1989
SUNFLOWER[1]	7·17m	23ft 6½in	F. Kelland	Exeter, Devon	1976
UMBRELLA PLANT	6·4m	20ft 11in	B. Lavery	Llanharry, Mid Glam	1992

[1] *A sunflower with a head diameter of 82cm 32¼in was grown by Emily Martin of Maple Ridge, British Columbia, Canada in Sep 1983. A fully mature sunflower measuring just 56mm 2⅕in was grown by Michael Lenke of Lake Oswego, Oregon, USA in 1985 using a patented bonsai technique.*

Longest daisy chain

The longest daisy chain measured 2·12km *6980ft 7in* and was made in 7hr by villagers of Good Easter, Chelmsford, Essex on 27 May 1985. The team is limited to 16.

and California, USA and Mexico. The green fluted column is surmounted by candelabra-like branches rising to a height of 17·67m *57ft 11¾in* in a specimen discovered in the Maricopa Mountains, near Gila Bend, Arizona on 17 Jan 1988.

An armless 24m *78ft* tall cactus was measured in April 1978 by Hube Yates in Cave Creek, Arizona, USA. It was toppled in a windstorm in July 1986 at an estimated age of 150 years. (⇔ also Flowers Table)

Largest rhododendron

Examples of the scarlet *Rhododendron arboreum* reach a height of 20m *65ft* on Mt Japfu, Nagaland, India.

The cross-section of a trunk of *Rhododendron giganteum* with a reputed height of 27·5m *90ft* from Yunnan, China is preserved at Inverewe Gardens, Highland.

British Isles The largest rhododendron in Britain is a specimen 7·6m *25ft* tall and 82·9m *272ft* in circumference at Government House, Hillsborough, Co. Down. Another example 13m *42ft 8in* high and 1·8m *6ft* in circumference has been measured at Fernhill, Dublin, Republic of Ireland.

Largest rose tree

A 'Lady Banks' rose tree at Tombstone, Arizona, USA has a trunk 101cm *40in* thick, stands 2·74m *9ft* high and covers an area of 499m² *5380ft²*. It is supported by 68 posts and several thousand feet of piping, which

Hanging basket

A giant hanging basket measuring 6·1 m *20ft* in diameter and containing about 600 plants was created by Rogers of Exeter Garden Centre in 1987. Its volume was approximately 118 m³ *4167ft³* and it weighed an estimated 4 tonnes. Another example from France with the same diameter but more conical in shape was smaller by volume.

---

enables 150 people to be seated under the arbour. The cutting came from Scotland in 1884.

Oldest pot plant The world's oldest and rarest pot plant is the cycad *Encephalartos altensteinii* brought from South Africa in 1775 and now housed at the Royal Botanic Gardens at Kew, Surrey. It is the only example of the species. (⬦ Species on the Brink)

Fruits and Vegetables

Most nutritive An analysis of 38 fruits commonly eaten raw (as opposed to dried) shows that the avocado (*Persea americana*) has the highest calorific value, with 163 kilocalories per edible 100 g *741 kilocal/lb*; it also contains vitamins A, C and E and 2·2 per cent protein. Avocados originated in Central and South America.

Least nutritive The fruit with the lowest calorific value is the cucumber (*Cucumis sativus*), with 16 kilocal/100 g *73 kilocal/lb*.

Vines and Vineyards

Largest vine This was planted in 1842 at Carpinteria, California, USA. By 1900 it was yielding more than 9 tonnes of grapes in some years, and averaged 7 tonnes per year until it died in 1920.

UK Britain's largest vine is the Great Vine at Hampton Court, Greater London, planted in 1768. It has a circumference of 2·16 m *7ft 1in*, branches up to 34·7 m *114ft* long and produces an average yield of 318·8 kg *703lb*.

In 1990 Leslie Stringer of Dartford, Kent obtained a yield of over 2300 kg *5071lb*

Most conquering conker

The most victorious untreated conker— the fruit of the common horse-chestnut (*Aesculus hippocastanum*)—was a 'five thousander plus', which won the BBC Conker Conquest in 1954. However, a professor of botany believes that this heroic specimen might well have been a 'ringer', probably an ivory or tagua nut (*Phytelephas macrocarpa*). The Guinness Book of Records *will not publish any category for the largest collection of conkers for fear that trees might suffer wholesale damage.*

Grape catching

The greatest distance at which a grape thrown from level ground has been caught in the mouth is 99·82 m *327ft 6 in*, by Paul J. Tavilla at East Boston, Massachusetts, USA on 27 May 1991. The grape was thrown by James Deady.

Most expensive fruit

John Synnott of Ashford, Co. Wicklow, Republic of Ireland sold 453 g *1lb* of strawberries (a punnet of 30 berries) for £530 or £17·70 a berry on 5 Apr 1977. The buyer was restaurateur Leslie Cooke, at an auction by Walter L. Cole Ltd in the Dublin Fruit Market.

---

from the Dartford Wondervine, planted in 1979. The plant was grown from a cutting taken from a vine planted in Banstead, Surrey in 1962.

Largest vineyard The world's largest vineyard extends over the Mediterranean slopes between the Pyrenees and the Rhône in the *départements* Gard, Hérault, Aude and Pyrénées-Orientales. It covers a total area of 840 000 ha *2075685 acres*, 52·3 per cent of which is *monoculture viticole*.

UK The largest vineyard in the UK is Denbies Wine Estate in Dorking, Surrey, covering 101 ha *250 acres*. Planting began in 1986 and the 300 000 vines planted have a projected annual production capacity of over 1 million bottles.

Most northerly vineyard There is a vineyard at Sabile, Latvia just north of Lat. 57°N.

UK The most northerly commercial vineyard in the United Kingdom is at Whitworth Hall, Spennymoor, Co Durham at Lat. 54°42′N.

Most southerly vineyard The most southerly commercial vineyards are found in central Otago, South Island, New Zealand south of Lat. 45°S.

Leaves

Largest The largest leaves of any plant are those of the raffia palm (*Raphia farinifera = R. ruffia*) of the Mascarene Islands in the Indian Ocean, and the Amazonian bamboo palm (*R. taedigera*) of South America and Africa, whose leaf blades may be up to 20 m *65½ ft* long with petioles measuring 3·96 m *13 ft*.

UK The largest leaves found on outdoor plants in Great Britain are those of *Gunnera manicata* from Columbia, with rhubarb-like leaves measuring up to 3 m *10 ft* in diameter on prickly stems up to 2·5 m *8 ft* tall.

Undivided The largest undivided leaf is that of *Alocasia macrorrhiza*, from Sabah, Malaysia. A specimen found in 1966 was 3·02 m *9 ft 11 in* long, 1·92 m *6 ft 3½ in* wide, and had a surface area of 3·17 m² *34·12 ft²*. A specimen of the water lily plant *Victoria amazonica* (Longwood hybrid) in the grounds of the Stratford-upon-Avon Butterfly Farm, Warks was 2·4 m *8 ft* in diameter on 2 Oct 1989.

Clovers A fourteen-leafed white clover (*Trifolium repens*) was found by Randy Farland near Sioux Falls, South Dakota, USA on 16 Jun 1975. A fourteen-leafed red clover (*Trifolium pratense*) was reported by Paul Haizlip at Bellevue, Washington, USA on 22 Jun 1987.

Seeds

Largest The largest seed in the world is that of the giant fan palm *Lodoicea maldivica* (= *L. callipyge, L. sechellarum*),

commonly known as the double coconut or coco de mer, found wild only in the Seychelles. The single-seeded fruit weighs up to 20 kg *44 lb* and can take 10 years to develop.

Smallest The smallest seeds are those of epiphytic (non-parasitic plants growing on others) orchids, at 992·25 million seeds/g *35 million/oz* (cf. grass pollens at up to 170·1 billion grains/g *6 billion grains/oz*).

Most durable The most conclusive claim for the longevity of seeds is that made for the Arctic lupin (*Lupinus arcticus*) found in frozen silt at Miller Creek, Yukon, Canada in July 1954 by Harold Schmidt. The seeds were germinated in 1966 and were radiocarbon dated to at least 8000 BC, and more probably to 13000 BC.

Ferns

Largest The largest of over 6000 species of fern is the tree fern (*Alsophila excelsa*), the trunk of which can reach heights of 18–25 m *60–80 ft*. It is found on Norfolk Island in the South Pacific.

UK The tallest fern in Britain is the bracken *Pteridium aquilinum*, examples of which measuring over 4·8 m *16 ft* were found in Ruislip, Middlesex in 1970.

Smallest The world's smallest ferns are *Hecistopteris pumila* of Central America, and *Azolla caroliniana* of the United States, which have fronds measuring only 12 mm *½ in*.

Grasses

Tallest A specimen of thorny bamboo culm (*Bambusa arundinacea*) felled at Pattazhi, Travancore, India in November 1904 was 37 m *121½ ft* tall. The tallest of the 160 different grasses found in Great Britain is the common reed (*Phragmites communis*), which reaches a height of 3 m *9¾ ft*.

Shortest The shortest grass native to Britain is the very rare sand bent (*Mibora minima*) found in Anglesey, Gwynedd, with a maximum height of less than 15 cm *6 in*.

Commonest The world's commonest grass is Bermuda grass (*Cynodon dactylon*), which is native to tropical Africa and the Indo-Malaysian region but which extends from Lat. 45°N to 45°S. It

109

Fruits and Vegetables

In the interests of fairness and to minimize the risk of mistakes being made, all plants should, where possible, be entered in official international, national or local garden contests. Only produce grown primarily for human consumption will be considered for publication. The assistance of Garden News and the World Pumpkin Confederation is gratefully acknowledged.

WORLD RECORDS

Type	Size		Grower	Location	Year
APPLE	1.43kg	3lb 2oz	Miklovic family	Caro, Michigan, USA	1992
BEETROOT	17.46kg	38lb 8oz	G. Wheeler	Holbury, Hants	1992
CABBAGE	56.24kg	124lb	B. Lavery	Llanharry, Mid Glam	1989
CARROT [1]	7kg	15lb 7oz	I. Scott	Nelson, New Zealand	1978
CELERY	20.89kg	46lb 1oz	B. Lavery	Llanharry, Mid Glam	1990
COURGETTE	29.25kg	64lb 8oz	B. Lavery	Llanharry, Mid Glam	1990
CUCUMBER [2]	9.1kg	20lb 1oz	B. Lavery	Llanharry, Mid Glam	1991
GARLIC	1.19kg	2lb 10oz	R. Kirkpatrick	Eureka, California, USA	1985
GRAPEFRUIT	2.97kg	6lb 8½oz	J. and A. Sosnow	Tucson, Arizona, USA	1984
GRAPES (bunch)	9.4kg	20lb 11½ oz	Bozzolo y Perut Ltda	Santiago, Chile	1984
LEEK (pot)	5.5kg	12lb 2oz	P. Harrigan	Linton, Northumberland	1987
LEMON	3.88kg	8lb 8oz	C. and D. Knutzen	Whittier, California, USA	1983
MARROW	49.04kg	108lb 2oz	B. Lavery	Llanharry, Mid Glam	1990
MELON (cantaloupe)	28.12kg	62lb	G. Daughtridge	Rocky Mount, North Carolina, USA	1991
ONION	5.05kg	11lb 2oz	R. Holland	Cumnock, Strathclyde	1992
PARSNIP	4.36m	171 ¾ in	B. Lavery	Llanharry, Mid Glam	1990
PETUNIA	4.16m	13ft 8in	B. Lawrence	Windham, New York, USA	1985
PINEAPPLE [3]	7.96kg	17lb 8oz	Dole Philippines Inc.	South Cotabato, Philippines	1984
POTATO [4]	3.2kg	7lb 1oz	J. East	Spalding, Lincs	1963
	3.2kg	7lb 1oz	J. Busby	Atherstone, Warks	1982
PUMPKIN	375.1kg	827lb	J. Holland	Puyallup, Washington, USA	1992
RADISH	17.2kg	37lb 15oz	Litterini family	Tanunda, South Australia	1992
RHUBARB	2.67kg	5lb 14oz	E. Stone	East Woodyates, Wilts	1985
RUNNER BEAN	100.3cm	39 ½ in	J. Taylor	Shifnal, Shrops	1986
SQUASH	250.24kg	821lb	L. Stellpflug	Rush, New York, USA	1990

STRAWBERRY	231 g	8·17 oz	G. Anderson	Folkestone, Kent	1983
SWEDE	22·11 kg	48 lb 12 oz	A. Foster	Anwick, Northumberland	1980
TOMATO	3·51 kg	7 lb 12 oz	G. Graham	Edmond, Oklahoma, USA	1986
TOMATO PLANT[7]	16·3 m	53 ft 6 in	G. Graham	Edmond, Oklahoma, USA	1985
WATERMELON	118·84 kg	262 lb	B. Carson	Arrington, Tennessee, USA	1990

UK NATIONAL RECORDS

CARROT[1]	4·65 kg	10 lb 4 oz	E. Stone	East Woodyates, Wilts	1984
GOOSEBERRY	58·5 g	2·06 oz	A. Dingle	Macclesfield, Cheshire	1978
GRAPEFRUIT	1·67 kg	3 lb 11 oz	Willington G.C.	Willington, Beds	1986
LEMON	2·13 kg	4 lb 11 oz	Pershore College	Pershore, Hereford & Worcester	1986
LUPIN	1·9 m	6 ft 3 in	K. Barnes	Guildford, Surrey	1988
MELON (cantaloupe)	8·33 kg	18 lb 5¾ oz	B. Lavery	Llanharry, Mid Glam	1991
PEACH	411 g	14½ oz	J. Bird	London	1984
PUMPKIN	322 kg	710 lb	B. Lavery	Llanharry, Mid Glam	1989
SQUASH	228·61 kg	504 lb	B. Lavery	Llanharry, Mid Glam	1991
TOMATO	2·54 kg	5 lb 9½ oz	R. Burrows	Huddersfield, W Yorks	1985
TOMATO PLANT[5]	13·96 m	45 ft 9½ in	Chosen Hill School	Gloucester	1981
TURNIP[6]	16·78 kg	37 lb	G. Farquhar	Tillyfourie, Grampian	1987
WATERMELON[7]	16·33 kg	36 lb	B. Lavery	Llanharry, Mid Glam	1990

1 A 5·14 m 16 ft 10½ in long carrot was grown by Bernard Lavery of Llanharry, Mid Glam in 1991.

2 A Vietnamese variety 1·83 m 6 ft long was reported by L. Szabó of Debrecen, Hungary in September 1976. A.C. Rayment of Chelmsford, Essex grew one measuring 1·10 m 43½ in in 1984–6.

3 Pineapples weighing up to 13 kg 28 lb 11 oz were reported from Tarauaca, Brazil in 1978.

4 One weighing 8·275 kg 18 lb 4 oz reported dug up by Thomas Siddal in his garden in Chester on 17 Feb 1795. A yield of 233·5 kg 515 lb was achieved from a 1·1 kg 2½ lb parent seed by Bowcock planted in April 1977.

5 It was reported at the Tsukuba Science Expo Centre, Japan on 28 Feb 1988 that a single plant produced 16 897 tomatoes.

6 A 33·1 kg 73 lb turnip was reported in December 1768 and one weighing 23·1 kg 51 lb was reported from Alaska in 1981, but this was not measured in competition.

7 Bill Rogerson of Robersonville, North Carolina, USA grew one weighing 126·5 kg 279 lb on 3 Oct 1988, but this was not measured in competition.

NUT TREE

PLUMP PUMPKIN
World Record
827 Pounds
Winner, Joel Holland
Puyallup, 1992

This monster 375·1 kg *827 lb* pumpkin was grown by Joel Holland of Puyallup, Washington, USA in 1992. One of its seeds is 25 mm *1 in* long.

(Photo: Nut Tree, California, USA/Dudley Owens)

is possibly the most troublesome weed of the grass family, affecting 40 crops in over 80 countries. The 'Callie' hybrid, selected in 1966, grows as much as 15 cm *6 in* a day and stolons reach 5·5 m *18 ft* in length.

Fastest growing Some species of bamboo have a growth rate of 91 cm *3 ft* per day. (⬦ General records)

Mosses The world's tallest moss is the Australian species *Dawsonia superba*, which can reach a height of 60 cm *24 in*. The longest is the mainly aquatic species *Fontinalis*, especially *F. antipyretica*, which forms streamers well over 1 m *3 ft 3 in* long in flowing water.

The smallest variety of moss is the microscopic pygmy moss (*Ephemerum*) which appears to the naked eye as a mere greenish stain until closer examination. Its leaves are notable, however, for their large cells, which can be up to 120 μm long and 25 μm wide.

Weeds

Largest The largest weed is the giant hogweed (*Heracleum mantegazzianum*), originally from the Caucasus. It reaches 3·65 m *12 ft* tall and has leaves 91 cm *3 ft* long.

Most damaging The virulence of weeds tends to be measured by the number of crops they affect and the number of countries in which they occur. On this basis the worst would appear to be the purple nut sedge, nutgrass or nutsedge (*Cyperus rotundus*), a land weed native to India but which attacks 52 crops in 92 countries.

UK The most damaging and widespread cereal weeds in Britain are the wild oats *Avena fatua* and *A. ludoviciana*. Their seeds can withstand temperatures of 115·6°C *240°F* for 15 min and remain viable, and up to 50 per cent losses have been recorded in crops affected by them.

Most spreading The greatest area covered by a single clonal growth is that of the wild box huckleberry (*Gaylussacia brachycera*), a mat-forming evergreen shrub first reported in 1796. A colony covering about 40 ha *100 acres* was found on 18 Jul 1920 near the Juniata River, Pennsylvania, USA. It has been estimated that this colony began 13 000 years ago.

112

Apple peeling

The longest single unbroken apple peel on record is one of 52·51m *172ft 4in*, peeled by Kathy Wafler of Wolcott, New York, USA in 11hr 30min at Long Ridge Mall, Rochester, New York on 16 Oct 1976. The apple weighed 567g *20oz*.

Apple picking

The greatest recorded performance is 7180·3kg *15830lb* picked in 8hr by George Adrian of Indianapolis, Indiana, USA on 23 Sep 1980.

Cucumber slicing

Norman Johnson of Blackpool College, Lancs set a record of 13·4sec for slicing a 30·5cm *12in* cucumber, 3·8cm *1½in* in diameter, at 22 slices to the inch (total 264 slices) at West Deutscher Rundfunk in Cologne, Germany on 3 Apr 1983.

Potato peeling

The greatest quantity of potatoes peeled by five people to an institutional cookery standard with standard kitchen knives in 45min is 482·8kg *1064lb 6oz* (net) by Marj Killian, Terry Anderson, Barbara Pearson, Marilyn Small and Janene Utkin at the 64th Annual Idaho Spud Day celebration, held at Shelley, Idaho, USA on 19 Sep 1992.

Aquatic weeds The worst aquatic weed of the tropics and subtropics is the water hyacinth (*Eichhornia crassipes*), a native of the Amazon Basin, but which extends from Lat. 40°N to 45°S. The intransigence of aquatic plants in manmade lakes is illustrated by the matforming water weed *Salvinia auriculata*, found in Africa. It was detected when Lake Kariba, which straddles the border of Zimbabwe and Zambia, was filled in May 1959 and within 13 months it had choked an area of 518km² *200 miles²*, rising to 1002km² *387 miles²* by 1963.

Seaweed

Longest The longest species of seaweed is the Pacific giant kelp (*Macrocystis pyrifera*), which, although it does not exceed 60m *196ft* in length, can grow 45cm *18in* in a day.

UK The longest of the 700 species of British seaweed is the brown seaweed (*Chorda filum*), which grows to a length of 6·10m *20ft*. The Japanese species *Sargassum muticum*, introduced into Britain c. 1970, can reach 9·0m *30ft*.

Trees and Wood

Earliest The earliest surviving species of tree is the maidenhair (*Ginkgo biloba*) of Zhejiang, China, which first appeared about 160 million years ago during the Jurassic era. It was 'rediscovered' by Kaempfer (Netherlands) in 1690 and reached England c. 1754. It has been grown in Japan since c. 1100, where it was known as *ginkyo* ('silver apricot') and is now known as *icho*.

Oldest Dendrochronologists estimate the *potential* life-span of a bristlecone pine (*Pinus longaeva*) to be nearly 5500 years, and that of a giant sequoia (*Sequoiadendron giganteum*) at perhaps 6000 years, although no single cell lives more than 30 years. The oldest recorded tree was a bristlecone pine designated WPN-114 and found to be 5100 years old. It grew at 3275m *10750ft* above sea level on the north-east face of Mt Wheeler, Nevada, USA.

Living The oldest recorded living tree is another bristlecone pine named 'Methuselah', growing at 3050m *10000ft* on the California side of the White Mountains, USA and confirmed as 4700 years old. In March 1974 it was reported to have produced 48 live seedlings.

UK The longest-lived British tree is the yew (*Taxus baccata*), for which a maximum age of well over 1000 years is usually conceded. The oldest known is the Fortingall yew near Aberfeldy, Tayside, part of which still grows. In 1777 this tree was over 15m *50ft* in girth and it cannot be much less than 3500 years old.

Most massive The world's most massive single tree is 'General Sherman' the giant sequoia (*Sequoiadendron gigan-*

113

Tallest Trees in the British Isles

Species	Location	m	ft
ALDER (Italian)	Westonbirt, Glos	34	*111*
ASH	Old Roar Ghyll, St. Leonards, E Sussex	41	*135*
BEECH	Hallyburton House, Tayside	46	*150*
BIRCH (Silver)	Ballogie, Grampian	30	*98*
CEDAR (of Lebanon)	Leaton Knolls, Shrops	42	*140*
CHESTNUT (Horse)	Ashford Chase, Petersfield, Hants	39	*130*
CYPRESS (Lawson)	Strone House, Strathclyde	40	*133*
DOUGLAS FIR[1]	The Hermitage, Perth, Tayside	+61	*200*
	Moniac Glen, Inverness, Highland	+61	*200*
ELM[2] (Wych)	Castle Howard, N Yorks	41	*134*
EUCALYPTUS (Blue gum)	Glencormack, Co. Wicklow	44	*144*
GRAND FIR[3]	Strone, Cairndow, Strathclyde	63	*206*
GINKGO	Sezincote, Glos	30	*98*
HEMLOCK (Western)	Benmore, Argyll, Strathclyde	51	*167*
HOLLY	Ashburnham Park, Battle, E Sussex	24	*80*
LARCH (European)	Glenlee, Dumfries & Galloway	46	*150*
LIME	Duncombe Park, Helmsley, N Yorks	45	*150*
MONKEY PUZZLE	Lochnaw, Dumfries & Galloway	29	*95*
OAK (Turkey)	Knightshayes, Tiverton, Devon	44	*144*
PEAR	Tickard's Manor, Guildford, Surrey	21	*69*
PINE (Corsican)	Adhurst, St. Mary, Petersfield, Hants	46	*150*
PLANE	Bryanston School, Blandford, Dorset	48	*156*
POPLAR (Black Italian)	Bowood, Wilts	46	*150*
SEQUOIA[4] (Giant)	Castle Leod, Strathpeffer, Highland	53	*174*
SILVER FIR	Armadale Castle, Skye, Highland	50	*164*
SPRUCE[5] (Sitka)	Strath Earn, Tayside	61	*200*
SYCAMORE	Lennoxlove, Haddington, Lothian	40	*132*
WALNUT (Black)	Much Hadham Rectory, Herts	36	*118*
WELLINGTONIA	Castle Leod, Strathpeffer, Highland	53	*173*
WILLOW (Weeping)	Ashford Chase, Petersfield, Hants	24	*79*
YEW	Belvoir Castle, Leics	29	*95*

[1] *The English record-holders are Douglas firs at Broadwood, Dunster, Somerset and Cragside, Northumberland, each measuring 57m 187ft.* [2] *It was estimated in 1980 that more than 17 million of the 23 million elms in southern England had been killed since 1968 by the fungus Ceratocystis ulmi that causes Dutch elm disease.* [3] *This is the UK record-holder. The Welsh record is a grand fir of 62m 203ft at Leighton Park, Powys.* [4] *The record for Northern Ireland is 50m 164ft at Caledon Castle, Co Tyrone.* [5] *The record for the Republic of Ireland is one of 50·6m 166ft at Currarmore, Co Waterford. On the night of 16–17 Oct 1987 an estimated 15 million trees were destroyed by high winds, at an estimated cost of £15 million.*

teum) growing in the Sequoia National Park, California, USA. It stands 83·8 m *275ft* tall and has a girth of 25·3 m *83ft* measured 1·4 m *4½ ft* above the ground. This tree is estimated to contain the equivalent of 600 120 board feet of timber, enough to make 5 billion matches, and its red-brown bark may be up to 61 cm *24 in* thick in parts. Its weight, including the root system, is estimated at 2500 tonnes but the timber is light (288·3 kg/m³ *18 lb/ft³*). The seed of a 'big tree' weighs only 4·7 mg *⅙₀₀₀ oz*

and its growth at maturity may therefore represent an increase in weight of 13×10^{11}. (⇔ General records)

Greatest spread The tree canopy covering the greatest area is that of the great banyan (*Ficus benghalensis*) in the Indian Botanical Garden, Calcutta, with 1775 prop or supporting roots and a circumference of 412 m *1350ft*. It covers some 1·2 ha *3 acres* and dates from before 1787. However, it is reported that a 550-year-old banyan tree known as 'Thimmamma

Hedge laying

John Williams of Sennybridge and David James of Llanwern, Brecon, hedged by the 'stake and pleach' method a total of 241·4m *264yd* in 11hr 24min on 28 Apr 1986.

Largest hedges

The world's tallest and longest hedge is the Meikleour beech hedge in Perthshire, planted in 1746 by Jean Mercer and her husband Robert Murray Nairne. Its tapered height when trimmed now varies from 24·4m *80ft* to 36·6m *120ft* along its length of 550m *1804ft*. Trimming takes place every 10 years or so and was last completed in six weeks in 1988.

A yew hedge planted in 1720 in Earl Bathurst's Park, Cirencester, Glos runs for 155·5m *510ft*, reaches 11m *36ft* in height and is 4·5m *15ft* thick at its base. The hedge takes about 20 days to trim.

The tallest box hedge is 12m *40ft* high and dates from the 18th century at Birr Castle, Co. Offaly, Republic of Ireland.

Marrimanu' in Gutibayalu village near Kadiri Taluk, Andrha Pradesh, India spreads over 2·1ha *5·2 acres*.

Greatest girth A circumference of 57·9m *190ft* was recorded for the pollarded (trimmed to encourage a more bushy growth) European chestnut (*Castanea sativa*) known as the 'Tree of the Hundred Horses' (*Castagno di Cento Cavalli*) on Mt Etna, Sicily, Italy in 1770 and 1780. It is now in three parts, widely separated.

'El Arbol del Tule' in Oaxaca state, Mexico is a 41m *135ft* tall Montezuma cypress (*Taxodium mucronatum*) with a girth in 1982 of 35·8m *117½ft*, measured 1·52m *5ft* above the ground. Generally speaking, however, the largest girths are attributed to African baobab trees (*Adansonia digitata*), with measurements of 54·5m *180ft* recorded.

UK A specimen of sweet (Spanish) chestnut (*Castanea sativa*) in the grounds of Canford School, near Poole, Dorset has a trunk with a circumference of 13·33m *43ft 9in*.

Tallest A *Eucalyptus regnans* at Mt Baw Baw, Victoria, Australia is believed to have measured 143m *470ft* in 1885. According to the researches of Dr A.C. Carder, the tallest tree ever measured was another Australian eucalyptus at Watts River, Victoria, Australia, reported in 1872 by forester William Ferguson. It measured 132·6m *435ft* tall and was almost certainly over 150m *500ft* originally.

Living The tallest tree currently standing is the 'National Geographic Society' coast redwood (*Sequoia sempervirens*) in the Redwood National Park, California, USA. Its revised height, following earlier miscalculations, was 111·25m *365ft* in October 1991, according to Ron Hildebrant of California.

The tallest non-coniferous, flowering tree is the Australian mountain ash, or giant gum, (*Eucalyptus regnans*) which can grow to over 96m *315ft*. The tallest is currently one of 95m *312ft* in the Styx Valley, Tasmania.

British Isles The best claimant for Britain's tallest tree is a Grand fir (*Abies grandis*) at Strone, Strathclyde which stood at 63m *206ft* in 1993. (⇔ Table)

Christmas tree The world's tallest cut Christmas tree was a 67·36m *221ft* Douglas fir (*Pseudotsuga menziesii*) erected at Northgate Shopping Center, Seattle, Washington, USA in December 1950.

UK A 26·3m *86ft 5in* tall Norway spruce (*Picea abies*) was grown on Viscount Weymouth's Longleat estate in Wiltshire and given to the King's College, Cambridge Choir School Development Appeal for Christmas 1989.

Fastest growing Discounting bamboo, which is classified as a woody grass, the fastest recorded rate of growth is 10·74m *35ft 3in* in 13 months (about 28mm *1¹⁄₁₀in* per day) by an *Albizzia falcata* planted on 17 Jun 1974 in Sabah, Malaysia.

Slowest growing Excluding *bonsai*, the 14th century Oriental art of cultivating miniature trees, the extreme in slow

The bristlecone pine has an estimated potential life-span of about 5500 years and this species represents both the oldest tree ever recorded (5100 years) and the oldest living tree, 4700-year-old 'Methuselah' in the White Mountains, California, USA.

(Photo: Planet Earth Pictures/William Smithey Jr)

growth is represented by the *Dioon edule* (Cycadaceae) measured in Mexico between 1981 and 1986 by Dr Charles M. Peters, who found the average annual growth rate to be 0·76mm *0·03in*; a 120-year-old specimen was just 10cm *4in* tall.

Most leaves Little work has been done on the laborious task of establishing which species has the most leaves. A large oak has perhaps 250 000, but a cypress may have some 45–50 million leaf scales.

Remotest The most remote tree is believed to be a solitary Norwegian spruce on Campbell Island, Antarctica, whose nearest companion would be over 222km *120 nautical miles* away on the Auckland Islands.

Largest forest The largest afforested areas in the world are the vast coniferous forests of northern Russia, lying between Lat. 55°N and the Arctic Circle. The total wooded area covers 1·1 billion ha *2·7 billion acres* (25 per cent of the world's forests), of which 38 per cent is Siberian larch. The

---

Tree climbing

The fastest time up a 30·5m *100ft* fir spar pole and back down to the ground is 24·82sec, by Guy German of Sitka, Alaska, USA on 3 Jul 1988 at the World Championship Timber Carnival in Albany, Oregon, USA.

The fastest time up a 9m *29ft 6in* coconut tree barefoot is 4·88sec, by Fuatai Solo, 17, in Sukuna Park, Fiji on 22 Aug 1980.

Tree sitting

The duration record for staying in a tree is more than 22 years, by Bungkas, who went up a palm tree in the Indonesian village of Bengkes in 1970 and has been there ever since. He lives in a nest which he made from branches and leaves. Repeated efforts have been made to persuade him to come down, but without success.

Tree topping

Guy German climbed a 30·5m *100ft* spar pole and sawed off the top (circumference of 100cm *40in*) in a record time of 53·35 sec at Albany, Oregon, USA on 3 Jul 1989.

---

former USSR is 34 per cent afforested. In comparison, the largest area of forest in the tropics is the Amazon basin, covering some 330 million ha *815 million acres*.

UK The largest forest in Britain is the Kielder Forest District in Northumber-land, covering an area of 39 380ha *97 309 acres*.

Longest avenue The world's longest avenue is the Nikko Cryptomeria Avenue comprising three parts converging on Imaichi City in the Tochigi Prefecture of Japan, with a total length of 35·41km *22 miles*. Planted in 1628–48, over 13 500 of its original 200 000 Japanese cedar (*Cryptomeria japonica*) trees survive, at an average height of 27m *88½ft*.

UK The longest avenue of trees in Great Britain is the privately-owned stretch of 1750 beeches covering a distance of 5·8km *3·6 miles* in Savernake Forest, near Marlborough, Wilts.

Wood cutting The first recorded lumberjack sports competition was held in 1572 in the Basque region of Spain.

The following records were set at the Lumberjack World Championships at Hayward, Wisconsin, USA (founded 1960):

Power saw (three slices of a 51cm *20in* diameter white-pine log with a single-engine saw from dead start)—8·71 sec by Ron Johnson (US) in 1986.

Bucking (one slice from a 51cm 20in diameter white-pine log with a crosscut saw)—one-man, 18·96 sec by Rolin Eslinger (US) in 1987; two-man, 7·27 sec by Jim Colbert and Mike Sullivan (both US) in 1988.

Standing block chop (chopping through a vertical 35·5cm *14in* diameter white-pine log 76cm *30in* in length)—22·05 sec by Melvin Lentz (US) in 1988.

Underhand block chop (chopping through a horizontal 35·5cm *14in* diameter white-pine log 76cm *30in* in

117

length)—17·84 sec by Laurence O'Toole (Australia) in 1985.

Springboard chopping (scaling a 2·7m *9ft* spar pole on springboards and chopping a 35·5cm *14in* diameter white-pine log)—1 min 18·45 sec by Bill Youd (Australia) in 1985.

Kingdom Protista

Discovered in 1676 by microscopist Antony van Leeuwenhoek of Delft, Netherlands (1632–1723), protista are single-celled or acellular organisms with characteristics common to both plants and animals. The more plant-like are termed Protophyta (protophytes), including unicellular algae, and the more animal-like are placed in the phylum Protozoa (protozoans), including amoeba and flagellates.

Largest The largest known protozoans in terms of volume were calcareous foraminifera (Foraminiferida) of the genus *Nummulites*, one species of which, known from Middle Eocene rocks of Turkey, attained a diameter of 22cm *8½in*.

The largest existing protozoan, a species of the fan-shaped *Stannophyllum* (Xenophyophorida), can exceed this in length (25cm *9¾in* has been recorded) but not in volume.

Smallest protophytes The marine microflagellate alga *Micromonas pusilla* has a diameter of less than 2μm *0·00008in*.

Fastest The protozoan *Monas stigmatica* has been found to move a distance equivalent to 40 times its own length in a second. No human can cover even seven times his own length in a second.

Fastest reproduction The protozoan *Glaucoma*, which reproduces by binary fission, divides as frequently as every three hours. Thus in the course of a day it could become a great-great-great-great-great-great grandparent and the progenitor of 512 descendants.

Kingdom Fungi

Fungi were once classified in the sub-kingdom Protophyta of the kingdom Protista.

Largest The world's largest fungus is a single living clonal growth of the underground fungus *Armillaria ostoyae*, reported in May 1992 as covering some 600 ha *1500 acres* in the forests of Washington state, USA. Estimates based on its size suggest that the fungus is 500–1000 years old, but no attempts have been made to estimate its weight. Also known as the honey or shoestring fungus, it fruits above ground as edible gilled mushrooms.

Heaviest Another similar clonal growth, but of the fungus *Armillaria bulbosa*, reported on 2 Apr 1992 to be covering about 15 ha *37 acres* of forest in Michigan, USA, was calculated to weigh over 100 tonnes, which is comparable with blue whales. The organism is thought to have originated from a single fertilized spore at least 1500 years ago.

Largest edible A giant puffball (*Langermannia gigantea*) measuring 2·64 m *8ft 8in* in circumference and weighing 22kg *48½lb* was found by Jean-Guy Richard of Montreal, Canada in 1987.

Heaviest An example of the edible chicken of the woods mushroom (*Laetiporus sulphureus*) weighing 45·4kg *100 lb* was found in the New Forest, Hants by Giovanni Paba of Broadstone, Dorset on 15 Oct 1990.

Fungi

Differing in most aspects from other plants, fungi perform the essential task of decomposing dead plants and animals, with some becoming parasitic. Forty species cause disease in humans, ranging from ringworm and athlete's foot to serious lung infections. More positively, however, fungi have been developed into vital antibiotic drugs such as penicillin.

Viruses

The first chemical description of a living entity was published in December 1991 by A. Molla, A.V. Paul and Eckard Wimmer of the State University of New York, USA.

The formula for the organic matter of poliovirus is $C_{332,652} H_{492,388} N_{98,245} O_{131,196} P_{7,501} S_{2,340}$ and it is believed to be the largest empirical formula ever reported.

Oldest DNA

Proteins, the building blocks of life, normally disappear rapidly from carcasses. Original proteins are only rarely found in fossils but in 1992 DNA, the specialized genetic-coding protein, was recovered from a termite which had become trapped in amber 25–30 million years ago in the Dominican Republic.

The largest recorded tree fungus is the bracket fungus *Rigidoporus ulmarius* growing from dead elm wood in the grounds of the International Mycological Institute at Kew, Surrey. It measured 150×144cm *59×56¾ in* with a circumference of 454cm *178¾ in*. In 1992 it was growing at a rate of 22·5cm *9 in* per year but this has now slowed.

Most poisonous The yellowish-olive death cap (*Amanita phalloides*), which can be found in England, is the world's most poisonous fungus, responsible for 90 per cent of fatal poisonings caused by fungi. Its total toxin content is 7–9mg dry weight, whereas the estimated lethal amount of amatoxins for humans, depending on bodyweight, is only 5–7mg—equivalent to less than 50g *1¾ oz* of a fresh fungus. From 6–15 hours after eating, the effects are vomiting, delirium, collapse and death. Among its victims was Cardinal Giulio de' Medici, Pope Clement VII (b. 1478) on 25 Sep 1534.

Aeroflora The highest recorded total fungal spore count was 161 037/m³ 5 686 861/ft³ near Cardiff, S Glam on 21 Jul 1971. The lowest counts of airborne allergens are nil.

Kingdom Procaryota

The earliest life-form reported from Britain is *Kakabekia barghoorniana*, a micro-organism similar in form to an orange slice, found near Harlech, Gwynedd in 1964 and dated in July 1986 to 4000 million years ago.

Bacteria

Antony van Leeuwenhoek (1632–1723) was the first to observe bacteria, in 1675.

Oldest Viable bacteria were reported in 1991 to have been recovered from sediments 3–4 million years old from the sea of Japan.

Living In 1991 it was reported that live bacteria were found in the carcass of a mastodon (an ancestor of the elephant) from Ohio, USA which died 12000 years earlier and which, on the evidence of spear marks found in the ribs, represented the first proof of humans killing a prehistoric animal. The bacteria gave the flesh 'a bad smell' even after such a long time.

Largest The largest bacterium is *Epulopiscium fishelsoni*, described in 1993 as a symbiont inhabiting the intestinal tract of the brown surgeonfish (*Acanthurus nigrofuscus*) from the Red Sea and the Great Barrier Reef off the coast of Australia. Measuring 80×600μm or more and therefore visible to the naked eye, this mega-micro-organism, first discovered by Israeli researchers in 1985, is so big it was originally thought to be a protozoan. At 1 million times larger than the human gut organism *Escherichia coli*, it is a reminder of the strange new life-forms we have yet to discover.

Smallest free-living entity The smallest of all free-living organisms are pleuro-pneumonia-like organisms (PPLO) of the genus *Mycoplasma*. One of these, *Mycoplasma laidlawii*, first discovered in sewage in 1936, has a

119

Microscopist Antony van Leeuwenhoek (1632–1723) and his simple, (single-lens) microscope, which he began to make in the 1670s. Later developments led to his production of increasingly powerful ground lenses for these tiny, hand-held instruments, enabling him to be the first to observe bacteria and protozoa.

(Photo: Ann Ronan Picture Library)

diameter during its early existence of only 10^{-7} m. Examples of the strain known as H.39 have a maximum diameter of 3×10^{-7} m and weigh an estimated 10^{-16} g. Thus a 190-tonne blue whale would weigh 1.9×10^{24} times as much.

Highest In April 1967 the US National Aeronautics and Space Administration (NASA) reported that bacteria had been discovered at an altitude of 41·13 km *25½ miles.*

Fastest By means of a polar flagellum rotating 100 times/sec, the rod-shaped bacillus *Bdellovibrio bacteriovorus* can travel 50 times its own length of 2μm per sec. This would be the equivalent of a human sprinter reaching 320 km/h *200 mph* or a swimmer crossing the English Channel in 6 min.

Toughest The bacterium *Micrococcus radiodurans* can withstand atomic radiation of 6·5 million röntgens, or 10 000 times that fatal to the average human.

In March 1983 John Barras of the University of Oregon, USA reported bacteria from sulphurous seabed vents thriving at 306°C *583°F* in the East Pacific Rise at Lat. 21°N.

Dmitriy Ivanovsky (1864–1920) first reported filterable objects in 1892, but Martinus Willem Beijerink (1851–1931) was the first to confirm the nature of viruses in 1898. These are now defined as aggregates of two or more types of chemical (including either DNA or RNA) which are infectious and potentially pathogenic.

Largest The longest known virus is the rod-shaped *Citrus tristeza*, with particles measuring 2×10^{-5} m.

Smallest The smallest known viruses are the nucleoprotein plant viruses such as the satellite of tobacco necrosis virus, with spherical particles 17×10^{-9} m in diameter.

Viroids

Viroids were discovered by Theodor O. Diener (USA) in February 1972. They are infectious agents of plants, are smaller than viruses and consist only of nucleic acid (RNA) cores.

A putative new infectious submicroscopic organism without nucleic acid and named a 'prion' was announced from the University of California in February 1982.

Parks, Zoos, Oceanaria, Aquaria

Parks

Largest The world's largest national park is the National Park of North-Eastern Greenland, covering some 972 000 km² *375 289 miles²* and stretching from Liverpool Land in the south to the northernmost island, Odaaq Ø, off Pearyland. Established in 1974 and enlarged in 1988, much of the park is covered by ice and is home to a variety of protected flora and fauna, including polar bears, musk ox and birds of prey.

UK The largest park in the United Kingdom is the Lake District National Park (designated as such in 1951), which covers 2292 km² *885 miles²* and lies wholly in Cumbria. Britain's largest private park is Woburn Park (1200 ha *3000 acres*), near Woburn Abbey, the seat of the Dukes of Bedford.

Largest game reserve The largest zoological reserve in the world is the Etosha National Park in Namibia. Established in 1907, it now covers an area of 99 525 km² *38 427 miles².*

Zoos

There are an estimated 757 zoos worldwide, attracting some 350 million visitors per year.

Oldest The earliest known collection of animals was established by Shulgi, a 3rd-dynasty ruler of Ur from 2097–2094 BC at Puzurish, Iraq. The oldest known zoo is at Schönbrunn, Vienna, Austria, built in 1752 by the Holy Roman Emperor Franz I for his wife Maria Theresa.

The oldest existing public zoological collection is that of the Zoological Society of London, founded in 1826. In January 1989 the collection comprised 11 108 specimens housed in Regent's Park, London (14·5 ha *36 acres*) and at Whipsnade Park, Beds (219 ha *541 acres*, opened 23 May 1931), representing the most comprehensive in the United Kingdom. The record annual attendances are 3 031 571 in 1950 for Regent's Park and 756 758 in 1961 for Whipsnade.

Without bars The earliest zoo without bars was at Stellingen, near Hamburg, Germany. It was founded in 1907 by Carl Hagenbeck (1844–1913), who used deep pits and large pens instead of cages to separate the exhibits from the visitors.

Oceanaria

Earliest The world's first oceanarium was Marineland of Florida, opened in 1938 at a site 29 km *18 miles* south of St Augustine, Florida, USA. Up to 26·3 million litres *5 800 000 gal* of sea-water are pumped daily through two major tanks, one rectangular (30·5 m *100 ft* long by 12·2 m *40 ft* wide by 5·5 m *18 ft* deep) containing 1·7 million litres *375 000 gal*, and one circular (71 m *233 ft* in circumference and 3·65 m *12 ft* deep) containing 1·5 million litres *330 000 gal*. The tanks are seascaped and include coral reefs and even a shipwreck.

Aquaria

Largest In terms of the volume of water held, the Living Seas Aquarium, opened in 1986 at the EPCOT Center, Florida, USA, is the world's largest, with a total capacity of 23·66 million litres *6·25 million gal*. It contains over 3000 fish representing 65 species.

The largest in terms of marine-life is the Monterey Bay Aquarium opened on 20 Oct 1984 in California, USA, which houses 6500 specimens (525 species) of flora and fauna in its 95 tanks. The volume of water held is 3 375 000 litres *750 000 gal*.

Human *Being*

- Origins
- Dimensions
- Reproductivity
- Longevity
- Anatomy and Physiology

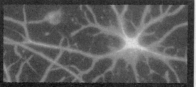

Origins

If the age of the Earth-Moon system (latest estimate 4540 ± 40 million years) is likened to a single year, hominids appeared on the scene at about 7:40p.m. on 31 December. Britain's earliest traceable inhabitants arrived at about 10:50p.m., the Christian era began nearly 14 seconds before midnight and the life span of a 120-year-old person would be 8⁄100th of a second. Present calculations indicate that the Sun's increased heat, as it becomes a 'red giant', will make life on Earth insupportable in about 5500 million years. Meanwhile there may well be colder epicycles.

Man (*Homo sapiens*) is a species in the sub-family Homininae of the family Hominidae of the super-family Hominoidea of the sub-order Simiae (or Anthropoidea) of the order Primates of the infra-class Eutheria of the sub-class Theria of the class Mammalia of the sub-phylum Vertebrata (Craniata) of the phylum Chordata of the sub-kingdom Metazoa of the animal kingdom.

Earliest Primates These appeared in the late Cretaceous epoch about 65 million years ago. The earliest members of the sub-order Anthropoidea are known from both Africa and South America in the early Oligocene, 30–34 million years ago, when the two infra-orders, Platyrrhini and Catarrhini, from the New and Old Worlds respectively, were already distinct. Finds from Faiyûm, Egypt, are being studied and may represent primates from the early Oligocene period, 37 million years.

Earliest hominoid The earliest hominoid fossil is a jaw-bone with three molars discovered by Martin Pickford (b. 18 Oct 1943) of the Muséum National d'Histoire Naturelle, Paris in the Otavi Hills, Namibia on 4 Jun 1991. It had been provisionally dated at 10–15 million years old but later refined to 12–13 million years and named *Otavi pithecus namibiensis*.

Earliest hominid The characteristics typical of the Hominidae include a large brain and bipedal locomotion. The earliest hominid relic is an Australopithecine jaw-bone, with two molars 5 cm *2 in* long, found by Kiptalam Chepboi near Lake Baringo, Kenya in February 1984. It has been dated to four million years ago by associated fossils and to 5·4–5·6 million years ago through rock correlation by potassium-argon dating.

Of early hominid material, one of the most complete is the skeleton of 'Lucy' (40 per cent complete) found by Dr Donald C. Johanson and T. Gray at Locality 162 by the Awash River, Hadar, in the Afar region of Ethiopia on 30 Nov 1974. She was estimated to be 106 cm *3ft 6 in* tall and *c.*40 years old when she died 3 million years ago.

Parallel tracks of hominid footprints extending over 24 m *80ft* were discovered by Paul Abell and Dr Mary

Oldest mummy

Mummification (from the Persian word *mūm*, wax) dates from 2600 BC or the 4th dynasty of the Egyptian pharaohs. The oldest known mummy is that of a high-ranking young woman who was buried *c.* 2600 BC on a plateau near the Great Pyramid of Cheops at Giza, or Al-Gizeh, Egypt. Her remains, which appear to represent an early attempt at mummification, were discovered in an excavation on 17 Mar 1989, but only her skull was intact. She is believed to have lived in the lost kingdom of Ankh Ptah.

The oldest complete mummy is of Wati, a court musician of *c.* 2400 BC from the tomb of Nefer in Saqqâra, Egypt, found in 1944.

Oldest human body

The body of a Late Stone Age man who is thought to have died *c.* 3300 BC, was found almost perfectly preserved in an Austrian glacier in September 1991.

Leakey at Laetoli, Tanzania in 1978, in volcanic ash dating to 3·6 million years ago. The height of the smallest, of what were believed to be three individuals, was estimated to be 120cm *3ft 11in*.

Earliest genus (Homo) The earliest species of this genus is *Homo habilis*, or 'Handy Man', from Olduvai Gorge, Tanzania, named by Louis Leakey, Philip Tobias and John Napier in 1964 after a suggestion from Prof. Raymond Arthur Dart (1893–1988).

The greatest age attributed to fossils of this genus is about 2·4 million years for a piece of cranium found in western Kenya in 1965. At the time it could not be positively identified, but scientists in the USA were able to confirm the identification in 1991. The date was provided by Alan Deino of the Geochronology Center of the Institute of Human Origins, Berkeley, California, USA, who analysed volcanic material in a layer just above the fossil site.

The earliest stone tools are abraded core-choppers dating from *c*.2·7 million years ago. They were found at Hadar, Ethiopia in November–December 1976 by Hélène Roche (France). Finger-held (as opposed to fist-held) quartz slicers found by Roche and Dr John Wall (New Zealand) close to the Hadar site by the Gona River can also be dated to *c*.2·7 million years ago.

Earliest Homo erectus This species (upright man), the direct ancestor of *Homo sapiens*, was discovered by Kamoya Kimeu on the surface at the site of Nariokotome III to the west of Lake Turkana, Kenya in August 1985. This skeleton of a 12-year-old boy 1·65m *5ft 5in* in length is the most complete of this species yet found; only a few small pieces are missing. It is dated to 1·6 million years ago.

Europe A *Homo erectus* skull from a site at Bilzingsleben, Germany, has been dated by uranium dating techniques and electron-spin resonance to not less than 350 000 and possibly more than 400 000 years.

UK Lower Palaeolithic hand-axes from the Waverley Wood Farm site, Warwicks and the hand-axe factory and occupation site at Boxgrove, W Sussex may date from an age earlier than 600 000 years. Sites such as these with an Acheulian culture represent the earliest evidence of a human presence in Britain.

The oldest actual human remains ever found in Britain are pieces of a brain case from a specimen of *Homo sapiens*, recovered in June 1935 and March 1936 by Dr Alvan T. Marston from the Boyn Hill Terrace in the Barnfield Pit, near Swanscombe, Kent. The remains were associated with a Middle Acheulian tool culture and probably date from either the Hoxnian or an earlier Interglacial Stage. Amino-acid dates for the Swanscombe deposits suggest an age of 400 000 years.

Three hominid teeth, mandible fragments and vertebra of *Homo sapiens neanderthalensis* were found in Pontnewydd Cave, Lower Elwy Valley, north Wales in October 1980. The stalagmite enclosing these bones has been dated by the thorium/uranium disequilibrium method to a little over 200 000 years.

In 1988 a jaw-bone of *Homo sapiens sapiens* (i.e. anatomically modern man) from a cave near Torquay, Devon was found to be 31 000 years old by radio-carbon dating: this is 13 000 years older than a previously dated skeleton of this species.

Dimensions

Giants

Growth of the body is determined by growth hormone. This is produced by the pituitary gland set deep in the brain. Over production in childhood produces abnormal growth and true gigantism is the result. The true height of human giants is frequently obscured by exaggeration and commercial dishonesty. The only admissible evidence on the actual height of giants is that collected since 1870 under impartial medical supervision. Unfortunately even medical authors themselves are not always blameless and can include fanciful, as opposed to measured heights.

Giants exhibited in circuses and exhibitions are routinely under contract not to be measured and are, almost tradition-

Goliath

Goliath of Gath (c. 1060 BC) is attributed in the Bible to have stood 6 cubits with an arm span of 290 cm *9 ft 6½ in* but this is open to doubt.

The Jewish historian Flavius Josephus (AD 37/38–c. 100) and some of the manuscripts of the Septuagint (the earliest Greek translation of the Old Testament) attribute to Goliath the wholly credible height of 4 Greek cubits and an arm span of 208 cm *6 ft 10 in*.

ally, billed by their promoters at heights up to 45 cm *18 in* in excess of their true heights.

Tallest Men

The tallest man in medical history of whom there is irrefutable evidence is Robert Pershing Wadlow, born at 6:30 a.m. on 22 Feb 1918 in Alton, Illinois, USA and who died at 1:30 a.m. on 15 Jul 1940 in a hotel in Manistee, Michigan, as a result of a septic blister on his right ankle, caused by a poorly fitting brace.

He was last measured on 27 Jun 1940 and was found to be 8 ft 11·1 in *272 cm* tall (arm-span 9 ft 5¾ in *288 cm*). Wadlow was still growing during his terminal illness and would probably have ultimately reached or just exceeded 9 ft *274 cm* in height if he had survived for another year.

His greatest recorded weight was 35 st 1 lb *222·7 kg* on his 21st birthday and when he died he weighed 31 st 5 lb *199 kg*. His shoes were size 37AA (18½ in *47 cm*) and his hands measured 12¾ in *32·4 cm* from the wrist to the tip of the middle finger.

England William Bradley (1787–1820), born in Market Weighton, East Riding, now Humberside, stood 7 ft 9 in *236 cm*.

John Middleton (1578–1623), the famous Childe of Hale, from near Liverpool, was credited with a height of 9 ft 3 in *282 cm* but a life-size impression of his right hand

Robert Wadlow

Weighing 3·85 kg *8½ lb* at birth, the abnormal growth of Robert Wadlow started at the age of 2 following a double hernia operation. His height progressed as follows:

Age	Height		Weight		
	cm	ft	in	kg	lb
5	163	5	4	48	105
8	183	6	0	77	169
9	189	6	2¼	82	180
10	196	6	5	95	210
11	200	6	7	–	–
12	210	6	10½	–	–
13	218	7	1¾	116	255
14	226	7	5	137	301
15	234	7	8	161	355
16	240	7	10¼	170	374
17	245	8	0½	143*	315
18	253	8	3½	–	–
19	258	8	5½	218	480
20	261	8	6¾	–	–
21	265	8	8¼	223	491
22·4**	272	8	11¹⁄₁₀	199	439

* Following severe influenza and infection of the foot.
** Still growing during his terminal illness.

(length 11½ in *29·2 cm*, cf. Wadlow's 12¾ in *32·4 cm*) painted on a panel in Brasenose College, Oxford indicates his true stature was nearer 7 ft 9 in *236 cm*.

Scotland The world's tallest recorded 'true' (non-pathological) giant was Angus Macaskill (1823–63), born on the island of Berneray in the Sound of Harris, Western Isles. He stood 7 ft 9 in *236 cm* and died in St Ann's, Cape Breton Island, Nova Scotia, Canada. His grandfather was also a giant.

Wales William Evans (1599–1634) of Monmouthshire, now Gwent, who was porter to King James I, stood 7 ft 6 in *228·6 cm*.

Republic of Ireland Patrick Cotter (O'Brien) (1760–1806), born in Kinsale, Co. Cork, was 8 ft 1 in *246 cm* tall. He died at Hotwells, Bristol.

Isle of Man The tallest Manxman on record was Arthur Caley of Sulby. He was variously credited with heights of 8 ft 2 in *249 cm* and 8 ft 4 in *254 cm*, but actually stood 7ft 6in *228·6 cm*. He died at Clyde, New Jersey, USA on 12 Feb 1889 aged 60.

Living Claims for the tallest person in the world can be disputed by Haji Mohammad Alam Channa (b. 1956) of Bachal Channa, Sehwan Sharif, Pakistan

Robert Wadlow (b. 1918) seen here with his two brothers, Eugene (b. 1922) (left) and Harold Jr (b. 1932). (Photo: Alton Telegraph)

Chris Greener, Britain's tallest man.

(Photo: Rex Features)

and the world's tallest living woman, Sandy Allen (USA) (b. 18 Jun 1955) (◊Tallest women), both are around 7ft 7¼in *231·7cm* tall.

UK The tallest man living in the UK is Christopher Paul Greener (b. New Brighton, Merseyside, 21 Nov 1943) of Hayes, Kent, who measures 7ft 6¼in *229cm* (weight 26st *165kg*).

Scotland The tallest Scotsman now living is George Gracie (b. 1938) of Forth, Lanarks, now in Strathclyde. He stands 7ft 3in *221cm* and weighs 32st

---

Married couple

Anna Hanen Swan (1846–88) of Nova Scotia, Canada was said to be 8ft 1in *246cm* but actually measured 7ft 5½in *227cm*. At the church of St Martin-in-the-Fields, London on 17 Jun 1871 she married Martin van Buren Bates (1845–1919) of Whitesburg, Letcher County, Kentucky, USA, who stood 7ft 2½in *220cm*, making them the tallest married couple on record.

Most dissimilar couple

Nigel Wilks (198cm *6ft 6in*) (b. 1963) of Kingston-upon-Hull, Humberside married Beverley Russell (119cm *4ft*) (b. 1963) who suffers from a skeletal disorder on 30 Jun 1984.

Most variable stature

Adam Rainer, born in Graz, Austria in 1899, measured 118cm *3ft 10½in* at the age of 21. He then suddenly started growing at a rapid rate, and by 1931 he had reached 218cm *7ft 1¾in*. He became so weak as a result that he was bedridden for the rest of his life. At the time of his death on 4 Mar 1950, aged 51, he measured 234cm *7ft 8in* and was the only person in medical history to have been both a dwarf and a giant.

203kg. His brother Hugh (b. 1941) is 7ft ½in *214cm*.

Wales Matthew Langmaid (b. Cardiff, Wales, 3 Oct 1968) is 7ft 1½in *217cm* tall.

Tallest Women

The tallest woman in medical history was the giantess Zeng Jinlian (b. 26 Jun 1964) of Yujiang village in the Bright Moon Commune, Hunan Province, central China, who measured 8ft 1¾in *248cm* when she died on 13 Feb 1982. This figure, however, represented her height with assumed normal spinal curvature because she suffered from severe scoliosis (curvature of the spine) and could not stand up straight. She began to grow abnormally from the age of four months and stood 5ft 1½in *156cm* before her fourth birthday and 7ft 1½in *217cm* when she was 13. Her hands measured 10in *25·5cm* and her feet 14in *35·5cm* in length. Both her parents and her brother were of normal size.

The giantess Ella Ewing (1875–1913) of Gorin, Missouri, USA was billed at 8ft 2in *249cm*, but this height was exaggerated. She measured 7ft 4½in *224cm* at the age of 23, and may have attained 7ft 6in *228·6cm* at the time of her death.

UK The tallest woman in British medical history was Jane ('Ginny') Bunford, (b. 26 Jul 1895) at Bartley Green, Northfield, Birmingham. Her skeleton, now preserved in the Anatomical Museum in the Medical School at Birmingham University, has a height of 7ft 4in *223·5cm*. Her abnormal growth started at the age of 11 following a head injury, and on her 13th birthday she measured 6ft 6in *198cm*. Shortly before her death on 1 Apr 1922 she stood 7ft 7in *231cm* tall, but she had severe kyphoscoliosis and would have measured at least 7ft 11in *241cm* if she had been able to stand fully erect.

Living The world's tallest woman is Sandy Allen, (b. 18 Jun 1955) of Chicago, Illinois, USA. A 6½lb *2·95kg* baby, her abnormal growth began soon after birth. At 10 years of age she stood 6ft 3in *190·5cm*, and measured 7ft 1in *216cm* when she was 16. On 14 Jul 1977 this giantess underwent a pituitary gland operation, which inhibited further growth at 7 ft 7¼ in *231·7 cm*. She now weighs 33 st *209·5 kg* and takes a size 16 EEE American shoe (14½ UK).

Tallest Twins

World The world's tallest identical twins are Michael and James Lanier (b. 27 Nov 1969) from Troy, Michigan, USA. They measured 7 ft 1 in *216 cm* at the age of 14 years and both now stand 7 ft 4 in *223·5 cm*. Their sister Jennifer is 5 ft 2 in *157 cm* tall.

The world's tallest female identical twins are Heather and Heidi Burge (b. 11 Nov 1971) from Palos Verdes, California, USA; they are both 6 ft 4¾ in *195 cm* tall.

UK The tallest identical male twins recorded in Britain were the Knipe brothers (b. 1761) of Magherafelt, near Londonderry, who both measured 7 ft 2 in *218 cm*.

The tallest living male twins are Andrew and Timothy Hull (b. 23 and 24 Oct 1968 respectively) of Redditch, Worcs, who are 6 ft 9·3 in *206·5 cm* and 6 ft 10·3 in *209 cm* respectively.

The tallest identical female twins are Daphne Turner and Evelyn Staniford (*née* Gould) (b. 28 Apr 1931) who both measure 6 ft ½ in *184 cm*. Each has a son who is over 6 ft 5 in *195·5 cm*.

Dwarfs

The strictures that apply to giants apply equally to dwarfs, insofar that exaggeration gives way to understatement. In the same way as 9 ft *274 cm* may be regarded as the limit towards which the tallest giants tend, so 22 in *56 cm* must be regarded as the limit towards which the shortest adult dwarfs or midgets tend (cf. the average length of new-born babies is 18–20 in *46–50 cm*). In the case of child dwarfs, their *ages* are often exaggerated by their agents or managers.

There are many causes of short stature in humans. They include genetic abnormalities, lack of appropriate hormones (e.g. growth hormones) and malnutrition. Dwarfism produced smaller stature in the past due to lower nutritional standards. There are an estimated 3000 people of

severely restricted growth (i.e. under 4 ft 8 in *142 cm*) living in Britain today.

Shortest person The shortest mature human of whom there is independent evidence is Gul Mohammed (b. 15 Feb 1957) of New Delhi, India. On 19 Jul 1990 he was examined at Ram Manohar Hospital, New Delhi, and found to measure 22½ in *57 cm* in height (weight 17 kg *37½ lb*). The other members of his immediate family are of normal height.

The shortest ever female has been Pauline Musters ('Princess Pauline'), a Dutch dwarf. She was born at Ossendrecht on 26 Feb 1876 and measured 12 in *30 cm* at birth. At nine years of age she was 55 cm *21·65 in* tall and weighed only 1·5 kg *3 lb 5 oz*. She died of pneumonia with meningitis on 1 Mar 1895 in New York City, USA at the age of 19. A post mortem examination showed her to be exactly 24 in *61 cm* (there was some elongation after death). Her mature weight varied from 7½–9 lb *3·4–4 kg* and her 'vital statistics' were 18½–19–17 in *47–48–43 cm*, which suggest she was overweight.

British Isles The shortest mature human ever recorded in Britain was Joyce Carpenter (1929–73), of Charford, now Hereford & Worcester, who stood 29 in *74 cm* tall and weighed 30 lb *13·6 kg*. She suffered from Morquio's disease which causes deformities of the spine and shortening of the neck and trunk.

Hopkins Hopkins (1737–54) of Llantrisant, Mid-Glamorgan, who suffered from progeria, was 31 in *79 cm* tall. He weighed 19 lb *8·6 kg* at the age of 7 and 13 lb *6 kg* at the time of his death.

Shortest living Female Madge Bester (b. 26 Apr 1963) of Johannesburg, South Africa, is only 65 cm *25·5 in* tall. However, she suffers from Osteogenesis imperfecta and is confined to a wheelchair. This disease means there is an inherited abnormality of collagen, which with calcium salts, produces a rigid structure within bones. It is characterized by brittle bones and other deformities of the skeleton. Her mother Winnie is not much taller, measuring 70 cm *27½ in*, and is also confined to a wheelchair.

UK The shortest adult living is Michael Henbury-Ballan (b. 26 Nov 1958) of

Tribes

The tallest major tribes in the world are the slender Tutsi, (also known as the Watusi) of Rwanda and Burundi, Central Africa, and the Dinka of the Sudan. In some groups of the Tutsi, adult males average 6 ft 5 in *195·5 cm* and females 5 ft 10 in *177·8 cm*.

The smallest pygmies are the Mbuti of the Ituri forest, Zaïre, Central Africa, with an average height of 4 ft 6 in *137 cm* for men and 4 ft 5 in *135 cm* for women.

Greatest differential in weight

The greatest weight difference recorded for a married couple is *c.* 589 kg *92 st 12 lb* in the case of Jon Brower Minnoch (⊳ Heaviest male) and his 50 kg *7 st 12 lb* wife Jeannette in March 1978.

The UK record is held by the wrestler Martin Ruane, alias Luke McMasters ('Giant Haystacks') and his 48 kg *7½ st* wife Rita, where their weight differential at one time may have been 270 kg *42½ st*.

Bassett, Southampton, Hants who is 94 cm *37 in* tall and weighs 35 kg *5½ st*. A 2·66 kg *5 lb 14 oz* baby, he stopped growing at the age of 13. His twin brother Malcolm is 175 cm *5 ft 9 in* tall and weighs 73 kg *11 st 7 lb*.

Patrick Scanlan (b. 1966) of Maida Vale, London stands 91 cm *36 in* tall and weighs only 19 kg *42 lb*, but he suffers from MPS, an enzyme disease that causes severe bone abnormalities, including curvature of the spine, and cannot stand erect. He stopped growing at the age of 4 years.

Twins The shortest twins ever recorded were the dwarfs Matjus and Bela Matina (b. 1903–*fl*.1935) of Budapest, Hungary, who later became naturalized American citizens. They both measured 76 cm *30 in*.

Living The world's shortest living identical twins are John and Greg Rice (b. 3 Dec 1951) of West Palm Beach, Florida, USA, who both measure 86·3 cm *34 in*.

The shortest identical twin sisters are Dorene Williams of Oakdale and Darlene McGregor of Almeda, California, USA (b. 1949), who each stand 124·4 cm *4 ft 1 in*.

Oldest There are only two centenarian dwarfs on record. The older was Hungarian-born Susanna Bokoyni (b. 6 Apr 1879), alias 'Princess Susanna', of Newton, New Jersey, USA, who died aged 105 years on 24 Aug 1984. She was 3 ft 4 in *101·5 cm* tall.

The other was Miss Anne Clowes of Matlock, Derbys, who died on 5 Aug 1784 aged 103 years. She was 3 ft 9 in *114 cm* tall.

Weight

Heaviest male The heaviest human in medical history was Jon Brower Minnoch (1941–83) of Bainbridge Island, Washington State, USA, who had suffered from obesity since childhood. The 6 ft 1 in *185 cm* tall former taxi-driver was 28 st *178 kg* in 1963, 50 st *317 kg* in 1966 and 69 st 9 lb *442 kg* in September 1976.

In March 1978, Minnoch was rushed to University Hospital, Seattle, saturated with fluid and suffering from heart and respiratory failure. It took a dozen firemen and an improvized stretcher to move him from his home to a ferry-boat. When he arrived at the hospital he was put in two beds lashed together. It took 13 people just to roll him over. By extrapolating his intake and elimination rates, consultant endocrinologist Dr Robert Schwartz calculated that Minnoch must have weighed more than 100 st *635 kg* when he was admitted, a great deal of which was water accumulation due to his congestive heart failure. After nearly two years on a 1200-calories-a-day diet the choking fluid had gone, and he was discharged at 34 st *216 kg*. In October 1981 he had to be readmitted, after putting on over 14 st *89 kg*. When he died on 10 Sep 1983 he weighed more than 57 st *362 kg*.

UK Peter Yarnall of East Ham, London weighed 58 st *368 kg* and was 5 ft 10 in *178 cm* tall. The former docker began putting on weight at a rapid rate in 1978 and for the last two years of his life he was bedridden. He died on 30 Mar 1984 aged 34 years and it took ten firemen five hours to demolish the wall of his bedroom and winch his body down to street level. His coffin measured 7ft 4in *223cm* in length, 4ft *122cm* across and had a depth of 2ft 9in *84cm*.

Republic of Ireland The heaviest is reputed to have been Roger Byrne, who was buried in Rosenallis, Co. Laoighis (Leix), on 14 Mar 1804. He died in his 54th year, and his coffin and its contents weighed 52st *330kg*.

Living The heaviest living man is T. J. Albert Jackson (b. 1941 as Kent Nicholson), also known as 'Fat Albert', of Canton, Mississippi, USA. He has weighed 63st 9lb *404kg*. He has a 120in *305cm* chest, a 116in *294cm* waist, 70in *178cm* thighs and a 29½in *75cm* neck.

UK The professional wrestler Martin Ruane, alias Luke McMasters ('Giant Haystacks'), who was born in Camberwell, London in 1946 once claimed to be 50st *317kg*. His weight fluctuates between 45st *286kg* and 46st *292kg* and he is 6ft 11in *211cm* tall.

Heaviest female The heaviest female ever recorded is Roselie Bradford (USA) (b. 1944), who it is claimed registered a peak weight of 75st *476kg* in January 1987. In August of that year she developed congestive heart failure and was rushed to hospital. She was consequently put on a carefully controlled diet and by September 1992 weighed 22st 6lb *142kg* (⊳Weight loss). Her target weight is 10st 10lb *68kg*.

UK The heaviest woman ever recorded was Mrs Muriel Hopkins (b. 1931) of Tipton, W Mids, who weighed 43st 11lb *278kg* (height 5ft 11in *180cm*) in 1978. Shortly before her death on 22 Apr 1979 she reportedly weighed 52st *330kg*, but this proved to be an over-estimate, and her actual weight was found to be 47st 7lb *301kg*. Her coffin measured 6ft 3in *190cm* in length, 4ft 5in *134cm* in width and was 3ft 9in *114cm* deep.

Heaviest twins Billy Leon (1946–79) and Benny Loyd (b. 7 Dec 1946) McCrary, alias McGuire, of Hendersonville, North Carolina, USA were normal in size until the age of six when they both contracted German measles. In November 1978 they weighed 53st 1lb

337kg (Billy) and 51st 9lb *328kg* (Benny) and had 84in *213cm* waists. As professional tag wrestling performers they were billed at weights up to 55st *349kg*. Billy died at Niagara Falls, Ontario, Canada on 13 Jul 1979.

Weight loss *Dieting* The greatest recorded slimming feat by a male was that of Jon Brower Minnoch (⊳ Heaviest male) who had reduced to 34st *216kg* by July 1979, thus indicating a weight loss of at least 66st *419kg* in 16 months.

Female Roselie Bradford (⊳Heaviest female) went from a weight of 1050lb *476kg* in January 1987 to 314lb *142kg* in September 1992, a loss of a record 736lb *334kg*.

The female champion in Britain is Mrs Dolly Wager (b. 1933) of Charlton, London, who, between September 1971 and 22 May 1973 reduced her weight from 31st 7lb *200kg* to 11st *70kg*, so losing 20st 7lb *130kg* with Weight Watchers.

Sweating Ron Allen (b. 1947) sweated off 21½lb *9·7kg* of his weight of 17st 1lb *113kg* in Nashville, Tennessee, USA in 24 hours in August 1984.

Weight gain The reported record for weight gain is held by Jon Brower Minnoch (⊳ Heaviest male) at 14st *89kg* in 7 days in October 1981 before readmittance to University of Washington Hospital, Seattle, USA. Arthur Knorr (USA) (1916–60) gained 21st *133kg* in the last six months of his life.

Miss Doris James of San Francisco, California, USA is alleged to have gained 23st 3lb *147kg* in the 12 months before her death in August 1965, aged 38, at a weight of 48st 3lb *306kg*. She was only 5ft 2in *157cm* tall.

Lightest The lightest adult on record was Lucia Xarate (1863–89) of San Carlos, Mexico, an emaciated ateleiotic dwarf of 26½in *67cm*, who weighed 2·13kg *4·7lb* at the age of 17. She 'fattened up' to 13lb *5·9kg* by her 20th birthday. At birth she weighed 2½lb *1·1kg*.

Edward C. Hagner (1892–1962), alias Eddie Masher, USA is alleged to have weighed only 3st 6lb *22kg* at a height of

5ft 7in *170cm*. He was also known as 'Skeleton Dude'.

The thinnest recorded adults of normal height are those suffering from anorexia nervosa. Losses of up to 65 per cent of the original bodyweight have been recorded in females, with a 'low' of 3st 3lb *20kg* in the case of Emma Shaller (1868–90) of St Louis, Missouri, USA, who was 5ft 2in *157cm* tall.

In August 1825 the biceps measurement of Claude-Ambroise Seurat (1797–1826) of Troyes, France was 4in *10cm* and the distance between his back and his chest was less than 3in *8cm*. According to one report he stood 5ft 7½in *171cm* and weighed 5st 8lb *35kg*, but in another account he was described as being 5ft 4in *163cm* and only 2st 8lb *16kg*.

British Isles The lightest adult was Hopkins Hopkins (⬦ Dwarfs).

Robert Thorn (b. 1842) of March, Cambs weighed 49lb *22kg* at the age of 32. He was 4ft 6in *137cm* tall and had a 27in *68cm* chest (expanded), 4½in *11cm* biceps, and a 3in *8cm* wrist. A doctor who examined him said he had practically no muscular development, 'although he could run along the road'.

Reproductivity

Motherhood

Most children The greatest officially recorded number of children born to one mother is 69, by the wife of Feodor Vassilyev (b. 1707–*fl*.1782), a peasant from Shuya, 240km *150 miles* east of Moscow, Russia. In 27 confinements she gave birth to 16 pairs of twins, seven sets of triplets and four sets of quadruplets. The case was reported to Moscow by the Monastery of Nikolskiy on 27 Feb 1782. Only two of these, who were born in the period *c*. 1725–65, failed to survive their infancy.

The world's most prolific mother is currently Leontina Albina (*née* Espinosa) (b. 1925) of San Antonio, Chile, who in 1981 produced her 55th and last child. Her husband Gerardo Secunda Albina (variously Alvina) (b. 1921) states that they were married in Argentina in 1943

and had 5 sets of triplets (all boys) before coming to Chile. Only 40 (24 boys and 16 girls) survive.

UK Elizabeth, wife of John Mott whom she married in 1676, of Monks Kirby, Warks, produced 42 live-born children. She died in 1720, 44 years after her marriage.

Today's champion mothers are believed to be Mrs Margaret McNaught (b. 1923), of Balsall Heath, Birmingham, 12 boys and 10 girls, all single births – two boys died in infancy and Mrs Mabel Constable (b. 1920), of Long Itchington, Warwicks, who also has had 22 children, including a set of triplets and two sets of twins.

Scotland Mrs Jessie Campbell (b. 1946) of Struan, Isle of Skye, Scotland, gave birth to her 20th child on 22 Jan 1990.

Ireland In December 1949 it was reported that Mrs Mabel Murphy (b. 1898) of Lisnaskea, Co. Fermanagh had produced 28 children (12 stillborn) in a 32 year marriage, but this claim has not been fully substantiated. Mrs Kathleen Scott (b. 4 Jul 1914) of Dublin gave birth to her 24th child on 9 Aug 1958.

Oldest mother Many apparently very late maternities may be cover-ups for illegitimate grandchildren. Post-menopausal women have been rendered fertile by recent hormonal techniques. Medical literature contains extreme but unauthenticated cases of septuagenarian mothers, such as Mrs Ellen Ellis, aged 72, of Four Crosses, Clwyd, who allegedly produced a stillborn 13th child on 15 May 1776 in her 46th year of marriage.

The oldest recorded mother for whom the evidence satisfied medical verification was Mrs Ruth Alice Kistler (*née* Taylor), formerly Mrs Shepard (1899–1982), of Portland, Oregon, USA. A birth certificate indicated that she gave birth to a daughter, Suzan, at Glendale, near Los Angeles, California, USA on 18 Oct 1956, when her age was 57 years 129 days.

In the *Gazette Médicale de Liège* (1 Oct 1891) Dr E. Derasse reported the case of one of his patients who gave birth to a healthy baby at the age of 59 years 5 months. The woman already had a married daughter aged 40 years.

UK Mrs Kathleen Campbell (b. 23 Apr 1932) of Ilkeston, Derbys, gave birth to a 2·92 kg *6 lb 7 oz* baby boy at Nottingham City Hospital on 9 Sep 1987 at the age of 55 years 141 days. She already had six children aged 16 to 22 years.

It was reported in the *British Medical Journal* (June 1991) that a mother gave birth at the age of 59 years. According to a report in the *Lancet* (1867) a woman reputedly aged 62 gave birth to triplets. She had previously had 10 children.

Ireland Mrs Mary Higgins (b. 7 Jan 1876) of Cork, Co. Cork gave birth to a daughter, Patricia, on 17 Mar 1931 when aged 55 years 69 days.

Babies

Heaviest single birth Big babies (i.e. over 10 lb *4·5 kg*) are usually born to mothers who are large, overweight or have a medical problem such as diabetes. The heaviest baby of a healthy mother was a boy weighing 10·2 kg *22 lb 8 oz* who was born to Sig. Carmelina Fedele of Aversa, Italy in September 1955.

Mrs Anna Bates (*née* Swan) (1846–88), the 7 ft 5½ in *227 cm* Canadian giantess, gave birth to a boy weighing 23 lb 12 oz *10·8 kg* (length 30 in *76 cm*) at her home in Seville, Ohio, USA on 19 Jan 1879, but the baby died 11 hours later.

UK It was reported in a letter to the *British Medical Journal* (1 Feb 1879) from a doctor in Torpoint, Cornwall that a child born on Christmas Day 1852 weighed 21 lb *9·5 kg*.

The only other reported birthweight in excess of 20 lb *9 kg* is 20 lb 2 oz *9·13 kg* for a boy with a 14½ in *37 cm* chest born to a 33-year-old schoolmistress in Crewe, Cheshire on 12 Nov 1884.

Guy Warwick Carr was born on 9 Mar 1992, the eighth child of Andrew and

Fastest triplet birth
Bradley, Christopher and Carmon were born naturally to Mrs James E. Duck of Memphis, Tennessee, USA in two minutes on 21 Mar 1977.

Nicola Carr (5 ft 2 in *157 cm* tall) of Kirkby-in-Furness, Cumbria, weighing 15 lb 8 oz *7 kg*. He was 25 in *63 cm* in length and midwives at the Maternity Unit had to raid the Children's Ward for nappies and clothes large enough to fit him.

Twins The world's heaviest twins, weighing 27 lb 12 oz *12·6 kg*, were born to Mrs J.P. Haskin, Fort Smith, Arkansas, USA on 20 Feb 1924.

Triplets The unconfirmed report of the world's heaviest triplets was a case from Iran (2 male, 1 female) weighing 26 lb 6 oz *12 kg* born on 18 Mar 1968.

UK The heaviest triplets in the UK, weighing 24 lb *10·9 kg*, were born to Mrs Mary McDermott of Bearpark, Co Durham on 18 Nov 1914.

Quadruplets The world's heaviest quadruplets (4 girls), weighing 22 lb 13 oz *10·4 kg*, were born to Mrs Ayako Takeda Tsuchihashi at the Maternity Hospital in Kagoshima, Japan on 4 Oct 1978.

Quintuplets Two cases have been recorded for heaviest quintuplets, with both recording a weight of 25 lb *11·35 kg*: on 7 Jun 1953 to Mrs Liu Saulian of Zhejiang, China; and on 30 Dec 1956 to Mrs Kamalammal of Pondicherry, India.

Lightest single births A premature baby girl weighing 280 g *9·9 oz* was reported to have been born on 27 Jun 1989 at the Loyola University Medical Center, Illinois, USA.

UK The lowest birthweight recorded for a surviving infant, of which there is definite evidence, is 10 oz *283 g* in the case of Mrs Marian Taggart (*née* Chapman) (1938–83). This baby was born six weeks premature in South Shields, Tyne & Wear. She was born unattended (length 12 in *30 cm*) and was nursed by Dr D.A. Shearer, who fed her hourly for the first 30 hours with brandy, glucose and water through a fountain-pen filler. At three weeks she weighed 1 lb 13 oz

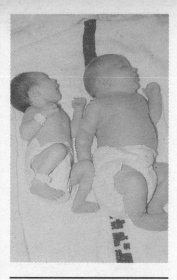

Guy Carr (right) at two days old with a baby of the same age. Guy was delivered naturally, i.e. per vagina, and suffered no trauma during delivery except for a little difficulty due to his broad shoulders.

(Photo: Donald Bell)

821g and by her first birthday 13 lb 14 oz *6·3 kg*. Her weight on her 21st birthday was 7 st 8 lb *48 kg*.

Test-tube babies There are various methods by which babies can be conceived outside of the mother's body. These children are usually known as 'test-tube' babies and the technique as I.V.F. (In vitro fertilization).

First The world's first test tube baby was born to Lesley Brown, 31, who gave birth by Caesarean section to Louise (5 lb 12 oz *2·6 kg*) in Oldham General Hospital, Lancs, at 11:47 p.m. on 25 Jul 1978. Louise was externally conceived on 10 Nov 1977.

Twins The world's first test-tube twins, Stephen and Amanda, were delivered by Caesarean section to Mrs Radmila Mays, 31, at the Queen Victoria Medical Centre,

Melbourne, Australia on 5 Jun 1981. Amanda weighed in at 5 lb 6 oz *2·4 kg* and Stephen 5 lb 3 oz *2·3 kg*.

Triplets The world's first test-tube triplets (two girls and one boy) were born at Flinders Medical Centre, Adelaide, Australia on 8 Jun 1983. At the request of the parents, no names were released.

Quintuplets The first test-tube quintuplets were Alan, Brett, Connor, Douglas and Edward, born to Linda and Bruce Jacobssen at University College Hospital, London on 26 Apr 1985.

Most premature babies James Elgin Gill was born to Brenda and James Gill, on 20 May 1987 in Ottawa, Ontario, Canada, 128 days premature and weighing 624g *1 lb 6 oz*.

UK Rukaya Bailey was born to Joanne Bailey 122 days premature on 26 Jun 1989 at Salford, Greater Manchester, and weighed 600g *1 lb 3 oz*.

Twins Arron and Laura Gaskarth (non-identical twins) were born on 15 Jul 1991 in Bishop Auckland General Hospital, Co Durham 107 days premature. Arron weighed 760g *1 lb 11 oz* and Laura 650g *1 lb 7 oz*.

Quadruplets Tina Piper of St Leonards-on-Sea, E Sussex, was delivered of quadruplets on 10 Apr 1988, at exactly 26 weeks' term. Oliver 2 lb 9 oz *1·16 kg*, (died February 1989), Francesca 2 lb 2 oz *0·96 kg*, Charlotte 2 lb 4½ oz *1·03 kg* and Georgina 2 lb 5 oz *1·05 kg* were all born at the Royal Sussex County Hospital, Brighton, Sussex.

Multiple Births

'Siamese' twins Conjoined twins derive the name 'Siamese' from the celebrated Chang and Eng Bunker ('Left' and 'Right' in Thai) born at Meklong on 11 May 1811 of Chinese parents. They were joined by a cartilaginous band at the chest. They married (in April 1843) the Misses Sarah and Adelaide Yates of Wilkes County, North Carolina, USA, and fathered 10 and 12 children respectively. They died within three hours of each other on 17 Jan 1874, aged 62.

Britain's first known pair were the 'Scottish brothers', who were born near Glasgow in 1490. They were brought to

The term 'Siamese' for conjoined twins is derived from the famous twins, Chang and Eng Bunker, born in Meklong, Siam (now Thailand) in 1811.

(Photo: Ann Ronan Picture Library)

Longest interval between twins

Mrs Danny Petrungaro (*née* Berg) (b. 1953) of Rome, Italy, who had been on hormone treatment after suffering four miscarriages, gave birth normally to a baby girl, Diana, on 22 Dec 1987, but she was not delivered of the other twin, Monica, by Caesarean section, until 27 Jan 1988, 36 days later.

Longest separated twins

Through the help of New Zealand's television programme *Missing* on 27 Apr 1989, Iris (*née* Haughie) Johns and Aro (*née* Haughie) Campbell (b. 13 Jan 1914) were reunited after 75 years' separation.

Lightest twins

Mary, 16oz 453g, and Margaret, 19oz 538g, were born on 16 Aug 1931 to Mrs Florence Stimson, Old Fletton, Peterborough, Cambs.

---

the Court of King James IV (1488–1513) of Scotland in 1491, and lived under the king's patronage for the rest of his reign. They died in 1518 aged 28 years, one brother succumbing five days before the other, who 'moaned piteously as he crept about the castle gardens, carrying with him the dead body of the brother from whom only death could separate him and to whom death would again join him'.

The only British example of pygopagus (joined at the buttocks back to back) twins to reach maturity were Daisy and Violet Hilton born in Brighton, E Sussex, on 5 Feb 1908. They died in Charlotte, North Carolina, USA on 5 Jan 1969, aged 60, from Hong Kong flu.

Rarest The most extreme form of conjoined twins is dicephales tetrabrachius dipus (two heads, four arms and two legs). The only fully reported example is Masha and Dasha Krivoshlyapovy, born in the USSR on 4 Jan 1950.

Earliest successful separation The earliest successful separation of Siamese twins was performed on xiphopagus (joined at the sternum) girls at Mount Sinai Hospital, Cleveland, Ohio, USA by Dr Jac S. Geller on 14 Dec 1952.

Quindecaplets It was announced by Dr Gennaro Montanino of Rome that he had removed by hysterotomy after four months of the pregnancy the foetuses of ten girls and five boys from the womb of a 35-year-old housewife on 22 Jul 1971. A fertility drug was responsible for this unique instance of quindecaplets.

Highest number at a single birth Ten children (decaplets) (two males, eight females) were reported to have been born at Bacacay, Brazil on 22 Apr 1946. Reports were also received from Spain in 1924 and China on 12 May 1936.

The highest number medically recorded is nine (nonuplets) born to Mrs. Geraldine Brodrick at Royal Hospital for Women, Sydney, Australia on 13 Jun 1971. None of the five boys (two stillborn) and four girls lived for more than 6 days. The birth of nine children has also been reported on at least two other occasions; Philadelphia, Pennsylvania, USA, 29 May 1971, and Bagerhat, Bangladesh, c. 11 May 1977, and in both cases none survived.

In Britain, the greatest number recorded is seven (septuplets) (four boys, three girls) born to Mrs Susan Halton (b. 1960) at Liverpool Maternity Hospital on 15 Aug 1987, none survived.

The birth of six children (sextuplets) has occurred on a number of occasions, but sadly, very rarely do all children survive. The most recent case in Great Britain of all surviving is the three boys and three girls born to Mrs Susan Coleman at Homerton, Greater London on 12 Nov 1986.

Most sets of multiple births in a family

Quintuplets There is no recorded case of more than single set.

Quadruplets Four sets to Mde Feodor Vassilyev, Shuya, Russia (died *ante* 1770) (⇔ Motherhood).

Triplets 15 sets to Maddalena Granata, Italy (b. 1839–*fl.* 1886).

Twins 16 sets to Mde Vassilyev (⇔ above). Mrs Barbara Zulu of Barbeton, South Africa bore 3 sets of girls and 3 mixed sets in seven years (1967–73). Mrs Anna Steynvaait of Johannesburg, South Africa produced 2 sets within 10 months in 1960.

UK–Twins 15 sets to Mrs Mary Jonas of Chester (died 4 Sep 1899), all sets were mixed.

Descendants

In polygamous countries, the number of a person's descendants can become incalculable. The last Sharifian Emperor of Morocco, Moulay Ismail (1672–1727), known as 'The Bloodthirsty', was reputed to have fathered a total of 525 sons and 342 daughters by 1703 and achieved a 700th son in 1721.

At the time of his death on 15 Oct 1992, Samuel S. Mast, aged 96, of Fryburg, Pennsylvania, USA, had 824 living descendants. The roll call comprised 11 children, 97 grandchildren, 634 great-grandchildren and 82 great-great-grandchildren.

Mrs Sarah Crawshaw (died 25 Dec 1844) left 397 descendants according to her gravestone in Stones Church, Ripponden, Halifax, W Yorks.

Seven-generation family Augusta Bunge (*née* Pagel) (b. 13 Oct 1879) of Wisconsin, USA, learned that she had become a great-great-great-great-grandmother when her great-great-great-granddaughter gave birth to a son, Christopher John Bollig, on 21 Jan 1989.

Great-great-great grandmother Harriet Holmes of Newfoundland, Canada (b. 17 Jan 1899) became the youngest living great-great-great-grandmother on 8 Mar 1987 at the age of 88 years 50 days.

Most living ascendants Megan Sue Austin of Bar Harbor, Maine, USA had a full set of grandparents and great-grandparents and five great-great-grandparents, making 19 direct ascendants when born on 16 May 1982.

Family tree The lineage of K'ung Ch'iu or Confucius (551–479 BC) can be traced back further than that of any other family. His four greats grandfather K'ung Chia is known from the 8th century BC. This man's 85th lineal descendants, Wei-yi (b. 1939) and Wei-ning (b. 1947), live today in Taiwan.

Longevity

No single subject is more obscured by vanity, deceit, falsehood and deliberate fraud than human longevity. Apart from the traces left by accidental 'markers' (e.g. the residual effects of established dated events such as the Chernobyl incident), there is no known scientific method of checking the age of any part of the living body.

Centenarians surviving beyond their 113th year are in fact extremely rare and the present absolute proven limit of human longevity does not yet admit of anyone living to celebrate their 121st birthday.

From data on documented centenarians, actuaries have shown that only one 115-year life can be expected in 2·1 billion lives (cf. world population which was estimated to be *c*.5480 million by mid-1992).

The height of credulity was reached on 5 May 1933, when a news agency filed a story from China, with a Beijing source that Li Zhongyun, the 'oldest man on earth' born in 1680, had died after 253 year (*sic*).

The latest census in China revealed only 3800 centenarians, of whom two-thirds were women. According to a 1985 census carried out in the Chinese province of Xinjiang Uygur Zizhiqu, there were 850 centenarians in the area, one of whom was returned at a highly improbable 125. In the USA as of 1 Jul 1990 the figure was 36 306. The number of UK centenarians announced on 23 Dec 1992 comprised a total of 263 men and 2090 women.

With an estimated world-wide population of some 40 000 centenarians, only

---

Longest pension

Miss Millicent Barclay was born on 10 Jul 1872, three months after the death of her father, Col. William Barclay, and became eligible for a Madras Military Fund pension to continue until her marriage. She died unmarried on 26 Oct 1969, having drawn the pension for every day of her life, 97 years 3 months.

Authentic National Longevity Records

Country	Years	Name	Days	Born			Died		
Japan	120	Shigechiyo Izumi	237	29	Jun	1865	21	Feb	1986
France	118	Jeanne Louise Calment	40	21	Feb	1875	fl.	April	1993
United States[1]	116	Carrie White (Mrs) (née Joyner)	88	18	Nov	1874	14	Feb	1991
United Kingdom	115	Charlotte Hughes (Mrs) (née Milburn)	229	1	Aug	1877	17	Mar	1993
Canada	113	Pierre Joubert	124	15	Jul	1701	16	Nov	1814
Australia	112	Caroline Maud Mockridge	330	11	Dec	1874	6	Nov	1987
Wales	112	John Evans	292	19	Aug	1877	10	Jun	1990
Spain[2]	112	Josefa Salas Mateo	228	14	Jul	1860	27	Feb	1973
Norway	112	Maren Bolette Torp	61	21	Dec	1876	20	Feb	1989
Morocco	112	El Hadj Mohammed el Mokri (Grand Vizier)	+			1844	16	Sep	1957
Poland	112	Rosalia Mielczarek (Mrs)	+			1868	7	Jan	1981
Netherlands	111	Thomas Peters	354	6	Apr	1745	26	Mar	1857
Ireland	111	The Hon. Katherine Plunket	327	22	Nov	1820	14	Oct	1932
Scotland	111	Kate Begbie (Mrs)	238	9	Jan	1877	5	Sep	1988
South Africa[3]	111	Johanna Booyson	151	17	Jan	1857	16	Jun	1968
Sweden[4]	111	Wilhelmine Sande (Mrs)	90	24	Oct	1874	21	Jan	1986
Czechoslovakia	111	Marie Bernatková	+	22	Oct	1857	fl.	October	1968
Germany[5]	111	Maria Corba	+	15	Aug	1878	fl.	March	1990
Finland	111	Fanny Matilda Nystrom	+	30	Sep	1878			1989
Channel Islands	110	Margaret Ann Neve (née Harvey)	321	18	May	1792	4	Apr	1903
Northern Ireland	110	Elizabeth Watkins (Mrs)	234	10	Mar	1863	31	Oct	1973
Yugoslavia	110	Demitrius Philipovitch	+	9	Mar	1818	fl.	August	1928
Greece	110	Lambrini Tsiatoura (Mrs)	+			1870	19	Feb	1981
USSR	110	Khasako Dzugayev	+	7	Aug	1860	fl.	August	1970
Italy	110	Damiana Sette (Sig.)	+			1874	25	Feb	1985

[1] Mrs Rena Glover Brailsford died in Summerton, South Carolina, on 6 July 1977 reputedly aged 118 yrs. The 1900 US Federal Census for Crawfish Springs Militia District of Walker County, Georgia, records an age of 77 for a Mark Thrash (reputedly born in Georgia in December 1822) who died near Chattanooga, Tennessee on 17 Dec 1943 and, the age attributed earlier was accurate, then he would have survived for 121 years. In 1991 it was reported that Jackson Pollard of Georgia was born on 15 Dec 1869 according to his social security payments, but no birth certificate or family Bible records are available.

[2] Señor Benita Medrana of Avila died on 28 Jan 1979 allegedly aged 114 years 335 days.

[3] Mrs Susan Johanna Deporter of Port Elizabeth, South Africa was reputedly 114 years old when she died on 4 Aug 1954.

[4] Mrs Sande was born in present-day Norway.

[5] An unnamed female died in Germany in 1979 aged 112 years, and an unnamed male aged also 112 years, in 1969.

Note: fl. is the abbreviation for the Latin = floruit, (at the relevant date).

Madame Jeanne Calment on her 116th birthday outside the nursing home at Arles, France, where she stays. Madame Calment continues to thrive but had a narrow escape shortly after her 118th birthday, when the home was badly damaged by a fire which killed two, but she escaped unharmed.

(Photo: Sipa Press)

22 per cent are male. While husbands have a better chance than bachelors, it appears that spinsters have a better chance than wives of reaching 100 years.

Oldest authentic centenarian The greatest *authenticated* age to which any human has ever lived is 120 years 237 days in the case of Shigechiuyo Izumi of Asan on Tokunoshima, an island 1320 km *820 miles* south-west of Tokyo, Japan. He was born at Asan on 29 Jun 1865, and recorded as a 6-year old in

THE OLDEST MAN IN LONDON DIES

LIVED THROUGH TEN REIGNS

London was mourning the death of its oldest resident, Thomas Carn, last night. Having lived to 107 years of age and seen off most illnesses in his remarkable life, he passed away quietly yesterday morning, a result of it is believed, influenza.

Older readers will remember 'Old Tom', as he was affectionately known, coming to the public's attention some seven years ago when he reached 100. It was thought at the time that he may be unique in having lived through the reigns of ten Kings and Queens of England—a fact which has yet to be contested or bettered, and one it is felt never will.

Born in 1471 just before the usurption of Henry VI by his third cousin, Edward (who became Edward IV). Tom saw a succession of monarchs come and go. The full list is as follows:

Henry VI	(usurped later murdered, 1471)
Edward IV	(d. pneumonia, 1483)
Edward V	(usurped later murdered ?, 1483)
Richard III	(d. Battle of Bosworth Field, 1485)
Henry VII	(d. arthritis and gout, 1509)
Henry VIII	(d. sinusitis and periostitis, 1547)
Edward VI	(d. tuberculosis, 1553)
Lady Jane Grey	(deposed later beheaded, 1553)
Mary I	(d. influenza, 1558)
Elizabeth I	

Asked in 1571 who is favourite monarch was, he replied, 'After Elizabeth, it has to be Henry the Eighth. He was such fun, always marrying, divorcing, beheading. Never a dull moment.'

Japan's first census of 1871. He died in his double-glazed bungalow at 12:15 GMT on 21 Feb 1986 after developing pneumonia. He worked until 105. His wife died aged only 90. He drank *sho-chu* (firewater, distilled from sugar) and took up smoking when aged 70. He attributed his long life to 'God, Buddha and the Sun'.

Oldest living The oldest living person in the world whose date of birth can be reliably authenticated is Jeanne Louise Calment who was born in France on 21 Feb 1875. She now lives in a nursing home in Arles, southern France where she celebrated her 118th birthday. She met Vincent van Gogh (died 29 Jul 1890) in her father's shop.

UK The oldest living person in Britain is Daisy Adams (b. 30 Jun 1880), who lives in Church Gresley, Derbys. The oldest living man is Edgar Sharpe (b. 18 Jan 1886) who lives in Dewsbury, W Yorks.

The only other UK citizens with birth and death certificated more than 112 years apart have been Mrs Charlotte Hughes (1877–1993) (115 years 229 days), Mrs Anna Williams (1873–1987) (114 years 208 days), John Evans (1877–1990) (112 years 292 days) Miss Alice Stevenson (1861–1973) (112 years 39 days) and Miss Janetta Thomas (1869–1982) (112 years 35 days).

Family centenarians The first recorded case in the UK of four siblings being centenarians occurred on 2 Apr 1984 when Mrs Lily Beatrice Parsons (*née* Andrews) reached her 100th birthday. Her three sisters were Mrs Florence Eliza White (1874–1979), Mrs Maud Annie Spencer (1876–1978), Mrs Eleanor Newton Webber (1880–1983). The family came from Teignmouth, Devon.

Oldest twins The chances of identical twins both reaching 100 are now probably about one in 50 million.

Eli Shadrack and John Meshak Phipps were born on 14 Feb 1803 at Affington, Virginia, USA. Eli died at Hennessey, Oklahoma on 23 Feb 1911 at the age of 108 years 9 days, on which day John was still living in Shenandoah, Iowa.

On 17 Jun 1984, identical twin sisters Mildred Widman Philippi and Mary Widman Franzini of St Louis, Missouri, USA celebrated their 104th birthday. Mildred died on 4 May 1985, 44 days short of the twins' 105th birthday.

UK Identical twin spinsters, Alice Maria and Emily Edith Weller were born within 15 minutes of each other on 20 Apr 1888 in Epsom, Surrey. Alice died on 21 Feb 1991 when aged 102.

Oldest triplets The longest-lived triplets recorded in Great Britain were Faith Alice, Hope Fanny and Charity Sarah Stockdale of Cracoe, near Skipton, N Yorks, born on 28–29 Dec 1857. Charity was the first to die, on 30 Jul 1944, aged 86 years 213 days.

Living The oldest living triplets in the UK are 82-year-old Pamela, Phyllis and Priscilla Laybourne (b. 27 Oct 1910, Newport, Gwent).

Oldest quadruplets The Ottman quads of Munich, Germany, Adolf, Anne-Marie, Emma and Elisabeth, were born on 5 May 1912. Adolf was the first to die, on 17 Mar 1992, aged 79 years 316 days.

Long spans The father of Baroness Elliot of Harwood (b. 15 Jan 1903), Sir Charles Tennant Bt, was born in Glasgow on 4 Nov 1823 in the reign of King George IV.

Anatomy and Physiology

Hydrogen (63 per cent) and oxygen (25·5 per cent) constitute the commonest of the 24 elements normally regarded as being in the human body. Potassium, carbon, sodium, calcium, sulphur, chlorine (as chlorides), phosphorus, iron and zinc are all present in significant quantities. Present in 'trace' quantities, but generally regarded as normal in a healthy body (even if the question of whether they are essential is a matter of controversy), are iodine, fluorine, copper, cobalt, chromium, manganese, selenium, molybdenum, and probably vanadium, nickel, silicon, tin and arsenic.

Hands, Feet and Hair

Touch The extreme sensitivity of the fingers is such that a vibration with a movement of 0·02 of a micron can be detected.

Longest fingernails Fingernails grow about 0·05 cm *0·02 in* a week—four times faster than toenails. The aggregate measurement of those of Shridhar Chillal (b. 1937) of Pune, Maharashtra, India on 3 Mar 1993 was 205 in *520 cm* for the five nails on his left hand (thumb 48 in *122 cm*, first finger 36 in *91 cm*, second finger 39 in *99 cm*, third finger 42 in *106 cm*, and the fourth 40 in *102 cm*). He last cut his nails in 1952.

Balancing on one foot

The longest recorded duration for balancing on one foot is 55 hr 35 min by Girish Sharma at Deori, India from 2–4 Oct 1992. The disengaged foot may not be rested on the standing foot nor may any object be used for support or balance.

Most fingers and toes (polydactylism) At an inquest held on a baby boy at Shoreditch in the East End of London on 16 Sep 1921 it was reported that he had 14 fingers and 15 toes.

Least toes The two-toed syndrome exhibited by some of the members of the Wadomo tribe of the Zambezi Valley, Zimbabwe and the Kalanga tribe of the

Vice Admiral Lord Nelson
(Photo: Bridgeman Art Library)

Human hair usually stops growing at 2½–3 ft 75–90 cm long, but at 12 ft 8 in 3·86 m, Diane Witt's hair is over twice as long as she is tall. This exceptional growth of hair is inexplicable: since 1981, when she last had it cut, it has more than doubled in length. Shampooing and combing her hair can take several hours at a time. To keep it out of her way, Diane normally wears it in a complicated braided arrangement piled on top of her head, held up by just two hairpins.
(Photo: R. H. Witt)

eastern Kalahari Desert, Botswana is hereditary via a single mutated gene. These 'ostrich people', as they are known, are not handicapped by their deformity, and can walk great distances without discomfort.

Largest feet If cases of elephantiasis are excluded, then the biggest feet currently known are those of Matthew McGrory (b. 17 May 1973) of Pennsylvania, USA, who wears size 23 US (22½ UK) shoes.

The owner of Britain's largest feet is John Thrupp (b. 1964) of Stratford-

143

The longest moustache, Kalyan Ramji Sain (Photo: Dilip Mehta)

upon-Avon, Warks, who wears a size 21 shoe. He is 2·11 m *6 ft 11 in* tall.

Longest hair Human hair grows at the rate of about 0·5 in *1·2 cm* in a month. If left uncut it will usually grow to a maximum of 2–3 ft *61–91 cm*.

In 1780 a head of hair measuring 12 ft *3·65 m* in length and dressed in a style known as the *plica candiforma* (hair forming matted spikes) was sent to Dresden after adorning the head of a Polish peasant woman for 52 years. The plait of hair was almost 12 in *30 cm* in circumference.

The longest documented length of hair belongs to Diane Witt of Worcester, Massachusetts, USA which measured over 12 ft 8 in *3·86 m* in March 1993.

Most valuable hair On 18 Feb 1988 a bookseller from Cirencester, Glos, paid £5575 for a lock of hair belonging to Vice Admiral Lord Nelson (1758–1805) at an auction held at Crewkerne, Somerset.

Longest beard The beard of Hans N. Langseth (b. 1846 near Eidsroll, Norway) measured 533 cm *17½ ft* at the time of his burial at Kensett, Iowa in 1927 after 15 years' residence in the United States. It was presented to the Smithsonian Institution, Washington, DC, in 1967.

Shaving

The fastest barbers on record are Denny Rowe and Gerry Harley. Denny Rowe shaved 1994 men in 60 min with a retractor safety razor in Herne Bay, Kent on 19 Jun 1988, taking on average 1·8 sec per volunteer, and drawing blood four times. Gerry Harley, of Gillingham, Kent shaved 235 even braver volunteers in 60 min with a cut-throat razor on 13 Aug 1984, averaging 15·3 sec per face. He drew blood only once.

Hair splitting

The greatest reported achievement in hair splitting has been that of the former champion cyclist and craftsman Alfred West (UK) (1901–85), who succeeded in splitting a human hair 17 times into 18 parts on eight occasions.

Longest hair

Claims of hair measuring up to 26 ft *8 m* in length have been reported. However, insufficient verification has been available to comfirm these claims.

The beard of the 'bearded lady' Janice Deveree (b. 1842) of Bracken County, Kentucky, USA was measured at 14 in *36 cm* in 1884.

Longest moustache

The moustache of Kalyan Ramji Sain of Sundargarth, India grown since 1976, reached a span of 327 cm *128¾ in* (right side 167 cm *65¾ in* and left side 160 cm *63 in*) in July 1992.

The longest moustache in Great Britain was that of John Roy (1910–88), of Weeley, near Clacton, Essex. It attained a peak span of 6ft 2½ in *189 cm* on 2 Apr 1976 (began growing in 1939). He accidentally sat on it in the bath in 1984 and lost 16½ in *42 cm*. He then took off the same amount from the other side to even the moustache.

The current UK champion is Ted Sedman of St Albans, Herts whose handlebar moustache measures 56 in *142 cm*.

Dentition

Earliest Tooth enamel is the only part of the human body which basically remains unchanged throughout life. It is also the hardest substance in the body, with a Knoop number of over 300. The first deciduous or milk teeth normally appear in infants at 5–8 months, these being the upper and lower jaw first incisors. There are many records of children born with teeth, the most distinguished example being Prince Louis Dieudonné, later Louis XIV of France, who was born with two teeth on 5 Sep 1638. Molars usually appear at 24 months, but in Pindborg's case published in Denmark in 1970, a six-week premature baby was documented with eight teeth at birth, of which four were in the molar region.

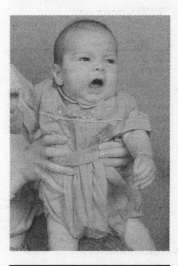

Shaun Keaney of Newbury, Berks was born on 10 Apr 1990 with 12 teeth. However, three days later, they were extracted to prevent possible feeding problems, especially for his mum!
(Photo: Rex Features)

Lifting and pulling with teeth

Walter Arfeuille of Ieper-Vlamertinge, Belgium lifted weights totalling 281·5kg *621lb* a distance of 17cm *6¾in* off the ground with his teeth in Paris, France on 31 Mar 1990.

Robert Galstyan of Masis, Armenia pulled two railway wagons coupled together, weighing a total of 219175kg *483197lb*, a distance of 7m *23ft* along a railway track with his teeth at Shcherbinka, Greater Moscow, Russia on 21 Jul 1992.

Most valuable tooth

In 1816 a tooth belonging to Sir Isaac Newton (1642–1727) was sold in London for £730. It was purchased by a nobleman who had it set in a ring, which he wore constantly.

Earliest false teeth

From discoveries made in Etruscan tombs, partial dentures of bridge-work type were being worn in what is now Tuscany, Italy as early as 700 BC. Some were permanently attached to existing teeth and others were removable.

Most set of teeth Cases of the growth in late life of a third set of teeth have been recorded several times. A reference to a case in France of a *fourth* dentition, known as Lison's case, was published in 1896.

Most dedicated dentist Brother Giovanni Battista Orsenigo of the Ospedale Fatebenefratelli, Rome, a monk who was also a dentist, conserved all the teeth he extracted in three enormous cases during the time he exercised his profession from 1868 to 1904. In 1903 the number was counted and found to be 2000744 teeth, indicating an average of 185 teeth, or nearly six total extractions a day.

Highest hyperacuity The human eye is capable of judging relative position with remarkable accuracy, reaching limits of between 3 and 5 seconds of arc.

In April 1984 Dr Dennis M. Levi of the College of Optometry, University of Houston, Texas, USA, repeatedly identified the relative position of a thin bright green line within 0·85 sec of arc. This is equivalent to a displacement of some ¼in *6 mm* at a distance of 1 mile *1·6 km*.

Colour sensitivity The unaided human eye, under the best possible viewing conditions, comparing large areas of colour, in good illumination, using both eyes, can distinguish surfaces of 10 million different colours. The most accurate photo-electric spectrophotometers possess a precision probably only 40 per cent as good as this. About 7·5 per cent of men and 0·1 per cent of women are colour blind. The most extreme form, monochromatic vision, is very rare.

Light sensitivity Working in Chicago, Illinois, USA in 1942, Maurice H. Pirenne detected a flash of blue light of 500nm in total darkness, when as few as five quanta or photons of light were available to be absorbed by the rod photo-receptors of the retina.

Longest Excluding a variable number of sesamoids (small rounded bones), there are 206 bones in the adult human body, compared with 300 for children (as they grow, some bones fuse together). The thigh bone or femur is the longest. It constitutes usually 27·5 per cent of a person's stature, and may be expected to be 19¾in *50cm* long in a 6ft *183cm* tall man. The longest recorded bone was the 76cm *29·9in* femur of the German giant Constantine, who died in Mons, Belgium on 30 Mar 1902, aged 30. The femur of Robert Wadlow, the tallest man ever recorded, measured an estimated 29½in *75cm* (⇔ Tallest men).

Smallest The stapes or stirrup bone, one of the three auditory ossicles in the middle ear, measures 2·6–3·4mm *0·10–0·13in* in length and weighs from 2·0 to 4·3mg *0·03–0·066grains*.

Largest and smallest biceps

Denis Sester (b. 18 Jul 1952) of Bloomington, Minnesota, USA has biceps 28¼ in *71·7 cm* cold (not pumped).

The biceps of Robert Thorn (⇔ Lightest adult) measured 4¼ in *10·8 cm* when pumped up.

Most alcoholic person

The California University Medical School, Los Angeles, USA reported in December 1982 the case of a confused but conscious 24-year-old female, who was shown to have a blood alcohol level of 1510 mg per 100 ml—nearly 19 times the UK driving limit (80 mg of alcohol per 100 ml of blood) and triple the normally lethal limit. After two days she discharged herself.

Tommy Johns of Brisbane, Queensland, Australia died in April 1988 from a brain tumour at the age of 66 years, after having been arrested nearly 3000 times for being drunk and disorderly in a public place.

Muscles

Largest Muscles normally account for 40 per cent of human bodyweight—and bulkiest of the 639 named muscles in the human body is usually the *gluteus maximus* or buttock muscle, which extends the thigh. However, in pregnant women the uterus or womb can increase its weight from about 30 g *1 oz* to over 1 kg *2·2 lb* and becomes larger than even the most successful body builder's buttock.

Smallest The stapedius, which controls the stapes (⇔ above), is less than 0·127 cm *0·05 in* long.

Longest The longest muscle in the human body is the *sartorius* which is a narrow ribbon-like muscle which runs from the pelvis and across the front of the thigh to the top of the tibia below the knee. Its action is to draw the lower limb into the cross-legged sitting posi-

tion, proverbially associated with tailors (Latin = *sartor*).

Strongest The strongest muscle in the human body is the masseter (one on each side of the mouth) which is responsible for the action of biting. In August 1986, Richard Hofmann (b. 1949) of Lake City, Florida, USA, achieved a bite strength of 975 lb *442 kg* for approximately 2 seconds in a research test using a gnathodynamometer at the College of Dentistry, University of Florida, USA. This figure is more than six times the normal biting strength.

Most active It has been estimated that the eye muscles move more than 100 000 times a day. Many of these eye movements take place during the dreaming phase of sleep. (⇔ Longest and shortest dreams)

Longest name The muscle with the longest name is the *levator labii superioris alaeque nasi* which runs inwards and downwards on the face, with one branch running to the upper lip and the other to the nostril. It is the muscle that everts or curls the upper lip and its action was particularly well demonstrated in the performances of Elvis Presley (1935–77).

Largest chest measurements The largest are among endomorphs (those with a tendency towards a thick chunky well-rounded body). In the extreme case of Robert Earl Hughes (1926–58) (USA) this was 124 in *315 cm*, and T. J. Albert Jackson, currently the heaviest living man (⇔ Heaviest men) has a chest measurement of 120 in *305 cm*.

The largest chest ever recorded in Britain was that of William Campbell (⇔ Heaviest men) which measured 96 in *244 cm*. Among muscular subjects (mesomorphs) of normal height, *expanded* chest measurements above 56 in *142 cm* are extremely rare.

The largest muscular chest measurement is that of American power-lifter Bruce Wayne Richardson (b. 23 Sep 1948) of Salt Lake City, Utah, USA at 72½ in *184 cm* who has admitted using anabolic steroids. He is 5 ft 8 in *175 cm* tall and weighs 18 st 4 lb *116 kg*.

147

Most expensive skull

The skull of Emanuel Swedenborg (1688–1772), the Swedish philosopher and theologian, was bought in London by the Royal Swedish Academy of Sciences for £5500 on 6 Mar 1978.

Jamie Reeves (b. 1962) of Sheffield, S Yorks, has a chest measurement of 152·4cm *60in*. At a height of 193cm *6ft 4in* he weighs 146kg *23st*.

Waists

Largest The largest waist ever recorded was that of Walter Hudson (1944–91) of New York, USA, which measured 119in *302cm* at his peak weight of 85st 7lb *545kg*.

Smallest The smallest waist of normal stature was that of Mrs Ethel Granger (1905–82) of Peterborough, Cambs, reduced from a natural 22in *56cm* to 13in *33cm* over the period 1929–39. A measurement of 13in *33cm* was also claimed for the French actress Mlle Polaire (real name Emile Marie Bouchand) (1881–1939).

Queen Catherine de Medici (1519–89) decreed a waist measurement of 13¾in *35cm* for ladies of the French court, but this was at a time when the human race was markedly more diminutive.

Necks

Longest The maximum measured extension of the neck by the successive fitting of copper coils, as practised by the women of the Padaung or Kareni tribe of Myanmar (Burma), is 40cm *15¾ in*. When the rings are removed, the muscles developed to support the head and neck shrink to their normal length.

Brains

Heaviest In normal brains there is little correlation between intelligence and size.

The heaviest brain ever recorded was that of a 50-year-old male, which weighed 2049g *4lb 8·3oz* and was reported by Dr Thomas F. Hegert, chief medical examiner for District 9, State of Florida, USA on 23 Oct 1975.

In January 1891 the *Edinburgh Medical Journal* reported the case of a 75-year-old man in the Royal Edinburgh Asylum whose brain weighed 1829g *4lb 0·5oz*.

The largest female brain on record weighed 1565g *3lb 7·3oz*. It belonged to a murderess.

Lightest The lightest 'normal' or non-atrophied brain on record was one weighing 1096g *2lb 6·7oz* reported by Dr P. Davis and Prof. E. Wright of King's College Hospital, London in 1977. It belonged to a 31-year-old woman.

Computation Mrs Shakuntala Devi of India demonstrated the multiplication of two 13-digit numbers 7 686 369 774 870 × 2 465 099 745 779 which were randomly selected by the Computer Department of Imperial College, London on 18 Jun 1980, in 28 seconds. Her correct answer was 18 947 668 177 995 426 462 773 730. Some experts on prodigies in calculation refuse to give credence to Mrs Devi on the grounds that her achievements are so vastly superior to the calculating feats of any other invigilated prodigy that the invigilation must have been defective.

Memory Bhanddanta Vicittabi Vumsa (1911–93) recited 16 000 pages of Buddhist canonical texts in Yangon (Rangoon), Myanmar (Burma) in May 1974.

Gon Yangling, 26, has memorized more than 15 000 telephone numbers in Harbin, China according to the Xinhua News Agency. Rare instances of eidetic memory (the ability to re-project and hence 'visually' recall material) are known to science.

Card memorizing Frost McKee of Georgetown, Texas, USA memorized a random sequence of 36 separate packs of cards (1872) (with eight errors) all of which had been shuffled together on a single sighting, at the Ramada Inn, Georgetown, Texas on 17–18 Oct 1992.

Dominic O'Brien of Buntingford, Herts memorised a single pack of shuffled cards in a time of 55·62 seconds at the *Guinness World of Records*, Piccadilly, London on 29 May 1992.

The greatest number of places of π Hideaki Tomoyori (b. 30 Sep 1932) of Yokohama, Japan recited 'pi' from memory to 40000 places in 17hr 21min, including breaks totalling 4hr 15min on 9–10 Mar 1987 at the Tsukuba University Club House.

The British record is 20013 by Creighton Herbert James Carvello (b. 19 Nov 1944) on 27 Jun 1980 in 9hr 10min at Saltscar Comprehensive School, Redcar, Cleveland.

Voice

Greatest range The normal intelligible outdoor range of the male human voice in still air is 180m *200yd*. The *silbo*, the whistled language of the Spanish-speaking Canary Island of La Gomera, is intelligible across the valleys, under ideal conditions, at 8km *5 miles*. There is a recorded case, under optimal acoustic conditions, of the human voice being detectable at a distance of 17km *10½ miles* across still water at night.

Screaming The highest scientifically measured emission has been one of 128dbA at 2½m *8ft 2in* by the screaming of Simon Robinson of McLaren Vale, South Australia at 'The Guinness Challenge' at Adelaide, Australia on 11 Nov 1988.

Whistling Roy Lomas achieved 122·5 dbA at 2½m *8ft 2in* in the Deadroom at the BBC studios in Manchester on 19 Dec 1983.

Shouting Annalisa Wray (b. 21 Apr 1974) of Comber, Co. Down, Northern Ireland achieved 119·4 dbA in shouting at the 7th International Rally Arura held in Coleraine Academical Institution, Coleraine, Londonderry, Northern Ireland on 11 Aug 1992.

Donald H. Burns of St George's, Bermuda achieved 119 dbA in shouting when he appeared on the Fuji TV film of *Narvhodo the World* at Liberty State Park, New Jersey, USA on 18 Jan 1989.

Town crier The greatest number of wins in the national Town Criers' Contest is 11 (between 1939–73) by Ben Johnson of Fowey, Cornwall.

Yodelling Yodelling has been defined as 'repeated rapid changes from the chest voice to falsetto and back again'. The most rapid recorded is twenty-two tones (fifteen falsetto) in 1sec, by Peter Hinnen of Zürich, Switzerland on 9 Feb 1992.

Highest detectable pitch The upper limit is accepted to be 20000Hz (cycles per sec), although it has been alleged that children with asthma can detect sounds of 30000 Hz. Bats emit pulses at up to 90000Hz. It was announced in February 1964 that experiments in the USSR had conclusively proved that oscillations as high as 200000 Hz can be detected if the oscillator is pressed against the skull.

Fastest talker Few people are able to speak *articulately* at a sustained speed above 300 words per min. The fastest broadcaster has been regarded as Gerry Wilmot (b. 6 Oct 1914, Victoria, British Columbia), an ice hockey commentator in the late forties.

Raymond Glendenning (1907–74), the BBC commentator, once spoke 176 words in 30 sec while commentating on a greyhound race.

In public life the highest speed recorded was a burst in excess of 300 words per min in a speech made in December 1961 by President John Fitzgerald Kennedy (1917–63).

Steve Woodmore of Orpington, Kent spoke 595 words in a time of 56·01 sec or 637·4 words per minute on the ITV Programme *Motor Mouth* on 22 Sep 1990.

Hamlet's soliloquy Sean Shannon a Canadian residing in Oxford recited Hamlet's soliloquy 'To be or not to be' (259 words) in a time of 24 sec (647·5 words per min) on BBC Radio Oxford on 26 Oct 1990.

Backwards talking Steve Briers of Kilgetty, Dyfed recited the entire lyrics of Queen's album *A Night at the Opera* at BBC North-West Radio 4's *Cat's Whiskers* on 6 Feb 1990 in a time of 9min 58·44sec.

Blood

Groups The preponderance of blood groups varies greatly from one locality to another. On a world basis Group O is the most common (46 per cent), but in

Recipient of blood

A 50-year-old haemophiliac, Warren C. Jyrich, required 2400 donor units of blood equivalent to 1080 litres, of blood when undergoing open-heart surgery at the Michael Reese Hospital, Chicago, Illinois, USA in December 1970.

Most infective poison

The rickettsial disease Q-fever, can be instituted by a *single* organism, though it is fatal in only 1 in 1000 cases. About 10 organisms of *Francisella tularenesis* (formerly *Pasteurella tularenesis*) can institute tularaemia, variously called alkali disease, Francis disease or deerfly fever. This is fatal in upwards of 10 cases in 1000.

Cardiopulmonary resuscitation

Brent Shelton and John Ash completed a CPR marathon (cardio-pulmonary resuscitation, 15 compressions alternating with two breaths) of 130 hr from 28 Oct–2 Nov 1991 at Regina, Saskatchewan, Canada.

Lung power

The inflation of a standard 1000 g *35 oz* meteorological balloon to a diameter of 2·44 m *8 ft* against time was achieved by Nicholas Mason in 45 min 7 sec for the *Tarm Pai Du* television programme in Thailand on 6 Nov 1992.

---

some areas, for example Norway, Group A predominates.

The full description of the commonest sub-group in Britain is O MsNs, P+, Rr, Lu(a−), K−, Le(a−b+), Fy(a+b+), Jk(a+b+), which occurs in one in every 270 people.

The rarest blood group of the ABO system, one of 14 systems, is AB, which occurs in less than 3 per cent of persons in the British Isles.

The rarest type in the world is a type of Bombay blood (sub-type h-h) found so far only in a Czechoslovak nurse in 1961, and in a brother (Rh positive) and sister (Rh negative) named Jalbert in Massachusetts, USA, reported in February 1968.

Largest vein The largest is the inferior vena cava, which returns the blood from the lower half of the body to the heart.

Largest artery The largest is the *aorta*, which is 3 cm *1·18 in* in diameter where it leaves the heart. By the time it ends at the level of the fourth lumbar vertebra it is about 1·75 cm *0·68 in* in diameter.

Cells

Largest The largest is the megakaryocyte, a blood cell, measuring 200 microns. It spends its life in the bone marrow rarely venturing out in the main stream of the blood itself. In the marrow it produces the 'stickiest' particles in the body—the platelets, which play an important role in stopping bleeding.

Smallest Some of the smallest cells are brain cells in the cerebellum and measure about 0·005 mm.

Longest The longest cells are neurons of the nervous system. Motor neurons some 1·3 m *4·26 ft* long have cell bodies (grey matter) in the lower spinal cord with axons (white matter) that carry nerve impulses from the spinal cord down to the big toe. Even longer are the cell systems which carry certain sensations (vibration and positional sense) back from the big toe to the brain. Their uninterrupted length, from the toe, and up the posterior part of the spinal cord to the medulla of the brain, is about equal to the height of the body.

Fastest turnover of body cells The fastest turnover of body cells i.e. the shortest life, is in the lining of the alimentary tract (gut) where the cells are shed every 3 days.

Longest life Those with the longest life are brain cells which last for life. They may be three times as old as bone cells which may live to 25–30 years.

Longest memory The lymphocyte (type of white blood cell) has the longest memory of any cell in the body.

The Heaviest Organ

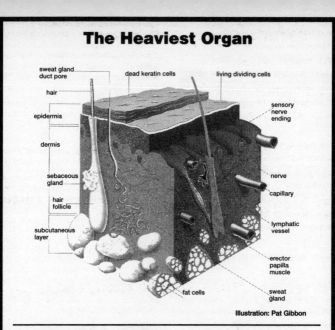

sweat gland duct pore

dead keratin cells

living dividing cells

hair

epidermis

dermis

sebaceous gland

hair follicle

subcutaneous layer

fat cells

sensory nerve ending

nerve

capillary

lymphatic vessel

erector papilla muscle

sweat gland

Illustration: Pat Gibbon

The skin is medically considered to be an organ and it weighs around 2·7 kg *5·9 lb* in an average adult. It covers the body completely acting as the first barrier against invading organisms. It also has sensory and excretory functions and plays an important part in regulating body temperature. Shown here (above) is a cross section through the skin. The outer layer is the epidermis, which can roughly be divided into two parts: an outer protective layer of flattened, dead cells impregnated with keratin and a lower layer of living dividing cells. Below this are the dermis and a subcutaneous layer of fat. Within the dermis are blood capillaries, sensory nerve endings, hair follicles (with associated sebaceous glands and erector muscles), lymph vessels and sweat glands.

The photo (left) shows the distinctive, but unique, patterns of skin ridges on a finger, i.e. fingerprint. The tiny depressions that can be seen on these ridges are sweat pores.

(Photo: Science Picture Library)

As successful generations of these cells, which are part of the body's immune defence system, are produced during one's life, they never forget an enemy.

Body Temperature

Highest Willie Jones, 52, was admitted to Grady Memorial Hospital, Atlanta, Georgia, USA on 10 Jul 1980 with heat-stroke on a day when the temperature reached 32·2°C *90°F* with 44 per cent humidity. His temperature was found to be 46·5°C *115·7°F*. After 24 days he was discharged 'at prior baseline status'.

Lowest People may die of hypothermia with body temperatures of 35°C *95°F*. The lowest authenticated body temperature is 18°C *64·4°F* (rectal temperature) for a newborn baby boy born unexpectedly in an unheated house in Peterborough, Cambs on 19 Apr 1992. After a delay the baby was taken to hospital presumed dead, however, a pulse rate of around ten beats per minute was found. The boy was then resuscitated and over the next four hours his temperature rose to normal. The boy has made a full recovery and is perfectly healthy.

There are also three reported cases of individuals surviving body temperatures as low as 16°C *60·8°F*.

Illness and Disease

Commonest *Non-contagious* The commonest non-contagious disease are periodontal diseases, such as gingivitis (inflammation of the gums). In their lifetime few people completely escape the effects of tooth decay.

Contagious The commonest contagious disease in the world is coryza (acute nasopharyngitis), or the common cold.

Rarest Medical literature periodically records hitherto undescribed diseases. A disease as yet undiagnosed but predicted by a Norwegian doctor is podocytoma of the kidney. This is a potential of the cells lining that part of the kidney (glomerulus) which acts as a sieve or filter for the blood to develop tumours.

Highest mortality There have been no reported recoveries from 'full blown' AIDS (Acquired Immune Deficiency Syndrome) which is caused by the Human Immunodeficiency Virus (HIV). The virus attacks the body's immune defence system, leaving the body wide open to attack from infections, which, to a healthy person, would be fought off without any problem. Many people who are carriers of the virus (HIV) may have none of the signs or symptoms associated with the disease AIDS. It may develop later. The World Health Organization (WHO) reported 611589 cases of AIDS as of 31 Jan 1993. The WHO estimate there are actually 2·5 million cases of AIDS and 13 million HIV positive cases worldwide.

Most infectious and most often fatal The pneumonic form of plague, as evidenced by the Black Death of 1347–51, killed everyone who caught it— a quarter of the population of Europe and some 75 million worldwide.

Leading cause of death In industrialized countries arteriosclerosis (thickening of the arterial wall) underlies much coronary (heart attacks and strokes) and cerebrovascular disease. Deaths from these diseases of the circulatory system totalled 264600 in England and Wales in 1989.

Medical Extremes

Cardiac arrest The longest is four hours in the case of a Norwegian fisherman, Jan Egil Refsdahl (b. 1936), who fell overboard in the icy waters off Bergen on 7 Dec 1987. He was rushed to nearby Haukeland Hospital after his body temperature fell to 24°C *75°F* and his heart stopped beating, but he made a full recovery after he was connected to a heart-lung machine normally used for heart surgery.

Longest coma Elaine Esposito (b. 3 Dec 1934) of Tarpon Springs, Florida, USA, never stirred after an appendectomy on 6 Aug 1941, when aged 6. She died on 25 Nov 1978 aged 43 years 357 days, having been in a coma for 37 years 111 days.

Longest and shortest dreams Dreaming sleep is characterized by rapid eye movements known as REM, first described in 1953 by William Dement of the University of Chicago, USA. The longest recorded period of REM is one of 2 hr 23 min on 15 Feb 1967 at the Department of Psychology, University of

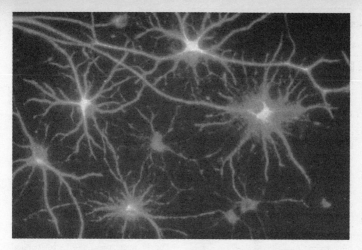

Illinois, Chicago by Bill Carskadon, who had had his previous sleep interrupted. In July 1984 the Sleep Research Centre, Haifa, Israel recorded nil REM in a 33-year-old male who had a shrapnel brain injury. (⊳ Muscles, most active)

g forces Racing driver David Purley (1945–85) survived a deceleration from 173 km/h *108 mph* to zero in 66 cm *26 in* in a crash at Silverstone, Northants on 13 Jul 1977 which involved a force of 179·8 g. He suffered 29 fractures, three dislocations and six heart stoppages.

The highest g value voluntarily endured is 82·6 g for 0·04 sec by Eli L. Beeding Jr on a water-braked rocket sled at Holloman Air Force Base, New Mexico, USA on 16 May 1958. He was subsequently hospitalized for three days.

Hiccoughing The longest recorded attack of hiccoughing was that which afflicted Charles Osborne (1894–1991) of Anthon, Iowa, USA. He started in 1922 while attempting to weigh a hog before slaughtering it. He was unable to find a cure, but led a reasonably normal life in which he had two wives and fathered eight children. He hiccoughed every 1½ seconds until a morning in February 1990. He died on 1 May 1991.

Human salamanders The highest dry-air temperature endured by naked men in US Air Force experiments in 1960 was

Impulses within the human nervous system can be conducted at up to 360 km/h *223 mph*. These impulses are carried on fibres known as processes which trail out in all directions from the nerve cell body which contains the nucleus. The processes are of varying size and it is the larger ones, which are insulated by a fatty substance known as myelin, that conduct at such high speeds.

(Photo: Science Photo Library)

205° C *400°F*, and for heavily clothed men 260° C *500°F*. Steaks require only 162° C *325°F* to cook. Temperatures of 140° C *284°F* have been found quite bearable in saunas.

Most injections Samuel L. Davidson (b. 30 Jul 1912) of Glasgow, has had at a conservative estimate 76 500 insulin injections since 1923.

Longest in 'iron lung' John Prestwich (b. 24 Nov 1938) of King Langley, Herts has been dependent on a negative pressure respirator since 24 Nov 1955.

Fastest nerve impulses The results of experiments published in 1966 have shown that the fastest messages transmit-

Motionlessness

António Gomes dos Santos of Zare, Portugal continuously stood motionless for 15hr 2min 55sec on 30 Jul 1988 at the Amoreiras Shopping Centre, Lisbon.

Fire breathers

Reg Morris blew a flame from his mouth to a distance of 9·4m *31ft* at the Miner's Rest, Chasetown, Staffs on 29 Oct 1986.

Fire extinguishers

Inge Widar Svingen, alias 'Benifax' of Norway on 10 Aug 1990 extinguished 25 270 torches of flame in his mouth in 2 hrs at Kolvereid in Nord-Trøndelag, Norway.

On 26 Jul 1986 at Port Lonsdale, Victoria, Australia, Sipra Ellen Lloyd set a female record by extinguishing 8357 torches.

Fire-eating is potentially a highly dangerous activity.

---

ted by the human nervous system can travel at 360 km/h *223 mph*. With advancing age, impulses are carried 15 per cent more slowly.

Heaviest organ The heaviest internal organ is the liver at 1·5kg *3·3lb*. This is four times heavier than the heart.

Pill-taking The highest recorded total of pills swallowed by a patient is 565 939 between 9 Jun 1967 and 19 Jun 1988 by C.H.A. Kilner (1926–88) of Bindura, Zimbabwe.

Post mortem birth The longest gestation interval in a post mortem birth was one of 84 days in the case of a baby girl born on 5 Jul 1983 to a brain-dead woman in Roanoke, Virginia, USA who had been kept on a life support machine since April.

Pulse rates A normal adult rate is 70–78 beats per min at rest for males and 75–85 for females. The heart rate may increase to 200 or more during vigourous exercise. However, an abnormal heart may beat as fast as 300 times per min or be so slow as to be virtually undetectable.

Sleeplessness Research indicates that on the Circadian (Latin: *circa* = around; *dies* = a day) cycle, for the majority peak efficiency is attained between 8 and 9p.m. and the low point comes at 4a.m. Victims of the very rare condition chronic colestites (total insomnia) have been known to go without definable sleep for many years.

Sneezing The longest lasting fit ever recorded is that of Donna Griffiths (b. 1969) of Pershore, Hereford & Worcester. She started sneezing on 13 Jan 1981 and surpassed the previous duration record of 194 days on 27 Jul 1981. She sneezed an estimated million times in the first 365 days. She achieved her first sneeze-free day on 16 Sep 1983—the 978th day.

The highest speed at which expelled particles have ever been measured to travel is 167km/h *103·6 mph*.

Snoring Melvyn Switzer of Dibden, Southampton, Hants recorded peak levels of 91–92 dBA whilst sleeping at the South View Hotel, Lyndhurst, Hants on the evening of 29 Oct 1992; the microphone was placed 60cm *2ft* above his head.

Swallowing The worst reported case of compulsive swallowing involved an insane female, Mrs H. aged 42, who complained of a 'slight abdominal pain'. She proved to have 2533 objects, including

---

Eating

Michel Lotito (b. 15 Jun 1950) of Grenoble, France, known as Monsieur Mangetout, has been eating metal and glass since 1959. Gastroenterologists have X-rayed his stomach and have described his ability to consume 900g *2lb* of metal per day as unique. His diet since 1966 has included 10 bicycles, a supermarket trolley in 4½ days, 7 TV sets, 6 chandeliers, a low-calorie Cessna light aircraft and a computer. He is said to have provided the only example in history of a coffin (handles and all) ending up inside a man.

Most tattoos

The ultimate in being tattooed is represented by Tom Leppard of Isle of Skye. He has gone for a leopard skin design, with all the skin between the dark spots tattooed saffron yellow. The area of his body covered is approximately 99·2 per cent of totality.

Bernard Moeller of Pennsylvania, USA has 14 000 individual tattoos up to January 1993.

The world's most decorated woman is strip artiste 'Krystyne Kolorful' (b. 5 Dec 1952, Alberta, Canada). Her 95 per cent body suit took 10 years to complete. Britain's most decorated woman is Rusty Field (b.1944) of Norfolk, who after 12 years under the needle of Bill Skuse has reached 85 per cent of totality.

Longest without food and water

The longest recorded case of survival without food *and* water is 18 days by Andreas Mihavecz, then 18, of Bregenz, Austria, who was put into a holding cell on 1 Apr 1979 in a local government building in Höchst, but was totally forgotten by the police. On 18 Apr 1979 he was discovered close to death having had neither food nor water. He had been a passenger in a crashed car.

947 bent pins, in her stomach. These were removed by Drs Chalk and Foucar in June 1927 at the Ontario Hospital, Canada. In a more recent case, 212 objects were removed from the stomach of a man admitted to Groote Schuur Hospital, Cape Town, South Africa in May 1985. They included 53 tooth-brushes, two telescopic aerials, two razors and 150 handles of disposable razors.

Another compulsive swallower in the USA, a 24-year-old psychoneurotic woman, gulped down a 12·7 cm *5 in*

long iron hinge bolt from a hospital door which amazingly passed through the curve of the duodenum and the intestinal tract and broke the bedpan when the patient successfully passed the object.

The heaviest object extracted from a human stomach has been a 2·53 kg *5 lb 3 oz* ball of hair from a 20-year-old female compulsive swallower in the South Devon and East Cornwall Hospital on 30 Mar 1895.

Underwater submergence

In 1986 two-year-old Michelle Funk of Salt Lake City, Utah, USA, made a full recovery after spending 66 minutes underwater. The toddler fell into a swollen creek near her home while playing. When she was eventually discovered, rescue workers found she had no pulse or heartbeat. Her life was saved by the first successful bypass machine which warmed her blood, which had dropped to 19°C *66°F*. Doctors at the hospital described the time she had spent under water as the 'longest documented submergence with an intact neurological outcome'.

Operations

Longest The most protracted reported operation has been one of 96 hr performed from 4–8 Feb 1951 in Chicago, Illinois, USA on Mrs Gertrude Levandowski for the removal of an ovarian cyst. During the operation her weight fell 280 kg *44 st* to 140 kg *22 st*. The patient suffered from a weak heart and surgeons had to exercise the utmost caution during the operation.

Most performed Dr M.C. Modi, a pioneer of mass eye surgery in India since 1943, has performed as many as 833 cataract operations in one day, visited 46 120 villages and 12 118 630 patients, performing a total of 610 564 operations to February 1993.

Dr Robert B. McClure (b. 1901) of Toronto, Canada performed a career total of 20 423 major operations from 1924 to 1978.

Most endured Since 22 Jul 1954 Charles Jensen of Chester, South Dakota, USA has had 925 operations (to February 1993) to remove the tumours associated with basal cell naevus syndrome. This is a rare genetically determined disorder

155

characterized by multiple skin lesions which are usually first noticed in childhood and increase in size and number in late adolescence. Each one resembles a skin malignancy better known as rodent ulcer. They do not spread to other parts of the body, and each lesion can be treated individually by surgical removal if and when it causes a specific problem.

Oldest patient The greatest recorded age at which anyone has undergone an operation is 111 years 105 days in the case of James Henry Brett, Jr (1849–1961) of Houston, Texas, USA. He had a hip operation on 7 Nov 1960.

The greatest age in Britain for an operation was in the case of Miss Mary Wright (b. 28 Feb 1862) who died during a thigh operation at Boston, Lincs on 22 Apr 1971 aged 109 years 53 days.

Earliest general anaesthesia The earliest recorded operation under general anaesthesia was for the removal of a cyst from the neck of James Venable by Dr Crawford Williamson Long (1815–78) using diethyl ether ($C_2H_5)_2O$, in Jefferson, Georgia, USA on 30 Mar 1842.

Tracheostomy Winifred Campbell (1902–92) of Wanstead, London breathed through a silver tube in her throat for 88 years.

Haemodialysis patient Raymond Jones (1929–91) of Slough, Berks, suffered from kidney failure from the age of 34, and received continuous haemodialysis for 28 years. He averaged three visits per week to the Royal Free Hospital, Hampstead, London.

Munchausen's syndrome The most extreme recorded case of the rare and incurable condition known as 'Munchausen's syndrome' (a continual desire to have medical treatment) was William McIlroy (b. 1906), who cost the National Health Service an estimated £2·5 million during his 50-year career as a hospital patient. During that time he had 400 major and minor operations, and stayed at 100 different hospitals using 22 aliases. The longest period he was ever out of hospital was six months. In 1979 he hung up his bedpan for the last time, saying he was sick of hospitals, and retired to an old people's home in Birmingham, W Mids where he died in 1983.

Hospital stay

The longest stay in a hospital was by Miss Martha Nelson who was admitted to the Columbus State Institute for the Feeble-Minded in Ohio, USA in 1875. She died in January 1975 at the age of 103 years 6 months in the Orient State Institution, Ohio after spending more than 99 years in hospitals.

Fastest amputation

The shortest time recorded for a leg amputation in the pre-anaesthetic era was 13–15 seconds by Napoleon's chief surgeon, Dominique Larrey. There could have been no ligation of blood vessels.

Largest tumour The largest tumour ever reported was Dr Arthur Spohn's case of an ovarian cyst which he estimated weighed 148·7 kg *23 st 6 lb* taken from a woman in Texas, USA in 1905. She made a full recovery.

A better documented and more recently recorded tumour was a multicystic mass of the ovary which weighed 137·6 kg *303 lb*. The one metre diameter growth was removed intact in October 1991 from the abdomen of an unnamed 35-year-old woman by Professor Katherine O'Hanlan of Stanford University Medical Center, California, USA. The operation took over 6 hours, and the patient left the operating theatre on one stretcher and the cyst on another. The patient weighed 95 kg *210 lb* after the operation and made a full recovery.

Largest gall bladder On 15 Mar 1989 at the National Naval Medical Center in Bethesda, Maryland, USA, Prof. Bimal C. Ghosh removed a gall bladder which weighed 10·4 kg *23 lb* from a 69-year-old woman. The patient had been complaining of increasing swelling around the abdomen, and after taking away this enlarged gall bladder, which weighed more than three times the average new born baby, the patient felt perfectly well and left hospital 10 days after the operation.

Gallstones The largest gallstone reported in medical literature was one of

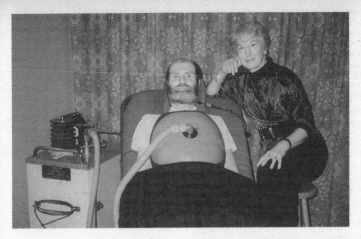

6·29kg *13lb 14oz* removed from an 80-year-old woman by Dr Humphrey Arthure at Charing Cross Hospital, London on 29 Dec 1952.

In August 1987 it was reported that 23 530 gallstones had been removed from an 85-year-old woman by Mr K. Whittle Martin at Worthing Hospital, W Sussex, after she complained of severe abdominal pain.

Surgical instruments *Largest* The largest instruments are robot retractors used in abdominal surgery, introduced by Abbey Surgical Instruments of Chingford, Essex in 1968 and weighing 5kg *11lb*. Some bronchoscopic forceps measure 60cm *23½in* in length.

Smallest The smallest instrument is the Microcystotome, a microknife used for cutting the lens in eye microsurgery. The length of the working part is 0·1mm *0·004in* and 0·08mm *0·0003in* wide. The smallest blade is one of natural diamond with a cutting edge of 200 Å. Both are licenced by the Microsurgery Research and Technology Complex, Moscow, Russia and patented by Svyatoslav Fyodorov, director of the Institute of Microsurgery.

Transplants

Heart The first operation was performed on Louis Washkansky, aged 55, at the Groote Schuur Hospital, Cape

Since contracting polio on his 17th birthday (24 Nov 1955) and as a result being paralysed from the chin down, John Prestwich has used a negative pressure respirator to keep him breathing. Cared for by his wife Maggie since their marriage in December 1971, John has worked out that his respirator has mechanically operated his chest over 315 500 000 times. Truly breathtaking!

Town, South Africa between 1 a.m. and 6 a.m., on 3 Dec 1967, by a team of 30 headed by Prof. Christiaan Neethling Barnard (b. 8 Oct 1922). The donor was Miss Denise Ann Darvall, aged 25. Washkansky lived for 18 days.

Britain's first heart transplant operation took place at the National Heart Hospital, London on 3 May 1968. The patient, Frederick West, survived for 46 days.

Longest surviving William George van Buuren of California, USA (1929–91), who received an unnamed person's heart at the Stanford Medical Center, Palo Alto, California, USA on 3 Jan 1970, survived for 21 years 10 months 24 days. The surgeon who performed the operation was Dr Edward Stinson.

Currently living Arthur F. Gay (b. 3 Oct 1936) is the longest-surviving heart transplant patient. The surgery was performed by Dr Richard Lower on 11 Jan 1973 at the Medical College of Virginia, USA.

Britain's longest-surviving heart transplant patient is Derrick H. Morris (b. 24 Mar 1930) who underwent surgery at Harefield Hospital, Greater London on 23 Feb 1980.

Youngest Paul Holt of Vancouver, British Columbia, Canada underwent a heart transplant at Loma Linda Hospital in California, USA on 16 Oct 1987 at the age of 2 hr 34 min. He was born six-weeks premature and weighed 2·9 kg *6 lb 6 oz*.

The youngest in the UK was Hollie Roffey, who received a new heart when aged only 10 days at the National Heart Hospital in London on 29 Jul 1984. She survived for only 10 days.

Five-organ Tabatha Foster (1984–88) of Madisonville, Kentucky, USA, at the age of 3 years 143 days, received a transplanted liver, pancreas, small intestine, portions of stomach and large intestine in a 15-hour operation at the Children's Hospital, Pittsburgh, on 31 Oct 1987. Before the operation, she had never eaten solid food.

Heart-lung-liver The first triple transplant took place on 17 Dec 1986 at Papworth Hospital, Cambridge, when Mrs Davina Thompson (b. 28 Feb 1951) of Rawmarsh, S Yorks, underwent surgery for seven hours by a team of 15 headed by chest surgeon Mr John Wallwork and Prof. Sir Roy Calne.

Artificial heart On 1–2 Dec 1982 at the Utah Medical Center, Salt Lake City, Utah, USA Dr Barney B. Clark, 61, of Des Moines, Washington, was the first recipient of an artificial heart. The surgeon was Dr William C. DeVries. The heart was a Jarvik 7 designed by Dr Robert K. Jarvik (b. 11 May 1946). Dr Clark died on 23 Mar 1983, 112 days later. William J. Schroeder survived for 620 days in Louisville, Kentucky from 25 Nov 1984 to 7 Aug 1986.

Britain's first artificial heart patient was Raymond Cook of Hucknall, Notts who temporarily received a Jarvik 7 on 2 Nov 1986 at Papworth Hospital, Cambridge, Cambs.

Kidney R.H. Lawler (b. 1895) (USA) performed the first transplant of the kidney in a human at Little Company of May Hospital, Chicago, Illinois, USA on 17 Jun 1950.

The longest surviving kidney transplant patient is Johanna Leonora Rempel (*née* Nightingale) (b. 24 Mar 1948) of Red Deer, Alberta, Canada who was given a kidney from her identical twin sister Lana Blatz on 28 Dec 1960. The operation was performed at the Peter Bent Brigham Hospital, Boston, Massachusett, USA. Both Johanna and her sister have continued to enjoy excellent health and both have born healthy children. (⇨First transplantee to give birth)

First transplantee to give birth Johanna Rempel gave birth to a baby boy, Kerry Melvin Ross 3·47 kg *7 lb 12 oz* at Winnipeg General Hospital, Manitoba, Canada on 7 Sep 1967. She had received a donor kidney in December 1960. (⇨ Longest surviving kidney transplant patient)

Science & Technology

- Elements
- Chemical Extremes
- Physical Extremes
- Mathematics
- Computers
- Power
- Engineering
- Borings and Mines
- Time Pieces
- Telephones & Facsimiles
- Telescopes
- Rocketry
- Space Flight

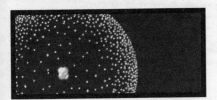

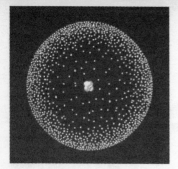

Elements

Although ordinary matter can be described in terms 94 naturally-occurring elements, the dynamics of galaxies suggest that over 90 per cent of all mass in the Universe is in an unknown form called 'cold dark matter'. This is thought to be an exotic form of matter unknown on Earth, but it is possible that it is ordinary matter which is too dim to be detected by present intruments. About 99 per cent of all visible matter exists as ionised plasma in which negatively charged electrons and positively charged ions are in flux. Hydrogen (H) is the most common element, accounting for over 90 per cent of all known matter in the Universe and 70·68 per cent by mass in the Solar System.

Sub-Nuclear Particles

Electron volt (eV) — mass-energy unit equivalent to $1·7826627 \times 10^{-36}$ kg.

Quarks are a set of at least six (up, down, charmed, strange, top and bottom) elementary particles and their corresponding antiparticles postulated to be the basic constituents of all baryons and mesons. Evidence for all except the top quark is now available. The lightest is the up quark with a short-range mass of 6 MeV and a long-range mass of 350 MeV, and the heaviest is the top quark with a predicted mass of 140 GeV.

It is currently thought that there are only three 'families' of quarks and leptons. The theoretical masses of the graviton (the as yet unobserved gravitational gauge boson), the photon, and the three neutrino leptons should all be zero. Current experimental limits are less than $7·6 \times 10^{-67}$ g for the graviton, less than $5·3 \times 10^{-60}$ g for the photon and less than 10 eV (less than $1·8 \times 10^{-32}$ g) for the electron neutrino.

As of April 1990 the existence was accepted of four gauge bosons, seven leptons and 136 hadron multiplets (77 meson multiplets and 59 baryon multiplets), representing the eventual discovery of 256 particles and an equal number of antiparticles.

Heaviest The heaviest particle is Z°, the neutral gauge boson discovered in May 1983 at CERN, Geneva, Switzerland, with a mass of 91·17 GeV. (⇨ Least stable)

Most stable The 'grand unified theory' of weak, electromagnetic, and strong forces predicts that the proton will not be stable, but experiments show that the

Longest index

The 11th collective index of *Chemical Abstracts*, completed in December 1987, contains 29406094 entries in 162992 pages and 93 volumes and weighs 184·5kg *407lb*. It provides references to 2812413 published documents in chemistry.

Longest echo

The longest echo produced in any building is 15sec following the closing of the Chapel door of the Mausoleum in Hamilton, Strathclyde, built 1840−55.

lifetime of the most likely decay mode (to a positron and a neutral pion) has a lower limit of 3.1×10^{32} years, which is over 40 times longer than the maximum lifetime predicted by the theory.

Least stable The shortest-lived subatomic particle is the Z^0 particle with a lifetime of 2.65×10^{-25} sec. (⟺ Heaviest particle)

Isotopes

Most The highest number is 36 for the gas xenon (Xe), with 9 stable and 27 radioactive isotopes, and caesium (Cs) (1 stable and 35 radioactive).

The greatest number of stable isotopes is 10 for the metallic element tin (Sn).

Least Hydrogen has only three confirmed isotopes, two of which are stable (protium and deuterium) and one radioactive (tritium). Twenty elements exist naturally only as single nuclides.

Most stable The most stable radioactive isotope is the double-beta decaying tellurium 128 (Te-128), with a half-life of 1.5×10^{24} years, a property confirmed in 1968, 44 years after its identification.

The alpha-decay record is 8×10^{15} years for samarium 148 (Sm-148) and the beta-decay record is 9×10^{15} years for cadmium 113 (Cd-113).

Least stable Lithium 5 (Li-5), discovered in 1950, has a lifetime of just 4.4×10^{-22} sec.

The 109 Elements

Of the 109 known elements, 94 exist naturally and 15 transuranium elements (numbers 95 to 109) have been produced artificially. At room temperature they comprise 2 liquids, 11 gases and 96 solids (assuming that elements 101 to 109 would prove to be solid if obtained as more than a few atoms at a time). On this basis 88 elements are considered metallic.

Most common The commonest element in the atmosphere is nitrogen (N), which is present at 78.08 per cent by volume (75.52 per cent by mass).

Rarest (natural) The least abundant element in the atmosphere is the radioactive gas radon (Rn), at 6×10^{-18} parts by volume. This is only 2.4 kg 5.3 lb

overall, but concentrated amounts of this radioactive gas in certain granitic areas have been blamed for a number of cancer deaths.

Most dense The densest solid at room temperature is osmium (Os), at 22.59 g/cm³ 0.8161 lb/in³.

Gas The heaviest gas is radon (Rn) at 0.01005 g/cm³ 0.6274 lb/ft³ (at NTP).

Least dense *Solid* The least dense element at room temperature is the metal lithium (Li) at 0.5334 g/cm³ 0.01927 lb/in³, although the density of solid hydrogen at its melting point of $-259.192°C$ $-434.546°F$ is only 0.0871 g/cm³ 0.00315 lb/in³.

Gas The lightest gas at NTP is hydrogen at just 0.00008989 g/cm³ 0.005612 lb/ft³.

Highest melting point The metallic element tungsten, or wolfram, (W) melts at $3420°C$ $6188°F$. On the assumption that graphite transforms to carbyne forms above $2300°C$ $4172°F$, then the non-metal with the highest melting and boiling points would be carbon (C) at $3530°C$ $6386°F$ and $3870°C$ $6998°F$ respectively. This is disputed, however, and one alternative suggestion is that graphite remains stable at high temperatures, subliming directly to vapour at $3720°C$ $6728°F$, and can only be obtained in liquid form above $4730°C$ $8546°F$ and a pressure of 10 MPa 100 atmospheres.

Lowest melting point Mercury (Hg) has the lowest melting point of the metals, namely $-38.829°C$ $-37.892°F$. Helium (He) cannot be obtained as a solid at atmospheric pressure, requiring a minimum pressure of 2.532 MPa 24.985 atmospheres at a temperature of $-272.375°C$ $-458.275°F$.

Highest boiling point The highest boiling point is $5860°C$ $10580°F$ for tungsten.

Lowest boiling point The lowest boiling point is $-268.928°C$ $-452.070°F$ for helium. The lowest for a metal is $356.62°C$ $673.92°F$ for mercury.

Purest In April 1978 P.V.E. McClintock of the University of Lancaster reported success in obtaining the isotope helium

4 (He-4) with impurity levels at less than two parts in 10^{15}.

Hardest The carbon (C) allotrope diamond has a Knoop value of 8400.

Thermal expansion Caesium (Cs) has the highest thermal expansion of a metallic element, at $9\cdot4\times10^{-5}$ per deg C, while the diamond allotrope of carbon (C) has the lowest expansion at 1×10^{-6} per deg C.

Most ductile One gram of gold (Au) can be drawn to 2·4km, or *1oz to 43miles*.

Highest tensile strength The strongest element is boron (B), with a tensile strength of 5·7GPa *8·3x10⁵lb/in²*.

Newest Element 108, provisionally named unniloctium (Uno) by IUPAC (the International Union of Pure and Applied Chemistry) but with the name hassium (Hs) proposed, was announced in April 1984 based on the observations of only three atoms at the Gesellschaft für Schwerionenforschung (GSI) in Darmstadt, Germany.

Liquid range Based on the differences between melting and boiling points, the element with the shortest liquid range (on the Celsius scale) is the inert gas neon (Ne) at only 2·542 degrees (from $-248\cdot594$ to $-246\cdot052$°C *-415·469 to -410·894°F*). The radioactive element neptunium (Np) has the longest range, at 3453 degrees (from 637 to 4090°C *1179 to 7394°F*).

Based on the true range of liquids from melting point to critical point, the shortest range is for helium (He) at 5·195 degrees, from absolute zero (i.e. $-273\cdot15$°C) to $-267\cdot955$°C *-459·67 to -450·319°F*. The longest range is for tungsten (W) at 10 200 degrees (from 3420 to 13620°C *6188 to 24548°F*).

Toxicity The most stringent restriction placed on a non-radioactive element is for beryllium (Be), with a threshold limit in air of only $2\,\mu g/m^3$.

For radioactive isotopes occurring naturally or produced in nuclear installations and having half-lives of over six months, the severest restriction in air is placed on thorium 228 (Th-228) or radiothorium, at $2\cdot4\times10^{-16}\,g/m^3$ (equivalent radiation intensity 0·0074 Bq/m³). The severest restriction in water is placed on radium 228 (Ra-228) or mesothorium I, at $1\cdot1\times10^{-13}\,g/litre$ of water (equivalent radiation intensity 1·1 Bq/litre).

Chemical Extremes

Smelliest substance The most evil of the 17000 smells so far classified is obviously a matter of opinion, but ethyl mercaptan (C_2H_5SH) and butyl selenomercaptan (C_4H_9SeH) are pungent claimants, each with a smell reminiscent of a combination of rotting cabbage, garlic, onions, burnt toast and sewer gas.

Most powerful nerve gas Ethyl S-2-diisopropylaminoethylmethyl phosphonothiolate, or VX, developed at the Chemical Defence Experimental Establishment, Porton Down, Wilts in 1952, is 300 times more powerful than the phosgene ($COCl_2$) used in World War I and has a lethal dosage of 10mg-minute/m³ airborne, or 0·3mg orally.

Most lethal man-made chemical The compound 2, 3, 7, 8-tetrachlorodibenzo-p-dioxin), or TCDD, the most deadly of the 75 known dioxins, is admitted to be 150000 times more lethal than cyanide, at $3\cdot1\times10^{-9}$ moles/kg.

Strongest acid and alkaline solutions Normal solutions of strong acids such as perchloric acid $HClO_4$ and strong alkalis such as sodium hydroxide NaOH, potassium hydroxide KOH and tetramethylammonium hydroxide $N(CH_3)_4OH$ tend towards pH values of 0 and 14 respectively. However, this scale is inadequate for describing the 'superacids', the strongest of which is estimated to be an 80 per cent solution of antimony pentafluoride in hydrofluoric acid (fluoroantimonic acid $HF:SbF_5$). The acidity function, H_o, of this solution has not been measured, but even a 50 per cent solution has an acidity function of -30, so that this acid mixture is 10^{18} times stronger than concentrated sulphuric acid.

Bitterest substance The bitterest-tasting substances are based on the denatonium cation N-(2-[2, 6-dimethyl phenyl amino]-2-oxoethyl)-N, N-diethyl-benzemethanaminium and have been produced commercially as benzoate and saccharide. Taste detection levels are as low as one part in 500 million, and a dilution of one part in 100 million will leave a lingering taste.

Sweetest substance Talin obtained from arils (appendages found on certain seeds) of the katemfe plant (*Thaumatococcus daniellii*) discovered in West Africa is 6150 times as sweet as a one per cent sucrose solution.

Most absorbent substance The US Department of Agriculture Research Service announced on 18 Aug 1974 that 'H-span' or Super Slurper composed of one half starch derivative and one quarter each of acrylamide and acrylic acid can, when treated with iron, retain water at 1300 times its own weight.

Finest powder The ultimate is solid helium, which was first postulated to be a monatomic powder as early as 1964.

Most refractory substance The most refractory compound is tantalum carbide $TaC_{0.88}$ which melts at 3990°C *7214°F*.

Least dense solids The solid substances with the lowest density are silica aerogels in which tiny spheres of bonded silicon and oxygen atoms are joined into long strands separated by pockets of air. The lightest of these aerogels, with a density of only $0.005 g/cm^3$ *5oz/ft³* was produced at the Lawrence Livermore Laboratory, California, USA. The main use will be in space to collect micrometeoroids and the debris present in comets' tails.

Highest superconducting temperature In May 1991 bulk superconductivity with a transition to zero resistance at −146.3°C *−231.3°F* was obtained at the Superconducting Research Laboratory, International Superconducting Technology Centre, Tokyo, Japan for a mixed oxide of thallium, barium, calcium and copper, i.e. $Tl_{1.7}Ba_2Ca_{2.3}Cu_3O_x$.

Most magnetic substance The most magnetic substance is neodymium iron boride $Nd_2Fe_{14}B$, with a maximum energy product (the highest energy that a magnet can supply when operating at a particular operating point) of up to $280 kJ/m^3$.

Physical Extremes

Highest temperature The highest temperatures are produced at the centres of thermonuclear fusion explosions, namely of the order of 400 000 000° C. This temperature was attained in 1990 under controlled conditions in the Tokamak Fusion Test Reactor at the Princeton Plasma Physics Laboratory, New Jersey, USA by deuterium injection into a deuterium plasma.

Lowest temperature The absolute zero of temperature, 0K on the Kelvin scale, corresponds to −273.15°C *−459.67°F*. The lowest temperature reached is 28×10^{-11} K, achieved in a nuclear demagnetization device at the Low Temperature Laboratory of the Helsinki University of Technology, Finland and announced in April 1993.

Highest pressures A sustained laboratory pressure of 170 GPa *11 000 tons force/in²* was reported from the giant hydraulic diamond-faced press at the Carnegie Institution's Geophysical Laboratory, Washington, DC, USA in June 1978.

Momentary pressures of 7000 GPa *498 000 tonnes/in²* were reported from the United States in 1958 using dynamic methods and impact speeds of up to 29 000 km/h *18 000 mph*.

Lowest friction The lowest coefficient of static and dynamic friction of any solid is 0.04 for polytetrafluoroethylene, or PTFE, $([-C_2F_4-]_n)$, which is the equivalent of wet ice on wet ice. First mass-produced by E.I. du Pont de Nemours & Co. Inc. in 1943, it is marketed from the USA under the trade name Teflon.

In the centrifuge at the University of Virginia, USA a 13.6 kg *30lb* rotor magnetically supported has been spun at 1000 rev/sec in a vacuum of 10^{-6} mm of mercury pressure. It loses only one revolution per second per day, thus spinning for years.

Highest velocity The highest velocity at which any solid object has been projected is 150 km/sec *93 miles/sec*, reported in August 1980 for a plastic

Slowest machine

A nuclear environ- mental machine for testing stress corrosion that can be controlled at a speed as slow as one million millionth of a millimetre per minute (1m *3·3ft* in about 2000 million years) has been developed by Nene Instruments of Wellingborough, Northants.

Pharmaceutical companies

The world's largest pharmaceutical company is Johnson & Johnson of New Brunswick, New Jersey, USA. The company employed a workforce of 84900, generating sales of $13·75 billion in 1992. Total assets for the year were $11·88 billion.

Britain's largest pharmaceutical company is Glaxo, with sales in 1991/92 of £4·1 billion.

---

disc at the Naval Research Laboratory, Washington, DC, USA.

Most powerful electric current

If fired simultaneously, the 4032 capacitors comprising the Zeus capacitor at the Los Alamos Scientific Laboratory, New Mexico, USA would produce, for a few microseconds, double the current generated elsewhere on Earth.

Hottest flame

The hottest flame is produced by carbon subnitride (C_4N_2) which, at one atmosphere pressure, can generate a flame calculated to reach 4988°C *9010°F*.

Highest frequency

The highest frequency measured *directly* is a visible yellow-green light at 520·2068085 terahertz for the o-component of the 17–1 P (62) transition line of iodine-127.

The highest measured frequency determined by precision metrology is a green light at 582·491703 terahertz for the b_{21} component of the R (15) 43−0 transition line of iodine-127.

Smallest hole

Holes corresponding to a diameter of 3·16Å ($3·16 \times 10^{-10}$ m) were produced on the surface of molybdenum disulphide by Dr Wolfgang Heckl (University of Munich) and Dr John Maddocks (University of Sheffield) using a chemical method involving a mercury drill. The holes were drilled on 17 Jul 1992 at the University of Munich, Germany.

Brightest light

The brightest artificial sources are laser pulses generated at the Los Alamos National Laboratory, New Mexico, USA announced in March 1987. An ultra-violet flash lasting 1 picosecond (1×10^{-12} sec) is intensified to a power of 5×10^{15} W.

The most powerful searchlight ever was produced during World War II by The General Electric Company Ltd at the Hirst Research Centre, Wembley, London. It had a consumption of 600 kW and gave an arc luminance of 46500 candelas/cm² *300000 candles/in²* and a maximum beam intensity of *2·7 billion candles* from its parabolic mirror of 3·04m *10ft* diameter.

Of continuously burning light sources, the most powerful is a 313kW high-pressure argon arc lamp of 1200000 candles, completed by Vortek Industries Ltd of Vancouver, British Columbia, Canada in March 1984.

Shortest light pulse

In April 1988 it was announced that Charles V. Shank and colleagues at the AT&T Laboratories in New Jersey, USA generated light pulses lasting just 6 femtoseconds (6×10^{-15} sec) and containing 3 or 4 optical cycles.

Magnetic fields

The strongest continuous field strength achieved was a total of $35·3 \pm 0·3$ teslas at the Francis Bitter National Magnet Laboratory, Massachusetts Institute of Technology, USA on 26 May 1988 by a hybrid magnet with holmium pole pieces. These had the effect of enhancing the central magnetic field of 31·8 teslas generated by the hybrid magnet.

The weakest magnetic field measured is one of 8×10^{-15} teslas in the heavily shielded room at the same laboratory. It is used for research into the very weak magnetic fields generated in the heart and brain.

Highest vacuum A vacuum of the order of 10^{-14} torr was obtained in October 1976 at the IBM Thomas J. Watson Research Center, Yorktown Heights, New York, USA using a cryogenic system with temperatures down to $-269°C$ $-452°F$. This degree of vacuum is equivalent to depopulating (baseball-sized) molecules from 1m apart to 80km apart, or from *1yard to 50miles*.

Lowest viscosity The California Institute of Technology first announced on 1 Dec 1957 that there was no measurable viscosity, i.e. perfect flow, in liquid helium II, which exists at temperatures close to absolute zero, i.e. $-273·15°C$ $-459·67°F$.

Highest voltage The highest-ever potential difference obtained in a laboratory has been $32±1·5MV$ by the National Electrostatics Corporation at Oak Ridge, Tennessee, USA on 17 May 1979.

Scientific Instruments

Largest The largest scientific instrument (and arguably the world's largest machine) so far created is the Large Electron Positron (LEP) storage ring at CERN, housed in a ring tunnel measuring 27km *16·8miles* in circumference. The tunnel, which is 3·8m *12½ft* in diameter, runs between 50 and 150m *164 – 492ft* beneath the Franco-Swiss border near Geneva and is accessible through 18 vertical shafts. Over 60000 tons of technical equipment have been installed in the tunnel and its eight underground work zones. It is intended to be a Z° particle factory, producing up to 10000 of these neutral weak gauge bosons every day in order to obtain a deeper understanding of the subatomic nature of matter. (⇔ Heaviest particle)

Finest balance The Sartorius Microbalance Model 4108, manufactured in Göttingen, Germany, can weigh objects of up to 0·5g *0·018oz* to an accuracy of 0·01g, or $1×10^{-8}$ g $3·5×10^{-10}$ oz, which is equivalent to little more than one sixtieth of the weight of the ink on this full stop.

Largest bubble chamber The \$7 million installation recorded its first tracks on 29 Sep 1973 at Fermilab, Batavia,

Largest barometer

An oil-filled barometer, of overall height 13m *42ft*, was constructed by Allan Mills and John Pritchard of the Department of Physics and Astronomy, University of Leicester in 1991. It attained a *standard* height of 12·20m *40ft* (at which pressure mercury would stand at 0·76m *2½ft*).

Smallest thermometer

Dr Frederich Sachs, a biophysicist at the State University of New York at Buffalo, USA, has developed an ultra-microthermometer for measuring the temperature of single living cells. The tip is one micrometre in diameter, about ¹⁄₅₀ that of a human hair.

Illinois, USA. It was 4·57m *15ft* in diameter, contained 33000litres *7259gal* of liquid hydrogen at a temperature of $-247°C$ $-413°F$, and had a superconducting magnet of 3tesla. The last tracks were recorded on 1 Feb 1988.

Fastest centrifuge Ultracentrifuges were invented by the Swedish Nobel prize-winning chemist Theodor Svedberg (1884–1971) in 1923. The highest manmade rotary speed ever achieved is 7250 km/h *4500mph* by a tapered 15·2cm *6in* carbon fibre rod rotating in a vacuum at Birmingham University, reported on 24 Jan 1975.

Most powerful laser Albert Einstein (1879–1955) formulated the principle of light amplification by stimulated emissions of radiation in 1917, but the first practical device was a gas maser (microwave amplification by stimulated emissions of radiation) produced in 1954 by J. Gordon, H. Zeiger and C. Townes. The first laser (a term coined by Richard Gould) was constructed in 1960 by Theodore Maiman of the Hughes Research Laboratory in California, USA, with similar devices developed independently by Soviet physicists N. Bassov and A. Prokhorov.

The most powerful laser is the 'Nova' at the Lawrence Livermore National

Laboratory, California, USA. Its 10 arms produce laser pulses capable of generating 100×10^{12} W of power, much of which is delivered to a target the size of a grain of sand in 1×10^{-9} sec. For this brief instance, that power is 200 times greater than the combined output of all the electrical generating plants in the US. Fitted with two target chambers, the laser itself is 91 m *300 ft* long and about three storeys high.

Heaviest magnet The heaviest magnet is in the Joint Institute for Nuclear Research at Dubna, near Moscow, Russia for the 10 GeV synchrophasotron. It weighs 36 000 tonnes and is 60 m *196 ft* in diameter.

Largest electromagnet The world's largest electromagnet is part of the L3 detector, an experiment on LEP (large electron–positron collider). The octagonal magnet consists of 6400 tons of low carbon steel yoke and 1100 tons of aluminium coil. The yoke elements are welded pieces weighing some 30 tons each and the coil consists of 168 turns welded together to form the eight-sided frame. Thirty thousand ampères of current flow through the aluminium coil to create a uniform magnetic field of 5 kilogauss. The magnet is higher than a four-storey building of about 1728 m³ *59 320 ft³* volume. Its total weight, including the frame, coil and inner support tube, is 7810 tons and

Ten laser beams generated by 'Nova' bombarding a pellet containing deuterium and tritium in a vacuum chamber at the Lawrence Livermore National Laboratory produce temperatures found at the Sun's core, triggering a fusion reaction.

(Photo: Science Photo Library)

it is composed of more metal than the Eiffel Tower.

Most powerful microscope The scanning tunnelling microscope (STM) invented at the IBM Zürich, Switzerland research laboratory in 1981 has a magnification ability of 100 million and a resolving power down to one hundredth the diameter of an atom (3×10^{-10} m). The fourth generation STM now being developed is said to be 'about the size of a finger tip'.

By using field ion microscopy the tips of probes of scanning tunnelling microscopes have been shaped to end in a single atom—the last three layers constituting the world's smallest man-made pyramid, consisting of 7, 3 and 1 atoms. Since the announcement in January 1990 that D.M. Eigler and E.K. Schweizer of the IBM Almaden Research Center, San Jose, California, USA had

Finest cut

The $13 million Large Optics Diamond turning Machine at the Lawrence Livermore National Laboratory in California, USA was reported in June 1983 to be able to sever a human hair 3000 times lengthways.

Thinnest glass

Type D263 glass, made by Deutsche Spezialglas AG of Grünenplan, Germany for use in electronic and medical equipment, has a minimum thickness of 0·025 mm *0·00098 in* and a maximum thickness of 0·035 mm *0·00137 in*.

Glass blowing

A bottle standing 2·3 m *7 ft 8 in* tall with a capacity of about 712 litres *188 gal* was blown at Wheaton Village, Millville, New Jersey, USA on 26 Sep 1992 by a team led by glass artist Steve Tobin. The attempt was made during the 'South Jersey Glass Blast', part of a celebration of the local glassmaking heritage.

Scientific instrument

The highest auction price paid for a scientific instrument is £385000 for a 34·29 cm *13½ in* Dutch gilt-brass astrolabe of 1559 by Walter Arsenius at Christie's, London on 6 Dec 1983.

used an STM to move and reposition single atoms of xenon on a nickel surface in order to spell out the initials 'IBM', other laboratories around the world have used similar techniques on single atoms of other elements.

Most powerful particle accelerator

The world's highest energy 'atomsmasher' is the 2 km *1·25 miles* diameter proton synchroton 'Tevatron' at the Fermi National Accelerator Laboratory (Fermilab) near Batavia, Illinois, USA. On 3 Jan 1987 a centre of mass energy of 1·8 TeV ($1·8 \times 10^{12}$ eV)

was achieved by colliding beams of protons and antiprotons.

The projected US Department of Energy superconducting supercollider (SSC) at Waxahachie, Texas, USA of 87·12 km *54·14 miles* circumference and using two 20 TeV proton colliding beams is due to become fully operational in the late 1990s.

Smallest prism

A glass prism with sides measuring 0·004 mm *0·001 in*, barely visible to the naked eye, was created at the National Institute of Standards and Technology in Boulder, Colorado, USA in 1989.

Sharpest objects and smallest tubes

The sharpest manufactured objects are glass micropipette tubes whose bevelled tips have outer and inner diameters of 0·02 μm and 0·01 μm respectively, the latter being 6500 times thinner than a human hair. They are used in intracellular work on living cells in techniques developed in 1977.

Smallest microphone

A microphone with a frequency response of 10 Hz–10 kHz and measuring 1·5×0·76 mm *0·06×0·03 in* was developed in 1967 by Prof. Ibrahim Kavrak of Bogazici University, Istanbul, Turkey as a new technique in measuring pressure in fluid flow.

Mathematics

In dealing with large numbers, the notation of 10 raised to various powers is used to eliminate a profusion of noughts. For example, 19 160 000 000 000 km would be expressed as $1·916 \times 10^{13}$ km. Similarly, a very small number, for example 0·000015 4324 g, would be written as a negative power, i.e $1·543 24 \times 10^{-5}$. Of the prefixes used with numbers, the smallest is 'yocto' (y), of power 10^{-24} and the largest is 'yotta' (Y), of power 10^{24}. Both are based on the Greek octo, eight (for the eighth power of 10^3).

Highest numbers

The highest lexicographically accepted named number in the system of successive powers of ten is the centillion, first recorded in 1852. It is the hundredth power of a million, or 1 followed by 600 noughts (although apparently only in the UK and Germany).

The number 10^{100} is designated a googol. The term was suggested by the nine-year old nephew of Dr Edward Kasner (USA). Ten raised to the power of a googol is described as a googolplex. Some conception of the magnitude of such numbers can be gained when it is said that the number of electrons in some models of the observable Universe is of the order of 10^{87}.

The highest named number outside the decimal notation is the Buddhist *asankhyeya*, which is equal to 10^{140} and mentioned in Jain works of *c*. 100 BC.

The highest number ever used in a mathematical proof is a bounding value published in 1977 and known as Graham's number. It concerns bichromatic hypercubes and is inexpressible without the special 'arrow' notation, devised by Knuth in 1976 and then extended to 64 layers.

Prime numbers A prime number is any positive integer (excluding unity 1) having no integral factors other than itself and unity, e.g. 2, 3, 5, 7 or 11. The lowest prime number is thus 2.

The highest *known* prime number (which has the form of a Mersenne prime) is $2^{756\,839} -1$, discovered in February 1992 by analysts at AEA Technology's Harwell Laboratory, Oxon. The number contains 227 832 digits (enough to fill over 18 pages of *The Guinness Book of Records*) and was found by means of a CRAY-2 supercomputer. (⇨ Perfect numbers)

The largest known twin primes are $1706595\times2^{11\,235} -1$ and $1706595\times2^{11\,235} +1$, found on 6 Aug 1989 by a team in Santa Clara, California, USA using an Amdahl 1200 supercomputer.

Composite numbers The lowest of the non-prime, or composite, numbers (excluding 1) is 4.

Perfect numbers A number is said to be perfect if it is equal to the sum of all divisors of the number other than itself, for example $1+2+4+7+14 = 28$. The lowest perfect number is therefore 6, as in $1+2+3$.

The highest known perfect number, and the 32nd so far discovered, is $(2^{756\,839}-1) \times 2^{756\,838}$. It has a total of 455663 digits (enough to fill over 36 pages of *The*

Oldest mathematical puzzle

'As I was going to St Ives, I met a man with seven wives. Every wife had seven sacks, and every sack had seven cats. Every cat had seven kits. Kits, cats, sacks and wives, how many were going to St Ives?'

Apart from slight differences in wording, this is identical to a puzzle found in the Rhind papyrus, an Egyptian scroll bearing mathematical tables and problems, copied by the scribe Ahmes *c*. 1650 BC.

Most accurate version of 'pi'
The most decimal places to which *pi* (π) has been calculated is 1073740000 by Yasumasa Kanada and Yoshiaki Tamura of the University of Tokyo, Japan on 19 Nov 1989 using a Hitac S-820/80E computer.

Most inaccurate In 1897 the General Assembly of Indiana, USA enacted in Bill No. 246 stating that *pi* was *de jure* 4, when even the Bible manages to imply that *pi* equals 3.

In 1853 William Shanks published his calculation of π to 707 decimal places, all calculated by hand. Ninety-two years later, in 1945, it was discovered that the last 180 digits were in fact all incorrect.

Guinness Book of Records) and it is derived from the largest known Mersenne prime (also the largest prime known), namely $2^{756\,839} -1$, discovered in February 1992. (⇨ Prime numbers)

Newest mathematical constant The study of turbulent water, the weather and other chaotic phenomena has revealed the existence of a new universal constant, the Feigenbaum number, first calculated by Mitchell J. Feigenbaum of the US. It is approximately equal to 4·669201609102990.

Most-proved theorem A book published in 1940 and entitled *The Pythagorean Proposition* contained 370 different proofs of Pythagoras' theorem including one by American President James Garfield (1831–81).

Longest proof The proof of the classification of all finite simple groups is spread over more than 14000 pages in nearly 500 papers in mathematical journals, contributed by more than 100 mathematicians over a period of more than 35 years.

Most prolific mathematician The prolific output of Swiss mathematician Leonard Euler (1707–83) was such that his papers were still being published for the first time more than 50 years after his death. His collected works have been printed bit by bit since 1910 and will eventually occupy more than 75 large quarto volumes.

Largest mathematical prize Dr Paul Wolfskell left prize money in his will for the first person to solve the last theorem of Pierre Fermat (1601–65). This prize was worth 100 000 deutschmarks in 1908. As a result of inflation, the prize is now just over 10 000 deutschmarks.

Earliest measures The earliest known measure of weight is the *beqa* of the Amratian period of Egyptian civilization *c.*3800 BC, found at Naqada, Egypt. The weights are cylindrical, with rounded ends and weigh from 188·7–211·2 g 6·65–7·45 oz.

The unit of length used by the megalithic tomb-builders in north-western Europe *c.* 3500 BC, and generally known as the megalithic yard, was deduced by Prof. Alexander Thom (1894–1985) in 1966 to have been 82·90 ± 0·09 cm 2·72 ± 0·003 ft.

Time measure Owing to variations in the length of a day, which is estimated to be increasing irregularly at an average rate of about a millisecond per century due to the Moon's tidal drag, the second has been redefined. Instead of being 1/86 400th part of a mean solar day, it has, since 1960, been reckoned as 1/31 556 9259 747th part of the solar (or tropical) year at AD 1900, January 0·12 hr, Ephemeris time (⟺ The Universe, Light-year). In 1958 the second of Ephemeris time was computed to be equivalent to 9 192 631 770 ± 20 cycles of the radiation corresponding to the transition of caesium-133 atoms when unperturbed by

exterior fields. The greatest diurnal change recorded has been 10 milliseconds on 8 Aug 1972, due to the most violent solar storm recorded in 370 years of observations.

The accuracy of the caesium beam frequency standard approaches eight parts in 10^{14}, compared to two parts in 10^{13} for the methane-stabilized helium-neon laser and six parts in 10^{13} for the hydrogen maser.

The longest measure of time is the *kalpa* in Hindu chronology. It is equivalent to 4320 million years. In astronomy a cosmic year is the period of rotation of the Sun around the centre of the Milky Way galaxy, i.e. 225 million years. In the Late Cretaceous Period of *c.* 85 million years ago the Earth rotated faster, resulting in 370·3 days per year, while in Cambrian times *c.* 600 million years ago there is evidence that the year comprised 425 days.

Computers

Earliest The earliest programmable electronic computer was the 1500-valve Colossus formulated by Prof. Max H.A. Newman (1897–1985) and built by T.H. Flowers. It was run in December 1943 at Bletchley Park, Bucks to break the German coding machine Enigma. It arose from a concept published in 1936 by Dr Alan Mathison Turing (1912–54) in his paper *On Computable Numbers with an Application to the Entscheidungsproblem.* Colossus was declassified on 25 Oct 1975.

The world's first stored-programme computer was the Manchester University Mark I, which incorporated the Williams storage cathode ray tube (patented 11 Dec 1946). It ran its first program, by Prof. Tom Kilburn (b. 1921), for 52 min on 21 Jun 1948.

Computers were greatly advanced by the invention of the point-contact transistor by John Bardeen and Walter Brattain (announced in July 1948), and the junction transistor by R.L. Wallace, Morgan Sparks and Dr William Bradford Shockley (1910–89) in early 1951.

The concept of the integrated circuit, which has enabled micro-miniaturisation,

The world's smallest robot is the 'Monsieur' microbot, developed by the Seiko Epson Corporation of Japan in 1992. The light-sensitive robot measures less than 1 cm³ *0·06 in³*, weighs 1·5 g *0·05 oz* and is made of 97 separate watch parts (equivalent to two ordinary watches). Capable of speeds of 11·3 mm/sec *0·4 in/sec* for about 5 min when charged, the 'Monsieur' has earned a design award at the International Contest for Hill-Climbing Micromechanisms.
(Photo: Seiko Epson Corporation)

was first published on 7 May 1952 by Geoffrey W.A. Dummer (b. 1909) in Washington, DC, USA.

The invention of the microcomputer was attributed to a team led by M.E. Hoff, Jr of Intel Corporation with the production of the microprocessor chip '4004' in 1969–71. On 17 Jul 1990, however, priority was accorded to Gilbert Hyatt (b. 1938), who devised a single chip microcomputer at Micro Computer Inc. of Van Nuys, Los Angeles in 1968–71 with the award of US Patent No. 4942516.

Most powerful The world's most powerful computer is the liquid-cooled CRAY-2 from Cray Research Inc. Minneapolis, Minnesota, USA. Its memory has a capacity of 256 million 64-bit words, resulting in a capacity of 2·12 gigabytes of main memory (a byte being a unit of storage comprising eight bits, and which may represent an alphanumeric character, instruction code or other information to the computer). It attains speeds of 250 million floating point operations per second (flops).

Computer company

The world's largest computer firm is International Business Machines (IBM) Corporation of Armonk, New York, USA. At December 1992, it had assets of $96·705 billion, and in the year ending 1992 it had gross revenues of $64·523 billion but net losses of $4·965 billion—the third highest ever. The company has 301 542 employees world-wide (compared with a peak of 407 000 in 1986) and 764 630 stockholders.

Fastest In 1992 it was reported that Cray Research had developed a parallel vector system, the Y-MP C90 supercomputer, with 2 gigabytes of central memory and with 16 CPUs (central processing units) giving a combined peak performance of 16 gigaflops.

On 18 Mar 1988 Sandia National Laboratory, New Mexico, USA announced a 'massively parallel' hypercube computer with 1024 parallel processors, which, by breaking down problems into parts for simultaneous solution, proved 1019 times faster than a conventional mainframe computer.

Fastest chip In March 1992 it was reported that DEC of Maynard, Massachusetts, USA had developed an all-purpose, a 64-bit processor known as Alpha, which could run at speeds of up to 150 MHz (compared to 25 MHz for many modern personal computers). One Alpha chip is claimed to have about the same processing power as a CRAY-1, which went on sale in 1976 as the Cray company's first supercomputer at a cost of $7·5 million. (⟷ Computer Data)

Fastest transistor A transistor capable of switching 230 billion times per second was announced by the University of Illinois at Urbana-Champaign in October 1986. The devices were made of indium, gallium arsenide and aluminium gallium arsenide and were developed in collaboration with General Electric Company.

Computer Data

The position of IBM as the world's top computer company is under increasing threat from leading software house Microsoft, developers of the Windows operating system running some 120 million PCs world-wide, and chip-makers Intel.

In 1992 IBM's market value fell by 63 per cent from its peak in February 1991 and, while it has registered the third highest corporate loss ever, representing a 74 per cent drop in profits, Intel has increased its performance by 30 per cent and Microsoft by 53 per cent.

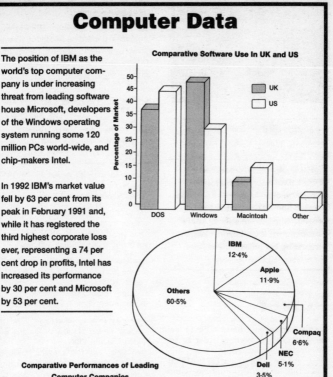

Comparative Software Use In UK and US

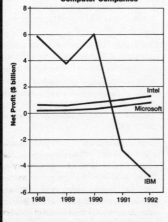

Comparative Performances of Leading Computer Companies

Although IBM still retains its lead in the PC market, the development of increasingly powerful micro-processors such as Intel's Pentium has resulted in a shift away from the mainframe computers on which IBM was built and towards fast, powerful and relatively inexpensive personal computers. As the largest semiconductor company, Intel's chips are fitted to some 70 per cent of the world's PCs.

Digital Equipment Corporation's Alpha 21064 microprocessor contains 1·7 million transistors and can process 400 million instructions per second. It is beaten only by Intel's Pentium chip, launched in 1993, comprising 3·1 million transistors.

(Photo: Digital Equipment Corporation)

Power

Steam engines *Oldest* The oldest steam engine in working order is the Smethwick Engine dating from 1779. Designed by James Watt (1736–1819) and built by the Birmingham Canal Company at a cost of £2000, the pump—originally a 60 cm *24 in* bore with a stroke of 2·4 m *8 ft*—worked on the canal locks at Smethwick, W Mids until 1891. The engine was presented to the Birmingham Museum of Science and Industry in 1960 and is regularly steamed for the public.

The oldest engine working as such and on its original site is the 1812 Boulton & Watt 26-hp, 1066 mm *42 in* bore beam engine on the Kennet and Avon Canal at Great Bedwyn, Wilts. It was restored by the Crofton Society in 1971 and still runs periodically.

Largest The largest ever single-cylinder steam engine was designed by Matthew Loam of Cornwall and built by the Hayle Foundry Co. in 1849 for land draining at Haarlem, Netherlands. The cylinder was 3·65 m *12 ft* in diameter and each stroke,

also of 3·65 m *12 ft*, lifted 61 096 litres *13 440 gal* of water.

Most efficient The most efficient steam engine recorded was Taylor's engine built by Michael Loam for United Mines of Gwennap, Cornwall in 1840. It registered only 0·8 kg *1·7 lb* of coal per horsepower per hour.

Largest power plant The most powerful installed power station is the Itaipu hydro-electric plant on the Paraná River near the Brazil-Paraguay border. Opened in 1984, the station's 18th turbine was put into operation in May 1991, giving a total capacity of 12600 MW from a projected 13 320 MW. A 20 000 MW power station project on the Tunguska River, Russia was announced in February 1982.

UK The power station with the greatest installed capacity in Great Britain is the Drax installation in North Yorkshire, with six 660 MW sets yielding 4000 MW.

Earliest atomic pile The world's first atomic pile was built in a disused squash court at Stagg Field, University of Chicago, Illinois, USA. It went 'critical' at 3:25 p.m. local time on 2 Dec 1942.

Nuclear power stations The first nuclear power station producing electricity was the EBR-1 in the USA on 20 Dec 1951. The first nuclear power station in Britain was Calder Hall (Unit 1), Cumbria which opened on 27 Aug 1956. It was also the first nuclear power station in the world to produce commerical nuclear power.

The world's largest nuclear power station, consisting of 10 reactors giving a net output of 8814 MW, is in Fukushima, Japan.

Nuclear reactors The world's largest single nuclear reactor is the Ignalina station, Lithuania, with a net capacity of 1380 MW. It became fully operational in January 1984.

Work began on the 1455 MW planned net capacity CHOOZ-B1 reactor in France in July 1982, and the first reactor became operational in 1991.

UK The largest capacity AGR (advanced gas-cooled reactor) in the UK is Tooness, near Dunbar, Lothian which has a net capacity of 625 MW.

Largest battery

The 10 MW lead-acid battery at Chino, California, USA has a design capacity of 40 MWh and will be used at an electrical sub-station for levelling peak demand loads. This $13 million project is a co-operative effort by Southern California Edison Co. Electric Power Research Institute and International Lead Zinc Research Organization Inc.

The zinc foil and sulfur (the former spelling 'sulphur' is not recommended by the IUPAC, the ruling body on chemical nomenclature) dry-pile batteries made by Watlin and Hill of London in 1840 have powered ceaseless tintinnabulation inside a bell jar at the Clarendon Laboratory, Oxford since that year.

Fusion power

In January 1982 the Tokamak-7 experimental thermonuclear apparatus was announced from the former USSR as operating 'reliably for months on end'. However, an economically viable thermonuclear reactor is not anticipated until 'about 2030'.

The first significant controlled fusion power production was achieved on 9 Nov 1991 at the Joint European Torus (JET) at Culham, Oxon by tritium injection into a deuterium plasma. Optimum fusion was sustained for about 2 sec and produced a power rating of 1·7 MW. Temperatures at the centre of thermonuclear fusion explosions have been found to be about 400 000 000°C *752 000 000°F*. (⇔ Highest temperature)

Solar power

The largest solar furnace in the world is LUZ in the Mojave Desert, California, USA, producing 354 MW and operating the world's nine largest solar electric generating systems (SEGS), which account for over 92 per cent of the world's solar electricity. A $1·5 billion solar development programme due for completion in 1994 will increase the capacity to 675 MW.

The $30 million thermal solar energy system at the Packerland Packing Co.

Bellevue Plant, Green Bay, Wisconsin, USA, completed in January 1984, comprises 9750 1·21×2·43 m *4×8 ft* collectors covering 28 985 m² *7·16 acres*. It will yield up to 8·44 MJ per month.

Tidal power stations

The world's first major station was the Usine marémotrice de la Rance, opened on 26 Nov 1966 on the Rance estuary in Brittany, France. It has an installed power of 240 MW, a net annual output of 544 million kWh and the 804 m *2640 ft* barrage contains 24 turbo alternators.

Boilers

The world's largest boilers had a capacity of 1330 MW involving the evaporation of 4 232 000 kg *9 330 000 lb* of steam per hour. They were ordered in the United States from Babcock & Wilcox Ltd of London. The largest boilers installed in the UK are six 660 MW units, also designed and constructed by Babcock & Wilcox, for the Drax power station, N Yorks.

Generators

The largest operational is a turbo-generator of 1450 MW (net) under installation at the Ignalina atomic power station in Lithuania. However, generators in the 2000 MW range are now in the planning stages both in the UK and the USA.

Transformers

The largest single-phase transformers are rated at 1 500 000 kVA. Of the eight in service with the American Electric Power Service Corporation, five step down from 765 to 345 kV. Britain's largest transformers are rated at 1 million kVA. Commissioned for the CEGB (Central Electric Generating Board) in October 1968, they were built by Hackbridge & Hewittic of Walton-on-Thames, Surrey.

Transmission lines

The longest span of any power line between pylons is 4888 m *16 040 ft* across the Søgne Fjord between Rabnaberg and Fatlaberg, Norway. Supplied in 1955 by Whitecross of Warrington, Cheshire and erected by A.S. Betonmast of Oslo as part of the high-tension power cable from Refsdal power station at Vik, the line weighs 12 tonnes. In 1967 two slightly shorter high-tensile steel/aluminium lines weighing 33 tonnes, manufactured by Whitecross and BICC, were added.

173

Biggest black-out

The greatest power failure in history struck seven north-eastern US states and Ontario, Canada on 9–10 Nov 1965. About 30 million people over an area of 207 200 km² *80 000 miles²* were plunged into darkness and only two were killed.

The longest in Britain are the 1618 m *5310 ft* lines built by J.L. Eve across the Severn, with main towers each 148 m *488 ft* high.

Highest The world's highest power lines span 3627 m *11 900 ft* across the Straits of Messina, Italy from towers at heights of 205 m *675 ft* (Sicily side) and 224 m *735 ft* (Calabria).

The highest lines in Britain are suspended from 192 m *630 ft* tall towers at a minimum height of 76 m *250 ft* across the Thames estuary. They are 1371 m *4500 ft* apart, have a breaking load of 130 tonnes and were made by BICC at West Thurrock, Essex.

Highest voltages The most powerful lines carry 1330 kV for 1970 km *1224 miles* on the DC Pacific Inter-tie in the USA. The Ekibastuz DC transmission lines in Kazakhstan are planned to be 2400 km *1490 miles* long with a 1·5 MV capacity.

Turbines The largest hydraulic turbines are rated at 815 MW. They are 9·7 m *32 ft* in diameter, have a 407-tonne runner, a 317·5-tonne shaft and were installed by Allis-Chalmers at the Grand Coulee Third Powerplant, Washington, USA.

A self-sustaining gas turbine with compressor and turbine wheels measuring just 5 cm *2 in* and an operating speed of 50 000 rev/min was built by Geoff Knights of London.

Wind generators The \$14·2 million GEC MOD-5A installation on the north shore of Oahu, Hawaii, USA produces 7·3 MW when the wind reaches 51·5 km/h *32 mph* through its 122 m *400 ft* rotors. Installation began in March 1984.

UK The 3 MW aerogenerator LS-1, with 60 m *196 ft 10 in* blades on a 37 m *121 ft* tall tower on Burgar Hill, Evie, Orkney, was

---

The Drax power station, N Yorks covers 368 ha *909 acres* overall and has a production capacity of 4000 MW. The plant also has the tallest chimney in Britain (259 m *850 ft*), the tallest cooling towers (115 m *377 ft*) and the largest boilers (six 660 MW units).

(Photo: National Power plc)

switched on in a gale on 10 Nov 1987. Built by the Wind Energy Group consortium of Taylor Woodrow, British Aerospace and GEC at a cost of £12 million, it will generate about 9 million kWh per year, enough for 2000 average houses.

Largest gasworks The flow of natural gas from the North Sea has replaced the manufacture of gas by the carbonization of coal and the reforming process using petroleum derivatives. Britain's largest ever gasworks, covering 120 ha *300 acres*, were at Beckton, Newham, London. The largest gasworks are now the Breakwater Works at Oreston, Plymouth, Devon, covering 7·6 ha *19 acres* and opened in 1966–7. Complex hydrocarbons are converted into methane at a rate of 1·4 million m³ *50 million ft³* per day.

Tidal mill The world's only surviving mill harnessing the power of the tide for regular production of wholemeal flour is the Eling Tide Mill, Hants, which attained 16 hr 7 min rotation of the waterwheel in one day on 12 Nov 1989.

Water mill The oldest water mill in continuous commercial use is Priston Mill near Bath, Avon, first mentioned in AD 931 in a charter of King Athelstan (reigned 924/5–939). It is driven by the Conygre Brook and is the only remaining working water mill of the 5700 recorded in the Domesday Book of 1086.

Windmills *Earliest* Although usually associated with the Netherlands, the earliest recorded windmills were used for grinding corn in Iran in the 7th century AD. The oldest Dutch mill is the towermill at Zeddam, Gelderland, built c.1450.

The earliest known windmill in England dates from 1185 at Weedley, near Hull, Humberside. The oldest working mill in England is the post-mill at Outwood, near Redhill, Surrey, built in 1665. However, the Ivinghoe Mill in Pitstone Green Farm, Bucks, dating from 1627, has been restored.

Largest At 33·33 m *109 ft 4 in*, the De Noord windmill in Schiedam, Netherlands is the tallest in Europe. The country's largest is the Dijkpolder in Maasland, built in 1718, with sails measuring 29 m *95 ft 9 in* from tip to tip.

The largest extant windmill in the British Isles is the Blennerville mill at Tralee, Co. Kerry, Republic of Ireland. Built c.1796, it is 196 m *60 ft* high and has sails 24·2 m *74 ft* in diameter.

Engineering

Oldest machinery The earliest mechanism st·ll in use is the *dâlu*—a water-raising instrument known to have been in use in the Sumerian civilization, which originated c. 3500 BC in lower Iraq.

UK The oldest piece of machinery (excluding clocks) operating in Britain is the snuff mill driven by a water-wheel at Wilson & Co. Sharrow Mill in Sheffield, S Yorks. It is known to have been operating in 1797 and more probably since 1730.

Blast furnace The world's largest blast furnace, with a volume of 5500 m³, is the no. 5 furnace at the Cherepovets works in Russia.

Catalytic cracker The world's largest catalytic cracker is Exxon's Bayway Refinery plant at Linden, New Jersey, USA, with a fresh feed rate of 19 million litres *4·2 million gal* per day.

Conveyor belts The world's longest single-flight conveyor belt stretches across 29 km *18 miles* in Western Australia and was installed by Cable Belt Ltd of Camberley, Surrey. Great Britain's longest, also installed by Cable Belt, runs for 8·9 km *5½ miles* underground at Longannet power station, Fife.

The world's longest multi-flight conveyor measured 100 km *62 miles* between the phosphate mine near Bucraa and the port of El Aiún, Morocco. Built by Krupps and completed in 1972, it had 11 flights of

---

Largest nut
The largest nuts ever made have an outer diameter of 132 cm *52 in*, a 63·5 cm *25 in* thread and weigh 4·74 tonnes. Known as 'Pilgrim Nuts', they are manufactured by Pilgrim Moorside Ltd of Oldham, Lancs for use on the columns of large forging presses.

Steel production

The world's largest producer of steel is the Nippon Steel Corporation of Japan, which produced 27·687 million tonnes of crude steel in the year ending March 1992, compared with 28·993 million tonnes in 1991. It now employs 37388 staff, compared with 51441 in 1988.

The Pohang works of the Pohang Iron & Steel Co. Ltd (POSCO) of South Korea produced 9 million tonnes of crude steel in 1988, the highest amount produced by a single integrated works.

Escalator riding

The record distance travelled on a pair of 'up' and 'down' escalators is 214·34km *133·18 miles*, by David Beattie and Adrian Simons at Top Shop, Oxford Street, London from 17–21 Jul 1989. They each completed 7032 circuits.

9–11 km *6–7 miles* and was driven at 4·5m/sec *10mph* before its closure.

Most powerful crane The greatest single load lifted by cranes is 10750tonnes during the positioning of an integrated module onto the Piper Bravo platform in the North Sea off Aberdeen, Grampian in December 1991. The lift was carried out by twin AmClyde 6000 cranes, designed and built by AmClyde Engineered Products Inc. of St Paul, Minnesota, USA and installed aboard the vessel *Derrick Barge 102*. (⇔ Greatest load raised)

Gantry crane The 28·14m *92·3ft* wide Rahco (R.A. Hanson Disc Ltd) gantry crane at the Grand Coulee Dam, Washington, USA Third Powerplant was tested in 1975 to lift a load weighing 2232 tonnes. It lowered an 1789-tonne generator rotor with an accuracy of 0·8mm *1·32in*.

Tallest mobile crane The 810-tonne Rosenkranz K10001, with a lifting capacity of 1000tonnes and a combined boom and jib height of 202m *663ft*, is carried on 10 trucks each limited to a length of 23·06m *75ft 8in* and an axle weight of

118tonnes. The crane can lift 30tonnes to a height of 160m *525ft*.

Greatest load raised The heaviest operation in engineering history was the raising (as opposed to lifting from above) of the entire 1·6km *1mile* long offshore Ekofisk complex in the North Sea on 17–18 Aug 1987 because of subsidence of the sea bed. The complex, consisting of eight platforms weighing some 40000tonnes, was raised 6·5m *21ft 4in* by 122 hydraulic jacks run by computer-controlled hydraulic system developed and supplied by the Dutch Mannesmann-Texroth company Hydraudyne Systems & Engineering bv of Boxtel, Netherlands. (⇔ also Most powerful cranes)

Most powerful diesel engines Five 12RTA84 type diesel engines each with a 12 cylinder power unit giving a maximum continuous output of 41920kW *57000bhp* at 95rev/min were constructed by Sulzer Brothers of Winterthur, Switzerland for container ships built for the American President Lines. The first of these ships, the *President Truman*, was delivered in April 1988.

Dragline The Ural Engineering Works in Yekaterinburg (formerly Sverdlovsk, Russia), completed in March 1962, has a dragline known as the ES-25(100) with a boom of 100m *328ft* and a bucket of 24m³ *31½yd³* capacity.

The world's largest walking dragline is 'Big Muskie', the Bucyrus-Erie 4250W, with a weight of 12000tonnes and a bucket capacity of 168m³ *220yd³* on a 94·4m *310ft* boom. This is the largest mobile land machine and is now operating on the Central Ohio Coal Co. Muskingum site in Ohio, USA.

UK The largest dragline excavator in Britain is 'Big Geordie', the Bucyrus-Erie at 1550W, 3000tonnes and with a forward mast 48·7m *160ft* high. It can strip 100tonnes of overburden in 65sec with its 49·7m³ *65yd³* bucket on a 80·7m *265ft* boom, and is owned by Derek Crouch (Contractors) Ltd of Peterborough, Cambs.

Earthmover The giant wheeled loader developed for open-air coal mining in Australia by SMEC, a consortium of 11 manufacturers in Tokyo, Japan, is 16·8m

Top spinning

The duration record for spinning a clock-balance wheel by unaided hand is 5 min 26·8 sec by Philip Ashley, 16, of Leigh, Lancs on 20 May 1968.

The record using 91·4 cm *36 in* of string with a 205·5 g *7¼ oz* top is 58 min 20 sec, by Peter Hodgson at Southend-on-Sea, Essex on 4 Feb 1985.

A team of 25 from the Mizushima Plant of Kawasaki Steel Works in Okayama, Japan spun a giant top 2 m *6 ft 6¾ in* tall and 2·6 m *8 ft 6¼ in* in diameter, weighing 360 kg *793·6 lb*, for 1 hr 21 min 35 sec on 3 Nov 1986.

55 ft long, weighs 180 tonnes, has a bucket capacity of 19 m³ *671 ft³* and is fitted with rubber tyres 3·5 m *11½ ft* in diameter.

Escalators The earliest 'Inclined Escalator' was installed by Jesse W. Reno on the pier at Coney Island, New York, USA in 1896, but the term was not registered in the USA until 28 May 1900.

UK Britain's first 'moving staircase' was installed at Harrods department store, Knightsbridge, London in November 1898, running 12 m *40 ft* from the ground to the first floor. The 'contraption', as it was known, could carry 4000 people per hour and was replaced by lifts in 1909.

The longest escalators in Britain are three flights at the Angel underground station, London, each measuring 60 m *197 ft*. Built by French engineers and installed as part of a £70 million facelift at the station, they caused great embarrassment to the management but no real surprise to London's commuters by breaking down three days after being put into operation on 12 Aug 1992.

The escalators at the station formerly named Lenin Square on the underground in St Petersburg (Leningrad), Russia have 729 steps and a vertical rise of 59·68 m *195 ft 9½ in*.

The world's longest *ride* is on the four-section outdoor escalator at Ocean Park, Hong Kong, which has an overall length

of 227 m *745 ft* and a total vertical rise of 115 m *377 ft*.

Moving walkways The world's longest moving walkways (also known as 'Travelators') are those installed in 1970 in the Neue Messe Centre, Düsseldorf, Germany, which measure 225 m *738 ft* between comb plates. The longest in Great Britain is the 110·3 m *362 ft 2 in* long Dunlop Starglide at London's Heathrow Airport Terminal 3, installed between March and May of 1970.

The ultimate in pampering to weary shoppers is the moving walkway at the Shopping Mall at Kawasaki-shi, Japan, which has a vertical height of 83·4 cm *32·83 in*. It was installed by Hitachi Ltd.

Forging The largest forging on record was a 204·4 tonnes *450600 lb*, 16·76 m *55 ft* long generator shaft for Japan, forged by the Bethlehem Steel Corporation of Pennsylvania, USA in October 1973.

Fork lift truck In 1991 Kalmar LMV of Lidhult, Sweden manufactured three counterbalanced fork lift trucks capable of lifting loads up to 90 tonnes at a load centre of 2400 mm *90·5 in*. They were built to handle the great man-made river project comprising two separate pipelines, one 998 km *620 miles* long running from Sarir to the Gulf of Sirte and the other 897 km *557 miles* from Tazirbu to Benghazi, Libya.

Lathe The largest is the 38·4 m *126 ft* long 416·2-tonne lathe built by Waldrich Siegen of Germany in 1973 for the South African Electricity Supply Commission at Rosherville. It has a capacity for 300 tonnes work pieces and swing-over beds of 5 m *16 ft 5 in* diameter.

Lifts The world's fastest domestic passenger lifts are the express lifts to the 60th floor of the 240 m *787 ft* tall 'Sunshine 60' building, Ikebukuro, in Tokyo, Japan, completed 5 Apr 1978. Built by Mitsubishi Corporation, they operate at a speed of 37 km/h *23 mph*.

Much higher speeds are achieved in the winding cages of mine shafts. A hoisting shaft 2072 m *6800 ft* deep, owned by Western Deep Levels Ltd in South Africa, winds at speeds of up to 65 km/h *41 mph*. Otitis media (popping of the ears) presents problems above even 16km/h *10mph*.

UK The longest fast lifts are the two 15-passenger cars in the British Telecom Tower, London, which travel 164m *540ft* at up to 18km/h *11mph*. The longest lift in the UK is one 283·4m *930ft* long in the BBC television tower at Bilsdale, West Moor, N Yorks. Built by J.L. Eve Construction, it runs at 2·4km/h *1·5mph*.

Pipelines *Earliest* The world's earliest pipeline, of 5cm *2in* diameter cast iron, laid at Oil Creek, Pennsylvania, USA in 1863 was torn up by Luddites.

Oil The world's longest crude oil pipeline is the Interprovincial Pipe Line Co. installation from Edmonton, Alberta, Canada to Buffalo, New York, USA, a distance of 2856km *1775 miles*. A series of 13 pumping stations maintain a flow of 31367145litres *6 900000gal* of oil per day along the pipe. The eventual length of the Trans-Siberian pipeline will be 3732km *2319 miles*, from Tuimazy through Omsk and Novosibirsk to Irkutsk. The first 48km *30 mile* section was opened in July 1957.

Gas The longest natural gas pipeline in the world is the Trans-Canada pipeline, which by 1974 had 9099km *5654 miles* of pipe up to 106·6cm *42in* in diameter. The world's longest submarine pipeline is that of 425km *264 miles* for natural gas from the Union Oil platform to Rayong, Thailand, opened on 12 Sep 1981.

The longest North Sea pipeline is the Ekofisk–Emden line, covering 418km *260 miles* and completed in July 1975. The deepest North Sea pipeline is from the Cormorant Field to Firths Voe, Shetland, at 162m *530ft*.

The large-calibre Urengoi-Nzhgorod line to Western Europe, begun in November 1982, covers 4451km *2765 miles* and was completed on 25 Jul 1983. Its capacity is 32000 million m³ *42000 million yd³* per year.

Water The world's longest water pipeline stretches 563km *350 miles* to the Kalgoorlie goldfields from near Perth, Western Australia. Constructed in 1903, the system has since been extended five-fold by branches.

Most expensive The world's most expensive pipeline is the Alaska pipeline running 1287km *800 miles* from Prudhoe Bay to Valdez. On completion of the first phase in 1977, it had cost $8 billion. The pipe is 1·21m *48in* in diameter and its capacity is now 2·1 million barrels per day.

Press The world's two most powerful production machines are forging presses in the USA. The Loewy closed-die forging press, in a plant leased from the US Air Force by the Wyman-Gordon Company at North Grafton, Massachusetts, weighs 9469tonnes and stands 34·79m *114ft 2in* high, of which 20·1m *66ft* is sunk below the operating floor. It has a rated capacity of 44600tonnes and became operational in October 1955. The second press is at the plant of the Aluminum Company of America in Cleveland, Ohio, USA.

The greatest press force of any sheet metal forming press is 106000tonnes for a QUINTUS fluid cell press delivered by ASEA to BMW AG in Munich, Germany in January 1986. The Bêché & Grohs counter-blow forging hammer, manufactured in Germany, is rated at 60000tonnes.

The most powerful press in Great Britain is the closed-die forging and extruding press installed in 1967 at the Cameron Iron Works, Livingston, West Lothian. The press is 28m *92ft* tall (8·2m *27ft* below ground) and exerts a force of 30000tonnes.

Printer The world's fastest printer was the Radiation Inc. electro-sensitive system at the Lawrence Livermore Radiation Laboratory in Livermore, California, USA. High-speed recording of up to 36000 lines per minute, each containing 120 alphanumeric characters, was attained by controlling electronic pulses through chemically-impregnated recording paper moving rapidly under closely-spaced fixed styluses. Thus the Bible (up to 773 746 words) could be printed in 65 seconds; 3048 times as fast as the peak rate of the world's fastest typist. (⇔ Fastest Typist)

Radar installation The largest of the three installations in the US Ballistic Missile Early Warning System (BMEWS) is that near Thule, Greenland, 1498km *931 miles* from the North Pole. It was completed in 1960 at a cost of $500 million. Its sister stations are at Cape Clear, Alaska, USA, completed in 1961, and the $115 million radar installation at Fylingdales Moor, N Yorks which was completed in June 1963.

The largest scientific radar installation is the 84 000 m² *21 acre* ground array at Jicamarca, Peru.

Ropes The largest rope ever made was a coir fibre launching rope with a diameter of 119cm *47 in* made in 1858 for the British liner *Great Eastern* by John and Edwin Wright of Birmingham, W Mids. It consisted of four strands, each of 3780 yarns.

Wire ropes The world's longest wire ropes are four made at British Ropes Ltd, Wallsend, Tyne & Wear, each measuring 24km *15 miles*. The ropes are 35 mm *1·3 in* in diameter, weigh 108·5 tonnes each and were ordered by the CEGB for use in the construction of the 2000 MW cross-Channel power cable.

The suspension cables on the Seto Grand Bridge, Japan, completed in 1988, are 104cm *41 in* in diameter.

A 56cm *22 in* diameter cable-laid rope with a calculated breaking strength of 11 000 tonnes was manufactured for demonstration purposes only by Franklin Offshore Supply & Engineering PTE LTD of Singapore in 1992. They also have the capacity to produce 63·5cm *25 in* cable. The largest cable-laid sling made for practical use measures 41cm *16 in* in diameter and has a minimum breaking load of 6600 tonnes. It was made in 1992 by United Ropes of Ridderkerk, Netherlands for Heeremac of Leiden.

Ropeway (téléphérique) The world's longest ropeway in the world is the COMILOG (Compagnie Minière de l'Ogooué) installation, built in 1959–62 for the Moanda manganese mine in Gabon, and extending 76km *47 miles*. It has 858 towers and 2800 buckets, with 155km *96 miles* of wire rope running over 6000 idler pulleys. The longest single-span ropeway is the 4114m *13500 ft* span from the Coachella Valley to Mt San Jacinto (3298m *10821 ft*), California, USA, opened on 12 Sep 1963.

The highest and longest passenger-carrying aerial ropeway in the world is the Teleférico Mérida in Venezuela, from Mérida City (1639·5 m *5379 ft*) to the summit of Pico Espejo (4763·7 m *15629 ft*), a rise of 3124m *10250 ft*. The ropeway is in four sections, involving three car changes in the 12·8km *8 mile* ascent in one hour. The fourth span is 3069m *10070 ft* in length. The cars have a maximum capacity of 45 people and travel at 5 km/h *3 mph*.

Britain's longest cable car was opened in June 1969 at Llandudno, Gwynedd. It has 42 cabins with a capacity of 1000 people per hour and is 1621m *5320 ft* long.

Shovel The Marion 6360 has a reach of 72·16m *236·75 ft*, a dumping height of 46·63 m *153 ft* and a bucket capacity of 138m³ *4860 ft³*. Manufactured in 1964 by the Marion Power Shovel Co. Ohio, USA, it weighs 11 million kg *24250000 lb* and uses 20 electric motors that generate 45 000 hp to operate its 67·2m *220·5 ft* long boom arm. It is operated for open-cast coal mining near Percy in Illinois, USA by the Arch Mineral Corporation.

Snow-plough blade A snow-plough with a blade 15·3m *50·25 ft* long, 1·24m *4 ft* high and with a clearing capacity of 31m³ *1095 ft³* in one pass was made by Aero Snow Removal Corporation of New York, USA in 1992 for operation at JFK International Airport.

Valve The world's largest valve is the 9·75m *32 ft* diameter, 170-tonne butterfly valve designed by Boving & Co. Ltd of London for use at the Arnold Air Force Base engine test facility in Tennessee, USA.

Wind tunnel The world's largest wind tunnel is at the NASA Ames Research Center in Mountain View, Palo Alto, California, USA. The largest test section measures 36×24m *118×79 ft* and is powered by six 17000kW motors, giving a top speed of 200km/h *124 mph*.

Britain's largest is at the Defence Research Agency Establishment at Farnborough, Hants. It has a working section of 42m² *452 ft²*, but it is not currently in use.

179

Mine Records

Earliest
World 100000 BC—CHERT (silica) Nazlet Sabaha Garb, Egypt.

UK 3390 BC±150—FLINT, Church Hill, Findon, W. Sussex.

Deepest
World [1] 3777 m *12 391 ft*—GOLD, Western Deep Levels, Carletonville, South Africa.

UK 1315 m *4314 ft*—COAL, Plodder Seam, Bickershaw Colliery, Leigh, Lancs.

Coal
Oldest (UK) c. 1822, Wearmouth, Tyne and Wear.

Deepest (exploratory shaft) 2042 m *6700 ft*, Donbas field, Ukraine.

(open cast, lignite) 325 m *1066 ft*, near Bergheim, Germany.

Copper
Earliest (UK) 1700–2000 BC, Cwmystwyth, Dyfed.

Deepest (open pit) 800 m *2625 ft*, Bingham Canyon, near Salt Lake City, Utah, USA.

Longest (underground) 1600 km *994 miles*, Division El Teniente, Codelco, Chile.

Gold
Largest (world) [2] 4900 ha *12 107 acres*, East Rand Proprietary Mines Ltd, Boksburg, Transvaal, South Africa.

Richest 49·4 million fine oz (all-time yield), Crown Mines, Transvaal, South Africa.

UK 120 000 fine oz (1854–1914), Clogau, St David's (discovered 1836), Gwynedd.

Iron
Largest 20 300 million tonnes (45–65% ore), Lebedinsky, Kursk region, Russia.

Lead
Largest >10 per cent of world output, Viburnum Trend, Missouri, USA.

Platinum
Earliest 2nd century BC, La Tolita, Ecuador.

Largest 28 tonnes per year, Rustenburg Platinum Mines Group, Transvaal, South Africa.

Quarry
Largest (world) 7·21 km² *2·81 miles²*, 3355 million tonnes (extracted), Bingham Canyon, Utah, USA.

UK 150 m *500 ft* deep, 2·6 km *1·6 miles* circumference, Old Delabole Slate Quarry (from c. 1570), Cornwall.

Spoil Dump
Largest (world) 7·4 billion ft³ *210 million m³*, New Cornelia Tailings, Ten Mile Wash, Arizona, USA.

UK 141 ha *348 acres*, Allerton Tip, near Castleford, W Yorks.

Tungsten
Largest 2000 tonnes per day, Union Carbide Mount Morgan mine, near Bishop, California, USA.

Uranium
[3] *Productivity* 6350 tonnes (ore) per day, Rio Algom Co. mine, Grant, New Mexico, USA.

[1] *Sinking began in Jun 1957 and 4267 m 14 000 ft is regarded as the limit. Its No. 3 vertical ventilation shaft is the world's deepest shaft, at 2949 m 9675 ft. This mine requires 128 050 tonnes of air per day and enough refrigeration energy needed to make 33 600 tonnes of ice. An underground shift comprises 11 150 men.*

[2] *The world's most productive gold mine may be Muruntau, Kyzyl Kum, Uzbekistan, with an estimated 80 tonnes per year. It has been estimated that South Africa has produced in 96 years (1886–1982) more than 31 per cent of all gold mined since 3900 BC. Over 51 per cent of the world's output is produced at the 38 mines of the Witwatersrand fields, South Africa, first discovered in 1886.*

[3] *This has been shut down, but remains on standby. The Gas Hills mine in Wyoming, USA, at 2540 tonnes per day, is currently the most productive.*

Borings and Mines

Deepest Man's deepest penetration into the Earth's crust is a geological exploratory borehole near Zapolarny in the Kola peninsula of Arctic Russia, begun on 24 May 1970 and reported in April 1992 to have surpassed a depth of 12 262 m *40 230 ft*. The eventual target of 15 000 m *49 212 ft* is expected in 1995. The drill bit is mounted on a turbine driven by a mud pump and the temperature at 12 km *7·45 miles* was already 210° C *229° F*. Test drilling of the Erbendorf hole, Upper Bavaria, Germany was announced on 9 Oct 1986. The planned depth of the £150 million project is 14 km *8·6 miles or 45 900 ft*.

Ocean drilling The deepest recorded drilling into the sea bed is 1740 m *5709 ft*

Ice-core drilling

The deepest borehole in ice was drilled at the Vostok station (Central Antarctica) by specialists of the St Petersburg (then Leningrad) Mining Institute in September 1989, when a depth of 2540m *8333ft* was achieved. The 18th Expedition drilled the deepest 'dry' borehole (without antifreeze) in 1972, reaching a depth of 952·5m *3125ft*.

Coal cutting

The individual coal cutting record is 45·4tonnes per person in one shift (six hours) by five Soviet miners under the leadership of Aleksey Stakhanov at the Tsentralnaya-Irmino mine, Donetsk region, Ukraine (then USSR) on 19 Sep 1935.

Using machinery the record weekly output per man is 309·07tonnes from each miner on the coalface at Stillingfleet Colliery, in Yorkshire's Selby complex, in the week ending 23 Apr 1988. The record output from a colliery in a week is 101 203 tonnes produced at Wistow, another Selby mine, in September 1989.

Coal shovelling

The record for filling a ½ton *508kg* hopper with coal is 27·93sec, by Wayne Miller at the Fingal Valley Festival in Fingal, Tasmania, Australia on 27 Feb 1993.

The record by a team of two is 16·05 sec, by Wayne Miller and Ian Austin on the same occasion.

by the *Glomar Challenger* of the US Deep Sea Drilling Project off north-west Spain in 1976. The deepest site is now 7034m *23 077ft* below the surface on the western wall of the Marianas Trench, Pacific Ocean.

British Isles The deepest drilling in the North Sea is in 795·8m *2611ft* of water on 11–12 Jun 1986 by the British-built *Sovereign Explorer*, a propulsion-assisted semisubmersible drilling unit operated by Scotdrill Offshore Co. Aberdeen, and contracted to Chevron Petroleum.

Oil

Production The world's largest oil producer is the former USSR, with a production in 1991 of 10·26 million barrels per day (b/d), compared with a peak 12·5 million b/d in 1988, followed by Saudi Arabia (8·2 million b/d) and the USA with 7·4million. UK production is about 2 million barrels.

Fields The world's largest oil field is the Ghawar field in Saudi Arabia, developed by ARAMCO, and measuring 240×35km *150×22miles*.

UK The area of the parts of the UK Continental shelf designated for oil exploration as at mid-1989 was 651650km² *252000miles²* with proven and probable reserves of 1330 milliontonnes of oil and 634 000 millionm³ *22400000 millionft³* of gas.

The most productive field is BP's Forties Field, which on 3 Apr 1989 became the first oil field in western Europe to produce a total of 2 billion barrels of oil and natural gas liquids. Production peaked for the UK's 32 oil fields at 127·5million tonnes.

Refineries The world's largest oil refinery is the Petroleos de Venezuela S.A. refinery in Judibana, Falcón, Venezuela. It is operated by the Lagoven subsidiary of Petroleos and now processes 530000 barrels of crude per day, compared with 571000 in 1990.

UK The largest oil refinery in the UK is the Esso Refinery at Fawley, near Southampton, Hants. Opened in 1921 and much expanded in 1951, it has a capacity of 15·6 million tonnes per year. Together with the associated chemical plant, the total investment on the 1295ha *3200 acre* site is £2·5 billion on a replacement cost basis.

The area occupied by the Shell Stanlow Refinery at Ellesmere Port, Cheshire, founded in 1922 and now with a capacity of 18 milliontonnes per year, is 810ha *2000acres*.

Waves of **Destruction**

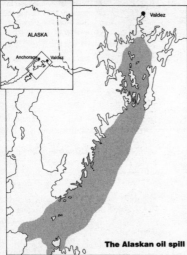

The Alaskan oil spill

Oil slicks always leave devastating images and are a constant reminder of the vulnerability of our environment. Many factors can affect the eventual impact of any spill, including location, weather conditions and temperature.

An estimated average of 2 million tonnes of oil is spilled from a total of some 1·5 billion tonnes shipped each year, i.e. about 0·13 per cent. The first major tanker spill, and the largest ever in British waters, was 120 000 tonnes from the grounding of the Torrey Canyon off Cornwall in 1967.

Despite our fears, the number of accidental tanker spills involving over 50 barrels (about 7 tonnes) has fallen from just over 120 in 1975 to under 40 in 1991.

Largest slick
644 km *400 miles* long (from 500 000 tonnes), *Ixtoc* (rig blow-out, 1979–80), Gulf of Mexico.

Oil from the *Exxon Valdez* spill (38 000 tonnes) in 1989 eventually affected 1700 km *1056 miles* of the Alaskan coastline.

Ecological damage

Although not ranking among even the top 20 largest spills, because of its environmentally sensitive location, the *Exxon Valdez* spillage off Alaska was an ecological disaster, with pollution eventually covering more than 2590 km *1000 miles* of land. An estimated 580 000 birds and 5500 otters are thought to have died as a result.

Generally speaking, in addition to already-endangered birds, marine mammals such as seals, porpoises and whales are also at risk, and crustaceans and molluscs are affected by oil sediment on the seabed. Long-term effects, for example, on the food chain and breeding patterns, have still to be evaluated fully.

The loss of some 84 000 tonnes from the tanker *Braer* off the Shetland Islands in January 1993, although relatively small, also great-

Oil-covered bird, Shetland Islands (Photo: Gamma)

ly affected a number of species, and estimates suggest that losses of shags, great northern divers and black guillemots could reach over 1 per cent of their total global populations.

Kuwait's sea of oil
(Photo: Gamma)

Record spillage
An estimated
816 000 tonnes were
deliberately released in
January 1991 during the
Gulf War. The oil, which
was up to 432 mm *17 in*
thick in places, spread
over some 644 km
400 miles of coastline.

Largest tanker, *Jahre Viking,* **485·45 m** *1504 ft*

Tanker *Braer,* **244 m** *800 ft*

Container lorry, 6 m *20 ft*

Largest tanker spills
300 000 tonnes, *Atlantic Empress/Aegean Captain*
(collision, 1979), Caribbean

250 000 tonnes, *Castillo de Bellver*
(fire, 1983), South Africa

220 000 tonnes, *Amoco Cadiz*
(grounded, 1978), France

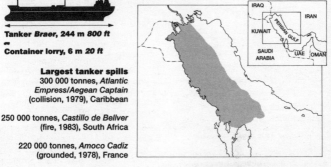

The tanker *Braer*
(Photo: Gamma)

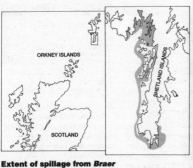

Extent of spillage from *Braer*

Oil gusher

The greatest wildcat ever recorded blew at Alborz No.5 well, near Qum, Iran on 26 Aug 1956. The uncontrolled oil gushed to a height of 52m *170ft* at 120000 barrels per day at a pressure of 62055kPa *9000lb/in²*. It was closed after 90 days' work by B. Mostofi and Myron Kinley of Texas, USA. On 15 Mar 1910 the Lake View No.1 gusher in California, USA may have yielded 125000 barrels in its first 24 hours.

Oil tanks

The largest oil tanks ever constructed are the five ARAMCO 1½-million-barrel storage tanks at Ju'aymah, Saudi Arabia. They are 21·94m *72ft* tall with a diameter of 117·6m *386ft* and were completed in March 1980.

Gas flare

The greatest gas fire burnt at Gassi Touil in the Algerian Sahara from noon on 13 Nov 1961 to 9:30a.m. on 28 Apr 1962. The pillar of flame rose 137m *450ft* and the smoke 182m *600ft*. It was eventually extinguished by Paul Neal ('Red') Adair (b. 1916) of Houston, Texas, USA, using 245kg *540lb* of dynamite, for a fee of about $1 million plus expenses.

Fastest drilling

The most footage drilled in one month is 10477m *34574ft* in June 1988 by Harkins & Company Rig Number 13 during the drilling of four wells in McMullen County, Texas, USA.

Platforms *Heaviest* The world's heaviest oil platform is the *Pampo* platform in the Campos Basin off Rio de Janeiro, Brazil, built and operated by the Petrobrás company. Opened in the

1970s, the platform weighs 24100tonnes, covers 3000m² *32292ft²* and produces 30000 barrels per day. It operates at a height of 115m *377ft* from the sea bed. (⟡ below)

Tallest The world's tallest production platform is the *Petrobrás 20* in the Marlim Field of the Campos Basin, operating 625m *2051ft* from the sea bed. The platform has been operational since July 1992 and produces 38000 barrels per day. (⟡ above)

Spills The world's worst oil spill occurred as a result of a marine blow-out beneath the drilling rig *Ixtoc I* in the Gulf of Campeche, Gulf of Mexico, on 3 Jun 1979. The slick reached 640km *400miles* by 5 Aug 1979. It was eventually capped on 24 Mar 1980 after an estimated loss of up to 500000tonnes.

The worst single assault ever made upon the eco-system was released on 19 Jan 1991 by the Iraqi President Saddam Hussein, who ordered the pumping of Gulf crude from the Sea Island terminal, Kuwait, and from seven large tankers. Provisional estimates put the loss at 816000tonnes.

The worst oil spill in history from a marine collision was 300000tonnes from the super-tankers *Atlantic Empress* and *Aegean Captain* after their collision off Tobago on 19 Jul 1979.

British Isles The worst spill in British waters was from the 118285dwt *Torrey Canyon* which struck the Pollard Rock off Land's End on 18 Mar 1967, resulting in the loss of up to 120000tonnes of oil.

Natural Gas

Gas in the UK was first discovered in the West Sole Field in October 1965 and oil in commercial quantities in the Forties Field (Block 21/10) at 2098m *6883ft* beneath the sea from the drilling rig *Sea Quest* on 18 Sep 1970, though a small gas field was discovered near Whitby, N Yorks in 1937.

Production The world's largest producer of natural gas is the former USSR with 816 billionm³ *28800 billionft³* in 1990, followed by the USA (520 billionm³ *18358 billionft³*), with the UK in 5th place with 48 billionm³ *1700 billionft³*.

Deposits The largest gas deposit in the world is at Urengoi, Russia, with an eventual production of 200 000 million m³ *261 600 million yd³* per year through six pipelines from proved reserves of about 7 000 000 million m³ *9 155 600 million yd³*. The trillionth (10¹²) cubic metre was produced on 23 Apr 1986.

Water wells The world's deepest water bore is the Stensvad Water Well 11-W1 of 2231 m *7320 ft* drilled by the Great Northern Drilling Co. Inc. in Rosebud County, Montana, USA in October and November 1961. The Thermal Power Co. geothermal steam well begun in Sonoma County, California, USA in 1955 is down to 2752 m *9029 ft*.

UK The deepest well in Great Britain is a water-table well 866 m *2842 ft* deep in the Staffordshire coal at Smestow, near Wolverhampton, W Mids.

The deepest artesian well in Britain is at the White Heather Laundry, Stonebridge Park, Brent, London, which was bored to a depth of 678 m *2225 ft* in 1911.

The deepest known hand-dug well is one dug to 391·6 m *1285 ft* between 1858 and March 1862 on the site of Fitzherbert School, Woodingdean, Brighton, Sussex.

Time Pieces

Most accurate The most accurate time-keeping device is a commercially available atomic clock manufactured by Hewlett-Packard of Palo Alto, California, USA, unveiled in December 1991. Designated the HP 5071A primary frequency standard with caesium-2 technology, the device, costing $54 000 and about the size of a desktop computer, is accurate to one second in 1·6 million years.

Mechanical The Olsen clock, completed for Copenhagen Town Hall, Denmark in December 1955 after 10 years, has more than 14 000 units and a mechanism which functions in 570 000 different ways. The celestial pole motion will take 25 753 years to complete a full circle and the clock is accurate to 0·5 sec in 300 years.

Clocks

Earliest The earliest mechanical clock, i.e. one with an escapement, was com-

The longest stoppage of the clock in the House of Commons clock tower, London since the first tick on 31 May 1859 has been 13 days, from noon on 4 April to noon on 17 Apr 1977. In 1945 a host of starlings slowed the minute hand by five minutes.

Pendulum

The world's longest pendulum measures 22·5 m *73 ft 9 ¾ in* and is part of the water-mill clock installed by the Hattori Tokeiten Co. in the Shinjuku NS building in Tokyo, Japan in 1983.

Astronomical clock

The entirely mechanical 'Planetarium Copernicus', made by Ulysse Nardin of Switzerland, is the only wrist-watch that indicates the time of day, the date, the phases of the Moon and the astronomical position of the Sun, Earth, Moon and the planets as known in Copernicus' day. It also represents the Ptolemaic universe showing the astrological 'aspects' at any given time.

pleted in China in AD 725 by Yi Xing and Liang Lingzan.

The world's oldest surviving working clock is the faceless clock dating from 1386, or possibly earlier, at Salisbury Cathedral, Wilts. It was restored in 1956, having struck the hours for 498 years and ticked more than 500 million times. Earlier dates, ranging back to *c.* 1335, have been attributed to the weight-driven clock in Wells Cathedral, Somerset, but only the iron frame is original.

A model of Giovanni de Dondi's heptagonal astronomical clock of 1348–64 was completed in 1962.

Largest The world's largest clock is the astronomical clock in the Cathedral of St Pierre, Beauvais, France, constructed between 1865 and 1868. It consists of

185

90 000 parts and is 12·1 m *40 ft* high, 6·09 m *20 ft* wide and 2·7 m *9 ft* deep.

The Su Song clock, built at Kaifeng, China in 1088–92, had a 20·3-tonne bronze armillary sphere for 1·52tonnes of water. It was installed in a 12·1 m *40 ft* high tower Beijing in 1126 and was last known to be working in 1136.

The largest by volume is 'Timepiece', which measures 15·54×15·54×15·54 m *51×51×51 ft* and is suspended over five floors in the International Square building in Washington, DC, USA. Computer driven and accurate to within ⅟₁₀₀ of a second, it weighs 2tonnes. It is lit by 122m *400 ft* of neon tubes, 12 of which light up to indicate the hour and minute. Designed by sculptor John Safer, it also shows when the sun is at its zenith in 12 international cities.

The largest digital clock measures 13·4×13·4×8·5 m *44×44×28 ft* and revolves on top of the Texas Building in Fort Worth, Texas, USA.

UK The largest clock in the United Kingdom is on the Royal Liver Building in Liverpool, Merseyside (built 1908–11). Its dials are 7·62m *25 ft* in diameter and it has four minute hands each measuring 4·26m *14 ft* long. It weighs 22·3tonnes overall and is 67m *220 ft* above street level.

Largest clock faces The world's largest clock face is that of the floral clock, which is 31m *101 ft* in diameter. It was installed on 18 Jun 1991 at Matsubara Park, Toi, Japan.

Highest The world's highest two-sided clock is 177m *580 ft* above street level on top of the Morton International Building, Chicago, Illinois, USA.

Largest sundial The world's largest sundial has a base diameter of 37·2m *122 ft* and is 36·6m *120 ft* high with a gnomon (projecting arm) of the same length. Designed by Arata Isozaki of

---

The 19th century astronomical clock in the Cathedral of St Pierre, Beauvais, France is 12·2m *40 ft* tall and consists of 90 000 parts.

(Photo: Rex Features)

Tokyo, Japan as the centre-piece of the Walt Disney World Co. headquarters in Orlando, Florida, USA, it was unveiled on 1 Mar 1991.

Most expensive The highest price paid for any clock is £905 882 at Christie's, New York, USA on 24 Apr 1991 by a private bidder for a rare 'Egyptian Revival' clock made by Cartier in 1927. Designed as an ancient Egyptian temple gate, with figures and hieroglyphs, the clock is made of mother-of-pearl, coral and lapis lazuli.

Watches

Earliest The oldest portable clockwork time-keeper is one made of iron by Peter Henlein in Nürnberg (Nuremberg), Bavaria, Germany *c.* 1504. The earliest wrist-watches were those of Jacquet-Droz and Leschot of Geneva, Switzerland, dating from 1790.

Largest The largest watch was a 'Swatch' 162m *531 ft 6 in* long and 20m *65 ft 7 ½ in* in diameter, made by D. Tomas Feliu, which was displayed on the Bank of Bilbao building, Madrid, Spain from 7–12 Dec 1985.

Heaviest The Eta 'watch' on the Swiss pavilion at Expo '86 in Vancouver, British Columbia, Canada from May to October weighed 35tonnes and was 24·3m *80 ft* high.

Smallest The smallest watches, measuring just over 12 mm *½ in* long and 4·76mm *3/16 in* wide, are produced by Jaeger le Coultre of Switzerland. They are equipped with a 15-jewelled movement and the movement and case weigh under 7g *0·25 oz*.

Most expensive The record price paid for a watch is SwFr4·95 million (£1 864 304) at Habsburg Feldman, Geneva, Switzerland on 9 Apr 1989 for a Patek Philippe 'Calibre '89' with 1728 separate parts.

Telephones and Facsimiles

Telephones It has been estimated by the International Telecommunication Union that there were approximately 537

million telephone subscribers in the world by the end of 1991. The country with the greatest number was the United States, with 130 110 000. This compares with the United Kingdom figure of 25 595 000 (March 1992), or 445 per 1000 people. Monaco has the most per head of poulation, with 810 per 1000. The greatest number of calls made in any country is in the United States, with 436 220 million per annum.

Busiest routes The busiest international telephone route is between the USA and Canada. In 1991 there were some 3·3 billion minutes of two-way traffic between the two countries. The country with which Britain has most telephone contact is also the USA, with 1·2 billion minutes of two-way traffic in 1991.

Longest telephone cable The world's longest submarine telephone cable is ANZCAN, which runs for 15 151 km *9415 miles* (8181 nautical miles) from Port Alberni, Canada to Auckland, New Zealand and Sydney, Australia via Fiji and Norfolk Island. It cost some US$379 million and was inaugurated by HM Queen Elizabeth II in November 1984.

Largest and smallest telephones The world's largest operational telephone was exhibited at a festival on 16 Sep 1988 to celebrate the 80th birthday of Centraal Beheer, an insurance company based in Apeldoorn, Netherlands. It was 2·47 m 8 ft 1 in high and 6·06 m *19 ft 11 in* long, and weighed 3·5 tonnes. The handset, being 7·14 m *23 ft 5 in* long, had to be lifted by crane in order to make a call.

The smallest operational telephone was created by Zbigniew Rózanek of Pleszew, Poland in September 1992. It measured just 6·7 × 1·9 × 2·8 cm *2⅝ × ¾ × 1⅛ in*.

Busiest telephone exchange GPT (GEC Plessey Telecommunications Ltd) demonstrated the ability of the 'System X' telephone exchange to handle 1 558 000 calls in an hour through one exchange at Beeston, Nottingham on 27 Jun 1989.

Optical fibre The longest distance at which signals have been transmitted without repeaters is 251·6 km *156·3 miles* at the British Telecom research laboratory at Martlesham Heath, Suffolk in February 1985. The laser wavelength

Largest switchboard

The world's biggest switchboard is that in the Pentagon, Washington, DC, USA, with 34 500 lines handling nearly 1 million calls per day through 322 000 km *200 000 miles* of telephone cable.

Smallest modem

Modems are devices that allow electron signals to be transmitted over large distances by MOdulating the signal at one end, and DEModulating the signal back to its original form at the destination. The smallest is the SRM-3A which is 61 mm *2·4 in* long, 31 mm *1·2 in* wide, and 19·8 mm *0·8 in* high, and weighs 31 g *1·1 oz*. It is currently manufactured by RAD Data Communications Ltd of Tel Aviv, Israel.

Morse code

The highest recorded speed at which anyone has received Morse code is 75·2 words per minute—over 17 symbols per second. This was achieved by Ted R. McElroy of the USA in a tournament at Asheville, North Carolina, USA on 2 Jul 1939.

The highest speed recorded for hand key transmitting is 175 symbols a minute by Harry A. Turner of the US Army Signal Corps at Camp Crowder, Missouri, USA on 9 Nov 1942.

Thomas Morris, a GPO operator, is reputed to have been able to send at 39–40 wpm *c.* 1919, but this has not been verifiable.

was 1525 nm and the rate was 35 megabits/sec. The longest unspliced ducted optical fibre link, with a capacity of 8000 telephone lines, was installed by BT in February 1991. The optical fibres, made by Optical Fibres of Deeside, are 13·6 km *8·45 miles* long and link Gloucester and Painswick exchanges.

Largest and smallest fax machines

The largest facsimile machine is manufactured by WideCom Group Inc of Ontario, Canada. 'WIDEfax 36' is able to transmit, print and copy documents up to 91 cm *36 in* in width.

The smallest is the Real Time Strategies Inc. hand-held device Pagentry, which combines various functions including the transmission of messages to facsimile machines. It measures just 7·6×12·7×1·9 cm *3×5×¾ in* and weighs 141·75 g *5 oz.*

Telescopes

Earliest It is not known for certain when the first telescope was made. Some of the refractive properties of lenses and reflection from mirrors were certainly known in ancient times, and spectacles were in use by the late 13th century. Roger Bacon (*c.* 1214–92) in England wrote about lenses, while Witelo (*c.* 1230–75) in Poland and John Pecham (*c.* 1230–92) in England covered both lenses and mirrors in detail.

In October 1608 three Dutch spectacle-makers stated that they had each invented a telescope and actually produced refracting telescopes. Credit is usually given to one of these, Hans Lippershey (*c.* 1570–1619), but Galileo (1564–1642) brought the invention to the notice of the scientific world, first constructing and using telescopes in 1609. However, recent examination of evidence for the claims by Thomas Digges (*c.* 1547–95) that his father Leonard Digges (*c.* 1520–59) had invented both a refractor and, it seems, a reflector as well, strongly indicates that a refractor at least existed in Elizabethan times. This is confirmed in William Bourne's work entitled *Inventions or Devises*, and also in a report which he wrote to Lord Burleigh, Queen Elizabeth I's chief adviser. Thomas Digges described in 1571 what seems to be a reflecting telescope, although the first detailed design known is that of Marin Mersenne (1588–1648). The first successful reflector to be made was that by Isaac Newton (1642–1727), constructed in 1668 or 1669. He presented it, or a copy of it, to the Royal Society in 1671.

Largest telescope The recently completed Keck telescope on Mauna Kea, Hawaii, USA has a 1000 cm *394 in* mirror, made up of 36 segments fitted together to produce the correct curve. Each segment is 183 cm *72 in* in aperture. An active support system holds each segment in place, and ensures that the images produced are brought to the same focus. The first image of the spiral galaxy NGC 1232 was obtained on 24 Nov 1990, when nine of the segments were in place. A twin Keck telescope is to be set up close to the first. When completed, Keck I and Keck II will be able to work together as an interferometer. Theoretically they would be able to see a car's headlights separately from a distance of 25 000 km *15 500 miles.*

Largest reflector The largest single-mirror telescope now in use is the 6 m *19 ft 8 in* reflector sited on Mount Semirodriki, near Zelenchukskaya in the Caucasus Mountains, Russia. It is at an altitude of 2080 m *6830 ft* and was completed in 1976. It has never come up to expectations, partly because it is not set up in a really good observing site. The largest satisfactory single-mirror telescope is the 508 cm *200 in* Hale reflector at Mount Palomar, California, USA. Though the Hale was completed in 1948, it is now much more efficient than it was, as it is used with electronic devices which are more sensitive than photographic plates. The CCD (Charged-Coupled Device) increases the sensitivity by a factor of around 100.

The largest British reflector is the 420 cm *165 in* William Herschel completed in 1987, which is set up at the Los Muchachos Observatory on La Palma, Canary Isles. Also at La Palma is the 256 cm *101 in* Isaac Newton telescope, transferred there from its old site at Herstmonceux in Sussex.

Metal-mirror A 183 cm *72 in* reflector was made by the third Earl of Rosse, and set up at Birr Castle, Republic of Ireland in 1845. The mirror was of speculum metal (an alloy of copper and tin). With it, Lord Rosse discovered the spiral forms of the galaxies. It was last used in 1909.

Largest planned The largest telescope of the century should be the VLT (Very Large Telescope) being planned by the

European Southern Observatory. It will consist of four 8m *26 ft 3 in* telescopes working together, providing a light-grasp equal to a single 16m *52 ft 6 in* mirror. The chosen site is Paranal, northern Chile, north of the La Silla Observatory (⟺ First telescope to use active optics). It is hoped to have the first units working by 1995, and the complete telescope by 2000.

Multiple-mirror The MMT (Multiple-Mirror telescope) at the Whipple Observatory at Mount Hopkins, Arizona, USA uses six 183cm *72 in* mirrors together, giving a light-grasp equal to a single 447cm *176 in* mirror. There are, however, considerable operational problems, and in 1995 a single circular 6·5m *256 in* mirror will be installed. Its proposed name is Mono Mirror Telescope, thus retaining the MMT.

Infrared The largest infrared telescope is the UKIRT (United Kingdom Infrared Telescope) on Mauna Kea, Hawaii, USA, which has a 374cm *147 in* mirror. It is, however, so good that it can be used for visual work as well as infrared.

Southern The largest southern hemisphere telescope is the 401cm *157⅞ in* reflector at Cerro Tololo in the Atacama Desert, northern Chile. The Anglo-Australian Telescope (AAT) at Siding Spring in New South Wales has a 389cm *153⅛ in* mirror.

Sub-millimetre The James Clark Maxwell telescope on Mauna Kea, Hawaii, USA has a 15m *49 ft 3 in* paraboloid primary, and is used for studies of the sub-millimetre part of the electromagnetic spectrum (0·3–1·0 mm *0·01–0·03 in*). It does not produce a visual image.

Solar The McMath solar telescope at Kitt Peak, Arizona, USA has a 2·1m *6 ft 11 in* primary mirror; the light is sent to it via a 32° inclined tunnel from a coelostat (rotatable mirror) at the top end. Extensive modifications to it are now being planned.

Largest refractor An 18·9m *62 ft* long 101·6cm *40 in* refractor completed in 1897 is situated at the Yerkes Observatory, Williams Bay, Wisconsin, USA and belongs to the University of Chicago, Illinois. Although nearly 100 years old, it is still in full use on clear nights. A larger refractor measuring 150cm *59 in* was built in France and shown at the Paris Exhibition in 1900. It was a failure and was never used for scientific work.

Britain's largest refractor is the 71·1cm *28 in* Great Equatorial Telescope of 1893 installed in the Old Royal Observatory, Greenwich, south-east London.

Largest radio dish Radio waves from the Milky Way were first detected by Karl Jansky of Bell Telephone Laboratories, Holmdel, New Jersey, USA in 1931 when he was investigating 'static' with an improvised 30·5m *100 ft* aerial. The only purpose-built radio telescope built before the outbreak of the war in 1939 was made by an amateur, Grote Reber, who detected radio emissions from the Sun. The diameter of the dish was 9·5m *31 ft 2 in*.

The pioneer large 'dish' was the 76m *250 ft* telescope at Jodrell Bank, Cheshire, now known as the Lovell Telescope, completed in 1957. It is part of the MERLIN network, which includes other dishes in various parts of Britain.

The world's largest dish radio telescope is the partially-steerable ionospheric assembly built over a natural bowl at Arecibo, Puerto Rico, completed in November 1963 at a cost of about $9000000. The dish has a diameter of 305m *1000 ft* and covers 7·48 ha *18½ acres*. Its sensitivity was raised by a factor of 1000 and its range to the edge of the observable Universe at some 15 billion light-years by the fitting of new aluminium plates at a cost of $8·8 million. It was rededicated on 16 Nov 1974.

The world's largest fully-steerable dish is the 100m *328 ft* diameter assembly at the Max Planck Institute for Radio Astronomy of Bonn in the Effelsberger Valley, Germany. It was completed in 1971 and weighs 3048 tonnes.

Largest radio installation The largest radio installation is the Australia Telescope which includes dishes at Parkes (64m *210 ft* diameter), Siding Spring (22m *72 ft*) and Culgoora (also 22m *72 ft*). There are also links with tracking stations at Usuada and Kashima, Japan, and the TDRS (Tracking and Data Relay Satellite), which is in a geosynchronous

Parkes radio telescope—part of the largest radio installation. The Australia telescope was completed in 1988, although the Parkes observatory had become
famous in 1962, as it was from there that the first quasar had been identified.
(⇨ Quasars)

(Photo: Science Photo Library)

Planetaria

The ancestor of the modern planetarium is the rotatable Gottorp Globe, built by Andreas Busch in Denmark about 1660. It was 10·54m *34ft 7in* in circumference and is now preserved in St Petersburg, Russia. The stars were painted on the inside. The first modern planetarium was opened in 1923 at Jena, Germany; it was designed by Walther Bauersfelt of the Carl Zeiss company. The world's largest planet-arium, in Miya-zaki, Japan, was completed on 30 Jun 1987. The dome has a diameter of 27m *88ft 7in*.

---

orbit. This is equivalent to a radio telescope with an effective diameter of 2·16 Earth diameters (27523km *17102miles*).

The VLA (Very Large Array) of the US National Science Foundation is Y-shaped, with each arm 20·9km *13miles* long and with 27 mobile antennae (each of 25m *82ft* diameter) on rails. It is 80km *50miles* west of Socorro in the Plains of San Augustin, New Mexico, USA and was completed on 10 Oct 1980.

First telescope to use active optics

Active optics involves automatic correction of the mirror curve as the telescope is moved around. It gives a great increase in resolution. The first major telescope to use active optics was the New Technology Telescope (NTT) at La Silla in the Atacama Desert of northern Chile, the observing site of the ESO (European Southern Observatory). The NTT, like all modern telescopes, has an altazimuth mount, and is probably the most effective ground-based telescope in use in the world today. It will shortly incorporate adaptive optics, which involves compensating the shape of the mirror for minor short-term variations in the atmosphere.

Observatory *Oldest* The oldest building extant is the 'Tower of the Winds', used by Andronichus of Cyrrhus in Athens, Greece *c.*100BC and equipped with sun-dials and clepsydra (water clock).

Highest The high-altitude observatory at Denver, Colorado, USA is at 4300m

14100ft and was opened in 1973. The main instrument is a 61cm *24in* reflector. It is slightly higher than the observatory at the summit of Mauna Kea, in Hawaii at 4194m *13760ft*.

Lowest The lowest 'observatory' is at Homestake Mine, South Dakota, USA, where the 'Telescope' is a tank of cleaning fluid (perchloroethylene), which contains chlorine, and can trap neutrinos from the Sun. The installation is 1·7km *1·1miles* below ground level, in the shaft of a gold-mine; the detector has to be at this depth, as otherwise the experiments would be confused by cosmic rays. The Homestake Observatory has been operating since 1964 and has provided results of tremendous value.

Largest Schmidt telescope A Schmidt telescope uses a spherical mirror with a correcting plate and can cover a very wide field with a single exposure. It is consequently invaluable in astronomy. The largest is the 2m *6ft 6in* instrument at the Karl Schwarzschild Observatory at Tautenberg, Germany. It has a clear aperture of 134cm *52¾in* with a 200cm *78¾in* mirror and a focal length of 4m *13ft*. It was brought into use in 1960.

Space telescope *Largest* The largest is the $1·55 billion NASA Edwin P. Hubble Space Telescope of 11tonnes and 13·1m *43ft* in overall length, with a 240cm *94½in* reflector. It was placed in orbit at 613km *381miles* altitude aboard a US space shuttle on 24 April 1990. When it had been launched, it was found to have a defective mirror, because of a mistake in the original construction—giving serious problems of spherical aberration. A repair mission is to go up in December 1993 with the aim of putting in compensatory equipment to allow for the fault in the main mirror. However, despite the faulty optics, the telescope can still outperform any ground-based telescope in some areas of astronomy.

Rocketry

Earliest uses War rockets, propelled by gun-powder (charcoal-saltpetre-sulfur), were described by Zeng Gongliang of China in 1042. This early form of rocket became known in Europe by 1258.

Progressive Rocket Altitude Records

Height				Launch Date	
Miles	Km	Rocket	Place		
0·71	1–14	A 7·62cm 3in rocket	Hackney, London, England	April	1750
1·25	2	Reinhold Tiling[1] (Germany) solid fuel rocket	Osnabrück, Germany	April	1931
1·9	3–1	'07' with liquid fuel engine '02' (USSR)	Nakhabino, Moscow region,USSR (now Russia)	16 Jul	1935
52·46	84·42	A4 rocket (Germany)[2]	Peenemünde, Germany	3 Oct	1942
c. 85	c. 136	A4 rocket (Germany)	Heidelager, Poland	early	1944
118	190	A4 rocket (Germany)	Heidelager, Poland	mid	1944
244	393	V2/WAC Corporal (2-stage) Bumper No. 5 (USA)	White Sands, New Mexico, USA[3]	24 Feb	1949
682	1097	Jupiter C (USA)	Cape Canaveral, Florida, USA	20 Sep	1956
>800	>1300	ICBM test flight R-7 (USSR)	Tyuratam, USSR (now Kazakhstan)	21 Aug	1957
>2700	>4345	Farside No. 5 (4-stage) (USA)	Eniwetok Atoll	20 Oct	1957
70700	113770	Pioneer 1-B Lunar Probe (USA)	Cape Canaveral, Florida, USA	11 Oct	1958
215300000*	346480000	Luna 1 or Mechtá (USSR)	Tyuratam, USSR (now Kazakhstan)	2 Jan	1959
242000000*	389450000	Mars 1 (USSR)	Tyuratam, USSR (now Kazakhstan)	1 Nov	1962
3666000000*[4]	5900000000	Pioneer 10 (USA)	Cape Canaveral, Florida, USA	2 Mar	1972

* Apogee in solar orbit.

FOOTNOTES
[1] There is some evidence that Tiling may shortly afterwards have reached 9·5 km 5·9 miles with a solid-fuel rocket at Wangerooge, East Friesian Islands, Germany.
[2] The A4 was latterly referred to as the V2 rocket, an acronym for second revenge weapon (Vergeltungswaffe) following upon the V1 'flying bomb'.
[3] The V2/WAC height may have been exceeded during the period 1950–6 to the time of the Jupiter C flight, as the Soviets reported in 1954 that a rocket had reached 386 km 240 miles at an unspecified date.
[4] Distance on crossing Pluto's orbit on 17 Oct 1986. Pioneer 11, Voyager 1 and Voyager 2 are also leaving the solar system.

Rocket engine

The most powerful rocket engine was built in the former USSR by the Scientific Industrial Corporation of Power Engineering in 1980. The RD–170 has a thrust of 806 tonnes in open space and 740 tonnes at the Earth's surface. It also has a turbopump rated at 190 MW, and burns liquid oxygen and kerosene.

The pioneer of military rocketry in Britain was Col. Sir William Congreve (1772–1828), Comptroller of the Royal Laboratory, Woolwich, London and Inspector of Military Machines. His '6lb rocket' was developed to a range of 1800 m *2000 yd* by 1805 and first used by the Royal Navy against Boulogne, France on 8 Oct 1806.

The first launching of a liquid-fuelled rocket (patented 14 Jul 1914) was by Dr Robert Hutchings Goddard (1882–1945) of the USA, at Auburn, Massachusetts, USA on 16 Mar 1926, when his rocket reached an altitude of 12·5 m *41 ft* and travelled a distance of 56 m *184 ft*.

The earliest Soviet rocket was the semi-liquid-fuelled GIRD–R1 (object 09), begun in 1931 and tested on 17 Aug 1933. The first fully liquid-fuelled rocket, GIRD–X, was launched on 25 Nov 1933.

Highest velocity The first space vehicle to achieve the Third Cosmic velocity sufficient to break out of the Solar System was *Pioneer 10*. The Atlas SLV–3C launcher with a modified Centaur D second stage and a Thiokol TE–364–4 third stage left the Earth at an unprecedented 51 682 km/h *32 114 mph* on 2 Mar 1972.

However, the fastest escape velocity from Earth was 54 614 km/h *34 134 mph*, achieved by the ESA *Ulysses* spacecraft, powered by an IUS–PAM upper stage after deployment from the Space Shuttle *Discovery* on 7 Oct 1990, en route to a solar polar orbit via Jupiter.

Mariner 10 reached a recorded Solar System speed of 211 126 km/h *131 954 mph* as it passed Mercury in September 1974, but the highest speed of approximately 252 800 km/h *158 000 mph* is recorded by the NASA–German *Helios B* solar probe

each time it reaches the perihelion of its solar orbit. Sister spaceship *Helios A* will also exceed *Mariner* 10's velocity. (⇔ Closest approach to the Sun by rocket)

Most powerful rocket The NI booster of the former USSR, first launched from the Baikonur Cosmodrome at Tyuratam, Kazakhstan on 21 Feb 1969, had a thrust of 4620 tonnes, but exploded at takeoff + 70 secs. Three other launch attempts also failed. Its booster *Energiya*, first launched on 15 May 1987 from the Baikonur Cosmodrome, weighed 2400 tonnes when fully loaded, with a thrust of 3483 tonnes. It was capable of placing 105 tonnes into low Earth orbit and was 58·7 m *192 ft 7 in* tall with a maximum diameter of 26 m *52 ft 6 in.* It comprised a core stage powered by four RD–0120 liquid oxygen and hydrogen engines— the first cryogenic units flown by the Russians. Four strap-on boosters powered by single RD–170 engines burning liquid oxygen and kerosene were used.

Closest approach to the Sun by a rocket The research spacecraft *Helios B* approached within 43·5 million km *27 million miles* of the Sun, carrying both US and West German instrumentation, on 16 Apr 1976. (⇔ Highest velocity)

Remotest man-made object *Pioneer 10*, launched from Cape Canaveral, Florida, USA, crossed the mean orbit of Pluto on 17 Oct 1986, being then at a distance of 5·91 billion km *3·67 billion miles.* In AD 34 593 it will make its nearest approach to the star *Ross 248*, 10·3 light years distant. *Voyager 1*, travelling faster, will have surpassed *Pioneer 10* in remoteness from the Earth by the end of the century. *Pioneer 11* and *Voyager 2* are also leaving the solar system.

Space Flight

The physical laws controlling the flight of artificial satellites were first propounded by Sir Isaac Newton (1642–1727) in his *Philosophiae Naturalis Principia Mathematica* ('Mathematical Principles of Natural Philosophy'), begun in March 1686 and first published in July 1687.

The first artificial satellite was successfully put into orbit by an inter-continental ballistic missile from the Baikonur

Away in space

How do the USSR and the USA compare in the so-called space race? The USSR's manned missions have actually totalled more than five times longer than those of the USA. Russia, in spite of only having been a separate sovereign country for a couple of years, comes third. Most people would know that astronauts and cosmonauts from other countries have sometimes accompanied Soviets or Americans on flights, but which country comes fourth in the list? The answer is in fact France, closely followed by Germany (excluding the former German Democratic Republic). These positions are determined by the number of days spent in space on missions by the leading nations. If the number of days spent in space by the individual astronauts and cosmonauts were taken into consideration instead, the top five countries would still be in the same order. The information is correct as at 31 March 1993, when the Soyuz TM 16 mission was in flight.

Russian cosmonaut Sergey Krikalyov made worldwide news in early 1992 when budget cuts and political wrangling prevented him from landing on schedule. He had gone up as a Soviet cosmonaut, but whilst in space his country broke up and the Soviet space programme effectively became the Russian space programme. For the first 221 days of his mission he was in effect a Soviet and the remaining 91 days a Russian — the totals in the illustrations include these two figures for the respective countries.

In addition to France and Germany many other countries have also had astronauts and cosmonauts on Soviet, American or Russian missions. In order of the time spent in space these are—

Countries	Days
Canada	26
Japan	15
Bulgaria	11
Belguim	8
Afghanistan	8
Italy	7
Switzerland	7
Syria	7
Czechoslovakia	7
Austria	7
Poland	7
India	7
United Kingdom	7
German Democratic Republic	7
Hungary	7
Cuba	7
Mongolia	7
Vietnam	7
Romania	7
Saudi Arabia	7
Netherlands	7
Mexico	6

USSR
3744 days

USA
674 days

Russia
491 days

France
53 days

Germany
33 days

USSR   USA   Russia   France   Germany

Lunar records

The first direct hit on the Moon was achieved at 2min 24sec after midnight (Moscow time) on 14 Sep 1959, by the Soviet space probe Lunar II near the Mare Serenitatis. The first photographic images of the hidden side of the Moon were collected by the Soviet Lunar III from 6:30a.m. on 7 Oct 1959 from a range of up to 70400km *43750miles*, and transmitted to the Earth from a distance of 470000km *292000miles*.

Most isolated human being

The farthest any human has been removed from his nearest living fellow human is 3596·4km *2233·2miles* in the case of the Command Module pilot Alfred M. Worden on the US *Apollo 15* lunar mission of 30 Jul–1 Aug 1971, while David Scott and James Irwin (1930–91) were at Hadley Base exploring the surface.

Suit

EVA suits for extra-vehicular activity worn by Space Shuttle crews from 1982 have a unit cost of $3·4 million.

Cosmodrome at Tyuratam, Kazakhstan, 275km *170miles* east of the Aral Sea and 250km *155* miles south of the town of Baikonur, on the night of 4 Oct 1957. It reached an altitude of between 228·5km (perigee or nearest point to Earth) and 946km (apogee or furthest point from Earth) *142miles and 588miles*, and a velocity of more than 28565km/h *17750mph*. This spherical satellite *Sputnik 1* ('Fellow Traveller'), officially designated 'Satellite 1957 Alpha 2', weighed 83·6kg *184·3lb*, with a diameter of 58cm *22¾in*. Its lifetime is believed to have been 92 days, ending on 4 Jan 1958. The 29·17m *95ft 8in* SL–1 launcher was designed under the direction of former Gulag prisoner Dr Sergey Pavlovich Korolyov (1907–66).

Earliest manned satellite

The earliest manned space flight ratified by the world governing body, the Fédération Aéronautique Internationale (FAI, founded 1905), was by Cosmonaut Flight Major (later Col.) Yuri Alekseyevich Gagarin (1934–68) in *Vostok 1* on 12 Apr 1961. Details filed showed take-off to be from the Baikonur Cosmodrome, Kazakhstan at 6:07a.m. GMT and the landing near Smelovka, near Engels, in the Saratov region of Russia, 108 minutes later. Col. Gagarin landed separately from his spacecraft, by parachute after ejecting as planned, as did all the *Vostok* pilots.

The maximum altitude during the 40868·6 km *25394½ mile* flight of *Vostok 1* was listed at 327km *203miles*, with a maximum speed of 28260km/h *17560mph*. Col. Gagarin, invested a Hero of the Soviet Union and awarded the Order of Lenin and the Gold Star Medal, was killed in a jet plane crash near Moscow on 27 Mar 1968.

There had been 158 manned spaceflights to 6 Apr 1993, of which 83 were American and 75 Soviet or former Soviet Union, including 3 Russian.

First woman in space

The first woman to orbit the Earth was Junior Lt (now Lt-Col. Eng) Valentina Vladimirovna Tereshkova (b. 6 Mar 1937). She was launched in *Vostok 6* from the Baikonur Cosmodrome, Kazakhstan at 9:30a.m. GMT on 16 Jun 1963, and landed at 8:16a.m. on 19 June, after a flight of 2 days 22hr 50min, during which she completed over 48 orbits (1971000km *1225000 miles*) and passed momentarily to within 5km *3 miles* of *Vostok 5*. As at 6 Apr 1993 a total of 21 women had flown into space—17 Americans, two Soviets, one from the UK (⇔ below) and one Canadian—out of the total of 286 people who have been into space.

First Briton in space

Helen Sharman (b. 30 May 1963) became the first Briton in space, in *Soyuz TM12* on 18 May 1991. She was the 15th woman in space, and was the first non-Soviet, non-US woman in space. Britain became the 21st 'space nation' as a result.

Astronaut

Oldest The oldest astronaut of the 286 people in space (to 6 Apr

1993) was Vance DeVoe Brand (USA) (b. 9 May 1931), aged 59, on 2 Dec 1990 while on the space shuttle mission aboard the STS 35 *Columbia*. The oldest woman was Shannon Lucid (USA), aged 48 years, on space shuttle mission STS 43 *Discovery* in July 1991. She is also the first woman to make three spaceflights, and is scheduled to make a fourth flight in July 1993.

Youngest The youngest has been Major (later Lt-Gen.) Gherman Stepanovich Titov (b. 11 Sep 1935), who was aged 25 years 329 days when launched in *Vostok 2* on 6 Aug 1961. The youngest woman in space was Valentina Tereshkova, who was 26. (⇨ First woman in space)

Longest and shortest manned space flight The longest manned flight was by Col. Vladimir Georgeyevich Titov (b. 1 Jan 1947) and Flight Engineer Musa Khiramanovich Manarov (b. 22 Mar 1951), who were launched to the Mir space station aboard *Soyuz TM4* on 21 Dec 1987 and landed, in *Soyuz TM6* (with French cosmonaut Jean-Loup Chretien), at a secondary recovery site near Dzhezkazgan, Kazakhstan on 21 Dec 1988, after a space flight lasting 365 days 22 hr 39 min 47 sec. The shortest manned flight was made by Cdr Alan Bartlett Shepard (b. 18 Nov 1923), USN aboard *Mercury Redstone 3* on 5 May 1961. His sub-orbital mission lasted 15 min 28 sec.

Although not spaceflights, the space shuttle *Challenger* flew for 73 sec before being destroyed on 28 Jan 1986, while the launch escape system of *Soyuz T10A* took Vladimir Titov and Gennady Strekalov on a 17 g ride lasting about 20 sec after the *Soyuz* booster caught fire and eventually exploded before lift-off on 27 Sep 1983.

The most experienced space traveller is the Soviet (now Azerbaijani) flight engineer Musa Manarov who has clocked up 541 days 31 min 10 sec on two space-flights in 1987–8 and 1990–1.

The longest US manned spaceflight, 84 days 1 hr 15 min 31 sec, was completed by *Skylab 4* astronauts Gerry Carr, Edward Gibson and Bill Pogue, in 1973–4. They are the most experienced US astronauts. The most experienced space shuttle flier is Daniel Brandenstein, with 32 days 22 hr 10 min.

Most journeys Capt. John Watts Young (b. 24 Sep 1930) (USN ret.) completed his sixth space flight on 8 Dec 1983, when he relinquished command of *Columbia* STS 9/Spacelab after a space career of 34 days 19 hr 41 min 53 sec. Young flew *Gemini 3*, *Gemini 10*, *Apollo 10*, *Apollo 16*, STS 1 and STS 9. The greatest number of flights by a Soviet cosmonaut is five by Vladimir Dzhanibekov (between 1978 and 1985). The most by a woman is three, by Shannon Lucid (STS 51G, 34 and 43), Kathryn Sullivan (STS 41G, 31 and 45) and Bonnie Dunbar (STS 61A, 32 and 50). Dunbar is also the woman with most space experience, at 31 days 17 hr 15 min. Lucid is scheduled to make a fourth flight in 1993.

Largest crew The most crew on a single space mission is eight. This included one female and was launched on space shuttle STS 61A *Challenger* on 30 Oct 1985, carrying the West German Spacelab D1 laboratory. The flight (the 22nd shuttle mission) was commanded by Henry Warren 'Hank' Hartsfield and lasted 7 days 44 min 51 sec. The most women in a space crew is three (of seven) during STS 40 *Columbia* in June 1991.

Most in space The greatest number of people in space at any one time has been 12, on three occasions. Seven Americans were aboard the space shuttle STS 35 *Columbia*, two Soviet cosmonauts aboard the Mir space station, and two cosmonauts and a Japanese journalist aboard *Soyuz TM11* on 2 Dec 1990. On 23–24 Mar 1992 six Americans and one Belgian were on space shuttle *Atlantis*, two CIS cosmonauts on Mir and two CIS cosmonauts and a German on *Soyuz TM14*, and most recently on 31 Jul 1992 four CIS cosmonauts and one Frenchman were aboard *Mir* at the same time as five US astronauts, one Swiss and one Italian were on STS46 *Atlantis*. A record five countries had astronauts or cosmonauts in space at the same time on 31 Jul 1992 – CIS, France, Italy, Switzerland and USA (⇨ above).

Lunar conquest Neil Alden Armstrong (b. Wapakoneta, Ohio, USA of Scottish

197

Progressive Speed Records

Speed Km/h	mph	Person and Vehicle	Place	Date
40	25	Sledging	Heinola, Finland	c.6500 BC
55	35	Horse-riding	Anatolia, Turkey	c.1400 BC
70	45	Mountain sledging	Island of Hawaii (now USA)	ante AD 1500
80	50	Ice yachts (earliest patent)	Netherlands	AD 1600
91	56·75	Grand Junction Railway 2-2-2: Lucifer	Madeley Banks, Staffs, England	13 Nov 1830
141·3	87·8	Tommy Todd, downhill skier	La Porte, California, USA	March 1873
144	90	Midland Railway 4-2-2 single	Ampthill, Bedford, England	March 1897
210·2	130·6	Siemens & Halske electric engine	Marienfeld-Zossen, near Berlin	27 Oct 1903
c.240	c.150	Frederick H. Marriott (fl. 1957) Stanley Steamer Wogglebug	Ormond Beach, Florida, USA	26 Jan 1907
339	210	Sadi Lecointe (France) Nieuport-Delage 29	Villesauvage, France	25 Sep 1921
668·2	415·2	Flt Lt (Later Wing Cdr) George Hedley Stainforth AFC Supermarine S.6B	Lee-on-Solent, England	29 Sep 1931
1004	623	Flugkapitän Heinz Dittmar Me. 163V-1	Peenemünde, Germany	2 Oct 1941
1078	670	Capt Charles Elwood Yeager, USAF Bell XS-1	Muroc Dry Lake, California, USA	14 Oct 1947
1556	967	Capt Charles Elwood Yeager, USAF Bell XS-1	Muroc Dry Lake, California, USA	26 Mar 1948
4675	2905	Maj Robert M. White, North American X-15	Muroc Dry Lake, California, USA	7 Mar 1961
c.28260	c.17560	Flt Maj Yuriy Alekseyevich Gagarin, Vostok 1	Earth orbit	2 Apr 1961
38988	24226	Col Frank Borman, USAF, Capt James Arthur Lovell, Jr, USN, Maj William A. Anders, USAF Apollo VIII	Trans-lunar injection	21 Dec 1968
39897	24790·8	Cdrs Eugene Andrew Cernan and John Watts Young, USN and Col Thomas P. Stafford, USAF Apollo X	Re-entry after lunar orbit	26 May 1969

[via Ireland] and German ancestry, on 5 Aug 1930), command pilot of the *Apollo 11* mission, became the first man to set foot on the Moon, on the Sea of Tranquillity, at 02:56 and 15 sec GMT on 21 Jul 1969. He was followed out of the lunar module *Eagle* by Col. Edwin Eugene 'Buzz' Aldrin, Jr, USAF (b. Montclair, New Jersey, USA of Swedish, Dutch and British ancestry, on 20 Jan 1930), while the command module *Columbia* piloted by Lt-Col. Michael Collins, USAF (b. Rome, Italy, of Irish and pre-Revolutionary American ancestry, on 31 Oct 1930) orbited above.

Eagle landed at 20:17 and 42 sec GMT on 20 July and lifted off at 17:54 GMT on 21 July, after a stay of 21 hr 36 min. *Apollo 11* had blasted off from Cape Canaveral, Florida, USA at 13:32 GMT on 16 July and was a culmination of the US space programme which at its peak employed 376 600 people and in 1966–67 attained a record budget of $5·9 billion.

There were six lunar landings altogether, and twelve people made a total of 14 EVAs on the moon totalling 79 hr 35 min between July 1969 and December 1972.

Altitude The greatest altitude attained by man was when the crew of the *Apollo 13* were at apocynthion (i.e. their furthest point) 254 km *158 miles* above the lunar surface, and 400 171 km *248 655 miles* above the Earth's surface at 1:21 a.m. BST on 15 Apr 1970. The crew were Capt. James Arthur Lovell, Jr, USN (b. 25 Mar 1928), Fred Wallace Haise, Jr (b. 14 Nov 1933) and John L. Swigert (1931–82).

The greatest altitude attained by a woman is 531 km *330 miles* by Kathryn Sullivan (USA) (b. 3 Oct 1951) during her flight on STS 31 on 24 Apr 1990.

Speed The fastest speed at which humans have travelled is 39 897 km/h *24 791 mph*. The command module of *Apollo 10* carrying Col. (now Brig. Gen.) Thomas Patten Stafford, USAF (b. 17 Sep 1930), Cdr Eugene Andrew Cernan (b. 14 Mar 1934) and Cdr (now Capt.) John Watts Young, USN (b. 24 Sep 1930), reached this maximum value at the 121·9 km *75·7 mile* altitude interface on its trans-Earth return flight on 26 May 1969.

Lunar conquest

A total of twelve men have walked on the Moon. They are:–

Neil Armstrong and Edwin Aldrin
Apollo 11, July 1969

Charles Conrad and Alan Bean
Apollo 12, November 1969

Alan Shepard and Edgar Mitchell
Apollo 14, February 1971

David Scott and James Irwin
Apollo 15, July 1971

John Young and Charles Duke
Apollo 16, April 1972

Eugene Cernan and Harrison Schmitt
Apollo 17, December 1972

The highest speed recorded by a woman is 28 582 km/h *17 864 mph* by Kathryn Sullivan at the start of re-entry at the end of the STS 31 *Discovery* shuttle mission on 29 Apr 1990. The highest recorded by a Soviet space traveller was 28 115 km/h *17 470 mph* by Valentina Tereshkova of the USSR (◇ First woman in space) in *Vostok 6* on 19 Jun 1963. However, because orbital injection of Soyuz spacecraft occurs at marginally lower altitude, it is probable that Tereshkova's speed was exceeded twice by Svetlana Savitskaya aboard *Soyuz 77* and *Soyuz T12* on 27 Aug 1982 and 28 Jul 1984, and also by Helen Sharman aboard *Soyuz TM12* on 18 May 1991.

Duration record on the Moon The crew of *Apollo 17* collected a record 114·8 kg *253 lb* of rock and soil during their three EVAs of 22 hr 5 min. They were Capt. Eugene Cernan (◇ Speed) and Dr Harrison Hagen 'Jack' Schmitt (b. 3 Jul 1935), who became the 12th man on the Moon. The crew were on the lunar surface for 74 hr 59 min during this longest of lunar missions, which took 12 days 13 hr 51 min on 7–19 Dec 1972.

Spacewalks Lt-Col. (now Maj. Gen.) Aleksey Arkhipovich Leonov (b. 20 May 1934) from *Voskhod 2* was the first per-

199

son to engage in EVA 'extra-vehicular activity' on 18 Mar 1965. Capt. Bruce McCandless II, USN (b. 8 Jun 1937), from the space shuttle *Challenger*, was the first to engage in untethered EVA, at an altitude of 264 km *164 miles* above Hawaii, on 7 Feb 1984. His MMU (Manned Manoeuvering Unit) back-pack cost $15 million to develop. The first woman to perform an EVA was Svetlana Savitskaya (b. 8 Aug 1948) from *Soyuz T12/Salyut 7* on 25 Jul 1984. The greatest number of spacewalks is eight, by Soviet cosmonauts Leonid Kizim and Vladimir Solovyov during two missions in 1984 and 1986.

The longest spacewalk ever undertaken was one of 8 hr 29 min, by Pierre Thuot, Rick Hieb and Tom Akers of STS 49 *Endeavour* on 13 May 1992. Anatoly Solovyov and Aleksandr Balandin of *Soyuz TM9* made a 7 hr 16 min EVA outside the Mir space station on 1 Jul 1990, which was the longest by Soviet cosmonauts. The longest spacewalk by a woman lasted 7 hr 49 min and was made by Kathryn Thornton (USA) of STS 49 *Endeavour* on 14 May 1992.

Space fatalities The greatest published number to perish in any of the 159 attempted manned space flights to 6 Apr 1993 is seven (five men and two women) aboard the *Challenger* 51L on 28 Jan 1986, when an explosion occurred 73 sec after lift-off, at a height of 14 300 m *47 000 ft*. *Challenger* broke apart under extreme aerodynamic overpressure.

Four people, all Soviet, have been killed during actual spaceflight—Vladimir Komarov of *Soyuz 1* which crashed on landing on 24 Apr 1967, and the un-spacesuited Georgi Dobrovolsky, Viktor Patsayev and Vladislav Volkov who died when their *Soyuz 11* spacecraft depressurized during the re-entry on 29 Jun 1971.

First extra-terrestrial vehicle The first wheeled vehicle landed on the Moon was the unmanned *Lunokhod I* which began its Earth-controlled travels on 17 Nov 1970. It moved a total of 10·54 km *6·54 miles* on gradients up to 30° in the Mare Imbrium and did not become non-functioning until 4 Oct 1971.

The lunar speed and distance record was set by the manned *Apollo 16* Rover, driven by John Young, with 18 km/h *11·2 mph* downhill and 33·8 km *22·4 miles*.

Heaviest and largest space objects The heaviest object orbited is the Saturn V third stage with Apollo 15 (spacecraft), which, prior to trans-lunar injection into parking orbit, weighed 140·51 tonnes. The 200 kg *440 lb* US RAE (Radio Astronomy Explorer) B, or *Explorer 49*, launched on 10 Jun 1973, was larger, with antennae 450 m *1500 ft* from tip to tip.

Most expensive projects The total cost of the US manned space programme by the spring of 1993 has been estimated to be $80·8 billion. The first 15 years of the Soviet space programme, from 1958 to September 1973, have been estimated to have cost $45 billion. The cost of the NASA shuttle programme has been $45·3 billion.

Buildings & Structures

- Origins
- Buildings for Living
- Buildings for Working
- Buildings for Leisure
- Towers and Masts
- Bridges
- Canals
- Dams
- Tunnels
- Specialized Structures

Origins

The earliest known human structure is a rough circle of loosely piled lava blocks found on the lowest cultural level at the Lower Palaeolithic site at Olduvai Gorge, Tanzania, and revealed by Dr Mary Leakey in January 1960. The structure was associated with artifacts and bones on a work-floor, dating from *c.* 1750000 BC.

The oldest free-standing structures in the world are now believed to be the megalithic temples at Mgarr and Skorba in Malta. With those at Ggantija in Gozo, they date from *c.* 3250 BC, some 3½ centuries earlier than the earliest Egyptian pyramid. (◇ Specialized structures)

UK Twelve small stone clusters, associated with broken bones and charcoal in stratum C of the early Palaeolithic site at Hoxne, near Eye, Suffolk may be

regarded as Britain's earliest structural remains, dated c. 250000 BC.

Wooden structures The world's oldest extant wooden buildings comprise the Pagoda, Chumanar Gate and Temple of Horyu (Horyu-ji) at Nara, Japan, dating from c. AD 670 and completed in 715.

What is believed to be the oldest complete wooden building in England, a burial chamber of the Neolithic period c. 3000 BC measuring 8×2m *26×6½ft*, was discovered in December 1986 in the Fenlands, Cambridge.

Buildings for Living

Earliest The earliest known evidence of a habitational structure is that of 21 huts with hearths or pebble-lined pits and delimited by stake-holes found in October 1965 at the Terra Amata site in Nice, France and thought to belong to the Acheulian culture of c. 400000 years ago. Excavation in 1966 revealed one hut with palisaded walls with axes of 15m *49ft* and 6m *20ft*.

Remains of the earliest dated stone habitation structures and cooking pits in Britain were discovered at Culverwell, Isle of Portland, Dorset and dated to 5200±135 BC (Mesolithic).

Greatest altitude The highest inhabited buildings in the world are those in the Indo-Tibetan border fort of Bāsisi by the Māna Pass (Lat. 31° 04'N, Long. 79° 24'E) at c. 5990m *19700ft*.

In April 1961, a three-room dwelling believed to date from the late pre-Columbian period c. 1480 was discovered at 6600 m *21650 ft* on Cerro

---

The tallest sand castle, built just with hands, buckets and shovels. It was made in 1991 at Harrison Hot Springs in Canada, and beat the record set at the same venue the previous year.

(Photo: The Harrison Hot Springs and Sculpture Society)

Sand castle

The tallest sand castle on record, constructed only with hands, buckets and shovels, was 5·94m *19ft 6in* high and was made by Team Totally in Sand and Freddie and the Sandblasters at Harrison Hot Springs, British Columbia, Canada on 15 Oct 1991.

The longest sand castle was 8·37km *5·2 miles* long, made by staff and pupils of Ellon Academy, near Aberdeen, Grampian on 24 Mar 1988.

Llullaillaco (6723m *22057ft*), on the Argentine–Chile border.

Northernmost The Danish scientific station set up in 1952 in Pearyland, northern Greenland is over 1450 km *900 miles* north of the Arctic Circle and is manned every summer.

The former USSR's drifting research station 'North Pole 15' passed within 2·8km *1¼ miles* of the North Pole in December 1967.

The most northerly continuously inhabited place is the Canadian Department of National Defence outpost at Alert on Ellesmere Island, Northwest Territories (Lat. 82° 30'N, Long. 62° W), set up in 1950.

Southernmost The most southerly permanent human habitation is the United States' Amundsen–Scott South Polar Station, completed in 1957 and replaced in 1975.

Earliest The castle at Gomdan, Yemen dates from before AD 100 and originally had 20 storeys.

Oldest The oldest stone castle in Great Britain is Chepstow Castle, Gwent, built c. 1067 on the west bank of the River Wye by William fitz Osbern.

Largest The largest ancient castle in the world is Hradčany Castle in Prague, Czech Republic, originating in the 9th century. It is an oblong irregular polygon with an axis of 570m *1870ft* and an

Largest moat

From plans drawn by French sources it appears that those which surround the Imperial Palace in Beijing (⇨ Palaces) measure 49 m *54 yd* wide and have a total length of 3290 m *3600 yd*. In all, the city's moats total 38 km *23½ miles*.

Most visited stately home

Warwick Castle near Stratford-on-Avon, Warks received 683 000 visitors in 1991. Built by the Beauchamp family, it dates from the 14th century.

---

average tranverse diameter of 128 m *420 ft*, giving a surface area of 7·28 ha *18 acres*.

The world's largest inhabited castle is the royal residence of Windsor Castle at Windsor, Berks. Primarily of 12th century construction, it is in the form of a waisted parallelogram measuring 576 × 164 m *1890 × 540 ft*. Carisbrooke Castle, Isle of Wight has overall dimensions of 110 × 137 m *360 × 450 ft*, or 411 × 251 m *1350 × 825 ft* including its earthworks. Dover Castle in Kent covers a total area of 13·75 ha *34 acres*, is 335 m *1100 ft* wide and has a curtain wall of 550 m *1800 ft*, or 700 m *2300 ft* including underground works.

The largest castle in Scotland is Edinburgh Castle, Lothian, with a major axis of 402 m *1320 ft* and measuring 1025 m *3360 ft* along its perimeter wall, including the Esplanade.

Palaces

Largest The Imperial Palace (Gugong) in the centre of Beijing, China covers a rectangle measuring 960 × 750 m *3150 × 2460 ft* over an area of 72 ha *178 acres*. The outline survives from the construction of the third Ming Emperor, Yongle (1402–24), but due to constant reconstruction work most of the intra-mural buildings (five halls and 17 palaces) are from the 18th-century.

The Palace of Versailles, 23 km *14 miles* south-west of Paris, is 580 m *1902 ft* long

and has a façade with 375 windows. The building, completed in 1682 for Louis XIV, occupied over 30 000 workmen under Jules Hardouin-Mansart (1646–1708).

Residential The palace (Istana Nurul Iman) of HM the Sultan of Brunei in the capital Bandar Seri Begawan was completed in January 1984 at a reported cost of £300 million. It is the largest residence in the world, with 1788 rooms and 257 lavatories. The underground garage accommodates the Sultan's 110 cars.

UK The largest-ever royal palace is Hampton Court, Greater London, acquired by Henry VIII from Cardinal Wolsey in 1525 and greatly enlarged by him and later by William III, Queen Anne and George I, whose son George II was its last resident monarch. It covers 1·6 ha *4 acres* of a 271 ha *669 acre* site.

The largest palace in the United Kingdom in royal use is Buckingham Palace, London, so named after its site, bought in 1703 by John Sheffield, the 1st Duke of Buckingham and Normanby (1648–1721). Buckingham House was reconstructed in the Palladian style between 1825 and 1836, following the design of John Nash (1752–1835). The 186 m *610 ft* long East Front was built in 1846 and refaced in 1912. The Palace, which stands in 15·8 ha *39 acres* of garden, has 600 rooms including a 34 m *111 ft* long ballroom used for investitures.

Housing

Earliest Eastry Court near Sandwich, Kent includes part of a Saxon building said to have been built in AD 603 by King Ethelbert, possibly as a palace. The present building is, however, in a much altered form.

Oldest inhabited Barton Manor in Pagham, W Sussex includes structures dating from Saxon times *c.* AD 800.

England's oldest inhabited house is reputed to be Little Dean Hall, Forest of Dean, Glos, dating from AD 1080. A Roman temple was found in its grounds in 1982.

Largest residence The largest non-palatial residence is St Emmeram Castle

The Forbidden City, Beijing, China across the 39·6 ha *98 acre* expanse of Tiananmen Square, the Temple of Heaven and a golden lion from within the City.

(Photos: Images Colour Library/Mike Langford)

in Regensburg, Germany. It has 517 rooms and a floor area of 21 460 m² *231 000 ft²*. It was owned by the late Prince Johannes von Thurn und Taxis, and his family only use 95 of the rooms. The castle is valued at more than 336 millionDM ($177 million).

UK The main part of Wentworth Woodhouse, near Rotherham, S Yorks, built over 300 years ago, has more than 240 rooms and its principal façade is 183m *600ft* long. Formerly the seat of the Earls Fitzwilliam, the house is now privately owned by Wensley Haydon-Baillie.

The house with the most rooms is Knole, near Sevenoaks, Kent, believed to have had 365 rooms, one for each day of the year, and now in the care of the National Trust. It is built round seven courtyards, the total depth from front to back being about 120m *400ft*. Thomas Bourchier, Archbishop of Canterbury (1454–86), bought the estate in 1456 and commenced building. Thomas Sackville, Earl of Dorset put the finishing touches between 1603–8. The royal residence of Sandringham House, Norfolk was reported to have had 365 rooms before the demolition of 73 surplus rooms in 1975.

The largest house in the Republic of Ireland is Castletown in Co. Kildare, owned and run by the Castletown Foundation, an independent foundation with charitable status set up by the Hon. Desmond Guinness. The house is approximately 121m *400ft* in length.

Scotland's largest house is Hopetoun House, West Lothian, built between 1696 and 1756 with a west façade 206m *675ft* long.

Forts

Fort George in Ardersier, Highland, built in 1748–69, is 640m *2100ft* long and has an average width of 189m *620ft* on a site covering a total of 17·2ha *42½ acres*.

Pole sitting

Modern records do not compare with that of St Simeon the Younger (*c.* AD 521–97), called Stylites, a monk who spent his last 45 years up a stone pillar on the Hill of Wonders, near Antioch, Syria.

The 'standards of living' at the top of poles can vary widely. Mellissa Sanders lived in a shack measuring 1·8×2·1m *6×7ft* at the top of a pole in Indianapolis, Indiana, USA from 26 Oct 1986–24 Mar 1988, a total of 516 days.

Rob Colley stayed in a barrel (maximum capacity 150 gal *682litres*) at the top of a pole 43ft *13·1m* high at Dartmoor Wildlife Park, near Plymouth, Devon for 42 days 35min from 13 Aug–24 Sep 1992.

Camping out

The silent Indian *fakir* Mastram Bapu ('contented father') remained on the same spot by the roadside in the village of Chitra for 22 years, from 1960 through to 1982.

Not even the most skilled estate agent could increase the dimensions of this decidedly bijou residence in Conwy, Gwynedd, offering full mod cons and short walk to front door.
(Photos: Gamma/Morgan-Spooner)

Smallest house The smallest house in Britain is the 19th-century fisherman's cottage at The Quay, Conwy, Gwynedd. Consisting of two tiny rooms and a staircase, it has a 182cm *72in* frontage, is 309cm *122in* high and measures 254cm *100in* from front to back.

The narrowest known house frontage is 119cm *47in* for 50 Stuart Street, Millport, on the island of Great Cumbrae, Strathclyde.

Most expensive The most expensive private house ever built is the Hearst Ranch at San Simeon, California, USA. It was built between 1922 and 1939 for William Randolph Hearst (1863–1951), at a total cost of more than $30 million. It has more than 100 rooms, a 32m *104ft* long heated swimming pool, a 25m *83ft* long assembly hall and a garage for 25 limousines. The house required 60 servants to maintain it.

The highest price for any house on the 1992 global residental property market was £50 million for the Casa Batlló in

THE GUINNESS TIMES

21st April, 1992

New house of cards record

—— 75 STOREYS AND 208 PACKS ——

Bryan Berg, a high school student at Spirit Lake in the USA, has just spent 30 hours creating the world's highest house of cards.

Berg, who achieved his record as part of a maths project, actually became interested in card houses some years ago, and has spent many hours practising and working on different construction methods.

Scaffolding and an adjustable platform enabled him to get higher and higher, but although he was aiming for 100 storeys, he stopped at 75, simply because he got scared.

If it's hard work building a 14-foot 6-inch (4.42-metre) house, seeing it come crashing down is easy, even if potentially dangerous!

---

central Barcelona, Spain. It was built for José Battló in 1887 and extensively remodelled by Antonio Gaudí (1852–1926).

Barracks Great Britain's oldest purpose-built barracks are those at Berwick-on-Tweed, Northumberland which date from 1719 and are still in part-time use. The oldest building to be converted into barracks is New Town Fort, Gravesend, Kent which dates from 1322.

Flats

Tallest The 218 m *716 ft* Metropolitan Tower on West 57th Street, New York City, USA has 78 storeys, of which the upper 48 are residential.

The tallest purely residential block of flats is the 195 m *639 ft*, 70-storey Lake Point Tower in Chicago, Illinois, USA which has 879 apartments.

UK The tallest residential block in Great Britain is Shakespeare Tower, Barbican, City of London. The 44-storey block, topped out on 24 Mar 1969, is 127·77 m *419 ft 2½ in* high and contains 116 flats.

Largest complex The largest aggregation of private blocks are those forming the Barbican Estate, designed by architects Chamberlain, Powell and Son, in the City of London. The site occupies 16ha *40 acres* and includes of 2011 flats and parking for 2000 cars.

Hotels

Largest The Excalibur Hotel/Casino in Las Vegas, Nevada, USA is built on a 47·3 ha *117 acres* site. Comprising 4032 deluxe rooms and employing 4000 staff, the hotel also offers 11 food outlets, including 7 themed restaurants. It opened in April 1990 and cost $290 million.

Most capacious The Hotel Rossiya in Moscow, Russia, opened in 1967, has 3200 rooms and 5300 beds.

The Izmailovo Hotel complex in Moscow, opened in July 1980 for the XXIInd Olympic Games, consists of five, 32-storey blocks and can accommodate 9500 people in 5000 rooms.

UK Britain's largest hotel is the Grosvenor House Hotel in Park Lane, London, opened in 1929. It is eight storeys high, covers 1ha *2½ acres* and caters for over 100000 visitors per year in 470 rooms. The Great Room is the largest single hotel room measuring 55×40m *181×131ft* with a height of 7m *23ft*. Banquets for 1500 can readily be held there.

The London Forum Hotel in Cromwell Road is Britain's most capacious, accommodating 1856 guests in 910 bedrooms. It employs 330 staff and was opened in 1973. (◇ Tallest)

Tallest Measured from the street level of its main entrance, the 73-storey Westin Stamford in Raffles City, Singapore was topped out in March 1985 at 226·1m *742ft*. The $235 million hotel is operated by Westin Hotel Co. and owned jointly by DBS Land and Overseas Chinese Banking Corporation. During 1990/1 it received a £54 million facelift. Measured from its rear entrance level, the Westin Stamford Detroit Plaza, USA is 227·9m *748ft* tall.

Britain's tallest hotel is the 27-storey, 132m *380ft* tall London Forum Hotel. (◇ Largest)

Most expensive room The Penthouse Suite in the Fairmont Hotel, San Francisco, California, USA can be rented for $6000 per night, plus taxes. The price includes a round-the-clock butler and maid, and airport limousine service. The suite was built in 1927 atop the Fairmont's main building. It has an immense drawing-room with grand piano, dining-room accommodating up to 50, a two-storey circular library with the celestial constellation in gold on a domed ceiling, a games room, three bedrooms and four bathrooms with 24-carat gold-plated fittings.

UK The Presidential Suite of the Hotel Hyatt Carlton Tower, London costs £2000 per night inclusive.

Largest hotel lobby The lobby at the Hyatt Regency in San Francisco, California USA is 107m *350ft* long, 49m *160ft* wide, and at 52m *170ft* is the height of a 17-storey building.

Most remote The Garvault Hotel in Kinbrace, Highland is claimed to be the most isolated hotel in mainland Britain, being some 26km *16 miles* from its nearest competitor at Forsinard, also in Highland.

Hoteliers Following its acquisition of Holiday Inns North America in February 1991, Bass plc, the UK's top brewing company, took ownership of the world's largest hotel chain. The company now owns, manages and franchises 1645 hotels totalling 327059 rooms in 52 countries. (◇ Brewers)

The largest hotel and catering group in Britain is Forte plc, with over 8500 outlets world-wide in over 40 countries (including 850 hotels), serving 300 million customers annually. It employs over 100000 staff in the Group and had a turnover of £2·641 billion (as at year ending 31 Jan 1991).

Hotel move The three-storey brick Hotel Fairmount (built 1906) in San Antonio, Texas, USA, which weighed 1451tonnes, was moved on 36 dollies with pneumatic tyres over city streets approximately five blocks and over a bridge, which had to be reinforced. The move by Emmert International of Portland, took six days, 30 Mar–4 Apr 1985, and cost $650000.

Buildings for Working

Construction project The largest public works project of modern times is the Madinat Al-Jubail Al-Sinaiyah project in Saudi Arabia, started in 1976 for an industrial city covering 10 146 m² *109 211 ft²*. At the peak of construction, nearly 52 000 workers were employed, representing 62 nationalities and a total volume of 270 million m³ *9535 million ft³* of earth has been dredged and moved, enough to construct a 1 m *3 ft 3 in* high belt around the Earth at the equator seven times.

Urban development The world's largest urban regeneration project is London Docklands, which covers 22 km² *8½ miles²*. Over 2·5 million m² *27 million ft²* of commercial development space and over 17 000 new homes have been completed or are under construction, and £3·5 billion is being invested in new public transport. By 1992 £8 billion had been invested by the private sector, together with a further £1·1 billion by the London Docklands Development Corporation, with more than 40 000 jobs created since 1981. The London Docklands Canary Wharf development is also the world's largest commercial development. (⬗ also Tallest offices)

Industrial The largest multi-level industrial building that is one discrete structure is the container freight station of Asia Terminals Ltd at Hong Kong's Kwai Chung container port. The gross floor area completed by March 1993 was 660 607 m² *7 110 719 ft²*, and the total area on completion of the 15-level building, scheduled for the end of 1994, will be 865 937 m² *9 320 867 ft²*. Building plan measurements of 276×292 m *906×958 ft* and a height of 109·5 m *359·25 ft* will give a volume of 5 853 092 m³ *206 699 993 ft³*. The entire area in each floor of the building is directly accessible by 14 m *46 ft* container trucks and the building will have 26·84 km *16·67 miles* of roadway and 2609 container truck parking spaces.

Commercial In terms of floor area, the world's largest commercial building under one roof is the flower auction

Buildings demolished by explosives

The largest has been the 21-storey Traymore Hotel, Atlantic City, New Jersey, USA on 26 May 1972 by Controlled Demolition Inc. of Towson, Maryland. This 600-room hotel had a cubic capacity of 181 340 m³ *6 403 926 ft³*.

The tallest chimney ever demolished by explosives was the Matla Power Station chimney, Kriel, South Africa, on 19 Jul 1981. It stood 275 m *902 ft* and was brought down by the Santon (Steeplejack) Co. Ltd of Greater Manchester.

In Great Britain Controlled Demolition Group Ltd of Leeds successfully demolished eight blocks of high rise flats at Kersal Vale, Salford, Manchester on 14 Oct 1990. The total cubic capacity of the tower blocks was 155 000 m³ *5 474 000 ft³*.

Surveyors

The world's largest firm of surveyors and real estate consultants is Jones, Lang Wootton of London, with more than 63 offices in 24 countries and a staff of 3250. Valuations completed in 1992 amounted to $134 billion, resulting in a world-wide fee income of over $300 million.

building of the Co-operative VBA (Verenigde Bloemenveilingen Aalsmeer) in Aalsmeer, Netherlands. The building now measures 776×631 m *2546×2070 ft*, giving an area of 689 656 m² *5·27 million ft²* compared with an original area of 343 277 m² *3·7 million ft²*.

The world's most capacious building is the Boeing Company's main assembly plant in Everett, Washington, USA, at 5 564 200 m³ *196 476 000 ft³* on completion in 1968. Subsequent expansion programmmes have increased the volume to

13·4 million m³ *472 million ft³*, with a
further increase in volume of 50 per cent
due for completion in 1993 in preparation for production of the new 777 airliner. The site covers some 410 ha
1025 acres.

UK The largest building in Britain is the
Ford Parts Centre at Daventry, Northants,
covering an area of 142674 m² *1·5 million ft²*. It was opened on 6 Sep 1972 at
a cost of nearly £8 million and employs
1300 people.

Administrative The largest ground
area covered by any office building is
that of the Pentagon, in Arlington,
Virginia, USA. Built to house the US
Defense Department's offices, it was
completed on 15 Jan 1943 and cost an
estimated $83 million. Each of the outer-
most sides is 281 m *921 ft* long and the
perimeter of the building is about 1405 m
4610 ft. Its five storeys enclose a floor
area of 604000 m² *149·2 acres*, the corridors total 27 km *17 miles* in length and
there are 7748 windows to be cleaned.
There are 29000 people working in the
building. (⇨ Telephones and Facsimiles)

Building contractor The largest construction company in the United
Kingdom is Tarmac. The company had
sales of £3·2 billion in 1991 and, despite
a severely depressed housing market,
sold 9569 houses at an average price of
£77100. It employs 31734 staff. Peak
sales turnover was £3·7 billion in 1990.

Brickworks The largest brickworks in
the world is the London Brick Co. Ltd
plant at Stewartby, Beds. Established in
1898, the site now covers 90 ha *221 acres*
and has a weekly production capacity of
10·5 million bricks and brick equivalent.

Offices

Largest The largest rentable office
complex is the World Trade Center in
New York City, USA, with a total of
1114800 m² *12 million ft²* of rentable
space available in the seven buildings,
including 406000 m² *4·37 million ft²* in

**The Pentagon in Arlington, Virginia,
USA and a small section of the building's 27 km *17 miles* of corridors.**

Stair climbing

The 100-storey record for stair climbing
was set by Dennis W. Martz in the
Detroit Plaza Hotel, Detroit, Michigan,
USA on 26 Jun 1978 at 11 min 23·8 sec.

Brian McCauliff ran a vertical mile
(ascending and descending eight times)
on the stairs of the Westin Hotel, Detroit,
Michigan, USA in 1 hr 38 min 5 sec on 2
Feb 1992.

Steve Silva climbed the 1172 steps of the
Westin Peachtree Plaza Hotel, Atlanta,
Georgia, USA 39 times (a total of 45708
steps and a vertical height of 8130·1 m
26676 ft) in 9 hr 50 min 43 sec on 27–28
Jan 1992. He went down by lift each time.

The record for the 1760 steps (vertical
height 342 m *1122 ft*) in the world's tallest
free- standing structure, Toronto's CN
Tower, Canada, is 7 min 52 sec by
Brendan Keenoy on 29 Oct 1989.

The record for the 1336 stairs of the
world's tallest hotel, the Westin Stamford
Hotel, Singapore, is 6 min 55 sec by
Balvinder Singh, in their 3rd Annual
Vertical Marathon on 4 Jun 1989.

Geoff Case raced up the 1575 steps of the
Empire State Building, New York City,
USA on 16 Feb 1993 in 10 min 18 sec.

Sunil Tamang of the 7th Gurkha Rifles
climbed up the 50 storeys of Canary
Wharf, Britain's tallest building, in a time
of 7 min 3·44 sec on 22 Aug 1992.

each of the twin towers. There are 99 lifts
in each tower and 43600 windows comprising 182880 m² *600000 ft²* of glass. There
are 50000 people working in the complex,
which attracts 90000 visitors daily.

UK The largest single open-plan office
in the United Kingdom is that of British

Gas West Midlands at Solihull, Warks, built by Spooners (Hull) Ltd in 1962. It now measures 230×49m *753×160ft*, and can accommodate 2125 staff.

Tallest The tallest office building in the world is the Sears Tower, national headquarters of Sears, Roebuck & Co. in Wacker Drive, Chicago, Illinois, USA, with 110 storeys rising to 443m *1454ft*. Its total height is 520m *1707ft* following the addition of two TV antennae. Construction began in August 1970 and the building was topped out on 4 May 1973, having surpassed the height of the World Trade Center in New York City at 2:35 p.m. on 6 Mar 1973 with the first steel column reaching to the 104th storey. The gross area of the tower is 418050m² *4·5 million ft²* and it is served by 104 lifts and 18 escalators. It has 16100 windows.

UK The tallest office building in Britain is the Canary Wharf tower in London Docklands, at 243·8m *800ft*. The tallest of three towers at the development, the 50-storey building, resembling an obelisk, was designed by US architect Cesar Pelli and consists of nearly 16000 pieces of steel. It overtook the National Westminster tower block by 61m *200ft* when it was topped out in November 1990.

Most expensive According to *World Rental Levels* by Richard Ellis of London, the highest rents in the world for prime offices are in Tokyo, Japan at £119.05 ($186.9) per ft² per annum (December 1992), compared with a peak of £127.20 ($206.68) in June 1991. Added service charges and rates raised the price to £131.08 ($205.79) per ft² (December 1992) and £137.35 ($225.34) at June 1991.

The UK equivalent for the same period was £40 per ft² per annum for offices in London's West End, rising to £69.12 with service charges included.

Embassies The former Soviet (now Russian) embassy on Bei Xiao Jie, Beijing occupies the whole 18·2 ha *45 acre* site of the old Orthodox Church Mission (established 1728), now known as the *Beiguan*. The building was handed over to the USSR in 1949.

UK The largest embassy in Great Britain is that of the United States in Grosvenor Square, London. The Chancery Building alone, completed in 1960, has a usable floor area of 22008m² *236895ft²*, 600 rooms on seven floors and can accommodate 700 staff.

Largest exhibition centre The International Exposition Center in Cleveland, Ohio, USA is situated on a 76ha *188 acre* site adjacent to Cleveland Hopkins International Airport in a building measuring 232250m² *2·5 million ft²*. An indoor terminal provides direct rail access and parking for 10000 cars.

UK The National Exhibition Centre, Birmingham, W Mids, which opened in February 1976, consists of 11 interconnecting halls covering 125000 m² *1·3 million ft²* with a volume of 1168466 m³ *41·26 million ft³*.

Buildings for Leisure

Largest The open Strahov Stadium in Prague, Czech Republic, completed in 1934, could accommodate 240000 spectators for mass displays of up to 40000 Sokol gymnasts.

Football The Maracaña Municipal Stadium in Rio de Janeiro, Brazil, has a normal capacity for 205000, of whom 155000 can be seated. A crowd of 199854 was accommodated for the World Cup final between Brazil and Uruguay on 16 Jul 1950. A dry moat, 2·13m *7ft* wide and more than 1·5m *5ft* deep, protects players from spectators and vice versa.

Britain's most capacious football stadium was Hampden Park, Glasgow, Strathclyde, home of Queen's Park Football Club, opened on 31 Oct 1903. Its record attendance was 149547 on 17 Apr 1937, but the current Ground Safety Certificate limits the capacity to 55746. The lowest recent attendance was 313 on 27 Mar 1984 for a Scottish Second Division League match between Queen's Park and Cowdenbeath.

The Toronto SkyDome showing part of the world's first and largest fully retractable roof. Operating on a system of steel tracks and 54 drive mechanisms, the 3·2 ha *8 acre*, 209 m *674 ft* wide roof moves at a rate of 21 m *71 ft* per minute and takes 20 minutes to open or close. It is overlooked by the CN Tower, the world's tallest self-supporting tower.

(Photo: Allsport/Rick Stewart)

Largest wooden building

Between 1942 and 1943 sixteen Navy airship wooden blimp hangars were built at various locations throughout the USA. They are 317m *1040ft* long, 51·91m *170ft 4in* high at the crown and 90·37m *296ft 6in* wide at the base. There are only nine remaining, two at each of Tillamook, Oregon; Moffett Field and Santa Ana, California, and Lakehurst, New Jersey and one at Elizabeth City, North Carolina.

Covered The Aztec Stadium in Mexico City, opened in 1968, has a capacity of 107000 for football, although a record attendance of 132274 was achieved for boxing on 20 Feb 1993. Nearly all seats are under cover. (▷ Boxing)

The largest covered stadium in Great Britain is the Empire Stadium, Wembley, Middx, opened in April 1923 and scene of the 1948 Olympic Games and the final of the 1966 World Cup. In 1962–3 the capacity under cover was increased to 100000, with 45000 seated and the original cost was £1250000. Following a refurbishment programme and new safety guidelines the capacity has been reduced to 81500 all seated.

Indoor The $173-million, 83·2m *273ft* tall Superdome in New Orleans, Louisiana, USA covering 5·26ha *13acres*, was completed in May 1975. Its maximum seating capacity is 97365 for conventions and 76791 for football. A gondola with six, 8m *26ft* TV screens produces instant replays.

Largest roof The transparent acryl glass 'tent' roof over the Munich Olympic Stadium, Germany measures 85000m² *914940ft²* in area and rests on a steel net supported by masts.

The longest roof span in the world is 240m *787ft 4in* for the major axis of the elliptical Texas Stadium, completed in 1971 at Irving, Texas, USA.

Retractable roof The world's largest retractable roof covers the SkyDome, home of the Toronto Blue Jays baseball team, near the CN Tower in Toronto,

Canada, completed in June 1989. The roof covers 3·2ha *8acres*, spans 209m *674ft* at its widest point and rises to 86m *282ft*. The stadium itself has a capacity of 67000 for concerts, 53000 for American football and 50600 for baseball. (▷ Baseball)

Largest air-supported building The octagonal Pontiac Silverdome Stadium in Detroit, Michigan, USA is 220m *722ft* long, 159m *522ft* wide and has a capacity for 80638. The air pressure is 34·4kPa *5 lb/ft²* supporting the 4ha *10 acre* translucent 'Fiberglas' roofing. The main floor measures 123×73m *402×240ft* and the roof is 62m *202ft* high. The structural engineers were Geiger-Berger Associates of New York City, USA.

The largest standard size airhall is 262m *860ft* long, 42·6m *140ft* wide and 19·8m *65ft* high, first sited at Lima, Ohio, USA and made by Irvin Industries of Stamford, Connecticut, USA.

Largest amusement resort Disney World is set in 11332ha *28000acres* of Orange and Osceola counties, 32km *20miles* south-west of Orlando, Florida, USA. It was opened on 1 Oct 1971 after a $400 million investment.

Most attended Disneyland at Anaheim, California, USA (opened 1955) received its 250-millionth visitor on 24 Aug 1985 at 9:52a.m. and its 300-millionth visitor in 1989.

Largest pleasure beach Virginia Beach, Virginia, USA has 45km *28miles* of beach front on the Atlantic and 16km *10miles* of estuary frontage. The area covers 803km² *310miles²* with 157 hotels and motels and 2230 campsites.

The most visited pleasure beach in Britain is at Blackpool, Lancs, attracting 17 million visitors annually.

Pleasure piers *Earliest* The earliest date attributed to a seaside 'jetty' is 1560 at Great Yarmouth, Norfolk; it was replaced by a new structure in 1808 which was washed away in 1953. The first 'proper' piers were constructed at Weymouth, Dorset in 1812, and Ryde, Isle of Wight in 1813–14. There is some doubt over the Weymouth date, though records show that a new reinforced concrete pier (pleasure/commercial) replaced an old 274m *900ft* wooden pier in 1933. They both remain *in situ* today although greatly altered over the years.

Longest The longest pleasure pier in the world is Southend Pier, Southend-on-Sea, Essex. The original wooden pier was opened in 1830 and extended in 1846. The present iron pier is 2·15km *1·34miles* long and was opened on 8 Jul 1889. In 1949–50 the pier had a peak 5·75 million visitors. The pier has been breached by 14 vessels since 1830 and there have been 3 major fires.

Most The resort with the most piers was Atlantic City, New Jersey, USA with seven, though currently only five remain, dating from 1883 to 1912. Of British resorts, Blackpool, Lancs now has three piers, the North, Central and South.

Naturist resorts *Oldest* The oldest naturist resort is Der Freilichtpark in Klingberg, Germany, established in 1903. The oldest recorded naturist club was the Fellowship of Naked Trust in British India in 1891. The first site in Britain was 'The Camp' at Wickford, Essex, opened in 1924.

Largest The largest naturist site is Domaine de Lambeyran, near Lodève in southern France, at 340ha *840acres*. The centre Helio Marin at Cap d'Agde, also in southern France, is visited by around 250000 people per annum. The largest naturist site in Great Britain is that of the Naturist Foundation in Orpington, Kent, at 20ha *50acres*.

Spas Spas are named after the watering place in the Liège province of Belgium, where hydropathy was developed from 1626. The largest spa in terms of available accommodation is Vichy, Allier, France, with 14000 hotel rooms. The highest French spa is Barèges, Hautes-Pyrénées, at 1240m *4068ft* above sea level.

Fairs

Earliest The earliest major international fair was the Great Exhibition of 1851 in the Crystal Palace, Hyde Park, London, which in 141 days attracted 6039195 admissions.

Largest The site of the Louisiana Purchase Exposition at St Louis, Missouri, USA in 1904 covered 514·66ha *1271·76 acres* and there was an attendance of 19694855. Events of the 1904 Olympic Games were staged in conjunction.

Big wheels The original Ferris Wheel, named after its constructor George W. Ferris (1859–96), was erected in 1893 at the Midway, Chicago, Illinois, USA at a cost of $385000. It was 76m *250ft* in diameter, 240m *790ft* in circumference, weighed 1087tonnes and carried 36 cars each seating 60 people, making a total of 2160 passengers. The structure was removed in 1904 to St Louis, Missouri, USA and was eventually sold as scrap for $1800.

In 1897 a Ferris Wheel with a diameter of 86·5m *284ft* was erected for the Earl's Court Exhibition, London. It had ten 1st-class and 30 2nd-class cars.

The largest diameter wheel now operating is the Cosmoclock 21 at Yokohama City, Japan. It is 105m *344½ft* high and 100m *328ft* in diameter, with 60 gondolas each with eight seats. There are such features as illumination by laser beams and acoustic effects by sound synthesizers, 60 arms holding the gondolas, each serve as a second hand for the 13m *42·65ft* long electric clock mounted at the hub.

Britain's largest is that of 61m *200ft* diameter with a capacity for 240 people at Margate, Kent.

Roller Coasters

The maximum speeds and dimensions claimed for switchbacks, scenic railways or roller coasters have long been exaggerated for commercial reasons.

Oldest operating The *Rutschbahnen* (Scenic Railway) Mk.2 was constructed at the Tivoli Gardens, Copenhagen, Denmark in 1913. This coaster opened to the public in 1914, and has remained open ever since.

UK The oldest operating roller coaster in Britain is the *Scenic Railway* at Dreamland Amusement Park, Margate, Kent. This wooden coaster has contin-

ued in operation it opened to the public on 3 Jul 1920.

Longest The longest roller coaster in the world is *The Ultimate* at Lightwater Valley, Theme Park in Ripon, N Yorks. The track measures is 2·29km *1·42miles*.

Greatest drop and fastest The *Steel Phantom*, opened in April 1991 at Kennywood Amusement Park, West Mifflin, Pennsylvania, USA, has a vertical drop of 68·55m *225ft* into a natural ravine, with a design speed of 128km/h *80mph*.

Tallest The tallest 'above ground' is the 63m *207ft* tall *Moonsault Scramble* at the Fujikyu Highland Park, near Kawaguchi Lake, Japan, opened on 24 Jun 1983.

This is due to be overtaken by a non-looping coaster under construction at Blackpool Pleasure Beach, Lancs, which will rise to a design height of 71·6m *235ft* when it opens in 1994. It is designed by Arrow Dynamics Inc. of Clearfield, Utah, USA.

Highest loop The first loop of the *Viper* at Six Flags Magic Mountain, Valencia, California, USA is 42·7m *140ft* above the ground. Riders are turned upside-down seven times over the 1167m *3830ft* track.

The arms holding the 60 gondolas serve as second hands on the 100m 328ft diameter Cosmoclock 21 big wheel in Yokahama City, Japan.
(Photo: Rex Features/Roy Garner)

Greatest number The most roller coasters at any amusement park is 10 at Cedar Point Amusement Park in Sandusky, Ohio, USA. There is a choice of 2 wood and 8 steel track coasters.

Shopping Centres

The world's first shopping centre was built in 1896 at Roland Park, Baltimore, Maryland, USA.

The world's largest centre is the $1·1 billion West Edmonton Mall in Alberta, Canada, which was opened on 15 Sep 1981 and completed four years later. It covers 483 080m² *5·2 million ft²* on a 49ha *121 acre* site and encompasses over 800 stores and services, as well as 11 major department stores. Parking is provided for 20 000 vehicles for more than 500 000 shoppers per week. (⬦ Car parks)

The world's largest wholesale merchandise mart is the Dallas Market Center on

Stemmons Freeway, Dallas, Texas, USA, covering nearly 864 000 m² *9·3 million ft²* in six buildings. Together with two further buildings under separate management, the whole complex covers 70 ha *175 acres* and houses some 2580 permanent showrooms displaying the merchandise of more than 30 000 manufacturers. The Center attracts 760 000 buyers each year to its 107 annual markets and trade shows.

UK The largest shopping complex in Britain and Europe is the MetroCentre in Gateshead, Tyne & Wear. The site covers an area of 54·63 ha *135 acres* housing 340 retail units (including the largest single-storey branch of Marks and Spencer at 17 279 m² *186 000 ft²*), giving a gross selling area of 204 380 m² *2·2 million ft²*. The complex also includes a leisure centre, 10-screen cinema, a 28-lane bowling alley, parking for 12 000 cars and its own purpose-built British Rail station.

Britain's largest covered city centre shopping complex is Manchester's Arndale Centre, which has a floor area of 209 000 m² *2 246 200 ft²* (gross retail area of 110 270 m² *1 187 000 ft²*) including a car park for 1800 cars. The centre was completed in 1979 after three years' work and was the first such centre in Europe with its own radio station, called 'Centre Sound' Radio.

Longest mall The world's longest shopping mall measures 650 m *2133 ft* and is part of the £40 million shopping centre at Milton Keynes, Bucks.

Nightclubs and Restaurants

Nightclubs The earliest nightclub (*botte de nuit*) was 'Le Bal des Anglais' at 6 rue des Anglais, Paris, France. Established in 1843, it closed *c.*1960.

Largest 'Gilley's Club' (formerly 'Shelly's'), built in 1955, was extended in 1971 on Spencer Highway, Houston, Texas, USA, with a seating capacity of 6000 under one roof covering 1·6 ha *4 acres*.

In the more classical sense the largest nightclub in the world is 'The Mikado' in the Akasaka district of Tokyo, Japan, with a seating capacity of 2000. Binoculars can be essential to an appreciation of the floor show.

Lowest The 'Minus 206' in Tiberias, Israel, on the shores of the Sea of Galilee is 206 m *676 ft* below sea level. An alternative candidate has been the oft-raided 'Outer Limits', opposite the Cow Palace, San Francisco, California, USA. It has been called 'The Most Busted Joint' and 'The Slowest to Get the Message'.

Restaurants *Earliest* The Casa Botin was opened in 1725 in Calle de Cuchilleros 17, Madrid, Spain.

Largest The Royal Dragon (Mang Gorn Luang) restaurant in Bangkok, Thailand, opened in October 1991, can seat 5000 customers served by 1200 staff. Because of the large service area (3·37 ha *8·35 acres*), the staff wear roller skates not only to get from place to place but also to speed the service.

Highest The highest restaurant in the world is at the Chacaltaya ski resort, Bolivia, at 5340 m *17 519 ft*.

The highest in Great Britain is the Ptarmigan Observation Restaurant at 1112 m *3650 ft* above sea level on Cairngorm, (1244 m *4084 ft*) near Aviemore, Highland.

Restaurateurs The world's largest restaurant chain is operated by McDonald's Corporation of Oak Brook, Illinois, USA founded in 1955 by Ray A. Kroc (1902–84) after buying out the brothers Dick and 'Mac' McDonald, pioneers of the fast-food drive-in. By December 1992 McDonald's licensed and owned 13 093 restaurants in 60 countries. Their largest outlet is on the Will Rogers Turnpike in Vinita, Oklahoma, covering 2707 m² *29 235 ft²* and the most capacious is the 700-seat restaurant opened in Beijing, China on 23 Apr 1992. World-wide sales in 1992 were $21·9 billion.

Fish and chip restaurant The world's largest fish and chip shop is Harry Ramsden's at White Cross, Guiseley, W Yorks, with 140 staff serving 1 million customers per year, who consume 213 tonnes of fish and 356 tonnes of potatoes. The Glasgow Branch sold and served a record 11 964 portions of fish and chips on 17 May 1992.

Bars and Public Houses

Oldest There are various claimants to the title of Great Britain's oldest inn. A foremost claimant is 'The Fighting Cocks', at St Albans, Herts, an 11th-century structure on an eighth-century site. The timber frame of the Royalist Hotel, Digbeth Street, Stow-on-the-Wold, Glos has been dated to even earlier, it was 'The Eagle and the Child' in the 13th century and known to exist in AD 947. An origin as early as AD 560 has been claimed for 'Ye Olde Ferry Boat Inn' at Holywell, Cambs. There is some evidence that it antedates the local church, built in 980, but no documentation is available earlier than AD 1100. The 'Bingley Arms', Bardsey, near Leeds, W Yorks, restored and extended in 1738, existed as the 'Priest's Inn', according to Bardsey Church records of AD 905.

Largest The largest beer-selling establishment in the world is the 'Mathäser', Bayerstrasse 5, Munich, Germany, where the daily sale reaches 48 000 litres *84 470 pints*. It was established in 1829, demolished in World War II and rebuilt by 1955. It now seats 5500 people.

UK The largest public house in Great Britain is the 'Downham Tavern',

The Casa Botin restaurant in Madrid, Spain was opened in 1725.

(Photo: ALER)

Downham Way, Bromley, Kent, built in 1930. Two large bars (counter length 13·7 m *45 ft*) accommodate 1000 customers and the pub employs 18–20 staff.

Longest The world's longest permanent continuous bar is the 123·7 m *405 ft 10 in* long counter in the 'Beer Barrel Saloon' at Put-in-Bay, South Bass Island, Ohio, USA opened in 1989. The bar is fitted with 56 beer taps and surrounded by 160 bar stools. The 'Bar at Erickson's', on Burnside Street, Portland, Oregon, USA in its heyday (1883–1920) possessed a bar measuring 208 m *684 ft*. The chief bouncer, Edward 'Spider' Johnson, had an assistant named 'Jumbo' Reilly who weighed 23 st and was said to resemble 'an ill-natured orang-utan'. Beer was five cents for 16 fluid ounces. Longer temporary bars have been erected, notably for beer festivals.

The longest bar in Great Britain with beer pumps is the Long Bar at the Cornwall Coliseum Auditorium at

Largest casino

The Trump Taj Mahal, Atlantic City, New Jersey, USA, which opened in April 1990, has a casino area of 11 100 m² *2·75 acres.*

Tallest bar

Humperdink's Seafood and Steakhouse Bar at Dallas, Texas, USA is 7·69 m *25 ft 3 in* high with two levels of shelving containing over 1000 bottles. The lower level has four rows of shelves approximately 12 m *40 ft* across and can be reached from floor level. If an order has to be met from the upper level, which has five rows of shelves, it is reached by climbing a ladder.

Carlyon Bay, St Austell, Cornwall. It measures 31·8 m *104¼ ft* and has 34 dispensers. The Grandstand Bar at Galway Racecourse, Republic of Ireland, completed in 1955, measures 64 m *210 ft*.

The longest pub bar is the 31·7 m *104⅓ ft* counter at 'The Horse Shoe', Drury Street, Glasgow, Scotland.

Smallest The ground floor of 'The Nutshell' in Bury St. Edmunds, Suffolk is 4·82×2·28 m *15 ft 10×7 ft 6 in.* It was granted a licence personally by a thirsty King Charles II (1630–1685) when passing by. The 'Lakeside Inn', The Promenade, Southport, Merseyside has a floor area of 6·7×4·87 m *22×16 ft* and is 4·57 m *15 ft* in height.

'The Smiths Arms' in Godmanstone, Dorset has external dimensions of 12·04×3·5 m *39½×11½ ft* and is 3·65 m *12 ft* in height.

The pub with the smallest bar room is the 'Dove Inn', Upper Mall, Chiswick, London measuring 127×239 cm *4 ft 2 in×7 ft 10 in.*

Most remote The Old Forge public house at Inverie, Knoydart, Inverness-shire is 32 km *20 miles* by ferry and 38·6 km *24 miles* 'as the crow flies' from its nearest contender; there are no roads into or out of Knoydart.

Longest pub name 'The Old Thirteenth Cheshire Astley Volunteer Rifleman Corps Inn' in Astley Street, Stalybridge, Manchester has 55 letters. A very contrived name consisting of 12822 letters and 1487 words was added to Bugsy's Amazin Downtown Diner/Bar at King's Stables Road, Edinburgh, Scotland.

Shortest name In Great Britain the shortest name was the 'X' at Westcott, Cullompton, Devon, but in October 1983 the name was changed to the 'Merry Harriers'.

Commonest name There are probably about 630 pubs in Britain called the 'Red Lion'. Arthur Amos of Bury St Edmunds, Suffolk, recorded 21516 pub names from 1938 to his death in June 1986. His son John took over the collection, which now numbers 25202.

Highest When open, the 'Snowdon Summit' licensed bar and cafeteria is the highest, at 1085 m *3560 ft.* In Great Britain the 'Tan Hill Inn' (licensee Margaret Baines) is 528 m *1732 ft* above sea level. It is just in N Yorks on the moorland road between Reeth, N Yorks and Brough, Cumbria.

Most visits Bruce Masters of Flitwick, Beds has visited a staggering 26756 pubs and a further 1209 other drinking establishments since 1960, partaking of the local brew in each case where available.

Towers and Masts

Tallest Structures

The tallest ever structure in the world was the guyed Warszawa Radio mast at Konstantynow, 96 km *60 miles* northwest of the capital of Poland. Prior to its fall during renovation work on 10 Aug 1991 it was 646·38 m *2120 ft 8 in* tall or more than four tenths of a mile. It was completed on 18 Jul 1974 and put into operation on 22 Jul 1974. It was designed by Jan Polak and weighed 550 tonnes. The mast was so high that anyone falling off the top would reach their terminal velocity and hence cease to be accelerating before hitting the ground.

The World's Tallest Structures PROGRESSIVE RECORDS

Height m	ft	Structure	Location	Material	Building or Completion Dates
62	204	Djoser step pyramid (earliest pyramid)	Saqqâra, Egypt	Tura limestone casing	c. 2650 BC
91·7	300·8	Pyramid of Meidum	Meidum, Egypt	Tura limestone casing	c. 2600 BC
101·1	331·6	Snefru Bent pyramid	Dahshûr, Egypt	Tura limestone casing	c. 2600 BC
104	342	Snefru North Stone pyramid	Dahshûr, Egypt	Tura limestone casing	c. 2600 BC
146·5	480·9 [1]	Great Pyramid of Cheops (Khufu)	El Gizeh, Egypt	Tura limestone casing	c. 2580 BC
160	525 [2]	Lincoln Cathedral, central tower	Lincoln, England	lead sheathed wood	c.1307–1548
149	489 [3]	St Paul's Cathedral spire	City of London, England	lead sheathed wood	1315–1561
141	465	Minster of Notre Dame	Strasbourg, France	Vosges sandstone	1420–1439
153	502 [4]	St Pierre de Beauvais spire	Beauvais, France	lead sheathed wood	–1568
144	475	St Nicholas Church	Hamburg, Germany	stone and iron	1846–1847
147	485	Rouen Cathedral spire	Rouen, France	cast iron	1823–1876
156	513	Köln Cathedral spires	Cologne, Germany	stone	–1880
169	555 [5]	Washington Monument	Washington, DC, USA	stone	1848–1884
300·5	985·9 [6]	Eiffel Tower	Paris, France	iron	1887–1889
318	1046	Chrysler Building	New York City, USA	steel and concrete	1929–1930
381	1250 [7]	Empire State Building	New York City, USA	steel and concrete	1929–1930
479	1572	KWTV Television Mast	Oklahoma City, USA	steel	November 1954
490	1610 [8]	KSWS Television Mast	Roswell, New Mexico, USA	steel	December 1956
493	1619	WGAN Television Mast	Portland, Maine, USA	steel	September 1959
510	1676	KFVS Television Mast	Cape Girardeau, Missouri, USA	steel	June 1960
533	1749	WTVM & WRBL Television Mast	Columbus, Georgia, USA	steel	May 1962
533	1749	WBIR-TV Mast	Knoxville, Tennessee, USA	steel	September 1963
628	2063	KTHI-TV Mast	Fargo, North Dakota, USA	steel	November 1963
646·38	2120·6 [9]	Warszawa Radio Mast	Płock, Poland	galvanized steel	18 Jul 1974

[1] Original height. With loss of pyramidion (topmost stone) height now 137m 449ft 6in.
[2] Fell in a storm in 1548.
[3] Struck by lightning and destroyed 4 Jun 1561.
[4] Fell April 1573, shortly after completion.
[5] Sinking at a rate of 0·0047ft per annum or 12·7cm 5in since 1884.
[6] Original height. With addition of TV antenna in 1957, now 320·75 m 1052 ft.
[7] Original height. With addition of TV tower on 1 May now 449 m 1472 ft. Exterior is clad in limestone from the Empire Quarry, Indiana.
[8] Fell in gale in 1960.
[9] Fell on 10 Aug 1991 during renovation as a result the KTHI-TV mast regained its status as the tallest structure.

Lego tower

The world's tallest Lego tower was 19·90m *65ft 2in* high, consisted of 248756 bricks and was built by the people of Auckland, New Zealand on 22–23 Feb 1992.

The tallest Lego tower in Britain measured 15·01m *49ft 2⅞in* and was built in the forecourt of Waterloo Station, London on 29–30 Oct 1985.

Work was begun in July 1970 on this tubular steel construction, with its 15 steel guy ropes. It recaptured for Europe, after 45 years, a record held in the USA since the Chrysler Building surpassed the Eiffel Tower in 1929. After 1991 it was described by the Poles as the 'world's longest tower'.

As a result, the tallest structure is now a stayed television transmitting tower 628m *2063ft* tall, between Fargo and Blanchard, North Dakota, USA. It was built at a cost of about $500 000 for Channel 11 of KTHI-TV, owned by the Pembina Broadcasting Company of North Dakota, a subsidiary of the Polaris Corporation from Milwaukee, Wisconsin, USA. The tower was erected in 30 days (2 Oct to 1 Nov 1963) by 11 men of the Kline Iron and Steel Company of Columbia, South Carolina, USA, who designed and fabricated the tower. From then until the completion of the mast at Konstantynow it was the tallest structure in the world, and remained the second tallest between 1974 and 1991.

The tallest structure in Great Britain is the Independent Television Commission's mast north of Horncastle, Lincs, completed in 1965 to a height of 385m *1265ft* with 2·13m *7ft* added by meteorological equipment installed in September 1967. It serves Yorkshire TV and weighs 210 tonnes.

Tallest Towers

The tallest free-standing structure (as opposed to a guyed wire) in the world is the $63 million CN Tower in Toronto, Canada, which rises to 553·34m *1815ft*

5in*. Excavation began on 12 Feb 1973 for the erection of the 130000-tonne reinforced, post-tensioned concrete structure, which was 'topped out' on 2 Apr 1975. The 416-seat restaurant revolves in the Sky Pod at 351m *1150ft*, from which the visibility extends to hills 120km *74½ miles* distant. Lightning strikes the top about 75 times per annum.

The tallest tower built before the era of television masts is the Eiffel Tower in Paris, France, designed by Alexandre Gustav Eiffel (1832–1923) for the Paris Exhibition and completed on 31 Mar 1889. It was 300·51m *985ft 11in* tall, now extended by a TV antenna to 320·75m *1052ft 4in*, and weighs 7340 tonnes. The maximum sway in high winds is 12·7cm *5in*. The whole iron edifice, which has 1792 steps, took 2years, 2months and 2days to build and cost 7799 401 francs 31 centimes.

The tallest self-supported tower in Great Britain is the 329m *1080ft* tall National Transcommunications transmitter at Emley Moor, W Yorks, completed in September 1971. The structure, which cost £900000, has an enclosed room at the 264m *865ft* level and weighs with its foundations more than 15000tonnes.

The tallest tower of the pre-television era was the New Brighton Tower of 171m *562ft* built on Merseyside in 1897–1900 and dismantled in 1919–21.

Bridges

Oldest Arch construction was understood by the Sumerians as early as 3200 BC and a reference exists to the bridging of the Nile in 2650 BC.

The oldest surviving datable bridge in the world is the slab stone single-arch bridge over the River Meles in Izmir (formerly Smyrna) Turkey, which dates from *c.* 850 BC.

The clapper bridges of Dartmoor and Exmoor (e.g. the Tarr Steps over the River Barle, Exmoor, Somerset) are thought to be of prehistoric types although none of the existing examples can be certainly dated. They are made of large slabs of stone placed over boulders.

Bridge sale

The largest antique ever sold was London Bridge in March 1968. Ivan F. Luckin (d. 1992) of the Court of Common Council of the Corporation of London sold it to the McCulloch Oil Corporation of Los Angeles, California, USA for £1 029 000. The 10 000 tonnes of façade stonework were re-assembled at a cost of £3 million at Lake Havasu City, Arizona, USA and 're-dedicated' on 10 Oct 1971.

Bridge building

A team of British soldiers from 21 Engineer Regiment based at Nienburg, Germany constructed a bridge across a 8 m *26 ft* gap using a five-bay single-storey MGB (medium girder bridge) in a time of 7 min 12 sec at Hameln, Germany on 3 Nov 1992.

The Romans built stone bridges in England and remains of these have been found at Corbridge, Northumberland, dating to the 2nd century AD, and at Chesters, Northumberland and Willow-

The longest cycleway bridge is over the 17 railway tracks of Cambridge Station, Cambs. It has a tower 35 m *115 ft* high and two 50 m *164 ft* long approach ramps, and is 237·6 m *779 ft 6 in* in length.

(Photo: Woodward Staton Croft)

ford, Cumbria. Remains of a very early wooden bridge have been found at Aldwinkle, Northants.

Longest Cable suspension The world's longest bridge span is the main span of the Humber Estuary Bridge, Humberside, at 1410 m *4626 ft*. Work began on 27 Jul 1972, after a decision announced on 22 Jan 1966. The towers are 162·5 m *533 ft 1⅝ in* tall from datum and are 36 mm *1⅜ in* out of parallel to allow for the curvature of the Earth. Including the Hessle and the Barton side spans, the bridge stretches 2220 m or *1·37 miles*. It was structurally completed on 18 Jul 1980 at a cost of £96 million and was opened by HM the Queen on 17 Jul 1981.

The Akashi-Kaikyo road bridge linking Honshu and Shikoku, Japan was started in 1988 and completion is planned for 1998. The main span will be 1990 m *6528 ft* in length with an overall suspended length with side spans totalling 3910 m *12828 ft.* Two towers will rise 297 m *974 ft 5 in* above water level, and the two main supporting cables will be 1100 mm *43¼ in* in diameter, making both tower height and span world records.

The Seto-Ohashi double-deck road and rail bridge linking Kojima, Honshu with Sakaide, Shikoku, Japan opened on 10 Apr 1988 at a cost of £4·9 billion and 17 lives. The tolls for cars are £33 each way. The overall length of the Seto-Ohashi Bridge is 12 306 m *43 374 ft*, making it the longest combined road/railway bridge in the world. The Minami-Bisanseto Bridge on this link has the world's longest suspension bridge span, at 1100 m *3609 ft* for combined road/railway traffic.

Cable-stayed The longest cable-stayed bridge span in the world is the 530 m *1739 ft* Skarnsundet Bridge over the Trondheim Fjord in Norway, completed in 1991.

The Pont de Normandie, in Le Havre, France, planned for completion in 1994, will have a cable-stayed main span of 856 m *2808 ft.*

Currently the longest cable-stayed bridge in the UK is the £86 million Queen Elizabeth II Bridge on the M25 motorway over the river Thames at Dartford, Kent with a span of 450 m *1476 ft* and opened to traffic in 1991.

The United Kingdom's longest long-span cable-stayed bridge will be the second Severn Bridge, due for completion in 1996, with a main span of 456 m *1496 ft.* It will join Avon with Gwent.

Cantilever The Quebec Bridge (Pont de Québec) over the St Lawrence River in Canada has the longest cantilever truss span of any in the world, measuring 549 m *1800 ft* between the piers and 987 m *3239 ft* overall. It carries a railway track and two carriageways. Work started in 1899, and it was finally opened to traffic on 3 Dec 1917 at a cost of $Can22·5 million and 87 lives.

Great Britain's longest cantilever bridge is the Forth Bridge. Its two main spans are 521 m *1710 ft* long. It carries a double railway track over the Firth of Forth 47·5 m *156 ft* above the water level. Work began in November 1882 and the first

---

The longest covered bridge is that over the St John River at Hartland, New Brunswick, Canada. It measures 390·8 m *1282 ft* overall, and was completed in 1899.

(Photo: Images Colour Library/Robert Estall)

Longest viaduct

The longest railway viaduct in the world is the rock-filled Great Salt Lake Railroad Trestle, carrying the Southern Pacific Railroad 19 km *11·85 miles* across the Great Salt Lake, Utah, USA. It was opened as a pile and trestle bridge on 8 Mar 1904, but converted to rock fill in 1955–60.

test trains crossed on 22 Jan 1890 after an expenditure of £3 million. It was officially opened on 4 Mar 1890. Of the 4500 workers who built it, 57 were killed in various accidents. To commemorate the centenary of the Forth Bridge HRH Prince Edward switched on the ScottishPower floodlights on 7 Oct 1990. Consisting of over 1000 lights, they illuminate the bridge from span to span. Over 40 km *25 miles* of cable were laid, making the structure the biggest illuminated bridge in the world.

Floating The longest floating bridge is the Second Lake Washington Bridge, Evergreen, Seattle, Washington State, USA. Its total length is 3839 m *12 596 ft* and its floating section measures 2291 m *7518 ft*. It was built at a total cost of $15 million and completed in August 1963.

Railway The world's longest rail/road bridge is the Seto-Ohashi Bridge. (⇨ Cable suspension, above)

Britain's longest is the second Tay Bridge 3552 m *11 653 ft*, across the Firth of Tay at Dundee, Scotland, opened on 20 Jun 1887. It has 85 spans, of which 74—with a length of 3136 m *10 289 ft*—are over the waterway.

The 878 brick arches of the former London–Greenwich Railway viaduct between London Bridge and Deptford Creek, built in 1836, extend for 6 km *3¾ miles*.

Steel arch bridge The longest steel arch bridge is the New River Gorge bridge, near Fayetteville, West Virginia, USA, completed in 1977, with a span of 520 m *1700 ft*.

The longest in Great Britain is the Runcorn–Widnes bridge, Cheshire

opened on 21 Jul 1961, with a span of 329·8 m *1082 ft*.

Stone arch bridge The longest stone arch bridge is the 1161 m *3810 ft* long Rockville Bridge north of Harrisburg, Pennsylvania, USA, with 48 spans containing 196 000 tonnes of stone. It was completed in 1901.

The longest stone arch span is the Planen Bridge in Germany at 89·9 m *295 ft*.

The longest in the United Kingdom is the Grosvenor Bridge at Chester, Cheshire (61 m *200 ft*) completed in 1830. At the time of its construction this was the longest such span in the world.

Longest bridging The Second Lake Pontchartrain Causeway was completed on 23 Mar 1969, joining Lewisburg and Metairie, Louisiana, USA. It has a length of 38 422 m *126 055 ft*. It cost $29·9 million and is 69 m *228 ft* longer than the adjoining First Causeway completed in 1956.

Widest The widest long-span bridge is the 503 m *1650 ft* Sydney Harbour Bridge, Australia (48·8 m *160 ft* wide). It carries two electric overhead railway tracks, eight lanes of roadway and a cycle track and footway. It was officially opened on 19 Mar 1932.

The Crawford Street Bridge in Providence, Rhode Island, USA has a width of 350 m *1148 ft*.

The River Roch is bridged for a distance of 445 m *1460 ft* where the culvert passes through the centre of Rochdale, Greater Manchester and this is sometimes claimed to be a breadth.

Highest The highest bridge in the world is over the Royal Gorge of the Arkansas River in Colorado, USA, at 321 m *1053 ft* above the water level. It is a suspension bridge with a main span of 268 m *880 ft* and was constructed in six months, ending on 6 Dec 1929.

The tallest multispan cantilever construction viaduct in the United Kingdom is over the Dee on the A483 Newbridge Bypass, Clwyd. It is 57·3 m *188 ft* high. The Crumlin viaduct (61 m *200 ft*) held the United Kingdom record between 1857 until its demolition in 1966.

Railway The highest railway bridge in the world is the Mala Rijeka viaduct of Yugoslav Railways at Kolasin on the Belgrade–Bar line. It is 198m *650 ft* high and was opened on 1 Jun 1976. It consists of steel spans mounted on concrete piers.

The highest railway bridge in Great Britain is the Ballochmyle viaduct over the river Ayr, Strathclyde, built 51·5m *169 ft* over the river bed in 1846–8. At that time it had the world's longest masonry railway arch span of 55·2m *181ft*.

Road The road bridge at the highest altitude in the world, 5602m *18 380 ft*, is the 30 m *98·4 ft* long Bailey Bridge designed and erected by Lt Col. S.G. Vombatkere and an Indian Army team in August 1982 near Khardung-La, in Ladakh, India.

Tallest The tallest bridge towers in the world are those of the Golden Gate Bridge, which connects San Francisco and Marin County, California, USA. The towers of this suspension bridge extend 227m *745 ft* above the water. Completed in 1937, the bridge has an overall length of 2733m *8966 ft*. These will be over-topped after 60 years by the Akashi-Kaikyo towers (⇨ Cable suspension bridges, longest).

Lowest Britain's lowest bridge over a public road is just 1·61m *5 ft 3½ in* high and is under a railway line and next to a level crossing at Hoddesdon, Herts.

Longest ancient The greatest of ancient aqueducts was that of Carthage in Tunisia, which ran 141km *87·6 miles* from the springs of Zaghouan to Djebel Djougar. It was built by the Romans during the reign of Publius Aelius Hadrianus (AD 117–138). In 1895, 344 arches still survived. Its original capacity has been calculated at 31·8 million litres *7 million gal* per day.

The triple-tiered aqueduct Pont du Gard, built in AD 19 near Nîmes, France, is 48m *157 ft* high.

The tallest of the 14 arches of the Aguas Livres aqueduct, built in Lisbon, Portugal in 1784, is 65m *213 ft*.

Longest modern The world's longest aqueduct, in the non-classical sense of water conduit, excluding irrigation canals, is the California State Water Project aqueduct, with a length of 1329km *826 miles*, of which 619km *385 miles* is canalized. It was completed in 1974.

The longest bridged aqueduct in Great Britain is the Pont Cysylltau in Clwyd on the Frankton to Llantisilio branch of the Shropshire Union Canal, generally known as the Llangollen or Welsh Canal. It is 307m *1007 ft* long, and has 19 arches up to 36m *118 ft* high above low water on the Dee. Designed by Thomas Telford (1757–1834), it was opened in 1805. It is still in use today by pleasure craft.

Canals

Earliest Relics of the oldest canals in the world, dated by archaeologists *c.* 4000 BC, were discovered near Mandali, Iraq early in 1968.

The earliest canals in Britain were first cut by the Romans. In the Midlands the 17 km *11 mile* long Fossdyke Canal between Lincoln and the River Trent at Torksey, Lincs was built *c.* AD 65 and was scoured in 1122. It is still in use today.

Though the Exeter Canal was cut as early as 1564–6, the first wholly artificial major navigation canal in the United Kingdom was the 29·7km *18½ mile* long canal with 14 locks from Whitecoat Point to Newry, Northern Ireland, opened on 28 Mar 1742.

The Sankey Navigation Canal in Lancashire was opened in November 1757. It is 12·8km *8 miles* in length, with 10 locks.

Longest The longest canal in the ancient world was the Grand Canal of China from Beijing to Hangzhou. It was begun in 540 BC and not completed until 1327, by which time it extended (including canalized river sections) for 1781 km *1107 miles*. The estimated workforce *c.* AD 600 reached 5 million on the Bian section. Having been allowed by 1950 to silt up to the point that it was nowhere more than 1·8m *6 ft* deep, it is now, however, plied by vessels of up to 2000 tonnes.

225

A ship passes through the Suez Canal, the longest big-ship canal and also the busiest in terms of tonnage carried.

(Photo: Spectrum Colour Library/ D & J Heaton)

The Beloye More (White Sea) Baltic Canal from Belomorsk to Povenets, Russia is 227 km *141 miles* long and has 19 locks. It was completed with the use of forced labour in 1933 but cannot accommodate ships of more than 5 m *16 ft* in draught.

The world's longest big-ship canal is the Suez Canal linking the Red and Mediterranean Seas, opened on 16 Nov 1869. It is 161·9 km *100·6 miles* in length from Port Said lighthouse to Suez Roads, and 60 m *197 ft* wide. The canal was planned by the French diplomat Comte Ferdinand de Lesseps (1805–94) and work began on 25 Apr 1859. The workforce consisted of 8213 men and 368 camels.

The largest vessel to transit the Suez Canal has been SS *Settebello*, of 322 446 tonnes (length 338·43 m *1110 ft 4 in*; beam 57·35 m *188 ft 2 in* at a maximum draught of 22·35 m *73 ft 4 in*). This was southbound in ballast on 6 Aug 1986. The USS *Shreveport* transited southbound on 15–16 Aug 1984 in a record 7 hr 45 min. There are over 15 000 transits annually or some 41 per day.

Canals and river navigations in Great Britain amount to approximately 5630 km *3500 miles* with a further 290 km *180*

Longest artificial seaway

The St Lawrence Sea-way is 304 km *189 miles* in length along the New York State–Ontario border from Montreal to Lake Ontario. It enables ships up to 222 m *728 ft* long and 8 m *26·2 ft* draught to sail 3769 km *2342 miles* from the North Atlantic up the St Lawrence estuary and across the Great Lakes to Duluth, Minnesota, USA. The project, begun in 1954, cost $470 million and the seaway was opened on 25 Apr 1959.

Largest canal system

The seawater cooling system of the Madinat Al-Jubail Al-Sinaiyah construction project in Saudi Arabia is believed to be the world's largest canal system. It brings 10 million m³ *353 million ft³* of seawater per day to cool the industrial establishments. (⇨ Construction project)

miles being restored. Of these, 4000km *2500 miles* are inter-linked.

Busiest The busiest ship canal is the Kiel Canal linking the North Sea with the Baltic Sea in Germany. Over 45000 transits are recorded annually. The busiest in terms of tonnage of shipping is the Suez Canal, with nearly 338 million grt in 1992.

Longest irrigation The Karakumsky Canal stretches 1200 km *745 miles* from Haun-Khan to Ashkhabad, Turkmenistan. The 'navigable' length in 1993 was 800km *500 miles*.

Locks

Largest The Berendrecht lock, which links the River Scheldt with docks of Antwerp, Belgium, is the largest sea lock in the world. First used in April 1989, it has a length of 500m *1640ft*, a width of 68m *223ft* and a sill level of 13·5m *44ft*. Each of its four sliding lock gates weighs 1500 tonnes. The cost of construction was approximately BFr 12 000 million (£180 million).

The largest and deepest lock in the United Kingdom is the Royal Portbury Lock, Bristol, which measures 366·7×43m *1199·8 × 140 ft* and has a depth of 20·2m *66 ft*. It was opened on 8 Aug 1977 by HM the Queen.

Deepest The deepest lock, although not operational, is the Zaporozhe on the Dnieperbug Canal, Ukraine, which can raise or lower barges at 39·2m *128 ft*.

Highest rise and longest flight The world's highest lock elevator overcomes a head of 68·6m *225 ft* at Ronquières on the Charleroi–Brussels Canal, Belgium. Two 236-wheeled caissons are each able to carry 1370 tonnes, and take 22 minutes to cover the 1432m *4698 ft* long inclined plane.

The highest rise of any boat-carrying plane in Britain was the 68·6m *225 ft* of the 285m *935 ft* long Hobbacott Down plane on the Bude Canal, Cornwall.

The longest flight of locks in the United Kingdom is on the Worcester and Birmingham Canal at Tardebigge, Hereford & Worcester, where in a 4km *2½ mile* stretch there are the Tardebigge (30 locks) and Stoke (six locks) flights

which together drop the canal 78·9m *259 ft*.

The flight of locks on the 11·6 km *7¼ mile* stretch to Marsden of the Huddersfield Canal (closed in 1944), numbered 42.

Largest cut The Corinth Canal, Greece, opened in 1893, was 6·34km *3·94 miles* long, 8 m *26 ft* deep, had an average depth of cutting of 306m *1003 ft* over some 4·2km *2·6 miles*, and an extreme depth of 459m *1505 ft*. The Gaillard Cut (known as 'the Ditch') on the Panama Canal is 82m *270 ft* deep between Gold Hill and Contractor's Hill with a bottom width of 152m *500 ft*. In one day in 1911 as many as 333 trains each carrying 363 tonnes of earth left this site—a total of more than 120 000 tonnes of spoil.

Dams

Earliest The earliest known dams were those uncovered by the British School of Archaeology in Jerusalem in 1974 and at Jawa in Jordan. These stone-faced earthen dams are dated to *c.* 3200 BC.

Most massive Measured by volume, the Itaipú dam on the Paraná river, on the boundary between Brazil and Paraguay, has a volume of 29 billion m³ *1024 billion ft³*. Its barrage is 7·7km *4·8 miles* in length and 196m *643 ft* high at its highest point. The dam was estimated to have cost $18 billion to construct.

The most massive dam in Britain is the Northumbrian Water Authority's Kielder dam, a 52m *170 ft* high earth embankment measuring 1140m *3740 ft* in length and 5 300 000m³ *6 932 000 yd³* in volume.

Britain has longer low dams or barrages of the valley cut-off type, notably the Hanningfield dam, Essex, built from July 1952 to August 1956 to a length of 2088m *6850 ft* and a height of 19·7m *64½ ft*.

Largest concrete The Grand Coulee dam on the Columbia River, Washington State, USA was begun in 1933 and became operational on 22 Mar 1941. It was finally completed in 1942 at a cost of $56 million. It has a crest length of 1272m *4173 ft* and is 167m *550 ft* high. The volume of concrete poured was

Largest polder (reclaimed land)

Of the five great polders in the old Zuider Zee, Netherlands, the largest will be the Markerwaard, if it is completed, at 60000 ha *148 250 acre* (603 km² *231 miles²*). However, for the time being the project has been abandoned. Work on the 106 km *65 mile* long surrounding dyke began in 1957. The water area remaining after the erection of the dam (32 km *20 miles* in length), built between 1927–32, is called IJsselmeer, which is due to have a final area of 1262·6 km² *487½ miles²*.

Largest levees

The most massive ever built are the Mississippi levees, begun in 1717 but vastly augmented by the US Federal Government after the disastrous floods of 1927. These extend for 2787 km *1732 miles* along the main river from Cape Girardeau, Missouri, USA to the Gulf of Mexico and comprise more than 765 million m³ *1000 million yd³* of earthworks. Levees on the tributaries comprise an additional 3200 km *2000 miles*.

Concrete pumping

The world record distance for pumping ready mixed concrete without a relay pump is 1520 m *4986 ft*, set on the Lake Chiemsee, Bavaria, Germany sewage tunnels project in 1989.

8092000 m³ *10 585 000 yd³* to a weight of 19595000 tonnes.

Highest The highest will be the 335 m *1098 ft* high Rogunskaya earth-filled dam across the river Vakhsh, Tajikistan, with a crest length of only 602 m *1975 ft* and a volume of 71 million m³ *2·5 billion ft³*. Preparations for building started in 1976, and construction began in March 1981. The completion date was set for 1992

but owing to the financial situation with the break-up of the Soviet Union it has yet to be met.

Meanwhile the tallest dam completed is the Nurek which is 300 m *984 ft* high on the river Vakhsh, Tajikistan, of 58 million m³ *2·05 billion ft³* volume.

The rock-fill Llyn Brianne dam, Dyfed is Great Britain's highest dam, reaching 91 m *298½ ft* in November 1971. It became operational on 20 Jul 1972.

Longest The 41 m *134½ ft* high Yacyreta–Apipe dam across the Paraná on the Paraguay–Argentina border will extend for 69·6 km *43·2 miles*. It was due for completion in 1992.

The Kiev dam across the Dniepr, Ukraine, completed in 1964, has a crest length of 412 km *256 miles*.

In the early 17th century an impounding dam of moderate height was built in Lake Hongze, Jiangsu province, China, of a reputed length of 100 km *62 miles*.

The longest sea dam in the world is the Afsluitdijk stretching 32·5 km *20·2 miles* across the mouth of the Zuider Zee in two sections of 2·5 km *1·6 miles* (mainland of North Holland to the Isle of Wieringen) and 30 km *18·6 miles* from Wieringen to Friesland. It has a sea-level width of 89 m *293 ft* and a height of 7·5 m *24 ft 7 in*.

Strongest Completed, but not operational, is the 245 m *803 ft* high Sayano-Shushenskaya dam on the River Yenisey, Russia, which is designed to bear a load of 18 million tonnes from a fully-filled reservoir of 31 300 million m³ *41000 million yd³* capacity.

<hr>

Reservoirs

Largest The most voluminous man-made reservoir is the Bratskoe reservoir, on the Angara river in Siberia, Russia with a volume of 169·3 km³ *40·6 miles³* and an area of 5470 km² *2111 miles²*. It extends for 599 km *372 miles* in length with a width of 33 km *21 miles*. It was filled in 1961–7.

The world's largest artificial lake measured by surface area is Lake Volta, Ghana, formed by the Akosombo dam, completed in 1965. By 1969 the lake had filled to an area of 8482 km² *3275 miles²*, with a shoreline 7250 km *4500 miles* in length.

The completion in 1954 of the Owen Falls Dam near Jinja, Uganda, across the northern exit of the White Nile from the Victoria Nyanza marginally raised the level of that *natural* lake by adding 204·8 km³ *218·9 million acre-feet*, and technically turned it into a reservoir with a surface area of 69 484 km² *26 828 miles²*.

The $4-billion Tucuruí dam in Brazil had, by 1984, converted the Tocantins River into a 1900 km *1180 mile* long chain of lakes.

UK The most capacious reservoir in Britain is Kielder Water in the North Tyne Valley, Northumberland, which filled to 200 billion litres *44 billion gal* from 15 Dec 1980 to mid-1982, and which acquired a surface area of 1086 ha *2684 acres* and a perimeter of 43·4 km *27 miles* to become England's second largest lake.

Rutland Water has a lesser capacity (124·1 billion litres *27·3 billion gal*) and a lesser perimeter (38·6 km *24 miles*) but a greater surface area of 1254 ha *3100 acres*.

The largest wholly artificial reservoir in Great Britain is the Queen Mary reservoir, built between August 1914 and June 1925 at Littleton, near Staines, Surrey, with an available storage capacity of 36·96 billion litres *8·13 billion gal* and a water area of 286 ha *132 acres*. The length of the perimeter embankment is 6·33 km *3·93 miles*.

Deepest The deepest reservoir in Britain is Loch Morar, Highland, with a maximum depth of 310 m *1017 ft*.

Tunnels

Water-supply tunnel The longest tunnel of any kind is the New York City West Delaware water-supply tunnel, begun in 1937 and completed in 1944. It has a diameter of 4·1 m *13½ ft* and runs for 169 km *105 miles* from the Rondout reservoir into the Hillview reservoir, on the border of Yonkers and New York City, USA.

The United Kingdom's longest is the London Water Ring Main, construction of which started in March 1986 and was completed in February 1993. When fully operational, the 80 km *50 mile* long Ring Main will carry 1300 million litres *285 million gal* of drinking water a day — half of London's requirements.

Rail The 53·85 km *33·46 mile* long Seikan rail tunnel was bored to 240 m *787 ft* beneath sea level and 100 m *328 ft* below the sea bed of the Tsugaru Strait between Tappi Saki, Honshū and Fukushima, Hokkaidō, Japan. Tests started on the sub-aqueous section (23·3 km *14½ miles*) in 1964 and construction in June 1972. It was holed through on 27 Jan 1983 after a loss of 34 lives. The first test run took place on 13 Mar 1988.

Proposals for a Brenner Pass Tunnel between Innsbruck, Austria and Italy envisage a rail tunnel between 58–63 km *36–39 miles* long.

Construction of the £9 billion Channel Tunnel under the English Channel between Folkestone, Kent and Calais, France began on 1 Dec 1987 and was completed in the spring of 1993. Road traffic using the Shuttle is due to begin in early 1994 with through passenger trains starting in mid-1994. A land link was created between Great Britain and France when the service tunnel drives met under the channel on 1 Dec 1990. The length of the twin rail tunnels of 7·6 m *24 ft 11 in* diameter are 49·94 km *31·03 miles*.

Great Britain's longest main-line railway tunnel is the Severn Tunnel 7 km *4 miles*, linking Avon and Gwent, constructed with 76 400 000 bricks between 1873 and 1886.

Continuous subway The Moscow metro Kaluzhskaya underground railway line from Medvedkovo to Bittsevsky Park is *c.* 37·9 km *23·5 miles* long and was completed in early 1990.

Road tunnel *Longest* The 16·32 km *10·14 mile* long two-lane St Gotthard road tunnel from Göschenen to Airolo, Switzerland opened to traffic on 5 Sep 1980. Nineteen lives were lost during its construction, begun in autumn 1969, at a cost of 690 million Swiss francs (then £175 million).

The longest road tunnel in the United Kingdom is the Mersey (Queensway) Tunnel, joining Liverpool and Birkenhead, Merseyside. It is 3·43 km *2·13 miles* long, or 4·62 km *2·87 miles* including branch tunnels. Work commenced in December 1925 and it was opened by HM King George V on 18 Jul 1934. The total cost was £7¾ million. The 11 m *36 ft* wide four-lane roadway carries nearly 7½ million vehicles a year. The first tube of the second Mersey (Kingsway) Tunnel was opened on 24 Jun 1971, with the breakthrough of the second in 1972.

Largest The largest diameter road tunnel in the world is that blasted through Yerba Buena Island, San Francisco, California, USA. It is 24 m *77 ft 10 in* wide, 17 m *56 ft* high and 165 m *540 ft* long. Around 250 000 vehicles pass through on its two decks every day.

Hydro-electric irrigation The 82·9 km *51½ mile* long Orange–Fish Rivers tunnel, South Africa, was bored between 1967 and 1973 at an estimated cost of £60 million. The lining to a minimum thickness of 23 cm *9 in* gave a completed diameter of 5·33 m *17 ft 6 in*.

The Majes dam project in Peru involves 98 km *60·9 miles* of tunnels for hydro-electric and water-supply purposes. The dam is at 4200 m *13780 ft* altitude.

Sewerage The Chicago TARP (Tunnels and Reservoir Plan) in Illinois, USA when complete will involve 211 km *131 miles* of sewerage tunnelling. Phase I will comprise 175·4 km *109 miles* when complete. As of April 1993, 81·3 km *50·5 miles* are operational, 55·5 km *34·5 miles* are under construction, and the remaining 38·6 km *24 miles* are unfunded. The system will provide pollution control to the area and will service 3·9 million people in 52 communities over a 971 km² *375 miles²* area. The estimated cost for the project is $3·6 billion ($2·4 billion for Phase I, $1·2 billion for Phase II).

The Henriksdal plant in Stockholm, Sweden was the world's first major waste-water plant to be built underground. It was built between 1941 and 1971, and involved the excavation of nearly 1 million m³ *35 300 000 ft³* of rock.

It is now being enlarged, with the extension due for completion in 1997.

Bridge-tunnel The Chesapeake Bay bridge-tunnel extends 28·40 km *17·65 miles* from Eastern Shore, Virginia Peninsula to Virginia Beach, Virginia, USA. It cost $200 million and was completed after 42 months. It opened to traffic on 15 Apr 1964. The longest bridged section is Trestle C (7·34 km *4·56 miles* long) and the longest tunnel is the Thimble Shoal Channel Tunnel (1·75 km *1·09 miles*).

Longest and largest canal-tunnel The Rove tunnel on the Canal de Marseille au Rhône in the south of France was completed in 1927 and is 7120 m *23 359 ft* long, 22 m *72 ft* wide and 11·4 m *37 ft* high. Built to be navigated by sea-going ships, it was closed in 1963 following a collapse of the structure and has not been re-opened.

Great Britain The longest canal tunnel is the Standedge (more properly Stanedge) Tunnel in W Yorks on the Huddersfield Narrow Canal, built from 1794 to 4 Apr 1811. It measures 5·1 km *3 miles* in length and was closed on 21 Dec 1944. However, it is currently undergoing restoration.

The British canal system contained 84 tunnels exceeding 30 yd *27·4 m*, of which 49 are open today. The longest of these is the 2·88 km *1·79 mile* long Dudley Tunnel on the Birmingham & Black Country canals, although navigation is restricted.

Oldest navigable The Malpas tunnel on the Canal du Midi in south-west France was completed in 1681 and is 161 m *528 ft* long. Its completion enabled vessels to navigate from the Atlantic Ocean to the Mediterranean Sea via the river Garonne to Toulouse and the Canal du Midi to Sète.

Tunnelling The longest unsupported example of a machine-bored tunnel is the Three Rivers water tunnel, 9·37 km *5·82 miles* long with a 3·2 m *10 ft 6 in* diameter, constructed for the city of Atlanta, Georgia, USA from April 1980 to February 1982.

The National Coal Board record of 251·4 m *824·8 ft* for a 3·80 m *12½ ft* wide,

2m *6½ft* high roadway, constructed by a team of 35 pitmen in five days, was set at West Cannock, Staffs, No. 5 Colliery from 30 Mar–3 Apr 1981.

Specialized Structures

Advertising signs The highest is the logo 'I' at the top of the First Interstate World Centre building, Los Angeles, California, USA, a 73-storey building 310m *1017ft* high.

The most conspicuous sign ever erected was the electric Citroën sign on the Eiffel Tower, Paris. It was switched on on 4 Jul 1925, and could be seen 38km *24 miles* away. It was in six colours with 250 000 lamps and 90km *56 miles* of electric cables. The letter 'N' which terminated the name 'Citroën' between the second and third levels measured 20·8m *68ft 5in* in height. The whole apparatus was taken down in 1936.

The largest advertisement on a building measured 3879m² *41756 ft²* and was erected to promote Emirates, the international airline of the United Arab Emirates. It was located by the M4 motorway, near Chiswick, London and was displayed from November 1992 to January 1993.

The UK's largest permanent advertising sign is 86·56×25m *284×82ft*, produced by Heritage Hampers. It is sited on the roof of one of the stands at Ayresome Park, the home ground of Middlesbrough Football Club, in Cleveland.

Animated The world's most massive animated advertising sign is that outside the Circus Circus Hotel, Reno, Nevada, USA, which is named Topsy the Clown. It is 38·7m *127ft* tall and weighs over 40·8tonnes, with 2·25km *1·4 miles* of neon tubing. His smile measures 4·26m *14ft* across.

Hoarding The world's largest hoarding is that of the Bassat Ogilvy Promotional Campaign for Ford España, measuring 145m *475ft 9in* in length and 24m *78ft 9in* in width. It is sited at Plaza de Toros

---

The huge advertisement for Emirates, which was located next to the M4 motorway between central London and Heathrow airport in late 1992 and early 1993.

(Photo: Emirates Airline)

Airborne sign

Reebok International Ltd of Massachusetts, USA flew a banner from a single seater plane which read 'Reebok Totally Beachin'. The banner measured 15m *50ft* in height and 30m *100ft* in length, and was flown from 13–16 and 20–23 Mar 1990 for four hours each day.

Grave digging

It is recorded that Johann Heinrich Karl Thieme, sexton of Aldenburg, Germany, dug 23311 graves during a 50-year career. In 1826 his understudy dug *his* grave.

Monumental de Barcelona, Barcelona, Spain and was installed on 27 Apr 1989.

Illuminated The world's longest illuminated sign measures 60×20m *197×66ft*. It is lit by 62400W metal-halide projectors and was erected by Abudi Signs Industry Ltd of Israel.

The UK's longest illuminated sign is the name VOLVO LEX measuring 57·93m *190ft 1in*. It was installed in 1989 by Herbert & Sons Signs Ltd of Surrey at Lex, a Volvo dealer in Edgware Road, Colindale, London NW9.

Neon The longest neon sign is the letter 'M' installed on the Great Mississippi River Bridge. It is 550m *1800ft* long and comprises 200 high-intensity lamps.

The largest measures 64×16·7m *210×55ft* and was built for Marlboro cigarettes at Hung Hom, Kowloon, Hong Kong in May 1986. It contains 10700m *35000ft* of neon tubing and weighs 114·7tonnes.

An interior-lit fascia advertising sign in Clearwater, Florida, USA completed by the Adco Sign Corp in April 1983 measured 356·17m *1168ft 6½in* in length.

Barn The largest barn in Great Britain is one at Frindsbury, Kent. Its length is 66·7m *219ft* and it is still wholly roofed.

The longest tithe barn in Britain is one measuring 81m *268ft* long at Wyke Farm, near Sherborne, Dorset.

The Ipsden Barn, Oxon, is 117m *385½ft* long but 9m *30ft* wide (1074m² *11565ft²*).

Bonfire The largest was constructed in Espel, in the Noordoost Polder, Netherlands. It stood 27·87m *91ft 5in* high with a base circumference of 84·40m *276ft 11in* and was lit on 19 Apr 1987.

The largest in Great Britain was the Coronation bonfire at the top of Arrowthwaite Brows, Whitehaven, Cumbria, lit in 1902 with 812tonnes of timber, and 4550litres *1000gal* each of petroleum and tar. It was octagonal in shape and built to a height of 37m *120ft*, with a base circumference of 47m *155ft* tapering to 6m *20ft*.

Breakwater The world's longest breakwater is that which protects the Port of Galveston, Texas, USA. The granite South Breakwater is 10·85km *6·74miles* in length.

Great Britain's longest is the North Breakwater at Holyhead, Anglesey, which is 2·395km *1·488miles* in length and was completed in 1873.

Cemeteries *Largest* Ohlsdorf Cemetery in Hamburg, Germany is the largest cemetery, covering an area of 400ha *990acres*, with 965000 burials and 393000 cremations as at 31 Dec 1992. It has been in continuous use since 1877.

Great Britain's largest cemetery is Brookwood Cemetery, Brookwood, Surrey, owned by Mr Ramadan Güney. It is 200ha *500acres* in extent and has more than 231000 interments.

Tallest The permanently illuminated Memorial Necropole Ecuméncia, located in Santos, near São Paulo, Brazil, is 10 storeys high, occupying an area of 1·8ha *4·4acres*.

Chimneys *Tallest* The coal power-plant No. 2 stack at Ekibastuz, Kazakhstan is 420m *1377ft* tall. The diameter tapers from 44m *144ft* at the base to 14·2m *46ft 7in* at the top and it weighs 60000tonnes. It was built by the Soviet Building Division of the Ministry of Energy between 15 Nov 1983 and 15 Oct 1987 at a cost of 7·89 million roubles and became operational in 1991.

The cooling towers at Uentrop.

(Photo: Sgt G.E.M. Coffin)

The tallest chimney in Great Britain is one of 259m *850ft* at Drax Power Station, N Yorks. It has an untapered diameter of 26m *85ft* and also has the greatest capacity of any British chimney. Building started in 1966 and the chimney was topped out on 16 May 1969. The architects were Clifford Tee & Gale of London.

Most massive The world's most massive chimney in terms of internal volume was built by M.W. Kellog Co. for Empresa Nacional de Electricidad S.A at Puentes de Garcia Rodriguez, Spain. The chimney is 353m *1148ft* tall, contains 15570m³ *556 247ft³* of concrete and 1315tonnes of steel and has an internal volume of 189744m³ *6·7 millionft³*.

Oldest The oldest known industrial chimney in Britain is the Stone Edge chimney near Chesterfield, Derbys, built to a height of 16·76m *55ft ante* 1771.

Columns The tallest columns are the thirty-six 27·5m *90ft* tall fluted pillars of Vermont marble in the colonnade of the Education Building, Albany, New York State, USA. Their base diameter is 1·98m *6ft 6in.*

The tallest load-bearing stone columns in the world are those measuring 21m *69ft* in the Hall of Columns of the Temple of Amun at Karnak, opposite Thebes on the Nile, the ancient capital of Upper Egypt. They were built in the 19th dynasty in the reign of Rameses II *c.*1270BC.

Cooling towers The largest cooling tower is 180m *590ft* tall and is adjacent to the nuclear power plant at Uentrop, Germany. It was completed in 1976.

UK The largest in the United Kingdom are 114m *374ft* tall, 91m *300ft* across the base and are of the Ferrybridge and Didcot type.

Crematorium The largest crematorium in the world is at the Nikolo-Arkhangelskiy Crematorium, east Moscow, Russia with seven twin cremators of British design, completed in March 1972. It covers an area of 210ha *519acres* and has six Halls of Farewell for atheists.

The oldest crematorium in Great Britain was built in 1879 at Woking, Surrey. The first cremation took place there on 26

Longest fence

The dingo-proof wire fence enclosing the main sheep areas of Australia is 1·8 m *6 ft* high, 30 cm *1 ft* underground and stretches for 5531 km *3437 miles*. The Queensland state government discontinued full maintenance in 1982.

Tallest fence

The world's tallest fences are security screens 20 m *65 ft* high erected by Harrop-Allin of Pretoria, South Africa in November 1981 to protect fuel depots and refineries at Sasolburg from terrorist rocket attack.

Mar 1885, the practice having been found legal after the cremation of Iesu Grist Price on Caerlan Fields, Llantrisant, Mid Glamorgan on 13 Jan 1884.

Domes The largest is the Louisiana Superdome, New Orleans, USA, which has a diameter of 207·26 m *680 ft*.

The largest dome of ancient architecture is that of the Pantheon, built in Rome in AD 112, with a diameter of 43·2 m *142 ft*.

Britain's largest is that of the Bell Sports Centre, Perth, Tayside with a diameter of 67 m *222 ft*. It was designed by D.B. Cockburn and constructed in Baltic whitewood by Muirhead & Sons Ltd of Grangemouth, Central.

Doors *Largest* The four doors in the Vehicle Assembly Building near Cape Canaveral, Florida, USA have a height of 140 m *460 ft*.

Great Britain's largest are those of the Britannia Assembly Hall, at Filton airfield, Avon. The doors are 315 m *1035 ft* in length and 20 m *67 ft* high, divided into three bays each 105 m *345 ft* across.

The largest simple hinged door in Great Britain is that of Ye Old Bull's Head, Beaumaris, Anglesey, which is 3·35 m *11 ft* wide and 3·96 m *13 ft* high.

Heaviest The heaviest door is that of the laser target room at Lawrence Livermore National Laboratory, California, USA. It weighs 326·5 tonnes, is up to 2·43 m *8 ft*

thick and was installed by Overly Manufacturing Company.

Oldest Great Britain's oldest are those of Hadstock Church, near Saffron Walden, Essex, which date from *c.*1040 AD and exhibit evidence of Danish workmanship.

Earthworks The largest earthworks prior to the mechanical era were the Linear Earth Boundaries of the Benin Empire (*c.*1300) in the Edo state (formerly Bendel) of Nigeria. Their existence was first reported in 1900 and they were partially surveyed in 1967. In March 1993 it was estimated by Dr Patrick Darling that the total length of the earthworks was probably around 16 000 km *10 000 miles*, with the amount of earth moved estimated at 75 million m³ *100 million yd³*.

The greatest prehistoric earthwork in Britain is Wansdyke, originally Wodensdic, which ran 138 km *86 miles* from Portishead, Avon to Inkpen Beacon and Ludgershall, south of Hungerford, Berks. It was built by the Belgae (*c.*150 BC) as their northern boundary.

The most extensive single-site earthwork is the Dorset Cursus near Gussage St Michael, 8 km *5 miles* south-west of Cranborne, dating from *c.*1900 BC. The workings are 9·7 km *6 miles* in length, involving an estimated 191 000 m³ *250 000 yd³* of excavations.

The largest of the Celtic hill-forts is Mew Dun, or Maiden Castle, 3 km *2 miles* south west of Dorchester, Dorset. It covers 46·5 ha *115 acres* and was abandoned shortly after AD 43.

Flagpoles The tallest flagpole was erected outside the Oregon Building at the 1915 Panama-Pacific International Exposition in San Francisco, California, USA. It stood 91 m *299 ft 7 in* in height and weighed 47 tonnes, and was trimmed from a Douglas fir.

The tallest unsupported flagpole in the world is the 86 m *282 ft* tall steel pole weighing 54 400 kg *120 000 lb*, which was erected on 22 Aug 1985 at the Canadian Expo 86 exhibition in Vancouver, British Columbia. This supports a gigantic ice hockey stick 62·5 m *205 ft* in length.

Great Britain's tallest flagpole is a 68 m *225 ft* tall Douglas fir staff at Kew,

The world's tallest fountain, located at the town which takes its name from its centrepiece—Fountain Hills.

(Photo: MCO Properties Inc.)

Richmond-upon-Thames, Surrey. Cut in Canada, it was shipped across the Atlantic and towed up the river Thames on 7 May 1958, to replace the old 65 m *214 ft* tall staff erected in 1919.

Fountains The tallest is the fountain at Fountain Hills, Arizona, USA, built at a cost of $1·5 million for McCulloch Properties Inc. At full pressure of 26·3 kg/cm² *375 lb/in²* and at a rate of 26 500 litres/min *5850 gal/min*, the 171·2 m *562 ft* tall column of water weighs over 8 tonnes. When all three pumps are on, it can reach 190 m *625 ft*, if conditions are right (for example, no wind). The nozzle speed achieved by the three 600 hp pumps is 236 km/h *146·7 mph*.

Britain's tallest is the Emperor Fountain at Chatsworth, Bakewell, Derbyshire. When first tested on 1 Jun 1844, it attained the then unprecedented height of 79 m *260 ft*. In recent years it has not been played to more than 76 m *250 ft* and rarely beyond 55 m *180 ft*.

Fumigation The largest fumigation carried out was during the restoration of the Mission Inn complex in Riverside, California, USA on 28 Jun–1 Jul 1987 to rid the buildings of termites. It was performed by Fume Masters Inc. of Riverside. Over 350 tarpaulins were used, each weighing up to 160 kg *350 lb*, and the operation involved completely covering the 6500 m² *70 000 ft²* site and buildings—domes, minarets, chimneys and balconies, some of which exceeded 30 m *100 ft* in height.

Gasholders The largest gasholders are at Fontaine L'Evêque, Belgium, where disused mines have been adapted to store up to 500 million m³ *17650 million ft³* of gas at ordinary pressure.

The largest known remaining conventional gasholder is that at Simmering, Vienna, Austria, completed in 1968, with a height of 84 m *275 ft* and a capacity of 300 000 m³ *10·6 million ft³*.

Great Britain's largest was at the East Greenwich Gas Works. The No. 2 holder was built in 1891 with an original capacity for 346 000 m³ *12 200 000 ft³*. It was later reconstructed with a capacity of 252 000 m³ *8·9 million ft³*, a water tank 92 m *303 ft* in diameter and a full inflated

height of 45 m *148 ft*. However, it has been demolished in the meantime and the record is now held by the No. 1 holder, built in 1885, also at Greenwich. It has a capacity of 229 000 m³ *8·1 million ft³* and a height of 61 m *200 ft*.

The River Tees Northern Gas Board's 361 m *1186 ft* deep underground storage, in use since January 1959, has a capacity of 9300 m³ *330 000 ft³*.

Globe The largest revolving globe is a sphere 10 m *33 ft* in diameter, weighing 30 tonnes. It is called 'Globe of Peace' and was built between 1982 and 1987 by Orfeo Bartolucci from Apecchio, Pesaro, Italy.

Grain elevator The single-unit elevator operated by the C-G-F Grain Co. at Wichita, Kansas, USA consists of a triple row of storage tanks, 123 on each side of the central loading tower or 'head house'. The unit is 828 m *2717 ft* long and 30·48 m *100 ft* wide. Each tank is 37 m *120 ft* high and has an internal diameter of 9·14 m *30 ft*, giving a total storage capacity of 7·3 million hl *20 000 000 bushels* of wheat.

The world's largest collection of elevators are the 23 on Lake Superior at Thunder Bay, Ontario, Canada, with a combined capacity of 37·4 million hl *103·9 million bushels*.

Greenhouse Britain's biggest greenhouse complex is that adjacent to the power station at Drax, N Yorks, which yields some 5000 tonnes of fruit a year. The area under glass covers 144 836 m² *37·78 acres*.

Jetty The longest deep-water jetty is the Quai Hermann du Pasquier at Le Havre, France, with a length of 1520 m *5000 ft*. It is part of an enclosed basin and has a constant depth of water of 9·8 m *32 ft* on both sides.

Kitchen An Indian government field kitchen set up in April 1973 at Ahmadnagar, Maharashtra, then a famine area, daily provided 1·2 million subsistence meals.

Lamp-post The tallest lighting columns are the four made by Petitjean & Cie of Troyes, France and installed by Taylor Woodrow at Sultan Qaboos Sports

Maypoles

The tallest reported and erected in England was one of Sitka spruce 32·12 m *105 ft 7 in* tall, put up in Pelynt, Cornwall on 1 May 1974.

The permanent pole at Paganhill, near Stroud, Glos, is 27·5 m *90 ft* tall.

Mazes

The oldest datable representation of a labyrinth is that on a clay tablet from Pylos, Greece c. 1200 BC.

The world's largest hedge maze is that at Longleat, near Warminster, Wilts, designed for Lord Weymouth by Greg Bright, which has 2·72 km *1·69 miles* of paths flanked by 16 180 yew trees. It was opened on 6 Jun 1978 and measures 116×57 m *381×187 ft*.

'Il Labirinto' at Villa Pisani, Stra, Italy, in which Napoleon was 'lost' in 1807, had 6·4 km *4 miles* of pathways.

Britain's oldest surviving hedge maze is at Hampton Court Palace, Greater London. It was designed by George London and Henry Wise in 1690 and measures 68×25 m *222×82 ft*.

Complex, Muscat, Oman. They stand 63·5 m *208 ft 4 in* high.

Lighthouses

Tallest The steel tower near Yamashita Park in Yokohama, Japan is 106 m *348 ft* high. It has a power of 600 000 candelas and a visibility range of 32 km *20 miles*.

The tallest lighthouse in Great Britain is the 49 m *160 ft 9 in* tall Bishop Rock Lighthouse, 6·4 km *4 miles* west of the Isles of Scilly. Established in 1858, it was converted to automatic operation on 21 Dec 1992.

The tallest lighthouse in Scotland is Skerryvore Lighthouse south-west of Tiree, Strathclyde, which is 48 m *157·4 ft*

high. Established in 1844, there are 151 steps to the top of the tower.

Most powerful The lighthouse in Great Britain with the most powerful light is Strumble Head Lighthouse on Ynysmeicl (St Michael's Island), 4·8 km *3 miles* west of Fishguard, Dyfed, Wales. Its intensity is 6 000 000 candela and its range is 39 km *24 miles*, characterized by four white flashes every 15 seconds. Electrified in 1965, the lighthouse was converted to unmanned automatic operation in 1980.

Greatest range The lights with the greatest range are those 332 m *1089 ft* above the ground on the Empire State Building, New York City, USA. Each of the four-arc mercury bulbs has a rated candle-power of 450 000 000, visible 130 km *80 miles* away on the ground and 490 km *300 miles* away from aircraft.

Remotest The remotest lighthouse in Great Britain is Sule Skerry, 56 km *35 miles* off shore and 72 km *45 miles* north-west of Dunnet Head, Highland. Established in 1895, the lighthouse was made fully automatic in December 1982.

The remotest in the Republic of Ireland is Blackrock, 14 km *9 miles* off the Mayo coast.

Marquees

Largest A marquee covering an area of 17 500 m² *188 350 ft²* (1·7 ha *4·32 acres*) was erected by the firm of Deuter from Augsburg, Germany for the 1958 'Welcome Expo' in Brussels, Belgium.

Britain's largest marquee was one made by Piggot Brothers in 1951 and used by the Royal Horticultural Society at their annual show (first held in 1913) in the grounds of the Royal Hospital in Chelsea, London. It measured 94×146 m *310×480 ft* and consisted of 30 km *18¾ miles* of 91 cm *36 in* wide canvas covering a ground area of 13 820 m² *148 800 ft²*.

The largest single-unit tent in Britain covers a ground area of c. 12 000 m² *130 000 ft²* and was manufactured by Clyde Canvas Ltd of Edinburgh, Lothian.

Manor Marquees Ltd of Maidstone, Kent erected a 143 m *470 ft* long marquee in one lift on 16 May 1987.

The Offshore Europe 1983 exhibition at Bridge of Don, Aberdeenshire, Scotland was housed in 15 contiguous air tents covering 27964 m² *6·91 acres.*

Menhir The tallest known menhir is the 380-tonne Grand Menhir Brisé, now in four pieces, which originally stood 22 m *72 ft* high at Locmariaquer, Brittany, France. Recent research suggests a possible 22·8 m *75 ft* for the height of a menhir, in three pieces, weighing 250 tonnes, also at Locmariaquer.

Great Britain's tallest is one of 7·6 m *25 ft* at Rudston, Humberside.

Monuments *Tallest* The tallest monument is the stainless-steel Gateway to the West arch in St Louis, Missouri, USA, completed on 28 Oct 1965 to commemorate the westward expansion after the Louisiana Purchase of 1803. It is a sweeping arch spanning 192 m *630 ft* and rising to the same height. It cost $29 million and was designed in 1947 by the Finnish-American architect Eero Saarinen (1910–61).

The tallest momumental column is that commemorating the Battle of San Jacinto (21 Apr 1836), on the bank of the San Jacinto River near Houston, Texas, USA. Constructed from 1936–39, at a cost of $1·5 million, the tapering column is 173 m *570 ft* tall, 14 m *47 ft* square at the base, and 9 m *30 ft* square at the observation tower, which is surmounted by a star weighing 199·6 tonnes. It is built of concrete with buff limestone, and weighs 31 888 tonnes.

Great Britain's largest megalithic prehistoric monument and largest existing henge are the 11·5 ha *28½ acre* earthworks and stone circles of Avebury, Wilts, 'rediscovered' in 1646. The earliest calibrated date in the area of this Neolithic site is *c.* 4200 BC. The work is 365 m *1200 ft* in diameter with a 12 m *40 ft* ditch around the perimeter. It required an estimated 15 million man-hours of work.

The henge of Durrington Walls, Wilts, obliterated by road building, had a diameter of 472 m *1550 ft.* It was built *c.* 2500 BC and required some 900 000 man-hours.

The largest trilithons exist at Stonehenge, to the south of Salisbury Plain, Wilts, with single sarsen blocks weighing over 45 tonnes and requiring over 550 men to drag them up a 9 degree gradient. The earliest stage of the construction of the ditch has been dated to 2800 BC. Whether Stonehenge, which required some 30 million man-years, was built as a place of worship, sky worship, as a lunar calendar, an eclipse-predictor or a navigation school, is still debated.

Oldest The oldest scheduled ancient monument is Kent's Cavern, near Torquay, Devon, which is a cave site containing deposits more than 300 000 years old dating from the Lower Palaeolithic period.

Newest The newest scheduled ancient monument is a hexagonal pillbox and 48 concrete tank-traps south of Christchurch, Dorset, built in World War II and protected since 1973.

Mound The largest artificial mound is the gravel mound built as a memorial to the Seleucid King Antiochus I (reigned 69–34 BC), which stands on the summit of Nemrud Dagi (2494 m *8182 ft*), southeast of Malatya, eastern Turkey. It is 59·8 m *197 ft* tall and covers 3 ha *7·5 acres.*

The largest in Great Britain is Silbury Hill, 9·7 km *6 miles* west of Marlborough, Wilts, which involved the moving of an estimated 680 000 tonnes of chalk, at a cost of 18 million man-hours to make a cone 39 m *130 ft* high with a base of 2 ha *5½ acres.* Prof. Richard Atkinson, who was in charge of the 1968 excavations, showed that it is based on an innermost central mound, similar to contemporary round barrows, and it is now dated to 2745 ± 185 BC.

The largest long barrow in England is that inside the hill-fort at Maiden Castle near Dorchester, Dorset. It originally had a length of 550 m *1800 ft* and several enigmatic features such as a ritual pit with pottery, limpet shells and animal bones. (⇨ Earthworks)

The longest long barrow containing a megalithic chamber is that at West Kennet near Silbury Hill, Wilts, (*c.* 2200 BC) measuring 117 m *385 ft* in length.

Obelisk (monolithic) *Largest* The 'skewer' or 'spit' (from the Greek *obeliskos*) of Tuthmosis III brought from Aswan, Egypt by Emperor Constantius in the spring of AD 357 was repositioned in the Piazza San Giovanni in Laterane, Rome on 3 Aug 1588. Once 36m *118ft 1in* tall, it now stands 32·81m *107ft 7in* and weighs 455tonnes.

The unfinished obelisk, probably commissioned by Queen Hatshepsut *c*.1490BC and *in situ* at Aswan, Egypt, is 41·75m *136ft 10in* long and weighs 1168 tonnes.

The longest time a raised obelisk has remained *in situ* is that still at Heliopolis, near Cairo, erected by Senusret I *c*. 1750BC.

Tallest The world's tallest obelisk is the Washington Monument in Washington, DC, USA. Situated in a 43ha *106 acre* site and standing 169·3m *555ft 5⅛in* high, it was built to honour George Washington (1732–99), the first President of the United States.

The United Kingdom's tallest is Cleopatra's Needle on the Embankment, London, which at 20·88m *68ft 5in* is the world's 11th tallest. Weighing 189·35 tonnes, it was towed up the Thames from Egypt on 21 Jan 1878 and positioned on 13 September.

Piers The origin of piers goes back to the origin of man-made harbours. That at Caesarea reputedly had the first free-standing breakwaters in 13 BC. However, it is possible that the structures associated with the 'great harbours' of the ancient world in Crete, Alexandria and Carthage pre-date this.

The Dammam Pier, Saudi Arabia, on the Persian Gulf, is the longest in the world with an overall length of 10·93 km *6·79 miles*. It was begun in July 1948 and completed on 15 Mar 1950. The area was subsequently developed by 1980 into the King Abdul Aziz Port, with 39 deep-water berths. The original causeway, much widened, and the port extends to 12·8km *7·95 miles* including other port structures.

Seven Wonders of the World

The Seven Wonders of the World were first designated by Antipater of Sidon in the 2nd century BC. They were:– the Pyramids of Giza, the Hanging Gardens of Babylon, the Statue of Zeus at Olympia, the Temple of Artemis at Ephesus, the Tomb of King Mausolus, the Colossus of Rhodes and the Pharos of Alexandria.

Only the Pyramids of Giza still exist substantially today. They are to be found near El Giza (El Gizeh), south-west of El Qāhira (Cairo) in Egypt. They were built by three Fourth Dynasty Egyptian Pharaohs: Khwfw (Khufu or Cheops), Kha-f-Ra (Khafre, Khefren or Chepren) and Menkaure (Mycerinus). The great pyramid (The 'Horizon of Khufu') was finished under Rededef *c*.2580 BC. Its original height was 146·7m *481ft 3in* (now, since the loss of its topmost stones and the pyramidion, reduced to 137·5m *451ft 1in*) with a base line of 230m *756ft*, thus covering slightly more than 5ha *13acres*. It has been estimated that a permanent work force of 4000 required 30 years to manoeuvre into position the 2300000 limestone blocks averaging 2½tonnes each, totalling about 5840000 tonnes and a volume of 2595000m³ *91640000ft³*. Some blocks weigh 15tonnes. A costing exercise published in December 1974 indicated that the work would require 405 men six years at a cost of $1·13billion.

Of the other six wonders only fragments remain of the Temple of Artemis (Diana) of the Ephesians, built *c*.350BC at Ephesus, Turkey (destroyed by the Goths in AD262), and of the Tomb of King Mausolus of Caria, built at Halicarnassus, now Bodrum, Turkey, *c*.325BC.

No trace remains of:– the Hanging Gardens of Semiramis, at Babylon, Iraq *c*.600BC; the statue of Zeus (Jupiter), by Phidias (5th century BC) at Olympia, Greece (lost in a fire at Istanbul) in marble, gold and ivory and 12m *40ft* tall; the figure of the god Helios (Apollo), a 35m *117ft* tall statue sculptured 292–280BC, by Chares of Lindus (destroyed by an earthquake in 224BC); and the world's earliest lighthouse, 122m *400ft* tall built by Sostratus of Cnidus (*c*.270BC) as a pyramid shaped tower of white marble, on the island of Pharos (Greek, *pharos*=lighthouse), off the coast of El Iskandariya (Alexandria), Egypt (destroyed by earthquake in AD1375).

Scarecrow

The tallest scarecrow was 'Stretch II', constructed by the Speers family of Paris, Ontario, Canada and a crew of 15 at the Paris Fall Fair on 2 Sep 1989. It measured 31·56m *103ft 6¾in* in height.

Great Britain's longest is the Bee Ness Jetty, completed in 1930, which stretches 2500m *8200ft* along the west bank of the river Medway, 8·8km *5½ miles* below Rochester, at Kingsnorth, Kent.

Promenade The longest covered promenade is the Long Corridor in the Summer Palace in Beijing, China, running for 728m *2388ft*. It is built entirely of wood and divided by crossbeams into 273 sections. These crossbeams, as well as the ceiling and side pillars, have over 10000 paintings of famous Chinese landscapes, depicting episodes from folk tales flowers and birds.

Pyramids *Largest* The largest pyramid, and the largest monument ever constructed, is the Quetzalcóatl at Cholula de Rivadabia, 101km *63 miles* south-east of Mexico City. It is 54m *177ft* tall and its base covers an area of nearly 18·2ha *45 acres*. Its total volume has been estimated at 3·3 million m³ *4·3 milion yd³* compared with the current volume of 2·4 million m³ *3·1 million yd³* for the

The Stickney Water Reclamation Plant in Chicago. There are 166 tanks of different sizes serving specific purposes on the 231 ha *570 acre* site, which also has its own railway with 50 km *30 miles* of track.

Pyramid of Khufu or Cheops. (⇔ Seven Wonders of the World)

The largest known single block in pyramid-building is from the Third Pyramid (Pyramid of Mycerinus) at El Gizeh, Egypt and weighs 290tonnes.

Oldest The Djoser Step Pyramid at Saqqâra, Egypt, was constructed by Imhotep to a height of 62m *204ft*, and originally had a Tura limestone casing dating from *c.*2900BC.

The oldest New World pyramid is that on the island of La Venta in south-eastern Mexico built by the Olmec people *c.*800BC. It stands 30m *100ft* tall with a base dimension of 128m *420ft*.

Scaffolding The tallest scaffolding was erected by SGB Contracts Division of Surrey at 53·24m *174ft 8in* high. It was erected around the statue of the Albert Memorial in Kensington, London in 1990 and will be there until restoration work has been completed. It was free-standing and cladded, and could have resisted wind forces of up to 90mph *145km/h*.

Sewage works The Stickney Water Reclamation Plant, Stickney, Illinois, USA (formerly the West-Southwest Sewage Treatment Works) began operation in 1939 on a 231ha *570acre* site in suburban Chicago, Illinois, and serves an area containing 2380000 people. A total of 651 staff are employed at the plant, which treated an average of 3028 million litres *666 million gal* of waste per day in 1992.

UK The largest full treatment works in Britain and Europe is the Beckton Works, east London, which serves a 2966000 population and handles a daily flow of 941 million litres *207 million gal* in a tank capacity of 21 400 m³ *757000ft³*.

Snow and ice constructions A snow palace 26·5m *87ft* high, one of four structures which together spanned 214·2m *702 ft 8in*, was unveiled on 7 Feb 1987 at Asahikawa City, Hokkaidō, Japan.

The world's largest ice construction was the ice palace built in January 1986, using 9000 blocks of ice, at St Paul, Minnesota, USA during the Winter Carnival. Designed by Ellerbe Associates Inc., it was 37×27m *120×90ft* and stood

39·24m *128ft 9in* high—the equivalent of a 13-storey building.

Snowman The tallest stood 23·22m *76ft 2in* high and was named Prince William. It was built by Philip and Colleen Price,

co-ordinators, with 10 others at Prince William Sound Community College, Valdez, Alaska, USA on 2 Apr 1992.

Stairway The longest service staircase is for the Niesenbahn funicular near Spiez,

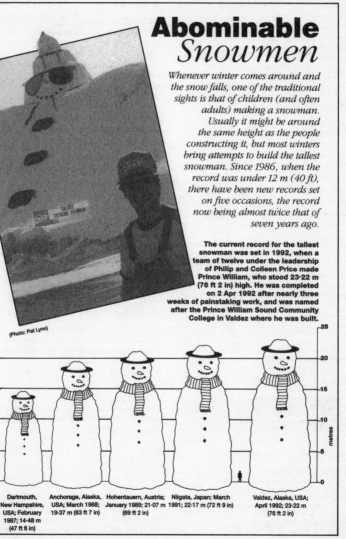

Abominable
Snowmen

Whenever winter comes around and the snow falls, one of the traditional sights is that of children (and often adults) making a snowman. Usually it might be around the same height as the people constructing it, but most winters bring attempts to build the tallest snowman. Since 1986, when the record was under 12 m (40 ft), there have been new records set on five occasions, the record now being almost twice that of seven years ago.

The current record for the tallest snowman was set in 1992, when a team of twelve under the leadership of Philip and Colleen Price made Prince William, who stood 23·22 m (76 ft 2 in) high. He was completed on 2 Apr 1992 after nearly three weeks of painstaking work, and was named after the Prince William Sound Community College in Valdez where he was built.

(Photo: Pat Lynn)

Dartmouth, New Hampshire, USA; February 1987; 14·48 m (47 ft 6 in)

Anchorage, Alaska, USA; March 1988; 19·37 m (63 ft 7 in)

Hohentauern, Austria; January 1989; 21·07 m (69 ft 2 in)

Niigata, Japan; March 1991; 22·17 m (72 ft 9 in)

Valdez, Alaska, USA; April 1992; 23·22 m (76 ft 2 in)

metres

241

Switzerland, which rises to 2365m *7759ft*. It has 11674 steps and a bannister.

The stone-cut Tai Shan temple stairs of 6600 steps in the Shandong Mountains, China ascend 1428m *4700ft*.

The longest stairs in Great Britain are those from the transformer gallery to the surface, 324m *1065ft*, in the Cruachan Power Station, Argyll. They have 1420 steps and the plant's work-study unit allows 27min 41·4sec for the ascent.

Spiral The tallest spiral staircase is on the outside of the chimney Bobila Almirall located in Angel Sallent in Terrasa, Barcelona, Spain. Built by Mariano Masana i Ribas in 1956, it is 63·2 m *207ft* high and has 217 steps.

The longest spiral staircase is one 336m *1103ft* deep with 1520 steps installed in the Mapco–White–County Coal Mine, Carmi, Illinois, USA by Systems Control Inc. in May 1981.

Statues *Longest* Near Bamiyan, Afghanistan there are the remains of the recumbent Sakya Buddha, built of plastered rubble, which was 'about 305m' *1000ft* long and is believed to date from the 3rd or 4th century AD.

Tallest A bronze statue of Buddha 120m *394ft* high was completed in Tokyo, Japan in January 1993. It is 35m *115ft* wide and weighs 100tonnes. The statue took seven years to make, and was a joint Japanese–Taiwanese project.

The statue of Maitreya, which stands 26m *85ft* high, is carved out of a single

---

Largest swing

A glider swing 9·1m *30ft* high was constructed by Kenneth R. Mack, Langenburg, Saskatchewan, Canada for Uncle Herb's Amusements in 1986. The swing is capable of taking its four riders to a height of 7·6m *25ft* off the ground.

Tallest totem pole

A 52·73m *173ft* tall pole was raised on 6 Jun 1973 at Alert Bay, British Columbia, Canada. It tells the story of the Kwakiutl and took 36 man-weeks to carve.

piece of white sandalwood tree. It is located at the Lama Temple (Yonghegong), built in 1649, in the north-west of Beijing. The Imperial Court allowed two years for the carving of the statue in the Pavilion House of Ten Thousand Fortunes and finished the project in 1750.

Tidal river barrier The largest tidal river barrier is the Oosterscheldedam, a storm surge barrier in the south-western corner of the Netherlands. It has 65 concrete piers and 62 steel gates, and covers a total length of 9km *5½ miles*. It was opened by HM Queen Beatrix on 4 Oct 1986.

Tombs The Mount Li tomb, the burial place of Qin Shi Huangdi, the 1st Emperor of Qin, dates to 221BC and is situated 40km *25 miles* east of Xianyang, China. The two walls surrounding the grave measure 2173×974m *7129× 3195ft* and 685×578m *2247×1896ft*. Several pits in the tomb contained a vast army of an estimated 8000 life-size terracotta soldiers.

A tomb housing 180000 World War II dead on Okinawa, Japan was enlarged in 1985 to accommodate another 9000 bodies thought to be buried on the island.

Vats *Largest* The largest wooden wine cask in the world is the Heidelberg Tun, completed in 1751, in the cellar of the Friedrichsbau, Heidelberg, Germany. Its capacity is 221726 litres *48 773 gal*.

'Strongbow', used by H.P. Bulmer Ltd, the English cider-makers of Hereford, measures 19·65m *64½ft* in height and 23m *75½ft* in diameter, with a capacity of 7·41million litres *1·63 million gal*.

Oldest The world's oldest known vat is still in use at Hugel et Fils (founded 1639) in Riquewihr, Haût-Rhin, France. Twelve generations of the family have used it since 1715.

Walls *Longest* The Great Wall of China is the longest in the world and has a main-line length of 3460km *2150 miles* —nearly three times the length of Britain. Completed during the reign of Qin Shi Huangdi (221–210BC), it has a further 2860km *1780 miles* of branches and spurs. Its height varies from 4·5–12m *15–39ft* and it is up to 9·8m

The walls of the Great Tower or Donjon of Flint Castle, Clwyd, built in 1277–80, are 7 m *23 ft* thick.

Indoor waterfall The tallest indoor waterfall measures 34·75 m *114 ft* in height and is backed by 840 m² *9000 ft²* of marble. It is situated in the lobby of Greektown's International Center Building, Detroit, Michigan, USA.

Water tower The Waterspheroid at Edmond, Oklahoma, USA, built in 1986, rises to a height of 66·5 m *218 ft*, and has a capacity of 1 893 000 litres *416 000 gal*. The tower was manufactured by Chicago Bridge and Iron.

Waterwheel The Mohammadieh Noria wheel at Hamah, Syria has a diameter of 40 m *131 ft* and dates from Roman times.

The largest waterwheel in Great Britain is the 15·36 m *50 ft 5 in* diameter wheel built in 1870 at Caernarfon, Gwynedd, and 1·5 m *5 ft* in width. It can be seen at the Welsh Slate Museum at Padarn Country Park, Llanberis, Gwynedd.

The largest in the British Isles is the Lady Isabella at Laxey, Isle of Man with a circumference of 69·5 m *228 ft* and an axle weight of 10 tonnes. It was completed on 24 Sep 1854 for draining the local lead mine but has not been used since 1929.

Windows The largest sheet of glass ever manufactured was one of 50 m² *540 ft²*, or 20 m×2·5 m *65 ft 7 in×8 ft 2¼ in*, exhibited by the Saint Gobin Co. in France at the *Journées Internationales de Miroiterie* in March 1958.

The largest single windows in the world are those in the Palace of Industry and Technology at Rondpoint de la Défense, Paris, France, with an extreme width of 218 m *715 ft* and a maximum height of 50 m *164 ft*.

The United Kingdom record was a sheet made by Pilkington of St Helens, Merseyside for the Festival of Britain in

32 ft thick. It runs from Shanhaiguan, on the Gulf of Bohai, to Yumenguan and Yangguan, and was kept in repair up to the 16th century. Some 51·5 km *32 miles* of the wall have been destroyed since 1966 and part of the wall was blown up to make way for a dam in July 1979. On 6 Mar 1985 a report from China stated that a five-year survey proved that its total length was once 9980 km *6200 miles*. It was reported in October 1990 that after two years of exertion Lin Youdian had become the first person to walk its entire length.

The longest of the Roman walls in Britain was the 4·5–6 m *15–20 ft* tall Hadrian's Wall, built AD 122–26. It crossed the Tyne-Solway isthmus for 118 km *73½ miles* from Bowness-on-Solway, Cumbria, to Wallsend-on-Tyne, Tyne & Wear, and was abandoned in AD 383.

Thickest Urnammu's city walls at Ur (now Muqayyar, Iraq), destroyed by the Elamites in 2006 BC, were 27 m *88 ft* thick and made of mud brick.

1951, measuring 2·5×15·2 m *8 ft 2¼ in ×49 ft 10½ in.*

The largest sheet of tempered (safety) glass ever processed was one made by P.T. Sinar Rasa Kencana of Jakarta, Indonesia, which measures 7 m *23 ft* long by 2·13 m *7 ft* wide and is 12 mm *½ in* thick.

Stained glass The tallest piece of stained glass is the 41·14 m *135 ft* high back-lit glass mural installed in 1979 in the atrium of the Ramada Hotel, Dubai. (⇨ Religions, Stained glass)

The largest single stained-glass window in the UK is one with an area of 746·9 m² *8039 ft²*, designed by Brian Clarke and installed at the Victoria Quarter, Leeds, W Yorks in 1990. (⇨ Religions, Stained glass)

Wine cellar The cellars at Paarl of the Ko-operative Wijnbouwers Vereeniging, known as KWV, in Cape Province, in the centre of the wine-growing district of South Africa, cover an area of 10 ha *25 acres* and have a capacity of 136 million litres *30 million gal.*

Ziggurat The largest ziggurat (from the Assyrian *ziqqurati*, = summit, height) ever built was that of the Elamite King Untas, *c.* 1250 BC. known as the Ziggurat of Choga Zambil, 30 km *18·6 miles* from Haft Tepe, Iran. The outer base was 105×105 m *344×344 ft* and the fifth 'box' 28×28 m *92×92 ft*, nearly 50 m *164 ft* above.

The largest partially surviving ziggurat is the Ziggurat of Ur (now Muqayyar, Iraq) with a base 61×45·7 m *200×150 ft*, built to three storeys and surmounted by a summit temple. The first and part of the second storeys now survive to a height of 18 m *60 ft*. It was built in the reign of Ur-nammu (*c.* 2113–2096 BC).

Transport

- Ships
- Coaching
- Bicycles
- Motorcycles
- Motorcars
- Roads
- Railways
- Aviation

Ships

Aborigines are thought to have been able to cross the Torres Strait from New Guinea to Australia, then at least 70 km *43½ miles* across, as early as *c.* 55 000 BC. It is believed that they may have used double canoes.

The earliest surviving vessel is a pine dug-out found in Pesse, Netherlands and dated to *c.* 6315 ± 275 BC. It is now in the Provincial Museum, Assen. A fleet of 12 funerary boats discovered in 1991 at Abydos, Egypt have been tentatively dated to *c.* 3000 BC. The vessels are up to 18 m *60 ft* long.

The oldest surviving boat in Britain was found in 1984 on Hasholme Hall Farm, Holme upon Spalding Moor, Humberside. The 2300-year-old boat, which is 13·71 m *45 ft* long, will require special conservation until the late 1990s.

The oldest shipwreck ever found is of a Cycladic trading vessel off the islet of Dhókós, near the Greek island of Hydra, reported in May 1975 and dated to 2450 BC ± 250.

A 45 cm *18 in* long paddle was found at the Star Carr site in North Yorkshire in 1948. Dated to *c.* 7600 BC, it is now in the Cambridge Museum of Archaeology.

Oldest active The world's oldest active paddle steamer continuously operated as such is *Skibladner*, which has plied Lake Mjøsa, Norway since 1856. She was built in Motala, Sweden and has had two major refits.

The screw propeller was invented and patented by a Kent farmer, Sir Francis Pettit Smith (1808–71), on 31 May 1836 (British Patent No. 7104).

Ocean-going The world's oldest active ocean-going ship is the *MV Doulos* (Greek for 'servant'), built in 1914 in the USA and first named *Medina*. She is currently operating as an international Educational and Christian service vessel with approximately 300 crew, staff and passengers on board from 30 different nations.

Longest canoe

The 35·7 m *117 ft* long kauri wood Maori war canoe *Nga Toki Matawhaorua* of 20·3 tonnes was shaped with adzes at Kerikeri Inlet, New Zealand in 1940. The crew numbered 70 or more.

The 'Snake Boat' *Nadubhagóm* 41·1 m *135 ft* long from Kerala, southern India has a crew of 109 rowers and nine 'encouragers'.

Largest human powered vessel

The giant ship *Tessarakonteres*, a three-banked catamaran galley built for Ptolemy IV *c.* 210 BC in Alexandria, Egypt, measured 128 m *420 ft*. The ship was built for 4000 rowers, with up to eight men to an oar of 38 cubits (17·4 m *57 ft*) length.

Largest propeller

The largest propeller ever is the 11 m *36 ft 1 in* diameter triple-bladed screw made by Kawasaki Heavy Industries of Japan and delivered on 17 Mar 1982 for the 208 739 dwt bulk carrier *Hoei Maru* (now *New Harvest*).

Most landings

The greatest number on an aircraft carrier in one day was 602, achieved by Marine Air Group 6 of the United States Pacific Fleet Air Force aboard the USS *Matanikau* on 25 May 1945 between 8 a.m. and 5 p.m.

UK The oldest extant British vessel is the *Foudroyant*, built of teak in Bombay in 1817 as HMS *Trincomalee*, and for many years a familiar sight moored in Portsmouth Harbour, Hants. Used as a training ship since 1897, the *Foudroyant* was moved from Portsmouth to Hartlepool, Cleveland in 1987 for repairs and restoration as a typical naval frigate of the Nelson era before eventually being displayed in a specially constructed dry-dock at Hartlepool.

Earliest powered vessels Marine propulsion by steam engine was first achieved in 1783 when the Marquis Jouffroy d'Abbans (1751–1832) ascended a reach of the river Saône near Lyon, France, in the 180-tonne paddle steamer *Pyroscaphe*.

The first successful power-driven vessel was the tug *Charlotte Dundas*, a stern paddle-wheel steamer built for the Forth and Clyde Canal in 1801–2 by William Symington (1763–1831), using a double-acting condensing engine constructed by James Watt (1736–1819).

Earliest turbine The *Turbinia* was designed by the Hon. Sir Charles Parsons (1854–1931) and built in 1894 at Wallsend-on-Tyne, Tyne & Wear. She was 30 m *100 ft* long, had a displacement of 45·2 tonnes and was powered by three steam turbines totalling about 2000 shp. First publicly demonstrated in 1897, when a speed of 34·5 knots *64 km/h* was achieved, the ship is now preserved at Newcastle-upon-Tyne.

Wooden ships Heaviest The 8662-tonne, 101·7 m *333 ⅔ ft* long *Richelieu* was launched in Toulon, France on 3 Dec 1873.

HM battleship *Lord Warden*, completed in 1869, displaced 8060 tonnes.

Longest The longest wooden ship ever constructed was the 115 m *377 ft 4 in Rochambeau* formerly the *Dunderberg*, built in New York (1867–72). By comparison, the biblical length of Noah's Ark was 300 cubits or, at 45·7 cm *18 in* to a cubit, 137 m *450 ft*.

Largest battleships The largest battleships ever commissioned were the Japanese vessels *Yamato* (completed on 16 Dec 1941 and sunk south-west of Kyūshū, Japan by US planes on 7 Apr 1945) and *Musashi* (sunk in the Philippine Sea by 11 bombs and 16 torpedoes on 24 Oct 1944). Both ships had a full load displacement of 73 977 tonnes, an overall length of 263 m *863 ft*, a beam of 38·7 m *127 ft* and a full load draught of 10·8 m *35 ½ ft*. They were armed with nine 460 mm *18·1 in* guns in three triple turrets. Each gun weighed 164·6 tonnes, was 22·8 m *75 ft* long and fired 1451 kg *3200 lb* projectiles.

The last battleships in active service were the USS *Missouri* and USS *Wisconsin*, 270 m *887 ft* long and with a full load displacement of 58 000 tonnes. Both were first commissioned in 1944

The USS *Nimitz* is one of a fleet of six US Navy Nimitz class nuclear-powered aircraft carriers. (Photo: Sygma)

247

and later recommissioned in 1986 and 1988 respectively following major refits. Armaments include nine, 16 inch guns used in the Gulf War in 1991 and capable of firing 1225 kg *2700 lb* projectiles a distance of 39 km *23 miles*. Both ships, together with two others of the same class, USS *New Jersey* and USS *Iowa*, are now in reserve.

UK Britain's largest and last battleship was HMS *Vanguard* (1944–60), which had a full load displacement of 52 245 tonnes, was 248.1 m *814 ft* long overall and was armed with eight 15 in guns, which were originally mounted in the battlecruisers *Courageous* and *Glorious* in 1917. *Vanguard* was completed too late for service in World War II, and spent a lot of time in the Home Fleet's Training Squadron before being broken up at Faslane, Strathclyde in 1960.

Smallest Royal Navy warships The Attacker Class Fast Patrol boats, built by Allday in 1983–4, have an overall length of 20 m *65.6 ft* and a displacement of 38 tonnes. HMS Chaser, one of five of these vessels, is used by students of the University of Aberdeen for training.

Fastest warship On 25 Jan 1980 a US Navy hovercraft, the 23.7 m *78 ft* long, 100-tonne test vehicle SES-100B, achieved a speed of 91.9 knots *170 km/h*. (⇔ Hovercraft)

Fastest destroyer The highest speed attained by a destroyer was 45.25 knots *83.42 km/h* by the 2830-tonne French ship *Le Terrible* in 1935. Built in Blainville, France and powered by four Yarrow small tube boilers and two

---

Guns and armour

The largest guns mounted in any of HM ships were the 18 in pieces in the light battlecruiser (later aircraft carrier) HMS *Furious* in 1917. In 1918 they were transferred to the monitors HMS *Lord Clive* and *General Wolfe*.

The thickest armour ever carried was in HMS *Inflexible* (completed 1881), measuring 60 cm *24 in* backed by teak up to a maximum thickness of 107 cm *42 in*.

Rateau geared turbines, giving 100 000 shp, she was decommissioned at the end of 1957.

Largest aircraft carriers The warships with the largest full load displacement in the world are the Nimitz class US Navy aircraft carriers USS *Nimitz, Dwight D. Eisenhower, Carl Vinson, Theodore Roosevelt, Abraham Lincoln* and *George Washington*, the last two of which displace 102 000 tons. They are 332.9 m *1092 ft* long, have 1.82 ha *4½ acres* of flight deck and, driven by four nuclear-powered 260 000 shp geared steam turbines, can reach speeds of well over 30 knots *56 km/h*. Their complement is 5986.

UK The Royal Navy's largest fighting ship is the aircraft carrier HMS *Ark Royal*, commissioned on 1 Nov 1985. She has a 167.6 m *550 ft* long flight deck, is 209.3 m *685.8 ft* long overall and is powered by four Rolls-Royce Olympus TM3B gas turbines delivering 94 000 shp to give a top speed of 28 knots *51.8 km/h*.

Submarines

Largest The world's largest submarines are of the Russian Typhoon class. The launch of the first at the secret covered shipyard at Severodvinsk in the White Sea was announced by NATO on 23 Sep 1980. The vessels are believed to have a dived displacement of 26 500 tonnes, to measure 170 m *558 ft* overall and to be armed with 20, multiple warhead SS-NX-20 missiles with a range of 8895 km *4800 nautical miles*. By late 1987 two others built in Leningrad (now St Petersburg), Russia were operational, each deploying 140 warheads.

UK The largest submarines ever built for the Royal Navy will be four nuclear-powered vessels of the Vanguard class, the first three of which, *Vanguard, Victorious* and *Vigilant* were laid down in 1986–91, with HMS *Vanguard* commissioned in 1992 at a cost of £600 million. They are 150 m *491 ft 8 in* long, have a beam of 12.8 m *42 ft*, a draught of 12 m *39.4 ft* and will have a dived displacement of about 15 000 tonnes.

Fastest The Russian Alpha class nuclear-powered submarines have a reported maximum speed of over

Fastest underwater human-powered vehicle

The fastest speed attained by a human-powered propeller submarine is 4·72±0·06 knots *2·43 m/sec* by *Subhuman II*, designed and built by the Mare Island Naval Shipyard, San Francisco, California, USA, using a counter-rotating propeller propulsion system, on 24 Oct 1992. The crew were Dennis Hamilton, Christopher Reno and team leader Jim Richardson.

The record by a human-powered non-propeller submarine is 2·9±0·1 knots *1·49 m/sec* by *SubDUDE*, designed by the Scripps Institution of Oceanography, University of California, San Diego, USA using a horizontal oscillating foil propulsion system on 21 Aug 1992. It was crewed by Kimball Millikan and Ed Trevino, with team leader Kevin Hardy.

45 knots *83·4 km/h*. With the use of titanium alloy, they are believed to be able to dive to 762 m *2500 ft*. A US spy satellite over the naval yard in Leningrad (now St. Petersburg) on 8 Jun 1983

showed that they were being lengthened and they are now 81·5 m *267·4 ft* long.

Deepest dive The 30-ton US Navy deep submergence vessel *Sea Cliff* (DSV 4), commissioned in 1973, reached a depth of 6000 m *20 000 ft* in March 1985.

Longest submarine patrol The longest submerged and unsupported patrol made public is 111 days (57 085 km *30 804 nautical miles*) by HM Submarine *Warspite* (Cdr J.G.F. Cooke RN) in the South Atlantic from 25 Nov 1982 to 15 Mar 1983.

Cargo Vessels

Largest The world's largest ship of any kind is the oil tanker *Jahre Viking* (formerly the *Happy Giant* and *Seawise Giant*), at 564 739 tonnes deadweight. The tanker is 485·45 m *1504 ft* long overall, has a beam of 68·8 m *226 ft* and a draught of 24·61 m *80 ft 9 in*. Declared a total loss after being disabled by severe bombardment in 1987–8 during the Iran-Iraq war, the tanker underwent extensive renovation in Singapore and Dubai, United Arab Emirates costing some $60 million and was relaunched under its new name in November 1991.

The largest ship carrying dry cargo is the ore carrier *Berge Stahl* of 364 767 tonnes deadweight, built in South Korea for its Norwegian owner Sig Bergesen. The vessel is 343 m *1125 ft* long, has a beam of 63·5 m *208 ft* and was launched on 5 Nov 1986.

Barges The world's largest RoRo (roll-on, roll-off) ships are four *El Rey* class barges of 16 700 tons and 176·78 m *580 ft* in length. They were built by the FMC Corp of Portland, Oregon, USA and are operated by Crowley Maritime Corp of San Francisco, USA between Florida, USA and Puerto Rico with tri-level lodging of up to 376 truck-trailers.

Car ferries The world's largest car and passenger ferries are *Silja Serenade* and *Silja Symphony*, which entered service between Stockholm, Sweden and Finland in 1990 and 1991. Operated by the Silja Line, they are of 58 376 grt, with a length of 203 m *666 ft*, a beam of 31·5 m *103·34 ft* and can carry 2500 passengers and 450 cars.

Fastest The fastest car ferry is the 24 065 grt gas-turbine powered *Finnjet*, built in 1977, operating in the Baltic between Helsinki, Finland and Travemünde, Germany and capable of exceeding 30 knots *55·5 km/h.*

Container ships *Earliest* Shipborne containerization began in 1955 when the tanker *Ideal X* was converted by Malcolm McLean of the United States to carry containers on deck only.

Largest American President Lines has built five ships in Germany, *President Adams*, *President Jackson*, *President Kennedy*, *President Polk* and *President Truman*, which are termed post-Panamax, being the first container vessels too large for transit of the Panama Canal. They are 275·14 m *902·69 ft* in length and 39·41 m *129·29 ft* in beam; the maximum beam for the Panama transit is 32·3 m *106 ft*. These vessels have a quoted capacity of 4300 TEU (standard length Twenty foot (i.e. 6·096 m) Equivalent Unit containers);

they have, however, carried more than this in normal service.

Longest Although of smaller registered tonnage, *Dresden Express*, built in South Korea in 1991 for the German Hapag-Lloyd company, is longer, at 294 m *964 ft* and has a quoted capacity of 4422 TEU.

Most powerful dredger The 142·7 m *468·4 ft* long *Prins der Nederlanden* of 10 586 grt can dredge 20 000 tonnes of sand from a depth of 35 m *115 ft* via two suction tubes in less than an hour.

Largest hydrofoil The 64·6 m *212 ft* long *Plainview* (314 tonnes full load) naval hydrofoil was launched by the Lockheed Shipbuilding and Construction Co. at Seattle, Washington, USA on 28 Jun 1965. She has a service speed of 92 km/h *57·2 mph.*

Most powerful icebreakers The most powerful purpose-built icebreakers are the *Rossiya* and her sister ships *Sovetskiy Soyuz* and *Oktyabryskaya Revolutsiya*. Built in Leningrad (now St. Petersburg), Russia and completed in 1985, *Rossiya* is of 23 460 tonnes, is 148 m *485 ft* long and is powered by 55·95 kW *75 000 hp* nuclear engines.

The largest *converted* icebreaker was the 306·9 m *1007 ft* long SS *Manhattan* (43 000 shp), which was converted into a 152 407-tonne icebreaker by the Humble Oil Co. She made a double voyage through the North-West Passage in arctic Canada from 24 August to 12 November 1969.

The North-West Passage was first navigated by Roald Engebereth Gravning Amundsen of Norway (1872–1928) in the sealing sloop *Gjøa* in 1906.

Light vessels The earliest station still marked by a light vessel is the Sunk in the North Sea, off Harwich, Essex, established in 1802. A Nore light vessel was first placed in the Thames estuary in 1732. *Note:* By 1989 all Trinity House manned light vessels around the coasts of England and Wales had been withdrawn and replaced by automatic vessels or LANBYs (Large Automatic Navigation Buoys).

Rail ferries The largest international rail ferries are the *Klaipeda*, *Vilnius*, *Mukran* and *Greifswald*, operating in the

Illustration: Dick Millington

Bath Tub Kings

For many years motorized bath tub racing has been a popular activity. A race using motorized baths over 34 miles *54·7 km* was first held in 1967 in Canada and before long similar events also began to taken place in Australia.

Before long 36 miles *57·9 km* had become the standard distance for championships. Two races which took place on a regular basis were across the Strait of Georgia, British Columbia, Canada and on a river at Grafton, New South Wales, Australia.

Regardless of location, however, it was Australians who set records. Phil Holt did so in 1976 with a time of 1 hr 36 min 4 sec, which he achieved at Nanaimo. At the same venue in 1978 Gary Deathbridge lowered the record to 1 hr 29 min 40 sec. This record stood for eight years until Greg Mutton recorded a time of 1 hr 27 min 48 sec at the Grafton festival in Australia in 1986, and a year later he beat his own record, with a time of 1 hr 22 min 27 sec. Since then he has remained the king of the bath tubs.

Largest wreck

The 312186-tonne deadweight VLCC (very large crude carrier) *Energy Determination* blew up and broke in two in the Strait of Hormuz, Persian Gulf on 12 Dec 1979. Her full value was $58 million.

The largest wreck removal was carried out in 1979 by Smit Tak International, who removed the remains of the 120000-ton French tanker *Betelgeuse* from Bantry Bay, Republic of Ireland within 20 months.

Most massive collision

The closest approach to an irresistible force striking an immovable object occurred on 16 Dec 1977, 35 km *22 miles* off the coast of southern Africa, when the tanker *Venoil* (330954 dwt) struck her sister ship *Venpet* (330869 dwt).

River boat

The world's largest inland boat is the 116 m *382 ft Mississippi Queen*, designed by James Gardner of London. The vessel was commissioned on 25 Jul 1976 in Cincinnati, Ohio, USA and is now in service on the Mississippi river.

Message in a bottle

The longest recorded interval between drop and pick-up is 73 years in the case of a message thrown from the SS *Arawatta* out of Cairns, Queensland, Australia on 9 Jun 1910 in a lotion bottle and reported to be found on Moreton Island Queensland, on 6 Jun 1983.

Baltic sea between Klaipeda, Lithuania and Mukran, Germany. Built in Wismar, Germany, each ferry is 11700 tons deadweight and has two decks measuring 190·5 m *625 ft* in length and 91·86 m

301·4 ft wide. Each vessel can lift 103 standard 14·83 m *48·65 ft*, 84-ton railcars and can cover 506 km *273 nautical miles* in 17 hr.

Most powerful tugs

The *Nikolay Chiker* (SB 135) and *Fotiy Krylov* (SB 135), commissioned in 1989 and built by Hollming Ltd of Finland for V/O Sudoimport of the former USSR, are of 24480 hp and 250 tons bollard pull at full power. They are 98 m *321 ft* long and 19·45 m *64 ft* wide. SB 135 is now owned and operated by the Tsavliris Group of Companies of Piraeus, Greece, and has been renamed *Tsavliris Giant*.

Largest whale factory

The Russian *Sovietskaya Ukraina* (32034 gross tons) with a summer deadweight of 46738 tonnes was completed in October 1959. She is 217·8 m *714 ½ ft* in length and 25·8 m *84 ft 7 in* in the beam.

Passenger Ships

Largest liners

The RMS *Queen Elizabeth* (finally 82998 but formerly 83673 gross tons), of the Cunard fleet, was the largest passenger vessel ever built and had the largest displacement of any liner in the world. She had an overall length of 314 m *1031 ft*, was 36 m *118 ft 7 in* in breadth and was powered by steam turbines which developed 168000 hp. Her last passenger voyage ended on 15 Nov 1968. In 1970 she was removed to Hong Kong to serve as a floating marine university and renamed *Seawise University*. She was burnt out on 9 Jan 1972 when three *simultaneous* outbreaks of fire strongly pointed to arson. The gutted hull had been cut up and removed by 1978. *Seawise* was a pun on the owner's initials, C.Y. Tung (1911–82).

The largest in current use and the longest ever is the *Norway* of 76049 gross register tons 315·53 m *1035 ft 7 ½ in* in overall length, with a passenger capacity of 2022 and 900 crew. She was built as the SS *France* in 1960 and renamed after purchase in June 1979 by Knut Kloster of Norway. She is normally employed on cruises in the Caribbean and is based at Miami, USA. Work undertaken during an extensive refit during the autumn of 1990 increased the number of passenger decks to 11. She draws 10·5 m *34 ½ ft*, has a beam of

33·5 m *110 ft* and cruises at 18 knots *33 km/h* for the Royal Viking Line.

The largest liner under the British Flag is MV *Queen Elizabeth 2* of 69 053 grt and an overall length of 293 m *963 ft*. Her maiden vogage for the Cunard Line was on 2 May 1969 and she set a 'turn round' record of 5 hr 47 min at New York City, USA on 21 Nov 1983. Built by John Brown & Co. (Clydebank) Ltd, Scotland, she was refitted by Lloyd Werft, Bremerhaven, Germany with diesel electric engines in 1986–7 to give a maximum speed of 32½ knots *60 km/h*. She is the last passenger liner to be regularly employed on transatlantic service between Southampton, Hants and New York, USA and can accommodate 1929 passengers and 1007 crew.

Yachts *Largest* The largest yacht is the Saudi Arabian royal yacht *Abdul Aziz*, which is 147 m *482 ft* long. Built in Denmark and completed on 22 Jun 1984 at Vospers Yard, Southampton, Hants, it was estimated in September 1987 to be worth over $100 million.

Private The largest private (non-Royal) yacht is the 122 m *400 ft* former ferry *Alexander*, converted in 1986.

Hydrofoils The largest passenger hydrofoils are three 165-ton Supramar PTS 150 Mk IIIs, which carry 250 passengers at 40 knots *74 km/h* across the Öre Sound between Malmö, Sweden and Copenhagen, Denmark. They were built by Westermoen Hydrofoil Ltd of Mandal, Norway.

Sailing Ships

Oldest active The oldest active square-rigged sailing vessel in the world is the restored SV *Maria Asumpta*, (formerly the *Ciudad de Inca*), built near Barcelona, Spain in 1858. She is 29·8 m *98 ft* overall and of 127 gross registered tonnage. She was restored in 1981–2 and is used for film work, promotional appearances at regattas and sail training. She is operated by The Friends of *Maria Asumpta* of Lenham, Maidstone, Kent.

Largest The largest vessel ever built in the era of sail was the *France II* (5806 gross tons), launched at Bordeaux, France in 1911. This was a steel-hulled, five-masted barque (square-rigged on four masts and fore and aft rigged on the aftermost mast). Her hull was 127·4 m *418 ft* overall. Although principally designed as a sailing vessel with a stump top gallant rig, she was also fitted with two auxiliary engines; however these were removed in 1919 and she became a pure sailing vessel. She was wrecked off New Caledonia on 12 Jul 1922.

The only seven-masted sailing schooner ever built was the 114·4 m *375·6 ft* long *Thomas W. Lawson* (5218 gross tons), built at Quincy, Massachusetts, USA in 1902 and wrecked off the Isles of Scilly, Cornwall on 15 Dec 1907. (⊳ Largest junks)

Largest in service The largest sailing ship now in service is the *Sedov* at 109 m *357 ft*, built in 1921 at Kiel, Germany and used for training by the Russians. She is 14·6 m *48 ft* in width, with a displacement of 6300 tonnes, 3556 grt and a sail area of 4192 m² *45 123 ft²*.

The world's only surviving First Rate Ship-of-the-Line is the Royal Navy's 104-gun battleship HMS *Victory*, laid down at Chatham, Kent on 23 Jul 1759 and constructed from the wood of some 2200 oak trees. She bore the body of Admiral Nelson from Gibraltar to Portsmouth, Hants arriving 44 days after serving as his victorious flagship at the Battle of Trafalgar on 21 Oct 1805. In 1922 she was moved to No. 2 dock at Portsmouth—site of the world's oldest graving dock. The length of her cordage (both standing and running rigging) is 30·77 km *19·12 miles*.

Longest The longest sailing ship is the 187 m *613 ft* French-built *Club Med 1*, with five aluminium masts and 2800 m² *3013 ft²* of computer-controlled polyester sails. Operated as a Caribbean cruise vessel for 425 passengers for Club Med, with the small sail area and powerful engines she is really a motor-sailer. A sister-ship *Club Med II* has been commissioned.

Junks A river junk 110 m *361 ft* long, with treadmill-operated paddle-wheels, was recorded in AD 1161.

The largest on record was the sea-going *Zheng He*, flagship of Admiral Zheng He's 62 treasure ships, of c. 1420, with a displacement of 3150 tonnes and a

Fastest shipbuilding

The fastest times in which complete ships of more than 10000 tons were ever built were achieved at Kaiser's Yard, Portland, Oregon, USA during the wartime programme for building 2742 Liberty ships in 18 shipyards from 27 Sep 1941. In 1942 No. 440, named *Robert E. Peary*, had her keel laid on 8 November, was launched on 12 November and was operational after 4 days 15½ hr on 15 November. She was broken up in 1963.

Riveting

The world record for riveting is 11 209 in 9 hr, by John Moir at the Workman Clark Ltd shipyard, Belfast in June 1918. His peak hour was his 7th, with 1409 rivets, an average of nearly 23½ per min.

Model boats

Members of the Lowestoft Model Boat Club crewed a radio controlled scale model boat on 17–18 Aug 1991 at Dome Leisure Park, Doncaster to a 24-hr distance record of 178·92 km *111·18 miles.*

David and Peter Holland of Doncaster, S. Yorks, members of the Conisbrough and District Modelling Association, crewed a 71 cm *28 in* long scale model boat of the Bridlington trawler *Margaret H* continuously on one battery for 24 hours for a distance of 53·83 km *33·45 miles* also at the Dome Leisure Park on 15–16 Aug 1992.

length variously estimated up to 164 m *538 ft.* She is believed to have had nine masts. In *c.* AD 280 a floating fortress 183 m *600 ft* square, built by Wang Jun on the Yangzi river, took part in the Jin-Wu river war. Present-day junks do not, even in the case of the Jiangsu traders, exceed 52 m *170 ft* in length.

Largest sails Sails are known to have been used for marine propulsion since 3500 BC. The largest spars ever carried were those in HM Battleship *Temeraire*, completed at Chatham, Kent on 31 Aug 1877. She was broken up in 1921. The fore and main yards measured 35 m *115 ft* in length. The foresail contained 1555 m *5100 ft* of canvas, weighing 2·03 tonnes and the total sail area was 2322 m² *25 000 ft².*

Tallest mast The *Velsheda*, a J class sailing vessel, is the tallest known single masted yacht in the world, at 51·6 m *169¼ ft* measured from heel fitting to mast truck. Built in 1933, the second of the four British J-class yachts, she is unusual in being the only one ever built that was not intended for the America's Cup race. With a displacement of 145 tonnes, she supports a sail area of 696·75 m² *7500 ft².*

Merchant Shipping

Total At 1 Jul 1992 the world total of merchant shipping, excluding vessels of less than 100 gross tonnage, sailing vessels and barges, was 79 845 ships of 444 304 999 gross tonnage.

Shipbuilding World-wide production completed in 1992 was 18·6 million gross tonnage of ships, excluding sailing ships, non-propelled vessels and vessels of less than 100 gross tonnage. The figures for Russia, Romania and the People's Republic of China are incomplete.

Japan completed 7·3 million gross tonnage (45 per cent of the world total) in 1992 and UK completions totalled 31 ships of 152 307 gross tonnage.

The world's leading shipbuilder in 1992 was Hyundai of South Korea, which completed 28 ships of 1·85 million gross tonnage.

Biggest owner The largest ship owners are the Japanese NYK Group, whose fleet of owned vessels totalled 1 279 022 gross tonnage at 1 Feb 1993.

Largest fleet The largest merchant fleet in the world at mid-1992 was that under the flag of Liberia, totalling some 55 166 948 gross tonnage. The equivalent figure for the UK was 1747 ships of 6016 868 gross tonnage. Though the UK numbered register ranks only 24th in the world, beneficial ownership of ships on 40 other flags (some of these flags of convenience) brings the UK controlled fleet to 7th among maritime nations, with at least 10·9 million gross tonnage.

Hovercraft
(skirted air-cushion vehicles)

Earliest The ACV (air-cushion vehicle) was first made a practical proposition by Sir Christopher Sydney Cockerell (b. 4 Jun 1910), a British engineer who had the idea in 1954, published his Ripplecraft report 1/55 on 25 Oct 1955 and patented it on 12 Dec 1955.

The earliest patent relating to air-cushioned craft was applied for in 1877 by Sir John I. Thornycroft (1843–1928) of London, and the idea was developed by Toivo Kaario of Finland in 1935.

The first flight by a hovercraft was made by the 4 tonne Saunders-Roe SRN1 at Cowes, Isle of Wight on 30 May 1959. With a 680 kg *1500 lb* thrust Viper turbo-jet engine, this craft reached 68 knots *126 km/h* in June 1961.

The first hovercraft public service was run across the Dee estuary between Rhyl, Clwyd and Wallasey, Merseyside by the 60 knot *111 km/h* 24-passenger Vickers-Armstrong VA-3 between 20 July and September 1962.

Largest The SRN4 Mk III, a British-built civil hovercraft, weighs 305 tons and can accommodate 418 passengers and 60 cars. It is 56·38 m *185 ft* in length, and is powered by four Bristol Siddeley Marine Proteus engines, giving a maximum speed in excess of the scheduled permitted cross-Channel operating speed of 65 knots *120·25 km/h.*

Fastest The world's fastest warship is the 23·7 m *78 ft* long 100 tonnes US Navy test hovercraft SES-100B. She attained a world record 91·9 knots *170 km/h* on 25 Jan 1980 on the Chesapeake Bay Test Range, Maryland, USA. As a result of the success of this test craft, a 3000-tonne US Navy Large Surface Effect Ship (LSES) was built by Bell Aerospace under contract from the Department of Defense in 1977–81. (⇔ Warships)

Squadron Leader Michael Cole, leader of a ten-strong expedition which, in 1990, reached the navigable source of the Yangzi River, China in the hovercraft *Neste Enterprise*.
(Photo: Michael Cole)

Transatlantic Marine Records

(More detailed marine tables compiled from information supplied by Nobby Clarke and Richard Boehmer can be found in earlier editions)

Category	Vessel	Skipper/Crew	Start	Finish	Duration
FIRST SOLO SAILING E–W	15-ton gaff sloop	Josiah Shackford (US)	Bordeaux, France, 1786	Surinam (Guiana)	35 days
FIRST ROWING	Ship's boat c. 6·1 m 20 ft	John Brown and five British deserters from garrison	St Helena 10 Jun 1799	Belmonte, Brazil (fastest-ever row)	28 days (83 mpd)
FIRST SOLO SAILING W–E	Centennial 6·1 m 20 ft	Alfred Johnson (US)	Shag Harbor, Maine, USA 1876	Wales	46 days
FIRST MOTOR-BOAT	Abiel Abbott Low 11·6 m 38 ft (10hp kerosene engine)	William C. Newman (US) Edward (son)	New York, USA 1902	Falmouth, Cornwall	36 days (83·3 mpd)
FIRST WOMAN SOLO W–E	Lugger 5·5 m 18 ft	Gladys Gradeley (US)	Nova Scotia 1903	Hope Cove, Devon	60 days
FIRST SOLO ROWING E–W	Britannia 6·7 m 22 ft	John Fairfax (GB)	Las Palmas, Canary Island 20 Jan 1969	Ft Lauderdale, Florida, USA, 19 Jul 1969	180 days
FIRST SOLO ROWING W–E	Super Silver 6·1 m 20 ft	Tom McClean (Ireland)	St John's, Newfoundland, Canada 1969	Black Sod Bay, Republic of Ireland 27 Jul 1969	70·7 days
FIRST OUTBOARD	Trans-Atlantic 7·9 m 26 ft (2·65 hp Evinrudes)	Al Grover (US) Dante (son)	St Pierre, Newfoundland, Canada 1985 (via Azores)	Lisbon, Portugal	34 days (88 mpd approx.)
FIRST ROW Both directions	QE III 6·05 m 19 ft 10 in	Don Allum (GB)	Canary Islands 1986 St John's, Canada	Nevis, West Indies Ireland 1987	114 days 77 days

FASTEST POWER W–E	*Gentry Eagle* 33.5m 110ft	Tom Gentry (US)	Ambrose Light Tower, USA 13:49 BST 24 Jul 1989	Bishop Rock Light 03:56 BST 27 Jul 1989	2 days 14 hr 7 min 47 sec (45.7 knots smg)
FASTEST SAIL W–E Non-solo	*Jet Services 5* 22.9m 75ft catamaran sloop	Serge Madec (France)	Ambrose Light Tower, USA 2 Jun 1990	Lizard Point, Cornwall 9 Jun 1990	6 days 13 hr 3 min 32 sec (18.4 knots smg)
FASTEST SAIL W–E Solo	*Pierre 1er* 18.3m 60ft trimaran sloop	Florence Arthaud (France)	Ambrose Light Tower, USA 24 Jul 1990	Lizard Point, Cornwall 3 Aug 1990	9 days 21 hr 42 min (12.2 knots smg)
FASTEST SAIL E–W Solo (beats non-solo)	*Fleury Michon (IX)* 18.3m 60ft trimaran	Philippe Poupon (France)	Plymouth, Devon (STAR) 5 Jun 1988	Newport, Rhode Island, USA 15 Jun 1988	10 days 9 hr (11.6 knots smg)

Transpacific Marine Records

FIRST ROWING	*Britannia II* 10.7m 35ft	John Fairfax (GB) Sylvia Cook (GB)	San Francisco, USA 26 Apr 1971	Hayman Island, Australia 22 Apr 1972	362 days
FIRST SOLO ROWING E–W	*Hele-on-Britannia* 9.75m 32ft	Peter Bird (GB)	San Francisco, USA 23 Aug 1982	Gt Barrier Reef, Australia 14 Jun 1983	294 days 14 480km *9000 miles*
FIRST SOLO ROWING W–E	*Sector* 8m 26ft	Gérard d'Aboville (France)	Choshi, Japan 11 Jul 1991	Ilwaco, Washington, USA 21 Nov 1991	133 days 10 150km *6300 miles*
FASTEST SAIL California–Japan	*Pen Duick V* 10.7m 35ft sloop	Eric Tabarly (France)	San Francisco, USA 15 Mar 1969	Tokyo, Japan 24 Apr 1969	39 days 15 hr 44 min (4.66 knots smg)

N.B. — The earliest single-handed Pacific crossings were achieved East–West by Bernard Gilboy (US) in 1882 in the 5.48m 18ft double-ender Pacific to Australia, and West–East by Fred Rebel (Latvia) in the 5.48m 18ft Elaine (from Australia) and Edward Miles (US) in the 11.2m 36¾ft Sturdy II (from Japan), both in 1932, the latter via Hawaii. STAR is a transatlantic race. smg = speed made good.

Marine Circumnavigation Records

(More detailed marine tables compiled from information supplied by Nobby Clarke and Richard Boehmer can be found in earlier editions)

Strictly speaking, a circumnavigation involves passing through a pair of antipodal points and all the records listed below are known to have met this requirement unless marked with an asterisk. A non-stop circumnavigation is entirely self-maintained; no water supplies, provisions, equipment or replacements of any sort may be taken aboard en route. Vessels may anchor, but no physical help may be accepted apart from passing mail or messages. All distances refer to nautical miles.

Category	Vessel	Skipper	Start	Finish
FIRST	Vittoria Expedition of Fernão de Magalhães (Ferdinand Magellan)	Juan Sebastián de Elcano or del Cano (d. 1526) and 17 crew	Seville, Spain 20 Sep 1519	San Lucar, Italy 6 Sep 1522 30 700 miles
FIRST BRITISH	Golden Hind (ex Pelican) 100 tons	Francis Drake (c. 1540–96) (knighted 4 Apr 1581)	Plymouth, Devon 13 Dec 1577	26 Sep 1580
*FIRST WOMAN	Etoile (Storeship for Bougainville's La Boudeuse)	Jeanne Baret, crypto-female valet of M. de Commerson	St Malo, France 1766	1769 (revealed as female on Hawaii)
FIRST SOLO	Spray 11·2 m 36 ft 9 in gaff yawl	Capt Joshua Slocum (US) (a non-swimmer)	Newport, RI, USA via Magellan Straits, Chile 24 Apr 1895	3 Jul 1898 46 000 miles
*FIRST MOTOR BOAT	Speejacks 29·9 m 98 ft	Albert Y. Gowen (US) plus wife and crew	New York City, USA 1921	New York City, 1922
FIRST SUBMERGED	Triton Nuclear submarine	Capt Edward L. Beach USN plus 182 crew	New London, Connecticut, USA 16 Feb 1960	10 May 1960 84 days 19 hr, 36 300 miles
FIRST NON-STOP SOLO W–E	Suhaili 9·87 m 32 ft 4 in Bermudan ketch	Robin Knox-Johnston (GB)	Falmouth, Cornwall 14 Jun 1968	22 Apr 1969 (312 days)
FIRST NON-STOP SOLO E–W	British Steel 18 m 59 ft ketch	Chay Blyth (GB)	Hamble River, Hants 18 Oct 1970	6 Aug 1971 (292 days)

Category	Vessel	Skipper	Start	Finish	Duration
FIRST WOMAN SOLO	Express Crusader 16·15m 53ft cutter	Dame Naomi James (New Zealand)	Dartmouth, Devon 9 Sep 1977	Dartmouth, 8 Jun 1978	265 sailing days + 7 days in port
FIRST SOLO IN BOTH DIRECTIONS (via Cape Horn)	Ocean Bound 12·5m 41ft Bermudan sloop	David Scott Cowper (GB)	Plymouth, Devon 1979 (W–E) / Plymouth 1981 (E–W)	Plymouth, 1980 / Plymouth 1982	
MOST SOLO (same yacht)	Tarmin 7·5m 24ft 7in Bermudan sloop	John Sowden (US)	Various ports 1966, 1974, 1983	1970, 1977, 1986	

Eduard Roditi, author of *Magellan of the Pacific*, advances the view that Magellan's slave, Enrique, was the first circumnavigator. He had been purchased in Malacca and it was shown that he already understood the Filipino dialect Vizayan, when he reached the Philippines from the east. He 'tied the knot' off Limasawa on 28 Mar 1521.

British Isles Records

Category	Vessel	Skipper	Start	Finish	Duration
AROUND BRITISH ISLES *Fastest power*	Ilan Voyager 21·3m 70ft trimaran	Mark Pridie (GB)	Brighton, E Sussex 9 May 1989	Brighton 12 May 1989	3 days 42 min (21·6 knots smg)
AROUND BRITISH ISLES *Fastest multihull*	Saab Turbo 22·9m 75ft catamaran	François Boucher (France)	Plymouth, Devon (RB & I) 18 Jun 1989	Plymouth (4 stops) 3 Jul 1989	7 days 7 hr 30min (+ 8 days in port)
AROUND BRITISH ISLES *Fastest monohull*	Vootreckker II 18·3m 60ft ULDB sloop	Bertie Reed (South Africa)	Plymouth, Devon (RB & I) 10 Jul 1982	Plymouth (4 stops) 29 Jul 1982	10 days 16hr 10min (+ 8 days in port)
ENGLISH CHANNEL *both ways* *Fastest multihull*	Fleury Michon VIII 22·9m 75ft trimaran	Philippe Poupon (France)	Calais, France Dec 1986	Calais via Dover, Kent Dec 1986	2 hr 21 min 57 sec (18·6 knots smg)
ENGLISH CHANNEL *both ways* *Fastest sailboard*	Hi Fly Board Gaastra sail	Pascal Maka (France)	Cape Blanc-Nez, France 1985	Cape Gris-Nez via Dover 1985	1 hr 59 min 57 sec (18·5 knots smg)

ULDB = Ultra-light displacement boat. RB & I = Round Britain & Ireland Race. smg = speed made good. All mileages are nautical miles.

(More detailed marine tables compiled from information supplied by Richard Boehmer can be found in earlier editions) For speed records ⇨Yachting.

Category	Vessel	Skipper	Start	Finish	Duration
DURATION AND DISTANCE / Non-stop by sail	Parry Endeavour* / 13·9 m 44 ft Bermudan sloop	Jon Sanders (Australia)	Fremantle, W Australia / 25 May 1986	Fremantle / 13 Mar 1988	71 000 miles in 658 days (av. speed 4-5 knots)
BEST DAY'S RUN* / Non-solo in multihull	Jet Services 5 / 18·3 m 60 ft catamaran sloop	Serge Madec (France)	42·638° N, 62·626° W / 22:22 GMT 3 Jun 1990	45·750° N, 51·480° W / 21:58 GMT 4 Jun 1990	514·01 miles (GCD)/23 hr 36 min (21·8 knots smg)
BEST DAY'S RUN / Solo in multihull	Laiterie Mont St Michel / 18·3 m 60 ft trimaran	Olivier Moussy (France)	50°13' N, 11°30' W / 18:18 GMT 6 Jun 1988	48°18' N, 23°30' W / 21:17 GMT 7 Jun 1988	430·8 miles (GCD)/24 hr (18·0 knots smg)
BEST DAY'S RUN / Solo in monohull	Generali Concorde / 18·3 m 60 ft sloop	Alain Gautier (France)	50·300° S, 42·550° E / 15:39 GMT 2 Dec 1990	51·800° S, 50·617° E / 15:16 GMT 3 Dec 1990	317·1 miles (GCD)/23 hr 37 min (13·43 knots smg)
BEST DAY'S RUN / Sailboard	Fanatic board / Gaastra sail	Françoise Canetos (France)	Sète, France / 13 Jul 1988	14 Jul 1988	227 miles/24 hr (9·46 knots smg)

* Best day's run for any vessel under sail. GCD = Great circle distance. smg = speed made good. All mileages are nautical miles.

Longest journey The longest hovercraft journey was one of 8047 km *5000 miles* by the British Trans-African Hovercraft Expedition, under the leadership of David Smithers, through eight West African countries in a Winchester class SRN6, between 15 Oct 1969 and 3 Jan 1970.

Cross-Channel The fastest scheduled crossing of the Channel was achieved by an SRN 4 Mark II Mountbatten class Hovercraft, operated by Hoverspeed, on 1 Sep 1984, when *The Swift* completed the Dover–Calais run in 24 min 8·4 sec to average more than 54½ knots *101 km/h*.

Highest The highest altitude reached by a hovercraft was on 11 Jun 1990 when *Neste Enterprise* and her crew of ten reached the navigable source of the Yangzi river, China at 4983 m *16 050 ft*.

The greatest altitude at which a hovercraft is operating is on Lake Titicaca, Peru, where since 1975 an HM2 Hoverferry has been hovering 3811 m *12 506 ft* above sea level.

Ocean Crossings

Earliest Atlantic The earliest crossing of the Atlantic by a power vessel, as opposed to an auxiliary-engined sailing ship, was a 22-day voyage begun in April 1827, from Rotterdam, Netherlands, to the West Indies, by the *Curaçao*. She was a 38·7 m *127 ft* wooden paddle boat of 438 tons, built as the *Calpe* in Dover, Kent in 1826 and purchased by the Dutch Govern- ment for a West Indian mail service.

The earliest Atlantic crossing made entirely under steam (with intervals for desalting

Around the World in 79 Days

On 20 Apr 1993 skipper Bruno Peyron of France and his four-man crew arrived back in France to a hero's welcome after circling the globe non-stop in 79 days 6 hr 16 min in the catamaran *Commodore Explorer*, beating Philéas Fogg's fictional voyage of 1873. Their prize was the new Jules Verne Trophy put up by the French Government.

Peyron, 37-year-old veteran of some 27 Atlantic crossings, set out on 31 Jan 1993 from the departure line between Ushant, France and Lizard Point, Cornwall with crewmen Olivier Despaignes, Marc Vallin, Jack Vincent (all France) and Cameron Lewis (US).

In winning this challenge, *Commodore Explorer*, the lengthened former *Jet Services 5*, also breaks the records for the fastest multihull, the fastest W–E and the fastest crewed circumnavigation.

---

the boilers) was by HMS *Rhadamanthus*, from Plymouth, Devon to Barbados, West Indies in 1832.

The earliest crossing under continuous steam power was by the condenser-fitted packet ship *Sirius*, 714 tonnes from Queenstown (now Cóbh), Republic of Ireland to Sandy Hook, New Jersey, USA, in 18 days 10 hr from 4–22 Apr 1838.

Fastest Atlantic Under the rules of the Hales Trophy or 'Blue Riband', which recognize the highest average speed rather than the shortest duration, the record is held by the 68 m *222 ft* Italian powerboat *Destriero* with an average speed of 53·09 knots between the Nantucket Light Buoy, USA and Bishop Rock Lighthouse, Isles of Scilly between 6–9 Aug 1992, in a time of 58 hr 34 min 4 sec. *Destriero* is classified as a yacht by the trophy's trustees and traditionalists still feel that the 'Blue Riband' should be held by the vessel making the best passage in regular liner service.

That distinction goes to the liner *United States* (then 51 988, now 38 216 gross tons), former flagship of the

United States Lines. On her maiden voyage between 3–7 Jul 1952 from New York, USA to Le Havre, France and Southampton, Hants, she averaged 35·39 knots, *65·95 km/h* for three days 10 hr 40 min (6:36 p.m. GMT, 3 July to 5:16 a.m., 7 July) on a route of 5465 km *2949 nautical miles* from the Ambrose light vessel to the Bishop Rock lighthouse, Isles of Scilly, Cornwall. During this run, on 6–7 July, she steamed the greatest distance ever covered by any ship in a day's run (24 hr) — 1609 km *868 nautical miles*, averaging 36·17 knots *67·02 km/h*. The maximum speed attained from her 240 000 shaft horsepower engines was 38·32 knots *71·01 km/h* in trials on 9–10 Jun 1952.

Fastest Pacific The fastest crossing from Yokohama, Japan to Long Beach, California, USA (4840 nautical miles *8960 km*) took 6 days 1 hr 27 min (30 Jun–6 Jul 1973) by the container ship *Sea-Land Commerce* 50 315 tons, at an average speed of 33·27 knots *61·65 km/h*.

Water speed The highest speed ever achieved on water is an estimated 300 knots *556 km/h* by Kenneth Peter Warby (b. 9 May 1939) on the Blowering Dam Lake, New South Wales, Australia on 20 Nov 1977 in his unlimited hydroplane *Spirit of Australia*.

The official world water speed record is 277·57 knots *514·389 km/h* set on 8 Oct 1978 by Warby on Blowering Dam Lake.

Youngest and oldest solo transatlantic crossings

Youngest sailing
17 yr 176 days David Sandeman (GB)
43 days, 1976

Oldest sailing
76 yr 165 days Stefan Szwarnowski (GB)
72 days, 1989

Youngest rowing
25 yr 306 days Sean Crowley (GB)
95 days 22 hr, 1988

Oldest rowing
51 yr Sidney Genders (GB)
160 days 8 hr, 1970

Fiona, Countess of Arran (b. 1918) drove her 4·57 m *15 ft* three-point hydroplane *Stradag* (Gaelic 'The Spark') to the first world water speed record for electrically propelled powerboats at a speed of 83·64 km/h *51·97 mph*, at the National Water Sports Centre, Holme Pierrepont, Notts on 22 Nov 1989.

Ports

Largest The Port of New York and New Jersey, USA is the world's largest, with a navigable waterfront of 1215 km *755 miles* (474 km *295 miles* in New Jersey) stretching over 238 km² *92 miles²*. A total of 261 general cargo berths and 130 other piers gives a total berthing capacity of 391 ships at any one time and the total warehousing floor space is 170·9 ha *422·4 acres*.

The largest British port by tonnage is London (including Tilbury), which handled 58 148 000 tonnes in 1990. The largest container port is Felixstowe, Suffolk which handled 1 019 000 units in 1990 carrying 16 448 000 tonnes.

Busiest The world's busiest port and largest artificial harbour is Rotterdam, Netherlands, which covers 100 km² *38 miles²*, with 122·3 km *76 miles* of quays. It handled 292 million tonnes of sea-going cargo in 1991.

Although the port of Singapore handled less tonnage in total seaborne cargo (than Rotterdam), it is the world's leading container port, handling a record 6·35 million TEU in 1991.

Britains busiest port in terms of ship movements is Dover, Kent which handled 25 832 ship arrivals in 1990. It also handled the highest value of trade at £34·5 billion (1991) and the largest number of accompanied passenger vehicles at 1 964 000 (1990).

Dry dock With a maximum shipbuilding capacity of 1 200 000 tons dwt, the Daewoo Okpo No. 1 Dry Dock, Koje Island in South Korea measures 530 m *1740 ft* long by 131 m *430 ft* wide and was completed in 1979. The dock gates, 14 m *46 ft* high and 10 m *33 ft* thick at the base, are the world's most massive.

Britain's largest dry dock is the Harland & Wolff building dock, Queen's Island, Belfast. It was excavated by George Wimpey Ltd to a length of 556 m *1825 ft* and a width of 93 m *305 ft* and can accommodate tankers of 1 million tons dwt. Work was begun on 26 Jan 1968 and completed on 30 Nov 1969; this involved the excavation of 306 000 m³ *400 000 yd³* of soil.

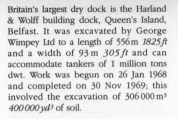

Coaching

Before the widespread use of tarred road surfaces from 1845, coaching was slow and hazardous. The zenith was reached on 13 Jul 1888 when James William Selby drove the *Old Times* coach 108 miles *173 km* from London to Brighton and back with eight teams and 14 changes in 7 hr 50 min, to average 13·8 mph *22·2 km/h*. A four-horse carriage could maintain a speed of 21⅓ mph *34 km/h* for nearly an hour.

The *Border Union* stagecoach, built *c.* 1825, ran four in hand from Edinburgh to London (393 miles *632 km*). When it ceased in 1845, due to competition from railways, the allowed schedule was 42 hr 23 min to average better than 9¼ mph *14·9 km/h*.

The record for changing a team of four horses by 12 ostlers is 21·32 sec, set by the Norwich Union Charity Mail Coach team led by driver John Parker, at Donnington Race Circuit, Leics on 9 Aug 1990.

The longest horse-drawn procession was a cavalcade of 68 carriages, which measured 920 m *3018 ft* 'nose to tail', organized by the Spies Travelling Company of Denmark on 7 May 1986. It

---

Carriage driving

The only man to drive 48 horses in a single hitch is Dick Sparrow of Zearing, Iowa, USA, between 1972 and 1977. The lead horses were on reins 41 m *135 ft* long.

Floyd Zopfi of Stratford, Wisconsin, USA has driven 52 llamas in a hitch on several occasions since 1990, with the lead llamas (four abreast) on reins 46 m *150 ft* long.

carried 810 people through the woods around Copenhagen to celebrate the coming of spring.

Bicycles

Earliest The earliest machine propelled by cranks and pedals with connecting rods and actually built, was in 1839–40 by Kirkpatrick Macmillan (1810–78) of Dumfries, Scotland. A copy of the machine is now in the Science Museum, Kensington, London.

The continuous history of cycling began with the *vélocipède* built in March 1861 by Pierre Michaux and his son Ernest of Rue de Verneuil, Paris, France.

In 1870, James Starley of Coventry, W. Midlands constructed the first penny-farthing or Ordinary bicycle. It had wire-spoked wheels for lightness and was later available with an optional-speed gear.

Smallest The world's smallest wheeled rideable bicycle is one with wheels of 1·9 cm *0·76 in* in diameter which was ridden by its constructor Neville Patten of Gladstone, Queensland, Australia for a distance of 4·1 m *13 ft 5½ in* on 25 Mar 1988.

Jacques Puyoou of Pau, Pyrénées-Atlantiques, France has built a tandem 36 cm *14 in* long, which has been ridden by him and Madame Puyoou.

Largest The largest bicycle, as measured by the wheel diameter, is 'Frankencycle', built by Dave Moore of Rosemead, California, USA and first ridden by Steve Gordon of Moorpark, California, on 4 Jun 1989. The wheel diameter is 3·05 m *10 ft* and it is 3·35 m *11 ft 2 in* high.

Penny-farthing

G.P. Mills of Anfield Bicycle Club holds the record for an Ordinary from Land's End to John o' Groats. Starting on Sunday 15 Aug 1886 he arrived at John o' Groats having ridden 1417 km *881 miles* in 5 days 10 hr on his Humber tricycle.

Longest The longest true bicycle ever built (i.e. without a third stabilizing wheel) is one designed and built by Terry Thessman of Pahiatua, New Zealand. It measures 22·24 m *72·96 ft* in length and weighs 340 kg *750 lb*. It was ridden by four riders a distance of 246 m *807 ft* on 27 Feb 1988. Cornering is a problem.

Wheelie A duration record for a bicycle wheelie is 5 hr 12 min 33 sec set by David Robilliard at the Beau Sejour Leisure Centre, St Peter Port, Guernsey, Channel Islands on 28 May 1990.

Human-powered vehicles (HPVs)
Fastest land The world speed records for human-powered vehicles (HPVs) over a 200 m flying start are: 105·36 km/h *65·48 mph* (single rider) by Fred Markham at Mono Lake, California, USA on 11 May 1986; and 101·3 km/h *62·92 mph* (multiple riders) by Dave Grylls and Leigh Barczewski at the Ontario Speedway, California on 4 May 1980. The one-hour standing start (single rider) record is held by Pat Kinch, riding *Kingcycle Bean*, averaging a speed of 75·57 km/h *46·96 mph* on 8 Sep 1990 at Millbrook Proving Ground, Bedford.

Water cycle The men's 2000 m record (single rider) is 20·66 km/h *12·84 mph* by Steve Hegg on *Flying Fish* at Long Beach, California, USA on 20 Jul 1987.

Unicycles

Tallest The tallest unicycle ever mastered is one 31·01 m *101 ft 9 in* tall ridden by Steve McPeak (with a safety wire suspended by an overhead crane) for a distance of 114·6 m *376 ft* in Las Vegas, USA in October 1980. The freestyle riding (i.e. without any safety harness) of ever taller unicycles must inevitably lead to serious injury or fatality.

Smallest Peter Rosendahl (Sweden) rode a 20·4 cm *8 in* high unicycle with a wheel diameter of 4·8 cm *1⅞ in*, with no attachments or extensions fitted, a distance of 10 m *9 ft 9½ in* on 20 Nov 1992 at Tangier Theater, Busch Gardens, Tampa, Florida, USA.

Fastest sprint Peter Rosendahl set a sprint record for 100 m from a standing start of 12·74 secs *(28·25 km/h*

Smallest unicycle (Photo: Busch Gardens, Tampa/Jim Tuten)

17·55 mph) at the Wet 'N Wild Show, Las Vegas, USA on 1 Jul 1990.

100 miles Takayuki Koike of Kanagawa, Japan set a record for 100 miles *160·9 km* of 6 hr 44 min 21·84 sec on 9 Aug 1987 (average speed 23·87 km/h *14·83 mph*).

Endurance Akira Matsushima (Japan) unicycled 5248 km *3260 miles* from Newport, Oregon to Washington DC, USA from 10 Jul–22 Aug 1992.

Land's End to John o' Groats Mike Day (b. 13 Mar 1965) of Southgate, London and Michel Arets (b. 9 Sep 1959) of Brussels, Belgium rode 1450 km *901 miles* from Land's End, Cornwall to John o' Groats, Highland, in 14 days 12 hr 41 min, 27 Aug–10 Sep 1986.

Backwards Peter Rosendahl of Las Vegas, Nevada, USA rode backwards for a distance of 74·75 km *46·7 miles* in 9 hr 25 min on 19 May 1990.

Motorcycles

Earliest The earliest internal combustion-engined motorized bicycle was a

The longest distance ever achieved for motorcycle long-jumping is 76·5 m *251 ft*, by Doug Danger on a 1991 Honda CR500 at Loudon, New Hampshire, USA on 22 Jun 1991.

wooden-framed machine built at Bad Cannstatt, Germany between October–November 1885 by Gottlieb Daimler (1834–1900) and first ridden by Wilhelm Maybach (1846–1929). It had a top speed of 19 km/h *12 mph* and developed one-half of one horsepower from its single-cylinder 264cc four-stroke engine at 700 rpm. Known as the 'Einspur', it was lost in a fire in 1903.

The first motorcycles of entirely British production were the 1046cc Holden flat-four and the 2¾ hp Clyde single both produced in 1898.

The earliest factory which made motorcycles in large numbers was opened in 1894 by Heinrich and Wilhelm Hildebrand and Alois Wolfmüller at Munich, Germany. In its first two years this factory produced over 1000 machines, each having a water-cooled 1488cc twin-cylinder four-stroke engine developing about 2·5 bhp at 600 rpm—the highest capacity motorcycle engine ever put into production.

Fastest production road machine
The 151 hp 1-litre Tu Atara YB6 EI has a road-tested top speed of 300 km/h *186 mph*.

Fastest racing machine There is no satisfactory answer to the identity of the fastest track machine other than to say that the current Honda, Suzuki and Yamaha machines have all been geared to attain speeds marginally in excess of 300 km/h *186 mph* under race conditions.

Highest speeds Official world speed records must be set with two runs over a measured distance made in opposite directions within a time limit of 1 hr for FIM records and of 2 hr for AMA records.

Donald A. Vesco (USA) (b. 8 Apr 1939), riding his 6·4 m *21 ft* long *Lightning Bolt* streamliner, powered by two 1016cc Kawasaki engines on Bonneville Salt Flats, Utah, USA on 28 Aug 1978 set AMA and FIM absolute records with an overall average of 512·733 km/h *318·598 mph* and completed the faster run at an average of 513·165 km/h *318·865 mph*.

The highest speed achieved over two runs in the UK is 332·30 km/h *200·9 mph* by Michel Booys riding a streamliner motorcycle, built by Alexander Macfadzean and powered by a turbo-charged 588cc Norton rotary engine, at Bruntingthorpe Proving Ground, Leics on 24 Aug 1991.

The fastest time for a single run over 440 yd from a standing start is 7·08 sec by Bo O'Brechta (USA) riding a super-charged 1200cc Kawasaki-based machine at Ontario, California, USA in 1980.

The highest terminal velocity recorded at the end of a 440 yd run from a standing start is 321·14 km/h *199·55 mph* by Russ Collins (USA) at Ontario, California, USA on 7 Oct 1978.

Longest *World* Gregg Reid of Georgia, Atlanta, USA designed and built a 4·57 m *15 ft 6 in* long 250cc motorbike weighing 235 kg *520 lb*. It is street legal.

UK Les Nash of Coventry, W Mids constructed a 'self made' 3500cc machine with a Rover V-8 engine. It measures 3·81 × 1·22 m *12 ft 6 in × 4 ft* and weighs more than 220 lb *500 lb*.

Smallest Simon Timperley and Clive Williams of Progressive Engineering Ltd, Ashton-under-Lyne, Lancs designed and constructed a motorcycle with a wheelbase of 10·79 cm *4·25 in*, a seat height of 49 mm *3·75 in* and with a wheel diameter of 1·90 cm *0·75 in* for the front and 2·41 cm *0·95 in* for the back. The bike was ridden a distance of 1 m *3·2 ft*.

Magnor Mydland of Norway has constructed a motorcycle with a wheelbase of 120 mm *4·72 in*, a seat height of 148 mm *5·82 in* and with wheels 38 mm *1·49 in* for the front and 49 mm *1·39 in* for the back in diameter. He rode a distance of 570 m *1870 ft* reaching a speed of 11·6 km/h *7·2 mph*.

Duration The longest time a motor scooter, a Kinetic Honda DX 100cc, has been kept in non-stop motion is 1001 hr when ridden by Har Parkash Rishi,

Jari Saarelainen (b. 4 Apr 1959) of Finland travelled a distance of 108 000 km *67 109 miles* and visited 43 countries on his Honda Gold Wing. He set off from Helsinki, Finland on 1 Dec 1989 and returned, 742 days later, on 12 Dec 1991. He only had two minor incidents along the way, a collision with a donkey and, as seen here, when his bike fell off a ferry and into the River Siak at Pekanbaru, Indonesia.

(Photo: Jari Saarelainen)

Amarjeet Singh and Navjot Chadha of India. The team covered a distance of 30 965 km *19 241 miles* at Traffic Park, Pune, Maharashtra, India between 22 April and 3 Jun 1990.

Longest ride Jari Saarelainen (b. 4 Apr 1959) of Finland riding his Honda Gold Wing 1500cc motorcycle travelled a distance of 108 000 km *67 109 miles* through 43 countries. He set off from Helsinki, Finland on 1 Dec 1989 and returned 742 days later on 12 Dec 1991.

The first woman to circumnavigate the world solo was Moniika Vega (b. 9 May

Wall of death
The greatest endurance feat on a 'wall of death' was 7 hr 0 min 13 sec, by Martin Blume at Berlin, Germany on 16 Apr 1983. He rode over 12 000 laps on the 10 m *33 ft* diameter wall on a Yamaha XS 400, averaging 45 km/h *30 mph* for the 292 km *181½ miles*.

1962) of Rio de Janeiro, Brazil riding her Honda 125cc motorcycle. Her journey commenced at Milan, Italy on 7 Mar 1990 and she returned to Italy on 24 May 1991 having covered a distance of 83 500 km *51 885 miles* and visited 53 countries.

Jim Rogers and Tabitha Eastabrook of New York, USA travelled a distance of 91 766 km *57 022 miles* on their motorcycles covering six continents. They set off from New York, USA in March 1990 and returned in November 1991.

Pyramid The Royal Signals White Helmets, established a world record with a pyramid of 54 men on eight motorcycles. The pyramid which was held together by muscle and determination only, with no straps, harnesses or any other aids, travelled a distance of 100 m *328 ft* at RAF Catterick, N Yorks on 24 Oct 1992.

Backwards riding Steering a motorcycle facing backwards from the top of a 10 ft *3·3 m* ladder, over a continuous period of 1 hr 30 min, Signalman Dewi Jones of the Royal Signals White Helmets covered a distance of 33 km *20·5 miles* at RAF Catterick, N Yorks on 30 Nov 1988.

Wheelie *Distance* Yasuyuki Kudoh covered 331 km *205·7 miles* non-stop on the rear wheel of his Honda TLM220R motorcycle at the Japan Automobile Research Institute proving ground, Tsukuba, near Tsuchiura, Japan on 5 May 1991.

Speed The highest speed attained on a back wheel of a motorcycle is 241 km/h *150 mph* by Steve Burns on a Spondon 1425 Turbo at Bruntingthorpe Proving Ground, Leics on 3 Jul 1989.

Two-wheel sidecar riding Konstantin Matveyev (Russia) rode a distance of 338·8 km *210·5 miles* on a Ural at Irbit Stadium, Sverdloskaya, Russia on 7–8 Jun 1992.

Most on one machine The record for the most people on a single machine is all 46 members of the Illawarra Mini Bike Training Club, New South Wales, Australia. They rode on a 1000cc motorcycle and travelled a distance of 1 mile *1·609 km* on 11 Oct 1987.

Oldest motorcyclist Arthur Merrick Cook (b. 13 Jun 1895) of Exeter, Devon still regularly rides his Suzuki 125 GS Special motorcycle every day.

Motorcars

Earliest

Model The earliest automobile of which there is a record is a two-foot-long steam-powered model constructed by Ferdinand Verbiest (died 1687), a Belgian Jesuit priest, and described in his *Astronomia Europaea*. His model of 1668 was possibly inspired either by Giovanni Branca's description of a steam turbine, published in his *La Macchina* in 1629, or even by Nan Huairen (writings on 'fire carts') in the Chu kingdom (*c.* 800 BC).

Passenger-carrying The earliest full-scale automobile was the first of two military steam tractors, completed at the Paris Arsenal in October 1769 by Nicolas-Joseph Cugnot (1725–1804). This reached 3·6 km/h *2¼ mph*. Cugnot's second, larger tractor, completed in May 1771, today survives in the Conservatoire Nationale des Arts et Métiers in Paris.

The world's first passenger-carrying automobile was a steam-powered road vehicle carrying eight passengers and built by Richard Trevithick (1771–1833). It first ran at Camborne, Cornwall on 24 Dec 1801.

Internal combustion Isaac de Rivaz (Switzerland) (died 1828) built a carriage powered by his 'explosion engine' in 1805. The first practical internal combustion engined vehicle was that built by

Registrations
The world's first plates were introduced by the Paris police in 1893 and in Britain in 1903.

The original A1 plate was secured by the 2nd Earl Russell (1865–1931) for his 12hp Napier.

Licence plate No. 8 was sold at a Hong Kong government auction for HK$5 million on 13 Feb 1988 to Law Ting-pong, a textile manufacturer. For the Chinese the number 8 is considered lucky.

Traffic lights
Semaphore-type traffic *signals* were set up in Parliament Square, London in 1868 with red and green gas lamps for night use. It was not an offence to disobey traffic signals until assent was given to the 1930 Road Traffic Act. Traffic *lights* were introduced in Great Britain with a one-day trial in Wolverhampton on 11 Feb 1928. They were first permanently operated in Leeds, W Yorks on 16 Mar 1928 and in Edinburgh, Scotland on 19 Mar 1928.

The first vehicle-actuated lights were installed by Plessey at the Cornhill–Gracechurch junction, City of London in April 1932.

the Londoner Samuel Brown (Brit. Pat. No. 5350, 25 Apr 1826), whose 4hp two-cylinder atmospheric gas 88 litre engined carriage climbed Shooters Hill, Blackheath, Kent in May 1826.

The first successful petrol-driven car, the Motorwagen, built by Karl-Friedrich Benz (1844–1929) of Karlsruhe, Germany, ran at Mannheim, in late 1885. The three-wheeler weighed 254 kg *5 cwt* and could reach a speed of 13–16 km/h *8–10 mph*. Its single-cylinder engine (bore 91·4 mm *3·6 in*, stroke 160 mm

6·3 in) delivered 0·85 hp at 400 rpm. It was patented on 29 Jan 1886. Its first 1 km *0·6 mile* road test was reported in the local newspaper, the *Neue Badische Landeszeitung*, of 4 Jun 1886, under the heading 'Miscellaneous'.

Britain's continuous motoring history started in November 1894 when Henry Hewetson drove his imported Benz Velo in the south-eastern suburbs of London.

Production

The number of vehicles constructed world-wide in 1991 was 46 420 410, of which 34 998 534 were motorcars. The peak year for production was 1989 when 47 697 698 vehicles (35 195 749 cars) were manufactured, although the peak for cars only was 1990 when 35 277 986 were produced.

The UK production figure for 1992 was 1 540 333 vehicles of which 1 291 880 were cars. The peak year for production was 1964 when 2 332 376 vehicles (1 867 640 cars) were manufactured.

The world's largest manufacturer of motor vehicles and parts (and the largest manufacturing company) is General Motors Corporation of Detroit, Michigan, USA. The company has on average 756 300 employees. A peak figure of 948 000 vehicles were produced in 1978 and the Company's highest yearly income was $126 billion in 1989.

The largest British manufacturer is the Rover Group plc, which produced 404 971 vehicles in 1992. The company produced three out of every 10 cars built in Britain and accounted for nearly half of the number of cars exported from the UK.

Largest car plant The largest single automobile plant in the world is the Volkswagenwerk at Wolfsburg, Germany, with approx 60 000 employees and a facility for producing 4000 vehicles every week. The factory buildings cover an area of 150 ha *371 acres* and the whole plant covers 760 ha *1878 acres*, with 74 km *46 miles* of rail sidings.

Longest in production The Morgan 4/4 celebrated its 57th birthday on 27 Dec 1992. Built by the Morgan Motor Car Co. of Malvern, Hereford & Worcester

Parade of Rolls Royce cars

A parade of 114 Rolls Royce motorcars assembled on the north bound carriageway of the Tolo Harbour Highway in the New Territories of Hong Kong on 8 Sep 1991. The average length of the cars participating was 5·23 m *17 ft 2 in* and the total length of the parade was 1629 m *1 mile 22 yd*.

Skid marks

The longest recorded on a public road were 290 m *950 ft* long left by a Jaguar car involved in an accident on the M1 near Luton, Beds on 30 Jun 1960. Evidence given in the subsequent High Court case *Hurlock* v. *Inglis et al.* indicated a speed 'in excess of 100 mph before the application of the brakes'.

The skid marks made by the jet-powered *Spirit of America*, driven by Norman Craig Breedlove, after the car went out of control at Bonneville Salt Flats, Utah, USA on 15 Oct 1964, were nearly 6 miles *9·6 km* long.

Longest car

A 30·5 m *100 ft* long 26-wheeled limo was designed by Jay Ohrberg of Burbank, California, USA. It has many features, including a swimming pool with diving board and a king-sized water bed. It is designed to drive as one piece or it can be changed to bend in the middle. Its main purpose is for use in films and exhibitions.

(founded 1910), there is still a six to eight-year waiting list for delivery.

The 21 millionth Volkswagen 'Beetle' rolled off the last remaining production line, at Puebla, Mexico in December 1991.

Britain's champion seller has been the Mini (5·26 million produced), designed by

Fastest standard production road car

Sir Alec Issigonis (1906–88), which originally sold for £496 19s 2d in August 1959.

Largest Of cars produced for private use, the largest was the Bugatti 'Royale' type 41, known in Britain as the 'Golden Bugatti', of which only six were assembled at Molsheim, France by the Italian Ettore Bugatti (1882–1947). First built in 1927, this machine has an eight-cylinder engine of 12·7 litres capacity, and measures over 6·7 m *22 ft* in length. The bonnet is over 2 m *7 ft* long.

Largest engines The highest engine capacity of a production car was 13·5 litres, for the US Pierce-Arrow 6–66

Raceabout of 1912–18, the US Peerless 6–60 of 1912–14 and the Fageol of 1918.

Most powerful The most powerful current production car is the Bugatti EB110 Super Sports which develops in excess of 610 bhp.

Heaviest The heaviest car recently in production (up to twenty-five were made annually) appears to be the Soviet-built Zil–41047 limousine with a 3·88 m *12·72 ft* wheel-base. It weighs 3335 kg *7352 lb*. A 'stretched' Zil (two to three made annually) was used by former President Mikhail Gorbachev until December 1991. It weighed 6 tonnes

Most expensive car (Photo: Bob Masters)

and was made of 75 mm *3 in* armour-plated steel. The eight-cylinder, 7-litre engine guzzled fuel at the rate of 9·6 km *6 miles* to the gallon.

Lightest Louis Borsi of London has built and driven a 9·5 kg *21 lb* car with a 2·5 cc engine. It is capable of 25 km/h *15 mph*.

Most expensive *Standard* The most expensive list-price British standard car is the XJ220 Jaguar quoted at £402 418.

Used The greatest confirmed price paid is $15 million for the 1931 Bugatti Type 41 Royale Sports Coupé by Kellner, sold by Nicholas Harley to the Meitec Corporation of Japan, completed on 12 Apr 1990.

Most inexpensive The cheapest car of all time was the 1922 Red Bug Buckboard, built by the Briggs & Stratton Co. of Milwaukee, Wisconsin, USA, listed at $125–$150. It had a 1·57 m *62 in* wheel-base and weighed 111 kg *245 lb*. Early models of the King Midget cars were sold in kit form for self-assembly for as little as $100 in 1948.

In March 1993 the cheapest listed new car in Britain was the Lada Riva 1·5E at £3905.

Fastest

Land speed The *official* one-mile land-speed record is 1019·467 km/h *633·468 mph*, set by Richard Noble (b. 6 Mar 1946) on 4 Oct 1983 over the Black Rock Desert, Nevada, USA in his 17 000 lb thrust Rolls-Royce Avon 302 jet-powered *Thrust 2*, designed by John Ackroyd.

The highest speed attained in Britain is 444 km/h *276 mph* by Poutiaiten Risto (Finland) in a Top Fuel dragster on 27 May 1991 at the Santa Pod County Raceway, Beds.

Rocket-engined The highest speed attained by any wheeled land vehicle is 1016·086 km/h *631·367 mph* over the first measured kilometre by *The Blue Flame*, a rocket powered four-wheeled vehicle driven by Gary Gabelich (b. 23 Aug 1940) (USA) on the Bonneville Salt Flats, Utah, USA on 23 Oct 1970. Momentarily Gabelich exceeded 1046 km/h *650 mph*. The car was powered by a liquid natural gas/hydrogen

peroxide rocket engine which could develop thrust up to 22 000 lb.

The highest reputed land speed figure in one direction is 1190·377 km/h *739·666 mph* or Mach 1·0106 by Stan Barrett (USA) in the *Budweiser Rocket*, a rocket-engined three-wheeled car, at Edwards Air Force Base, California, USA on 17 Dec 1979. *This published speed of Mach 1·0106 is* not *officially sanctioned by the USAF as the Digital Instrument Radar was not calibrated or certified. The radar information was not generated by the vehicle directly but by an operator aiming a dish by means of a TV screen.*

The highest land speed recorded by a woman is 843·323 km/h *524·016 mph* by Mrs Kitty Hambleton (*née* O'Neil) (USA) in the rocket-powered three-wheeled SM1 *Motivator* over the Alvard Desert, Oregon, USA on 6 Dec 1976. Her official two-way record was 825·126 km/h *512·710 mph* and she probably touched 965 km/h *600 mph* momentarily.

Piston-engined The highest speed measured for a wheel-driven car is 696·331 km/h *432·692 mph* by Al Teague (USA) in *Speed-O-Motive/Spirit of 76* on Bonneville Salt Flats, Utah, USA on 21 Aug 1991 over the final 132 ft of a mile run (425·230 mph for the whole mile).

Diesel-engined The prototype 3 litre Mercedes C 111/3 attained 327·3 km/h *203·3 mph* in tests on the Nardo Circuit, southern Italy on 5–15 Oct 1978, and in April 1978 averaged 314·5 km/h *195·4 mph* for 12 hours, so covering a world record 3773·5 km *2344·7 miles*.

Electric car *UK Land speed* On 22 Jun 1991 Max Rink (18) of Oundle School, Peterborough achieved a speed of 111·37 km/h *69·21 mph* over a one km flying start, at Bruntingthorpe Proving Ground, Leics. Over the two runs the average speed achieved was 106·43 km/h *66·14 mph*. The vehicle weighed only 60 kg *132 lb* and was built in 1986 by four 14-year-old pupils from Oundle School.

Steam car On 19 Aug 1985 Robert E. Barber broke the 79-year-old record for a steam car when *Steamin' Demon*, built by the Barber-Nichols Engineering Co., reached 234·33 km/h *145·607 mph* at Bonneville Salt Flats, Utah, USA.

Road cars Various de-tuned track cars have been licensed for road use but are not normal production models.

The highest speed ever attained by a standard production car is 349·21 km/h *217·1 mph* for a Jaguar XJ220, driven by Martin Brundle at the Nardo test track, Italy on 21 Jun 1992.

The highest acceleration reported for a standard production car is 0–60 mph *0–96·5 km/h* in 3·275 sec for a Ford RS200 Evolution, driven by Graham Hathaway at the Boreham Proving Ground, Essex on 28 Apr 1993.

The fastest lap on a UK circuit by a production car was achieved in a Ferrari 512TR at an average speed of 282·2 km/h *175·4 mph*, and a peak speed over ½ mile of 285·2 km/h *177·3 mph* by Andrew Frankel of *Autocar & Motor* Magazine at Millbrook on 10 Jun 1992.

Driving

Highest mileage The highest recorded mileage for a car is 1 442 044 miles *2 320 745 km* up to 25 Jan 1993 for a 1963 Volkswagen 'Beetle' owned by Albert Klein of Pasadena, California, USA.

Six continents The fastest drive taking in the six continents, with a total distance of more than an equator's length (40 075 km *24 901 miles*), is one of 39 days 20 hr. Driving a Nissan Sunny 1·4 car, Saloo and Neena Choudhury of Calcutta, India left New Delhi, on 7 Nov 1991 and returned to the same place on 17 Dec 1991. On their journey they travelled through 25 countries.

Amphibious circumnavigation The only circumnavigation by an amphibious vehicle was by Ben Carlin (Australia) (died 7 Mar 1981) in the amphibious jeep, Half-Safe. He completed the last leg of the Atlantic crossing (the English Channel) on 24 Aug 1951. He arrived back in Montreal, Canada on 8 May 1958, having completed a circumnavigation of 39 000 miles *62 765 km* over land and 9600 miles *15 450 km* by sea and river. He was accompanied on the transatlantic stage by his ex-wife Elinore (USA) and on the long trans-Pacific stage (Tokyo to Anchorage, Alaska) by Broye Lafayette De-Mente (USA) (b. 1928).

Visiting the 12 capital cities of the European Community

Three members of the Welwyn Round Table Number 821, Stephen Long, Andrew Nation and John Orlandi, driving a Granada Scorpio Estate, visited the 12 capital cities of the European Community, covering a distance of 8802 km *5469 miles* in a time of 117 hr 52 min between 2–7 Dec 1992.

Ramp jumping (car)

The longest ramp jump in a car, with the car landing on its wheels and being driven on, is 70·73 m *232 ft*, by Jacqueline De Creed (*née* Creedy) in a 1967 Ford Mustang at Santa Pod Raceway, Beds on 3 Apr 1983.

Worst driver

It was reported that a 75-year-old male driver received ten traffic tickets, drove on the wrong side of the road four times, committed four hit-and-run offences and caused six accidents, all within 20 minutes, in McKinney, Texas, USA on 15 Oct 1966.

The most comprehensively banned driver in Britain was John Hogg, 28, who, in the High Court, Edinburgh on 27 Nov 1975, received 5¾ years in gaol and his 3rd, 4th and 5th life bans for drunken driving in a stolen car while disqualified. For his previous 40 offences he had received bans of 71½ years plus two life bans.

One-year duration record The greatest distance ever covered in one year is 573 029 km *354 257 miles* by two Opel Rekord 2-litre passenger sedans, both of which covered this distance between 18 May 1988 and the same date in 1989 without any major mechanical breakdowns. The vehicles were manufactured by the Delta Motor Corporation, Port Elizabeth, South Africa, and were driven on tar and gravel roads in the Northern Cape by a team of company drivers from

Highest recorded mileage for a car

Delta. The entire undertaking was monitored by the Automobile Association of South Africa.

Trans-Americas Garry Sowerby (Canada), with Tim Cahill (USA) as co-driver and navigator, drove a 1988 GMC Sierra K3500 four-wheel-drive pick-up truck powered by a 6·2 litre V8 Detroit diesel engine from Ushuaia, Tierra del Fuego, Argentina to Prudhoe Bay, Alaska, USA, a distance of 23720 km *14739 miles*, in a total elapsed time of 23 days 22 hr 43 min from 29 September to 22 Oct 1987. The vehicle and team were surface freighted from Cartagena, Colombia to Balboa, Panama so as to by-pass the Darién Gap.

The Darién Gap was first traversed by the LandRover *La Cucaracha Carinosa* (The Affectionate Cockroach) of the Trans-Darién Expedition 1959–60, crewed by former SAS man Richard E. Bevir (UK) and engineer Terence John Whitfield (Australia). They left Chepo, Panama on 3 Feb 1960 and reached Quibdó, Colombia on 17 June, averaging 660 ft *200 m* per hour of indescribable difficulty.

Cape to London The record time for the 18787 km *11 674 mile* road route from Cape Town, South Africa to London is 14 days 19 hr 26 min, set by husband and wife team Brig. John and Dr Lucy Hemsley from 8–22 Jan 1983 in a Range Rover. Apart from the Channel crossing they were the first to drive entirely overland from Cape Town to London.

British counties Kevin Sinclair, Richard Gamble, Jonathan Busst and Ian Canning of the London Ambulance Service completed a tour of the 73 counties of the United Kingdom, covering a distance of 5632·5 km *3500 miles* in a time of 95 hr 13 min between 2–6 Nov 1991 averaging 59·15 km/h *36·75 mph*.

Around Ireland Larry Mooney (driver), Paul Gleeson and Alan Park (navigators), all of Northern Ireland drove around the 32 counties of Ireland in a time of 12 hr 19 min between 21–22 Jun 1991, covering a distance of 917·7 km *570·2 miles* an average speed of 74 km/h *46 mph*.

Round Britain economy A Daihatsu Charade 1·0 turbo diesel driven by Helen Horwood, Joanne Swift and John Taylor around a 5827 km *3621 mile* course from 7–14 Oct 1991 returned a fuel consumption of 103·01 mpg.

The record for a petrol engined car is 78·90 mpg for a Honda Civic VEi driven by Team Mad Scientist and Crazy Guys, led by Dr. Shigeru Miyano, from 3–10 Jun 1992.

Petrol consumption A 'car' specially designed by a team of students from Lycée St Joseph la Joliverie, St Sébastien sur Loire, France achieved a performance of 7591 mpg in the Shell Mileage Marathon at Silverstone, Northants on 17 Jul 1992.

Most economical Amongst production cars available in the United Kingdom both the Citroen AX 14DTR and the Daihatsu Charade Diesel Turbo could make this claim. The Department of Transport figures are: Citroen 54·3 mpg (urban cycle), 78·5 mpg (steady 56 mph), 56·5 mpg (steady 75 mph); Daihatsu 57·6 mpg (urban cycle) 78·5 mpg (steady 56 mph), 49·6 mpg (steady 75 mph). *(Because of current standard practice metric figures have not been added).*

On 9 Aug 1989 motoring writer Stuart Bladon drove a Citroen AX 14DTR a distance of 180·26 km *112·01 miles* using one gallon of fuel driving on the M11 Motorway in a test run arranged by Lucas Diesel Systems.

Longest fuel range The greatest distance driven without refuelling in a standard vehicle is 2724 km *1691·6 miles* by a 1991 Toyota LandCruiser diesel station wagon (factory optional twin fuel tanks, capacity 174 litres *38·2 gal*). The Toyota was driven by Ewan Kennedy with Ian Lee (observer) from Nyngan, New South Wales, Australia to Winton, Queensland and back between 18–21 May 1992. The average speed was 60 km/h *37 mph.*

The greatest distance travelled by a vehicle on the contents of a standard fuel tank is 2153·4 km *1338·1 miles* by an Audi 100 TDI diesel car (capacity 17·62 gal *80·1 litres*). Stuart Bladon, with RAC observer Robert Proctor, drove from John o' Groats to Land's End and returned to Scotland between 26–28 Jul 1992.

Driving in reverse Charles Creighton (1908–70) and James Hargis of Maplewood, Missouri, USA drove their Model A Ford 1929 roadster in reverse from New York, USA 5375 km *3340 miles* to Los Angeles, California, from 26 Jul–13 Aug 1930 without once stopping the engine. They arrived back in New

The record for persistence in taking the Department of Transport's driving test is held by Mrs Git Kaur Randhawa (b. 7 Feb 1937) of Hayes, Middlesex, who triumphed at her 48th attempt, after more than 330 lessons, on 19 Jun 1987.

The world's easiest tests have been those in Egypt, in which the ability to drive 6 m *19·6 ft* forward and the same in reverse has been deemed sufficient. In 1979 it was reported that accurate reversing between two rubber traffic cones had been added. 'High cone attrition' soon led to the substitution of white lines.

York in reverse on 5 September, so completing 11 555 km *7180 miles* in 42 days.

Brian 'Cub' Keene and James 'Wilbur' Wright drove their Chevrolet Blazer 14 533 km *9031 miles* in 37 days (1 August–6 Sep 1984) in reverse through 15 US states and Canada. Though it was prominently named 'Stuck in Reverse', law enforcement officers in Oklahoma refused to believe it and insisted they drove in reverse reverse, i.e. forwards, out of the state.

The highest average speed attained in any non-stop reverse drive exceeding 800 km *500 miles* was achieved by Gerald Hoagland, who drove a 1969 Chevrolet Impala 806·2 km *501 miles* in 17 hr 38 min at Chemung Speed Drome, New York, USA on 9–10 Jul 1976, to average 45·72 km/h *28·41 mph.*

Battery-powered vehicle David Turner and Tim Pickhard of Turners of Boscastle Ltd, Cornwall, travelled 1408 km *875 miles* from Land's End to John o' Groats in 63 hr in a Freight Rover Leyland Sherpa powered by a Lucas electric motor from 21–23 Dec 1985.

Two-side-wheel driving *Car* Bengt Norberg (b. 23 Oct 1951) of Äppelbo, Sweden drove a Mitsubishi Colt GTi-16V on two side wheels non-stop for a distance of 310·391 km *192·873 miles* in a time of 7 hr 15 min 50 sec. He also achieved a distance of 44·808 km

27·842 miles in 1 hr at Rattvik Horse Track, Sweden on 24 May 1989.

Sven-Erik Söderman (Sweden) (b. 26 Sep 1960) achieved a speed of 164·38 km/h *102·14 mph* over a 100 m flying start on the two wheels of an Opel Kadett at Mora Siljan airport, Mora, Sweden on 2 Aug 1990. Söderman achieved a record speed for the flying kilometre of 152·96 km/h *95·04 mph* at the same venue on 24 Aug 1990.

Truck Sven-Erik Söderman drove a Daf 2800 7·5 ton truck on two wheels for a distance of 10·83 km *6·73 miles* at Mora Siljan airport on 19 May 1991.

Bus Bobby Ore (b. Jan 1949) drove a double-decker bus a distance of 246 m *810 ft* on two-wheels at North Weald airfield, Essex on 21 May 1988.

Wheelie Steve Murty drove a Pirelli High Performer truck on its rear wheels for 547·1 m *1794·9 ft* at the National Power Sports Festival, Blackpool, Lancs on 28 Jun 1991.

Most durable driver Goodyear Tire and Rubber Co. test driver Weldon C. Kocich drove 5 056 472 km *3 141 946 miles* from 5 Feb 1953 to 28 Feb 1986, so averaging 153 226 km *95 210 miles* per year.

Oldest driver Roy M. Rawlins (b. 10 Jul 1870) of Stockton, California, USA was warned for driving at 95 mph *152 km/h* in

The greatest distance covered by a battery-powered car on a single charge is 547·014 km *339·898 miles* by the Horlacher Na-S Sport, driven by Paul Schweizer. The car, designed by Horlacher AG of Möhlin, Switzerland, was driven on public roads from Zurich to Geneva, via Berne and Lausanne, on 4 Mar 1992.

a 55 mph *88·5 km/h* zone in June 1974. On 25 Aug 1974 he was awarded a California State licence valid until 1978, but Mr Rawlins died on 9 Jul 1975, one day short of his 105th birthday.

Mrs Maude Tull of Inglewood, California, USA, who took to driving aged 91 after her husband died, was issued a renewal on 5 Feb 1976 when aged 104.

Britain's oldest known drivers have been Benjamin Kagan (1878–1988) of Leeds and Rev. Albert Thomas Humphrey (1886–1988) from Pawlett, near Bridgwater, Somerset; both drove up to the age of 102.

The greatest age at which an individual has first passed the Department of Transport driving test has been 90 years 229 days by Mrs Gerty Edwards Land (b.

9 Sep 1897) on 27 Apr 1988 in Colne, Lancs. The oldest man to pass was David Coupar (b. 9 Feb 1898) on 4 Mar 1987 in Perth, Perthshire. He was aged 89 years 2 months .

Youngest driver Stephen Andrew Blackbourn of Lincoln, Lincs having passed his driving test on his 17th birthday, went on to pass the advanced test less than five hours later on 20 Feb 1989. His brother Mark previously held the record.

Specialized Vehicles

Largest The most massive automotive land vehicle is 'Big Muskie' built by Bucyrus Erie. (⬦ Engineering, dragline)

Longest The Arctic Snow Train has 54 wheels and is 174·3 m *572 ft* long. It was built by R.G. Le Tourneau Inc. of Longview, Texas, USA for the US Army. Its gross train weight is 400 tons, with a top speed of 32 km/h *20 mph*, and it was driven by a crew of six when used as an 'overland train' for the military. It generates 4680 shaft horsepower and has a fuel capacity of 29 648 litres *6522 gal*. It is owned by the world-famous wirewalker Steve McPeak (USA) who makes all repairs, including every punctured wheel, single-handed in often sub-zero temperatures in Alaska.

Ambulance The world's largest ambulances are the 18 m *59 ft* long articulated Alligator Jumbulances Marks VI, VII, VIII and IX, operated by the ACROSS Trust to convey the sick and handicapped on holidays and pilgrimages across Europe. They are built by Van Hool of Belgium with Fiat engines at a cost £200 000 and carry 44 patients and staff.

Buses *Earliest* The first municipal motor omnibus service in the world was inaugurated on 12 Apr 1903 and ran between Eastbourne railway station and Meads, E Sussex.

Longest The longest are the articulated DAF Super CityTrain buses of Zaïre, with 110 passenger seats and room for 140 'strap-hangers' in first trailer and 60 seated and 40 'strap-hangers' in the second, making a total of 350. Designed by the President of the Republic of Zaïre, Citoyen Mobutu Sese Seko Kuku Ngbendu wa za Banga (b. 14 Oct 1930).

Bus travelling Tony Wallis of London travelled on 112 different numbered London buses, using each route only once, from dawn to dusk on 21 Jun 1991.

They are 32·20 m *105·64 ft* long and weigh 28 tonnes unladen.

The longest rigid single bus is 14·96 m *49 ft* long, carries 69 passengers and is built by Van Hool of Belgium.

Largest fleet The 6580 single-decker buses in Rio de Janeiro, Brazil make up the world's largest bus fleet.

The largest fleet in the UK is operated by London Buses. At 26 Nov 1992, 5096 buses and coaches were operated of which 3686 were double deckers, 219 were single deckers and coaches and 1191 were mini/midibuses; 747 of the familiar Routemasters (in service since 1958) survive.

Longest route The longest regularly scheduled bus route is operated by Group Ormeño, which since August 1978 has run a regular scheduled service between Tumbes, Peru and Buenos Aires, Argentina. The route is 5727 km *3559 miles* long, taking 116 hr with two hours stop over in Lima and 12 hours in Santiago, Chile.

The longest route in Britain is route 806 between Penzance, Cornwall and Dundee, Tayside at 1102 km *685 miles*, operated by Western National Ltd and Tayside Travel Services Ltd, each company allocating coaches on alternate days.

Caravans Largest The largest two-wheeled five-storey caravan was built in 1990 for H.E Sheik Hamad Bin Hamdan Al Nahyan of Abu Dhabi, United Arab Emirates. It is 20 m *66 ft* long, 12 m *39 ft* wide and weighs 120 tons. There are eight bedrooms and bathrooms, four garages and water storage for 24 000 litres *5279 gal*.

Longest journey The continuous motor caravan journey of 231 288 km *143 716 miles* by Harry B. Coleman and Peggy Larson in a Volkswagen Camper from 20 Aug 1976 to 20 Apr 1978 took them through 113 countries.

275

Manchester's Metrolink. (Photo: Margaret Robinson)

Fastest The world speed record for a caravan tow is 204·02 km/h *126·77 mph* for a Roadstar caravan towed by a 1990 Ford EA Falcon saloon and driven by 'Charlie' Kovacs, at Mangalore Airfield, Seymour, Victoria, Australia on 18 Apr 1991.

Crawler The most massive vehicle ever constructed is the Marion eight-caterpillar crawler used for conveying Saturn V rockets to their launch pads at Cape Canaveral, Florida, USA. The two built cost $12·3 million, each measuring 131 ft 4 in × 114 ft *40 × 34·7 m*. The loaded train weight is 8165 tonnes.

The windscreen wiper blades are 106 cm *42 in* long and are the world's largest.

Dumper truck The world's largest is the Terex Titan 33–19 manufactured by General Motors Corporation and now in operation at Westar Mine, British Columbia, Canada. It has a loaded weight of 548·6 tonnes and a capacity of 317·5 tonnes. When tipping its height is 17 m *56 ft*. The 16-cylinder engine delivers 3300 hp. The fuel tank holds 5910 litres *1300 gal*.

Fire engines The fire appliance with the greatest pumping capacity is the 860 hp eight-wheel Oshkosh firetruck

Fire pumping

The greatest volume of water stirrup-pumped by a team of eight in 80 hours is 143 459 litres *31 557 gal*, by fire-fighters based at Knaresborough Fire Station, N Yorks, from 25–28 Jun 1992.

Fire pump manhandling

The longest unaided tow of a fire appliance in excess of 10 cwt *508 kg* in 24 hr on a closed circuit is 358·8 km *223 miles*, by a 32-man team of the Dublin Fire Brigade with a 520 kg *1144 lb* fire pump on 20–21 Jun 1987.

Tractor marathon

The longest journey by tractor on record is 23 335 km *14 500 miles*. The Young Farmers Group of Devon left England on 18 Oct 1990 and drove overland to Zimbabwe arriving on 4 Mar 1991.

(manufactured by Oshkosh Truck Corporation, Oshkosh, Wisconsin, USA), weighing 60 tonnes and used for aircraft and runway fires. It can discharge 189 000 litres *41 600 gal* of foam through two turrets in just 150 sec.

Fastest The fastest on record is the Jaguar XJ12 'Chubb Firefighter', which on 2 Nov 1982 atttained a speed of 210·13 km/h *130·57 mph* in tests when servicing the *Thrust 2* land speed record trials. (<> Fastest cars, land speed)

Go-Karting The highest mileage recorded in 24 hours on a outdoor circuit by a four-man team is 1638 km *1018 miles* on a one-mile track at the Erbsville Kartway, Waterloo, Ontario, Canada. The 5 hp 140cc Honda engined kart was driven by Owen Nimmo, Gary Ruddock, Jim Timmins and Danny Upshaw on 4–5 Sep 1983.

The highest mileage recorded in 24 hours on an indoor track by a four-man team driving 160cc karts is 1358·669 km *844·25 miles* on a 186·4 m *204 yd* track at the Welsh Karting Centre, Newport, Gwent. The drivers were Ken Denscombe, Gerry Austin, Kevin Blanch and Mark Bowden (Costain Civil Engineering team) who completed 7289 laps on 19–20 Nov 1992.

Lawn mowers The widest gang mower in the world is the 5 ton 60 ft *18 m* wide 27-unit 'Big Green Machine' used by the turf farmer Jay Edgar Frick of Monroe, Ohio, USA. It mows an acre in 60 sec.

The longest drive on a lawn mower was a distance of 4882 km *3034 miles*, when Ian Ireland of Harlow, Essex drove an Iseki SG15 between Harlow, and Southend Pier, Essex from 13 Aug to 7 Sep 1989. He was assisted by members of 158 Round Table, Luton, Beds and raised over £15 000 in aid of the Leukaemia Research Fund.

A 12-hour run-behind record of 169·1 km *105·1 miles* was set at Wisborough Green, W Sussex on 28–29 Jul 1990 by the 'Doctor's Flyers' team.

The greatest distance covered in the annual 12-hour Lawn Mower Race (under the rules of the British Lawn Mower Racing Association) is 468 km *291 miles* by John Gill, Robert Jones and Steve Richardson of Team Gilliams at

Wisborough Green, W Sussex on 1 and 2 Aug 1992.

Pedal car The record from Marble Arch, London to the Arc de Triomphe, Paris, France, including a Channel crossing by ferry, is 21 hr 24 min, for a distance of 383 km *238 miles*, by a team of six members from NCH (National childcare charity) on 30 Aug 1991.

Rocket-powered sleds The highest speed recorded on ice is 399·00 km/h *247·93 mph* by *Oxygen*, driven by Sammy Miller (b. 15 Apr 1945) on Lake George, New York, USA on 15 Feb 1981.

Snowmobiles John Outzen, Carl and Denis Boucher drove snowmobiles a distance of 16 499·5 km *10 252·3 miles* in 56 riding days from Anchorage, Alaska, USA to Dartmouth, Nova Scotia, Canada from 2 Jan–3 Mar 1992.

Solar powered The highest speed attained by a solely solar-powered land vehicle is 78·39 km/h *48·71 mph* by Molly Brennan driving the General Motors *Sunraycer* at Mesa, Arizona, USA on 24 Jun 1988. The highest speed of 135 km/h *83·88 mph* using solar/battery power was achieved by Star Micronics solar car *Solar Star* driven by Manfred Hermann on 5 Jan 1991 at Richmond RAAF Base, Richmond, NSW, Australia.

Taxis The largest taxi fleet is that in Mexico City, with 60 000 'normal' taxis, *pesaros* (communal fixed route taxis) and *settas* (airport taxis).

Currently there are 16 565 taxis and 20 220 taxi-drivers in London.

The longest fare on record is one of 23 196 km *14 413 miles* at a cost of 70 000 FIM (approximately £9000). Mika Lehtonen and Juhani Saramies left Nokia, Finland on 2 May 1991 and travelled through Scandinavia down to Spain and arrived back in Nokia on 17 May 1991.

Charles Kerslake (b. 27 Jun 1895) held a London Metropolitan cab licence from February 1922 until his retirement in May 1988 aged 92 years 11 months.

Trams *Longest journey* The longest now possible is from Krefeld St Tönis to Witten Annen Nord, Germany. With luck at the eight inter-connections, the

277

105·5 km *65·5 mile* trip can be achieved in 5½ hours.

The city of St Petersburg, Russia has the most extensive tramway system with 2402 cars on 64 routes with 690·6 km *429·1 miles* of track.

The first phase of Manchester's Metrolink system, England's only street-operated Light Rapid Transport (LRT) opened on 6 Apr 1992. The system is estimated to cost £140 million and will incorporate some 25 stations. It will eventually encompass the whole of the Greater Manchester area. The vehicles are 29 m *95 ft* long, seating 86 passengers with a capacity for an additional 120 standing.

The Glasgow system was scrapped in 1962 and that in London in 1952.

Oldest The oldest trams in revenue service in the world are motorcars 1 and 2 of the Manx Electric Railway, dating from 1893. These run regularly on the 28·5 km *17¾ miles* railway between Douglas and Ramsey, Isle of Man.

Trolleybuses The last trolleybus in Britain, owned by Bradford Corporation, ran in 1972. Plans have been made to reintroduce trolleybuses by both West and South Yorks Passenger Transport Executives.

Truck Les Shockley of Galena, Kansas, USA drove his Jet Truck *ShockWave* powered by three Pratt & Whitney jet engines developing 36 000 hp to a record speed of 412 km/h *256 mph* in 6·36 sec over a quarter-mile standing start on 4 Jun 1989 at Autodrome of Monterrey, Monterrey, Mexico. He set a further record for the standing mile at 605 km/h *376 mph* at Paine Field, Everett, Washington, USA on 18 Aug 1991.

Wrecker The world's most powerful wrecker is the Twin City Garage and Body Shop's 20·6 tonnes, 11 m *36 ft* long International M6-23 'Hulk' 1969 stationed at Scott City, Missouri, USA. It can lift in excess of 295 tonnes on its short boom.

Services

Car parks The world's largest is the West Edmonton Mall, Edmonton, Alberta, Canada, which can hold 20 000 vehicles. There are overflow facilities on an adjoining lot for 10 000 more cars.

Parking meters

The earliest were installed in the business district of Oklahoma City, Oklahoma, USA on 19 Jul 1935. They were invented by Carl C. Magee (USA) and reached London in 1958.

Car wrecking

In a career lasting 25 years from 1968 to 1993 Dick Sheppard of Gloucester wrecked a total of 2003 cars.

Slot car racing

The longest slot car track measures 292 m *958 ft* and was built at Mallory Park Circuit, Leicester on 22 Nov 1991 using pieces collected from enthusiasts. One lap was successfully completed by a car.

Tyre supporting

The greatest number of motor tyres supported in a free-standing 'lift' is 96, by Gary Windebank of Romsey, Hants in February 1984. The total weight was 653 kg *1440 lb*. The tyres used were Michelin XZX 155×13.

The largest parking area in Great Britain is that for 15 000 cars and 200 coaches at the National Exhibition Centre, Birmingham, West Midlands (▷ Buildings for Working, exhibition centres).

Britain's highest-capacity underground car park is at the Victoria Centre, Nottingham, with space for 1650 cars, opened in June 1972. The deepest underground car park in Britain and Europe is Aldersgate, City of London at 26 m *85 ft* below street level, comprising 14 split levels of parking and a capacity of 670 car parking spaces.

Filling stations The largest concentration of pumps are 204 — 96 of them Tokheim Unistar (electronic) and 108 Tokheim Explorer (mechanical) — in Jeddah, Saudi Arabia.

The highest filling station in the world is at Leh, Ladakh, India, at 3658 m *12 001 ft*,

The world's largest tyres are manufactured by the Goodyear Tire & Rubber Co. for giant dumper trucks. They measure 12 ft *3·65 m* in diameter, weigh 12 500 lb *5670 kg* and cost $74 000. A tyre 17 ft *5·2 m* in diameter is believed to be the limitation of what is practical.

(Photo: Rex Features/Sipa Press)

The highest filling station in the world is at Leh, Ladakh, India, at 3658 m *12 001 ft*, operated by the Indian Oil Corporation.

The commonest brand of petrol in the United Kingdom is Shell, with 2587 retail outlets or 13·4% of the total.

Garage   The largest private garage is one of two storeys built outside Bombay for the private collection of 176 cars owned by Pranlal Bhogilal (b. 1939).

The KMB Overhaul Centre, operated by the Kowloon Motor Bus Co. (1933) Ltd, Hong Kong, is the world's largest multi-storey service centre. Purpose built for double decker buses, its four floors occupy in excess of 47 000 m² *11·6 acres*.

Tow   The longest on record was one of 7658 km *4759 miles* from Halifax, Nova Scotia to Canada's Pacific coast, when Frank J. Elliott and George A. Scott of Amherst, Nova Scotia persuaded 168 passing motorists in 89 days to tow their Model T Ford (in fact engineless) to win a $1000 bet on 15 Oct 1927.

After his 1969 MGB broke down in the vicinity of Moscow, Russia (formerly USSR) the late Eddie McGowan of Chipping Warden, Oxfordshire was towed by Mark Steven Morgan driving his 1968 MGC a distance of 1569 km *975 miles* of the 2343 km *1456 miles* from Moscow to West Berlin on a single 2 m *7 ft* nylon tow rope from 12–17 Jul 1987.

Heaviest load   On 14–15 Jul 1984 John Brown Engineers & Contractors BV moved the Conoco Kotter Field production deck with a roll-out weight of 3805 tonnes for the Continental Netherlands Oil Co. of Leidsenhage, Netherlands.

The heaviest road load moved in the United Kingdom has been the 2045 tonnes, 79 m *259 ft* long Ingst motorway bridge on the M4 near Bristol, redundant after 26 years of use. The operation closed the Motorway from late on 28 Feb to 3 Mar 1992 and was conducted by Edmund Nuttall civil engineering firm and Econfreight, contractors.

Longest   The longest item moved by road was a high-pressure steel gas storage vessel 83·8 m *275 ft* long and weighing 233 tonnes transported to a new site at Beckton gasworks in east London on 10 Jul 1985. The overall train length was 99 m *325 ft*.

The longest item moved has been a 91·21 m *299 ft 3 in* horizontal bridge-like structure for use in an aircraft hangar. It weighed 62 tonnes and was transported to the paint spraying facility at Stansted airport, London on 29 Nov 1990. The overall train length was 101·12 m *331·54 ft*, and the steel structure was built and erected by Fabriweld Ltd (Ireland).

Non-stop duration   A Scalextric Jaguar XJ8 ran non-stop for 866 hr 44 min 54 sec and covered a distance of 2850·39 km *1771·2 miles* from 2 May to 7 Jun 1989. The event was organized by the Rev. Bryan G. Apps, and church members of Southbourne, Bournemouth, Dorset.

Distance, 24 hours   On 5–6 Jul 1986 the North London Society of Model Engineers team at the ARRA club in Southport, Merseyside achieved a 24-hour distance record for a 1:32 scale car of 492·364 km *305·949 miles*, 11 815 laps of the track driving a Rondeau M482C Group C Sports car, built by Ian Fisher. This was under the rules of the B.S.C.R.A (British Slot Car Racing Association). A team of eight set a new distance record of 271·126 km *168·56 miles* for the H: scale 24-hour Le Mans Slot Car Race driving a Mercedes at the Welfare Sports Centre, Derby on 20–21 Jun 1992.

Roads

Trackway   *Oldest*   The oldest known trackway in England is the Sweet Track in the Somerset Levels near Shapwick. Dendrochronologists in 1990 indicated that the road was built from trees felled in the winter of 3807–3806 BC.

The oldest in the Republic of Ireland are at Corlea and Derryoghil bogs, near Lanesborough, Co. Roscommon, where prehistoric tracks made of oak and ash logs, which have been radiocarbon dated to c. 2500–2300 BC, have been discovered.

Road mileages

The country with the greatest length of road is the United States (all 50 states), with 6 244 497 km *3 880 151 miles* of graded roads. Great Britain has 384 188 km *238 723 miles* of road, including 3210 km *1995 miles* of motorway.

Longest and shortest gaps

The greatest error a motorway driver can make when missing an exit is travelling southbound on the M11 in Hertfordshire. The gap between junctions 10 (Duxford) and 8 (Bishop's Stortford) is 28·6 km *17·8 miles*. Junction 9 is open only to northbound drivers. The shortest gap between two exits is less than 160 m *174 yd*, between junctions 19 (Clydebank) and 18 (Charing Cross), on the eastbound M8 in central Glasgow.

Milestone

Britain's oldest milestone *in situ* is a Roman stone dating from AD 150 on the Stanegate, at Chesterholme, near Bardon Mill, Northumberland.

Longest ford

The longest ford on any classified road in England is on Violet's Lane, north of Furneux Pelham, Herts, and measures 903 m *987½ yd* in length.

Longest ring-road

Work on the M25 six lane London Orbital Motorway, 195·5 km *121½ miles* long commenced in 1972 and was completed on 29 Oct 1986 at an estimated cost of £909 million, or £7·5 million per mile.

Longest motorable road The Pan-American Highway, from north-west Alaska, USA to Santiago, Chile, thence eastward to Buenos Aires, Argentina and terminating in Brasilia, Brazil is over 24 140 km *15 000 miles* in length. There is, however, a small incomplete section in Panama and Colombia known as the Darién Gap. The first all-land crossing of this was achieved by Loren Lee Upton and Patricia Mercier in a 1966 CJ 5 Jeep. Their journey began at Yaviza, Panama on 22 Feb 1985 and ended on 4 Mar 1987 at Riosuico, Columbia.

Great Britain The longest designated road in Great Britain is the A1 from London to Edinburgh, of 648 km *403 miles*.

Britain's longest uninterrupted dual carriageway is from Plymouth to Exeter (A38) and then by the M5 and M6, A74, M74, M73, M8 and A8 for a total of 827 km *514 miles* ending at Port Glasgow (west of Glasgow).

The longest Roman roads were Watling Street, from Dubrae (Dover), 346 km *215 miles* through Londinium (London) to Viroconium (Wroxeter), and Fosse Way, which ran 350 km *218 miles* from Lindum (Lincoln) through Aquae Sulis (Bath) to Isca Dumnoniorum (Exeter). However, a 16 km *10 mile* section of Fosse Way between Ilchester and Seaton remains indistinct.

Highest The highest trail in the world is a 13 km *8 mile* stretch of the Gangdise, Tibet between Khaleb and Xinjifu, Tibet, which in two places exceeds 6080 m *20 000 ft*.

The highest road in the world is in Khardungla pass at an altitude of 5682 m *18 640 ft*. This is one of the three passes of the Leh–Manali road completed in 1976 by the Border Roads Organization, New Delhi, India; motor vehicles have been able to use it from 1988.

Europe The highest motor road is the Pico de Veleta in the Sierra Nevada, southern Spain. The shadeless climb of 36 km *22·4 miles* brings the motorist to 3469 m *11 384 ft* above sea level and became, on completion of a road on its southern side in 1974, arguably Europe's highest 'pass'.

Great Britain The highest unclassified road in the United Kingdom is the A6293 tarmaced private extension at Great Dun Fell, Cumbria (847 m *2780 ft*), leading to a Ministry of Defence and Air Traffic

Control installation. A permit is required to use it.

The highest public classified road in England is the A689 at Killhope Cross (626 m *2056 ft*) on the Cumbria–Durham border near Nenthead.

The highest classified road in Scotland is the A93 road over the Grampians through Cairnwell, a pass between Blairgowrie, Perthshire and Braemar, Aberdeenshire, which reaches a height of 670 m *2199 ft*. An estate track exists to the summit of Ben a'Bhuird 1176 m *3860 ft* in Grampian.

The highest classified road in Wales is the Rhondda Afan inter-valley road (A4107), which reaches 533 m *1750 ft* in height 4 km *2½ miles* east of Abergwynfi, Mid Glamorgan.

The highest motorway in Great Britain is the trans-Pennine M62, which, at the Windy Hill interchange, reaches an altitude of 371 m *1220 ft*. Its Dean Head cutting is the deepest roadway cutting in Europe, at 55·7 m *183 ft*.

Lowest The lowest road is along the Israeli shores of the Dead Sea at 393 m *1290 ft* below sea level.

The lowest surface roads in Great Britain are just below sea level in the Holme Fen area of Cambridgeshire 2·75 m *9 ft* below sea level.

Widest The widest road in the world is the Monumental Axis, running for 2·4 km *1½ miles* from the Municipal Plaza to the Plaza of the Three Powers in Brasilia, the capital of Brazil. The six-lane boulevard was opened in April 1960 and is 250 m *820·2 ft* wide.

The San Francisco–Oakland Bay Bridge Toll Plaza has 23 lanes (17 westbound) serving the bridge in Oakland, California, USA.

The only instance of 17 carriageway lanes side by side in Britain occurs on the M61 at Linnyshaw Moss, Worsley, Greater Manchester.

Traffic volume The most heavily travelled stretch of road is Interstate 405 (San Diego Freeway), in Orange County, California, USA, which has a peak-hour volume of 25 500 vehicles. This volume occurs on a 0·9 mile stretch between

Garden Grove Freeway and Seal Beach Boulevard.

The greatest traffic density at any one point in Great Britain is at Hyde Park Corner, London. The peak flow (including the underpass) for 24 hours in 1990 was 240 000 vehicles.

Motorway Britain's busiest and most heavily travelled motorway is the M25; with the section between Junctions 13 (Staines) and 14 (Heathrow) having an average traffic flow of 168 000 vehicles over a 24 hour period.

Traffic density The territory with the highest traffic density in the world is Hong Kong. In 1992 there were 418 vehicles per mile of serviceable roads, i.e. a density of 3·84 m *4·21 yd* per vehicle.

The comparative figure for Great Britain was 14·8 m *16·2 yd* per vehicle in 1991.

Traffic jams The longest ever reported was that which stretched 176 km *109·3 miles* northwards from Lyon towards Paris, France on 16 Feb 1980. A record traffic jam was reported of 1½ million cars crawling bumper-to-bumper over the East-West German border on 12 Apr 1990.

The longest in Britain were two of 40 miles *64·3 km*: on the M1 from Junction 13 (Milton Keynes) to Junction 18 (Rugby) on 5 Apr 1985; and on the M6 between Charnock Richard and Carnforth, Lancs on 17 Apr 1987 involving 200 000 people and a tailback of 50 000 cars and coaches.

The longest of solid stationary traffic was 22 miles *35·40 km* on the M25 from midway between Junction 9 (Leatherhead) and Junction 8 (Reigate) on 17 Aug 1988.

Most complex interchange The most complex interchange on the British road system is that at Gravelly Hill, north of Birmingham on the Midland Link Motorway section of the M6, opened on 24 May 1972. Popularly known as 'Spaghetti Junction', it includes 18 routes on six levels (together with a diverted canal and river). Its construction needed 26 000 tonnes of steel, 250 000 tonnes of concrete and 300 000 tonnes of earth, and cost £8·2 million.

Longest viaduct The longest elevated viaduct on the British road system is the 4·78 km *2·97 mile* Gravelly Hill to Castle Bromwich section of the M6 in the West Midlands. It was completed in May 1972. (⊳ Most complex interchange)

Streets *Longest* The longest designated street in the world is Yonge Street, running north and west from Toronto, Canada. The first stretch, completed on 16 Feb 1796, ran 55 km *34 miles*. Its official length, now extended to Rainy River on the Ontario–Minnesota border, is 1896·3 km *1178·3 miles*.

Narrowest The world's narrowest street is in the village of Ripatransone in the Marche region of Italy. It is called Vicolo della Virilita ('Virility Alley') and is 43 cm *16·9 in* wide.

Shortest The title of 'The Shortest Street in the World' is claimed by the town of Bacup in Lancashire, where Elgin Street, situated by the old market ground, measures just 17 ft *5·2 m*.

Steepest The steepest street in the world is Baldwin Street, Dunedin, New Zealand, which has a maximum gradient of 1 in 1·266.

Britain's steepest motorable road is the unclassified Chimney Bank at Rosedale Abbey, N Yorks which is signposted '1 in 3'. The county surveyor states it is 'not quite' a 33 per cent gradient. Unclassified road No. 149 at Ffordd Penllech, Harlech which is narrow and twisting, is at its steepest gradient 1 in 2·91.

Squares *Largest* Tiananmen 'Gate of Heavenly Peace' Square in Beijing, described as the navel of China, covers 39·6 ha *98 acres*.

Great Britain The largest square in Great Britain is the 2·82 ha *6·99 acre* Ladbroke Square (open to residents only), constructed in 1842–5, while Lincoln's Inn Fields covers 2·76 ha *6·84 acres*.

Railways

Trains

Earliest Wagons running on wooden rails were used for mining as early as 1550 at Leberthal, Alsace, and in Britain

---

Model railway

A standard 'Life-Like' BL2 HO scale electric train pulled six eight-wheel coaches for 1207½ hr from 4 Aug–23 Sep 1990 covering a distance of 1463·65 km *909½ miles*. The event was organized by Ike Cottingham and Mark Hamrick of Mainline Modelers of Akron, Ohio, USA.

The longest recorded run by a model *steam* locomotive is 231·7 km *144 miles* in 27 hr 18 min by the 18·4 cm *7¼ in* gauge 'Winifred', built in 1974 by Wilf Grove at Thames Ditton, Surrey, on 8–9 Sep 1979. 'Winifred' works on 5·6 kg/cm² *80 lb/in²* pressure and is coal-fired, with cylinders 54 mm *2⅛ in* in diameter and 79 mm *3⅛ in* stroke.

The most miniature model railway ever built is one of 1:1000 scale by Jean Damery (b. 1923) of Paris, France. The engine runs on a 4½ volt battery and measures 7·9 mm *5/16 in* overall.

---

for conveying coal from Strelley to Wollaton near Nottingham from 1604–15 and at Broseley Colliery, Shrops in October 1605.

Richard Trevithick built his first steam locomotive for the 914 mm *3 ft* gauge iron plateway at Coalbrookdale, Shrops in 1803, but there is no evidence that it ran. His second locomotive drew wagons in which men rode on a demonstration run at Penydarren, Mid Glamorgan on 22 Feb 1804, but it broke the plate rails.

The earliest commercially successful steam locomotive worked in 1812 on the Middleton Colliery Railway to Leeds, Yorks, and was authorized by Britain's first Railway Act of 9 Jun 1758.

The first permanent public railway to use steam traction was the Stockton & Darlington, from its opening on 27 Sep 1825 from Shildon to Stockton via Darlington, in Cleveland. The 7-tonne *Locomotion* could pull 48 tonnes at a

speed of 24 km/h *15 mph*. It was designed and at times driven by George Stephenson (1781–1848).

The first regular steam passenger service was inaugurated over a one-mile section (between Bogshole Farm and South Street in Whitstable, Kent) on the 10·05 km *6¼ mile* Canterbury & Whitstable Railway on 3 May 1830, hauled by the engine *Invicta*.

The first practical electric railway was Werner von Siemens' oval metre gauge demonstration track, about 300 m *984 ft* long, at the Berlin Trades Exhibition on 31 May 1879.

Fastest The highest speed attained by a railed vehicle is 9851 km/h *6121 mph*, or Mach 8, by an unmanned rocket sled over the 15·2 km *9½ mile* long rail track at White Sands Missile Range, New Mexico, USA on 5 Oct 1982.

The highest speed recorded on any national rail system is 515 km/h *320 mph* by the French SNCF high-speed train TGV (Train à Grande Vitesse) between Courtalain and Tours on 18 May 1990. It

A dramatic shot of the Trans-Siberian Railway, the world's longest railway. The first section was opened at the end of the last century, and a link from Moscow to the Sea of Japan established in 1901. Additional stretches have been added from time to time since then to make the journey faster, most recently in 1984.
(Photo: Sygma/D. Kirkland)

was brought into service on 27 Sep 1981. By September 1983 it had reduced its scheduled time for the Paris–Lyon run of 425 km *264 miles* to two hours exactly, so averaging 212·5 km/h *132 mph*.

The highest speed ever ratified for a steam locomotive was 201 km/h *125 mph* over 402 m *440 yd* by the LNER 4–6–2 No. 4468 *Mallard* (later numbered 60022), which hauled seven coaches weighing 243 tonnes gross down Stoke Bank, near Essendine, between Grantham, Lincs, and Peterborough, Cambs, on 3 Jul 1938. Driver Joseph Duddington was at the controls with Fireman Thomas Bray. The engine suffered damage to the middle big-end bearing.

British Rail inaugurated their HST (High Speed Train) daily services between London–Bristol and South Wales on 4 Oct 1976. The electric British Rail APT-P (Advanced Passenger Train-Prototype) attained 261 km/h *162 mph* between Glasgow and Carlisle on its first revenue-earning run on 7 Dec 1981. It covered the 644 km *400 miles* from Glasgow to London in 4¼ hr, but was subsequently withdrawn from service because of technical problems.

The fastest scheduled train on British Rail is the Edinburgh–London *Flying Scotsman*, which covers the 633·2 km *393·5 miles* in 249 minutes, at an average speed of 152·6 km/h *94·8 mph* including two stops. This train is powered by the fastest locomotives in current service, the Class 91 25kV electric type, one of which reached 260 km/h *162 mph* between Grantham and Peterborough on 18 Sep 1989.

Longest non-stop run The longest run on British Rail without a publicly-advertized stop is the *Night Scotsman* sleeping car service between London Euston and Edinburgh, a distance of 644 km *400 miles*, taking 6 hr 27 min. The longest journey without any scheduled stop is the *Newcastle Pullman*, which covers the 374·1 km *232·5 miles* between Darlington and London in 2 hr 22 min.

Most powerful The world's most powerful steam locomotive, measured by tractive effort, was No. 700, a triple-articulated or triplex six-cylinder 2–8–8–8–4 engine built by the Baldwin Locomotive Works in 1916 for the Virginian Railway, USA. It had a tractive force of 75 434 kg *166 300 lb* when working compound and 90 520 kg *199 560 lb* when working simple.

Probably the heaviest train ever hauled by a single engine was one of 15 545 tonnes made up of 250 freight cars stretching 2·5 km *1·6 miles* by the *Matt H. Shay* (No. 5014), a 2–8–8–8–2

engine, which ran on the Erie Railroad from May 1914 until 1929.

In September 1990 a single locomotive hauled a 5220-tonne train with 50 wagons carrying limestone from Merehead Quarry, Somerset to Acton, Greater London — the heaviest on record in Britain. (⇨ Freight trains)

Largest steam locomotive The largest operating steam locomotive is the Union Pacific RR *Challenger* type 4–6–6–4 No. 3985, built by the American Locomotive Co. in 1943. In working order, with tender, it weighs 485 tonnes. It is used on enthusiasts' specials in the USA.

Greatest load The world's strongest rail carrier, with a capacity of 807 tonnes, is the 336-tonne 36-axle 'Schnabel'. It is 92 m *301 ft 10 in* long and was built for a US railway by Krupp, Germany in March 1981.

The heaviest load carried by British Rail was a boiler drum weighing 279 tonnes and 37·1 m *122 ft* long which was carried from Immingham Dock to Killingholme, Humberside in September 1968.

The heaviest load ever moved on rails is the 10 860-tonne Church of the Virgin Mary (built in 1548 in Most, now Czech Republic), in October–November 1975, because it was in the way of coal workings. It was moved 730 m *800 yd* at 0·002 km/h *0·0013 mph* over four weeks, at a cost of £9 million.

Freight trains The world's longest and heaviest freight train on record, with the largest number of wagons recorded, made a run on the 1065 mm *3 ft 6 in* gauge Sishen–Saldanha railway in South Africa on 26–27 Aug 1989. The train consisted of 660 wagons each loaded to 105 tons gross, a tank car and a caboose, moved by nine 50 kV electric and seven diesel-electric locomotives distributed along the train. The train was 7·3 km *4½ miles* long and weighed 69 393 tons excluding locomotives. It travelled 861 km *535 miles* in 22 hr 40 min.

British Rail's heaviest freight train runs from Merehead Quarry, Somerset to Acton, Greater London, usually with 5100 tonnes of limestone in 50 wagons. The train is hauled by a single 'Class 59' diesel locomotive. (⇨ Most powerful above)

285

The longest regular freight train journey on British Rail is the twice-weekly china clay train from Burngullow, Cornwall to Irvine, Scotland, a round trip of 1834 km *1140 miles*, hauled by the same pair of diesel locomotives throughout.

Longest passenger train The longest passenger train measured 1732 m *1894 yd*, consisting of 70 coaches. It was pulled by one electric locomotive and the total weight was 2786 tonnes. The train of the National Belgian Railway Company took 1 hr 11 min 5 sec to complete the 62 km *38·5 mile* journey from Ghent to Ostend on 27 Apr 1991.

Tracks

Longest The world's longest run is one of 9438 km *5864½ miles* on the Trans-Siberian line from Moscow to Nakhodka, Russia, on the Sea of Japan. There are 97 stops on the journey, which is scheduled to take 8 days 4 hr 25 min.

The longest and newest cross-country railway in the world is the 3145 km *1954 mile* Baikal–Amur Mainline (BAM), begun in 1938, restarted in 1974 and put into service on 27 Oct 1984. It runs from Ust-Kut, Eastern Siberia to Komsomolsk on the Amur River in Russia. The volume of earth and rock which had to be

The highest railway line is the Central Railway of the Peruvian State Railways, which reaches an altitude of 4818 m *15 806 ft*. There are 67 tunnels and 59 bridges, some of which are engineering works in themselves.
(Photo: Chris Kapolka)

moved was estimated at 382 million m³ *13 500 million ft³*.

Longest straight The Commonwealth Railways Trans-Australian line over the Nullarbor Plain, from Mile 496 between Nurina and Loongana, Western Australia to Mile 793 between Ooldea and Watson,

Spike driving
In the World Championship Professional Spike Driving Competition held at the Golden Spike National Historic Site in Utah, USA, Dale C. Jones, 49, of Lehi, Utah, USA drove six 17·8 cm *7 in* railroad spikes in a time of 26·4 sec on 11 Aug 1984. He incurred no penalty points under the official rules.

South Australia, is 478 km *297 miles* dead straight, although not level.

The longest straight on British Rail is the 29 km *18 miles* between Barlby Junction and Brough, N Yorks on the 'down' line from Selby to Kingston-upon-Hull, Humberside.

Widest and narrowest gauge The widest in standard use is 1·676 m *5 ft 6 in.* This width is used in Spain, Portugal, India, Pakistan, Bangladesh, Sri Lanka, Argentina and Chile.

The narrowest gauge on which public services are operated is 260 mm *10¼ in* on the Wells Harbour (1·12 km *0·7 mile*) and the Wells Walsingham Railways (6·5 km *4 miles*) in Norfolk.

Highest line At 4818 m *15 806 ft* above sea level, the standard gauge (1435 mm *4 ft 8½ in*) track on the Morococha branch of the Peruvian State Railways at La Cima is the highest in the world.

The highest point on the British Rail system is at Drumochter Pass on the old Perthshire-Inverness border, where the track reaches an altitude of 452 m *1484 ft* above sea-level.

The highest railway in Britain is the Snowdon Mountain Railway, which rises from Llanberis, Gwynedd to 1064 m *3493 ft* above sea-level, just below the summit of Snowdon (*Yr Wyddfa*). It has a gauge of 800 mm *2 ft 7½ in.*

Lowest line The world's lowest is in the Seikan Tunnel between Honshu and Hokkaido, Japan. The rails are 240 m *786 ft* below the Tsugaro Straits. The tunnel was opened on 13 Mar 1988 and is 53·8 km *33½ miles* long.

The lowest in Europe is the Channel Tunnel, where the rails are 127 m *417 ft* below mean sea level.

On British Rail, the Severn Tunnel descends to 43·8 m *144 ft* below sea level.

Steepest railway The world's steepest railway is the Katoomba Scenic Railway in the Blue Mountains of NSW, Australia. It is 310 m *1020 ft* long with a gradient of 1 in 0·82. A 220 hp electric winding machine hauls the car by twin steel cables 22 mm diameter. The ride takes about 1 min 40 sec and carries around 420 000 passengers a year.

Steepest gradient The world's steepest standard-gauge gradient by adhesion is 1:11, between Chedde and Servoz on the metre-gauge SNCF Chamonix line, France.

The steepest sustained adhesion-worked gradient on a main line in the United Kingdom is the 3·2 km *2 mile* Lickey incline of 1:37·7, just south-west of Birmingham, W. Midlands.

Slightest gradient The mildest gradient posted on the British Rail system is one indicated as 1:14 400 between Pirbright, Surrey Junction and Farnborough, Hants. This could be described alternatively as England's most obtuse summit.

Busiest system The railway carrying the largest number of passengers is the East Japan Railway Co., which in 1992 carried 16 306 000 daily.

Greatest length of railway The country with the greatest length of railway is the United States with 286 814 km *178 223 miles* of route.

The farthest anyone can get from a railway on the mainland island of Great Britain by road is 156·6 km *97¼ miles* in the case of Southend, Mull of Kintyre, Strathclyde.

The number of journeys made on British Rail in 12 months to 31 Mar 1992 was 739 700 000 (average 43·3 km *27 miles*) compared with the peak year of 1957, when 1101 million journeys (average 33 km *20½ miles*) were made.

Stations

Largest The world's largest station is Grand Central Terminal, Park Avenue and 42nd Street, New York City, USA, built from 1903–13. It covers 19 ha *48 acres* on two levels with 41 tracks on the upper level and 26 on the lower. On average more than 550 trains and 200 000 people per day use it.

The largest railway station on the British Rail system is Waterloo, London (11·4 ha *28¼ acres*). Following completion of five new platforms in 1993 for international trains using the Channel Tunnel, its 24 main and two Waterloo and City Line

287

platforms have a total length of 6357 m *20 866 ft*.

Oldest Liverpool Road Station, Greater Manchester was first used on 15 Sep 1830. Part of the original station is now a museum.

Busiest The busiest railway junction in the world is Clapham Junction, London, on the Southern Region of British Rail, with an average of 2200 trains passing through each 24 hours. All trains from Waterloo and all the Brighton line trains from Victoria pass through.

Highest The Condor station in Bolivia at 4786 m *15 705 ft* on the metre gauge Rio Mulato to Potosi line is the highest in the world.

The highest passenger station on British Rail is Corrour, Inverness-shire at an altitude of 410·5 m *1347 ft* above sea level.

Waiting-rooms The world's largest waiting-rooms are the four in Beijing Station, Chang'an Boulevard, Beijing, China, opened in September 1959, with a total standing capacity of 14 000.

Platforms The longest railway platform in the world is the Kharagpur platform, West Bengal, India, which measures 833 m *2733 ft* in length.

The State Street Center subway platform on 'The Loop' in Chicago, Illinois, USA measures 1066 m *3500 ft* in length.

The longest in the British Rail system is the 602·7 m *1977 ft 4 in* long platform at Gloucester.

The two platforms comprising the New Misato railway station on the Musashino line, Saitama, Japan are 300 m *984 ft* apart and are connected by a bridge.

Underground Railways

Most extensive The subway with most stations in the world is the New York City Metropolitan Transportation Authority subway, USA (first section opened on 27 Oct 1904). There are 469 subway stations in a network which covers 380 km *238 route miles*. It serves an estimated 5 million underground and bus passengers per day.

The most extensive underground or rapid transit railway systems of the 94 in the world is the London Underground, with 408 km *254 miles* of route, of which 135 km *85 miles* is bored tunnel and 32 km *20 miles* is 'cut and cover'. The whole system is operated by a staff of 21 200 serving 273 stations. The 4146 cars forming a fleet of 570 trains carried 751 million passengers in 1991–2.

The longest underground journey without a change is on the Central Line from Epping to West Ruislip — 54·9 km *34·1 miles*.

Busiest The world's busiest ever metro system has been the Greater Moscow Metro (opened 1935) in Russia. At its peak there were 3·3 billion passenger journeys in a year, although by 1991 the figure had declined to 2·5 billion. It has 3500 railcars and a workforce of 25 000. There are 141 stations (18 of which have more than one name, being transfer stations) and 226·7 km *140 miles* of track. A 5 kopek fare was maintained for the first 56 years from 1935–91, but the fare has now been increased to 3 roubles.

Rail Travel

Calling all stations Alan M. Witton of Chorlton, Manchester visited every open British Rail station (2362) in a continuous tour for charity of 26 703 km *16 593 miles* in 452 hr 26½ min from 13 Jul–28 Aug 1980.

Colin M. Mulvany and Seth N. Vafiadis of west London visited every open British Rail station (2378) embracing also the Tyne & Wear, Glasgow and London underground systems (333 stations) for charity in 31 days 5 hr 8 min 58 sec. They travelled over 24 989 km *15 528 miles* to average 61·2 km/h *38·1 mph* from 4 Jun–5 Jul 1984.

Four points of the compass Norma and Ronald Carter and their children Jonathan and Nicola of Whitkirk, Leeds, W Yorks visited the northernmost, southernmost, westernmost and easternmost stations in Great Britain in a time of 40 hr 5 min from 15–16 Aug 1991. These are Thurso, Scotland (north), Lowestoft, Suffolk (east), Penzance, Cornwall (south) and Arisaig, Scotland (west).

Most miles in 7 days Andrew Kingsmell and Sean Andrews of Bromley, Kent together with Graham Bardouleau of

Train spotting

Bill Curtis of Clacton-on-Sea, Essex is acknowledged as the world champion train spotter—or 'gricer' (after Richard Grice, the first champion). His totals include some 60 000 locomotives, 11 200 electric units and 8300 diesel units, clocked up over a period of 40 years in a number of different countries.

Longest issued railway ticket

A rail ticket measuring 34 m *111 ft 10½ in* was issued to Ronald, Norma and Jonathan Carter for a series of journeys on British Rail throughout England between 15–23 Feb 1992.

Suggestion boxes

The most prolific example on record of the use of any suggestion box scheme is that of John Drayton (1907–87) of Newport, Gwent, who plied the British rail system with a total of 31 400 suggestions from 1924 to August 1987. More than one in seven were adopted and 100 were accepted by London Transport. In 1983 he was presented with a chiming clock by British Rail to mark almost 60 years of suggestions.

Underground tour

The record time for doing a tour of the London Underground taking in all of the 273 stations is 18 hr 41 min 41 sec by a team of five—Robert A. Robinson, Peter D. Robinson, Timothy J. Robinson, Timothy J. Clark and Richard J. Harris—on 30 Jul 1986.

Crawley, W Sussex travelled 21 090 km *13 105 miles* on the French national railway system in 6 days 22 hr 38 min from 28 Nov–5 Dec 1992.

Most miles in 24 hours The greatest distance travelled on British Rail in 24 hours (without duplicating any part of the journey) is 2842·5 km *1766¼ miles* by Norma and Jonathan Carter, 15, from 3–4 Sep 1992.

The greatest distance on British Rail in 24 hours using environmentally friendly electric trains is 2817·2 km *1750½ miles*, by Ronald and Jonathan Carter on 16–17 Jul 1992.

Longest journey In the course of some 73 years commuting by British Rail from Kent to London, Ralph Ransome of Birchington travelled an equivalent of an estimated 39 times round the world. He retired early, aged 93, on 5 Feb 1986.

Most countries travelled through in 24 hours The record number of countries travelled through entirely by train in 24 hours is ten, by Aaron Kitchen on 16–17 Feb 1987. His route started in Yugoslavia and continued through Austria, Italy, Liechtenstein, Switzerland, France, Luxemburg, Belgium and the Netherlands, arriving in West Germany 22 hr 42 min later.

Handpumped railcars A speed of 33 km/h *20½ mph* for a 300 m *984 ft* course was achieved by Gold's Gym, Surrey, British Columbia, Canada at the Annual World Championship Handcar Races, Port Moody, British Columbia with their five-man team (one pusher, four pumpers) in a time of 32·71 sec on 5 Jul 1986.

Aviation

The first controlled and sustained power-driven flight occurred near the Kill Devil Hill, Kitty Hawk, North Carolina, USA at 10:35 a.m. on 17 Dec 1903, when Orville Wright (1871–1948) flew the 12-hp chain-driven *Flyer I* for a distance of 36·5 m *120 ft* at an airspeed of 48 km/h *30 mph*, a ground speed of 10·9 km/h *6·8 mph* and an altitude of 2·5–3·5 m *8–12 ft* for about 12 seconds, watched by his brother Wilbur (1867–1912), four men and a boy. Both brothers, from Dayton, Ohio, were bachelors because, as Orville put it, they had not the means to 'support a wife as well as an aeroplane'. The *Flyer I* was first exhibited in

the National Air and Space Museum at the Smithsonian Institution, Washington DC, USA on 17 Dec 1948.

The first hop by a man-carrying aeroplane entirely under its own power was made when Clément Ader (1841–1925) of France flew in his *Éole* for about 50 m *164 ft* at Armainvilliers, France on 9 Oct 1890. It was powered by a lightweight steam engine of his own design, which developed about 15 kW *20 hp*.

The earliest 'rational design' for a flying machine, according to the Royal Aeronautical Society, was that published by Emanuel Swedenborg (1688–1772) in Sweden in 1717.

Great Britain The first officially recognized flight in the British Isles was made by the US citizen Samuel Franklin Cody (1861–1913) who flew 423 m *1390 ft* in his own biplane at Farnborough, Hants on 16 Oct 1908.

Horatio Frederick Phillips (1845–1924) almost certainly covered 152 m *500 ft* in his *Multiplane* 'Venetian blind' aeroplane at Streatham, Surrey in 1907.

The first Briton to fly was George Pearson Dickin (1881–1909), a journalist from Southport, Lancs as a passenger to Wilbur Wright at Auvour, France on 3 Oct 1908.

The first resident British citizen to fly in Britain was J.T.C. Moore-Brabazon (later Lord Brabazon of Tara) (1884–1964),

The Hughes H.4 Hercules flying-boat *Spruce Goose* has the largest wing span of any aircraft, at 97·51 m *319 ft 11 in*. It flew just once, in a test run in 1947.
(Photo: Sygma)

with three short but sustained flights from 30 Apr–2 May 1909.

Cross-Channel The earliest crossing was made on 25 Jul 1909 when Louis Blériot (1872–1936) of France flew his Blériot XI monoplane, powered by a 23-hp Anzani engine, 41·8 km *26 miles* from Les Baraques, France to Northfall Meadow, near Dover Castle, Kent in 36½ minutes, after taking off at 4:41 a.m.

Jet-engined Proposals for jet propulsion date back to Capt. Marconnet (1909) of France, and Henri Coanda (1886–1972) of Romania, and to the turbojet proposals of Maxime Guillaume (France) in 1921.

The earliest tested run was that of British Power Jets' experimental WU1 (Whittle Unit No. 1) at Rugby on 12 Apr 1937, invented by Flying Officer (later Air Commodore) Sir Frank Whittle (b. 1 Jun 1907), who had applied for a patent on jet propulsion in 1930.

The first flight by an aeroplane powered by a turbojet engine was made by the

Heinkel He 178, piloted by Flugkapitän Erich Warsitz, at Marienehe, Germany on 27 Aug 1939. It was powered by a Heinkel He S3b engine weighing 378 kg *834 lb* (as installed with long tailpipe) designed by Dr Hans Pabst von Ohain. First bench tests were made in 1937.

The first British jet flight of 17 minutes was made by Flt Lt P.E.G. 'Jerry' Sayer (killed 1942) in the Gloster-Whittle E.28/39 (wing span 8·84 m *29 ft*, length 7·70 m *25 ft 3 in*) fitted with an 390 kg *860 lb* s.t. Whittle W-1 engine at Cranwell, Lincs on 15 May 1941. The maximum speed was *c.* 560 km/h *350 mph*. This aircraft (W4041/G) is now in the Science Museum, London.

Supersonic flight The first was achieved on 14 Oct 1947 by Capt. (later Brig Gen) Charles ('Chuck') Elwood Yeager (b. 13 Feb 1923), over Edwards Air Force Base, Muroc, California, USA in a Bell XS-1 rocket plane ('Glamorous Glennis' named after Yeager's wife) at Mach 1·015 (1078 km/h *670 mph*) at an altitude of 12 800 m *42 000 ft*. The XS-1 is now in the National Air and Space Museum at the Smithsonian Instutution, Washington, DC, USA.

The first British aircraft to attain Mach 1 in a dive was the de Havilland D.H.108 tail-less research aircraft on 9 Sep 1948, piloted by John Derry (killed 1952).

The former Soviet Tupolev T-144, first flown on 31 Dec 1968 and therefore the world's first supersonic airliner to fly, entered service initially carrying cargo only.

London–New York

The record from central London to downtown New York City, New York, USA—by helicopter and Concorde—is 3 hr 59 min 44 sec and the return 3 hr 40 min 40 sec, set by David J. Springbett and David Boyce on 8–9 Feb 1982.

Round the world

The fastest time for a circumnavigation under FAI regulations using scheduled flights is 44 hr 6 min by David J. Springbett (b. 2 May 1938) of Taplow, Bucks. His route took him from Los Angeles, California, USA eastabout via London, Bahrain, Singapore, Bangkok, Manila, Tokyo and Honolulu from 8–10 Jan 1980 over a 37 124 km *23 068 mile* course.

Trans-Atlantic The first crossing of the North Atlantic by air was made by Lt Cdr. (later Rear Admiral) Albert Cushion Read (1887–1967) and his crew (Stone, Hinton, Rodd, Rhoads and Breese) in the 84-knot *155 km/h* US Navy/Curtiss flying-boat NC-4 from Trepassey Harbor, Newfoundland, Canada via the Azores, to Lisbon, Portugal from 16–27 May 1919. The whole flight of 7591 km *4717 miles*, originating from Rockaway Air Station, Long Island, New York, USA on 8 May, required 53 hr 58 min, terminating at Plymouth, Devon on 31 May. The Newfoundland–Azores flight of 1930 km *1200 miles* took 15 hr 18 min at 81·7 knots *151·4 km/h*.

Non-stop The first non-stop transatlantic flight was achieved 18 days later. The pilot, Capt. John Williams Alcock (1892–1919), and navigator, Lt Arthur Whitton Brown (1886–1948) left Lester's Field, St John's, Newfoundland, Canada at 4:13 p.m. GMT on 14 Jun 1919, and landed at Derrygimla bog near Clifden, Co. Galway, Republic of Ireland at 8:40 a.m. GMT, 15 June, having covered a distance of 3154 km *1960 miles* in their Vickers Vimy, powered by two 360-hp Rolls-Royce Eagle VIII engines. Both men were created civil KBES on 21 Jun

1919, when Alcock was aged 26 years 227 days, and they shared a *Daily Mail* prize of £10000.

Solo The first solo trans-Atlantic flight was achieved by Capt. (later Brigadier) Charles Augustus Lindbergh (1902–74) who took off in his 220 hp Ryan monoplane *Spirit of St Louis* at 12:52 p.m. GMT on 20 May 1927 from Roosevelt Field, Long Island, New York, USA. He landed at 10:21 p.m. GMT on 21 May 1927 at Le Bourget Airfield, Paris, France. His flight of 5810 km *3610 miles* lasted 33 hr 29½ min and he won a prize of $25000. The *Spirit of St Louis* is now in the National Air and Space Museum at the Smithsonian Institution, Washington DC, USA.

North-Atlantic The first solo, two-way staged crossing of the North Atlantic in an open-cockpit home-built biplane was achieved by 70-year-old former US Air Force pilot Burdon L. ('Dave') Davidson. Flying his Marquart MA5 Charger (registration N13DD) eastbound from Goose Bay, Newfoundland on 6 Jul 1991, via Greenland and Iceland, he reached Stornoway, Lewis on 16 July. The westbound flight over the same route was recorded between 16–28 Aug 1991.

Trans-Pacific The first non-stop flight was by Major Clyde Pangborn and Hugh Herndon in the Bellanca cabin monoplane *Miss Veedol*. They took off from Sabishiro Beach, Japan and covered the distance of 7335 km *4558 miles* to Wenatchee, Washington State, USA in 41 hr 13 min from 3–5 Oct 1931. (For earliest crossing, ⊳ Circumnavigational flights)

Circumnavigational flights Strict circumnavigation of the globe requires the aircraft to pass through two antipodal points, thus covering a minimum distance of 40 007·86 km *24 859·73 miles*.

Earliest The earliest such flight, of 42398 km *26 345 miles*, was by two US Army Douglas DWC amphibians in 57 'hops' between 6 April and 28 Sep 1924, beginning and ending at Seattle, Washington State, USA. The *Chicago* was piloted by Lt Lowell H. Smith and Lt Leslie P. Arnold, and the *New Orleans* by Lt Erik H. Nelson and Lt John Harding. Their flying time was 371 hr 11 min.

Fastest The fastest flight under the FAI (Fédération Aéronautique Internationale) rules, which permit flights that exceed the length of the Tropic of Cancer or Capricorn (36787·6 km *22858·8 miles*), was that of the eastabout flight of 32 hr 49 min by an Air France Concorde (Capts. Claude Delorme and Jean Boyé) from Lisbon, Portugal via Santo Domingo, Acapulco, Honolulu, Guam, Bangkok and Bahrain on 12–13 Oct 1992. The AF 1492 flight was undertaken to celebrate the 500th anniversary of Christopher Columbus' discovery of the New World.

First without refuelling Richard G. 'Dick' Rutan and Jeana Yeager, in their specially constructed aircraft *Voyager*, designed by Dick's brother Burt Rutan, flew from Edwards Air Force Base, California, USA from 14–23 Dec 1986. Their flight took 9 days 3 min 44 sec and they covered a distance of 40212 km *24987 miles* averaging 186·11 km/h *115·65 mph*. The plane, with a wing span of 33·77 m *110 ft 10 in*, was capable of carrying 5636 litres *1240 gal* of fuel weighing 4052 kg *8934 lb*. It took over two years to construct. The pilot flew in a cockpit measuring 1·71 × 0·55 m *5 ft 7 in × 1 ft 10 in* and the off-duty crew member occupied a cabin 2·29 × 0·61 m *7 ft 6 in × 2 ft*. *Voyager* is now in the National Air and Space Museum at the Smithsonian Institution, Washington DC, USA.

First circum-polar Capt. Elgen M. Long, 44, achieved the first circum-polar flight in a Piper PA-31 Navajo from 5 Nov–3 Dec 1971. He covered 62597 km *38 896 miles* in 215 flying hours. The cabin temperature sank to −40°C *−40°F* over Antarctica.

First single-engined flight Richard Norton, an American airline captain, and Calin Rosetti, head of satellite navigation systems at the European Space Agency, made the first single-engined circumpolar flight in a Piper PA-46-310P Malibu. This began and finished at Le Bourget airport, Paris, France, from 21 Jan–15 Jun 1987. They travelled 55266 km *34342 miles* in a flying time of 185 hr 41 min.

Largest wing span The aircraft with the largest wing span ever constructed is the $40-million Hughes H.4 Hercules flying-boat *Spruce Goose*. She was raised 70 ft *21·3 m* into the air in a test run of 1000 yd *914 m*, piloted by Howard Hughes (1905–76), off Long Beach Harbor, California, USA on 2 Nov 1947, but after this she never flew again. The eight-engined 193-tonne aircraft has a wing span of 97·51 m *319 ft 11 in* and a length of 66·64 m *218 ft 8 in*. In a delicate engineering feat she was moved bodily by the Goldcoast Corporation, aided by the US Navy barge crane YD-171, on 22 Feb 1982 to a hall across the harbour. In the summer of 1992 it was put up for sale, and the plan now is to make it the centrepiece of a new museum in McMinnville, Oregon, USA.

Among current aircraft, the Russian Antonov An-124 has a wing span of 73·3 m *240 ft* and the Boeing 747-400 one of 64·92 m *213 ft*.

A modified six-engine version of the An-124, known as An-225 which was built to carry the former Soviet space shuttle *Buran*, has a wing span of 88·4 m *290 ft*. (⇨ Heaviest below)

The $34-million Piasecki Heli-Stat, comprising a framework of light-alloy and composite materials, to mount four Sikorsky SH-34J helicopters and the envelope of a Goodyear ZPG-2 patrol airship, was exhibited on 26 Jan 1984 at Lakehurst, New Jersey, USA. Designed for use by the US Forest Service and designated Model 94-37J Logger, it had an overall length of 104·55 m *343 ft* and was intended to carry a payload of 21·4 tons. It crashed on 1 Jul 1986.

Heaviest The aircraft with the highest standard maximum take-off weight is the Antonov An-225 *Mriya* (Dream) of 600 tonnes *1 322 750 lb*. Such an aircraft lifted a payload of 156 300 kg *344 579 lb* to a height of 12 410 m *40 715 ft* on 22 Mar 1989. The flight was made by Capt. Alexander Galunenko with his crew of seven pilots along the route Kiev–Leningrad–Kiev. The flight, which was non-stop, covered a distance of 2100 km *1305 miles* and took 3 hr 47 min. (⇨ Most capacious)

Electric plane The MB-E1 is the first electrically propelled aircraft. A Bosch 8-kW *10·7 hp* motor is powered by Varta FP25 nickel-cadmium 25 Ah batteries. The aircraft, with a wing span of 12 m *39·4 ft*, is 7 m *23 ft* long and weighs 400 kg *882 lb*. It was designed by the model aircraft constructor Fred Militky (USA) and made its maiden flight on 21 Oct 1973.

Ultralight On 3 Aug 1985 Anthony A. Cafaro (b. 30 Nov 1951) flew an ultra-light aircraft (maximum weight 111 kg *245 lb*, maximum speed 104·6 km/h *65 mph*, fuel capacity 19 litre *4¼ gal*) single-seater Gypsy Skycycle for 7 hr 31 min at Dart Field, Mayville, New York, USA. Nine fuel 'pick-ups' were completed during the flight.

Smallest The smallest biplane ever flown was *Bumble Bee Two*, designed and built by Robert H. Starr of Arizona, USA. It was 2·64 m *8 ft 10 in* long, with a wing span of 1·68 m *5 ft 6 in*, and weighed 179·6 kg *396 lb* empty. The highest speed attained was 306 km/h *190 mph*. On 8 May 1988 after flying to a height of 120 m *400 ft* it crashed, and was totally destroyed.

The smallest monoplane ever flown is the *Baby Bird*, designed and built by Donald R. Stits. It is 3·35 m *11 ft* long, with a wing span of 1·91 m *6 ft 3 in* and weighs 114·3 kg *252 lb* empty. It is powered by a 55-hp two-cylinder Hirth engine, giving a top speed of 177 km/h *110 mph*. It was first flown by Harold Nemer on 4 Aug 1984 at Camarillo, California, USA.

The smallest *twin-engined* aircraft may be the Colomban MGI5 Cricri (first flown 19 Jul 1973), which has a wing span of 4·9 m *16 ft* and measures 3·91 m *12 ft 10 in* long overall. It is powered by two JPX PUL engines and is rated at 11 kW *15 hp*.

The smallest jet is the 450 km/h *280 mph* Silver Bullet, weighing 196 kg *432 lb*, with a 5·2 m *17 ft* wing span, built by Bob Bishop (USA).

Bombers Heaviest The eight-jet Boeing B-52H Stratofortress has a maximum take-off weight of 221 400 kg *488 000 lb*, a wing span of 56·4 m *185 ft* and is 48·02 m *157 ft 6¾ in* in length. It has a

The smallest jet is the _Silver Bullet_, with a wing span of just 5·2 m _17 ft_.

(Photo: Rex Features/Oxley)

speed of over 1046 km/h _650 mph_. The B-52 can carry twelve SRAM thermo-nuclear short-range attack missiles or twenty-four 340 kg _750 lb_ bombs under its wings and eight more SRAMs or eighty-four 226 kg _500 lb_ bombs in the fuselage.

The ten-engined Convair B-36J, weighing 185 tonnes, had a greater wing span at 70·1 m _230 ft_, but it is no longer in service. Its top speed was 700 km/h _435 mph_. The use of both piston engines (driving propellers) and jet engines (providing thrust) led to the epithet 'six turning, four burning'.

Fastest The world's fastest operational bombers include the French Dassault Mirage IV, which can fly at Mach 2·2 (2333 km/h _1450 mph_) at 11 000 m _36 000 ft_.

The American variable-geometry or 'swing-wing' General Dynamics FB-111A has a maximum speed of Mach 2·5, and the former Soviet swing-wing Tupolev Tu-22M, known to NATO as 'Backfire', has an estimated over-target speed of Mach 2·0 but could be as fast as Mach 2·5.

Largest airliner The highest capacity jet airliner is the Boeing 747-400, which entered service with Northwest Airlines on 26 Jan 1989; it has a wing span of 64·4 m _211 ft 5 in_, a range exceeding 12 500 km _8000 miles_ and can carry up to 567 passengers. The Boeing 'Jumbo Jet' was first flown on 9 Feb 1969. It can carry from 385 to more than 560 passengers and has a maximum speed of 969 km/h _602 mph_. Its wing span is 59·6 m _195 ft 5 in_ and its length 70·7 m _231 ft 10 in_. It entered service on 22 Jan 1970.

The largest ever British aircraft was the experimental Bristol Type 167 Brabazon, which had a maximum take-off weight of 131·4 tonnes, a wing span of 70·10 m _230 ft_ and a length of 53·94 m _177 ft_. This eight-engined aircraft first flew on 4 Sep 1949. The four-jet Super VC10, the last design constructed by Vickers, weighed 149·5 tons and had a wing span of 44·55 m _146 ft 10 in_.

Passenger load The greatest passenger load carried by any single commercial airliner was 1087 during _Operation Solomon_ which began on 24 May 1991 when Ethiopian Jews were evacuated from Addis Ababa to Israel on a Boeing 747 of El Al airlines.

Fastest airliner The supersonic BAC/Aérospatiale Concorde, first flown on 2 Mar 1969, with a designed capacity of 128 (and potentially 144) passengers, cruises at up to Mach 2·2 (2333 km/h

Round the world—antipodal points
Brother Michael Bartlett of Balham, London travelled round the world on scheduled flights, taking in exact antipodal points, in a time of 87 hr 40 min from 4–8 Mar 1993. Leaving from London he flew via Singapore and Auckland, New Zealand continuing by car to Ti Tree Point, on Highway 52. He later changed planes at Madrid airport, Spain (the point exactly opposite Ti Tree Point on the other side of the world). His journey took him a total distance of 45 738 km *28 420 miles*.

He also achieved a record time for flying round the world on scheduled flights, but just taking in the airports closest to antipodal points, when he flew via Shanghai, China and Buenos Aires, Argentina in a time of 68 hr 28 min. On this trip he travelled a distance of 41 682 km *25 901 miles* between 16–19 Nov 1992.

1450 mph). It has a maximum take-off weight of 185 065 kg *408 000 lb*. It flew at Mach 1·05 on 10 Oct 1969, exceeded Mach 2 for the first time on 4 Nov 1970, and became the first supersonic airliner used on passenger services on 21 Jan 1976. In service with Air France and British Airways, Concorde has been laid out for 100 passengers. The New York–London record is 2 hr 54 min 30 sec, set on 14 Apr 1990.

Most capacious The Aero Spacelines Super Guppy has a cargo hold with a usable volume of 1410 m³ *49790 ft³* and a maximum take-off weight of 79·38 tonnes. Its wing span is 47·62 m *156 ft 3 in* and its length 43·05 m *141 ft 3 in*. Its cargo compartment is 33·17 m *108 ft 10 in* long with a cylindrical section 7·62 m *25 ft* in diameter.

The Russian Antonov An-124 *Ruslan* has a cargo hold with a usable volume of 1014 m³ *35800 ft³* and a maximum take-off weight of 405 tonnes. It is powered

by four Lotarev D-18T turbofans giving a cruising speed of up to 850 km/h *528 mph* at 12 000 m *39 370 ft* and a range of 4500 km *2796 miles*. A special-purpose heavy-lift version of the An-124, known as An-225 *Mriya* (Dream), has been developed with a stretched fuselage providing as much as 1190 m³ *42 000 ft³* usable volume. Its cargo compartment includes an unobstructed 43 m *141 ft* hold length, with maximum width and height of 6·4 m *21 ft* and 4·4 m *14 ft 5 in* respectively. A new wing centre section carries an additional two engines, permitting an estimated total 141 tonnes *310 000 lb* thrust. Having flown first on 21 Dec 1988, the aircraft was used to carry the Soviet space shuttle *Buran* for the first time on 13 May 1989 when it was airborne for 13 hr 13 min. (▷ Heaviest above)

Heaviest commercial cargo movement The Russian manufacturer Antonov and the British charter company Air Foyle carried out the heaviest commercial air cargo movement, by taking three transformers weighing 43 tonnes each and other equipment from Barcelona, Spain to Nouméa, New Caledonia between 10–14 Jan 1991. The total weight carried in the An-124 *Ruslan* (▷ above) was 133·485 tonnes.

Antonov and the then Soviet state airline Aeroflot carried the heaviest single piece of cargo, in taking a one-piece newsprint press weighing 55 tonnes from Helsinki, Finland to Melbourne, Australia, in November 1989 on behalf of forwarding agent Röhlig Australia. The aircraft, an Antonov An-124, weighed 175 tonnes empty.

Largest propeller The largest ever used was the 6·9 m *22 ft 7½ in* diameter Garuda propeller, fitted to the Linke-Hofmann R II built in Breslau, Germany (now Wrocław, Poland) which flew in 1919. It was driven by four 193 kW *260-hp* Mercedes engines and turned at only 545 rpm.

Most flights by propeller-driven airliner A Convair CV-580 turboprop airliner was reported by the manufacturer in April 1991 to have achieved 139 368 flights. Exact age was not announced but even if it were the first such airframe the figure equates to more than nine flights a day since 1952.

Most scheduled flights as a passenger in 24 hours

Brother Michael Bartlett of London made 42 scheduled passenger flights with Heli Transport of Nice, southern France between Nice, Sophia Antipolis, Monaco and Cannes in 13 hr 33 min on 13 Jun 1990.

Visiting 12 EC countries by scheduled flights

Brother Michael Bartlett of London visited the 12 European community countries as a passenger on 12 different scheduled flights in a time of 29 hr 11 min on 22–23 Jan 1993.

Solar-powered aeroplane

The *Solar Challenger*, designed by a team led by Dr Paul MacCready, was flown for the first time entirely under solar power on 20 Nov 1980. On 7 Jul 1981, piloted by Steve Ptacek (USA), the *Solar Challenger* became the first aircraft of this category to achieve a crossing of the English Channel. Taking off from Pontoise-Cormeilles, Paris, France the 262 km *163 mile* journey to Manston, Kent was completed in 5 hr 23 min at a maximum altitude of 3350 m *11000 ft*. The aircraft has a wing span of 14·3 m *47 ft*.

Most flights by a jet airliner

A survey of ageing airliners or so-called 'geriatric jets' published in May 1993 in the weekly *Flight International* magazine reported a McDonnell Douglas DC-9 still in service which had logged 95 396 flights in under 27 years. This equates to more than nine flights a day, averaging 43 min 12 sec each, but after allowing for 'downtime' for maintenance the real daily average is higher.

The most hours recorded by a jet airliner still in service is the 94 431 hours reported for a Boeing 747 in the same issue of *Flight International* (⟺ above).

Oldest jet airliner

According to the London-based aviation information and consultancy company Airclaims, a first-generation airliner built in 1958—a Boeing 707—was still in service in April 1993.

Scheduled flights

Longest The longest non-stop scheduled flight currently operating is one of 12 847 km *7983 miles* by South African Airways for their flight from Johannesburg, South Africa to New York, USA. In terms of time taken, the longest is 15 hr 5 min, for London Heathrow to Osaka, Japan with British Airways and also for Los Angeles, USA to Hong Kong with Delta Air Lines.

The longest non-stop delivery flight by a commercial jet is 18 105 km *11 250 miles* from London to Sydney, Australia by the Qantas Boeing 747-400 *Longreach*, using 179 500 kg *176·6 tons* of specially formulated Shell Jet A-1 high-density fuel, in 20 hr 9 min on 16–17 Aug 1989. The flight originated in Washington State, USA.

A Boeing 767-200ER flight from Seattle, Washington, USA to Nairobi, Kenya on 8–9 Jun 1990 set a new speed and endurance record for the longest delivery flight by a twin-engined commercial jet. The Royal Brunei Airlines Boeing 767 flew 14 890 km *8040 nautical miles* great-circle distance in 18 hr 29 min, consuming 75·4 tonnes of fuel.

Shortest The shortest scheduled flight is by Loganair between the Orkney Islands of Westray and Papa Westray. This has been flown with Britten-Norman BN-2 Islander twin-engined 10-seat transports since September 1967. Though scheduled for 2 minutes, in favourable wind conditions it was once accomplished in 58 sec by Capt. Andrew D. Alsop. The check-in time for the flight is 20 minutes.

Alaska Airlines has provided the shortest scheduled flight by jet, by McDonnell Douglas MD-80 between San Francisco and Oakland, California, USA. The return flight averaged 5 minutes for the 19·3 km *12 mile* journey. Some 25 minutes were allowed in the airline timetable.

Highest Speed

Official record The airspeed record is 3529·56 km/h *2193·17 mph*, by Capt. Eldon W. Joersz and Major George T. Morgan, Jr, in a Lockheed SR-71A

'Blackbird' near Beale Air Force Base, California, USA over a 25 km *15½ mile* course on 28 Jul 1976.

Air-launched record The fastest fixed-wing aircraft in the world was the US North American Aviation X-15A-2, which flew for the first time (after modification from the X-15A) on 25 Jun 1964, powered by a liquid oxygen and ammonia rocket propulsion system. Ablative materials on the airframe enabled it to withstand a temperature of 3000°F *1650°C*. The landing speed was momentarily 389·1 km/h *242 mph*. The highest speed attained was 7274 km/h *4520 mph* (Mach 6·7) when piloted by Major William J. Knight, USAF (b. 1930), on 3 Oct 1967.

An earlier version piloted by Joseph A. Walker (1920–66) reached 107 960 m *354 200 ft* over Edwards Air Force Base, California, USA on 22 Aug 1963. The final flight (the 199th) was on 24 Oct 1968 after which the programme, which had begun on 8 Jun 1959, was suspended.

United States NASA Rockwell International space shuttle orbiter *Columbia*, commanded by Capt. John W. Young, USN, and piloted by Capt. Robert L. Crippen, USN was launched from the Kennedy Space Center, Cape Canaveral, Florida, USA on 12 Apr 1981 after expenditure of $9·9 billion since 1972. *Columbia* broke all records in space by a fixed-wing craft, with 26 715 km/h *16 600 mph* at main engine cut-off. After re-entry from 122 km *400 000 ft*, experiencing temperatures of 2160°C *3920°F*, she glided home weighing 97 tonnes, and with a landing speed of 347 km/h *216 mph*, on Rogers Dry Lake, California, USA on 14 Apr 1981.

Under the FAI (Fédération Aéronautique Internationale) regulations for Category P for aerospacecraft, *Columbia* is holder of the current absolute world record for duration—13 days 19 hr 30 min to main gear touchdown when launched on its 12th mission, STS 50, with seven crewmen on 9 Jul 1992.

Orbiter *Discovery* holds the shuttle altitude record of 532 km *332 miles* achieved on 24 Apr 1990 on its 10th flight.

The greatest mass lifted by the shuttle and placed in orbit was 132 912 kg *293 019 lb*. This was the lift-off weight of *Discovery* STS 41, launched on 6 Oct 1990 carrying the *Ulysses* solar polar orbiter and an IUS/PAM solid propellant upper stage.

Fastest jet The USAF Lockheed SR-71, a reconnaissance aircraft, has been the world's fastest jet (⇨ official record, above). First flown in its definitive form on 22 Dec 1964, it was reportedly capable of attaining an altitude ceiling of close to 100 000 ft *30 000 m*. It has a wing span of 16·94 m *55 ft 7 in* and a length of 32·73 m *107 ft 5 in* and weighs 77·1 tonnes *170 000 lb* at take-off. Its reported range at Mach 3 was 4800 km *3000 miles* at 24 000 m *79 000 ft*. At least 30 are believed to have been built before the plane was retired by the US Air Force.

Fastest combat jet The fastest combat jet is the USSR Mikoyan MiG-25 fighter (NATO code name 'Foxbat'). The reconnaissance 'Foxbat-B' has been tracked by radar at about Mach 3·2 (3395 km/h *2110 mph*). When armed with four large underwing air-to-air missiles known to NATO as 'Acrid', the fighter 'Foxbat-A' is limited to Mach 2·8 (2969 km/h *1845 mph*). The single-seat 'Foxbat-A' has a wing span of 13·95 m *45 ft 9 in*, is 23·82 m *78 ft 2 in* long and has an estimated maximum take-off weight of 37·4 tonnes *82 500 lb*.

Fastest biplane The fastest is the Italian Fiat CR42B, with a 753 kW *1010 hp* Daimler-Benz DB601A engine, which attained 520 km/h *323 mph* in 1941. Only one was built.

Fastest piston-engined aircraft On 21 Aug 1989, in Las Vegas, Nevada, USA, the Rare Bear, a modified Grumman F8F Bearcat piloted by Lyle Shelton, set the FAI approved world record for a 3 km *1⅞ mile* course of 850·24 km/h *528·33 mph*.

Fastest propeller-driven aircraft The fastest propeller-driven aircraft in use is the former Soviet Tu-95/142 *Bear* with four 14 795 hp *11 033 kW* engines driving eight blade contra-rotating propellers with a maximum level speed of Mach 0·82 or 925 km/h *575 mph*.

The turboprop-powered Republic XF-84H prototype US Navy fighter which flew on 22 Jul 1955 had a top *design*

297

The fastest propeller-driven aircraft is *Bear*, which can fly at a speed of 925 km/h *575 mph*. (Photo: Aviation Picture Library)

speed of 1078 km/h *670 mph*, but was abandoned.

Fastest transatlantic flight The flight record is 1 hr 54 min 56·4 sec by Major James V. Sullivan, 37, and Major Noel F. Widdifield, 33, flying a Lockheed SR-71A 'Blackbird' eastwards on 1 Sep 1974. The average speed, slowed by refuelling from a Boeing KC-135 tanker aircraft, for the New York–London stage of 5570·80 km *3461·53 miles* was 2908·3 km/h *1806·96 mph*.

The solo record (Gander, Newfoundland, Canada to Gatwick, W Sussex) is 8 hr 47 min 32 sec, an average speed of 426·7 km/h *265·1 mph*, by Capt. John J.A. Smith in a Rockwell Commander 685 twin-turboprop on 12 Mar 1978 achieving an average speed of 426·71 km/h *265·214 mph*.

Fastest climb Heinz Frick of British Aerospace took a Harrier GR5 powered by a Rolls-Royce Pegasus 11-61 engine from a standing start to 12 000 m *39 370 ft* in 2 min 6·63 sec above the Rolls-Royce flight test centre, Filton, Bristol, Avon on 15 Aug 1989.

Aleksandr Fedotov (USSR) in a Mikoyan E 266M (MiG-25) aircraft established the fastest time to height record on 17 May

Time zones parties
On 31 Dec 1992 a group of 97 Atlantic Time Tunnellers saw the New Year in twice by having a party at Shannon, Republic of Ireland and leaving at 00:10 on Concorde for Bermuda, where they arrived at 23:21 in time for a second New Year's celebration. In so doing they achieved the fastest west–east Atlantic crossing for a passenger aircraft.

Touchdown in the 12 EC countries
On 13 Jun 1989 pilots Michael Hamlin and Robert Noortman of Hamlin Jet Ltd flew a Cessna Citation *Biz Jet One* a distance of 5950 km *3700 miles*. They touched down at 12 different landing strips of the 12 EC countries in a time of 18 hrs 55 min.

1975, reaching 35 000 m *114 830 ft* in 4 min 11·7 sec after take off from Podmoscovnoe, Russia.

Duration The duration record is 64 days 22 hr 19 min 5 sec, set by Robert

John o' Groats–Land's End

The record time for an 'End to End' flight over Great Britain where supersonic overflying is banned is 46 min 44 sec by a McDonnell F-4K Phantom (Wing Commander John Brady and Flt Lt Mike Pugh) on 24 Feb 1988.

Fastest time to refuel

The record time for refuelling an aeroplane (with 390 litres *85 gal* of 100 octane avgas) is 3 min 24 sec, for a 1975 Cessna 310 (N92HH), by the Sky Harbor Air Service Line Crew. It had landed at Cheyenne airport, Wyoming, USA on 5 Jul 1992 during an around the world air race.

Timm and John Cook in the Cessna 172 *Hacienda*. They took off from McCarran Airfield, Las Vegas, Nevada, USA just before 3:53 p.m. local time on 4 Dec 1958 and landed at the same airfield just before 2:12 p.m. on 7 Feb 1959. They covered a distance equivalent to six times round the world, being refuelled without any landings.

Airports

Largest The £2·1 billion King Khalid international airport outside Riyadh, Saudi Arabia covers an area of 225 km² *55 040 acres*. It was opened on 14 Nov 1983. It also has the world's tallest control tower, 81 m *265 ft* in height.

The Hajj Terminal at the £2·8 billion King Abdul-Aziz airport near Jeddah, Saudi Arabia is the world's largest roofed structure, covering 1·5 km² *370 acres*.

The world's largest airport terminal is Hartsfield Atlanta international airport, Georgia, USA, opened on 21 Sep 1980, with floor space covering 20·43 ha *50½ acres* and still expanding. In 1992 the terminal serviced 42 032 988 passengers using 145 gates, although it has a capacity for 75 million.

UK Over 80 airline companies from 65 countries operate scheduled services into Heathrow airport, London (1197 ha *2958 acres*). Between 1 Jan–31 Dec 1992 there were 381 200 air transport movements, including 380 753 passenger flights, handled by a staff of 53 000 employed by the various companies, government departments and Heathrow Airport Ltd, a subsidiary of BAA plc. The total number of passengers, both incoming and outgoing, was 44 964 million including transit passengers.

One day records at Heathrow were set on 6 Jul 1990 with 1232 flights handled and on 31 Jul 1992 with 160 333 passengers. The airport's busiest single hour of two way passenger flow was recorded on 18 Aug 1990 when 12 434 passengers travelled through the terminal building.

Busiest The Chicago international airport, O'Hare Field, Illinois, USA had a total of 64 441 087 passengers and 808 759 aircraft movements in the year 1991. This represents a take-off or landing every 39 sec around the clock.

Heathrow Airport, London handles more international traffic than any other, with 38 245 900 international passengers in 1992.

The busiest landing area ever has been Bien Hoa Air Base, South Vietnam, which handled approximately 1 000 000 take-offs and landings in 1970.

Helipad The heliport at Morgan City, Louisiana, USA, one of a string used by helicopters flying energy-related offshore operations into the Gulf of Mexico, has pads for 46 helicopters. The world's largest helipad has been An Khe, South Vietnam, during the Vietnam War.

Landing fields Highest The highest is La Sa (Lhasa) airport, Tibet, People's Republic of China, at 4363 m *14 315 ft*.

Lowest The lowest landing field is El Lisan on the east shore of the Dead Sea, 360 m *1180 ft* below sea level, but during World War II BOAC Short C-class flying boats operated from the surface of the Dead Sea at 394 m *1292 ft* below sea level.

The lowest international airport is Schiphol, Amsterdam, Netherlands at 4·5 m *15 ft* below sea level.

Farthest and nearest to capital or city The airport farthest from the city centre it allegedly serves is Viracopos,

Paris–London

The fastest time to travel the 344 km *214 miles* from central Paris, France, to central London (BBC TV centre) is 38 min 58 sec by David Boyce of Stewart Wrightson (Aviation) Ltd on 24 Sep 1983. He travelled by motorcycle and helicopter to Le Bourget; Hawker Hunter jet (piloted by the late Michael Carlton) to Biggin Hill, Kent; and by helicopter to the TV centre car park.

Longest air ticket

A 12 m *39 ft 4½ in* air ticket was issued for $4500 to M. Bruno Leunen of Brussels, Belgium in December 1984 for a 85 623 km *53 203 mile* trip on 80 airlines with 109 stopovers.

Plane pulling

Dave Gauder single-handedly pulled Concorde 12·2 m *40 ft* across the tarmac at Heathrow Airport, London on 11 Jun 1987.

A team of 59 Qantas personnel pulled a Boeing 747 weighing 205 tonnes a distance of 100 metres in 62·1 sec at Perth airport, Australia on 22 Oct 1988.

Wing walking

Roy Castle, host of the BBC TV *Record Breakers* programme, flew on the wing of a Boeing Stearman biplane for 3 hr 23 min on 2 Aug 1990, taking off from Gatwick, W Sussex and landing at Le Bourget, near Paris, France.

Brazil, which is 96 km *60 miles* from São Paulo. Gibraltar airport is a mere 800 m *880 yd* from the city centre.

The London City airport, built on a redeveloped former docklands site, is 9·65 km *6 miles* east of the principal financial district.

Longest runways The longest runway in the world is at Edwards Air Force Base on the west side of Rogers dry lakebed at Muroc, California, USA, and is 11·92 km *7·41 miles* in length. The *Voyager* aircraft, taking off for its round-the-world unrefuelled flight (⊳ Circumnavigational flights), used 4·3 km *14 200 ft* of the 4·6 km *15 000 ft* long main base concrete runway.

The world's longest civil airport runway is one of 4·89 km *3·04 miles* at Pierre van Ryneveld airport, Upington, South Africa, constructed in five months from August 1975 to January 1976.

A paved runway 6·24 km *3·88 miles* long appears on maps of Jordan at Abu Husayn.

The longest runway normally available to civil aircraft in the United Kingdom is No. 1 at Heathrow Airport, London, measuring 3·90 km *2·42 miles*.

The most southerly major runway (2·57 km *1·6 miles*) in the world is at Mount Pleasant, East Falkland (Lat 51°50′S), built in 16 months to May 1985.

Largest hangars Hangar 375 ('Big Texas') at Kelly Air Force Base, San Antonio, Texas, USA, completed on 15 Feb 1956, has four doors each 76 m *250 ft* wide, 18·3 m *60 ft* high, and weighing 608 tonnes. The high bay is 610 × 90 × 27·5 m *2000 × 300 × 90 ft* in area and is surrounded by a 17·8 ha *44 acre* concrete apron. It is the largest free-standing hangar in the world.

Delta Airlines' jet base on a 56·6 ha *175 acre* site at Hartsfield International Airport, Atlanta, Georgia, USA has 14·5 ha *36 acres* roof area. A recent addition to the hangar gives it a high-bay area of 317 × 74 × 27 m *1041 × 242 × 90 ft*.

UK The largest hangar building in the United Kingdom is the Brabazon assembly hall at the former Bristol Aeroplane Company's works at Filton, Avon, now part of British Aerospace. The overall width of the hall is 321 m *1054 ft* and the overall depth of the centre bay is 128 m *420 ft*. It encloses a floor area of 3 ha *7½ acres*. The cubic capacity of the hall is 934 000 m³ *33 000 000 ft³*. The building

Stowaway

The most rugged stowaway in an aeroplane was Socarras Ramirez, who escaped from Cuba on 4 Jun 1969 by stowing away in an unpressurized wheel well in the starboard wing of a Douglas DC-8. The aircraft, belonging to Iberia Airlines, was on a flight from Havana, Cuba to Madrid, Spain, a distance of 9000 km *5600 miles*.

was begun in April 1946 and completed by September 1949. (⬦ also Largest doors)

Airlines

Busiest The country with the busiest airlines system is the United States, where the total number of passengers for air carriers in scheduled domestic operations exceeds 450 million annually.

On 31 Mar 1992 British Airways operated a fleet of 230 aircraft. Average staff employed totalled 50409, and 25422000 passengers were carried in 1991–2 on 584000 km *363000 miles* of unduplicated routes.

Busiest international route The city-pair with the highest international scheduled passenger traffic is London/Paris. More than 3 million passengers fly between the two cities annually, or more than 4100 each way each day (although London-bound traffic is higher than that bound for Paris).

Largest The USSR state airline Aeroflot, so named since 1932, was instituted on 9 Feb 1923 and has been the largest airline of all-time. In its last complete year of formal existence (1990) it employed 600000 (more than the top 18 US airlines put together) and flew 139 million passengers with 20000 pilots along 1000000 km *620000 miles* of domestic routes across 11 time zones. The peak size of its fleet remains unknown with estimates ranging up to 14700, if 'bush' aircraft and helicopters were included. By late 1991 their fleet was operated by at least 46 domestic operators.

Oldest Koninklijke-Luchtvaart-Maatschappij NV (KLM), the national airline of the Netherlands, opened its first scheduled service (Amsterdam–London) on 17 May 1920, having been established on 7 Oct 1919.

Delag (Deutsche Luftschiffahrt AG) was founded at Frankfurt am Main, Germany on 16 Oct 1909 and started a scheduled airship service on 17 Jun 1910.

Chalk's International Airline has been flying amphibious planes from Miami, Florida, USA to the Bahamas since July 1919. Albert 'Pappy' Chalk flew from 1911–75.

Aerospace company The world's largest aerospace company is Boeing of Seattle, Washington, USA, with 1992 sales of $30·2 billion and a workforce of 148600 world-wide. Cessna Aircraft Company of Wichita, Kansas, USA has produced more than 177800 aircraft since Clyde Cessna's first was built in 1911.

Personal Aviation Records

Oldest and youngest passengers Airborne births are reported every year.

The oldest person to fly has been Mrs Jessica S. Swift (b. Anna Stewart, 17 Sep 1871), aged 110 years 3 months, from Vermont to Florida, USA in Dec 1981.

The oldest Briton to fly is Charlotte Hughes of Redcar, Cleveland (b. 1 Aug 1877). She was given a flight on Concorde from London to New York as a 110th birthday present on 4 Aug 1987, returning four days later. In February 1992 she became the oldest Briton of all-time. (⬦ Longevity)

Most experienced passenger Edwin A. Shackleton of Bristol, Avon has flown as a passenger in 462 different categories of aircraft. His first flight was in March 1943 in D.H. Dominie R9548; other aircraft have included helicopters, gliders, microlights, gas and hot air ballons.

Pilots Youngest The youngest age at which anyone has ever qualified as a military pilot is 15 years 5 months in the case of Sgt Thomas Dobney (b. 6 May 1926) of the RAF. He had overstated his age (14 years) on entry.

Wholly untutored, James A. Stoodley aged 14 years 5 months took his 13-year-old brother John on a 29-minute joy ride in an unattended US Piper Cub trainer

301

aircraft near Ludgershall, Wilts in December 1942.

Oldest The world's oldest pilot is Stanley Wood (b. 22 Sep 1896) of Shoreham, W Sussex, who flew a US-built Harvard trainer plane on 8 Apr 1993 at the age of 96. His first solo flight had been an unofficial one during World War I.

Mrs Peggy Follis (b. 7 Aug 1913) of London qualified as a pilot on 8 Aug 1991 when aged 78 years.

Longest serving military pilot Squadron Leader N.E. Rose, AFC and bar, AMN (RAF Retd) (b. 30 May 1924) flew military aircraft without a break in service for 47 years from 1942 to 1989 achieving 11 539 hours of flying in 54 different categories of aircraft. He first learnt to fly in a Tiger Moth in Southern Rhodesia then flew Hurricanes in World War II. He last flew with the RAF in a Chipmunk of No. 10 Air Experience Flight.

Most flying hours Pilot John Edward Long (b. 10 Nov 1915) (USA) logged a total of 58 205 hr of flying as a pilot between 1 May 1933 and 1 Apr 1993—cumulatively more than six years airborne.

Passenger The record as a supersonic passenger is held by Fred Finn, who made his 700th Concorde crossing in 1992 commuting regularly from New Jersey, USA to London. In April 1991 he became the first passenger to achieve 10 million miles *16 million km.*

Up until her retirement in 1988 Maisie Muir of Orkney, Scotland flew over 8400 times with Loganair in connection with her business duties for the Royal Bank of Scotland.

Most planes flown James B. Taylor, Jr (1897–1942) flew 461 different categories of powered aircraft during his 25 years as an active experimental test and demonstration pilot for the US Navy and a number of American aircraft manufacturing companies. He was one of the few pilots of the 1920s and 1930s qualified to perform terminal-velocity dives. During one dive in 1939, he may have become the first pilot in history to fly faster than 500 mph *804 km/h* and live.

Most Trans-Atlantic flights Between March 1948 and his retirement on 1 Sep 1984 Flight Service Manager Charles M. Schimpf logged a total of 2880 Atlantic crossings—a rate of 6·4 per month.

Human-powered flight The first man-powered Channel crossing was achieved on 12 Jun 1979 by Bryan Allen (USA) in the *Gossamer Albatross,* designed by Dr Paul MacCready. The 35·82 km *22·26 mile* flight from Folkestone, Kent to Cap Gris Nez, France set the duration record of 2 hr 49 min.

The Daedalus Project, centred on the Massachusetts Institute of Technology, achieved its goal of human-powered flight, when Kanellos Kanellopoulos (b. 25 Apr 1957) averaged 29·7 km/h *18·5 mph* in his 34·1 m *112 ft* wing span machine from Crete to the island of Santoríni on 23 Apr 1988 flying 119 km *74 miles.*

Earliest Leonardo da Vinci (1452–1519) proposed the idea of a helicopter-type craft, although it is known that the Chinese had built helicopter-like toys as early as the 4th century BC.

A craft bearing a resemblance to a helicopter was built in France by Paul Cornu and flown on 13 Sep 1907, but it was not until 1936 that the Focke-Achgelis (designated the FA 61) was flown, making it the first practical helicopter.

Fastest Under FAI rules, the world's speed record for helicopters was set by John Trevor Eggington with co-pilot Derek J. Clews, who averaged 400·87 km/h *249·09 mph* over Glastonbury, Somerset on 11 Aug 1986 in a Westland Lynx company demonstrator helicopter.

Largest The former Soviet Mil Mi-12 (NATO code-name 'Homer') is powered by four 6500 hp *4847 kW* turboshaft engines and has a span of 67 m *219 ft 10 in* over its rotor tips, with a length of 37 m *121 ft 4½ in.* It weighs 103·3 tonnes.

Smallest The Aerospace General Co. one-man rocket-assisted minicopter weighs about 72·5 kg *160 lb* and can cruise for 400 km *250 miles* at 297 km/h *185 mph.*

Greatest load lifted On 3 Feb 1982 at Podmoscovnoe in the USSR, a Mil Mi-26 heavy-lift helicopter (NATO code-name

The world record speed for a helicopter was achieved by a Westland Lynx helicopter, which reached a speed of 400·87 km/h _249·09 mph_ in 1986. It had taken ten years to design and develop the helicopter in such a way as to reach this speed.

(Photo: Westland)

'Halo'), crewed by G.V. Alfeurov and L.A. Indeyev (co-pilot), lifted a total mass of 56·77 tonnes to 2000 m _6560 ft._

Highest altitude The record for helicopters is 12 442 m _40 820 ft_ by an Aérospatiale AS 315 B Lama, flown by Jean Boulet over Istres, France on 21 Jun 1972.

The highest recorded landing has been at 7000 m _23 000 ft_, below the southeast face of Everest in a rescue flight in May 1971.

Longest hover Doug Daigle, Brian Watts and Dave Meyer of Tridair Helicopters, together with Rod Anderson of Helistream, Inc. of California, USA maintained a continuous hovering flight in a 1947 Bell B model for 50 hr 50 sec during 13–15 Dec 1989.

Circumnavigation H. Ross Perot Jr and Jay Coburn made the first helicopter circumnavigation in _Spirit of Texas_ in 29 days 3 hr 8 min 13 sec from 1–30 Sep 1982 leaving from and returning to Dallas, Texas, USA.

The first solo round-the-world flight in a helicopter was completed by Dick Smith

(Australia) on 22 Jul 1983. Taking off from and returning to the Bell Helicopter facility at Fort Worth, Texas, USA, in a Bell Model 206L-3, LongRanger III, his unhurried flight began on 5 Aug 1982 and covered a distance of 56 742 km _35 258 miles._

Autogyros

Earliest The autogyro or gyroplane, a rotorcraft with an unpowered rotor turned by the airflow in flight, preceded any practical helicopter with its engine-driven rotor.

Juan de la Cierva (Spain) designed the first successful gyroplane with his model C.4 (commercially named an 'Autogiro') which flew at Getafe, Spain on 9 Jan 1923.

Speed, altitude and distance records Wing Cdr. Kenneth H. Wallis (GB) holds the straight-line distance record of 874·32 km _543·27 miles_ set in his WA-116/F autogyro on 28 Sep 1975 with a non-stop flight from Lydd, Kent to Wick, Highland.

On 20 Jul 1982, flying from Boscombe Down, Wilts, he established a new autogyro altitude record of 5643·7 m *18 516 ft* in his WA-121/Mc.

Wing Cdr. Wallis flew his WA-116/F/S, with a 60-hp Franklin aero-engine, to a record speed of 193·6 km/h *120·3 mph* over a 3 km *1⅞ mile* straight course at Marham, Norfolk on 18 Sep 1986.

Flying-Boat

Fastest The fastest flying-boat ever built was the Martin XP6M-1 Seamaster, the US Navy four-jet-engined minelayer flown in 1955–9, with a top speed of 1040 km/h *646 mph*. In September 1946 the Martin JRM-2 Mars flying-boat set a payload record of 30 992 kg *68 327 lb*.

The official flying-boat speed record is 911·98 km/h *566·69 mph*, set up by Nikolay Andreyevskiy and crew of two in a Soviet Beriev M-10, powered by two AL-7 turbojets, over a 15–25 km *9·3–15½ mile* course at Joukovsky-Petrovskoye, USSR on 7 Aug 1961.

The M-10 holds all 12 records listed for jet-powered flying-boats, including an altitude record of 14 962 m *49 088 ft* set by Georgiy Buryanov and crew over the Sea of Azov, USSR on 9 Sep 1961.

Airships

Earliest The earliest flight in an airship was by Henri Giffard from Paris to Trappes in his steam-powered coal-gas airship 2500 m³ *88 300 ft³* in volume and 43·8 m *144 ft* long, on 24 Sep 1852.

The earliest British airship was a 566 m³ *20 000 ft³* craft, 22·8 m *75 ft* long built by Stanley Spencer. Her maiden flight was from Crystal Palace, London on 22 Sep 1902.

Largest *Rigid* The largest was the 213·9-tonne German *Graf Zeppelin II* (LZ 130), with a length of 245 m *804 ft* and a capacity of 200 000 m³ *7 062 100 ft³*. She made her maiden flight on 14 Sep 1938 and in May and August 1939 made radar spying missions in British air space. She was dismantled in April 1940. Her sister ship *Hindenburg* was 1·70 m *5 ft 7 in* longer.

The largest British airship was the R101 built by the Royal Airship Works, Cardington, Beds, which first flew on 14 Oct 1929. She was 237 m *777 ft* in length

and had a capacity of 155 995 m³ *5 508 800 ft³*. She crashed near Beauvais, France, killing all but six of the 54 aboard, on 5 Oct 1930.

Non-rigid The largest ever constructed was the US Navy ZPG 3-W, which had a capacity of 42 950 m³ *1 516 300 ft³*, was 123 m *403 ft* long and 25·9 m *85 ft 1 in* in diameter, and had a crew of 21. She first flew on 21 Jul 1958, but crashed into the sea in June 1960.

Greatest passenger load The most people ever carried in an airship was 207, in the US Navy *Akron* in 1931. The transatlantic record is 117, by the German *Hindenburg* in 1937. She exploded into a fire-ball at Lakehurst, New Jersey, USA on 6 May 1937.

The largest airship currently certificated for the public transport of passengers (13) is the 59 m *193 ft 7 in* long non-rigid Skyship 600 series of 6650 m³ *235 400 ft³* capacity, built by the UK company Airship Industries. The maiden flight was on 27 Mar 1984.

Distance records The FAI accredited straight-line distance record for airships is 6384·5 km *3967·1 miles*, set up by the German *Graf Zeppelin* (LZ 127), captained by Dr Hugo Eckener, between 29 Oct–1 Nov 1928.

From 21–25 Nov 1917 the German Zeppelin L59 flew from Yambol, Bulgaria to south of Khartoum, Sudan, and returned to cover a minimum of 7250 km *4500 miles*.

Duration record The longest recorded flight by a non-rigid airship (without refuelling) is 264 hr 12 min by a US Navy Goodyear-built ZPG-2 class ship (Commander J.R. Hunt, USN) from South Weymouth Naval Air Station, Massachusetts, USA from 4–15 Mar 1957, landing back at Key West, Florida, USA after having flown 15 205 km *9448 miles*.

Ballooning

Earliest The earliest recorded ascent was by a model hot-air balloon invented by Father Bartolomeu de Gusmão (*né* Lourenço) (1685–1724), which was flown indoors at the Casa da India, Terreiro do Paço, Portugal on 8 Aug 1709.

Distance record The record distance travelled by a balloon is 8382·54 km *5208·68 miles*, by the Raven experimental helium-filled balloon *Double Eagle V* (capacity 11 300 m³ *399 100 ft³*) from 9–12 Nov 1981. The journey started from Nagashima, Japan and ended at Covello, California, USA. The crew for this first manned balloon crossing of the Pacific Ocean were Ben L. Abruzzo, 51, Rocky Aoki, 43 (Japan), Ron Clark, 41, and Larry M. Newman, 34.

Duration record Richard Abruzzo, 29, together with Troy Bradley, 28, set a duration record of 144 hr 16 min in *Team USA* in crossing the Atlantic Ocean from Bangor, Maine, USA to Ben Slimane, Morocco on 16–22 Sep 1992. The previous record had been set by Richard's father, Ben, in *Double Eagle II* in 1978.

Atlantic crossing Col. Joe Kittinger, USAF (⇔ Parachuting) became the first man to complete a solo trans-atlantic crossing by balloon. In the 2850 m³ *101 000 ft³* helium-filled balloon *Rosie O'Grady*, Kittinger lifted off from Caribou, Maine, USA on 14 Sep 1984 and completed a distance of 5701 km *3543 miles* before landing at Montenotte, near Savona, Italy 86 hours later on 18 Sep 1984.

Highest *Unmanned* The highest altitude attained by an unmanned balloon was 51 800 m *170 000 ft* by a Winzen balloon of 1·35 million m³ *47·8 million ft³* launched at Chico, California, USA in October 1972.

Manned The greatest altitude reached in a manned balloon is an unofficial 37 750 m *123 800 ft* by Nicholas Piantanida (1933–66) of Bricktown, New Jersey, USA, from Sioux Falls, South Dakota on 1 Feb 1966. He landed in a cornfield in Iowa but did not survive.

The official record (closed gondola) is 34 668 m *113 740 ft* by Commander Malcolm D. Ross, USNR and the late Lt Cdr. Victor A. Prother, USN in an ascent from the deck of USS *Antietam* over the Gulf of Mexico on 4 May 1961 in a balloon of 339 800 m³ *12 million ft³*.

Owing to an oversight, Keith Lang and Harold Froelich, scientists from Minneapolis, USA, ascended in an open gondola and without the protection of pressure

Most to jump from a balloon
On 12 Sep 1992 a record fifteen people (a group of Royal Marines plus friends) all parachuted from a hot air balloon over the Somerset/Devon county boundary. The same group made a similar ascent on 1 Oct 1992 and this time a record ten people jumped *simultaneously*, from a height of 1800 m *6000 ft*.

Largest balloons
The largest balloons ever built, by Winzen Research Inc., Minnesota, USA, have an inflatable volume of 2 million m³ *70 million ft³* and are 300 m *1000 ft* in height. They are unmanned.

Most passengers in a balloon
A balloon of 73 600 m³ *2·6 million ft³* capacity named *Miss Champagne* was built by Tom Handcock of Portland, Maine, USA. Tethered, it rose to height of 12·25 m *50 ft* with 61 passengers on board on 19 Feb 1988. The Dutch balloonist Henk Brink made an unthethered flight of 200 m *656 ft* in the 24 000 m³ *850 000 ft³* *Nashua Number One* carrying a total of 50 passengers and crew. The flight, on 17 Aug 1988, lasted 25 min, commenced from Lelystad airport, Netherlands, and reached an altitude of *100 m* 328 ft.

suits to an altitude of 12·84 km *7·98 miles*, on 26 Sep 1956. During their 6½-hour flight, at maximum altitude and without goggles, they observed the Earth and measured a temperature of −58°C *−72°F*.

Hot-air The modern revival of this form of ballooning began in the USA in 1961, and the first World Championships were held in Albuquerque, New Mexico, USA on 10–17 Feb 1973.

Mass ascent The greatest mass ascent of hot-air balloons from a single site took place when 128 participants at the Ninth

Parachuting Records

It is estimated that the human body reaches 99 per cent of its low-level terminal velocity after falling 573 m 1880 ft, which takes 13–14 sec. This is 188–201 km/h 117–125 mph at normal atmospheric pressure in a random posture, but up to 298 km/h 185 mph in a head-down position.

FIRST Tower [1] Louis-Sébastien Lenormand (1757–1839), quasi-parachute, Montpellier, France, 1783.
Balloon André-Jacques Garnerin (1769–1823), 680 m 2230 ft Monceau Park, Paris, France, 22 Oct 1797.
Aircraft *Man:* 'Captain' Albert Berry, an aerial exhibitionist, St Louis, Missouri, USA, 1 Mar 1912. *Woman:* Mrs Georgina 'Tiny' Broadwick (b. 1893), Griffith Park, Los Angeles, USA, 21 Jun 1913.

LONGEST DURATION FALL Lt Col. Wm H. Rankin, USMC, 40 min due to thermals, North Carolina, USA, 26 Jul 1956.

LONGEST DELAYED DROP World *Man:* Capt. Joseph W. Kittinger [2], 25 820 m 84 700 ft or 16·04 miles, from balloon at 31 330 m 102 800 ft, Tularosa, New Mexico, USA, 16 Aug 1960. *Woman:* E. Fomitcheva (USSR) 14 800 m 48 556 ft, over Odessa, USSR, 26 Oct 1977.
Over UK *Man (Civilian):* M. Child, R. McCarthy, 10 180 m 33 400 ft from balloon at 10 850 m 35 600 ft, Kings Lynn, Norfolk, 18 Sep 1986. *Woman (Civilian):* Francesca Gannon and Valerie Slattery, 6520 m 21 391 ft from aircraft at 7600 m 24 900 ft, Netheravon, Wilts, 11 Mar 1987. *Group:* S/Ldr J. Thirtle AFC, Fl. Sgt A.K. Kidd AFM, Sgts L. Hicks (died 1971), P.P. Keane AFM BEM, K.J. Teesdale AFM, 11 943 m 39 183 ft from aircraft at 12 613 m 41 383 ft, Boscombe Down, Wilts, 16 Jun 1967.

BASE JUMP Highest Nicholas Feteris and Dr Glenn Singleman from a ledge (the 'Great Trango Tower') at 5880 m 19 300 ft in the Karakoram, Pakistan, 26 Aug 1992.
Jumps from buildings and claims for lowest base jumps will not be accepted.

MID-AIR RESCUE Earliest Miss Dolly Shepherd (1886–1983) brought down Miss Louie May on her single 'chute from balloon at 3350 m 11 000 ft, Longton, Staffs, 9 Jun 1908.
Lowest Gregory Robertson saved Debbie Williams (unconscious), collision at 2750 m 9000 ft, pulled her ripcord at 1070 m 3500 ft —10 secs from impact, Coolidge, Arizona, USA, 18 Apr 1987.

HIGHEST ESCAPE Flt Lt J. de Salis, RAF and Fg Off. P. Lowe, RAF, 17 100 m 56 000 ft, Moynash, Derby, 9 Apr 1958.
Lowest S/Ldr Terence Spencer DFC, RAF, 9–12 m 30–40 ft, Wismar Bay, Baltic, 19 Apr 1945.

HIGHEST LANDING Ten USSR parachutists [3], 7133 m 23 405 ft, Lenina Peak, USSR May 1969.

MOST SOUTHERLY T/Sgt Richard J. Patton (died 1973), Operation Deep Freeze, South Pole, 25 Nov 1956.

MOST NORTHERLY Six members of the Canadian Armed Forces were the first people to jump at Lat. 90° 00′ N, 27 Apr 1974.

CROSS-CHANNEL (LATERAL FALL) Sgt Bob Walters with three soldiers and two Royal Marines, 35·4 km 22 miles from 7600 m 25 000 ft, Dover, Kent to Sangatte, France, 31 Aug 1980.

TOTAL SPORT PARACHUTING DESCENTS *Man:* Don Kellner, 18 000, various locations in the USA up to 31 Oct 1992. *Woman:* Valentina Zakoretskaya (USSR), 8000, over USSR, 1964–September 1980.

24-HOUR TOTAL *Man:* Dale Nelson (USA), 301 (in accordance with United States Parachute Association rules), Pennsylvania, USA, 26–27 May 1988. *Woman:* Cheryl Stearns (USA), 255 at Lodi, California, USA 26–27 Nov 1987.

MOST TRAVELLED Kevin Seaman from a Cessna Skylane (pilot Charles E. Merritt), 19 611 km 12 186 miles, jumps in all 50 US States, 26 Jul–15 Oct 1972.

HEAVIEST LOAD US Space Shuttle *Columbia*, external rocket retrieval, 80 ton capacity, triple array, each 36·5 m 120 ft diameter, Atlantic, off Cape Canaveral, Florida, USA, 12 Apr 1981.

HIGHEST STACK 38, by a team of American parachutists at Richland, Washington, USA; held for 10·3 sec on 10 Oct 1992.

LARGEST FREE FALL FORMATION 200, from 10 countries held for 6·47 sec, from 5030 m 16 500 ft, over Myrtle Beach, California, USA, 23 Oct 1992. *Women:* 100, from 20 countries held for 5·97 sec, from 5200 m 17 000 ft, Aéreodrome du Cannet des Maures, France, 14 Aug 1992. *UK* 60, held for 4 sec, from 4600 m 15 000 ft, Peterborough, Cambs, 8 Jun 1989.

OLDEST *Man:* Edwin C. Townsend (died 7 Nov 1987), 89 years, Vermillion Bay, Louisiana, USA, 5 Feb 1986. *Woman:* Sylvia Brett (GB), 80 years 166 days, Cranfield, Beds, 23 Aug 1986. *Tandem, Man:* Frank Blazek (USA), 91 years 312 days, Westhampton Beach, New York, USA, 21 Jul 1992. *Woman:* Corena Leslie (USA), 89 years 326 days, Buckeye airport, Arizona, USA, 8 Jun 1992.

LONGEST FALL WITHOUT PARACHUTE World Vesna Vulovic (Yugoslavia), air hostess in DC-9 which blew up at 10 160 m 33 330 ft over Srbská Kamenice, Czechoslovakia (now Czech Republic), 26 Jan 1972.
UK Flt-Sgt Nicholas Stephen Alkemade (died 22 Jun 1987), from blazing RAF Lancaster bomber, at 5500 m 18 000 ft over Germany (near Oberkürchen), 23 Mar 1944.

FOOTNOTES
[1] *The king of Ayutthaya, Siam in 1687 was reported to have been diverted by an ingenious athlete parachuting with two large umbrellas. Faustus Verancsis is reputed to have descended in Hungary with a framed canopy in 1617.*
[2] *Maximum speed in rarefied air was 1006 km/h 625·2 mph at 90 000 ft 27 400 m — hence marginally supersonic.*
[3] *Four were killed.*

Cheryl Stearns made 255 parachute jumps in 24 hours in November 1987, which at the time was a joint overall record (shared with Russell Fish), and remains the most in a 24 hour period by a woman.

Bristol International Balloon Festival at Ashton Court, Bristol, Avon took off within 1 hour on 15 Aug 1987.

Atlantic crossing Richard Branson (GB) with his pilot Per Lindstrand (GB) were the first to cross the Atlantic in a hot-air balloon, from 2–3 Jul 1987. They ascended from Sugarloaf, Maine, USA and covered the distance of 4947 km *3075 miles*, to Limavady, Co. Londonderry, Northern Ireland in 31 hr 41 min.

Pacific crossing Richard Branson and Per Lindstrand crossed the Pacific in the *Virgin Otsuka Pacific Flyer* from the southern tip of Japan to Lac la Matre, Yukon, north-western Canada on 15–17 Jan 1991 in a 73 600 m³ *2·6 million ft³* hot-air balloon (the largest ever flown) to set FAI records for duration (46 hr 15 min) and distance (great circle 7671·9 km *4768 miles*). Unofficial world best performances were additionally set

for the fastest speed from take-off to landing of 237 km/h *147 mph*. A speed of 385 km/h *239 mph* was sustained over one hour.

Altitude Per Lindstrand achieved the altitude record of 19 800 m *65 000 ft* in a Colt 600 hot-air balloon over Laredo, Texas, USA on 6 Jun 1988.

Gas The FAI endurance and distance record for a gas and hot-air balloon is 144 hr 16 min and 5340·2 km *3318·2 miles* by *Team USA*, crewed by Richard Abruzzo and Troy Bradley on 16–22 Sep 1992. (⇔ above)

First flight over Mount Everest Two balloons achieved the first overflight of the summit of Mount Everest at the same time on 21 Oct 1991. They were *Star Flyer 1*, piloted by Chris Dewhirst (Australia) with cameraman Leo Dickinson, and *Star Flyer 2*, piloted by Andy Elson and cameraman Eric Jones (all British). The two 6800 m³ *240 000 ft³* balloons set hot-air balloon records for the highest launch at 4735 m *15 536 ft* and touch-down at 4940 m *16 200 ft*.

Model Aircraft

Altitude Maynard L. Hill (USA), flying a radio-controlled model, established the world record for altitude, reaching a height of 8208 m *26 922 ft* on 6 Sep 1970.

Distance Gianmaria Aghem (Italy) holds the closed-circuit distance record, with 1239 km *769·9 miles*, achieved on 26 Jul 1986.

Speed The speed record is 390·92 km/h *242·92 mph*, set by W. Sitar (Austria) on 10 Jun 1977.

Duration The record duration flight is one of 33 hr 39 min 15 sec by Maynard Hill (⇔ above), with a powered model on 1–2 Oct 1992.

An indoor model with a wound rubber motor designed by J. Richmond (USA) set a duration record of 52 min 14 sec on 31 Aug 1979.

Jean-Pierre Schiltknecht flew a solar driven model airplane for a duration record of 10 hr 43 min 51 sec at Wetzlar, Germany on 10 Jul 1991.

Largest model glider In January 1990 *Eagle III*, a radio controlled glider

Longest paper aircraft flight

The level flight duration record for a hand-launched paper aircraft is 17·20 sec by Ken Blackburn at Milwaukee, Wisconsin, USA on 28 Jul 1987.

Distance record

An indoor distance of 58·82 m *193 ft* was recorded by Tony Felch at the La Crosse Center, Wisconsin, USA on 21 May 1985. A paper plane was reported and witnessed to have flown 2 km *1¼ miles* by 'Chick' C.O. Reinhart from a tenth-storey office window at 60 Beaver Street, New York City, USA across the East River to Brooklyn in August 1933, helped by a thermal from a coffee-roasting plant.

Largest paper aircraft

The largest flying paper aeroplane, with a wing span of 9·15 m *30 ft 6 in*, was constructed by pupils from various schools in Hampton, Virginia, USA and flown on 25 Mar 1992. It was launched indoors from a 3 m *10 ft* high platform and flown for a distance of 35 m *114 ft 9 in*.

weighing 6·5 kg *14 lb 8 oz* with a wing span of 9·80 m *32 ft 6 in*, was designed and constructed by Carlos René Tschen and Carlos René Tschen Jr of Colonia San Lázaro, Guatemala. It is capable of reaching a maximum speed of *c*. 28 km/h *17 mph*.

Cross-Channel The first model helicopter cross channel flight was achieved by a 5 kg *11 lb* model Bell 212, radio controlled by Dieter Zeigler. It flew a distance of 52 km *32 miles* between Ashford, Kent and Ambleteuse, France on 17 Jul 1974.

Smallest The smallest model aeroplane to fly is one weighing 0·1 g *0·004 oz* powered by an attached horsefly and designed by insectonaut Don Emmick of Seattle, Washington State, USA. On 24 Jul 1977 it flew for 5 minutes at Kirkland, Washington State, USA.

Business World

- **Commerce**
- **Economics**
- **Agriculture**

Commerce

Oldest industry The oldest known industry is flint knapping, involving the production of chopping tools and hand axes, dating from 2·5 million years ago in Ethiopia. The earliest evidence of trading in exotic stone and amber dates from *c.* 28000 BC in Europe. Agriculture is often described as 'the oldest industry in the world', whereas in fact there is no firm evidence yet that it was practised before *c.* 11000 BC.

Oldest company Although not strictly a company, the Royal Mint has origins dating back to AD 287. The Aberdeen Harbour Board started collecting tithes from shipping in 1136 on the authority of King David I of Scotland (reigned 1124–53). The Faversham Oyster Fishery Co. is referred to in the Faversham Oyster Fishing Act of 1930 as existing 'from time immemorial', i.e. in English law, from before 1189. The first bill of adventure, signed by the English East India Co., was dated 21 Mar 1601.

The oldest existing documented company is Stora Kopparbergs Bergslags of Falun, the Swedish industrial and forestry enterprise, which has been in continuous operation since the 11th century. It is first mentioned in historical records in the year 1288, when a Swedish bishop bartered an eighth share in the enterprise, and it was granted a charter in 1347. It is the largest privately-owned power producer in Sweden but in June 1991 it was reported that the company was closing down its 1000-year old copper mine at Falun.

Largest companies The first company to have assets in excess of $1 billion was the United States Steel (now USX) Corporation of Pittsburgh, Pennsylvania, with $1·5 billion at the time of its creation by merger in 1902.

The largest manufacturing company in the world in terms of assets, sales and employees is General Motors Corporation of Detroit, Michigan, USA, with operations throughout the world and a workforce of 750000. In addition to its core business of motor vehicles and components, the company also produces defence and aerospace materials and

310

Oldest UK family business
John Brooke & Sons Holdings Ltd, spinners and clothiers of Huddersfield, W Yorks has been run by the same family since 1541. The present directors, brothers E.L.M. and M.R.H. Brooke, are of the 16th generation.

Faux pas
If measured by financial consequence, the greatest *faux pas* on record was that of the young multi-millionaire James Gordon Bennett (1841–1918), committed on 1 Jan 1877 at the family mansion of his demure fiancée, one Caroline May, in Fifth Avenue, New York, USA. Bennett arrived in a two-horse cutter late and obviously in wine. By dint of intricate footwork, he gained the portals to enter the withdrawing room, where he was the cynosure of all eyes. He mistook the fireplace for a plumbing fixture more usually reserved for another purpose. The May family broke the engagement and Bennett was obliged to spend the rest of his foot-loose and fancy-free life based in Paris with the resultant non-collection of millions of dollars in tax by the US Treasury.

Companies
The number of limited companies registered in Great Britain at 31 Mar 1993 was 956314 (221766 less than in 1992), of which 11680 were public limited companies and the balance private.

provides computer and communication services. Its assets in 1992 were $191·012 billion, with sales totalling $132·4 billion. Despite these figures, however, the company announced a loss of $23·5 billion for the year, representing the largest loss ever. (⇨ Greatest loss)

UK The net assets of Shell Transport and Trading Co. plc at 31 Dec 1992 were £13·644 billion, mainly comprising its 40 per cent share in the net assets of the Royal Dutch Shell Group of companies which stood at £34·11 billion. Group companies employ some 127 000 staff. Shell Transport was formed in 1897 by Marcus Samuel (1853–1927), later the 1st Viscount Bearsted.

The biggest British manufacturing company is Imperial Chemical Industries (ICI) plc, which had assets of £11 billion at 1 Jan 1993 and an average workforce of 117 500 during the year. Its peak turnover was £13·2 billion for the year ending 1989. The company, which has more than 400 UK and overseas subsidiaries, was formed on 7 Dec 1926 by the merger of four concerns—British Dyestuffs Corporation Ltd; Brunner, Mond & Co. Ltd; Nobel Industries Ltd and United Alkali Co. Ltd. The first chairman was Sir Alfred Moritz Mond (1868–1930), later the 1st Lord Melchett. The company split into ICI and Zeneca in 1993.

Largest employer The world's largest commercial or utility employer is Indian Railways, with 1 646 704 staff at 31 Mar 1990. The largest employer in the UK is the National Health Service, with 1 245 000 staff (excluding general practitioners) at 30 Sep 1991.

Greatest sales The first company to surpass the $1 billion mark in annual sales was the United States Steel (now USX) Corporation of Pittsburgh, Pennsylvania in 1917. There are now 570 corporations with sales exceeding £1 billion, including 272 from the United States. The *Fortune* 500 List of leading industrial corporations at April 1993 is headed by General Motors Corporation of Detroit, Michigan, USA, with sales of $132·4 billion for 1992.

Sales per unit area The record for the greatest sales based on square footage of selling space is held by Richer Sounds plc, the hi-fi retail chain, with sales at their busiest outlet at London Bridge Walk reaching a peak of £17 553 per square foot for the year ending 31 Jan 1992.

Greatest profit The greatest net profit ever made by a corporation in 12 months is $7·6 billion by American Telephone and Telegraph Co. (AT&T) from 1 Oct 1981 to 30 Sep 1982.

BP (British Petroleum) announced UK record net profits of £7·053 billion for the year 1985/6.

Greatest loss The world's worst annual net trading loss is $23·5 billion (£15·5 billion) reported for 1992 by General Motors. The bulk of this figure was, however, due to a single charge of some $21 billion for employees' health costs and pensions and disclosed because of new US accountancy regulations.(⇔ also Largest companies)

UK The greatest annual loss made by a British company is £3·91 billion by the National Coal Board (now British Coal) in the year ending 31 Mar 1984.

Take-overs The highest bid in a corporate take-over was $21 billion for RJR Nabisco Inc., the tobacco, food and beverage company, by the Wall Street leveraged buyout firm Kohlberg Kravis Roberts, who offered $90 a share on 24 Oct 1988. By 1 Dec 1988 the bid, led by Henry Kravis, had reached $109 per share to aggregate $25 billion.

UK The largest bid ever made for a British company is £13 billion for BAT Industries on 11 Jul 1989 by Hoylake, led by Sir James Goldsmith, Jacob Rothschild and Kerry Packer. Hanson Trust won control of Consolidated Gold Fields (founded 1897) on 7 Aug 1989 with a bid of £3·5 billion.

Bankruptcies On 3 Sep 1992 Kevin Maxwell, son of the former press magnate Robert Maxwell (1923–91), became the world's biggest bankrupt with debts of £406·8 million. The announcement followed a private hearing in the High Court on a presentation by the liquidators of the Bishopsgate Investment Management company, from which millions of pounds of Maxwell employees' pension funds were misappropriated.

Corporate The biggest corporate bankruptcy in terms of assets was $35·9 billion filed by Texaco in 1987.

The number of business failures in the UK reached a record 47 777 in 1991, representing an increase of over 60 per cent on the previous record set in 1990.

Accountants The world's largest firm of accountants and management consultants is KPMG, with a world-wide fee income

311

Largest Toyshop

Hamleys of Regent Street, London is the world's oldest, largest and best-stocked toyshop. Shown here is a small selection of the 50 000 different items on sale, ranging from simple plastic dinosaurs to high-tech simulators. Guarding the stuffed toy department is the largest toy, a magnificent giant rhinoceros priced at £2000. The smallest is a 10 mm *0·4 in* teacup for a doll's house, at £2·99 for a set of four. The comic department includes the most expensive item, an original 1939 copy of *Detective Comics 27*, available for £106 000.

(Photos: Peter Greenhalf for Guinness Publishing)

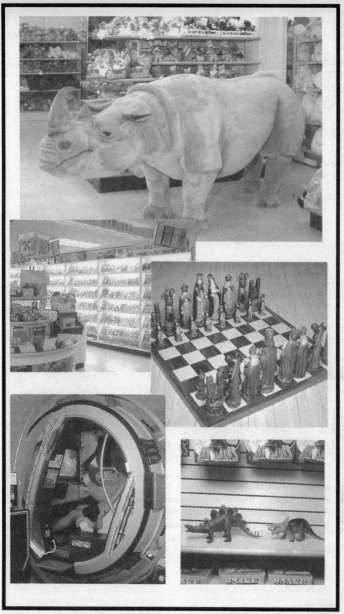

Most expensive doll

The highest price paid for a doll is £90 200 for a 1909 bisque Kämmer and Reinhardt doll at Sotheby's, London on 16 Feb 1989. It was bought by Mme Dina Vierny, who had planned to open a Museum of Childhood in France.

Most expensive Teddy bear

The highest price paid for a Teddy bear is £55 100 for a dual-plush brown bear made by Steiff of Germany c. 1920, bought at Sotheby's, London on 19 Sep 1989 by dealer James Fox.

---

of $6·154 billion at 30 Sep 1992. The company had over 73 000 employees in 834 cities in 124 countries.

Banks The world's largest multilateral development bank is the International Bank for Reconstruction and Development, founded on 27 Dec 1945 and known as the World Bank. Based in Washington, DC, USA, the bank had an authorized share capital of $152·2 billion at 30 Jun 1992. There were 159 members with a subscribed capital of $126·2 billion at 30 Jun 1992, at which time the World Bank also had unallocated reserves and accumulated net income of $11·2 billion.

The world's biggest commercial bank by assets is the Dai-Ichi Kangyo Bank Ltd of Japan, with $427·1 billion at 31 Mar 1993. The bank with most branches is the State Bank of India, which had 12664 outlets at 1 Jan 1993 and assets of $36 billion.

UK The UK's oldest independent bank is C. Hoare & Co., founded in 1672 by Richard Hoare, a goldsmith, in London. Child & Co. of Fleet St, although now part of the Royal Bank of Scotland, can trace its origins back to 1584 when its founder William Wheeler became formally apprenticed as a goldsmith.

The bank with the largest network in the United Kingdom is the National Westminster, with consolidated total assets of £143·2 billion and 2684 branches at 31 Dec 1992.

Building societies The biggest lender in the world is the Japanese government-controlled House Loan Corporation. The biggest building society in the world is the Halifax Building Society of Halifax, W Yorks with assets of £62 billion in 1992 and lending in that year of £8·3 billion. The Society has 20621 employees and 2707 offices. Established in 1853, two in every five households in the UK now have a Halifax account.

Chemists The largest chain of chemist stores in the world is Rite Aid Corporation of Shiremanstown, Pennsylvania, USA which had 2341 branches throughout the US in 1992. The Walgreen Co. of Deerfield, Illinois, USA has fewer shops, but a larger volume of sales, totalling $7·474 billion in 1992.

Britain's largest chain of pharmacies is Boots The Chemists, which had 1085 retail stores at March 1993. The firm was founded by Jesse Boot (1850–1931), later the 1st Baron Trent.

Department stores The world's largest department store is R.H. Macy & Co. Inc. at Herald Square, New York City, USA. It covers 20·3ha *50·5 acres* and employed 14000 staff handling 400000 items. Total sales for the company's 150 stores in 1990 were $7·3 billion. Rowland Hussey Macy's sales on his first day at his fancy goods store on 6th Avenue, on 27 Oct 1858, were recorded as $11·06. Macy's is, however, now undergoing bankruptcy proceedings.

The store with the highest sales volume was Nordstrom, based in Seattle, Washington, USA, with 70 stores generating $3·4 billion in 1992.

UK The largest department store in the United Kingdom is Harrods Ltd of Knightsbridge, London, named after Henry Charles Harrod (1800–85), who opened a grocery in Knightsbridge in 1849. It now has a total selling floor space of 10·5 ha *25 acres*, with 50 lifts and 36 flights of stairs and escalators, employs 3500–4500 people depending on the time of year and achieved record sales of over £346 million in the year ending 30 Jan 1993. The record for one day is almost £9 million in the January 1993 sale, with over £19 million taken in the first four days and £50 million taken during the month.

Company directorships

The all-time record for directorships was set by Hugh T. Nicholson (1914–85), formerly senior partner of Harmood Banner & Sons of London, who, as a liquidating chartered accountant, became director of all 451 companies of the Jasper group in 1961 and had seven other directorships.

The director with the most listings in the 1992 *Directory of Directors* is Peter Michael George, with 212.

Jumble sale

The Cleveland Convention Center, Ohio, USA White Elephant Sale (instituted 1933) on 18–19 Oct 1983 raised $427935·21. The greatest amount of money raised at a one-day sale is $195388·53 at the 59th one-day rummage sale organized by the Winnetka Congregational Church, Illinois, USA on 9 May 1991.

Britain's largest jumble sale was Jumbly '79, sponsored by *Woman's Own*, at Alexandra Palace, London from 5–7 May 1979 in aid of the Save the Children Fund. The attendance was 60000 and the gross takings in excess of £60000.

Insurance The company with the highest volume of insurance in force in the world is the Metropolitan Life Insurance Co. of New York City, USA, with $908·6 billion at year end 1990. The Prudential Insurance Company of America of Newark, New Jersey has the greatest volume of consolidated assets, totalling $200 billion in 1992.

The world's largest single insurance association is the Blue Cross and Blue Shield Association, the hospital insurance organization, with 67·5 million members in 1992 and $63·1 billion in total benefits paid out.

The largest life assurance group in the United Kingdom is the Prudential Corporation plc with total assets at 1 Jan 1993 of £52·6 billion.

Policies The largest life assurance policy ever issued was for $100 million, bought by a major US entertainment corporation on the life of a leading US entertainment industry figure. The policy was sold in July 1990 by Peter Rosengard of London and was placed by Shel Bachrach of Albert G. Ruben & Co. Inc. of Beverly Hills, California, USA and Richard Feldman of the Feldman Agency, East Liverpool, Ohio with nine insurance companies to spread the risk.

The highest payout on a single life was reported on 14 Nov 1970 to be some $18 million to Linda Mullendore, widow of an Oklahoma, USA rancher. Her murdered husband had paid $300000 in premiums in 1969.

Marine insurance The largest ever marine insurance loss was approximately $836million for the Piper Alpha Oil Field in the North Sea. On 6 Jul 1988 a leak from a gas compression chamber underneath the living quarters ignited and triggered a series of explosions which blew Piper Alpha apart. Of the 232 people on board, only 65 survived.

The largest sum claimed for consequential losses is £890 million against owning, operating and building corporations and Claude Phillips resulting from the loss of up to 200000tonnes of oil from the tanker *Amoco Cadiz* on the Brittany coast on 16 Mar 1978.

Paper company The world's largest producer of paper, fibre and wood products is International Paper of Purchase, New York, USA, with sales in 1992 of $13·5 billion. The company employs 70500 workers.

The largest uncoated wood-free paper machine in the United Kingdom is the PM6 at New Thames Paper Co. Ltd in Kemsley, near Sittingbourne, Kent, which has a capacity of more than 160 000 tonnes per year. The paper manufacturing and converting complex covers an area of 60·7ha *150acres*.

Retailers Woolworth Corporation now operates more than 9000 retail stores world-wide, giving a net income for 1992 of $280 million. Frank Winfield

Woolworth opened his first store, 'The Great Five Cent Store', in Utica, New York, USA on 22 Feb 1879.

The world's largest retailing firm is Wal-Mart Inc. of Bentonville, Arizona, USA, founded by Sam Walton (1920–92) in 1962, with sales of $44 billion at 31 Jan 1992 from some 1750 outlets.

Economics

Monetary and Financial

Largest budget The greatest governmental expenditure ever made by any country was $1382 billion by the US government for the fiscal year 1992.

The highest-ever revenue figure was $1091·6 billion by the US in the same year. An expenditure budget of $1468 billion was sent to Congress on 30 Jan 1993 for the fiscal year 1994 which starts on 1 Oct 1993.

The greatest fiscal surplus ever was $8 419 469 844 in the United States in 1947/8. The worst deficit was $290 billion in the US fiscal year 1992.

UK The greatest general UK government expenditure was £236·5 billion planned for the fiscal year 1991/2. The highest general government receipts are expected to be £222 billion for the same fiscal year. The public sector borrowing requirement was at a peak of £44 622 million in 1992/3 compared with a debt repayment of £7588 million in 1988/9.

Foreign aid The greatest donor of foreign aid has been the United States—the total net foreign aid given by its government between 1 Jul 1945 and 1 Jan 1991 was $312·7 billion. The country receiving most US aid in 1991 was Israel with $3·65 billion. US foreign aid began with $50 000 to Venezuela for earthquake relief in 1812.

Least taxed The sovereign countries with the lowest income tax are Bahrain and Qatar, where the rate, regardless of income, is nil. No tax is levied on the Sarkese (inhabitants of Sark) in the Channel Islands. There is no taxation in Tristan da Cunha apart from a nominal 65p a year paid by all males between the ages of 18 and 65.

Highest taxation The country with the highest taxation is Norway, where the highest rate of income tax in 1992 was 65 per cent, although additional personal taxes make it possible to be charged in excess of 100 per cent. In January 1974 the 80 per cent limit was abolished there and some 2000 citizens were then listed in the *Lignings Boka* as paying more than 100 per cent of their taxable income. The shipping magnate Hilmar Reksten (1897–1980) was assessed at 491 per cent.

In Denmark the highest rate of income tax is 68 per cent, but a net wealth tax of 1 per cent can also result in tax of over 100 per cent on income in extreme situations.

UK In the UK until 1979 the former top earned and unearned rates were 83 per cent and 98 per cent. The standard rate of tax was reduced to 25 per cent and the higher rate to 40 per cent in the 1988 Budget. The all-time record was set in 1967/8, when a 'special charge' of up to 9s. (45p) in the £ additional to surtax brought the top rate to 27s 3d in the £ (or 136 per cent) on investment income.

Highest tax demands The highest recorded personal tax demand was for $336 million on 70 per cent of the estate of American Howard Hughes.

The highest disclosed UK personal income tax demand raised is one for £5 371 220 for 1981 against merchant banker Nicholas van Hoogstraten.

Lowest rates (UK) Income tax was first introduced in Great Britain in 1799 for incomes above £60 per annum. It was discontinued in 1815, only to be reintroduced in 1842 at the rate of 7d (2·91p) in the £. It was at its lowest at 2d (0·83p) in the £ in 1875, gradually climbing to 1s 3d (6·24p) by 1913. From April 1941 until 1946 the record peak of 10s (50p) in the £ was maintained to assist in the financing of the war effort.

Balance of payments (current account) The record deficit for any country for a calendar year was $163·5 billion reported by the US in 1987. The record surplus was Japan's $126·1 billion for the year to March 1992.

The most favourable current balance of payments figure for the UK has been a surplus of £6748 million in 1981 (best quarter January–March, with a surplus of £2935 million). The worst figure was a deficit of £21726 million in 1989 (worst quarter July–September, with a deficit of £6065 million).

National debt The largest national debt of any country in the world is that of the United States, where the gross federal public debt surpassed the trillion (10^{12}) dollar mark on 30 Sep 1981. By the end of 1992 it had reached a record $4071 billion, with net interest payments on the debt of a record $199·4 billion.

The national debt in Great Britain was less than £1 million during the reign of James II in 1687. The UK's national debt in March 1992 was £213457 million.

Most foreign debt The country most heavily in overseas debt at year end 1991 was the United States, with $443·4 billion, although the size of its debt is small relative to its economic strength. Among developing countries, Brazil has the highest foreign debt, with $123 billion at the end of 1990.

Gross national product The country with the largest gross national product is the United States, with a record $5963 billion for the year ending 31 Dec 1992. The GNP of the UK at factor cost in 1992 was £518602 million.

National wealth The richest territory as listed in the 1992 *World Bank Atlas* is Switzerland, with a gross national product (GNP) per capita of $33510 for 1991. The USA, which led the rankings from 1910 to 1973, was 10th with $22560. The UK stood 17th with $16750. It has been estimated that the gross physical assets of the USA totalled $26·7 trillion ($26·7 \times 10^{12}$) at the end of 1991, equivalent to $105659 per capita.

The latest estimated figure for private wealth in the UK is £1160000 million or £59000 per household.

Poorest country According to the same source, Mozambique had the lowest GNP per capita in 1991, with only $70, but figures were unavailable for several countries.

Gold reserves The world's greatest monetary gold reserves are those of the United States Treasury at 261·81 million fine oz at the end of 1992, equivalent to $86·39 billion at the current price of $300 per fine oz. The United States Bullion Depository at Fort Knox, 48km *30 miles* south-west of Louisville, Kentucky, USA, has been the principal federal depository of US gold since December 1936. Gold is stored in 446000 standard mint bars of 12·4414kg *400troy oz* measuring $17·7 \times 9·2 \times 4·1$ cm $7 \times 3⅝ \times 1⅝$ *in*. Gold's peak price was $850 on 21 Jan 1980.

The UK's gold reserves totalled 18·67 million fine oz at October 1992.

Minimum lending rate The highest-ever figure for the British bank rate (since 13 Oct 1972, the minimum lending rate) was 17 per cent from 15 Nov 1979 to 3 Jul 1980. The longest period without a change was the 12 years 13 days from 26 Oct 1939 to 7 Nov 1951, during which time the rate stayed at 2 per cent. This lowest-ever rate had been first attained on 22 Apr 1852.

Worst inflation The world's worst inflation occurred in Hungary in June 1946, when the 1931 gold pengö was valued at 130 million trillion ($1·3 \times 10^{20}$) paper pengös. Notes were issued for 'Egymillard billion' (one milliard billion or 10^{21}) pengös on 3 Jun and withdrawn on 11 Jul 1946. Vouchers for 1000 billion billion (10^{27}) pengös were issued for taxation payment only. The circulation of the Reichsbank mark on 6 Nov 1923 reached 400338326350700000000 and inflation was 755700 millionfold on 1913 levels.

The country with the worst inflation in 1992 was Zaire, where consumer price increases rose to 7058 per cent. Inflation in the CIS (formerly USSR) totalled 1181·8 per cent in 1992 according to IMF data.

The UK's worst rate in a year was for August 1974 to August 1975, when inflation ran at a rate of 26·9 per cent. The increase in the Tax and Price Index (allowing for tax reliefs) was 8·1 per cent for the 12 months to June 1990. The largest 12 month increase in the TPI (extrapolated) was 31·9 per cent, also recorded in August 1975.

Least inflation The country with the least inflation in 1992 was Gabon, where prices fell by 4·2 per cent.

Wealth and Poverty

The comparison and estimation of extreme personal wealth are beset with intractable difficulties. Quite apart from reticence and the element of approximation in the valuation of assets, as Jean Paul Getty (1892–1976) once said: 'If you can count your millions you are not a billionaire.' The term millionaire was coined *c.* 1740 and billionaire (in the original American sense of one thousand million) in 1861. The earliest dollar centi-millionaire was Cornelius Vanderbilt (1794–1877), who left $100 million in 1877. The first billionaires were John Davison Rockefeller (1839–1937) and Andrew William Mellon (1855–1937), with Rockefeller believed to be the first to a billion dollars. In 1937, the last year in which all three were alive, a billion US dollars were worth £205 million, but that amount of sterling would today have a purchasing power exceeding £5 billion.

Richest men Much of the wealth of the world's monarchs represents national rather than personal assets. The richest person in the world is HM Sir Muda Hassanal Bolkiah Mu'izzaddin Waddaulah (b. 15 Jul 1946) of Brunei, self-appointed Prime Minister and Finance and Home Affairs Minister, who has a fortune estimated at $37billion by *Fortune* magazine in September 1992.

The same source estimates the richest private individual to be John Werner Kluge of Metromedia, with $8·1 billion. The only other estimated deca-billionaire among private citizens was the Japanese real estate owner Taikichiro Mori (1904–93), whose fortune was revised from $15 billion to $10 billion during 1991.

The richest man in Great Britain is reputed to be the 6th Duke of Westminster (b. 22 Dec 1951), whose assets were estimated in April 1993 to be worth £1·5 billion from £3·5billion in 1992.

Richest women HM the Queen is asserted by some to be the wealthiest woman, with a fortune estimated at

His Majesty the Sultan of Brunei, whose fortune is estimated at $37 billion.
(Photo: Sygma/T. Matsumoto)

£6·75 billion ($11·7 billion) in April 1993. However, few of her assets under the perpetual succession of the Crown are personal, disposable or alienable, and her personal wealth was estimated at £500 million. An alternative estimate published by *The Economist* in January 1992 placed her personal wealth at much closer to £150 million.

The cosmetician Madame C.J. Walker (*née* Sarah Breedlove) (1857–1919 of Delta, Louisiana, USA) is reputed to have become the first self-made millionairess. She was an uneducated Negro orphan whose fortune was founded on a hair straightener.

Richest families It was tentatively estimated in 1974 that the combined value of the assets nominally controlled by the Du Pont family of some 1600 members may be of the order of $150000 million. The family arrived in the USA from France on 1 Jan 1800. Capital from Pierre Du Pont (1730–1817) enabled his son Eleuthère Irénée Du Pont to start his explosives company in the United States.

A more conclusive claimant is the Walton retailing family, worth an estimated $24 billion, compared with Britain's retailing giants, the Sainsbury family, with an estimated $5·2 billion.

Youngest millionaires The youngest person ever to accumulate a million dollars was the American child film actor Jackie Coogan (1914–84), co-star with Sir Charles Chaplin (1889–1977) in *The Kid*, made in 1921.

The youngest of the 101 dollar billionaires reported in the US in 1992 was William Gates, 36, co-founder of software house Microsoft of Seattle, Washington. Gates was 20 when he set up his company in 1976 and was a billionaire in 11 years. (⊳ Computers)

The youngest millionairess was Shirley Temple (b. USA, 23 Apr 1928) now Mrs Charles Black, who accumulated wealth exceeding $1 million before she was 10 from a childhood acting career spanning 1934–9.

Highest incomes The largest incomes derive from the collection of royalties per barrel by rulers of oil-rich

---

Piggy bank

A giant pink piggy bank measuring 2·31×3·61 m 7½ ×12ft with a capacity of 7·2 m³ 254·25 ft³ was made by Mercian Housing Association Ltd in May 1990.

Lecture fees

Dr Ronald Dante was paid $3 080 000 for lecturing students on hypnotherapy at a two-day course held in Chicago, USA on 1–2 Jun 1986. He was teaching for 8 hours each day, and thus earned $192 500 per hour.

---

sheikhdoms who have not formally revoked personal entitlement. Shaikh Zayid ibn Sultan an-Nuhayan (b. 1918), Head of State of the United Arab Emirates, arguably has title to some $9 billion of the country's annual gross national product.

Greatest wills The highest-valued will ever proved in the UK was worth £118 221 949 net, left by the 6th Marquess of Cholmondeley (1919–90). He was the former Lord Great Chamberlain, and as such was the figure who walked backwards in front of the Queen at the State Opening of Parliament.

On 29 Apr 1985 the estate of Sir Charles Clore (1904–79) was agreed by a court hearing at £123 million. The Inland Revenue initially claimed £84 million in duties, but settled for £67 million.

The largest fortune proved in the will of a woman in the UK was £92 814 057 net by Dorothy de Rothschild (1895–1988), matriarch of the leading family in world Jewry.

Largest dowry The largest recorded dowry was that of Elena Patiño, daughter of Don Simón Iturbi Patiño (1861–1947), the Bolivian tin millionaire, who in 1929 bestowed £8 million from a fortune at one time estimated to be worth £125 million.

Return of cash The largest amount of cash ever found and returned to its

4 July, 1916

THE GUINNESS TIMES

You can't take it with you

WORLD'S GREATEST MISER DIES LEAVING A FORTUNE

Hetty Green, reputedly America's wealthiest woman and arguably the world's most miserly, died yesterday leaving an estate worth $95 million.

Mrs Green, a New York financier who, at the age of 30 inherited $10 million following the deaths of her father and aunt, increased this tenfold by careful management and avoiding unnecessary expenditure.

Despite keeping over $31¼ million in one bank alone, Mrs Green ate cold porridge through being too thrifty to

Photo: Library of Congress, Washington, DC , USA.

heat it, and her son's leg had to be amputated because of her delays in finding a clinic offering free medical treatment.

Henrietta Howland Green (née Robinson), born 21 Nov 1835, New Bedford, Massachusetts; died 3 July 1916, New York City.

owners was $500 000, discovered by Lowell Elliott, 61, on his farm at Peru, Indiana, USA. It had been dropped in June 1972 by a parachuting hijacker. Jim Priceman, 44, assistant cashier at Doft & Co. Inc., returned an envelope containing $37·1 million in *negotiable* bearer certificates found outside 110 Wall Street to A.G. Becker Inc. of New York, USA on 6 Apr 1982. In announcing a reward of $250 Beckers were acclaimed as 'being all heart'.

Greatest bequests The largest single bequest in the history of philanthropy

was the $1 billion art collection of the American publisher Walter Annenberg, who, on 12 Mar 1991, announced his intention to leave the collection to the Metropolitan Museum of Art in New York City, USA.

The largest single cash bequest was the $500 million gift, announced on 12 Dec 1955, to 4157 educational and other institutions by the Ford Foundation (established 1936) of New York, USA.

UK The greatest benefactions of a British millionaire were those of William Richard Morris, later the Viscount

Nuffield (1877–1963), which totalled more than £30 million between 1926 and his death on 22 Aug 1963.

Highest salary It was reported by the US government that Michael Milken, the 'junk bond king' at Drexel Burnham Lambert Inc., was paid an all-time high of $550 million in salary and bonuses in 1987. (⇔ Fines).

The world's highest paid executive in 1991 was Leon Hirsch, chief executive of U.S. Surgical, who received $118 million including $109 million for stock options.

Britain's highest-paid man is William Brown, an insurance broker with Walsham Brothers, whose salary and dividends for 1991 was reported to be £17 million, compared with £9360000 in 1990. David John Sainsbury, deputy chairman of J. Sainsbury plc. supermarket chain in 1990 was recorded as having received £24 570 527 gross in dividends

Highest fees The highest-paid investment consultant in the world is Harry D. Schultz, who lives in Monte Carlo and Zurich, Switzerland. His standard consultation fee for 60 minutes is $2400 on weekdays and $3400 at weekends. Most popular are the five-minute phone consultations at $200 (i.e. $40 a minute). His 'International Harry Schultz Letter', instituted in 1964, sells at $50 per copy. A life subscription costs $2400.

Golden handshake *Business Week* magazine reported in May 1989 that the largest golden handshake ever given was one of $53·8 million, to F. Ross Johnson, who left RJR Nabisco as chairman in February 1989.

In the UK, Robert Noonan was reported on 25 Apr 1989 to stand to receive £2 270 000 in a pay-off under the £82 million terms of a bid for Marler Estates, of which he was chairman, by Conrad Holdings.

Stock Exchanges

The oldest of the world's Stock Exchanges is that of Amsterdam, Netherlands, founded in 1602 with dealings in printed shares of the United East India Company of the Netherlands in the Oude Zijds Kapel. The largest trading

volume in 1992 was New York with £1161 billion, ahead of London with £1045 billion and the Federation of German Stock Exchanges with £891 billion.

London Stock Exchange *Most bargains* The highest number of equity bargains in one day was 114973 on 22 Oct 1987. The record for a year is 13557455 bargains in 1987. There were 7367 securities listed at 31 Dec 1992 (cf. the 9749 peak in June 1973). Their total nominal value was £511·6 billion (gilt-edged £172 billion), with a market value of £2579·3 billion (gilt-edged £186·5 billion).

Trading volume The busiest session on the London market was on 28 Jan 1993, when 1·3 billion shares were traded.

FT-SE 100 share index *Closing prices* The highest closing figure for the FT-SE 100 index was 2957·3, reached on 8 Mar 1993, with an all-time high of 2980·9 reached on 9 Mar 1993. The lowest closing figure was 986·9 on 23 Jul 1984.

Greatest rise and fall The greatest rise in a day has been 142·2 points to 1943·8 on 21 Oct 1987, and the greatest fall in a day's trading was 250·7 points to 1801·6 on 20 Oct 1987.

New York Stock Exchange The market value of stocks listed on the New York Stock Exchange reached an all-time high of $3200 billion at the end of March 1991. The record day's trading was 608148710 shares on 20 Oct 1987, compared with 16410030 shares traded on 29 Oct 1929, the 'Black Tuesday' of the famous 'crash', a record unsurpassed until April 1968.

The largest stock trade in the history of the NYSE took place on 10 Apr 1986, and involved a 48788800-share block of Navistar International Corporation stock traded at $10 in a transaction worth $487888000.

The highest price paid for a seat on the New York Stock Exchange was $1·15 million in 1987. The lowest 20th-century price was $17000, set in 1942.

Closing prices The highest closing figure on the Dow Jones Industrial average (instituted 8 Oct 1896) of selected stocks was 3523·28 on 20 May 1993. The index closed above 3000 points for the first time on 17 Apr 1991, at 3004·46, although it had edged past the 3000 barrier for the first time on Friday 13 Jul 1990 after a strong run.

The Depression caused the Dow Jones average to plunge from 381·71 on 3 Sep 1929 to its lowest ever closing figure of 41·22 on 2 Jul 1932.

Greatest rise and fall The record daily rise is 186·84 points, to 2027·85, achieved on 21 Oct 1987. The largest decline in a day's trading was 508 points (22·6 per cent) on 19 Oct 1987 (Black Monday). The total lost in security values from 1 Sep 1929 to 30 Jun 1932 was $74 billion. The greatest paper loss in a year was $210 billion in 1974.

Most valued companies The greatest aggregate market value of any corporation at April 1993 was £78·5 billion for Exxon of Irving, Texas, USA.

UK The largest wholly British company in terms of market capitalization is currently BT, valued at £25·2 billion at 20 May 1993.

Largest flotation The largest ever flotation in stock-market history was the £5·2 billion sale of the 12 UK regional electricity companies to 5·7 million shareholders. The offer was heavily oversubscribed, with a total of 12·75 million applications processed. Trading began on 11 Dec 1990 and ended with Manweb, which covers Merseyside and north Wales, producing the highest premium—66p on the 100p partly-paid price of 240p. The flotation of British Gas plc had an equity offer which produced the record sum of £7·75 billion, but to only 4·5 million shareholders. Allotment letters were dispatched on 15 Dec 1986.

The record number of investors for a single issue is 5·9 million in the Mastergain '92 equity fund floated by the Unit Trust of India, Bombay in April and May 1992.

AGM attendance A world record total of 20109 shareholders attended the AGM in April 1961 of the American Telephone and Telegraph Co. (AT&T).

Rights issue The largest recorded rights issue in Britain was one of £921 million by Barclays Bank, announced on 7 Apr 1988.

322

Smallest company equity
Britain's smallest ever company was Frank Davies Ltd, incorporated on 22 Aug 1924 with a ½d share capital divided into two ¼d shares. Converting to decimal coinage (£0·002 divided into two shares of £0·001), it was finally dissolved in 1978 without ever having increased its share capital.

Highest par value The highest denomination of any share quoted in the world is a single share in Moeara Enim Petroleum Corporation, worth £50586 (165000 Dutch florins) on 22 Apr 1992.

Greatest personal loss The highest recorded personal paper losses on stock values were incurred by Ray A. Kroc (1902–84), former chairman of the McDonald's Corporation, amounting to $65 million on 8 Jul 1974. (⇨ Restaurateurs)

Company names The longest company name on the Index registered under the Companies Acts is 'The Only Ordinary People Trying to Impress the Big Guys with Extraordinary Ideas, Sales, Management, Creative Thinking and Problem Solving Consultancy Company Ltd', company number 2660603. This is the specially adopted name of 'The Planet Hollywood Restaurant Company Ltd' owned by Arnold Schwarzenegger, Sylvester Stallone and Bruce Willis.

The shortest names on the Index are D Ltd, E Ltd, H Ltd, Q Ltd, U Ltd, X Ltd and Y Ltd.

Paper Money

Earliest Paper money was an invention of the Chinese, first tried in AD812 and prevalent by AD970. The world's earliest banknotes (*banco-sedler*) were issued in Stockholm, Sweden in July 1661, the oldest survivor being one of five dalers dated 6 Dec 1662. The oldest surviving printed Bank of England note is one for £555 to bearer, dated 19 Dec 1699, measuring 11·4 × 19·1 cm 4½ × 7½ in.

Largest The largest paper money ever issued was the one-guan note of the

Chinese Ming Dynasty issue of 1368–99, which measured 22·8 × 33·0 cm 9 × 13 in. In October 1983 one sold for £340.

Smallest The smallest national note ever issued was the 10-bani note of the Ministry of Finance of Romania in 1917. It measured (printed area) 27·5 × 38 mm 1¹/₁₆ × 1¹/₂ in. Of German *Notgeld*, the smallest were the 1–3 pfg notes of Passau (1920–21), which measured 18 × 18·5 mm ¹¹/₁₆ × ³/₄ in.

Highest values The highest-value notes in circulation are US Federal Reserve $10 000 banknotes, bearing the head of Salmon P. Chase (1808–73). It was announced in 1969 that no further notes higher than $100 would be issued, and only 345 $10 000 bills remain in circulation or unretired. The highest value ever issued by the US Federal Reserve System is a note for $100 000, bearing the head of President Woodrow Wilson (1856–1924), which is only used for transactions between the Federal Reserve and the Treasury Department.

Two Bank of England notes for £1 million still exist, dated before 1812, but these were used only for internal accounting. There are also two Treasury £1 million notes dating from 1948 in existence, one of which was sold to dealer Brian Dawson for £23 100 at Christie's, London on 9 Oct 1990.

The highest-value notes in Great Britain which have been *issued* are £1000 notes, first printed in 1725, discontinued on 22 Apr 1943 and withdrawn on 30 Apr 1945. Just over 100 of these notes were still unretired up to April 1993.

Lowest values The lowest-value (and the lowest-denomination) legal tender banknote is the one-sen (or 1/100th of a rupiah) Indonesian note. Its exchange value in early 1993 was 327 170 to the £.

The lowest-denomination Bank of England notes ever printed were the black on pale blue half-crown (now 12½p) notes in 1941, signed by the late Sir Kenneth Peppiatt. Very few examples survive and they are valued at not less than £1500.

Highest circulation The highest ever Bank of England note circulation in the UK was £19 059 million worth on 24 Dec 1992 — equivalent to a pile 381 km 237 miles high in new £5 notes.

Most expensive The record price paid for a single lot of banknotes was £240 350 (including buyer's premium) by

323

Richard Lobel, on behalf of a consortium, at Phillips, London on 14 Feb 1991. The lot consisted of a cache of British military notes which were found in a vault in Berlin, Germany, and contained more than 17 million notes.

Banknote collection Chris Boyd of New Malden, Surrey has accumulated banknotes from 204 different countries since he started collecting in 1990.

Cheques and Coins

Largest The greatest amount paid by a single cheque in the history of banking was £1 425 000 000. Issued on 11 Jul 1989 and signed by D. Gareth Jones, Abbey National Building Society Treasurer and Assistant General Manager, and Jonathan C. Nicholls, Abbey National Building Society Assistant Treasurer, the cheque represented a payment from the expiring Abbey National Building Society in favour of the newly created Abbey National plc. A much larger one, for $4 176 969 623·57, was drawn on 30 Jun 1954, although this was an internal US Treasury cheque.

Collection—record price The highest price ever paid for a coin collection was $25 235 360 for the Garrett family collection of US and colonial coins collected between 1860 and 1942, which had been donated to Johns Hopkins University, Baltimore, Maryland, USA. The sales were made at four auctions held on 28–29 Nov 1979 and 25–26 Mar 1981 at the Bowers & Ruddy Galleries in Wolfeboro, New Hampshire, USA.

Hoards The most valuable hoard of coins was one of about 80 000 aurei in Brescello near Modena, Italy in 1714, believed to have been deposited *c.* 37 BC. The largest deliberately buried hoard ever found was the Brussels hoard of 1908 containing *c.* 150 000 coins.

The largest hoard of English coins was the Tutbury (Staffs) hoard of 1831 containing over 20 000 silver coins, the majority of which were pence of Edward I (1271–1307).

The largest accidental hoard on record was from the 1715 Spanish Plate Fleet, which sank off the coast of Florida, USA. A reasonable estimate of its contents would be some 60 million coins, about

Coin balancing

Hiem Shda of Kiriat Mozkien, Israel stacked a pyramid of 847 coins on the edge of a coin free-standing vertically on the base of a coin which was on a table on 30 Jul 1989.

The tallest single column of coins ever stacked on the edge of a coin was made up of 253 Indian one rupee pieces on top of a vertical five rupee coin, by Dipak Syal of Yamuna Nagar, India on 3 May 1991. He also balanced 10 one rupee coins and 10 ten paise coins alternately horizontally and vertically in a single column on 1 May 1991.

Column of coins

The most valuable column of coins was worth £18701 and was 1·90m *6 ft 3 in* high. It was built by Robert Young and a team of helpers at Notton, W Yorks on 18 Jun 1992.

Pile of coins

The most valuable pile of coins had a total value of $126 463·61 and consisted of 1 000 298 American coins of various denominations. It was constructed by the YWCA of Seattle-King County, Washington, USA at Redmond, Washington on 28 May 1992.

half of which were recovered by Spanish authorities shortly after the event. Of the remaining 30 million pieces, perhaps 500 000 have been recovered by modern salvors, presumably leaving the other 29½ million coins still awaiting recovery.

The record in terms of weight is 43 tonnes of gold, from the White Star Liner HMS *Laurentic*, which was mined in 40·2 m *132 ft* of water off Fanad Head, Donegal, Ireland in 1917. Of the 3211 gold ingots 3191 have been recovered since then by the Royal Navy, Cossum

Coins

Oldest
World: c. 630 BC electrum staters of King Gyges (now Lydia), Turkey[1]. *British:* c. 90 BC Westerham-type gold stater[2].

Earliest Dated
World: Samian silver tetradrachm struck in Zankle (now Messina), Sicily, dated year 1, viz 494 BC — shown as 'A'. *Christian Era:* MCCXXXIIII (1234) Bishop of Roskilde coins, Denmark (6 known). *British:* 1539 James V of Scotland gold 'bonnet piece'. *Earliest English:* 1548 Edward VI gold ten shillings (MDXLVIII).

Heaviest
World: 19·71 kg *43lb 7¼ oz* Swedish 10-daler copper plate 1644[3]. *British:* 121·1 g *4¼ oz* Shrewsbury silver pound of 1644, the heaviest of the Charles I silver pounds from the English Civil War[4].

Lightest
World: 0·002 g *14000 to the oz* Nepalese silver ¼ jawa c.1740. *British:* 2·66 grains *180 to the oz* Henry VIII 2nd coinage silver farthings (1526–42).

Most Expensive
World: $3190000 for the King of Siam Proof Set, a set of 1804 and 1834 US coins which had once been given to the King of Siam, purchased by Iraj Sayah and Terry Brand at Superior Galleries, Beverly Hills, California, USA on 28 May 1990. Included in the set of nine coins was the 1804 silver dollar, which had an estimated value of about $2000000. The record price paid for an individual coin is $1500000, for the US 1907 Double Eagle Ultra High Relief $20 gold coin, sold by MTB Banking Corporation of New York, USA to a private investor on 9 Jul 1990. *British:* £124300 (including buyer's premium) bid for a Victoria gothic crown in gold (2 known), at a joint auction between Spink & Son, London and the Taisei Stamp and Coin Co., in Tokyo, Japan on 3 Jul 1988.

Footnotes
[1] *Chinese uninscribed 'spade' money of the Zhou Dynasty has been dated to c.550BC.*
[2] *Bellovaci-type gold staters, which were struck in northern France and not in Britain, circulated as early as c.130BC.*
[3] *The largest coin-like medallion was completed on 21 Mar 1986 for the World Exposition in Vancouver, British Columbia, Canada, Expo 86 — a $1000000 gold piece. Its dimensions were 95·25cm 37½ in diameter and 19·05mm¾ in thick, and it weighed 166kg 365lb 15oz or 5337oz (troy) of gold.*
[4] *The heaviest current British coin is the 39·94g 1⅜oz gold £5 piece.*

Line of coins
The most valuable line of coins was made up of 1724000 US quarters to a value of $431000. It was 41·68km *25·9miles* long and was laid at the Atlanta Marriott Marquis Hotel, Georgia, USA by members of the National Exchange Club on 25 Jul 1992. The most valuable line of coins in Britain was the 'Golden Mile' of £1 coins with a value of £71652, laid at the Town Hall at Romford, Essex on 22 Apr 1990. The attempt was carried out under the supervision of Pauline Obee, assisted by volunteers from Havering-atte-Bower, Essex.

The longest line of coins on record had a total length of 48·89km *30·38 miles* and was made using 1886975 2p coins. It was laid by the Friends of the Samaritans at the Great Park, Windsor, Berks on 16 Aug 1992.

Coin snatching
The greatest number of new 10p pieces clean-caught from being flipped from the back of a forearm into the same downward palm is 328, by Dean Gould of Felixstowe, Suffolk on 6 Apr 1993.

Diving Syndicate and Consortium Recovery Ltd.

Mints Largest The largest mint in the world is that of the US Treasury. It was built from 1965–69 on Independence Mall, Philadelphia, Pennsylvania, covers 4·7ha *11·5acres* and has an annual production capacity of 12 billion coins (down from 15 billion). One new high-speed stamping machine called *Graebner Press* can produce coins at a rate of 42000 per hour and the record production was 19·5 billion coins produced between the Philadelphia and Denver mints in 1982.

Smallest The smallest issuing mint in the world belongs to the Sovereign Military

Order of Malta, in the City of Rome. Its single-press mint is housed in one small room and has issued proof coins since 1961. (⇨ Smallest countries)

Charity fund-raising Profits from sales of the single *Do They Know It's Christmas*, recorded by Band Aid in 1984, and other related projects in support of the Ethiopian Famine Relief Fund raised £110 million at the close of the account in 1992. (⇨ Recorded Sound)

The greatest recorded amount raised by a charity walk or run is $Can 24·7 million by Terry Fox (1958–81) of Canada who, with an artificial leg, ran from St John's, Newfoundland to Thunder Bay, Ontario in 143 days from 12 Apr–2 Sep 1980. He covered 5373km *3339 miles*.

Charity credit cards The Leeds Permanent Building Society Visa affinity credit card has raised some £4 million since its launch in 1988, the main beneficiary being the Imperial Cancer Research Fund with £2 million.

Labour

Trade unions *Oldest* The oldest of the 71 trade unions affiliated to the Trades Union Congress (founded 1868) at May 1993 is the Educational Institute of Scotland (EIS), founded in Edinburgh on 18 Sep 1847, with 47169 members.

Part of the continuous line of coins which had a total value of $431000. When the record was set in July 1992 this was equal to just under £227000.

(Photo: Marquette Industries/Jerry Stahl)

Largest The world's largest union is the Professionalniy Soyuz Rabotnikov Agro-Promyshlennogo Kompleksa (Agro-Industrial Complex Workers' Union) in Russia, with 15·2 million members in January 1993.

The largest union in the UK is the Transport and General Workers' Union (TGWU), with 1126631 members at 1 Jan 1992, compared to a peak membership of 2086281 in 1979.

Smallest The ultimate in small unions was the Jewelcase and Jewellery Display Makers Union (JJDMU), founded in 1894. It was dissolved on 31 Dec 1986 by its general secretary, Charles Evans. The motion was seconded by Fergus McCormack, its only surviving member. The smallest union is currently the 16-member Sheffield Wool Shear Workers.

Longest name The union with the longest name is the International Association of Marble, Slate and Stone

Employment agency

The world's largest employment services group is Manpower, with world-wide sales of all their brand units of $3·5 billion at year end 31 March 1992.

Polishers, Rubbers and Sawyers, Tile and Marble Setters' Helpers and Marble Mosaic and Terrazzo Workers' Helpers, or the IAMSSPRSTMSHMMTWH of Washington, DC, USA.

Labour disputes *Earliest* A labour dispute concerning monotony of diet and working conditions was recorded in 1153 BC in Thebes, Egypt. The earliest recorded strike was one by an orchestra leader named Aristos from Greece, in Rome *c.* 309 BC. The dispute concerned meal breaks.

Largest The most serious single labour dispute in the UK was the General Strike of 4–12 May 1926, called by the Trades Union Congress in support of the Miners' Federation. During the nine days of the strike 1 580 000 people were involved and 14 220 000 working days were lost. In the year 1926 as a whole a total of 2 750 000 people were involved in 323 different labour disputes and the working days lost during the year amounted to 162 300 000, the highest figure ever recorded.

The number of working days lost to strikes in 1991 was the lowest since records began in the 1890s, with 761 000 in 369 separate stoppages. The highest number of stoppages in a wartime year was 2194 in 1944.

Longest strike The world's longest recorded strike ended on 4 Jan 1961, after 33 years. It concerned the employment of barbers' assistants in Copenhagen, Denmark. The longest recorded major strike was that at the plumbing fixtures factory of the Kohler Co. in Sheboygan, Wisconsin, USA, between April 1954 and October 1962. The strike is alleged to have cost the United Automobile Workers' Union about $12 million to sustain.

Britain's most protracted national strike was called by the National Union of Mineworkers from 8 Mar 1984 to 5 Mar

Oldest club

Britain's oldest gentlemen's club is White's, St James's, London, opened *c.* 1697 by Francis White (died 1711) as a Chocolate House. It moved to its present site in 37 St James's in 1755. It has been described as an 'oasis in a desert of democracy'. Britain's oldest known dining club founded in 1626 is the Charterhouse School Founder's Day Dinner, held annually on 12 December. London clubland's most senior member was Sir Walter Howard (1888–1992) who joined the United Oxford and Cambridge University Club in 1912.

1985. HM Treasury estimated the cost to be £2625 million or £118·93 per household.

Unemployment *Highest* The highest recorded percentage unemployment in Great Britain was on 23 Jan 1933, when the total of unemployed persons on the Employment Exchange registers was 2903065, representing 22·8 per cent of the insured working population. The peak figure for the post-war period in the UK has been 12·3 per cent of the workforce (3 407 729) on 9 Jan 1986.

Lowest In December 1973 in Switzerland the total number of unemployed was reported to be 81 from a population of 6·6 million. The lowest recorded peace-time level of unemployment in Britain was 0·9 per cent on 11 Jul 1955, when 184929 persons were registered. The peak figure for the employed labour force in the UK has been 26 948 000 in December 1989.

Working career The longest working life has been that of 98 years by Mr Izumi who began work goading draught animals at a sugar mill at Isen, Tokunoshima, Japan in 1872. He retired as a sugar cane farmer in 1970 aged 105. (⬦ Oldest authentic centenarian)

The longest working life recorded in the UK was that of Susan O'Hagan (1802–1909) who was in domestic service with three generations of the Hall family of Lisburn, near Belfast, Co.

Antrim for 97 years from the age of 10 to light duties at 107.

The longest recorded industrial career in one job in Britain was that of Miss Polly Gadsby, who started work with Archibald Turner & Co. of Leicester at the age of nine. In 1932, after 86 years' service, she was still at her bench wrapping elastic at the age of 95. Theodore C. Taylor (1850–1952) served 86 years with J.T. & J. Taylor of Batley, W Yorks including 56 years as chairman. The longest serving company chairman on record was James Todd of Findlater Mackie Todd & Co. Ltd, a wine and spirits company. He was chairman of the London-based firm for 63 years from 1893 through to his death in 1956 at the age of 89, having joined in 1884. Edward William Beard (1878–1982), a builder of Swindon, Wilts retired in October 1981 after 85 years with the firm he had founded in 1896. Commissioner Catherine Bramwell-Booth (1883–1987) had been serving the Salvation Army since 1903. Richard John Knight (b. 20 Apr 1881) was company secretary to seven companies at the time of his death on 12 Nov 1984, aged 103 years.

Working week A case of a working week of 142 hours (with an average each day of 3hr 42min 51sec for sleep) was recorded in June 1980 by Dr Paul Ashton, the anaesthetics registrar at Birkenhead General Hospital, Merseyside. He described the week in question as 'particularly bad but not untypical'. Some non-consultant doctors are contracted to work 110 hours a week or be available for 148 hours. Some contracts for fully salaried university lecturers call for a three-hour week or a 72-hour year spread over 24 weeks.

Energy Consumption

To express the various forms of available energy (coal, liquid fuels and water power etc., but omitting vegetable fuels and peat), it is the practice to convert them all into terms of a fuel equivalent.

According to *World Bank Atlas* data for 1990, the highest energy consumption was in Qatar, at 15·26 tonnes oil equivalent per capita. The UK figure was 3·646tonnes per capita. The lowest consumption from the available figures was

less than 0·5 kg *18 oz* per capita in Lesotho and Namibia.

Postal Services

Largest mail The country with the largest volume of mail in the world is the United States, whose population posted 166·4 billion letters and packages in the fiscal year ending 1992. At that time the US Postal Service employed 725 290 people and had the world's largest civilian vehicle fleet of 178925 cars and trucks.

The UK total was 16 364 million letters and 183·6 million parcels in the year ending 31 Mar 1992. The record day was 16 Dec 1991 with 121·1 million items, when Christmas cards coincided with share certificates following the privatization of BT.

Postal addresses The practice of numbering houses began on the Pont Notre Dame, Paris, France in 1463. The highest-numbered house in Britain is No. 2679 Stratford Road, Hockley Heath, W Mids, owned since 1977 by Mr and Mrs Malcolm Aldridge. The highest-numbered house in Scotland is No. 2631 London Road, Mount Vernon, Glasgow, which has been owned since 1986 by Mr and Mrs Norman Brown.

Oldest pillar boxes The first orthodox system of roadside posting-boxes was

---

Stamp licking

John Kenmuir of Hamilton, Strathclyde licked and affixed 393 stamps in 4min at the BBC TV studios on 26 Sep 1990, later shown on the *Record Breakers* programme.

Most personal mail

The highest confirmed amount of mail received by any private citizen in a year is 900000 letters by the baseball star Henry Louis 'Hank' Aaron (b. 1934), reported by the US Postal Department in June 1974. About a third were letters of hate engendered by his bettering of George Herman 'Babe' Ruth's career record for home runs. (⇨ Baseball)

Postage Stamps

(Auction records unless stated otherwise and all prices include buyer's premium)

Earliest
Put on sale at GPO 1 May 1840. Penny Black 1d of Great Britain, Queen Victoria, 68158080 printed.

Highest Price (World)
£1350000 (Sw.Fr. 3400000). Penny Black, 2 May 1840 cover, bought at Harmers, Lugano, Switzerland on behalf of a Japanese buyer on 23 Mar 1991.

Highest Price (UK)
£374000. China 1878 5candarins 'wide spacing' unique mint sheet of 25, sold at Sotheby's, London on 11 Sep 1991 and bought by a Hong Kong collector. Single stamp. £203500, Bermuda 1854 Perot Postmaster (1d red on blueish wove paper on 1855 letter) at Christie's, London on 13 Jun 1991.

Highest Total (UK)
£2201463. The Major James Starr collection of Chinese stamps on 11–13 Sep 1991, with all 993 lots sold.

Largest Purchase
$11 million. Marc Haas collection of 3000 US postal and pre-postal covers to 1869, bought by Stanley Gibbons Ltd, London in August 1979.

Largest (Special Purpose)
247·7 x 69·8mm 9¾ x 2¾ in. China 1913. 10 cent letter stamp.

Largest (Standard Postage)
160 x 110mm 6⁵⁄₁₆ x 4⁵⁄₁₆ in. Marshall Islands 75 cents issued 30 Oct 1979.

Smallest
8 x 9·5mm ⁵⁄₁₆ x ⅜ in. Colombian State of Bolivar, 1863–6. 10 cent and 1 peso value.

Highest Denomination (World)
£100. Red and black, Kenya, Uganda and Tanganyika 1925.

Highest Denomination (UK)
£10. Grey-white, issued 2 Feb 1993, depicting Britannia and embossed with Braille markings for the first time.

Lowest Denomination
3000 pengö of Hungary. Issued 1946 when 150 million million pengö=1p.

Rarest (World)
Unique examples include: British Guiana 1 cent black on magenta of 1856 (last on the market in 1980), Swedish 3 skilling-banco yellow colour error of 1855; and the US postmasters' stamps from Boscawen, New Hampshire and Lockport, New York, USA.

Largest Issue (UK)
A total of 751·25 million of the 1929 1½ d Postal Union Congress commemorative stamps were sold.

established in 1653 in Paris, France to facilitate the interchange of correspondence in the city. They were erected at the intersection of main thoroughfares and were emptied three times a day.

A cast iron posting box dating from c. 1690 was found at the White Hart coaching inn, Spilsby, Lincs in January 1988. The oldest pillar box still in service in the British Isles is one dating from 8 Feb 1853 in Union Street, St Peter Port, Guernsey, Channel Islands. Cast by John Vaudin in Jersey, it was restored to its original maroon livery in October 1981. The oldest box in mainland Britain is at Barnes Cross, Holwell (postally in Bishop's Caundle), Dorset, dating from probably later in 1853. The oldest in the Republic of Ireland is a hexagonal-roofed pillar box in Kent Railway Station, Glanmire, Co. Cork, dating from 1857.

Post offices The country with the greatest number of post offices is India, with 144829 in 1988. At 31 Mar 1992 there were 20160 post offices in the UK, the oldest of which is at Sanquhar, Dumfries & Galloway, first referred to in 1763. The northernmost post office in the British Isles is at Haroldswick, Unst, Shetland Islands and the most southerly is at Samarès, Jersey, Channel Islands, although it is not run by the British Post Office. The most southerly in mainland Britain is the Lizard subpost office, Cornwall. The highest post office in England is at Quarnford, Buxton, Derbys at 359·9m *1181ft*.

The longest post office counter in Britain measured 56·4m *185ft* and had 33 positions when opened in 1962 at Trafalgar Square, London. The longest is currently one of 47·85m *157ft* with 17 positions at George Square, Glasgow, Strathclyde. The post office with the greatest number of positions is London Chief Office, near St Paul's Cathedral, with 25.

Agriculture

Origins It has been estimated that about 21 per cent of the world's land surface is cultivable and that only 7·6 per cent is actually under cultivation.

Evidence adduced in 1971 from Nok Nok Tha and Spirit Cave, Thailand tends

Appropriate transport is well-advised when patrolling Australia's record sized sheep stations, the largest of which, at Commonwealth Hill, South Australia, covers 10567 km² *4080 miles²*.

(Photo: Rex Features)

to confirm that plant cultivation was part of the Hoabinhian culture *c.* 11 000 BC, but it is still likely that hominids (humans and their human-like ancestors) probably survived for 99·93 per cent of their known history without cultivating plants or domesticating animals.

Various species of plant were being domesticated in the Near East by 8000–7500 BC, for example, in Iraq, Syria, Iran and Jordan. It is argued that maize was grown around 5000 BC in the Tehuacan Valley of Mexico, and rice was being grown at about the same date at Hemudu, near Shanghai, China.

Animal husbandry It has been suggested that reindeer (*Rangifer tarandus*) may have been domesticated as early as 18000 BC, but definite proof is still lacking. The earliest known domesticated animal was probably of the order Carnivora (dogs) used in hunting about 9000–9500 years ago at sites such as Cayönü, Turkey and Star Carr in England.

The earliest known animals domesticated for food were probably descendants of the wild goats of Bezoar (*Capra aegagrus = hircus*), which were herded at Asiah, Iran *c.* 7700 BC. Sheep (*Ovis aries*) have been dated to *c.* 7200 BC at Argissa Magula in Thessaly,

Greece, and pigs (*Sus domestica*) and cattle (*Bos primigenius = taurus*) to *c.* 7000 BC at the same site. Chickens were domesticated before 6000 BC in Indochina and by 5900–5400 BC had spread to North China, as shown by radiocarbon dating from a Neolithic site at Peiligang, near Zhengzhou, and also at Wu'an Cishan and Tengxian Beixin. Chickens did not reach Britain until *c.* 150 BC.

Fisheries

United Nations Food and Agricultural Organization figures for 1990 (the last year for which comparable data is available) showed the world's leading fishing nation to be China, with a total catch of 12 million tonnes, followed by the former USSR (10·39 million tonnes) and Japan (10·35 million). The US was in 5th place with 5·87 million tonnes and the figure for the UK was 803 500 tonnes. The world total for the year was 97·2 million tonnes, down from a record 100 million tonnes in 1989.

The record for a single trawler is £278 798 from a 37 897-tonne catch by the Icelandic vessel *Videy* landed at Hull, Humberside on 11 Aug 1987. The greatest catch ever recorded from a single throw is 2471 tonnes by the purse seine-net boat M/S *Flømann* from Hareide, Norway in the Barents Sea on 28 Aug 1986. It was estimated that more than 120 million fish were caught in this shoal.

Real Estate

The world's largest landowner is the United States Government, with a holding of 295 million ha *728 million acres*, which represents an area 12 times larger than the United Kingdom. It has been suggested that the former Soviet Government constitutionally owned all the land in the entire country, with the exception, perhaps, of that on which foreign embassies stand—a total of 22·4 million km² *8·6 million miles²*.

British Isles The largest landowner is the Forestry Commission (instituted 1919), which has 1 127 594 ha *2 786 285 acres* throughout England, Scotland and Wales. The largest private landowner is the National Trust in England, Wales and

Smallest holding

The Electricity Trust of South Australia are the proprietors of a registered and separately-delineated piece of land in Adelaide measuring just 25·4mm *1in* on all four sides, i.e. one square inch.

Northern Ireland, with 232 029 ha *573 335 acres*. The UK's greatest-ever private landowner, however, was George Granville Sutherland-Leveson-Gower, 3rd Duke of Sutherland (1828–92), who owned 550 000 ha *1·4 million acres* in 1883. The individual with the largest acreage is currently the 9th Duke of Buccleuch (b. 28 Sep 1923), who owns 136 035 ha *336 000 acres*.

The longest accepted land tenure is that held by St Paul's Cathedral, London of land at Tillingham, Essex, given by Aethelbert, King of Kent no later than AD 616.

Prices The most expensive piece of property ever recorded, the land around the central Tokyo retail food store Mediya Building in the Ginza district, was quoted in October 1988 by the Japanese National Land Agency at a peak 33·3 million yen per m[2] (then equivalent to $248000).

The record price per acre paid for agricultural land in Great Britain is £12000 for a site at Elm Road, March, Cambs sold by J. Collingwood & Son of March on 31 Dec 1973.

Farms

Earliest The earliest mainland site in Britain is at Freshwater West, Dyfed, dated 5000–4680 BC.

Largest The largest farms in the world are *kolkhozy* collective farms in the former USSR. These were reduced in number from 235 500 in 1940 to 26 900 in 1988 and represented a total cultivated area of 169·2 million ha *417·6 million acres*. Units of over 25 000 ha *60000 acres* were not uncommon.

The pioneer farm owned by Laucidio Coelho near Campo Grande, Mato Grosso, Brazil c.1901 covered 8700km[2] *3358 miles[2]*

and supported 250000 head of cattle at the time of the owner's death in 1975.

British Isles The UK has about 18·5 million ha *45·7 million acres* of farmland on 241 400 holdings, the largest of which are the Scottish hill farms in the Grampians. The largest arable holding is that of the Earls of Iveagh at Elveden, Suffolk, where 4500 ha *11000 acres* are farmed on an estate covering 9100 ha *22 500 acres*. Production in 1991 included 9613 tonnes of grain and 42495 tonnes of sugar beet. Other vegetable crops, including potatoes, peas and carrots, produced a yield of over 25 186 tonnes. The livestock includes 1000 ewes and 6795 pigs.

Foot-and-mouth disease This first appeared in Britain at Stratford, east London in August 1839. The worst outbreak of the disease in Britain was in Shropshire from 25 Oct 1967 to 25 Jun 1968, when there were 2364 outbreaks and 429 632 animals slaughtered at a direct and consequential loss of £150 million. The outbreak of 1871, when farms were much smaller, affected 42 531 farms.

Cattle station Until 1915 the Victoria River Downs Station in Northern Territory, Australia covered an area of 90650km[2] *35000 miles[2]*, which is equivalent to the combined area of England's 20 largest counties.

The world's largest cattle station is currently the Anna Creek station of South Australia owned by the Kidman family. It covers 30000 km[2] *11600 miles[2]*, or 23 per cent the size of England, with the biggest component being Strangway at 14000km[2] *5500 miles[2]*.

Chicken ranch The Agrigeneral Company L.P. in Ohio, USA has 4·8 million hens laying some 3·7 million eggs daily.

Community garden The largest such project is that operated by the City Beautiful Council and the Benjamin Wegerzyn Garden Center at Dayton, Ohio, USA. It comprises 1173 allotments, each measuring 74·5m[2] *812 ft[2]*.

Hop farm The world's leading private hop growers are John I. Haas Inc., with farms in Oregon and Washington, USA, Tasmania and Victoria, Australia and

331

Knitting

The Exeter Spinners— Audrey Felton, Christine Heap, Eileen Lancaster, Marjorie Mellis, Ann Sandercock and Maria Scott—produced a jumper by hand from raw fleece in 1 hr 55 min 50·2 sec on 25 Sep 1983 at BBC Television Centre, London.

Sheep to shoulder

At the International Wool Secretariat Development Centre, Ilkley, W Yorks, a team of eight using commercial machinery produced a jumper—from shearing sheep to the finished article—in 2 hr 28 min 32 sec on 3 Sep 1986.

Kent, covering a net area of 2487 ha *6146 acres*. The UK has 3527 ha *8715 acres* under hop production.

Mushroom farm The world's largest mushroom farm is owned by Moonlight Mushrooms Inc. and was founded in 1937 in a disused limestone mine near Worthington, Pennsylvania, USA. The farm employs 1106 people who work in a maze of underground galleries 251 km *156 miles* long, producing 24 500 tonnes of mushrooms per year. The French annual consumption is unrivalled at 3·17 kg *7 lb* per person.

Piggery The world's largest piggery is the Sljeme pig unit in Yugoslavia, which is able to process 300 000 pigs per year.

Sheep station The largest sheep station in the world is Commonwealth Hill, in the north-west of South Australia. It grazes between 50 000 and 70 000 sheep, along with 24 000 uninvited kangaroos, in an area of 10 567 km² *4080 miles²* enclosed by 221 km *138 miles* of dog-proof fencing. The head count on Sir William Stevenson's 16 579 ha *40 970 acre* Lochinver station in New Zealand was 127 406 sheep on 1 Jan 1993.

The largest sheep drive on record involved the movement of 43 000 sheep from Barcaldine to Beaconsfield station, Queensland, Australia (a distance of 64 km *40 miles*) by 27 horsemen in 1886.

332

Turkey farm The farms of Bernard Matthews plc produce 10 million turkeys per year and employ a staff of 2500. The largest farm, at North Pickenham, Norfolk, produces 1 million turkeys.

Some exceptionally high livestock auction prices are believed to result from collusion between buyer and seller to raise the ostensible price levels of the breed concerned. Others are marketing and publicity exercises with little relation to true market prices.

Cattle The highest price ever paid was $2·5 million for the beefalo (a ⅜ bison, ⅜ Charolais, ¼ Hereford) 'Joe's Pride', sold by D. C. Basalo of Burlingame, California to the Beefalo Cattle Co. of Calgary, Canada on 9 Sep 1974.

UK A 14-month-old Canadian Holstein bull 'Pickland Elevation B. ET' was bought by Premier Breeders of Stamfordham, Northumberland for £233 000 in September 1982.

The highest price paid for any farm animal at auction in the UK is 65 000 guineas (£68 250) for 'Grantchester Heather VIII', a Holstein Friesian cow sold to Brian Draper of Shrewsbury, Shrops by John Suenson-Taylor of Audlem, Cheshire at the Grantchester sale on 12 Aug 1992.

Cow The highest price paid for a cow is $1·3 million for a Holstein at auction in East Montpelier, Vermont, USA in 1985. The British record is £68 250, also for a Holstein Friesian. (⬦ above)

Goat On 25 Jan 1985 an Angora buck bred by Waitangi Angoras of Waitangi, North Island, New Zealand was sold to Elliott Brown Ltd of Waipu, New Zealand for NZ $140 000.

Horse The highest price paid for a draught horse is $47 000 by C.G. Good of Ogden, Iowa, USA for the seven-year-old Belgian stallion 'Farceur' at Cedar Falls, Iowa on 16 Oct 1917.

A Welsh mountain pony stallion named 'Coed Cock Bari' was sold to an Australian bidder in Wales in September 1978 for 21 000 guineas (£22 050).

Chicken and turkey plucking

Ernest Hausen (1877– 1955) of Fort Atkinson, Wisconsin, USA died undefeated after 33 years as champion. On 19 Jan 1939 he was timed at 4·4 sec for plucking a chicken.

Vincent Pilkington of Cootehill, Co. Cavan, Republic of Ireland killed and plucked 100 turkeys in 7 hr 32 min on 15 Dec 1978. His record for a single turkey is 1 min 30 sec, set on RTE Television in Dublin on 17 Nov 1980.

Lowest price

The lowest price ever realized for livestock was at a sale at Kuruman, Cape Province, South Africa in 1934, where donkeys were sold for less than 2p each.

Pig The highest price ever paid for a pig is $56 000 for a cross-bred barrow named 'Bud', owned by Jeffrey Roemisch of Hermleigh, Texas, USA and bought by E.A. 'Bud' Olson and Phil Bonzio on 5 Mar 1983. The British record is 3300 guineas (£3465) paid by Malvern Farms for a Swedish Landrace gilt 'Bluegate Ally 33rd', owned by the Davidson Trust, in a draft sale at Reading, Berks on 2 Mar 1955.

Sheep The highest price ever paid for a sheep is $A450 000 (£205 000) by Willogoleche Pty Ltd for the Collinsville stud 'JC&S 43' at the 1989 Adelaide Ram Sales, South Australia.

The British record is £32 000 for a Scottish Blackface lamb ram named 'Old Sandy', sold by Michael Scott at Lanark, Strathclyde on 14 Oct 1988.

Wool The highest price ever paid for wool is $A3008·5 per kg greasy for a bale of Tasmania superfine at the wool auction in Tasmania, Australia on 23 Feb 1989 by Fujii Keori Ltd of Osaka, Japan— top bidders since 1973.

Cattle

The country with the largest stock of cattle is India, with an estimated 271·4 million head from a world total of 1 billion head in 1991. The estimated UK stock is 11·9 million. The leading producer of milk in 1992 was the US, with 68·8 million tonnes.

Largest The heaviest breed of cattle is the Chianini, which was brought to the Chiana Valley in Italy from the Middle East in pre-Roman times. Four types of the breed exist, the largest of which is the Val di Chianini, found on the plains and low hills of Arezzo and Sienna. Bulls average 1·73m *5ft 8in* at the forequarters and weigh 1300 kg *2865 lb*, but Chianini oxen have been known to attain heights of 1·9m *6ft 2¾in*. The sheer expense of feeding such huge cattle has put the breed under threat of extinction in Italy, but farmers in North America, Mexico and Brazil are still enthusiastic buyers of the breed.

The heaviest cattle on record was a Holstein–Durham cross named 'Mount Katahdin', which, from 1906 to 1910, frequently weighed 2267 kg *5000 lb*. He stood 1·88m *6ft 2in* at the shoulder and had a girth measuring 3·96m *13ft*. The cattle was exhibited by A.S. Rand·of Maine, USA and died in a barn fire c.1923.

UK Britain's largest breed of cattle is the South Devon, bulls of which measure up to 1·55m *5ft 1in* at the withers and weigh about 1250 kg *2755 lb*. The heaviest example on record weighed 1678 kg *3700 lb*.

The British record for any breed is 2032 kg *4480 lb* recorded for 'The Bradwell Ox', owned by William Spurgin of Orpland Farm, Bradwell-on-Sea, Essex. In 1830, when six years old, this bull measured 4·57m *15ft* from nose to tail and had a maximum girth of 3·35m *11ft*.

Smallest The smallest breed of domestic cattle is the Ovambo of Namibia, with bulls and cows averaging 225 kg *496 lb* and 160 kg *353 lb* respectively.

UK The smallest British breed is the miniature Dexter, bulls of which weigh 450 kg *992 lb* and stand 1·1m *3ft 3⅓in* at the withers. In May 1984 a height of just 86·3 cm *34 in* was reported for an adult Dexter cow named 'Mayberry', owned by R. Hillier of Church Farm, South Littleton, Evesham, Worcs.

Crop Production

Barley is just one of the cereal crops grown in record amounts in the republics of the former USSR, which together produce an estimated 57 million tonnes from an area of about 26 million ha *64·2 million acres*.

(Photo: Images Colour Library)

A yield of 12·2 tonnes/ha of winter barley was achieved on 2 Aug 1989 by Gordon Rennie of Edington Mains, Chirnside, Borders from 21·29 ha *52·6 acres*.

Cotton The total area of land used for cotton production was about 33·6 million ha *83 million acres*, giving a total estimated production in 1991/2 of 90·5 million bales weighing 217·72 kg *480 lb* each.

The leading cotton producer is China, with figures estimated at 22 million such bales.

Corn The total amount of land used for growing corn in 1990/91 was 128·2 million ha *316·8 million acres*, producing an estimated 472 million tonnes, 88 million tonnes of which were produced by China from an estimated 21 million ha *51·9 million acres*.

Oats The world-wide production of oats in 1990/91 was an estimated 42·8 million tonnes harvested from about 21·6 million ha *53·4 million acres*, most of which, 17·5 million tonnes, is produced by the former USSR from some 10·5 million ha *26 million acres*.

Potatoes Norfolk farmer Roger Southwell harvested 205·65 tonnes of potatoes in four hours from an area of 2·46 ha *6·07 acres* at Watermill Farm, Northwold, Norfolk on 1 Nov 1989. The machinery used was made by Standen Engineering Ltd of Ely, Cambs.

Rice About half of the world's population, including virtually the whole of

Barley The total amount of land farmed for barley production in the 1990/91 season was estimated to be 73·2 million ha *18 million acres*, with total production of 181·5 million tonnes and an average yield of 2·48 tonnes/ha. The world's leading grower of barley is the former USSR, which is estimated to produce 57 million tonnes from about 26 million ha *64·2 million acres*.

Bale rolling

Michael Priestley and Marcus Stanley of Heckington Young Farmers Club rolled a 1·2 m *3ft 11in* wide cylindrical bale over a 50 m *164ft* course in 18·06 sec at the Lincolnshire Federation of Young Farmers' Clubs annual sports day at Sleaford, Lincs on 25 Jun 1989.

East Asia, is totally dependent on rice as the staple food. The total amount of land used for rice production is 146·8 million ha *362·7 million acres*, with India leading on the area farmed, at 42·2 million ha *104·3 million acres*.

The world's leading producer, however, is China with estimated yields of 185 million tonnes from 32·7 million ha *80·8 million acres*.

Wheat An estimated 230·3 million ha *569 million acres* of land is used for wheat production world-wide, giving a yield of 590·1 million tonnes.

The leading grower is the former USSR, which produces 108 million tonnes from about 47·5 million ha *117·4 million acres* farmed.

The largest single fenced field sown with wheat measured 14 160 ha *35 000 acres* and was sown in 1951 south-west of Lethbridge, Alberta, Canada. The British record yield is 13·99 tonnes/ha *111·4 cwt/acre* from 17·49 ha *43·24 acres* by Gordon Rennie of Clifton Mains, Newbridge, Lothian in 1981.

Baling *Largest rick* A rick of 40 400 bales of straw was built between 22 Jul and 3 Sep 1982 by Nick and Tom Parsons with a gang of eight at Cuckoo Pen Barn Farm, Birdlip, Glos. The completed rick measured 45·7×9·1×18·2 m *150×30×60 ft* high and weighed some 711 tonnes. The team baled, hauled and ricked 24 200 bales in seven consecutive days from 22–29 July.

Fastest Svend Erik Klemmensen of Trustrup, Djursland, Denmark baled 200 tonnes of straw in 9 hr 54 min using a Hesston 4800 baling machine on 30 Aug 1989.

Combine harvesting Philip Baker of West End Farm, Merton, Bicester, Oxon harvested 165·6 tonnes of wheat in eight hours using a Massey Ferguson MF 38 combine on 8 Aug 1989.

On 9 Aug 1990 an international team from CWS Agriculture, led by estate manager Ian Hanglin, harvested 358·09

Field to loaf

The fastest time for producing 13 loaves (a baker's dozen) from growing wheat is 12 min 11 sec, by representatives from the villages of Clapham and Patching in West Sussex on 23 Aug 1992. They used 13 microwaves to bake the loaves.

Using a traditional baker's oven to actually bake the bread, the record time is 19 min 45 sec, by a team organized by John Haynes of millers Read Woodrow at Alpheton, Suffolk on 19 Sep 1992.

tonnes of wheat in eight hours from 44 ha *108·72 acres* at Cockayne Hatley Estate, Sandy, Beds. The equipment consisted of a Claas Commandor 228 combine fitted with a Shelbourne Reynolds SR 6000 stripper head.

Ploughing The world championship (instituted 1953) has been staged in 18 countries and won by competitors from 12 nations. The United Kingdom has been the most successful country, winning 10 championships. The only person to take the title three times is Hugh B. Barr of Northern Ireland, in 1954–6.

The fastest recorded time for ploughing an acre *0·404 ha* to United Kingdom Society of Ploughmen rules is 9 min 49·88 sec by Joe Langcake at Hornby Hall Farm, Brougham, Penrith, Cumbria on 21 Oct 1989. He used a case IH 7140 Magnum tractor and Kverneland four-furrow plough.

The greatest area ploughed with a six-furrow plough to a depth of 22·86 cm *9 in* in 24 hours is 70 ha *173 acres*. This was achieved by Richard Gaisford and Peter Gooding of Wiltshire Young Farmers, using a Case IH tractor and Lemken plough, at Manor Farm, Pewsey, Wilts on 25–26 Sep 1990.

Oldest 'Big Bertha' (b. 17 Mar 1944), a Dremon owned by Jerome O'Leary of Blackwatersbridge, Co. Kerry, Republic of Ireland, celebrated her 49th birthday in 1993. (⇨ also Most prolific)

Most prolific On 25 Apr 1964 it was reported that a cow named 'Lyubik' had given birth to seven calves in the former Soviet town of Mogilev. A case of five live calves at one birth was reported in 1928 by T.G. Yarwood of Manchester.

The lifetime breeding record is 39 in the case of 'Big Bertha'. (⇨ Oldest)

Sires 'Soender Jylland's Jens', a Danish black-and-white bull, left 220000 surviving progeny by artificial insemination when he was put down at the age of 11 in Copenhagen in September 1978. 'Bendalls Adema', a Friesian bull, died at the age of 14 in Clondalkin, Dublin, Republic of Ireland on 8 Nov 1978, having sired an estimated 212000 progeny by artificial insemination.

Birthweights On 28 May 1986 a Holstein cow owned by Sherlene O'Brien of Simitar Farms, Henryetta, Oklahoma, USA gave birth to a perfectly formed stillborn calf weighing 122·4kg *270lb*. The sire was an Aberdeen-Angus bull which had 'jumped the fence'. The heaviest recorded live birthweight for a calf is 102kg *225lb* from a British Friesian cow at Rockhouse Farm, Bishopston, Swansea, W Glam in 1961.

Lightest The lowest live birthweight accurately recorded for a calf is 6·5kg *14lb 5oz* for a healthy female born on 27 Oct 1991 on the farm of Ole Willumsgaard Lauridsen and Roos Verhoven in Hemmet, Denmark. It was a cross between a Danish SDM and a Belgian blue-white. A crossbred Angus calf owned by Leroy and Jo Seiner of Humansville, Missouri, USA weighed 7·6kg *16lb 12oz* at two weeks old and an estimated 4kg *9lb* at birth on 12 Sep 1991.

Milk yields The highest recorded world lifetime yield of milk is 211025kg *465224lb* to 1 May 1984 from the unglamorously named cow No. 289, owned by M.G. Maciel & Son of Hanford, California, USA. The greatest yield from any British cow was 165000kg *363759lb* by 'Winton Pel Eva 2', owned by John Waring of Glebe House, Kilnwick, near Pocklington, Humberside.

The greatest recorded yield for one lactation (maximum 365 days) is 25247kg *55661lb* in 1975 by the Holstein 'Beecher Arlinda Ellen', owned by Mr and Mrs Harold Beecher of Rochester, Indiana, USA.

British Isles 'Oriel Freda 10' (b. 21 Feb 1978), a Friesian owned by the Mellifont Abbey Trust of Collon, Co. Louth, Republic of Ireland, produced 21513kg *47427½lb* in 305 days in 1986. The British lactation record (305 days) is 19400kg *42769lb*, produced in 1984–5 by 'Michaelwood Holm Emoselle 25' (b. 1 Aug 1973), a Friesian owned by Mr and Mrs M.T. Holder of Aylesmore Farm, Newent, Glos. (⇨ also Butterfat yields)

The highest reported milk yield in a day is 109·3kg *241lb* by 'Urbe Blanca' in Cuba on or about 23 Jun 1982.

Butterfat yields The world record lifetime yield is 7425kg *16370lb* by the US Holstein 'Breezewood Patsy Bar Pontiac' in 3979 days. The British record butterfat yield in a lifetime is 5518kg *12166 lb* (from 123865kg *273072lb* at 4·45 per cent) by the Ayrshire cow 'Craighead Welma', owned by W. Watson Steele.

The world record for 365 days is 1418kg *3126 lb* by 'Roybrook High Ellen', a Holstein owned by Yashuhiro Tanaka of Tottori, Japan.

The British record for 365 days is 852kg *1878lb* by the Friesian 'Michaelwood Holm Emoselle 25'. This cow went on to milk for a total of 395 days in her eighth lactation, producing 1012kg *2231lb* of butterfat. She also holds the British record for butterfat yield in one day, at 4·53kg *10lb*. (⇨ also Milk yields)

Cow shed

The longest cow shed in Britain is that of the Yorkshire Agricultural Society at Harrogate, N Yorks. It is 139m *456ft* long and can cater for 686 cows. The National Agricultural Centre at Kenilworth, Warks, completed in 1967, can house 782 animals.

Hand-milking of cow

Joseph Love of Kilifi Plantations Ltd, Kenya milked 531 litres *117 gal* from 30 cows on 25 Aug 1992.

Cheese

The oldest and most primitive cheeses are the Arabian *kishk*, made of the dried curd of goats' milk. Today there are some 450 named cheeses in 18 major varieties, but many are merely named after different towns and differ only in shape or the method of packing. France has 240 varieties, with England and Wales producing over 125 varieties. The world's biggest producer of cheese is the US, with an estimated 2·9 million tonnes in 1992.

The most active cheese-eaters are the people of France, with an annual average in 1983 of 20 kg *44 lb* per person. The most popular cheese in Britain is Cheddar, accounting for about 60 per cent of total consumption.

Goats

Largest The largest goat ever recorded was a British Saanen named 'Mostyn Moorcock', owned by Pat Robinson of Ewyas Harold, Hereford & Worcester, which reached a weight of 181·4 kg *400 lb* (shoulder height 111·7 cm *44 in* and overall length of 167·6 cm *66 in*). He died in 1977 at the age of four.

Smallest Some pygmy goats weigh only 15–20 kg *33–44 lb*.

Oldest The oldest goat on record is a Toggenburg feral cross named 'Hongi' (b. August 1971), belonging to April Koch of Glenorchy, near Otago, New Zealand, which was still alive in mid-March 1989 aged 17 years 8 months. The oldest goat currently living in Britain is 'Emmahazelina' (b. 20 Apr 1972), a British Toggenburg owned by Michael C. Johnston of Farrington, Blandford Forum, Dorset.

Most prolific According to the British Goat Society, at least one or two cases of quintuplets are recorded annually out of the 10 000 goats registered, but some breeders only record the females born. On 14 Jan 1980 a nanny named 'Julie', owned by Galen Cowper of Nampah, Idaho, USA, gave birth to septuplets, but they all died, including the mother.

Milk yields The highest recorded milk yield for any goat is 3499 kg *7714 lb* in 365 days by 'Osory Snow-Goose', owned by Mr and Mrs G. Jameson of Leppington, New South Wales, Australia, in 1977.

'Snowball', owned by Don Papin of Tipton, California, USA, lactated continuously for 12 years 10 months between 1977 and 1989.

Pigs

The world's leading producer of hogs is China, with 365 million head in 1991 from a world total of 768·1 million.

Largest The heaviest pig ever recorded was a Poland–China hog named 'Big Bill', weighing 1157·5 kg *2552 lb* just before being put down after accidently breaking a leg en route to the Chicago World Fair for exhibition in 1933. Other statistics included a height of 1·52 m *5 ft* at the shoulder and a length of 2·74 m *9 ft*. At the request of his owner, W.J. Chappall, 'Bill' was mounted and displayed in Weekly County, Tennessee, USA until his acquisition in 1946 by a travelling carnival. On the death of the carnival's proprietor his family allegedly donated 'Big Bill' to a museum, but no trace has been found of him since.

UK The British Gloucester Old Spot breed is known to have exceeded 635 kg *1400 lb* in weight. The heaviest on record was a boar bred by Joseph Lawton of Astbury, Cheshire (and possibly owned by Joseph Bradbury of Little Hay Wood, Staffs), which weighed 639·5 kg *1410 lb*, stood 1·43 m *4 ft 8¼ in* at the shoulder and was 2·94 m *9 ft 8 in* long.

Smallest The smallest breed of pig is the Mini Maialino, developed by Stefano Morini of St Golo d'Enza, Italy after 10 years' experimentation with Vietnamese pot-bellied pigs. The piglets weigh 400 g *14 oz* at birth and 9 kg *20 lb* at maturity.

Most prolific A breeding sow will live 12 years or more before it is slaughtered, but the maximum potential lifespan is 20 years. The highest recorded number of piglets in one litter is 34, farrowed on 25–26 Jun 1961 by a sow owned by Aksel Egedee of Denmark. In February 1955 a Wessex sow belonging to E.C. Goodwin of Paul's Farm, Leigh, near Tonbridge Kent also had a litter of 34, of which 30 were stillborn.

The highest number of live births in Britain is 30 from a White Wessex sow reported by W. Ives of Dane End Fruit Farm, near Ware, Herts in September 1979.

A Large White owned by H.S. Pedlingham farrowed 385 pigs in 22 litters from December 1923 to September 1934. During the period 1940–52 a Large Black sow belonging to A.M. Harris of Lapworth, Warks farrowed 26 litters. A Newsham Large White×Landrace sow from Meeting House Farm, Staintondale, near Scarborough, N Yorks farrowed 189 piglets (seven stillborn) in nine litters up to 22 Mar 1988. Between 6 May 1987 and 9 Feb 1988 she gave birth to 70 piglets.

Birthweights A Hampshire×Yorkshire sow belonging to Rev. John Schroeder of Mountain Grove, Missouri, USA farrowed a litter of 18 on 26 Aug 1979. Five were stillborn, including one male weighing 2·38kg *5lb 4oz,* compared with he average birthweight of 1·36kg *3lb.*

The highest recorded weight for a piglet at weaning (eight weeks) is 36·7kg *81lb* for a boar, one of a litter of nine farrowed on 6 Jul 1962 by the Landrace gilt 'Manorport Ballerina 53rd' ('Mary'), and sired by a Large White named 'Johnny' at Kettle Lane Farm, West Ashton, Trowbridge, Wilts.

In Nov 1957 a total weight of 514·3kg *1134 lb* was reported at weaning for a litter of 18 farrowed by an Essex sow owned by B. Ravell of Seaton House, Thorugumbald, Hull, Humberside.

Poultry

Figures for 1991 showed the United States to be the largest producer of chicken meat, with 11·84 milliontonnes from a world total of 39 milliontonnes. The leading egg producer, however, is China, where 159 billion were laid in 1990, compared with 69 billion in the United States.

Chickens *Largest* The heaviest breed of chicken is the White Sully, a hybrid of large Rhode Island Reds and other varieties developed by Grant Sullens of West Point, California, USA. The largest, a rooster named 'Weirdo', reportedly weighed 10kg *22lb* in January 1973 and was so aggressive that he killed two cats and maimed a dog which ventured too close.

The largest recorded chicken is 'Big Snow', a rooster weighing 10·51kg *23lb 3oz* on 12 Jun 1992, with a chest girth of 84 cm *2ft 9in* and standing 43·2cm *1ft 5in* at the shoulder. Owned and bred by Ronald Alldridge of Deuchar, Queensland, Australia, 'Big Snow' died of natural causes on 6 Sep 1992.

Most prolific The highest authenticated rate of egg-laying is 371 in 364 days by a White Leghorn (No. 2988) in an official test conducted by Prof. Harold V. Biellier ending on 29 Aug 1979 at the College of Agriculture, University of Missouri, USA.

The British record is 353 eggs in 365 days in a national laying test at Milford, Surrey in 1957 by a Rhode Island Red 'Wonderful Lady', owned by W. Lawson of Welham Grange, Retford, Notts.

The highest annual average per bird for a flock is 315 eggs in 52 weeks (August 1991–August 1992) from 5997 free-range ISA Brown layers, owned by Vernon Wride of Park Farm, Heol-y-Cyw, Pencoed, Mid Glam.

Largest egg The heaviest egg reported is one of 454g *16 oz,* with a double yolk and double shell, laid by a White Leghorn at Vineland, New Jersey, USA on 25 Feb 1956. The largest recorded was a five-yolked egg measuring 31cm *12¼ in* around the long axis, 22·8 cm *9 in* around the short and weighing 'nearly 12oz' , laid by a Black Minorca at Mr Stafford's Damsteads Farm, Mellor, Lancs in 1896.

Most yolks The highest claim for the number of yolks in a hen's egg is nine, reported by Diane Hainsworth of Hainsworth Poultry Farms, Mount Morris, New York, USA in July 1971, and also from a hen in Kyrgyzstan in August 1977.

Egg shelling

Two kitchen hands, Harold Witcomb and Gerald Harding, shelled 1050 dozen eggs in a 7¼hr shift at Bowyers, Trowbridge, Wilts on 23 Apr 1971. Both men were blind.

Crochet

Barbara Jean Sonntag (b. 1938) of Craig, Colorado, USA crocheted 330 shells plus five stitches (equivalent to 4412 stitches) in 30 min at a rate of 147 stitches per min on 13 Jan 1981.

Ria van der Honing of Wormerveer, Netherlands completed a crochet chain 62·50 km *38·83 miles* in length on 14 Jul 1986.

Tailoring

The highest speed in which the manufacture of a three-piece suit has been executed from sheep to finished article is 1 hr 34 min 33·42 sec, by 65 members of the Melbourne College of Textiles, Pascoe Vale, Victoria, Australia on 24 Jun 1982. Catching and fleecing took 2 min 21 sec, and carding, spinning, weaving and tailoring occupied the remaining time.

Fine spinning

The longest thread of wool, hand-spun and plied to weigh 10g *0·35 oz*, was one with a length of 553·03 m *1815 ft 3 in*, achieved by Julitha Barber of Bull Creek, Western Australia, Australia at the International Highland Spin-In, Bothwell, Tasmania on 1 Mar 1989.

Flying 'Sheena', a barnyard bantam owned by Bill and Bob Knox, flew 192·07 m *630 ft 2 in* at Parkesburg, Pennsylvania, USA on 31 May 1985.

Ducks Most prolific An Aylesbury duck belonging to Annette and Angela Butler of Princes Risborough, Bucks laid 457

eggs in 463 days, including an unbroken run of 375 in as many days. The duck died on 7 Feb 1986. Another duck of the same breed owned by Edmond Walsh of Gormanstown, Co. Kildare, Republic of Ireland laid eggs every year until her 25th birthday. She died on 3 Dec 1978 aged 28 yr 6 months.

Goose The heaviest goose egg weighed 680 g *24 oz*, measured 34 cm *13½ in* round the long axis and a maximum of 24 cm *9½ in* around the short axis. It was laid on 3 May 1977 by a white goose named 'Speckle', owned by Donny Brandenberg of Goshen, Ohio, USA. The average weight is 283–340 g *10–12 oz*.

Turkey The greatest dressed weight recorded for a turkey is 39·09 kg *86 lb* for a stag named 'Tyson' reared by Philip Cook of Leacroft Turkeys Ltd, Peterborough, Cambs. It won the last annual 'heaviest turkey' competition, held in London on 12 Dec 1989, and was auctioned for charity for a record £4400. Stags of this size have been so overdeveloped for meat production that they are unable to mate because of their shape and the hens have to be artificially inseminated.

Sheep

The world's leading producer of sheep is Australia, with a total of 177·8 million head in 1990.

Largest The largest sheep ever recorded was a Suffolk ram named 'Stratford Whisper 23H', which weighed 247·2 kg *545 lb* and stood 1·09 m *43 in* tall in March 1991. It is owned by Joseph and Susan Schallberger of Boring, Oregon, USA.

Smallest The smallest breed of sheep is the Ouessant, from the Ile d'Ouessant, Brittany, France at 13–16 kg *29–35 lb* in weight and standing 45–50 cm *18–20 in* at the withers. The species was saved from extinction by breeding programmes.

Most prolific The record for lambs at a single birth is eight (five rams and three ewes) on 4 Sep 1991 from a Finnish Landrace ewe owned by the D.M.C. Partnership (comprising Trevor and Diane Cooke, Stephen and Mary Moss and Ken and Carole Mihaere) of Feilding, Manawatu, New Zealand. On 2

Dec 1992 a Charolais ewe owned by Graham and Jo Partt of Wem, Shrops also gave birth to eight lambs, seven of which survived.

Birthweights The highest recorded birthweight for a lamb is 17·2 kg *38 lb* at Clearwater, Sedgwick County, Kansas, USA in 1975, but neither lamb nor ewe survived. Another lamb of the same weight was born on 7 Apr 1975 on the Gerald Neises Farm, Howard, South Dakota, USA but died soon afterwards.

UK On 13 Apr 1990 it was reported that a Kent ewe had given birth to a live lamb weighing 12·7 kg *28 lb* on the Belton estate, near Grantham, Lincs, farmed by Les Baker. A crossbred Suffolk lamb of the same weight was delivered on 22 Jan 1992 at Stoupergate Farm, owned by D. and E. Brooke, in Hatfield, S Yorks.

Combined weight A four-year-old Suffolk ewe owned by Gerry H. Watson of Augusta, Kansas, USA gave birth to two live sets of triplets on 30–31 Jan 1982. The total weight of the lambs was 22·4 kg *49½ lb*. The greatest combined birthweight for lambs in Britain is 21·1 kg *43½ lb* for live quadruplets produced on 20 Feb 1990 by a Friezland × Exmoor Horn owned by John and Margaret Sillick of South Stursdon Farm, Bude, Cornwall.

Lightest The lowest live birthweight recorded for a lamb is 900 g *1 lb 15¾ oz* for a female Texel (one of twins), born on 28 Mar 1991 at the farm owned by Verner and Esther Jensen in Rødekro, Denmark. This record was equalled on 8 Jun 1991 by a badger-faced Welsh mountain lamb named 'Lyle' (also a twin), born at Thorpe Park, Chertsey, Surrey.

Oldest A crossbred sheep owned by Griffiths & Davies of Dolclettwr Hall, Taliesin, near Aberystwyth, Dyfed gave birth to a healthy lamb in 1988 at the age of 28, after lambing successfully more than 40 times. She died on 24 Jan 1989 just one week before her 29th birthday.

Shearing The highest speed for sheep shearing in a working day was recorded by Alan McDonald, who machine-sheared 805 lambs in nine hours (an average of 89·4) at Waitnaguru, New Zealand on 20 Dec 1990.

Peter Casserly of Christchurch, New Zealand achieved a solo blade (i.e. hand-shearing) record of 353 lambs in nine hours on 13 Feb 1976. The women's record is 390 lambs in eight hours by Deanne Sarre of Pingrup at Yealering, Western Australia on 1 Oct 1989.

UK The British record set under National Shearing Competitions Committee rules (9 hours, sheep caught by shearers) is 1869 by the four-man team of William Workman, Ian Matthews, Howell Havard and Philip Evans at Pant Farm, Merthyr Cynog, Powys on 30 Jun 1990, when Philip Evans also set a new solo record of 535.

The record for lambs is 973 by Robert Bull and Barry Godsell at Winchelsea Beach, E Sussex on 17 Jun 1989. A solo record of 817 was set by Philip Evans at Pant Farm, Merthyr Cynog, Powys on 20 Jul 1991. Although this exceeds the world record set in New Zealand, the attempts are not directly comparable because of differing rules.

In a 24-hour shearing marathon, Alan MacDonald and Keith Wilson machine-sheared 2220 sheep at Warkworth, Auckland Province, New Zealand on 26 Jun 1988. Godfrey Bowen of New Zealand sheared a Cheviot ewe in 46 sec at the Royal Highland Show in Dundee, Tayside in June 1957.

Longest survival On 24 Mar 1978 Alex Maclennan found one ewe still alive after he had dug out 16 sheep buried in a snowdrift for 50 days near the River Skinsdale on Mrs Tyser's Gordonbush Estate in Sutherland, Highland after the great January blizzard. The sheep's hot breath creates air-holes in the snow, and the animals gnaw their own wool for protein.

Longest fleece A Merino wether found on the K.P. & B.A. Reynolds Company's Willow Springs Station, South Australia in November 1990 produced 29·5 kg *65 lb* of wool from a fleece 63·5 cm *25 in* long, representing an estimated 7-year growth.

Arts & Entertainment

Art

Origins

Origins Engravings showing circles, dots, lines and arcs have been dated by thermoluminescence (TL) and other techniques to 60000–50000 years old at the Malunkunanja II site in northern Australia. A piece of ox rib found in 1973 at Pech de l'Aze, Dordogne, France in an early Middle Palaeolithic layer of the Riss glaciation of c. 105000 BC has several engraved lines on one side, thought to be possibly intentional.

The oldest known extant and dated examples of representational art are from layers dated to c. 25000 BC from La Ferrassie, near Les Eyzies in the Périgord, France, where blocks of stone engraved with animals and female symbols were found. Some blocks were also decorated with symbols painted in red ochre.

British Isles The earliest example of an engraving found in Britain is of a horse's head on a piece of rib-bone from Robin Hood Cave, Creswell Crag, Derbys. It dates from the Upper Palaeolithic period of c. 15000–10000 BC.

Painting

Earliest Ochre and haematite pieces found in Australia from c. 60000–50000 years ago and later from Swaziland suggest that some form of painting was practised, but none has survived to indicate what form it took.

Largest The largest-ever painting measures 6727·56 m² *72437 ft²* after allowing for shrinkage of the canvas. It is made up of brightly coloured squares superimposed by a 'Smiley' face and was painted by students of Robb College at Armidale, New South Wales, Australia, aided by local schoolchildren and students from neighbouring colleges. The canvas was completed by its designer, Australian artist Ken Done, and unveiled at the University of New England at Armidale on 10 May 1990.

UK The oval painting *Triumph of Peace and Liberty* by Sir James Thornhill (1676–1734) on the ceiling of the Painted Hall in the Royal Naval College, Greenwich measures 32·3×15·4 m *106×51 ft* and took 20 years (1707–27) to complete.

Finest paint brush

The finest standard brush sold is the 000 in Series 7 by Winsor and Newton, known as a 'triple goose'. It is made of 150–200 Kolinsky sable hairs weighing 15 mg *0·000529 oz.*

Largest poster

A poster measuring 20000 m² *215280 ft²* was made by the Sendai Junior Chamber Inc. of Sendai City, Japan on 18 Aug 1991.

Auction The largest painting ever auctioned was Carl Larsson's *Midvinterblot*, painted in Stockholm, Sweden from 1911 to 1915 and sold at Sotheby's, London on 25 Mar 1988 for £880000 to the Umeda Gallery of Japan. The painting measured 13·4×2·7 m *44×9 ft.*

Most valuable The 'Mona Lisa' (*La Gioconda*) by Leonardo da Vinci (1452–1519) in the Louvre, Paris, France was assessed for insurance purposes at $100 million for its move to Washington, DC, USA and New York City for exhibition from 14 Dec 1962 to 12 Mar 1963. However, insurance was not concluded because the cost of the closest security precautions was less than that of the premiums. It was painted c. 1503–07 and measures 77×53 cm *30·5×20·9 in.* It is believed to portray either Mona (short for Madonna) Lisa Gherardini, the wife of Francesco del Giocondo of Florence, or Constanza d'Avalos, coincidentally nicknamed La Gioconda, mistress of Giuliano de Medici. King Francis I of France bought the painting for his bathroom in 1517 for 4000 gold florins, or 15·3 kg *92 oz* of gold.

Most prolific painter Pablo Diego José Francisco de Paula Juan Nepomuceno Crispin Crispiano de la Santisima Trinidad Ruiz y Picasso (1881–1973) of Spain was the most prolific of all painters, in a career which lasted 78 years. It has been estimated that Picasso produced about 13500 paintings or designs, 100000 prints or engravings, 34000 book illustrations and 300 sculptures or ceramics. His life-time *oeuvre* has been valued at £500 million.

Oldest RA The oldest ever Royal Academician was (Thomas) Sidney Cooper, who died on 8 Feb 1902 aged 98 yr 136 days having exhibited 266 paintings over the record span of 69 consecutive years (1833–1902).

Youngest RA Mary Moser (later Mrs Hugh Lloyd, 1744–1819) was elected on the foundation of the Royal Academy in 1768 when aged 24.

Youngest exhibitor The youngest exhibitor at the Royal Academy of Arts Annual Summer Exhibition was Lewis Melville 'Gino' Lyons (b. 30 Apr 1962). His *Trees and Monkeys* was painted on 4 Jun 1965, submitted on 17 Mar 1967 and exhibited on 29 Apr 1967.

Largest galleries The world's largest art gallery is the Winter Palace and the neighbouring Hermitage in St Petersburg, Russia. One has to walk 24 km *15 miles* to visit each of the 322 galleries, which house nearly 3 million works of art and objects of archaeological interest.

Most heavily endowed The J. Paul Getty Museum at Malibu, California, USA was established with an initial £700 million budget in January 1974 and now has an annual budget of £104 million for acquisitions to stock its 38 galleries.

Murals

Earliest The earliest known murals on man-made walls are the clay relief leopards at Çatal Hüyük in southern Anatolia, Turkey, discovered by James Malaart at level VII in 1961 and dating from *c.* 6200 BC.

Largest A mural on the 23-storey Vegas World Hotel, Las Vegas, Nevada, USA covers an area of 8867 m² *95 442 ft²*.

Britain's largest mural covers 1709 m² *18 396 ft²* and is painted on the Stage V wall of BBC Television Centre, London.

'Smiley' face on canvas, designed by Australian artist Ken Done and painted with the help of students of Robb College, local schoolchildren and other college students from Armidale, New South Wales, Australia in aid of UNICEF.
(Photo: Robb College, U.N.E.)

Commissioned as the result of a competition run by the *Going Live* programme, the mural was painted in September 1991 by the Scenic Set company to a design by Vicky Askew.

Mosaics

Largest The world's largest mosaic is on the walls of the central library of the Universidad Nacional Autónoma de Mexico in Mexico City. Of the four walls, the two largest measure 1203 m² *12949 ft²*, and the scenes on each represent the pre-Hispanic past.

UK The largest Roman mosaic in Britain is the Woodchester Pavement in Gloucester of *c.* AD 325. It measures 14·3 m² *47 ft²* and comprises 1·6 million tesserae (tiles). Excavated in 1793 and now re-covered with protective earth, a total reconstruction was carried out by Robert and John Woodward of Stroud, Glos and completed in June 1987.

Sculpture

Earliest The earliest known examples of sculpture date from the Aurignacian culture of *c.* 28 000–22 000 BC and include the so-called 'Venus' figurines from Austria and others from northern Italy and central France.

Largest The mounted figures of Jefferson Davis (1808–89), Gen. Robert

Sand sculpture

The longest sand sculpture ever made was the 26 375·9 m *86 535 ft* long sculpture named 'The GTE Directories Ultimate Sand Castle', built by more than 10 000 volunteers at Myrtle Beach, South Carolina, USA on 31 May 1991. The tallest was the 'Invitation to Fairyland', which was 17·12 m *56 ft 2 in* high, and was built by 2000 local volunteers at Kaseda, Japan on 26 Jul 1989 under the super-vision of Gerry Kirk of Sand Sculptors International of San Diego and Shogo Tashiro of Sand Sculptors International of Japan.

Edward Lee (1807–70) and Gen. Thomas Jonathan (Stonewall) Jackson (1824–63) are 27·4 m *90 ft* high and cover 0·5 ha *1·33 acres* on the face of Stone Mountain, near Atlanta, Georgia, USA. Roy Faulkner was on the mountain face for 8 years 174 days with a thermo-jet torch, working with the sculptor Walker Kirtland Hancock and other helpers, from 12 Sep 1963 to 3 Mar 1972.

The largest scrap-metal sculpture was built by Sudhir Deshpande of Nashik, India and unveiled in February 1990. Named *Powerful*, the colossus weighs 27 tonnes and stands 17 m *55¾ ft* tall.

Ground figures In the Nazca Desert, 300 km *185 miles* south of Lima, Peru there are straight lines (one more than 11·2 km *7 miles* long), geometric shapes and outlines of plants and animals drawn on the ground some time between 100 BC and AD 600 for probably religious, astronomical or even economic purposes by an imprecisely identified civilization. They were first detected from the air *c.* 1928 and have been described as the world's longest works of art.

Powerful, created by Sudhir Deshpande of Nashik, India and unveiled in February 1990, stands 17 m 55¾ ft tall and weighs 27 tonnes.
(Photo: Sudhir Deshpande)

Hill figures In August 1968 a 100 m *330 ft* tall figure was found on a hill above Tarapacá, Chile.

UK The largest human hill carving in Britain is the 'Long Man' of Wilmington, E Sussex, at 68 m *226 ft* in length.

The oldest of Britain's 'White Horses' is the Uffington horse in Oxfordshire, dating from the late Iron Age (*c.* 150 BC) and measuring 114 m *374 ft* from nose to tail and 36 m *120 ft* high.

Most expensive The record price paid for a sculpture at auction is £6·82 million at Sotheby's, London on 7 Dec 1989 for a bronze garden ornament, *The Dancing Faun*, made by the Dutch-born sculptor Adrien de Vries (1545/6–1626). London dealer Cyril Humpris bought the figure from an unnamed Brighton, W Sussex couple who had paid £100 for it in the 1950s and in whose garden it had stood unremarked upon for 40 years.

The highest price paid for the work of a sculptor during his lifetime is £1 265 000 at Sotheby's, New York, USA on 21 May 1982 for the 190·5 cm *75 in* long elmwood *Reclining Figure* by Henry Moore (1898–1986).

Highest Prices

Sales were at auction unless stated otherwise and include the buyer's premium.

Painting On 15 May 1990 *Portrait of Dr Gachet* by Vincent (Willem) van Gogh (1853–90) was sold within three minutes for $82·5 million at Christie's, New York, USA. The painting depicts Van Gogh's physician and was completed only weeks before the artist's suicide in 1890. It was bought by Ryoei Saito of Japan.

UK The highest auction price for a painting by a British artist is £10·78 million for *The Lock* (1824) by John Constable (1776–1837) at Sotheby's, London on 14 Nov 1990. The buyer was Baron Hans Heinrich Thyssen-Bornemisza, a director of Sotheby's.

The University of London privately sold their Turner painting *Van Tromp Going About to Please His Masters* for £11 million in February 1993 to the Getty Museum to raise funds for the college.

Miniature The record price is £352 000 paid by the Alexander Gallery of New York, USA at Christie's, London on 7 Nov 1988 for a 54 mm *2⅛ in* high miniature of George Washington, painted by the Irish-American miniaturist John Ramage (*c.* 1748–1802) in 1789.

20th-century painting The record bid for a 20th-century painting is $47·8 million at Sotheby's, New York on 9 May 1989 for *Yo Picasso* (1901), a self-portrait by Pablo Picasso (1881–1973).

Living artist The record for a work by a living artist is $20·68 million (£13 million) for *Interchange*, an abstract by the American painter Willem de Kooning (b. Rotterdam, Netherlands, 1904) at Sotheby's, New York on 8 Nov 1989. Painted in 1955, it was bought by Japanese dealer/collector 'Mountain Tortoise'.

UK The highest price paid during his lifetime for any painting by an artist born in the United Kingdom was $6·27 million for *Triptych May–June* by Francis Bacon (1909–92, born in Dublin, Republic of Ireland when still part of the United Kingdom) on 2 May 1989 at Sotheby's, New York, USA.

Print The record price for a print was £561 600 for the 1655 etching *Christ Presented to the People* by Rembrandt (1606–69) at Christie's, London on 5 Dec 1985. It was sold by the Chatsworth Settlement Trustees.

Drawing The highest price ever paid for a drawing is $8·36 million (£4·27 million) for the pen-and-ink scene *Jardin de Fleurs*, drawn by Vincent Van Gogh at Arles, France in 1888 and sold at Christie's, New York on 14 Nov 1990 to an anonymous buyer.

Poster The record for a poster is £68 200 at Christie's, London on 4 Feb 1993 for an advertisement for the 1895 Glasgow exhibition. The artist was Charles Rennie Mackintosh (1868–1928).

Antiques

All prices quoted are inclusive of the buyer's premium and all records were set at public auction unless stated otherwise.

345

Auctioneering

The longest one-man auction on record is one of 60 hr, conducted by Reg Coates at Gosport, Hants from 9–11 Sep 1988.

Most valuable carpet

The most valued carpet ever made was the Spring carpet of Khusraw made for the audience hall of the Sassanian palace at Ctesiphon, Iraq. It consisted of about 650 m² *7000 ft²* of silk and gold thread encrusted with emeralds. It was cut up as booty by looters in AD 635 and, from the known realization value of the pieces, must have had an original value of some £100 million.

Jewelled egg

The largest and most elaborate jewelled egg stands 70 cm *2 ft* tall and was fashioned from 16·8 kg *37 lb* of gold studded with 20000 pink diamonds. Designed by London jeweller, Paul Kutchinsky, the Argyle Library Egg took six British craftsmen 7000 man-hours to create and has a price tag of £7 million. It was unveiled on 30 Apr 1990 before going on display at the Victoria and Albert Museum, London.

Shoes

A pair of women's cream kid and braid high-heeled slap-soled shoes of *c.* 1660, sold by Lord Hereford at Sotheby's, London in September 1987 to Sonia Bata, fetched £21000. An export licence was reportedly refused on 20 Jun 1988.

Auctioneers The oldest firm of art auctioneers in the world is the Stockholms Auktionsverk of Sweden, which was established on 27 Feb 1647. Christie's of London held their first art auction in 1766. The largest firm is the Sotheby Group of London and New York, founded in 1744 although trading until 1778 was primarily in books. Sotheby's turnover in 1989 was a record $2·9 billion and their New York sales set a single series record of $360·4 million in May 1990.

Art nouveau The highest auction price for any piece of art nouveau is $1·78 million (£1·1 million) for a standard lamp in the form of three lotus blossoms by the Daum Brothers and Louis Majorelle of France, sold at Sotheby's, New York, USA on 2 Dec 1989.

Blanket The most expensive blanket was a Navajo Churro hand-spun serape of *c.* 1852 sold for $115500 at Sotheby's, New York, USA on 22 Oct 1983.

Carpet In 1946 the Metropolitan Museum in New York City, USA privately paid $1 million for the 8·07 × 4·14m *26·5 × 13·6 ft* Anhalt Medallion carpet made in Tabriz or Kashan, Persia (now Iran) *c.* 1590.

The highest price paid at auction is £441500 for a 17th century Persian rug at Christie's, London on 29 Apr 1993.

Ceramics The highest price for any ceramic is £3·74 million for a Chinese Tang dynasty (AD 618–906) horse sold by the British Rail Pension Fund and bought by a Japanese dealer at Sotheby's, London on 12 Dec 1989. The horse was stolen from a warehouse in Hong Kong on 14 November, but was recovered on 2 December in time for the sale.

Chamber pot A 935 g *33 oz* silver pot, made by David Willaume and engraved for the 2nd Earl of Warrington, sold for £9500 at Sotheby's, London on 14 Jun 1984.

Furniture The highest price ever paid for a single piece of furniture is £8·58 million ($15·1 million) at Christie's, London on 5 Jul 1990 for the 18th-century Italian 'Badminton Cabinet' owned by the Duke of Beaufort. It was bought by Barbara Piasecka Johnson of Princeton, New Jersey, USA.

The highest price paid for an item of English furniture was £1·1 million at Christie's, London on 6 Jul 1989 for a George III ormolu-mounted mahogany dressing and writing commode, attributed to John Channon and made *c.* 1760.

Glass The record is £520 000 for a Roman glass cage-cup of c. AD 300, measuring 18 cm 7 *in* in diameter and 10 cm 4 *in* in height, sold at Sotheby's, London on 4 Jun 1979 to Robin Symes.

Guns A .45 calibre Colt single-action army revolver, Serial No. 1 from 1873, sold for $242 000 (£151 250) at Christie's, New York, USA on 14 May 1987.

Jewellery The world's largest jewellery auction, which included a Van Cleef and Arpels 1939 ruby and diamond necklace, realized £31 380 197 when the collection belonging to the Duchess of Windsor (1896–1986) was sold at Sotheby's, Geneva, Switzerland on 3 Apr 1987.

The record for individual items of jewellery is £3·1 million for two pear-shaped diamond drop earrings of 58·6 and 61 carats bought and sold anonymously at Sotheby's, Geneva on 14 Nov 1980.

Musical box The highest price paid for a musical box is £20 900 for a Swiss example made for a Persian prince in 1901 and sold at Sotheby's, London on 23 Jan 1985.

Playing cards The highest price for a deck of playing cards is $143 352 by the Metropolitan Museum of Art, New York City, USA at Sotheby's, London on 6 Dec 1983.

Silver The record for English silver is £1 485 000 for the 'Maynard' sideboard dish made by the Huguenot silversmith Paul de Lamerie in 1736 and sold at Christie's, London on 22 May 1991.

Snuff box The highest price paid for a snuff box is 2·53 million Swiss francs (£1 155 250) at Sotheby's, Geneva, Switzerland on 17 Nov 1992 for a gold box decorated with diamonds, rubies and emeralds made for Frederick the Great of Prussia c. 1770. It was one of 297 lots sold for 19·7 million Swiss francs (£9 million) by Princess Gloria von Thurn und Taxis of Germany and was bought by London dealers S.J. Phillips.

Sword The highest price paid for a sword is £823 045 for the Duke of Windsor's Royal Navy officer's sword (presented to him by King George V in 1913) at Sotheby's, Geneva, Switzerland on 3 Apr 1987.

Tapestry The record price for a tapestry is £638 000, paid by Swiss dealer Peter Kleiner at Christie's, London on 3 Jul 1990 for a fragment of a rare Swiss example woven near Basle in the 1430s. The tapestry was in the Benedictine Abbey at Muri until 1840 before descending through the Vischer family.

Thimble The record for a thimble is £18 000 at Phillips' Midland branch on 13 Dec 1992 for a late 16th century gold jewelled thimble reputed to have belonged to Queen Elizabeth I. It was bought by Asprey's on behalf of a client.

Toys The most expensive antique toy was sold for $231 000 (£128 333) by the trustees in bankruptcy of London dealers Mint & Boxed to a telephone bidder at Christie's, New York City, USA on 14 Dec 1991. The work is a hand-painted tin plate replica of the 'Charles' hose reel, a piece of fire-fighting equipment, measuring 381 × 584 mm *15 × 23 in* and built c. 1870 by George Brown & Co. of Forestville, Connecticut, USA. Claims that this toy had been sold privately for $1 million in 1990 were subsequently refuted.

The highest price paid for a single toy soldier is £3375 for a uniformed scale figure of Hitler's deputy, Rudolf Hess, made by the Lineol company of Brandenburg, Germany. The figure was among several sold by the Danish auction house Boyes in London on 23 Apr 1991.

Language

There is no actual agreement on the number of languages spoken today. Most reference books give 4000–5000, but estimates have varied from 3000 to as many as 10 000.

Earliest The ability to speak is thought to be dependent upon physiological changes in the height of the larynx between *Homo erectus* and *Homo sapiens sapiens* as developed c. 45 000 BC. The discovery of a hyoid bone (from the base of the tongue) from a cave site on Mt Carmel, Israel shows that Neanderthal man may have been capable of speech 60 000 years ago, but the usual dating is 50 000–30 000 BC.

The view from an interpreter's booth at an assembly of the United Nations in New York City, USA, where many of the world's most versatile linguists have perfected their skills.

(Photo: Gamma/J. Turpin)

Oldest English words It was first suggested in 1979 that languages ancestral to English (Indo-European) split *c.* 3500 BC. According to researches completed in 1989, about 40 words of a proto-Indo-European (the parent of Indo-European) substratum survive in English, e.g. apple (apal), bad (bad), gold (gol) and tin (tin). The parent language is thought to have been spoken before 3000 BC and to have split into different languages over the period 3000–2000 BC.

There are eight indigenous languages older than English still in use in the British Isles. These are: Welsh, Cornish, Scots, Irish, Manx, Channel Isles patois, Sheldru or Shelta and Romani.

Commonest language The language used by more people than any other is Chinese, spoken by an estimated 1000 million people. The so-called 'common language' (*pǔtōnghuà*) is the standard form of Chinese, with a pronunciation based on that of Beijing. It is known in Taiwan as *guoyu* ('national speech') and

in the West as Mandarin. After various attempts to write Chinese in the Roman alphabet, *Hanyu Pinyin*, the term used on mainland China and meaning 'spell sound', was adopted on 11 Feb 1958 as a writing system of 58 symbols.

The most widespread and the second most commonly spoken language is English, with a conservative estimate of 800 million speakers, rising to a liberal 1500 million. Of these, some 350 million are native speakers, mainly in the US (about 220 million), the UK (55 million), Canada (17 million) and Australia (15 million).

Most languages The former Australian territory of Papua New Guinea has, owing to its many isolated valleys, the greatest concentration of separate languages in the world, with an estimated 869, i.e. each language has about 4000 speakers.

Most complex The following extremes of complexity have been noted: The Amele language of Papua New Guinea has the most verb forms, with over

Debating

Students of St Andrews Presbyterian College in Laurinburg, North Carolina, USA, together with staff and friends, debated the motion 'There's No Place Like Home' for 517 hr 45 min from 4–26 Apr 1992. The aim of the debate was to increase awareness of the problems of being homeless.

Most synonyms

The condition of being inebriated has more synonyms than any other condition or object. Paul Dickson of Garrett Park, Maryland, USA has compiled and published a list of 2660 words and phrases in his book *Word Treasury*.

69 000 finite forms and 860 infinitive forms of the verb; Haida, the North American Indian language, has the most prefixes (70); Tabassaran, a language of Daghestan, Azerbijan, uses the most noun cases (48), the Eskimo language used by the Inuit has 63 forms of the present tense and simple nouns have as many as 252 inflections.

Least irregular verbs The artificial language Esperanto was published by its inventor Dr Ludwig Zamenhof (1859–1917) of Warsaw in 1887 without irregular verbs. It is estimated to have about 1 million speakers. The earlier interlanguage Volapük, invented by Johann Martin Schleyer (1831–1912), also has absolutely regular configuration. The Turkish language has a single irregular verb—*olmak*, meaning 'to be'.

Most irregular verbs According to *The Morphology and Syntax of Present-day English* by Prof. Olu Tomori, English has 283 irregular verbs, 30 of which are merely formed with prefixes.

Rarest sounds The rarest speech sound is probably that written 'ř' in Czech and termed a 'rolled post-alveolar fricative'. It occurs in very few languages and is the last sound mastered by Czech children. In the southern Bushman language /xo there is a click articulated with both lips, which is written ☉. This character is usually referred to as a 'bull's eye' and the sound, essentially a kiss, is termed a 'velaric ingressive bilabial stop'. In some contexts the 'l' sound in the Arabic word *Allah* is pronounced uniquely in that language.

Commonest sound No language is known to be without the vowel 'a' (as in the English 'father'.

Vocabulary The English language contains about 616 500 word forms plus another 400 000 technical terms, the most in any language, but it is doubtful if any individual uses more than 60000. UK residents who have undergone a full 16 years of education use perhaps 5000 words in speech and up to 10000 words in written communications. The membership of the International Society for Philosophical Enquiry (no admission for IQs below 148) have an average vocabulary of 36250 words, and Shakespeare employed a vocabulary of *c.* 33000 words.

Greatest linguist If the yardstick of ability to speak with fluency and reasonable accuracy is maintained, it is doubtful whether any human being could maintain fluency in more than 20–25 languages concurrently or achieve fluency in more than 40 in a lifetime.

The world's greatest linguist is believed to be have been Dr Harold Williams of New Zealand (1876–1928), a journalist and one-time foreign editor of *The Times*. Self-taught in Latin, Greek, Hebrew and many of the European and Pacific island languages as a boy, Dr Williams spoke 58 languages and many dialects fluently. He was the only person to attend the League of Nations in Geneva, Switzerland and converse with every delegate in their own language.

In terms of oral fluency the most multilingual living person is Derick Herning of Lerwick, Shetland, whose command of 22 languages earned him victory in the inaugural 'Polyglot of Europe' contest held in Brussels, Belgium in May 1990.

Alphabets

Earliest The earliest example of alphabetic writing, clay tablets showing the 32 cuneiform letters of the Ugaritic alphabet,

349

were found in 1929 at Ugarit (now Ras Shamra), Syria and dated to *c.* 1450 BC.

Oldest letter The letter 'O' is unchanged in shape since its adoption in the Phoenician alphabet *c.* 1300 BC.

Newest letters Until about 1600 there was no clear distinction in the English alphabet between the letters 'i' and 'j' or 'u' and 'v'. After 1600 'i' and 'u' came to represent vowels only, while 'j' and 'v' became consonants. Even as recently as the 19th century some dictionaries did not distiguish between 'i' and 'j' and in Alexander Cruden's *Concordance to the Holy Scriptures* (1815), the next word after *I* is *Jacinth*, while *Joyous* is followed by *Iron*. There are 65 alphabets now in use world-wide.

Longest The language with the most letters is Khmer (Cambodian), with 74 (including some without any current use).

Shortest Rotokas of central Bougainville Island, Papua New Guinea has least letters, with 11 (a, b, e, g, i, k, o, p, ř, t and u).

Most and least consonants The language with most distinct consonantal sounds is that of the Ubykhs in the Caucasus, with 80–85, and that with the least is Rotokas, which has only six consonants.

Most and least vowels The language with the most vowels is Sedang, a central Vietnamese language with 55 distinguishable vowel sounds, and that with the least is the Caucasian language Abkhazian with two.

Smallest letters Scanning tunnelling microscope (STM) techniques pioneered in April 1990 by physicists Donald Eigler and Erhard Schweizer at IBM's Almaden Research Center in San Jose, California, USA have enabled single atoms of various elements to be manipulated to form characters and pictures.

Words

Longest Lengthy concatenations and some compound or agglutinative words or nonce words can be been written in the closed-up style of a single word. The longest known example is a compound 'word' of 195 Sanskrit characters (transliterating to 428 letters in the Roman alphabet) describing the region near Kanci, Tamil Nadu, India, which appears in a 16th-century work by Tirumalāmbā, Queen of Vijayanagara.

The longest word in the *Oxford English Dictionary* is *pneumonoultramicroscopicsilicovolcanoconiosis (-koniosis)*, with 45 letters, describing 'a lung disease caused by the inhalation of very fine silica dust'. It is described as 'factitious' by the editors of the dictionary.

Longest scientific name The systematic name for *deoxyribonucleic acid* (DNA) of the human mitochondria contains 16 569 nucleotide residues and is thus *c.* 207 000 letters long. It was published in key form in *Nature* on 9 Apr 1981.

Longest palindromes The world's longest known palindromic word is *saippuakivikauppias* (19 letters), which is Finnish for 'a dealer in lye' (caustic soda or potash). The longest in English is *tattarrattat* (12 letters), a nonce-word meaning rat-a-tat, appearing in the *Oxford English Dictionary*.

Some baptismal fonts in Greece and Turkey bear the circular 25-letter inscription ΝΙΨΟΝ ΑΝΟΜΗΜΑΤΑ ΜΗ ΜΟΝΑΝ ΟΨΙΝ, meaning 'wash (my) sins not only (my) face'. This appears at St Mary's Church, Nottingham, St Paul's, Woldingham, Surrey and other churches.

Longest anagrams The longest non-scientific English words which can form anagrams are the 17-letter transpositions *representationism* and *misrepresentation*. The longest scientific transposals are *hydroxydesoxycorticosterone* and *hydroxydeoxycorticosterones*, with 27 letters.

Abbreviations The longest abbreviation is S.K.O.M.K.H.P.K.J.C.D.P.W.B., the initials of the Syarikat Kerjasama Orang-orang Melayu Kerajaan Hilir Perak Kerana Jimat Cermat Dan Pinjam-meminjam Wang Berhad. This is the Malay name for The Cooperative Company of the Lower State of Perak Government's Malay People for Money Savings and Loans Ltd, in Teluk Anson, Perak, West Malaysia (formerly Malaya). The abbreviation for this abbreviation is Skomk.

Shortest The 55-letter full name of Los Angeles (El Pueblo de Nuestra Señora la

Longest Words

JAPANESE[1]	Chi-n-chi-ku-ri-n (12 letters) *a very short person (slang)*
SPANISH	Superextraordinarisimo (22) *extraordinary*
FRENCH	Anticonstitutionnellement (25) *anticonstitutionally*
ITALIAN	Precipitevolissimevolmente (26) *as fast as possible*
PORTUGUESE	Inconstitucionalissimamente (27) *with the highest degree of unconstitutionality*
ICELANDIC	Haecstaréttarmálaflutningsmaður (29) *supreme court barrister*
RUSSIAN	Ryentgyenoelyektrokardiografichyeskogo (33 Cyrillic letters, transliterating as 38) *of the X-ray electrocardiographic*
HUNGARIAN	Megszentségtelenithetetlenségeskedéseitekért (44) *for your unprofanable actions*
DUTCH[4]	Kindercarnavalsoptochtvoorbereidingswerkzaamheden (49) *preparation activities for a children's carnival procession*
DANISH	Speciallægepraksisplanlægningsstabiliseringsperiode (51) *the stabilization period of the planning of medical specialist's practices*
FINNISH	Lentokonesuihkuturbiinimoottoriapumekaanikkoaliupseerioppilas (61) *apprentice corporal, working as assistant mechanic in charge of aeroplane turbine engines*
GERMAN[2,3]	Donaudampfschiffahrtselektrizitaetenhauptbetriebswerkbauunterbeamtengesellschaft (80) *the club for subordinate officials of the head office management of the Danube steamboat electrical services (name of a pre-war club in Vienna)*
SWEDISH[3]	Nordöstersjökustartilleriflygspaningssimulatoranläggningsmateriel-underhåll suppföljningssystemdiskussionsinläggsförberedelse-arbeten (130) *preparatory work on the contribution to the discussion on the maintaining system of support of the material of the aviation survey simulator device within the north-east part of the coast artillery of the Baltic*

[1] *Patent applications sometimes harbour long compound 'words'. An extreme example is one of 13 kana (Japanese syllabary) which transliterates to the 40-letter Kyukitsurohekimenfuchakunenryosekisanryo meaning 'the accumulated amount of fuel condensed on the wall face of the air intake passage'.*

[2] *The longest dictionary word in everyday usage is Rechtsschutzversicherungsgesellschaften (39) meaning 'insurance companies which provide legal protection'.*

[3] *Agglutinative words are limited only by imagination and are not found in standard dictionaries. The first 100-letter such word was published in 1975 in Afrikaans.*

Reina de los Angeles de Porciuncula) is abbreviated to L.A., or 3·63 per cent of its length.

Longest acronym The longest acronym is NIIOMTPLABOPARMBETZHEL-BETRABSBOMONIMONKONOTDTEKH-STROMONT with 56 letters (54 in Cyrillic) in the *Concise Dictionary of Soviet Terminology, Institutions and Abbreviations* (1969), meaning: the laboratory for shuttering, reinforcement, concrete and ferroconcrete operations for composite-monolithic and monolithic constructions of the Department of the Technology of Building-assembly operations of the Scientific Research Institute of the Organization for mechanization and technical aid to building of the Academy of Building and Architecture of the USSR.

Commonest words and letters The most frequently used words in written English are, in descending order of frequency: *the, of, and, to, a, in, that, is, I, it, for* and *as*. The most commonly used in conversation is *'I'*. The commonest

351

Most succinct word

The most challenging word for any lexicographer to define briefly is the Fuegian (southernmost Argentina and Chile) word *mamihlapinatapai*, meaning 'looking at each other hoping that either will offer to do something which both parties desire but are unwilling to do'.

letter is 'e'. More words begin with the letter 's' than any other, but the most commonly *used* initial letter is 't' as in 'the', 'to', 'that' or 'there'.

Most meanings The most overworked word in English is 'set', which Dr Charles Onions (1873–1965) of Oxford University Press gave 58 noun uses, 126 verbal uses and ten as a participial adjective.

Personal Names

Earliest The earliest surviving personal name is seemingly that of a predynastic king of Upper Egypt *ante* 3050 BC, who is indicated by the hieroglyphic sign for a scorpion. It has been suggested that the name should be read as Sekhem.

UK The earliest known name of any resident of Britain is Divitiacus, King of the Suessiones, the Gaulish ruler of the Kent area *c.* 100 BC under the name Prydhain. Scotland, unlike England, was never fully conquered by the Roman occupiers (AD 43–410) and Calgācus (b. *c.* AD 40), who led the final resistance in Scotland, was the earliest native whose name has been recorded.

Longest pedigree It is claimed on behalf of the Clan Mackay that their clan can be traced to Loarn, the Irish invader of south-west Pictland, now Argyll, *c.* AD 501. The only non-royal English pedigree that can show with certainty a clear pre-Conquest descent is that of the Arden family, which includes Mary Arden, Shakespeare's mother.

Longest personal name The longest name on a birth certificate is that of Rhoshandiatellyneshiaunneveshenk Koyaanfsquatsiuty Williams, born to Mr and Mrs James Williams in Beaumont, Texas, USA on 12 Sep 1984. On 5 Oct 1984 the father filed an amendment

Most surnames

A six-barrelled surname was borne by Major L.S.D.O.F. (Leone Sextus Denys Oswolf Fraudatifilius) Tollemache-Tollemache de Orellana-Plantagenet-Tollemache-Tollemache (1884–1917). At school he was known as Tolly. Of non-repetitious surnames, the last example of a five-barrelled one was that of the Lady Caroline Jemima Temple-Nugent-Chandos-Brydges-Grenville (1858–1946).

The longest single English surname is Featherstonehaugh (17 letters), variously pronounced Featherstonehaw, Festonhaw, Fessonhay, Freestonhugh, Feerstonhaw or Fanshaw.

In Scotland the surname Nin (feminine of Mac) Achinmacdholicachinskerray (29 letters) was recorded in an 18th-century parish register.

which expanded his daughter's first name to 1019 letters and the middle name to 36 letters.

Most Christian names Laurence Watkins (b. 9 Jun 1965) of Auckland, New Zealand claims a total of 2310 Christian names, added by deed poll in 1991 after official opposition by the Registrar and a prolonged court battle. The great-great-grandson of Carlos III of Spain, Don Alfonso de Borbón y Borbón (1866–1934), had 94 Christian names, several of which were lengthened by hyphenation.

UK John and Margaret Nelson of Chesterfield, Derbys gave their daughter Tracy (b. 13 Dec 1985) a total of 139 other Christian names. In November 1986 the names were recorded in a document separate from the birth certificate.

Shortest surnames The commonest single-letter surname is 'O', prevalent in Korea but with 52 examples in US telephone books (1973–81) and 12 in Belgium. This name causes most distress

Longest Place-names

In its most scholarly transliteration, Krungthep Mahanakhon, the 167-letter official name for Bangkok, the capital of Thailand, has 175 letters. The official short version (without capital letters which are not used in Thai) is included below.

World

krungthepphramahanakhon bowonratanakosin mahintharayuthaya mahadilokphiphobnovpharad radchataniburirom udomsantisug (111 letters)

Longest in use

Taumatawhakatangihangakoauauotamateaturipukakapikimaungahoronukupokaiwhenuakitanatahu (85 letters, Southern Hawke's Bay, New Zealand)[1]

British Isles

Gorsafawddachaidraigddanheddogleddollônpenrhynareurdraethceredigion (67 letters, Fairbourne Steam Railway, near Barmouth, Gwynedd)[2]

Llanfairpwllgwyngyllgogerychwyrndrobwllllantysiliogogogoch (58 letters, Anglesea, Gwynedd)[3]

Lower Llanfihangel-y-Creuddyn (26 letters, near Aberystwyth, Dyfed)[4]

England

Saint Mary le More and All Hallows with Saint Leonard and Saint Peter (57 letters, Wallingford, Oxon)[5]

North Leverton with Habblesthorpe (30 letters, Notts)[6]

Sutton-under-Whitestonecliffe/Sutton-under-the-Whitestonecliff (27/29 letters, N Yorks)[7]

Cottonshopeburnfoot (19 letters, Northumberland)[8]

Scotland

Meallan Liath Coire Mhic Dhubhghaill (32 letters, near Aultanrynie, Highland)

Coignafeuinternich (18 letters, Highland)

Kirkcudbrightshire (18 letters)[9]

Republic of Ireland

Muckanaghederdauhalia (21 letters, near Oughterard, Co Galway)[10]

[1] Unofficial name of a hill, the Maori translation meaning 'The place where Tamatea, the man with the big knees, who slid, climbed and swallowed mountains, known as landeater, played his flute to his loved one'. [2] Commercially-motivated creation on a station board 19·5 m 64 ft long. [3] Concocted version of a name translated as 'St Mary's Church by the pool of the white hazel trees, near the rapid whirlpool, by the red cave of the Church of St Tysilio'. This is the name used for the reopened (April 1973) village railway station in Anglesey, Gwynedd and was coined by a local bard, Y Barddd Cocos (John Evans, 1827–95) as a hoax. The official name consists of the first 20 letters. [4] The longest Welsh place-name in the Ordnance Survey Gazetteer. [5] A parish formed on 5 Apr 1971. [6] Longest unhyphenated. [7] Longest hyphenated. [8] Longest single word. [9] Became merged into Dumfries & Galloway on 16 May 1975. [10] Literally meaning 'the piggery between two briny inlets'.

to those concerned with the prevention of cruelty to computers.

British Isles There exist among the 47 million names on the Department of Social Security index six examples of a one-letter surname—'A', 'B', 'J', 'N', 'O' and 'X'. The Christian name 'A' has been used for five generations in the Lincoln Taber family of Fingringhoe, Essex.

Commonest surname The Chinese name Zhang is borne, according to estimates, by between 9·7 and 12·1 per cent of the Chinese population, so indicating even on the lower estimate that there are at least some 113 million Zhangs—almost twice the population of the United Kingdom.

The commonest surname in the English-speaking world is Smith. The most recent published count showed 659050 nationally insured Smiths in Great Britain, of whom 10102 were plain John Smith and another 19502 were John (plus one or more names) Smith. Including uninsured persons there were over 800000 Smiths in England and Wales alone, of whom 81493 were called A. Smith.

'Macs' There are estimated to be some 1·6 million people in Britain with M', Mc or Mac (Gaelic genitive of 'son') as part of their surnames. The commonest of these is Macdonald, which accounts for about 55000 of the Scottish population.

Place-names

Earliest The world's earliest known place-names are pre-Sumerian, e.g. Kish, Ur and the now lost Attara, and therefore earlier than *c.* 3600 BC.

British Isles The earliest recorded British place-name is Belerion, the Penwith peninsula of Cornwall, referred to as such by Pytheas of Massilia *c.* 308 BC. The name Salakee (meaning 'tin island') on St Mary's, Isles of Scilly is, however, arguably of a pre-Indo-European substrate. The earliest distinctive name for what is now Great Britain was Albion, used by Himilco *c.* 500 BC. The oldest name among England's 46 counties is Kent, first mentioned in its Roman form of Cantium (from the Celtic *canto*, meaning a rim, i.e. a coastal district), also from the cir-

Place-names

The most common place-name in Great Britain is Newton, meaning 'new settlement', occurring 467 times (151 in its simple form and 316 in compound names). Of the basic form, 90 are found in Scotland, and 40 of these are in the Grampian region alone.

cumnavigation by Pytheas of Massilia. The earliest mention of England is the form *Angelcymn*, which appeared in the *Anglo-Saxon Chronicle* in AD 880.

Shortest The shortest place-names consist of just single letters and examples can be found in various countries around the world, and include the villages of Y, France, Å in Denmark, Norway and Sweden and the River E, Highland.

Most spellings The spelling of the Dutch town of Leeuwarden has been recorded in 225 versions since AD 1046. Bromsberrow, Glos is recorded in 161 spellings since the 10th century, as reported by local historian Lester Steynor.

Literature

Earliest The earliest form of writing was pictographic and appears on Sumerian clay tablets from *c.* 3400–3300 BC found at Uruk and Kish, Iraq. This form developed into the cuneiform style by *c.* 2500 BC, which was capable of communicating true literature. Written signs in the form of tokens or tallies from Iran have been dated to 8500 BC.

Paper dated to between 71 BC and AD 21, i.e. 100 years earlier than the previous presumed date for paper's invention, has been found in north-west China.

Oldest book The oldest handwritten book, still intact, is a Coptic Psalter dated to about 1600 years ago, found in 1984 at Beni Suef, Eygpt.

UK The earliest known manuscript written in Britain is a bifolium of Eusebius' *Historia Ecclesiastica* from *c.* AD 625, possibly from the Jarrow library. Fragments of Roman wooden writing tablets found in the 1970s at Vindolanda

Nobel Prizes

The Nobel Prize is the most valuable award for literature, and was worth SwKr6·7 million (about £589000) in 1993. To date 32 different countries (counting Germany as two) have produced winners, the latest being St Lucia, birthplace of poet Derek Walcott, the 1992 winner.

The last British winner was William Golding (b. 19 Sep 1911) in 1983, and the award has been declined twice, by Boris Pasternak (1890–1960) in 1958 and by Jean-Paul Sartre (1905–80) in 1964.

The table shows those countries with more than one winner (to 1992).

France	12
USA	10
UK	8
Sweden	6
Germany*	5
Italy	5
Spain	5
Denmark	3
Netherlands	3
Poland	3
USSR (former)	3
Chile	2
Greece	2
Republic of Ireland	2
Switzerland	2

*Before 1948

(Chesterholme), Northumberland have been shown to make up the earliest known substantial written records in British history. These contain letters and a quotation from the Roman poet Virgil (70–19 BC) and are dated to c. AD 100.

Oldest mechanically printed The oldest surviving printed work is the Dharani scroll or *sutra* from wooden printing blocks found in the foundations of the Pulguk Sa pagoda, Kyŏngju, South Korea on 14 Oct 1966. It has been dated to no later than AD 704.

It is widely accepted that the earliest mechanically printed full-length book was the Gutenberg Bible, printed in Mainz, Germany, c. 1454 by Johann Henne zum Gensfleisch zur Laden, called 'zu Gutenberg' (c. 1398–1468). The earliest exactly dated printed work is the Psalter completed on 14 Aug 1457 by Johann Fust (c. 1400–66) and Peter Schöffer (1425–1502), Gutenberg's chief assistant.

The earliest printing by William Caxton (c. 1422–91), though undated, would appear to be *The Recuyel of the Historyes of Troye* in Cologne in late 1473 to spring 1474.

Smallest book The smallest marketed, bound and printed book is one printed on 22 gsm paper measuring 1mm×1mm ½s×½sin, comprising the children's story *Old King Cole!* and published in 85 copies in March 1985 by The Gleniffer Press of Paisley, Strathclyde. The pages can be turned (with care) only by the use of a needle.

Largest publications The largest publication ever compiled was the *Yongle Dadian* (the great thesaurus of the Yongle reign) of 22937 manuscript chapters (370 still survive) in 11095 volumes. It was written by 2000 Chinese scholars in 1403–08. The entire Buddhist scriptures are inscribed on 729 marble slabs measuring 1·5×1m *5×3½ft* housed in 729 stupas in the Kuthodaw Pagoda, south of Mandalay, Myanmar (Burma). They were incised in 1860–68.

UK The 1112-volume set of *British Parliamentary Papers* was published by the Irish University Press in 1968–72. A complete set weighs 3·3 tonnes, costs £50000 and would take six years to read at ten hours per day. The production involved the skins of 34000 Indian goats and the use of £15000 worth of gold ingots. The total print is 500 sets and the price per set in 1987 was £49500. In 1990 The British Library published its *General Catalogue of Printed Books to 1975* on a set of three CD-ROMs, priced at £9000. Alternatively, readers can spend six months scanning 178000 catalogue pages in 360 volumes.

Dictionaries Deutsches Wörterbuch, started by Jacob and Wilhelm Grimm in 1854, was completed in 1971 and consists of 34519 pages and 33 volumes costing DM5425 in 1988.

The largest English-language dictionary is the 20-volume *Oxford English*

Longest literary gestation

The standard German dictionary *Deutsches Wörterbuch* was begun by the brothers Grimm (Jacob and Wilhelm, 1785–1863 and 1786–1859 respectively) in 1854 and finished in 1971. *Acta Sanctorum*, begun by Jean Bolland in 1643, arranged according to saints' days, reached the month of November in 1925 and an introduction for December was published in 1940.

Oxford University Press received back their proofs of *Constable's Presentments* from the Dugdale Society in December 1984. They had been sent out for correction 35 years earlier in December 1949.

Christmas card exchange

Frank Rose of Burnaby, British Columbia, Canada and Gordon Loutet of Lake Cowichan, British Columbia have deliberately exchanged the same Christmas card every year since 1929.

Pen pals

The longest sustained correspondence on record is one of 75 years from 11 Nov 1904 between Mrs Ida McDougall of Tasmania, Australia and Miss R. Norton of Sevenoaks, Kent until Mrs McDougall's death on 24 Dec 1979.

Dictionary, with 21728 pages. The first edition, edited by Sir James Murray, was published between 1884 and 1928. The second edition, published in March 1989, defines 616500 word-forms and contains 2412400 illustrative quotations and approximately 350 million letters and figures (equivalent to 70 million words of a nominal five letters long). The longest entry is that for the verb *set*, with over 75000 words of text. The greatest outside contributor has been Marghanita Laski (1915–88), with a reputed 250000 quotations from 1958 until her death.

Encyclopedias The largest encyclopedia was the Chinese *Yongle Dadian*. (⇨ Largest publications)

Currently, the largest encyclopedia is *La Enciclopedia Universal Ilustrada Europeo-Americana* (J. Espasa & Sons, Madrid and Barcelona) totalling 105000 pages and an annual supplement since 1935 comprising 165·2 million words. The number of volumes in the set in August 1983 was 104, and the price $2325.

The most comprehensive English-language encyclopedia is *The New Encyclopedia Britannica*, the current 32-volume 16th edition of which contains 32030 pages and costs £1398.

Fiction The novel *Tokuga-Wa Ieyasu* by Sohachi Yamaoka has been serialized in Japanese daily newspapers since 1951, requiring nearly 40 volumes. The longest published novel of note is *Les hommes de bonne volonté* by Louis Henri Jean Farigoule (1885–1972), alias Jules Romains, of France, in 27 volumes in 1932–46. The English version *Men of Good Will* was published in 14 volumes in 1933–46 as a 'novel-cycle'. The 4959-page edition published by Peter Davies Ltd has an estimated 2070000 words, excluding the 100-page index.

Who's Who The longest entry in *Who's Who* (founded 1848 and first published 1949) was that of the Rt Hon. Sir Winston Leonard Spencer Churchill (1874–1965), who appeared in 67 editions from 1899 (18 lines) and had 211 lines by the 1965 edition. The longest entry in the book's current wider format is that of Dame Barbara Cartland, who is allocated 199 lines in the 1993 edition (⇨ Most prolific author). Apart from those who qualify for inclusion by hereditary title, the youngest entrant has been Sir Yehudi Menuhin (b. New York City, USA, 22 Apr 1916), the concert violinist, who first appeared in the 1932 edition at the age of 15.

Maps

Oldest A clay tablet depicting the river Euphrates flowing through northern Mesopotamia, Iraq dates to *c.* 2250 BC. The earliest printed map in the world is one of western China dated to AD 1115.

UK The earliest surviving product of English map-making is the Anglo-Saxon *Mappa Mundi*, known as the Cottonian manuscript, from the late 10th century. The earliest printed map of Britain was Ptolemy's outline printed in Bologna, Italy in 1477.

Largest The largest permanent, two-dimensional atlas measures 4552 m² *49 000 ft²* and was painted by students of O'Hara Park School, Oakley, California, USA in the summer of 1992.

The Challenger relief map of British Columbia, Canada, measuring 575 m² *6080 ft²*, was designed and built in the period 1945–52 by the late George Challenger and his son Robert. It is now on display at the Pacific National Exhibition in Vancouver, British Columbia.

Most expensive The highest price paid for an atlas is $1 925 000 for a copy of Ptolemy's *Cosmographia* at Sotheby's, New York City, USA on 31 Jan 1990.

Highest Prices

Books The highest price paid for any book is £8·14 million for the 226-leaf manuscript *The Gospel Book of Henry the Lion, Duke of Saxony* at Sotheby's, London on 6 Dec 1983. The book, which measures 34·3 × 25·4 cm *13½ × 10 in*, was illuminated *c.* 1170 by the monk Herimann at Helmershansen Abbey, Germany with 41 full-page illustrations and was bought by Hans Kraus for the Hermann Abs consortium.

The record for a *printed* book is $5·39 million for an Old Testament (Genesis to Psalms) of the Gutenberg Bible printed in 1455 in Mainz, Germany. It was bought by Tokyo booksellers Maruzen Co. Ltd at Christie's, New York, USA on 22 Oct 1987.

Broadsheet The highest price ever paid for a printed page was $2 420 000 for a copy of *The Declaration of Independence*, printed in Philadelphia, Pennsylvania, USA in 1776 by John Dunlap. It was sold by Samuel T. Freeman & Co. to Donald Scheer of Atlanta, Georgia on 13 Jun 1991.

Manuscripts The highest price ever paid for a manuscript is £2·97 million by London dealers Quaritch at Sotheby's, London on 29 Nov 1990 for the 13th-century *Northumberland Bestiary*, a colourful and highly illustrated encyclopedia of real and imaginary animals. The book was sold by the Duchess of Northumberland, whose family had owned it for over 200 years.

Musical The auction record for a musical manuscript is £2 585 000 paid by London dealer James Kirkman at Sotheby's, London on 22 May 1987 for a 508-page, 21·6 × 16·5 cm *8½ × 6½ in* bound volume of nine complete symphonies in Mozart's hand. The record for a single musical manuscript is £1·1 million paid at Sotheby's, London on 6 Dec 1991 for the autograph copy of the Piano Sonata in E minor, opus 90 by Ludwig van Beethoven (1770–1827).

Diaries and Letters

Longest kept diary Col. Ernest Loftus of Harare, Zimbabwe began his daily diary on 4 May 1896 at the age of 12 and continued it until his death on 7 Jul 1987 aged 103 years 178 days, a total of 91 years.

Most letters Uichi Noda, former Vice Minister of Treasury and Minister of Construction in Japan, from July 1961 until his bedridden wife Mitsu's death in March 1985, wrote her 1307 letters amounting to 5 million characters during his overseas trips. These letters have been published in 25 volumes totalling 12 404 pages. Rev. Canon Bill Cook and his fiancée/wife Helen of Diss, Norfolk exchanged 6000 love letters during their 4½-year separation from March 1942—May 1946.

Longest letter to an editor The *Upper Dauphin Sentinel* of Pennsylvania, USA published a letter of 25 513 words over eight issues from August to November 1979, written by John Sultzbaugh of Lykens, Pennsylvania.

Most letters to an editor David Green, author and solicitor of Castle Morris, Dyfed, had his 131st letter published in the main correspondence columns of *The Times* on 31 May 1993. His record year was 1972 with 12.

Shortest correspondence The shortest correspondence on record was that between Victor Marie Hugo (1802–85) and his publisher, Hurst and Blackett, in 1862. The author was on holiday and anxious to know how his new novel *Les Misérables* was selling. He wrote '?' and received the reply '!'.

The shortest letter to *The Times* comprised the single abbreviated symbol 'Dr?' in the interrogative from R. S. Cookson of London NW11 on 30 Jul 1984 in a correspondence on the correct form of recording a plurality of academic doctorates. On 8 Jan 1986 a letter was sent to *The Times* by a seven-year-old girl from the Isle of Man. It read 'Sir, Yours faithfully Caroline Sophia Kerenhappuch Parkes'. The brief epistle was intended to inform readers of her unusual name, Kerenhappuch, mentioned in a letter the previous week from Rev. John Ticehurst on the subject of uncommon 19th-century names.

Christmas cards The earliest known Christmas card was sent out by Sir Henry Cole (1808–82) in 1843 but this practice did not become an annual ritual until 1862.

The greatest number of personal Christmas cards sent out is believed to be 62 824 by Werner Erhard of San Francisco, California, USA in December 1975. Many must have been to unilateral acquaintances.

Autographs and Signatures

Earliest The earliest surviving examples of autographs are those made by scribes on cuneiform clay tablets from Tell Abu Salābīkh, Iraq dated to the early Dynastic III A period c. 2600 BC. A scribe named 'a-du' has added 'dub-sar' after his name, thus translating to 'Adu, scribe'. The earliest surviving signature on a papyrus is that of the scribe Amen'aa, held in the Leningrad (St Petersburg) Museum, Russia and dated to the Egyptian middle kingdom, which began c. 2130 BC.

UK A signum exists for William I (the Conqueror) from c. 1070. The earliest English sovereign whose handwriting is known to have survived is Edward III (1327–77). The earliest full signature extant is that of Richard II, dated 26 Jul 1386. The Magna Carta does not bear even the mark of King John (reigned 1199–1216), but carries only his seal affixed on 19 Jun 1215.

Most expensive The highest price ever paid on the open market for a single signed autograph letter has been $360 000 on 29 Oct 1986 at Sotheby's, New York, USA for a letter by Thomas Jefferson condemning prejudice against Jews in 1818. It was sold by Charles Rosenbloom of Pittsburgh, Pennsylvania, USA.

The highest price paid for an autograph letter signed by a living person is $12 500 at the Hamilton Galleries on 22 Jan 1981 for a letter from President Ronald Reagan praising Frank Sinatra.

Rarest and most valuable Only one example of the signature of Christopher Marlowe (1564–93) is known. It is in the Kent County Archives on a will of 1583.

Authors

Most prolific A lifetime output of 72–75 million words has been calculated for Charles Harold St John Hamilton, alias Frank Richards (1876–1961), the creator of Billy Bunter. In his peak years (1915–26) he wrote up to 80 000 words a week for the boys' school weeklies *Gem* (1907–39), *Magnet* (1908–40) and *Boys' Friend*.

Novels The greatest number of novels published is 904 by Kathleen Lindsay (Mrs Mary Faulkner) (1903–73) of Somerset West, Cape Province, South Africa. She wrote under two other married names and eight pen names. Baboorao Arnalkar (b. 9 Jun 1907) of Maharashtra State, India published 1092 short mystery stories in book form and several non-fiction books between 1936 and 1984.

UK The most prolific author is currently Dame Barbara Cartland, with 583 titles published in 30 languages to date. She has averaged 23 titles per year for the last 19 years and was made a Dame of the Order of the British Empire by HM The Queen in the 1991 New Year's Honours List for services to literature and the community.

Enid Mary Blyton (1898–1968) (Mrs Darrell Waters) completed 700 children's stories, many of them brief, with 59 in

358

Most pseudonyms

The writer with the greatest number of pseudonyms is the minor Russian humorist Konstantin Arsenievich Mikhailov (b. 1868), whose 325 pen names are listed in the *Dictionary of Pseudonyms* by I.F. Masanov, published in Moscow in 1960. The names, ranging from Ab. to Z, were mostly abbreviations of his real name.

1955. Her books have been translated into about 40 languages.

Text books Britain's most successful writer of text books is ex-schoolmaster Ronald Ridout (b. 23 Jul 1916) who has had 515 titles published since 1958, with sales of 91·35 million. His *The First English Workbook* has sold 5·6 million copies.

Greatest advance The greatest advance for a single book is $14 million (£7·3 million), reported in August 1992 to have been paid by Berkeley Putnam for the North American rights to *Without Remorse* by Tom Clancy. On 9 Feb 1989 the American horror writer Stephen King (b. 21 Sep 1947) was reported to have scooped a £26 million advance for his next four books.

On 6 May 1992 the British journalist and author Barbara Taylor Bradford (b. 10 May 1933) concluded a deal with HarperCollins for £17 million (over some five years) for three novels.

Highest paid author In 1958 Deborah Schneider of Minneapolis, Minnesota, USA wrote 25 words to complete a sentence in a competition for the best blurb for Plymouth cars. She beat about 1·4 million entrants to the prize of $500 every month for life. On normal life expectations she should collect $12 000 per word. No known anthology includes Mrs Schneider's deathless prose but it is in her deed box at her bank 'Only to be opened after death'. She passed $8000 a word by 1991.

Top-selling authors The world's top-selling fiction writer is Dame Agatha Christie (*née* Miller, later Lady Mallowan, 1890–1976), whose 78 crime novels have sold an estimated 2 billion copies

in 44 languages. Agatha Christie also wrote 19 plays and six romantic novels under the pseudonym Mary Westmacott. Royalty earnings are estimated to be worth £2·5 million per year.

The top-selling living author is Dame Barbara Cartland with global sales of over 650 million for her 583 titles published. (⊳ Most prolific author)

Non-fiction It has been reported that 800 million copies of the red-covered booklet *Quotations from the Works of Mao Zedong* (*Tse-tung*) were sold or distributed between June 1966, when possession became virtually mandatory in China, and September 1971, when its promoter Marshal Lin Biao died in an air crash.

Biography Georges Simenon wrote 22 autobiographical books from 1972. The longest biography in publishing history is that of Sir Winston Churchill by his son Randolph (4832 pages) and Martin Gilbert (17811 pages), to date comprising 22 volumes and 9694000 words.

Most rejections The record for rejections of a manuscript before publication is 176 (and non-acknowledgement from many other publishers) in the case of Bill Gordon's *How Many Books Do You Sell in Ohio?* from October 1983 to November 1985. The record was then spoiled by Mr Gordon's rejection of a written offer from Aames-Allen. British novelist John Creasey (1908–73) received 743 rejection slips before becoming the best-selling author of 564 books.

Oldest The oldest author in the world was Alice Pollock (*née* Wykeham-Martin, 1868–1971) of Haslemere, Surrey, whose first book *Portrait of My Victorian Youth* (Johnson Publications) was published in March 1971 when she was aged 102 years 8 months. *Cofio Canrif*, the autobiography of Griffith R. Williams of Llithfaen, Gwynedd, was published on his 102nd birthday on 5 Jun 1990.

Youngest Poet Laureate Laurence Eusden (1688–1730) 'received the bays' on 24 Dec 1718 at the age of 30 years and 3 months.

Oldest Poet Laureate The greatest age at which a poet has succeeded is 73 in the case of William Wordsworth (1770–1850)

on 6 Apr 1843. The longest-lived Laureate was John Masefield, who died on 12 May 1967 aged 88 years 345 days. The longest any poet has worn the laurel is 41 years 322 days in the case of Alfred (later the 1st Lord) Tennyson (1809–92), who was appointed on 19 Nov 1850 and died in office on 6 Oct 1892.

Longest poem The lengthiest poem ever published has been the Kirghiz folk epic *Manas*, which appeared in printed form in 1958 but which has never been translated into English. According to the *Dictionary of Oriental Literatures*, this three part epic runs to about 500 000 lines. Short translated passages appear in *The Elek Book of Oriental Verse*.

The longest poem in English is one on the life of King Alfred by John Fitchett (1766–1838) of Liverpool, Merseyside, which ran to 129 807 lines and took 40 years to write. His editor, Robert Riscoe, added the concluding 2585 lines.

Best-selling Books

The world's best-selling and most widely distributed book is the Bible, with an estimated 6·1 billion copies printed between 1815 and 1992. Since 1976 combined global sales of Today's English Version (*Good News*) New Testament and Bible (which is copyright of the Bible Societies) have exceeded 236·9 million copies. Apart from the King James version (averaging some 13 million copies printed annually), there are at least 14 other copyrights on other versions of the Bible and it has been translated into 2009 languages, with portions of it into a further 910, compared with 222 languages for Lenin. The oldest publisher of bibles is the Cambridge University Press, which began with the Geneva version in 1591. (⬡ Oldest publisher)

Excluding versions of the Bible, the world's all-time best-selling book is *The Guinness Book of Records*, first published in October 1955 by Guinness Superlatives, a subsidiary of Arthur Guinness Son & Co. (Park Royal) Ltd, and edited by Norris Dewar McWhirter (b. 12 Aug 1925) and his twin brother Alan Ross McWhirter (killed 27 Nov 1975). Global sales in some 43 languages have reached 74 million to May 1993.

Slowest seller
The accolade for the world's slowest-selling book (known in US publishing as slooow sellers) probably belongs to David Wilkins' translation of the New Testament from Coptic into Latin, published by Oxford University Press (OUP) in 1716 in 500 copies. Selling an average of one each 20 weeks, it remained in print for 191 years.

Fiction It is difficult to state with certainty which single work has the highest sales, but two novels are considered contenders. *Valley of the Dolls* (first published March 1966) by Jacqueline Susann (Mrs Irving Mansfield) (1921–74) had a world-wide total of 28 712 000 to 30 Mar 1987. In the first six months Bantam sold 6·8 million copies. *Gone With the Wind* by Margaret Mitchell, published in 1936, is also credited with sales of over 28 million copies.

Alistair Stuart MacLean (1922–87) wrote 30 books, 28 of which each sold over a million copies in the UK alone. His books have been translated into 28 languages and 13 have been filmed. It has been estimated that a 'MacLean' novel is purchased every 18 seconds.

Best-seller lists The longest duration on the *New York Times* best-seller list (founded 1935) has been for *The Road Less Traveled* by M. Scott Peck, which on 2 Oct 1988 had its 258th week on the lists.

UK A Brief History of Time (Transworld/Bantam Press) by Prof. Stephen Hawking (b. 8 Jan 1942) has appeared in *The Sunday Times* best-seller list (which excludes books published annually) for a record 212 weeks to 30 May 1993. *The Country Diary of an Edwardian Lady* (Michael Joseph, Webb & Bower) by Edith Holden (1871–1920) held the No. 1 position for 64 weeks.

Publishers and Printers

Oldest publisher Cambridge University Press has a continuous history of printing and publishing since 1584. The University received Royal Letters Patent to print and sell all manner of books on 20 Jul 1534.

In 1978 the Oxford University Press (OUP) celebrated the 500th anniversary of the printing of the first book in the City of Oxford in 1478. This was before OUP itself was in existence.

Most prolific publisher In terms of new titles per annum, Britain's most prolific publisher in 1989 was Oxford University Press with 1922.

In 1992 the UK published a record 78 835 new titles and editions, an increase of 16·44 per cent on the 1991 total.

At its peak in 1989, Progress Publishers (founded in 1931 as the Publishing Association of Foreign Workers in the USSR) of Moscow, USSR printed over 750 titles in 50 languages annually.

Largest publisher The world's largest publisher of magazines and books is Time Inc., a division of Time Warner of New York, USA. Revenues in 1992 totalled $3·123 billion.

Fastest publishing One thousand bound copies of *William and his Adventures*, published by the Royal Marsden Hospital Appeal and Scriptmate and printed by Booksprint, were produced from raw disk in 12hr 18min on 5 Jun 1992.

Largest printer The largest printers in the world are believed to be R.R. Donnelley & Sons Co. of Chicago, Illinois, USA. The company, founded in 1864, has nearly 100 manufacturing facilities, offices, service centres and subsidiaries world-wide, turning out $4·1 billion worth of work per year.

The largest printer under one roof is the United States Government Printing Office (founded 1861) in Washington, DC, USA. Encompassing 13·92 ha *34·4 acres* of floor space, the central office processes an average of 1464 print orders daily, uses 42 276 tonnes of paper annually and maintains an inventory of over 16 000 titles in print.

Highest Printings

It is believed that in the USA, Van Antwerp Bragg and Co. printed some 60 million copies of the 1879 edition of *The McGuffey Reader*, compiled by Henry Vail in the pre-copyright era for distribution to public schools.

The initial print order for the 1990/91 Automobile Association *Members' Handbook* was 6 153 000 copies, representing a stack seven times the height of Mt Everest. The total print since 1908 is 101 673 000 and it is currently printed by Petty & Sons Ltd of Leeds, W Yorks and Jarrolds Printing Ltd of Norwich, Norfolk.

The aggregate print of *The Highway Code* (instituted 1931) has reached 111 million, with 2 million copies of the new edition sold in three months to April 1993.

Fiction The highest print order for a work of fiction in the UK was 3 million by Penguin Books Ltd for their paperback edition of *Lady Chatterley's Lover*, by D.H. (David Herbert) Lawrence (1885–1930). Total world-wide sales to April 1993 were 4 898 241 copies.

Bookshops The bookshop with most titles and the longest shelving (48 km *30 miles*) in the world is W.&G. Foyle Ltd of London. Established in 1904 in a small shop in Islington, the company is now at 113–119 Charing Cross Road in premises measuring 7044 m² *75 825 ft²*. The most capacious individual bookstore in the world measured by square footage is the Barnes & Noble Bookstore at 105 Fifth Ave at 18th Street, New York City, USA. It covers 14 330 m² *154 250 ft²* and has 20·71 km *12·87 miles* of shelving.

Libraries and Museums

Earliest One of the earliest known collections of archival material was that of King Ashurbanipal held at Nineveh (668–627 BC). He had clay tablets referring to events, personages and religious ideas as far back as the Early Dynastic times of Sumer *c.* 2700 BC.

Largest library The United States Library of Congress (founded on 24 Apr 1800) in Washington, DC, USA contains 101 395 257 items, including 15 700 905 books in the classified collections and 85 694 352 items in non-classified. The library occupies 265 000 m² *2·85 million ft²* of space in the Capitol Hill buildings, and has additional offices and branches world-wide. At May 1992 there were 925 km *575 miles* of shelving and 5050 employees.

The largest non-statutory library is the New York Public Library (founded 1895) on Fifth Avenue, New York City, USA with a floor space covering 48 800 m² *525 276 ft²* and 141·6 km *88 miles* of shelving, plus an underground extension with the capacity for an additional 148 km *92 miles*. Its collection, including 82 branch libraries embraces 13 887 774 volumes, 18 349 585 manuscripts and 381 645 maps.

UK The largest library in the United Kingdom is the British Library, comprising 19 buildings in London and a 24·3 ha *60 acre* site at Boston Spa, W Yorks, and with a total staff of some 2500. The Library contains over 18 million volumes. Stock increases involve over 12·8 km

8 miles of new shelving annually. The Newspaper Library at Colindale, north London, opened in 1932, has 583 000 volumes and parcels comprising 70 000 different titles on 35·4 km *22 miles* of shelving. The Document Supply Centre in West Yorks (shelf capacity 157·7 km *98 miles*) runs the largest library inter-

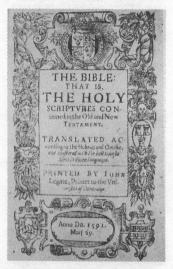

The heart of the University of Cambridge. The building in the background with the square tower and flagpole is Cambridge University Press, the world's oldest publisher. Also shown is CUP's 1591 Geneva version of the Bible.

(Photos: CUP/Tim Rawle)

Overdue books

The record for an unreturned and overdue library book was set when a book in German on the Archbishop of Bremen, published in 1609, was borrowed from Sidney Sussex College, Cambridge by Colonel Robert Walpole in 1667–68. It was found by Prof. Sir John Plumb in the library of the then Marquess of Cholmondeley at Houghton Hall, Norfolk and returned 288 years later. No fine was exacted.

Library books

Public libraries in the UK issued 580 million books in 1991/2, representing 10·1 issues per person.

---

lending operation in the world; it handles annually over 3 million requests from other libraries (UK and overseas) for items they do not hold in stock. The National Sound Archive holds 1 million discs and 62000 hours of recorded tape. The largest public reference library in Europe is the extended Mitchell Library in Glasgow, Strathclyde, which has a floor area of 50000 m² *538 200 ft²*, or 4·9 ha *12·3 acres*, and an ultimate capacity for 4 million volumes.

Oldest museum The world's oldest extant museum is the Ashmolean in Oxford, built between 1679 and 1683 and named after the collector Elias Ashmole (1617–92). Since 1924 it has housed an exhibition of historic scientific instruments.

Largest museum The Smithsonian Institution comprises 16 museums and the National Zoological Park in Washington, DC, USA. It contains over 140 million items and has over 6000 employees.

The American Museum of Natural History in New York City, USA, founded in 1869, comprises 23 interconnected buildings. The buildings of the Museum and the Planetarium contain 11 148 m² *1·2 million ft²* of floor space, accommodating more than 30 million artifacts and specimens and the museum attracts over 3 million visitors each year.

UK The largest and most visited museum in the United Kingdom is the British Museum (founded in 1753), which was opened to the public in 1759. The main building in Bloomsbury, London was begun in 1823 and has a total floor area of 8·7 ha *21·5 acres*. In 1992, 6 725 192 people passed through its doors.

Most popular The highest attendance for any museum is over 118 437 (with the doors temporarily closed) on 14 Apr 1984 at the Smithsonian's National Air and Space Museum, Washington, DC, USA, opened in July 1976.

Newspapers

Oldest A copy has survived of a news pamphlet published in Cologne, Germany in 1470. The oldest existing newspaper in the world is the Swedish official journal *Post och Inrikes Tidningar*, founded in 1645 and published by the Royal Swedish Academy of Letters. The oldest existing commercial newspaper is the *Haarlems Dagblad/Oprechte Haarlemsche Courant*, published in Haarlem, Netherlands. First issued as the *Weeckelycke Courante van Europa* on 8 Jan 1656, a copy of issue No. 1 survives.

UK The *London Gazette* (originally the *Oxford Gazette*) was first published on 16 Nov 1665. The newspaper with the earliest origins still published is *Berrow's Worcester Journal* (originally the *Worcester Post Man*), published in Worcester. It was traditionally founded in 1690 and has appeared weekly since June 1709. No complete file exists. The earliest foundation date for any British newspaper published under the same title is the *Stamford Mercury*, printed since 1712 and traditionally even 1695.

The oldest Sunday newspaper is *The Observer*, first issued on 4 Dec 1791.

Largest The most massive single issues of a newspaper have been of the *Sunday New York Times*, which by August 1987 had reached 6·35 kg *14 lb*, with a prediction that 7·7 kg *17 lb* was a probability. The largest page size ever used was 130×89 cm *51×35 in* for *The Constellation*, printed in 1859 by George

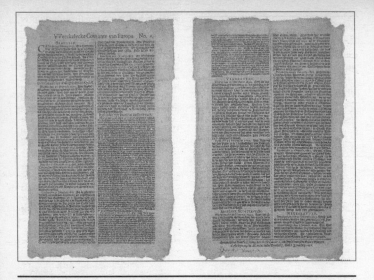

Pages from issue No. 1 of the Dutch newspaper *Weeckelycke Courante van Europa* of 8 Jan 1656, giving news from Spain, Germany, Prussia, France, England and Scotland, as well as the Netherlands.

Most misprints

The record for misprints in *The Times* was set on 22 Aug 1978 when on page 19 there were 97 in 5½ single column inches. The passage concerned 'Pop' (Pope) Paul VI.

Most durable advertiser

The Jos Neel Co., a clothing store in Macon, Georgia, USA (founded 1880) has run an 'ad' in the *Macon Telegraph* every day in the upper left corner of page 2 since 22 Feb 1889.

Roberts as part of the 4 July celebrations in New York City, USA.

The *Worcestershire Chronicle* was the largest British newspaper, and a surviving issue of 16 Feb 1859 measures 82×57cm *32¼ × 22½ in*.

Smallest

The smallest original page size was 7·6 × 9·5 cm *3 × 3¾ in* for the *Daily Banner* (25 cents per month) of Roseberg, Oregon, USA. Issues dated 1 and 2 Feb 1876 survive. The British Library Newspaper Library contains the *Watford News and Advertiser* of 1 Apr 1899, which measures 7·5×10 cm *2·9×3·9in*.

Most expensive

Britain's most expensive newpaper is *The Sunday Times* at 90 p.

Longest editorship

Sir Etienne Dupuch (1899–91) of Nassau, Bahamas was editor-in-chief of *The Tribune* from 1 Apr 1919 to 1972, and contributing editor until his death on 23 Aug 1991, a total of 72 years. The longest editorship of any UK national newspaper was 57 years by C.P. (Charles Prestwich) Scott (1846– 1932) of the *Manchester Guardian* (the *Guardian* from 1959), who occupied the post from the age of 26 in 1872 until his retirement in 1929.

Cartoon strips

The earliest cartoon is 'The Yellow Kid', which first appeared in the *New York Journal* on 18 Oct 1896.

The longest-lived newspaper comic strip is the 'Katzenjammer Kids' (Hans and Fritz), created by Rudolph Dirks and first published in the *New York Journal* on 12 Dec 1897.

The most syndicated strip is 'Peanuts' by Charles Schulz of Santa Rosa, California, USA. First published in October 1950, it currently appears in 2300 newspapers in 68 countries and 26 languages. In 1990 Schulz's income was estimated at $5 million per month.

Most durable feature Mary MacArthur of Port Appin, Strathclyde has contributed a regular feature to *The Oban Times and West Highland Times* since 1926.

Most syndicated columnist Ann Landers (*née* Eppie Lederer, b. 4 Jul 1918) appears in over 1200 newspapers with an estimated readership of 90 million. Her only serious rival is 'Dear Abby' (Mrs Pauline Phillips), her identical twin sister based in Beverly Hills, California, USA.

Circulation

Earliest million The first newspaper to achieve a circulation of 1 million copies was *Le Petit Journal*, published in Paris, France, which reached this figure in 1886, when selling at 5 centimes. Sales of the *Daily Mail* first reached a million on 2 Mar 1900.

Highest The highest circulation for any newspaper in the world was that for *Komsomolskaya Pravda* (founded 1925), the youth paper of the former Soviet Communist Party, which reached a peak daily circulation of 21 975 000 copies in May 1990. The eight-page weekly newspaper *Argumenty i Fakty* (founded 1978) of Moscow, Russia attained a figure of 33 431 100 copies in May 1990,

when it had a estimated readership of over 100 million.

UK The *News of the World* (founded 1 Oct 1843) attained peak sales of 8 480 878 copies in April 1951 and had an estimated readership of over 19 million. The latest sales figure is 4·6 million copies per issue, with an estimated readership of 12·5 million. The highest net sale of any daily newspaper in the UK is 3·5 million for *The Sun*, with an estimated readership of 10·1 million at March 1993.

Most read The national newspaper achieving the closest to a saturation circulation is the *Sunday Post*, established in Glasgow, Strathclyde in 1914. In 1992 its estimated readership in Scotland of 1 905 000 represented 47 per cent of the entire population aged 15 and over, compared to 54 per cent in 1989. The *Arran Banner* (founded March 1974) has a readership of 97+ per cent on Britain's seventh largest offshore island.

Periodicals

Oldest The oldest continuing periodical in the world is *Philosophical Transactions of the Royal Society*, published in London, which first appeared on 6 Mar 1665. Britain's oldest weekly periodical is *The Lancet*, first published in 1823.

Annual The most durable annual is *Old Moore's Almanack*, published since 1697, when it appeared as a broadsheet produced by Dr Francis Moore (1657–1715) of Southwark, London to advertise his 'physiks'. Published by W. Foulsham & Co. Ltd of Slough, Berks, its aggregate sales to date are over 113 million.

Largest circulations Total sales through non-commercial channels by Jehovah's Witnesses of *The Truth that Leads to Eternal Life*, published by the Watchtower Bible and Tract Society of New York City, USA on 8 May 1968, reached 107 562 995 in 117 languages by April 1993.

The peak circulation of any weekly periodical was achieved by the US *TV Guide* which, in 1974, became the first magazine to sell a billion copies in a year. In its 41 basic international editions, *Reader's Digest* (established February 1922) circulates 28·5 million copies monthly in 17 languages, including a US edition of more than 16·31 million copies and a UK edition (established 1939) of over 1·5 million copies.

Parade, the US syndicated colour magazine, has been distributed with 352 newspapers every Sunday since 18 Jul 1993, giving a peak circulation of 36·73 million.

UK Before deregulation of the listings market in March 1991, the highest circulation of any periodical in Britain was that of the *Radio Times* (instituted on 28 Sep 1923). Average weekly sales for July–December 1989 were 3 037 129 copies, with a readership of 9 031 000. The highest sales figure for any issue was 11 037 139 copies for the 1989 Christmas edition.

Largest The bulkiest consumer magazine ever published was the 10 Jan 1990 issue of *Shukan Jutaku Joho* (Weekly Housing Information), running to 1940 pages. Published in Japan by the Recruit Company Ltd, it retailed for 350 yen.

Most advertising pages The greatest number of pages of advertisements sold in a single issue of a periodical is 829·54 by the October 1989 edition of *Business Week*.

Crosswords

Earliest Opinions differ on what constitutes a true crossword as distinct from other forms of word puzzle, but the earliest contender is considered to be a 25-letter acrostic of Roman provenance discovered on a wall in Cirencester, Glos in 1868. Another possible contender is an example of 'blended squares', published in the women's magazine *The People's Home Journal* in September 1904. The modern crossword is believed to have evolved from Arthur Wynne's 'Word Cross', published in the Sunday *New York World* on 21 Dec 1913. The first British publication to use a regular puzzle was *Pearson's Magazine* with a 'Word Square' in February 1922. The first crossword published in a British newspaper was devised by C.W. Shepherd in the *Sunday Express* of 2 Nov 1924.

Largest published In July 1982 Robert Turcot of Québec, Canada compiled a crossword comprising 82 951 squares. It

Fastest crossword solution
The fastest recorded time for completing *The Times* crossword under test conditions is 3 min 45 sec by Roy Dean of Bromley, Kent in the BBC *Today* radio studio on 19 Dec 1970.

Dr John Sykes won *The Times/Collins Dictionaries* championship 10 times between 1972 and 1990, when he solved each of the four puzzles in an average time of 8 min and beat the field by a record margin of 9½ min on 8 Sep at the Hilton hotel, London. He set a championship best time of 4 min 28 sec in 1989.

Slowest solution
In May 1966 *The Times* of London received an announcement from a Fijian woman that she had just succeeded in completing their crossword No. 673 in the issue of 4 Apr 1932. As disclosed by her husband, D.T. Lloyd in a letter to *The Times* on 8 Feb 1990, the woman was stationed in Fiji as the wife of a Civil Servant, and far from being fiendishly difficult, the puzzle was in an edition which was used to wrap a parcel and had subsequently lain uncompleted for 34 years.

contained 12 489 clues across, 13 125 down and covered 3·55 m² *38·28 ft²*.

Compilers The most prolific crossword compiler is Roger F. Squires of Ironbridge, Shrops, who devises 39 published puzzles single-handedly each week. His total output to September 1993 was over 41 900 crosswords, and his millionth clue was published in the *Daily Telegraph* on 6 Sep 1989.

Music

Whistles and flutes made from perforated phalange bones have been found at Upper Palaeolithic sites of the Aurignacian period (*c.* 25 000–22 000 BC), e.g. at Istallóskö, Hungary and in Moldova. Musical history can, however, be traced back to the 3rd millennium BC, when the yellow bell (*huang zhong*) had a recognized standard musical tone in Chinese temple music.

The world's earliest surviving musical notation dates from *c.* 1800 BC. A heptatonic scale deciphered from a clay tablet by Dr Duchesne-Guillemin in 1966–67 was found at a site in Nippur, Sumer, now Iraq.

The human voice Before this century the extremes were a staccato E in *alt altissimo* (e^{iv}) by Ellen Beach Yaw (USA) (1869–1947) in Carnegie Hall, New York, USA on 19 Jan 1896, and an A₁ (55 Hz) by Kasper Foster (1617–73).

Madeleine Marie Robin (1918–60), the French operatic coloratura, could produce and sustain the B above high C in the Lucia mad scene in Donizetti's *Lucia di Lammermoor*. Since 1950 singers have achieved high and low notes far beyond the hitherto accepted extremes. However, notes at the bass and treble extremities of the register tend to lack harmonics and are of little musical value.

Ivan Rebroff, the German bass, has a voice which extends easily over four octaves from low F to high F, 1¼ octaves above C. Dan Britton of Branson, Missouri, USA can produce the note E-0 (18·84 Hz).

The highest note put into song is G^{iv} first occurring in Mozart's *Popoli di Tessaglia*. The lowest vocal note in the classical repertoire is in Mozart's *Die Entführung aus dem Serail* in Osmin's aria which calls for a low D (73·4 Hz).

Songs

Oldest The *shaduf* chant has been sung since time immemorial by irrigation workers on the man-powered, pivoted-rod bucket raisers of the Nile water mills (or *saqiyas*) in Egypt. An Assyrian love song, from *c.* 1800 BC to an Ugaritic god from a tablet of notation and lyric was reconstructed for an 11-string lyre at the University of California, Berkeley, USA on 6 Mar 1974.

Longest rendering of national anthem

'God Save the King' was played non-stop 16 or 17 times by a German military band on the platform of Rathenau railway station, Brandenburg, Germany on the morning of 9 Feb 1909. The reason was that King Edward VII was struggling inside the train with the uniform of a German field-marshal before he could emerge.

Worst singer

While no agreement exists as to the identity of history's greatest singer, there is unanimity on the worst. The excursions of the soprano Florence Foster Jenkins (1868–1944) into lieder and even high coloratura culminated on 25 Oct 1944 in her sell-out concert at the Carnegie Hall, New York City, USA. The diva's (already high) high F was said to have been made higher in 1943 by a crash in a taxi. It is one of the tragedies of musicology that Madame Jenkins' *Clavelitos*, accompanied by Cosme McMoon, was never recorded for posterity.

The oldest known harmonized music performed today is the English song *Sumer is icumen in*, which dates from *c.* 1240.

National anthems The oldest national anthem is the *Kimigayo* of Japan, the words of which date from the 9th century, whilst the oldest music belongs to the anthem of the Netherlands. The shortest anthems are those of Japan, Jordan and San Marino, each with only four lines. Of the 11 wordless national anthems, the oldest is that of Spain, dating from 1770.

Top songs The most frequently sung songs in English are *Happy Birthday to You* (based on *Good Morning to All*), by Kentucky Sunday School teachers Mildred Hill and Patty Smith Hill of New York, USA (written in 1893 and under copyright from 1935 to 2010); *For He's a Jolly Good Fellow* (originally the French *Malbrouk*), known at least as early as

367

the US wrote 8500 hymns, and is reputed to have finished one hymn in 15 minutes. Charles Wesley (1707–88) wrote about 6000 hymns.

Bells

Oldest The world's oldest bell is the tintinnabulum found in the Babylonian Palace of Nimrod in 1849 by Austen (later Sir) Henry Layard (1817–94), dating from *c.* 1100 BC. The oldest known tower bell is one in St Benedict Church, Rome, Italy dated 'anno domini millesimo sexagesimo IX (1069).

UK The fragile hand bell known as the Black or Iron Bell of St Patrick is dated *c.* AD 450. The oldest tower bell in Great Britain is one of 50 kg *1 cwt* at St Botolph, Hardham, Sussex, still in use and dated *ante* 1100. The oldest inscribed bell is the Gargate bell at Caversfield church, Oxon, which is dated *c.* 1200–1210. The oldest *dated* bell in England is one hanging in Lissett church, near Bridlington, Humberside discovered in October 1972 to bear the date MCCLIIII (1254).

Heaviest The Tsar Kolokol, cast by Russian brothers I.F. and M.I. Motorin on 25 Nov 1735 in Moscow, weighs 202 tonnes and measures 6·6 m *22 ft* in diameter, 6·14 m *20 ft* high and 60 cm *24 in* at its thickest point. The bell was cracked in a fire in 1737 and a fragment, weighing about 11·5 tonnes, was broken off. The bell has stood, unrung, on a platform in the Kremlin in Moscow since 1836 with the broken section alongside.

The heaviest bell still in use is the Mingun bell, weighing 92 tonnes with a diameter of 5·09 m *16 ft 8½ in* at the lip, in Mandalay, Myanmar (Burma). The bell is struck by a teak boom from the outside. It was cast at Mingun late in the reign of King Bodawpaya (1782–1819). The heaviest swinging bell is the Petersglocke in the south-west tower of

1781, and *Auld Lang Syne* (originally the Strathspey *I Fee'd a Lad at Michaelmass*), some words of which were written by Robert Burns (1759–96). *Happy Birthday* was sung in space by the *Apollo IX* astronauts on 8 Mar 1969.

Songwriters The most successful songwriters in terms of number one singles are John Lennon (1940–80) and Paul McCartney (b. 18 Jun 1942). McCartney is credited as writer on 32 number one hits in the US to Lennon's 26 (with 23 co-written), whereas Lennon authored 29 UK number ones to McCartney's 28 (25 co-written).

Earliest hymn There are over 950 000 Christian hymns in existence. The music and parts of the text of a hymn in the *Oxyrhynchus Papyri* from the 2nd century are the earliest known hymnody. The earliest exactly datable hymn is the *Heyr Himna Smiður (Hear, the Maker of Heaven)* from 1208 by the Icelandic bard and chieftain Kolbeinn Tumason (1173–1208).

Longest hymn The *Hora novissima tempora pessima sunt; vigilemus* by Bernard of Cluny (mid 12th century) runs to 2966 lines. The longest in English is *The Sands of Time are Sinking* by Anne Ross Cousin (*née* Cundell, 1824–1906), which has 152 lines, but only 32 lines appear in the Methodist Hymn Book.

Most prolific hymnists Frances (Fanny) Jane van Alstyne (1820–1915) of

Cologne Cathedral, Germany, cast in 1923 with a diameter of 3·40m *11ft 1¾in* weighing 25·4tonnes.

UK The heaviest bell hung in Great Britain is 'Great Paul' in the south-west tower of St Paul's Cathedral, London. Cast in 1881, it weighs 17tonnes, has a diameter of 2·9m *9ft 6½in* and sounds the note E-flat. 'Big Ben', the hour bell in the clock tower of the House of Commons, London was cast in 1858 and weighs 13·8tonnes. It is the most broadcast bell in the world and is note E.

Peals A ringing peal is defined as a diatonic 'ring' of five or more bells hung for full-circle change ringing. Of 5517 rings so hung, only 92 are outside the British Isles. Only one of these has more than 12 bells, namely St Martin's Church in Birmingham, W Mids, which has 16. The heaviest ring in the world is that of 13 bells cast in 1938–99 for the Anglican Cathedral in Liverpool, Merseyside. The total bell weight is 16·76tonnes, of which Emmanuel, the tenor bell note A, weighs 4170·8kg *82cwt 11lb*.

Largest carillon The largest carillon (minimum of 23 bells) is the Laura Spelman Rockefeller Memorial Carillon in Riverside Church, New York City, USA, with 74 bells weighing 103·6tonnes. The bourdon, giving the note lower C, weighs 18·6tonnes. Cast in England, it has a diameter of 3·09m *10ft 2in* and is the largest *tuned* bell in the world.

UK The carillon in St Nicholas Church, Aberdeen, Grampian consists of 48 bells weighing 25·8tonnes. The bourdon bell weighs 4·6tonnes and is the note G-sharp.

Bell ringing Eight bells have been rung to their full 'extent' (40320 unrepeated changes of Plain Bob Major) only once without relays. This took place in a bell foundry at Loughborough, Leics, beginning at 6:52a.m. on 27 Jul 1963 and ending at 12:50a.m. on 28 July, after 17hr 58min. The peal was composed by Kenneth Lewis of Altrincham, Manchester and the eight ringers were conducted by Robert B. Smith of Marple, Manchester. Theoretically it would take 37years 355days to ring 12 bells (maximus) to their full extent of 479001600 changes. The greatest number of peals

(minimum of 5000 changes, all in tower bells) rung in a year is 303, by Colin Turner of Abingdon, Oxon in 1989.

As at 1 Jan 1992 both Peter Border of Barford, Warks and John Mayne of St Albans, Herts had rung more than 2800 peals. George Symonds (1875–1974) of Ipswich, Suffolk was a regular bell-ringer for 89 years. He conducted a peal at the age of 97 and rang his last peal in 1973 at the age of 98. He is thus the oldest ringer ever to have conducted a rung a peal, and also the longest-serving ringer.

Instruments

Earliest piano The earliest pianoforte in existence is one built in Florence, Italy in 1720 by Bartolommeo Cristofori (1655–1731) of Padua, and now preserved in the Metropolitan Museum of Art, New York City, USA.

Grandest piano The grandest grand piano was one of 1·25tonnes and 3·55m *11ft 8in* in length made by Chas H. Challen & Son Ltd of London in 1935. The longest bass string measured 3·02m *9ft 11in*, with a tensile strength of 30tonnes.

Most expensive piano The highest price ever paid for a piano was $390000 at Sotheby Parke Bernet, New York, USA on 26 Mar 1980 for a Steinway grand of *c.* 1888 sold by the Martin Beck Theater. It was bought by a non-pianist.

Largest organ The largest and loudest musical instrument ever constructed is the now only partially functional Auditorium Organ in Atlantic City, New Jersey, USA. Completed in 1930, this heroic instrument had two consoles (one with seven manuals and another movable one with five), 1477 stop controls and 33112 pipes, ranging in tone from 4·7mm *⅓in* to the 19·5m *64ft* tone. It had the volume of 25 brass bands, with a range of seven octaves.

The world's largest fully functional organ is the six manual 30067 pipe Grand Court Organ installed in the Wanamaker Store, Philadelphia, Pennsylvania, USA in 1911 and enlarged between then and 1930. It has a 19·5m *64ft* tone gravissima pipe.

The world's largest church organ is that in Passau Cathedral, Germany. It was completed in 1928 by D. F. Steinmeyer & Co. and has 16000 pipes and five manuals.

The chapel organ at West Point US Military Academy, New York, USA has, since 1911, been expanded from 2406 to 18200 pipes.

UK The largest organ in Great Britain is that completed in Liverpool Anglican Cathedral on 18 Oct 1926, with two five-manual consoles and 9704 speaking pipes (originally 10936) ranging from tones 1·9 cm to 9·75 m ¾ in to 32 ft.

Loudest organ stop The Ophicleide stop of the Grand Great in the Solo Organ in the Atlantic City Auditorium (see above) is operated by a pressure of water 24 kPa *3½ lb/in²* and has a pure trumpet note of ear-splitting volume, more than six times the volume of the loudest locomotive whistles.

Largest pan pipes The world's largest pan pipes created by Simon Desorgher and Lawrence Casserley consist of five contra-bass pipes, each 100 mm in diameter with lengths of 4790 mm, 4160 mm, 3606 mm, 3104 mm and 2666 mm, respectively and five bass pipes of 50 mm diameter with lengths of 2395 mm, 2080 mm, 1803 mm, 1522 mm and 1333 mm. Their first public appearance was at Jubilee Gardens, London on 9 Jul 1988.

Most durable musicians The Romanian pianist Cella Delavrancea (1887–1991) gave her last public recital, receiving six encores, at the age of 103. Yiannis Pipis (b. 25 Nov 1889) of Nicosia, Cyprus has been a professional Folkloric violinist since 1912.

The world's oldest active musician is Jennie Newhouse (b. 12 Jul 1889) of High Bentham, N Yorks, who has been the regular organist at the church of St Boniface in Bentham since 1920.

Largest brass instrument The largest recorded brass instrument is a tuba standing 2·28 m *7½ ft* tall, with 11·8 m *39 ft* of tubing and a bell 1 m *3 ft 4 in* across. This contrabass tuba was constructed for a world tour by the band of American composer John Philip Sousa (1854–1932), *c.*

1896–98. It is now owned by a circus promoter in South Africa.

Largest stringed instrument The largest movable stringed instrument ever constructed was a pantaleon with 270 strings stretched over 4·6 m² *50 ft²* used by George Noel in 1767. The greatest number of musicians required to operate a single instrument was the six required to play the gigantic orchestrion, known as the Apollonican, built in 1816 and played until 1840.

Largest double bass A double bass measuring 4·26 m *14 ft* tall was built in 1924 in Ironia, New Jersey, USA by Arthur K. Ferris, allegedly on orders from the Archangel Gabriel. It weighed 590 kg *1301 lb* with a sound box 2·43 m *8 ft* across, and had leathern strings totalling 31·7 m *104 ft*. Its low notes could be felt rather than heard. Sixteen musicians from Blandford, Dorset played a double bass simultaneously (five fingering and eleven bowing) in a rendition of Strauss' *Perpetuum Mobile* at Blandford Town Hall on 6 Jun 1989.

Largest guitar The largest (and possibly the loudest) playable guitar in the world is 11·63 m *38 ft 2 in* tall, 4·87 m *16 ft* wide and weighs 446 kg *1865 lb*. Modelled on the Gibson 'Flying V', it was made by students of Shakamak High School in Jasonville, Indiana, USA. The instrument was unveiled on 17 May 1991 when, powered by six amplifiers, it was played simultaneously by six members of the school.

Most expensive guitar A Fender Stratocaster belonging to Jimi Hendrix (1942–70) was sold by his former drummer 'Mitch' Mitchell for £198 000 at Sotheby's, London on 25 Apr 1990.

Most valuable violin The highest price paid at auction for a violin, or any instrument, is £902 000 ($1·7 million) for the 1720 'Mendelssohn' Stradivarius, named after the German banking family who were descendants of the composer. It was sold to a mystery buyer at Christie's, London on 21 Nov 1990.

Most valuable 'cello The highest ever auction price for a violoncello is £682 000 paid at Sotheby's, London on 22 Jun 1988 for a Stradivarius known as

'The Cholmondeley', which was made in Cremona, Italy c. 1698.

Largest drum A drum with a 3·96m *13ft* diameter was built by the Supreme Drum Co., London and played at the Royal Festival Hall, London on 31 May 1987.

Largest drum kit A drum kit consisting of 112 pieces—88 drums, 18 cymbals, 4 hi-hats, 1 gong, 1 cowbell and various other assorted accessories—was made by Jeffrey Carlo of Brentwood, New York, USA in 1990.

Longest alphorn A 47m *154ft 8in* (excluding mouthpiece) long alphorn weighing 103kg *227lb* was completed by Swiss-born Peter Wutherich, of Boise, Idaho, USA in December 1989. The diameter at the bell is 62cm *24½in* and the sound takes 105·7 milliseconds to emerge from the bowl after entry into the mouthpiece.

Highest and lowest notes The extremes of orchestral instruments (excluding the organ) range between a handbell tuned to g^v (6272 cycles/sec) and the sub-contrabass clarinet, which can reach C_{11} or 16·4 cycles/sec. In 1873 a sub double bassoon able to reach $B_{111}\pm$ or 14·6 cycles/sec was constructed but no surviving specimen is known.

The extremes for the organ are g^{vi} (the sixth G above middle C) (12544 cycles/sec) and C_{111} (8·12 cycles/sec) obtainable from 1·9cm *¾in* and 19·5m *64ft* pipes respectively.

Orchestras

Oldest The first modern symphony orchestra—basically four sections consisting of woodwind, brass, percussion and bowed string instruments—was founded at the court of Duke Karl Theodor at Mannheim, Germany in 1743. The oldest existing symphony orchestra, the Gewandhaus Orchestra of Leipzig, Germany, was also established in 1743. Originally known as the Grosses Concert and later as the Liebhaber-Concerte, its current name dates from 1781.

Largest On 17 Jun 1872, Johann Strauss the younger (1825–99) conducted an orchestra of 987 pieces supported by a choir of 20 000, at the World Peace Jubilee in Boston, Massachusetts, USA.

Bottle orchestra

In an extraordinary display of oral campanology, the Brighton Bottle Orchestra—Terry Garoghan and Peter Miller—performed a musical medley on 444 miniature Gordon's gin bottles at the Brighton International Festival, E Sussex on 21 May 1991. It took 18 hours to tune the bottles, and about 10 times the normal rate of puff (90 breaths/min) to play them. Apparently there is no risk of intoxication, as the bottles are filled with water.

Orchestral instrument

The harp is the only solely finger-plucked instrument capable of creating enough sound to merit a regular place in a symphony orchestra. Tension in the strings can reach 1000lb and the sound board is often up to 10mm *0·4in* thick to withstand the strain.

Musical chairs

The largest game on record was one starting with 8238 participants, ending with Xu Chong Wei on the last chair, which was held at the Anglo-Chinese School, Singapore on 5 Aug 1989.

Drumming

Four hundred separate drums were played in 20·50 sec by Carl Williams at the Alexander Stadium, Birmingham, W Mids on 4 Oct 1992.

The number of first violinists was 400. On 14 Dec 1991 the 2000-piece 'Young People's Orchestra and Chorus of Mexico', consisting of 53 youth orchestras from Mexico plus musicians from Venezuela and the former USSR, gave a full classical concert conducted by Fernando Lozano and others at the Magdalena Mixhiuca Sports Centre, Mexico City.

Largest band The most massive band ever assembled was one of 20 100 bandsmen at the Ullevaal Stadium, Oslo, Norway from Norges Musikkorps Forbund bands on 28 Jun 1964.

One-man Rory Blackwell, aided by his double left-footed perpendicular percussion-pounder, plus his three-tier right-footed horizontal 22-pronged differential beater, and his 12-outlet bellow-powered horn-blower, played 108 different instruments (19 melody and 89 percussion) simultaneously in Dawlish, Devon on 29 May 1989. He also played 314 instruments in a single rendition in 1 min 23·07 sec, again at Dawlish, on 27 May 1985.

Marching band The largest marching band was one of 4524, including 1342 majorettes, under the direction of Danny Kaye (1913–87) at Dodger Stadium, Los Angeles, California, USA on 15 Apr 1985.

Musical march The longest recorded musical march was one of 75·2 km *46·7 miles*, by members of Showband Marum, a Dutch marching band, who walked in time from Assen to Marum, Netherlands on 9 May 1992. Of the 60 people who started, 52 completed the march, in 13 hr 50 min.

Conductors The Austrian Herbert von Karajan (1908–89), principal conductor of the Berlin Philharmonic Orchestra for 35 years before his retirement shortly before his death, was the most prolific conductor ever, having made over 800 recordings of all the major works. Von Karajan also conducted the Philharmonia Orchestra of London, the Vienna State Opera and La Scala Opera of Milan.

The longest-serving conductor was Dr Aloys Fleischmann (1910–92), who conducted the Cork Symphony Orchestra for 58 consecutive seasons, ending in 1991–92. Sir Georg Solti (b. 21 Oct 1912), the Hungarian-born principal conductor of the Chicago Symphony Orchestra, has won a record 31 Grammy awards for his recordings, with the orchestra itself winning 46. (⇨ also Grammy awards)

Largest choir Excluding 'sing alongs' by stadium crowds, the greatest choir is one of 60 000, which sang in unison as a finale of a choral contest among 160 000

participants in Breslau, Germany on 2 Aug 1937.

Estimating the size of audiences at open-air events where no admission is paid is often left to the police, media reporters, promoters and publicity agents. Estimates therefore vary widely and it is very difficult to check the accuracy of claims.

Classical An estimated record 800 000 attended a free open-air concert by the New York Philharmonic conducted by Zubin Mehta, on the Great Lawn of Central Park, New York, USA on 5 Jul 1986, as part of the Statue of Liberty Weekend.

Rock/pop festival The best claim is believed to be 725 000 for Steve Wozniak's 1983 US Festival in San Bernardino, California. The Woodstock Music and Art Fair held on 15–17 Aug 1969 at Bethel, New York, USA is thought to have attracted an audience of 300–500 000. The attendance at the 3rd Pop Festival at East Afton Farm, Freshwater, Isle of Wight, Hants on 30 Aug 1970 was claimed by its promoters, Fiery Creations, to be 400 000.

Solo performer The largest *paying* audience ever attracted by a solo performer was an estimated 180–184 000 in the Maracaña Stadium, Rio de Janeiro, Brazil to hear Paul McCartney (b. 1942) on 21 Apr 1990.

Jean-Michel Jarre, the *son et lumière* specialist, entertained an estimated audience of 2 million in Paris, France at a free concert on Bastille day (14 July) 1990.

Most successful tour The Rolling Stones 1989 'Steel Wheels' North American tour earned an estimated £185 million ($310 million) and was attended by 3·2 million people in 30 cities.

Wembley Stadium Michael Jackson sold out seven nights at Wembley Stadium, performing to a total audience of 504 000 on 14, 15, 16, 22, 23 Jul and 26, 27 Aug 1988.

Largest concert On 21 Jul 1990 Potsdamer Platz, straddling East and West Berlin, was the site of the largest single rock concert in terms of participants and organisation ever staged.

372

Fastest tour

As a finale to their 25th anniversary year, Status Quo played four major UK venues in under 12 hours on the 'Rock 'Til You Drop' tour on 21 Sep 1991. Starting in London, the tour moved to the International Arena in Sheffield, N Yorks, the SE&CC in Glasgow, Strathclyde and the NEC in Birmingham, W Mids and ended at Wembley Arena, London.

Roger Waters' production of Pink Floyd's *The Wall* involved 600 people performing on a stage measuring 168×25m *551 ×82ft* at its highest point. An estimated 200 000 people gathered for the building and demolition of a wall made of 2500 styrofoam blocks symbolizing the demise of the Berlin Wall.

Composers

Most prolific The most prolific composer was Georg Philipp Telemann (1681–1767) of Germany. He wrote 12 complete sets of services (one cantata every Sunday) for a year, 78 services for special occasions, 40 operas, 600 to 700 orchestral suites, 44 passions, plus concertos, sonatas and other chamber music. The most prolific symphonist was Johann Melchior Molter (*c.* 1695–1765) of Germany with over 170. Franz Joseph Haydn (1732–1809) of Austria wrote 108 numbered symphonies, many of which are regularly played today.

Longest symphony The longest single classical symphony is the orchestral symphony No. 3 in D minor by Gustav Mahler (1860–1911) of Austria. Composed in 1896, the work requires a contralto, a women's and a boys' choir, in addition to a full orchestra. A full performance requires 1 hr 40 min, of which the first movement alone takes between 30 and 36 min.

The Symphony No. 2 (the Gothic), composed from 1919–22 by William Havergal Brian (1876–1972), was played by over 800 performers (four brass bands) in the Victoria Hall, Hanley, Staffs

The spectacular sight of an estimated 2 million people at La Defense, Paris, France for Jean-Michel Jarre's free *son et lumière* show on Bastille Day 1990.
(Photo: Sygma/Jean Jean)

Most Grammy awards

An all-time record 31 awards to an individual (including a special Trustees' award presented in 1967) have been won since 1958 by the British conductor, Sir Georg Solti (b. Budapest, Hungary, 21 Oct 1912).

The Chicago Symphony Orchestra, whose principal conductor is Sir Georg Solti, has won 46 awards.

The greatest number won in a year is eight by Michael Jackson in 1984.

Best-selling albums

The best-selling classical album is *In Concert*, with global sales of 5 million copies to date. It was recorded by José Carreras, Placido Domingo and Luciano Pavarotti at the 1990 World Cup Finals in Rome, Italy.

on 21 May 1978 (conductor Trevor Stokes). A recent broadcast required 1hr 45½ min. Brian wrote an even vaster work based on Shelley's 'Prometheus Unbound' lasting 4hr 11min, but the full score has been missing since 1961. The symphony *Victory at Sea*, written by Richard Rodgers for the documentary film of the same name and arranged by Robert Russell Bennett for NBC TV in 1952, lasted 13hours.

Longest piano composition
The longest continuous non-repetitive piano piece ever published has been *The Well-Tuned Piano* by La Monte Young, first presented by the Dia Art Foundation at the Concert Hall, Harrison St, New York, USA on 28 Feb 1980. The piece lasted 4hr 12min 10sec. *Symphonic Variations*, composed in the 1930s for piano and orchestra by the British-born Kaikhosru Shapurji Sorabji (1892–1988) on 500 pages of close manuscript in three volumes, would last for six hours at the prescribed tempo.

Longest The longest of commonly performed operas is *Die Meistersinger von Nürnberg* by Wilhelm Richard Wagner (1813–83) of Germany. A normal uncut version as performed by the Sadler's Wells company between 24 Aug and 19 Sep 1968 entailed 5hr 15min of music. *The Heretics* by the Hungarian-American Gabriel von Wayditch (1888–1969) is orchestrated for 110 pieces and lasts 8½hr.

Shortest The shortest opera published is *The Sands of Time* by Simon Rees and Peter Reynolds, first performed by Rhian Owen and Dominic Burns on 27 Mar 1993 at The Hayes, Cardiff, S Glam and lasting for 4min 9sec.

Longest aria The longest single aria, in the sense of an operatic solo, is Brünnhilde's immolation scene in Wagner's *Götterdämmerung*, a well-known recording of which has been timed at 14min 46sec precisely.

Youngest opera singers Ginetta Gloria La Bianca, born in Buffalo, New York, USA on 12 May 1934, sang Rosina in *The Barber of Seville* at the Teatro

Longest silence

The longest interval between the known composition of a major composer and its performance in the manner intended is from 3 Mar 1791 until 9 Oct 1982 (over 191 years), in the case of Mozart's *Organ Piece for a Clock*, a fugue fantasy in F minor (K 608), arranged by the organ builders Wm Hill & Son and Norman & Beard Ltd at Glyndebourne, E Sussex.

Most recordings

In the largest ever recording project, 180 compact discs containing the complete set of authenticated works by Mozart were released by Philips Classics in 1990–91 to commemorate the bicentenary of the composer's death. The complete set comprises over 200 hours of music and would occupy 2m 6½ft of shelving.

Longest operatic encore

The listed in the *Concise Oxford Dictionary of Opera*, was of the entire opera Cimarosa's *Il Matrimonio Segreto* at its première in 1792. This was at the command of the Austro-Hungarian Emperor Leopold II (reigned 1790–92).

dell'Opera, Rome, Italy on 8 May 1950 aged 15 years 361 days, having appeared as Gilda in *Rigoletto* at Velletri 45 days earlier on 24 March.

Oldest opera singers

The tenor Giovanni Martinelli sang the part of Emperor Altoum in *Turandot* in Seattle, Washington, USA on 4 Feb 1967 when aged 81. Danshi Toyotake (b. Yoshie Yokota, 1891–1989) of Hyogo, Japan sang *Musume Gidayu* (traditional Japanese narrative) for 91 years from the age of seven. Her professional career spanned 81 years.

Most curtain calls

On 24 Feb 1988 Luciano Pavarotti (b. 12 Oct 1935) received 165 curtain calls and was applauded for 1 hr 7 min after singing the part of Nemorino in Gaetano Donizetti's *L'elisir d'amore* at the Deutsche Oper in Berlin, Germany.

Placido Domingo (b. 21 Jan 1941) was applauded for 1 hr 20 min through 101 curtain calls after a performance of *Othello* at the Vienna Staatsoper on 30 Jul 1991.

Largest opera houses

The Metropolitan Opera House at the Lincoln Center, New York City, USA, completed in September 1966 at a cost of $45·7 million, has a seating and standing room capacity of 4065, with seating for 3800 in the 137m *451ft* deep auditorium. The stage is 70m *230ft* wide and 45m *148ft* deep.

The tallest opera house is housed in a 42-storey building on Wacker Drive in Chicago, Illinois, USA. The Teatro della Scala (La Scala) in Milan, Italy shares with the Bolshoi Theatre in Moscow, Russia the most tiers, namely six.

Ballet

Fastest 'entrechat douze'

In the *entrechat* (a vertical spring from the fifth position with the legs extended criss-crossing at the lower calf), the starting and finishing position each count as one, such that in an *entrechat douze* there are 5 crossings and uncrossings. This was performed by Wayne Sleep (b. 17 Jul 1948) for the BBC *Record Breakers* programme on 7 Jan 1973. He was in the air for 0·71 sec.

Grands jetés

On 28 Nov 1988 Wayne Sleep completed 158 *grands jetés* along Dunston Staiths, Gateshead, Tyne & Wear in 2 min.

Most turns

The greatest number of spins called for in classical ballet choreography is 32 *fouettés rond de jambe en tournant* in *Swan Lake* by Pyotr Ilyich Chaykovskiy (Tchaikovsky) (1840–93). Delia Gray (b. 30 Oct 1975) of Bishop's Stortford, Herts achieved 166 such turns

---

Largest Contracts

Michael Jackson	$890 million* (Sony, March 1991)
Prince	$100 million (Time Warner, September 1992)
Paul McCartney	$65 million (£100)(Capitol–EMI, 1993)
Madonna	$60 million (Time Warner, 1992)
Barbra Streisand	$40–60 million (Sony, December 1992)
Elton John/Bernie Taupin	$41 million (Time Warner, November 1992)
Rolling Stones	$30–40 million (Virgin, November 1991)
Mötley Crüe	+$35 million (Elektra Records)
Janet Jackson	±$32–35 million (Virgin, March 1991)
Aerosmith	+$30 million (Columbia Records)

*Prospective earnings of $1 billion were reported.

during the Harlow Ballet School's summer workshop at The Playhouse, Harlow, Essex on 2 Jun 1991.

Most curtain calls The greatest recorded number of curtain calls ever received is 89 by Dame Margot Fonteyn de Arias (*née* Margaret Evelyn Hookham (1919–91) and Rudolf Hametovich Nureyev (1938–93) after a performance of *Swan Lake* at the Vienna Staatsoper, Austria in October 1964.

Largest cast The largest number of ballet dancers used in a production in Britain has been 2000 in the London Coster Ballet of 1962, directed by Lillian Rowley, at the Royal Albert Hall, London.

Recorded Sound

Origins The gramophone (phonograph) was first conceived by Charles Cros (1842–88), a French poet and scientist, who described his idea in sealed papers deposited in the French Academy of Sciences on 30 Apr 1877. However, a practical device was first achieved by Thomas Alva Edison (US, 1847–1931). The first successful wax cylinder machine was on 4–6 Dec 1877 constructed by his mechanic, John Kruesi, demonstrated on 7 Dec and patented on 19 Feb 1878. The horizontal disc was introduced by Emile Berliner (1851–1929) and first demonstrated in Philadelphia on 18 May 1888.

Earliest records The oldest existing recording was made in 1878 by Augustus Stroh, but it remains on the mandrel of his machine and has never been played. The oldest playable record is believed to be an engraved metal cylinder made by Frank Lambert in 1878 or 1879 and voicing the hours on the clock. The recording is owned by Aaron Cramer of New York City, USA.

Tape recording Magnetic recording was invented by Valdemar Poulsen (1869–1942) of Denmark with his steel wire Telegraphone in 1898 (US Pat. No. 661619). Fritz Pfleumer (German Patent 500900) introduced tape in 1928. Tapes were first used at the Blattner Studios, Elstree, Herts in 1929. Plastic tapes were devised by BASF of Germany in 1932–35, but not generally marketed until 1950 by Recording Associates of New York. In April 1983 Olympic Optical Industry Co. of Japan marketed a micro-cassette recorder measuring 10·7 × 5·1 × 0·4 cm *4⅕ × 2 × ½ in* and weighing 125 g *4·4 oz.*

Smallest cassette The NT digital cassette made by the Sony Corporation of Japan for use in dictating machines measures just 30×21×5 mm *1⅕×⅘×⅕ in.*

Smallest functional record Six titles of 33·3 mm *1$\frac{5}{16}$ in* diameter were recorded by HMV's studio at Hayes, Middx on 26 Jan 1923 for Queen Mary's Dolls' House. Some 92 000 of these miniature records were pressed including 35 000 of *God Save The King* (Bb 2439).

Most successful solo recording artist No independently audited figures have ever been published for Elvis Aron Presley (1935–77) but he has had over 170 major hit singles and over 80 top-selling albums since 1956.

On 9 Jun 1960 the Hollywood Chamber of Commerce presented Harry Lillis (alias Bing) Crosby Jr (1904–77) with a platinum disc to commemorate the alleged sale of 200 million records from the 2600 singles and 125 albums he had recorded. On 15 Sep 1970 he received a second platinum disc when Decca claimed sales of 300 650 000 discs. No independently audited figures of his global lifetime sales have ever been published and these figures are considered exaggerated.

Most successful group The Beatles have amassed the greatest sales for any group. The band, from Liverpool, Merseyside, comprised George Harrison (b. 25 Feb 1943), John Ono (formerly John Winston) Lennon (b. 9 Oct 1940–killed 8 Dec 1980), James Paul McCartney (b. 18 Jun 1942) and Richard Starkey, *alias* Ringo Starr (b. 7 Jul 1940). All-time sales have been estimated by EMI at over 1 billion discs and tapes. All four ex-Beatles sold many million further records as solo artists.

Earliest golden discs The first actual golden disc was one sprayed by RCA Victor for the US trombonist and bandleader Alton 'Glenn' Miller (1904–44)

Diana Ross, the most successful female chart singer, with over 50 UK solo and accompanied hit singles, some 35 albums and 12 No. 1 US singles. In 1993 she celebrates 30 years in showbusiness.

(Photo: Rogers and Cowan International)

for his *Chattanooga Choo Choo* on 10 Feb 1942.

The first actual piece eventually to aggregate a total sale of a million copies was of performances by Enrico Caruso (b. Naples, Italy, 1873, d. 2 Aug 1921) of the aria *'Vesti la giubba'* ('On with the Motley') from the opera *I Pagliacci* by Ruggiero Leoncavallo (1858–1919), the earliest version of which was recorded with piano on 12 Nov 1902. The first single recording to surpass the million

mark was Alma Gluck's *Carry Me Back to Old Virginny* on the Red Seal Victor label on the 12 in *30·48 cm* single faced (later backed) record No. 74420.

Most golden discs The only *audited* measure of gold, platinum and multiplatinum singles and albums within the United States is certification by the Recording Industry Association of America (RIAA), introduced on 14 Mar 1958.

The Rolling Stones have 55 (34 gold, 15 platinum, 6 multiplatinum (2 million or more), the most for any group. The group with the most multiplatinum albums is the Beatles with 11.

In August 1992, following new audit figures, the estate of Elvis Presley was presented with 110 gold and platinum records, making him the most certified

Most UK Hit Singles In One Year

ELVIS PRESLEY 1957			THE WEDDING PRESENT 1992		
Date	Title	Chart position	Chart position	Title	Date
Feb	Mystery Train	25	26	Blue Eyes	Jan
Mar	Rip It Up	27	20	Go-go Dancer	Feb
May	Too Much	6	14	Three	Mar
Jun	All Shook Up	*24/1	14	Silver Shorts	Apr
Jul	Teddy Bear	3	10	Come Play With Me	May
Aug	Paralysed	8	16	California	Jun
Oct	Party	2	22	Flying Saucer	Jul
Oct	Got A Lot o' Lovin' To Do	17	19	Boing!	Aug
Nov	Loving You	24	17	Love Slave	Sep
Nov	Trying To Get To You	16	17	Sticky	Oct
Nov	Lawdy Miss Clawdy	15	23	Queen of Outer Space	Nov
Nov	Santa Bring My Baby Back To Me	7	25	No Christmas	Dec

Reached number one after re-release.

The Wedding present had 12 new hits in the year, a record for any act. However, unlike Presley, who spent a total of 108 weeks in the chart in 1957, five of The Wedding Present's hits were 'one week wonders' and none of them stayed more than two weeks.

Phonographic identification

Dr Arthur B. Lintgen (b. 1932) of Rydal, Pennsylvania, USA, has an as yet unique and proven ability to identify the music on phonograph records purely by visual inspection without hearing a note.

recording artist ever. The female solo artist to receive the most awards is Barbra Streisand, with 56 (7 gold singles, 30 gold albums and 19 platinum albums).

The first platinum album was awarded to the Eagles for *Greatest Hits, 1971–75* in 1976. The group Chicago holds the record for most platinum albums, with 17. Barbra Streisand holds the record for a solo artist, with 19, and the record for most multiplatinum, with seven. Paul McCartney holds the record for a male solo artist, with 12, while Billy Joel holds the record for the most multiplatinum albums for an individual, with eight.

Biggest sellers (Singles) The biggest-selling record to date is *White Christmas* written by Irving Berlin (b. Israel Bailin, 1888–1989) and recorded by Bing Crosby on 29 May 1942. It was announced in 1987 that North American sales alone reached 170884207 copies by 30 Jun 1987.

The highest claim for any 'pop' record is an unaudited 25 million for *Rock Around the Clock*, copyright in 1953 by James E. Myers under the name Jimmy DeKnight and the late Max C. Freedmann and recorded on 12 Apr 1954 by Bill Haley (1927–1981) and his Comets.

Record shop

HMV opened the world's largest record store at 150 Oxford Street, London on 24 Oct 1986. Its trading area measures $3408\,m^2$ $36684\,ft^2$.

Fastest rapper

Rebel X.D. of Chicago, Illinois, USA rapped 674 syllables in 54·9sec at the Hair Bear Recording Studio, Alsip, Illinois on 27 Aug 1992.

UK The top-selling British single is *I Want to Hold Your Hand* by The Beatles, released in 1963, with world sales of over 13 million. The top-selling single in the UK is *Do They Know It's Christmas*, written and produced by Bob Geldof and Midge Ure and recorded by Band Aid in 1984, with sales of 3·6 million by May 1987 and a further 8·1 million world-wide. The profits went to the Ethiopian Famine Relief Fund.

Biggest sellers (Albums) The best-selling album of all time is *Thriller* by Michael Jackson (b. 29 Aug 1958), with global sales of over 47 million copies to date. The best-selling album by a group is Fleetwood Mac's *Rumours* with over 21 million sales to May 1990.

The best selling album by a British group is *Dark Side of the Moon* by Pink Floyd with sales audited at 19·5 million to December 1986. The best-selling album in Britain is *Sgt Pepper's Lonely Hearts Club Band* by The Beatles, with an 'official' figure of 4·25 million sales since its release in June 1967.

Whitney Houston by Whitney Houston, released in 1985 and with sales of over 14 million copies (including over 9 million in the US, 1 million in the UK and a further million in Canada), is the best-selling debut album of all time.

Soundtrack The best-selling movie soundtrack is *Saturday Night Fever*, with sales of over 26·5 million to May 1987.

The charts (UK Singles) Singles record charts were first published in Britain on 14 Nov 1952 by *New Musical Express*. *I Believe* by Frankie Laine (b. 30 Mar 1913) held the No. 1 position for 18 weeks (non-consecutive) from April 1953. Bryan Adams (b. 5 Nov 1959) spent a record 16 consecutive weeks at No. 1 with *(Everything I Do) I Do It For You*, taken from the film *Robin Hood: Prince of Thieves*. The run ended at the end of October 1991.

The longest stay is 122 weeks for *My Way* by Francis Albert Sinatra (b. 12 Dec 1915) in nine separate runs from 2 Apr 1969 to 1 Jan 1972. The record for most consecutive weeks on the chart is 56 weeks for Engelbert Humperdinck's *Release Me*, from 26 Jan 1967.

The Beatles and Elvis Presley hold the record for the most No. 1 hits with 17 each, with Presley also having an overall record 109 hits in the UK singles chart from May 1956 to date and the longest time on the charts, at 1145 weeks.

Cliff Richard (b. 14 Oct 1940) holds the record for the most hit singles, with 110 to November 1992.

The most successful female vocalist to feature in the British charts is Diana Ross (b. Detroit, Michigan, USA, 26 Mar 1944), with some 51 solo hits. She has also had another 22 hits with the Supremes (Mary Wilson and Florence Ballard) until her departure in 1970, plus several other hit recordings with singers such as Marvin Gaye, Michael Jackson, Smokey Robinson and Stevie Wonder.

The charts (UK Albums) The first British album chart was published on 8 Nov 1958 by Melody Maker.

The first No. 1 LP was the film soundtrack *South Pacific*, which held the position for a record 70 consecutive weeks, eventually achieving a record 115 weeks at No. 1.

The album with the most total weeks on chart is *Rumours* by Fleetwood Mac with 433 weeks by December 1991. The recording of Vivaldi's *Four Seasons* by the English Chamber Orchestra directed by Nigel Kennedy had topped the classical chart for over one year since its release on 25 Sep 1989.

The Beatles have had most the No.1 albums with 12, and Elvis Presley the most hit albums, a total of 91.

Kylie Minogue (b. 28 May 1968), whose debut album *Kylie* topped the chart in July 1988, holds the record for the best-ever start to a singles chart career, with her first 10 singles reaching the Top 5.

The charts (US Singles) Singles record charts were first published by *Billboard* on 20 Jul 1940, when the No. 1 was *I'll Never Smile Again* by Tommy Dorsey (1905–56). *Near You* by Francis Craig topped the chart for 17 weeks in 1947.

The Beatles have had the most No. 1 hits, with 20. Elvis Presley has had the most hit singles on *Billboard* Hot 100, namely 149 from 1956 to May 1990.

Bing Crosby's *White Christmas* spent a total of 72 weeks in the chart between 1942 and 1962, while *Tainted Love* by Soft Cell stayed on the chart for 43 *consecutive* weeks from January 1982.

The charts (US Albums) *Billboard* first published an album chart on 15 Mar 1945 when the No. 1 was *King Cole Trio* featuring Nat 'King' Cole (1919–65). The soundtrack *South Pacific* was No. 1 for 69 weeks (non-consecutive) from May 1949. *Dark Side of the Moon* by Pink Floyd enjoyed 730 weeks on the *Billboard* charts to April 1989.

The Beatles had the most No. 1s (15), Elvis Presley was the most successful soloist, with nine No. 1 albums. Elvis Presley also had the most hit albums (94 from 1956 to April 1989). The best-selling female singer of all time, with the most No. 1 albums (6), and most hit albums (40 between 1963 and April 1989), is Barbra Streisand. (⇔ Most golden discs)

Fastest-selling The fastest-selling non-pop record of all time is *John Fitzgerald Kennedy—A Memorial Album* (Premium Albums), recorded on 22 Nov 1963, the day of President Kennedy's assassination, which sold 4 million at 99 cents in six days (7–12 Dec 1963). The fastest-selling British record is the Beatles' double album *The Beatles* (Apple) with 'nearly 2 million' sold in its first week in November 1968.

Advance sales The greatest advance sale for a single world-wide is 2·1 million for *Can't Buy Me Love* by the Beatles, released on 21 Mar 1964. The UK record for advance sales of an album is 1·1 million for *Welcome to the Pleasure Dome*, the debut album by Frankie Goes To Hollywood, released in 1984.

Most song titles—DJ challenge Disc-jockey John Murray of Kirkcaldy, Fife played 37 song titles from two decks in two minutes on the BBC Record Breakers programme broadcast on 16 Nov 1990.

Compact discs Developed jointly by Philips and Sony in 1978 and introduced in 1982, the compact disc (CD) increasingly challenges the LP and cassette as a recording medium. The first CD to sell a million copies world-wide was Dire

Straits' *Brothers in Arms* in 1986. It subsequently topped a million sales in Europe alone including over 250000 in Britain.

Dancing

Marathon dancing must be distinguished from dancing mania, or tarantism, which is a pathological condition. The worst outbreak of the latter was at Aachen, Germany in July 1374, when hordes of men and women broke into a frenzied and compulsive choreomania in the streets. It lasted for many hours until injury or complete exhaustion ensued.

Largest and longest dances An estimated 30 000 people took part in a Madison/Electric Slide line dance held during the 1991 Comin' Home African American Holiday Celebration in Columbus, Ohio, USA on 12 Jul 1991.

The most taxing marathon dance staged as a public spectacle was one by Mike Ritof and Edith Boudreaux, who logged 5148 hr 28½ min to win $2000 at Chicago's Merry Garden Ballroom, Belmont and Sheffield, Illinois, USA from 29 Aug 1930 to 1 Apr 1931. Rest periods were progressively cut from 20 to 10 to 5 to nil minutes per hour, with 10-inch steps and a maximum of 15 seconds for closure of eyes.

Cathy McConochie led an ensemble of 18 dancers through the streets of Sacramento, California, USA on 30 May 1992 during the Sacramento Children's Festival in a choreographed routine, covering a distance of 14·2km *8·8 miles*.

Ballroom The world's most successful professional ballroom dancing champions have been Bill and Bobbie Irvine, who won 13 world titles between 1960 and 1968. The oldest competitive ballroom dancer was Albert J. Sylvester (1889–1989) of Corsham, Wilts, who retired at the age of 94.

Conga The longest recorded conga was the Miami Super Conga, held in conjunction with Calle Ocho—a party to which Cuban-Americans invite the rest of Miami for a celebration of life together. Held on 13 Mar 1988, the conga consisted of 119986 people.

Dancing dragon
The longest dancing dragon, created by South Yorkshire Cubscouts, measured 1061 m *3481ft* from the end of its tongue to the tip of its tail. A total of 1118 people brought the dragon to life, making it dance for 5 minutes at the Don Valley stadium, Sheffield, S Yorks on 27 Jun 1992.

Square dance calling
Alan Covacic called for 26 hr 2 min for the Wheelers and Dealers Square Dance Club at RAF Halton, Aylesbury, Bucks from 18–19 Nov 1988.

The longest in Britain comprised a 'snake' of 8659 people from the South-Eastern Region of the Camping and Caravanning Club of Great Britain and Ireland. It took place on 4 Sep 1982 at Brands Hatch, Kent.

Country dancing The largest genuine Scottish country dance ever staged was a 512-some reel, held in Toronto, Canada on 17 Aug 1991 and organized by the Toronto branch of the Royal Scottish Country Dance Society.

Flamenco The fastest flamenco dancer ever measured is Solero de Jerez, aged 17, who in Brisbane, Australia in September 1967 attained 16 heel taps per second, in an electrifying routine.

Limbo The lowest height for a bar (flaming) under which a limbo dancer has passed is 15·25 cm *6 in* off the floor, by Dennis Walston, alias King Limbo, at Kent, Washington State, USA on 2 Mar 1991.

Junior J. Renaud (b. 7 Jun 1954) became the first Official World Limbo Champion at the inaugural International Limbo Competition on 19 Feb 1974 at Port of Spain, Trinidad.

The record for a performer on roller skates is 13 cm *5⅛ in*, achieved by Amitesh Purohit at the National Sub-Junior School Championships held at Indore, Madhya Pradesh, India on 19 Jul 1991.

Tap The fastest *rate* ever measured for tap dancing is 32 taps per second by Stephen Gare of Sutton Coldfield, W Mids, at the Grand Hotel, Birmingham, W Mids on 28 Mar 1990.

Roy Castle, host of the BBC TV *Record Breakers* programme, achieved one million taps in 23hr 44min at the Guinness World of Records exhibition, London on 31 Oct–1 Nov 1985.

The greatest-ever assemblage of tap dancers in a single routine numbered 6008 outside Macy's Store in New York City, USA on 23 Aug 1992.

Theatre

Oldest Theatre in Europe has its origins in Greek drama performed in honour of a god, usually Dionysus, and a small theatre was built on several sites by the 5th century BC.

Oldest indoor theatre The oldest indoor theatre in the world is the Teatro Olimpico in Vicenza, Italy. Designed in the Roman style by Andrea di Pietro, alias Palladio (1508–80), it was begun three months before his death and finished by his pupil Vicenzo Scamozzi (1552–1616) in 1583. It is preserved today in its original form.

UK The earliest London theatre was James Burbage's 'The Theatre', built in 1576 near Finsbury Fields, London.

The oldest theatre still in use in Great Britain is The Royal in Bristol, Avon. The foundation stone was laid on 30 Nov 1764, and the theatre was opened on 30 May 1766 with a 'Concert of Musick and a Specimen of Rhetorick'. The City Varieties Music Hall in Leeds, W Yorks was a singing room in 1762 and so claims to outdate the Theatre Royal. Actors had the legal status of rogues and vagabonds until the passing of the Vagrancy Act in 1824.

The oldest amateur dramatic society is the Old Stagers, inaugurated in Canterbury, Kent in 1841. They have performed in every year except the years of World Wars I and II.

Largest The world's largest building used for theatre is the National People's Congress Building (*Ren min da hui tang*) on the west side of Tiananmen Square, Beijing, China. It was completed in 1959 and covers an area of 5·2ha *12·9 acres*. The theatre seats 10000 and is occasionally used as such, as in 1964 for the play *The East is Red*. The most capacious purpose-built theatre is the Perth Entertainment Centre, Western Australia, with 8500 seats and a main stage measuring 21·3 × 13·7m *70 × 45ft*. It was opened on 26 Dec 1974.

Smallest The world's smallest regularly operated professional theatre is the Piccolo in Juliusstrasse, Hamburg, Germany. It was founded in 1970 and has a maximum capacity of 30 seats.

Largest amphitheatre The Flavian amphitheatre or Colosseum of Rome, Italy, completed in AD 80, covers 2ha *5acres* and has a capacity of 87000. It has a maximum length of 187m *612ft* and a maximum width of 175m *515ft*.

Largest stage The world's largest stage is in the Ziegfeld Room in Reno, Nevada, USA with a 53·6m *176ft* passerelle, three main lifts each capable of raising 1200 show girls (65·3tonnes), two 19·1m *62½ft* circumference turntables and 800 spotlights.

Longest runs The longest continuous run of any show in the world is *The Mousetrap* by Dame Agatha Christie (1890–1976), which opened on 25 Nov 1952 at the Ambassadors Theatre, London (capacity 453) and moved after 8862 performances to the St Martin's Theatre next door on 25 Mar 1974. The 16000th performance was on 6 May 1991, and the box office has grossed £20 million from more than 9 million attenders. The Vicksburg Theater Guild, Mississippi, USA has been playing *Gold in the Hills* by J. Frank Davis discontinuously but every season since 1936.

Revue The greatest number of performances of any theatrical presentation is 47250 (to April 1986) for *The Golden Horseshoe Revue*, a show staged at Disneyland Park, Anaheim, California, USA from 16 Jul 1955 to 12 Oct 1986. It was seen by 16 million people.

Broadway The musical *A Chorus Line* opened on 25 Jul 1975 and closed on 28 Apr 1990 after a record run of almost 15

Most ardent theatre-goers

Dr H. Howard Hughes (b. 1902), Prof. Emeritus of Texas Wesleyan College, Fort Worth, Texas, USA attended 6136 shows in the period 1956–87.

Britain's leading 'first nighter' Edward Sutro (1900–78) saw 3000 first-night productions from 1916–56 and possibly more than 5000 shows in his 60 years of theatre-going. The highest precisely recorded number of theatre attendances in Britain is 3687 shows in 33 years from 28 Mar 1953 until his death on 10 Sep 1986 by John Iles of Salisbury, Wilts.

years and 6137 performances. It was created by Michael Bennet (1943–87).

Musical shows The off-Broadway musical show *The Fantasticks* by Tom Jones and Harvey Schmidt opened on 3 May 1960, and the total number of performances to 5 May 1993 is 13 680 at the Sullivan Street Playhouse, Greenwich Village, New York, USA.

UK The longest-running musical show performed in Britain was *The Black and White Minstrel Show*, later *Magic of the Minstrels*. The aggregate but discontinuous number of performances was 6464 with a total attendance of 7 794 552. The show opened at the Victoria Palace, London on 25 May 1962 and closed on 4 Nov 1972. It reopened for a season in June 1973 at the New Victoria and finally closed on 8 Dec 1973.

The longest running West End musical is *Cats* which has been playing at the New London Theatre, Drury Lane since 12 May 1981. The aggregate box office gross is estimated at over £250 million.

Comedy The longest-running comedy in Britain was *No Sex Please We're British*, written by Anthony Marriott and Alistair Foot and presented by John Gale. It opened at the Strand Theatre on 3 Jun 1971, transferred to the Duchess Theatre on 2 Aug 1986 and finally ended on 5 Sep 1987 after 17 years and 6761

performances. It was directed by Allan Davis throughout its run.

Shortest runs The shortest theatrical run on record was of *The Intimate Revue* at the Duchess Theatre, London, on 11 Mar 1930. Anything which could go wrong did. With scene changes taking up to 20 min apiece, the management scrapped seven scenes to get the finale on before midnight. The run was described as 'half a performance'.

Greatest loss The largest loss sustained by a theatrical show was borne by the American producers of the Royal Shakespeare Company's musical *Carrie*, which closed after five performances on Broadway on 17 May 1988 at a cost of $7 million.

King, the musical about Martin Luther King, lost £3 million in a six-week run ending on 2 Jun 1990, equalling the London record losses of *Ziegfeld* in 1988.

One-man shows The longest run of one-man shows is 849, by Victor Borge (b. Copenhagen, 3 Jan 1909) in *Comedy in Music* from 2 Oct 1953 to 21 Jan 1956 at the Golden Theater, Broadway, New York City, USA.

The world aggregate record for one-man shows is 1700 performances of *Brief Lives* by Roy Dotrice (b. Guernsey, 26 May 1923), including 400 straight at the

---

Gurning

The only gurner to have won six national titles is Ron Looney of Egremont, Cumbria, from 1978–83.

Magician, fastest

Eldon D. Wigton, alias Dr Eldoonie, performed 225 different tricks in 2 min at Kilbourne, Ohio, USA on 21 Apr 1991.

Gladiatorial combat

Emperor Trajan of Rome (AD 98–117) staged a display involving 4941 pairs of gladiators over 117 days. Publius Ostorius, a freedman, survived 51 combats in Pompeii.

THE GUINNESS TIMES REVIEW

17th May 1993

Zero Attendance at First Night

It's a good thing nobody's turned up - I've forgotten my lines!

In these recessionary times with shows facing early closure and large losses, we reflect on the unfortunate case of the play *Bag*, described as 'an unusual comedy', which opened to a completely empty house at the Grantham Leisure Centre on 24 Nov 1983. Things did, however, improve for the second of its two performances the following night when a small audience was in attendance, presumably out of curiosity.

Ten years on the organizers, Grantham Live Productions, are still at a loss to explain the underwhelming enthusiasm as, although the miserable weather was certainly a factor, it could not be totally to blame.

The production, written by Bryony Lavery and directed by Michele Frankel, included among its cast of five a youthful Josie Lawrence, who, unhindered by distractions such as audiences in her formative years, now features regularly on Channel 4's *Whose Line Is It Anyway?*

Mayfair Theatre, London ending on 20 Jul 1974. He was on stage for more than 2½ hr per performance of this 17th-century monologue and required 3 hr for make-up and 1 hr for removal of make-up, so aggregating 40 weeks in the chair.

Most durable performers Kanmi Fujiyama (b. 1929) played the lead role in 10 288 performances by the comedy company Sochiku Shikigeki from November 1966 to June 1983.

UK David Raven played Major Metcalfe in *The Mousetrap* on 4575 occasions between 22 Jul 1957 and 23 Nov 1968. Dame Anna Neagle (1904–86) played the lead role in *Charlie Girl* at the Adelphi Theatre, London for 2062 of 2202 performances between 15 Dec 1965 and 27 Mar 1971. She played the role a further 327 times in 327 performances in Australasia.

Jack Howarth (1896–1984) was an actor on the stage and later in television for 76 years from 1907 until his last appearance after 23 years as Albert Tatlock in *Coronation Street* on 25 Jan 1984. Frances Etheridge has played Lizzie, the housekeeper, in *Gold in the Hills* more than 660 times over a span of 47 years since 1936. (⬦ Longest runs)

Advance sales The musical *Miss Saigon*, produced by Cameron Mackintosh and starring Jonathan Pryce and Lea Salonga, opened on Broadway in April 1991 after generating record advance sales of $36 million.

Most roles The greatest recorded number of theatrical, film and television roles is 3385 since 1951 by Jan Leighton of New York City, USA.

Theatrical roles Kanzaburo Nakamura (b. July 1909) has performed in 806 Kabuki titles from November 1926 to January 1987. As each title in this classical Japanese theatrical form lasts 25 days, he has therefore played 20 150 performances.

Shakespeare The longest of the 37 plays written by William Shakespeare (1564–1616) is *Hamlet* (1604), comprising 4042 lines and 29 551 words. Of Shakespeare's 1277 speaking parts, the longest is that of Hamlet, at 1569 lines and 11 610 words.

Longest chorus line The longest chorus line in performing history numbered up to 120 in some of the early Ziegfeld's Follies. In the finale of *A Chorus Line* on the night of 29 Sep 1983, when it broke the record as the longest-running Broadway show ever, 332 top-hatted 'strutters' performed on stage.

On 28 Mar 1992 at the Swan Centre, Eastleigh 543 members of the cast of *Showtime News*, a major production by Hampshire West Girl Guides, performed a routine choreographed by professional dancer Sally Horsley.

Arts festival The world's largest arts festival is the annual Edinburgh Festival Fringe (instituted in 1947). In 1992, its record year, 540 groups gave 12 132 performances of 1103 shows between 16 August and 5 September. Prof. Gerald Berkowitz of Northern Illinois University attended a record 145 separate performances at the 1979 Festival between 15 August and 8 September.

Fashion shows The greatest distance covered by a model on a catwalk is 133·7 km *83·1 miles* by Eddie Warke at Parke's Hotel, Dublin, Republic of Ireland from

19–21 Sep 1983. The record by female models is 114·4 km *71·1 miles*, by Roberta Brown and Lorraine McCourt on the same occasion. The compère was Marty Whelan of Radio 2.

Beauty contests The first international beauty contest was staged by P.T. Barnum (with the public to be the judges) in the USA in June 1855.

The world's largest annual beauty pageants are the Miss World and Miss Universe contests (inaugurated in 1951 and 1952 respectively). The most successful country in the latter contest has been the USA, with winners in 1954, 1956, 1960, 1967 and 1980. The greatest number of countries represented in the Miss Universe contest was 81 in 1983.

The country which has produced the most winners in the Miss World contest is the United Kingdom, with five. They were Rosemarie Frankland (1961); Ann Sidney (1964); Lesley Langley (1965); Helen Morgan (1974), who resigned, and Sarah-Jane Hutt (1983). The maximum number of contestants was 84 in November 1988. The shortest reign as Miss World was 18 hr, by Miss Germany (Gabriella Brum) in 1980.

Circus

The oldest permanent circus building is Cirque d'Hiver (originally Cirque Napoléon), which opened in Paris, France on 11 Dec 1852. The largest travelling circus tent was that of Ringling Bros and Barnum & Bailey, which they used on USA tours from 1921 to 1924. It covered 8492 m² *91 415 ft²*, consisting of a round top 61 m *200 ft* in diameter with five middle sections 18 m *60 ft* wide.

The largest audience for a circus was 52 385 for Ringling Bros and Barnum & Bailey, at the Superdome, New Orleans, Louisiana, USA on 14 Sep 1975, and the largest in a tent was 16 702 (15 686 paid), also for Ringling Bros and Barnum & Bailey, at Concordia, Kansas, USA on 13 Sep 1924.

Aerial acts The highest trapeze act was performed by Ian Ashpole (Great Britain) at a height of 5005 m *16 420 ft*, suspended from a hot-air balloon

Plate spinning

The greatest number of plates spun simultaneously is 108, by Dave Spathaky of London for the *Tarm Pai Du* television programme in Thailand on 23 Nov 1992.

Trampolining

Trampolines were used in show business at least as early as 'The Walloons' of the period 1910–12. The sport of trampolining (from the Spanish word *trampolin*, a springboard) dates from 1936, when the prototype 'T' model trampoline was developed by George Nissen (USA).

between St. Neots, Cambs and Newmarket, Suffolk on 16 May 1986. Janet May Klemke (USA) performed a record 305 one arm planges at Medina Shrine Circus, Chicago, Illinois, USA on 21 Jan 1938. A single-heel hang on a swinging bar was first performed by Angela Revelle in Australia in 1977.

Flying return trapeze

A flying return trapeze act was first performed by Jules Léotard (France) at Cirque Napoléon, Paris, France on 12 Nov 1859. A triple back somersault on the flying trapeze was first performed by Lena Jordan (Latvia) to Lewis Jordan (USA) in Sydney, Australia in April 1897. The back somersault record is a quadruple back, by Miguel Vasquez (Mexico) to Juan Vasquez at Ringling Bros and Barnum & Bailey Circus, Tucson, Arizona, USA on 10 Jul 1982.

The greatest number of consecutive triple back somersaults successfully carried out is 135, by Jamie Ibarra (Mexico) to Alejandro Ibarra, between 23 July–12 Oct 1989, at various locations in the USA.

Flexible pole

The first and only publicly performed quadruple back somersault on the flexible pole was accomplished by Maxim Dobrovitsky (USSR) of the Egorov Troupe at the International Circus Festival of Monte Carlo in Monaco on 4 Feb 1989. Corina Colonelu Mosoianu (Romania) is the only person to have performed a triple full twisting somersault, on 17 Apr 1984

at Madison Square Garden, New York City, USA.

High wire

A seven person pyramid (three layers) was achieved by the Great Wallendas (Germany) at Wallenda Circus, USA in 1947. The highest highwire feat (ground supported) was at a height of 411 m *1350 ft* by Philippe Petit (France) between the towers of the World Trade Center, New York City, USA on 7 Aug 1974.

Horseback riding

The record for consecutive somersaults on horseback is 23, by James Robinson (USA) at Spalding & Rogers Circus, Pittsburgh, Pennsylvania, USA in 1856. Willy, Beby and Rene Fredianis (Italy) performed a three high column at Nouveau Cirque, Paris, France in 1908, a feat not since emulated. 'Poodles' Hanneford (Ireland) (b. England) holds the record for running leaps on and off, with 26 at Barnum & Bailey Circus, New York, USA in 1915.

Human cannonball

The first human cannonball was Eddie Rivers (USA) billed as 'Lulu', from a Farini cannon at Royal Cremorne Music Hall, London in 1871. The record distance a human has been fired from a cannon is 53·4 m *175 ft* in the case of Emanuel Zacchini (Italy) in the USA in 1940.

Human pyramid

The weight record is 771 kg *1700 lbs*, when Tahar Douis supported twelve members of the Hassani Troupe (three levels in height) at the BBC TV studios, Birmingham, W Mids on 17 Dec 1979.

The height record is 12 m *39 ft*, when Josep-Joan Martinez Lozano of the Colla Vella dels Xiquets mounted a nine-high pyramid at Valls, Spain on 25 Oct 1981.

Risley

A back somersault feet to feet was first performed by Richard Risley Carlisle and son (USA) at the Theatre Royal, Edinburgh in February 1844.

Teeter board

The Kehaiovi Troupe (Bulgaria) achieved a seven-person high perch pole column at Blackpool Tower Circus, Blackpool, Lancs on 16 Jul 1986.

Trampoline

Marco Canestrelli (USA) performed a septuple twisting back somersault to bed at Ringling Bros and Barnum & Bailey Circus, St Petersburg, Florida, USA on 5 Jan 1979. He also achieved a quintuple twisting back somersault to a two high column, to Belmonte Canestrelli at Ringling Bros and Barnum & Bailey Circus, New York City, USA on 28 Mar 1979. Richard Tison (France) achieved a triple twisting triple back somersault at Berchtesgaden, Germany on 30 Jun 1981.

Stilt-walking The fastest stilt-walker on record is Roy Luiking, who covered 100m *328ft* on 30·5cm *1ft* high stilts in 13·01 sec at Didam, Netherlands on 28 May 1992. Over a long distance, the fastest is M. Garisoain of Bayonne, France, who in 1892 walked the 8km *4·97miles* from Bayonne to Biarritz on stilts in 42min, an average speed of 11·42km/h *7·10mph*.

The greatest distance ever walked on stilts is 4804km *3008 miles*, from Los Angeles, California, USA to Bowen, Kentucky, USA by Joe Bowen from 20 Feb–26 Jul 1980. In 1891 Sylvain Dornon stilt-walked from Paris, France to Moscow, Russia in 50 stages, covering 2945km *1830miles*. Another source gives his time as 58 days. Either way, although Bowen's distance was greater, Dornon walked at a much higher speed.

Even with a safety or Kirby wire, very high stilts are *extremely* dangerous—25 steps are deemed to constitute 'mastery'. The tallest stilts ever mastered measured 12·36m *40ft 9½in* from ground to ankle. Eddy Wolf ('Steady Eddy') of Loyal, Wisconsin, USA walked a distance of 25 steps without touching his safety handrail wires on 3 Aug 1988 using aluminium stilts of this length.

The heaviest stilts ever mastered weighed 25·9kg *57lb* each, and were the ones used by Eddy Wolf in his successful attempt on the height record. (⇨ above)

Wild animal presentations Willy Hagenbeck (Germany) worked with 70 polar bears in a presentation at the Paul Busch Circus, Berlin, Germany in 1904.

The greatest number of lions mastered and fed in a cage by an unaided lion-tamer was 40, by 'Captain' Alfred Schneider in 1925.

Clyde Raymond Beatty (USA) handled 43 'cats' (lions and tigers) simultaneously in 1938. Beatty was the featured attraction

The Cirque d'Hiver in Paris is the world's oldest permanent circus building. Crowds have been flocking in to see performances there since it opened in 1852.

(Photos: Ann Ronan Picture Library and James Clift for Guinness Publishing)

at every show he appeared in for more than 40 years. He insisted upon being called a lion-trainer. More than 20 lion-tamers have died of injuries since 1900.

Photography

Origins The earliest reference to a photographic image is in a letter dated 19 Jul 1822 to French scientist Joseph Niépce (1765–1833) from his brother Claude (1763–1828), referring to a photograph of an engraving of Pope Pius VII taken at Gras, near Châlon-sur-Saône, France.

Earliest photographs The earliest known surviving photograph, also by Niépce, was taken in 1827 using a camera obscura and shows the view from the window of his home. Rediscovered by Helmut Gernsheim in

1952, it is now in the Gernsheim Collection at the University of Texas, Austin, USA.

UK The oldest surviving photograph taken in England is as negative image of a window in Lacock Abbey, Wilts, taken in August 1835 by William Henry Fox Talbot (1800–77), inventor of the negative-positive process. Donated to the Science Museum, London, it is now at the National Museum of Photography, Film and Television, Bradford, W Yorks.

Aerial photograph The earliest aerial photograph was taken in 1858 by Gaspard Felix Tournachon (1820–1910), *alias* Nadar, from a balloon near Villacoublay, on the outskirts of Paris, France.

Cameras

Largest The largest and most expensive industrial camera ever built is the 27-tonne Rolls-Royce camera commissioned in 1956 and now owned by BPCC Graphics Ltd of Derby. It is 2·69m *8ft 10in* high, 2·51m *8¼ft* wide and 14·02m *46ft* long. The lens is a 160cm *63in* f16 Cooke Apochromatic and the bellows were made by Camera Bellows Ltd of Birmingham, W Mids.

A pinhole camera was created from a Portakabin unit measuring 10·4 × 2·9 × 2·64m *34 × 9½ × 9ft* by photographers John Kippen and Chris Wainwright at the National Museum of Photography, Film and Television in Bradford, W Yorks on 25 Mar 1990. The unit produced a direct positive measuring 10·2 × 1·27m *33 × 4ft 2 in.*

Smallest Excluding those built for intracardiac surgery and espionage, the smallest marketed camera has been the circular Japanese 'Petal' camera, with a diameter of 2·9cm *1·14in* and a thickness of 1·65cm *0·65in*. It has a focal length of 12mm *0·47in.*

Fastest A camera built for research into high-power lasers by The Blackett Laboratory of Imperial College of Science and Technology, London registering images at a rate of 33 billion frames per sec. The fastest production camera is currently the Imacon 675, made by Hadland Photonics Ltd of Bovington, Herts, operating at up to 600 million frames per sec.

Most expensive photograph

The black and white print of a woman's face dotted with glass tears, taken in about 1930 by Man Ray, sold for £122500 (about $192325) at Sotheby's, London on 7 May 1993.

Largest lens

The National Museum of Photography, Film and Television in Bradford, W Yorks has the largest lens on display, made by Pilkington Special Glass Ltd of St Asaph, Clwyd. Its dimensions are: focal length 8·45m *333in*, diameter 1·372m *54in*, weight 215kg *474lb*. Its focal length enables writing on the museum's walls to be read from a distance of 12·19m *40ft*.

Most expensive The most expensive camera equipment in the world is that of Nikon Corporation of Tokyo, Japan, whose complete range of 29 cameras, 90 lenses and 659 accessories sold for £155361.49 excluding VAT in May 1992. The highest auction price for any camera is £29700 for a lady's patent watch camera of *c.* 1890 made by Lancaster and Son of Birmingham, W Mids, sold at Christie's, London on 12 Mar 1992.

Longest negative On 6 May 1992 Thomas Bleich of Austin, Texas, USA produced a negative image measuring 712·47×25·4cm *23ft 4½×10½in* using a 26·67cm *10½ in* focal length Turner-Reich lens and Kodak No. 10 Cirkut Camera. The photograph, a portrait of about 3500 attendants at a concert in Austin, achieved a view of over 1440 degrees in a single shot.

Cinema

Films

The earliest motion pictures were made by Louis Aimé Augustin Le Prince (1842–90), who was attested to have achieved dim moving outlines on a whitewashed wall at the Institute for the Deaf, Washington Heights, New York,

USA as early as 1885–87. The earliest surviving film (sensitized 53·9mm 2⅛ in wide paper roll) is from his camera, patented in Britain on 16 Nov 1888, taken in early October 1888 of the garden of his father-in-law, Joseph Whitley, in Roundhay, Leeds, W Yorks at 10–12 frames/sec.

The first commercial presentation of motion pictures was at Holland Bros' Kinetoscope Parlor at 1155 Broadway, New York City, USA on 14 Apr 1894. Viewers could see five films for 25 cents or 10 for 50 cents from a double row of Kinetoscopes developed by William Kennedy Laurie Dickson (1860–1935), assistant to Thomas Edison (1847–1931), in 1889–91.

The earliest publicly presented film on a *screen* was *La Sortie des Ouvriers de l'Usine Lumière*, probably shot in August or September 1894 in Lyon, France. It was exhibited at 44 rue de Rennes, Paris, France on 22 Mar 1895 by the Lumière brothers, Auguste Marie Louis Nicholas (1862–1954) and Louis Jean (1864–1948).

Earliest feature film The world's first full-length feature film was *The Story of the Kelly Gang*, made in Melbourne, Victoria, Australia in 1906. Produced on a budget of £450, this biopic of the notorious armoured bushranger Ned Kelly (1855–80) ran for 60–70min and opened at the Melbourne Town Hall on 26 Dec 1906. It was produced by the local theatrical company J. and N. Tait.

Earliest 'talkie' The earliest sound-on-film motion picture was achieved by Eugene Augustin Lauste (1857–1935), who patented his process on 11 Aug 1906 and produced a workable system using a string galvanometer in 1910 at Benedict Road, Stockwell, London. The earliest public presentation of sound on film was by the Tri-ergon process at the Alhambra cinema, Berlin, Germany on 17 Sep 1922.

Largest output India's production of feature-length films was a record 948

Even with revised estimates of $95 million, *Terminator 2: Judgement Day* is still the world's costliest film. Non-stop action has title star Arnold Schwarzenegger chancing more than an arm for his reported $15 million fee.
(Photos: Sygma)

Most film extras

It is believed that over 300 000 extras appeared in the funeral scene of *Gandhi*, the 1982 epic directed by Sir Richard Attenborough.

Largest film première

A Few Good Men, starring Tom Cruise, Demi Moore and Jack Nicholson, was released simultaneously in over 50 countries by Columbia Pictures in December 1992.

Highest-paid stunt performer

Stuntman Dar Robinson was paid $100 000 for the 335 m *1100 ft* leap from the CN Tower, Toronto, Canada in November 1979 for *High Point*. His parachute opened just 91 m *300 ft* above ground. He died on 21 Nov 1986 aged 39.

---

in 1990, and its annual output has exceeded 700 every year since 1979.

Most expensive film At the time of its release in July 1991, *Terminator 2: Judgement Day*, was reported to have cost Carolco Pictures $95 million (revised from earlier reports of $104), plus print and advertising costs of about $20 million. Its star, Arnold Schwarzenegger, was believed to have received a fee of $15 million for the film.

In terms of real costs adjusted for inflation, the most expensive film ever made was *Cleopatra* (USA, 1963), whose $44 million budget would be equivalent to over $200 million in 1993.

Least expensive full-length feature film The total cost of production for the 1927 film *The Shattered Illusion*, by Victorian Film Productions, was £300. It took 12 months to complete and included spectacular scenes of a ship being overwhelmed by a storm.

Most expensive film rights The highest price ever paid for film rights was $9·5 million announced on 20 Jan 1978 by Columbia for *Annie*, the Broadway musical by Charles Strouse starring Andrea McCardle, Dorothy Loudon and Reid Shelton. The highest price paid for an 'untried' script is $3 million to Joe Eszterhas for the controversial *Basic Instinct*, the film of which, directed by Paul Verhoeven, was released to protests in the US in March 1992.

Longest film The longest film commercially-released in its entirety was Edgar Reitz's 25 hr 32 min *Die Zweite Heimat* (Germany, 1992), premièred in Munich on 5–9 Sep 1992.

Fastest film production The shortest time ever taken to make a feature-length film from scripting to screening is 13 days for *The Fastest Forward*, produced by Russ Malkin and directed by John Gore. The all-star British cast, the crew, technicians and cinemagraphic suppliers accepted the charity challenge and the 75-minute thriller was given a gala premiere at London's Dominion Theatre on 27 May 1990 to raise money for Telethon '90.

Highest box office gross The box office gross champion is Steven Spielberg's *ET: The Extra-Terrestrial*, released on 11 Jun 1982, which had grossed over $700 million (including videos) by December 1989. Its UK television premiere on Christmas day 1990 attracted 17·5 million viewers.

Batman Returns (Warner Bros) set a new opening day record of $16·1 million on 19 Jun 1992 and also a single day record of $16·8 million on 20 June during its US opening weekend at a record 2644 cinemas.

UK In January 1991 UIP's *Ghost*, starring Patrick Swayze, Demi Moore and Oscarwinner Whoopi Goldberg, became the highest-ever grossing film in the UK, with box office takings of £20·7 million.

Largest loss The greatest loss incurred by a film is $57 million by Columbia TriStar's *Hudson Hawk* (USA, 1991), starring Bruce Willis (b. 19 Mar 1955) and directed by Michael Lehmann. Costing $65 million, this James Bond-type spoof returned $8 million in North America — and hardly anything elsewhere.

Highest earnings Jack Nicholson stood to receive up to $60 million for playing 'The Joker' in Warner Brothers' $50 mil-

High diving

Col. Harry A. Froboess (Switzerland) jumped 120m *394ft* into the Bodensee from the airship *Graf Hindenburg* on 22 Jun 1936. The greatest height reported for a dive into an air bag is 99·4m *326ft* by stuntman Dan Koko, who jumped from the top of Vegas World Hotel and Casino on to a 6·1×12·2×4·2m *20×40×14ft* target on 13 Aug 1984. His impact speed was 141km/h *88mph*.

Kitty O'Neil dived 54·8m *180ft* from a helicopter over Devonshire Downs, California, USA on 9 Dec 1979 on to an air cushion measuring 9·15×18·3m *30×60ft* for a TV film stunt.

Most expensive prop

The highest price paid at auction for a film prop is $275000 at Sotheby's, New York City, USA on 28 Jun 1986 for James Bond's Aston Martin DB5 from *Goldfinger* (UK, 1964).

---

lion *Batman*, through a percentage of the film's receipts in lieu of salary. Barbra Streisand received a record $6 million for an actress for the Oscar-nominated *Prince of Tides* (1991).

The highest paid child performer is Macaulay Culkin (b. 26 Aug 1980), who, at the age of 11, was paid $1 million for *My Girl* (1991). This was followed by a contract for $5 million (plus 5 per cent of ticket sales) for *Home Alone II: Lost in New York* (1992), the sequel to his 1990 box-office hit.

Most durable series The longest series of films is the 100 features made in Hong Kong about the 19th century martial arts hero Huang Fei-Hong, starting with *The True Story of Huang Fei-Hong* (1949) and continuing with *Once Upon a Time in China 2* (1992). The most durable continuing series with the same star is Shochiku Studios of Japan's 46 *Tora-San* comedy films, featuring Kiyoshi Atsumi (b. 1929) in a 'Chaplin-esque' rôle from August 1969 to December 1992.

UK The longest British series is the 'Carry On' films, starting with *Carry On Sergeant* (1958) and continuing to *Carry On Columbus*, which featured some survivors of the earlier films. Kenneth Williams (1926–87) appeared in 25 of the films.

Most profitable series The most successful movie series is the 18 James Bond films, from *Dr No* (GB, 1962) starring Sean Connery (b. 25 Aug 1930) to *Licence to Kill* (1989) with Timothy Dalton (b. 21 Mar 1944). The series has grossed over $1 billion worldwide to date.

Largest studios The largest film studio complex in the world is that at Universal City, Los Angeles, California, USA. The back lot contains 476 buildings and there are 34 sound stages on the 170ha *420acre* site. The largest studio in Britain is Pinewood Studios in Iver, Bucks, covering 36·8ha *91acres*. Built in 1936, it includes 75 buildings and 18 stages.

Largest studio stage The world's largest studio stage is the 007 stage at Pinewood Studios, designed by Michael Brown for producer Albert R. Broccoli and set creator Ken Adam and built in 1976 for the James Bond film *The Spy Who Loved Me*. The set measures 102×42×12m *336×139×41ft* and accommodated 4·54 million litres *1·2 million gal* of water, a full-scale section of a 600000-ton supertanker and three scaled-down nuclear submarines.

Largest film set The largest-ever film set, measuring 400×230m *1312×754ft*, was the Roman Forum, designed by Veniero Colosanti and John Moore for Samuel Bronston's production of *The Fall of the Roman Empire* (1964). It was built on a 22·25ha *55acre* site outside Madrid, Spain. 1100 workmen spent seven months laying the surface of the Forum with 170000 cement blocks, erecting 6705m *22000ft* of concrete stairways, 601 colums and 350 statues, and constructing 27 full-size buildings.

Longest directorial career The directorial career of King Vidor (1894–1982) lasted for 67 years, beginning with the two-reel comedy *Hurricane in Galvaston* (1913) and culminating in

another short, a documentary called *The Metaphor* (1980).

Oldest director The Dutch director Joris Ivens (1898–1989) directed the Franco-Italian co-production *Une Histoire de Vent* in 1988 at the age of 89. He made his directorial debut with the Dutch film *De Brug* in 1928. Hollywood's oldest director was George Cukor (1899–1983), who made his 50th

---

Most portrayed character

The character most frequently appearing on the screen is Sherlock Holmes, created by Sir Arthur Conan Doyle (1859–1930). The Baker Street sleuth has been portrayed by some 75 actors in 211 films since 1900.

In horror films the character most often portrayed is Count Dracula, created by Bram Stoker (1847–1912). Representations of the Count or his immediate descendants outnumber those of his closest rival, Frankenstein's creation, by 160 to 115.

and final film, MGM's *Rich and Famous* in 1981 at the age of 81.

Oldest performers The oldest screen performer in a speaking rôle was Jeanne Louise Calment (b. 1875–*fl.* March 1993), who portrayed herself at the age of 114 in the 1990 Canadian film *Vincent and Me*. She is the last living person to have known Vincent van Gogh. (⇔ Human Being)

UK The oldest British film performer was Dame Gwen Ffrancon-Davies (1891–1992), who appeared in the Sherlock Holmes TV movie *The Master Blackmailer* (UK, 1991) at the age of 100. She died one month after the film was screened.

Most durable performers The record for the longest screen career is 83 years by German actor Curt Bois (1900–91), who made his debut in *Der Fidele Bauer* at the age of eight and whose last film was *Wings of Desire* (1988). The American actress Helen Hayes (1900-93) first appeared on screen at the age of 10 in *Jean and the Calico Doll*, with much of her later work being for television. Her last screen rôle was in *Divine Mercy, No Escape* (1988) in a career lasting 78 years. The most enduring star of the big screen was Lillian Gish (1893–1993)— although her birthdate is usually given as 1896. She made her debut in *An Unseen Enemy* (1912) and her last film in a career spanning 75 years was *The Whales of August* (1987).

Most generations of screen actors in a family There are four generations of screen actors in the Redgrave family. Roy Redgrave (1872–1922) made his screen debut in 1911 and continued to appear in Australian films until 1920. Sir Michael Redgrave married actress Rachel Kempson and their two daughters Vanessa and Lynn and son Corin are all actors. Vanessa's two daughters Joely and Natasha and Corin's daughter

Oscar winners

Fifteen performers have won two Oscars in starring roles (the year the award was presented is given in each case):–

Ingrid Bergman 1945/56

Marlon Brando 1955/73

Gary Cooper 1942/53

Bette Davis 1936/39

Olivia de Havilland 1947/50

Sally Field 1980/85

Jane Fonda 1972/79

Jodie Foster 1989/92

Dustin Hoffman 1980/89

Glenda Jackson 1971/74

Vivien Leigh 1940/52

Frederic March 1933/47

Luise Rainer 1937/38

Elizabeth Taylor 1961/67

Spencer Tracy 1938/39

Jemma are already successful actresses with films such as *Wetherby*, *A Month in the Country* and *The Dream Demon* to their respective credit.

Costumes The largest number of costumes used for any one film was 32 000 for the 1951 film *Quo Vadis*.

Most changes Elizabeth Taylor changed costume 65 times in *Cleopatra* (1963). The costumes were designed by Irene Sharaff and cost $130 000.

Most expensive Constance Bennett's sable coat in *Madam X* (1965) was valued at $50 000. The most expensive costume designed and made specially for a film was Edith Head's mink and sequins dance costume worn by Ginger Rogers in *Lady in the Dark* (1944), which cost Paramount $35 000 (⋄ Oscar winners). The ruby slippers worn by Judy Garland in the 1939 film *The Wizard of Oz* were sold on 2 Jun 1988 to a mystery buyer at Christie's, New York, USA for $165 000.

Oscar winners Walter (Walt) Elias Disney (1901–66) has won more 'Oscars'—the awards of the United States Academy of Motion Picture Arts and Sciences, instituted on 16 May 1929 and named after Oscar Pierce of Texas, USA—than any other person. The count comprises 20 statuettes and 12 other plaques and certificates, including posthumous awards.

The only person to win four Oscars in a starring role is Katharine Hepburn (b. USA, 8 Nov 1909) for *Morning Glory* (1932–3), *Guess Who's Coming to Dinner* (1967), *The Lion in Winter* (1968) and *On Golden Pond* (1981). The awards were made in 1934, 1968, 1969 and 1982 respectively. She has been nominated 12 times. Edith Head (1907–81) won eight individual awards for costume design. (⋄ Costumes)

The film with most awards is *Ben Hur* (1959) with 11. The film receiving the highest number of nominations is *All About Eve* (1950) with 14. It won six— Best Supporting Actor: George Sanders; Best Picture, Best Costume Design; Edith Head, Charles Le Maire, Best Director; Joseph L. Mankiewicz, Best Sound Recording, Best Screenplay; Joseph L. Mankiewicz.

Youngest winners The youngest winner in competition is Tatum O'Neal (b. 5 Nov 1963), who was aged 10 when she received the award in 1974 for Best Supporting Actress in *Paper Moon* (1973). Shirley Temple (b. 23 Apr 1928) was awarded an honorary Oscar at the age of five for achievements in 1934.

Oldest winners The oldest recipients, George Burns (b. 20 Jan 1896), Best Supporting actor for *The Sunshine Boys* in 1976, and Jessica Tandy (b. 7 Jun 1909), Best Actress for *Driving Miss Daisy* in 1990, were both 80 at the time of their presentation, although Miss Tandy was the elder by five months.

Most versatile personalities The only three performers to have won Oscar, Emmy, Tony and Grammy awards have been actress Helen Hayes (1900–93) in 1932–1976; composer Richard Rodgers (1902–1979) and actress/singer/dancer

Rita Moreno (b. 1931) in 1961–1977. Barbra Streisand has received Oscar, Grammy and Emmy awards, in addition to a special 'Star of the Decade' Tony award.

Most honoured entertainer The world's most honoured entertainer is Bob Hope (*né* Leslie Townes Hope, London, 29 May 1903). He has been uniquely awarded the USA's highest civilian honours—the Medal of Freedom (1969); the Congressional Gold Medal (1963); the Medal of Merit (1966); the Distinguished Public Service Medal (1973); the Distinguished Service Gold Medal (1971). Awarded an Hon. CBE (1976) and appointed Hon. Brigadier of the US Marine Corps, he also has 44 honorary degrees.

Cinemas

Earliest The earliest structure designed and exclusively used for exhibiting projected films is believed to be one erected at the Atlanta Show, Georgia, USA in October 1895 to exhibit C. F. Jenkins' phantoscope. The earliest attempt at establishing a cinema in Britain was made by Birt Acres, whose Kineopticon opened at 2 Piccadilly Mansions at the junction of Piccadilly Circus and Shaftesbury Avenue on 21 Mar 1896. After only a few weeks, the cinema was gutted by fire.

Largest The largest cinema in the world is the Radio City Music Hall, New York City, USA, opened on 27 Dec 1932 with 5945 (now 5874) seats. Kinepolis, the first eight screens of which opened in Brussels, Belgium in 1988, is the world's largest cinema complex. It has 24 screens and a total seating capacity of 7000. The Odeon, Leicester Square, London has 1983 seats.

Highest cinema-going The largest cinema audience is that of China, with mainland attendance figures of 14 billion in 1991, compared with a peak 21·8 billion in 1988. Admissions in the UK were a record 103·6 million in 1992.

Biggest screen The largest permanently installed cinema screens, measuring 29·3 × 21·5 m *70½ × 96 ft*, are IMAX screens in the Keong Emas Imax Theatre, Taman Mini Park, Jakarta, Indonesia and at the Six Flags Great America in Gurnee, Illinois, USA. A temporary screen measuring 90·5 × 10 m *297 × 33 ft* was used at the 1937 Paris Exposition.

Most films seen Gwilym Hughes of Dolgellau, Gwynedd has seen 20 064 films at the cinema since 1953.

Radio

The earliest patent for telegraphy without wires (wireless) was received by Dr Mahlon Loomis (USA) (1826–86). It was entitled 'Improvement in Telegraphy' and was dated 20 Jul 1872 (US Pat. No. 129971). He in fact demonstrated only potential differences on a galvanometer between two kites 22 km *14 miles* apart in Loudoun County, Virginia, USA in October 1866.

Earliest patent A public demonstration of wireless transmission of speech was given in the town square of Murray, Kentucky, USA in 1892 by Nathan B. Stubblefield, who died destitute on 28 Mar 1928. The first patent for a system of communication by means of electromagnetic waves, numbered No. 12039, was granted on 2 Jun 1896 to the Italian-Irish Marchese Guglielmo Marconi (1874–1937).

The first permanent wireless installation was constructed at The Needles, Isle of Wight by Marconi's Wireless Telegraph Co. Ltd in November 1897.

Earliest broadcast The world's first advertised broadcast was made on 24 Dec 1906 by the Canadian-born Prof. Reginald Aubrey Fessenden (1868–1932) from the 128 m *420 ft* mast of the National Electric Signalling Company at Brant Rock, Massachusetts, USA. The transmission included Handel's *Largo*. Fessenden had achieved the broadcast of speech as early as November 1900 but this was highly distorted.

UK The first experimental broadcasting transmitter in Great Britain was set up at the Marconi Works in Chelmsford, Essex in December 1919, and broadcast a news service in February 1920. The earliest regular broadcast was made from the

Brain of Britain quiz

The youngest person to become 'Brain of Britain' on BBC radio was Anthony Carr of Anglesey, Gwynedd in 1956 at the age of 16. The oldest contestant has been the author and translator Hugh Merrick (1898–1980) in his 80th year in August 1977.

The record score is 35 by the 1981 winner Peter Barlow of Richmond, Surrey and Peter Bates of Taunton, Somerset who won the title in 1984.

Marconi transmitter '2MT' at Writtle, Essex on 14 Feb 1922.

Transatlantic transmissions The earliest transatlantic wireless signal (the letter S in Morse Code) was transmitted from a 10kW station at Poldhu, Cornwall to Signal Hill, St John's, Newfoundland, Canada and received by Guglielmo Marconi and his assistants George Stephen Kemp and Percy Paget at 12:30p.m. on 12 Dec 1901.

Speech was first heard across the Atlantic in November 1915 when a transmission from the US Navy station at Arlington, Virginia was received by US radio-telephone engineers on the Eiffel Tower in Paris, France.

Earliest radio-microphones The radio-microphone, which was in essence also the first 'bug', was devised by Reg Moores (GB) in 1947 and first used on 76 MHz in the ice show *Aladdin* at Brighton Sports Stadium, E Sussex in September 1949.

Longest BBC national broadcast The reporting of the Coronation of Queen Elizabeth II on 2 Jun 1953 began at 10:15 a.m. and finished at 5:30p.m., after 7hr 15min.

Longest continuous broadcast Radio Telefís éireann transmitted an unedited reading of Ulysses by James Joyce (1882–1941) lasting 29hr 38min 47sec on 16–17 Jul 1982.

Topmost prize Mary Buchanan, 15, on WKRQ, Cincinnati, USA, won a prize of $25000 for 40 years (viz. $1 million) on 21 Nov 1980.

Most durable programmes *Rambling with Gambling*, the early morning WOR-NY programme, began in March 1925 and has been continued by three generations of the Gambling family. As of 30 Apr 1993, there had been 21281 shows.

BBC The longest-running BBC radio series is *The Week's Good Cause*, which began on 24 Jan 1926. The St Martin-in-the-Fields Christmas appeal by Canon Geoffrey Brown on 14 Dec 1986 raised a record £138039.

The longest running record programme is *Desert Island Discs* which began on 29 Jan 1942 and originally presented by its creator Roy Plomley, who died on 28 May 1985 having presented 1791 editions. It is now hosted by Sue Lawley. The record number of appearances is four by Arthur Askey (1900–82), the last time being on the 1572nd show on 20 Dec 1980.

The longest-running solo radio feature is *Letter from America* by (Alfred) Alistair Cooke (b. 20 Nov 1908), first broadcast on 24 Mar 1946. The original broadcaster of the series was Raymond Gram Swing.

The longest-running radio serial is *The Archers*, created by Godfrey Baseley and first broadcast on 1 Jan 1951. The only role played without interruption from the start is that of Philip Archer by Norman Painting (b. 23 Apr 1924).

Most stations The country with the greatest number of radio broadcasting stations is the United States, where there were 11334 authorized stations at 31 Dec 1992.

Highest listening Surveys carried out in 90 countries showed that, in 1993, the global estimated audience for the BBC World Service, broadcast in 39 languages, was 124 million regular listeners—greater than the combined listenership of Voice of America, Radio Moscow and *Deutsche Welle*. This is, however, a conservative estimate because figures are unavailable for several countries, including China, Cuba, Myanmar (Burma), Iran, Afghanistan and Vietnam.

The peak recorded listenership on BBC Radio was 30 million on 6 Jun 1950 for the boxing match between Lee Savold (US) and Bruce Woodcock (GB) (b. Doncaster, S Yorks, 1921).

Highest response The highest recorded response from a radio show was on 27 Nov 1974 when, on a 5-hr talk show on WCAU, Philadelphia, Pennsylvania, USA, astrologer Howard Sheldon registered a call count of 388 299 on the *Bill Corsair Show*.

Television

Origins The invention of television, the instantaneous viewing of distant objects by electrical transmissions, was not an act but a process of successive and inter-dependent discoveries. The first commercial cathode ray tube was introduced in 1897 by Karl Ferdinand Braun (1850–1918), but was not linked to 'electric vision' until 1907 by Prof. Boris Rosing (disappeared 1918) of Russia in St Petersburg.

A.A. Campbell Swinton (1863–1930) published the fundamentals of television transmission on 18 Jun 1908 in a brief letter to *Nature* entitled 'Distant Electric Vision'.

The earliest public demonstration of television was given on 27 Jan 1926 by John Logie Baird (1888–1946) of Scotland, using a development of the mechanical scanning system patented by Paul Gottlieb Nipkow (1860–1940) on 6 Jan 1884. He had achieved the transmission of a Maltese Cross over 3·05 m *10ft* at 8 Queen's Arcade, Hastings, E Sussex, by February 1924 and the first facial image (of William Taynton, 15) at 22 Frith Street, London on 30 Oct 1925. Taynton had to be bribed with 2s6d. A patent application for the Iconoscope had been filed on 29 Dec 1923 by Dr Vladimir Kuzmich Zworykin (1889–1982) but was not issued until 20 Dec 1938.

Earliest service John Logie Baird launched his first television 'service' via a BBC transmitter on 30 Sep 1929 and marketed the first sets, Baird Televisors, at 26 guineas in May 1930.

Most expensive television rights
In November 1991 it was reported that a group of US and European investors, led by CBS, had paid $8 million for the television rights to *Scarlett*, the sequel to Margaret Mitchell's *Gone With the Wind*, written by Alexandra Ripley. The proposed eight-hour mini-series is scheduled for screening in 1993.

Best-selling video
Walt Disney's Oscar-winning animated film *Beauty and the Beast* has sold a record 20 million units in the US and another 5 million copies in the UK since its release in October 1992. Sales revenue in North America alone reached $22 million by March 1993.

The world's first high-definition (i.e. 405 lines) television broadcasting service was opened from Alexandra Palace, London on 2 Nov 1936, when there were about 100 sets in the United Kingdom.

Transatlantic transmissions On 9 Feb 1928 the images of J.L. Baird and a Mrs Howe was transmitted from Station 2 KZ at Coulsdon, Surrey to Station 2 CVJ, Hartsdale, New York, USA.

The earliest transatlantic transmission by satellite was achieved at 1 a.m. on 11 Jul 1962, via the active satellite *Telstar 1* from Andover, Maine, USA to Pleumeur Bodou, France. The picture was of Frederick R. Kappell, chairman of the American Telephone and Telegraph Company (AT & T), owners of the satellite. The first 'live' broadcast was made on 23 Jul 1962.

Longest telecast The longest pre-scheduled telecast on record was a continuous transmission for 163 hr 18 min by GTV 9 of Melbourne, Australia, covering the *Apollo XI* moon mission from 19–26 Jul 1969.

Earliest video-tape recording Alexander Mikhailovich Poniatoff first demonstrated video-tape recording known as Ampex (his initials plus 'ex' for excellence) in 1956. The earliest

'Mastermind' records

Jennifer Keaveney (on 'The life and work of E. Nesbit') scored a record 40 points in a 1986 semi-final and equalled her semi-final score of 40 points when she won the 1986 final with 'The life and works of Elizabeth Gaskell'. Mary Elizabeth Raw ('The life and reign of Charles I') also scored 40 points in the first programme of the 1989 series.

Quizzes

The greatest number of participants was 80799 in the All-Japan High School Quiz Championship televised by NTV on 31 Dec 1983.

In the most successful quiz, 34532 questions were answered correctly. The final scores were 17064 for Team A and 17468 for Team B in the quiz organized by Shrewsbury Junior Chamber at Shrewsbury, Shropshire from 12–17 Apr 1990.

demonstration of a home video recorder was on 24 Jun 1963 at the BBC News Studio at Alexandra Palace, London of the Telcan, developed by Norman Rutherford and Michael Turner of the Nottingham Electronic Valve Co.

Fastest video production Tapes of the Royal Wedding of HRH Prince Andrew and Miss Sarah Ferguson on 23 Jul 1986 were produced by Thames Video Collection. Live filming ended with the departure of the honeymoon couple from Chelsea Hospital by helicopter at 4:42 p.m., and the first fully edited and packaged VHS tapes were bought at 10:23 p.m., 5 hr 41 min later from the Virgin Megastore, Oxford Street, London.

Most durable shows The world's most durable TV show is NBC's *Meet the Press*, first transmitted on 6 Nov 1947 and weekly since 12 Sep 1948, originated by Lawrence E. Spivak, who appeared weekly as either moderator or panel member until 1975. As of 23 May 1993, 2294 shows had been aired. Tim Russert has succeeded as the show's new host since Derrick Utley left in December 1991.

UK Britain's most durable surviving television programme is the seasonal ballroom dancing show *Come Dancing*, first transmitted on 29 Sep 1950. The children's show *Andy Pandy* was first transmitted on 11 Jul 1950 but consisted of repeats of a cycle of 26 shows until 1970. Thirteen new episodes were then made, which were repeated until 1976.

The *BBC News* was inaugurated in vision on 5 Jul 1954. Richard Baker read the news from 1954 to Christmas 1982. Of current affairs programmes BBC's weekly *Panorama* was first transmitted on 11 Nov 1953 but has summer breaks. The monthly *Sky at Night* has been presented by Patrick Moore without a break or a miss since 24 Apr 1957.

Serial The longest-running domestic drama serial is Granada's *Coronation Street* which ran twice weekly from 9 Dec 1960 until 20 Oct 1989, after which viewers were treated to a third weekly episode. William Roache has played Ken Barlow without a break since the outset.

Most sets The global total of homes with television surpassed 500 million in 1987, led by the USA with 89·13 million. The USA had, by January 1989, 90·4 million TV households, with 50·24 million on cable TV. The number of homes with colour sets was 8·3 million (97 per cent) by January 1989 and more than 60 per cent of the total homes own two or more TV sets. On 15 Feb 1988 the new China News Agency announced that China's number of TV viewers had risen to 600 million from 100 million sets. There are 8250 TV transmitting stations world-wide, of which 1241 are in the USA.

UK The proportion of households in Great Britain with colour sets was 93 per cent in 1989. Just over half (51 per cent) of all households had two or more sets. The number of licences in force was 20067114 at 31 Mar 1993, of which 19030794 were for colour sets.

The number of monochrome licences continues to decline in line with the trend towards colour viewing and at 31

Mar 1993 there were only 1 036 320 black-and-white licences in force.

TV watching In June 1988 it was reported that the average US child sees at least 26 000 murders on TV by his or her 18th birthday. Between the ages of 2 and 11 the average viewing time is 31 hours 52 minutes per week. In 1988 the average British person watched 25 hr 21 min of television per week.

Greatest audience The estimated global audience for the 1990 World Cup finals played in Italy from 8 June to 8 July is 26·5 billion. An estimated 2·5 billion viewers tuned into the live and recorded transmissions of the XXIIIrd Olympic Games in Los Angeles, California, USA from 27 Jul to 13 Aug 1984. The American Broadcasting Co. airing schedule comprised 187½ hours of coverage on 56 cameras.

The estimated viewership for the 'Live Aid' concerts organized by Bob Geldof and Bill Graham, via a record 12 satellites, was 1·6 billion, or nearly one third of the world's population.

The highest ever audience for a single programme was 133·4 million viewers watching the NBC transmission of Super Bowl XXVII on 31 Jan 1993. The *Muppet Show* is the most widely viewed programme in the world, with an estimated audience of 235 million in 106 countries at August 1989.

UK The biggest audience for a single broadcast on British television is 25·21 million for the England *v.* West Germany World Cup semi-final match on 4 Jul 1990.

An aggregate audience of 39 million was estimated to have watched the wedding of TRH the Prince and Princess of Wales in London on 29 Jul 1981.

Most expensive production The *Winds of War*, a seven-part Paramount World War II saga aired by ABC, was the most expensive ever TV production costing $42 million over 14 months' shooting. The final episode on 13 Feb 1983 attracted a rating of 41 per cent of the total number of viewers, and a share of 56 per cent share of total sets turned on that were tuned in.

Largest contracts John William Carson (b. 23 Oct 1925), formerly the host of

Most takes

The highest number of 'takes' for a TV commercial is 28 by comedienne Pat Coombs in 1973. Her explanation was 'Every time we came to the punch line I just could not remember the name of the product'.

Shortest advertisement

An advertisement for the 1993 Guinness Book of Records lasting just 3 sec was devised by agency Leo Burnett and broadcast on UK satellite stations up to Christmas 1992.

The Tonight Show, had a contract with NBC reportedly worth $5 million per year for his one-hour evening shows aired four times weekly.

UK The largest contract in British television was one of a reported £9 million, inclusive of production expenses, signed by Tom Jones (b. Thomas Jones Woodward, 7 Jun 1940) of Treforest, Mid Glam in June 1968 with ABC-TV of the United States and ATV in London for 17 one-hour shows per annum from January 1969 to January 1974.

Highest-paid entertainer The highest paid television performer is the comedian Bill Cosby, who was reported in October 1991 to have an estimated income of $115 million for 1990 and 1991.

Most successful telethon The world record for a telethon is $78 438 573 in pledges in 21½ hours by the 1989 Jerry Lewis Labor Day Telethon on 4 Sep.

The Comic Relief '89 Appeal, the second 'Red Nose Day' hosted by comedians Lenny Henry and Griff Rhys-Jones, raised a UK record £26 660 145.

Biggest sale The greatest number of episodes of any TV programme ever sold was 1144 episodes of *Coronation Street* by Granada Television to CBKST Saskatoon, Saskatchewan, Canada on 31 May 1971. This constituted 20 days 15 hr 44 min continuous viewing. A further 728 episodes (Jan 1974–Jan 1981) were sold to CBC in August 1982.

Most prolific scriptwriter The most prolific television writer in the world was the Rt Hon. Lord Willis (1918–92). Since 1949 he created 41 series, including the first seven years and 2·25 million words of *Dixon of Dock Green*, which ran on BBC television from 1955 to 1976, 37 stage plays and 39 feature films. He had 29 plays produced and his total output since 1942 is estimated to be 20 million words.

Highest TV advertising rates The highest TV advertising rate is $800 000 per 30 sec for NBC network prime-time during the transmission of Super Bowl XXV on 27 Jan 1991, watched by over 120 million viewers.

Longest commercial The longest advertisement broadcast on British television was 7 min 10 sec by Great Universal Stores on TV-AM's *Good Morning Britain* on 20 Jan 1985, at a cost of £100 000.

Most expensive commercial It was reported in March 1988 that Pepsi Cola had paid Michael Jackson £7 million to do four TV commercials for them.

Largest sets The Sony Jumbo Tron colour TV screen at the Tsukuba International Exposition '85 near Tokyo, Japan in March 1985 measured 24·3 × 45·7 m *80×150 ft*.

The largest cathode ray tubes for colour sets are 94 cm *37 in* models manufactured by Mitsubishi Electric of Japan.

Smallest sets The Seiko TV-Wrist Watch, launched on 23 Dec 1982 in Japan, has a 30·5 mm *1·2 in* screen and weighs only 80 g *2·8 oz*. Together with the receiver unit and headphones, the entire black and white system, costing 108 000 yen, weighs only 320 g *11·3 oz*.

The smallest single-piece set is the Casio-Keisanki TV-10 weighing 338 g *11·9 oz* with a 6·85 cm *2·7 in* screen, launched in Tokyo in July 1983.

The smallest and lightest colour set, measuring 60 × 24 × 91 mm *2·4 × 0·9 × 3·6 in* and weighing 168·5 g *6 oz* with battery, is the Casio CV-1, launched by the Casio Computer Co. Ltd of Japan in July 1992. It has a screen size of 35 mm *1·4 in* and retails in Japan for 40 000 yen (about £200).

Human World

Political and Social

The world comprises 191 sovereign countries and 62 non-sovereign or other territories (dependencies of sovereign states, territories claimed in Antarctica and disputed territories), making a total of 253 as at May 1993.

Largest The country with the greatest area is Russia, with a total area of 17 075 400 km² *6 592 800 miles²*, or 11·5 per cent of the world's total land area. It is 70 times larger than the UK, but with a population in 1992 of 149·47 million has only 2·6 times more people than the UK.

The UK covers 244 100 km² *94 247 miles²* (including 3218 km² *1242 miles²* of inland water), or 0·16 per cent of the total land area of the world. Great Britain is the world's eighth largest island, with an area of 229 979 km² *88 795 miles²* and a coastline 7930 km *4928 miles* long, of which Scotland accounts for 4141 km *2573 miles*, England 3104 km *1929 miles* and Wales 685 km *426 miles*.

Smallest The smallest independent country in the world is the State of the Vatican City or Holy See (Stato della Città del Vaticano), which was made an enclave within the city of Rome, Italy on 11 Feb 1929. The enclave has an area of 44 ha *108·7 acres*. The maritime sover-

eign country with the shortest coastline is Monaco, with 5·61 km *3½ miles*, excluding piers and breakwaters. The world's smallest republic is Nauru, less than 1 degree south of the equator in the western Pacific, which became independent on 31 Jan 1968. It has an area of 2129 ha *5263 acres* and a population of 9600 (latest estimate 1992).

The smallest colony in the world is Gibraltar (since 1969, the City of Gibraltar), with an area of 5·8 km² *1440 acres/2¼ miles²*. However, Pitcairn Island, the only inhabited island (56 people in mid-1992) of a group of four (total area 48 km² *18½ miles²*), has an area of 388 ha *960 acres/1½ miles²*. It was named after Midshipman Robert Pitcairn of HMS *Swallow* in July 1767.

Before it was forcibly incorporated into Dahomey (now Benin) in 1961, the smallest colony was the Portuguese enclave of Ouidah, consisting of the Fort of St John the Baptist of Ajuda, with an area of just 2 ha *5 acres*.

The seat of the Sovereign Military Order of Malta and the official residence of the Grand Master have been in Rome, Italy since 1834. The order has a territory of 1·2 ha *3 acres*, including the Villa Malta on the Aventine and the Malta Palace at 68 Via Condotti. It maintains diplomatic relations with a number of foreign governments, through accredited representatives, and its legal status is the same as other states. Consequently it is sometimes called the 'smallest state in the world'.

Flattest and most elevated The country with the lowest 'high point' is Maldives; it attains 2·4 m *8 ft*. The country with the highest 'low point' is Lesotho, where the egress of the Senqu (Orange) river-bed is 1381 m *4530 ft* above sea level.

Largest political division The Commonwealth, a free association of 50 independent states and their dependencies, covers an area of 29 328 947 km² *11 323 906 miles²* with a population estimated to be 1 443 128 000. Almost all

Monaco has the shortest coastline of any sovereign country.

(Photo: Images Colour Library)

National boundaries

The frontier which is crossed most frequently is that between the United States and Mexico. It extends for 3110km *1933 miles* and in the year to 30 Sep 1992 there were 268 795 652 crossings.

member countries once belonged to the former British Empire. They believe in democracy and equal rights for all men and women regardless of race, colour, religion or politics. The Commonwealth promotes world peace, international understanding and an end to poverty and racism.

National boundaries There are 319 national land boundaries in the world. The continent with the greatest number is Africa, with 109. Of the estimated 420 maritime boundaries, only 140 have so far been ratified. The ratio of boundaries to area of land is greatest in Europe.

Longest boundary The longest *continuous* boundary in the world is that between Canada and the United States, which (including the Great Lakes boundaries) extends for 6416km *3987 miles* (excluding the frontier of 2547km *1538 miles* with Alaska). If the Great Lakes boundary is excluded, the longest land boundary is that between Chile and Argentina, which is 5255km *3265 miles* in length.

The UK's boundary with the Republic of Ireland measures 358km *223 miles*.

Shortest boundary The 'frontier' of the Holy See in Rome measures 4·07km *2·53 miles*. The land frontier between Gibraltar and Spain at La Linea, closed between June 1969 and February 1985, measures 1·53km *1672 yd*. In Africa, Zambia, Zimbabwe, Botswana and Namibia, almost meet at a single point on the Zambezi river.

Most boundaries The country with the most land boundaries is China, with 16 — Mongolia, Russia, North Korea, Hong Kong, Macau, Vietnam, Laos, Myanmar (Burma), India, Bhutan, Nepal, Pakistan, Afghanistan, Tajikistan, Kyrgyzstan and Kazakhstan. These extend for 24000km *14900 miles*. The country with the largest number of maritime boundaries is Indonesia, with 19. The longest maritime

boundary is that between Greenland and Canada at 2697km *1676 miles*.

World The average daily increase in the world's population is rising towards 263 000 or an average of approximately 182 per minute. There are, however, seasonal variations in the numbers of births and deaths throughout the year. For past, present and future estimates, ⇔ table on next page.

Most populous country The most populated country is China, which in *pinyin* is written Zhongguo (meaning 'central land'). It had an estimated population of 1 165 888 000 in mid-1992 and has a rate of natural increase of nearly 14·6 million per year or just under 40 000 a day. Its population is more than that of the whole world 200 years ago. India (mid-1992 population of 889 700 000) is predicted to overtake China in size of population by AD 2050, with 1591 million against 1555 million for China.

Least populous The independent state with the smallest population is the Vatican City or the Holy See (⇔ Smallest country above), with 750 inhabitants in 1992 and a nil return for births.

Most densely populated The most densely populated territory in the world is the Portuguese province of Macau, on the southern coast of China. It has an estimated population of 367 000 (1992) in an area of $18·0km^2$ *6·9 miles²*, giving a density of $20389/km^2$ *53 188/mile²*. The principality of Monaco, on the south coast of France, has a population of 30 300 (1992) in an area of just $1·95km^2$ *0·75 miles²*, a density equal to $15538/km^2$ *40 400/mile²*.

Of territories with an area of more than $1000km^2$, Hong Kong ($1075km^2$ *415 miles²*) contains an estimated 5 799 000 people (1992), giving the territory a density of $5394/km^2$ *13 973/mile²*. Hong

---

World population

Matej Gaspar, born 11 Jul 1987 in Yugoslavia, was symbolically named the world's five billionth inhabitant by the United Nations Secretary-General.

World Population

Date	Millions	Date	Millions
8000 BC	c. 6	1970	3698
AD 1	c. 255	1975	4080
1000	c. 254	1980	4450
1250	416	1985	4854
1500	460	1986	4936
1600	579	1987	5023
1700	679	1988	5111
1750	770	1989	5201
1800	954	1990	5292
1900	1633	1991	5385
1920	1862	1992	5480
1930	2070	1993	5576
1940	2295	2000*	6261
1950	2515	2025*	8504
1960	3019	2050*	10019

*These projections are from the UN publication 'World Population Prospects 1990'.

Note: The all-time peak annual increase of 2·06 per cent in the period 1965–70 had declined to 1·74 per cent by 1985–90. By 2025 this should decline to 0·99 per cent. In spite of the reduced percentage increase, world population is currently growing by 96 million people every year. Projections issued by the UN Population Fund on 29 Apr 1992 estimated that the population would stabilize at around 11 600 million c. 2150.

Using estimates made by the French demographer J. N. Biraben and others, A. R. Thatcher, a former Director of the Office of Population Censuses and Surveys, has calculated that the number of people who died between 40 000 BC and AD 1990 was nearly 60 000 million. This estimate implies that the current world population is about one eleventh of those who have ever lived.

Kong is the most populous of all colonies. The transcription of the name is from a local pronunciation of the Beijing dialect version of Xiang gang (meaning 'a port for incense'). The 1976 by-census showed that the West Area of the urban district of Mong Kok on the Kowloon Peninsula had a density of 252 090/km² *652 910/mile²*.

Of countries over 2500 km² or *1000 miles²* the most densely populated is Bangladesh, with a population of 110 602 000 (1992) living in 143 998 km² *55 598 miles²* at a density of 768/km² *1989/mile²*. The Indonesian island of Java (with an area of 132 186 km² *51 037 miles²*) had a population of 107 525 520 in 1990, giving a density of 813/km² *2107/mile²*.

The UK (244 100 km² *94 247 miles²*) had an estimated population of 57 919 000 in early 1993, giving a density of 237/km² *615/mile²*. The 1992 population density for the Borough of Islington, London was 11 812/km² *30 588/mile²*.

Most sparsely populated Antarctica became permanently occupied by relays of scientists from 1943. The population varies seasonally and reaches 2000 at times.

The least populated territory, apart from Antarctica, is Greenland, with a population of 56 600 (1992) in an area of 2 175 600 km² *840 000 miles²*, giving a density of one person to every 38·44 km² *14·84 miles²*. Some 84·3 per cent of the island comprises an ice-cap.

The lowest population density for any administrative area in the UK is that of Highland, Scotland with 8·0/km² *20·7/mile²*. The most sparsely populated county in England is Northumberland, with a density of 59·7/km² *154·7/mile²*.

Emigration More people emigrate from Mexico than from any other country, mainly to the USA. The Soviet invasion of Afghanistan in December 1979 caused an influx of 2 900 000 refugees into Pakistan and a further 2 200 000 into Iran. By 1989 the number of Afghan refugees in Pakistan had increased to 3 622 000. In late 1992 there were some 27 million refugees worldwide.

A total of 137 000 British citizens emigrated from the UK in 1991. The largest number of emigrants from the British

Most densely populated

In 1959, at the peak of the housing crisis in Hong Kong, it was reported that in one house designed for 12 people the number of occupants was 459, including 104 in one room and four living on the roof.

Immigration

In the fiscal year to September 1986, a record 1 615 854 people were arrested by US patrols on the Mexican border.

Isles in any one year was 360 000 in 1852, mainly from Ireland.

France is the most popular destination for tourists, with winter sports being just as much an attraction as summer holidays.
(Photo: Sygma/B. Annebicque)

Immigration The country which regularly receives the most legal immigrants is the United States. It has been estimated that between 1820 and 1991 the USA received 58 821 181 *official* immigrants. One in 76 of the US population is, however, an *illegal* immigrant.

The peak year for immigration into the UK was the 12 months from 1 Jul 1961 to 30 Jun 1962, when about 430 000 Commonwealth citizens arrived. The number of foreign immigrants in the year 1991 was 150 000.

Tourism The most popular tourist destination is France, which in 1991 received 55 731 000 foreign tourists. The country with the greatest receipts from tourism is the United States, with $45·6 billion in 1991. The biggest spenders on foreign tourism are Americans, who in the same year spent $39·4 billion abroad.

A record 18·1 million foreign tourists visited the United Kingdom in 1992. The highest level of expenditure, however, was £7785 million in 1990.

Birth rate Highest and lowest The crude birth rate—the number of births per 1000 population—for the whole world was estimated to be 27·1 per 1000 in 1985–90. The highest rate estimated by the United Nations for 1985–90 was 56·3 per 1000 for Malawi. Excluding the Vatican City, where the rate is negligible, the lowest recorded rate was 9·5 per 1000 for San Marino for the same period.

The crude birth rate for the UK was 13·8 registered live births per 1000 population in 1991 (13·7 for England and Wales, 13·1 for Scotland and 16·5 for Northern Ireland), while for the Republic of Ireland it was 15·1 in 1990. The annual number of births in England and Wales was highest this century in 1920 at 957 782, and lowest in 1977 at 569 259. After falling each year since 1964 when there were 875 972 births, the number started to rise again in 1978. In 1991 there were 699 200 births (on average 1916 per day or 80 per hour). The number outside marriage is now more than five times what it was in 1961, when the figure was 6 per cent, having passed 30 per cent in 1991.

Death rate The crude death rate—the number of deaths per 1000 population of all ages—for the whole world was an estimated 9·8 per 1000 in 1985–90. East Timor had a rate of 45·0 per 1000 from 1975–80, although this had subsided to 21·5 in 1985–90. The highest estimated rate in the same period was 23·4 for Sierra Leone. The lowest estimated rate for 1985–90 was 3·8 deaths per 1000 for Bahrain and the United Arab Emirates.

The crude death rate for the UK was 11·3 in 1991 (11·2 for England and Wales, 12·0 for Scotland and 9·5 for Northern Ireland). The local authority districts with the highest SMR (Standard Mortality Ratio, where the national average is 100) in 1991 were Middlesbrough and Derwentside, both of which had a SMR of 123. East Dorset had the lowest SMR, at 76. The 1990 rate for the Republic of Ireland was 9·1 registered deaths per 1000.

Natural increase The rate of natural increase for the whole world was estimated to be 17·3 (27·1 births less 9·8 deaths) per 1000 in 1985–90 compared with a peak 22 per 1000 in 1965. The highest of the latest available recorded rates was 37·4 (51·1 less 13·7) for Zambia in 1985–90. The lowest rate of natural increase in any major independent country in recent times was in the former West Germany, which experienced a decline in the same period, with a figure of −1·5 per 1000 (10·7 births and 12·2 deaths).

The 1991 rate for the UK was 2·5 (2·5 in England and Wales, 1·1 in Scotland and 7·0 in Northern Ireland). The rate for the first time in the first quarter of 1975 became temporarily one of natural decrease. The 1990 figure for the Republic of Ireland was 6·0.

Suicide The estimated daily rate of suicides throughout the world surpassed 1000 in 1965. The country with the highest rate is Sri Lanka, with 47 per 100000 population in 1991. The country with the lowest recorded rate is Jordan, with just a single case in 1970 and hence a rate of 0·04 per 100000.

In England and Wales the rate in 1991 was 7·8 per 100000 population.

Marriage and divorce The marriage rate for the Northern Mariana Islands, in the Pacific Ocean, is 31·2 per 1000 population. In the UK there were 375400 marriages in 1990—a rate of 6·6 per 1000 population. The average (median) age

for first marriages in England and Wales in 1990 was 26·1 years (men) and 24·3 years (women).

The country with most divorces is the United States, with a total of 1168000 in 1991—a rate of 4·6 per thousand population. The all-time high rate was 5·4 per thousand in 1979. There were 167500 divorces in 1990 in the UK—more than four in ten UK marriages end in divorce.

Sex ratio There were estimated to be 1014 males in the world for every 1000 females in 1990. The country with the largest recorded shortage of women is the United Arab Emirates, which in 1990 had an estimated 493 to every 1000 males. The country with the largest recorded shortage of males is Ukraine, with an estimated 1153 females to every 1000 males.

The ratio in the UK, which was 1069 females to every 1000 males in 1961, had become 1048 to every 1000 males by 1991, and is expected to be 1034 per 1000 by the turn of the century.

Infant mortality The world infant mortality rate—the number of deaths at ages under one year per 1000 live births—was 71·0 per 1000 for 1985–90. The lowest of the latest recorded rates is 5·0 in Japan in 1987.

In Ethiopia the infant mortality rate was unofficially estimated to be nearly 550 per 1000 live births in 1969. The highest rate recently estimated is 172·1 per 1000 in Afghanistan (1985–90).

The rate of infant mortality for the UK was a record low of 7·4 in 1991. The corresponding rate in 1989 for the Republic of Ireland was 7·5.

Expectation of life at birth World expectation of life has risen from 47·5 years (1950–5) towards 63·9 years (1985–1990). There is evidence that expectation of life in Britain in the 5th century AD was 33 years for males and 27 years for females. In the decade 1890–1900 the expectation of life among the population of India was 23·7 years.

The highest average expectation of life at birth is in Japan, with 82·1 years for women and 76·1 years for men in 1991. The lowest estimated for the period 1985–90 is 39·4 years for males in Sierra

Hospitals

The country with the greatest number of hospitals is China, with 61929 in 1989. Nauru has the most hospital beds per person (250 for every 10000 people), and Bangladesh and Ethiopia the fewest (3 per 10000).

Medical families

The four sons and five daughters of Dr Antonio B. Vicencio of Los Angeles, California, USA all qualified as doctors during the period 1964–82. The Barcia family of Valencia, Spain have had the same medical practice for seven generations since 1792. Eight sons of John Robertson of Benview, Dumbarton, Strathclyde graduated as medical doctors between 1892 and 1914.

Leone and 42·0 years for females in Afghanistan.

The latest available figures for the UK (1988–90) are 72·7 years for males and 78·3 years for females (73·0 years for males and 78·5 years for females in England and Wales, 70·8 and 76·6 in Scotland, and 71·3 and 77·2 in Northern Ireland). The Republic of Ireland figures for 1985–7 were 71·0 for males and 76·7 for females. The British figures for 1901 were 45·5 years for males and 49·0 years for females.

Housing For comparison, dwelling units are defined as a structurally separated room or rooms occupied by private households of one or more people and having separate access or a common passageway to the street.

The country with the greatest number of dwelling units is China, with 276947962 in 1990.

Great Britain had an estimated stock of 23046000 dwellings at the end of 1991, of which 67·7 per cent were owner-occupied. The record number of permanent houses built in a year was 425835 in 1968.

Physicians The country with the greatest number of physicians is China, which had 1763000 physicians in 1990, including those practising dentistry and those of traditional Chinese medicine.

There were 147412 doctors on the General Medical Council's Principal List, and therefore entitled to practise in the UK, as at 1 Jan 1993.

Chad has the highest number of people per physician, with 47640, whilst at the other extreme in Italy there is one physician for every 225 people. The United Kingdom has one physician to every 393 people.

Dentists The country with the most dentists is the United States, where 139625 were registered members of the American Dental Association at the end of 1992.

The number of dentists registered in the UK as at 1 Jan 1992 was 26561.

Mental health The country with the most psychiatrists and psychologists is the United States. The registered membership of the American Psychiatric Association (instituted in 1844) was 37982 in 1993, and the membership of the American Psychological Association (instituted in 1892) was 118000.

Political Unrest

Biggest demonstration A figure of 2·7 million was reported from China for a demonstration against the USSR in Shanghai on 3–4 Mar 1969 following border clashes.

Saving of life The greatest number of people saved from extinction by one man is estimated to be nearly 100000 Jews in Budapest, Hungary from July 1944 to January 1945 by the Swedish diplomat Raoul Wallenberg (b. 4 Aug 1912). After escaping an assassination attempt by the Nazis, he was imprisoned without trial in the Soviet Union. On 6 Feb 1957 Andrey Gromyko, Deputy Foreign Minister, said prisoner 'Walenberg' had died in a cell in Lubyanka Jail, Moscow on 16 Jul 1947. Sighting reports within the Gulag system persisted for years after his disappearance. He was made an Honorary Citizen of the USA on 5 Oct 1981 and on 7 May 1987 a statue was unveiled to him in

Budapest to replace an earlier one which had been removed.

Mass killings *China* The greatest massacre ever imputed by the government of one sovereign nation against the government of another is that of 26·3 million Chinese between 1949 and May 1965, during the regime of Mao Zedong (Mao Tse-tung, 1893–1976). This accusation was made by an agency of the Soviet government in a radio broadcast on 7 Apr 1969. The broadcast broke down the figure into four periods: 2·8 million (1949–52); 3·5 million (1953–7); 6·7 million (1958–60); and 13·3 million (1961–May 1965).

The Walker Report, published by the US Senate Committee of the Judiciary in July 1971, placed the parameters of the total death toll within China since 1949 between 32·25 and 61·7 million. An estimate of 63·7 million was published by Jean-Pierre Dujardin in *Figaro* magazine of 19–25 Nov 1978.

In the 13th–17th centuries there were three periods of wholesale massacre in China. The numbers of victims attributed to these events are assertions rather than reliable estimates. The figure put on the Mongolian invasions of northern China from 1210–19 and from 1311–40 are

Mystery still surrounds the fate of Raoul Wallenberg, who is estimated to have saved the lives of approaching 100 000 people during World War II. This photograph shows him in Swedish military uniform.

(Photo: Popperfoto)

Mass killings

As a percentage of a nation's total population the worst genocide appears to have been that in Cambodia (formerly Kampuchea). According to the Khmer Rouge Foreign Minister, Ieng Sary, more than a third of the 8 million Khmers were killed between 17 Apr 1975, when the Khmer Rouge captured Phnom Penh, and January 1979, when they were overthrown. Under the rule of Saloth Sar, alias Pol Pot, a founder member of the CPK (Communist Party of Kampuchea, formed in September 1960), towns, money and property were abolished and economical execution by bayonet and club introduced. Deaths at the Tuol Sleng interrogation centre reached 582 in a day.

both of the order of 35 million, while the number of victims of the bandit leader Zhang Xianzhong (*c.* 1605–47), known as the 'Yellow Tiger', from 1643–7 in the Sichuan province has been put at 40 million.

USSR Scholarly estimates for the number of human casualties of Soviet communism focus on some 40 million, excluding those killed in the 'Great Patriotic War'. Larger figures are claimed in Moscow today but these are not necessarily more authoritative. Nobel prizewinner Aleksandr Solzhenitsyn (b. 11 Dec 1918) put the total as high as 66 700 000 for the period between October 1917 and December 1959.

Towns and Cities

Oldest The oldest known walled town in the world is Arihã (Jericho). The radiocarbon dating on specimens from the lowest levels reached by archaeologists indicates habitation there by perhaps 2700 people as early as 7800 BC.

The settlement of Dolní Věstonice, Czech Republic has been dated to the Gravettian culture *c.* 27000 BC.

The oldest capital city in the world is Dimashq (Damascus), Syria. It has been continuously inhabited since *c.* 2500 BC.

Great Britain *Towns, villages, hamlets and boroughs* The oldest town in Great Britain is often cited as Colchester, the old British Camulodunum, headquarters of Belgic chiefs in the first century BC. However, the name of the tin trading post Salakee, St Mary's, Isles of Scilly is derived from pre-Celtic roots and hence *ante* 550 BC.

Many towns and villages in England can claim occupation during early prehistoric times, e.g. Thatcham, Berks, but continual occupation is difficult to prove. However, from the Iron Age onwards archaeological and historical evidence is more satisfactory and there are a number of places which were undoubtedly occupied without a break. One such place is, collectively, the six villages on the Isle of Portland, which also have the distinction of having been a Royal Manor continuously from 1078 up to the present day.

It is extremely difficult to interpret the evidence which can be derived from early charters granted to towns and boroughs and the archival evidence is often not complete. There are also several possible interpretations of the concept of a 'borough' (from burg or burgh). The following 'boroughs' claim to have had charters granted to them before AD 1000: Barnstaple, Colchester, Dover and Malmesbury. Towns or places, still extant and clearly identifiable, which are mentioned in the Anglo-Saxon Chronicles (compiled in the 9th century by monks in Winchester), associated with the events between AD 485–600 are: Bamburgh (Northumberland), Bath (Avon), Carisbrooke (Isle of Wight, Hants), Cirencester (Gloucs), Durham (Co. Durham), Gloucester (Gloucs), Iona (Scotland), Pevensey (East Sussex), Portsmouth (Hants), Salisbury (Wilts) and Wimbledon (London).

Poverty is rife in Mexico City, the world's most populous city.

(Photo: Sygma/D. Goldberg)

407

Worst Disasters in the World

Disaster	Number killed	Location	Date
Pandemic	75000000	Eurasia: The Black Death (bubonic, pneumonic and septicaemic plague)	1347–51
Genocide	c. 35000000	Mongol extermination of Chinese peasantry	1311–40
Famine	c. 30000000[1]	Northern China	1959–61
Influenza	21640000	World-wide	1918–19
Circular Storm[2]	1000000	Ganges Delta Islands, Bangladesh	12–13 Nov 1970
Flood	900000	Huang He River, China	Oct 1887
Earthquake	830000	Shaanxi, Shanxi and Henan provinces, China	2 Feb 1556
Landslides (Triggered off by single earthquake)	180000	Gansu Province, China	16 Dec 1920
Atomic Bomb	155200	Hiroshima, Japan (including radiation deaths within a year)	6 Aug 1945
Conventional Bombing[3]	c. 140000	Tokyo, Japan	10 Mar 1945
Volcanic Eruption	92000	Tambora, Sumbawa, Indonesia	5–10 Apr 1815
Avalanches	c. 18000[4]	Yungay, Huascarán, Peru	31 May 1970
Marine (Single ship)	c. 7700	*Wilhelm Gustloff* (25 484 tons) German liner torpedoed off Danzig by Soviet submarine S-13 (only 903 survivors)	30 Jan 1945
Dam Burst	c. 5000[5]	Machhu River Dam, Morvi, Gujarat, India	11 Aug 1979
Panic	c. 4000	Chongqing, China, air raid shelter	6 Jun 1941
Smog	3500–4000	London fog, England (excess deaths)	4–9 Dec 1952
Industrial (Chemical)	3350	Union Carbide methylisocyanate plant, Bhopal, India	2–3 Dec 1984
Tunnelling (Silicosis)	c. 2500	Hawk's Nest hydroelectric tunnel, W. Virginia, USA	1931–35
Fire[6] (Single building)	1670	The Theatre, Guangdong (Canton), China	May 1845
Explosion	1635[7]	Halifax, Nova Scotia, Canada	6 Dec 1917
Mining[8]	1549	Honkeiko (Benxihu) Colliery, China (coal dust explosion)	26 Apr 1942
Tornado	c. 1300	Shaturia, Bangladesh	26 Apr 1989
Riot	c. 1200	New York anti-conscription riots	13–16 Jul 1863
Mass Suicide[9]	960	Jewish Zealots, Masada, Israel	73
Railway	>800	Bagmati River, Bihar, India	6 Jun 1981
Fireworks	>800	Dauphin's wedding, Seine, Paris, France	16 May 1770
Aircraft (Civil)[10]	583	KLM-Pan Am Boeing 747 ground crash, Tenerife	27 Mar 1977
Man-eating Animal	436	Champawat district, India, tigress shot by Col. Jim Corbett (1875–1955)	1902–10
Terrorism	329	Bomb aboard Air-India Boeing 747, crashed into Atlantic south-west of Ireland. Sikh extremists suspected	23 Jun 1985

Hail[1]	246	Moradabad, Uttar Pradesh, India	20 Apr 1888
Road[11]	176	Petrol tanker explosion inside Salang Tunnel, Afghanistan	3 Nov 1982
Offshore Oil Platform	167	Piper Alpha oil production platform, North Sea	6 Jul 1988
Submarine	130	Le Surcouf rammed by US merchantman Thompson Lykes in Caribbean	18 Feb 1942
Lightning	81	Boeing 707 jet airliner, struck by lightning near Elkton, Maryland, USA	8 Dec 1963
Helicopter	61	Russian military helicopter carrying refugees shot down near Lata, Georgia	14 Dec 1992
Mountaineering	43	Lenin Peak, Tajikistan/Kyrgyzstan border (then USSR)	13 Jul 1990
Ski Lift (Cable car)	42	Cavalese resort, northern Italy	9 Mar 1976
Nuclear Reactor	31[12]	Chernobyl No. 4, Ukraine (then USSR)	26 Apr 1986
Elevator (Lift)	31	Gold mine lift at Vaal Reefs, South Africa fell 1·9km 1:2 miles	27 Mar 1980
Yacht Racing	19	28th Fastnet Race—23 boats sank or abandoned in Force 11 gale	13–15 Aug 1979
Space Exploration	7[13]	US Challenger 51L Shuttle, Cape Canaveral, Florida, USA	28 Jan 1986
Nuclear Waste Accident	high but undisclosed[14]	Venting of plutonium extraction wastes, Kyshtym, Russia (then USSR)	c. Dec 1957

FOOTNOTES

[1] It has been estimated that more than 5 million died in the post-World War I famine of 1920–1 in the USSR. The Soviet government in July 1923 informed Mr (later President) Herbert Hoover that the ARA (American Relief Administration) had since August 1921 saved 20 million lives from famine and famine-related diseases.

[2] This figure disputed—1972 for the Bangladeshi disaster was from Dr Afzal, Principal Scientific Officer of the Atomic Energy Authority Centre, Dacca. One report asserted that less than half of the population of the four islands of Bhola, Charjabbar, Hatia and Ramagati (1961 Census 1·4 million) survived. The most damaging hurricane recorded was Hurricane Andrew from 23–26 Aug 1992, which was estimated to have done c. $22 billion worth of damage.

[3] The number of civilians killed by the bombing of Germany has been put variously at 593 000 and 'over 635 000'; including some 35 000 deaths in the raids on Dresden, Germany from 13–15 Feb 1945. Total Japanese fatalities were 600 000 (conventional) and 220 000 (nuclear).

[4] A total of 18 000 Austrian and Italian troops were reported to have been lost in the Dolomite valleys of northern Italy on 13 Dec 1916 in more than 100 snow avalanches. Some of the avalanches were triggered by gunfire.

[5] The dynamiting of a Yangzi Jiang dam at Huayuan Kow by Guomindang (GMD) forces in April 1938 during the Sino-Japanese war is reputed to have resulted in 890 000 deaths.

[6] >200 000 killed in the sack of Moscow, as a result of fires started by the invading Tatars in May 1571. Worst-ever hotel fire, 162 killed, Hotel Daeyungak, Seoul, South Korea 25 Dec 1971. Worst circus fire, 168 killed, Hartford, Connecticut, USA 6 Jul 1944.

[7] Some sources maintain that the final death toll was over 3000 on 6–7 December. Published estimates of the 11 000 killed at the BASF chemical plant explosion at Oppau, Germany on 21 Sep 1921 were exaggerated. The most reliable estimate is 561 killed.

[8] The worst gold-mining disaster in South Africa was when 182 were killed in Kinross gold mine on 16 Sep 1986.

[9] As reported by the historian Flavius Josephus (c. 37–100). In modern times, the greatest mass suicide was on 18 Nov 1978 when 913 members of the People's Temple cult died of mass cyanide poisoning near Port Kaituma, Guyana. Some 7000 Japanese committed suicide, many of them jumping off cliffs to their deaths, in July 1944 during the US Marines' assault of the island of Saipan.

[10] The crash of JAL's Boeing 747, flight 123, near Tokyo on 12 Aug 1985, in which 520 passengers and crew perished, was the worst single plane crash in aviation history.

[11] Western estimates gave the number of deaths at c. 1100. Latvia has the highest fatality rate in road accidents, with 34·7 deaths per 100 000 population, and Malta the lowest, with 1·6 per 100 000.

[12] Explosion at 0123 hrs local time. Thirty-one was the official Soviet total of immediate deaths. It is not known how many of the c. 200 000 people involved in the clean-up operation died in the five-year period following the disaster since no systematic records were kept. The senior scientific officer Vladimir Chernousenko, who gave himself two to four years to live owing to his exposure to radiation, put the death toll as between 7000 and 10 000 in a statement on 13 Apr 1991.

[13] In the greatest space disaster on the ground 91 people were killed when an R-16 rocket exploded during fuelling at the Baikonur Space Center, Kazakhstan on 24 Oct 1960.

[14] More than 30 small communities in a 1200km² 460mile² area were eliminated from maps of the USSR in the years after the accident, with 17 000 people evacuated. It was possibly an ammonium nitrate-hexone explosion. A report released in 1992 indicated that 8015 people had died over a 32-year period of observation as a direct result of discharges from the complex.

Worst Disasters in the British Isles

Disaster	Number killed	Location	Date
Famine	1500000[1]	Ireland (famine and typhus)	1846–51
Pandemic (the Black Death)	800000		1347–50
Influenza	225000		Sep–Nov 1918
Circular Storm	c. 8000	'The Channel Storm'	26 Nov 1703
Smog	3500–4000	London fog	4–9 Dec 1952
Flood	c. 2000[2]	Severn Estuary	20 Jan 1606
Bombing	1436	London	10–11 May 1941
Marine (single ship)	c. 800[3]	HMS Royal George off Spithead, Hants	29 Aug 1782
Riot	565 (min)	London anti-Catholic Gordon riots	2–13 Jun 1780
Mining	439	Universal Colliery, Senghenydd, Mid Glam	14 Oct 1913
Terrorism (aircraft)	270[4]	Bomb aboard Pan Am Boeing 747, crashed over Lockerbie, Dumfries & Galloway	21 Dec 1988
Dam Burst	250	Bradfield Reservoir, Dale Dyke, near Sheffield, S Yorks (embankment burst)	12 Mar 1864
Railway	227[5]	Triple collision, Quintinshill, Dumfries & Galloway	22 May 1915
Fire (single building)	188[6]	Theatre Royal, Exeter	5 Sep 1887
Panic	183	Victoria Hall, Sunderland, Tyne and Wear	16 Jun 1883
Offshore Oil Platform	167	Piper Alpha oil production platform, North Sea	6 Jul 1988
Landslide	144	Pantglas coal tip No. 7, Aberfan, Mid Glam	21 Oct 1966
Explosion	134[7]	Chilwell, Notts (explosives factory)	1 Jul 1918
Nuclear Reactor	footnote[8]	Cancer deaths; Windscale (now Sellafield), Cumbria	10 Oct 1957
Submarine	99	HMS Thetis, during trials, Liverpool Bay	1 Jun 1939
Tornado	75	Tay Bridge collapsed under impact of 2 tornadic vortices	28 Dec 1879
Helicopter	45	Chinook, off Sumburgh, Shetland Islands	6 Nov 1986
Road	33[9]	Coach crash, River Dibb, near Grassington, N Yorks	27 May 1975
Lightning	31	(Annual total) Worst year on record	1914
Yacht Racing	19	28th Fastnet Race—23 boats sank or abandoned in Force 11 gale. Of 316 starters only 128 finished	13–15 Aug 1979
Avalanches	8	Lewes, E Sussex	27 Dec 1836
Mountaineering	6	On Cairn Gorm, near Aviemore (1245 m 4084ft)	21 Nov 1971
Earthquake	2	London earthquake, Christ's Hospital (Newgate)	6 Apr 1580

The smallest place with a town council is Fordwich, in Kent (population 252). England's largest village is Lancing, W Sussex, with an estimated population of 18100.

The most remote village on mainland Great Britain is Inverie, Highland, which is a walk of 43·5 km *27 miles* from Arnisdale, also in Highland, its nearest village.

Of the 32 new towns set up in Great Britain, that with the largest eventual planned population is Milton Keynes, Bucks, with a projected 210000 for the end of the century.

Most populous The most populous urban agglomeration in the world as listed in the United Nations *Prospects of World Urbanization 1990* is Mexico City, with a population of 20200000. By 2000 this was expected to have increased to 25600000. Tokyo-Yokohama, Japan, which until the late 1980s had been the most populous, is expected to have declined to third in the list by the turn of the century, with São Paulo in Brazil second. Censuses from individual countries and other surveys may give slightly different figures.

Great Britain The most populous conurbation in Britain is London, with 6806000 people (1992). The peak figure for London was 8615050 in 1939. The residential population of the City of London (274 ha *677·3 acres* plus 24·9 ha *61·7 acres* foreshore) is 4300 (1990 estimate) compared with 129000 in 1851. The daytime figure is 285000.

Largest in area The world's largest city, in area, is Mount Isa, Queensland, Australia. The area administered by the City Council is 41225 km² *15917 miles²*.

The largest conurbation in the UK is Greater London, with an area of 1579·5 km² *609·8 miles²*.

Highest The highest capital in the world, before the domination of Tibet by China, was Lhasa, at an elevation of 3684 m *12087 ft* above sea level. La Paz, administrative and *de facto* capital of Bolivia, stands at an altitude of 3631 m *11916 ft* above sea level. Its airport, El Alto, is at 4080 m *13385 ft*. The city was founded in 1548 by Capt. Alonso de

411

Mendoza on the site of an Indian village named Chuquiapu. It was originally called Ciudad de Nuestra Señora de La Paz (City of Our Lady of Peace), but in 1825 was renamed La Paz de Ayacucho, its present official name. Sucre, the legal capital of Bolivia, stands at 2834 m *9301 ft* above sea level.

The new town of Wenchuan, founded in 1955 on the Qinghai–Tibet road north of the Tangla range, is the highest town in the world at 5100 m *16 730 ft* above sea level.

A settlement on the T'e-li-mo trail in southern Tibet is sited at an altitude of 6019 m *19 800 ft*.

The highest village in Great Britain is Flash, Staffs at 462·7 m *1518 ft* above sea level.

The highest in Scotland is Wanlockhead, in Dumfries & Galloway, at 420 m *1378 ft* above sea level.

Lowest The Israeli settlement of Ein Bokek, which has a synagogue, on the shores of the Dead Sea is the lowest in the world, at 393·5 m *1291 ft* below sea level.

Most remote from sea The large town most remote from the sea is Urumqi (Wu-lu-mu-ch'i) in Xinjiang, the capital of China's Xinjiang Uygur Autonomous Region, at a distance of about 2500 km *1500 miles* from the nearest coastline. Its population was estimated to be 1 160 000 in late 1990.

Royalty and Heads of State

Oldest ruling house The Emperor of Japan, Akihito (b. 23 Dec 1933), is the 125th in line from the first Emperor, Jimmu Tenno or Zinmu, whose reign was traditionally from 660 to 581 BC, but more probably dates from *c.* 40 BC to *c.* 10 BC.

Her Majesty Queen Elizabeth II (b. 21 Apr 1926) represents dynasties historically traceable back at least 54 generations to the 4th century AD in the case of Tegid, great grandfather of Cunedda, founder of the House of Gwynedd in Wales. If the historicity of some early Scoto-Irish and Pictish kings were acceptable, the lineage could be extended to about 70 generations.

Reigns *Longest all-time* The longest recorded reign of any monarch is that of Phiops II (also known as Pepi II), or Neferkare, a Sixth Dynasty pharaoh of ancient Egypt. His reign began *c.* 2281 BC, when he was 6 years of age, and is believed to have lasted *c.* 94 years. Minhti, King of Arakan, which is now part of Myanmar (Burma), is reputed to have reigned for 95 years between 1279 and 1374. Musoma Kanijo, chief of the Nzega district of western Tanganyika (now part of Tanzania), reputedly reigned for more than 98 years from 1864, when aged 8, until his death on 2 Feb 1963. The longest reign of any European monarch was that of Afonso I Henriques of Portugal, who ascended the throne on 30 Apr 1112 and died on 6 Dec 1185 after a reign of 73 years 220 days, first as a count and then as king.

Longest current The King of Thailand, Bhumibol Adulyadej (Rama IX) (b. 5 Dec 1927), is currently the world's longest-reigning monarch, having succeeded to the throne following the death of his older brother on 9 Jun 1946. The longest-reigning queen is HM Queen Elizabeth II (⟨⟩ above), who succeeded to the throne on 6 Feb 1952 on the death of her father.

Shortest The Crown Prince Luis Filipe of Portugal was mortally wounded at the same time that his father was killed by a bullet which severed his carotid artery, in the streets of Lisbon on 1 Feb 1908. He was thus technically King of Portugal (Dom Luis III) for about 20 minutes.

Highest post-nominal numbers The highest post-nominal number ever used to designate a member of a royal house was 75, briefly enjoyed by Count Heinrich LXXV Reuss zu Schleiz (1800–1801). All male members of this branch of the German family are called Heinrich and are successively numbered from I upwards in three sequences. The first began in 1695 (and ended with Heinrich LXXV), the second began in 1803 (and ended with Heinrich XLVII) and the third began in 1910. These are

The enthronement of Akihito, the Emperor of the oldest ruling house in the world, on 12 Nov 1990.

(Photo: Sygma)

purely *personal* numbers and should not be confused with *regnal* numbers.

British regnal numbers date from the Norman Conquest. The highest is 8, used by Henry VIII (1509–47) and by Edward VIII (1936) who died as HRH the Duke of Windsor on 28 May 1972. Jacobites liked to style Henry Benedict, Cardinal York (b. 1725), the grandson of James II, as Henry IX in respect of his 'reign' from 1788 to 1807, when he died as last survivor in the male line of the House of Stuart.

Longest-lived 'royals' The longest life among the blood royal of Europe was that of the Princess Pauline Marie Madeleine of Croy (1887–1987), who celebrated her 100th birthday in her birthplace of Le Roeulx, Belgium on 11 Jan 1987.

The greatest age among European royal consorts is the 101 years 268 days of HSH Princess Leonilla Bariatinsky (b. 9 Jul 1816 in Moscow), who married HSH Prince Louis of Sayn-Wittgenstein-Sayn and died in Ouchy, Switzerland on 1 Feb 1918.

The longest-lived queen on record was Zita, Empress of Austria and Queen of Hungary, whose husband reigned as Emperor Charles I of Austria and King Charles IV of Hungary from 1916–18; she died on 14 Mar 1989 aged 96 years 309 days.

HRH Princess Alice (b. 25 Feb 1883) became the longest-lived British 'royal' ever on 15 Jul 1977 and died aged 97 years 313 days on 3 Jan 1981. She ful-

British Monarchy Records

Longest Reign or Tenure
Kings: 59 years 96 days[1] George III, from 1760–1820
Queens Regnant: 63 years 216 days Victoria, from 1837–1901
Queens Consort: 57 years 70 days Charlotte, from 1761–1818 (Consort of George III)

Shortest Reign or Tenure
Kings: 77 days[2] Edward V, in 1483
Queens Regnant: 13 days[3] Jane, from 6–19 Jul 1553
Queens Consort: 154 days Yoleta, from 1285–6 (Second Consort of Alexander III)

Longest Lived
Kings: 81 years 239 days[4] George III (1738–1820)
Queens Regnant: 81 years 243 days Victoria (1819–1901)
Queens Consort: 92 years Lady Elizabeth Bowes Lyon, Queen Elizabeth, the Queen Mother (b. 4 Aug 1900)

Oldest to Start Reign or Consortship
Kings: 64 years 10 months William IV (reigned 1830–7)
Queens Regnant: 37 years 5 months Mary I (reigned 1553–8)
Queens Consort: 56 years 53 days Alexandra (1844–1925) (Consort of Edward VII, reigned 1901–10)

Youngest to Start Reign or Consortship
Kings: 269 days Henry VI in 1422
Queens Regnant: 6 or 7 days Mary, Queen of Scots in 1542
Queens Consort: 6 years 11 months Isabella (Second Consort of Richard II) in 1396

FOOTNOTES
[1] *James Francis Edward, the Old Pretender, known to his supporters as James III, styled his reign from 16 Sep 1701 until his death on 1 Jan 1766 (i.e. 64 years 109 days).*
[2] *There is a strong probability that in pre-Conquest times Sweyn 'Forkbeard', the Danish King of England, reigned for only 40 days in 1013–14.*
[3] *She accepted the allegiance of the Lords of the Council (9 July) and was proclaimed on 10 July so is often referred to as the 'Nine-day Queen'.*
[4] *Richard Cromwell (b. 4 Oct 1626), the 2nd Lord Protector from 3 Sep 1658 until his abdication on 24 May 1659, lived under the alias John Clarke until 12 Jul 1712, aged 85 years 9 months and was thus the longest-lived head of state.*

Roman occupation

During the 369-year-long Roman occupation of England, Wales and parts of southern Scotland, there were 40 sole and 27 co-emperors of Rome. Of these the longest-reigning was Constantinus I (The Great) from 31 Mar 307 to 22 May 337—30 years 2 months.

filled 20000 engagements, including the funerals of five British monarchs.

Youngest king and queen Of the world's 191 sovereign states, 45 are not republics. They are headed by 1 emperor, 13 kings, 3 queens, 2 sultans, 1 grand duke, 2 princes, 3 amirs, an elected monarch, the Pope, a president chosen from and by 7 hereditary sheiks, a head of state currently similar to a constitutional monarch, and 2 nominal non-hereditary 'princes' in one country. Queen Elizabeth II is head of state of 15 Commonwealth countries in addition to the UK. The country with the youngest king is Swaziland, where King Mswati III (⊳ below) was crowned on 25 Apr 1986 aged 18 years 6 days. He was born Makhosetive, the 67th son of King Subhusa II. The country with the youngest queen is Denmark, with Queen Margrethe II (b. 16 Apr 1940).

Heads of State *Oldest and youngest* The oldest head of state in the world is Félix Houphouët-Boigny, president of the Ivory Coast (b. 18 Oct 1905). The youngest is King Mswati III of Swaziland (b. 19 Apr 1968) (⊳ above).

First female presidents Isabel Perón (b. 4 Feb 1931) of Argentina became the world's first female president when she succeeded her husband on his death on 1 Jul 1974. She held office until she was deposed in a bloodless coup on 24 Mar 1976. President Vigdis Finnbogadottir (b. 15 Apr 1930) of Iceland became the world's first democratically elected female head of state on 30 Jun 1980.

Meeting The summit segment of the United Nations Conference on Environment and Development, on 12–13 Jun 1992, was attended by 92 heads of state and heads of government—the largest gathering of world leaders. The summit had 103 participants altogether and was one of the meetings at the 'Earth Summit', which was held in Rio de Janeiro, Brazil from 3–14 Jun 1992.

Legislatures

Earliest and oldest The earliest known legislative assembly or *ukkim* was a bicameral one in Erech, Iraq *c.*2800 BC. The oldest recorded legislative body is the Icelandic *Althing*, founded in AD 930. This body, which originally comprised 39 local chieftains at Thingvellir, was abolished in 1800, but restored by Denmark to a consultative status in 1843 and a legislative status in 1874. The legislative assembly with the oldest *continuous* history is the Isle of Man Tynwald which may have its origins in the late ninth century and hence possibly pre-date the *Althing*. All new laws are proclaimed in Manx and English.

Largest The largest legislative assembly in the world is the National People's Congress of the People's Republic of China, which has 2978 single-party members who are indirectly elected for a five-year term. The eighth congress convened in March 1993.

Smallest quorum The House of Lords has the smallest quorum, expressed as a percentage of eligible voters, of any legislative body in the world, namely less than one-third of 1 per cent. To transact business there must be three peers present, including the Lord Chancellor or his deputy. The House of Commons' quorum of 40 MPs (out of 651 members), including the Speaker or his deputy, is 13 times as exacting.

Constitutions

The world's oldest comprehensive written constitution still in uninterrupted use is that of the United States of America, ratified by the necessary Ninth State (New Hampshire) on 21 Jun 1788 and declared to be in effect on 2 July of that year.

Handshaking

The record number of hands shaken by a public figure at an official function was 8513 by President Theodore Roosevelt (1858–1919) at a New Year's Day White House presentation in Washington, DC, USA on 1 Jan 1907. Scott Killon of Vancouver, Canada shook hands with 25289 different people in 8 hours during Expo 92 in Seville, Spain on 8 Aug 1992.

Stair climbing

In the line of duty, Brian Davis has mounted 334 of the 364 steps of the tower in the Houses of Parliament 4291 times in nine years to 31 Mar 1993— equivalent to 26 ascents of Mt Everest.

Whilst Theodore Roosevelt holds the handshaking record for a politician, Scott Killon shook hands with over 25000 visitors in just eight hours at Expo 92 in Seville. He began at the pavilion of his own country, Canada, and visited a number of other areas of the exhibition in the course of the evening.

(Photo: Government of Canada)

Greatest petitions The greatest petition on record was signed by 13 078 935 people in South Korea between 11 Nov–23 Dec 1991. They were protesting against efforts by advanced agricultural exporting countries to open their country's rice market to foreign imports.

In Great Britain the largest theoretically has been the Great Chartist Petition of 1848, but of the 5 706 000 'signatures' only 1 975 496 were valid. Otherwise the largest in Britain was in support of ambulance workers in their pay dispute, when a national petition containing 4 680 727 signatures was delivered to the House of Commons on 14 Dec 1989. Since 1974, the signatures on petitions which have been presented have not been counted at the House of Commons.

Longest membership The longest span as a legislator was 83 years, by József Madarász (1814–1915). He first attended the Hungarian Parliament from 1832–86 as *oblegatus absentium* (i.e. on behalf of an absent deputy). He was a full member from 1848–50 and from 1861 until his death on 31 Jan 1915.

Longest speeches The longest speech made was one by Chief Mangosuthu Buthelezi, the Zulu leader, when he gave an address to the KwaZulu legislative assembly between 12 and 29 Mar 1993.

He spoke on 11 of the 18 days, averaging nearly 2½ hours on each of the 11 days.

United Nations The longest speech made in the United Nations has been one of 4hr 29min on 26 Sep 1960 by President Fidel Castro Ruz (b. 13 Aug 1927) of Cuba.

Oldest treaty The oldest treaty still in force is the Anglo-Portuguese Treaty, which was signed in London over 620 years ago on 16 Jun 1373, making Portugal the UK's oldest ally. The text was confirmed 'with my usual flourish' by John de Banketre, Clerk.

Women's suffrage As far back as 1838 the Pitcairn Islands incorporated female suffrage in its constitution, although this was only *de facto* and not legally binding. The earliest legislature with female voters was the Territory of Wyoming, USA in 1869, followed by the Isle of Man in 1881. The earliest country to have universal suffrage was New Zealand in 1893. The attempted exercise of the franchise by Mrs Lily Maxwell in Manchester on 26 Nov 1867 was declared illegal on 9 Nov 1868.

Parliaments—United Kingdom

Earliest The earliest known use of the term 'parliament' is in an official royal document, in the meaning of a summons to the King's (Henry III's) Council, dating from 19 Dec 1241. The Houses of Parliament of the United Kingdom in the Palace of Westminster, London had 1856 members (House of Lords 1205, of whom *c.* 650 are active; House of Commons 651) in April 1993.

Longest The longest English Parliament was the 'Pensioners' Parliament of Charles II, which lasted from 8 May 1661 to 24 Jan 1679, a period of 17 years 8 months and 16 days. The longest United Kingdom Parliament was that of George V, Edward VIII and George VI, lasting from 26 Nov 1935 to 15 Jun 1945, a span of 9 years 6 months and 20 days.

Shortest The parliament of Edward I, summoned to Westminster for 30 May 1306, lasted only 1 day. That of Charles II at Oxford lasted 7 days, from 21–28 Mar 1681. The shortest United Kingdom Parliament was that of George III, lasting from 15 Dec 1806 to 29 Apr 1807, a period of only 4 months and 14 days.

Longest sittings The longest sitting in the House of Commons was one of 41½hr from 4p.m. on 31 Jan 1881 to 9:30a.m. on 2 Feb 1881, on the question of better Protection of Person and Property in Ireland. The longest sitting of the Lords has been 19hr 16min from 2:30p.m. on 29 Feb to 9:46a.m. on 1 Mar 1968 on the Commonwealth Immigrants Bill (committee stage). The longest sitting of a standing committee was from 10:30a.m. on 11 May to 12:08p.m. on 13 May 1948, when Standing Committee D considered the Gas Bill through two nights for 49hr 38min.

Longest speeches The longest recorded continuous speech in the Chamber of the House of Commons was that of Rt Hon Henry Peter Brougham (1778–1868) on 7 Feb 1828, when he spoke for 6hours on Law Reform. He ended at 10:40p.m. and the report of this speech occupied 12 columns of the next day's *Times.* Brougham, created the 1st Lord Brougham and Vaux on 22 Nov 1830, then set the House of Lords record, also with 6 hours, on 7 Oct 1831, when speaking on the second reading of the Reform Bill, 'fortified by 3 tumblers of spiced wine'.

The longest back-bench speech under present, much stricter standing orders has been one of 4hr 23min by Sir Ivan Lawrence (b. 24 Dec 1936), Conservative Member for Burton, opposing the Water (Fluoridation) Bill on 6 Mar 1985. John Golding (b. 9 Mar 1931) (then Labour, Newcastle-under-Lyme) spoke for 11 hr 15 min in committee on small amendments to the British Telecommunications Bill on 8–9 Feb 1983.

Most and least time-consuming legislation The most profligate use of parliamentary time was on the Government of Ireland Bill of 1893–4, which required 82 days in the House of Commons of which 46 days were in committee. The record for a standing committee is 59 sittings for the Police and Criminal Evidence Bill, from 17 Nov 1983 to 29 Mar 1984.

The Abdication Bill (of King Edward VIII) passed all its stages in the Commons (2hr) and the Lords (8min) on 11–12 Dec 1936 and received the Royal Assent at 1:52a.m. on the latter date. Several Bills have gone through the Commons without debate—most notably the Protection of Birds (Amendment) Bill 1976, which took just 67 sec in July 1976.

Private Members' Bills Balloting by private members for parliamentary time was in being at least as early as 1844. The highest recorded number of public Bills introduced by private members was 226 in 1908, but the highest number to receive Royal Assent was 27 in the Commons and 7 in the Lords in 1963–4. The least productive session was 1973–4, with nil from 42 Bills presented in the Commons and nil from 10 in the Lords.

Divisions The record number of divisions in a House of Commons day is 64 on 23–24 Mar 1971, including 57 in succession between midnight and noon. The greatest number of votes in a division was 660, with a majority of 40 (350–310) against the government of the Marquess of Salisbury on the vote of no confidence on 11 Aug 1892.

Elections—World

Largest The largest elections in the world were those beginning on 20 May 1991 for the Indian *Lok Sabha* (Lower

The Mongolian People's Revolutionary Party has held power since 1924, until three years ago without any opposition but since then in a multi-party system. The 1990 elections gave the people the opportunity to reject Communism, but they voted in favour of it. Procedures in rural regions were very different from what people in the west are used to.

(Photo: Sygma/L. Zilberman)

House), which has 543 elective seats. A total of 315 439 908 people cast their votes in the 511 constituencies where the seats were being contested, out of an eligible electorate of 488 678 993. The elections were contested by 359 parties, and there were nearly 565 000 polling stations manned by 3 million staff. As a result of the election a new government was formed under the leadership of P. V. Narasimha Rao of the Congress (I) Party.

Closest The ultimate in close political elections occurred in Zanzibar (now part of Tanzania) on 18 Jan 1961, when the Afro-Shirazi Party won by a single seat, after the seat of Chake-Chake on Pemba Island had been gained by a single vote.

The narrowest recorded percentage win in an election would seem to be for the office of Southern District Highway Commissioner in Mississippi, USA on 7 Aug 1979. Robert E. Joiner was declared the winner over W. H. Pyron, with 133 587 votes to 133 582. The loser thus obtained more than 49·999 per cent of the votes.

Most decisive North Korea recorded a 100 per cent turn-out of electors and a 100 per cent vote for the Workers' Party of Korea in the general election of 8 Oct 1962. The next closest approach was in Albania on 14 Nov 1982, when a single voter spoiled national unanimity for the official (and only) Communist candidates, who consequently obtained 99·999 93 per cent of the poll in a reported 100 per cent turn-out of 1 627 968.

Longest in power In Mongolia the Communists (Mongolian People's Revolutionary Party) have been in power since 1924, although only in the last three years within a multi-party system. In February 1992 the term 'People's Republic' was dropped from the name, and all Russian troops have now left the country.

Most bent In the Liberian presidential election of 1927 President Charles D.B. King (1875–1961) was returned with a majority over his opponent, Thomas J.R. Faulkner of the People's Party, officially announced as 234 000. President King thereby claimed a 'majority' more than 15½ times greater than the entire electorate.

Highest personal majority The highest ever personal majority for any politician has been 4 726 112 in the case of Boris Yeltsin, the unofficial Moscow candidate, in the parliamentary elections held in the former Soviet Union on 26 Mar 1989. Yeltsin received 5 118 745 votes out of the 5 722 937 which were cast in the Moscow constituency, his closest rival obtaining 392 633 votes. Benazir Bhutto achieved 96·71 per cent of the poll in the Larkana-III constituency at the 1988 general election in Pakistan, with 82 229 votes. The next highest candidate obtained just 1979 votes.

Largest party The largest political party is the Chinese Communist Party, formed in 1920, which has a membership estimated in 1991 to be 50 320 000.

Largest ballot paper On 5 Mar 1985 in the State Assembly (*Vidhan Sabha*) elections in Karnataka, India there were 301 candidates for Belgaum City.

Political instability El Salvador has averaged one government every eighteen months since it obtained its independence in 1821, whilst Syria had 17 governments in the space of just 33

417

European Parliament Records

★ The Parliament was first constituted as the Assembly of the European Coal and Steel Community, and adopted the name of European Parliament in 1962. Direct elections were introduced in 1979, and the first such elections were held between 7 and 10 June of that year. The next elections will be held between 9 and 12 Jun 1994.

★ There are 518 members (usually referred to as MEPs) of the European Parliament.

★ France, Germany, Italy and the United Kingdom have most members, with 81 each, whilst Luxembourg has the fewest, with 6.

★ The President of the Parliament is directly elected by its members, for a term of 2½ years. France is the only country to have had more than one President—Simone Veil, who was elected in 1979, and Pierre Pflimlin, who was elected in 1984.

★ Currently the largest grouping in the Parliament is the Socialist Group, with 198 members, whilst the smallest is the non-attached, with 21.

★ The best turnout has been in Belgium in 1989, when 93 per cent of the electorate voted (although voting is compulsory there), and the lowest has been in the United Kingdom in 1984,

The European Parliament plays an important part in the life of the European community, having legislative, budgetary and supervisory roles. Every five years people in the member countries of the European Community are given the chance to have their say and choose its members.
(Photo: Rex Features/Boccon Gibod)

when just 32·5 per cent of the electorate cast their votes.

★ In Europe as a whole, the highest turnout was in 1979, when 62·5 per cent voted. The turnout has declined at both of the subsequent elections.

months between March 1949 and December 1951, thus averaging a change every other month. Some statisticians contend that Bolivia, since it became a sovereign country in 1825, has had a record 191 attempted coups. Only 23 of these, however, have been successful.

Prime Ministers and Statesmen

Oldest The longest-lived Prime Minister of any country was Naruhiko

Higashikuni (Japan), who was born on 3 Dec 1887 and died on 20 Jan 1990, aged 102 years 48 days. He was his country's first Prime Minister after World War II, but held office for less than two months, resigning in October 1945.

El Hadji Muhammad el Mokri, Grand Vizier of Morocco, died on 16 Sep 1957 at a reputed age of 116 Muslim (*Hijri*) years, equivalent to 112½ Gregorian years.

Prime Ministerial Records

Though given legal warrant in the instrument of the Congress of Berlin in 1878 and awarded official recognition in a Royal Warrant of 1905, the first statutory mention of the title of Prime Minister was only in 1917. All previous acknowledged First Ministers had tenure as First Lords of the Treasury with the exception of No. 11, William Pitt, Earl of Chatham, who controlled his ministers as Secretary of State of the Southern Department or as Lord Privy Seal. The first to preside over his fellow King's ministers was Sir Robert Walpole. His ministry began in 1721, although it was not until 15 May 1730, when Viscount Townshend resigned from his position as Secretary of State, that Walpole gained absolute control of the Cabinet.

Record	No.	Figure	Name	Date / Note
LONGEST SERVING	16th	17 years 47 days	Hon. William Pitt (1759–1806)	19 Dec 1783–3 Feb 1801
LONGEST SERVING (20th century)	51st	11 years 203 days	Margaret Thatcher (née Roberts) (b. 13 Oct 1925)	3 May 1979–22 Nov 1990
MOST MINISTRIES	40th	5	Earl Baldwin (1867–1947)	22 May 1923–28 May 1937
SHORTEST SERVICE IN OFFICE	21st	120 days	George Canning (1770–1827)	10 Apr–8 Aug 1827
YOUNGEST TO ASSUME OFFICE	16th	24 years 205 days	Hon. William Pitt (1759–1806)	19 Dec 1783 (declined when 23 years 275 days)
YOUNGEST TO ASSUME OFFICE (20th century)	52nd	47 years 244 days	John Major (b. 29 Mar 1943)	28 Nov 1990
OLDEST FIRST TO ASSUME OFFICE	30th	70 years 109 days	Viscount Palmerston (1784–1865)	6 Feb 1855
GREATEST AGE IN OFFICE	32nd	84 years 64 days	William Gladstone (1809–98)	3 Mar 1894 (elected at 82 years 171 days)
LONGEST LIVED	46th	92 years 322 days	Earl of Stockton (1894–1986)	from 6 Apr 1984 (so surpassing No. 43)
LONGEST SURVIVAL AFTER OFFICE	12th	41 years 45 days	Duke of Grafton (1735–1811)	from 28 Jan 1770
SHORTEST LIVED	6th	44 years	Duke of Devonshire (1720–64)	died 2 Oct 1764 (exact birth date unknown)
SHORTEST MINISTRY	23rd	22 days	Duke of Wellington (1769–1852)	17 Nov–9 Dec 1834
SHORTEST POSSESSION OF SEALS	4th	c. 48 hours	Earl of Bath (1684–1764)	10–12 Feb 1746
SHORTEST PRIOR SERVICE AS MP	16th	2 years 11 months	Hon. William Pitt (1759–1806)	19 Dec 1783
LONGEST PRIOR SERVICE AS MP	30th	47 years	Viscount Palmerston (1784–1865)	1807–6 Feb 1855
LONGEST SUBSEQUENT SERVICE AS MP	38th	22 years 156 days	Earl Lloyd George (1863–1945)	22 Oct 1922–26 Mar 1945
LONGEST SPAN AS MP (broken)	43rd	63 years 360 days approx.	Sir Winston Churchill (1874–1965)	1 Oct 1900–25 Sep 1964
RICHEST	28th	£7¼ million (now approx. £210 million)	Earl of Derby (1799–1869)	Annual rent roll in 1869 £170000
POOREST	16th	£40000 (now >£1 million) in debt	Hon. William Pitt (1759–1806)	Level of personal debt by 1800
TALLEST	50th	1·85m 6ft 1 in	Lord Callaghan (b. 27 Mar 1912)	
SHORTEST	27th	1·64m 5ft 4¾ in	Lord John Russell (1792–1878)	Seven-month baby: max. wt. 50·7 kg 8 stone
MOST LIVING SIMULTANEOUSLY	8th, 11–26th, 29–30th; 12th, 14th–31st		Bute, Chatham, Grafton, North, Shelburne, Portland (Pitt) till Chatham died	5 Feb–11 May 1788
				21 Dec 1804–7 May 1805
				19 Dec 1783–11 May 1788
MOST LIVING EX-PRIME MINISTERS	6	34–35th, 37–38th, 40th–41st	Rosebery, Balfour, Asquith, Lloyd-George, Baldwin, Macdonald (Baldwin's second term) till Asquith died	4 Nov 1924–15 Feb 1928
ASSASSINATED	1	19th	Hon. Spencer Perceval (1762–1812)	4 Oct 1809–11 May 1812

Prime ministerial children

The Duke of Grafton (1735–1811), who was Prime Minister from 14 Oct 1768 to 28 Jan 1770, fathered more children than any other British Prime Minister. He had three children by his first wife and twelve or possibly thirteen by his second.

Most principal offices

Lord Callaghan (b. 27 Mar 1912), Prime Minister from 16 Oct 1964 to 4 May 1979, uniquely served also as Foreign and Home Secretary and as Chancellor of the Exchequer.

The oldest age at *first* appointment has been 81, in the case of Morarji Ranchhodji Desai of India (b. 29 Feb 1896) in March 1977.

Longest term of office The longest-serving Prime Minister of a sovereign state is currently Khalifa bin Sulman al-Khalifa (b. 3 Jul 1933) of Bahrain, who has held office since Bahrain became independent in August 1971. By then he had already been in office for 1½ years.

Marshal Kim Il Sung (*né* Kim Sung Chu) (b. 15 Apr 1912) has been head of government or head of state of the Democratic People's Republic of Korea since 25 Aug 1948.

Andrey Andreyevich Gromyko (1909–89) had been Minister of Foreign Affairs of the USSR since 15 Feb 1957 (having been Deputy Foreign Minister since 1946), when he was elected President of the USSR in 2 Jul 1985, a position he held until 30 Sep 1988. Pyotr Lomako (1904–90) served in the government of the former USSR as Minister for Non-Ferrous Metallurgy from 1940–1986. He was relieved of his post after 46 years on 1 Nov 1986, aged 82, having served on the Central Committee of the CPSU since 1952.

Woman Sirimavo Bandaranaike (b. 1916) of Ceylon (now Sri Lanka) became the first woman Prime Minister when her party, the Sri Lanka ('Blessed Ceylon') Freedom Party, won the gen-

eral election in July 1960. (⇔ also Longest hearings)

Youngest Currently the youngest head of government is HM Druk Gyalpo ('dragon king') Jigme Singye Wangchuk of Bhutan (b. 11 Nov 1955), who has been head of government since March 1972, when he was 16 years old.

Majorities—United Kingdom

Largest The largest majority, in 1931 by the coalition of Conservatives, Liberals and National Labour, was 491 seats and 60·5 per cent of the vote. The largest majority in the era before universal suffrage was 288 by a 'Liberal' alliance of Whigs, Radicals and Irish supporters of O'Connell in 1832.

Smallest The narrowest majority was that of Labour in 1964, with four over the Conservatives and Liberals combined. In the two elections of 1910 the Liberals had a majority of two in February and there was a dead heat in December, but in both cases they had the support of the Irish Nationalists and Labour, which gave them in practice majorities of 122 and 126.

Division The largest majority on a division was one of 529 in favour of the government (563–34) on 21 Jan 1991, on a vote against its motion expressing full support for British forces in the Gulf during the Gulf War.

House of Lords

Oldest member The oldest member ever was the Rt Hon. Lord Shinwell (1884–1986), who first sat in the Lower House in November 1922 and lived to be 101 years 202 days. The oldest peer to make a maiden speech was Lord Maenan (1854–1951) at the age of 94 years 123 days (⇔ Peerage).

Youngest member The youngest potential member of the House of Lords is currently the Earl of Craven (b. 12 Jun 1989). The youngest current member to have taken his seat is the Earl of Hardwicke (b. 3 Feb 1971).

Political Office Holders

Party The longest period of party ascendancy in British political and parlia-

United Kingdom Electoral Records

Votes (electorate)

MOST: 33 610 399, general election 9 Apr 1992.

MOST (party): 14 094 116 (Con.), general election 9 Apr 1992.

Votes (individual)

MOST: 75 205, Sir Cooper Rawson (Con.), Brighton, Sussex, 1931.

LEAST: Nil, F.R. Lees (Temperance Chartist), Ripon, Yorks, Dec 1860.

LEAST SINCE UNIVERSAL FRANCHISE: 5, Lt. Cdr W. Boaks (Public Safety Democratic Monarchist White Resident), Glasgow, Hillhead, 25 Mar 1982; Dr Kailish Trivedi (Independent Janata), Kensington by-election, 14 Jul 1988.

LEAST SINCE UNIVERSAL FRANCHISE IN GENERAL ELECTION: 13, B.C. Wedmore (Belgrano), Finchley, 9 Jun 1983.

Majority

HIGHEST: *Man*: 62 253, Sir Cooper Rawson (Con.), Brighton, Sussex, 1931. *Woman*: 38 823, Countess of Iveagh (Con.), Southend, Essex, 1931.

HIGHEST (current): 36 230 by Rt Hon. John Major (Con., Huntingdon).

NARROWEST: 1 vote, Matthew Fowler (Lib.), Durham, 1895; 1 vote, H.E. Duke (Unionist), Exeter, Devon, Dec 1910. *Since Universal Franchise*: 2 votes, A.J. Flint (National Labour), Ilkeston, Derbyshire, 1931.

NARROWEST (current): 19 by Walter Sweeney (Con., Vale of Glamorgan).

Oldest MP

EVER: Aged 97 or 98, Sir Francis Knollys, Reading (c. 1550–1648).

SINCE 1832: Aged 96 years 13 days, Hon. Charles Pelham Villiers, Wolverhampton South (1802–98).

Youngest MP

EVER: Aged 15 or 16, Edmund Waller (1606–87), Amersham, Bucks, 1621.

SINCE 1832: James Dickson (Lib.) (1859–1941), returned for Dungannon, Co. Tyrone on 25 Jun 1880, at the age of 21 years 67 days.

Most Recounts

7: Brighton, Kemptown 1964 and Peterborough 1966.

General Election Poll

HIGHEST: 93·42%, Fermanagh & S Tyrone, 1951.

LOWEST: 29·7%, Kennington, London, 1918.

Last Unopposed Returns

GENERAL ELECTION: 25 Oct 1951, Antrim N and S: R.W.H. O'Neill and D.L. Savory; Armagh: Major J.R.E. Horden; Londonderry: W. Wellwood (all Ulster Unionists).

BY-ELECTION: 20 Nov 1954, Armagh: C.W. Armstrong.

Largest Constituency by Area

Ross, Cromarty & Skye, 954 680 ha *2 472 260 acres*.

Largest Electorate

217 900, Hendon (Barnet), 1941.

Smallest Electorate

10 851, City of London, 1945.

Most Rotten Borough

(8 Electors for 2 unopposed members) 1821 Old Sarum, Wiltshire. No elections contested 1295–1831.

Most Parliamentary Contests

16 by Rt Hon. Tony Benn (formerly A.N. Wedgwood-Benn) (b. 3 Apr 1925) since November 1950.

Most By-Election Candidates

19: Newbury, 6 May 1993, won by David Rendel (Lib. Dem.).

Longest Gap Between By-Elections

No writ was moved for any by-election between that for Truro on 12 Mar 1987 and that for Kensington and Chelsea on 14 Jul 1988—1 year 125 days later.

---

mentary history is definitional. The Whig Ascendancy ran from 17 Mar 1715 to the death of King George II on 25 Oct 1760, and followed until the assuming of office of the Earl of Bute on 26 May 1762—47 years 2 months, in which time there were eight general elections. The Tory Ascendancy ran from the appointment of William Pitt (the Younger) on 19 Dec 1783, as confirmed by the general elec-

Speakership— longest tenure

Arthur Onslow (1691–1768) was elected Mr Speaker on 23 Jan 1728, aged 36. He held the position for 33 years 43 days, until 18 Mar 1761, allowing for the 'lost' 11 days (3–13 Sep 1752).

Lowest election expenses

When James Maxton retained his seat in the Glasgow (Bridgeton) constituency at the 1935 general election, his expenses totalled just £54.

Fastest election result

In the 1959 general election, the result from Billericay, Essex was announced as early as 57 minutes after the polls closed, at 9:57 p.m.

Heaviest and tallest MP

The heaviest MP of all time is believed to be Sir Cyril Smith, Liberal member for Rochdale from October 1972 to April 1992, when in January 1976 his peak reported weight was 189·6kg *29st 12lb*.

Sir Louis Gluckstein (1897–1979), Conservative member for East Nottingham (1931–45), was an unrivalled 2·02m *6ft 7½in*. Currently the tallest is the Hon. Archie Hamilton (b. 30 Dec 1941), Conservative member for Epsom and Ewell, at 1·98m *6ft 6in*.

---

tion of March–May 1784, until the fall of the Duke of Wellington's second administration on 21 Nov 1830—46 years 11 months, during which time there were seven general elections.

Prime Ministers The only Prime Minister to retain power for four successive general elections was Lord Liverpool, in 1812 (30 Sep–24 Nov), 1818 (11 Jun–4 Aug), 1820 (1 Mar–21 Apr) and 1826 (3 Jun–23 Jul).

Since the reduction of the term of Parliaments from seven years to five years in 1911, the only Prime Minister to have been returned to power in three successive general elections is Margaret Thatcher (◇ table), on 3 May 1979, 9 Jun 1983 and 11 Jun 1987.

Chancellorship *Longest and shortest tenures* The Rt Hon. Sir Robert Walpole, later the 1st Earl of Orford (1676–1745), served for 22 years 5 months as Chancellor of the Exchequer, holding office continuously from 12 Oct 1715 to 12 Feb 1742, except for the period from 16 Apr 1717 to 2 Apr 1721.

The briefest tenure of this office was 26 days in the case of the Baron (later the 1st Earl of) Mansfield (1705–93), from 11 Sep to 6 Oct 1767. The only man to serve four terms as Chancellor was the Rt Hon. William Ewart Gladstone (1809–98).

The longest budget speech was that of the Rt Hon. David (later Earl) Lloyd George (1863–1945) on 29 Apr 1909, which lasted 4hr 51min but was interrupted by a 30-min laryngeal tea-break. He announced *inter alia* the introduction of car tax and petroleum duty. Mr Gladstone spoke for 4¾hours on 18 Apr 1853.

Foreign Secretaryship *Longest tenures* The longest continuous term of office of any Foreign Secretary has been the 10 years 359 days of Sir Edward Grey (later Viscount Grey of Fallodon) from 11 Dec 1905 to 5 Dec 1916. The Rt Hon. Sir Henry John Temple, 3rd Viscount Palmerston aggregated 15 years 296 days in three spells in 1830–34, 1835–41 and 1846–51.

MPs *Youngest* Henry Long (1420–90) was returned for an Old Sarum seat at the age of 15. His precise date of birth is unknown. Minors were debarred in law in 1695 and in fact in 1832.

The youngest ever woman MP has been Josephine Bernadette Devlin, now Mrs Michael McAliskey (b. 23 Apr 1947), elected for Mid Ulster (Independent Unity) aged 21 years 359 days on 17 Apr 1969.

The youngest current member is Matthew Taylor, MP (Liberal Democrat) for Truro (b. 3 Jan 1963).

Oldest Sir Francis Knollys (*c*. 1550–1648), 'the ancientest Parliament man in England', was re-elected for Reading in

Women MPs

A record 59 women were voted in to the House of Commons in the general election of 9 Apr 1992.

1640 when apparently aged 90, and was probably 97 or 98 at the time of his death.

The oldest of 20th-century members has been Samuel Young (b. 14 Feb 1822), Nationalist MP for East Cavan (1892 to 1918), who died on 18 Apr 1918, aged 96 years 63 days.

Father of the House The title is nowadays bestowed on the Member who has the longest unbroken service in the Commons. The earliest occurrence of the phrase dates from 1816.

The oldest Father was the Rt Hon. Charles Pelham Villiers (Wolverhampton South) when he died on 16 Jan 1898, aged 96 years 13 days. The current Father is the Rt Hon. Sir Edward Heath, MP (Old Bexley and Sidcup), who took the oath on 2 Mar 1950.

Longest span Sir Francis Knollys (⬦ above) was elected for Oxford in 1575 and died a sitting member for Reading 73 years later in 1648.

The longest span of service of any 20th-century MP is 63 years 11 months (1 Oct 1900 to 25 Sep 1964) by the Rt Hon. Sir Winston Leonard Spencer Churchill (1874–1965), with breaks only in 1908 and from 1922–4. The longest continuous span was that of C.P. Villiers (⬦ above). The longest living of all parliamentarians was Theodore Cooke Taylor (1850–1952), Liberal MP for Batley from 1910–18.

Briefest span There are two 18th-century examples of posthumous elections. Capt. the Hon. Edward Legge, RN (1710–47) was returned unopposed for Portsmouth on 15 Dec 1747. News came later that he had died in the West Indies 87 days before polling. In 1780 John Kirkman, standing for the City of London, expired before polling had ended but was nonetheless duly returned. A.J. Dobbs (Lab, Smethwick), elected on 5 Jul 1945, was killed on the way to take his seat.

Women The first woman to be elected to the House of Commons was Mme Constance Georgine Markievicz (*née* Gore Booth). She was elected as member (Sinn Fein) for St Patrick's Dublin on 28 Dec 1918. The first woman to take her seat was the Viscountess Astor (1879–1964) (*née* Nancy Witcher Langhorne at Danville, Virginia, USA; formerly Mrs Robert Gould Shaw), who was elected Unionist member for the Sutton division of Plymouth, Devon on 28 Nov 1919, and took her seat 3 days later. The first woman to take her seat from the island of Ireland was Lady Fisher (*née* Patricia Smiles) as unopposed Ulster Unionist for North Down on 15 Apr 1953, as Mrs Patricia Ford.

The first woman cabinet minister was the Rt Hon. Margaret Grace Bondfield (1873–1953), appointed Minister of Labour in 1929.

Weight of legislation The greatest amount of legislation in a year has been 11 453 pages (83 Public General Acts and 2251 Statutory Instruments) in 1975. This compares with 46 Acts and 1130 Instruments (1998 pages) in 1928. The most Acts were 123 in 1939 and the fewest 39 in 1929 and 1942. The peak for Statutory Instruments was 2916 in 1947.

Mayoralties The longest recorded mayoralty was that of Edmond Mathis (1852–1953), *maire* of Ehuns, Haute-Saône, France for 75 years (1878–1953). The mayoralty of the City of London dates from 1192, with the 20-year term of Henry Fitz Ailwyn until 1212. Since the practice of annual elections was instituted in 1215, the longest-serving Mayor was Gregory de Rokesley, who held office for eight years (1274/75–1280/81 and 1284/85). The earliest recorded mayor of the City of York, Nigel, dates from 1142. Anthony Jennings served as Mayor of Fordwich, Kent for 44 consecutive years from 1785–1829. Councillor Denis Martineau was Lord Mayor of Birmingham in 1986/87, following in office his father, grandfather, great-grandfather and great-great-grandfather.

Local government service duration records

The oldest local office was that of reeve, to supervise villeins. First mentioned in AD 787, it evolved to that of shire reeve, hence sheriff.

Major Sir Philip Barber (1876–1961) served as county councillor for Nottinghamshire for 63 years 41 days, from 8 Mar 1898 to 18 Apr 1961. Matthew Anderson was a member of the Borough Council of Abingdon, Oxon for 69 years 4 months, from April 1709 until August 1778. Henry Winn (1816–1914) served as parish clerk for Fulletby, near Horncastle, Lincs for 76 years. Clifford Tasker (1906–1980) of Pontefract, W Yorks was appointed as presiding officer for elections in 1921 when aged 15, and served for 59 years until March 1980.

Judicial

Legislation and Litigation

Statutes *Oldest* The earliest surviving judicial code was that of King Ur-Hammu during the third dynasty of Ur, Iraq, *c.* 2250 BC. The oldest English statute in the Statute Book is a section of the Statute of Marlborough of 18 Nov 1267, re-entitled in 1948 'The Distress Act 1267' and most recently cited in the High Court in 1986. Some statutes enacted by Henry II (died 1189) and earlier kings are even more durable as they have been assimilated into the Common Law. An extreme example is Ine's Law concerning the administration of shires. Ine reigned over the West Saxons from AD 689–726.

Longest in the UK The weightiest piece of legislation ever written is the Income and Corporation Taxes Act 1988 of more than 1000 pages and weighing 2·5 kg 5½ lb. Lord Houghton of Sowerby appealed to fellow peers in November 1987 'not to walk about with it' for fear

Most inexplicable statutes

Certain pieces of legislation have always defied interpretation and the most inexplicable must be a matter of opinion. A judge of the Court of Session of Scotland once sent the Founding Editors his candidate, which reads: *'In the Nuts (unground), (other than ground nuts) Order, the expression nuts shall have reference to such nuts, other than ground nuts, as would but for this amending Order not qualify as nuts (unground) (other than ground nuts) by reason of their being nuts (unground).'*

of ruptures. Of old statutes, 31 George III XIV, the Land Tax Act of 1791, written on parchment, consists of 780 skins forming a roll 360m *1170ft* long.

Shortest The shortest statute is the Parliament (Qualification of Women) Act 1918, which runs to 27 operative words: 'A woman shall not be disqualified by sex or marriage from being elected to or sitting or voting as a Member of the Commons House of Parliament.' Section 2 contains a further 14 words giving the short title.

Patents The earliest of all known English patents was that granted by Henry VI in 1449 to Flemish-born John of Utyman for making coloured glass for the windows of Eton College. The peak number of applications for patents filed in the UK in any one year was 63614 in 1969. The shortest patent is one of 48 words filed on 14 May 1956 and concerned a harrow attachment. The longest, comprising 2290 pages of text and 495 sheets of drawings, was filed on 31 Mar 1965 by IBM to cover a computer.

Thomas Alva Edison (1847–1931) has had the most patents, with 1093 either on his own or jointly. They included the microphone, the motion-picture projector and the incandescent electric lamp.

Most protracted litigation The dispute over the claim of the Prior and Convent (now the Dean and Chapter) of Durham Cathedral to administer the spiritualities of the diocese during a vacancy in the See grew fierce in 1283. It flared up again in 1672 and 1890; an attempt in November 1975 to settle the issue, then 692 years old, was unsuccessful. Neither side admits the legitimacy of writs of appointment issued by the other even though identical persons are named.

Gaddam Hanumantha Reddy, a civil servant, brought a series of legal actions against the Hyderabad state government and the Indian government covering a total period of 44 years 9 months and 8 days from April 1945 through to January 1990. The litigation outlasted the entire period of his employment in the Indian Administrative Service. He complained that his results in the entrance examination for the Hyderabad Civil Service entitled him to greater seniority and higher pay.

Fastest English hearings The law's shortest delay occurred in *Duport Steels and Others* v. *Sirs and Others*, which was heard in the High Court on 25 Jan 1980. The case was heard on appeal on 26 January, and the full hearing in the House of Lords took place on the morning of 1 February with the decision given in the afternoon.

Sir Stephen Brown, President of the High Court Family Division, authorised an emergency Caesarean operation on a woman on 12 Oct 1992 in order to save her life (and in a vain attempt to save the life of her unborn child). The judge said: 'This application came to the notice of the court officials at 1.30 pm, it has come on for hearing just before 2 o'clock and now at 2.18 pm I propose to make the declaration which is sought'.

Longest hearings The longest civil case heard before a jury is *Kemner* v. *Monsanto Co.*, which concerned an alleged toxic chemical spill in Sturgeon, Missouri, USA in 1979. The trial started on 6 Feb 1984, at St Clair County Court House, Belleville, Illinois, USA before Circuit Judge Richard P. Goldenhersh, and ended on 22 Oct 1987. The testimony lasted 657 days, following which the jury deliberated for two months. The residents of Sturgeon were awarded $1 million nominal compensatory damages and $16 280 000 punitive damages, but these awards were overturned by the Illinois Appellate Court on 11 Jun 1991 because the jury in the original trial had not found that any damage had resulted from the spill.

The Supreme Court of Sri Lanka spent a record 527 days hearing a challenge to the election of President Ranasinghe Premadasa as head of state in 1988. A total of 977 witnesses gave evidence over a three year period, from 19 Jun 1989 to 30 Jun 1992. The challenge, brought by the opposition leader Sirimavo Bandaranaike (⇨ Prime Ministers and Statesmen, Woman), was rejected by the court on 1 Sep 1992.

Longest British hearings The longest trial in the annals of British justice was the Tichborne personation case. The civil trial began on 11 May 1871, lasted 103 days and collapsed on 6 Mar 1872. The criminal trial went on for 188 days, resulting in a sentence on 28 Feb 1874 for two counts of perjury (two 7-year consecutive terms of imprisonment with hard labour) on London-born Arthur Orton, alias Thomas Castro (1834–98), who claimed to be Roger Charles Tichborne (1829–54), the elder brother of Sir Alfred Joseph Doughty-Tichborne, 11th Bt (1839–66). The whole case thus spanned 1025 days. The jury were out for only 30 minutes.

Best-attended trial

The greatest attendance at any trial was at that of Major Jesús Sosa Blanco, aged 51, for an alleged 108 murders. At one point in the 12½ hr trial (5:30 p.m. to 6 a.m., 22–23 Jan 1959), 17 000 people were present in the Havana Sports Palące, Cuba. He was executed on 18 Feb 1959.

Greatest damages—breach of promise

The largest sum involved in a breach of promise suit in the UK was £50 000, accepted in 1913 by Miss Daisy Markham, alias Mrs Annie Moss (died 20 Aug 1962, aged 76), in settlement against the 6th Marquess of Northampton (1885–1978).

The impeachment of Warren Hastings (1732–1818), which began in 1788, dragged on for 7 years until 23 Apr 1795, but the trial lasted only 149 days. Hastings was appointed a member of the Privy Council in 1814.

The longest single fraud trial was the Britannia Park trial, which began on 10 Sep 1990 and ended on 4 Feb 1992 after 252 working days. The case centred on the collapse of the Britannia theme park near Heanor, Derbys in 1985. The fraud case *R*. v. *Bouzaglo and Others* ended before Judge Brian Gibbens (1912–85) on 1 May 1981 having lasted 274 days, but with two separate trials. They appealed on 10 Dec 1981. Trial costs were estimated at £2·5 million.

The fluoridation case *McColl* v. *Strathclyde Regional Council* lasted 204 days ending on 27 Jul 1982 before Lord Jauncey, whose judgment in the £1 million case ran to 400 pages. The longest case in the House of Lords was *Armstrong Patents* v. *British Leyland*, which ended on 27 Feb 1986 having occupied the Lords of Appeal in Ordinary for seven weeks.

Murder The longest murder trial in Britain was that at the Old Bailey, London of Reginald Dudley, 51, and Robert Maynard, 38, in the Torso Murder of Billy Moseley and Micky Cornwall which ran before Mr Justice Swanwick from 11 Nov 1976 to 17 Jun 1977 with 136 trial days. Both men were sentenced to life imprisonment (minimum 15 years). Costs were estimated to exceed £500000 and the evidence amounted to 3500000 words.

The case of Stephen Miller, Yusef Abdullahi and Tony Paris lasted longer, but there were two hearings. They were accused of murdering Lynette White, a Cardiff prostitute, on 14 Feb 1988. The first hearing in 1989 lasted 82 days, but ended with the death of the judge, Mr Justice McNeill. The second one lasted 115 days, ending on 20 Nov 1990. The three men were found guilty and sentenced to life imprisonment, but were cleared by the Court of Appeal on 10 Dec 1992.

Divorce The longest trial of a divorce case in Britain was *Gibbons* v. *Gibbons*

and Roman and Halperin. On 19 Mar 1962, after 28 days, Mr Alfred George Boyd Gibbons was granted a decree *nisi* against his wife Dorothy for adultery with Mr John Halperin of New York City, USA.

Shortest trials The shortest recorded British murder hearings were *R*. v. *Murray* on 28 Feb 1957 and *R*. v. *Cawley* at Winchester assizes on 14 Dec 1959. Proceedings occupied only 30 seconds on each occasion.

Litigants in person Since the Union of the Parliaments in 1707 the only Scot to win an appeal in person before the House of Lords has been Mr Jack Malloch, an Aberdeen schoolmaster. In 1971 he was restored to his employment with costs under the dormant but unrepealed Teachers Act 1882.

Dr Mark Feldman, a chiropodist, of Lauderhill, Florida, USA became the first litigant in person to secure seven figures ($1 million) before a jury in compensatory and punitive damages, in September 1980. The case concerned conspiracy and fraud alleged against six other doctors.

Longest address The longest address in a British court was in *Globe and Phoenix Gold Mining Co. Ltd* v. *Amalgamated Properties of Rhodesia*. Mr William Henry Upjohn KC (1853–1941) concluded his speech on 22 Sep 1916, having addressed the court for 45 days.

Highest bail The highest bail figure in a British court is £3·5 million, which was set for Asil Nadir, the chairman of Polly Peck International, on 17 Dec 1990. He had developed the company over 20 years from a small clothing concern into an international group, but it collapsed in September 1990 and he subsequently faced 18 charges of theft and false accounting amounting to £25 million.

Longest inquiry The longest and most expensive public inquiry has been that over the projected £1200 million Sizewell B nuclear power station, Suffolk under Sir Frank Layfield QC. It began on 11 Jan 1983 and finished after 340 days of hearings on 7 Mar 1985 in the Snape Maltings, Aldeburgh. The cost to public funds was £20 million and the 3000-page eight-volume report weighed 13·6 kg *30 lb* and cost £30.

Greatest damages *Civil damages* The largest damages awarded in legal history were $11120 million to Pennzoil Co. against Texaco Inc. concerning the latter's allegedly unethical tactics in January 1984 to break up a merger between Pennzoil and Getty Oil Co., by Judge Solomon Casseb, Jr in Houston, Texas, USA on 10 Dec 1985. An out-of-court settlement of $5500 million was reached after a 48-hour negotiation on 19 Dec 1987.

The largest damages awarded against an individual were $2100 million. On 10 Jul 1992 Charles H Keating Jr, the former owner of Lincoln Savings and Loan of Los Angeles, California, USA, was ordered by a federal jury to pay this sum to 23000 small investors who were defrauded by his company. The figure was subject to final approval by the judge.

Personal injury The greatest personal injury damages ever awarded were $78183000, to the model Marla Hanson, 26, on 28 Sep 1987, against three men responsible for a razor attack on her face in Manhattan, New York City, USA. The award was uncontested and included $40000000 in punitive damages. The three men were sentenced to imprisonment. Since they were without assets Miss Hanson was empowered to claim 10 per cent of their post-prison earnings.

The greatest sum awarded in compensatory personal injury damages was $65086000, awarded on 18 Jul 1986 to Mrs Agnes Mae Whitaker against the New York City Health and Hospitals Corporation for malpractice. A misdiagnosis of food poisoning led to major surgery and severe disablement.

The compensation for the disaster on 2–3 Dec 1984 at the Union Carbide Corporation plant in Bhopal, India was agreed at $470 million. The Supreme Court of India passed the order for payment on 14 Feb 1989 after a settlement between the corporation and the Indian government, which represented the interests of more than 500000 claimants including the families of 3350 people who died. On 27 Mar 1992 the Bhopal Court ordered the extradition of Walter Anderson, retired chairman of Union Carbide, on charges of 'culpable homicide', stating the death toll as more than 4000, with 20000 injured and the number of claimants rising to 600000.

The British record is potentially £100 million, awarded in the High Court on 31 Oct 1991 to Rebecca Field of Hampton Park, Hereford & Worcester, who was left severely disabled as a result of a hospital blunder when she was born in 1984. Herefordshire Health Authority agreed to pay record damages of £1·7 million under a structured settlement. Of this, it was agreed that £1042413 would be invested to provide an annual income for life. If she lives to the age of 76, her damages will total an estimated £100 million, which will attract no tax.

Defamation The record award in a libel case is $58 million, to Vic Feazell, a former district attorney, on 20 Apr 1991 at Waco, Texas, USA. He claimed that he had been libelled by a Dallas-based television station and one of its reporters in 1985, and that this had ruined his reputation. The parties reached a settlement on 29 Jun 1991, but neither side would disclose the amount.

The record damages for libel in Great Britain was the £1·5 million award to Lord Aldington, a former brigadier and former chairman of the Sun Alliance insurance company, against Count Nikolai Tolstoy, a historian, and Nigel Watts, a property developer. The award was made by a High Court jury on 30 Nov 1989 following accusations that Lord Aldington had

The Union Carbide plant in Bhopal, where the gas leak disaster in 1984 resulted in compensation to the victims amounting to $470 million.

(Photo: Sygma/Baldev)

been a war criminal. However, he did not actually receive this amount.

The most expensive defamation trial in Great Britain has been the 87-day-long case of *Gee* v. *British Broadcasting Corporation*, which ran before Lord Justice Croom-Johnson from 22 Oct 1984 to 2 May 1985. The costs have been estimated at £1·5 million, excluding the BBC's internal costs, over the 681 days from the offending transmission of *That's Life* on 26 Jun 1983. Dr Gee, who was in the witness box for 27 days, received a then record settlement of £100 007.

Greatest compensation for wrongful imprisonment
Robert McLaughlin, 29, was awarded $1 935 000 in October 1989 for wrongful imprisonment as a result of a murder in New York City, USA in 1979 which he did not commit. He had been sentenced to 15 years in prison and actually served six years, from 1980 to 1986, when he was released after his foster father succeeded in showing the authorities that he had nothing to do with the crime.

Greatest alimony suit
Belgian-born Sheika Dena Al-Fassi, 23, filed the highest-ever alimony claim of $3 billion against her former husband, Sheik Mohammed Al-Fassi, 28, of the Saudi Arabian royal family, in Los Angeles, California, USA in February 1982. Mr Marvin Mitchelson, explaining the size of the settlement claim, alluded to the Sheik's wealth, which included 14 homes in Florida alone and numerous private aircraft. On 14 Jun 1983 she was awarded $81 million and declared she would be 'very very happy' if she were able to collect.

Greatest divorce settlement
The largest publicly declared settlement was that achieved in 1982 by the lawyers of Soraya Khashóggi from her husband Adnan—£500 million plus property. Mrs Anne Bass, former wife of Sid Bass of Texas, USA, was reported to have rejected $535 million as inadequate to live in the style to which she had been made accustomed.

The highest divorce award in Great Britain was one of £1 295 000 (£1 000 000 in cash plus a £295 000 maisonette), made to Yugoslavian-born Radojka Gojkovic against her former husband in the High Court Family Division on 17 Feb 1989. The settlement was upheld by the Court of Appeal on 12 Oct 1989.

Patent case
Polaroid Corporation was awarded $909·5 million in Boston, Massachusetts, USA on 12 Oct 1990 in a suit involving Eastman Kodak Co. for infringing patents for instant photography cameras and films. Polaroid had filed suit in 1976, claiming that Kodak had infringed patents used in Polaroid's 1972 SX-70 system. Both companies filed appeals and eventually it was agreed that Kodak would pay $925 million.

Largest suit
The highest amount of damages ever sought to date is $675 000 000 000 000 (then equivalent to 10 times the US national wealth) in a suit by Mr I. Walton Bader brought in the US District Court, New York City, USA on 14 Apr 1971 against General Motors and others for polluting all 50 states.

Highest costs
The Blue Arrow trial, involving the illegal support of the company's shares during a rights issue in 1987, is estimated to have cost approximately £35 million. The trial at the Old Bailey, London lasted a year and ended on 14 Feb 1992 with four of the defendants being convicted. Although they received suspended prison sentences, they were later cleared on appeal.

The most expensive man-hunt in police history was one costing £4 million. It terminated on 13 Jun 1981 with the arrest of Peter William Sutcliffe (the 'Yorkshire Ripper'), in Sheffield, S Yorks. His trial at the Old Bailey, London cost £250 000 and resulted in his being sentenced to life imprisonment for 13 murders (which orphaned 25 children) and seven attempted murders.

Wills
The shortest valid will in the world is 'Vše zene', the Czech for 'All to wife', written and dated 19 Jan 1967 by Herr Karl Tausch of Langen, Germany.

The shortest will contested but subsequently admitted to probate in English law was the case of *Thorne* v. *Dickens* in 1906. It consisted of the three words 'All for mother' in which 'mother' was not his mother but his wife. The smallest will preserved by the Record Keeper is an identity disc 3·8 cm *1½ in* in diameter belonging to A.B. William Skinner, killed aboard HMS *Indefatigable* at Jutland in 1916. It had 40 words engraved on it including the signatures of two witnesses and was proved on 24 Jun 1922.

The longest will on record was that of Mrs Frederica Evelyn Stilwell Cook (b. USA), proved at Somerset House, London on 2 Nov 1925. It consisted of four bound volumes containing 95 940 words, primarily concerning some $100 000 worth of property.

The oldest written will dates from 2061 BC, and is that of Nek'ure, the son of the Egyptian pharaoh Khafre. The will was carved onto the walls of his tomb, and indicated that he would bequeath 14 towns, 2 estates and other property to his wife, another woman and three children.

The largest number of codicils (supplements modifying the details) to a will admitted to probate is 21, in the case of the will of J. Paul Getty. The will was dated 22 Sep 1958 and it had 21 codicils dating from 18 Jun 1960 through to 11 Mar 1976. Getty died on 6 Jun 1976.

Most durable judges The oldest recorded active judge was Judge Albert R. Alexander (1859–1966) of Plattsburg, Missouri, USA. He was enrolled as a member of the Clinton County Bar in 1926, and was later the magistrate and probate judge of Clinton County until his retirement aged 105 years 8 months on 9 Jul 1965.

The greatest recorded age at which any British judge has sat on a bench was 93 years 9 months in the case of Sir William Francis Kyffin Taylor (later Lord Maenan), who was born on 9 Jul 1854 and retired as presiding judge of the Liverpool Court of Passage in April 1948, having held that position since 1903. Sir Salathiel Lovell (1619–1713) was still sitting when he died on 3 May 1713 in his 94th or 95th year. The greatest age at which a House of Lords judgment has been given is 92 in the case of the 1st Earl of Halsbury (b. 3 Sep 1823) in 1916. Lord Chief Baron of Exchequer in Ireland, the Rt Hon. Christopher Palles (1831–1920) served for 42 years, from 17 Feb 1874 until 1916.

Longest lease

There is a lease concerning a plot for a sewage tank adjoining Columb Barracks, Mullingar, Co. Westmeath, Republic of Ireland, which was signed on 3 Dec 1868 for 10 million years. It is to be assumed that a future civil servant will bring up the matter for review early in AD 10 001 868. Leases in Ireland lasting 'for ever' are quite common.

Master of the Rolls

The longest tenure of the Mastership of the Rolls since the office was inaugurated in 1286 has been 24 years 7 months by David de Wollore, from 2 Jul 1346 to 27 March 1371. The longest tenure since the Supreme Court Judicature Act of 1881 has been that of 20 years 5 months by the Rt Hon. Lord Denning (b. 23 Jan 1899), from 19 Apr 1962 to 30 Sep 1982. He had been first appointed a High Court judge in 1944. William Morland held the office for 77 days, while Sir Humphrey May died 'soon after' his appointment on 10 Apr 1629.

Most offices

Viscount Simon (1873– 1954) was appointed Solicitor General in 1910, Attorney General in 1913, Home Secretary in 1915 and 1935, Foreign Secretary in 1931, Chancellor of the Exchequer in 1937 and Lord Chancellor in 1940.

Youngest judge No collated records on the ages of judicial appointments exist. However, David Elmer Ward had to await the legal age of 21 before taking office after nomination in 1932 as Judge of the County Court at Fort Myers, Florida, USA.

Muhammad Ilyas passed the examination enabling him to become a Civil Judge in July 1952 at the age of 20 years

9 months, although formalities such as medicals meant that it was not until eight months later that he started work as a Civil Judge in Lahore, Pakistan.

The youngest certain age at which any English judge has been appointed is 28, in the case of Sir Ernest Wild KC (b. 1 Jan 1869) who was appointed Judge of the Norwich Guildhall Court of Record in 1897 at that age.

Most judges Lord Balmerino was found guilty of treason by 137 of his peers on 28 Jul 1746. In the 20th century, 24 judges of the European Court of Human Rights in Strasbourg, France passed judgment in *The Sunday Times* v. *the United Kingdom (no. 2)* and *Observer and Guardian* v. *the United Kingdom* ('the Spycatcher cases') on 26 Nov 1991. The verdict was unanimous in favour of the newspapers.

Most offices The most high judicial offices held by one man were by Alexander Wedderbarn (1733–1805), later Lord Loughborough and Earl of Rosslyn, who was Solicitor-General in 1771, Attorney-General in 1778, Chief Justice of common pleas from 1780–93, and finally Lord Chancellor from 27 Jan 1793 until he resigned in 1801.

Youngest English QC The earliest age at which a barrister has taken silk this century is 33 years 8 months in the case of Mr (later the Rt Hon. Sir) Francis Raymond Evershed (1899–1966) in April 1933. He was later Lord Evershed, Master of the Rolls. In the 18th century Sir Francis Buller was nepotistically given silk at the age of 31 in 1777, being a nephew of the Lord Chancellor of the time, Lord Bathurst.

Most successful lawyer Sir Lionel Luckhoo, senior partner of Luckhoo and Luckhoo of Georgetown, Guyana, succeeded in getting 245 successive murder charge acquittals between 1940 and 1985.

Most durable solicitors William George (1865–1967), brother of Prime Minister David Lloyd George, passed his preliminary law examination in May 1880 and was practising until December 1966 at the age of 101 years 9 months. The most durable firm is Pickering Kenyon of London, which was founded by William Umfreville in 1561.

Law firms The world's largest law firm in terms of billings is Skadden, Arps, Slate, Meagher & Flom of New York, with sales of about $500 million as at 31 Dec 1991. The largest firm based on practices is Baker & McKenzie, employing 1651 lawyers, 540 of whom are partners, in 28 countries at 31 Mar 1993. The firm was founded in Chicago, Illinois, USA in 1949.

Crime

Largest criminal organizations In terms of profit, the largest syndicate of organized crime is the Mafia, which has its origins in Sicily and dates from the 13th century, and which has infiltrated the executive, judiciary and legislature of the United States. It consists of some 3000 to 5000 individuals in 25 'families' federated under 'The Commission', with an annual turnover in vice, gambling, protection rackets, tobacco, bootlegging, hijacking, narcotics, loan-sharking and prostitution which was estimated by US News & World Report in December 1982 at $200 billion, with a profit estimated in March 1986 by the Attorney Rudolph Giuliani at $75 billion.

In terms of numbers, the Yamaguchi-gumi gang of the *yakuza* in Japan has 30 000 members. There are some 90 000 *yakuza* or gangsters altogether, in more than 3000 groups. They go about their business openly and even advertize for recruits. On 1 Mar 1992 new laws were brought in to combat their activities, which include drug trafficking, smuggling, prostitution and gambling.

There are believed to be more than 250 000 triad members worldwide, but they are fragmented into many groups which often fight each other and compete in disputed areas. Hong Kong alone has some 100 000 triads.

Assassinations The most frequently assassinated heads of state in modern times have been the Tsars of Russia. In the two hundred years from 1718 to 1918 four Tsars and two heirs apparent were assassinated, and there were many other unsuccessful attempts.

The target of the highest number of *failed* assassination attempts on an individual head of state in modern times was Charles de Gaulle (1890–1970), President of France from 1958 to 1969. He was reputed to have survived no fewer than 31 plots against his life between 1944, when the shadow government which he had formed returned to Paris from Algeria, and 1966 (although some plots were foiled before culminating in actual physical attacks).

Most prolific murderers It was established at the trial of Behram, the Indian Thug, that he had strangled at least 931 victims with his yellow and white cloth strip or *ruhmal* in the Oudh district between 1790 and 1840. It has been estimated that at least 2 000 000 Indians were strangled by Thugs (*burtotes*) during the reign of the Thugee (pronounced tugee) cult from 1550 until its final suppression by the British raj in 1853.

The greatest number of victims ascribed to a murderess has been 610, in the case of Countess Erzsébet Báthory (1560–1614) of Hungary. At her trial, which began on 2 Jan 1611, a witness testified to seeing a list of Countess Báthory's victims in her own handwriting totalling this number. All were alleged to be young girls from near her castle at Csejthe, where she died on 21 Aug 1614. She had been

Charles de Gaulle, who was the target of a record 31 assassination attempts. Frederick Forsyth's novel *The Day of the Jackal*, later made into a film, gave a vivid idea of the lengths to which people went in the pursuit of such an objective.
(Photo: Popperfoto)

Crime prevention
A team of ten officers from Essex Police in Chelmsford succeeded in postcoding 500 bicycles in four hours on 14 Apr 1991 as part of the national Crime Prevention Week.

Largest object stolen by a single man
On a moonless night at dead calm high water on 5 Jun 1966, armed with only a sharp axe, N. William Kennedy slashed free the mooring lines at Wolfe's Cove, St Lawrence Seaway, Canada of the 10 639-dwt SS *Orient Trader* owned by Steel Factors Ltd of Ontario. The vessel drifted to a waiting blacked-out, tug thus escaping a ban on any shipping movements during a violent wildcat waterfront strike. She then sailed for Spain.

walled up in her room for 3½ years after being found guilty.

20th century A total of 592 deaths was attributed to one Colombian bandit leader, Teófilo ('Sparks') Rojas, between 1948 and his death in an ambush near Armenia, Colombia on 22 Jan 1963. Some sources attribute 3500 slayings to him during *La Violencia* of 1945–62.

In a drunken rampage lasting 8 hours on 26–27 Apr 1982, policeman Wou Bom-Kon, 27, killed 57 people and wounded 35 with 176 rounds of rifle ammunition and hand grenades in the Kyong Sang-Namdo province of South Korea. He blew himself up with a grenade.

United Kingdom The biggest murder in the UK this century was committed by the unknown person or people who planted the bomb on Pan Am flight PA103, which crashed over Lockerbie, Dumfries & Galloway on 21 Dec 1988, killing a total of 270 people in the aeroplane and on the ground.

The self-confessed arsonist Bruce Lee was sent to a mental hospital by Leeds Crown Court in January 1981, but on 14 Mar 1982 he retracted his confessions to starting fires in which 26 perished. On 2 Dec 1983 the Court of Appeal quashed charges of causing 11 of the deaths.

Mary Ann Cotton (*née* Robson) (b. 1832 at East Rainton, Co. Durham), hanged in Durham Jail on 24 Mar 1873, is believed to have poisoned 14, possibly 20, people.

Dennis Andrew Nilsen (b. 1948), then of 23 Cranley Gardens, Muswell Hill, north London, admitted to 15 one-at-a-time murders between December 1978 and February 1983. He was sentenced to life imprisonment, with a 25-year minimum, on 4 Nov 1983 at the Old Bailey by Mr Justice Croom-Johnson for six murders and two attempted murders.

Dominic McGlinchey (b. 1955) in November 1983 admitted in a press interview to at least 30 killings in Northern Ireland. He was jailed for 10 years at Dublin's Special Criminal Court on 11 Mar 1986 for shooting with intent to resist arrest in Co. Clare, Republic of Ireland on 17 Mar 1984.

On 7 May 1981 John Thompson of Hackney, London was found guilty at the Old Bailey of the 'specimen' murder by arson of Archibald Campbell and jailed for life. There were 36 other victims at the Spanish Club, Denmark Street, London.

The worst armed rampage in Britain was at Hungerford, Berks on 19 Aug 1987, during which Michael Ryan, 27, shot dead 14 people and wounded 16 others before shooting and killing himself. Two people subsequently died from injuries sustained, bringing the total to 16.

Lynching The worst year in the 20th century for lynchings in the United States was 1901, with 130 lynchings, while the first year with no reported cases was 1952. The last lynching case recorded in Britain was that of *R.* v. *Caskie and Stevenson* on 29 Dec 1922. The accused were discharged after a verdict of not proven for murder by assault of Robert Alexander Stewart, 32, at Dalmarnock Bridge, Glasgow on 11 Sep 1922. Stewart was falsely thought by a tram conductor to be kidnapping Alistair John Sinclair, aged five, who gave evidence not under oath and standing on a seat.

Mass poisoning On 1 May 1981 an 8-year-old boy became the first of more than 600 victims of the Spanish cooking oil scandal. On 12 June it was discovered that his cause of death was the use

The worst case of mass poisoning occurred in Spain in 1981 through using adulterated cooking oil, resulting in over 600 deaths. The photographs show angry scenes at the start of the trial and samples of the oil being analysed.

(Photos: Sygma/Nova and Sygma/J Pavlovsky)

of 'denatured' industrial colza from rape seed. The trial of 38 defendants, including the manufacturers Ramón and Elías Ferrero, lasted from 30 Mar 1987 to 28 Jun 1988. The 586 counts on which the prosecution demanded jail sentences totalled 60000 years.

Robbery The greatest robbery on record was that of the Reichsbank following Germany's collapse in April–May 1945. The Pentagon in Washington described the event, first published in *The Guinness Book of Records* in 1957, as 'an unverified allegation'. *Nazi Gold* by Ian Sayer and Douglas Botting, published in 1984, however, finally revealed full details and estimated that the total haul would have been equivalent to £2500 million at 1984 values.

The government of the Philippines announced on 23 Apr 1986 that it had succeeded in identifying $860·8 million 'salted' by the former President Ferdinand Edralin Marcos (1917–89) and his wife Imelda. The total national loss from November 1965 was believed to be $5–$10 billion.

Treasury Bills and certificates of deposit worth £292 million were stolen when a mugger attacked a money-broker's messenger in the City of London on 2 May 1990. As details of the documents stolen were quickly flashed on the City's market dealing screens and given to central banks world-wide, the chances of anyone being able to benefit from the theft were considered to be very remote.

The robbery in the Knightsbridge Safety Deposit Centre, London on 12 Jul 1987 was estimated at £30 million by the Metropolitan Police and has been said to be nearer to £60 million by the robbers themselves. Of the 126 boxes broken into, property was stolen from 113. The managing director Parvez Latif, 30, was among those charged on 17 Aug 1987.

At 6:40a.m. on 26 Nov 1983 six masked men raided the Brinks Mat Unit 7 warehouses at the Heathrow Trading Estate, Middx, removing 6800 bars of gold and platinum together with diamonds and travellers' cheques worth £26 369 778. Michael McAvoy, 32, of East Dulwich and Brian Robinson, 41, of Lewisham were each sentenced to 25 years at the Old Bailey on 3 Dec 1984.

Art It is arguable that the *Mona Lisa*, though never valued, is the most valuable object ever stolen. It disappeared from the Louvre, Paris on 21 Aug 1911. It was recovered in Italy in 1913, when Vincenzo Perugia was charged with its theft.

On 14 Apr 1991 twenty paintings, estimated to be worth $500 million, were stolen from the Van Gogh Museum in Amsterdam, Netherlands. However, only 35 minutes later they were found in an abandoned car not far from the museum. On 18 Mar 1990, eleven paintings by Rembrandt, Vermeer, Degas, Manet and Flinck, plus a Chinese bronze beaker of about 1200 BC and a finial in the form of an eagle, worth in total an estimated $200 million, had been stolen from the Isabella Stewart Gardner Museum in Boston, Massachusetts, USA. Unlike the Van Gogh paintings, these have not been recovered in the meantime.

On 24 Dec 1985 a total of 140 'priceless' gold, jade and obsidian artifacts were stolen from the National Museum of Anthropology, Mexico City. The majority of the stolen objects were recovered in June 1989 from the Mexico City home of a man described by officials as the mastermind of the theft.

Bank During the extreme civil disorder prior to 22 Jan 1976 in Beirut, Lebanon, a guerrilla force blasted the vaults of the British Bank of the Middle East in Bab Idriss and cleared out safe deposit boxes with contents valued by former Finance Minister Lucien Dahdah at $50 million and by another source at an 'absolute minimum' of $20 million.

Train The greatest recorded train robbery occurred between 3:03 a.m. and 3:27 a.m. on 8 Aug 1963, when a General Post Office mail train from Glasgow, Strathclyde was ambushed at Sears Crossing and robbed at Bridego Bridge near Mentmore, Bucks. The gang escaped with about 120 mailbags containing £2 631 784 worth of banknotes being taken to London for destruction. Only £343 448 was recovered.

Jewels The greatest recorded theft of jewels was from the bedroom of the 'well-guarded' villa of Prince Abdel Aziz bin Ahmed Al-Thani near Cannes, France on 24 Jul 1980. They were valued at $16 000 000.

The biggest theft of jewels in Britain was that from Bond Jewellers, Conduit Street, London on 20 Jun 1983, when the haul was estimated to be worth £6 million.

Greatest kidnapping ransom

Historically the greatest ransom paid was that for Atahualpa by the Incas to Francisco Pizarro in 1532–3 at Cajamarca, Peru, which constituted a hall full of gold and silver, worth in modern money some $170 million.

The greatest ransom ever reported in modern times is 1500 million pesos ($60 million) for the release of the brothers Jorge Born, 40, and Juan Born, 39, of Bunge and Born, paid to the left-wing urban guerrilla group Montoneros in Buenos Aires, Argentina on 20 Jun 1975.

Greatest hijack ransom

The highest amount ever paid to aircraft hijackers has been $6 million, by the Japanese government, in the case of a JAL DC-8 at Dacca Airport, Bangladesh on 2 Oct 1977, with 38 hostages. Six convicted criminals were also exchanged. The Bangladesh government had refused to sanction any retaliatory action.

Largest narcotics haul

The greatest drug haul in terms of value was achieved on 28 Sep 1989, when cocaine with an estimated street value of $6–7 billion was seized in a raid on a warehouse in Los Angeles, California, USA. The haul of 20 tonnes was prompted by a tip-off from a local resident who had complained about heavy lorry traffic and people leaving the warehouse 'at odd hours and in a suspicious manner'. The greatest haul in terms of weight was by the authorities in Bilo, Pakistan on 23 Oct 1991. The seizure comprised 38·9 tonnes *85 846 lb* of hashish and 3·23 tonnes *7128 lb* of heroin.

In Britain, cocaine with a value of £160 million and weighing 1·1 tonne was seized at Woolwich Reach, London on 23 Nov 1992 after the Panamanian-registered oil rig support vessel *Fox Trot Five* had arrived from South America. The operation, codenamed 'Operation Emerge', followed a long period of intelligence-gathering and surveillance. The largest amount of drugs seized in one operation by weight was from the *Britannia Gazelle*, a British-registered oil rig support ship just a couple of days earlier. The vessel had been boarded in the North Sea on 20 Nov 1992 and brought back to Hull, Humberside where more than 1000 sacks containing a total of 20 tonnes of cannabis were recovered the next day.

Largest narcotics operation

The bulkiest drugs seizure was 2903 tonnes of Colombian marijuana in a 14-month-long project codenamed 'Operation Tiburon', carried out by the Drug Enforcement Administration and Colombian authorities. The arrest of 495 people and the seizure of 95 vessels was announced on 5 Feb 1982.

Biggest bank fraud

The Banca Nazionale del Lavoro, Italy's leading bank, admitted on 6 Sep 1989 that it had been defrauded of an estimated $3 billion, with the disclosure that its branch in Atlanta, Georgia, USA had made unauthorized loan commitments to Iraq. Both the bank's chairman, Nerio Nesi, and its director general, Giacomo Pedde, resigned following the revelation.

Computer fraud

Between 1964 and 1973, 64000 fake insurance policies were created on the computer of the Equity Funding Corporation in the USA, involving $2 billion.

Greatest banknote forgery

The greatest forgery was the German Third Reich's forging operation, code name 'Operation Bernhard', run by Major Friedrich Krüger during the World War II. It involved £150 million worth of British notes, about half of which were £5 notes, although various other denominations were also printed. They were produced by 140 Jewish prisoners at Sachsenhausen concentration camp.

Maritime fraud

A cargo of 180 000 tonnes of Kuwaiti crude oil on the supertanker *Salem* at Durban was sold without title to the South African government in December 1979. The ship mysteriously sank off Senegal on 17 Jan 1980 leaving the government to pay £148 million to Shell International, who owned the shipment.

Stanley Mark Rifkin (b. 1946) was arrested in Carlsbad, California, USA by the FBI on 6 Nov 1978 and charged with defrauding a Los Angeles bank of $10·2 million by manipulation of a computer system. He was sentenced to 8 years' imprisonment in June 1980.

Capital Punishment

The discovery of Tollund man in a bog near Silkeborg, Denmark in 1950 showed that capital punishment dates at least from the Iron Age. The countries in which capital punishment is still prevalent include China, Iran, Iraq, Saudi Arabia, Malaysia, USA (36 states) and some of the independent countries which were formerly in the USSR. Capital punishment was first abolished *de facto* in 1798 in Liechtenstein.

Capital punishment in the British Isles had been widely practised up until the reign of William I (1066–87), but was virtually abolished by him. It was then brought back for murder and a growing number of other crimes by Henry I in the next century. It reached a peak in the reign of Edward VI (1547–53), when an average of 560 persons were executed annually at Tyburn (near the point where Marble Arch now stands, in London) alone. It has been estimated that as many as 50 000 people may have been done to death at Tyburn by the time the last execution took place there in 1783.

The notorious Black Act of 1723, popularly known as the Bloody Code, gave rise to a seemingly infinite variety of capital crimes, mostly against property, and many of these remained on the statute books even into the 19th century. The last man to be executed under the Black Act was William Potter, an Essex man who was hanged in 1814 for cutting down his neighbour's orchard.

By 1861, the number of capital offences had been reduced to four. These were murder, treason, arson in dockyards and piracy with violence. Between 1868 — when public executions were abolished — and 1964 the most murderers hanged in a year was 27 (24 men, 3 women) in 1903. In 1956 there were no executions. The death penalty for murder was suspended in the UK in 1965 for an experimental period of five years, and formally abolished on 18 Dec 1969.

Largest hanging The most people hanged from one gallows were 38 Sioux Indians by William J. Duly outside Mankato, Minnesota, USA on 26 Dec 1862 for the murder of a number of unarmed citizens. The Nazi Feldkommandant simultaneously hanged 50 Greek resistance men as a reprisal measure in Athens on 22 Jul 1944.

Last hangings The last public execution in England took place outside Newgate Prison, London at 8 a.m. on 26 May 1868, when Michael Barrett was hanged for his part in the Fenian bomb outrage on 13 Dec 1867, when 12 were killed outside the Clerkenwell House of Detention, London. The last public hanging in Scotland was that of the murderer Robert Smith outside Dumfries Prison on 12 May 1868 by the hangman Thomas Askern.

The first non-public hanging was that of the murderer Thomas Wells at Maidstone on 13 Aug 1868. The last executions in the UK were those of Peter Anthony Allen (b. 4 Apr 1943), hanged at Walton

Prison, Liverpool by Robert L. Stewart, and of John Robson Walby (b. 1 Apr 1940), alias Gwynne Owen Evans, by Harry B. Allen at Strangeways Gaol, Manchester, both on 13 Aug 1964. They had been found guilty of the capital murder of John Alan West on 7 April 1964. The 15th, youngest and last woman executed this century was Mrs Ruth Ellis (*née* Neilson) for the murder of David Blakely, 25, shot outside the Magdala public house, Hampstead, London on 10 Apr 1955. She was executed on 13 July at Holloway Prison, London (⇨ Last death sentences).

The last public hanging in the United States occurred at Owensboro, Kentucky on 14 Aug 1936, when Rainey Bethea was executed in the presence of a crowd of more than 10000. The following year a 'private' hanging was performed which was actually witnessed by some 500 people although the number of official witnesses was limited to just 12—Roscoe 'Red' Jackson was hanged on 21 May 1937 at Galena, Missouri.

Youngest The lowest reliably recorded age was of a girl aged seven, hanged at King's Lynn, Norfolk in 1808. In Britain the death penalty for persons under 16 was excluded in the Children Act of 1908, although no person under that age had been executed for many years prior to this. The youngest persons hanged since 1900 have been six 18-year-olds, the most recent of whom was Francis Robert George ('Flossie') Forsyth on 10 Nov 1960.

Oldest The oldest person hanged in the UK since 1900 was a man of 71 named Charles Frembd (*sic*) at Chelmsford Gaol on 4 Nov 1914, for the murder of his wife at Leytonstone, London. In 1843 Allan Mair was executed at Stirling, Central for murder. He was 82, and was hanged sitting in a chair as he was incapable of standing up.

Treason The last person executed for treason in the UK was William Joyce (dubbed 'Lord Haw-Haw'), who was hanged at Wandsworth Prison by Albert Pierrepoint on 3 Jan 1946.

Last death sentences The last woman to be sentenced to death in the UK was Mary Wilson, 66, who was convicted at

Witchcraft

The last legal execution of a witch occurred at Glarus, Switzerland in 1782. It is estimated that at least 200000 witches were executed during the European witchcraze of the 16th and 17th centuries.

The last person executed in Britain for witchcraft was Jenny Horn, burned alive at Dornoch, Highland in 1722. The last convicted witch executed in England was Alice Molland, hanged at Exeter, Devon in 1685. The last person condemned to death for witchcraft in England was Jane Wenham, of Walkern, Herts. She was found guilty in 1712 of bewitching a 16-year-old girl, Ann Thorn, but was granted a royal pardon by Queen Anne. The crime of witchcraft was removed from the Statute Book by an Act of 1736 which repealed the Witchcraft Act of 1563.

Hanging in chains

The last recorded use of a gibbet occurred at Leicester in August 1832, when a local bookbinder, James Cook, was hanged for murder, and his corpse suspended in iron hoops, 10m *33ft* above the ground, with the head shaved and tarred. Public protests led the Home Secretary to order its removal after hanging for three days. Hanging in chains had been in use for centuries as a mark of peculiar infamy to distinguish murder as the most heinous of crimes.

Leeds, W Yorks in 1958 of murdering two of her three husbands by poisoning. The sentence was commuted to life imprisonment, three years after the execution of Ruth Ellis. (⇨ Last hangings)

The last person to be sentenced to death in the British Isles was Tony Teare, 22, who was convicted at Douglas, Isle of Man of murdering a 22-year-old woman, Corinne Bentley, and sentenced on 10 Jul 1992 to be hanged. The sentence was duly commuted to life imprisonment, and later that year the Manx parliament formally abolished the death penalty on the island, the last part of the British Isles to do so.

Last beheadings The last person to be publicly guillotined in France was the murderer Eugen Weidmann, before a large crowd at Versailles, near Paris at 4:50 a.m. on 17 Jun 1939. The executioner was Henri Desfourneaux. Dr Joseph Ignace Guillotin (1738–1814) died a natural death. He had advocated the use of the machine designed by Dr Antoine Louis in 1789 in the French constituent assembly. The last use before abolition on 9 Sep 1981 was on 10 Sep 1977 at Baumettes Prison, Marseille, for torturer and murderer Hamida Djandoubi, aged 28.

The last man to be executed by beheading in Britain was Simon Fraser, Lord Lovat, who was beheaded in his eightieth year on Tower Hill, London in March 1747, for his part in the Jacobite rebellion. The axe and block believed to have been used by the executioner John Thrift on this occasion are preserved in the Tower.

Busiest prison The prison in which most death sentences have been carried out in Britain is Wandsworth, London. Between 1878, when Wandsworth became the hanging prison for London south of the Thames, and 1965, when the death penalty was abolished, 134 executions took place there.

Death Row The longest sojourn on Death Row was the 39 years of Sadamichi Hirasawa (1893–1987) in Sendai Jail, Japan. He was convicted in 1948 of poisoning 12 bank employees with potassium cyanide to effect a theft of £100, and died aged 94. Willie Jasper Darden, 54, survived a record six death warrants in 14 years on Death Row for the murder of a shopkeeper in 1973. His final TV interview was interrupted by a power failure caused by a test of the Florida electric chair in which he died on 15 Mar 1988. On 31 Oct 1987 Liong Wie Tong, 52, and Tan Tian Tjoen, 62, were executed for robbery and murder by firing squad in Jakarta, Indonesia after 25 years on Death Row.

Executioners The longest period of office of a public executioner was that of William Calcraft (1800–79), who was in action from 1829 to 25 May 1874 and officiated at nearly every hanging outside and later inside Newgate Prison, London. On 2 Apr 1868 he hanged the murderess Mrs Frances Kidder, 25, outside Maidstone Jail, Kent—the last public execution of a woman.

The oldest active executioner in British history was John Murdoch, who was already 64 when he was retained as an assistant hangman in Scotland in 1831. He carried out his last exexcution in Glasgow twenty years later, aged 84, and was able to mount the scaffold only with the aid of a staff.

For 55 years from 1901 to the resignation of Albert Pierrepoint in February 1956, the Pierrepoint family largely monopolized the task of executing murderers in Britain. Henry Albert Pierrepoint officiated from 1901 to 1910. The longest-serving of the Pierrepoints was his elder brother Thomas, who was in action from 1906 to 1946. Albert (1905–92), son of Henry, himself claims to have officiated at the hanging of 550 men and women in several countries, including a record 27 war criminals in one day in Germany. Britain's last executioners were Harry B. Allen and Robert L. Stewart, who were on call until the abolition of hanging for murder in 1969, and probably for some time afterwards, as the death penalty remained on the statute book for treason and other offences against the state.

Corporal punishment The last use of corporal punishment in one of HM Prisons was on 26 Jun 1962 and it was abolished in the UK by the Criminal Justice Act 1967. The treadmill and the crank machine, widely used for punishing prisoners sentenced to hard labour, were abolished by the Prisons Act of 1898.

Prison Sentences

Longest sentences Chamoy Thipyaso, a Thai woman known as the queen of underground investing, and seven of her associates were each jailed for 141 078 years by the Bangkok Criminal Court, Thailand on 27 Jul 1989 for swindling the public through a multi-million dollar deposit-taking business. A sentence of 384912 years was *demanded* at the prosecution of Gabriel March Grandos, 22, at Palma de Mallorca, Spain on 11 Mar 1972 for failing to deliver 42768 letters, or 9 years per letter.

The longest sentence imposed on a mass murderer was 21 consecutive life sentences and 12 death sentences in the case of John Gacy, who killed 33 boys and young men between 1972 and 1978 in Illinois, USA. He was sentenced by a jury in Chicago, Illinois on 13 Mar 1980.

Kevin Mulgrew from the Ardoyne district of Belfast was sentenced on 5 Aug 1983 to life imprisonment for the murder of Sergeant Julian Connolley of the Ulster Defence Regiment. In addition he was given a further 963 years to be served concurrently on 84 other serious charges, including 13 conspiracies to murder and 8 attempted murders.

The longest single period served by a reprieved murderer in Great Britain this century was 40 years 11 months by John Watson Laurie, the Goat Fell or Arran murderer, who was reprieved on the grounds of insanity in November 1889. He died in Perth Penitentiary on 4 Oct 1930.

The longest prison sentence imposed by a judge under British law was one of 45 years on 24 Oct 1986 in the case of Jordanian terrorist Nezar Hindawi for his abortive bomb plot against an El Al airliner on 17 Apr 1986.

The longest single sentence passed on a woman under English law was 20 years for Mrs Lorna Teresa Cohen (*née* Petra) (1913–92) at the Old Bailey on 22 Mar 1961 for conspiring to commit a breach of the Official Secrets Act 1911. Her sentence was remitted on 24 Jul 1969. Judith Minna Ward was sentenced to 20 years for a single offence and an aggregate 30 years on 4 Nov 1974 as a result of an explosion in an army coach near Drighlington, W Yorks on 4 Feb 1974. On 11 May 1992 she was freed having served 18 years, and reports indicate that she may receive £215000 compensation for having been wrongfully imprisoned.

Longest time served Paul Geidel (1894–1987) was convicted of second-degree murder on 5 Sep 1911 when a 17-year-old porter in a hotel in New York, USA. He was released from the Fishkill Correctional Facility, Beacon, New York aged 85 on 7 May 1980, having served 68 years, 8 months and 2 days—the longest recorded term in US history. He first refused parole in 1974.

Oldest Bill Wallace (1881–1989) was the oldest prisoner on record, spending the last 63 years of his life in Aradale Psychiatric Hospital, at Ararat, Victoria, Australia. He had shot and killed a man at a restaurant in Melbourne, Victoria in December 1925, and having been found unfit to plead, was transferred to the responsibility of the Mental Health Department in February 1926. He remained at Aradale until his death on 17 Jul 1989, shortly before his 108th birthday.

Longest in Broadmoor Special Hospital The longest period for which any person has been detained in Broadmoor Hospital, Crowthorne, Berks, which provides conditions of maximum security for patients with criminal, violent or dangerous propensities, is 76 years in the case of William Giles. He had been charged with arson but found insane, and was admitted to Broadmoor Hospital in May 1885 at the age of 10. He died there in March 1962 at the age of 87.

The longest escape from Broadmoor was one of 39 years by James Kelly, who got away on 23 Jan 1888, using a pass key made from a corset spring. After an adventurous life in Paris, France, in New York, USA and at sea he returned in April 1927 to ask for readmission. After some difficulties this was arranged. He died back in Broadmoor in September 1929.

Most arrests A record for arrests was set by Tommy Johns (1922–88) in Brisbane, Queensland, Australia on 9 Sep 1982 when he faced his 2000th conviction for drunkenness since 1957. His total at the time of his last drink on 30 Apr 1988 was 'nearly 3000'.

Greatest mass arrests The greatest mass arrest reported in a democratic country was of 15617 demonstrators on 11 Jul 1988, rounded up by South Korean police to ensure security in advance of the 1988 Olympic Games in Seoul.

The largest in the UK occurred on 17 Sep 1961, when 1314 demonstrators supporting unilateral nuclear disarmament were arrested for obstructing highways leading to Parliament Square, London by sitting down. As a consequence of the 1926 General Strike there were 3149 prosecutions, for incitement (1760) and violence (1389).

Fines

Heaviest The largest fine ever was one of $650 million, which was imposed on the US securities house Drexel Burnham Lambert in December 1988 for insider trading. This figure represented $300 million in direct fines, with the balance to be put into an account to satisfy claims of parties that could prove they were defrauded by Drexel's actions.

The record for an individual is $200 million, which Michael Milken (⇨ also Highest salary) agreed to pay on 24 Apr 1990. In addition, he agreed to settle civil charges filed by the Securities and Exchange Commission. The payments were in settlement of a criminal racketeering and securities fraud suit brought by the US government. He was released from a 10-year prison sentence in January 1993.

The heaviest fine ever imposed in the UK was £5 million on Gerald Ronson (b. 26 May 1939), the head of Heron International, announced on 28 Aug 1990 at Southwark Crown Court, London. Ronson was one of four defendants in the Guinness case concerning the company's takeover bid for Distillers.

The highest fine ever imposed on a UK company is 10 million ECUs (equivalent to £5·7 million) on ICI by the EEC for irregular trading concerning polypropylene from 1977–83, on 24 Apr 1986.

Prisons

Largest The largest prison built in Britain, and the first to be built and run by the state instead of local authorities, was Millbank Penitentiary in London. Completed in 1821, it covered 3 ha *7 acres* of ground and had 5 km *3 miles* of passages. It was closed in 1890 as an expensive failure, and demolished in 1903. The site is now partly occupied by the Tate Gallery. The most capacious prison in Great Britain is Wandsworth, south London, with a certified normal accommodation of 965. A peak occupancy of 1556 was reached on 17 Aug 1990. The highest prison walls in Great Britain are those of Lancaster Prison, measuring 11–15·8 m *36–52 ft*. The Maze Prison, near Lisburn, Northern Ireland, was opened in 1974 and covers 53·8 ha *133 acres*, with eight 100-cell blocks surrounded by a 9·1 m *30 ft* wall. The largest prison in Scotland is Barlinnie, Glasgow, with 750 single cells. The largest prison in the Republic of Ireland is Mountjoy Prison, Dublin, with 808 cells.

Highest population The country with the highest per capita prison population is the USA, with 455 prisoners per 100 000 people.

The peak average prison population, including police cell occupation, for England and Wales was 51 239 for the week beginning 17 Jul 1987. In Scotland the prison population record was 5872 on 24 Feb 1993 and in Northern Ireland 2934 on 16 Nov 1975.

Most secure prison After it became a maximum security federal prison in 1934, no convict was known to have lived to tell of a successful escape from the prison of Alcatraz Island in San Francisco Bay, California, USA. A total of 23 men attempted it but 12 were recaptured, five were shot dead, one drowned and five were presumed drowned. On 16 Dec 1962, just before the prison was closed on 21 Mar 1963, one man reached the mainland alive, only to be recaptured on the spot. John Chase held the record with 26 years there.

Most expensive prison Spandau Prison, in Berlin, Germany originally built in 1887 for 600 prisoners, was used solely for the Nazi war criminal Rudolf Hess (1894–1987) for the last twenty years of his life. The cost of maintenance of the staff of 105 was estimated in 1976 to be $415 000 per annum. On 19 Aug 1987 it was announced that Hess had strangled himself two days earlier with a piece of electrical flex and that he had left a note in old German script. Two months after his death, the prison was demolished.

Longest prison escape The longest recorded escape by a recaptured prisoner was that of Leonard T. Fristoe, 77, who escaped from Nevada State Prison, USA on 15 Dec 1923 and was turned in by his son on 15 Nov 1969 at Compton, California. He had had 46 years of freedom under the name of Claude R. Willis. He had killed two sheriff's deputies in 1920.

Greatest gaol break In February 1979 a retired US Army colonel, Arthur 'Bull' Simons, led a band of 14 to break into Gasre prison, Tehran, Iran to rescue two fellow Americans. Some 11 000 other prisoners took advantage of this and the Islamic revolution in what became history's largest ever gaol break. It was arranged by H. Ross Perot, the employer of the two Americans. Over 20 years later he was to make the news again in connection with the 1992 American presidential election.

In September 1971 Raúl Sendic and 105 other Tupamaro guerillas, plus five non-political prisoners, escaped from a Uruguayan prison through a tunnel 91 m *298 ft* long.

The greatest gaol break in the UK was that from the Maze Prison on 25 Sep 1983, when 38 IRA prisoners escaped from Block H-7.

Honours, Decorations and Awards

Oldest order The earliest honour known was the 'Gold of Honour' for extraordinary valour awarded in the 18th Dynasty *c.*1440–1400 BC. A statuette was found at Qan-el-Kebri, Egypt. The oldest true order was the Order of St John of Jerusalem (the direct descendant of which is the Sovereign Military Order of Malta), legitimized in 1113. The prototype of the princely Orders of Chivalry is thought to be the Most Noble Order of the Garter, founded by King Edward III *c.*1348.

Versatility The only person to have been awarded a Victoria Cross and win an

Most titles

The most titled person in the world is the 18th Duchess of Alba, Doña María del Rosario Cayetana Fitz-James Stuart y Silva (b. 28 Mar 1926). She is 6 times a duchess, once a countess-duchess, once a viscountess, 18 times a marchioness, 19 times a countess and 17 times a Spanish grandee.

Youngest awards

Kristina Stragauskaite of Skirmantiskes, Lithuania was awarded a medal 'For Courage in Fire' when she was just 4 years 252 days old. She had saved the lives of her younger brother and sister when a fire had broken out on 7 April 1989 in the family's home while her parents were out. The award was decreed by the Presidium of the Lithuanian Soviet Socialist Republic.

The youngest age at which an official gallantry award has ever been won is eight years in the case of Anthony Farrer, who was given the Albert Medal on 23 Sep 1916 for fighting off a cougar at Cowichan Lake, Vancouver Island, Canada to save Doreen Ashburnham. She was also awarded the Albert Medal, which she exchanged in 1974 for the George Cross.

Olympic Gold Medal has been Lt-Gen. Sir Philip Neame (1888–1978). He received the VC in 1914 and was an Olympic gold medallist for Britain for rifle shooting in 1924, though under the illusion at the time that he was shooting for the British Empire. The only George Cross holder who was also a Fellow of the Royal Society was Prof. Peter Victor Danckwerts (1916–85), who as a sub-lieutenant RNVR defused 16 parachute mines in under 48 hr in the London docks during the Battle of Britain in August 1940.

Victoria Cross *Double awards* The only three men ever to have been awarded a bar to the Victoria Cross (instituted 29 Jan 1856) are:

Surg.-Capt. (later Lt-Col.) Arthur Martin-Leake VC*, VD, RAMC (1874–1953) (1902 and bar 1914).

Capt. Noel Godfrey Chavasse VC*, MC, RAMC (1884–1917) (1916 and bar posthumously 1917).

Second-Lt. (later Capt.) Charles Hazlitt Upham VC*, NZMF (b. 21 Sep 1908) (1941 and bar 1942).

The most VCs awarded in a war were the 634 in World War I (1914–18). The greatest number gained exclusively in a single action was 11 at Rorke's Drift in the Zulu War on 22–23 Jan 1879. The school with most recipients is Eton College, Lt Col. Herbert 'H' Jones being the 36th (posthumously in the Falklands campaign, in 1982).

Youngest The earliest established age for a VC is 15 years 100 days for hospital apprentice Andrew (wrongly gazetted as Arthur) Fitzgibbon (b. 13 May 1845 at Peteragurh, northern India) of the Indian Medical Services for bravery at the Taku Forts in northern China on 21 Aug 1860. The youngest living VC is Capt. Rambahadur Limbu (b. 1 Nov 1939 at Chyangthapu, Nepal) of the 10th Princess Mary's Own Gurkha Rifles. The award was for his courage as a lance-corporal while fighting in the Bau district of Sarawak, east Malaysia on 21 Nov 1965. He retired on 25 Mar 1985 as a Captain.

Oldest Capt. William Raynor was the oldest person to receive the medal. It was awarded when he was 62, for the part he played in blowing up an arms store besieged by insurgents on 11 May 1857, the second day of the Indian Mutiny. The medal was retrieved on behalf of the family at a London auction in 1987, and is displayed at the RAOC Museum, Camberley, Surrey.

Longest-lived The longest-lived of all the 1351 recipients of the Victoria Cross has been Lt-Col. Harcus Strachan. He was born in Bo'ness, West Lothian on 7 Nov 1884 and died in Vancouver, British Columbia, Canada on 1 May 1982 aged 97 years 175 days.

Record price The highest price ever paid for a Victoria Cross was £132 000 for the VC—and other medals—awarded to Major Edward 'Mick' Mannock (⟺ Top-scoring air aces) posthumously in 1919, in recognition of bravery of the first order in aerial combat. It was sold to a private collector at Billingshurst, W Sussex on 19 Sep 1992.

The record for a George Cross is £20 250 at Christie's on 14 Mar 1985, for that of Sgt Michael Willets (3rd Battalion Parachute Regiment), killed by an IRA bomb in Ulster in 1971.

Most highly decorated The four living persons to have been twice decorated with any of the UK's topmost decorations are Capt. C. H. Upham VC and bar; HM the Queen Mother CI, GCVO, GBE, who is a Lady of the Garter and a Lady of the Thistle; HRH the Duke of Edinburgh KG, KT, OM, GBE and HRH Prince Charles KG, KT, GCB. Britain's most highly decorated woman is the World War II British agent Mrs Odette Hallowes GC, MBE, Légion d'Honneur, Ordre St George (Belge), who survived imprisonment and torture at the hands of the Gestapo from 1943–5. Violette Reine Elizabeth Szabo (*née* Bushell) GC (1921–45), killed by the Gestapo, lost her husband in the French Legion at El Alamein in 1942. He was Etienne Szabo, Médaille Militaire, Légion d'Honneur and Croix de Guerre.

Most lifeboat medals Sir William Hillary (1771–1847), founder of the Royal National Lifeboat Institution in 1824, was personally and uniquely awarded four RNLI Gold Medals, in 1825, 1828 and 1830 (twice). The only triple award this century has been to Coxswain Henry Blogg GC, BEM (1876–1954) of Cromer, Norfolk, who also had four Silver Medals. The record for Silver

Lifesaving

The greatest single rescue in Britain was on 17 Mar 1907, when four lifeboats lifted 456 shipwreck survivors to safety off the Lizard, Cornwall.

The greatest number of awards gained by a member of the Royal Life Saving Society is 219 by Eric Deakin of Hightown, Lancs since 1960.

Medals is five, by Sydney Harris of Great Yarmouth and Gorleston, Norfolk (1905—twice, 1909, 1912 and 1916).

Most mentions in despatches The record number of 'mentions' is 23 by Field Marshal the Rt Hon. Sir Frederick Sleigh Roberts Bt, the Earl Roberts VC, VD (1832–1914).

Most post-nominal letters HRH the Duke of Windsor (1894–1972) when Prince of Wales had 10 sets and was also a privy counsellor, viz. KG, PC, KT, KP, GCB, GCSI, GCMG, GCIE, GCVO, GBE, MC. He later appended the ISO but never did so in the cases of the OM, CH or DSO, of which orders he had also been sovereign. Lord Roberts, who was also a privy counsellor, was the only non-royal holder of eight sets of *official* post-nominal letters.

Civilian gallantry Reginald H. Blanchford of Guernsey has received the following awards for life saving on land and at sea: MBE for gallantry in 1950; Queen's Commendation in 1957; Life Saving Medal of The Order of St John in Gold in 1957 with gold bar in 1963; George Medal in 1958; Carnegie Hero Fund's Bronze Medallion in 1959; OBE 1961. He was made a Knight of Grace of The Order of St John in 1970 and most recently received the American Biographical Institute's Silver Shield of Valor in 1992.

USA The highest US military decoration is the Medal of Honor, usually referred to as the Congressional Medal of Honor. Five marines received both the Army and Navy Medals of Honor for the same deeds in 1918, and 14 officers and men received the medal on two occasions between 1864 and 1915 for two distinct acts. The Defense Department refuses to recognize any military hero as having the most awards, but various heroes have been nominated by unofficial groups. Since medals and decorations cannot be compared in value, the title of most decorated is only a matter of subjective evaluation. General Douglas

Military awards were a matter of great pride when the USSR was the leading superpower along with the USA, and Marshal Zhukov uniquely received the Gold Star of a Hero of the Soviet Union four times. He is seen here with Pandit Nehru, the Indian Prime Minister, in 1957.

(Photo: Popperfoto)

MacArthur (1880–1964), because of his high rank and his years of military service spanning three wars, would seem to hold the best claim to 'Most Decorated American Soldier'. In addition to the Congressional Medal of Honor, he also received 58 separate awards and decorations with 16 Oak Leaf Clusters (for repeat awards), plus 18 campaign stars.

USSR The USSR's highest award for valour was the Gold Star of a Hero of the Soviet Union, 11040 of which were awarded in World War II. The only wartime triple awards of the Gold Star were to Marshal Georgiy Konstantinovich Zhukov (1896–1974), and to the leading air aces Guards Colonel (later Marshal of Aviation) Aleksandr Ivanovich Pokryshkin (1913–85) and Aviation Maj. Gen. Ivan Nikitovich Kozhedub (1920–91). Zhukov was subsequently awarded a fourth Gold Star.

Germany The Knight's Cross of the Iron Cross with swords, diamonds and golden oak-leaves was uniquely awarded to Col. Hans Ulrich Rudel (1916–82) for 2530 operational flying missions on the Eastern Front in the period 1941–5. He destroyed 519 Soviet armoured vehicles.

428 574 sec

The International Committee of the Red Cross has won the most Nobel Prizes, with three awards. Its headquarters are in Geneva, where it has an independent council of 25 Swiss nationals. The statues in front of the building represent unknown prisoners of war.

(Photo: James Clift for Guinness Publishing)

Order of Merit The Order of Merit (instituted on 23 Jun 1902) is limited to 24 members at any one time. The longest-lived of the 162 holders has been the Rt Hon. Bertrand Arthur William Russell, 3rd Earl Russell, who died on 2 Feb 1970 aged 97 years 260 days. The oldest recipient was Dame Ninette de Valois (b. 6 Jun 1898), who received the Order at the age of 94 years 179 days on 2 Dec 1992. The youngest recipient has been HRH the Duke of Edinburgh, who was appointed on his 47th birthday on 10 Jun 1968.

Most valuable annual prize The most valuable annual prize is the Louis Jeantet Prize for Medicine, which in 1993 was worth SFr 2 000 000 (equivalent to approximately £867 000). It was first awarded in 1986 and is intended to 'provide substantial funds for the support of biomedical research projects'.

Nobel Prizes

Earliest 1901 for Physics, Chemistry, Physiology or Medicine, Literature and Peace.

Most Prizes USA has won 210, outright or shared, including most for Physiology or Medicine (71); Physics (55); Chemistry (37), Peace (18); Economics (19). France has most for Literature (12). The United Kingdom total is 89, outright or shared, comprising Chemistry (23); Physiology or Medicine (22); Physics (20); Peace (10); Literature (8); Economics (6).

Oldest Laureate Professor Francis Peyton Rous (US) (1879–1970) in 1966 shared in the Physiology or Medicine prize at the age of 87.

Youngest Laureates *At time of award:* Professor Sir Lawrence Bragg (1890–1971) 1915 Physics prize at 25. *At time of work:* Bragg, and Theodore W. Richards (US) (1868–1928), 1914 Chemistry prize for work done when 23. *Literature:* Rudyard Kipling (UK) (1865–1936) 1907 prize at 41. *Peace:* Mrs Mairead Corrigan-Maguire (Northern Ireland) (b. 27 Jan 1944) 1976 prize (shared) at 32.

Most 3 Awards: International Committee of the Red Cross, Geneva (founded 1863) Peace 1917, 1944 and 1963 (shared); 2 Awards: Dr Linus Carl Pauling (US) (b. 28 Feb 1901) Chemistry 1954 and Peace 1962; Mme Marja Sklodowska Curie (Polish-French) (1867–1934) Physics 1903 (shared) and Chemistry 1911; Professor John Bardeen (US) (1908–91) Physics 1956 (shared) and 1972 (shared); Professor Frederick Sanger (b. 13 Aug 1918) Chemistry 1958 and 1980 (shared); Office of the United Nations' High Commissioner for Refugees, Geneva (founded 1951) Peace 1954 and 1981.

Highest Prize Swedish Krona 6 700 000 (for 1993), equivalent to £589 000.

Lowest Prize Swedish Krona 115 000 (for 1923), equivalent to £6620.

Most statues The world record for raising statues to oneself was set by Joseph Vissarionovich Dzhugashvili, alias Stalin (1879–1953), the leader of the Soviet Union from 1924–53. It is estimated that

443

at the time there were *c.* 6000 statues to him throughout the USSR and in many cities in eastern Europe. The country's highest mountain was named Pik Stalina (Stalin Peak), although it was renamed in 1962. In addition numerous enterprises, schools, institutes and theatres were named after him, as were 15 Soviet towns or cities. The last statue of Stalin was demolished in 1992 in Ulan Bator, the capital of Mongolia. The man to whom most statues have been raised is Buddha. The 20th-century champion is Vladimir Ilyich Ulyanov, alias Lenin (1870–1924), busts of whom have been mass-produced, as also has been the case with Mao Zedong (Mao Tse-tung) (1893–1976) and Ho Chi Minh (1890–1969).

Most honorary degrees The greatest number of honorary degrees awarded to any individual is 127, given to Rev. Father Theodore M. Hesburgh (b. 25 May 1917), president of the University of Notre Dame, Indiana, USA. These have been accumulated since 1954.

The Royal Society The longest term as a Fellow of the Royal Society (founded 1660) has been approximately 68 years in the case of Sir Hans Sloane (1660–1753), who was elected in 1685. The longest-lived Fellow was Sir Rickard Christophers (1873–1978), who died aged 104 years 84 days. The youngest Fellow is believed to have been Sir Joseph Hodges, who was born *c.* 1704 and elected on 5 Apr 1716 at about 12 years of age. The oldest person to have been elected as a Fellow was Sir Rupert Edward Cecil Lee Guinness, the 2nd Earl of Iveagh (1874–1967), who was elected in 1964 at the age of 90.

Erasmus Darwin was elected on 9 Apr 1761 and was followed by his son Robert (1788 to 1848), *his* son Charles (1839 to 1882), his sons Sir George (1879 to 1912), Francis (1882 to 1925) and Horace (1903 to 1928) and Sir George's son Sir Charles (1922 to 1962), so spanning over 200 years with five generations.

Peerage

Most ancient The oldest extant peerage is the premier Earldom of Scotland, held by the Rt Hon. Margaret of Mar, the Countess of Mar and 31st holder of this Earldom (b. 19 Sep 1940), who is the

Most prolific peers

The most prolific peers of all time are believed to be the 1st Earl Ferrers (1650–1717) and the 3rd Earl of Winchilsea (*c.* 1627–89), each with 27 legitimate children. In addition, the former reputedly fathered 30 illegitimate children.

heir-at-law of Roderick or Rothri, 1st Earl (or Mormaer) of Mar, who witnessed a charter in 1114 or 1115 as 'Rothri *comes*'.

Oldest creation The greatest age at which any person has been raised to the peerage is 93 years 337 days in the case of Sir William Francis Kyffin Taylor (b. 9 Jul 1854), who was created Baron Maenan of Ellesmere, Shrops on 10 Jun 1948, and died aged 97 on 22 Sep 1951. The oldest elevation to a life peerage has been that of Emanuel Shinwell (1884–1986) on 2 Jun 1970 when aged 85 years 227 days.

Longest-lived peer The longest-lived peer ever recorded was the Rt Hon. Emanuel Shinwell (<> above), who was created a life baron in 1970 and died on 8 May 1986 aged 101 years 202 days. The oldest peeress recorded was the Countess Desmond, who was alleged to be 140 when she died in 1604. This claim is patently exaggerated but it is accepted that she may have been 104. Currently the oldest peer is the Rt Hon. Jeffery Amherst, 5th Earl Amherst (b. 13 Dec 1896).

Youngest peers Twelve Dukes of Cornwall became (in accordance with the grant by the Crown in Parliament) peers at birth as the eldest sons of a sovereign; and the 9th Earl of Chichester inherited his earldom at his birth on 14 Apr 1944, 54 days after his father's death. The youngest age at which a person has had a peerage conferred on him is 7 days old in the case of the Earldom of Chester on HRH the Prince George (later George IV) on 19 Aug 1762. The youngest to be created a life peer or peeress is Baroness Masham of Ilton, Countess of Swinton (b. 19 Apr 1935) aged 34, in 1970.

Longest peerage The longest tenure of a peerage has been 87 years 10 days in the case of Charles St Clair, Lord Sinclair, born 30 Jul 1768, succeeded 16 Dec 1775 and died aged 94 years 243 days on 30 Mar 1863.

The shortest enjoyment of a peerage was the 'split second' by which the law assumes that the Hon. Wilfrid Carlyl Stamp (b. 28 Oct 1904), the 2nd Baron Stamp, survived his father, Sir Josiah Charles Stamp, the 1st Baron Stamp, when both were killed as a result of German bombing of London on 16 Apr 1941. Apart from this legal fiction, the shortest recorded peerage was one of 30 min in the case of Sir Charles Brandon, the 3rd Duke of Suffolk, who died aged 13 or 14 just after succeeding his brother Henry, when both were suffering a fatal illness, at Buckden, Cambs on 14 Jul 1551.

Highest numbering The highest succession number borne by any peer is that of the present 35th Baron Kingsale (John de Courcy, b. 27 Jan 1941), who succeeded to the then 746-year-old barony on 7 Nov 1969. His occupations have included barman, bingo-caller and plumber.

Most creations The largest number of new hereditary peerages created in any year was 54 in 1296. The record for all peerages (including 40 life peerages) is 55 in 1964. The greatest number of extinctions in a year was 16 in 1923 and the greatest number of deaths was 44 in 1935.

Most prolific Currently the peer with the largest family is Robert Keith Rous, 6th Earl of Stradbroke (b. 25 Mar 1937), with seven sons and seven daughters by two different wives. The most prolific peeress is believed to be Mary Fitzgerald, wife of Patrick, 19th Baron Kingsale, who bore 23 children (no twins) who survived to baptism. She died in 1663.

Baronets The greatest age to which a baronet has lived is 101 years 188 days, in the case of Sir Fitzroy Donald Maclean, 10th Bt (1835–1936). He was the last survivor of the Crimean campaign of 1853–6. Capt. Sir Trevor Wheler, 13th Bt (1889–1986) was a baronet for a record

82 years 156 days. The only baroness is Dame Maureen Dunbar of Hempriggs, who succeeded in her own right as 8th in line of a 1706 baronetcy in 1965. There are nearly 1400 baronets.

Knights *Youngest and oldest* The youngest age for the conferment of a knighthood is 29 days for HRH the Prince George (b. 12 Aug 1762) (later George IV) by virtue of his *ex officio* membership of the Order of the Garter consequent upon his creation as Prince of Wales on 17 or 19 Aug 1762. The greatest age for the conferment of a knighthood is on a 100th birthday, in the case of the Knight Bachelor Sir Robert Mayer (1879–1985), who was also made a KCVO by the Queen at the Royal Festival Hall, London on 5 Jun 1979.

Most brothers George and Elizabeth Coles of Australia had four sons knighted—Sir George (1885–1977); Sir Arthur (1892–1982); Sir Kenneth (1896–1985) and Sir Edgar (1899–1981). George re-married and had a fifth son who was also knighted—Sir Norman (1907–89).

Military and Defence

War

Earliest conflict The oldest known offensive weapon is a broken wooden spear found in April 1911 at Clacton-on-Sea, Essex by S. Hazzledine Warren. This is much beyond the limit of radiocarbon dating but is estimated to have been fashioned before 200 000 BC.

Longest The longest war which could be described as continuous was the Thirty Years War, between various European countries from 1618 to 1648. As a result the map of Europe was radically changed. The so-called 'Hundred Years War' between England and France, which lasted from 1338 to 1453 (115 years), was in fact an irregular succession of wars rather than a single one. The *Reconquista*—the series of campaigns in the Iberian Peninsula to recover the region from the Islamic Moors—began in

28th August 1896

THE GUINNESS TIMES

BRITAIN & ZANZIBAR AT WAR

Conflict lasts 38 minutes

WHAT DID YOU DO IN THE WAR, DADDY?

ACTUALLY, I MISSED IT, M'BOY— HAVIN' BREAKFAST AT THE TIME!

Britain went to war with Zanzibar yesterday, but only for 38 minutes. Following the death of the Sultan under somewhat suspicious circumstances three days ago, Sa'id Khalid and his supporters seized the palace and barricaded it, with Khalid proclaiming himself as the new Sultan.

British forces landed men at the custom house and an ultimatum was issued to Khalid that the palace would be bombarded if he did not surrender and take down his flag by 9 a.m. yesterday. At 7.30 Rear Admiral Harry Rawson repeated the ultimatum, and two minutes after the deadline had passed, with no response, Her Majesty's ships 'Rangoon',

'Sparrow' and 'Thrush' opened fire on the palace. Fire was returned and there was a violent exchange, but less than 40 minutes later the palace was reduced to ruins and the occupants fled, with Khalid surrendering to the German consulate. Later in the day Hamud ibn Muhammad was appointed as the new Sultan.

The shortest war on record had finished almost as soon as it had begun.

718 and continued intermittently until 1492, when Granada, the last Moorish stronghold, was finally conquered.

Bloodiest By far the most costly war in terms of human life was World War II (1939–45), in which the total number of fatalities, including battle deaths and civilians of all countries, is estimated to have been 54·8 million, assuming 25 million Soviet fatalities and 7·8 million Chinese civilians killed. The country which suffered most was Poland, with 6 028 000 or 17·2 per cent of its population of 35 100 000 killed. The total combatant death toll from World War I was 9·7 million, compared with the 15·6 million from World War II. In the case of the UK, however, the heavier armed

forces fatalities occurred in World War I (1914–18), with 765 399 killed out of some 5 500 000 engaged (13·9 per cent), compared with 265 000 out of 5 896 000 engaged (4·49 per cent) in World War II.

In the Paraguayan war of 1864–70 against Brazil, Argentina and Uruguay, the population of Paraguay was reduced from 1 400 000 to 220 000 survivors, of whom only 30 000 were adult males. Dr William Brydon (1811–73) and two natives were the sole survivors of a seven-day retreat of 13 000 soldiers and camp-followers from Kabul, Afghanistan. Dr Brydon's horse died 2 days after his arrival at Jellalabad, some 115 km *70 miles* to the east on the route to the Khyber Pass, on 13 Jan 1842.

Most costly war

The material cost of World War II far transcended that of the rest of history's wars put together and has been estimated at $1·5 trillion. The total cost to the Soviet Union was estimated in May 1959 at 2·5 trillion roubles, while a figure of $530 billion has been estimated for the USA.

In the case of the UK the cost of £34 423 million was over five times as great as that of World War I (£6700 million) and 158·6 times that of the Boer War of 1899–1902 (£217 million).

Bloodiest civil

The bloodiest civil war in history was the *Taiping* ('Great Peace') rebellion, which was a revolt against the Chinese Qing Dynasty between 1851 and 1864. The rebellion was led by the deranged Hong Xiuquan (executed), who imagined himself to be a younger brother of Jesus Christ. His force was named *Taiping Tianguo* ('Heavenly Kingdom of Great Peace'). According to the best estimates the loss of life was some 20 million, including more than 100 000 killed by government forces in the sack of Nanjing on 19–21 Jul 1864.

Last battle on British soil

The last pitched land battle in Britain was at Culloden Field, Drummossie Moor, near Inverness on 16 Apr 1746. The last clan battle in Scotland was between Clan Mackintosh and Clan MacDonald at Mulroy, Inverness-shire in 1689. The last battle on English soil was the Battle of Sedgemoor, Somerset on 6 Jul 1685, when the forces of James II defeated the supporters of Charles II's illegitimate son, James Scott (formerly called Fitzroy or Crofts), the Duke of Monmouth (1649–85). During the Jacobite rising of 1745–6, there was a skirmish at Clifton Moor, Cumbria on 18 Dec 1745, when forces under Prince William, Duke of Cumberland (1721–65) brushed with the rebels of Prince Charles Edward Stuart (1720–88). About 12 men were killed on the King's side and five Highlanders.

This was a tactical victory for the Jacobites under Lord George Murray.

Bloodiest battle

Modern It is difficult to compare the major battles of World Wars I and II because of the timescales. The 142-day long first battle of the Somme, France (1 Jul–19 Nov 1916) produced an estimated total number of casualties of over 1·22 million, of which 398 671 were British (57 470 on the first day) and more than 600 000 German. Gunfire was heard on Hampstead Heath, London. The losses of the German Army Group Centre on the Eastern Front between 22 Jun and 8 Jul 1944 (17 days) totalled 350 000.

The greatest death toll in a battle has been estimated at *c.* 1 109 000 in the Battle of Stalingrad, USSR (now Volgograd, Russia), ending with the German surrender on 31 Jan 1943 by Field Marshal Friedrich von Paulus (1890–1957). The Soviet garrison commander was Gen. Vasiliy Chuikov. The Soviet army also lost *c.* 650 800 soldiers who were injured but survived. Additionally, only 1515 civilians from a pre-war population of more than 500 000 were found alive after the battle. The final drive on Berlin, Germany by the Soviet Army and the battle for the city which followed, from 16 Apr–2 May 1945, involved 3·5 million men, 52 000 guns and mortars, 7750 tanks and 11 000 aircraft on both sides.

Ancient Modern historians give no credence, on logistic grounds, to the casualty figures attached to ancient battles, such as the 250 000 reputedly killed at Plataea (Greeks *v.* Persians) in 479 BC or the 200 000 allegedly killed in a single day at Châlons-sur-Marne, France (Huns *v.* Romans) in AD 451.

British The bloodiest battle fought on British soil was the battle of Towton, near Tadcaster, N Yorks on 29 Mar 1461, when 36 000 Yorkists defeated 40 000 Lancastrians. The total loss has been estimated at between 28 000 and 38 000 killed. A figure of 80 000 British dead was attributed by Tacitus to the battle of AD 61 between Queen Boudicca (Boadicea) of the Iceni and the Roman Governor of Britain Suetonius Paulinus, for the reputed loss of only 400 Romans in an army of 10 000. The site of the battle is unknown but may have been near Borough Hill, Daventry, Northants, or more probably near Hampstead Heath, London. Prior to this battle the Romans had lost up to 70 000 in Colchester and London.

Greatest naval battle The greatest number of ships and aircraft ever involved in a sea–air action was 231 ships and 1996 aircraft in the Battle of Leyte Gulf, in the Philippines. It raged from 22–27 Oct 1944, with 166 Allied and 65 Japanese warships engaged, of which 26 Japanese and six US ships were sunk. In addition, 1280 US and 716 Japanese aircraft were engaged. The greatest purely naval battle of modern times was the Battle of Jutland on 31 May 1916, in which 151 Royal Navy warships were involved against 101 German warships. The Royal Navy lost 14 ships and 6097 men and the German fleet 11 ships and 2545 men. The greatest of ancient naval battles was the Battle of Salamis, Greece in September 480 BC. There were an estimated 800 vessels in the defeated Persian fleet and 380 in the victorious fleet of the Athenians and their allies, with a possible involvement of 200 000 men. The death toll at the Battle of Lepanto on 7 Oct 1571 has been estimated at 33 000.

Greatest invasion *Seaborne* The greatest invasion in military history was the Allied land, air and sea operation against the Normandy coasts of France on D-day, 6 Jun 1944. Thirty-eight convoys of 745 ships moved in on the first three days, supported by 4066 landing craft, carrying 185 000 men, 20 000 vehicles and 347 minesweepers. The air assault comprised 18 000 paratroopers from 1087 aircraft. The 42 available divisions had air support from 13 175 aircraft. Within a month 1 100 000 troops, 200 000 vehicles and 750 000 tons of stores were landed. The Allied invasion of Sicily from 10–12 Jul 1943 involved the landing of 181 000 men in three days.

Airborne The largest airborne invasion was the Anglo-American assault of three divisions (34 000 men), with 2800 aircraft and 1600 gliders, near Arnhem, in the Netherlands, on 17 Sep 1944.

Last on the soil of Great Britain The last invasion of Great Britain occurred on 12 Feb 1797, when the Irish-American adventurer General Tate landed at Carreg Wastad Point, Pembroke (now Dyfed) with 1400 French troops. They surrendered outside Fishguard, a few miles away, to Lord Cawdor's force of the Castlemartin Yeomanry and some local inhabitants armed with pitchforks. The UK Crown Dependency of the Falkland Islands was invaded by Argentine troops on 2 Apr 1982. British troops re-landed at San Carlos on 21 May and accepted the surrender of Brig. Gen. Mario Menéndez 24 days later, on 14 Jun 1982.

Longest range attacks The longest range attacks in air history were those undertaken by seven B-52G bombers, which took off from Barksdale air force base, Louisiana, USA on 16 Jan 1991 to deliver air-launched cruise missiles against targets in Iraq shortly after the start of the Gulf War. Each flew a distance of 22 500 km *14 000 miles*, refuelling four times in flight, with the round-trip mission lasting some 35 hours.

Greatest evacuation The greatest evacuation in military history was that carried out by 1200 Allied naval and civil craft from the beach-head at Dunkerque (Dunkirk), France between 27 May and 4 Jun 1940. A total of 338 226 British and French troops were taken off.

Worst sieges The worst siege in history was the 880-day siege of Leningrad, USSR (now St Petersburg, Russia), by the German Army from 30 Aug 1941 until 27 Jan 1944. The best estimate is that between 1·3 and 1·5 million defenders and citizens died. This included 641 000 people who died of hunger in the city and 17 000 civilians killed by shelling. More than 150 000 shells and 100 000 bombs were dropped on the city. The

---

Largest civilian evacuation

Following the Iraqi invasion of Kuwait in August 1990, Air India evacuated 111 711 of its nationals who were working in Kuwait. Beginning on 13 August, 488 flights took the ex-patriates back to India over a two-month period.

longest recorded siege was that of Azotus (now Ashdod), Israel which according to Herodotus was besieged by Psamtik I of Egypt for 29 years in the period 664–610 BC.

Chemical warfare The greatest number of people killed through chemical warfare were the estimated 4000 Kurds who died at Halabja, Iraq in March 1988 when President Saddam Hussein used chemical weapons against Iraq's Kurdish minority for the support it had given to Iran in the Iran–Iraq war.

Defence Spending

In 1991 it was estimated that the world's spending on armaments was running at an annual rate of some $600 billion. In 1992 there were 24 714 000 full-time armed forces regulars or conscripts plus 38 341 000 reservists, totalling 63 055 000. The budgeted expenditure on defence by the US government for the fiscal year 1992 was $270·9 billion. The defence budget of Russia was given as 411·3 billion roubles in 1992. The UK defence budget for 1992/93 is £24·4 billion.

Armed Forces

Largest China's People's Liberation Army's strength in 1992 was estimated to be 3 030 000 (comprising land, sea and air forces), with reductions continuing. Her reserves number around 1·2 million. Prior to its break-up, the USSR had the largest regular armed force in the world, with 3 400 000 personnel in 1991. It is not possible to give the size of Russian armed forces, as it is constantly changing as former republics convert Russian units into national forces, but plans are to maintain forces of about 1·5 million. The USA's military manpower is 1 914 000 (1992) and that of the UK 293 500 (also 1992).

Navies ***Largest*** The largest navy in the world in terms of manpower is the United States Navy, with 546 600 plus 193 000 Marines in mid-1992. The active strength in 1992 included six nuclear-powered aircraft carriers, with six others, 25 Ballistic Missile submarines, 87 nuclear attack submarines and one diesel attack submarine, 48 cruisers, 45 destroyers, 83 frigates and 65 amphibious warfare ships. The navy of the former

Including reserves, China has the largest armed forces in the world. A small proportion of them are seen here parading through Guangzhou.
(Photo: Gamma/V. Clavieres)

USSR had a larger submarine fleet, of 250 vessels (including 55 ballistic missiles). It also had four aircraft carriers, 33 cruisers, 26 destroyers, 129 frigates and 80 amphibious warfare ships. This includes the Black Sea Fleet which has 18 submarines but none with ballistic missiles and 36 surface combatants. The Black Sea Fleet will be split between Ukraine, Russia and Georgia. The rest of the navy is based at Russian ports.

The strength of the Royal Navy in mid-1992 included 3 *Invincible* class carriers, 3 (but probably only two seaworthy) nuclear submarines with strategic nuclear missiles and one of the new *Trident* armed class still under trial, 13 other nuclear and 6 diesel attack submarines, 12 guided weapon destroyers and 29 frigates. The uniformed strength was 62 100, including The Fleet Air Arm and Royal Marines (7600), in 1992. In 1914 the Royal Navy had 542 warships including 72 capital ships with 16 building, making it the largest navy in the world at the time.

Longest-serving admiral Admiral of the Fleet Sir Provo Wallis (1791–1892) first served on HMS *Cleopatra* in October 1804. Because of his service on the ship in 1805 against the French, he was kept on the active list in 1870 for life. He was thus 87 years 4 months on paid active service, though he was earlier on the books as a volunteer for a further nine years from 1795–1804—a system by which even infants could gain seniority on joining.

Youngest conscripts

President Francisco Macias Nguema of Equatorial Guinea (deposed in August 1979) decreed in March 1976 compulsory military service for all boys aged between seven and 14. The edict stated that any parent refusing to hand over his or her son 'will be imprisoned or shot'.

Armies *Oldest* The oldest army in the world is the 80–90 strong Pontifical Swiss Guard in the Vatican City, with a regular foundation dating back to 21 Jan 1506. Its origins, however, predate 1400.

Largest Numerically, the world's largest army is that of the People's Republic of China, with a total strength of some 2·3 million in mid-1992. The total size of the former USSR's army in mid-1991 was estimated by the International Institute for Strategic Studies at 1 400 000 men believed to be organized into 139 divisions (tank, motor rifle and airborne).

The strength of the British Army in early 1993 was 134 583. The basic strength maintained in Northern Ireland was 12 527 plus 5938 from the Ulster Defence Regiment. Between 1969 and the spring of 1993, 2130 civilians and 930 armed forces and police personnel were killed in the province.

Oldest soldiers The oldest 'old soldier' of all time was probably John B. Salling of the army of the Confederate States of America and the last accepted survivor of the US Civil War (1861–5). He died in Kingsport, Tennessee, USA on 16 Mar 1959, aged 113 years 1 day.

The oldest Chelsea pensioner, based *only* on the evidence of his tombstone, was 111-year-old William Hiseland (6 Aug 1620–7 Feb 1732). George Ives (b. Brighton, E. Sussex, 17 Nov 1881, d. 12 Apr 1993) of the 1st Imperial Yeomanry fought in the Boer War, and also lived to the age of 111. After the war he emigrated to Canada, where he lived for some 90 years. The longest-serving British soldier has been Field Marshal Sir William Gomm (1784–1875), who was an ensign in 1794 and Constable of the

Tower of London over 80 years later at his death aged 91.

Youngest soldiers Marshal Duke of Caxias (25 Aug 1803–7 May 1880), Brazilian military hero and statesman, entered his infantry regiment at the age of five in 1808. Fernando Inchauste Montalvo (b. 18 Jun 1930), the son of a major in the Bolivian air force, went to the front with his father on his 5th birthday during the war between Bolivia and Paraguay (1932–5). He had received military training and was subject to military discipline.

The youngest enlistment in Britain in the 20th century is believed to be that of William Frederick Price (b. 1 Jun 1891), who was enlisted into the army at Aldershot on 23 May 1903, when aged 11 years 356 days.

Tallest soldiers The tallest soldier of all time was Väinö Myllyrinne (1909–63), who was conscripted into the Finnish Army when he was 2·21 m 7 ft 3 in and later grew to 2·51 m 8 ft 3 in. The British Army's tallest soldier was Benjamin Crow, who was signed on at Lichfield, Staffs in November 1947 when he was 2·15 m 7 ft 1 in tall. Edward Evans (1924–58), who later grew to 2·35 m 7 ft 8½ in, was in the army when he was 2·08 m 6 ft 10 in.

British regimental records The oldest regular regiment in the British Army is the Royal Scots, raised in French service in 1633, though the Buffs (Royal East Kent Regiment) can trace their origin to independent companies in Dutch pay as early as 1572. The Coldstream Guards, raised in 1650, were, however, placed on the establishment of the British Army before the Royal Scots and the Buffs. The oldest armed body in the UK is the Queen's Bodyguard of the Yeomen of the Guard, formed in 1485. The Honourable Artillery Company, senior regiment of the Territorial Army, formed from the Fraternity of St George, Southwark, London received its charter from Henry VIII in 1537 but this lapsed until it was re-formed in 1610. The infantry regiment with most battle honours is the Royal Highland Fusiliers (Princess Margaret's Own Glasgow and Ayrshire Regiment), with 208. The most senior regiment of the Reserve Army is the Royal Monmouthshire Royal

Speed march

A team of nine representing II Squadron RAF Regiment from RAF Hullavington, Wilts, each man carrying a pack weighing at least 40lb 18·1kg, including a rifle, completed the London marathon in 4hr 33min 58sec on 21 Apr 1991.

Flt Sgt Chris Chandler set an individual record in the RAF Swinderby Marathon at Swinderby, Lincs on 25 Sep 1992, with a pack weighing 40lb 18·1kg. His time was 3hr 56min 10sec.

Army drill

On 8–9 Jul 1987 a 90-man squad of the Queen's Colour Squadron, RAF performed a total of 2722662 drill movements (2001384 rifle and 721278 foot) at RAF Uxbridge, Middx from memory and without a word of command in 23hr 55min.

Armour

The highest auction price paid for a suit of armour was £1925000, by B.H. Trupin (US) on 5 May 1983 at Sotheby's, London for a suit made in Milan by Giovanni Negroli in 1545 for Henri II of France. It came from the Hever Castle Collection in Kent.

Military feast

It was estimated that some 30000 guests attended a military feast given at Radewitz, Poland on 25 Jun 1730 by King August II (1709–33).

Engineers (Militia), formed on 21 Mar 1577 and never disbanded, with battle honours at Dunkirk, 1940 and Normandy, 1944.

Conscientious objector *Most obdurate* The only conscientious objector to be six times court-martialled in World War II was Gilbert Lane of Wallington, Surrey. He served 31 months' detention and 183 days' imprisonment.

Greatest mutiny In World War I, 56 French divisions comprising some 650000 men and their officers, refused orders on the Western Front sector of General Robert Nivelle in April 1917 after the failure of his offensive.

Longest march The longest march in military history was the famous Long March by the Chinese Communists in 1934–5. In 368 days, of which 268 days were days of movement, from October to October, their force of some 100000 covered 9700km *6000miles* from Ruijin, in Jiangxi, to Yan'an, in Shaanxi. They crossed 18 mountain ranges and 24 rivers, and eventually reached Yan'an with only about 8000 surviors following continual rearguard actions against nationalist Guomindang (GMD) forces.

On the night of 12–13 Sep 1944 a team of nine from B Company 4th Infantry Battalion of the Irish Army made a night march of 67·6km *42miles* in full battle order carrying 18·1kg *40lb* in 11hr 49min.

Air forces *Oldest* The earliest autonomous air force is the Royal Air Force, which can be traced back to 1878, when the War Office commissioned the building of a military balloon. The Royal Engineers Balloon Section and Depot was formed in 1890 and the Air Battalion of the Royal Engineers followed on 1 Apr 1911. On 13 May 1912 the Royal Flying Corps was formed, with both Military and Naval Wings, the latter being renamed the Royal Naval Air Service. The Royal Air Force was formed on 1 Apr 1918 from the RFC and the RNAS, and took its place alongside the Royal Navy and the Army as a separate service with its own Ministry. Balloons had been used for military observation by both sides during the American Civil War (1861–5).

Largest The greatest air force of all time was the United States Army Air Corps (now the US Air Force), which had 79908 aircraft in July 1944 and 2411294 personnel in March 1944. The US Air Force, including strategic missile forces, had 499400 personnel and 8718 aircraft in mid-1992. The Air Force of the former USSR had 895000 personnel (including some 200000 manning surface-to-air missiles) in mid-1991. It had 11370 aircraft. Russia has inherited some 6200 of the Soviets' combat aircraft and the majority of the other types such as trainers and transport. In addition, in mid-1991 the USSR's Offensive Strategic Rocket Forces had about 164 000 operational personnel. Eventually only Russia will have strategic rocket forces.

The strength of the Royal Air Force in 1992 was 86 000, with 40 operational squadrons.

Top jet ace The greatest number of kills in jet-to-jet battles is 16, by Capt. Joseph Christopher McConnell, Jr, of the United States Air Force, in the Korean war (1950–3). He was killed on 25 Aug 1954. Lt-Col. Heinz Bär (Germany) also achieved 16 kills as a jet pilot, in 1945, although against propeller driven aeroplanes. It is possible that an Israeli ace may have surpassed this total in the period 1967–70, but the identity of pilots is subject to strict security.

Top woman ace The record score for any woman fighter pilot is 12, by Jnr-Lt Lydia Litvak (USSR) (b. 1921) on the Eastern Front between 1941 and 1943. She was killed in action on 1 Aug 1943.

Top-scoring air aces (World Wars I and II) The 'scores' of air aces in both wars are *still* disputed. The highest figures officially attributed are:

World	United Kingdom
World War I	
80 Rittmeister Manfred Freiherr (Baron) von Richthofen (Germany)	57[1] Major James T.B. McCudden VC, DSO*, MC*, MM
World War II	
352[2] Major Erich Hartmann (Germany)	38 Group-Capt. (now Air Vice Marshal) James Edgar Johnson DSO**, DFC*

[1] 73 'victories' are frequently attributed to Major Edward Mannock VC, DSO**, MC*, although he actually claimed no more than 50—the total stated in his VC citation. The figure of 73 is thought to be used so that he would appear to beat the 72 'victories' which were claimed by the Canadian pilot Lt-Col. William 'Billy' Bishop VC, although many of these are considered to be unsubstantiated.

[2] The highest total in one sortie is 13 in 17 min by Major Erich Rudorffer, on the Russian front on 6 Nov 1943.

[3] The greatest number of successes against flying bombs (V1s) was by Sqn Ldr Joseph Berry DFC** (b. Nottingham, 1920, killed 2 Oct 1944), who brought down 60 during the V1 campaign between 13 Jun and 1 Sep 1944, 57 of them at night. The most successful fighter pilot in the RAF was Sqn Ldr Marmaduke Thomas St John Pattle DFC*, of South Africa, with a known total of at least 40 enemy aircraft.

Anti-submarine successes The highest number of U-boat kills attributed to one ship in World War II was 15, to HMS *Starling* (Capt. Frederic John Walker DSO***, RN). Captain Walker was in command at the sinking of a total of 25 U-boats between 1941 and the time of his death on 9 Jul 1944. The US Destroyer Escort *England* sank six Japanese submarines in the Pacific between 18 and 30 May 1944.

Most successful submarine captains The most successful of all World War II submarine commanders was Leutnant Otto Kretschmer, captain of the U.23 and U.99, who up to March 1941 sank one destroyer and 44 Allied merchantmen totalling 266629 gross registered tons.

In World War I Kapitänleutnant (later Vizeadmiral) Lothar von Arnauld de la Périère, in the U.35 and U.139, sank 195 Allied ships totalling 458856 gross registered tons. The most successful boats were the U.35, which in World War I sank 54 ships of 90350 grt in a single voyage and 224 ships of 539711 grt all told, and the U.48, which sank 51 ships of 310 007 grt in World War II. The largest target ever sunk by a submarine was the Japanese aircraft carrier *Shinano* (59994 tonnes) by USS *Archerfish* (Cdr Joseph F. Enright, USN) on 29 Nov 1944.

Bombs

Heaviest The heaviest conventional bomb ever used operationally was the Royal Air Force's *Grand Slam*, weighing 9980 kg *22 000 lb* and 7·74 m *25 ft 5 in* long, dropped on Bielefeld railway viaduct, Germany on 14 Mar 1945. In

1949 the United States Air Force tested a bomb weighing 19050 kg *42000 lb* at Muroc Dry Lake, California, USA. The heaviest known nuclear bomb was the MK 17 carried by US B-36 bombers in the mid-1950s. It weighed 19050 kg *42000 lb* and was 7·47m *24ft 6in* long.

Atomic The first atom bomb dropped on Hiroshima, Japan by the United States at 8:16a.m. on 6 Aug 1945 had an explosive power equivalent to that of 12·5 kilotons of trinitrotoluene ($C_7H_5O_6N_3$), called TNT. Code-named *Little Boy*, it was 3·04 m *10 ft* long and weighed 4080 kg *9000 lb*. It burst 565m *1850 ft* above the city centre.

The most powerful thermonuclear device so far tested is one with a power equivalent to that of 57 megatons of TNT, detonated by the former USSR in the Novaya Zemlya area at 8:33a.m. GMT on 30 Oct 1961. The shock-wave circled the world three times, taking 36 hr 27 min for the first circuit. Some estimates put the power of this device at between 62 and 90 megatons.

The largest US H-bomb tested was the 18–22 megaton *Bravo* at Bikini Atoll, Marshall Islands on 1 Mar 1954. On 9 Aug 1961, Nikita Khrushchev, then the Chairman of the Council of Ministers of the USSR, declared that the Soviet Union was capable of constructing a 100-megaton bomb, and announced the possession of one during a visit to what was then East Berlin, East Germany on 16 Jan 1963. Such a device could make a crater in rock 107m *355ft* deep and 2·9 km *1·8 miles* wide, with a fireball 13·9 km *8·6 miles* in diameter.

Largest nuclear weapons The most powerful ICBM (inter-continental ballistic missile) is the former USSR's SS-18 (Model 5), believed to be armed with 10 750-kiloton MIRVs (multiple independently targetable re-entry vehicles). SS-18 ICBMs are located on the territories of both Russia and Kazakhstan — they are now controlled by the Commonwealth of Independent States. Earlier models had a single 20-megaton warhead. START 2 (START = Strategic Arms Reduction Talks) requires all SS-18, and all other ICBMs with more than one warhead, to be eliminated. The US Titan II carrying a W-53 warhead was

rated at 9 megatons but was withdrawn, leaving the 1·2 megaton W-56 as the most powerful US weapon.

Largest 'conventional' explosion The largest use of conventional explosives was by a team of Chinese army engineers who blew up a mountain to allow for the expansion of an airport in Zhuhai, an economic development zone near Macao. A total of nearly 12 200 tonnes of TNT were detonated on 28 Dec 1992 after 1000 technicians had spent several months preparing for the explosion.

Tanks

Earliest The first tank was *No. 1 Lincoln*, modified to become *Little Willie*, built by William Foster & Co. Ltd of Lincoln. It first ran on 6 Sep 1915. Tanks first saw action with the Heavy Section, Machine Gun Corps, later the Tank Corps, at the Battle of Flers-Courcelette, France on 15 Sep 1916. The Mark I Male tank, armed with a pair of 6-pounder guns and three machine guns, weighed 28·4 tonnes and was powered by a 105 hp motor, giving a maximum road speed of 4·8–6·4 km/h *3–4mph*.

Heaviest The heaviest tank ever constructed was the German Panzer Kampfwagen Maus II, which weighed 192 tonnes. By 1945 it had reached only the experimental stage and was abandoned. The heaviest operational tank used by any army was the 75·2 tonne 13-man French Char de Rupture 2C bis of 1922. It carried a 155mm *6⅛ in* howitzer and was powered by two 250 hp engines giving a maximum speed of 12 km/h *8mph*.

The heaviest British tank was the Experimental Heavy Tank TOG 2 built in 1914. It weighed 80 tonnes, was 10·13m *33ft 3in* long, had a crew of six and a top speed of 13·7 km/h *8½mph*. It is on permanent display at the Tank Museum, Bovington, Dorset. The heaviest British tank to enter service was *Conqueror*, at 66 tonnes.

The most heavily armed tank since 1972 has been the Soviet T-72, with a 125mm *4⅞ in* high-velocity gun. The American Sheridan light tank mounts a 152mm

453

6 in weapon which is both a gun and a missile launcher combined but this is not a long barrelled, high-velocity gun of the conventional type. The British AVRE *Centurion* has a 165 mm *6½ in* low-velocity demolition gun.

Fastest The fastest armoured reconnaissance vehicle is the British *Scorpion*, which can touch 80 km/h *50 mph* with a 75 per cent payload. The American experimental tank M1936 built by J. Walter Christie was clocked at 103·4 km/h *64·3 mph* during official trials in Britain in 1938.

Most prolific The greatest production of any tank was that of the Soviet T-54/55 series, of which more than 50 000 were built between 1954 and 1980 in the USSR alone, with further production in the one-time Warsaw Pact countries and China.

Guns

Earliest Although it cannot be accepted as proven, it is believed that the earliest guns were constructed in both China and in north Africa in *c.* 1250. The earliest representation of an English gun is

Gun running

The record for the Royal Tournament Naval Field Gun Competition (instituted 1907, with present rules since 1913) is 2 min 40·6 sec, by the Portsmouth Command Field Gun crew at Earl's Court, London on 19 Jul 1984. The barrel alone weighs 406 kg *8 cwt*. The wall is 1·52 m *5 ft* high and the chasm 8·53 m *28 ft* across.

Field gun pull

Three teams of eight members from 72 Ordnance Company (V) RAOC pulled a 25-pounder field gun over a distance of 177·98 km *110·6 miles* in 24 hours at Donnington, Shrops on 2–3 Apr 1993.

Military engines

The largest military catapults, or onagers, could throw a missile weighing 27 kg *60 lb* a distance of 460 m *500 yd*.

contained in an illustrated manuscript dated 1326, now at Oxford. The earliest anti-aircraft gun was an artillery piece on a high-angle mounting used in the Franco-Prussian War of 1870 by the Prussians against French balloons.

Largest The largest gun ever constructed was used by the Germans in the siege of Sevastopol, USSR (now Russia) in July 1942. It was of a calibre of 800 mm *31 in* with a barrel 28·87 m *94 ft 8½ in* long. Internally it was named *Schwerer Gustav*, and was one of three guns which were given the general name of *Dora*, although the other two were not finished and so were not used in action. It was built by Krupp, and its remains were discovered near Metzenhof, Bavaria in August 1945. The whole assembly of the gun was 42·9 m *141 ft* long and weighed 1344 tonnes, with a crew of 1500. The range for an 8·1 tonne projectile was 46·67 km *29 miles*.

During World War I the British Army used a gun of 457 mm *18 in* calibre. The barrel alone weighed 127 tonnes. In World War II the *Bochebuster*, a train-mounted howitzer with a calibre of 457 mm *18 in* firing a 1130 kg *2500 lb* shell to a maximum range of 20850 m *22 800 yd*, was used from 1940 onwards as part of the Kent coast defences.

Greatest range The greatest range ever attained by a gun was achieved by the HARP (High Altitude Research Project) gun, consisting of two 420 mm *16½ in* calibre barrels in tandem 36·4 m *119 ft 5 in* long and weighing 150 tonnes, at Yuma, Arizona, USA. On 19 Nov 1966 an 84 kg *185 lb* projectile was fired to an altitude of 180 km *112 miles*.

The static V3 underground firing tubes built in 50° shafts during World War II near Mimoyècques, not far from Calais, France, to bombard London were never operative. This would have been a distance of some 150 km *95 miles*.

The famous long-range gun which shelled Paris in World War I was the *Paris-Geschütz* (Paris Gun), with a calibre of 210 mm *8¼ in*, a designed range of 127·9 km *79½ miles* and an achieved range of 122 km *76 miles* from the Forest of Crépy in March 1918.

Mortars The largest mortars ever constructed were Mallet's mortar (Woolwich Arsenal, London, 1857) and the *Little David* of World War II, made in the USA. Each had a calibre of 914mm *36in*, but neither was ever used in action.

The heaviest mortar employed was the tracked German 600mm *23½in* siege piece *Karl*, of which there were seven such mortars built. Only six of these were actually used in action, although never all at the same time, at Sevastopol, USSR in 1942, at Warsaw, Poland in 1944, and at Budapest, Hungary, also in 1944.

Largest cannon The highest-calibre cannon ever constructed is the *Tsar Pushka* (*King of Cannons*), now housed in the Kremlin, Moscow, Russia. It was built in the 16th century with a bore of 890mm *35in* and a barrel 5·34m *17ft6in* long. It weighs 39·3 tonnes or 2400 *poods* (sic).

The Turks fired up to seven shots per day from a bombard 7·92m *26ft* long, with an internal calibre of 1066mm *42in*, against the walls of Constantinople (now Istanbul) from 12 Apr–29 May 1453. The cannon was dragged by 60 oxen and 200 men and fired a 540kg *1200lb* stone ball.

Nuclear delivery vehicles As of September 1990 the USSR deployed 2500 nuclear delivery launchers compared to the USA's 2246 as counted under the START rules and compared to the proposed limit of 1600. Again under START counting rules, the former USSR could deliver a maximum of 10271 warheads and the USA 10563, but this is a theoretical total and not necessarily the number held. The START limit for nuclear warheads is 6000. There are four republics of the former USSR (Russia, Ukraine, Belarus and Kazakhstan) which hold strategic nuclear weapons, but the latter three nations are committed to giving up their nuclear weapons. A second START treaty agreed between the USA and Russia will reduce warhead numbers to between 3000 and 3500 each.

Education

Compulsory education was first introduced in 1819 in Prussia. It became compulsory in the UK in 1870.

University *Oldest* The Sumerians had scribal schools or *É-Dub-ba* soon after 3500 BC. The oldest existing educational institution in the world is the University of Karueein, founded in AD 859 in Fez, Morocco. The University of Bologna, the oldest in Europe, was founded in 1088.

The oldest university in the UK is the University of Oxford, which came into being *c.* 1167. The oldest of the existing colleges is probably University College (1249), though its foundation is less well documented than that of Merton in 1264. The earliest college at Cambridge University is Peterhouse, founded in 1284. The largest college at either university is Trinity College, Cambridge, founded in 1546. The oldest university in Scotland is the University of St Andrews, Fife. Established as a university in 1410, theology and medicine may have been taught there since *c.* AD 900.

Greatest enrolment The university with the greatest enrolment in the world is the State University of New York, USA, which had 404065 students at 64 campuses throughout the state in late 1992. The greatest enrolment at a university centred in one city is at the University of Rome (*La Sapienza*), in Italy. It was built in the 1920s as a single-site campus, and still is mainly based there although some faculties are now outside the campus. Its peak number of students was 180000 in 1987, although the number has dropped slightly in the past few years.

Britain's largest university is the University of London, with 69640 internal students and 23100 external students (1992/3), totalling 92740. The Open University at Walton Hall near Milton Keynes, Bucks was first called the University of the Air and was granted a Royal Charter on 30 May 1969. In 1992 it supported 91793 undergraduate and associate registered students following undergraduate or diploma in education courses, 7448 postgraduate students and 21161 student-course registrations for associate short-courses. There were 3162 full-time staff and 6588 tutorial and counselling staff, most of whom held full-time posts with other universities and colleges.

Largest The largest existing university building in the world is the M.V. Lomonosov State University on the Lenin Hills, south of Moscow, Russia. It stands 240 m 787 ft 5 in tall, and has 32 storeys and 40 000 rooms. It was constructed from 1949–53.

Professor *Youngest* The youngest at which anybody has been elected to a chair in a university is 19 years in the case of Colin MacLaurin (1698–1746), who was elected to Marischal College, Aberdeen as Professor of Mathematics on 30 Sep 1717. In 1725 he was made Professor of Mathematics at Edinburgh University on the recommendation of Sir Isaac Newton (1642–1727), who was a professor at Cambridge at the age of 26. Henry Phillpotts (1778–1869) became a don at Magdalen College, Oxford on 25 Jul 1795 aged 17 years 80 days.

Most durable Dr Joel Hildebrand (1881–1983), Professor Emeritus of Physical Chemistry at the University of California, Berkeley, USA, first became an assistant professor in 1913 and published his 275th research paper 68 years later in 1981.

The longest period for which any professorship has been held in Britain is 63 years in the case of Thomas Martyn (1735–1825), Professor of Botany at Cambridge University from 1762 until his death. The last professor-for-life was the pathologist Prof. Henry Roy Dean (1879–1961) for his last 39 years at Cambridge.

Youngest undergraduate and graduate Michael Tan (⊳ Youngest A level pass below) started studying for a BSc degree in mathematics at Canterbury University, New Zealand in March 1992 at the age of 7 years 11 months.

In Britain, the most extreme recorded cases of undergraduate juvenility were those of Alexander Hill (1785–1867), who entered St Andrews University at the age of 10 years 4 months in November 1795, and William Thomson (1824–1907), later Lord Kelvin, who entered Glasgow

Schools

The country with the greatest number of primary schools is China, with 938 394 in 1990. San Marino has the lowest pupil to teacher ratio, with 5·5 children per teacher.

At general secondary level India has the most schools, with 214 380 in 1990, whilst the Australian external territory of Cocos (Keeling) Islands has the best pupil to teacher ratio, at 6·0 pupils per teacher. Among sovereign countries San Marino has the best ratio—6·5 pupils per teacher.

Higher education

India has the greatest number of institutions, with 6600, whilst the USA has both the greatest number of students (13 711 000) and the highest ratio, at 5596 tertiary level students per 100 000 population.

Most graduates in a family

Mr and Mrs Harold Erickson of Naples, Florida, USA saw all of their 14 children—11 sons and three daughters— obtain university or college degrees between 1962 and 1978.

University also at the age of 10 years 4 months, in October 1834.

Adragon Eastwood De Mello (b. 5 Oct 1976) of Santa Cruz, California, USA obtained his BA in mathematics from the University of California in Santa Cruz on 11 Jun 1988 at the age of 11 years 8 months.

Ganesh Sittampalam (b. 11 Feb 1979) of Surbiton, Surrey became Britain's youngest undergraduate this century when he started a BSc mathematics degree course at the University of Surrey at the age of 11 years 8 months in October 1990. Less than two years later, in July 1992, he became Britain's youngest graduate this century, obtaining his degree at the age of 13 years 5 months.

Youngest doctorate On 13 Apr 1814 the mathematician Carl Witte of Lochau was made a Doctor of Philosophy of the University of Giessen, Germany when aged 12.

School *Oldest* The title of the oldest existing school in Britain is contested. It is claimed that King's School in Canterbury, Kent was a foundation of St Augustine, some time between his arrival in Kent in AD 597 and his death *c.* 604.

Cor Tewdws (College of Theodosius) at Llantwit Major, South Glamorgan, reputedly burnt down in AD 446, was refounded, after a lapse of 62 years, by St Illtyd in 508, and flourished into the 13th century.

Winchester College was founded in 1382. Lanark Grammar School claims to have been referred to in a papal bull drawn up in 1183 by Lucius III.

Most expensive Excluding schools catering for specialist needs, the most expensive school which is a member of the Headmasters' Conference in Great Britain is Harrow School, Middx (headmaster Nicholas. R. Bomford). The maximum annual fee for boarders in 1992/3 is £11925.

The most expensive school which is a member of the Girls' School Association is Roedean School, Brighton, East Sussex (headmistress Mrs A.R. Longley), with annual fees in 1992/3 of £11655 for boarders.

In the academic year 1992/3 St Andrew's Private Tutorial Centre, Cambridge (directors A.K. Easterbrook and M.J. Martin) charges £13230 for full-time science students (predominantly individual tuition plus accommodation).

Internationally the most expensive schools in the world tend to be prestigious international finishing schools, such as those in Switzerland.

Largest In 1988/89 Rizal High School, Pasig, Manila, Philippines had an enrolment of 16458 regular students, although numbers have slightly declined since then.

The school with the most pupils in Great Britain was Banbury Comprehensive,

Oldest PTA

The parent–teacher association with the earliest known foundation date in Britain is that for Lawrence Sheriff School, Rugby, Warks, formed in 1908.

Highest endowment

The greatest single gift in the history of higher education has been $125 million, to Louisiana State University by C.B. Pennington in 1983.

Oxon with 2767 in the 1975 summer term. In 1992/3 Exmouth Community College, Devon had the most pupils, with 2133. The highest enrolment in Scotland has been at Our Lady's Roman Catholic High School, Motherwell, Lanarkshire, with a peak of 2317 in August 1977. The highest enrolment in 1992/3 was at Holyrood School, Glasgow, Strathclyde, with 1852 pupils. The total in the Holy Child School, Belfast, Northern Ireland reached 2752 in 1973 before the school was split up. The highest enrolment in 1992/3 was 2449 at St Louise's Comprehensive College, Belfast.

Earliest comprehensive school Windermere Grammar School (then in Westmorland), adopted the non-selective comprehensive principle as early as 1945. It closed in 1965, and together with two other schools in the area, formed a new comprehensive school— The Lakes School, in Troutbeck Bridge, Cumbria. The Calder High School, near Hebden Bridge, W Yorks, opened as a comprehensive school in 1950, and was established through the amalgamation of Hebden Bridge Grammar School and various 'through schools' which served the vicinity. The earliest purpose-built was Kidbrooke Comprehensive for Girls, in south-east London, opened in 1954.

Most schools The greatest documented number of schools attended by a pupil is 265, by Wilma Williams, now Mrs R.J. Horton, from 1933–43 when her parents were in show business in the USA.

Most O and A levels Since 1965 Dr Francis L. Thomason of Hammersmith,

La Maestra Chucha still commands the attention of most of her pupils, more than 81 years after she set up a school with her sisters and began teaching children how to read and write.

London has accumulated 70 O and O/A levels, 16 A levels and 1 S level, making a total of 87, of which 36 have been in the top grade. David Biggins of Sheffield, S Yorks has passed a total of 18 A levels since 1982.

The highest number of top-grade A levels attained at one sitting is seven, by Stephen Murrell of Crown Woods School, Eltham, London in June 1978, out of eight passes. Robert Pidgeon (b. 7 Feb 1959) of St Peter's School, Bournemouth, Dorset secured 13 O level passes at grade A at one sitting in the summer of 1975, and subsequently passed three A levels at grade A and two S levels with firsts. Nicholas Barberis achieved a total of 27 top grades while at Eltham College, London, passing 20 O/AO levels and 7 A levels, all at grade A, between 1984 and 1988.

Youngest A level pass Ganesh Sittampalam (b. 11 Feb 1979) of Surbiton, Surrey is the youngest person to have passed an A level, achieving grade A in both Mathematics and Further Mathematics in June 1988, when aged 9 years 4 months.

Michael Tan (b. 4 Apr 1984) of Christchurch, New Zealand took and passed his New Zealand bursary examination in mathematics—equivalent to an A level in the UK—in November 1991 at the age of 7 years 11 months.

Oldest A level pass George Lush of Hatfield, Herts passed A level Italian in 1969, obtaining a grade D, just a few months before his 89th birthday.

Youngest headmaster The youngest headmaster of a major public school in Great Britain was Henry Montagu Butler (b. 2 Jul 1833), appointed Headmaster of Harrow School on 16 Nov 1859 at the age of 26 years 137 days. His first term in office began in January 1860.

Most durable don Dr Martin Joseph Routh (1755–1854) was President of Magdalen College, Oxford from April 1791 for 63 years 8 months, until his death in his 100th year on 22 Dec 1854. He had previously been a Fellow for 16 years and was thus a don for a span of 79 years.

Most durable Fellow Tressilian Nicholas (1888–1989) was a Fellow of Trinity College, Cambridge for a total of 76 years, from 1912 to 1918 and 1919 until his death in 1989.

Most durable teachers Medarda de Jesús León de Uzcátegui, alias La Maestra Chucha, has been teaching in Caracas, Venezuela for a total of 81 years. In 1911, at the age of 12, she and her two sisters set up a school there which they named *Modelo de Aplicación*. Since marrying in 1942, she has run her own school, which she calls the *Escuela Uzcátegui*, from her home in Caracas.

David Rhys Davies (1835–1928) taught as a pupil teacher and subsequently a teacher and headmaster for a total of 76 years. Most of his teaching was done at Talybont-on-Usk School, near Brecon, Powys (1856–79) and at Dame Anna Child's School, Whitton, Powys. The teaching career of Col. Ernest Achey Loftus (1884–1987) spanned a total of 73 years. He started teaching in May 1901 in York, and in 1953, four years after retiring, went out to Africa. There he served as an assistant master in schools in Kenya, Malawi and finally Zambia, retiring as the world's oldest civil servant at the age of 91 years 38 days on 18 Feb 1975. Elsie Marguerite Touzel (1889–1984) of Jersey, Channel Islands began her teaching career aged 16 in 1905 and taught at various schools in Jersey until her retirement 75 years later on 30 Sep 1980.

Religions

Oldest Human burial, which has religious connotations, is known from c. 60 000 BC among *Homo sapiens neanderthalensis* in the Shanidar cave, northern Iraq.

Largest Religious statistics are necessarily only tentative, since the test of adherence to a religion varies widely in rigour, while many individuals, particularly in the East, belong to two or more religions.

Christianity is the world's prevailing religion, with some 1833 million adherents in 1992, or 33·4 per cent of the world's population. There were 1026 million Roman Catholics in the same year. The largest non-Christian religion is Islam (Muslim), with some 971 million followers in 1992.

In the UK the Roman Catholic population is 5615 million, while the Anglicans have an actual membership of 1924 000. They comprise members of the Established Church of England, the Dis-established Church in Wales, the Scottish Episcopal Church and the Church of Ireland. The Church of England has 2 provinces (Canterbury and York), 44 dioceses, 10957 full-time diocesan clergy, including 707 women, and 13060 parishes as at 31 Dec 1992. In Scotland the largest membership is that of the Church of Scotland (46 presbyteries), which had 752719 members at the end of 1992.

Largest clergies The world's largest religious organization is the Roman Catholic Church, with 155 cardinals, 785 archbishops, 3273 bishops, 403173 priests and 882111 nuns at the end of 1990.

Places of Worship

Earliest Many archaeologists are of the opinion that the decorated Upper Palaeolithic caves of Europe (c. 30000– 10000 BC) were used as places of worship or religious ritual. Claims have been made that the El Juyo cave, northern Spain contains an actual shrine, dated to c. 12000 BC. A similar age is given to a wooden platform, discovered in 1992. On the edge of an ancient lake near the northern Polish village of Tlokowo wooden carved figurines were apparently thrown from the platform as ritual offerings. Small shrines preceded the building of larger temples in the Near East, for example at Tell Aswad, Syria c. 5200 BC. The earliest complex temple in the Near East was the one in level XVII at Eridu, Iraq c. 3700 BC. The oldest surviving Christian church in the world is a converted house in Qal'at es Salihiye (formerly Douro-Europos) in eastern Syria, dating from AD 232.

Oldest Great Britain The oldest places of worship are the enigmatic stone circles or henges of the Neolithic period, for example Avebury, Wilts, dating from c. 3000–2800 BC. The earliest Christian church in the UK was at Colchester, Essex and was built c. AD 320. Its ruins can still be seen next to the modern police station. The oldest surviving ecclesiastical building in the UK is a 6th-century cell built by St Brendan in AD 542 on Eileachan Naoimh (pronounced 'Noo'), Garvelloch Islands, Strathclyde. The church in Great Britain with the oldest origins is St Martin's Church in Canterbury, Kent. It was built in AD 560 on the foundations of a first-century Roman temple. The chapel of St Peter on the Wall, Bradwell-on-Sea, Essex was built from AD 654–660. The oldest church in Ireland is the Gallerus Oratory, built c. AD 750 at Ballyferriter, near Kilmalkedar, Co. Kerry. Britain's oldest nunnery is Minster Abbey, on the Isle of Sheppey, Kent. It was founded c. AD 670 by Sexburga, the widow of Ercombert, King of Kent. The oldest Roman Catholic church is St Etheldreda, Ely Place, Holborn, London, founded in 1251. The oldest non-conformist chapel is the thatched chapel at Horningsham, Wilts, dated 1566.

Largest temple The largest religious structure ever built is Angkor Wat ('City Temple'), enclosing 162·6 ha *402 acres* in Cambodia (formerly Kampuchea), south-east Asia. It was built to the Hindu god Vishnu by the Khmer King Suryavarman II in the period 1113–50. Its curtain wall measures 1280 × 1280 m *4199 × 4199 ft* and its population, before it was abandoned in 1432, was 80000. The whole complex of 72 major monuments, begun c. AD 900, extends over 24 × 8 km *15 × 5 miles*.

The largest Buddhist temple in the world is Borobudur, near Jogjakarta, Indonesia,

The tallest cathedral spire is at Ulm in Germany, and can be seen particularly clearly from beyond the River Danube.

(Photo: James Clift for Guinness Publishing)

built in the 8th century. It is 31·5m *103ft* tall and 123m *403ft* square.

The largest Mormon temple is the Salt Lake Temple, Utah, USA, dedicated on 6 Apr 1893, with a floor area of 23505m² *253015ft²* or *5·8* acres.

Cathedrals *Largest* The world's largest cathedral is the cathedral church of the Diocese of New York, St John the Divine, with a floor area of 11240m² *121000ft²* and a volume of 476350m³ *16822000ft³*. The cornerstone was laid on 27 Dec 1892, and work on the Gothic building was stopped in 1941. Work restarted in earnest in July 1979. In New York it is referred to as 'St John the Unfinished'. The nave is the longest in the world at 183·2m *601ft* in length, with a vaulting 37·8m *124ft* in height.

The cathedral covering the largest area is that of Santa Maríá de la Sede in Sevilla (Seville), Spain. It was built in Spanish Gothic style between 1402 and 1519, and is 126·2m *414ft* long, 82·6m *271ft* wide and 30·5m *100ft* high to the vault of the nave.

The largest cathedral in the British Isles is the Cathedral Church of Christ in Liverpool. It was built in modernized Gothic style, and work was begun on 18 Jul 1904; it was finally consecrated on 25 Oct 1978 after 74 years (cf. Exeter Cathedral, 95 years). Half a million stone blocks and 12 million bricks were used in its construction and the actual cost was some £6 million. The building

encloses 9687m² *104275ft²* and has an overall length of 193·9m *636ft*. The Vestey Tower is 100·9m *331ft* high. It contains the highest vaulting in the world—53·3m *175ft* maximum at undertower, and the highest Gothic arches ever built, being 32·6m *107ft* at apexes.

Smallest The smallest church in the world designated as a cathedral—the seat of a diocesan bishop—is that of the Christ Catholic Church, Highlandville, Missouri, USA. It was consecrated in July 1983. It measures 4·3 × 5·2m *14 × 17ft* and has seating for 18 people.

The smallest cathedral in use in the UK is Cumbrae Cathedral (the Cathedral of the diocese of the Isles) at Millport on the isle of Cumbrae, Strathclyde, which was built in 1849–51. The nave measures only 12·2 × 6·1m *40 × 20ft* and the total floor area is 197·3m² *2124ft²*.

Largest church The largest church in the world is the Basilica of St Peter, built between 1506 and 1614 in the Vatican City, Rome, Italy. Its length, including the walls of the apse and façade, is 218·7 m *717ft 6in*. The area is 23 000 m² *247572ft²*. The inner diameter of the famous dome is 42·56m *139ft 8in* and its centre is 119·88m *393ft 4in* high. The external height is 136·57m *448ft 1in*. Taller, although not as tall as the cathedral in Ulm, Germany (⇨ Tallest spire), is the Basilica of Our Lady of Peace (Notre Dame de la Paix) at Yamoussoukro, Ivory Coast, completed in 1989. Including its golden cross, it is 158m *519ft* high.

The elliptical basilica of St Pie X at Lourdes, France, completed in 1957 at a cost of £2 million, has a capacity of

---

Cathedral visits

Richard Marr, Peter Brown and Roy Emery of Coventry, W Mids, together with Nicholas Tooby of Nuneaton, Warks, went to all of the 65 Anglican Cathedrals in England, Scotland, Wales and Northern Ireland in a time of 110hr 10min between 23–27 May 1992. Using a Citroen BX19 TZD diesel saloon car, they covered a distance of 4988km *3100miles*.

20000 under its giant span arches and a length of 200m *660ft*.

The largest church in the UK is the Collegiate Church of St Peter in Westminster, usually referred to as Westminster Abbey, which was built between AD 1050–1745. Its maximum length is 161·5m *530ft*, the breadth across the transept 61·9m *203ft* and the internal height 30·98m *101ft 8in*. The largest parish church is the Parish Church of the Most Holy and Undivided Trinity at Kingston-upon-Hull, Humberside covering 2530m² *27235ft²* and with an external length and width of 87·7 × 37·7m *288 × 124ft*. It is also believed to be the country's oldest brick building serving its original purpose, dating from *c*. 1285. Both the former Cathedral of St Mungo, Glasgow and Beverley Minster, Humberside are now used as parish churches. The largest school chapel is that of Lancing College, W Sussex. It is 45·7m *150ft* high and has a capacity of 600.

Longest The crypt of the underground Civil War Memorial Church in the Guadarrama Mountains, 45km *28 miles* from Madrid, Spain, is 260m *853ft* in length. It took 21 years (1937–58) to build, at a reported cost of £140 million, and is surmounted by a cross 150m *492ft* tall.

Smallest church The world's smallest church is the chapel of Santa Isabel de Hungría, in Colomares, a monument to Christopher Columbus at Benalmádena, Málaga, Spain. It is an irregular shape and has a total floor area of 1·96m² *21⅛ft²*.

Largest synagogue The largest synagogue in the world is Temple Emanu-El on Fifth Avenue at 65th Street, New York City, USA. The temple, completed in September 1929, has a frontage of 45·7m *150ft* on Fifth Avenue and 77·1m *253ft* on 65th Street. The sanctuary proper can accommodate 2500 people, and the adjoining Beth-El Chapel seats 350. When all the facilities are in use, more than 6000 people can be accommodated.

The largest synagogue in Great Britain is the Edgware Synagogue, Barnet, London, completed in 1959, with seating for 1630. That with the highest registered membership is Ilford Synagogue, London with 2210 members.

Largest mosque The largest mosque is Shah Faisal Mosque, near Islamabad, Pakistan. The total area of the complex is 18·97ha *46·87acres*, with the covered area of the prayer hall being 0·48ha *1·19acres*. It can accommodate 100000 worshippers in the prayer hall and the courtyard, and a further 200000 people in the adjacent grounds.

Tallest minaret The tallest minaret in the world is that of the Great Hassan II Mosque, Casablanca, Morocco, measuring 175·6m *576ft*. The cost of construction of the mosque was £218 million. Of ancient minarets the tallest is the Qutb Minar, south of New Delhi, India, built in 1194 to a height of 72·54m *238ft*.

Tallest and oldest stupa The now largely ruined Jetavanarama dagoba in the ancient city of Anuradhapura, Sri Lanka, is some 120m *400ft* in height. The 99·3m *326ft* tall Shwedagon pagoda, in Yangon (Rangoon), Myanmar (Burma), is built on the site of a pagoda dating from 585BC which was 8·2m *27ft* tall.

Sacred object The sacred object with the highest intrinsic value is the 15th-century gold Buddha in Wat Trimitr Temple in Bangkok, Thailand. It is 3m *10ft* tall and weighs an estimated 5½ tonnes. At the April 1993 price of £223 per fine ounce, its intrinsic worth was £28·2 million. The gold under the plaster exterior was found only in 1954.

Tallest spire The tallest cathedral spire in the world is that of the Protestant Cathedral of Ulm in Germany. The building is early Gothic and was begun in 1377. The tower, in the centre of the west façade, was not finally completed until 1890 and is 160·9m *528ft* high. The world's tallest church spire is that of the

---

Chicago Temple of the First Methodist Church on Clark Street, Chicago, Illinois, USA. The building consists of a 22-storey skyscraper (erected in 1924) surmounted by a parsonage at 100·5m *330ft*, a 'Sky Chapel' at 121·9m *400ft* and a steeple cross at 173·1m *568ft* above street level.

The highest spire in Great Britain is that of the church of St Mary, called Salisbury Cathedral, Wilts. The Lady Chapel was built in the years 1220–5 and the main fabric of the cathedral was finished and consecrated in 1258. The spire was added later, *ante* 1305, and reaches a height of 123·1m *404ft*. The central spire of Lincoln Cathedral, which was completed *c.* 1307 and fell in 1548, was 160m *525ft* tall.

Stained glass *Oldest* Pieces of stained glass dated before AD 850, some possibly even to the 7th century, excavated by Prof. Rosemary Cramp, were set into a window of that date in the nearby St Paul's Church, Jarrow, Co. Durham. The oldest complete stained glass in the world represents the Prophets in a window of the Cathedral of Augsburg, Germany, dating from the second half of the 11th century. The oldest datable stained glass in the UK is represented by a figure of St Michael in All Saints Church, Dalbury, Derbys of the late 11th century.

Largest The largest stained-glass window is that of the Resurrection Mausoleum in Justice, Illinois, USA, measuring 2079m² *22381ft²* in 2448 panels, completed in 1971. Although not one continuous window, the Basilica of Our Lady of Peace (Notre Dame de la Paix) at Yamoussoukro, Ivory Coast contains a number of stained-glass windows covering a total area of 7430m² *80000ft²*.

The largest single ecclesiastical stained-glass window in Great Britain is the east window in Gloucester Cathedral measuring 21·9 × 11·6m *72 × 38ft*, set up to commemorate the Battle of Crécy (1346), while the largest area of stained glass comprises the 128 lights, totalling 2320m² *25000ft²*, in York Minster. (⇨ Largest window)

Brasses The world's oldest monumental brass is that commemorating Bishop Yso von Wölpe in the Andreaskirche, Verden, near Hanover, Germany, dating

The record price for an icon is $150000 paid at Christie's, New York, USA on 17 Apr 1980 for the *Last Judgement* (from the George R. Hann collection, Pittsburgh, Pennsylvania), made in Novgorod, Russia in the 16th century.

Singing

Rev. Acharya Prem Bhikshuji (d. 18 Apr 1970) started chanting the Akhand Rama-Dhoon at Jamnagar, Gujarat, India on 1 Aug 1964, and devotees were still continuing in May 1992.

from 1231. An engraved coffin plate of St Ulrich (died 973), laid in 1187, was found buried in the Church of SS Ulrich and Afra, Augsburg, Germany in 1979.

The oldest brass in Great Britain is that of Sir John D'Abernon (died 1277) at Stoke D'Abernon, near Leatherhead, Surrey, dating from *c.* 1320. A dedication brass dated 24 Apr 1241 in Ashbourne Church, Derbys has been cited as the earliest arabic writing extant in Britain.

Church Personnel

There are more than 2000 'registered' saints, of whom around two-thirds are either Italian or French.

Most rapidly canonized The shortest interval that has elapsed between the death of a saint and his or her canonization was in the case of St Peter of Verona, Italy, who died on 6 Apr 1252 and was canonized 337 days later on 9 Mar 1253. For the other extreme of 857 years, ⇨ table of Popes and Cardinals.

Bishopric *Longest tenure* The longest tenure of any Church of England bishopric is 57 years in the case of the Rt Rev. Thomas Wilson, who was consecrated Bishop of Sodar and Man on 16 Jan 1698 and died in office on 7 Mar 1755. Of English bishoprics, the longest tenures—if one excludes the unsubstantiated case of Aethelwulf, reputedly Bishop of Hereford from 937 to 1012—are those of 47 years by Jocelin de Bohun of Salisbury

Popes and Cardinals

Longest Papal Reign
Pius IX—Giovanni Maria Mastai-Ferretti (1846–78). 31 years 236 days

Shortest Papal Reign
Stephen II (died 752). 2 days

Longest-Lived Popes
St Agatho (died 681) (probably exaggerated) ?106 years. Leo XIII—Gioacchino Pecci (1810–1903). 93 years 140 days

Youngest Elected
John XII—Ottaviano (c. 937–64) in 955. 18 years old

Last Married
Adrian II (pre-celibacy rule). Elected 867

Last With Children
Gregory XIII—Ugo Buoncompagni (1502–85). One son. Elected 1572

Last Non-Cardinal
Urban VI—Bartolomeo Prignano (1318–89), Archbishop of Bari. Elected 8 Apr 1378

Last Briton
Adrian IV—Nicholas Breakspear (c. 1100–59) (b. Abbots Langley, Herts). Elected 4 Dec 1154

Last Previous Non-Italian
Adrian VI—Adrian Florensz Boeyens (Netherlands). Elected 9 Jan 1522

Slowest Election
Gregory X—Teobaldi Visconti. 31 months, Feb 1269–1 Sep 1271

Fastest Election
Julius II—on first ballot, 21 Oct 1503

Slowest Canonization
St Leo III—over span of 857 years, 816–1673

Oldest Cardinal
(all-time)
Georgio da Costa (b. Portugal 1406, died Rome, Italy aged 102 years). Elected 18 Sep 1508
(current)
Antonelli Ferdinando Giuseppe (b. Subbiano, Italy, 14 Jul 1896)

Youngest Cardinal
(all-time)
Luis Antonio de Bourbon (b. 25 Jul 1727). 8 years 147 days. Elected 19 Dec 1735
(current)
Alfonso Lopez Trujillo of Colombia (b. 18 Nov 1935). 47 years 76 days

Longest-Serving Cardinal
Cardinal Duke of York, grandson of James VII of Scotland and II of England. 60 years 10 days, 1747–1807

Longest-Serving Bishop
Bishop Louis François de la Baume de Suze (1603–90). 76 years 273 days from 6 Dec 1613

(1142–89) and Nathaniel Crew or Crewe of Durham (1674–1721).

Bishops *Oldest* The oldest serving bishop (excluding suffragans and assistants) in the Church of England as at April 1993 was the Rt Rev. Eric Kemp, Bishop of Chichester, who was born on 27 Apr 1915.

The oldest Róman Catholic bishop in recent years has been Archbishop Edward Howard, formerly Archbishop of Portland-in-Oregon, USA (b. 5 Nov 1877), who died aged 105 years 58 days on 2 Jan 1983. He had celebrated mass about 27800 times. Bishop Herbert Welch of the United Methodist Church, who was elected a Bishop for Japan and Korea in 1916, died on 4 Apr 1969 aged 106.

Youngest The youngest bishop of all time was HRH the Duke of York and Albany, the second son of George III, who was elected Bishop of Osnabrück, through his father's influence as Elector of Hanover, at the age of 196 days on 27 Feb 1764. He resigned 39 years later. The youngest serving bishop (excluding suffragans and assistants) in the Church of England is the Rt Rev. Nigel McCulloch, Bishop of Wakefield, who was born on 17 Jan 1942. When suffragans and assistants are counted, the youngest is the Rt Rev. Graham James, Suffragan Bishop of St Germans, who was born on 19 Jan 1951.

Oldest parish priest Father Alvaro Fernandez (8 Dec 1880–6 Jan 1988) served as a parish priest at Santiago de Abres, Spain from 1919 until he was 107 years old. The oldest Anglican clergyman, Rev. Clement Williams (b. 30 Oct 1879), died aged 106 years 3 months on 3 Feb 1986. He lined the route at Queen Victoria's funeral and was ordained in 1904.

Longest service Rev. K.M. Jacob (b. 10 Jul 1880) was made a deacon in the Marthoma Syrian Church of Malabar in Kerala, southern India in 1897. He served his church until his death on 28 Mar 1984, 87 years later.

The longest Church of England incumbency on record is one of 75 years 357 days by Rev. Bartholomew Edwards, Rector of St Nicholas, Ashill, Norfolk from 1813 to 1889. There is some doubt as to whether Rev. Richard Sherinton was

Saints

The school in Britain which has produced the most saints is Stonyhurst College, in Lancashire. St Thomas Garnet SJ (executed in 1608), St John Plessington (executed in 1679) and St Philip Evans SJ (also executed in 1679) all attended St Omers in France, which is where Stonyhurst was based at the time.

Martyrs

The first Christian martyr was St Stephen, executed c. AD 36. Britain's first was St Alban, executed c. AD 209.

Sunday school

The pioneer of the Sunday school movement is generally accepted to be Robert Raikes (1736–1811). In 1780 he engaged a number of women in his home city of Gloucester to teach children on Sundays. Reading and religious instruction were from the outset the main activities, and by 1785 the Sunday School Society had been formed.

F. Otto Brechel (1890–1990) of Mars, Pennsylvania, USA completed 88 years (4576 Sundays) of perfect attendance at church school at three different churches in Pennsylvania—the first from 1902 to 1931, the second from 1931 to 1954, and the third from 1954 onwards.

---

installed at Folkestone from 1524 or 1529 to 1601. If the former is correct it would surpass the Edwards record (◇ above). The parish of Farrington, Hants had only two incumbents in a period of 122 years: Rev. J. Benn (28 Mar 1797 to 1857) and

Rev. T.H. Massey (1857 to 5 Apr 1919). From 1675 to 1948 the incumbents of Rose Ash, Devon were from eight generations of the family of Southcomb.

Longest-serving chorister John Love Vokins (1890–1989) was a chorister for 92 years. He joined the choir of Christ Church, Heeley, Sheffield, S Yorks in 1895 and that of St Michael's, Hathersage, Derbys, 35 years later, and was still singing in 1987.

Oldest warden Having become a chorister in 1876 at the age of nine, Thomas Rogers was appointed vicar's warden in 1966 at Montacute, Somerset, aged 99.

Oldest parish register The oldest part of any parish register surviving in England contains entries from the summer of 1538. There is a sheet from that of Alfriston, E Sussex recording a marriage on 10 Jul 1504, but it is thought that this is possibly a reference to 1544 as it is among entries from 1547. Scotland's oldest surviving register is that for Anstruther-Wester, Fife, with burial entries from 1549.

Largest crowds The greatest recorded number of human beings assembled with a common purpose was an estimated 15 million at the Hindu festival of Kumbh mela, which was held at the confluence of the Yamuna (formerly the Jumna), the Ganges and the invisible 'Saraswathi' at Allahabad, Uttar Pradesh, India on 6 Feb 1989. (◇ also Largest funerals)

Largest funerals The funeral of the charismatic C.N. Annadurai (died 3 Feb 1969), Madras Chief Minister, was attended by 15 million people, according to a police estimate. The queue at the grave of the Russian chansonnier and guitarist Vladimir Visotsky (died 28 Jul 1980), stretched for 10 km *6 miles*. The longest funeral in Britain was probably that of Vice-Admiral Viscount Nelson on 9 Jan 1806. Ticket-holders were seated in St Paul's Cathedral by 8:30 a.m. Many were unable to leave until 9 p.m.

Human

Achievements

Endurance and Endeavour

Most travelled The world's most travelled man is Parke G. Thompson, from Akron, Ohio, USA, who has visited all of the sovereign countries and all but five of the non-sovereign or other territories which existed in the spring of 1993 (⬦ Countries).

The most travelled couple are Dr Robert and Carmen Becker of East Northport, New York, USA, both of whom have visited all of the sovereign countries apart from Iraq and all but six of the non-sovereign or other territories.

Longest walks The first person reputed to have 'walked round the world' is George Matthew Schilling (USA) from 3 Aug 1897 to 1904, but the first verified achievement was by David Kunst (b. 1939, USA) from 20 Jun 1970 to 5 Oct 1974.

Tomás Carlos Pereira (b. Argentina, 16 Nov 1942) spent 10 years, from 6 Apr 1968 to 8 Apr 1978, walking 48000 km *29 800 miles* around five continents. Steven Newman of Bethel, Ohio, USA spent four years, from 1 Apr 1983 to 1 Apr 1987, walking 36 200 km *22 500 miles* around the world, covering 20 countries and five continents.

Rick Hansen (b. Canada, 1957), who was paralysed from the waist down in 1973 as a result of a motor accident, wheeled his wheelchair 40 074·06 km *24 901·55 miles* through four continents and 34 countries. He started his journey from Vancouver on 21 Mar 1985 and arrived back there on 22 May 1987.

George Meegan (b. 2 Oct 1952) from Rainham, Kent walked 30 431 km *19 019 miles* from Usuaia, the southern tip of South America, to Prudhoe Bay in northern Alaska, taking 2426 days from 26 Jan 1977 to 18 Sep 1983. He thus completed the first traverse of the Americas and the western hemisphere.

Sean Eugene McGuire (USA; b. 15 Sep 1956) walked 11791 km *7327 miles* from the Yukon River, north of Livengood, Alaska to Key West, Florida in 307 days, from 6 Jun 1978 to 9 Apr 1979. The trans-Canada (Halifax to Vancouver) record walk of 6057 km *3764 miles* is 96 days by Clyde McRae, aged 23, from 1 May to 4 Aug 1973. John Lees (b. 23 Feb 1945) of Brighton, E Sussex walked 4628 km *2876 miles* across the USA from City Hall, Los Angeles, California to City Hall, New York in 53 days 12 hr 15 min (averaging 86·49 km *53·75 miles* a day) between 11 April and 3 Jun 1972.

The longest walk round the coast of the British Isles was one of 15 239 km *9469 miles* by John Westley of Cheshunt, Herts from 5 Aug 1990 to 20 Sep 1991. His walk began and ended at Tower Bridge, London. Vera Andrews set a record for the longest walk in mainland Britain, when she covered a total distance of 11 777 km *7318 miles* between 2 Jan and 24 Dec 1990, taking in all of the British Gas showrooms. She started and finished at her home town of Clacton-on-Sea, Essex.

Most travelled man

The most travelled man in the horseback era was believed to be the Methodist preacher Bishop Francis Asbury (b. Handsworth, W Mids, 1745), who travelled 425 000 km *264 000 miles* in North America between 1771 and 1815. During this time he preached some 16 000 sermons and ordained nearly 3000 ministers.

First to see both Poles

The first people to see both Poles were Capt. Roald Engebereth Gravning Amundsen (⬦ South Pole conquest) and Oskar Wisting when they flew aboard the airship Norge over the North Pole on 12 May 1926, having previously been to the South Pole on 14 Dec 1911.

North Pole conquest The claims of the two Arctic explorers Dr Frederick Albert Cook (1865–1940) and Cdr (later Rear-Ad.) Robert Edwin Peary (1856–1920), of the US Naval Civil Engineering branch, to have reached the North Pole lack irrefutable proof, and several recent surveys have produced conflicting con-

Two major Antarctic expeditions took place in late 1992/early 1993, with records set by Erling Kagge (left) through his solo trek, and Sir Ranulph Fiennes (below left) together with Dr Michael Stroud.

(Photos: Rex Features and Sygma/Fiennes-Stroud-Howell)

clusions. On excellent pack ice and modern sledges, Wally Herbert's 1968–9 expedition (⟷ Arctic crossing, below) attained a best day's route mileage of 37km *23 miles* in 15hr. Cook (⟷ above) claimed 42km *26 miles* twice, while Peary claimed an average of 61km *38 miles* over eight consecutive days, which many glaciologists regard as quite unsustainable.

The first people indisputably to have reached the North Pole at ground level—the exact point Lat. 90° 00′ 00″ N (±300 metres)—were Pavel Afanasyevich Geordiyenko, Pavel Kononovich Sen'ko, Mikhail Mikhaylovich Somov and Mikhail Yemel' yenovich Ostrekin (all of the former USSR), on 23 Apr 1948. They arrived and departed by air.

The earliest indisputable attainment of the North Pole by surface travel over the sea-ice took place at 3 p.m. (Central Standard Time) on 19 Apr 1968, when expedition leader Ralph Plaisted (US), accompanied by Walter Pederson, Gerald Pitzel and Jean Luc Bombardier, reached the Pole after a 42-day trek in four skidoos (snowmobiles). Their arrival was independently verified 18hr later by a US Air Force weather aircraft. The party returned by aircraft.

Naomi Uemura (1941–84), the Japanese explorer and mountaineer, became the first person to reach the North Pole in a solo trek across the Arctic sea-ice at 4:45a.m. GMT on 1 May 1978. He had travelled 725km *450miles*, setting out on 7 Mar from Cape Edward, Ellesmere Island in northern Canada. He averaged nearly 13km *8 miles* per day with his sled *Aurora* drawn by 17 huskies. He also left by aircraft.

The first people to ski to the North Pole were the seven members of a Soviet expedition, led by Dmitry Shparo. They reached the Pole on 31 May 1979 after a trek of 1500km *900 miles* which took them 77 days.

Dr Jean-Louis Etienne, aged 39, was the first to reach the Pole solo and without dogs, on 11 May 1986 after 63 days. He left by aircraft.

On 20 Apr 1987 Shinji Kazama, aged 36, of Tokyo, Japan reached the North Pole from Ward Hunt Island, northern Canada in 44 days, having started on his 200 cc motorcycle on 8 March. He also left by aircraft.

The first woman to set foot on the North Pole was Mrs Fran Phipps (Canada) on 5 Apr 1971. She flew there by ski-plane with her husband, a bush pilot. Galina Aleksandrovna Lastovskaya (b. 1941) and Lilia Vladislavovna Minina (b. 1959) were crew members of the Soviet atomic icebreaker *Arktika*, which reached the Pole on 17 Aug 1977.

South Pole conquest The first men to cross the Antarctic Circle (Lat. 66° 33′ S) were the 193 crew members of the *Resolution* (462 tons) (Capt. James Cook,

RN, 1728–79) and *Adventure* (336 tons) (Lt Tobias Furneaux, RN) on 17 Jan 1773 at 39°E. The first person known to have sighted the Antarctic ice shelf was Capt. Fabian Gottlieb Benjamin von Bellingshausen (Russia) (1778–1852) on 27 Jan 1820 from the vessel *Vostok* accompanied by *Mirnyy*. The first people known to have sighted the mainland of the continent were Capt. William Smith (1790–1847) and Master Edward Bransfield, RN, in the brig *Williams*. They saw the peaks of Trinity Land three days later, on 30 Jan 1820.

The South Pole (alt. 2779 m *9186 ft* on ice and 102 m *336 ft* bedrock) was first reached at 11 a.m. on 14 Dec 1911 by a Norwegian party of five men led by Amundsen (1872–1928), after a 53-day march with dog sledges from the Bay of Whales, into which he had penetrated in the vessel *Fram*. Subsequent calculations showed that Olav Olavson Bjaaland and Helmer Hanssen probably passed within 400–600 m *1300–2000 ft* of the exact location of the South Pole. The other two members were Sverre H. Hassell (died 1928) and Oskar Wisting (died 1936). (⊳ First to see both Poles)

The first person to reach the South Pole solo and unsupported was Erling Kagge, aged 29 (Norway), on 7 Jan 1993 after a 50-day trek of 1400 km *870 miles* from Berkner Island.

The longest unsupported trek in Antarctica was by team-leader Sir Ranulph Fiennes, 48, with Dr Michael Stroud, 37, who set off from Gould Bay on 9 Nov 1992, reached the South Pole on 16 Jan 1993 and finally abandoned their walk on the Ross ice shelf on 11 February. They covered a distance of 2170 km *1350 miles* during their 94-day trek. (⊳ Longest sledge journeys)

The first woman to set foot on Antarctica was Mrs Karoline Mikkelsen, the wife of a whaling captain, on 20 Feb 1935. It was not until 11 Nov 1969 that a woman stood at the South Pole. On that day Lois Jones, Eileen McSaveney, Jean Pearson, Terry Lee Tickhill (all US), Kay Lindsay (Australia) and Pam Young (NZ) arrived by air at Amundsen-Scott station and walked to the exact point from there.

First to visit both Poles Dr Albert Paddock Crary (US) (1911–87) reached the North Pole in a Dakota aircraft on 3 May 1952. On 12 Feb 1961 he arrived at the South Pole by Sno Cat on a scientific traverse party from the McMurdo Station.

Pole to pole circumnavigation The first pole to pole circumnavigation was achieved by Sir Ranulph Fiennes, Bt and Charles Burton of the British Trans-Globe Expedition, who travelled south from Greenwich (2 Sep 1979), via the South Pole (15 Dec 1980) and the North Pole (10 Apr 1982), and back to Greenwich, arriving on 29 Aug 1982 after a 56 000 km *35 000 mile* trek. (⊳ Arctic crossing and Antarctic crossing)

First to walk to both Poles The first man to walk to both the North and the South Pole was Robert Swan (b. 28 Jul 1956). He led the three-man Footsteps of Scott expedition, which reached the South Pole on 11 Jan 1986, and three years later headed the eight-man Icewalk expedition, which arrived at the North Pole on 14 May 1989.

Arctic crossing The first crossing of the Arctic sea-ice was achieved by the British Trans-Arctic Expedition, which left Point Barrow, Alaska on 21 Feb 1968 and arrived at the Seven Island archipelago north-east of Spitzbergen 464 days later, on 29 May 1969. This involved a haul of 4699 km *2920 statute miles* with a drift of 1100 km *700 miles*, compared with the straight-line distance of 2674 km *1662 miles*. The team comprised Wally Herbert (leader), 34, Major Ken Hedges, RAMC, 34, Allan Gill, 38, and Dr Roy Koerner (glaciologist), 36, and 40 huskies.

The only crossing achieved in a single season was that by Fiennes and Burton (⊳ Pole to pole circumnavigation and Antarctic crossing) from Alert via the North Pole to the Greenland Sea in open snowmobiles. Both reached the North Pole and returned by land.

Antarctic crossing The first surface crossing of the Antarctic continent was completed at 1:47 p.m. on 2 Mar 1958, after a trek of 3473 km *2158 miles* lasting 99 days from 24 Nov 1957, from Shackleton Base to Scott Base via the Pole. The crossing party of 12 was led

THE GUINNESS TIMES

12th May, 1992

Record survival at sea

177 days adrift with the sharks

Tabwai Mikaie and Arenta Tebeitabu, two fishermen from the island of Nikunau in Kiribati, have been found alive after surviving for a record 177 days adrift at sea in their fishing boat - a 13-foot (4-metre) open dinghy.

They were apparently caught in a cyclone shortly after setting out on a trip on 17 November last year, and although their boat overturned, they were able to set it upright and drift. They have survived on fish caught by a spear and fishing line, and the occasional floating coconut, with

rain water to drink. Twice they managed to catch turtles as they swam past. However, most of the time they had nothing at all to eat. A third man set off with them, but he died just a few days ago, although it is not known how. Barely conscious, the two men have now been washed ashore on the island of Upolu, in Western Samoa, some 1100 miles (1800 kilometres) away. It has emerged that their families and friends have even held a funeral for them. The local police commissioner has described the men as 'just skin and bone'.

---

by Dr (now Sir) Vivian Ernest Fuchs (b. 11 Feb 1908).

The 4185km *2600 mile* trans-Antarctic leg from Sanae to Scott Base of the 1980–2 Trans-Globe Expedition was achieved in 67 days, from 28 Oct 1980 to 11 Jan 1981, having reached the South Pole on 15 Dec 1980. The three-man party on snowmobiles comprised Sir Ranulph Fiennes, Bt (b. 1944), Oliver Shepard and Charles Burton. (↔ Pole to pole circumnavigation and Arctic crossing)

Longest sledge journeys The longest polar sledge journey was that undertaken by the International Trans-Antarctica Expedition (six members), who sledged a distance of some 6040km *3750 miles* in 220 days from 27 Jul 1989 (Seal Nunataks)

to 3 Mar 1990 (Mirnyy). The expedition was accompanied by a team of 40 dogs, but a number of them were flown out from one of the staging posts for a period of rest before returning to the Antarctic. The expedition was supported by aircraft throughout its duration.

The longest *totally self-supporting* polar sledge journey ever made was one of 2170km *1350 miles* from Gould Bay to the Ross ice shelf by Sir Ranulph Fiennes and Dr Michael Stroud. (↔ South Pole conquest)

Greatest ocean descent The record ocean descent was achieved in the Challenger Deep of the Marianas Trench, 400km *250 miles* south-west of Guam in the Pacific Ocean, when the Swiss-built

469

US Navy bathyscaphe *Trieste*, manned by Dr Jacques Piccard (Switzerland) (b. 28 Jul 1922) and Lt Donald Walsh, USN reached a depth of 10916m *35813ft* at 1:10 p.m. on 23 Jan 1960 (⇨ Oceans deepest). The pressure of the water was 1187kgf/cm^2 *16883lbf/in^2* and the temperature 3°C *37°F*. The descent took 4hr 48min and the ascent 3hr 17min.

Deep-diving records The record depth for the *ill-advisedly* dangerous activity of breath-held diving is 107m *351ft* by Angela Bandini (Italy) on a marked cable off Elba, Italy on 3 Oct 1989. She was under water for 2 min 46 sec.

The record dive with scuba (self-contained under-water breathing apparatus) is 133m *437ft* by John J. Gruener and R. Neal Watson (US) off Freeport, Grand Bahama on 14 Oct 1968.

The record dive utilizing gas mixtures was a simulated dive to a depth of 701m *2300ft* of sea-water by Théo Mavrostomos as part of the HYDRA 10 operation at the Hyperbaric Center of Comex in Marseilles, France on 20 Nov 1992, during a 43-day dive. He was breathing 'hydreliox' (hydrogen, oxygen and helium).

Arnaud de Nechaud de Feral performed a saturation dive of 73 days from 9 Oct–21 Dec 1989 in a hyperbaric chamber simulating a depth of 300m *985ft*, as part of the HYDRA 9 operation carried out by Comex at Marseilles, France. He was breathing 'hydrox', a mixture of hydrogen and oxygen.

Longest on a raft

The longest recorded survival alone on a raft is 133 days (4½ months) by Second Steward Poon Lim (b. Hong Kong) of the UK Merchant Navy, whose ship, the SS *Ben Lomond*, was torpedoed in the Atlantic 910km *565 miles* west of St Paul's Rocks in Lat. 00°30′N, Long. 38°45′W at 11:45 a.m. on 23 Nov 1942. He was picked up by a Brazilian fishing boat off Salinópolis, Brazil on 5 Apr 1943 and was able to walk ashore. In July 1943 he was awarded the BEM. He now lives in New York City, USA.

High altitude diving

The record for high altitude diving is 5032m *16 509ft*, in a lake in the crater of Popocatépetl, a dormant volcano in Mexico. Roger Weihrauch (Germany) spent 20 minutes exploring the 5m *16ft* deep lake on 20 Nov 1983.

Submergence

The *continuous* duration record (i.e. no rest breaks) for scuba (i.e. self-contained underwater breathing apparatus, used without surface air hoses) is 212hr 30min, by Michael Stevens of Birmingham in a Royal Navy tank at the National Exhibition Centre, Birmingham from 14–23 Feb 1986. Measures have to be taken to reduce the numerous health risks in such endurance trials.

Richard Presley spent 69 days 19 min in a module underwater at a lagoon in Key Largo, Florida, USA from 6 May to 14 Jul 1992. The test was carried out as part of a mission entitled Project Atlantis which had as its aim to explore the human factors of living in an undersea environment.

Deepest underwater escapes The deepest underwater rescue ever achieved was of the *Pisces III*, in which Roger R. Chapman (28), and Roger Mallinson (35), were trapped for 76 hours when it sank to 480m *1575ft*, 240km *150 miles* south-east of Cork, Republic of Ireland on 29 Aug 1973. It was hauled to the surface on 1 September by the cable ship *John Cabot* after work by *Pisces V*, *Pisces II* and the remote-control recovery vessel US CURV.

The greatest depth from which an actual escape without any equipment has been made is 68·6m *225ft*, by Richard A. Slater from the rammed submersible *Nekton Beta* off Catalina Island, California, USA on 28 Sep 1970.

The record for an escape with equipment was by Norman Cooke and Hamish Jones on 22 Jul 1987. During a naval exercise they escaped from a depth of 183m *601ft* from the submarine HMS

When a US Navy UH-46 Sea Knight helicopter crashed at sea in August 1991 killing all its crew members, a major operation began to locate and recover it to ascertain the cause of the accident. Once identified, the USS Salvor (ARS 52) was chosen to take responsibility for the operation, and a painstaking operation ended in February 1992 with a record for the deepest salvage. Not surprisingly, handshakes and celebratory cigars were the order of the day afterwards.

Otus in Bjornefjorden, off Bergen, Norway. They were wearing standard suits with a built-in lifejacket, from which air expanding during the ascent passes into a hood over the escaper's head.

Deepest salvage The greatest depth at which salvage has been successfully carried out is 5258m *17251ft*, in the case of a helicopter which had crashed into the Pacific Ocean in August 1991 with the loss of four lives. Crew of the USS *Salvor* and personnel from Eastport International managed to raise the wreckage to the surface on 27 Feb 1992

so that the authorities could try to determine the cause of the accident.

The deepest salvage operation ever achieved with divers was on the wreck of HM cruiser *Edinburgh*, sunk on 2 May 1942 in the Barents Sea off northern Norway, inside the Arctic Circle, in 245m *803ft* of water. Over 32 days (from 17 Sep–7 Oct 1981), 12 divers dived on the wreck in pairs, using a bell from the *Stephaniturm* (1446 tonnes), under the direction of former RN officer Michael Stewart. A total of 460 gold ingots (the only 100 per cent salvage to date) was recovered, John Rossier being the first person to touch the gold.

Greatest penetration into the earth
The deepest penetration made into the ground by human beings is in the Western Deep Levels Mine at Carletonville, Transvaal, South Africa, where a record depth of 3581m *11749ft* was attained on 12 Jul 1977. The virgin rock temperature at this depth is 55°C *131°F*. (⇨ Borings and mines)

Shaft-sinking record The one-month (31 days) world record is 381·3m *1251ft* for a standard shaft 7·9m *26ft* in diameter at Buffelsfontein Mine, Transvaal, South Africa, in March 1962.

The British record of 131·2m *430ft* for a shaft 7·9m *26ft* in diameter was set in No. 2 Shaft of the NCB's Whitemoor Mine near Selby, N Yorks in 31 days (15 Nov–16 Dec 1982).

Marriage

Most marriages The greatest number of marriages contracted by one person in the monogamous world is 27, by former Baptist minister Glynn 'Scotty' Wolfe (b. 1908) of Blythe, California, USA, who first married in 1927. He thought that he had a total of 41 children.

The greatest number of monogamous marriages by a woman is 22, by Linda Essex of Anderson, Indiana, USA. She has had 15 different husbands since 1957, her most recent marriage being in October 1991. However, that also ended in a divorce.

The record for bigamous marriages is 104, by Giovanni Vigliotto, one of many aliases used by either Fred Jipp (b. New York City, 3 Apr 1936) or Nikolai

Most married

Richard and Carole Roble of South Hempstead, New York, USA have married each other 52 times, with their first wedding being in 1969. They have chosen a different location each time, with ceremonies in all of the states of the USA.

Peruskov (b. Siracusa, Sicily, 3 Apr 1929) during 1949–81 in 27 US states and 14 other countries. Four victims were aboard one ship in 1968 and two in London. On 28 Mar 1983 in Phoenix, Arizona, USA he received 28 years for fraud and six for bigamy, and was fined $336 000. He died in February 1991.

In Britain, the only woman to contract eight legal marriages is Olive Joyce Wilson of Marston Green, Birmingham, W Mids. She has consecutively been Mrs John Bickley, Mrs Don Trethowan, Mrs George Hundley, Mrs Raymond Ward, Mrs Harry Latrobe, Mrs Leslie Harris, Mrs Ray Richards, and now Mrs John Grassick. All were divorced except Mr Hundley, who died.

Oldest bride and bridegroom The oldest recorded bridegroom has been Harry Stevens, aged 103, who married Thelma Lucas, 84, at the Caravilla Retirement Home, Wisconsin, USA on 3 Dec 1984. The oldest recorded bride is Minnie Munro, aged 102, who married Dudley Reid, 83, at Point Clare, New South Wales, Australia on 31 May 1991.

The British record was set by Sir Robert Mayer (1879–1985), who married Jacqueline Noble, 51, in London on 10 Nov 1980 when aged 101 years. Mrs Winifred Clark (b. 13 Nov 1871) became Britain's oldest recorded bride when she married Albert Smith, 80, at St Hugh's Church, Cantley, S Yorks the day before her 100th birthday.

Longest marriage The longest recorded marriages were both of 86 years. Sir Temulji Bhicaji Nariman and Lady Nariman, who were married from 1853 to 1940, were cousins and the marriage took place when both were aged five. Sir Temulji (b. 3 Sep 1848) died, aged 91 years 11 months, in August 1940

at Bombay, India. Lazarus Rowe (b. Greenland, New Hampshire, USA in 1725) and Molly Webber were recorded as marrying in 1743. He died first, in 1829, also after 86 years of marriage.

The British record is for a marriage of 82 years between James Frederick Burgess (b. 3 Mar 1861, died 27 Nov 1966) and his wife Sarah Ann, née Gregory (b. 11 Jul 1865, died 22 Jun 1965). They were married on 21 Jun 1883 at St James's, Bermondsey, London.

Golden weddings The greatest number of golden weddings in a family is 10, the six sons and four daughters of Joseph and Sophia Gresl of Manitowoc, Wisconsin, USA all celebrating golden weddings between April 1962 and September 1988, and the six sons and four daughters of George and Eleonora Hopkins of Patrick County, Virginia, USA all celebrating their golden weddings between November 1961 and October 1988.

The British record is seven, the three sons and four daughters of Mr and Mrs F. Stredwick of East Sussex all celebrating their golden weddings between May 1971 and April 1981.

Wedding ceremonies The largest mass wedding ceremony was one of 20 825 couples officiated over by Sun Myung Moon (b. 1920) of the Holy Spirit Association for the Unification of World Christianity in the Olympic Stadium in Seoul, South Korea on 25 Aug 1992. In addition a further 9800 couples around the world took part in the ceremony through a satellite link.

Most expensive The wedding of Mohammed, son of Shaik Rashid Bin Saeed Al Maktoum, to Princess Salama in Dubai in May 1981 lasted seven days and cost an estimated £22 million. It was held in a purpose-built stadium for 20 000 people.

Greatest attendance At the wedding of cousins Menachem Teitelbaum and Brucha Sima Meisels at Uniondale, Long Island, New York City, USA on 4 Dec 1984, the attendance of the Satmar sect of Hasidic Jews was estimated to be 17–20 000.

Longest engagement The longest engagement on record was between

Octavio Guillen and Adriana Martinez. They finally took the plunge after 67 years in June 1969 in Mexico City. Both were then aged 82.

Youngest married It was reported in 1986 that an 11-month-old boy was married to a 3-month-old girl in Bangladesh to end a 20-year feud between two families over a disputed farm.

Oldest divorced The oldest aggregate age for a couple to be divorced is 188. On 2 Feb 1984 a divorce was granted in Milwaukee, Wisconsin, USA to Ida Stern, aged 91, and her husband Simon, 97. The British record is 166, Harry Bidwell of Brighton, E Sussex, who was 101, divorcing his 65-year-old wife on 21 Nov 1980.

Best man The world champion 'best man' is Ting Ming Siong, from Sibu, Sarawak, in Malaysia, who officiated at a wedding for the 808th time since 1976 in March 1993.

Feasts and Celebrations

Banquets The most lavish menu ever served was for the main banquet at the Imperial Iranian 2500th Anniversary gathering at Persepolis in October 1971. The feast, which lasted 5½hr, comprised quails' eggs stuffed with Iranian caviar, a mousse of crayfish tails in Nantua sauce, stuffed rack of roast lamb, a main course of roast peacock stuffed with *foie gras*, fig rings and raspberry sweet champagne sherbet. The wines included *Château Lafite-Rothschild* 1945 at £40 (now £235) per bottle from Maxime's, Paris.

The largest feast was attended by 150000 guests on the occasion of the renunciation ceremony of Atul Dalpatlal Shah, when he became a monk, at Ahmedabad, India on 2 Jun 1991.

The greatest number of people served indoors at a single sitting was 18000 municipal leaders at the Palais de l'Industrie, Paris, France on 18 Aug 1889.

Dining out The world champion for eating out was Fred E. Magel of Chicago, Illinois, USA, who over a period of 50 years dined out 46000 times in 60 countries as a restaurant grader. He claimed that the restaurant which served the largest helpings was Zehnder's Hotel,

Dining out
The greatest altitude at which a formal meal has been held is 6768 m *22205ft*, at the top of Mt Huascaran, Peru, when nine members of the Ansett Social Climbers from Sydney, Australia scaled the mountain on 28 Jun 1989 with a dining table, chairs, wine and three-course meal. At the summit they put on top hats, thermal black ties and ball-dresses for their dinner party, which was marred only by the fact that the wine turned to ice.

Frankenmuth, Michigan, USA. Mr Magel's favourite dishes were South African rock lobster and mousse of fresh English strawberries.

Party-giving The International Year of the Child children's party in Hyde Park, London on 30–31 May 1979 was attended by the royal family and 160000 children.

The world's biggest birthday party was attended by 75000 people at Buffalo, New York, USA on 4 Jul 1991 as part of the 1991 Friendship Festival, an annual event held every July to celebrate the national birthdays of the USA and Canada.

The largest in Britain was attended by an estimated 10000 people on 5 Aug 1989 at Douglas, Isle of Man. The party was held to mark the 50th birthday of Trevor Baines, a well-known local businessman.

The largest Christmas party ever staged was that thrown by the Boeing Co. in the 65000-seat Kingdome, Seattle, Washington State, USA. The party was held in two parts on 15 Dec 1979, and a total of 103152 people attended.

On 25 Sep 1992 a total of 240451 people attended 4841 coffee mornings held simultaneously throughout Great Britain as part of the Macmillan Nurse Appeal, raising more than £464000 in the process.

The largest teddy bears' picnic ever staged was attended by 9750 bears together with their owners in Auckland, New Zealand on 14 Feb 1993.

Miscellaneous Endeavours

We are phasing out such categories in the 'Human Achievements' area where the duration of the event is the only criterion for inclusion, and will not be adding any new marathon records or reintroducing ones which have been in the book in the past but are no longer included. If you are planning an attempt on an endurance marathon you should contact us at a very early stage to check whether the entry is going to be retained.

Balloon sculpture The largest balloon sculpture was a reproduction of Van Gogh's *Fishing Boats on the Beach of Les Saintes Maries*, made out of 25344 coloured balloons on 28 Jun 1992. Students from Haarlem Business School created the picture at a harbour in Ouddorp in the Netherlands.

Barrel rolling The record for rolling a full 36gal *1·64hl* metal beer barrel over a measured mile is 8min 7·2sec, by Phillip Randle, Steve Hewitt, John Round, Trevor Bradley, Colin Barnes and Ray Glover of Haunchwood Collieries Institute and Social Club, Nuneaton, Warks on 15 Aug 1982. A team of 10 rolled a 63·5kg *140lb* barrel 241km *150miles* in 30hr 31min at Chlumčany, Czech Republic on 27–28 Oct 1982.

Barrow pushing The heaviest loaded one-wheeled barrow pushed for a minimum 200 level feet *61 level metres* was one loaded with bricks weighing a gross 3·753tonnes *8275lb*. It was pushed a distance of 74·1m *243ft* by John Sarich at London, Ontario, Canada on 19 Feb 1987.

Barrow racing The fastest time attained in a 1mile *1·6km* wheelbarrow race is 4min 48·51sec, by Piet Pitzer and Jaco Erasmus at the Transvalia High School, Vanderbijlpark, South Africa on 3 Oct 1987. Brothers-in-law Malcolm Shipley and Adrian Freebury pushed each other from John o' Groats to Land's End for charity in 30 days from 28 Jul–26 Aug 1980.

Baton twirling The greatest number of complete spins done between tossing a baton into the air and catching it is 10 by Donald Garcia, on the BBC *Record Breakers* programme on 9 Dec 1986. The record for women is seven, by Lisa Fedick on the same programme, by Joanne Holloway at the UK National Baton Twirling Association Championships in Paignton, Devon on 29 Oct 1987, and by Rachel Hayes on 18 Sep 1988, also later shown on the BBC *Record Breakers* programme.

Bed making The pair record for making a bed with 1 blanket, 2 sheets, an undersheet, an uncased pillow, 1 counterpane and 'hospital' corners is 17·3sec, by Sister Sharon Stringer and Nurse Michelle Benkel of the Royal Masonic Hospital, London on 19 Sep 1990, shown on BBC TV's *Record Breakers* programme. The record time for one person to make a bed is 28·2sec, by Wendy Wall, 34, of Hebersham, Sydney, Australia on 30 Nov 1978.

Bed pushing The longest recorded push of a normally sessile object is of 5204km *3233 miles 1150 yd*, in the case of a wheeled hospital bed by a team of nine employees of Bruntsfield Bedding Centre, Edinburgh from 21 Jun–26 Jul 1979.

Bed race The record time for the annual Knaresborough Bed Race (established 1966) in N Yorks is 12min 9sec for the 3·27km *2mile 63yd* course crossing the River Nidd by the Vibroplant team on 9 Jun 1990. The course record for the 10mile *16·1km* Chew Valley Lake race (established 1977) in Avon is 50min, by the Westbury Harriers' three-man bed team.

Beer keg lifting George Olesen raised a keg of beer weighing 62·5kg *137lb 13oz* above his head 670 times in the space of six hours at Horsens, Denmark on 25 Jun 1992.

Beer tankard The largest tankard was made by the Selangor Pewter Co. (now known as Royal Selangor International Sdn.BHD) of Kuala Lumpur, Malaysia and unveiled on 30 Nov 1985. It measures 198·7cm *6½ ft* in height and has a capacity of 2796litres *615gal*.

The scene at Ouddorp harbour in the Netherlands on 28 Jun 1992, when more than 25 000 balloons were used to recreate this Van Gogh picture.

Beer mat flipping Dean Gould of Felixstowe, Suffolk flipped a pile of 111 mats (1·2mm thick 490gsm wood pulp board) through 180 degrees and caught them on 13 Jan 1993.

Beer stein carrying Barmaid Rosie Schedelbauer covered a distance of 15m *49ft 2½in* in 4sec with five full steins in each hand in a televised contest at Königssee, Germany on 29 Jun 1981.

Brick carrying The greatest distance achieved for carrying a 9lb *4·08kg* brick in a nominated ungloved hand in an uncradled downward pincher grip is 99·4km *61¾ miles*, by Reg Morris of Walsall, W Mids on 16 Jul 1985. The women's record for a 9lb 12oz *4·42kg* brick is 36·2km *22½ miles*, by his wife Wendy Morris on 28 Apr 1986.

Bricklaying Tony Gregory of Horndon on the Hill, Essex laid 747 bricks, each weighing 2 kg *4lb 7oz*, in 60 min at Grays, Essex on 18 Apr 1987. This was achieved in accordance with the rules of the Brick Development Association and the Guild of Bricklayers.

Brick lifting Russell Bradley of Worcester lifted 31 bricks laid side by side off a table, raising them to chest height and holding them there for two seconds on 14 Jun 1992. The greatest weight of bricks lifted was also by Russell Bradley, on 17 Nov 1990, when he succeeded in lifting 26 far heavier bricks weighing a total of 86kg *189lb 9oz*, again holding them for two seconds.

Bubble David Stein of New York City, USA created a 15·2m *50ft* long bubble on 6 Jun 1988. He made the bubble using a bubble wand, washing-up liquid and water.

Bubble-gum blowing The greatest reported diameter for a bubble-gum bubble under the strict rules of this highly competitive activity is 55·8cm *22in*, by Susan Montgomery Williams of Fresno, California, USA in June 1985.

The British record is 42cm *16½ in* by Nigel Fell, 13, from Derryaghy, Co. Antrim in November 1979. This was equalled by John Smith of Willingham, Cambs on 25 Sep 1983.

Bucket chain The longest fire service bucket chain stretched over 3496·4 m *11 471ft*, with 2271 people passing 50 buckets along the complete course at the Centennial Parade and Muster held at Hudson, New York, USA on 11 Jul 1992.

Catapulting The greatest recorded distance for a catapult shot is 415m *1362 ft* by James M. Pfotenhauer, using a patented 5·22m *17ft 1½in* Monarch IV Supershot and a 53-calibre lead musket ball on Ski Hill Road, Escanaba, Michigan, USA on 10 Sep 1977.

Cigar box balancing Terry Cole of Walthamstow, London balanced 220 unmodified cigar boxes on his chin for nine seconds on 24 Apr 1992.

Coal carrying In the greatest non-stop bag carrying feat, 1cwt *50·8kg* of household coal in an open bag was carried 54·7km *34miles* by Neil Sullivan, 37, of Small Heath, Birmingham, in 12hr 45min on 24 May 1986.

David Jones of Huddersfield, W Yorks holds the record for the annual race at Gawthorpe, W Yorks, carrying a 50kg *110lb* bag over the 1012·5m *1107·2yd* course in 4min 6sec on 1 Apr 1991.

Crate climbing Philip Bruce stacked 38 beer crates in a single column and climbed up them to a height of 9·65m *31 ft 8in* at Sowerby Bridge, West Yorks on 26 Aug 1991.

Crawling The longest continuous voluntary crawl (progression with one or other knee in unbroken contact with the ground) is 50·6km *31½ miles*, by Peter

Crawling

Over a space of 15 months ending on 9 Mar 1985, Jagdish Chander, 32, crawled 1400 km *870 miles* from Aligarh to Jamma, India to propitiate his revered Hindu goddess, Mata.

Escapology

A manufacturer of strait-jackets acknowledges that an escapologist 'skilled in the art of bone and muscle manipulation' could escape from a standard jacket in seconds. There are, however, methods by which such circumvention can itself be circumvented.

McKinlay and John Murrie, who covered 115 laps of an athletics track at Falkirk, Central on 28–29 Mar 1992.

Demolition work Fifteen members of the Black Leopard Karate Club demolished a seven-room wooden farmhouse west of Elnora, Alberta, Canada in 3 hr 18 min by foot and empty hand on 13 Jun 1982.

Egg and spoon racing Dale Lyons of Meriden, W Mids ran the London marathon (42·195 km *26 miles 385 yd*) while carrying a dessert spoon with a fresh egg on it in 3 hr 47 min on 23 Apr 1990.

Egg dropping The greatest height from which fresh eggs have been dropped (to earth) and remained intact is 198 m *650 ft*, by David S. Donoghue from a helicopter on 2 Oct 1979 on a golf course in Tokyo, Japan.

Escapology Nick Janson of Benfleet, Essex has escaped from handcuffs locked on him by more than 1400 different police officers over the period since 1954.

Footbag The world record for keeping a footbag airborne is 48825 consecutive kicks or hacks by Ted Martin (USA) in Memphis, Tennessee, USA on 4 Jun 1988. The women's record is held by Francine Beaudry (Canada), with 15458 on 28 Jul 1987 at Golden, Colorado, USA.

The greatest number of kicks in five minutes is 912 by Kenny Shults (USA) also at Golden, Colorado on 30 Jul 1991 and for women the record is 705 by Sam Lundberg (USA) on 28 Jul 1992, again at Golden, Colorado.

Hitch-hiking The title of world champion hitch-hiker is claimed by Bill Heid of Allen Park, Michigan, USA who since 1964 has obtained free rides totalling an estimated 673 200 km *418 300 miles.*

Hod carrying Russell Bradley of Worcester carried bricks weighing 164 kg *361 lb 9 oz* up a ladder of the minimum specified length of 12 ft *3·65 m* on 28 Jan 1991 at Worcester City Football Club. The hod weighed 43 kg *94 lb 13 oz* and he was thus carrying a total weight of 207 kg *456 lb 6 oz.* He also carried bricks weighing 260·4 kg *574 lb 1 oz* in a hod weighing 48 kg *105 lb 13 oz* a distance of 5 m *16 ft 5 in* on the flat, before ascending a runged ramp to a height of 7 ft *2·13 m* at Worcester Rugby Club on 17 Mar 1991. This gave a total weight of 308·4 kg *679 lb 14 oz.*

Hop-scotch The greatest number of games of hop-scotch successfully completed in 24 hr is 307, by Ashrita Furman of Jamaica, New York, USA in Zürich, Switzerland on 5–6 Apr 1991.

Human centipede The largest 'human centipede' to move 30 m *98 ft 5 in* (with ankles firmly tied together) consisted of 1189 people (pupils from Archbishop Holgate and Fulford schools in York and students from York University) at York on 16 Oct 1991. Nobody fell over in the course of the walk.

Kissing Alfred A.E. Wolfram of New Brighton, Minnesota, USA kissed 8001 people in 8 hours at the Minnesota Renaissance Festival on 15 Sep 1990— one every 3·6 seconds.

Kite flying The following records are all recognized by *Kite Lines* magazine:–

The longest kite flown was 1034·45 m *3394 ft* in length. It was made and flown by Michel Trouillet and a team of helpers at Nîmes, France on 18 Nov 1990.

The largest kite flown was one of 553 m² *5952 ft².* It was first flown by a Dutch team on the beach at Scheveningen, Netherlands on 8 Aug 1981.

Knitting

Gwen Matthewman's technique (<> right-hand column) has been filmed by the world's only Professor of Knitting—a Japanese.

French knitting

Ted Hannaford of Sittingbourne, Kent has produced a piece of French knitting 7·25km *4miles 890yd* long since he started work on it in April 1989.

Blanket

The largest hand-knitted blanket was made in 1991 by Friends of St Catherine's Hospice in Crawley, West Sussex. It measured 45·11×7·42 m *148×54ft*, giving an area of 3492·4m² *37592ft²*.

Scarf

The longest scarf ever knitted was 32km 1·9m *20miles 13ft*. It was made by residents of Abbeyfield Houses for the Abbeyfield Society of Potters Bar, Herts and was completed on 29 May 1988.

A record height of 9740m *31955ft* was reached by a train of eight kites over Lindenberg, Germany on 1 Aug 1919.

The altitude record for a single kite is 3801m *12471ft*, in the case of a kite flown by Henry Helm Clayton and A.E. Sweetland at the Blue Hill Weather Station, Milton, Massachusetts, USA on 28 Feb 1898.

The fastest speed attained by a kite was 193 km/h *120mph* flown by Pete DiGiacomo at Ocean City, Maryland, USA on 22 Sep 1989.

The greatest number of figure-of-eights achieved with a kite in an hour is 2911, by Stu Cohen at Ocean City, Maryland, USA on 25 Sep 1988.

The greatest number of kites flown on a single line is 11 284 by Sadao Harada and a team of helpers at Sakurajima, Kagoshima, Japan on 18 Oct 1990.

The longest recorded flight is one of 180hr 17min by the Edmonds Community College team at Long Beach, Washington State, USA from 21–29 Aug 1982. Managing the flight of this J-25 parafoil was Harry N. Osborne.

Knitting The world's most prolific hand-knitter of all time has been Mrs Gwen Matthewman of Featherstone, W Yorks. She attained a speed of 111 stitches per min in a test at Phildar's Wool Shop, Central Street, Leeds, W Yorks on 29 Sep 1980.

Knot-tying The fastest recorded time for tying the six Boy Scout Handbook Knots (square knot, sheet bend, sheep shank, clove hitch, round turn and two half hitches, and bowline) on individual ropes is 8·1sec by Clinton R. Bailey, Sr, 52, of Pacific City, Oregon, USA on 13 Apr 1977.

Land rowing The greatest distance covered by someone on a land rowing machine is 5278·5km *3280miles*, by Rob Bryant of Fort Worth, Texas, USA, who 'rowed' across the USA. He left Los Angeles, California on 2 Apr 1990, reaching Washington, DC on 30 July.

Leap-frogging The greatest distance covered was 1603·2km *996·2miles*, by 14 students from Stanford University, California, USA, who started leap-frogging on 16 May 1991 and stopped 244hr 43min later on 26 May.

Litter collection The greatest number of volunteers involved in collecting litter in one location on one day is 19924, who cleaned up the city of Wellington, New Zealand in the Keep Wellington Beautiful campaign on 6 Oct 1991.

Log rolling The record number of International Championships won is 10, by Jubiel Wickheim of Shawnigan Lake, British Columbia, Canada, between 1956 and 1969. At Albany, Oregon, USA on 4 Jul 1956 Wickheim rolled on a 35·5cm *14in* log against Chuck Harris of Kelso, Washington State, USA for 2hr 40min before losing.

Milk bottle balancing The greatest distance walked by a person continuously balancing a milk bottle on the head is

104·2km *64¾ miles* by Milind Deshmukh at Pune, India on 14–15 May 1993. It took him 20hr 43min to complete the walk.

Milk crate balancing Terry Cole of Walthamstow, London managed to balance 25 crates on his chin for 10·3sec on the Isle of Dogs, London on 28 Jul 1991.

John Evans of Marlpool, Derbys balanced 84 crates (weighing a total of 125kg *275lb*) on his head for 10 seconds on 8 Dec 1992.

Needle threading The record number of times that a strand of cotton has been threaded through a number 13 needle (eye 12·7×1·6mm *½×¹⁄₁₆in*) in 2 hours is 11796, achieved by Sujay Kumar Mallick of Bhopal, India on 5 Apr 1992.

Oyster opening The record for opening oysters is 100 in 2 min 20·07sec, by Mike Racz in Invercargill, New Zealand on 16 Jul 1990.

Paper chain A paper chain 59·05km *36·69 miles* long was made by 60 students from University College Dublin as part of UCD Science Day in Dublin, Republic of Ireland on 11–12 Feb 1993. The chain consisted of nearly 400000

links and was made over a period of 24 hours.

Pass the parcel The largest game of pass the parcel involved 3464 people who removed 2000 wrappers in two hours from a parcel measuring 1·5×0·9× 0·9m *5×3×3ft* at Alton Towers, Staffs on 8 Nov 1992. The event was organized by Parcelforce International and the final present was an electronic keyboard, won by Sylvia Wilshaw.

Pogo stick jumping The greatest number of jumps achieved is 177737, by Gary Stewart at Huntington Beach, California, USA on 25–26 May 1992. Ashrita Furman of Jamaica, New York, USA set a distance record of 24·125km *14·99 miles* in 5hr 33min on 25 May 1991 in Seoul, South Korea.

Pram pushing The greatest distance covered in pushing a pram in 24hr is 563·62km *350·23 miles* by 60 members of the Oost-Vlanderen branch of Amnesty International at Lede, Belgium on 15 Oct 1988. A ten-man team from the Royal Marines School of Music, Deal, Kent, with an adult 'baby', covered a distance of 437·2km *271·7 miles* in 24hr from 22–23 Nov 1990.

Riding in armour The longest recorded ride in armour is one of 334·7 km *208 miles* by Dick Brown, who left Edinburgh, Lothian on 10 Jun 1989 and arrived in his home town of Dumfries four days later. His total riding time was 35hr 25min.

Rope slide The greatest distance recorded in a rope slide is from near the top of Blackpool Tower, Lancs—at a height of 126·8m *416ft*—to a fixed point 343·8m *1128ft* from the base of the tower. Set up by the Royal Marines, the rope was descended on 8 Sep 1989 by Sgt Alan Heward and Cpl Mick Heap of the Royal Marines, John Herbert of Blackpool Tower, and Cheryl Baker and Roy Castle of the BBC *Record Breakers*

Shorthand

Morris I. Kligman, official court reporter of the US Court House, New York has taken 50 000 words in 5 hr (a sustained rate of 166·6wpm). Rates are much dependent upon the nature, complexity and syllabic density of the material.

Tightrope walking

Charles Blondin made a crossing of the Niagara Falls giving Harry Colcord a piggyback ride on 15 Sep 1860. Though many artistes would still find it difficult to believe, Colcord was his agent.

The oldest wirewalker was 'Professor' William Ivy Baldwin (1866–1953), who crossed the South Boulder Canyon, Colorado, USA on a 97·5m *320ft* wire with a 38·1m *125ft* drop on his 82nd birthday on 31 Jul 1948.

---

programme. The total length descended was 366·4m *1202ft*.

Shorthand The highest recorded speeds ever attained under championship conditions are 300 words per min (99·64 per cent accuracy) for five minutes and 350wpm (99·72 per cent accuracy, that is, two insignificant errors) for two minutes, by Nathan Behrin (US) in tests in New York in December 1922. Behrin (b. 1887) used the Pitman system, invented in 1837. Mr G.W. Bunbury of Dublin, Ireland held the unique distinction of writing at 250wpm for 10 minutes on 23 Jan 1894. Arnold Bradley achieved a speed of 309 wpm without error using the Sloan-Duployan system, with 1545 words in 5 minutes in a test in Walsall, W Mids on 9 Nov 1920.

Spitting The greatest recorded distance for a cherry stone is 26·96m *88ft 5½in*, by Horst Ortmann at Langenthal, Germany on 29 Aug 1992. The record for projecting a water-melon seed is 20·96m *68ft 9⅛ in* by Lee Wheelis at Luling, Texas, USA on 24 Jun 1989. Randy Ober of Bentonville, Arkansas, USA spat a tobacco wad 14·50m *47ft*

7in at the Calico 5th Annual Tobacco Chewing and Spitting Championships, held north of Barstow, California on 4 Apr 1982.

Standing The longest period on record that anyone has stood continuously is more than 17 years in the case of Swami Maujgiri Maharaj when performing the *Tapasya* or penance from 1955 to 1973 in Shahjahanpur, Uttar Pradesh, India. When sleeping he would lean against a plank. He died in September 1980 at the age of 85.

Stone skipping (Ducks and drakes) The video-verified stone skipping record is 38 skips, achieved by Jerdone at Wimberley, Texas, USA on 20 Oct 1992.

Stretcher bearing The longest distance a stretcher with a 63·5kg *10st* 'body' has been carried is 254·6km *158·2miles*, in 46hr 35min from 27–29 May 1992. This was achieved by two four-man teams from the 85th Medical Batallion, Ft Meade, Maryland, USA.

String ball, largest The largest ball of string on record is one 4·03m *13ft 2½ in* in diameter and 12·65m *41ft 6 in* in circumference, amassed by J.C. Payne of Valley View, Texas, USA between 1989 and 1992.

Tightrope walking The greatest 19th-century tightrope walker was Jean-François Gravelet, alias Charles Blondin (1824–97), of France, who made the earliest crossing of the Niagara Falls on a 76mm *3in* rope, 335m *1100ft* long, 48·8m *160ft* above the Falls on 30 Jun 1859.

The world tightrope endurance record is 185 days, by Henri Rochatain (b. 1926) of France, on a wire 120m *394ft* long, 25m *82ft* above a supermarket in Saint Etienne, France from 28 Mar–29 Sep 1973. Doctors have remained puzzled about his ability to sleep on the wire.

Ashley Brophy of Neilborough, Victoria, Australia walked 11·57km *7·18miles* on a wire 45m *147ft 8in* long and 10m *32ft 10in* above the ground at the Adelaide Grand Prix, Australia on 1 Nov 1985 in 3½hr.

Steve McPeak (b. 21 Apr 1945) of Las Vegas, Nevada, USA ascended the 46·6mm *1⅞in* diameter Zugspitzbahn cable on the Zugspitze, Germany for a vertical height of 705 m *2313 ft* in three stints aggregating 5 hr 4 min on 24, 25 and 28 Jun 1981. The maximum gradient over the stretch of 2282 m *7485 ft* was more than 30 degrees.

The greatest drop over which anyone has walked on a tightrope is 3150 m *10335 ft*, above the French countryside, by Michel Menin of Lons-le-Saunier, France, on 4 Aug 1989.

Typewriting The highest recorded speeds attained with a ten-word penalty per error on a manual machine are: five min—176 wpm net Mrs Carole Forristall Waldschlager Bechen at Dixon, Illinois, USA on 2 Apr 1959; and one hour—147 wpm net Albert Tangora (US) (Underwood Standard), 22 Oct 1923.

The official hour record on an electric typewriter is 9316 words (40 errors) on an IBM machine, giving a net rate of 149 words per min, by Margaret Hamma, now Mrs Dilmore (US), in Brooklyn, New York, USA on 20 Jun 1941. In an official test in 1946, Stella Pajunas, now Mrs Garnand, attained a rate of 216 words in a minute on an IBM machine.

Gregory Arakelian of Herndon, Virginia, USA set a speed record of 158 wpm, with two errors, on a personal computer in the Key Tronic World Invitational Type-Off, which attracted some 10 000 entrants worldwide. He recorded this speed in the semi-final, in a three-minute test, on 24 Sep 1991.

Typewriting

Les Stewart of Mudjimba Beach, Queensland, Australia has typed the numbers 1 to 775 000 in *words* on 15 390 quarto sheets as of 20 Mar 1993. His target is to become a 'millionaire'.

Typewriters

The first patent for a typewriter was by Henry Mill in 1714 but the earliest known working machine was made by Pellegrine Turri (Italy) in 1808.

Mihail Shestov set a numerical record by typing spaced *numbers* from 1 to 785 in 5 minutes in Frederiksberg, Denmark on 17 Oct 1991.

Unsupported circle The highest recorded number of people who have demonstrated the physical paradox of all being seated without a chair is an unsupported circle of 10 323 employees of the Nissan Motor Co. at Komazawa Stadium, Tokyo, Japan on 23 Oct 1982. The British record is 7402 participants at Goodwood Airfield, W Sussex on 25 May 1986, as part of a Sport Aid event.

Whip cracking The longest whip ever 'cracked' is one of 56·24 m *184 ft 6 in* (excluding the handle), wielded by Krist King of Pettisville, Ohio, USA on 17 Sep 1991.

Window cleaning Keith Witt of Amarillo, Texas, USA cleaned three standard 1079 × 1194 mm *42½ × 47 in* office windows with a 300 mm *11·8 in* long squeegee and 9 litres *2 gal* of water in 10·13 sec on 31 Jan 1992. The record was achieved at the International Window Cleaning Association convention at San Antonio, Texas, USA.

Writing, minuscule In 1926 an account was published of Alfred McEwen's pantograph record in which the 56-word version of the Lord's Prayer was written by diamond point on glass in the space of 0·04 × 0·02 mm *0·0016 × 0·0008 in*.

Surendra Apharya of Jaipur, India wrote 10 056 characters (speeches by Nehru) within the size of a definitive Indian postage stamp, measuring 19·69 × 17·82 mm *0·78 × 0·70 in*, in December 1990, and also wrote 1749 characters (names of various countries, towns and regions) on a single grain of rice on 19 May 1991. Chang Shi-Qi of Wuhan, China wrote 308 characters ('God bless you' 28 times) on a human hair 2 cm *⁸/₁₀ in* long at the Guinness World of Records Exhibition, Singapore on 2 Jun 1992.

Yo-yo A yo-yo was a toy in Grecian times and is depicted on a bowl dated 450 BC. It was also a Filipino jungle fighting weapon recorded in the 16th century, weighing 1·8 kg *4 lb* with a 6 m *20 ft* thong. The word means 'come-come'. Though illustrated in a book in 1891 as a

Yo-yo

The largest yo-yo ever constructed was one measuring 1·83m *6ft* in diameter made by the woodwork class of Shakamak High School in Jasonville, Indiana, USA. It weighed 372kg *820lb* and was launched from a 48·76m *160ft* crane on 29 Mar 1990, when it 'yo-yoed' 12 times.

bandalore, the craze did not begin until Donald F. Duncan of Chicago, Illinois, USA initiated it in 1926. The most difficult modern yo-yo trick is the 'whirlwind', incorporating both inside and outside horizontal loop-the-loops. 'Fast' Eddy McDonald of Toronto, Canada completed 21663 loops in 3 hr on 14 Oct 1990 at Boston, Massachusetts, USA, having previously set a 1 hr speed record of 8437 loops at Cavendish, Prince Edward Island, Canada on 14 Jul 1990.

Juggling

11 rings (juggled) Albert Petrovski (USSR), 1963–6; Eugene Belaur (USSR), 1968; Sergey Ignatov (USSR), 1973.

12 rings (flashed) Albert Lucas (US), 1985.

7 clubs (juggled) Albert Petrovski (USSR), 1963; Sorin Munteanu (Romania), 1975; Jack Bremlov (Czechoslovakia), 1985; Albert Lucas (US), 1985; Anthony Gatto (US), 1988.

8 clubs (flashed) Anthony Gatto (US), 1989.

11 bean bags (flashed) Bruce Serafian (US), 1992.

10 balls Enrico Rastelli (Italy), 1920s; Albert Lucas (US), 1984.

8 plates Enrico Rastelli (Italy), 1920s; Albert Lucas (US), 1984.

7 flaming torches Anthony Gatto (US), 1989.

Bounce juggling Tim Nolan (US), 10 balls, 1988.

Basketball spinning Bruce Crevier (US), 16 basketballs (whole body), 1992.

Ball spinning (on one hand) François Chotard (France), 9 balls, 1990.

Duration: 5 clubs without a drop 45min 2sec, Anthony Gatto (US), 1989.

Duration: 3 objects without a drop Jas Angelo (GB), 8hr 57min 31sec, 1989.

7 ping-pong balls with mouth Tony Ferko (Czechoslovakia), 1987.

Pirouettes with 3 cigar boxes Kris Kremo (Switzerland) (quadruple turn with 3 boxes in mid-air), 1977.

5 balls inverted Bobby May (US), 1953.

Most objects aloft 821 jugglers kept 2463 objects in the air simultaneously, each person juggling at least three objects at Seattle, Washington, USA in 1990.

3 objects while running (Joggling) Owen Morse (US), 100m in 11·68sec, 1989 and 400m in 57·32sec, 1990; Kirk Swenson (US), 1 mile *1·6 km* in 4 min 43 sec, 1986 and 5000m *3·1 miles* in 16 min 55 sec, 1986; Ashrita Furman (US), marathon—42·195km *26 miles 385 yd*— in 3hr 22min 32·5sec, 1988 and 50miles *80·5 km* in 8 hr 52 min 7 sec, 1989; Michael Hout (US), 110m hurdles in 20·00sec, 1992; Albert Lucas (US), 400m hurdles in 1min 10·37sec, 1989; Owen Morse, Albert Lucas, Tuey Wilson and John Wee (all US), 1mile *1·6 km* relay in 3min 57·38sec, 1990.

5 objects while running (Joggling) Owen Morse (US), 100m in 13·8 sec, 1988. Bill Gillen (US), 1 mile *1·6 km* in 7 min 41·01sec, 1989 and 5000m *3·1 miles* in 28min 11sec, 1989.

Count them! One, two ... fifteen, sixteen. Bruce Crevier sets a new basketball spinning record.

Food

Apple pie The largest apple pie ever baked was that made by ITV chef Glynn Christian in a 12×7 m *40 × 23 ft* dish at Hewitts Farm, Chelsfield, Kent from 25–27 Aug 1982. Over 600 bushels of apples were included in the pie, which weighed 13·66 tonnes *30 115 lb*. It was cut by Rear-Admiral Sir John Woodward.

Banana split The longest banana split ever created measured 7·32 km *4·55 miles* in length, and was made by residents of Selinsgrove, Pennsylvania, USA on 30 Apr 1988.

Barbecue The record attendance at a one-day barbecue was 35 072, at the Iowa State Fairgrounds, Des Moines, Iowa, USA on 21 Jun 1988. The greatest meat consumption ever recorded at a one-day barbecue was at the same event—9·13 tonnes *20 130 lb* of pork consumed in 5 hr. The greatest quantity of meat consumed at any barbecue was 9·58 tonnes *21 112 lb* of beef at the Sertoma Club Barbecue, New Port Richey, Florida, USA, from 7–9 Mar 1986.

Cakes The largest cake ever created weighed 58·08 tonnes *128 238 lb 8 oz*, including 7·35 tonnes *16 209 lb* of icing. It was made to celebrate the 100th birthday of Fort Payne, Alabama, USA, and was in the shape of Alabama. The cake

---

Dish

The largest item on any menu in the world is roasted camel, prepared occasionally for Bedouin wedding feasts. Cooked eggs are stuffed into fish, the fish stuffed into cooked chickens, the chickens stuffed into a roasted sheep's carcass and the sheep stuffed into a whole camel.

Condiment, rarest

The world's most prized condiment is Cà Cuong, a secretion recovered in minute amounts from beetles in North Vietnam. Owing to war conditions, the price had risen to $100 per 28 g *1 oz* before supplies virtually dried up in 1975.

was prepared by a local bakery, EarthGrains, the first cut being made by 100-year old resident Ed Henderson on 18 Oct 1989.

The tallest cake was 30·85 m *101 ft 2½ in* high, created by Beth Cornell Trevorrow and her team of helpers at the Shiawassee County Fairgrounds, Michigan, USA. It consisted of 100 tiers and was completed on 5 Aug 1990.

The Alimentarium, a museum of food in Vevey, Switzerland, has on display the world's oldest cake, which was sealed and 'vacuum-packed' in the grave of Pepionkh, who lived in Ancient Egypt around 2200 BC. The 11 cm *4·3 in* wide cake has sesame on it and honey inside, and was possibly made with milk.

Cheese The largest cheese ever created was a cheddar of 18·17 tonnes *40 060 lb*, made on 13–14 Mar 1988 at Simon's Specialty Cheese, Little Chute, Wisconsin, USA. It was subsequently taken on tour in a specially designed, refrigerated 'Cheesemobile'.

Cherry pie The largest cherry pie on record weighed 17·11 tonnes *37 740 lb 10 oz* and contained 16·69 tonnes *36 800 lb* of cherry filling. It measured 6·1 m *20 ft* in diameter, and was baked by members of the Oliver Rotary Club at Oliver, British Columbia, Canada on 14 Jul 1990.

Chocolate model The largest chocolate model was one weighing 4 tonnes *8818 lb*, in the shape of a traditional Spanish sailing ship. It was made by Gremi Provincial de Pastissería, Confitería i Bollería school, Barcelona, Spain in February 1991 and measured 13 × 8·5 × 2·5 m *42 ft 8 in × 27 ft 10½ in × 8 ft 2½ in*.

Christmas pudding The largest was one of 3·28 tonnes *7231 lb 1 oz*, made by the villagers of Aughton, Lancs and officially unveiled at the Famous Aughton Pudding Festival held on 11 Jul 1992. Work on the pudding had started on 3 July and it was ready the day before the festival.

Cocktail The largest cocktail on record was a 'Hurricane' consisting of 6056·7 litres *1332·3 gal*, made at the annual Bartenders' Ball held on Long Island, New York, USA on 15 Mar 1993. It was named after Hurricane Gloria, which had battered the island in 1985, and consisted of rum, triple sec, sour mix, orange juice and grenadine.

Doughnut The largest ever made was an American-style jelly doughnut weighing 1·7 tonnes *3739 lb*, which was 4·9 m *16 ft* in diameter and 40·6 cm *16 in* high in the centre. It was made by representatives from Hemstrought's Bakeries, Donato's Bakery and the radio station WKLL-FM at Utica, New York, USA on 21 Jan 1993.

Easter eggs The heaviest Easter egg on record, and also the tallest, was one weighing 4·76 tonnes *10482 lb 14 oz*, 7·1 m *23 ft 3 in* high, made by staff of Cadbury Red Tulip at their factory in Ringwood, Victoria, Australia. It was completed on 9 Apr 1992 and officially unveiled by the Australian test cricketer Merv Hughes.

Food, most expensive The most expensive food is saffron from Spain, which comes from the stamen or stigma of a crocus. It is sold at Harrods in London for £305 per 100g *3·5 oz*.

Haggis The largest haggis on record (encased in eight ox stomach linings) weighed 285·8 kg *630 lb* and was made for the ASDA Superstore, Corby, Northants by David A. Hall Ltd of Broxburn, Lothian on 6 Nov 1986.

Hamburger The largest hamburger on record was one of 2·50 tonnes *5520 lb*, made at the Outgamie County Fairgrounds, Seymour, Wisconsin, USA on 5 Aug 1989.

Ice-cream sundae The largest ice-cream sundae was one weighing 24·91 tonnes *54914 lb 13 oz*, made by Palm Dairies Ltd under the supervision of Mike Rogiani in Edmonton, Alberta, Canada on 24 Jul 1988. It consisted of 20·27 tonnes *44689 lb 8 oz* of ice-cream, 4·39 tonnes *9688 lb 2 oz* of syrup and 243·7 kg *537 lb 3 oz* of topping.

Jelly The world's largest jelly, a 35000 litre *7700 gal* water-melon flavoured pink jelly made by Paul Squires and Geoff Ross, was set at Roma Street Forum, Brisbane, Queensland, Australia on 5 Feb 1981 in a tank supplied by Pool Fab.

The huge raspberry-flavoured ice lolly made at Oostkapelle, Netherlands in August 1992.
(Photo: Ronald Vonk)

Kebab The longest kebab ever was one 630·0 m *2066 ft 11 in* long, made by the Namibian Children's Home at Windhoek, Namibia on 21 Sep 1991.

Lasagne The largest lasagne was one weighing 1·64 tonnes *3609 lb 10 oz* and measuring 15·2 × 1·5 m *50 × 5 ft*. It was made by Andreano Rossi and Ciro Geroso, along with a team of helpers, at the Royal Dublin Society Spring Show in Dublin, Republic of Ireland on 11 May 1990.

Loaf The longest loaf on record was a Rosca de Reyes 1064 m *3491 ft 9 in* long, baked at the Hyatt Regency Hotel in Guadalajara, Mexico on 6 Jan 1991. If a consumer of a 'Rosca', or twisted loaf, finds the embedded doll, that person has to host the Rosca party (held annually at Epiphany) the following year.

The largest pan loaf ever baked, by staff of Sasko in Johannesburg, South Africa on 18 Mar 1988, weighed 1·43 tonnes *3163 lb 10 oz* and measured 3 × 1·25 × 1·1 m *9 ft 10 in × 4 ft 1 in × 3 ft 7 in*.

Lollipop The world's largest ice lolly was one of 5·6 tonnes *12346 lb*, made by Eric Rotte, owner of a local cafe and bar, together with a team of helpers at Oostkapelle, Netherlands on 1 Aug 1992.

The largest 'regular' lollipop weighed 1·01 tonnes *2220 lb 11 oz* and was made by Stephen Spring and James Alexandrou of Lolly Pops/Johnson's Confectionery at Darling Harbour, Sydney, Australia on 18–19 Aug 1990.

483

The big Biscuit

I TRIED TO EAT THE WORLD'S LARGEST COOKIE

RIPON WISCONSIN

Cutting the pieces

The largest biscuit ever made was a chocolate chip cookie with an area of 84·35 m² 907·9 ft², made at the annual Riponfest at Ripon, Wisconsin, USA on 11 Jul 1992. It was 10·36 m 34 ft in diameter and contained nearly 4 million chocolate chips.

Serves 8163

1270 lb (576 kg) flour
600 lb (272 kg) sugar
760 lb (345 kg) soya oil
25 ½ lb (11·5 kg) table salt
12¾ lb (6 kg) vanilla essence
20 ½ lb (9 kg) powdered eggs
9 lb (4 kg) baking soda
27 gallons (123 litres) water

plus 664 lb (301 kg) chocolate chips
(equals 3 839 207 chocolate chips)

VERY HOT !
DO NOT
TOUCH OVEN

Baking the biscuit

484

Preheat oven to 220°F (105°C).

Mix all of the ingredients in a large bowl.

Add the chocolate chips and beat thoroughly.

Transfer dough mixture to biscuit tin via semi trailer lorry carrying 70 containers, each filled with 50 lb (23 kg) of the dough mixture.

Bake on top of a rotating tin for approx 2½ hours.

Remove oven top and allow to cool.

Slice using ten pizza cutters soldered together at 4 inch (10 centimetre) intervals.

The best bit!

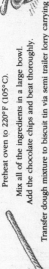

Measuring the depth

The idea to make a huge biscuit was first discussed by the organizing committee eight months before the festival. Samples of different types of chocolate chip cookie were tasted and a recipe selected for the attempt. At the next meeting the team discussed how dough would be prepared and transported, and the biscuit baked and distributed. Safety and sanitation were also dealt with.

A test run with a small oven and a comparatively small biscuit revealed some problems, notably that the biscuit was not evenly baked as

the heat source was stationary. This was resolved by rotating the tray over the heat source.

Next a direct fired burner was constructed, and a gas line run to the location of the attempt. Before the big day a full trial run was done, but not successfully as it was cool and windy and thus not possible to generate any heat build-up in the oven.

Even on the day there were difficulties — the biscuit tray became very hard to turn and one section of the outside frame gave way. The

organizers were almost ready to announce to the crowd that the attempt would have to be abandoned, but just in time the cause of the problem was established, and once corrected the event could continue.

The biscuit actually took 2½ hours to bake, with a successful outcome, and then it was just a case of distributing, eating and enjoying. The day can best be summed up by one of the organizers, who commented "The project was a great amount of fun, but I don't think that we will bake a bigger one next year".

Noodle making

Happy Kuk made 4096 noodle strings (i.e 2^{12}, in twelve movements) from a single piece of noodle dough in 45·14sec at the launch of the Chinatown and Asian Food Festival in Melbourne, Victoria, Australia on 19 Jan 1993. This is more than 90 noodles per second.

Omelette making

The greatest number of two-egg omelettes made in 30min is 427, by Howard Helmer at the International Poultry Trade Show held at Atlanta, Georgia, USA on 2 Feb 1990.

Pancake tossing

The greatest number of times a pancake has been tossed in 2 minutes is 307, by Philip Artingstall at Durban, South Africa on 23 Feb 1993.

Meat pie The largest meat pie on record weighed 9·03tonnes *19908lb* and was the ninth in the series of Denby Dale, W Yorks pies. It was baked on 3 Sep 1988 to mark the bicentenary of Denby Dale pie-making, the first one in 1788 having been made to celebrate King George III's return to sanity. The fourth (Queen Victoria's Jubilee, 1887) went a bit 'off' and had to be buried in quicklime.

Milk shake The largest milk shake was a chocolate one of 7160·8 litres *1575·2gal*, made by the Smith Dairy Products Co. at Orrville, Ohio, USA on 20 Oct 1989.

Mince pie The largest mince pie recorded was one of 1·02tonnes *2260lb*, measuring 6·1 × 1·5m *20 × 5ft*, baked at Ashby-de-la-Zouch, Leics on 15 Oct 1932.

Omelette The largest omelette in the world had an area of 123 m² *1324ft²* and was made in a skillet 12·52m *41ft 1in* in diameter. It was cooked by staff and pupils of the Municipal School for Special Education at Opwijk, Belgium on 10 Jun 1990.

Paella The largest paella measured 20m *65ft 7in* in diameter and was made by Juan Carlos Galbis and a team of helpers in Valencia, Spain on 8 Mar 1992. It was eaten by 100000 people.

Pancake The largest pancake was 12·55m *41ft 2in* in diameter and 3cm *1¼ in* deep, and weighed 2·68tonnes *5908lb*. It was baked and flipped at Bloemfontein, South Africa on 7 Mar 1992.

Pastry The longest pastry was a mille-feuille (cream puff pastry) 1037·25m *3403ft* in length, made by employees of Pidy, a company based in Ypres, Belgium on 4–5 Sep 1992.

Pizza The largest pizza ever baked was one measuring 37·4m *122ft 8in* in diameter, made at Norwood Hypermarket, Norwood, South Africa on 8 Dec 1990.

Popcorn The largest container full of popcorn was one with 169.33 m³ *5979·33ft³* of popped corn. It was just over 6m *19ft 8in* in diameter and 5·81m *19ft 1in* in height. It took the staff from United Cinemas International in Derby three days to achieve the record, beginning their attempt on 23 Aug 1991 and completing it on 26 August.

Salami The longest salami on record was one 20·95m *68ft 9in* long with a circumference of 63·4cm *25in*, weighing 676·9kg *1492lb 5oz*, made by staff of A/S Svindlands Pølsefabrikk at Flekkefjord, Norway from 6–16 Jul 1992.

Sausage The longest continuous sausage on record was one of 21·12km *13⅛ miles*, made at the premises of Keith Boxley at Wombourne, near Wolverhampton, W Mids in 15 hr 33 min on 18–19 Jun 1988.

Spice, most expensive Prices for wild ginseng (root of *Panax quinquefolium*) from the Chan Pak Mountain area of China, thought to have aphrodisiac qualities, were reported in November 1979 to be as high as $23000 per ounce in Hong Kong. Total annual shipments from Jilin Province do not exceed 4kg *140oz* a year. A leading medical journal in the USA has likened its effects to 'corticosteroid poisoning'.

Spice, 'hottest' The hottest of all spices is believed to be habanero, belonging to the genus *capsicum*, found mainly in the Caribbean and the Yucatán area of Mexico. A single dried gram will produce detectable 'heat' in 200 kg *440 lb* of bland sauce.

Stick of rock The largest stick of rock was one weighing 413·6 kg *911 lb 13 oz*. It was 5·03 m *16 ft 6 in* long and 43·2 cm *17 in* thick, and was made by the Coronation Rock Company of Blackpool, Lancs on 20 Jul 1991.

Strawberry bowl The largest bowl of strawberries had a net weight of 2·19 tonnes *4832 lb*. The strawberries were picked at Walt Furlong's farm at New Ross, Co. Wexford, Republic of Ireland during the Enniscorthy Strawberry Fair on 9 Jul 1989.

Sweets The largest sweet on record was a marzipan chocolate weighing 1·85 tonnes *4078 lb 8 oz*, made at the Ven International Fresh Market, Diemen, Netherlands on 11–13 May 1990.

Trifle The largest sherry trifle on record was one weighing 3·13 tonnes *6896 lb*, including 91 litres *20 gal* of sherry, made on 26 Sep 1990 by students of Clarendon College of Further Education, Nottingham.

Yorkshire pudding The largest Yorkshire pudding was one with an area of 42·04 m² *452·2 ft²*, measuring 9·18 × 4·58 m *30 ft 1¼ in × 15 ft 0¼ in*. It was made by staff from Rotherham Council's catering department at Rotherham, S Yorks on 1 Aug 1991 to celebrate Yorkshire Day.

Drink

As from 1 Jan 1981 the strength of spirits has been expressed in terms of percentage volume of alcohol at 20°C *68°F*. Prior to 1981, strength was expressed in terms of proof spirit, which was defined in the Excise Act of 1880 as being the mixture which at 51°F *10·6°C* weighed exactly twelve thirteenths of an equal measure of water. Proof spirit contained 49 per cent by weight of alcohol or 57 per cent by volume at 20°C *68°F*. Absolute or pure alcohol is 100 per cent alcohol and was formerly expressed as 175 per cent proof or 75 per cent over

proof (OP). Since 1981, strengths in the EC have been quoted as percentage alcohol at 20°C *68°F*, but the term 'proof' is still encountered in some areas.

In the USA, proof spirit has a different meaning, and contains 50 per cent alcohol by volume at 60°F *15·6°C* so that absolute or pure alcohol is 200 per cent US proof spirit. The USA has also moved away from proof spirit and is now quoting strengths as percentage alcohol by volume at 60°F *15·6°C*.

Alcohol consumption France has the greatest consumption of alcohol per person, with 12·7 litres *22·3 pints* of pure alcohol per annum. The UK ranks 21st in the world, with 7·6 litres *13·4 pints* per person per annum.

Beer *Oldest* Written references to beer have been found dating from as far back as *c.* 5000 BC, as part of the daily wages of workers at the Temple of Erech in Mesopotamia. Physical evidence of beer dating from *c.* 3500 BC has been detected in remains of a jug found at Godin Tepe, Iran in 1973 during a Royal Ontario Museum expedition. It was only in 1991 that analysis of the remains was carried out, which established that residues in deep grooves in the jug were calcium oxalate, also known as beerstone and still created in barley-based beers.

Strongest Roger & Out brewed at the Frog & Parrot in Sheffield, S Yorks, from a recipe devised by W.R. Nowill and G.B. Spencer, has an alcohol volume of 16·9 per cent. It was first brewed in July 1985 and has been on sale ever since. The strongest lager is Samichlaus Dark 1987, brewed by Brauerei Hürlimann of Zürich, Switzerland. It is 14·93 per cent alcohol by volume at 20°C.

Bottles *Largest* A bottle 2·54 m *8 ft 4 in* tall and 2·17 m *7 ft 1½ in* in circumference was unveiled at the Shepherd Neame Brewery at Faversham, Kent on 27 Jan 1993. It took 13 minutes to fill the bottle, with 625·5 litres *137½ gal* of Kingfisher beer, the leading Indian lager.

The largest bottles normally used in the wine and spirit trade are the Jeroboam (equal to 4 bottles of champagne or, rarely, of brandy, and from 5–6½ bottles of claret according to whether blown or moulded) and the double magnum

THE GUINNESS TIMES

9th July, 1989

Oldest evidence of wine reported

New research reveals 5500-year-old vintage

The earliest physical evidence of wine is now known to date from as far back as 3500 BC, much earlier than was previously thought. This has been detected in remains of a Sumerian jar found at Godin Tepe, Iran in 1973 during an expedition organized by the Royal Ontario Museum from Toronto, Canada.

For many years the jar was simply stored in the museum, but recently Virginia Badler, a PhD student at the University of Toronto, has been carrying out an analysis of the jar in connection with her thesis. She has now established that a large red stain shows the presence of tartaric acid, a chemical which in nature is found predominantly in grapes. The jar also has a hole directly opposite the stain, in keeping with the normal procedure for winemaking in the past, so as to prevent the container from bursting after secondary fermentation.

A number of experts have said that they agree with the results of the analysis.

It is thought that Stone Age man may have been cultivating wine around 8000 BC, but no firm proof of this has ever been found.

(equal, since c.1934, to 4 bottles of claret or, more rarely, red Burgundy). A complete set of champagne bottles would consist of a quarter bottle, through the half bottle, bottle, magnum, Jeroboam, Rehoboam, Methuselah, Salmanazar and Balthazar, to the Nebuchadnezzar, which has a volume of 16 litres *28·14 pt*, and is equivalent to 20 bottles.

A bottle which contained 33·7 litres of Château Lalande Sourbet 1985 was sold at auction on 10 Oct 1989 in Copenhagen, Denmark. This was equal in volume to almost 45 standard wine bottles.

Smallest The smallest bottles of liquor now sold are of White Horse Scotch Whisky, which stand just over 5 cm *2 in* high and contain 1·3 ml *22 minims*. A mini case of 12 bottles costs about £8.00, and measures 5·3 × 4·8 × 3·4 cm *2¹⁄₁₆ × 1⁷⁄₈ × 1¹⁄₁₆ in*. The distributors are Cumbrae Supply Co. of Linwood, Strathclyde.

Brewers The oldest brewery in the world is the Weihenstephan Brewery, Freising, near Munich, Germany, founded in AD 1040.

The largest single brewing organization in the world is Anheuser-Busch Inc. of St Louis, Missouri, USA, with 12 breweries in the United States. In 1992 the company sold 10·18 billion litres *2·24 billion gal*, the greatest annual volume ever produced by any brewing company in a year. The company's St Louis plant covers 40·5 ha *100 acres* and has an annual capacity of 1·53 billion litres *336 million gal*. One of its brands,

Wine tasting

The largest ever reported was that sponsored by WQED, a San Francisco television station, in San Francisco, California, USA on 22 Nov 1986. Some 4000 tasters consumed 9360 bottles of wine.

Yard of ale

Peter Dowdeswell of Earls Barton, Northants drank a yard of ale (1·42 litres *2½ pints*) in 5·0 sec at RAF Upper Heyford, Oxon on 4 May 1975.

Distillers

Old Bushmills Distillery, Co. Antrim, licensed in 1608, claims to have been in production in 1276.

Budweiser, is the top-selling beer in the world, with 5633 million litres *1239 million gal* sold in 1991.

The largest brewery on a single site is that of the Coors Brewing Co. at Golden, Colorado, USA, where 2·26 billion litres *498 million gal* were produced in 1992. At the same location is the world's largest aluminium can manufacturing plant, with a capacity of more than 5 billion cans annually.

The largest brewing company in the United Kingdom is Bass plc, which has some 4400 public houses and 540 off-licences. The company has net assets of £3·3 billion, controls 10 breweries and has around 84 000 employees. Its turnover for the year ending 30 Sep 1992 was £4307 million. (⊳ Hoteliers)

Distillers The world's most profitable spirits producer is United Distillers, the spirits company of Guinness plc, having made a profit of £769 million in 1992. The largest blender and bottler of Scotch whisky is also United Distillers, their Shieldhall plant in Glasgow having the capacity to fill an estimated 144 million bottles of Scotch a year. This is equivalent to approximately 109 million litres *24 million gal*, most of which is exported. The world's best-selling

brands of Scotch and gin, Johnnie Walker Red Label and Gordon's, are both products of United Distillers.

Most alcoholic drinks When Estonia was independent between the two world wars, the Estonian Liquor Monopoly marketed 98 per cent alcohol distilled from potatoes (196 per cent US proof). In 31 US states Everclear, 190 per cent proof or 95 per cent volume alcohol, is marketed by the American Distilling Co. 'primarily as a base for home-made cordials'.

Spirits *Most expensive* A bottle of 50-year-old Glenfiddich whisky was sold for a record price of 99 999 999 lire (approx. £45 200) to an anonymous Italian businessman at a charity auction in Milan, Italy. The postal auction was held over a two-month period from October to December 1992. The most expensive spirit on sale is Springbank 1919 Malt Whisky, a bottle of which costs £6750 (including VAT) at Fortnum & Mason in London.

Vintners The world's oldest champagne firm is Ruinart Père et Fils, founded in 1729. The oldest cognac firm is Augier Frères & Cie, established in 1643.

Wine *Oldest* The oldest bottle of wine to have been sold at auction was a bottle of 1646 Imperial Tokay, which was bought by John A. Chunko of Princeton, New Jersey, USA and Jay Walker of Ridgefield, Connecticut, USA for SFr 1250 (including buyer's premium) at Sotheby's, Geneva, Switzerland on 16 Nov 1984. At the time the sum paid was equivalent to £405.

Most expensive £105 000 was paid for a bottle of 1787 Château Lafite claret, sold to Christopher Forbes (US) at Christie's, London on 5 Dec 1985. The bottle was engraved with the initials of Thomas Jefferson (1743–1826), 3rd President of the United States—'Th J'—a factor which greatly affected the bidding. In November 1986 its cork, dried out by exhibition lights, slipped, making the wine undrinkable. The record price for a half bottle of wine is FF180 000 (£18 000), for a 1784 Château Margaux, also bearing the initials of Thomas Jefferson, which was sold by Christie's at Vinexpo in Bordeaux, France on 26 Jun 1987.

Most alcoholic drinks

Royal Navy rum, introduced in 1655, was 40°OP (79 per cent volume) before 1948, but was later reduced to 4·5°UP (under proof) or 55 per cent volume. The daily rum ration for Royal Navy sailors was abolished on 31 Jul 1970. Full-strength British Navy Pusser's Rum is currently distributed by I.D.V. (UK) Ltd of Harlow, Essex. The Royal New Zealand Navy was the last navy in the world to issue rum on a daily basis, abolishing the traditional tot on 1 Mar 1990.

Champagne cork flight

The longest flight of a cork from an untreated and unheated bottle 1·22m *4ft* from level ground is 54·18m *177ft 9in*, reached by Prof. Emeritus Heinrich Medicus at the Woodbury Vineyards Winery, New York, USA on 5 Jun 1988.

Champagne fountain

The greatest number of storeys achieved in a champagne fountain, successfully filled from the top and using traditional long-stem glasses, is 44 (height 7·52m *24ft 8in*), achieved by Pascal Leclerc with 14404 glasses at the Biltmore Hotel, Los Angeles, California, USA on 18 Jun 1984.

Wine auction

The largest single sale of wine was conducted by Christie's of London on 10–11 Jul 1974 at Quaglino's Ballroom, London, when 2325 lots comprising 432000 bottles realized £962190.

The record price for a glass of wine is FF8500 (£1040), for the first glass of Beaujolais Nouveau 1992 released in Beaune (from Maison Jaffelin), in the wine region of Burgundy, France. It was bought by Patrick Thiébaut at Pickwick's, a British pub in Beaune, on 19 Nov 1992.

Soft drinks Pepsico of Purchase, New York, USA topped the *Fortune 500* table for beverage companies in April 1993, with total sales for 1992 of $22·1 billion, compared with $13·2 billion for the Coca-Cola Company of Atlanta, Georgia. Coca-Cola is, however, the world's most popular soft drink, with sales in 1992 of 506 million drinks per day, representing an estimated 46 per cent of the world market.

Mineral water The world's largest mineral water firm is Source Perrier, near Nîmes, France, with an annual production of more than 2·5billion bottles, of which 800million now come from Perrier. The French drink about 77litres *136pints* of mineral water per person per year, although the highest average consumption is in Italy, with 105litres *185pints* per person per year.

Manufactured Articles

Collections: Because of the infinite number of objects it is possible to collect, we can only include a small number of claims which reflect proven widespread interest.

We are more likely to consider claims for items accumulated on a personal basis over a significant period of time, made through appropriate established and recognized societies, as these are often better placed to comment authoritatively in record terms.

Axe A steel axe measuring 18·28m *60ft* long, 7m *23ft* wide and weighing 7tonnes was designed and built by BID Ltd of Woodstock, New Brunswick, Canada. The axe was presented to the town of Nackawic, in New Brunswick, on 11 May 1991 to commemorate the town's selection as Forestry Capital of Canada for 1991. Calculations suggested it would take a 140-tonne lumberjack to swing the axe, but a crane was used to lift it into its concrete 'stump'.

Basket The world's largest hand-woven basket measures 14·63 × 7·01 × 5·79m

48 × 23 × 19 ft and was made by the Longaberger Company of Dresden, Ohio, USA in 1990.

Beer cans John F. Ahrens of Mount Laurel, New Jersey, USA has a collection of nearly 15 000 different cans. A Rosalie Pilsner can sold for $6000 in the USA in April 1981. A collection of 2502 unopened bottles and cans of beer from 103 countries was bought for $25 000 by the Downer Club ACT of Australia at the Australian Associated Press Financial Markets Annual Charity Golf Tournament on 23 Mar 1990.

Beer mats (tegestology) The world's largest collection of beer mats is owned by Leo Pisker of Langenzersdorf, Austria, who has collected 140 180 different mats from 159 countries to date. The largest collection of British mats to date is 65 260, owned by Timothy Stannard of Birmingham, W Mids.

Beer labels (labology) Jan Solberg of Oslo, Norway has amassed 353 500 different beer labels from around the world to May 1992. The greatest collection of different British beer labels is 30 722 (to April 1987) by Keith Osborne, Hon. Sec. of The Labologists' Society (founded by Guinness Exports Ltd in 1958). His oldest is one from A.B. Walker & Co., Warrington, Cheshire of *c.* 1846.

Bottle caps Helge Friholm (b. 1909) of Søborg, Denmark has amassed 73 823 different bottle caps from 179 countries since 1950.

Pyramid A pyramid consisting of 362 194 bottle caps was constructed by a team of 11 led by Yevgeniy Lepechov at Chernigov, Kiev, Ukraine from 17–22 Nov 1990.

Bottle collections George E. Terren of Southboro, Massachusetts, USA had a collection of 31 804 bottles (miniatures) of distilled spirit and liquor at 31 May 1992. The record for beer is 3080 unduplicated full bottles from 102 countries collected by Ted Shuler of Germantown, Tennessee, USA. Ron Werner of Bothell, Washington, USA has a collection of 4414 different bottles from 71 countries, but some 2000 are empty.

David L. Maund of Upham, Hants has a collection of 9847 unduplicated miniature Scotch whisky bottles and 323 different miniature bottles of Guinness at April 1993.

Carpets The world's largest carpet was a gold-enriched silk carpet of Hashim (dated AD 743) of the Abbasid caliphate in Baghdad, Iraq, reputed to have measured 4950 m² *54 000 ft²*. A 4851 m² *52 225 ft²* red carpet weighing 28 tons was laid on 13 Feb 1982, by the Allied Corporation, from Radio City Music Hall to the New York Hilton along the Avenue of the Americas, New York City, USA.

The most finely-woven carpet is a silk hand-knotted example with 655 knots per cm² *4224 knots/in²*, measuring 35·5 × 55·8 cm *14 × 22 in*. It was made over a period of 22 months by the Kapoor Rug Corporation of Jaipur, India and completed in May 1993.

Chandeliers The world's largest set of chandeliers was created by the Kookje Lighting Co. Ltd of Seoul, South Korea. It is 12 m *39 ft* high, weighs 10·67 tonnes and has 700 bulbs. Completed in November 1988, it occupies three floors of the Lotte Chamshil Department Store in Seoul. Britain's largest chandelier measures 9·1 m *30 ft* and is in the Chinese Room at the Royal Pavilion, Brighton, E Sussex. It was made in 1818 and weighs one ton.

Cheque The world's physically largest cheque measured 21·36 × 9·58 m *70 × 31 ft*. It was presented by InterMortgage of Leeds, W Yorks to Yorkshire Television's 1992 Telethon Appeal on 4 Sep 1992 to the value of £10 000.

Christmas cracker The largest functional cracker ever constructed was 45·72 m *150 ft* long and 3·04 m *10 ft* in diameter. It was made by international rugby league footballer, Ray Price for Markson Sparks! of New South Wales, Australia and pulled at Westfield Shopping Town, Chatswood, Sydney, Australia on 9 Nov 1991.

Cigarettes The longest cigarettes ever marketed were *Head Plays*, each 27·9 cm *11 in* long and sold in packets of five in the United States from 1930, to save tax. The shortest were *Lilliput* cigarettes, each 31·7 mm *1¼ in* long and 3 mm *⅛ in* in diameter, made in Great Britain in 1956.

The world's largest collection of cigarettes was amassed by Robert E.
Kaufman, of New York, USA and consisted of 8390 different cigarettes from
173 countries and territories. Upon his
death in March 1992 his wife Naida took
over the collection. The oldest brand
represented is *Lone Jack* of *c.* 1885 and
both the longest and shortest are represented. (⇔ above)

Cigarette cards The largest known cigarette card collection is that of Edward

---

Can construction

A scale-model stadium-shaped structure
consisting of 2 million empty beverage
cans was built in Verona, Italy by 150
members of AVIS–AIDO with the co-
operation of Rail (producers of
aluminium cans). It was completed on
1 Dec 1989 after 18000 hours of work.

Quilt

The world's largest quilt was made by
7000 citizens of North Dakota for the
1989 centennial of North Dakota.
It measured 25·9 × 40·8m *85 × 134ft.*

The largest patchwork quilt made in the
UK measures 15·24 × 28·3m *50ft ×
92ft 10in* and was completed on 14 Aug
1990 by residents of Anchor Housing
Association sheltered schemes throughout the country.

Catherine wheel

A self-propelled horizontal firework
wheel of 14·4m *47ft 4in* diameter, built
by the Florida Pyrotechnic Arts Guild,
was displayed at the Pyrotechnics Guild
International Convention in Idaho Falls,
Idaho, USA on 14 Aug 1992. It functioned for 3min 45sec. A vertical wheel
at the same event, built by Essex
Pyrotechnics of Saffron Walden, Essex,
was 13·8m *45½ ft* in diameter and
functioned for 1min 20sec.

Wharton-Tigar (b. 1913) of London with
over 1 million cigarette and trade cards
in some 45000 sets. This collection has
been bequeathed to the British Museum,
who have agreed to make it available for
public study.

Cigarette lighters Frans Van der
Heyden of Vlijmen, Netherlands has collected a total of 51006 different lighters.

Cigarette packets The largest verified
private collection consists of 111870
packets from 260 countries and territories, accumulated by Claudio Rebecchi
of Modena, Italy since 1962.

Cigars The largest cigar ever made is
5·095m *16ft 8½in* long and weighs
262kg *577lb 9oz* (over ¼ton). It was
constructed in 243 hours using 3330 full
tobacco leaves by Tinus Vinke and Jan
Weijmer in February 1983 and is on display at the Tobacco Museum in Kampen,
Netherlands.

The largest marketed cigar is the 35·5cm
14in Valdez Emperador made by Fábrica
de Puros Santa Clara of San Andrés
Tuxtla, Veracruz, Mexico and distributed
exclusively by Tabacos San Andrés.

Credit cards The largest collection of
valid credit cards is one of 1356 all different) by Walter Cavanagh (b. 1943) of
Santa Clara, California, USA. The cost of
acquisition to 'Mr Plastic Fantastic' was
nil, but they are worth more than $1·6
million in credit. They are kept in the
world's longest wallet—76·2m *250ft* in
length and weighing 17·01kg *37½lb.*

Dress A wedding outfit created by
Hélène Gainville with jewels by Alexander Reza is estimated to be worth
$7301587·20. The dress is embroidered
with diamonds mounted on platinum
and was unveiled in Paris, France on 23
Mar 1989.

The world's longest wedding dress train
measured 157m *515ft* and was made by
the Hansel and Gretel bridal outfitters of
Gunskirchen, Germany in 1992. Britain's
longest wedding dress train measured
29·8m *97ft 7¾in* and was made by
Margaret Riley of Thurnby Lodge, Leics
for the blessing of the marriage of Diane
and Steven Reid in Thurmaston, Leics on
6 May 1990.

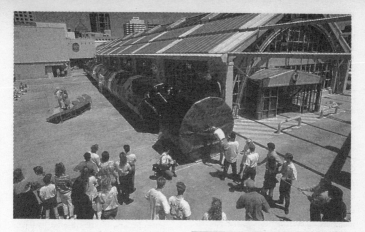

Earrings Carol McFadden of Oil City, Pennsylvania, USA has collected 14850 different pairs of earrings since 1951. Not having pierced ears is not a hindrance as special adaptors enable her to wear the earrings.

Fabrics The oldest surviving fabric, discovered at Çatal Hüyük, Turkey, has been radiocarbon dated to 5900 BC.

The most expensive wool fabric is manufactured by Fujii Keori Ltd of Osaka, Japan from bales of Tasmanian Superfine, which retailed at 3 million yen per metre in January 1989.

Fan A hand painted Spanish fan made of fabric and wood measuring 4·71 m *15·45 ft* when unfolded and 2·44 m *8 ft* high was completed by D. Juan Reolid González of Torrent, Valencia, Spain in June 1991.

Fireworks *Largest* The largest firework ever produced was *Universe I Part II*, exploded for the Lake Toya Festival, Hokkaido, Japan on 15 Jul 1988. The 700 kg *1543 lb* shell was 139 cm *54·7 in* in diameter and burst to a diameter of 1·2 km *0·75 miles*.

Display The longest fireworks display was produced by the Johore Tourism Department, the United Malaysian Youth Movement and Yap Seng Hock on 20 Feb 1988 at Pelangi Garden, Johore Bahru, Johore, Malaysia. The total length

of the display, which lasted for 9 hr 27 min, was 5723·3 m *18 777 ft* and it consisted of 3 338 777 firecrackers and 666 kg *1468 lb* of gunpowder.

Flags The largest flag in the world, one of the Republic of China presented to the city of Kaohsiung, Taiwan by Unichamps Inpe'l Corp. on 9 Apr 1989, measured 126 × 84 m *413 × 275½ ft* and weighed 820 kg *1807 lb*.

The largest Union Flag (or Union Jack) measured 73·15 × 32·91 m *240 × 108 ft* and was displayed at the Royal Tournament, Earl's Court, London in July 1976. It weighed more than a ton and was made by Form 4Y of Bradley Rowe School, Exeter, Devon.

The largest flag *flown* from a flagstaff is a Brazilian national flag measuring 70 × 100 m *229 ft 8 × 328 ft 1 in* in Brasilia.

Jigsaw puzzles The world's largest jigsaw puzzle covers an area of 1050 m² *11302·2 ft²* and consists of 2250 pieces. Assembled on 19 Mar 1991, it was devised by J.N. Nichols (Vimto) plc of Manchester, and designed and built by students from Manchester Polytechnic.

A puzzle consisting of 204 484 pieces was made by BCF Holland b.v. of Almelo,

Garden gnome

The earliest recorded garden gnome was one placed in the rockery at Lamport Hall, Northants in 1847 by Sir Charles Isham, Bt (1819–1903) who treated gnomes as if they were real people.

Silver

The largest single pieces of silver are a pair of water jugs of 242·7kg *10408troyoz* (4·77cwt) made by Gorind Narain in 1902 for the Maharaja of Jaipur (1861–1922). They are 1·6m *5ft 3in* tall, 2·48m *8ft 1½in* in circumference and have a capacity of 8182litres *1800gal*. They are now in the City Palace, Jaipur, India.

Netherlands and assembled by students of the local Gravenvoorde School on 25 May–1 June 1991. The completed puzzle measured 96·25m² *1036ft²*.

Custom-made Stave puzzles of 2640 pieces, created by Steve Richardson of Norwich, Vermont, USA, cost $8680 in June 1992.

Kettle The largest antique copper kettle was one standing 0·9m *3ft* high with a 1·8m *6ft* girth and a 90litre *20gal* capacity, built in Taunton, Somerset, for Fisher and Son *c.* 1800.

Knife The penknife with the greatest number of blades is the Year Knife made by cutlers Joseph Rodgers & Sons, of Sheffield, S Yorks, whose trade mark was granted in 1682. The knife was made in 1822 with 1822 blades and a blade was added every year until 1973 when there was no further space. It was acquired by Britain's largest hand tool manufacturers, Stanley Works (Great Britain) Ltd of Sheffield, S Yorks, in 1970.

Litter bin The world's largest litter bin was made by Natsales of Durban, South Africa for 'Keep Durban Beautiful Association Week' from 16–22 Sep 1991. The 6·01m *19ft 9in* tall fibre glass bin is a replica of the standard Natsales make and holds 43507 litres *9570 gal.*

Matchbox labels Teiichi Yoshizawa (b. 1904) of Chiba-Ken, Japan has amassed 712 118 matchbox labels (including advertising labels) from 150 countries since 1925. Phillumenist Robert Jones of Indianapolis, USA has a collection of some 280000 (excluding any pub/bar or other advertising labels).

Matchstick model Joseph Sciberras of Malta constructed an exact replica, including the interior, of St. Publius Parish Church, Floriana, Malta consisting of over 3 million matchsticks. Made to scale, the model measures 2 × 2 × 1·5m *6½ × 6½ × 5ft*.

Pens The most expensive writing pen is the 5003.002 Caran D'Ache 18-carat solid gold Madison slimline ballpoint pen incorporating white diamonds of 6·35 carats, exclusively distributed by Jakar International Ltd of London. Its recommended retail price in 1993 is £25995 (incl. VAT).

A Japanese collector paid 1·3 million French francs in Feb 1988 for the 'Anémone' fountain pen made by Réden, France. It was encrusted with 600 precious stones, including emeralds, amethysts, rubies, sapphires and onyx, and took skilled craftsmen over a year to complete.

The world's best-selling pen is the BiC Crystal, made by the BiC organization with daily global sales of over 15 million. Sales in the UK are over 600000 daily, containing enough ink to draw a line around the Earth 37 times.

Pottery The largest thrown vase on record is one measuring 5·345m *17ft 6in* in height (including a 1·30m *4ft 3in* tall lid), weighing 600kg *1322lb 12oz*. It was completed on 1 Jun 1991 by Faiarte Ceramics of Rustenberg, South Africa. The Chinese ceramic authority Chingwah Lee of San Francisco, California, USA was reported in August 1978 to have appraised a unique 99cm *39in* Kangxi four-sided vase at $60 million.

Shoes Emperor Field Marshal Jean Fedor Bokassa of the Central African Empire (now Republic) commissioned pearl-studded shoes at a cost of $85000 from the House of Berluti, Paris, France for his self-coronation at Bangui on 4 Dec 1977.

Exterior and interior views of a matchstick scale replica of St Publius Church, Florian, Malta, made by Joseph Sciberras.

(Photos: Joseph Sciberras)

The most expensive marketed shoes are mink-lined golf shoes with 18-carat gold embellishments and ruby-tipped spikes made by Stylo Matchmakers International of Northampton, Northants, costing £13 600 per pair in 1993.

Sofa The longest standard marketed sofa is the 3·74m *12ft 3in* long Augustus Rex, made by Dodge & Son of Sherborne, Dorset. The retail price in 1992 was £1850 plus 25 m *82ft* of fabric of the customer's choice.

In April 1990 a 6·63 m *21ft 9in* long jacquard fabric sofa with an estimated value of $8000 was specially manufactured by Mountain View Interiors of Collingwood, Ontario, Canada.

Stuffed toy *Longest* A 'bookworm' measuring 202·5 m *675ft* was completed in December 1992 by students of Kendall Central School, New South Wales, Australia.

Table The longest table was set up in Pesaro, Italy on 20 Jun 1988 by the US Libertas Scavolini Basketball team. It was 3070 m *3357yd* long and was used to seat 12000 people.

Table cloth The world's largest table cloth is 457·81 m *1502ft* long, 1·37 m *4½ft* wide and was made by the Sportex division of Artex International in Highland, Illinois, USA on 17 Oct 1990.

The UK record is a cloth 300·5 m *985·8ft* long by 1·83 m *6ft* wide made of damask by Tonrose Limited of Manchester in June 1988.

Tapestry and embroidery The largest tapestry ever woven is the *History of Iraq*, covering an area of 1242·1 m² *13370·7ft²*. It was designed by the artist Frane Delale and produced by the Zivtex Regeneracija Workshop in Zabok, Yugoslavia. Completed in 1986, it now adorns the wall of an amphitheatre in Baghdad, Iraq.

Britain's largest single tapestry is *Christ in Glory* which measures 22·77 × 11·59 m *74ft 8 × 38ft* and weighs just over 1 tonne. It was designed by Graham Vivian Sutherland (1903–80) for an altar-hanging in Coventry Cathedral, W Midlands and made by 12 weavers at Pinton Frères of Felletin, France in two years. It cost £10500 and was delivered on 1 Mar 1962 for the consecration of the cathedral on 25 May.

Longest The famous Bayeux *Telle du Conquest, dite tapisserie de la reine Mathilde* hanging depicting events of 1064–6 in 72 scenes is 70·40 m *231ft* long, 49·5 cm *19½ in* wide and was probably worked in Canterbury, Kent, *c.* 1086. It was 'lost' for 2½ centuries from 1476 until 1724.

Embroidery A 20·3 cm *8in* deep and 407·82 m *1338ft* long embroidery of scenes from C.S. Lewis's *Narnia* children's stories was made by Margaret S. Pollard of Truro, Cornwall to the order of Michael Maine. Its total area is about 82 m² *937ft²*.

Tartan The earliest evidence of tartan is the so-called Falkirk tartan, found stuffed in a jar of coins in Bells Meadow, Falkirk, Central. It is of a dark and light brown pattern and dates from *c.* AD245. The earliest reference to a specific named tartan is to a Murray tartan in 1618, although Mackay tartan was probably worn earlier. There are 2179 tartans known to The Tartans Museum at the headquarters of the Scottish Tartans Society in Comrie, Perth, Tayside. HRH Prince of Wales is eligible to wear 11, including the Balmoral, which has been exclusive to the royal family since 1852.

Time capsule The world's largest time capsule is the Tropico Time Tunnel of 283 m³ *10000ft³* in a cave in Rosamond, California, USA sealed by the Kern Antelope Historical Society on 20 Nov 1966 and intended for opening in AD2866.

Wallet The most expensive wallet is a platinum-cornered, diamond-studded crocodile creation made by Louis Quatorze of Paris and Mikimoto of Tokyo which sold in September 1984 for £56000.

Zip-fastener The world's longest zip-fastener was laid around the centre of Sneek, Netherlands on 5 Sep 1989. The brass zipper, made by Yoshida (Netherlands) Ltd, is 2851 m *9353·56ft* long and consists of 2565900 teeth.

Sports *&Games*

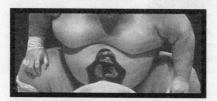

**Includes all major sports
from Aerobatics to Yachting.**

General Records

Fastest The fastest projectile speed in any moving ball game is *c.* 302 km/h *188 mph* in pelota. This compares with 273 km/h *170 mph* (electronically timed) for a golf ball driven off a tee.

Slowest In wrestling, before the rules were modified towards 'brighter wrestling', contestants could be locked in holds for so long that a single bout once lasted for 11 hr 40 min.

In the extreme case of the 2 hr 41 min pull in the regimental tug o' war in Jubbulpore, India, on 12 Aug 1889, the winning team moved a net distance of 3·6 m *12 ft* at an average speed of 0·00135 km/h *0·00084 mph*.

World record breakers *Youngest* The youngest at which anybody has broken a non-mechanical world record is 12 yr 298 days for Gertrude Caroline Ederle (USA) (b. 23 Oct 1906) with 13 min 19·0 sec for women's 880 yd freestyle swimming at Indianapolis, USA on 17 Aug 1919.

Oldest Gerhard Weidner (West Germany) (b. 15 Mar 1933) set a 20-mile walk record on 25 May 1974, aged 41 yr

The fastest speed reached in a non-mechanical sport is in sky-diving, in which a speed of 298 km/h *185 mph* is attained in a head-down free-falling position, even in the lower atmosphere. In delayed drops speeds of 1005 km/h *625 mph* have been recorded at high, rarefied altitudes.

(Photo: Allsport/Vandystadt/Didier Klein)

71 days, the oldest to set an official world record, open to all ages, recognized by an international governing body.

Most prolific Between 24 Jan 1970 and 1 Nov 1977 Vasiliy Alekseyev (USSR) (b. 7 Jan 1942) broke 80 official world records in weightlifting.

Champion *Youngest* The youngest successful competitor in a world title event was a French boy, whose name is not recorded, who coxed the Netherlands' Olympic pair at Paris on 26 Aug 1900. He was not more than ten and may have been as young as seven.

Fu Mingxia (China) (b. 16 Aug 1978) won the women's world title for platform diving at Perth, Australia on 4 Jan 1991, at the age of 12 yr 141 days.

The youngest individual Olympic winner was Marjorie Gestring (USA) (b. 18 Nov 1922), who took the springboard diving title at the age of 13 yr 268 days at the Olympic Games in Berlin on 12 Aug 1936.

Oldest Fred Davis (b. 14 Feb 1913) won (and retained) the world professional billiards title in 1980, aged 67.

Oldest competitor at major games William Edward Pattimore (b. 1 Mar 1892) competed for Wales at bowls at the 1970 Commonwealth Games in Edinburgh at the age of 78, the oldest competitor at such an international event open to competitors of all ages.

Britain's oldest Olympian was Hilda Lorna Johnstone (1902–90) who was 70 yr 5 days when she was placed twelfth in the Dressage competition at the 1972 Olympic Games.

Most versatile Charlotte 'Lottie' Dod (1871–1960) won the Wimbledon singles tennis title five times between 1887 and 1893, the British Ladies' Golf Championship in 1904, an Olympic silver medal for archery in 1908, and represented England at hockey in 1899. She also excelled at skating and tobogganing.

Mildred 'Babe' Zaharias (*née* Didrikson) (1914–56) (USA) won two gold medals (80 m hurdles and javelin) and a silver (high jump) at the 1932 Olympic Games. She set world records at those three events in 1930–32. She was an All-

Largest playing field

For any ball game, the largest playing field is 12·4 acres *5 ha* for polo, or a maximum length of 300 yd *274 m* and a width, without side boards, of 200 yd *182 m*. With boards the width is 160 yd *146 m*.

Twice a year in the Parish of St Columb Major, Cornwall, a game called hurling (not to be confused with the Irish game) is played on a 'pitch', which consists of the entire parish, approximately 25 square miles *64·7 km²*.

Youngest international

The youngest at which any person has won international honours is aged eight in the case of Joy Foster, the Jamaican singles and mixed doubles table tennis champion in 1958.

The youngest British international was diver Beverley Williams (b. 5 Jan 1957) who was 10 yr 268 days old when she competed against the USA at Crystal Palace, London on 30 Sep 1967.

American basketball player for three years and set the world record for throwing the baseball 90·22 m *296 ft*. Switching to golf she won the US Women's Amateur title in 1946 and the US Women's Open in 1948, 1950 and 1954. She also excelled at several other sports.

Charles Burgess Fry (GB) (1872–1956) was perhaps the most versatile male sportsman at the highest level. On 4 Mar 1893 he equalled the world long jump record of 7·17 m *23 ft 6½ in*. He represented England *v.* Ireland at soccer (1901) and played first-class rugby for the Barbarians. His greatest achievements, however, were at cricket, where he headed the English batting averages in six seasons and captained England in 1912. He was also an excellent angler and tennis player.

Longest reign

Jacques Edmond Barre (France) (1802–73) was a world champion for 33 years (1829–62) at real tennis. Although archer Alice Blanche Legh (1855–1948) did not compete every year, she was a British champion for a span of 41 years (1881–1922), during which she won 23 national titles, the last when she was aged 67.

Largest contract

In March 1990, the National Football League concluded a deal worth $3640 million for four years' coverage of American Football by the five major TV and cable networks, ABC, CBS, NBC, ESPN and TBS. This represented $26·1 million for each League team in the first year, escalating to $39·1 million in the fourth.

Largest crowd

The greatest number of live spectators for any sporting spectacle is the estimated 2 500 000 who have lined the route of the New York Marathon. However, spread over three weeks, it is estimated that more than 10 000 000 see the annual *Tour de France* cycling race.

Olympic The total attendance at the 1984 Summer Games was given as 5 526 782 plus an estimated 275 000 spectators at road cycling and marathon events. The total includes 1 421 627 for soccer and 1 129 465 for track and field athletics.

Stadium A crowd of 199 854 attended the Brazil *v.* Uruguay soccer match, in the Maracaña Municipal Stadium, Rio de Janeiro, Brazil on 16 Jul 1950.

Most participants

On 15 May 1988 an estimated 110 000 runners (including unregistered athletes) ran in the Examiner Bay to Breakers 12·2 km *7·6 mile* race in San Francisco, California, USA.

The 1988 Women's International Bowling Congress Championship tournament attracted 77 735 bowlers for the 96-day event held 31 March–4 July at Reno/Carson City, Nevada, USA.

Worst disasters

In recent history, the stands at the Hong Kong Jockey Club racecourse collapsed and caught fire on 26 Feb 1918, killing an estimated 604 people.

During the reign of Antoninus Pius (AD 138–161), 1112 spectators were quoted as being killed when the upper wooden tiers in the Circus Maximus,

Heaviest sportsman

Professional wrestler William J. Cobb of Macon, Georgia, USA, who in 1962 was billed as 'Happy Humphrey', weighed 364kg *802lb*. The heaviest player of a ball-game was Bob Pointer, the 221kg *487lb* US Football tackle formerly on the 1967 Santa Barbara High School Team, California, USA.

Loops

Joann Osterud achieved 208 outside loops in a 'Supernova' Hyperbipe over North Bend, Oregon, USA on 13 Jul 1989. On 9 Aug 1986, David Childs performed 2368 inside loops in a Bellanca Decathalon over North Pole, Alaska.

Brian Lecomber completed 180 consecutive inside loops in a Jaguar Extra 230 on 29 Jul 1988 over Plymouth, Devon.

Inverted flight

The duration record is 4hr 38min 10sec by Joann Osterud from Vancouver to Vanderhoof, Canada on 24 Jul 1991.

Rome collapsed during a gladiatorial combat.

Britain As a result of overcrowding just after the start of the FA Cup semi-final between Liverpool and Nottingham Forest at the Leppings Lane end of Hillsborough Stadium, Sheffield, S Yorks on 15 Apr 1989, 96 people were killed and 170 injured.

Aerobatics

World Championships Held biennially since 1960 (except 1974), scoring is based on a system originally devised by Col. José Aresti of Spain. The competition consists of a known and unknown compulsory and a free programme.

The men's team competition has been won a record six times by the USSR. Petr Jirmus (Czechoslovakia) is the only man to become world champion twice,

in 1984 and 1986. Betty Stewart (USA) won the women's competition in 1980 and 1982.

Lyubov Nemkova (USSR) won a record five medals: first in 1986, second in 1982 and 1984 and third in 1976 and 1978. The oldest ever world champion has been Henry Haigh (USA) (b. 12 Dec 1924), aged 63 in 1988.

British The only medal achieved by Britain has been a bronze in the team event in 1976. The highest individual placing by a Briton is fourth by Neil Williams (1935–77) in 1976.

American Football

Championships The Green Bay Packers won a record 11 NFL titles, 1929–31, 1936, 1939, 1944, 1961–2, 1965–7.

Most consecutive wins The record is 18 by: the Chicago Bears (twice), 1933–4 and 1941–2; the Miami Dolphins, 1972–3; and the San Francisco 49ers, 1988–9. The most consecutive games without defeat is 25 by Canton (22 wins and 3 ties) in 1921–3.

Most games played George Blanda (b. 17 Sep 1927) played in a record 340 games in a record 26 seasons in the NFL (Chicago Bears 1949–58, Baltimore Colts 1950, Houston Oilers 1960–66 and Oakland Raiders 1967–75). The most consecutive games played is 282 by Jim Marshall (Cleveland Browns 1960 and Minnesota Vikings 1961–79).

Longest run from scrimmage Tony Dorsett (b. 7 Apr 1954) scored on a touchdown run of 99yd for the Dallas Cowboys *v.* the Minnesota Vikings on 3 Jan 1983.

Longest pass completion A pass completion of 99yd has been achieved on six occasions and has always resulted in a touchdown. The most recent was a pass from Ron Jaworski (b. 23 Mar 1951) to Mike Quick (b. 14 May 1959) of the Philadelphia Eagles against the Atlanta Falcons on 10 Nov 1985.

NFL Records

Most Points

Career ....2002 George Blanda (Chicago Bears, Baltimore Colts, Houston Oilers, Oakland Raiders), 1949–75
Season ....176 Paul Hornung (Green Bay Packers), 1960
Game ....40 Ernie Nevers (Chicago Cardinals) v. Chicago Bears, 28 Nov 1929

Most Touchdowns

Career.............126 Jim Brown (Cleveland Browns), 1957–65
Season .... 24 John Riggins (Washington Redskins), 1983
Game .... 6 Ernie Nevers (Chicago Cardinals) v. Chicago Bears, 28 Nov 1929
William 'Dub' Jones (Cleveland Browns) v. Chicago Bears, 25 Nov 1951
Gale Sayers (Chicago Bears) v. San Francisco 49ers, 12 Dec 1965

Most Yards Gained Rushing

Career .....16726 Walter Payton (Chicago Bears), 1975–88
Season ......2105 Eric Dickerson (Los Angeles Rams), 1984
Game .... 275 Walter Payton (Chicago Bears) v. Minnesota Vikings, 20 Nov 1977

Most Yards Gained Receiving

Career ...... 13821 James Lofton (Breen Bay Packers, Los Angeles Raiders, Buffalo Bills), 1978–92
Season ....1746 Charley Hennigan (Houston Oilers), 1961
Game .... 336 Willie 'Flipper' Anderson (Los Angeles Rams),v. New Orleans Saints, 26 Nov 1989

Most Yards Gained Passing

Career ..... 47003 Fran Tarkenton (Minnesota Vikings, New York Giants), 1961–78
Season ...... 5084 Dan Marino (Miami Dolphins), 1984
Game ....554 Norm Van Brocklin (Los Angeles Rams) v. New York Yanks, 28 Sep 1951

Most Passes Completed

Career .... 3686 Fran Tarkenton (Minnesota Vikings, New York Giants), 1961–78
Season .... 404 Warren Moon (Houston Oilers), 1991
Game .... 42 Richard Todd (New York Jets) v. San Francisco 49ers, 21 Sep 1980

Pass Receptions

Career .... 847 Art Monk (Washington Redskins), 1980–92
Season .... 108 Sterling Sharp (Green Bay Packers), 1992
Game .... 18 Tom Fears (Los Angeles Rams) v. Green Bay Packers, 3 Dec 1950

Field Goals

Career .... 373 Jan Stenerud (Kansas City Chiefs, Green Bay Packers, Minnesota Vikings), 1967–85
Season .... 35 Ali Haji-Sheikh (New York Giants), 1983
Game .... 7 Jim Bakken (St Louis Cardinals), v. Pittsburgh Steelers, 24 Sep 1967
Rich Karlis (Minnesota Vikings) v. Los Angeles Rams, 5 Nov 1989
Longest ....63 Tom Dempsey (New Orleans Saints) v. Detroit Lions, 8 Nov 1970

Super Bowl

First held in 1967 between the winners of the NFL and the AFL. Since 1970 it has been contested by the winners of the National and American Conferences of the NFL.

The most wins is four by the Pittsburgh Steelers, 1975–6, 1979–80; and by the San Francisco 49ers, 1982, 1985, 1989–90.

The highest team score and record victory margin was when the San Francisco 49ers beat the Denver Broncos 55–10 at

Super Bowl Game & Career Records

POINTS	18	Roger Craig (San Francisco 49ers) 1985
		Jerry Rice (San Francisco 49ers) 1990
Career	24	Franco Harris (Pittsburgh Steelers) 1975–6, 1979–80
		Roger Craig (San Francisco 49ers) 1985, 1989–90
		Jerry Rice (San Francisco 49ers) 1989–90
TOUCHDOWNS	 3	Roger Craig (San Francisco 49ers) 1985
		Jerry Rice (San Francisco 49ers) 1990
Career	 4	Franco Harris (Pittsburgh Steelers) 1975–6, 1979–80
		Roger Craig (San Francisco 49ers) 1985, 1990
		Jerry Rice (San Francisco 49ers) 1989–90
TOUCHDOWN PASSES	5	Joe Montana (San Francisco 49ers) 1990
Career	11	Joe Montana (San Francisco 49ers) 1982, 1985, 1989–90
YARDS GAINED RUSHING	...204	Timmy Smith (Washington Redskins) 1988
Career	354	Franco Harris (Pittsburgh Steelers) 1975–6, 1979–80
YARDS GAINED PASSING	 357	Joe Montana (San Francisco 49ers) 1989
Career	 1142	Joe Montana (San Francisco 49ers) 1982, 1985, 1989–90
YARDS GAINED RECEIVING	215	Jerry Rice (San Francisco 49ers) 1989
Career	364	Lynn Swann (Pittsburgh Steelers) 1975–6, 1979–80
PASSES COMPLETED	 29	Dan Marino (Miami Dolphins) 1985
Career	83	Joe Montana (San Francisco 49ers) 1982, 1985, 1989–90
PASS RECEPTIONS	11	Dan Ross (Cincinnati Bengals) 1982
		Jerry Rice (San Francisco 49ers) 1989
Career	21	Andre Reed (Buffalo Bills) 1990–93
FIELD GOALS	 4	Don Chandler (Green Bay Packers) 1968
		Ray Wersching (San Francisco 49ers) 1982
Career	5	Ray Wersching (San Francisco 49ers) 1982, 1985
MOST VALUABLE PLAYER	 3	Joe Montana (San Francisco 49ers) 1982, 1985, 1990

Action from Super Bowl XXVII, when the Dallas Cowboys beat the Buffalo Bills 52–17.

(Photo: Allsport/Rick Stewart)

In a career spanning 13 seasons with the Washington Redskins, Art Monk made a record 847 receptions.

(Photo: Allsport/Rick Stewart)

Sterling Sharpe of the Green Bay Packers had a record 108 pass receptions during the 1992 season.

(Photo: Allsport/Rick Stewart)

New Orleans, Louisiana on 28 Jan 1990. The highest aggregate score was in 1993 when the Dallas Cowboys beat the Buffalo Bills 52–17. In their 42–10 victory over the Denver Broncos on 31 Jan 1988, the Washington Redskins scored a record 35 points in the second quarter.

Other Records

Highest team score Georgia Tech, Atlanta, Georgia scored 222 points, including a record 32 touchdowns, against Cumberland University, Lebanon, Tennessee (nil) on 7 Oct 1916.

Britain The premier competition is the Coca-Cola Bowl (formerly the Budweiser Bowl) which was inaugurated in 1986. It has been won twice by the London Ravens, 1986 and 1987, the Manchester Spartans, 1989 and 1990, and the Birmingham Bulls, 1988 and 1991.

Highest score The East Kent Cougars, based in Folkestone, beat the Maidstone M20's, 148–6 at Mote Park, Maidstone, Kent on 15 May 1988.

Angling

Oldest existing club The Ellem fishing club was formed by a number of Edinburgh and Berwickshire gentlemen in Scotland in 1829. Its first annual general meeting was held on 29 Apr 1830.

Largest single catch The largest officially ratified fish ever caught on a rod was a man-eating great white shark (*Carcharodon carcharias*) weighing 1208kg *2664lb* and measuring 5·13m *16ft 10in* long, caught on a 59kg *130lb* test line by Alf Dean at Denial Bay, near Ceduna, South Australia on 21 Apr 1959. A great white shark weighing 1537kg *3388lb* was caught by Clive Green off Albany, Western Australia on 26 Apr 1976 but will remain unratified as whale meat was used as bait.

The biggest ever rod-caught fish by a British angler is a 620kg *1366lb* great white shark, by Vic Samson at The Pales, South Australia on 8 Apr 1989.

In June 1978 a great white shark measuring 6·2m *20ft 4in* in length and weighing over 2268kg *5000lb* was harpooned and landed by fishermen in the harbour of San Miguel, Azores.

The largest marine animal killed by *hand* harpoon was a blue whale 29·56m *97ft* in length, by Archer Davidson in Twofold Bay, New South Wales, Australia in 1910. Its tail flukes measured 6·09m *20ft* across and its jaw bone 7·11m *23ft 4in*.

The largest fish ever taken underwater was an 804lb *364kg* giant black grouper or jewfish by Don Pinder of the Miami Triton Club, Florida, USA in 1955. The British spear-fishing record is 89lb *40·36kg* for an angler fish by James Brown (Weymouth Association Divers) in 1969.

British Angling Records

COARSE FISH: A selection of those fish recognized by the National Association of Specialist Anglers

Species	Weight				Name of Angler	Location	Date
	lb	oz	dr	kg			
Barbel	15	7	–	6.99	R. Morris	River Medway, Kent	1993
Bleak	–	4	4	0.12	B. Derrington	River Monnow, Wye Mouth	1982
Bream (Common, Bronze)	16	9	–	7.51	M. McKeown	Southern water	1991
Bream, Silver	–	15	0	0.425	D. E. Flack	Grime Spring, Lakenheath, Suffolk	1988
Carp	51	8	–	23.36	C. Yates	Redmire Pool, Herefordshire	1980
Carp, Grass	23	14	–	10.82	G. Wallis	Canterbury Lake	1991
Catfish (Wells)	43	8	–	19.73	R. J. Bray	Wilstone Reservoir, Tring, Herts	1970
Chub	8	4	–	3.74	G. F. Smith	Royalty Fishery, Hampshire Avon	1913
Dace	1	4	4	0.57	J. L. Gasson	Little Ouse, Thetford, Norfolk	1960
Eel	11	2	–	5.04	S. Terry	Kingfisher Lake, Ringwood, Hants	1978
Gudgeon	–	5		0.141	D. Hall	River Nadder, Salisbury, Wilts	1990
Perch	5	9	–	2.52	J. Shayler	Private water, Kent	1985
Pike	46	13	–	21.23	R. Lewis	Llandegfedd Reservoir, Pontypool, Gwent	1992
Roach	4	3	–	1.89	R. N. Clarke	Dorset Stour	1990
Tench	14	3	–	6.43	Philip Gooriah	Wraysbury No.1 Reservoir	1987
Zander (Pikeperch)	18	8	–	8.39	D. Litton	Cambridge stillwater	1988

FRESHWATER GAME FISH:

Species	Weight				Name of Angler	Location	Date
	lb	oz	dr	kg			
Salmon	64	–		29.03	Miss G. W. Ballantine	River Tay, Scotland	1922
Trout, American Brook	5	13	8	2.65	A. Pearson	Avington Fishery, Hants	1981
Trout, Brown	19	9	4	8.88	J. A. F. Jackson	Loch Quoich, Inverness	1978
Trout, Rainbow	24	2	13	10.96	J. Moore	Pennine Trout Fishery, Littleborough, Lancs	1990
Trout, Sea	22	8	–	10.20	S. Burgoyne	River Leven	1989

World Angling Records; Freshwater and Saltwater

A selection of All-Tackle records ratified by the International Game Fish Association as at 1 Jan 1993

Species	Weight			Name	Location	Date
	lb	oz	kg			
Barracuda, Great	85	0	38-55	John W. Helfrich	Christmas Island, Kiribati	11 Apr 1992
Bass, Striped	78	8	35-60	Albert R. McReynolds	Atlantic City, New Jersey, USA	21 Sep 1982
Catfish, Flathead	91	4	41-39	Mike Rogers	Lake Lewisville, Texas, USA	28 Mar 1982
Cod, Atlantic	98	12	44-79	Alphonse J. Bielevich	Isle of Shoals, New Hampshire, USA	8 Jun 1969
Halibut, Pacific	368	0	166-92	Celia H. Dueitt	Gustavus, Alaska, USA	5 Jul 1991
Mackerel, King	90	0	40-82	Norton I. Thornton	Key West, Florida, USA	16 Feb 1976
Marlin, Black	1560	0	707-61	Alfred C. Glassell Jr	Cabo Blanco, Peru	4 Aug 1953
Pike, Northern	55	1	25-00	Lothar Louis	Lake of Grefeern, Germany	16 Oct 1986
Sailfish (Pacific)	221	0	100-24	C. W. Stewart	Santa Cruz Island, Ecuador	12 Feb 1947
Salmon, Atlantic	79	2	35-89	Henrik Henriksen	Tana River, Norway	1928
Shark, Hammerhead	991	0	449-50	Allen Ogle	Sarasota, Florida, USA	30 May 1982
Shark, Porbeagle	465	0	210-92	Jorge Potier	Padstow, Cornwall	23 Jul 1976
Shark, Thresher	802	0	363-80	Dianne North	Tutukaka, New Zealand	8 Feb 1981
Shark, White	2664	0	1208-38	Alfred Dean	Ceduna, South Australia	21 Apr 1959
Snook	53	10	24-32	Gilbert Ponzi	Parasmina Ranch, Costa Rica	18 Oct 1978
Sturgeon, White	468	0	212-28	Joey Pallotta III	Benicia, California, USA	9 Jul 1983
Swordfish	1182	0	536-15	L. Marron	Iquique, Chile	17 May 1953
Trout, Brook	14	8	6-57	Dr W. J. Cook	Nipigon River, Ontario, Canada	July 1916
Trout, Brown	40	4	18-25	Howard L. Collins	Little Red River, Heber Springs, Arkansas, USA	9 May 1992
Trout, Lake	66	8	30-16	Rodney Harback	Great Bear Lake, NWT, Canada	19 Jul 1991
Trout, Rainbow	42	2	19-10	David Robert White	Bell Island, Alaska, USA	22 Jun 1970
Tuna, Bluefin	1496	0	679-00	Ken Fraser	Aulds Cove, Nova Scotia, Canada	26 Oct 1979
Tuna, Yellowfin	388	12	176-35	Curt Wiesenhutter	San Benedicto Island, Mexico	1 Apr 1977
Wahoo	155	8	70-53	William Bourne	San Salvador, Bahamas	3 Apr 1990

IGFA world records

The International Game Fish Association (IGFA) recognizes world records for a large number of species of game fish (both freshwater and saltwater). Their thousands of categories include all-tackle, various line classes and tippet classes for fly fishing. New records recognized by the IGFA reached an annual peak of 1074 in 1984.

The heaviest freshwater category recognized is for the sturgeon – record weight of 212·28kg *468lb* caught by Joey Pallotta on 9 Jul 1983 off Benicia, California, USA.

***

World Freshwater Championship The
Confédération Internationale de la Pêche Sportive (CIPS) championships were inaugurated as European championships in 1953 and recognized as World championships in 1957.

France won the European title in 1956 and 12 world titles between 1959 and 1990. Robert Tesse (France) took the individual title a record three times, 1959–60, 1965.

The record weight (team) is 34·71kg *76·52lb* in 3hr by West Germany on the Neckar at Mannheim, Germany on 21 Sep 1980. The individual record is 16·99kg *37·45lb* by Wolf-Rüdiger Kremkus (West Germany) at Mannheim on 20 Sep 1980. The most fish caught is 652 by Jacques Isenbaert (Belgium) at Dunaújváros, Hungary on 27 Aug 1967.

Fly fishing World fly fishing championships were inaugurated by the CIPS in 1981. The most team titles is five by Italy, 1982–4, 1986, 1992. The most individual titles is two by Brian Leadbetter (GB), 1987 and 1991.

Casting The longest freshwater cast ratified under ICF (International Casting Federation) rules is 175·01m *574ft 2in* by Walter Kummerow (West Germany), for the Bait Distance Double-Handed 30g event held at Lenzerheide, Switzerland in the 1968 Championships. The British

national record is 148·78m *488ft 1in* by Andy Dickison on the same occasion.

At the currently contested weight of 17·7g, known as 18g Bait Distance, the longest Double-Handed cast is 139·31m *457ft ½in* by Kevin Carriero (USA) at Toronto, Canada on 24 Jul 1984. The British national records are: Fixed spool reel, 138·79m *455ft 3in* by Hugh Newton at Peterborough, Cambs on 21 Sep 1985; and Multiplier reel, 108·97m *357ft 6in* by James Tomlinson at Torrington, Devon on 27 Apr 1985.

The longest Fly Distance Double-Handed cast is 97·28m 319ft 1in by Wolfgang Feige (West Germany) at Toronto, Canada on 23 Jul 1984. Hywel Morgan set a British national record of 91·22m *299ft 2in* at Torrington, Devon on 27 Apr 1985.

The UK Surfcasting Federation record (150g *5¼oz* weight) is 257·32m *844ft 3in* by Neil Mackellow at Peterborough, Cambs on 1 Sep 1985.

Archery

Oldest club The oldest archery body in the British Isles is the Society of Archers in Yorkshire, formed on 14 May 1673, though the Society of Kilwinning Archers, in Scotland, has contested the Pa-pingo Shoot since 1488.

Highest championship scores The highest scores achieved in either a World or Olympic championship for Double FITA rounds are: men, 2617 points (possible 2880) by Darrell Owen Pace (USA) (b. 23 Oct 1956) and Richard Lee McKinney (USA) (b. 20 Oct 1963) at Long Beach, California, USA on 21–22 Oct 1983; and women, 2683 points by Kim Soo-nyung (South Korea) (b. 5 Apr 1971) at Seoul, South Korea on 27–30 Sep 1988.

British records York round – possible 1296 pts: Single round, 1190 Steven Hallard (b. 22 Feb 1965); Double round, 2284 Steven Hallard.

Hereford (Women) – possible 1296 pts: Single round, 1206 Pauline Edwards (b. 23 Apr 1949); Double round, 2380 Joanne Franks (later Edens) (b. 1 Oct 1967) at the British Target Championships on 8 Sep 1987.

World Archery Records

MEN (Single FITA rounds)

Event	Points	Possible	Name and Country	Year
FITA	1352	1440	Vladimir Yesheyev (USSR)	1990
90m	330	360	Vladimir Yesheyev (USSR)	1990
70m	344	360	Hiroshi Yamamoto (Japan)	1990
50m	345	360	Richard McKinney (USA)	1982
30m	358	360	Antonio Vasquez (Spain)	1992
Final	345	360	Vladimir Yesheyev (USSR)	1990
Team	3963	4320	USSR (Stanislav Zabrodskiy, Vadim Shikarev, Vladimir Yesheyev)	1989
Final	1005	1080	South Korea (Kim Sun-bin, Yang Chang-hoon, Park Jae-pyo)	1990

WOMEN (Single FITA rounds)

Event	Points	Possible	Name and Country	Year
FITA	1370	1440	Lee Eun-kyung (South Korea)	1990
70m	*341	360	Kim Soo-nyung (South Korea)	1990
	338	360	Cho Youn-jeong (South Korea)	1992
60m	347	360	Kim Soo-nyung (South Korea)	1989
50m	337	360	Lee Eun-kyung (South Korea)	1990
30m	357	360	Joanne Edens (GB)	1990
Final	346	360	Kim Soo-nyung (South Korea)	1990
Team	4025	4320	South Korea (Kim Soo-nyung, Wang Hee-nyung, Kim Kyung-wook)	1989
Final	1030	1080	South Korea (Kim Soo-nyung, Lee Eun-kyung Lee Seon-hee)	1991

*unofficial

Indoor Double FITA rounds at 25m

	Points	Possible	Name and Country	Year
MEN	591	600	Erwin Verstegen (Holland)	1989
WOMEN	592	600	Petra Ericsson (Sweden)	1991

Indoor FITA round at 18m

	Points	Possible	Name and Country	Year
MEN	591	600	Vladimir Yesheyev (USSR)	1989
WOMEN	587	600	Denise Parker (USA)	1989

FITA round (Men): Single round, 1314 Steven Hallard; Double round, 2616 Steven Hallard, both at Lausanne, Switzerland in July 1989.

FITA round (Women): Single round, 1323 Alison Williamson (b. 3 Nov 1971) at the Olympics at Barcelona, Spain in August 1992; Double round, 2591 Alison Williamson at Belgian FITA Star on 5 Jun 1989.

World Championships The most titles won by a man is four by Hans Deutgen (Sweden) (1917–89) in 1947–50, and the most by a woman is seven by Janina Spychajowa-Kurkowska (Poland) (1901–79) in 1931–4, 1936, 1939 and 1947. The USA has a record 14 men's and 8 women's team titles.

Oscar Kessels (Belgium) (1904–68) participated in 21 world championships.

Olympic Games Hubert van Innis (Belgium) (1866–1961) won six gold and three silver medals at the 1900 and 1920 Olympic Games.

British Championships The most titles is 12 by Horace Alfred Ford (1822–80) in 1849–59 and 1867, and 23 by Alice Blanche Legh (1855–1948) in 1881, 1886–92, 1895, 1898–1900, 1902–9, 1913 and 1921–2. Miss Legh was inhibited from winning from 1882 to 1885–because her mother was champion–and for four further years 1915–18 because there were no Championships during World War I.

Greatest draw

Gary Sentman, of Roseberg, Oregon, USA drew a longbow weighing a record 79·83 kg *176 lb* to the maximum draw on the arrow of 72 cm *28¼ in* at Forksville, Pennsylvania, USA on 20 Sep 1975.

Athletics

Women's bests not yet officially recognised as world records.

Pole vault, 4·01 m *13 ft 1¾ in* Sun Caiyun (China) at Landau, Germany on 31 Jan 1993.

Hammer, 65·40 m *214 ft 7 in* Olga Kuzenkova (Russia) at Bryansk, Russia on 4 Jun 1992.

---

24 hours – target archery The highest recorded score over 24 hours by a pair of archers is 76 158 during 70 Portsmouth Rounds (60 arrows per round at 20 yd at 60 cm FITA targets) by Simon Tarplee and David Hathaway at Evesham, Worcs on 1 Apr 1991. During this attempt Simon Tarplee set an individual record of 38 500.

Athletics

Fastest speed An analysis of split times at each 10 metres in the 1988 Olympic Games 100 m final in Seoul on 24 Sep 1988 won by Ben Johnson (Canada) in 9·79 (average speed 36·77 km/h *22·85 mph* but later disallowed as a world record due to his positive drugs test for steroids) from Carl Lewis (USA) 9·92, showed that both Johnson and Lewis reached a peak speed (40 m–50 m and 80 m–90 m respectively) of 0·83 sec for 10 m, i.e. 43·37 km/h *26·95 mph*. In the women's final Florence Griffith-Joyner was timed at 0·91 sec for each 10 m from 60 m to 90 m, i.e. 39·56 km/h *24·58 mph*.

Highest jump above own head The greatest height cleared above an athlete's own head is 59 cm *23¼ in* by Franklin Jacobs (USA) (b. 31 Dec 1957), 1·73 m *5 ft 8 in* tall, who jumped 2·32 m *7 ft 7¼ in* at New York, USA on 27 Jan 1978. The greatest height cleared by a woman above her own head is 32 cm *12¾ in* by Yolanda Henry (USA) (b. 2 Dec 1964), 1·68 m *5 ft 6 in* tall, who jumped 2·00 m *6 ft 6¾ in* at Seville, Spain on 30 May 1990.

Most Olympic titles The most Olympic gold medals won is ten (an absolute Olympic record) by Raymond Clarence Ewry (USA) (1873–1937) in the standing high, long and triple jumps in 1900, 1904, 1906 and 1908.

Women The most gold medals won by a woman is four shared by: Francina 'Fanny' E. Blankers-Koen (Netherlands) (b. 26 Apr 1918) 100 m, 200 m, 80 m hurdles and 4 × 100 m relay, 1948; Elizabeth 'Betty' Cuthbert (Australia) (b. 20 Apr 1938) 100 m, 200 m, 4 × 100 m relay, 1956 and 400 m, 1964; Bärbel Wöckel (*née* Eckert) (GDR) (b. 21 Mar 1955) 200 m and 4 × 100 m relay in 1976 and 1980; and Evelyn Ashford (USA) (b. 15 Apr 1957) 100 m 1984, and 4 × 100 m relay in 1984, 1988 and 1992.

Most wins at one Games The most gold medals at one celebration is five by Paavo Johannes Nurmi (Finland) (1897–1973) in 1924; 1500 m, 5000 m, 10 000 m cross-country, 3000 m team and cross-country team. The most at individual events is four by Alvin Christian Kraenzlein (USA) (1876–1928) in 1900: 60 m, 110 m hurdles, 200 m hurdles and long jump.

Most Olympic medals The most medals won is 12 (nine gold and three silver) by Paavo Nurmi (Finland) in the Games of 1920, 1924 and 1928.

Women The most medals won by a woman athlete is seven by Shirley Barbara de la Hunty (*née* Strickland) (Australia) (b. 18 Jul 1925) with three gold, one silver and three bronze in the 1948, 1952 and 1956 Games. A re-read of the photo-finish indicates that she finished third, not fourth, in the 1948 200 metres event, thus unofficially increasing her medal haul to eight. Irena Szewinska (*née* Kirszenstein) (Poland) (b. 24 May 1946) won three gold, two silver and two bronze in 1964, 1968, 1972 and 1976, and is the only woman athlete to win a medal in four successive Games.

Dan O'Brien is the current world record holder for the decathlon. Here he is seen in action in four of the ten disciplines during his world record at Talence, France on 4–5 Sep 1992.

(Photo: Allsport/Vandystadt/Richard Martin)

World Records Men

World outdoor records for the men's events scheduled by the International Amateur Athletic Federation. Fully automatic electric timing is mandatory for events up to 400 metres.

Running

Date	min:sec	Name and Country	Venue		
100 metres	9·86*	Frederick Carleton 'Carl' Lewis (USA) (b. 1 Jul 1961)	Tokyo, Japan	25 Aug	1991
200 metres	19·72A	Pietro Paolo Mennea (Italy) (b. 28 Jun 1952)	Mexico City, Mexico	12 Sep	1979
400 metres	43·29	Harry Lee 'Butch' Reynolds Jr (USA) (b. 8 Aug 1964)	Zürich, Switzerland	17 Aug	1988
800 metres	1:41·73	Sebastian Newbold Coe (GB) (b. 29 Sep 1956)	Florence, Italy	10 Jun	1981
1000 metres	2:12·18	Sebastian Newbold Coe (GB)	Oslo, Norway	11 Jul	1981
1500 metres	3:28·82	Noureddine Morceli (Algeria) (b. 20 Feb 1970)	Rieti, Itlay	6 Sep	1992
1 mile	3:46·32	Steven Cram (GB) (b. 14 Oct 1960)	Oslo, Norway	27 Jul	1985
2000 metres	4:50·81	Said Aouita (Morocco) (b. 2 Nov 1959)	Paris, France	16 Jul	1987
3000 metres	7:28·96	Moses Kiptanui (Kenya) (b. 1 Sep 1971)	Cologne, Germany	16 Aug	1992
5000 metres	12:58·39	Said Aouita (Morocco)	Rome, Italy	22 Jul	1987
10000 metres	27:08·23	Arturo Barrios (Mexico) (b. 12 Dec 1963)	Berlin, Germany	18 Aug	1989
20000 metres	56:55·6	Arturo Barrios (Mexico)	La Flèche, France	30 Mar	1991
25000 metres	1 hr 13:55·8	Toshihiko Seko (Japan) (b. 15 Jul 1956)	Christchurch, New Zealand	22 Mar	1981
30000 metres	1 hr 29:18·8	Toshihiko Seko (Japan)	Christchurch, New Zealand	22 Mar	1981
1 hour	21 101m 13·111 miles	Arturo Barrios (Mexico)	La Flèche, France	30 Mar	1991

* Ben Johnson (Canada) (b. 30 Dec 1961) ran 100m in 9·79sec at Seoul, South Korea on 24 Sep 1988, but was subsequently disqualified on a positive drugs test for steroids. He later admitted to having taken drugs over many years, and this invalidated his ratified 9·83sec at Rome, Italy on 30 Aug 1987.
A This record was set at high altitude—Mexico City 2240m 7349ft. Best mark at low altitude: 200m: 19·73sec, Michael Lawrence Marsh (USA) (b. 4 Aug 1967), Barcelona, Spain, 5 Aug 1992.

Hurdling

	min:sec	Name and Country	Venue		
110 metres (3' 6" 106 cm)	12·92	Roger Kingdom (USA) (b. 26 Aug 1962)	Zürich, Switzerland	16 Aug	1989
400 metres (3' 0" 91·4 cm)	46·78	Kevin Curtis Young (USA) (b. 6 Sep 1966)	Barcelona, Spain	6 Aug	1992
3000 metres steeplechase	8:02·08	Moses Kiptanui (Kenya)	Zürich, Switzerland	19 Aug	1992

Relays

4×100 metres	37.40	USA		Barcelona, Spain	8 Aug 1992

(Michael Marsh, Leroy Russell Burrell, Dennis A Mitchell, Carl Lewis)

4×200 metres ... 1:19.11 ... Santa Monica Track Club (USA) ... Philadelphia, USA ...25 Apr 1992
(Michael Marsh, Leroy Burrell, Floyd Wayne Heard, Carl Lewis)

4×400 metres ... 2:55.74 ... USA ... Barcelona, Spain ...8 Aug 1992
(Andrew Valmon, Quincy Watts, Michael Duane Johnson, Steven Earl Lewis)

4×800 metres ... 7:03.89 ... Great Britain ... Crystal Palace, London ...30 Aug 1982
(Peter Elliott, Garry Peter Cook, Steven Cram, Sebastian Coe)

4×1500 metres ... 14:38.8 ... West Germany ... Cologne, Germany ...17 Aug 1977
(Thomas Wessinghage, Harald Hudak, Michael Lederer, Karl Fleschen)

Field Events

	m	ft	in	Name and Country	Venue	Date
High Jump	2.44	8	0½	Javier Sotomayor (Cuba) (b. 13 Oct 1967)	San Juan, Puerto Rico	29 Jul 1989
Pole Vault	6.13	20	1¼	Sergey Nazarovich Bubka (Ukraine) (b. 4 Dec 1963)	Tokyo, Japan	19 Sep 1992
Long Jump	8.95	29	4½	Michael Anthony 'Mike' Powell (USA) (b. 10 Nov 1963)	Tokyo, Japan	30 Aug 1991
Triple Jump	17.97	58	11½	William Augustus 'Willie' Banks (USA) (b. 11 Mar 1956)	Indianapolis, USA	16 Jun 1985
Shot 7.26 kg 16 lb	23.12	75	10¼	Eric Randolph 'Randy' Barnes (USA) (b. 16 Jun 1966)	Los Angeles, California, USA	20 May 1990
Discus 2 kg 4 lb 6.55 oz	74.08	243	0	Jürgen Schult (GDR) (b. 11 May 1960)	Neubrandenburg, Germany	6 Jun 1986
Hammer 7.26 kg 16 lb	86.74	284	7	Yuriy Georgyevich Sedykh (USSR) (b. 11 Jun 1955)	Stuttgart, Germany	30 Aug 1986
Javelin 800 g 28.22 oz	95.54	313	5	Jan Zelezny (Czech Republic) (b. 16 Jun 1966)	Pietersburg, South Africa	6 Apr 1993

Decathlon

	Name and Country	Venue	Date
8847 points	Dan Dion O'Brien (USA) (b. 18 Jul 1966)	Talence, France	4–5 Sep 1992

(1st day: 100m 10.43sec, Long Jump 8.06m 26ft 6¼in,
(2nd day: 110m hurdles 13.98sec, Discus 48.56m 159ft 4in,
Shot Put 16.69m 54ft 9¼in, High Jump 2.07m 6ft 9½in,400m 48.51 sec)
Pole Vault 5.00 m 16ft 4½in, Javelin 62.58m 205ft 4in, 1500m 4:42.10 sec)

World Records *Women*

World outdoor records for the women's events scheduled by the International Amateur Athletic Federation. Fully automatic electric timing is mandatory for all events up to 400 metres.

Running

	min:sec	Name and Country	Venue	Date
100 metres	10.49	Delorez Florence Griffith Joyner (USA) (b. 21 Dec 1959)	Indianapolis, Indiana, USA	16 Jul 1988
200 metres	21.34	Delorez Florence Griffith Joyner (USA)	Seoul, South Korea	29 Sep 1988
400 metres	47.60	Marita Koch (GDR) (b. 18 Feb 1957)	Canberra, Australia	6 Oct 1985
800 metres	1:53.28	Jarmila Kratochvílová (Czechoslovakia) (b. 26 Jan 1951)	Munich, Germany	26 Jul 1983

Event		Name and Country	Venue		Date
1000 metres	2:30·6	Tatyana Providokhina (USSR) (b. 26 Mar 1953)	Podolsk, USSR	20	Aug 1978
1500 metres	3:52·47	Tatyana Vasilyevna Kazankina (USSR) (b. 17 Dec 1951)	Zürich, Switzerland	13	Aug 1980
1 mile	4:15·61	Paula Ivan (Romania) (b. 20 Jul 1963)	Nice, France	10	Jul 1989
2000 metres	5:28·69	Maricica Puică (Romania) (b. 29 Jul 1950)	Crystal Palace, London	11	Jul 1986
3000 metres	8:22·62	Tatyana Kazankina (USSR)	Leningrad, USSR	26	Aug 1984
5000 metres	14:37·33	Ingrid Kristiansen (née Christensen) (Norway) (b. 21 Mar 1956)	Stockholm, Sweden	5	Aug 1986
10000 metres	30:13·74	Ingrid Kristiansen (Norway)	Oslo, Norway	5	Jul 1986

Hurdling

Event		Name and Country	Venue		Date
100 metres (2' 9" 84 cm)	12·21	Yordanka Donkova (Bulgaria) (b. 28 Sep 1961)	Stara Zagora, Bulgaria	20	Aug 1988
400 metres (2' 6" 76 cm)	52·94	Marina Stepanova (née Makeyeva) (USSR) (b. 1 May 1950)	Tashkent, USSR	17	Sep 1986

Relays

Event		Name and Country	Venue		Date
4×100 metres	41·37	GDR	Canberra, Australia	6	Oct 1985
		(Silke Gladisch (now Möller), Sabine Rieger (now Günther), Ingrid Auerswald (née Brestrich), Marlies Göhr (née Oelsner))			
4×200 metres	1:28·15	GDR	Jena, Germany	9	Aug 1980
		(Marlies Göhr (née Oelsner), Romy Müller (née Schneider), Bärbel Wöckel (née Eckert), Marita Koch)			
4×400 metres	3:15·17	USSR	Seoul, South Korea	1	Oct 1988
		(Tatyana Ledovskaya, Olga Nazarova, Maria Pinigina (née Grigoryeva), Olga Bryzgina (née Vladykina))			
4×800 metres	7:50·17	USSR	Moscow, USSR	5	Aug 1984
		(Nadezhda Olizarenko (née Mushta), Lyubov Gurina, Lyudmila Borisova, Irina Podyalovskaya)			

Field Events

	m	ft	in	Name and Country	Venue		Date
High Jump	2·09	6	10¼	Stefka Kostadinova (Bulgaria) (b. 25 Mar 1965)	Rome, Italy	30	Aug 1987
Long Jump	7·52	24	8¼	Galina Chistyakova (USSR) (b. 26 Jul 1962)	Leningrad, USSR	11	Jun 1988
Triple Jump	14·97	49	1¼	Yolanda Chen (Russia) (b. 26 Jul 1961)	Moscow, Russia	18	Jun 1993
Shot 4 kg 8 lb 13 oz	22·63	74	3	Natalya Venedictovna Lisovskaya (b. 16 Jul 1962)	Moscow, USSR	7	Jun 1987
Discus 1 kg 2 lb 3·27 oz	76·80	252	0	Gabriele Reinsch (GDR) (b. 23 Sep 1963)	Neubrandenburg, Germany	9	Jul 1988
Javelin 600 g 24·74 oz	80·00	262	5	Petra Felke (now Meier) (GDR) (b. 30 Jul 1959)	Potsdam, Germany	9	Sep 1988

Heptathlon

	Name and Country	Venue		Date
7291 points	Jacqueline Joyner-Kersee (USA) (b. 3 Mar 1962)	Seoul, South Korea	23–24	Sep 1988

(100 m hurdles 12·69 sec; High Jump 1·86 m 6 ft 1¼ in; Shot 15·80 m 51 ft 10 in; 200 m 22·56 sec; Long Jump 7·27 m 23 ft 10¼ in; Javelin 45·66 m 149 ft 10 in; 800 m 2 min 08·51 sec)

Sergey Bubka has set 34 pole vault world records (16 outdoor, 18 indoor) and dominated the discipline for over 10 years, but he failed to clear any height in the 1992 Olympic final.

(Photo: Allsport/Mike Hewitt)

Most Olympic titles British The most gold medals won by a British athlete (excluding tug of war and walking, *q.v.*) is two by: Charles Bennett (1871–1949) (1500m and 5000m team, 1900); Alfred Edward Tysoe (1874–1901) (800m and 5000m team, 1900); John Thomas Rimmer (1879–1962) (4000m steeplechase and 5000m team, 1900); Albert George Hill (1889–1969) (800m and 1500m, 1920); Douglas Gordon Arthur Lowe (1902–81) (800m 1924 and 1928); Sebastian Newbold Coe (b. 29 Sep 1956) (1500m 1980 and 1984) and Francis Morgan 'Daley' Thompson (b. 30 Jul 1958) (decathlon 1980 and 1984). Daley Thompson was also world champion at the decathlon in 1983.

Most Olympic medals British The most medals won by a British athlete is four by Guy Montagu Butler (1899–1981) gold for the 4 × 400m relay and silver for 400m in 1920 and bronze for each of these events in 1924, and by

Sebastian Coe, who also won silver medals at 800m in 1980 and 1984. Three British women athletes have won three medals: Dorothy Hyman (b. 9 May 1941) with a silver (100m, 1960) and two bronze (200m, 1960 and 4 × 100m relay, 1964), Mary Denise Rand (now Toomey, *née* Bignal), (b. 10 Feb 1940) with a gold (long jump), a silver (pentathlon) and a bronze (4 × 100m relay), all in 1964 and Kathryn Jane Cook (*née* Smallwood) (b. 3 May 1960), all bronze–at 4 × 100m relay 1980 and 1984, and at 400m in 1984.

Olympic champions Oldest and youngest The oldest athlete to win an Olympic title was Irish-born Patrick Joseph 'Babe' McDonald (*né* McDonnell) (USA) (1878–1954) who was aged 42yr 26days when he won the 56lb *25·4kg* weight throw at Antwerp, Belgium on 21 Aug 1920. The oldest female champion was Lia Manoliu (Romania) (b. 25 Apr 1932) aged 36yr 176days when she won the discus at Mexico City on 18 Oct 1968. The youngest gold medallist was Barbara Pearl Jones (USA) (b. 26 Mar 1937) who at 15yr 123days was a member of the winning 4 × 100m relay

Russian Irina Privalova, indoor world record holder for 50 and 60 metres.

(Photo: Allsport/Gray Mortimore)

World Indoor Records

Track performances around a turn must be made on a track of circumference no longer than 200 metres.

MEN

Running

	min:sec	Name and Country	Venue	Date
50 metres	5.61*	Manfred Kokot (GDR) (b. 3 Jan 1948)	East Berlin, Germany	4 Feb 1973
	5.61*	James Sanford (USA) (b. 27 Dec 1957)	San Diego, California, USA	20 Feb 1981
60 metres	6.41*	Andre Cason (USA) (b. 13 Jan 1969)	Madrid, Spain	14 Feb 1992
200 metres	20.36	Bruno Romal Marie-Rose (France) (b. 20 May 1965)	Liévin, France	22 Feb 1987
400 metres	45.02	Danny Joe Everett (USA) (b. 1 Nov 1966)	Stuttgart, Germany	2 Feb 1992
800 metres	1:44.84	Paul Ereng (Kenya) (b. 22 Aug 1967)	Budapest, Hungary	4 Mar 1989
1000 metres (2:16.4 officially)	2:16.62	Robert Druppers (Netherlands) (b. 29 Apr 1962)	The Hague, Netherlands	20 Feb 1988
1500 metres	3:34.16	Noureddine Morceli (Algeria) (b. 20 Feb 1970)	Seville, Spain	28 Feb 1991
1 mile	3:49.78	Eamonn Coghlan (Ireland) (b. 21 Nov 1952)	East Rutherford, New Jersey, USA	27 Feb 1983
3000 metres	7:37.31	Moses Kiptanui (Kenya) (b. 1 Sep 1971)	Seville, Spain	20 Feb 1992
5000 metres	13:20.4	Suleiman Nyambui (Tanzania) (b. 13 Feb 1953)	New York, USA	6 Feb 1983
50 metres hurdles	6.25	Mark McKoy (Canada) (b. 10 Dec 1961)	Kobe, Japan	5 Mar 1986
60 metres hurdles	7.36π	Greg Foster (USA) (b. 4 Aug 1958)	Los Angeles, USA	16 Jan 1987
	7.37	Roger Kingdom (USA) (b. 26 Aug 1962)	Piraeus, Greece	8 Mar 1989

* Ben Johnson (Canada) (b. 30 Dec 1961) ran 50 m in 5·55 sec at Ottawa, Canada on 31 Jan 1987 and 60m in 6·41 sec at Indianapolis, USA on 7 Mar 1987, but these were invalidated due to his admission of having taken drugs over many years, following his disqualification at the 1988 Olympics.

π adjudged by observers to have been with a rolling start, but officially ratified.

Relays

	min:sec	Name and Country	Venue	Date
4×200 metres	1:22.11	United Kingdom	Glasgow, Strathclyde	3 Mar 1991
		(Linford Christie, Darren Braithwaite, Ade Mafe, John Regis)		
4×400 metres	3:03.05	Germany	Seville, Spain	10 Mar 1991
		(Rico Lieder, Jens Carlowitz, Karsten Just, Thomas Schönlebe)		

Walking

5000 metres	18:11-41u	Ronald Weigel (GDR) (b. 8 Aug 1959)	Vienna, Austria	13 Feb 1988
	18:15-25	Grigory Kornev (Russia) (b. 14 Mar 1961)	Moscow, Russia	7 Feb 1992

u *not officially recognised.*

Field Events

	m	ft	in			
High Jump	2.43	7	11½	Javier Sotomayor (Cuba) (b. 13 Oct 1967)	Budapest, Hungary	4 Mar 1989
Pole Vault	6.15	20	2¼	Sergey Nazarovich Bubka (Ukraine) (b. 4 Dec 1963)	Donetsk, Ukraine	21 Feb 1993
Long Jump	8.79	28	10¼	Fredrick Carleton 'Carl' Lewis (USA) (b. 1 Jul 1961)	New York, USA	27 Jan 1984
Triple Jump	17.76	58	3¼	Michael Alexander Conley (USA) (b. 5 Oct 1962)	New York, USA	27 Feb 1987
Shot	22.66	74	4¼	Eric Randolph 'Randy' Barnes (USA) (b. 16 Jun 1966)	Los Angeles, California, USA	20 Jan 1989
Heptathlon	6476 points			Dan Dion O'Brien (USA) (b. 18 Jul 1966)	Toronto, Canada	13–14 Mar 1993

(60m 6·67 sec; Long Jump, 7·84m; Shot, 16-02m; High Jump, 2·13m;
60m hurdles, 7·85sec; Pole vault, 5·20m; 1000m 2:57·96)

WOMEN

Running

	min:sec			
50 metres	6·05	Irina Privalova (Russia) (b. 12 Nov 1968)	Moscow, Russia	2 Feb 1993
60 metres	6·92	Irina Privalova (Russia)	Madrid, Spain	11 Feb 1993
200 metres	21·87	Merlene Ottey (Jamaica) (b. 10 May 1960)	Lievin, France	13 Feb 1993
400 metres	49·59	Jarmila Kratochvílová (Czechoslovakia) (b. 26 Jan 1951)	Milan, Italy	7 Mar 1982
800 metres	1:56·40	Christine Wachtel (GDR) (b. 6 Jan 1965)	Vienna, Austria	13 Feb 1988
1000 metres	2:33·93	Inna Yevseyeva (Ukraine) (b. 14 Aug 1964)	Moscow, Russia	7 Feb 1992
1500 metres	4:00·27	Doina Melinte (Romania) (b. 27 Dec 1956)	East Rutherford, New Jersey, USA	9 Feb 1990
1 mile	4:17·14	Doina Melinte (Romania)	East Rutherford, New Jersey, USA	9 Feb 1990
3000 metres	8:33·82	Elly van Hulst (Netherlands) (b. 9 Jun 1957)	Budapest, Hungary	4 Feb 1989
5000 metres	15:03·17	Elizabeth McColgan (GB) (b. 24 May 1964)	Birmingham, W Midlands	22 Feb 1992
50 metres hurdles	6·58	Cornelia Oschkenat (GDR) (b. 29 Oct 1961)	Berlin, Germany	20 Feb 1988
60 metres hurdles	7·69	Lyudmila Narozhilenko (Russia) (b. 21 Apr 1964)	Chelyabinsk, Russia	4 Feb 1993

Relays

4×200 metres	1:32·55	S. C. Eintracht Hamm (West Germany)	Dortmund, Germany	19 Feb 1988

(Helga Arendt, Silke-Beate Knoll, Mechthild Kluth, Gisela Kinzel)

Continued

	m	ft	in			
4×400 metres	3:27·22			Germany	Seville, Spain	10 Mar 1991
	(Sandra Seuser, Katrin Schreiter, Annet Hesselbarth, Grit Breuer)					

Walking

3000 metres	11:44·00			Alina Ivanova (Ukraine) (b. 25 Jun 1969)	Moscow, Russia	7 Feb 1992

Field Events

	m	ft	in			
High jump	2·07	6	9½	Heike Henkel (Germany) (b. 5 May 1964)	Karlsruhe, Germany	9 Feb 1992
Long jump	7·37	24	2¼	Heike Drechsler (GDR) (b. 16 Dec 1964)	Vienna, Austria	13 Feb 1988
Triple jump	14·47	47	5¾	Inessa Kravets (Ukraine) (b. 5 Oct 1966)	Toronto, Canada	14 Mar 1993
Shot	22·50	73	10	Helena Fibingerová (Czechoslovakia) (b. 13 Jul 1959)	Jablonec, Czechoslovakia	19 Feb 1977
Pentathlon	4991 points			Irina Belova (Russia) (b. 27 Mar 1968)	Berlin, Germany	14–15 Feb 1992
	(60m hurdles 8·22sec; High jump 1·93m; Shot 13·25m; Long jump 6·67m; 800m 2:10·26)					

Ukrainian Inessa Kravets 'stepping' her way to a new indoor triple jump world record at the 1993 World Indoor Championships at Toronto.
(Photo: Allsport/Gray Mortimore)

team, at Helsinki, Finland on 27 Jul 1952. The youngest male champion was Robert Bruce Mathias (USA) (b. 17 Nov 1930) aged 17yr 263days when he won the decathlon at the London Games on 5–6 Aug 1948.

The oldest Olympic medallist was Tebbs Lloyd Johnson (GB) (1900–84), aged 48yr 115days when he was third in the 1948 50000m walk. The oldest woman medallist was Dana Zátopková (Czechoslovakia) (b. 19 Sep 1922) aged 37yr 348days when she was second in the javelin in 1960.

World Championships Quadrennial World Championships, distinct from the Olympic Games, were inaugurated in 1983, when they were held in Helsinki, Finland. The most medals won is nine by Frederick Carleton 'Carl' Lewis (b. 1 Jul 1961), a record eight gold, 100m, long jump and 4×100m relay 1983; 100m, long jump and 4×100m relay 1987; 100m and 4×100m relay 1991; and silver at long jump 1991. Lewis has also won eight Olympic golds, 1984–92. The most medals by a women is seven by Merlene Ottey (Jamaica) (b. 10 May 1960) gold, 4× 100m, one silver, five bronze, 1983–91. The most gold by a woman is three by: Marita Koch (GDR) (b. 18 Feb 1957), 200m, 4×100m and 4×400m relay 1983; Silke Gladisch (GDR) (b. 20 Jun 1964) 4×100m relay 1983, 100m and 200m 1987; Sabine Busch (GDR) (b. 21 Nov 1962) 4×400m relay 1983, 1987, 400m hurdles 1987; Tatyana Samolenko (now Dorovskikh) (USSR) (b. 12 Aug 1961) 1500 m 1987, 3000m 1987, 1991; and Jackie Joyner-Kersee (USA) (b. 3 Mar 1962) long jump 1987, 1991, heptathlon, 1987.

Indoor First held as the World Indoor Games in 1985, they are now staged biennially. The most individual titles is four by: Stefka Kostadinova (Bulgaria) (b. 25 Mar 1965) high jump 1985, 1987, 1989, 1993; and Mikhail Shchennikov (Russia) (b. 24 Dec 1967) 5000m walk 1987, 1989, 1991, 1993.

World record breakers *Oldest and youngest* For the greatest age at which anyone has broken a world record under IAAF jurisdiction, ⇨ General

Steve Smith, British high jump record holder, in action during the 1993 World Indoor Championships where he won a bronze medal, and set a Commonwealth indoor record of 2·37m.

(Photo: Allsport/Gray Mortimore)

Records. The female record is 36yr 139days for Marina Styepanova (*née* Makeyeva) (USSR) (b. 1 May 1950) with 52·94 sec for the 400 m hurdles at Tashkent, USSR on 17 Sep 1986. The youngest individual record breaker is Wang Yan (China) (b. 9 Apr 1971) who set a women's 5000m walk record at age 14yr 334days with 21 min 33·8 sec at Jian, China on 9 Mar 1986. The youngest male is 17yr 198days by Thomas Ray (GB) (1862–1904) when he pole-vaulted 3·42m *11ft 2¾in* on 19 Sep 1879 (prior to IAAF ratification).

Most records in a day Jesse Owens (USA) (1913–80) set six world records in 45min at Ann Arbor, Michigan on 25 May 1935 with a 9·4 sec 100 yd at 3:15p.m., a 8·13m *26ft 8¼ in* long jump at 3:25p.m., a 20·3sec 220yd (and 200m) at 3:45p.m. and a 22·6sec 220yd low hurdles (and 200m) at 4p.m.

Most national titles Great Britain The most national senior titles won by an athlete is 30 by Judith Miriam Oakes (b. 14 Feb 1958) at the shot with ten WAAA outdoor, 12 WAAA indoor and eight UK titles, 1977–91. The greatest number of senior AAA titles (excluding those in tug of war events) won by one athlete is 14 individual and one relay title by Emmanuel McDonald Bailey (Trinidad) (b. 8 Dec 1920), between 1946 and 1953. The most won outdoors in a single event is 13 by Denis Horgan (Ireland) (1871–1922) in the shot put between 1893 and 1912. Thirteen senior AAA titles were also won by: Michael Anthony Bull (b. 11 Sep 1946) at pole vault, eight indoor and five out, and by Geoffrey Lewis Capes (b. 23 Aug 1949) at shot, six indoor and seven out.

The greatest number of WAAA outdoor titles won by one athlete is 14 by Suzanne Allday (née Farmer) (b. 26 Nov 1934) with seven each at shot and discus between 1952 and 1962. She also won two WAAA indoor shot titles.

Most international appearances The greatest number of international matches contested for any nation is 89 by shot-putter Bjørn Bang Andersen (b. 14 Nov 1937) for Norway, 1960–81.

The greatest number of full Great Britain international appearances (outdoors and

United Kingdom (National) Records *Men*

Running

	min:sec	Name	Venue	Date
100 metres	9.92	Linford Christie (b. 10 Apr 1960)	Tokyo, Japan	25 Aug 1991
200 metres	20.09	Linford Christie	Seoul, South Korea	28 Sep 1988
	20.09	John Paul Lyndon Regis (b. 13 Oct 1966)	Barcelona, Spain	5 Aug 1992
400 metres	44.47	David Grindley (b. 3 Sep 1965)	Barcelona, Spain	3 Aug 1992
800 metres	1:41.73	Sebastian Newbold Coe (b. 29 Sep 1956)	Florence, Italy	10 Jun 1981
1000 metres	2:12.18	Sebastian Newbold Coe	Oslo, Norway	11 Jul 1981
1500 metres	3:29.67	Steven Cram (b. 14 Oct 1960)	Nice, France	16 Jul 1985
1 mile	3:46.32	Steven Cram	Oslo, Norway	27 Jul 1985
2000 metres	4:51.39	Steven Cram	Budapest, Hungary	4 Aug 1985
3000 metres	7:32.79	David Robert Moorcroft (b. 10 Apr 1953)	Crystal Palace, London	17 Jul 1982
5000 metres	13:00.41	David Robert Moorcroft	Oslo, Norway	7 Jul 1982
10000 metres	27:23.06	Eamonn Thomas Martin (b. 9 Oct 1958)	Oslo, Norway	2 Jul 1988
20 000 metres	57:28.7	Carl Edward Thackery (b. 14 Oct 1962)	La Flèche, France	31 Mar 1990
25000 metres	1hr 15:22.6	Ronald Hill	Bolton, Lancashire	21 Jul 1965
30000 metres	1hr 31:30.4	James Noel Carroll Alder (b. 10 Jun 1940)	Crystal Palace, London	5 Sep 1970
1 hour	12 miles 1688 yd 20855m	Carl Edward Thackery	La Flèche, France	31 Mar 1990

Hurdling

	min:sec	Name	Venue	Date
110 metres	13.04	Colin Ray Jackson (b. 18 Feb 1967)	Cologne, Germany	16 Aug 1992
400 metres	47.82	Kriss Kezie Uche Chukwu Duru Akabusi (b. 28 Nov 1958)	Barcelona, Spain	6 Aug 1991
3000 metres steeplechase	8:07.96	Mark Robert Rowland (b. 7 Mar 1963)	Seoul, South Korea	30 Sep 1988

Relays

	min:sec	Name	Venue	Date
4x100 metres	37.98	National Team: Darren Braithwaite, John Paul Lyndon Regis, Marcus Adam, Linford Christie	Split, Yugoslavia	1 Sep 1990
4x200 metres	1:21.29	National Team: Marcus Adam, Adeoye Mafe, Linford Christie, John Paul Lyndon Regis	Birmingham	23 Jun 1989
4x400 metres	2:57.53	National Team: Roger Anthony Black, Derek Redmond, John Regis, Kriss Akabusi	Tokyo, Japan	1 Sep 1991
4x800 metres	7:03.89	National Team: Peter Elliott, Gary Peter Cook, Steven Cram, Sebastian Newbold Coe	Crystal Palace, London	30 Aug 1982

4x1500 metres ......14:56-8 ......National Team: Alan David Mottershead, Geoffrey Michael Cooper, Stephen John Emson, Roy Wood ......Bourges, France ......24 Jun 1979

Field Events

	m	ft	in	Name	Venue	Date
High Jump	2-37	7	9¼	Stephen James Smith (b. 29 Mar 1973)	Seoul, South Korea	20 Sep 1992
Pole Vault	5-65	18	6½	Keith Frank Stock (b. 18 Mar 1957)	Stockholm, Sweden	7 Jul 1981
Long Jump	8-23	27	0	Lynn Davies (b. 20 May 1942)	Berne, Switzerland	30 Jun 1968
Triple Jump	17-57A	57	7¾	Keith Leroy Connor (b. 16 Sep 1957)	Provo, Utah, USA	5 Jun 1982
Shot 7-26 kg 16 lb	21-68	71	1½	Geoffrey Lewis Capes (b. 23 Aug 1949)	Cwmbran, Gwent	18 May 1980
Discus 2 kg 4 lb 6-55 oz	64-32*	211	0	William Raymond Tancred (b. 6 Aug 1942)	Woodford, Essex	10 Aug 1974
Hammer 7-26 kg 16 lb	77-54	254	5	Martin Girvan (b. 17 Apr 1960)	Wolverhampton, West Midlands	12 May 1984
Javelin 800 g 28-22 oz	91-46	300	1	Stephen James Backley (GB) (b. 12 Feb 1969)	Auckland, New Zealand	25 Jan 1992

A Record set at high altitude, best at low altitude: 17-43m 57ft 2¼in by Jonathon David Edwards (b. 10 May 1966) at Carlisle, Cumbria on 22 Jun 1991.

* William Raymond Tancred threw 64-94m 213ft 1in at Loughborough, Leicestershire on 21 Jul 1974 and Richard Charles Slaney (b. 16 May 1956) threw 65-16m 213ft 9in at Eugene, Oregon, USA on 1 Jul 1985 but these were not ratified.

Decathlon

	Name	Venue	Date
8847 points	Francis Morgan 'Daley' Thompson (b. 30 Jul 1958)	Los Angeles, California, USA	8-9 Aug 1984

(1st day: 100m 10-44 sec, Long Jump 8-01m 26ft 3½in, Shot Put 15-72m 51ft 7in, High Jump 2-03m 6ft 8in, 400m 46-97 sec)
(2nd day: 110m Hurdles 14-33 sec, Discus 46-56m 152ft 9in, Pole Vault 5-00m 16ft 4¾in, Javelin 65-24m 214ft 0in, 1500m 4:35-00 sec)

United Kingdom (National) Records Women

Running

	minsec	Name	Venue	Date
100 metres	11-10	Kathryn Jane Smallwood (now Cook) (b. 3 May 1960)	Rome, Italy	5 Sep 1981
200 metres	22-10	Kathryn Jane Cook (née Smallwood)	Los Angeles, California, USA	9 Aug 1984
400 metres	49-43	Kathryn Jane Cook (née Smallwood)	Los Angeles, California, USA	6 Aug 1984
800 metres	1:57-42	Kirsty Margaret McDermott (now Wade) (b. 6 Aug 1962)	Belfast, Northern Ireland	24 Jun 1985
1000 metres	2:33-70	Kirsty Margaret McDermott (now Wade)	Gateshead, Tyne and Wear	9 Aug 1985
1500 metres	3:59-96	Zola Budd (now Pieterse) (b. 26 May 1966)	Brussels, Belgium	30 Aug 1985
1 mile	4:17-57	Zola Budd (now Pieterse)	Zürich, Switzerland	21 Aug 1985

	m	ft	in	Name	Venue	Date
2000 metres	5:29·58			Yvonne Carol Grace Murray (b. 4 Oct 1964)	Crystal Palace, London	11 Jul 1986
3000 metres	8:28·83			Zola Budd (now Pieterse)	Rome, Italy	7 Sep 1985
5000 metres	14:48·07			Zola Budd (now Pieterse)	Crystal Palace, London	26 Aug 1985
10000 metres	30:57·07			Elizabeth McColgan (née Lynch) (b. 24 May 1964)	Hengelo, Netherlands	25 Jun 1991

Hurdling
	m			Name	Venue	Date
100 metres	12·82			Sally Jane Janet Gunnell (b. 29 Jul 1966)	Zürich, Switzerland	17 Aug 1988
400 metres	53·16			Sally Janet Jane Gunnell	Tokyo, Japan	29 Aug 1991

Relays
	m			Name	Venue	Date
4×100 metres	42·43			National Team: Heather Regina Hunte (now Oakes), Kathryn Jane Smallwood (now Cook), Beverley Lanita Goddard (now Callender), Sonia May Lannaman	Moscow, USSR	1 Aug 1980
4×200 metres	1:31·57			National Team; Donna-Marie Louise Hartley (née Murray), Verona Marolin Elder (née Bernard), Sharon Colyear (now Danville), Sonia May Lannaman	Crystal Palace, London	20 Aug 1977
4×400 metres	3:22·01			National Team: Phyllis Smith (née Watt), Lorraine I Hanson, Linda Keough, Sally Janet Jane Gunnell	Tokyo, Japan	1 Sep 1991
4×800 metres	8:19·90			National Team: Ann Margaret Williams, Paula Tracy Fryer, Yvonne Murray, Diane Delores Edwards	Sheffield, S Yorks	5 Jun 1992

Field Events
	m	ft	in	Name	Venue	Date
High Jump	1·95	6	4¾	Diana Clare Elliot (now Davies) (b. 7 May 1961)	Oslo, Norway	26 Jun 1982
Pole Vault	3·55	11	7¾	Katherine 'Kate' Staples (b. 2 Nov 1965)	Southampton, Hants	6 Jun 1993
Long Jump	6·90	22	7¾	Beverly Kinch (b. 14 Jan 1964)	Helsinki, Finland	14 Aug 1983
Triple Jump	13·72	45	0¼	Michelle Amanda Griffiths (b. 6 Oct 1971)	Crystal Palace, London	13 Jun 1993
Shot 4 kg 8 lb 13 oz	19·36	63	6¼	Judith Miriam Oakes (b. 14 Feb 1958)	Gateshead, Tyne and Wear	14 Aug 1988
Hammer 4 kg 8 lb 13 oz	56·76	186	3	Esther Augee (b. 1 Jan 1964)	Bromley, Kent	15 May 1993
Discus 1 kg 2 lb 3·27 oz	67·48	221	5	Margaret Elizabeth Ritchie (b. 6 Jul 1952)	Walnut, California, USA	26 Apr 1981
Javelin 600 g 21·16 oz	77·44	254	1	Fatima Whitbread (b. 3 Mar 1961)	Stuttgart, Germany	28 Aug 1986

Heptathlon
	Name	Venue	Date
6623 points	Judy Earline Veronica Simpson (née Livermore) (b. 14 Nov 1960)	Stuttgart, Germany	29-30 Aug 1986

(100 m hurdles 13·05 sec; High Jump 1·92 m 6ft 3½in; Shot 14·75 m 48ft 4in; 200 m 25·09 sec; Long Jump 6·56 m 21 ft 6¼ in; Javelin 40·92 m 134 ft 3 in; 800 m 2 min 11·70 sec)

indoors) is 73 by Verona Marolin Elder (née Bernard) (b. 5 Apr 1953), mostly at 400 m, from 1971 to 1983. The men's record is 67 by shot-putter Geoff Capes, 1969–80. At pole vault and decathlon Mike Bull had 66 full internationals or 69 including the European Indoor Games, before these were official internationals. The most outdoors is 61 by hammer thrower Andrew Howard Payne (b. South Africa, 17 Apr 1931) from 1960 to 1974.

Oldest and youngest internationals
The oldest full Great Britain international was Donald James Thompson (b. 20 Jan 1933), aged 58 yr 89 days, at 200 km walk at Bazencourt, France on 20–21 Apr 1991. In the same race Edmund Harold Shillabeer (b. 2 Aug 1939) became the oldest international débutant, aged 51 yr 260 days.

The oldest woman was Christine Rosemary Payne (née Charters, now Chimes) (b. 19 May 1933) at discus in the Great Britain v. Finland match on 26 Sep 1974, aged 41 yr 130 days. The youngest man was high jumper Ross Hepburn (b. 14 Oct 1961) v. the USSR on 26 Aug 1977, aged 15 yr 316 days, and the youngest woman was Janis Walsh (now Cue) (b. 28 Mar 1960) v. Belgium (indoor) at 60 m and 4 × 200 m relay on 15 Feb 1975, aged 14 yr 324 days.

Longest winning sequence Iolanda Balas (Romania) (b. 12 Dec 1936) won a record 150 consecutive competitions at high jump from 1956 to 1967. The record at a track event is 122 at 400 metres hurdles by Edwin Corley Moses (USA) (b. 31 Jul 1955) between his loss to Harald Schmid (West Germany) (b. 29 Sep 1957) at Berlin, Germany on 26 Aug 1977 and that to Danny Lee Harris (USA) (b. 7 Sep 1965) at Madrid, Spain on 4 Jun 1987.

'End to end' The fastest confirmed run from John o' Groats to Land's End is 10 days 15 hr 27 min by Donald Alexander Ritchie (GB) (b. 6 Jul 1944) from 1–12 Apr 1989. A faster 10 days 3 hr 30 min was claimed by Fred Hicks (GB) for 1410 km *876 miles* on 20–30 May 1977.

The fastest by a women is 13 days 17 hr 42 min by walker Ann Sayer (⬦ Walking). A relay team of 10 from Vauxhall Motors A.C. covered the distance in 76 hr 58 min 29 sec from 31 May–3 Jun 1990.

Longest running race The longest races ever staged were the 1928 (5507 km *3422 miles*) and 1929 (5898 km *3665 miles*) trans-continental races from New York City to Los Angeles, California, USA. The Finnish-born Johnny Salo (1893–1931) was the winner in 1929 in 79 days, from 31 March to 18 June. His elapsed time of 525 hr 57 min 20 sec (averaging 11·21 km/h *6·97 mph*) left him only 2 min 47 sec ahead of Englishman Pietro 'Peter' Gavuzzi (1905–81).

The longest race staged annually is the New York 1300 Mile race, held since 1987, at Flushing Meadow-Corona Park, Queens, New York. The fastest time to complete the race is 16 days 19 hr 31 min 47 sec by Al Howie (GB) (b. 16 Sep 1945) from 16 Sep–3 Oct 1991.

Longest runs Al Howie (GB) ran across Canada, from St Johns to Victoria, a distance of 7295·5 km *4533·2 miles*, in 72 days 10 hr 23 min, 21 Jun–1 Sep 1991. Robert J Sweetgall (USA) (b. 8 Dec 1947) ran 17071 km *10 608 miles* around the perimeter of the USA starting and finishing in Washington, DC, 9 Oct 1982–15 Jul 1983.

Ron Grant (Australia) (b. 15 Feb 1943) ran around Australia, 13383 km *8316 miles* in 217 days 3 hr 45 min, 28 Mar–31 Oct 1983. Max Telford (New Zealand) (b. Hawick, 2 Feb 1955) ran 8224 km *5110 miles* from Anchorage, Alaska to Halifax, Nova Scotia, in 106 days 18 hr 45 min from 25 Jul to 9 Nov 1977.

The fastest time for the cross-America run is 46 days 8 hr 36 min by Frank Giannino Jr (USA) (b. 1952) for the 4989 km *3100 miles* from San Francisco to New York from 1 Sep–17 Oct 1980. The women's trans-America record is 69 days 2 hr 40 min by Mavis Hutchinson (South Africa) (b. 25 Nov 1942) from 12 Mar–21 May 1978.

Greatest mileage Douglas Alistair Gordon Pirie (GB) (1931–91), who set five world records in the 1950s, estimated that he had run a total distance of 347 600 km *216 000 miles* in 40 years to 1981.

521

Ultra Long Distance World Records

MEN

Track

	hr:min:sec	Name	Venue		Date
50km	2:48:06	Jeff Norman (GB)	Timperley, Manchester	7	Jun 1980
50miles	4:51:49	Don Ritchie (GB)	Hendon, London	12	Mar 1983
100km	6:10:20	Don Ritchie (GB)	Crystal Palace, London	28	Oct 1978
100miles	11:30:51	Don Ritchie (GB)	Crystal Palace, London	15	Oct 1977
200km	15:11:10**	Yiannis Kouros (Greece)	Montauban, France	15–16	Mar 1985
200 miles	27:48:35	Yiannis Kouros (Greece)	Montauban, France	15–16	Mar 1985
500km	60:23:00	Yiannis Kouros (Greece)	Colac, Australia	26–29	Nov 1984
500 miles	105:42:09	Yiannis Kouros (Greece)	Colac, Australia	26–30	Nov 1984
1000km	136:17:00	Yiannis Kouros (Greece)	Colac, Australia	26 Nov–1	Dec 1984

kilometres

		Name	Venue		Date
24 hours	283·600	Yiannis Kouros (Greece)	Montauban, France	15–16	Mar 1985
48 hours	452·270	Yiannis Kouros (Greece)	Montauban, France	15–17	Mar 1985
6 days	1023·200	Yiannis Kouros (Greece)	Colac, Australia	26 Nov–1	Dec 1984
(indoors)	1030·000	Jean-Gilles Bossiquet (France)	La Rochelle, France	16–23	Nov 1992

Road*

	hr:min:sec	Name	Venue		Date
50km	2:43:38	Thompson Magawana (South Africa)	Claremont-Kirstenbosch	12	Apr 1988
50miles	4:50:21	Bruce Fordyce (South Africa)	London–Brighton	25	Sep 1983
1000miles	10d10hr30min35sec	Yiannis Kouros (Greece)	New York, USA	21–30	May 1988

kilometres

		Name	Venue		Date
24 hours	286·463	Yiannis Kouros (Greece)	New York, USA	28–29	Sep 1985
6 days	1028·370	Yiannis Kouros (Greece)	New York, USA	21–26	May 1988

WOMEN

Track

	hr:min:sec	Name	Venue		Date
15km	49:44·0	Silvana Cruciata (Italy)	Rome, Italy	4	May 1981
20km	1:06:55·5	Rosa Mota (Portugal)	Lisbon, Portugal	14	May 1983

WOMEN (continued)

Track	hr:min:sec				
25km	1:29:30	Karolina Szabo (Hungary)	Budapest, Hungary	23	Apr 1988
30km	1:47:06	Karolina Szabo (Hungary)	Budapest, Hungary	23	Apr 1988
50km	3:26:44	Carolyn Hunter-Rowe (GB)	Barry, S Glam	7	Mar 1993
50miles	6:14:34**	Ann Trason (USA)	Hayward, California, USA	3-4	Aug 1991
100km	7:48:15**	Ann Trason (USA)	Hayward, California, USA	3-4	Aug 1991
100miles	14:29:44	Ann Trason (USA)	Santa Rosa, California, USA	18-19	Mar 1989
200km	19:28:48	Eleanor Adams (GB)	Melbourne, Australia	19-20	Aug 1989
200miles	39:09:03	Hilary Walker (GB)	Blackpool, Lancashire	5-6	Nov 1988
500km	77:53:46	Eleanor Adams (GB)	Colac, Australia	13-15	Nov 1989
500miles	130:59:58	Sandra Barwick (New Zealand)	Campbelltown, Australia	18-23	Nov 1990

kilometres					
1hour	18·084	Silvana Cruciata (Italy)	Rome, Italy	4	May 1981
24hours	240·169	Eleanor Adams (GB)	Melbourne, Australia	19-20	Aug 1989
48hours	366·512	Hilary Walker (GB)	Blackpool, Lancashire	5-7	Nov 1988
6days	883·631	Sandra Barwick (New Zealand)	Campbelltown, Australia	18-24	Nov 1990

Road*	hr:min:sec				
30km	1:38:27	Ingrid Kristiansen (Norway)	London	10	May 1987
50km	3:08:13	Frith van der Merwe (South Africa)	Claremont-Kirstenbosch	25	Mar 1989
50miles	5:40:18	Ann Trason (USA)	Houston, Texas, USA	23	Feb 1991
100km	7:18:57	Birgit Lennartz (West Germany)	Hanau, Germany	28	May 1989
100miles	13:47:41	Ann Trason (USA)	Queens, New York	4	May 1991
200km	19:22:05	Ann Trason (USA)	Queens, New York	16-17	Sep 1989
	(indoors) 19:00:31	Eleanor Adams (GB)	Milton Keynes	3-4	Feb 1990
1000km	7d 11hr 11min 00sec	Sandra Barwick (New Zealand)	Queens, New York	16-23	Sep 1991
1000miles	12d 14hr 38in 40sec	Sandra Barwick (New Zealand)	Queens, New York	16-29	Sep 1991

*Where superior to track bests and run on properly measured road courses. It should be noted that road times must be assessed with care as course conditions can vary considerably.

**Timed on one running watch only.

Roof of the world run

Ultra runner Hilary Walker (b. 9 Nov 1953) ran the length of the Friendship Highway from Lhasa, Tibet to Kathmandu, Nepal, a distance of 950km *590 miles*, in 14 days 9 hrs 36 min from 18 Sep–2 Oct 1991. The run was made at an average altitude of 4200 m *13780 ft* with a maximum height attained of 5220 m *17126 ft* at Jia Tsuo La.

Backwards running

Timothy 'Bud' Badyna (USA) ran the fastest marathon in 4 hr 15 sec at Colombus, Ohio, USA on 10 Nov 1991. He also ran 10 km in 45 min 37 sec at Toledo, Ohio, USA on 13 Jul 1991. Donald Davis (USA) (b. 10 Feb 1960) ran 1 mile in 6 min 7·1 sec at the University of Hawaii on 21 Feb 1983. Ferdie Ato Adoboe (Ghana) ran 100 yd in 12·7 sec (100 m in 13·6 sec) at Smith's College, Northampton, Massachusetts, USA on 25 Jul 1991.

Dr Ron Hill (b. 21 Sep 1938), the 1969 European and 1970 Commonwealth marathon champion, has not missed a day's training since 20 Dec 1964. His meticulously compiled training log shows a total of 203059 km *126 202 miles* from 3 Sep 1956 to 17 May 1993. He has finished 114 marathons, all sub 2:52 and has raced in 54 nations.

The greatest competitive distance run in a year is 8855 km *5502 miles* by Malcolm Campbell (GB) (b. 17 Nov 1934) in 1985.

1000 hours Ron Grant (Australia) ran 3 km within an hour, every hour, for 1000 consecutive hours at New Farm Park, Brisbane, Australia on 6 Feb–20 Mar 1991.

Mass relay records The record for 100 miles *160·9 km* by 100 runners from one club is 7 hr 53 min 52·1 sec by Baltimore Road Runners Club, Towson, Maryland, USA on 17 May 1981. The women's record is 10 hr 47 min 9·3 sec on 3 Apr 1977 by the San Francisco Dolphins Southend Running Club, USA. The record for 100 × 100 m is 19 min 14·19 sec by a team from Antwerp at Merksem, Belgium on 23 Sep 1989.

The longest relay ever run was 17391 km *10 806 miles* by 23 runners of the Melbourne Fire Brigade, around Australia on Highway No. 1, in 50 days 43 min, 6 Aug–25 Sep 1991. The most participants is 6500, 260 teams of 25, for the Batavierenrace from Nijmegen to Enschede, Netherlands on 25 Apr 1992. The greatest distance covered in 24 hours by a team of ten is 450·978 km *280·224 miles* by Oxford Striders RC at East London, South Africa on 5–6 Oct 1990.

Highland Games The weight and height of cabers (Gaelic *cabar*) vary considerably. Extreme values are 7·62 m *25 ft* and 127 kg *280 lb*. The Braemar caber (5·86 m *19 ft 3 in* and 54·4 kg *120 lb*) in Grampian was untossed from 1891 until 1951 when George Clark (1907–86) succeeded in pitching it to revolve longitudinally, landing with its base away from the competitor, without deviation from a straight line.

The best authentic mark recorded for throwing the 56 lb weight for height, using one hand only is 5·23 m *17 ft 2 in* by Geoffrey Lewis Capes (GB) (b. 23 Aug 1949) at Lagos, Nigeria on 5 Dec 1982. The best throw recorded for the Scots hammer is 46·08 m *151 ft 2 in* by William Anderson (b. 6 Oct 1938) at Lochearnhead on 26 Jul 1969.

Marathon

Oldest The Boston marathon, the world's longest-lasting major marathon, was first held on 19 Apr 1897 and covered 39 km *24 miles 1232 yd*.

Fastest It should be noted that courses may vary in severity. The following are the best times recorded, all on courses whose distance has been verified.

The world records are: (men) 2 hr 6 min 50 sec by Belayneh Dinsamo (Ethiopia) (b. 28 Jun 1965) at Rotterdam, Netherlands on 17 Apr 1988 and (women) 2 hr 21 min 6 sec by Ingrid Kristiansen (*née* Christensen) (Norway) (b. 21 Mar 1956) at London on 21 Apr 1985.

The British records are: (men) 2hr 7min 13sec by Stephen Henry Jones (b. 4 Aug 1955) at Chicago, Illinois, USA on 20 Oct 1985 and (women) 2hr 25min 56sec by Véronique Marot (b. 16 Sep 1955) at London on 23 Apr 1989.

Most competitors The record number of confirmed finishers in a marathon is 25797 from 26900 starters in the New York City on 3 Nov 1991. A record 105 men ran under 2hr 20min and 46 under 2hr 15min in the World Cup marathon at London on 21 Apr 1991, and a record 6 men ran under 2hr 10min at Fukuoka, Japan on 4 Dec 1983 and at London on 23 Apr 1989. A record 9 women ran under 2hr 30min in the first Olympic marathon for women at Los Angeles, USA on 5 Aug 1984.

Most run by an individual Sy Mah (Canada) (1926–88) ran 524 marathons of 26miles 385yd or longer from 1967 to his death in 1988. He paced himself to take 3½hr each run.

John A. Kelley (USA) (b. 6 Sep 1907) has finished the Boston Marathon 61 times, winning in 1933 and 1945, to 1992.

Three in three days The fastest combined time for three marathons in three days is 8hr 22min 31sec by Raymond Hubbard (Belfast 2hr 45min 55sec, London 2hr 48min 45sec and Boston 2hr 47min 51sec) on 16–18 Apr 1988.

Oldest finishers The oldest man to complete a marathon was Dimitrion Yordanidis (Greece), aged 98, in Athens, Greece on 10 Oct 1976. He finished in 7 hr 33 min. Thelma Pitt-Turner (New Zealand) set the women's record in August 1985, completing the Hastings, New Zealand marathon in 7 hr 58 min at the age of 82.

Half marathon

The distance of a half the full marathon has become established in recent years as one of the most popular for road races. In 1992 the IAAF held the first official world championships at this distance.

The world best time on a properly measured course is 59min 47sec by Moses Tanui (Kenya) (b. 20 Aug 1965) at Milan, Italy on 3 Apr 1993. The British best is 60min 59sec by Steve Jones from Newcastle to South Shields, Tyneside on 8 Jun 1986.

Ingrid Kristiansen (Norway) ran 66min 40sec at Sandes, Norway on 5 Apr 1987, but the measurement of the course has not been confirmed. She holds the recognised best by a woman with 68min 32sec at New Bedford, USA on 19 Mar 1989. Liz McColgan ran 67min 11sec at Tokyo, Japan on 26 Jan 1992, but the course was 33m downhill, a little more than the allowable 1 in 1000 drop; she also ran a British best of 68min 42sec at Dundee, Tayside on 11 Oct 1992.

Walking

Most Olympic medals Walking races have been included in the Olympic events since 1906. The only walker to win three gold medals has been Ugo Frigerio (Italy) (1901–68) with the 3000m in 1920, and 10000m in 1920 and 1924. He also holds the record of most medals with four (he won the bronze medal at 50000m in 1932), a total shared with Vladimir Stepanovich Golubnichiy (USSR) (b. 2 Jun 1936), who won gold medals for the 20000m in 1960 and 1968, the silver in 1972 and the bronze in 1964.

The best British performance has been two gold medals by George Edward Larner (1875–1949) for the 3500m and the 10 miles in 1908, but Ernest James Webb (1872–1937) won three medals, being twice 'walker-up' to Larner and finishing second in the 10000m in 1912.

Most titles Four-time Olympian, Ronald Owen Laird (b. 31 May 1938) of the New York AC won a total of 65 US national titles from 1958 to 1976, plus four Canadian Championships.

The greatest number of UK national titles won by a British walker is 27 by Vincent Paul Nihill (b. 5 Sep 1939) from 1963 to 1975.

Longest race The Paris–Colmar, until 1980 Strasbourg–Paris, event in France (instituted 1926 in the reverse direction), now about 524km *325 miles*, is the world's longest annual race walk.

The fastest performance is by Robert Pietquin (Belgium) (b. 1938) who walked 507km *315 miles* in the 1980 race in 60hr 1min 10sec (after deducting

Double world champion and world record holder Maurizio Damilano.

(Photo: Allsport/Gray Mortimore)

4hr compulsory stops). This represents an average speed of 8·45 km/h *5·25 mph*. Roger Quémener (France) has won a record seven times, 1979, 1983, 1985–9. The first woman to complete the race was Annie van der Meer (Netherlands) (b. 24 Feb 1947), who was 10th in 1983 in 82hr 10min.

'End to end' The fastest Land's End to John o' Groats walk is 12days 3hr 45min for 1426·4 km *886·3 miles* by WO2 Malcolm Barnish of the 19th Regiment, Royal Artillery from 9–21 Jun 1986. The women's record is 13days 17hr 42min by Ann Sayer (b. 16 Oct 1936), 20 Sep–3 Oct 1980. The Irish 'end to end' record over the 644km *400·2miles* from Malin Head, Donegal to Mizen Head, Cork is 5days 22hr 30min, set by John 'Paddy' Dowling (b. 15 Jun 1929) on 18–24 Mar 1982.

24 hours The greatest distance walked in 24hr is 226·432km *140miles 1229yd* by Paul Forthomme (Belgium) on a road

Track Walking World Records

The International Amateur Athletic Federation recognises men's records at 20km, 30km, 50km and 2hours, and women's at 5km and 10km.

MEN

Event	hr:min:sec	Name, Country and Date of Birth	Venue	Date
10 km	38:02·60	Jozef Pribilinec (Czechoslovakia) (b. 6 Jul 1960)	Banská Bystrica, Czechoslovakia	30 Aug 1985
20 km	1:18:35·2	Stefan Johansson (Sweden) (b. 11 Apr 1967)	Fana, Norway	18 May 1992
30 km	2:01:44·1	Maurizio Damilano (Italy) (b. 6 Apr 1957)	Cuneo, Italy	4 Oct 1992
50 km	3:41:38·4	Raul Gonzalez (Mexico) (b. 29 Feb 1952)	Fana, Norway	25 May 1979
1 hour	15 447 m	Jozef Pribilinec (Czechoslovakia)	Hildesheim, Germany	6 Sep 1986
2 hours	29 572 m	Maurizio Damilano (Italy)	Cuneo, Italy	4 Oct 1992

WOMEN

Event	hr:min:sec	Name, Country and Date of Birth	Venue	Date
3 km	11:51·26	Kerry Ann Saxby (Australia) (b. 2 Jun 1961)	Melbourne, Australia	7 Feb 1991
5 km	20:07·52	Beate Anders (GDR) (b. 4 Feb 1968)	Rostock, Germany	23 Jun 1990
10 km	41:56·23	Nadezhda Ryashkina (USSR) (b. 1967)	Seattle, Washington, USA	24 Jul 1990

Road Walking

It should be noted that severity of road race courses and the accuracy of their measurement may vary, sometimes making comparisons of times unreliable.

WORLD BESTS

MEN

20 km: 1 hr 18 min 13 sec, Pavol Blazek (Czechoslovakia) (b. 9 Jul 1958) at Hildesheim, Germany on 16 Sep 1990.

30 km: 2 hr 2 min 41 sec, Andrey Perlov (USSR) (b. 12 Dec 1961) at Sochi on 19 Feb 1989.

50 km: 3 hr 37 min 41 sec, Andrey Perlov (USSR) at Leningrad, USSR on 5 Aug 1989.

WOMEN

10 km: 41 min 30 sec, Kerry Ann Saxby (Australia) (b. 2 Jun 1961) at Canberra, Australia on 27 Aug 1988.

20 km: 1 hr 29 min 40 sec, Kerry Saxby at Värnamo, Sweden on 13 May 1988.

50 km: 4 hr 50 min 51 sec, Sandra Brown (GB) (b. 1 Apr 1949) at Basildon, Essex on 13 Jul 1991.

BRITISH BESTS

MEN

20 km: 1 hr 22 min 03 sec, Ian Peter McCombie (b. 11 Jan 1961) at Seoul, South Korea on 23 Sep 1988.

30 km: 2 hr 7 min 56 sec, Ian Peter McCombie at Edinburgh, Lothian on 27 Apr 1986.

50 km: 3 hr 51 min 37 sec, Christopher Lloyd Maddocks (b. 28 Mar 1957) at Burrator, Devon on 28 Oct 1990.

WOMEN

10 km: 45 min 42 sec, Lisa Martine Langford (b. 15 Mar 1967) at New York, USA on 3 May 1987.

course at Woluwe, Belgium on 13–14 Oct 1984. The best by a woman is 211·25 km *131·27 miles* by Annie van der Meer-Timmermann (Netherlands) at Rouen, France on 10 Apr–11 May 1986.

Backwards walking The greatest ever exponent of reverse pedestrianism has been Plennie L. Wingo (b. 24 Jan 1895) then of Abilene, Texas, USA who completed his 12 875 km *8000 mile* trans-continental walk from Santa

---

Walking on hands

The distance record for walking on hands is 1400 km *870 miles*, by Johann Hurlinger of Austria, who in 55 daily 10-hr stints walked from Vienna to Paris in 1900, averaging 2·54 km/h *1·58 mph*. Shin Don-mok of South Korea completed a 50 m inverted sprint in 17·44 sec on 14 Nov 1986. A four-man relay team of David Lutterman, Brendan Price, Philip Savage and Danny Scannell covered 1 mile *1·6 km* in 24 min 48 sec on 15 Mar 1987 at Knoxville, Tennessee, USA.

Monica, California, USA to Istanbul, Turkey from 15 Apr 1931 to 24 Oct 1932. The longest distance recorded for walking backwards in 24 hr is 153·52 km *95·40 miles* by Anthony Thornton (USA) in Minneapolis, Minnesota, USA on 31 Dec 1988–1 Jan 1989.

Badminton

World championships *Individual (instituted 1977)* A record five titles have been won by Park Joo-bong (South Korea) (b. 5 Dec 1964), men's doubles 1985 and 1991 and mixed doubles 1985, 1989 and 1991. Three Chinese players have won two individual world titles: men's singles: Yang Yang (b. 8 Dec 1963) 1987 and 1989; women's singles: Li Lingwei 1983 and 1989; Han Aiping (b. 22 Apr 1962) 1985 and 1987.

Team The most wins at the men's World Team Badminton Championships for the Thomas Cup (instituted 1948) is eight by Indonesia (1958, 1961, 1964, 1970, 1973, 1976, 1979 and 1984). The most wins at the women's World Team Badminton Championships for the Uber Cup (instituted 1956) is five by: Japan (1966, 1969, 1972, 1978 and 1981); and China (1984, 1986, 1988, 1990 and 1992).

All-England Championships For long the most prestigious championships, they were instituted in 1899. A record eight men's singles were won by Rudy Hartono Kurniawan (Indonesia) (b. 18 Aug 1948), in 1968–74 and 1976. The greatest number of titles won (including

Shortest badminton game

Christine Magnusson (Sweden) beat Martine de Souza (Mauritius) 11–1, 11–0 in 8 min 30 sec at the 1992 Olympic Games at Barcelona, Spain.

Longest rallies

In the men's singles final of the 1987 All-England Championships between Morten Frost (Denmark) and Icuk Sugiarto (Indonesia) there were two successive rallies of over 90 strokes.

doubles) is 21 by George Alan Thomas (1881–1972) between 1903 and 1928. The most by a woman is 17 by: Muriel Lucas (later Mrs King Adams), 1899–1910; and Judith Margaret 'Judy' Hashman (*née* Devlin) (USA) (b. 22 Oct 1935) including a record ten singles, 1954, 1957–8, 1960–64, 1966–7.

Baseball

World Series

Origins Played annually between the winners of the National League and the American League, the World Series was first staged unofficially in 1903, and officially from 1905. The most wins is 22 by the New York Yankees between 1923 and 1978 from a record 33 series appearances from winning the American League titles between 1921 and 1981. The most National League titles is 19 by the Dodgers—Brooklyn 1890–1957, Los Angeles 1958–88.

Most valuable player The only men to have won this award twice are: Sanford 'Sandy' Koufax (b. 30 Dec 1935) (Los Angeles, NL 1963, 1965), Robert 'Bob' Gibson (b. 9 Nov 1935) (St. Louis NL, 1964, 1967) and Reginald Martinez 'Reggie' Jackson (b. 18 May 1946) (Oakland AL 1973, New York AL, 1977).

Attendance The record attendance for a series is 420 784 for the six games when the Los Angeles Dodgers beat the Chicago White Sox 4–2 between 1 and 8 Oct 1959. The single game record is 92 706 for the fifth game of this series at the Memorial Coliseum, Los Angeles on 6 Oct 1959.

Major League

Most games played Peter Edward 'Pete' Rose (b. 14 Apr 1941) played in a record 3562 games with a record 14 053 at bats for Cincinnati NL 1963–78 and 1984–6, Philadelphia NL 1979–83, Montreal NL 1984. Henry Louis 'Lou' Gehrig (1903–41) played in 2130 successive games for the New York Yankees (AL) from 1 Jun 1925 to 30 Apr 1939.

Most home runs *Career* Henry Louis 'Hank' Aaron (b. 5 Feb 1934) holds the major league career record with 755 home runs; 733 for the Milwaukee (1954–65) and Atlanta (1966–74) Braves in the National League and 22 for the Milwaukee Brewers (AL) 1975–6. On 8 Apr 1974 he had bettered the previous record of 714 by George Herman 'Babe' Ruth (1895–1948). Ruth hit his home runs from 8399 times at bat, the highest home run percentage of 8·5%. Joshua Gibson (1911–47) of Homestead Grays and Pittsburgh Crawfords, Negro League clubs, achieved a career total of nearly

World Series Records

Most series played 14	Lawrence Peter 'Yogi' Berra (New York, AL) 1947–63	
Most series played by pitcher ..11	Edward Charles 'Whitey' Ford (New York, AL) 1950–64	
Most home runs in a game 3	George Herman 'Babe' Ruth (New York, AL) ....6 Oct 1926	
....3	George Herman 'Babe' Ruth (New York, AL) ....9 Oct 1928	
....3	Reginald Martinez Jackson (New York, AL) ....18 Oct 1977	
Runs batted in 6	Robert C. Richardson (New York, AL) ....8 Oct 1960	
Strikeouts 17	Robert Gibson (St Louis, NL)................................ 2 Oct 1968	
Perfect game (9 innings)	Donald James Larson (New York, AL) v Brooklyn . 8 Oct 1956	

Note: AL - American League   *NL - National League*

US Major League Baseball Records

Batting

AVERAGE, Career, ·366 Tyrus Raymond 'Ty' Cobb (Detroit AL, Philadelphia AL) 1905–28. Season, ·440 Hugh Duffy (Boston NL) 1894.

RUNS, Career, 2245 Tyrus Raymond Cobb 1905–28. Season, 192 William Robert Hamilton (Phildelphia NL) 1894.

HOME RUNS, Career[*1], 755 Henry 'Hank' Aaron (Milwaukee NL, Atlanta NL, Milwaukee AL) 1954–76. Season, 61 Roger Eugene Maris (New York AL) 1961.

RUNS BATTED IN, Career, 2297 Henry 'Hank' Aaron 1954–76. Season, 190 Lewis Rober 'Hack' Wilson (Chicago NL) 1930. Game, 12 James LeRoy Bottomley (St Louis NL) 16 Sep 1924. Innings, 7 Edward Cartwright (St Louis AL) 23 Sep 1890.

BASE HITS, Career, 4256 Peter Edward Rose (Cincinnati NL, Philadelphia NL, Montreal NL, Cincinnati NL) 1963–86. Season, 257 George Harold Sisler (St Louis AL) 1920.

TOTAL BASES, Career, 6856 Henry 'Hank' Aaron 1954–76. Season, 457 George Herman 'Babe' Ruth (New York AL) 1921.

HITS, Consecutive, 12 Michael Franklin 'Pinky' Higgins (Boston AL) 19–21 Jun 1938; Walter 'Moose' Dropo (Detroit AL) 14–15 Jul 1952.

CONSECUTIVE GAMES BATTED SAFELY, 56 Joseph Paul DiMaggio (New York AL) 15 May–16 Jul 1941.

STOLEN BASES, Career, 1066 Rickey Henley Henderson (Oakland AL) 1979–93. Season, 130 Rickey Henderson 1982.

CONSECUTIVE GAMES PLAYED[*2], 2130 Henry Louis 'Lou' Gehrig (New York AL) 1 Jun 1925–30 April 1939.

GAMES WON, Career, 511 Denton True 'Cy' Young (Cleveland NL, St Louis NL, Boston AL, Cleveland AL, Boston NL) 1890–1911. Season, 60 Charles Gardner Radbourn (Providence NL) 1884.

CONSECUTIVE GAMES WON, 24 Carl Owen Hubbell (New York NL) 1936–7.

Pitching

SHUTOUTS, Career, 113 Walter Perry Johnson (Washington AL) 1907–27. Season, 16 George Washington Bradley (St Louis NL) 1876; Grover Cleveland Alexander (Philadelphia NL) 1916.

STRIKEOUTS, Career, 5678 Lynn Nolan Ryan (New York NL, California AL, Houston NL, Texas AL) 1966–92. Season, 383 Lynn Nolan Ryan (California AL) 1973. (513 Matthew Aloysius Kilroy (Baltimore AA) 1886). Game (9 innings), 20 Roger Clemens (Boston AL) v. Seattle 29 Apr 1986.

NO-HIT GAMES, Career, 7 Lynn Nolan Ryan 1973–91.

EARNED RUN AVERAGE, Season, 0·90 Ferdinand Schupp (140 inns) (New York NL) 1916; 0·96 Hubert 'Dutch' Leonard (222 inns) (Boston AL) 1914; 1·12 Robert Gibson (305 inns) (St Louis NL) 1968.

Note: AL - American League
NL - National League
* Japanese League records that are superior to those in the US major leagues;
[1]868 Sadaharu Oh (Yomiuri) 1959–80.
[2]2215 Sachio Kinugasa (Hiroshima) 1970–87.

---

800 homers including an unofficial record season's total of 75 in 1931.

Season The US major league record for home runs in a season is 61 by Roger Eugene Maris (1934–85) for New York Yankees in 162 games in 1961. 'Babe' Ruth hit 60 in 154 games in 1927 for the New York Yankees. The most official home runs in a minor league season is 72 by Joe Bauman of Roswell Rockets, New Mexico in 1954.

Game The most home runs in a major league game is four, first achieved by Robert Lincoln 'Bobby' Lowe (1868–1951) for Boston *v.* Cinncinnati on 30 May 1894. The feat had been achieved a further ten times since then.

Consecutive games The most consecutive games hitting home runs is eight by Richard Dale Long (b. 6 Feb 1926) for Pittsburgh (NL), 19–28 May 1956 and by

Longest throw of a baseball

Glen Edward Gorbous (b. Canada, 8 Jul 1930) threw 135·88m *445ft 10in* on 1 Aug 1957.

Women Mildred Ella 'Babe' Didrikson (later Mrs Zaharias) (USA) (1914–56) threw 90·2m *296ft* at Jersey City, New Jersey, USA on 25 Jul 1931.

Donald Arthur Mattingly (b. 21 Apr 1961) for New York (AL), July 1987.

Most games won by a pitcher Denton True 'Cy' Young (1867–1955) had a record 511 wins and a record 749 complete games from a total of 906 games and 815 starts in his career for Cleveland NL 1890–98, St Louis NL 1899–1900, Boston AL 1901–08, Cleveland AL 1909–11 and Boston NL 1911. He pitched a record total of 7357 innings.

Cigarette card

The most valuable card is one of the six known baseball series cards of Honus Wagner, who was a non-smoker, which was sold at Sotheby's, New York, USA for $451000 on 22 Mar 1991. The buyers were Bruce McNall, owner of the Los Angeles Kings ice hockey club, and team member Wayne Gretzky, the game's most successful player.

Fastest base runner

The fastest time for circling bases is 13·3sec by Ernest Evar Swanson (1902–73) at Columbus, Ohio, USA in 1932, at an average speed of 29·70km/h *18·45mph*.

Fastest pitcher

Lynn Nolan Ryan (then of the California Angels) (b. 31 Jan 1947) was measured to pitch at 162·3km/h *100·9mph* at Anaheim Stadium, California, USA on 20 Aug 1974.

The career record of most games pitching is 1070 by James Hoyt Wilhelm (b. 26 Jul 1923) for a total of nine teams between 1952 and 1972; he set the career record with 143 wins by a relief pitcher. The season's record is 106 games pitched by Michael Grant Marshall (b. 15 Jan 1943) for Los Angeles (NL) in 1974.

Most consecutive games won by a pitcher Carl Owen Hubbell (1903–88) pitched for the New York Giants to win 24 consecutive games, 16 in 1936 and 8 in 1937.

Most consecutive hits Michael Franklin 'Pinky' Higgins (1909–69) had 12 consecutive hits for Boston (AL) 19–21 Jun 1938. This was equalled by Walter 'Moose' Droppo (b. 30 Jan 1923) for Detroit (AL) 14–15 Jul 1952. Joseph Paul DiMaggio (b. 25 Nov 1914) hit in a record 56 consecutive games for New York in 1941; he was 223 times at bat, with 91 hits, scoring 16 doubles, 4 triples and 15 home runs.

Most consecutive scoreless games Orel Leonard Hershiser IV (b. 16 Sep 1958) pitched a record 59 consecutive shutout innings from 30 Aug to 28 Sep 1988.

Perfect game A perfect nine innings game, in which the pitcher allows the opposition no hits, no runs and does not allow a man to reach first base, was first achieved by John Lee Richmond (1857–1929) for Worcester against Cleveland in the NL on 12 Jun 1880. There have been 13 subsequent perfect games over nine innings, but no pitcher has achieved this feat more than once. On 26 May 1959 Harvey Haddix Jr. (b. 18 Sep 1925) for Pittsburgh pitched perfect game for 12 innings against Milwaukee in the National League, but lost in the 13th.

Cy Young award Awarded annually from 1956 to the outstanding pitcher on the major leagues, the most wins is four by Stephen Norman Carlton (b. 22 Dec 1944) (Philadelphia, NL) 1972, 1977, 1980, 1982.

Youngest player Frederick Joseph Chapman (1872–1957) pitched for Philadelphia in the American Association at 14 yr 239 days on 22 Jul 1887, but did not play again.

The youngest major league player of all time was the Cincinnati pitcher Joseph Henry Nuxhall (b. 30 Jul 1928), who played one game in June 1944, aged 15yr 314days. He did not play again in the NL until 1952. The youngest player to play in a minor league game was Joe Louis Reliford (b. 29 Nov 1939) who played for the Fitzgerald Pioneers against Statesboro Pilots in the Georgia State League, aged 12yr 234days on 19 Jul 1952.

Oldest player Leroy Robert 'Satchel' Paige (1906–82) pitched for Kansas City A's (AL) at 59 years 80 days on 25 Sep 1965.

Record attendances The all-time season record for attendances for both leagues is 56 888 512 in 1991. The record for an individual league is 32 117 588 for the American League in 1991. The record for an individual team is 4 028 318 for the home games of the Toronto Blue Jays at their all-weather SkyDome with its retractable roof in 1992.

An estimated 114 000 spectators watched a game between Australia and an American Services team in a demonstration event during the Olympic Games at Melbourne on 1 Dec 1956.

Longest home run In a minor league game at Emeryville Ball Park, California, USA on 4 Jul 1929, Roy Edward 'Dizzy' Carlyle (1900–56) hit a home run measured at 188·4m *618ft*.

In 1919 'Babe' Ruth hit a 178·9m *587ft* homer in a Boston Red Sox *v.* New York Giants exhibition match at Tampa, Florida, USA.

Basketball

Most titles *Olympic* The USA has won ten men's Olympic titles. From the time the sport was introduced to the Games in 1936 to 1972, they won 63 consecutive matches until they lost 50–51 to the USSR in the disputed Final in Munich. Since then they have won a further 29 matches and had another loss to the USSR (in 1988).

Basketball dribbling

Peter del Masto (USA) dribbled a basketball without 'travelling' from near Lee to Provincetown, Massachusetts, a distance of 426·8km *265·2 miles*, from 12–25 Aug 1989.

Bob Nickerson of Gallitzin, Pennsylvania, Dave Davlin of Garland, Texas and Jeremy Kable of Highspire, Pennsylvania, all USA, have each successfully demonstrated the ability to dribble four basketballs simultaneously.

The women's title has been won a record three times by the USSR in 1976, 1980 and 1992 (by the Unified team from the republics of the ex-USSR).

World The USSR has won most titles at both the men's World Championships (instituted 1950) with three (1967, 1974 and 1982) and women's (instituted 1953) with six (1959, 1964, 1967, 1971, 1975 and 1983). Yugoslavia have also won three men's world titles: 1970, 1978 and 1990.

European The most wins in the European Championships for men is 14 by the USSR, and in the women's event 21 also by the USSR, winning all but the 1958 championship since 1950, in this biennial contest.

The most European Champions Cup (instituted 1957) wins is seven by Real Madrid, Spain 1964–5, 1967–8, 1974, 1978 and 1980.

The women's title has been won 18 times by Daugava, Riga, Latvia between 1960 and 1982.

English The most English National Championship titles (instituted 1936) have been won by London Central YMCA, with eight wins in 1957–8, 1960, 1962–4, 1967 and 1969.

The English National League title has been won seven times by Crystal Palace 1974, 1976–8, 1980 and 1982–3. In the 1989/90 season Kingston won all five domestic trophies; the National League and Championship play-offs, the National Cup, League Cup and WIBC. The English Women's Cup (instituted 1965) has been won a record eight times by the Tigers, 1972–3, 1976–80 and 1982.

Highest score In a senior international match Iraq scored 251 against Yemen (33) at New Delhi in November 1982 at the Asian Games.

The highest in a British Championship is 125 by England v. Wales (54) on 1 Sep 1978. England beat Gibraltar 130–45 on 31 Aug 1978.

US College The NCAA aggregate record is 399 when Troy State (258) beat De Vry Institute, Atlanta (141) at Troy, Alabama on 12 Jan 1992. Troy's total is the highest individual team score in a match.

United Kingdom The highest score recorded in a match is 250 by the Nottingham YMCA Falcons v. Mansfield Pirates at Nottingham on 18 Jun 1974. It was a handicap competition and Mansfield received 120 points towards their total of 145.

The highest score in a senior National League match is 174 by Chiltern Fast Break v. Swindon Rakers (40) on 13 Oct 1990.

The highest in the National Cup is 157 by Solent Stars v. Corby (57) on 6 Jan 1991.

Individual Mats Wermelin (Sweden), age 13, scored all 272 points in a 272–0 win in a regional boys' tournament in Stockholm, Sweden on 5 Feb 1974.

The record score by a woman is 156 points by Marie Boyd (now Eichler) of Central HS, Lonaconing, Maryland, USA in a 163–3 defeat of Ursaline Academy, Cumbria on 25 Feb 1924.

The highest score by a British player is 124 points by Paul Ogden for St Albans School, Oldham (226) v. South Chadderton (82) on 9 Mar 1982.

The highest individual score in a league match for Britain is 108 by Lewis Young for Forth Steel in his team's 154–74 win over Stirling in the Scottish League Division One at Stirling on 2 Mar 1985.

The record in an English National League (Div. One) or Cup match is 73 points by Terry Crosby (USA) for Bolton in his team's 120–106 defeat by Manchester Giants at Altrincham,

532

The tallest in NBA history has been Manute Bol (Sudan) (b. 16 Oct 1962) of the Washington Bullets and Golden State Warriors at 2·30m *7ft 6¾in*. He made his pro début in 1985.

Cheshire on 26 Jan 1985; by Billy Hungrecker in a semi-final play-off for Worthing v. Plymouth at Worthing, W Sussex on 20 Mar 1988; and by Renaldo Lawrence for Stevenage in his team's 113–102 win against Gateshead on 30 Dec 1989.

National Basketball Association

Most titles Boston Celtics have won a record 16 NBA titles, 1957, 1959–66, 1968–9, 1974, 1976, 1981, 1984, 1986.

Highest score The highest aggregate score in an NBA match is 370 when the Detroit Pistons (186) beat the Denver Nuggets (184) at Denver on 13 Dec 1983. Overtime was played after a 145–145 tie in regulation time. The record in regulation time is 320, when the Golden State Warriors beat Denver 162–158 on 2 Nov 1990. The most points in a half is 107 by the Phoenix Suns in the first half against Denver on 11 Nov 1990. The most points in a quarter is 58 (fourth) by Buffalo at Boston on 20 Oct 1972.

Individual scoring Wilton Norman 'Wilt' Chamberlain (b. 21 Aug 1936) set an NBA record with 100 points for Philadelphia v New York at Hershey, Pennsylvania on 2 Mar 1962. This included a record 36 field goals and 28 free throws (from 32 attempts) and a record 59 points in a half (the second). The free throws game record was equalled by Adrian Dantley (b. 28 Feb 1956) for Utah v. Houston at Las Vegas on 5 Jan 1984. The most points scored in an NBA game in one quarter is 33 (second) by George Gervin for San Antonio v. New Orleans on 9 Apr 1978.

Most games Kareem Abdul-Jabbar (formerly Ferdinand Lewis Alcindor) (b. 16 Apr 1947) took part in a record 1560 NBA regular season games over 20 seasons, totalling 57 446 minutes played, for

In his career, 1979–91, for the Los Angeles Lakers, Magic Johnson had a NBA record 9921 assists.

(Photo: Allsport (USA)/Ken Levine)

the Milwaukee Bucks, 1969–75, and the Los Angeles Lakers, 1975–89. He also played a record 237 play-off games. The most successive games is 906 by Randy Smith for Buffalo, San Diego, Cleveland and New York from 18 Feb 1972 to 13 Mar 1983. The record for complete games played in one season is 79 by Wilt Chamberlain for Philadelphia in 1962, when he was on court for a record 3882 minutes. Chamberlain went through his entire career of 1045 games without fouling out.

Most points Kareem Abdul-Jabbar set NBA career records with 38 387 points (average 24·6 points per game), including 15 837 field goals in regular season games, and 5762 points, including 2356 field goals in play-off games. The previous record holder, Wilt Chamberlain, had an average of 30·1 points per game for his total of 31 419 for Philadelphia 1959–62, San Francisco 1962–5, Philadelphia 1964–8 and Los Angeles 1968–73. He scored 50 or more points in 118 games, including 45 in 1961/2 and 30 in 1962/3 to the next best career total of 17. He set season's records for points and scoring average with 4029 at 50·4 per game, and also for field goals, 1597, for Philadelphia in 1961/2. The highest career average for players exceeding 10 000 points is 32·3 by Michael Jordan (b. 17 Feb 1963), 21 541 points in 667 games for the Chicago Bulls, 1984–93. Jordan also holds the career scoring average record for play-offs at 36·4 for 4040 points in 111 games, 1984–93.

Winning margin The greatest winning margin in an NBA game is 68 points when the Cleveland Cavaliers beat the Miami Heat, 148–80 on 17 Dec 1991.

Winning streak Los Angeles Lakers won a record 33 NBA games in succession from 5 Nov 1971 to 7 Jan 1972, as during the 1971/2 season they won a record 69 games with 13 losses.

Youngest and oldest player The youngest NBA player has been Bill Willoughby (b. 20 May 1957), who made his début for Atlanta Hawks on 23 Oct 1975 at 18 yr 156 days. The oldest NBA regular player was Kareem Abdul-Jabbar, who made his last appearance for the Los Angeles Lakers at 42 yr 59 days in 1989.

Other Records

Most points The records for the most points scored in a college career are (women): 4061, Pearl Moore of Francis Marion College, Florence, South Carolina, USA, 1975–9; (men): 4045 by Travis Grant for Kentucky State, USA in 1969–72.

In the English National League, Russ Saunders (b. 25 Nov 1957) scored 5504 points, 1982–93. The most apperances in the League is 383 by Paul Philp (b. 23 Dec 1952), 1972–93.

Tallest players Suleiman 'Ali Nashnush (1943–91) was reputed to be 2·45m 8ft ¼ in when he played for the Libyan team in 1962.

British Christopher Greener of London Latvians was 2·29m 7ft 6¼ in and made his international début for England v. France on 17 Dec 1969.

Shooting speed The greatest goal-shooting demonstration has been by Ted St Martin of Jacksonville, Florida, USA who, on 25 Jun 1977, scored 2036 consecutive free throws. On 11 Jun 1992 Jeff Liles scored 231 out of 240 attempts in 10 minutes at Southern Nazarene University, Bethany, Oklahoma, USA. He repeated this total of 231 (241 attempts) on 16 June. This speed record is achieved using one ball and one rebounder.

In 24 hours Fred Newman scored 20371 free throws from a total of 22049 taken (92·39 per cent) at Caltech, Pasadena, California, USA on 29–30 Sep 1990.

Steve Bontrager (USA) (b. 1 Mar 1959) of Polycell Kingston scored 21 points in a minute from seven positions in a demonstration for BBC TV's *Record Breakers* on 29 Oct 1986.

Longest goal Christopher Eddy (b. 13 Jul 1971) scored a field goal, measured at 27·49m *90ft 2¼ in*, for Fairview High School *v.* Iroquois High School at Erie, Pennsylvania, USA on 25 Feb 1989. The shot was made as time expired in overtime and it won the game for Fairview, 51–50.

British A distance of 23·10m *75ft 9½ in* is claimed by David Tarbatt (b. 23 Jan 1949) of Altofts Aces *v.* Harrogate Demons at Featherstone, W Yorks on 27 Jan 1980.

Largest attendance The largest crowd for a basketball match is 80000 for the final of the European Cup Winners' Cup between AEK Athens (89) and Slavia Prague (82) at the Olympic stadium, Athens, Greece on 4 Apr 1968.

Billiards

Most titles *World* The greatest number of World Championships (instituted 1870) won by one player is eight by John Roberts Jr (GB) (1847–1919) in 1870 (twice), 1871, 1875 (twice), 1877 and 1885 (twice). The record for world amateur titles is four by Robert James Percival Marshall (Australia) (b. 10 Apr 1910) in 1936, 1938, 1951 and 1962.

Britain The greatest number of United Kingdom professional titles (instituted

Keith Sheard scored 28530 in 19min 5sec in a league game at the Crown and Thistle, Headington, Oxford on 9 Jul 1984. Sheard scored 1500 points in a minute on BBC TV's *Record Breakers* on 23 Sep 1986.

The highest score in 24 hours by a team of five is 1 754 730 by Les Green, Ricard Powell, Kevin Clark, Mick Lingham and Curt Driver of The Shipwrights Arms, Chatham, Kent on 26–27 May 1990.

Most three-cushion titles William F. Hoppe (USA) (1887–1959) won 51 billiards championships in all forms spanning the pre- and post-international era from 1906 to 1952.
UMB Raymond Ceulemans (Belgium) (b. 12 Jul 1935) has won 20 world three-cushion championships (1963–73, 1975–80, 1983, 1985, 1990).

1934) won is seven (1934–9 and 1947) by Joe Davis (1901–78), who also won four world titles (1928–30 and 1932). The greatest number of English Amateur Championships (instituted 1888) won is 15 by Norman Dagley (b. 27 Jun 1930) in 1965–6, 1970–75, 1978–84. The record number of women's titles is nine by Vera Selby (b. 13 Mar 1930), 1970–78. Uniquely, Norman Dagley has won the English Amateur Championships (as above), World Amateur Championships (1971, 1975), United Kingdom Professional Championship (1987) and World Professional Championship (1987).

Youngest champion The youngest winner of the world professional title is Mike Russell (b. 3 Jun 1969), aged 20yr 49days, when he won at Leura, Australia on 23 Jul 1989.

Highest breaks Tom Reece (1873–1953) made an unfinished break of 499135, including 249152 cradle cannons (two points each) in 85hr 49min against Joe Chapman at Burroughes' Hall, Soho Square, London between 3 Jun and 6 Jul 1907. This was not recognized because press and public were not continuously present.

The highest certified break made by the anchor cannon is 42746 by William Cook (England) from 29 May to 7 Jun 1907.

The official world record under the then baulk-line rule is 1784 by Joe Davis in the United Kingdom Championship on 29 May 1936.

Walter Albert Lindrum (Australia) (1898–1960) made an official break of 4137 in 2hr 55min against Joe Davis at Thurston's on 19–20 Jan 1932, before the baulk-line rule was in force. Geet Sethi (India) made a break of 1276 in the World Professional Championship in Bombay, India on 1 Oct 1992.

The highest break recorded in amateur competition is 1149 by Michael Ferreira (India) at Calcutta, India on 15 Dec 1978. Under the more stringent 'two pot' rule, restored on 1 Jan 1983, the highest break is Ferreira's 962 unfinished in a tournament at Bombay, India on 29 Apr 1986.

Fastest century Walter Lindrum made an unofficial 100 break in 27·5sec in Australia on 10 Oct 1952. His official record is 100 in 46·0sec set in Sydney, Australia in 1941.

Board Games

Chess

World Championships World champions have been officially recognized since 1886. The longest undisputed tenure was 26yr 337days by Dr Emanuel Lasker (1868–1941) of Germany, from 1894 to 1921.

The women's world championship title was held by Vera Francevna Stevenson-Menchik (USSR, later GB) (1906–44) from 1927 until her death, and was successfully defended a record seven times.

Team The USSR has won the biennial men's team title (Olympiad) a record 18 times between 1952 and 1990, and the women's title 11 times from its introduction in 1957 to 1986.

Youngest Gary Kimovich Kasparov (USSR) (b. 13 Apr 1963) won the title on 9 Nov 1985 at 22yr 210 days.

Maya Grigoryevna Chiburdanidze (USSR) (b. 17 Jan 1961) won the women's title in 1978 when only 17.

Oldest Wilhelm Steinitz (Austria, later USA) (1836–1900) was 58yr 10days when he lost his title to Lasker on 26 May 1894.

Most active Anatoliy Yevgenyevich Karpov (USSR) (b. 23 May 1951) in his tenure as champion, 1975–85, averaged 45·2 competitive games per year, played in 32 tournaments and finished first in 26.

Most British titles The most British titles have been won by Dr Jonathan Penrose (b. 7 Oct 1933) with ten titles in 1958–63, 1966–9. Rowena Mary Bruce (*née* Dew) (b. 15 May 1919) won 11 women's titles between 1937 and 1969.

Grand Masters The youngest individual to qualify as an International Grand Master is Judit Polgar (Hungary) (b. 23 Jul 1976), aged 15yr 150days on 20 Dec 1991.

The youngest Briton to qualify is Michael Adams (b. 17 Nov 1971), aged 17yr 216days on 21 Jul 1989.

The first British player to attain official International Grand Master status was Anthony John Miles (b. 23 Apr 1955) on 24 Feb 1976.

Highest rating The highest rating ever attained on the officially adopted Elo System (devised by Arpad E. Elo (1903–92)) is 2805 by Gary Kasparov (USSR) at the end of 1992.

The highest-rated woman player is Judit Polgar (Hungary), who achieved a peak rating of 2595 at the end of 1992.

The top British player on the Elo list is Nigel David Short (b. 1 Jun 1965) who reached a peak rating of 2685 at the end of 1991.

The top British woman is Susan Kathryn Arkell (*née* Walker) (b. 28 Oct 1965) who reached a peak of 2355 on 1 Jul 1988.

Least games lost by a world champion José Raúl Capablanca (Cuba) (1888–1942) lost only 34 games (out of 571) in his adult career, 1909–39. He

Gary Kasparov and Nigel Short will contest the World Championship at chess, beginning in September 1993. The prize money is a record £1·7 million with the winner receiving £1 million.

(Photos: Allsport/Howard Boylan & Shaun Botterill)

Slowest moves The slowest reported moving (before time clocks were used) in an official event is reputed to have been by Louis Paulsen (Germany) (1833–91) against Paul Charles Morphy (USA) (1837–84) at the first American Chess Congress, New York on 29 Oct 1857. The game ended in a draw on move 56 after 15 hours of play of which Paulsen used *c.* 11 hours.

Grand Master Friedrich Sämisch (Germany) (1896–1975) ran out of the allotted time (2 hr 30 min for 45 moves) after only 12 moves, in Prague, Czechoslovakia, in 1938.

The slowest move played, since time clocks were introduced, was at Vigo, Spain in 1980 when Francisco R. Torres Trois (b. 3 Sep 1946) took 2 hr 20 min for his seventh move *v.* Luis M. C. P. Santos (b. 30 Jun 1955).

The Master game with most moves on record was one of 269 moves, when Ivan Nikolić drew with Goran Arsović in a Belgrade, Yugoslavia tournament, on 17 Feb 1989. It took a total of 20 hr 15 min.

<hr>

Draughts

World champions Walter Hellman (USA) (1916–75) won a record eight world titles during his tenure as world champion 1948–75.

British titles The British Championship (biennial) was inaugurated in 1886 and has been won six times by Samuel Cohen (London) (1905–72), 1924, 1927, 1929, 1933, 1937 and 1939. John McGill (Kilbride) (b. 1936) won six Scottish titles between 1959 and 1974. William Edwards (b. 28 Jan 1915) of Abercynon, Wales won the English open title on a record five successive occasions – 1979, 1981, 1983, 1985 and 1987.

In 1986, Andrew Knapp (b. 19 Oct 1966), on his first attempt, became at 19 yr 322 days the youngest ever winner of the English Amateur Championship (instituted 1910).

Youngest and oldest national champion Asa A. Long (b. 20 Aug 1904) became the youngest US national champion, aged 18 yr 64 days, when he won in Boston, Massachusetts, USA on 23

was unbeaten from 10 Feb 1916 to 21 Mar 1924 (63 games) and was world champion 1921–7.

Most opponents The record for most consecutive games played is 663 by Vlastimil Hort (Czechoslovakia, later Germany) (b. 12 Jan 1944) over 32½ hours at Porz, Germany on 5–6 Oct 1984. He played 60–120 opponents at a time, scoring over 80 per cent wins and averaging 30 moves per game. He also holds the record for most games simultaneously, 201 during 550 consecutive games of which he only lost ten, in Seltjarnes, Iceland on 23–24 Apr 1977.

Eric G. J. Knoppert (Netherlands) (b. 20 Sep 1959) played 500 games of 10-minute chess against opponents averaging 2002 on the Elo scale on 13–16 Sep 1985. He scored 413 points (1 for win, ½ for draw), a success rate of 82·6 per cent.

Oldest chess pieces

The oldest pieces identified as chess pieces were found at Nashipur, datable to *c.*AD 900.

Domino stacking

David Coburn successfully stacked 291 dominoes on a single supporting domino on 19 Aug 1988 in Miami, Florida, USA.

Domino toppling

The greatest number set up single-handed and toppled is 281581 out of 320236 by Klaus Friedrich, 22, at Fürth, Germany on 27 Jan 1984. The dominoes fell within 12min 57·3sec, having taken 31 days (10 hr daily) to set up.

Thirty students at Delft, Eindhoven and Twente Technical Universities in the Netherlands set up 1500000 dominoes representing all of the European Community member countries. Of these, 1382101 were toppled by one push on 2 Jan 1988.

Solitaire

The shortest time taken to complete the game is 10·0sec by Stephen Twigge at Scissett Baths, W Yorks on 2 Aug 1991.

Biggest board game

The world's biggest board game was a version of the game, Goose, and was organized by 'Jong Nederland'. It stretched for 638m *697yd* and was played by 1631 participants at Someren, Netherlands on 16 Sep 1989.

___

Oct 1922. He became the oldest, aged 79yr 334days, when he won his sixth title in Tupelo, Mississippi, USA on 21 Jul 1984. He was also world champion 1934–8.

Most opponents Charles Walker played a record 229 games simultaneously, winning 227, drawing 1 and losing 1, at the International Checkers Hall of Fame, Petal, Mississippi, USA on 25 Jan 1992.

The largest number of opponents played without a defeat or draw is 172 by Nate Cohen of Portland, Maine, USA at Portland on 26 Jul 1981. This was not a simultaneous attempt, but consecutive play over a period of four hours.

Newell W. Banks (1887–1977) played 140 games simultaneously, winning 133 and drawing seven, in Chicago, Illinois in 1933. His playing time was 145min, so averaging about one move per sec. In 1947 he played blindfolded for 4hr per day for 45 consecutive days, winning 1331 games, drawing 54 and losing only two, while playing six games at a time.

Longest games In competition the prescribed rate of play is not less than 30 moves per hour with the average game lasting about 90min. In 1958 a game between Dr Marion Tinsley (USA) and Derek Oldbury (GB) lasted 7 hr 30min (played under the 5-minutes-a-move rule).

Scrabble (Crossword Game)

Highest scores The highest competitive game score is 1049 by Phil Appleby (b. 9 Dec 1957) in June 1989. His opponent scored 253 and the margin of victory, 796 points, is also a record.

His score included a single turn of 374 for the word 'OXIDIZERS'. The highest competitive single turn score recorded, however, is 392 by Dr Saladin Karl Khoshnaw (of Kurdish origin) in Manchester in April 1982. He laid down 'CAZIQUES', which means 'native chiefs of West Indian aborigines'.

Most titles British National Championships were instituted in 1971. Philip Nelkon (b. 21 Jul 1956) has won a record four times, 1978, 1981, 1990 and 1992.

World Championship The first world championship was held in London in 1991 and was played in English. The winner was Peter Morris (USA) (b. 1962) who collected a first prize of $10000.

Bobsleigh and Tobogganing

Bobsledding

Most titles The Olympic four-man bob title (instituted 1924) has been won five times by Switzerland (1924, 1936, 1956, 1972 and 1988).

The Olympic two-man bob title (instituted 1932) has been won three times by Switzerland (1948, 1980 and 1992).

The most gold medals won by an individual is three by Meinhard Nehmer (GDR) (b. 13 Jun 1941) and Bernhard Germeshausen (GDR) (b. 21 Aug 1951) in the 1976 two-man, 1976 and 1980 four-man events.

The most medals won is six (two gold, two silver, two bronze) by Eugenio Monti (Italy) (b. 23 Jan 1928), 1956 to 1968.

The only British victory was at two-man bob in 1964 by the Hon. Thomas Robin Valerian Dixon (b. 21 Apr 1935) and Anthony James Dillon Nash (b. 18 Mar 1936).

World and Olympic The world four-man bob title (instituted 1924) has been won 20 times by Switzerland (1924, 1936, 1939, 1947, 1954–7, 1971–3, 1975, 1982–3, 1986–90, 1993) including their five Olympic victories. Switzerland have won the two-man title 16 times (1935, 1947–50, 1953, 1955, 1977–80, 1982–3, 1987, 1990 and 1992) including their three Olympic successes.

Eugenio Monti was a member of eleven world championship crews, eight two-man and three four-man in 1957–68.

Tobogganing

Oldest club The St Moritz Tobogganing Club, Switzerland, founded in 1887, is the oldest toboggan club in the world. It is notable for being the home of the Cresta Run, which dates from 1884.

Cresta Run The course is 1212 m *3977 ft* long with a drop of 157 m *514 ft* and the record is 50·41 sec (av. 86·56 km/h *53·79 mph*) by Christian Bertschinger (Switzerland) (b. 8 Feb 1964) on 23 Feb 1992. On 20 Jan 1991 he set a record from Junction (890 m *2920 ft*) of 41·45 sec.

The greatest number of wins in the Grand National (instituted 1885) is eight by the 1948 Olympic champion Nino Bibbia (Italy) (b. 15 Mar 1922) in 1960–64, 1966, 1968 and 1973; and by Franco Gassner (Switzerland) (b. 2 May 1945) in 1981, 1983–6, 1988–9 and 1991. The greatest number of wins in the Curzon Cup (instituted 1910) is eight by Bibbia in 1950, 1957–8, 1960, 1962–4, and 1969. The only men to have won the four most important races (Curzon Cup, Brabazon Trophy, Morgan Cup and Grand National) in one season are, Bruno Bischofberger (1972), Paul Felder (1974), Nico Baracchi (1982), Franco Gansser (1988) and Christian Bertschinger (1992), all of Switzerland.

The oldest person to have ridden the Cresta Run successfully is Robin Todhunter (GB) (b. 10 Mar 1903), aged 83 yr 329 days on 2 Feb 1987.

Lugeing

Most titles The most successful riders in the World Championships (instituted 1953) have been Thomas Köhler (GDR) (b. 25 Jun 1940), who won the single-seater title in 1962, 1964 (Olympic) and 1967 and shared the two-seater title in 1965, 1967 and 1968 (Olympic).

Margit Schumann (GDR) (b. 14 Sep 1952) has won five women's titles, 1973–5, 1976 (Olympic) and 1977. Steffi Walter (*née* Martin) (GDR) (b. 17 Sep 1962) became the first rider to win two Olympic single-seater luge titles, with victories at the women's event in 1984 and 1988.

Fastest lugeing speed

The highest recorded, photo-timed speed is 137·4 km/h *85·38 mph* by Asle Strand (Norway) at Tandådalens Linbana, Sälen, Sweden on 1 May 1982.

Bowling (Tenpin)

World Championships The World (*Fédération Internationale des Quilleurs*)

Championships were instituted for men in 1954 and for women in 1963.

The highest pinfall in the individual men's event is 5963 (in 28 games) by Ed Luther (USA) at Milwaukee, Wisconsin, USA on 28 Aug 1971.

For the current schedule of 24 games the men's record is 5261 by Richard Clay 'Rick' Steelsmith (b. 1 Jun 1964) and women's record is 4894 by Sandra Jo Shiery (USA), both at Helsinki, Finland in June 1987.

The World Cup (instituted 1965) is contested annually by the national champions of the member countries of the FIQ. The most wins is three by Paeng Nepomuceno (Philippines) (b. 30 Jan 1957), 1976, 1980 and 1992.

Highest scores The highest individual score for three sanctioned games (possible 900) is 899 by Thomas Jordan (USA) (b. 27 Oct 1966) at Union, New Jersey, USA on 7 Mar 1989. The record by a woman is 864 by Jeanne Maiden (b. 10 Nov 1957) of Tacoma, Washington at Solon, Ohio, USA on 23 Nov 1986. This series included a record 40 consecutive strikes.

The maximum 900 for a three-game series was achieved by Glenn Richard Allison (b. 22 May 1930) at the La Habra Bowl in Los Angeles, California, USA on 1 Jul 1982, but this was not recognized by the ABC due to the oiling patterns on the boards. It has been recorded five times in unsanctioned games–by Leon Bentley at Lorain, Ohio, USA on 26 Mar 1931; by Joe Sargent at Rochester, New York, USA in 1934; by Jim Murgie in Philadelphia, Pennsylvania, USA on 4 Feb 1937; by Bob Brown at Roseville Bowl, California, USA on 12 Apr 1980 and by John Strausbaugh at York, Pennsylvania, USA on 11 Jul 1987. Such series must have consisted of 36 consecutive strikes (i.e. all pins down with one ball).

The highest number of sanctioned 300 games is 42 by Robert Learn Jr (b. 11 Apr 1962) of Erie, Pennsylvania, USA; the women's record is 20 by Jeanne Maiden.

Great Britain The British record for a three–game series is 806 by Philip Anthony Scammell (b. 8 May 1962) at Worthing, W Sussex on 26 Sep 1986. Army Sergeant Michael Langley scored

835 at S.H.A.P.E., Belgium on 15 Apr 1985.

The three–game series record for a woman player is 740 by Elizabeth Cullen at the Astra Bowl, RAF Brize Norton, Oxon on 15 Mar 1983.

The maximum score for a single game of 300 has been achieved on several occasions. The first man to do so was Albert Kirkham (b. 1931) of Burslem, Staffs on 5 Dec 1965. The first woman was Georgina Wardle (b. 24 Jul 1948) at the Sheffield Bowl, S Yorks on 20 Jan 1985. The first person to achieve the feat twice is Patrick Duggan (b. 26 May 1944), in 1972 and 1986, both at Bexleyheath Bowl, Kent.

PBA records Earl Roderick Anthony (b. 27 Apr 1938) was the first to win $1 million and won a record 41 PBA titles in his career.

The season's record earnings is $298 237 by Mike Aulby (b. 25 Mar 1960) in 1989. The career record is $1 592 966 by Marshall Holman (b. 29 Sep 1954) to end of 1992.

Bowls

Outdoor

World Championships (instituted 1966) The only man to win two or more singles titles is David John Bryant (England) (b. 27 Oct 1931), who won in 1966, 1980 and 1988. With the triples 1980, and the Leonard Trophy 1980 and 1988, he has won six World Championship gold medals.

At Johannesburg, South Africa, in February 1976, the South African team achieved an unprecedented clean sweep of all four titles plus the team competition (Leonard Trophy).

The Leonard Trophy has been won three times by Scotland, 1972, 1984 and 1992.

Elsie Wilke (New Zealand) won two women's singles titles, 1969 and 1974. Three women have won three gold medals: Merle Richardson (Australia) fours 1977, singles and pairs 1985; Dorothy Roche (Australia) triples 1985 and 1988, fours 1988; and Margaret

539

The successful Scottish bowls team who won the Leonard Trophy at the 1992 World Championships at Worthing, E Sussex. It was a record third success for Scotland.
(Photo: Allsport/Stephen Munday)

Johnston (Ireland) singles 1992 and pairs 1988 and 1992.

English and British Championships The record number of English Bowls Association (founded 8 Jun 1903) championships is 16 won or shared by David Bryant, including six singles (1960, 1966, 1971–3, 1975), three pairs (1965, 1969, 1974), three triples (1966, 1977, 1985) and four fours championships (1957, 1968, 1969 and 1971). He has also won seven British Isles titles (four singles, one pairs, one triple, one fours) in the period 1957–86. 1987.

The youngest ever EBA singles champion was David A. Holt (b. 9 Sep 1966) at 20yr 346 days in 1987.

Most international appearances By any bowler is 78 by Syd Thompson (b. 29 Aug 1912) for Ireland, 1947–73 and David Bryant for England, 1958–87. Thompson also had 51 indoor caps.

The youngest bowler to represent England was Gerard Anthony Smyth (b. 29 Dec 1960) at 20 yr 196 days on 13 Jul 1981.

Indoor

World Championships (instituted 1979) The most singles titles is three by: David Bryant, 1979–81 and Richard Corsie (GB), 1989, 1991 and 1993. Bryant with Tony Allcock (b. 11 Jun

Highest score–24 hours bowling
A team of six scored 212692 at Strykers Pleasure Bowl, Bushbury, Wolverhampton, W Mids on 20–21 Jun 1992. The highest individual total is 47 556 by Brian Larkins at the Hollywood Bowl, Bolton, Lancs on 9–10 Apr 1993.

Highest bowls score
In an international bowls match, Swaziland beat Japan by 63–1 during the World Championships at Melbourne, Australia on 16 Jan 1980.

1955) has won the pairs (instituted 1986) six times, 1986–7, 1989–92.

English Nationals (instituted 1960) This competition has been won most often by David Bryant with nine wins between 1964 and 1983. The youngest EIBA singles champion, John Dunn (b. 6 Oct 1963), was 17yr 117days when he won in 1981.

Highest score Joan Eggleton, Brenda King, Maureen Smith and Patricia Bain of Eastbourne & District Indoor Bowls Club beat a four from Egerton Park, 59–2 over 21 ends at Eastbourne, E Sussex on 7 Feb 1989.

The greatest 'whitewash' is 55–0 by C. Hammond and B. Funnell against A. Wise and C. Lock in the second round of the EIBA National Pairs Championships on 17 Oct 1983 at The Angel, Tonbridge, Kent.

Boxing

Longest fights The longest recorded fight with gloves was between Andy Bowen of New Orleans (1867–94) and Jack Burke at New Orleans, Louisiana, USA on 6–7 Apr 1893. It lasted 110 rounds, 7hr 19min (9:15p.m.–4:34a.m.), and was declared a no contest (later changed to a draw). Bowen won an 85-round bout on 31 May 1893.

The longest bare-knuckle fight was 6hr 15min between James Kelly and Jack Smith at Fiery Creek, Dalesford, Victoria, Australia on 3 Dec 1855.

The greatest number of rounds was 276 in 4 hr 30 min when Jack Jones beat Patsy Tunney in Cheshire in 1825.

Shortest fights There is a distinction between the quickest knock-out and the shortest fight. A knock-out in 10½ sec (including a 10 sec count) occurred on 23 Sep 1946, when Al Couture struck Ralph Walton while the latter was adjusting a gum shield in his corner at Lewiston, Maine, USA. If the time was accurately taken it is clear that Couture must have been more than half-way across the ring from his own corner at the opening bell.

The shortest fight on record appears to be one in a Golden Gloves tournament at Minneapolis, Minnesota, USA on 4 Nov 1947, when Mike Collins floored Pat Brownson with the first punch and the contest was stopped, without a count, 4 sec after the bell.

The shortest world title fight was 45 sec, when Lloyd Honeyghan (b. 22 Apr 1960) beat Gene Hatcher in an IBF welterweight bout at Marbella, Spain on 30 Aug 1987. Some sources also quote the Al McCoy (1894–1966) first round knockout of George Chip in a middleweight contest on 7 Apr 1914 as being 45 sec.

The shortest ever heavyweight world title fight was the James J. Jeffries (1875–1953)–Jack Finnegan bout at Detroit, USA on 6 Apr 1900, won by Jeffries in 55 sec.

The shortest ever British title fight was one of 40 sec (including the count), when Dave Charnley knocked out David 'Darkie' Hughes in a lightweight championship defence in Nottingham on 20 Nov 1961.

Eugene Brown, on his professional debut, knocked out Ian Bockes of Hull at Leicester on 13 Mar 1989. The fight

---

Most knock-downs in a title fight
Vic Toweel (South Africa) (b. 12 Jan 1929) knocked down Danny O'Sullivan of London 14 times in ten rounds in their world bantamweight fight at Johannesburg on 2 Dec 1950, before the latter retired.

---

was officially stopped after '10 seconds of the first round'. Bockes got up after a count of six but the referee stopped the contest.

Most British titles The most defences of a British heavyweight title is 14 by 'Bombardier' Billy Wells (1889–1967) from 1911 to 1919.

The only British boxer to win three Lonsdale Belts outright was heavyweight Henry William Cooper (b. 3 May 1934). He retired after losing to Joe Bugner (b. Hungary, 13 Mar 1950), having held the British heavyweight title from 12 Jan 1959 to 28 May 1969 and from 24 Mar 1970 to 16 Mar 1971.

The fastest time to win a Lonsdale Belt, for three successive championship wins, is 160 days by Colin McMillan at featherweight, 22 May–29 Oct 1991.

The longest time for winning a Lonsdale Belt outright is 8 yr 236 days by Kirkland Laing (b. 20 Jun 1954), 4 Apr 1979–26 Nov 1987.

Tallest The tallest boxer to fight professionally was Gogea Mitu (b. 1914) of Romania in 1935. He was 2·23 m 7 ft 4 in and weighed 148 kg 327 lb. John Rankin, who won a fight in New Orleans, Louisiana, USA in November 1967, was reputedly also 2·23 m 7 ft 4 in. Jim Culley, 'The Tipperary Giant', who fought as a boxer and wrestled in the 1940s is also reputed to have been 2·23 m 7 ft 4 in.

Most fights without loss Edward Henry (Harry) Greb (USA) (1894–1926) was unbeaten in a sequence of 178 bouts, but these included 117 'no decision', of which five were unofficial losses, in 1916–23.

Of boxers with complete records, Packey McFarland (USA) (1888–1936) had 97 fights (5 draws) in 1905–15 without a defeat.

Pedro Carrasco (Spain) (b. 7 Nov 1943) won 83 consecutive fights from 22 April 1964 to 3 Sep 1970, drew once and had a further nine wins before his loss to Armando Ramos in a WBC lightweight contest on 18 Feb 1972.

Most knock-outs The greatest number of finishes classed as 'knock-outs' in a career (1936–63) is 145 (129 in profes-

Lennox Lewis (left), Britain's first world heavyweight champion this century successfully defending his WBC title against America's Tony Tucker, holder of a world heavyweight title for the shortest time, at Las Vegas, Nevada on 8 May 1993.

(Photo: Allsport/Holly Stein)

sional bouts) by Archie Moore (USA) (b. Archibald Lee Wright, 13 Dec 1913 or 1916).

The record for consecutive KO's is 44 by Lamar Clark (USA) (b. 1 Dec 1934) from 1958 to 11 Jan 1960. He knocked out six in one night (five in the first

Youngest & oldest

Mike Tyson (USA) was 20 yr 144 days when he beat Trevor Berbick (USA) to win the WBC version at Las Vegas, Nevada, USA on 22 Nov 1986. He added the WBA title when he beat James 'Bonecrusher' Smith on 7 Mar 1987 at 20 yr 249 days. He became universal champion on 2 Aug 1987 when he beat Tony Tucker (USA) for the IBF title.

Jersey Joe Walcott (USA) (b. Arnold Raymond Cream, 31 Jan 1914) was 37 yr 168 days, when he knocked out Ezzard Mack Charles (1921–75) on 18 Jul 1951 in Pittsburgh, Pennsylvania, USA. He was also the oldest holder at 38 yr 236 days, losing his title to Rocky Marciano on 23 Sep 1952.

round) at Bingham, Utah, USA on 1 Dec 1958.

Attendances *Highest* The greatest paid attendance at any boxing match is 132 274 for four world title fights at the Aztec Stadium, Mexico City on 20 Feb 1993, headed by the successful WBC super lightweight defence by Julio César Chávez (Mexico) over Greg Haugen (USA).

The indoor record is 63 350 at the Ali *v.* Leon Spinks (b. 11 Jul 1953) fight in the Superdome, New Orleans, Louisiana, USA on 15 Sep 1978.

The British attendance record is 82 000 at the Len Harvey *v.* Jock McAvoy fight at White City, London on 10 Jul 1939.

The highest non-paying attendance is 135 132 at the Tony Zale *v.* Billy Pryor fight at Juneau Park, Milwaukee, Wisconsin, USA on 16 Aug 1941.

Lowest The smallest attendance at a world heavyweight title fight was 2434, at the Cassius (Muhammad Ali) Clay *v* Sonny Liston fight at Lewiston, Maine, USA on 25 May 1965.

World Heavyweight

Earliest title fight Long accepted as the first world heavyweight title fight, with gloves and 3-min rounds, was that between John Lawrence Sullivan (1858–1918) and 'Gentleman' James John Corbett (1866–1933) in New Orleans, Louisiana, USA on 7 Sep 1892. Corbett won in 21 rounds. However the fight between Sullivan, then the world bare-knuckle champion, and Dominick F. McCaffrey in Chester Park, Cincinnati, Ohio on 29 Aug 1885 was staged under Queensberry Rules with the boxers wearing gloves over six rounds. The referee Billy Tait left the ring without giving a verdict, but when asked two days later said that Sullivan had won.

Reign *Longest* Joe Louis (USA) (b. Joseph Louis Barrow, 1914–81) was champion for 11 years 252 days, from 22 Jun 1937, when he knocked out James Joseph Braddock in the eighth round at Chicago, Illinois, USA, until announcing his retirement on 1 Mar 1949. During his

Julio César Chavez is currently the most successful boxer with 87 victories from 87 fights in his professional career.

(Photo: Allsport/Holly Stein)

reign Louis made a record 25 defences of his title.

Shortest Tony Tucker (USA) (b. 28 Dec 1958) was IBF champion for 64 days, 30 May–2 Aug 1987, the shortest duration for a title won and lost in the ring.

Most recaptures Muhammad Ali is the only man to regain the heavyweight championship twice. Ali first won the title on 25 Feb 1964, defeating Sonny Liston. He defeated George Foreman on 30 Oct 1974, having been stripped of the title by the world boxing authorities on 28 Apr 1967. He won the WBA title from Leon Spinks on 15 Sep 1978, having previously lost to him on 15 Feb 1978.

Undefeated Rocky Marciano (USA) (b. Rocco Francis Marchegiano) (1923–69) is the only world champion at *any weight* to have won every fight of his complete professional career, from 17 Mar 1947–21 Sep 1955 (he announced his retirement on 27 Apr 1956); 43 of his 49 fights were by knock-outs or stoppages.

Heaviest Primo Carnera (Italy) (1906–67), the 'Ambling Alp', who won the title from Jack Sharkey in New York City, USA on 29 Jun 1933, scaled 118 kg *260 lb* for this fight but his peak weight was 122 kg *269 lb*. He had an expanded chest measurement of 137 cm *54 in* and the longest reach at 217 cm *85½ in* (fingertip to fingertip).

Lightest Robert James 'Bob' Fitzsimmons (1863–1917), from Helston, Cornwall weighed 75 kg *165 lb*, when he won the title by knocking out James J. Corbett at Carson City, Nevada, USA on 17 Mar 1897.

Tallest There is uncertainty as to the tallest world champion. Ernest Terrell (USA) (b. 4 Apr 1939), WBA champion 1965–67, was reported to be 1·98 m *6 ft 6 in*. Slightly higher figures had been given for earlier champions, but, according to measurements by the physical education director of the Hemingway Gymnasium, Harvard University, Cambridge, Massachusetts Primo Carnera was 1·966 m *6 ft 5·4 in*, although widely reported and believed to be up to 2·04 m *6 ft 8½ in*. Jess Willard (1881–1968), who won the title in 1915, often stated to be 1·99 m *6 ft 6¼ in*, was in fact 1·96 m *6 ft 5¼ in*.

Shortest Tommy Burns, world champion from 23 Feb 1906 to 26 Dec 1908, stood 1·70 m *5 ft 7 in* and weighed between 76–81 kg *168–180 lb*.

Longest-lived Jack Sharkey (b. Joseph Paul Zukauskas, 26 Oct 1902), champion from 21 Jun 1932 to 29 Jun 1933, surpassed the previous record of 87 yr 341 days held by Jack Dempsey (1895–1983) on 3 Oct 1990.

World Champions, any weight

Reign *Longest* The Joe Louis heavyweight duration record of 11 yr 252 days stands for all divisions.

Shortest Tony Canzoneri (USA) (1908–59) was world light-welterweight champion for 33 days, 21 May to 23 Jun 1933, the shortest period for a boxer to have won and lost the world title in the ring.

Youngest Wilfred Benitez (b. New York, 12 Sep 1958) of Puerto Rico, was 17 yr 176 days when he won the WBA light welterweight title in San Juan, Puerto Rico on 6 Mar 1976.

Oldest Archie Moore, who was recognized as a light heavyweight champion up to 10 Feb 1962 when his title was removed, was then believed to be between 45 and 48.

Longest career Bob Fitzsimmons had a career of over 31 years from 1883 to 1914. He had his last world title bout on 20 Dec 1905 at the age of 42 yr 208 days. Jack Johnson (USA) (1878–1946) also had a career of over 31 years, 1897–1928.

Longest fight The longest world title fight (under Queensberry Rules) was that between the lightweights Joe Gans (1874–1910), of the USA, and Oscar Matthew 'Battling' Nelson (1882–1954), the 'Durable Dane', at Goldfield, Nevada, USA on 3 Sep 1906. It was terminated in the 42nd round when Gans was declared the winner on a foul.

Most different weights The first boxer to have won world titles at four weight categories was Thomas Hearns (USA) (b. 18 Oct 1958), WBA welterweight in 1980, WBC super welterweight in 1982, WBC light heavyweight in 1987 and WBC middleweight in 1987. He added a fifth weight division when he won the super middleweight title recognized by the newly created World Boxing Organization (WBO) on 4 Nov 1988, and he won the WBA light heavyweight title on 3 Jun 1991.

Sugar Ray Leonard (USA) (b. 17 May 1956) has also claimed world titles in five weight categories. Having previously won the WBC welterweight in 1979 and 1980, WBA junior middleweight in 1981 and WBC middleweight in 1987, he beat Donny Lalonde (Canada) on 7 Nov 1988, for both the WBC light heavyweight and super middleweight titles. However, despite the fact that the WBC sanctioned the fight, it is contary to their rules to contest two divisions in the one fight. Consequently, although Leonard won, he had to relinquish one of the titles.

The feat of holding world titles at three weights *simultaneously* was achieved by Henry 'Homicide Hank' Armstrong (USA) (1912–88), at featherweight, lightweight and welterweight from August to December 1938. It is argued, however, that Barney Ross (b. Barnet David Rosofsky, USA) (1909–67) held the lightweight, junior-welterweight and welterweight, simultaneously, from 28 May to 17 Sep 1934 (although there is some dispute as to when he relinquished his lightweight title).

In recent years there has been a proliferation of weight categories and governing bodies but Armstrong was undisputed world champion at widely differing weights which makes his achievement all the more remarkable.

Most recaptures The only boxer to win a world title five times at one weight is 'Sugar' Ray Robinson (USA) (b. Walker Smith Jr, 1921–89), who beat Carmen Basilio (USA) in the Chicago Stadium on 25 Mar 1958, to regain the world middleweight title for the fourth time.

Dennis Andries (b. Guyana, 5 Nov 1953) became the first British boxer to regain a world title twice. He had initially won the WBC light-heavyweight title on 30 Apr 1986 and first regained the title on 22 Feb 1989 after being beaten in 1987. He regained the title for a second time on 28 Jul 1990.

Most title bouts The record number of title bouts in a career is 37, of which 18 ended in 'no decision', by three-time world welterweight champion Jack Britton (USA) (1885–1962) in 1915–22. The record containing no 'no decision' contests is 27 (all heavyweight) by Joe Louis between 1937–50.

Greatest weight difference When Primo Carnera (Italy) 122 kg *269 lb* fought Tommy Loughran (USA) 83 kg *183 lb* for the world heavyweight title at Miami, Florida, USA on 1 Mar 1934, there was a weight difference of 39 kg *86 lb* between the two fighters. Carnera won the fight on points.

Greatest 'tonnage' The highest aggregate weight recorded in any fight is 317 kg *699 lb* when Claude 'Humphrey' 'McBride (Oklahoma), 154 kg *339½ lb*, knocked out Jimmy Black (Houston), who weighed 163 kg *359½ lb* in the third round at Oklahoma City on 1 Jun 1971.

The greatest 'tonnage' in a world title fight was 221·5 kg *488¼ lb*, when Carnera, then 117·5 kg *259 lb* fought Paolino Uzcudun (Spain) 104 kg *229¼ lb* in Rome, Italy on 22 Oct 1933:

Amateur

Most Olympic titles Only two boxers have won three Olympic gold medals:

southpaw László Papp (Hungary) (b. 25 Mar 1926), middleweight 1948, light-middleweight 1952 and 1956; and Teofilo Stevenson (Cuba) (b. 23 Mar 1952), heavyweight 1972, 1976 and 1980.

The only man to win two titles in one celebration was Oliver L. Kirk (USA), who won both bantam and feather-weight titles in St Louis, Missouri, USA in 1904, but he needed only one bout in each class.

Another record that will stand forever is that of the youngest Olympic boxing champion: Jackie Fields (*né* Finkelstein) (USA) (b. 9 Feb 1908) who won the 1924 featherweight title at 16 years 162 days. The minimum age for Olympic boxing competitors is now 17.

Oldest gold medallist Richard Kenneth Gunn (GB) (1871–1961) won the Olympic featherweight gold medal on 27 Oct 1908 in London aged 37 yr 254 days.

World Championships A record four world titles (instituted 1974) have been won by Félix Savon (Cuba) heavyweight 1986, 1989, 1991 and 1993.

Most British titles The greatest number of ABA titles won by any boxer is eight by John Lyon (b. 9 Mar 1962) at light-flyweight 1981–4 and at flyweight 1986–9.

Alex 'Bud' Watson (b. 27 May 1914) of Leith, Scotland won the Scottish heavyweight title in 1938, 1942–3, and the light-heavyweight championship 1937–9, 1943–5 and 1947, making ten in all. He also won the ABA light-heavyweight title in 1945 and 1947.

Longest span The greatest span of ABA title-winning performances is that of the heavyweight Hugh 'Pat' Floyd (b. 23 Aug 1910), who won in 1929 and gained his fourth title 17 years later in 1946.

Canoeing

Most titles *Olympic* Gert Fredriksson (Sweden) (b. 21 Nov 1919) won a record six Olympic gold medals, 1948–60. He added a silver and a bronze for a record eight medals.

The most by a woman is four by Birgit Schmidt (*née* Fischer) (GDR) (b. 25 Feb 1962), 1980–92.

Birgit Schmidt (near lane) during the 500 m K1 final at the 1992 Olympics, which she went on to win by just 0·36sec. It was her 23rd world or Olympic title since 1978.

(Photo: Allsport/Nathan Bilow)

The most gold medals at one Games is three by Vladimir Parfenovich (USSR) (b. 2 Dec 1958) in 1980 and by Ian Ferguson (New Zealand) (b. 20 Jul 1952) in 1984.

World Including the Olympic Games a women's record 23 titles have been won by Birgit Schmidt, 1978–92.

Longest race

The Canadian Government Centennial Voyageur Canoe Pageant and Race from Rocky Mountain House, Alberta to the Expo 67 site at Montreal, Quebec was 5283km *3283 miles*. Ten canoes represented Canadian provinces and territories. The winner of the race, which took from 24 May to 4 Sep 1967, was the Province of Manitoba canoe *Radisson*.

Canoe raft

A raft of 568 kayaks and canoes, organized by the Notts County Scout Council with the assistance of scouts from Derbys, Leics and Lincs, was held together by hands only, while free floating for 30 seconds, on the River Trent, Nottingham on 30 Jun 1991.

Biggest tournament

The Epson World Bridge Championship, held on 20–21 Jun 1992, was contested by more than 102 000 players playing the same hands, at over 2000 centres worldwide.

Perfect deals

The mathematical odds against dealing 13 cards of one suit are 158 753 389 899 to 1, while the odds against a named player receiving a 'perfect hand' consisting of all 13 spades are 635 013 559 599 to 1. The odds against each of the four players receiving a complete suit (a 'perfect deal') are 2 235 197 406 895 366 368 301 599 999 to 1.

Possible auctions

The number of possible auctions with North as dealer is 128 745 650 347 030 683 120 231 926 111 609 371 363 122 697 557.

The men's record is 13 by Gert Fredriksson, 1948–60, Rüdiger Helm (GDR) (b. 6 Oct 1956), 1976–83, and Ivan Patzaichin (Romania) (b. 26 Nov 1949), 1968–84.

The most individual titles by a British canoeist is four by Richard Fox (b. 5 Jun 1960) at K1 slalom in 1981, 1983, 1985 and 1989. Fox also won four gold medals at K1 team, between 1981 and 1987.

Highest speed The German four-man kayak Olympic champions in 1992 at Barcelona, Spain covered 1000 m in 2min 52·17sec in a heat on 4 August. This represents an average speed of 20·90km/h *12·98mph*.

At the 1988 Olympics, the Norwegian four achieved a 250m split of 42·08sec between 500m and 750m in a heat, for a speed of 21·39km/h *13·29mph*.

Longest journey Father and son Dana and Donald Starkell paddled from Winnipeg, Manitoba, Canada by ocean and river to Belem, Brazil, a distance of 19 603km *12 181 miles* from 1 Jun 1980 to 1 May 1982. All portages were human powered.

Without portages or aid of any kind the longest is one of 9820km *6102 miles* by Richard H. Grant and Ernest 'Moose' Lassy circumnavigating the eastern USA via Chicago, New Orleans, Miami, New York and the Great Lakes from 22 Sep 1930 to 15 Aug 1931.

North Sea On 17–18 May 1989, Kevin Danforth and Franco Ferrero completed the Felixstowe to Zeebrugge route in 27hr 10min in a double sea kayak. The open crossing, over 177km *110 miles*, was self-contained and unsupported.

River Rhine The fastest time, solo and unsupported, is 10days 12hr 9min by Frank Palmer, 15–25 May 1988. The supported team record is 7days 23hr 31sec by the RAF Laarbruch Canoe Club, led by Andy Goodsell, 17–24 May 1989. The 'Rhine Challenge', as organized by the International Long River Canoeists Club, begins from an official marker post in Chur, Switzerland and ends at Willemstad, Netherlands, a distance of 1149km *714 miles*.

24 hours Zdzislaw Szubski paddled 252·9km *157·1 miles* in a Jaguar K1 canoe on the Vistula River, Włocklawek to Gdańsk, Poland on 11–12 Sep 1987.

Flat water Marinda Hartzenberg (South Africa) paddled, without benefit of current, 220·69km *137·13 miles* on Loch Logan, Bloemfontein, South Africa on 31 Dec 1990–1 Jan 1991.

Open sea Randy Fine (USA) paddled 194·1km *120·6 miles* along the Florida coast on 26–27 Jun 1986.

Greatest lifetime distance Fritz Lindner of Berlin, Germany, totalled 103 444km *64 277 miles* from 1928 to 1987.

Eskimo rolls Ray Hudspith (b. 18 Apr 1960) achieved 1000 rolls in 34min 43sec at the Elswick Pool, Newcastle upon Tyne on 20 Mar 1987. He completed 100 rolls in 3min 7·25sec at Killingworth Leisure Centre, Tyne and Wear on 3 Mar 1991. Randy Fine (USA) completed 1796 continuous rolls at Biscayne Bay, Florida, USA on 8 Jun 1991.

'Hand rolls' Colin Brian Hill (b. 16 Aug 1970) achieved 1000 rolls in 31min 55·62 sec at Consett, Co. Durham on 12 Mar

1987. He also achieved 100 rolls in 2min 39·2sec at Crystal Palace, London on 22 Feb 1987. He completed 3700 continuous rolls at Durham City Swimming Baths, Co. Durham on 1 May 1989.

Card Games

Contract Bridge

Most world titles The World Championship (Bermuda Bowl) has been won a record 13 times by Italy's Blue Team (*Squadra Azzurra*), 1957–9, 1961–3, 1965–7, 1969, 1973–5 and by the USA, 1950–51, 1953–4, 1970–71, 1976–7, 1979, 1981, 1983, 1985, 1987. Italy also won the team Olympiad in 1964, 1968 and 1972. Giorgio Belladonna (b. 7 Jun 1923) was in all the Italian winning teams.

The USA have a record six wins in the women's world championship for the Venice Trophy: 1974, 1976, 1978, 1987, 1989 and 1991, and three women's wins at the World Team Olympiad: 1976, 1980 and 1984.

Most hands In the 1989 Bermuda Bowl in Perth, Australia, Marcel Branco and Gabriel Chagas (both Brazil) played a record 752 out of a possible 784 boards.

Most master points In the latest ranking list based on Master Points awarded by the World Bridge Federation, the leading players in the world are (men) Robert Hamman (b. 1938) of Dallas, Texas, USA with 6046 and (women) Sandra Landy (GB) (b. 1938) with 3077.

Card throwing

Kevin St Onge threw a standard playing card 56·41m *185ft 1in* at the Henry Ford Community College Campus, Dearborn, Michigan, USA on 12 Jun 1979.

Card holding

Ralf Laue held 310 standard playing cards in a fan in one hand, so that the value and colour of each one was visible, at Zürich, Switzerland on 6 Apr 1991.

Cribbage

Rare hands Five maximum 29 point hands have been Sean Daniels of Astoria, Oregon, USA, 1989–92. Paul Nault of Athol, Massachusetts, USA had two such hands within eight games in a tournament on 19 Mar 1977.

Most points in 24 hours The most points scored by a team of four, playing singles in two pairs, is 126 414 by Mark Fitzwater, Eddie Pepper, Mark Perry and Gary Watson at The Green Man, Potton, Beds on 8–9 May 1993.

Cricket

Records in First-class matches

Batting Records Teams

Highest innings Victoria scored 1107 runs in 10hr 30min against New South Wales in an Australian Sheffield Shield match at Melbourne on 27–28 Dec 1926.

Test England scored 903 runs for seven wickets declared in 15hr 17min, *v.* Australia at The Oval, London on 20, 22 and 23 Aug 1938.

County Championship Yorkshire scored 887 in 10hr 50min, *v.* Warwickshire at Edgbaston, Birmingham on 7–8 May 1896.

Lowest innings The traditional first-class record is 12 by Oxford University (who batted a man short) *v.* the Marylebone Cricket Club (MCC) at Cowley Marsh, Oxford on 24 May 1877, and by Northamptonshire *v.* Gloucestershire at Gloucester on 11 Jun 1907. However, 'The Bs' scored 6 in their second innings *v.* England at Lord's, London on 12–14 Jun 1810 in one of the major matches of that era.

Test 26 by New Zealand *v.* England at Auckland on 28 Mar 1955.

Aggregate for two innings 34 (16 and 18) by Border *v.* Natal in the South African Currie Cup at East London on 19 and 21 Dec 1959. In an early match, Leicestershire totalled 23 (15 and 8) *v.* Nottinghamshire (61) at Leicester on 25 Aug 1800.

Individual Cricket Records

FIRST-CLASS (FC) AND TEST CAREER

Batting

		Name	Team	Date
Most runs	FC 61237	Sir John Berry 'Jack' Hobbs (1882–1963) (av. 50-65)	Surrey/England	1905–34
	Test 10262	Allan Robert Border (b. 27 Jul 1955) (av. 51-05)	Australia (141 Tests)	1978–93
Most centuries	FC 197	Sir Jack Hobbs (in 1315 innings)	Surrey/England	1905–34
	Test 34	Sunil Gavaskar (in 214 innings)	India	1971–87
Highest average	FC 95-14	Sir Donald George Bradman (b. 28 Aug 1908) (28 067 runs in 338 innings, including 43 not outs)	NSW/South Australia/Australia	1927–49
	Test 99-94	Sir Donald Bradman (6996 runs in 80 innings)	Australia (52 Tests)	1928–4

Bowling

		Name	Team	Date
Most wickets	FC 4187	Wilfred Rhodes (1877–1973) (av. 16-71)	Yorkshire/England	1898–1930
	Test 431	Sir Richard John Hadlee (b. 3 Jul 1951) (av. 22-29)	New Zealand (86 Tests)	1973–90
Lowest average (min 15 wkts)	Test 10-75	George Alfred Lohmann (1865–1901) (112 wkts)	England (18 Tests)	1886–96

Wicket-Keeping

		Name	Team	Date
Most dismissals	FC 649	Robert William Taylor (b. 17 Jul 1941)	Derbyshire/England	1960–88
	Test 355	Rodney William Marsh (b. 11 Nov 1947)	Australia (96 Tests)	1970–84
Most catches	FC 1473	Robert Taylor	Derbyshire/England	1960–88
	Test 343	Rodney Marsh	Australia	1970–84
Most stumpings	FC 418	Leslie Ethelbert George Ames (1905–90)	Kent/England	1926–51
	Test 52	William Albert Stanley Oldfield (1894–1976)	Australia (54 Tests)	1920–37

Fielding

		Name	Team	Date
Most catches	FC 1018	Frank Edward Woolley (1887–1978)	Kent/England	1906–38
	Test 140	Allan Robert Border	Australia (141 Tests)	1978–93

IN A TEST SERIES

Batting

		Name	Teams (No. of Tests)	Season
Most runs	974	Sir Donald Bradman (av. 139·14)	Australia v. England (5)	1930
Most centuries	5	Clyde Leopold Walcott (b. 17 Jan 1926)	West Indies v. Australia (5)	1954/5
Highest average	563·00	Walter Reginald Hammond (563 runs, 2 inns, 1 not out)	England v. New Zealand (2)	1932/3

Bowling

Most wickets	49	Sydney Francis Barnes (1873–1967) (av. 10·93)	England v. South Africa (4)	1913/14
Lowest average	5·80	George Alfred Lohmann (35 wkts)	England v. South Africa (3)	1895/6

(min 20 wkts)

Wicket-Keeping

Most dismissals	28	Rodney Marsh (all caught)	Australia v. England (5)	1982/3
Most stumpings	9	Percy William Sherwell (1880–1948)	South Africa v. Australia (5)	1910/11

Fielding

Most catches	15	Jack Morrison Gregory (1895–1973)	Australia v. England (5)	1920/21

All-Round

400 runs/30 wickets	475/34	George Giffen (1859–1927)	Australia v. England (5)	1894/5

IN A FIRST-CLASS SEASON IN ENGLAND

Batting

		Name (Team)	Year
Most runs	3816	Denis Charles Scott Compton (b. 23 May 1918) (av. 90·85) (Middlesex & England)	1947
Most centuries	18	Denis Compton (in 50 innings with 8 not outs) (Middlesex & England)	1947
Highest average	115·66	Sir Donald Bradman (2429 runs in 26 innings, with 5 not outs) (Australians)	1938

Bowling

Most wickets	304	Alfred Percy 'Tich' Freeman (1888–1965) (1976·1 overs, av. 18·05) (Kent & England)	1928
Lowest average	8·54	Alfred Shaw (1842–1907) (186 wkts) (Nottinghamshire & England)	1880

(min 100 wkts)

Wicket-Keeping

Most dismissals	128	Leslie Ames (79 caught, 49 stumped) (Kent & England)	1929
Most catches	96	James Graham Binks (b. 5 Oct 1935) (Yorkshire)	1960
Most stumpings	64	Leslie Ames (Kent)	1932

Fielding

Most catches	78	Walter Reginald Hammond (1903–65) (Gloucestershire & England)	1928

Successive sixes

Cedric Ivan James Smith (1906–79) hit nine successive sixes for a Middlesex XI *v.* Harrow and District at Rayner's Lane, Harrow in 1935. This feat was repeated by Arthur Dudley Nourse (1910–81) in a South African XI *v.* Military Police match at Cairo, Egypt in 1942–3. Nourse's feat included six sixes in one over.

Century on début and wicket with first ball

Frederick William Stocks (b. 6 Nov 1918) of Nottinghamshire achieved the unique feat of scoring a century on his first-class début, *v.* Kent at Trent Bridge on 13 May 1946, and of taking a wicket with his first ball in first-class cricket, *v.* Lancashire at Old Trafford on 26 Jun 1946.

Most runs off a ball

Albert Neilson Hornby (1847–1925) scored ten off James Street (1839–1906) for Lancashire v. Surrey at The Oval on 14 Jul 1873, a feat equalled by Samuel Hill Wood (later Sir Samuel Hill Hill-Wood) (1872–1949) off Cuthbert James Burnup (1875–1960) for Derbyshire v. MCC at Lord's on 26 May 1900.

Greatest victory

A margin of an innings and 851 runs was recorded, when Pakistan Railways (910 for 6 declared) beat Dera Ismail Khan (32 and 27) at Lahore on 2–4 Dec 1964.

In England England won by an innings and 579 runs (also the record for a Test) against Australia at The Oval on 20–24 Aug 1938 when Australia scored 201 and 123 with two men short in both innings. The most one-sided county match was when Surrey (698) defeated Sussex (114 and 99) by an innings and 485 runs at The Oval on 9–11 Aug 1888.

Most runs in a day

Australia scored 721 all out (ten wickets) in 5 hr 48 min against Essex at Southchurch Park, Southend-on-Sea on 15 May 1948.

Test 588 at Old Trafford, Manchester on 27 Jul 1936 when England added 398 and India were 190 for 0 in their second innings by the close.

Batting Records Individuals

Highest innings

Hanif Mohammad (b. 21 Dec 1934) scored 499 in 10 hr 35 min for Karachi against Balawalpur at Karachi, Pakistan on 8, 9 and 11 Jan 1959.

In England Archibald Campbell MacLaren (1871–1944) scored 424 in 7 hr 50 min for Lancashire *v.* Somerset at Taunton, Somerset on 15–16 Jul 1895.

Test Sir Garfield St Aubrun Sobers (b. 28 Jul 1936) scored 365 not out in 10 hr 14 min for West Indies *v.* Pakistan at Sabina Park, Kingston, Jamaica on 27 Feb–1 Mar 1958. The English Test record is 364 by Sir Leonard Hutton (1916–90) against Australia at The Oval on 20, 22 and 23 Aug 1938.

Longest innings

Hanif Mohammad (Pakistan) batted for 16 hr 10 min for 337 runs against the West Indies at Bridgetown, Barbados on 20–23 Jan 1958. The English record is 13 hr 17 min by Len Hutton in his record Test score of 364.

Most runs off an over

The first batsman to score 36 runs off a six ball over was Sir Garfield Sobers off Malcolm Andrew Nash (b. 9 May 1945) for Nottinghamshire *v.* Glamorgan at Swansea on 31 Aug 1968. His feat was emulated by Ravishankar Jayadritha Shastri (b. 27 May 1962) for Bombay *v.* Baroda at Bombay, India on 10 Jan 1985 off the bowling of Tilak Raj Sharma (b. 15 Jan 1960).

Playing in a Shell Trophy match for Wellington *v.* Canterbury at Christchurch on 20 Feb 1990, in a deliberate attempt to give away runs, Robert Howard Vance (b. 31 Mar 1955) bowled an over containing 22 balls, 17 of which were deliberate no-balls (the umpire losing count and declaring over one ball early!). From this over Lee Kenneth Germon (b. 4 Nov 1968) of Canterbury hit 70 runs, including eight sixes and five

Most balls

The most balls bowled in a match is 917 by Cottari Subbanna Nayudu (b. 18 Apr 1914), 6–153 and 5–275, for Holkar v. Bombay at Bombay on 4–9 Mar 1945. The most balls bowled in a Test match is 774 by Sonny Ramadhin (b. 1 May 1929) for the West Indies v. England, 7–49 and 2–179, at Edgbaston on 29 May–4 Jun 1957. In the second innings he bowled a world record 588 balls (98 overs).

Fastest

The highest electronically measured speed for a ball bowled by any bowler is 160·45 km/h *99·7 mph* by Jeffrey Robert Thomson (Australia) (b. 16 Aug 1950) against the West Indies in December 1975.

Most extras

The West Indies hold the record for having conceded the most extras in both a Test innings and a one-day international. The Test record is 71 in Pakistan's 1st innings at Georgetown, Guyana on 3–4 Apr 1988. The figure consisted of 21 byes, 8 leg byes, 4 wides and 38 no balls. The limited-overs record is 59 (8 byes, 10 leg byes, 4 no balls and 37 wides) also against Pakistan at Brisbane on 7 Jan 1989.

---

fours, Richard George Petrie (b. 23 Aug 1967) scored five runs including one four, and with two runs from no-balls off which no runs were hit, a total of 77 runs was conceded.

Most sixes in an innings John Richard Reid (b. 3 Jun 1928) hit 15 in an innings of 296, lasting 3 hr 40 min, for Wellington v. Northern Districts in a Plunket Shield match at Wellington, New Zealand on 14–15 Jan 1963.

Test Walter Hammond hit ten sixes in his 336 not out for England v. New Zealand at Auckland on 31 Mar and 1 Apr 1933.

Triple hundred and hundred The only batsman to have scored a triple hundred and a hundred in the same match is Graham Alan Gooch (b. 23 Jul 1953) for England v. India at Lord's in 1990. He scored 333 in the first innings on 26–27 July and 123 in the second on 30 July for a record Test aggregate 456 runs.

Double hundreds The only batsman to score double hundreds in both innings is Arthur Edward Fagg (1915–77), who made 244 and 202 not out for Kent v. Essex at Colchester, Essex from 13–15 Jul 1938. Sir Donald Bradman scored a career record 37 double hundreds, 1927–49.

Fastest scoring Cedric Ivan James 'Jim' Smith (1906–79) scored 50 in 11 minutes for Middlesex v. Gloucestershire at Bristol on 16 Jun 1938. He went on to score 66. A faster 50 was completed off 13 balls in 8 min (1:22 to 1:30 p.m.) in 11 scoring strokes by Clive Clay Inman (b. 29 Jan 1936) in an innings of 57 not out for Leicestershire v. Nottinghamshire at Trent Bridge, Nottingham on 20 Aug 1965 but full tosses were bowled to expedite a declaration.

Fastest 100 The fastest against genuine bowling was completed in 35 min off between 40 and 46 balls by Percy George Herbert Fender (1892–1985), in his 113 not out for Surrey v. Northamptonshire at Northampton on 26 Aug 1920. Thomas Masson Moody (Australia) (b. 2 Oct 1965) completed a century in 26 min off 36 balls for Warwickshire v. Glamorgan at Swansea on 27 Jul 1990.

The hundred in fewest recorded deliveries was by David William Hookes (b. 3 May 1955) in 34 balls, in 43 min, for South Australia v. Victoria at Adelaide on 25 Oct 1982. In all he scored 107 from 40 balls in this the second innings, following 137 in the first innings. The fastest hundred in a major one-day competition was by Graham David Rose (b. 12 Apr 1964) off 36 balls for Somerset against Devon in the NatWest Trophy first round at Torquay on 27 Jun 1990.

The fastest Test hundred was completed in 70 min off 67 balls by Jack Morrison Gregory (1895–1973), in his 119 for Australia v. South Africa at Johannesburg

551

The leading run scorer in Test cricket is Allan Border of Australia, who surpassed Sunil Gavaskar's record against New Zealand on 26 Feb 1993. The leading run scorers for each of the nine Test playing nations at 1 Jun 1993 are:

Australia	Allan Border 10262
India	Sunil Gavaskar 10122
Pakistan	Javed Miandad 8569
West Indies	Vivian Richards 8540
England	David Gower 8231
New Zealand	John Wright 5334
South Africa	Bruce Mitchell 3471
Sri Lanka	Arjuna Ranatunga 2122
Zimbabawe	Andrew Flower 341

(Photos: Allsport/Joe Mann & Adrian Murrell)

on 12 Nov 1921. The fastest in terms of fewest balls received was one off 56 balls by Isaac Vivian Alexander Richards (b. 7 Mar 1952) for the West Indies *v.* England at St John's, Antigua on 15 Apr 1986. His final score was 110 in 81 minutes.

Edwin Boaler Alletson (1884–1963) scored 189 runs in 90 min for Nottinghamshire *v.* Sussex at Hove on 20 May 1911. The most prolific scorer of hundreds in an hour or less was Gilbert Laird Jessop (1874–1955), with 14 between 1897 and 1913.

Fastest 200 Scored in 113 min by Ravi Shastri off 123 balls for Bombay *v.* Baroda at Bombay on 10 Jan 1985 (⇔ Most runs off an over). Clive Hubert Lloyd (b. 31 Aug 1944), for West Indians *v.* Glamorgan at Swansea on 9 Aug 1976, and Gilbert Jessop (286), for Gloucestershire *v.* Sussex at Hove on 1 Jun 1903, both scored 200 in 120 min. Lloyd received 121 balls, but the figure for Jessop is not known.

Fastest 300 Completed in 181 min by Denis Compton, who scored 300 for the MCC *v.* North-Eastern Transvaal at Benoni, South Africa on 3–4 Dec 1948.

Slowest scoring The longest time a batsman has ever taken to score his first run is 1 hr 37 min by Thomas Godfrey Evans (b. 18 Aug 1920), before he scored 10 not out for England *v.* Australia at Adelaide on 5–6 Feb 1947. The longest innings without scoring is 87 min by Vincent Richard Hogg (b. 3 Jul 1952) for Zimbabwe–Rhodesia 'B' *v.* Natal 'B' at Pietermaritzburg in the South African Castle Bowl competition on 20 Jan 1980.

The slowest hundred on record is by Mudassar Nazar (b. 6 Apr 1956) for Pakistan *v.* England at Lahore on 14–15 Dec 1977. He required 9 hr 51 min for 114, reaching the 100 in 9 hr 17 min. The slowest double hundred is one of 12 hr 57 min (548 balls) by Don Sardha Brendon Priyantha Kuruppu (b. 5 Jan 1962) during an innings of 201 not out for Sri Lanka *v.* New Zealand at Colombo on 16–19 Apr 1987.

Highest partnership For any wicket is the fourth–wicket stand of 577 by Gulzar Mahomed (1921–92), 319, and Vijay Samuel Hazare (b. 11 Mar 1915), 288, for Baroda *v.* Holkar at Baroda, India on 8–10 Mar 1947.

In England 555, for the first-wicket by Percy Holmes (1886–1971) (224 not out) and Herbert Sutcliffe (1894–1978) (313) for Yorkshire *v.* Essex at Leyton, Essex on 15–16 Jun 1932.

Test 467, for the third wicket by Martin David Crowe (b. 22 Sep 1962) (299) and Andrew Howard Jones (b. 9 May 1959) (186) for New Zealand *v.* Sri Lanka at Wellington on 3–4 Feb 1991.

Bowling

Most wickets *In an innings* Only one bowler has taken all ten wickets in an innings on three occasions—Alfred 'Tich' Freeman of Kent, 1929–31. The fewest runs scored off a bowler taking all ten wickets is ten, off Hedley Verity (1905–43) for Yorkshire *v.* Nottinghamshire at Leeds on 12 Jul 1932 though the full analyses for some early performances of the feat are unknown. The only bowler to bowl out all ten was John Wisden (1826–84) for North *v.* South at Lord's in 1850.

In a match James Charles 'Jim' Laker (1922–86) took 19 wickets for 90 runs (9–37 and 10–53) for England *v.* Australia at Old Trafford from 27–31 Jul 1956.

Most consecutive wickets No bowler in first-class cricket has yet achieved five wickets with five consecutive balls. The nearest approach was that of Charles Warrington Leonard Parker (1882–1959) (Gloucestershire) in his own benefit match against Yorkshire at Bristol on 10 Aug 1922, when he struck the stumps with five successive balls but the second was called as a no-ball. The only man to have taken four wickets with consecutive balls more than once is Robert James Crisp (b. 28 May 1911) for Western Province *v.* Griqualand West at Johannesburg, South Africa on 24 Dec 1931 and against Natal at Durban, South Africa on 3 Mar 1934.

Patrick Ian Pocock (b. 24 Sep 1946) took five wickets in six balls, six in nine balls and seven in eleven balls for Surrey *v.* Sussex at Eastbourne, E Sussex on 15 Aug 1972. In his own benefit match at Lord's on 22 May 1907, Albert Edwin Trott (1873–1914) of Middlesex took four Somerset wickets with four consecutive balls and then later in the same innings achieved a 'hat trick'.

Most consecutive maidens Hugh Joseph Tayfield (b. 30 Jan 1929) bowled 16 consecutive eight-ball maiden overs (137 balls without conceding a run) for South Africa *v.* England at Durban on 25–26 Jan 1957. The greatest number of consecutive six-ball maiden overs bowled is 21 (131 balls) by Rameshchandra Gangaram 'Bapu' Nadkarni (b. 4 Apr 1932) for India *v.* England at Madras on 12 Jan 1964. Alfred Shaw (1842–1907) of Nottinghamshire bowled 23 consecutive 4-ball maiden overs (92 balls) for North *v.* South at Trent Bridge, Nottingham on 17 Jul 1876.

Most expensive bowling The greatest number of runs hit off one bowler in an innings is 362, off Arthur Alfred Mailey (1886–1967) of New South Wales by

Victoria at Melbourne on 24–28 Dec 1926. The most runs conceded by a bowler in a match is 428 by Cottari Subbanna Nayudu (b. 18 Apr 1914) in the Holkar v. Bombay match above. The most runs conceded in a Test innings is 298 by Leslie O'Brien 'Chuck' Fleetwood-Smith (1908–71) for Australia v. England at The Oval on 20–23 Aug 1938.

All-Rounders

The double The 'double' of 1000 runs and 100 wickets in the same season was performed a record number of 16 times by Wilfred Rhodes between 1903 and 1926. The greatest number of consecutive seasons in which a player has performed the 'double' is 11 (1903–13) by George Herbert Hirst (1871–1954), of Yorkshire and England. Hirst is also the only player to score 2000 runs (2385) and take 200 wickets (208) in the same season (1906).

Test cricket *Career* The best all-round record is Kapil Dev Nikhanj (India) (b. 6 Jan 1959) who has scored 5069 runs (av. 31·29), 420 wickets (av. 29·66) and 63 catches in 124 matches, 1978–93. England's best is Ian Terence Botham (England) (b. 24 Nov 1955) with 5200 runs (av. 33·54), 383 wickets (av. 28·40) and 120 catches in 102 matches, 1977–92.

Match and innings Botham is the only player to score a hundred and take eight wickets in an innings in the same Test, with 108 and 8–34 for England v. Pakistan at Lord's on 15–19 Jun 1978. He scored a hundred (114) and took more than ten wickets (6–58 and 7–48) in a Test, for England v. India in the Golden Jubilee Test at Bombay on 15–19 Feb 1980. This feat was emulated by Imran Khan Niazi (b. 25 Nov 1952) with 117, 6–98 and 5–82 for Pakistan v. India at Faisalabad on 3–8 Jan 1983.

Wicket-Keeping

Most dismissals *Innings* The most dismissals is nine (eight catches and a stumping) by Tahir Rashid (b. 21 Nov 1960) for Habib Bank v. Pakistan Automobile Corporation at Gujranwala, Pakistan on 29 Nov 1992. Three other player have taken eight catches in an innings: Arthur Theodore Wallace 'Wally'

Grout (1927–68) for Queensland v. Western Australia at Brisbane on 15 Feb 1960; David Edward East (b. 27 Jul 1959) for Essex v. Somerset at Taunton on 27 Jul 1985; and Stephen Andrew Marsh (b. 27 Jan 1961) for Kent v. Middlesex on 31 May and 1 Jun 1991. The most stumpings in an innings is six by Henry 'Hugo' Yarnold (1917–74) for Worcestershire v. Scotland at Broughty Ferry, Tayside on 2 Jul 1951.

Match The most dismissals is 12 by: Edward Pooley (1838–1907), eight caught, four stumped, for Surrey v. Sussex at The Oval on 6–7 Jul 1868; nine caught, three stumped by both Donald Tallon (1916–84) for Queensland v. New South Wales at Sydney, Australia on 2–4 Jan 1939, and by Hedley Brian Taber (b. 29 Apr 1940) for New South Wales v. South Australia at Adelaide on 13–17 Dec 1968. The record for catches is 11 by: Arnold Long (b. 18 Dec 1940), for Surrey v. Sussex at Hove on 18 and 21 Jul 1964, by Rodney Marsh for Western Australia v. Victoria at Perth on 15–17 Nov 1975; by David Leslie Bairstow (b. 1 Sep 1951) for Yorkshire v. Derbyshire at Scarborough on 8–10 Sep 1982; by Warren Kevin Hegg (b. 23 Feb 1968) for Lancashire v. Derbyshire at Chesterfield on 9–11 Aug 1989; by Alec James Stewart (b. 8 Apr 1963) for Surrey v. Leicestershire at Leicester on 19–22 Aug 1989; and by Timothy John Neilsen (b. 5 May 1968) for South Australia v. Western Australia at Perth on 15–18 Mar 1991. The most stumpings in a match is nine by Frederick Henry Huish (1869–1957) for Kent v. Surrey at The Oval on 21–23 Aug 1911.

Most dismissals in Tests *Innings* The record is seven (all caught) by Wasim Bari (b. 23 Mar 1948) for Pakistan v. New Zealand at Auckland on 23 Feb 1979, by Bob Taylor for England v. India at Bombay on 15 Feb 1980, and by Ian David Stockley Smith (b. 28 Feb 1957) for New Zealand v. Sri Lanka at Hamilton on 23–24 Feb 1991.

Match The record is ten, all caught, by Bob Taylor for England v. India at Bombay, 15–19 Feb 1980.

Fielding

Most catches *Innings* The greatest number of catches in an innings is seven, by Michael James Stewart (b. 16 Sep 1932) for Surrey v. Northamptonshire at Northampton on 7 Jun 1957; and by Anthony Stephen Brown (b. 24 Jun 1936) for Gloucestershire v. Nottinghamshire at Trent Bridge on 26 Jul 1966.

Match Walter Hammond held ten catches (four in the first innings, six in the second) for Gloucestershire v. Surrey at Cheltenham on 16–17 Aug 1928.

The most catches in a Test match is seven by: Greg Chappell for Australia v. England at Perth on 13–17 Dec 1974; Yajurvindra Singh (b. 1 Aug 1952) for India v. England at Bangalore on 28 Jan–2 Feb 1977; Mohammad Azharuddin (b. 8 Feb 1963) for India v. Pakistan at Karachi on 15–16 Nov 1989; and Krishnamachari Srikkanth (b. 21 Dec 1959) for India v. Australia at Perth on 1–2 Feb 1992.

Longest throw A cricket ball (155 g *5½ oz*) was reputedly thrown 128·6 m *140 yd 2 ft* by Robert Percival, a left-hander, on Durham Sands racecourse on Easter Monday, 18 Apr 1882.

Test Records

Test appearances The most Test matches played is 141 by Allan Robert Border (Australia) (b. 27 Jul 1955), 1979–93. Border's total includes a record 138 consecutive Tests and a record 78 as captain. The English record for most Tests is 117 by David Ivon Gower (b. 1 Apr 1957), 1978–92; and for consecutive Tests is 65 by Alan Philip Eric Knott (b. 9 Apr 1946), 1971–7 and Ian Botham, 1978–84.

Longest match The lengthiest recorded cricket match was the 'timeless' Test between England and South Africa at Durban on 3–14 Mar 1939. It was abandoned after ten days (eighth day rained off) because the ship taking the England team home was due to leave. The total playing time was 43 hr 16 min and a record Test match aggregate of 1981 runs was scored.

Largest crowds The greatest attendance at a cricket match is about 394 000 for the Test between India and England at Eden Gardens, Calcutta on 1–6 Jan 1982. The record for a Test series is 933 513 for Australia v. England (five matches) in 1936/37. The greatest recorded attendance at a cricket match on one day was 90 800 on the second day of the Test between Australia and the West Indies at Melbourne on 11 Feb 1961. The English match record is 159 000 for England v. Australia at Headingley, Leeds on 22–27 Jul 1948, and the record for one day probably a capacity of 46 000 for Lancashire v. Yorkshire at Old Trafford on 2 Aug 1926. The English record for a Test series is 549 650 for the series against Australia in 1953. The highest attendance for a limited-overs game is an estimated 90 450 at Eden Gardens to see India play South Africa on the latter's return to official international cricket, on 10 Nov 1991.

Most successful Test captain Clive Hubert Lloyd (b. 31 Aug 1944) led the West Indies in 74 Test matches from 22 Nov 1974 to 2 Jan 1985. Of these, 36 were won, 12 lost and 26 were drawn. His team set records for most successive Test wins, 11 in 1984, and most Tests without defeat, 27, between losses to Australia in December 1981 and January 1985 (through injury Lloyd missed one of those matches, when the West Indies were captained by Vivian Richards).

One-Day Internationals

World Cup The World Cup was held in England in 1975, 1979 and 1983, in India and Pakistan in 1987, and in Australia and New Zealand in 1992. The West Indies are the only double winners, in 1975 and 1979. Matches were originally 60 overs per side, but since 1987 they have been of 50 overs.

One-day international records *Team* The highest innings score by a team is 363–7 (55 overs) by England v. Pakistan at Trent Bridge on 20 Aug 1992. The lowest completed innings total is 43 by Pakistan v. the West Indies at Newlands, Cape Town, South Africa on 25 Feb 1993. The largest victory margin is 232 runs by Australia v. Sri Lanka (323–2 to 91), at Adelaide, Australia on 28 Jan 1985.

Individual The highest individual score is 189 not out by Isaac Vivian Alexander

English One–Day Cricket Records

GC/NWT: Gillette Cup (1963–1980); NatWest Trophy (1981–)
      (60-over matches; 65-over matches 1963).
SL (Sunday League): John Player (1969–1986); Refuge Assurance (1987–91);
                  AXA Equity & Law (1993–) (50-over matches;
                  40-over matches 1969–92).
B & H: Benson & Hedges Cup (1972–) (55-over matches).

Most wins
GC/NWT	5	Lancashire 1970–2, 1975, 1990.
SL	3	Kent 1972–3, 1976; Essex 1981, 1984–5; Hampshire 1975, 1978, 1986;
		Worcestershire 1971, 1987–8; Lancashire 1969–70, 1989.
B & H	3	Kent 1973, 1976, 1978; Leicestershire 1972, 1975, 1985.

Highest innings total
GC/NWT	413–4	Somerset v. Devon, Torquay, 1990.
SL	360–3	Somerset v. Glamorgan, Neath, 1990.
B & H	388–7	Essex v. Scotland, Chelmsford, 1992.

Lowest innings total
GC/NWT	39	Ireland v. Sussex, Hove, 1985.
SL	23	Middlesex v. Yorkshire, Headingley, 1974.
B & H	50	Hampshire v. Yorkshire, Headingley, 1991.

Highest individual innings
GC/NWT	206	Alvin Isaac Kallicharran (b. 21 Mar 1949), Warwickshire v. Oxfordshire, Edgbaston, 1984.
SL	176	Graham Alan Gooch (b. 23 Jul 1953), Essex v. Glamorgan, Southend, 1983.
B & H	198*	Graham Gooch, Essex v. Sussex, Hove, 1982.

Best individual bowling
GC/NWT	8–21	Michael Anthony Holding (b. 16 Feb 1954), Derbyshire v. Sussex, Hove, 1988.
SL	8–26	Keith David Boyce (b. 11 Oct 1943), Essex v. Lancashire, Old Trafford, 1971; Alan Ward (b. 10 Aug 1947) took 4 wickets in 4 balls, Derbyshire v. Sussex, Derby, 1970.
B & H	7–12	Wayne Wendell Daniel (b. 16 Jan 1956), Middlesex v. Minor Counties (East), Ipswich, 1978.

Most dismissals in an innings
GC/NWT	6	Robert William Taylor (b. 17 Jul 1941), Derbyshire v. Essex, Derby, 1981; Terry Davies (b. 25 Oct 1960), Glamorgan v. Staffordshire, Stone, 1986.
SL	7	Bob Taylor, Derbyshire v. Lancashire, Old Trafford, 1975.
B & H	8	Derek John Somerset Taylor (b. 12 Nov 1942), Somerset v. Combined Universities, Taunton, 1982.

Runs in career
GC/NWT	2261	Graham Gooch, Essex 1973–92.
SL	7259	Graham Gooch, Essex 1973–93.
B & H	4456	Graham Gooch, Essex 1973–93.

Wickets in career
GC/NWT	81	Geoffrey Graham Arnold (b. 3 Sep 1944), Surrey, Sussex 1963–80.
SL	386	John Kenneth Lever (b. 24 Feb 1949), Essex 1969–89.
B & H	149	John Lever, Essex 1972–89.

Dismissals in career
GC/NWT	66	Bob Taylor, Derbyshire 1963–84.
SL	255	David Bairstow, Yorkshire 1972–90.
B & H	122	David Bairstow, Yorkshire 1972–90.

*Not out

English County Championship

The greatest number of victories since 1890, when the Championship was officially constituted, has been by Yorkshire with 29 outright wins (the last in 1968), and one shared (1949). The record number of consecutive title wins is seven by Surrey from 1952 to 1958. The greatest number of appearances in County Championship matches is 763 by Wilfred Rhodes for Yorkshire between 1898 and 1930, and the greatest number of consecutive appearances is 423 by Kenneth George Suttle (b. 25 Aug 1928) of Sussex between 1954 and 1969. James Graham 'Jimmy' Binks (b. 5 Oct 1935) played in all 412 County Championship matches for Yorkshire between his début in 1955 and his retirement in 1969.

Richards (b. 7 Mar 1952) for the West Indies v. England at Old Trafford on 31 May 1984. The best bowling analysis is 7–37 by Aqib Javed (b. 5 Aug 1972) for Pakistan v. India at Sharjah on 25 Oct 1991. The best partnership is 224 unbroken by Dean Mervyn Jones (b. 24 Mar 1961) and Allan Border for Australia v. Sri Lanka at Adelaide, Australia on 28 Jan 1985.

Career The most matches played is 255 by Allan Border (Australia), 1979–93. The most runs scored is 8195 (av. 41·81) by Desmond Leo Haynes (West Indies) (b. 15 Feb 1956) in 225 matches, 1977–93; this total includes a record 16 centuries. The most wickets taken is 241 (av. 26·65) by Kapil Dev (India) in 206 matches, 1978–93. The most dismissals is 204 (183 ct, 21 st) by Peter Jeffrey Leroy Dujon (West Indies) (b. 28 Mar 1956) in 169 matches, 1981–91. The most catches by a fielder is 117 by Border.

Oldest and Youngest

First-class The oldest player in first-class cricket was the Governor of Bombay, Raja Maharaj Singh (India) (1878–1959), aged 72yr 192days, when he batted, scoring 4, on the opening day of the match played on 25–27 Nov 1950

at Bombay for his XI v. Commonwealth XI. The youngest is reputed to be Esmail Ahmed Baporia (India) (b. 24 Apr 1939) for Gujarat v. Baroda at Ahmedabad, India on 10 Jan 1951, aged 11yr 261days. The oldest Englishman was Benjamin Aislabie (1774–1842) for MCC (of whom he was the secretary) v. Cambridge University at Lord's on 1–2 Jul 1841, when he was aged 67yr 169days. The youngest English first-class player was Charles Robertson Young (1852–?) for Hampshire v. Kent at Gravesend on 13 Jun 1867, aged 15yr 131days.

Test The oldest man to play in a Test match was Wilfred Rhodes, aged 52yr 165days, for England v. West Indies at Kingston, Jamaica on 12 April 1930. Rhodes made his Test début in the last Test of William Gilbert Grace (1848–1915), who at 50yr 320days at Nottingham on 3 Jun 1899 was the oldest ever Test captain. The youngest Test captain was the Nawab of Pataudi (later Mansur Ali Khan) at 21yr 77days on 23 Mar 1962 for India v. West Indies at Bridgetown, Barbados. The youngest Test player was Mushtaq Mohammad (b. 22 Nov 1943), aged 15yr 124days, for Pakistan v. West Indies at Lahore on 26 March 1959. England's youngest player was Dennis Brian Close (b. 24 Feb 1931) aged 18yr 149days v. New Zealand at Old Trafford on 23 Jul 1949.

Women's Cricket

Batting Individual The highest individual innings recorded is 224 not out by Mabel Bryant for Visitors v. Residents at Eastbourne, E Sussex in August 1901. The highest innings in a Test match is 193 by Denise Annetts (b. 30 Jan 1964), in 381 minutes, for Australia v. England at Collingham, Notts on 23–24 Aug 1987 in a four-day Test. With Lindsay Reeler (b. 18 Mar 1961), 110 not out, she added 309 for the third wicket, the highest Test partnership. The highest in a three-day Test is 189 (in 222 minutes) by Elizabeth Alexandra 'Betty' Snowball (1907–88) for England v. New Zealand at Christchurch, New Zealand on 16 Feb 1935.

Rachael Flint (*née* Heyhoe) (b. 11 Jun 1939) has scored the most runs in Test cricket, 1814 (av. 49·02) in 25 matches from December 1960 to July 1979.

Team The highest innings score by any team is 567 by Tarana v. Rockley, at Rockley, New South Wales, Australia in 1896. The highest Test innings is 525 by Australia v. India at Ahmedabad on 4 Feb 1984. The highest score by England is 503 for five wickets declared by England v. New Zealand at Christchurch, New Zealand on 16 and 18 Feb 1935. The most in a Test in England is 426 by India at Stanley Park, Blackpool, Lancs on 3–7 Jul 1986.

The lowest innings in a Test is 35 by England v. Australia at St Kilda, Melbourne, Australia on 22 Feb 1958. The lowest in a Test in England is 63 by New Zealand at Worcester on 5 Jul 1954.

Bowling Mary Beatrice Duggan (England) (1925–73) took a record 77 wickets (av. 13·49) in 17 Tests from 1949 to 1963. She recorded the best Test analysis with seven wickets for six runs for England v. Australia at St Kilda, Melbourne on 22 Feb 1958.

Rubina Winifred Humphries (b. 19 Aug 1915), for Dalton Ladies v. Woodfield SC, at Huddersfield, W Yorks on 26 Jun 1931, took all ten wickets for no runs. (She also scored all her team's runs.) This bowling feat was equalled by Rosemary White (b. 22 Jan 1938) for Wallington LCC v. Beaconsfield LCC in July 1962.

All-round Betty Wilson (Australia) (b. 1923) was the first Test player, man or woman, to score a century and take ten wickets in a Test match. She took 7–7, including a hat-trick, and 4–9 and scored exactly 100 in the second innings against England at St Kilda on 21–24 Feb 1958. Enid Bakewell (b. 18 Dec 1940) was the first English Test player, man or woman, to achieve this Test Match double. Playing against the West Indies at Edgbaston on 1–3 Jul 1979, she scored 112 not out and had match figures of 10–75.

Wicket-keeping Lisa Nye (b. 24 Oct 1966) claimed a Test record eight dismissals (six caught, two stumpings) in an innings for England v. New Zealand at New Plymouth on 12–15 Feb 1992. Christina Matthews (Australia) (b. 1959) has taken a record 53 dismissals (43 catches, 10 stumpings) in 19 Tests.

World Cup Four women's World Cups have been staged. Australia won in 1978, 1982 and 1988 and England in 1973. The highest individual score in this series is 143 not out by Lindsay Reeler for Australia v. Netherlands at Perth, Australia on 29 Nov 1988. The highest by an England player is 138 not out by Janette Brittin v. International XI at Hamilton, New Zealand on 14 Jan 1982.

Highest individual innings In a Junior House match between Clarke's House (now Poole's) and North Town, at Clifton College, Bristol, 22–23, 26–28 Jun 1899, Arthur Edward Jeune Collins (1885–1914) scored an unprecedented 628 not out in 6 hr 50 min, over five afternoons' batting, carrying his bat through the innings of 836. The scorer, E. W. Pegler, gave the score as '628–plus or minus 20, shall we say'.

Highest partnership During a Harris Shield match in 1988 at Sassanian Ground, Bombay, India, Vinod Kambli (b. 18 Jan 1972) (349 not out) and Sachin Tendulkar (b. 24 Apr 1973) (326 not out) put on an unbeaten partnership of 664 runs for the third wicket for Sharadashram Vidyamandir v. St Xavier's High School.

Fastest individual scoring Stanley Keppel 'Shunter' Coen (South Africa) (1902–67) scored 50 runs (11 fours and one six) in 7 min for Gezira v. the RAF in 1942. The fastest hundred by a prominent player in a minor match was by Vivian Frank Shergold Crawford (1879–1922) in 19 min at Cane Hill, Surrey on 16 Sep 1899. Lindsay Martin scored 100 off 20 deliveries (13 sixes, 5 fours and 2 singles) for Rosewater v. Warradale on 19 Dec 1987. David Michael Roberts Whatmore (b. 6 Apr 1949) scored 210 (including 25 sixes and 12 fours) off 61 balls for Alderney v. Sun Alliance at Alderney, Channel Islands on 19 Jun 1983. His first 100 came off 33 balls and his second off 25 balls.

Most runs off a ball Garry Chapman (partnered by Chris Veal) scored 17 (all run, with no overthrows) off a single delivery for Banyule against Macleod at Windsor Reserve, Victoria, Australia on 13 Oct 1990. Chapman had pulled the ball to mid-wicket where it disappeared into 25cm *10in* high grass.

Most runs off an over H. Morley scored 62, nine sixes and two fours, off an eight-ball over from R. Grubb which had four no-balls, in a Queensland country match in 1968–9.

Bowling Nine wickets with nine consecutive balls were taken by: Stephen Fleming, for Marlborough College 'A' XI *v.* Bohally Intermediate at Blenheim, New Zealand in December 1967; and by Paul Hugo for Smithfield School *v.* Aliwal North, South Africa in February 1931. In the Inter-Divisional Ships Shield at Purfleet, Essex on 17 May 1924, Joseph William Brockley (b. 9 Apr 1907) took all ten wickets, clean bowled, for two runs in 11 balls–including a triple hat trick. Jennings Tune took all ten wickets, all bowled, for 0 runs in five overs for Cliffe *v.* Eastrington in the Howden and District League at Cliffe, Yorkshire on 6 May 1922. Wynton Edwards of Queen's College took 10 for 0 (10 overs) against Selborne College at Queenstown, South Africa on 25 Mar 1950 and Errol Hall also took 10 for 0 (27 balls) for Australian *v.* Tannymorel at Warwick, Queensland on 2 Nov 1986.

In 1881 Frederick Robert Spofforth (1853–1926) at Bendigo, Victoria, Australia clean bowled all ten wickets in *both* innings. J. Bryant for Erskine *v.* Deaf Mutes in Melbourne on 15 and 22 Oct 1887, and Albert Rimmer for Linwood School *v.* Cathedral GS at Canterbury, New Zealand in December 1925, repeated the feat. In the 1910 season, H. Hopkinson, of Mildmay CC, London, took 99 wickets for 147 runs.

Wicket-keeping Welihinda Badalge Bennett (b. 25 Jan 1933) caught four and stumped six batsmen in one innings, on 1 March 1953 for Mahinda College *v.* Galle CC, at the Galle Esplanade, Sri Lanka.

Fielding In a Wellington, New Zealand secondary schools 11-a-side match on 16 Mar 1974, Stephen Lane, 13, held 14 catches in the field (seven in each innings) for St Patrick's College, Silverstream *v.* St Bernard's College, Lower Hutt.

Croquet

Most championships The greatest number of victories in the Open Croquet Championships (instituted at Evesham, Worcestershire, 1867) is ten by John William Solomon (b. 22 Nov 1931) (1953, 1956, 1959, 1961, 1963–8). He also won ten Men's Championships (1951, 1953, 1958–60, 1962, 1964–5, 1971–2), ten Open Doubles (with Edmond Patrick Charles Cotter) (1954–5, 1958–9, 1961–5 and 1969) and one Mixed Doubles (with Freda Oddie) in 1954, making a total of 31 titles. Solomon has also won the President's Cup (instituted 1934, an invitation event for the best eight players) on nine occasions (1955, 1957–9, 1962–4, 1968 and 1971), and was Champion of Champions on all four occasions that that competition was run (1967–70).

George Nigel Aspinall (b. 29 Jul 1946) has won the President's Cup a record 11 times, 1969–70, 1973–6, 1978, 1980, 1982, 1984–5.

Dorothy Dyne Steel (1884–1965), fifteen times winner of the Women's Championship (1919–39), won the Open Croquet Championship four times (1925, 1933, 1935–6). She had also five Doubles and seven Mixed Doubles for a total of 31 titles.

World championships The first World Championships were held at the Hurlingham Club, London in 1989 and have been held annually since. The only double winner is Robert Fulford (GB) (b. 1970), 1990 and 1992.

Cross-country Running

World Championships The inaugural International Cross-Country Championships took place at the Hamilton Park Racecourse, Scotland on 28 Mar 1903.

The greatest margin of victory is 56sec or 356m *390yd* by John 'Jack' Thomas Holden (England) (b. 13 Mar 1907) at Ayr Racecourse, Strathclyde on 24 Mar 1934.

Since 1973 the events have been official world championships under the auspices of the International Amateur Athletic Federation.

Most wins The greatest number of team victories has been by England with 45 for men, 11 for junior men and seven for women. The USA and USSR each has a record eight women's team victories. The greatest team domination was by Kenya at Auckland, New Zealand on 26 March 1988. Their senior men's team finished eight men in the first nine, with a low score of 23 (six to score) and their junior men's team set a record low score, 11 (four to score) with six in the first seven.

The greatest number of men's individual victories is five by John Ngugi (Kenya) (b. 10 May 1962), 1986–89 and 1992. The women's race has been won five times by: Doris Brown-Heritage (USA) (b. 17 Sep 1942), 1967–71; and by Grete Waitz (*née* Andersen) (Norway) (b. 1 Oct 1953), 1978–81 and 1983.

Most appearances Marcel van de Wattyne (Belgium) (b. 7 Jul 1924) ran in a record 20 races, 1946–65. The women's record is 16 by Jean Lochhead (Wales) (b. 24 Dec 1946), 1967–79, 1981, 1983–84.

English Championship The National Cross-Country Championship was inaugurated at Roehampton, London in 1877.

The most individual titles won is four by Percy Haines Stenning (1854–92) (Thames Hare and Hounds) in 1877–80 and Alfred E. Shrubb (1878–1964) (South London Harriers) in 1901–4. The most successful club in the team race has been Birchfield Harriers from Birmingham with 28 wins and one tie between 1880 and 1988.

The most individual wins in the English women's championships is six by Lillian Styles, 1928–30, 1933–4 and 1937; the most successful team is Birchfield Harriers with 13 titles.

The largest field was the 2195 finishers in the senior race in 1990 at Leeds, W Yorks on 24 February. In this race, a record 250 clubs scored (by having six runners finish).

Curling

Most titles Canada has won the men's World Championships (instituted 1959) 20 times, 1959–64, 1966, 1968–72, 1980, 1982–3, 1985–7, 1989–90.

The most Strathcona Cup (instituted 1903) wins is seven by Canada (1903, 1909, 1912, 1923, 1938, 1957, 1965) against Scotland.

The most women's World Championships (instituted 1979) is six by Canada (1980, 1984–7, 1989).

Fastest game Eight curlers from the Burlington Golf and Country Club curled an eight-end game in 47 min 24 sec, with time penalties of 5 min 30 sec, at

---

Croquet International trophy

The MacRobertson Shield (instituted 1925) has been won a record nine times by Great Britain, 1925, 1937, 1956, 1963, 1969, 1974, 1982, 1990 and 1993.

A record seven appearances have been made by John G. Prince (New Zealand) (b. 23 Jul 1945) in 1963, 1969, 1975, 1979, 1982, 1986 and 1990; on his début he was the youngest ever international at 17 yr 190 days.

Largest cross-country field

The largest recorded field in any cross-country race was 11 763 starters (10 810 finished) in the 30 km *18·6 miles* Lidingöloppet, near Stockholm, Sweden on 3 Oct 1982.

Longest curling throw

The longest throw of a curling stone was a distance of 175·66 m *576 ft 4 in* by Eddie Kulbacki (Canada) at Park Lake, Neepawa, Manitoba, Canada on 29 Jan 1989. The attempt took place on a specially prepared sheet of curling ice on frozen Park Lake, a record 1200 ft *365·76 m* long.

Burlington, Ontario, Canada on 4 Apr 1986, following rules agreed with the Ontario Curling Association. The time is taken from when the first rock crosses the near hogline until the game's last rock comes to a complete stop.

Largest bonspiel The largest bonspiel in the world is the Manitoba Curling Association Bonspiel held annually in Winnipeg, Canada. In 1988 there were 1424 teams of four men, a total of 5696 curlers, using 187 sheets of curling ice.

Largest rink The world's largest curling rink was the Big Four Curling Rink, Calgary, Alberta, Canada, opened in 1959 and closed in 1989. Ninety-six teams and 384 players were accommodated on two floors each with 24 sheets of ice.

Cycling

Highest speed The highest speed ever achieved on a bicycle is 245·077 km/h *152·284 mph* by John Howard (USA) behind a wind-shield at Bonneville Salt Flats, Utah, USA on 20 Jul 1985. It should be noted that considerable help was provided by the slipstreaming effect of the lead vehicle.

The British speed record is 158·05 km/h *98·21 mph* over 200 metres by David Le Grys (b. 10 Aug 1955) on a closed section of the M42 at Alvechurch, Warks on 28 Aug 1985.

The greatest distance ever covered in one hour is 122·771 km *76 miles 504 yd* by Leon Vanderstuyft (Belgium) (1890–1964) on the Montlhéry Motor Circuit, France on 30 Sep 1928, achieved from a standing start paced by a motorcycle.

The 24hr record behind pace is 1958·196 km *1216·8 miles* by Michael Secrest at Phoenix International Raceway, Arizona on 26–27 Apr 1990.

Most titles *Olympic* The most gold medals won is three by Paul Masson (France) (1874–1945) in 1896, Francisco Verri (Italy) (1885–1945) in 1906 and Robert Charpentier (France) (1916–66) in 1936. Daniel Morelon (France) (b. 28 Jul 1944) won two in 1968 and a third in 1972; he also won a silver in 1976 and a bronze medal in 1964. In the 'unofficial' 1904 cycling programme,

Roller cycling

James Baker (USA) achieved a record speed of 246·5 km/h *153·2 mph* at El Con Mall, Tucson, Arizona, USA on 28 Jan 1989.

Marcus Latimer Hurley (USA) (1885–1941) won four events.

World World Championships are contested annually. They were first staged for amateurs in 1893 and for professionals in 1895.

The most wins at a particular event is ten by Koichi Nakano (Japan) (b. 14 Nov 1955), professional sprint 1977–86.

The most wins at a men's amateur event is seven by Daniel Morelon (France), sprint 1966–7, 1969–71, 1973, 1975; and Leon Meredith (GB) (1882–1930), 100 km motor paced 1904–5, 1907–9, 1911, 1913.

The most women's titles is eight by Jeannie Longo (France) (b. 31 Oct 1958), pursuit 1986 and 1988–9; road 1985–7 and 1989 and points 1989.

British Beryl Burton (b. 12 May 1937), 25 times British all-round time trial champion (1959–83), won 72 individual road TT titles, 14 track pursuit titles and 12 road race titles to 1986. Ian Hallam (b. 24 Nov 1948) won a record 25 men's titles, 1969–82.

Chris Boardman, winner of the 1992 Olympic individual pursuit title, on the revolutionary Lotus bike with which he set a 5 km world record.
(Photo: Allsport/Davis Cannon)

World Cycling Records

These records are those recognized by the Union Cycliste Internationale (UCI). From 1 Jan 1993 their severely reduced list no longer distinguished between those set by professionals and amateurs, indoor and outdoor, or at altitude and sea level.

MEN

Distance	hr:min:sec	Name and Country	Venue	Date
Unpaced Standing Start				
1km	1:02·091	Maic Malchow (GDR)	Colorado Springs, USA	28 Aug 1986
4km	4:24·496	Christopher Boardman (GB)	Barcelona, Spain	28 Jul 1992
4km team	4:08·06	Germany	Stuttgart, Germany	16 Aug 1991
1hour (km)	51·15135	Francesco Moser (Italy)	Mexico City	23 Jan 1984
Unpaced Flying Start				
200metres	10·099	Vladimir Adamashvili (USSR)	Moscow, USSR	6 Aug 1990
500metres	26·649	Aleksandr Kirichenko (USSR)	Moscow, USSR	29 Oct 1988

WOMEN

Distance	hr:min:sec	Name and Country	Venue	Date
Unpaced Standing Start				
500m	33·438	Galina Yenyukhina (Russia)	Moscow, Russia	29 Apr 1993
3km	3:38·190	Jeannie Longo (France)	Mexico City	5 Oct 1989
1hour (km)	46·35270	Jeannie Longo (France)	Mexico City	1 Oct 1989
Unpaced Flying Start				
200metres	11·101	Galina Yenyukhina (Russia)	Moscow, Russia	2 Jul 1992
500metres	29·655	Erika Salumäe (USSR)	Moscow, USSR	6 Aug 1987

Tour de France The world's premier stage was first contested in 1903. Held over a three-week period, the longest race ever staged was over 5745 km *3570 miles* in 1926. The greatest number of wins in the *Tour de France* is five by Jacques Anquetil (France) (1934–1987), 1957, 1961–4; Eddy Merckx (Belgium) (b. 17 Jun 1945), 1969–72 and 1974; and Bernard Hinault (France) (b. 14 Nov 1954), 1978–9, 1981–2 and 1985.

The closest race ever was in 1989 when after 3267 km *2030 miles* over 23 days (1–23 Jul) Greg LeMond (USA) (b. 26 Jun 1960), who completed the Tour in 87hr 38min 35sec, beat Laurent Fignon (France) (b. 12 Aug 1960) in Paris by only 8sec.

The fastest average speed was 39·504 km/h *24·547 mph* by Miguel Induráin (Spain) (b. 16 Jul 1964) in 1992.

The longest ever stage was the 486km from Les Sables d'Olonne to Bayonne in 1919. The most participants were 210 starters in 1986.

Tour of Britain (Milk Race) Four riders have won the Tour of Britain twice each — Bill Bradley (GB) (1959–60), Leslie George West (GB) (1965, 1967), Fedor den Hertog (Netherlands) (1969, 1971) and Yuriy Kashurin (USSR) (1979, 1982).

The closest race ever was in 1976 when after 1665·67km *1035 miles* over 14days (30 May–12 Jun) Bill Nickson (GB) (b. 30 Jan 1953) beat Joe Waugh (GB) by 5sec.

The fastest average speed is 42·185km/h *26·213 mph* by Joey McLoughlin (GB) (b. 3 Dec 1964) in the 1986 race (1714km *1065 miles*).

Malcolm Elliott (b. 1 Jul 1961) won a record six stages in 1983 and had taken his total to 15 by 1987, after winning a record four in succession.

The longest Milk Race was in 1969 (2438·16 km *1515 miles*) although the longest ever Tour of Britain was in 1953 (2624·84km *1631 miles* starting and finishing in London).

Six-day races The most wins in six-day races is 88 out of 233 events by Patrick Sercu (b. 27 Jun 1944), of Belgium, 1964–83.

Longest one-day race The longest single-day 'massed start' road race is the 551–620 km *342–385 miles* Bordeaux–Paris, France event. Paced over all or part of the route, the highest average speed was in 1981 with 47·186km/h *29·32mph* by Herman van Springel (Belgium) (b. 14 Aug 1943) for 584·5km *363·1 miles* in 13hr 35min 18sec.

Cross-America The trans-America solo records recognized by the Ultra-Marathon Cycling Association are: men, Paul Selon 8days 8hr 45min; women, Susan Notorangelo 9days 9hr 9min, both in the Race Across America, Costa Mesa, California to New York, 5000km *3107 miles* in August 1989.

The trans-Canada record is 13days 9hr 6min by Bill Narasnek of Lively, Ontario, 6037km *3751 miles* from Vancouver, BC to Halifax, Nova Scotia on 5–18 Jul 1991.

Daniel Buettner, Bret Anderson, Martin Engel and Anne Knabe cycled the length of the Americas, from Prudhoe Bay, Alaska, USA to the Beagle Channel, Ushuaia, Argentina from 8 Aug 1986–13 Jun 1987. They cycled a total distance of 24 568km *15 266 miles.*

Endurance Thomas Edward Godwin (GB) (1912–75) in the 365 days of 1939 covered 120 805 km *75 065 miles* or an average of 330·96 km *205·65 miles* per day. He then completed 160 934 km *100 000 miles* in 500 days to 14 May 1940.

Jay Aldous and Matt DeWaal cycled 22 997km *14 290 miles* on a round-the-world trip from This is the Place Monument, Salt Lake City, Utah, USA in 106 days, 2 Apr–16 Jul 1984.

Tal Burt (Israel) circumnavigated the world (21 329km *13 253 road miles*) from Place du Trocadero, Paris, France in 77days 14hr, from 1 Jun–17 Aug 1992.

Cycle touring The greatest mileage amassed in a cycle tour was more than 646 960km *402 000 miles* by the itinerant lecturer Walter Stolle (b. Sudetenland, 1926) from 24 Jan 1959 to 12 Dec 1976. He visited 159 countries starting from Romford, Essex. From 1922 to 25 Dec 1973 Tommy Chambers (1903–84) of Glasgow, rode a verified total of 1 286 517km *799 405 miles.*

Visiting every continent, John W. Hathaway (b. England, 13 Jan 1925) of Vancouver, Canada covered 81 430km *50 600 miles* from 10 Nov 1974 to 6 Oct 1976. Veronica and Colin Scargill, of Bedford, travelled 29 000km *18 020 miles*

British Road Records

Type	Time (hr:min:sec)	Name	Date
100 Miles			
Men's bike	3:16:56	Ian Cammish (b. 1 Oct 1956)	1 Nov 1990
Men's trike	3:39:51	Dave Pitt (b. 3 Mar 1950)	18 Oct 1991
Women's bike	3:49:42	Pauline Strong (b. 19 Mar 1956)	18 Oct 1991
London to Brighton and Back			
Men's bike	4:15:08	Phil Griffiths (b. 18 Mar 1949)	20 Jul 1977
Men's trike	4:51:07	Dave Pitt	25 Jul 1979
Women's bike	4:55:28	Gill Clapton (b. 25 Sep 1942)	15 Jul 1972
London to Bath and Back			
Men's bike	9:03:07	John Woodburn (b. 22 Dec 1936)	13 Jun 1981
Men's trike	10:19:00	Ralph Dadswell (b. 28 Jul 1964)	22 Jun 1991
Women's bike	10:41:22	Eileen Sheridan (b. 18 Oct 1923)	22 Aug 1952
Land's End to John O' Groats			
Men's bike	1 day 21:02:18	Andy Wilkinson (b. 22 Aug 1963)	29 Sep–1 Oct 1990
Men's trike	2 days 5:29:01	Ralph Dadswell	10–12 Aug 1992
Women's bike	2 days 6:49:45	Pauline Strong	28–30 Jul 1990

Miguel Induráin (Spain), in the distinctive yellow jersey, won the 1992 Tour de France with a record average speed.

(Photo: Allsport/Vandystadt)

around the world on a tandem, 25 Feb 1974–27 Aug 1975.

The most participants in a bicycle tour are 31 678 in the 90 km *56 miles* London to Brighton Bike Ride on 19 Jun 1988. However, it is estimated that 45 000 cyclists took part in the 75 km *46 miles* Tour de l'Ile de Montréal, Canada on 7 Jun 1992.

The most participants in a tour in an excess of 1000 km are 2037 (from 2157 starters) for the Australian Bicentennial Caltex Bike Ride from Melbourne to Sydney from 26 Nov–10 Dec 1988.

Cyclo-Cross

The greatest number of World Championships (instituted 1950) has been won by Eric de Vlaeminck (Belgium) (b. 23 Aug 1945) with the Amateur and Open in 1966 and six Professional titles in 1968–73.

British titles (instituted 1955) have been won most often by John Atkins (b. 7 Apr 1942) with five Amateur (1961–2,

1966–8), seven Professional (1969–75) and one Open title in 1977.

Highest altitude Canadians Bruce Bell, Philip Whelan and Suzanne MacFadyen cycled at an altitude of 6960 m *22 834 ft* on the peak of Mt Aconcagua, Argentina on 25 Jan 1991.

Cycle Speedway

First mention of the sport is at Coventry in 1920 and it was first organized in 1945. The sport's governing body, the Cycle Speedway Council, was formed in 1973. The most British Senior Team Championships (instituted 1950) is eight by Poole, Dorset (1982, 1984, 1987–92).

The most individual titles is four by Derek Garnett (b. 16 Jul 1937) (1963, 1965, 1968 and 1972); he also won the inaugural British Veterans' Championship in 1987.

Darts

Most titles Eric Bristow (b. 25 Apr 1957) has most wins in the World Masters Championship (instituted 1974) with five, 1977, 1979, 1981 and 1983–4, the World Professional Championship (instituted 1978) with five, 1980–81 and 1984–6, and the World Cup Singles (instituted 1977), four, 1983, 1985, 1987 and 1989.

John Lowe (b. 21 Jul 1945) is the only other man to have won each of the four

Darts Scoring Records

24-Hour

MEN (8 players) 1 722 249 by Broken Hill Darts Club at Broken Hill, New South Wales, Australia on 28–29 Sep 1985. **WOMEN** (8 players) 744 439 by a team from the Lord Clyde, Leyton, London on 13–14 Oct 1990. **INDIVIDUAL** 518 060 by Davy Richardson-Page at Blucher Social Club, Newcastle on 6–7 Jul 1991. **BULLS AND 25s** (8 players) 510 625 by a team at the Kent and Canterbury Hospital Sports and Social Club, Canterbury on 20–21 Oct 1989.

10-Hour

MOST TREBLES 3056 (from 7992 darts) by Paul Taylor at the Woodhouse Tavern, Leytonstone, London on 19 Oct 1985. **MOST DOUBLES** 3265 (from 8451 darts) by Paul Taylor at the Lord Brooke, Walthamstow, London on 5 Sep 1987. **HIGHEST SCORE** (retrieving own darts) 465 919 by Jon Archer and Neil Rankin at the Royal Oak, Cossington, Leics on 17 Nov 1990. **BULLS** (individual) 1200 by Johnny Mielcarek (USA) at the Pete Rose Ballpark Cafe, Boca Raton, Florida, USA on 27 May 1993.

6-Hour

MEN 210 172 by Russell Locke at the Hugglescote Working Mens Club, Coalville, Leics on 10 Sep 1989. **WOMEN** 99 725 by Karen Knightly at the Lord Clyde on 17 Mar 1991.

Million and One Up

MEN (8 players) 36 583 darts by a team at the Buzzy's Pub and Grub, Lynn, Massachusetts, USA on 19–20 Oct 1991. **WOMEN** (8 players) 70 019 darts by The Delinquents darts team at the Top George, Combe Martin, Devon on 11–13 Sep 1987.

major titles: World Masters, 1976 and 1980; World Professional, 1979, 1987 and 1993; World Cup Singles, 1981; and *News of the World*, 1981.

World Cup The first World Cup was held at the Wembley Conference Centre, London in 1977. England has a record seven wins at this biennial tournament. Eric Bristow and John Lowe played on all seven teams.

A biennial World Cup for women was instituted in 1983 and has been won three times by England.

Speed records The fastest time taken to complete three games of 301, finishing on doubles, is 1 min 47 sec by Keith Deller (b. 24 Dec 1959) on BBC TV's *Record Breakers* on 22 Oct 1985.

The record time for going round the board clockwise in 'doubles' at arm's length is 9·2 sec by Dennis Gower at the Millers Arms, Hastings, E Sussex on 12 Oct 1975 and 14·5 sec in numerical order by Jim Pike (1903–60) at the Craven Club, Newmarket, Suffolk in March 1944.

The record for this feat at the 9ft *2·7 m* throwing distance, retrieving own darts, is 2 min 13 sec by Bill Duddy (b. 29 Sep 1932) at The Plough, Haringey, London on 29 Oct 1972.

Least darts Scores of 201 in four darts, 301 in six darts, 401 in seven darts and 501 in nine darts, have been achieved on various occasions.

The lowest number of darts thrown for a score of 1001 is 19 by: Cliff Inglis (b. 27 May 1935) (160, 180, 140, 180, 121, 180, 40) at the Bromfield Men's Club, Devon on 11 Nov 1975 and Jocky Wilson (b. 22

Least darts

Roy Edwin Blowes (Canada) (b. 8 Oct 1930) was the first person to achieve a 501 in nine darts, 'double-on, double-off', at the Widgeons pub, Calgary, Canada at 9 Mar 1987. His scores were: bull, treble 20, treble 17, five treble 20s and a double 20 to finish.

Record prize

John Lowe won £102 000 for achieving the first 501 scored with the minimum nine darts in a major event on 13 Oct 1984 at Slough in the quarter-finals of the World Match-play Championships. His darts were six successive treble 20s, treble 17, treble 18 and double 18.

John Lowe, one of only two darts players to have won all the major tournaments, won the World Professional Championship for a third time in 1993.

(Photo: Allsport/Simon Bruty)

Mar 1950) (140, 140, 180, 180, 180, 131, Bull) at The London Pride, Bletchley, Bucks on 23 Mar 1989.

A score of 2001 in 52 darts was achieved by Alan Evans (b. 14 Jun 1949) at Ferndale, Mid Glam on 3 Sep 1976; 3001 in 73 darts was thrown by Tony Benson at the Plough Inn, Gorton, Manchester on 12 Jul 1986. Linda Batten (b. 26 Nov 1954) set a women's 3001 record of 117 darts at the Old Wheatsheaf, Enfield, London on 2 Apr 1986 and a total of 100 001 was achieved in 3732 darts by Alan Downie of Stornoway on 21 Nov 1986.

Equestrian Sports

Show Jumping

Olympic Games The most Olympic gold medals is five by Hans Günter Winkler (West Germany) (b. 24 Jul 1926), four team in 1956, 1960, 1964 and 1972 and the individual Grand Prix in 1956. He also won team silver in 1976 and team bronze in 1968 for a record seven medals overall.

The most team wins in the Prix des Nations is six by Germany in 1936, 1956, 1960, 1964 and as West Germany in 1972 and 1988.

The lowest score obtained by a winner is no faults by Frantisek Ventura (Czechoslovakia) (1895–1969) on *Eliot*, 1928; Alwin Schockemöhle (West Germany) (b. 29 May 1937) on *Warwick Rex*, 1976 and Ludger Beerbaum (Germany) (b. 25 Aug 1963) on *Classic Touch*, 1992.

Pierre Jonquères d'Oriola (France) (b. 1 Feb 1920) uniquely won the individual gold medal twice, 1952 and 1964.

World Championships The men's World Championships (instituted 1953) have been won twice by Hans Günter Winkler (West Germany) (1954–5) and Raimondo d'Inzeo (Italy) (b. 8 Feb 1925) (1956 and 1960).

The women's title (1965–74) was won twice by Jane 'Janou' Tissot (*née* Lefebvre) (France) (b. Saigon, 14 May 1945) on *Rocket* (1970 and 1974).

A team competition was introduced in 1978 and the most wins is two by France, 1982 and 1990.

President's Cup Instituted in 1965 for Nations Cup teams, it has been won a record 14 times by Great Britain, 1965, 1967, 1970, 1972–4, 1977–9, 1983, 1985–6, 1989, 1991.

World Cup Instituted in 1979, double winners have been Conrad Homfeld (USA) (b. 25 Dec 1951), 1980 and 1985; Ian Millar (Canada) (b. 6 Jan 1947), 1988–9; and John Whitaker (GB) (b. 5 Aug 1955), 1990–91.

King George V Gold Cup and Queen Elizabeth II Cup David Broome (b. 1 Mar 1940) has won the King George V Gold Cup (first held 1911) a record six times, 1960 on *Sunsalve*, 1966 on *Mister Softee*, 1972 on *Sportsman*, 1977 on *Philco*, 1981 on *Mr Ross* and 1991 on *Lannegan*.

The Queen Elizabeth II Cup (first held 1949), for women, has been won five times by his sister Elizabeth Edgar (b. 28 Apr 1943), 1977 on *Everest Wallaby*, 1979 on *Forever*, 1981 and 1982 on *Everest Forever*, 1986 on *Everest Rapier*.

The only horse to win both these trophies is *Sunsalve* in 1957 (with Elisabeth Anderson) and 1960.

Only on three occasions has the winner of the individual Show jumping Olympic title registered 0 faults, the latest being German Ludger Beerbaum on *Classic Touch* in 1992.

(Photo: Allsport/Chris Cole)

Jumping records The official *Fédération Equestre Internationale* records are: high jump 2·47 m *8 ft 1¼ in* by *Huasó*, ridden by Capt. Alberto Larraguibel Morales (Chile) at Viña del Mar, Santiago, Chile on 5 Feb 1949; long jump over water 8·40 m *27 ft 6¾ in* by *Something*, ridden by André Ferreira (South Africa) at Johannesburg, South Africa on 25 Apr 1975.

The British high jump record is 2·32 m *7 ft 7¼ in* by the 16·2 hands *165 cm* grey gelding *Lastic* ridden by Nick Skelton (b. 30 Dec 1957) at Olympia, London on 16 Dec 1978.

On 25 Jun 1937, at Olympia, the Lady Wright (*née* Margery Avis Bullows) set the best recorded height for a British equestrienne on her liver chestnut *Jimmy Brown* at 2·23 m *7 ft 4 in*.

The greatest recorded height reached on bareback is 2·13 m *7 ft* by Michael Whitaker (b. 17 Mar 1960) on *Red Flight*

Carriage driving

World Championships were first held in 1972. Three team titles have been won by: Great Britain, 1972, 1974 and 1980; Hungary, 1976, 1978 and 1984; and the Netherlands, 1982, 1986 and 1988.

Two individual titles have been won by: György Bárdos (Hungary), 1978 and 1980; Tjeerd Velstra (Netherlands), 1982 and 1986; and Ijsbrand Chardon (Netherlands), 1988 and 1992.

at Dublin, Republic of Ireland on 14 Nov 1982.

Three-Day Event

Olympic Games and World Championships Charles Ferdinand Pahud de Mortanges (Netherlands) (1896–1971) won a record four Olympic gold medals, team 1924 and 1928, individual (riding *Marcroix*) 1928 and 1932, when he also won a team silver medal.

Bruce Oram Davidson (USA) (b. 13 Dec 1949) is the only rider to have won two world titles (instituted 1966), on *Irish Cap* in 1974 and *Might Tango* in 1978.

Richard John Hannay Meade (GB) (b. 4 Dec 1938) is the only British rider to win three Olympic gold medals—as an individual in 1972 with team titles in 1968 and 1972.

Badminton The Badminton Three-Day Event (instituted 1949) has been won six times by Lucinda Jane Green (*née* Prior-Palmer) (b. 7 Nov 1953), in 1973 (on *Be Fair*), 1976 (*Wide Awake*), 1977 (*George*), 1979 (*Killaire*), 1983 (*Regal Realm*) and 1984 (*Beagle Bay*).

Ian David Stark (GB) (b. 22 Feb 1954) became the first ever rider to ride first (*Sir Wattie*) and second (*Glenburnie*) in the same year at Badminton in May 1988.

Dressage

Olympic Games and World Championships Germany (West Germany 1968–90) have won a record eight team gold medals, 1928, 1936, 1964, 1968, 1976, 1984, 1988 and 1992, and have

most team wins, six, at the World Championships (instituted 1966). Dr Reiner Klimke (West Germany) (b. 14 Jan 1936) has won a record six Olympic golds (team 1964–88, individual, 1984). He also won individual bronze in 1976 for a record seven medals overall and is the only rider to win two world titles, on *Mehmed* in 1974 and *Ahlerich* in 1982. Henri St Cyr (Sweden) (1904–79) won a record two individual Olympic gold medals, 1952 and 1956. This was equalled by Nicole Uphoff (Germany) in 1992, having previously won in 1988.

World Cup Instituted in 1986, the only double winner is Christine Stückelberger (Switzerland) (b. 22 May 1947) on *Gauguin de Lully* in 1987–8.

Fencing

Most titles *World* The greatest number of individual world titles won is five by Aleksandr Romankov (USSR) (b. 7 Nov 1953), at foil 1974, 1977, 1979, 1982 and 1983, but Christian d'Oriola (France) won four world foil titles, 1947, 1949, 1953–4 as well as two individual Olympic titles (1952 and 1956).

Four women foilists have won three world titles: Helene Mayer (Germany) (1910–53), 1929, 1931, 1937; Ilona Schacherer-Elek (Hungary) (1907–88), 1934–35, 1951; Ellen Müller–Preis (Austria) (b. 6 May 1912), 1947, 1949–50; and Cornelia Hanisch (West Germany) (b. 12 Jun 1952), 1979, 1981, 1985. Of these only Ilona Schacherer-Elek also won two individual Olympic titles (1936 and 1948).

The longest span for winning an individual world or Olympic title is 20 years by Aladár Gerevich (Hungary) (b. 16 Mar 1910) at sabre, 1935–55.

Olympic The most individual Olympic gold medals won is three by Ramón Fonst (Cuba) (1883–1959) in 1900 and 1904 (two) and by Nedo Nadi (Italy) (1894–1952) in 1912 and 1920 (two). Nadi also won three team gold medals in 1920 making five gold medals at one celebration, the record for fencing and then a record for any sport. Aladár Gerevich (Hungary) won seven golds, one individual and six team, 1932–60; a span of 28 years, an Olympic record.

Edoardo Mangiarotti (Italy) (b. 7 Apr 1919) with six gold, five silver and two bronze, holds the record of 13 Olympic medals. He won them for foil and épée from 1936 to 1960.

The most gold medals by a woman is four (one individual, three team) by Yelena Dmitryevna Novikova (*née* Belova) (USSR) (b. 28 Jul 1947) from 1968 to 1976, and the record for all medals is seven (two gold, three silver, two bronze) by Ildikó Sági (formerly Ujlaki, *née* Retjö) (Hungary) (b. 11 May 1937) from 1960 to 1976.

British Three British fencers have won individual world titles: Gwen Neligan (1906–72) at foil in 1933; Henry William Furze 'Bill' Hoskyns (b. 19 Mar 1931) at épée in 1958; and Allan Louis Neville Jay (b. 30 Jun 1931) at foil in 1959, when he also won silver in épée. The only British fencer to win an Olympic gold medal is Gillian Mary Sheen (now Donaldson) (b. 21 Aug 1928) in the 1956 foil.

A record three Olympic medals were won by Edgar Isaac Seligman (1867–1958) with silver medals in the épée team event in 1906, 1908 and 1912.

Bill Hoskyns has competed most often for Great Britain with six Olympic appearances, 1956–76.

The most won at one weapon is ten at women's foil by Gillian Sheen, 1949, 1951–8, 1960. The men's records are: foil, 7 by John Emyrs Lloyd (1908–1987) 1928, 1930–33, 1937–8; épée, 6 by Edward Owen 'Teddy' Bourne (b. 30 Sep 1948) 1966, 1972, 1974, 1976–8 and William Ralph Johnson (b. 3 Jun 1948) 1968, 1982, 1984–5, 1987, 1990; and sabre, 6 by Dr Roger F. Tredgold (1912–75) 1937, 1939, 1947–9, 1955.

Field Sports

Pack The Old Charlton Hunt (later the Goodwood) in West Sussex (now extinct), the Duke of Monmouth and Lord Grey of Werke at Charlton, Sussex, and the Duke of Buckingham in North Yorks owned packs which were entered to fox only, during the reign (1660–85) of Charles II.

Largest The pack with the greatest number of hounds has been the Duke of Beaufort's hounds maintained at Badminton, Avon since 1786. At times hunting six days a week, this pack once had 120 couples of hounds. It now meets four days a week.

Longest mastership The 10th Duke of Beaufort (1900–84) was Master of Foxhounds from 1924 until his death in 1984 and hunted his hounds on 3895 days from 1920–67.

Longest hunt The longest recorded hunt was one held by Squire Sandys which ran from Holmbank, northern Lancs to Ulpha, Cumbria, a total of nearly 80 miles *128 km* in reputedly only 6hr, in January or February 1743.

Beagling
The longest mastership of a pack was by Jean Bethel 'Betty' McKeever (*née* Dawes) (1901–90), who was Master of the Blean Beagles in Kent from 1909 until her death. She was given her first pack by her father at the age of eight and remained the sole Master.

The longest duration hunt was one of 10 hr 5 min by Charlton Hunt of W Sussex, which ran from East Dean Wood at 7:45 a.m. to a kill over 57¼ miles *92 km* away at 5:50 p.m. on 26 Jan 1738.

Most widespread hunting Between 1969 and 1992, John N. P. Watson (b. 18 Jun 1927), hunting correspondent to *Country Life*, hunted with 283 different packs of foxhounds, staghounds and harehounds in Britain, Ireland, USA and Europe.

Record heads The world's finest head is the 23-pointer stag in the Maritzburg collection, Germany. The outside span is 192 cm *75½ in*, the length 120·5 cm *47½ in* and the weight 18·824 kg *41½ lb*.

The greatest number of points is probably 33 (plus 29) on the stag shot in 1696 by Frederick III (1657–1713), the Elector of Brandenburg, later King Frederick I of Prussia.

Largest tally to a single sportsman A record 556 813 head of game fell to the guns of the 2nd Marquess of Ripon (1852–1923) between 1867 and when he dropped dead on a grouse moor after shooting his 52nd bird on the morning of 22 Sep 1923. This figure included 241 234 pheasants, 124 193 partridge and 31 900 hares. (His game books are held by the gunmakers James Purdey and Sons.)

Thomas, 6th Baron Walsingham (1843–1919), bagged 1070 grouse, a one-day record for a single gun, in Yorkshire on 30 Aug 1888.

Football (Association)

Longest match The duration record for first-class fixtures is 3 hr 30 min (with interruptions), in the Copa Libertadores in Santos, Brazil, on 2–3 Aug 1962, when Santos drew 3–3 with Peñarol FC of Montevideo, Uruguay.

The longest British match on record was one of 3 hr 23 min between Stockport County and Doncaster Rovers in the

Eton Fives—Most titles

One pair has won the amateur championship (Kinnaird Cup) ten times—Brian C. Matthews (b. 15 Aug 1957) and John P. Reynolds (b. 9 Aug 1961), 1981–90. John Reynolds won an eleventh title with Manuel de Souza-Girao (b. 20 Aug 1970) in 1991.

Rugby Fives—Most titles

The greatest number of Amateur Singles Championships (instituted 1932) ever won is 19 by Wayne Enstone (b. 12 Jun 1951) in 1973–8 and 1980–92.

The record for the Amateur Doubles Championship (instituted 1925) is 10 by David John Hebden (b. 30 Jun 1948) and Ian Paul Fuller (b. 25 May 1953) in 1980–85 and 1987–90.

---

second leg of the Third Division (North) Cup at Edgeley Park, Stockport, Greater Manchester on 30 Mar 1946.

Longest unbeaten run Nottingham Forest were undefeated in 42 consecutive First Division matches from 20 Nov 1977 to 9 Dec 1978. In Scottish Football Glasgow Celtic were undefeated in 62 matches (49 won, 13 drawn), 13 Nov 1915–21 April 1917.

Most postponements The Scottish Cup tie between Inverness Thistle and Falkirk during the winter of 1978–9 was postponed a record 29 times due to weather conditions. Finally Falkirk won the game 4–0.

Goal Scoring

Teams The highest score recorded in a first-class match is 36. This occurred in the Scottish Cup match between Arbroath and Bon Accord on 5 Sep 1885, when Arbroath won 36–0 on their home ground. But for the lack of nets and the consequent waste of retrieval time the score must have been even higher. Seven further goals were disallowed for offside.

British Goal-Scoring Records

Scottish Cup
   13   John Petrie for Arbroath *v.* Bon Accord on 5 Sep 1885.

Football League
   10   Joe Payne (1914–77) for Luton Town *v.* Bristol Rovers (Div 3S) at Luton on 13 Apr 1936.

Football League Division One
   7   Ted Drake (b. 16 Aug 1912) for Arsenal *v.* Aston Villa at Birmingham on 14 Dec 1935; James David Ross for Preston North End *v.* Stoke at Preston on 6 Oct 1888.

Football League Cup
   6   Frankie Bunn (b. 6 Oct 1962) for Oldham Athletic *v.* Scarborough at Oldham on 25 Oct 1989.

FA Cup (Preliminary Round)
   10   Chris Marron for South Shields *v.* Radcliffe at South Shields on 20 Sep 1947.

FA Cup
   9   Edward 'Ted' MacDougall (b. 8 Jan 1947) for Bournemouth *v.* Margate (first round) at Bournemouth on 20 Nov 1971.

Scottish League
   8   James Edward McGrory (1904–82) for Celtic *v.* Dunfermline (Div 1) at Celtic Park, Glasgow on 14 Jan 1928.

Home International
   6   Joe Bambrick (b. 3 Nov 1905) for Ireland *v.* Wales at Belfast on 1 Feb 1930.

The highest margin recorded in an international match is 17, when England beat Australia 17–0 at Sydney on 30 Jun 1951. This match is not listed by England as a *full* international. The highest in the British Isles was when England beat Ireland 13–0 at Belfast on 18 Feb 1882.

The highest score between English clubs in any major competition is 26, when Preston North End beat Hyde 26–0 in an FA Cup tie at Deepdale, Lancs on 15

Oct 1887. The biggest victory in an FA Cup final is six when Bury beat Derby County 6–0 at Crystal Palace on 18 Apr 1903, in which year Bury did not concede a single goal in their five Cup matches.

The highest score by one side in a Football League (First Division) match is 12 goals when West Bromwich Albion beat Darwen 12–0 at West Bromwich, W Mids on 4 Apr 1892; when Nottingham Forest beat Leicester Fosse by the same score at Nottingham on 21 Apr 1909; and when Aston Villa beat Accrington 12–2 at Perry Barr, W Mids on 12 Mar 1892.

The highest aggregate in League Football was 17 goals when Tranmere Rovers beat Oldham Athletic 13–4 in a Third Division (North) match at Prenton Park, Merseyside, on Boxing Day, 1935. The record margin in a League match has been 13 in the Newcastle United 13, Newport County 0 (Second Division) match on 5 Oct 1946 and in the Stockport County 13, Halifax 0 (Third Division (North)) match on 6 Jan 1934.

The highest number of goals by any British team in a professional league in a season is 142 in 34 matches by Raith Rovers (Scottish Second Division) in the 1937/8 season. The English League record is 134 in 46 matches by Peterborough United (Fourth Division) in 1960/61.

Individual The most scored by one player in a first-class match is 16 by Stephan Stanis (*né* Stanikowski, b. Poland, 15 Jul 1913) for Racing Club de Lens *v.* Aubry-Asturies, in Lens, France, in a wartime French Cup game on 13 Dec 1942.

The record number of goals scored by one player in an international match is ten by Sofus Nielsen (1888–1963) for Denmark *v.* France (17–1) in the 1908 Olympics and by Gottfried Fuchs (1889–1972) for Germany who beat Russia 16–0 in the 1912 Olympic tournament (consolation event) in Sweden.

Most in a season The most goals in a League season is 60 in 39 games by William Ralph 'Dixie' Dean (1907–80) for Everton (First Division) in 1927/8 and 66 in 38 games by James Smith (1902–76) for Ayr United (Scottish Second Division)

Fastest own goal

Torquay United's Pat Kruse (b. 30 Nov 1953) equalled the fastest goal on record when he headed the ball into his own net only 6 sec after kick-off v. Cambridge United on 3 Jan 1977.

Goalkeeping

The longest that any goalkeeper has succeeded in preventing any goals being scored past him in top-class competition is 1275 mins by Abel Resino of Athletico Madrid to 17 Mar 1991. The record in international matches is 1142 min for Dino Zoff (Italy) (b. 22 Feb 1942), from September 1972 to June 1974.

The British club record in all competitive matches is 1196 min by Chris Woods (b. 14 Nov 1959) for Glasgow Rangers from 26 Nov 1986 to 31 Jan 1987.

Heaviest goalkeeper

The biggest goalkeeper in representative football was the England international Willie Henry 'Fatty' Foulke (1874–1916), who stood 1·90m *6 ft 3 in* and weighed 141 kg *22 st 3 lb*. His last games were for Bradford City, by which time he was 165 kg *26 st*. He once stopped a game by snapping the cross bar.

in the same season. With three more in Cup ties and 19 in representative matches Dean's total was 82.

Career Artur Friedenreich (Brazil) (1892–1969) scored an undocumented 1329 goals in a 26 year first-class football career, 1909–35. The most goals scored in a specified period is 1279 by Edson Arantes do Nascimento (Brazil) (b. 23 Oct 1940), known as Pelé, from 7 Sep 1956 to 1 Oct 1977 in 1363 games. His best year was 1959 with 126, and the *Milesimo* (1000th) came from a penalty for his club Santos in the Maracaña Stadium, Rio de Janeiro on 19 Nov 1969 when playing his 909th first-class match. He later added two more goals in special appearances. Franz 'Bimbo' Binder (b. 1 Dec 1911) scored 1006 goals in 756 games in Austria and Germany between 1930 and 1950.

The international career record for England is 49 goals by Robert 'Bobby' Charlton (b. 11 Oct 1937). His first was v. Scotland on 19 Apr 1958 and his last on 20 May 1970 v. Colombia.

The greatest number of goals scored in British first-class football is 550 (410 in Scottish League matches) by James McGrory of Glasgow Celtic (1922–38). The most scored in League matches is 434, for West Bromwich Albion, Fulham, Leicester City and Shrewsbury Town, by George Arthur Rowley (b. 21 Apr 1926) between 1946 and April 1965. Rowley also scored 32 goals in the F.A. Cup and one for England 'B'.

Fastest goals The fastest Football League goals on record were scored in 6 sec by Albert E. Mundy (b. 12 May 1926) (Aldershot) in a Fourth Division match v. Hartlepool United at Victoria Ground, Hartlepool, Cleveland on 25 Oct 1958, by Barrie Jones (b. 31 Oct 1938) (Notts County) in a Third Division match v. Torquay United on 31 Mar 1962, and by Keith Smith (b. 15 Sep 1940) (Crystal Palace) in a Second Division match v. Derby County at the Baseball Ground, Derby on 12 Dec 1964.

The fastest confirmed hat-trick is in 2½ minutes by Ephraim 'Jock' Dodds (b. 7 Sep 1915) for Blackpool v. Tranmere Rovers on 28 Feb 1942, and Jimmy Scarth (b. 26 Aug 1920) for Gillingham v. Leyton Orient in Third Division (Southern) on 1 Nov 1952. A hat-trick in 1 min 50 sec is claimed for Maglioni of Independiente v. Gimnasia y Escrima de la Plata in Argentina on 18 Mar 1973. John McIntyre (Blackburn Rovers) scored four goals in 5 min v. Everton at Ewood Park, Blackburn, Lancs on 16 Sep 1922. William 'Ginger' Richardson (West Bromwich Albion) scored four goals in 5 min from the kick-off against West Ham United at Upton Park on 7 Nov 1931. Frank Keetley scored six goals in 21 min in the second half of the Lincoln City v. Halifax Town league match on 16 Jan 1932. The international

record is three goals in 3½ min by George William Hall (Tottenham Hotspur) for England against Ireland on 16 Nov 1938 at Old Trafford, Greater Manchester.

The FIFA World Cup

The *Fédération Internationale de Football Association* (FIFA), which was founded on 21 May 1904, instituted the first World Cup on 13 Jul 1930, in Montevideo, Uruguay. It is held quadrennially. Three wins have been achieved by Brazil 1958, 1962 and 1970; Italy 1934, 1938 and 1982; and West Germany 1954, 1974 and 1990. Brazil, uniquely, have taken part in all 14 finals tournaments.

Appearances Antonio Carbajal (Mexico) (b. 7 Jan 1929) is the only player to have appeared in five World Cup finals tournaments, keeping goal for Mexico in 1950, 1954, 1958, 1962 and 1966, playing 11 games in all. The most appearances in finals tournaments is 21 by: Uwe Seeler (West Germany) (b. 5 Nov 1936), 1958–70; and by Wladyslaw Zmuda (Poland) (b. 6 Jun 1954), 1974–86. Pelé is the only player to have been with three World Cup-winning teams, in 1958, 1962 and 1970. The youngest ever to play in the World Cup is Norman Whiteside, who played for Northern Ireland v. Yugoslavia aged 17 yr 41 days on 17 Jun 1982.

Goal scoring Just Fontaine (b. Marrakech, Morocco, 18 Aug 1933) of France scored 13 goals in six matches in the final stages of the 1958 competition in Sweden. Gerd Müller (West Germany) (b. 3 Nov 1945) scored 10 goals in 1970 and four in 1974 for the highest aggregate of 14 goals. Fontaine, Jaïrzinho (Brazil) (b. 25 Dec 1944) and Alcide Ghiggia (Uruguay) are the only three players to have scored in every match in a final series. Jaïrzinho scored seven in six games in 1970 and Ghiggia, four in four games in 1950 .

The most goals scored in a final is three by Geoffrey Charles Hurst (b. 8 Dec 1941) for England v. West Germany on 30 Jul 1966. Three players have scored in two finals: Vava (real name Edwaldo Izito Neto) (Brazil) (b. 12 Nov 1934) in 1958 and 1962, Pelé in 1958 and 1970;

and Paul Breitner (West Germany) (b. 5 Sep 1951) in 1974 and 1982.

The highest score in a World Cup match occurred in a qualifying match in Auckland on 15 Aug 1981 when New Zealand beat Fiji 13–0. The highest score during the final stages is 10, scored by Hungary in a 10–1 win over El Salvador at Elche, Spain on 15 Jun 1982. The highest match aggregate in the finals tournament is 12, when Austria beat Switzerland, 7–5, in 1954.

The best defensive record belongs to England, who in six matches in 1966 conceded only three goals.

European Championship (Nations Cup) Held every four years from 1958. West Germany are the only country to have won twice, in 1972 and 1980. They also lost in the 1976 final, to Czechoslovakia and in 1992 to Denmark (as Germany).

European Champion Clubs Cup The European Cup for the league champions of the respective nations was approved by FIFA on 8 May 1955 and was run by the European governing body UEFA (Union of European Football Associations) which came into being in the previous year. Real Madrid won the first final, and have won a record six times 1956–60, 1966. The highest score in a final was Real Madrid's 7–3 win over Eintracht Frankfurt at Hampden Park, Glasgow on 18 May 1960.

Glasgow Celtic became the first British club to win the Cup, beating Inter-Milan 2–1 in Lisbon, Portugal on 25 May 1967. They also became the first British club to win the European Cup and three senior domestic tournaments (League, League Cup and FA Cup) in the same season. Liverpool, winners in 1977, 1978, 1981 and 1984, have been the most successful British club.

European Cup Winners Cup A tournament for national cup winners started in 1960/61. Barcelona have won a record three times, 1979, 1982 and 1989. Tottenham Hotspur were the first British club to win the trophy, when they set a record score for the final beating Atlético Madrid 5–1 in Rotterdam, Netherlands on 15 May 1963.

UEFA Cup Originally known as the International Inter-City Industrial Fairs Cup, this club tournament began in 1955. The first competition lasted three years, the second two years. In 1960/61 it became an annual tournament and since 1971/2 has been for the UEFA Cup. The most wins is three by Barcelona in 1958, 1960 and 1966. The first British club to win the trophy was Leeds United in 1968.

Most international appearances The greatest number of appearances for a national team is 150 by Hector Chumpitaz (Peru) (b. 12 Apr 1943) from 1963 to 1982. This includes all matches played by the national team. The record for full internationals against other national teams is 125 by Peter Shilton of England.

The most international appearances by a woman is 59 by Linda Curl (b. 1962) for England, 1977–90.

Oldest The oldest international has been William Henry 'Billy' Meredith (1874–1958) (Manchester City and United) who played outside right for Wales *v.* England at Highbury, London on 15 Mar 1920 when aged 45 yr 229 days. He played internationally for a record span of 26 years (1895–1920).

Youngest The youngest British international was Norman Whiteside, who played for Northern Ireland *v.* Yugoslavia at 17 yr 41 days on 17 Jun 1982.

England's youngest international was James Frederick McLeod Prinsep (1861–95) (Clapham Rovers) *v.* Scotland at Kennington Oval, London on 5 Apr 1879, at 17 yr 252 days. The youngest Welsh cap was Ryan Giggs (b. 29 Nov 1973) (Manchester United), *v.* Germany at Nuremburg, Germany on 16 Oct 1991, aged 17 yr 321 days. Scotland's youngest international has been John Alexander Lambie (1868–1923) (Queen's Park), at 17 yr 2 days *v.* Ireland on 20 Mar 1886. The youngest for the Republic of Ireland was James Holmes (b. 11 Nov 1953) (Coventry City), at 17 yr 200 days *v.* Austria in Dublin on 30 May 1971.

British International Appearances

ENGLAND 125, Peter Leslie Shilton (b. 18 Sep 1949) (Leicester City, Stoke City, Nottingham Forest, Southampton, Derby County) 1970–90.

NORTHERN IRELAND 119, Patrick A. Jennings (b. 12 Jun 1945) (Watford, Tottenham Hotspur, Arsenal) 1964–86

SCOTLAND 102, Kenneth M. Dalglish (b. 4 Mar 1951) (Celtic, Liverpool) 1971–86

WALES 73, Peter Nicholas (b. 10 Nov 1959) (Crystal Palace, Arsenal, Luton Town, Aberdeen, Chelsea, Watford) 1979–91

REPUBLIC OF IRELAND 72, William 'Liam' Brady (b. 13 Feb 1956) (Arsenal, Juventus, Sampdoria, Internazionale,

FA Challenge Cup and Scottish FA Cup

Most wins The greatest number of FA Cup wins is eight by Tottenham Hotspur, 1901, 1921, 1961, 1962, 1967, 1981, 1982 and 1991 (nine appearances). The most appearances in the final is 12 by Arsenal (six wins). The most goals in a final is seven; when Blackburn Rovers beat Sheffield Wednesday 6–1 in 1890 and when Blackpool beat Bolton Wanderers 4–3 in 1953.

The greatest number of Scottish FA Cup wins is 29 by Celtic in 1892, 1899, 1900, 1904, 1907–8, 1911–12, 1914, 1923, 1925, 1927, 1931, 1933, 1937, 1951, 1954, 1965, 1967, 1969, 1971–2, 1974–5, 1977, 1980, 1985 and 1988–9.

Youngest player The youngest player in an FA Cup final was Paul Allen (b. 28 Aug 1962) for West Ham United *v.* Arsenal on 10 May 1980, aged 17 yr 256 days. Derek Johnstone (Rangers) (b. 4 Nov 1953) was 16 yr 11 months old when he played in the Scottish League Cup final against Celtic on 24 Oct 1970. The youngest goal scorer in the FA Cup final was Norman Whiteside (b. 7 May 1965) for Manchester United *v.* Brighton at 18 yr 19 days on 26 May 1983. The youngest player ever in the FA Cup com-

Football League Cup

Instituted in 1960/1, the most wins is four by; Liverpool, 1981–4; and Nottingham Forest, 1978–9, 1989–90.

Scottish League Cup

Instituted in 1946/7, the most wins is 18 by Rangers between 1947 and 1992.

Olympic Games

The only country to have won the Olympic football title three times is Hungary in 1952, 1964 and 1968. The United Kingdom won the unofficial tournament in 1900 and the official tournaments of 1908 and 1912. The highest Olympic score is 17 by Denmark *v.* France 'A' (1) in 1908. A record 126 nations are taking part in qualifying for the 1992 tournament.

petition was full back Andrew Awford (b. 14 Jul 1972) at 15 yr 88 days for Worcester City in a qualifying round tie at Borehamwood, Herts on 10 Oct 1987.

Most medals Three players have won five FA Cupwinners' medals: James Henry Forrest (1864–1925) with Blackburn Rovers (1884–6, 1890–1); the Hon. Sir Arthur Fitzgerald Kinnaird (1847–1923) with Wanderers (1873, 1877–8) and Old Etonians (1879, 1882); and Charles Harold Reynolds Wollaston (1849–1926) with Wanderers (1872–3, 1876–8).

The most Scottish Cupwinners' medals won is eight by Charles Campbell (d. 1927) (Queen's Park) in 1874–6, 1880–82, 1884 and 1886.

Longest tie The most protracted FA Cup tie in the competition proper was that between Stoke City and Bury in the third round, with Stoke winning 3–2 in the fifth meeting after 9 hr 22 min of play in January 1955. The matches were at Bury (1–1) on 8 Jan; Stoke-on-Trent on 12 Jan (abandoned after 22 min of extra time with the score 1–1); Goodison Park (3–3) on 17 Jan; Anfield (2–2) on 19 Jan; and finally at Old Trafford on 24

Alex Ferguson (b. 31 Dec 1941) (left) holds aloft the FA Premier League Trophy won by Manchester United. Ferguson is the only manager to have won League, Cup and League Cup in both Scotland and England (his Scottish successes coming with Aberdeen). He is also the only manager to have won the European Cup-Winners' Cup with two clubs.

(Photo: Allsport/Shaun Botterill)

Jan. In the 1972 final qualifying round Alvechurch beat Oxford City after five previous drawn games (total playing time 11 hours).

League Championships

The record number of successive national league championships is nine by: Celtic (Scotland) 1966–74; CSKA, Sofia (Bulgaria) 1954–62; and MTK Budapest (Hungary) 1917–25. The Sofia club holds a European post–war record of 26 league titles, including two under the name CFKA Sredets (re-named CSKA).

English The greatest number of League Championships (First Division) is 18 by Liverpool in 1901, 1906, 1922–3, 1947, 1964, 1966, 1973, 1976–7, 1979–80, 1982–4, 1986, 1988 and 1990. The record number of wins in a season is 33 from 42 matches by Doncaster Rovers in Third Division (North) in 1946/7. The First Division record is 31 wins from 42 matches by Tottenham Hotspur in 1960/1. In 1893/4 Liverpool won 22 and drew 6 in 28 Second Division games. They also won the promotion match. The most points in a season under the current scoring system is 102 from 46 matches by Swindon in the Fourth Division in 1985/6. Under the new system the First Division record would have been Liverpool's 98 in 1978/9, when they won 30 and drew 8 of their 42 matches.

'Double' The only FA Cup and League Championship 'doubles' are those of Preston North End in 1889, Aston Villa in 1897, Tottenham Hotspur in 1961, Arsenal in 1971 and Liverpool in 1986. Preston won the League without losing a match and the Cup without having a goal scored against them throughout the whole competition.

Scottish Glasgow Rangers have won the Scottish League Championship 42 times (one shared 1891) between 1891 and 1992. Their 76 points in the Scottish

Ryan Giggs (b. 29 Nov 1973) of Manchester United, the youngest ever Welsh international, has won an unprecedented two Professional Footballers' Association Young Player of the Year awards, 1992–3.

(Photo: Allsport/Steve Morton)

First Division in 1920/1 (from a possible 84) represents a record in any division. However a better percentage was achieved by Rangers in 1898/9 when they gained the maximum of 36 by winning all their 18 matches.

Most durable Peter Leslie Shilton (b. 18 Sep 1949) has made a record 1347 senior UK appearances, including a record 968 League appearances, 286 for Leicester City (1966–74), 110 for Stoke City (1974–7), 202 for Nottingham Forest (1977–82), 188 for Southampton (1982–7), 175 for Derby County (1987–92) and 7 for Plymouth Argyle (1992), 87 FA Cup, 96 League Cup, 125 internationals, 13 Under-23, 5 Football League XI and 53 various European and other club competitons. Norman John Trollope (b. 14 Jun 1943) made 770

League appearances for one club, Swindon Town, between 1960 and 1980.

Transfer fees The highest transfer fee quoted for a player is a reported £13 million for Gianluigi Lentini (Italy), from Torino to AC Milan in June 1992.

The highest transfer fee for a British player is the £5·5 million paid by: Bari (Italy) to Aston Villa for David Platt (b. 10 Jun 1966) on 21 Jul 1991; and by Lazio (Italy) to Tottenham Hotspur for Paul Gascoigne (b. 27 May 1967) on 26 May 1992.

The record fee between two British clubs is a reported £3·6 million paid by Blackburn Rovers to Southampton for Alan Shearer (b. 13 Aug 1970).

Greatest crowds The greatest recorded crowd at any football match was 199 589 for the Brazil *v.* Uruguay World Cup match in the Maracaña Municipal Stadium, Rio de Janeiro, Brazil on 16 Jul 1950. The record attendance for a European Cup match is 136 505 at the semi-final between Glasgow Celtic and Leeds United at Hampden Park, Glasgow on 15 Apr 1970.

The British record paid attendance is 149 547 at the Scotland *v.* England inter-

Closest win

In 1923/4 Huddersfield won the First Division Championship over Cardiff by 0·02 of a goal with a goal average of 1·81. The 1988/9 League Championship was decided by the fact that Arsenal had scored more goals (73 to 65) than Liverpool, after both teams finished level on points and goal difference.

Most peripatetic fan

Edward Wood of Quarndon, Derbys watched a Football League match at all the League grounds in England and Wales (including Berwick Rangers) in just 243 days, 17 Aug 1991–15 Apr 1992.

He began at Gillingham v. Scunthorpe (4–0) and finished at Brighton v. Derby County (1–2). On four occasions he watched two matches in a day.

national at Hampden Park, Glasgow on 17 Apr 1937. It is, however, probable that this total was exceeded (estimated 160 000) at the FA Cup final between Bolton Wanderers and West Ham United at Wembley Stadium on 28 Apr 1923, when the crowd spilled onto the pitch and the start was delayed 40 min until it was cleared. The counted admissions were 126 047.

The Scottish Cup record attendance is 146 433 when Celtic played Aberdeen at Hampden Park on 24 Apr 1937. The record attendance for a League match in Britain is 118 567 for Rangers v. Celtic at Ibrox Park, Glasgow on 2 Jan 1939.

The highest attendance at an amateur match has been 120 000 in Senayan Stadium, Jakarta, Indonesia on 26 Feb 1976 for the Pre-Olympic Group II final, North Korea v. Indonesia.

Smallest crowd The smallest crowd at a full home international was 2315 for Wales v. Northern Ireland on 27 May 1982 at the Racecourse Ground, Wrexham, Clwyd. The smallest paying attendance at a Football League fixture

was for the Stockport County v. Leicester City match at Old Trafford, Manchester on 7 May 1921. Stockport's own ground was under suspension and the 'crowd' numbered 13 but an estimated 2000 gained free admission. When West Ham beat Castilla of Spain (5–1) in the European Cup Winners Cup at Upton Park, Greater London on 1 Oct 1980 and when Aston Villa beat Besiktas of Turkey (3–1) in the European Cup at Villa Park, Birmingham on 15 Sep 1982, there were no paying spectators due to disciplinary action by the European Football Union.

Penalties

The greatest number of penalty kicks taken to decide a cup game under the jurisdiction of the Football League occurred in a Freight Rover Trophy, Southern Section quarter-final between Aldershot and Fulham on 10 Feb 1987, at the Recreation Ground, Aldershot, Hants. After 90 minutes play the score was 1–1. A further 30 minutes of extra time produced no further scoring. It needed 28 penalty kicks, of which only seven were missed, before Aldershot won 11–10.

The record number of penalties awarded in a League match is five during the Crystal Palace v. Brighton & Hove Albion Second Division game on 27 Mar 1989. Palace missed three of their spot kicks and each side was successful once. Palace eventually won 2–1.

In the Cyprus First-Division match in which Omonia beat Olympiakos 6–4 in Nicosia on 15 February 1987, FIFA referee Stafanos Hadjistefanou awarded six penalties, three to each side, all of which were converted by George Savvides (Omonia) and Sylvester Vernon (Olympiakos).

Other Matches

Highest scores Teams Drayton Grange Colts beat Eldon Sports Reserves 49–0 in a Daventry and District Sunday League match at Grange Estate, Northants on 13 Nov 1988. Every member of the side including the goalkeeper scored at least one goal.

In an Under-14 League match between Midas FC and Courage Colts, in Kent, on

Ball control

Huh Nam Jin (South Korea) juggled a regulation soccer ball for 17hr 10min 57sec non-stop with feet, legs and head without the ball ever touching the ground at Swiss Grand Hotel, Seoul, South Korea on 24 May 1991. The heading record is 7hr 5min 5sec by Tomas Lundman (Sweden) at Nöjeskällan, Märsta, Sweden on 5 Sep 1992.

Jan Skorkovsky of Prague, Czechoslovakia kept a football up while he travelled a distance of 42·195km *26·219 miles* for the Prague City Marathon in 7hr 18min 55sec on 8 Jul 1990.

---

11 Apr 1976, the full-time score after 70minutes play was 59–1. Top scorer for Midas was Kevin Graham with 17 goals. Courage had scored the first goal.

Needing to improve their goal 'difference' to gain promotion in 1979, Ilinden FC of Yugoslavia, with the collusion of the opposition, Mladost, and the referee, won their final game of the season 134–1. Their rivals for promotion won their match, under similar circumstances, 88–0.

Individual Dean Goodliff scored 26 goals for Deleford Colts v. Iver Minors in the Slough Boys Soccer Combination Under-14 League at Iver, Bucks in his team's 33–0 win on 22 Dec 1985. The women's record is 22 goals by Linda Curl of Norwich Ladies in a 40–0 league victory over Milton Keynes Reserves at Norwich on 25 Sep 1983.

Season The greatest number of goals in a season reported for an individual player in junior professional league football is 96 by Tom Duffy (b. 7 Jan 1937), for Ardeer Thistle FC, Strathclyde in 1960/61. Paul Anthony Moulden (b. 6 Sep 1967) scored 289 goals in 40 games for Bolton Lads Club in Bolton Boys Federation intermediate league and cup matches in 1981/2. An additional 51 goals scored in other tournaments brought his total to 340, the highest season figure reported in any class of

competitive football for an individual. He made his Football League debut for Manchester City on 1 Jan 1986 and has played for the England Youth team.

Fastest goals *Individual* Goals scored in 3seconds and under after the kick-off have been achieved by a number of players.

Own goal The fastest own goal on record has been in 4sec 'scored' by Richard Nash of Newick v. Burgess Hill Reserves at Newick, E Sussex on 8 Feb 1992.

Team The shortest time for a semi-professional team to score three goals from the start of a game is 122sec by Burton Albion v. Redditch United in a Beazer Homes League Premier Division match on 2 Jan 1989.

Goalkeeping Craig Manktelow (b. 5 Mar 1967) of Kawerau Electrical Services in New Zealand played 15 matches without conceding a goal, a total of 1350min, from 6 May–19 Aug 1989.

Longest ties In the Hertfordshire Intermediate Cup, London Colney beat Leavesden Hospital after 12hr 41min play and seven ties from 6 Nov to 17 Dec 1971.

Largest tournament The Metropolitan Police 5-a-side Youth Competition in 1981 attracted an entry of 7008 teams, a record for an FA sanctioned competition.

Most and least successful teams Winlaton West End FC, Tyne & Wear, completed a run of 95 league games without defeat between 1976 and 1980. Penlake Junior Football Club remained unbeaten for 153 games (winning 152 including 85 in succession) in the Warrington Hilden Friendly League from 1981 until defeated in 1986. Stockport United FC, of the Stockport Football League, lost 39 consecutive League and Cup matches, September 1976 to 18 Feb 1978.

Most indisciplined In the local cup match between Tongham Youth Club, Surrey and Hawley, Hants, on 3 Nov 1969, the referee booked all 22 players including one who went to hospital, and one of the linesmen. The match, won by Tongham 2–0, was described by a player as 'a good, hard game'.

Largest crowd

The record crowd for a Gaelic football match is 90 556 for the Down v. Offaly final at Croke Park, Dublin in 1961.

In a Gancia Cup match at Waltham Abbey, Essex on 23 Dec 1973, the referee, Michael J. Woodhams, sent off the entire Juventus-Cross team and some club officials. Glencraig United, Faifley, near Clydebank, had all 11 team members and two substitutes for their 2–2 draw against Goldenhill Boys' Club on 2 Feb 1975 booked in the dressing room before a ball was kicked. The referee, Mr Tarbet of Bearsen, took exception to the chant which greeted his arrival. It was not his first meeting with Glencraig.

It was reported on 1 Jun 1993 that in a league match between Sportivo Ameliano and General Caballero in Paraguay, referee William Weiler sent off 20 players. Trouble flared after two Sportivo players were sent off, a ten-minute fight ensued and Weiler then dismissed a further 18 players, including the rest of the Sportivo team. Not suprisingly the match was abandonded.

Gaelic Football

All-Ireland Championships The greatest number of All–Ireland Championships won by one team is 30 by Ciarraidhe (Kerry) between 1903 and 1986. The greatest number of successive wins is four by Wexford (1915–18) and Kerry twice (1929–32, 1978–81).

The most finals contested by an individual is ten, including eight wins by the Kerry players Pat Spillane, Paudie O'Shea and Denis Moran, 1975–6, 1978–82, 1984–6.

The highest team score in a final was when Dublin, 27 (5 goals, 12 points) beat Armagh, 15 (3 goals, 6 points) on 25 Sep 1977. The highest combined score was 45 points when Cork (26) beat Galway (19) in 1973. A goal equals three points.

The highest individual score in an All-Ireland final has been 2 goals, 6 points by Jimmy Keaveney (Dublin) v. Armagh in 1977, and by Michael Sheehy (Kerry) v. Dublin in 1979.

Gambling

Bingo

Largest house The largest 'house' in Bingo sessions was 15 756 at the Canadian National Exhibition, Toronto on 19 Aug 1983. Staged by the Variety Club of Ontario Tent Number 28, there was total prize money of $C250 000 with a record one-game payout of $C100 000.

Earliest and latest Full House A 'Full House' call occurred on the 15th number by Norman A. Wilson at Guide Post Working Men's Club, Bedlington, Northumberland on 22 Jun 1978, by Anne Wintle of Brynrethin, Mid Glam, on a coach trip to Bath on 17 Aug 1982 and by Shirley Lord at Kahibah Bowling Club, New South Wales, Australia on 24 Oct 1983.

'House' was not called until the 86th number at the Hillsborough Working Men's Club, Sheffield, S Yorks on 11 Jan 1982. There were 32 winners.

Slot machines

The biggest beating handed to a 'one-armed bandit' was $9 357 489.41 by Delores Adams, 60, at the Harrah's Reno Casino-Hotel, Nevada, USA on 30 May 1992.

Biggest lottery win

The biggest individual gambling win is $40 million by Mike Wittkowski in the Illinois State Lottery, announced on 3 Sep 1984. From $35 worth of 'Lotto' tickets bought by his family, the winning six numbers bring him $2 million for the next 20 years.

Football Pools

The winning dividend paid out by Littlewoods Pools in their first week in February 1923 was £212s0d. In 1991/2 the three British Pools companies which comprise the Pool Promoters Association (Littlewoods, Vernons and Zetters) had a total record turnover of £840 415 000, of which Littlewoods contributed over 70 per cent.

Biggest win *British* The record individual payout, which is also the biggest ever individual prize paid in any British competition, is £2 246 113 paid by Littlewoods Pools to an anonymous Bournemouth man for matches played on 13 Jun 1992.

The record double payout is £2 677 650 by Littlewoods to an anonymous man and woman from Manchester, both of whom won £1 338 825 for matches on 4 Apr 1992. In that same week Littlewoods made the record total payout for a single week of £3 942 828.

Horse Racing

Highest ever odds The highest secured odds were 1 670 759 to 1 by George Rhodes of Aldershot, Hants. For a 5p bet, with a 10 per cent bonus for the ITV Seven, less tax, he was paid £86 024.42 by the William Hill Organization on 30 Sep 1984.

Edward Hodson of Wolverhampton, W Mids landed a 3 956 748 to 1 bet for a 55p stake on 11 Feb 1984, but his bookmaker had a £3000 payout limit.

The world record odds on a 'double' are 31 793 to 1 paid by the New Zealand Totalisator Agency Board on a five shilling tote ticket on *Red Emperor* and *Maida Dillon* at Addington, Christchurch in 1951.

Greatest payout Anthony A. Speelman and Nicholas John Cowan (both Great Britain) won $1 627 084.40, after federal income tax of $406 768.00 was withheld, on a $64 nine-horse accumulator at Santa Anita racecourse, California, USA on 19 Apr 1987. Their first seven selections won and the payout was for a jackpot, accumulated over 24 days.

The largest payout by a British bookmaker is £567 066.25 by Ladbrokes, paid

to Dick Mussell of Havant, Hants for a combination of an accumulator, trebles, doubles and singles on five horses at Cheltenham on 12 Mar 1992.

Biggest tote win The best recorded tote win was one of £341 2s 6d to 2s representing odds of 3410¼ to 1, by Catharine Unsworth of Blundellsands, Liverpool, Merseyside at Haydock Park on a race won by *Coole* on 30 Nov 1929.

The highest odds in Irish tote history were £289.64 for a 10p unit on *Gene's Rogue* at Limerick on 28 Dec 1981.

Largest bookmaker The world's largest bookmaker is Ladbrokes with a peak turnover from gambling in 1988 of £2107 million and the largest chain of betting shops, over 1990 in Great Britain and the Republic of Ireland at 1 Jul 1993, as well as outlets in Germany and Belgium.

Topmost tipster The only recorded instance of a racing correspondent forecasting ten out of ten winners on a race card was at Delaware Park, Wilmington, Delaware, USA on 28 Jul 1974 by Charles Lamb of the *Baltimore News American*.

The best performance by a British correspondent is seven out of seven winners for a meeting at Wolverhampton on 22 Mar 1982 by Bob Butchers of the *Daily Mirror*. This was repeated by Fred Shawcross of the *Today* newspaper at York on 12 May 1988. In greyhound racing the best performance is 12 out of 12 by Mark Sullivan of the *Sporting Life* for a meeting at Wimbledon on 21 Dec 1990.

Gliding

Most titles The most World Individual Championships (instituted 1937) won is four by Ingo Renner (Australia) in 1976 (Standard class), 1983, 1985 and 1987 (Open).

British The British National Championship (instituted 1939) has been won eight times by Ralph Jones (b. 29 Mar 1936).

The first woman to win this title was Anne Burns (b. 23 Nov. 1915) of Farnham, Surrey on 30 May 1966.

World & British Gliding Single-Seater Records

Category	Distance	Name	Type of Glider	Location	Date
Straight Distance	1460·8km 907·7 miles	Hans-Werner Grosse (West Germany)	ASK-12	Lübeck, Germany to Biarritz, France	25 Apr 1972
(British)	949·35km 589·9 miles	Karla Karel	LS-3	Australia	20 Jan 1980
Declared Goal Distance	1254·26km 779·36 miles	Bruce Lindsay Drake (New Zealand)	Nimbus 2	Te Anau to Te Araroa, New Zealand	14 Jan 1978
		David Wapier Speight (New Zealand)	Nimbus 2	Te Anau to Te Araroa, New Zealand	14 Jan 1978
		S. H. 'Dick' Georgeson (New Zealand)	Nimbus 2	Te Anau to Te Araroa, New Zealand	14 Jan 1978
(British)	859·2km 534 miles	M. T. Alan Sands	Nimbus 3	Ridge soaring to Chilhowee, Va, USA	23 Apr 1986
Goal and Return	1646·76km 1023·25 miles	Thomas L. Knauff (USA)	Nimbus 3	Williamsport, Pa to Knoxville, Tn, USA	25 Apr 1983
(British)	1127·68km 700·72 miles	M. T. Alan Sands	Nimbus 3	Lock Haven, Pa to Bluefield, Va, USA	7 May 1985
Absolute Altitude	14938m 49009ft	Robert R. Harris (USA)	Grob G102	California, USA	17 Feb 1986
(British)	11500m 37729ft	H. C. Nicholas Goodhart	Schweitzer 1-23	California, USA	12 May 1955
Height Gain	12894m 42303ft	Paul F. Bikle (USA)	Schweitzer SGS1-23E	Mojave, Lancaster, California, USA	25 Feb 1961
(British)	10065m 33022ft	David Benton	Nimbus 2	Portmoak, Scotland	18 Apr 1980

SPEED OVER TRIANGULAR COURSE

Distance	km/h	mph	Name	Type of Glider	Location	Date
100km	195·3	121·35	Ingo Renner (Australia)	Nimbus 3	Tocumwal, Australia	14 Dec 1982
(British)	166·38	103·38	Bruce Cooper	LS-6	Australia	4 Jan 1991
300km	169·49	105·32	Jean-Paul Castel (France)	Nimbus 3	Bitterwasser, South Africa	15 Nov 1986
(British)	146·8	91·2	Edward Pearson	Nimbus 2	S. W. Africa (now Namibia)	30 Nov 1976
500km	170·06	105·67	Beat Bunzli (Switzerland)	DG 400	Bitterwasser, South Africa	9 Jan 1988
(British)	141·3	87·8	Bradley James Grant Pearson	ASW-20	South Africa	28 Dec 1982
750km	158·40	98·43	Hans-Werner Grosse (West Germany)	ASW-22	Alice Springs, Australia	8 Dec 1985
(British)	109·8	68·2	Michael R. Carlton	Kestrel 19	South Africa	5 Jan 1975
1000km	145·32	90·29	Hans-Werner Grosse (West Germany)	ASW-17	Alice Springs, Australia	3 Jan 1979
(British)	112·15	69·68	George Lee	ASW 20	Australia	25 Jan 1989
1250km	133·24	82·79	Hans-Werner Grosse (West Germany)	ASW-17	Alice Springs, Australia	9 Dec 1980
(British)	109·01	67·73	Robert L. Robertson	Ventus A	USA	2 May 1986

Women's altitude records The women's single-seater world record for absolute altitude is 12 637 m *41 460 ft* by Sabrina Jackintell (USA) in an Astir GS on 14 Feb 1979.

The height gain record is 10 212 m *33 504 ft* by Yvonne Loader (New Zealand) at Omarama, New Zealand on 12 Jan 1988.

The British single-seater absolute altitude record is 10 550 m *34 612 ft* by Anne Burns in a Skylark 3B over South Africa on 13 Jan 1961, when she set a then world record and still a British record for height gain of 9119 m *29 918 ft*.

Hang Gliding

World Championships The World Team Championships (officially instituted 1976) have been won most often by Great Britain (1981, 1985, 1989 and 1991).

World records The *Fédération Aéronautique Internationale* recognizes world records for rigidwing, flexwing and multiplace flexwing. These records are the greatest in each category–all by flexwing gliders.

Men Greatest distance in straight line and declared goal distance: 488·19 km *303·35 miles* Larry Tudor (USA), Hobbs Airpark, New Mexico to Elkhart, Kansas, 3 Jul 1990. Height gain: 4343·4 m *14 250 ft* Larry Tudor (USA), Lone Pine, California, 8 Apr 1985.

Out and return distance: 310·302 km *192·812 miles* Larry Tudor (USA) and Geoffrey Loyns (GB), Lone Pine, 26 Jun 1988. Triangular course distance: 196 km *121·79 miles* James Lee (USA), San Pedro Mesa, Colorado, 4 Jul 1991.

Women Greatest distance: 335·75 km *208·63 miles* Kari Castle (USA), Lone Pine, 22 Jul 1991. Height gain: 3657·17 m *11 998·62 ft* Tover Buas-Hansen (Norway) Bishops Airport, California, 6 Jul 1989.

Out and return distance via single turn: 292·04 km *181·47 miles* Kari Castle (USA), Hobbs Airpark, 11 Jul 1990. Declared goal distance: 212·50 km *132·04 miles* Liavan Mallin (Ireland), Horseshoe Meadows, 13 Jul 1989.

Triangular course distance: Judy Leden (GB), 114·107 km *70·904 miles*, Konsen, Austria, 22 Jun 1991.

British The British record for distance is held by Geoffrey Loyns, 312·864 km *194·41 miles*, in Flagstaff, Arizona, USA on 11 Jun 1988. The best in Britain is 244 km *151·62 miles* by Gordon Rigg from Lords Seat to Witham Friary, Somerset on 4 Jun 1989.

Golf

Oldest club The oldest club of which there is written evidence is the Gentlemen Golfers (now the Honourable Company of Edinburgh Golfers) formed in March 1744–ten years prior to the institution of the Royal and Ancient Club of St Andrews, Fife. However, the Royal Burgess Golfing Society of Edinburgh claims to have been founded in 1735.

Highest course The Tuctu Golf Club in Morococha, Peru, is 4369 m *14 335 ft* above sea level at its lowest point. Golf has, however, been played in Tibet at an altitude of over 4875 m *16 000 ft*.

Largest green

Probably the largest green in the world is that of the par-6 635 m *695 yd* fifth hole at International GC, Bolton, Massachusetts, USA, with an area greater than 2600 m² *28 000 ft²*.

Golf club & ball

A Scottish iron golf club of *c.* 1700 sold for £92 400 at Sotheby's sale of golfing memorabilia at Loretto School, Musselburgh, Lothian, held on 13 Jul 1992 to coincide with the 121st Open Championship. It was bought by Titus Kendall on behalf of the Valderamma Golf Club in Sotte Grande, Spain.

On 14 Jul 1992 Titus Kendall also paid a record £19 250 at Philips, Edinburgh for a gutta (latex-type) ball made by Scot Alan Robertson in 1849.

Longest hole

The longest hole in the world is the 6th hole (par-7) of the Koolan Island GC, Western Australia, which measures 867 m *948 yd*.

The longest hole on a championship course in Great Britain is the sixth at Troon, Strathclyde, which stretches 528 m *577 yd*.

Most balls hit in one hour

The most balls driven in one hour, over 100 yards and into a target area, is 1536 by Noel Hunt at Shrigley Hall, Pott Shrigley, Cheshire on 2 May 1990.

Throwing the golf ball

The lowest recorded score for throwing a golf ball round 18 holes (over 5490 m *6000 yd*) is 82 by Joe Flynn (USA), 21, at the 5695 m *6228 yd* Port Royal course, Bermuda on 27 Mar 1975.

Golf ball balancing

Lang Martin balanced seven golf balls vertically without adhesive at Charlotte, North Carolina, USA on 9 Feb 1980.

Lowest score

The lowest four round total in a US LPGA Championship event is 267 (68, 66, 67, 66) by Betsy King (USA) (b. 13 Aug 1955) in the Mazda LPGA Championship on the par-71 5735 m *6272 yd* Bethesda Country Club course, Bethesda, Maryland, USA on 14–17 May 1992. She won by 11 strokes and was 17 under-par, both LPGA Championship records.

Great Britain The nine hole course at Leadhills, Strathclyde is 457 m *1500 ft* above sea level.

Highest shot on Earth Gerald Williams (USA) played a shot from the summit of Mt Aconcagua (6960 m *22 834 ft*), Argentina on 22 Jan 1989.

Biggest bunker The world's biggest bunker (called a trap in the USA) is Hell's Half Acre on the 535 m *585 yd* seventh hole of the Pine Valley course, Clementon, New Jersey, USA, built in 1912 and generally regarded as the world's most trying course.

Longest course The world's longest course is the par-77 7612 m *8325 yd* International GC, Bolton, Massachussetts, USA, from the 'Tiger' tees, remodelled in 1969 by Robert Trent Jones.

Floyd Satterlee Rood used the United States as a course, when he played from the Pacific surf to the Atlantic surf from 14 Sep 1963 to 3 Oct 1964 in 114 737 strokes. He lost 3511 balls on the 5468 km *3397.7 mile* trail.

Longest drives The greatest recorded drive on an ordinary course is one of 471 m *515 yd* by Michael Hoke Austin (b. 17 Feb 1910) of Los Angeles, California, USA, in the US National Seniors Open Championship at Las Vegas, Nevada on 25 Sep 1974. Austin, 1·88 m *6 ft 2 in* tall and weighing 92 kg *203 lb* drove the ball to within a yard of the green on the par-4 412 m *450 yd* fifth hole of the Winterwood Course and it rolled 59 m *65 yd* past the flagstick. He was aided by an estimated 56 km/h *35 mph* tailwind.

A drive of 2414 m *2640 yd (1½ miles)* across ice was achieved by an Australian meteorologist named Nils Lied at Mawson Base, Antarctica in 1962.

On the Moon the energy expended on a mundane 300 yd 274 m drive would achieve, craters permitting, a distance of 1 mile 1·6 km.

Longest putt The longest recorded holed putt in a major tournament is 110 ft by; Jack Nicklaus (b. 21 Jan 1940) in the 1964 Tournament of Champions; and Nick Price in the 1992 United States PGA.

Robert Tyre 'Bobby' Jones Jr, (1902–71) was reputed to have holed a putt in excess of 30 m *100 ft* at the fifth green in the first round of the 1927 Open at St Andrews.

Bob Cook (USA) sank a putt measured at 42·74 m *140 ft 2¾ in* on the 18th at St

Most Major Golf Titles

The Open	Harry Vardon (1870–1937)	6	1896, 1898–9, 1903, 11, 14
The Amateur	John Ball (1861–1940)	8	1888, 90, 92, 94, 99, 1907, 1910, 12
US Open	William 'Willie' Anderson (1880–1910)	4	1901, 03–05
	Robert Tyre 'Bobby' Jones Jr (1902–71)	4	1923, 26, 29–30
	William Benjamin Hogan (b. 13 Aug 1912)	4	1948, 50–51, 53
	Jack William Nicklaus (b. 21 Jan 1940)	4	1962, 67, 72, 80
US Amateur	Robert Tyre Jones Jr	5	1924–25, 27–8, 30
US PGA	Walter Charles Hagan (1892–1969)	5	1921, 24–7
	Jack William Nicklaus	5	1963, 71, 73, 75, 80
US Masters	Jack William Nicklaus	6	1963, 65–6, 72, 75, 86
US Women's	Elizabeth 'Betsy' Earle-Rawls (b. 4 May 1928)	4	1951, 53, 57, 60
Open	'Mickey' Wright (b. 14 Feb 1935)	4	1958–59, 61, 64
US Women's Amateur	Glenna Collett Vare (née Collett) (1903–89)	6	1922, 25, 28–30, 35
British Women's	Charlotte Cecilia Pitcairn Leitch (1891–1977)	4	1914, 20–21, 26
	Joyce Wethered (b. 17 Nov 1901) (Now Lady Heathcoat-Amory)	4	1922, 24–5, 29

Note: Nicklaus is the only golfer to have won 5 different major titles (The Open, US Open, Masters, PGA and US Amateur titles) twice and a record 20 all told (1959–86). In 1930 Bobby Jones achieved a unique 'Grand Slam' of the US and British Open and Amateur titles.

Andrews in the International Fourball Pro Am Tournament on 1 Oct 1976.

Scores

Lowest 9 holes Nine holes in 25 (4, 3, 3, 2, 3, 3, 1, 4, 2) was recorded by A. J. 'Bill' Burke in a round in 57 (32+25) on the 5842 m *6389 yd* par-71 Normandie course at St Louis, Missouri, USA on 20 May 1970.

The tournament record is 27 by Mike Souchak (USA) (b. 10 May 1927) for the second nine (par-35), first round of the 1955 Texas Open (⬦ 72 holes); Andy North (USA) (b. 9 Mar 1950) second nine (par-34), first round, 1975 BC Open at En-Joie GC, Endicott, New York; José Maria Canizares (Spain) (b. 18 Feb 1947), first nine, third round, in the 1978 Swiss Open on the 6228 m *6811 yd* Crans GC, Crans-sur-Seine; and Robert Lee (GB) (b. 12 Oct 1961) first nine, first round, in the Monte Carlo Open on the 5714 m *6249 yd* Mont Agel course on 28 Jun 1985.

Lowest 18 holes *Men* At least four players have played a long course (over 6000 m *6561 yd*) in a score of 58, most recently Monte Carlo Money (USA) (b. 3

Dec 1954) at the par-72, 6041 m *6607 yd* Las Vegas Municipal GC, Nevada, USA on 11 Mar 1981.

Alfred Edward Smith (1903–85) achieved an 18-hole score of 55 (15 under par 70) on his home course of 3884 m *4248 yd*, scoring 4, 2, 3, 4, 2, 4, 3, 4, 3=29 out, and 2, 3, 3, 3, 3, 2, 5, 4, 1=26 in, on 1 Jan 1936.

The United States PGA Tournament record for 18 holes is 59 by Al Geiberger (b. 1 Sep 1937) (30+29) in the second round of the Danny Thomas Classic, on the 72-par 6628 m *7249 yd* Colonial GC course, Memphis, Tennessee on 10 Jun 1977; and by Chip Beck in the third round of the Las Vegas Invitational, on the 72-par 6381 m *6979 yd* Sunrise GC course, Las Vegas, Nevada on 11 Oct 1991.

Other golfers to have recorded 59 over 18 holes in major non-PGA tournaments include: Samuel Jackson 'Sam' Snead (b. 27 May 1912) in the third round of the Sam Snead Festival at White Sulphur Springs, West Virginia, USA on 16 May 1959; Gary Player (South Africa) (b. 1 Nov 1935) in the second round of the Brazilian Open in Rio de Janeiro on 29

Nov 1974; David Jagger (GB) (b. 9 Jun 1949) in a Pro-Am tournament prior to the 1973 Nigerian Open at Ikoyi GC, Lagos; and Miguel Martin (Spain) in the Argentine Southern Championship at Mar de Plata on 27 Feb 1987.

Women The lowest recorded score on an 18-hole course (over 5120 m *5600 yd*) for a woman is 62 (30+32) by Mary 'Mickey' Kathryn Wright (USA) (b. 14 Feb 1935) on the Hogan Park Course (par-71, 5747 m *6286 yd*) at Midland, Texas, USA, in November 1964, Janice Arnold (New Zealand) (31+31) at the Coventry Golf Club, W Mids (5317 m *5815 yd*) on 24 Sep 1990, Laura Davies (GB) (32+30) at the Rail Golf Club, Springfield, Illinois, USA on 31 Aug 1991 and Hollis Stacy (b. 16 Mar 1954) at Meridian Valley Country Club, Seattle, Washington on 18 Sep 1992.

Wanda Morgan (b. 22 Mar 1910) recorded a score of 60 (31+29) on the Westgate and Birchington GC course, Kent, over 18 holes (4573 m *5002 yd*) on 11 Jul 1929.

Great Britain The lowest score recorded in a first-class professional tournament on a course of more than 5490 m *6000 yd* in Great Britain is 60 (30+30), by Paul Curry in the second round of the Bell's Scottish Open on the King's course (5899 m *6452 yd*), Gleneagles, Fife on 9 Jul 1992.

Lowest 36 holes The record for 36 holes is 122 (59+63) by Sam Snead in the 1959 Sam Snead Festival on 16–17 May 1959.

Horton Smith (1908–63), twice US Masters Champion, scored 121 (63+58) on a short course on 21 Dec 1928 (<> 72 holes).

The lowest score by a British golfer has been 124 (61+63) by Alexander Walter Barr 'Sandy' Lyle (b. 9 Feb 1958) in the Nigerian Open at the 5508 m *6024 yd* (par-71) Ikoyi GC, Lagos in 1978.

Lowest 72 holes The lowest recorded score on a first-class course is 255 (29 under par) by Leonard Peter Tupling (GB) (b. 6 Apr 1950) in the Nigerian Open at Ikoyi GC, Lagos in February 1981, made up of 63, 66, 62 and 64 (average 63·75 per round).

The lowest 72 holes in a US professional event is 257 (60, 68, 64, 65) by Mike Souchak in the 1955 Texas Open at San Antonio.

The 72 holes record on the European tour is 258 (64, 69, 60, 65) by David Llewellyn (b. 18 Nov 1951) in the Biarritz Open on 1–3 Apr 1988. This was equalled by Ian Woosnam (Wales) (b. 2 Mar 1958) (66, 67, 65, 60) in the Monte Carlo Open on 4–7 Jul 1990.

The lowest 72 holes in an open championship in Europe is 262 (67, 66, 66, 63) by Percy Alliss (GB) (1897–1975) in the 1932 Italian Open at San Remo, and by Lu Liang Huan (Taiwan) (b. 10 Dec 1935) in the 1971 French Open at Biarritz.

The lowest for four rounds in a British first-class tournament is 262 (66, 63, 66, 67) by Bernard Hunt in the Piccadilly Tournament on the par-68 5655 m *6184 yd* Wentworth East course, Virginia Water, Surrey on 4–5 Oct 1966.

Trish Johnson scored 242 (64, 60, 60, 58) (21 under par) in the Bloor Homes Eastleigh Classic at the Fleming Park Course (4025 m *4402 yd*) at Eastleigh, Hants on 22–25 Jul 1987.

Horton Smith scored 245 (63, 58, 61 and 63) for 72 holes on the 4297 m *4700 yd* course (par-64) at Catalina Country Club, California, USA, to win the Catalina Open on 21–23 Dec 1928.

World one-club record Thad Daber (USA), with a 6-iron, played the 5520 m *6037 yd* Lochmore GC, Cary, North Carolina, USA in 70 to win the 1987 World One-club Championship.

Most shots for one hole A woman player in the qualifying round of the Shawnee Invitational for Ladies at Shawnee-on-Delaware, Pennsylvania, USA, *c.* 1912, took 166 strokes for the short 118 m *130 yd* 16th hole. Her tee shot went into the Binniekill River and the ball floated. She put out in a boat with her exemplary but statistically-minded husband at the oars. She eventually beached the ball 2·4 km *1½ miles* downstream but was not yet out of the wood. She had to play through one on the home run.

The highest score for a single hole in the British Open is 21 by a player in the inaugural meeting at Prestwick in 1860.

Double figures have been recorded on the card of the winner only once, when Willie Fernie (1851–1924) scored a ten at Musselburgh, Lothian in 1883.

Fastest rounds *Individual* With such variations in lengths of courses, speed records, even for rounds under par, are of little comparative value. The fastest round played when the golf ball comes to rest before each new stroke is 27 min 9 sec by James Carvill (b. 13 Oct 1965) at Warrenpoint Golf Course, Co. Down (18 holes, 5628 m *6154 yd*) on 18 Jun 1987.

Team The 35 members of the Team Balls Out Diving completed the 18-hole 5516 m *6033 yd* John E. Clark course at Point Micu, California, USA in 9 min 39 sec on 16 Nov 1992. They scored 71!

Slowest rounds The slowest stroke-play tournament round was one of 6 hr 45 min taken by South Africa in the first round of the 1972 World Cup at the Royal Melbourne GC, Australia. This was a four-ball medal round; everything holed out.

Most holes in 24 hours *On foot* Ian Colston, 35, played 22 rounds and five holes (401 holes) at Bendigo GC, Victoria, Australia (par-73, 5542 m *6061yd*) on 27–28 Nov 1971.

The British record is 360 holes by Antony J. Clark at Childwall GC, Liverpool on 18 Jul 1983.

David Brett of Stockport played 218 holes in 12 hours at Didsbury GC, Greater Manchester (par-70, 5696 m *6230yd*) on 22 Jun 1990.

Using golf carts David Cavalier played 846 holes at Arrowhead Country Club, North Canton, Ohio, USA (9-hole course, 2755 m *3013yd*) on 6–7 Aug 1990.

Doug Wert played 440 holes in 12 hours on the 5526 m *6044 yd* course at the Tournament Players Club, Coral Springs, Florida, USA on 7 Jun 1993.

Most holes played in a week Steve Hylton played 1128 holes at the Mason Rudolph GC (5541m *6060yd*), Clarksville, Tennessee, USA from 25–31 Aug

1980. Using a buggy for transport, Colin Young completed 1260 holes at Patshull Park GC (5863 m *6412yd*), Pattingham, Shropshire from 2–9 Jul 1988.

Championship Records

The Open (inaugurated 1860, Prestwick, Strathclyde) *First nine holes* 28 by Denis Durnian (b. 30 Jun 1950), at Royal Birkdale, Southport, Merseyside in the second round on 15 Jul 1983.

Any round 63 by: Mark Stephen Hayes (USA) (b. 12 Jul 1949) at Turnberry, Strathclyde on 7 Jul 1977; Isao Aoki (Japan) (b. 31 Aug 1942) at Muirfield, Lothian on 19 Jul 1980; Gregory John Norman (Australia) (b. 10 Feb 1955) at Turnberry on 18 Jul 1986; Paul Broadhurst (GB) (b. 14 Aug 1965) at St Andrews, Fife on 21 Jul 1990; and Joseph Martin 'Jodie' Mudd (USA) (b. 23 Apr 1960) at Royal Birkdale on 21 Jul 1991.

First 36 holes Nicholas Alexander 'Nick' Faldo (GB) (b. 18 Jul 1957) completed the first 36 holes at Muirfield, Lothian in 130 strokes (66, 64) on 16–17 Jul 1992. (Faldo added a third round of 69 to equal the 54–hole record of 199 which he had set at St Andrews in 1990 (67, 65, 67)).

Total aggregate 268 (68, 70, 65, 65) by Thomas Sturges Watson (USA) (b. 4 Sep 1949) at Turnberry in July 1977.

US Open (inaugurated in 1895) *Any round* 63 by: Johnny Miller (b. 29 Apr 1947) on the 6328 m *6921yd* par-71 Oakmont Country Club course, Pennsylvania on 17 Jun 1973; by Jack Nicklaus and Tom Weiskopf (USA) (b. 9 Nov 1942) at Baltusrol Country Club (6414 m *7015yd*), Springfield, New Jersey, both on 12 Jun 1980.

First 36 holes 134 by: Jack Nicklaus (63, 71) at Baltusrol, 12–13 Jun 1980; Chen Tze-Chung (Taiwan) (65, 69) at Oakland Hills, Birmingham, Michigan in 1985; and Lee Janzen (USA) (67, 67) at Baltusrol, 17–18 Jun 1993.

Total aggregate 272 by Jack Nicklaus (63, 71, 70, 68), 12–15 Jun 1980 and Lee Janzen (67, 67, 69, 69), 17–20 Jun 1993, both at Baltusrol.

The Solheim Cup (first held in 1990 and won by the USA) is the women's equivalent to the Ryder Cup, with the match format being very much the same. Above, the European team celebrate their success over the USA in 1992.

(Photo: Allsport/David Cannon)

Above right, Davis Love III (left) and Fred Couples (both USA) celebrate their success in the 1992 World Cup. It was the USA's 18th win in the cup.

(Photo: Allsport/David Cannon)

Severiano Ballesteros has won a record 51 European Order of Merit events, 1974–92.

(Photo: Allsport/Stephen Munday)

Nick Faldo in action during the 1992 Johnnie Walker World Championship which has the highest total prize money of any tournament. Faldo won the event, rounding off a highly successful year in which he won a season's record earnings in European Order of Merit tournaments.

(Photo: Allsport/David Cannon)

Youngest and oldest hole-in-one

The youngest golfer recorded to have shot a hole-in-one is Coby Orr (5 years) of Littleton, Colorado on the 94 m *103 yd* fifth at the Riverside Golf Course, San Antonio, Texas, USA in 1975.

The British record was set by Mark Alexander, aged 6 yr 251 days, on the 99 m *109 yd* sixth at the Chessington Golf Centre, Greater London on 17 Sep 1989. The youngest girl to score an ace is Nicola Hammond, aged 10 yr 204 days on the 98 m *107 yd* third at Dereham GC, Norfolk on 17 June 1990.

The oldest golfers to have performed this feat are: (men) 99 yr 244 days Otto Bucher (Switzerland) (b. 12 May 1885) on the 119 m *130 yd* 12th at La Manga GC, Spain on 13 Jan 1985; (women) 95 yr 257 days Erna Ross (b. 9 Sep 1890) on the 102 m *112 yd* 17th at The Everglades Club, Palm Beach, Florida, USA on 23 Apr 1986.

The British records: (men) 92 yr 169 days Samuel Richard Walker (b. 6 Jan 1892) at the 143 m *156 yd* 8th at West Hove GC, E Sussex on 23 Jun 1984; (women) 90 yr 236 days Dorothy Huntley-Flindt (b. 19 Jun 1898) at the 102 m *112 yd* 13th at Barton-on-Sea GC, Hants on 10 Feb 1989.

The oldest player to score his age is C. Arthur Thompson (1869–1975) of Victoria, British Columbia, Canada, who scored 103 in 1973.

US Masters (played on the 6382 m 6980 yd Augusta National Golf Course, Georgia, first in 1934)   Any round 63 by Nicholas Raymond Leige Price (Zimbabwe) (b. 28 Jan 1957) in 1986.

First 36 holes 131 (65, 66) by Raymond Loran Floyd (b. 4 Sep 1942) in 1976.

Total aggregate 271 by: Jack Nicklaus (67, 71, 64, 69) in 1965 and Raymond Floyd (65, 66, 70, 70) in 1976.

Team Competitons

World Cup (formerly Canada Cup)

The World Cup (instituted as the Canada Cup in 1953) has been won most often by the USA with 18 victories between 1955 and 1992.

The only men to have been on six winning teams have been Arnold Palmer (b. 10 Sep 1929) (1960, 1962–4, 1966–7) and Jack Nicklaus (1963–4, 1966–7, 1971 and 1973). Only Nicklaus has taken the individual title three times (1963–4, 1971).

The lowest aggregate score for 144 holes is 544 by Australia, Bruce Devlin (b. 10 Oct 1937) and Anthony David Graham (b. 23 May 1946), at San Isidro, Buenos Aires, Argentina from 12–15 Nov 1970.

The lowest individual score has been 269 by Roberto de Vicenzo (Argentina) (b. 14 Apr 1923), also in 1970.

Ryder Cup

The biennial Ryder Cup professional match between the USA and Europe (British Isles or Great Britain prior to 1979) was instituted in 1927. The USA has won 22 to 5 (with 2 draws) to 1991.

Arnold Palmer has the record of winning most Ryder Cup matches with 22 from 32 played, with two halved and 8 lost. Christy O'Connor Sr (Ireland) (b. 21 Dec 1924) played in ten contests, 1955–73.

Walker Cup

The series was instituted in 1921 (for the Walker Cup since 1922 and now held biennially). The USA have won 29, Great Britain & Ireland 3 (in 1938, 1971 and 1989) and the 1965 match was tied.

Jay Sigel (USA) (b. 13 Nov 1943) has won a record 16 matches, with five halved and nine lost, 1977–91. Joseph Boynton Carr (GB & I) (b. 18 Feb 1922) played in ten contests, 1947–67.

Curtis Cup

The biennial ladies' Curtis Cup match between the USA and Great Britain and Ireland was first held in 1932. The USA have won 20 to 1992, GB

& I five (1952, 1956, 1986, 1988 and 1992) and two matches have been tied.

Mary McKenna (GB & I) (b. 29 Apr 1949) played in a record ninth match in 1986, when for the first time she was on the winning team. Carole Semple Thompson (USA) has won a record 12 matches in 7 contests, 1974–92.

Individual Records

Richest prize The greatest first place prize money ever won is $1 000 000 awarded annually from 1987 to 1991 to the winners of the Sun City Challenge, Bophuthatswana, South Africa; Ian Woosnam (Wales) was the first winner in 1987.

The greatest total prize money is $2 700 000 (including $550 000 first prize) for the Johnnie Walker World Championship at Tryall GC, Montego Bay, Jamaica on 17–20 Dec 1992.

Highest earnings *US PGA and LPGA circuits* The all-time career earnings record on the US PGA circuit is held by Thomas O. Kite Jr (USA) (b. 9 Dec 1949) with $8 299 794, 1982 to 21 Jun 1993. He also holds the earnings record for a year, $1 395 278 in 1989.

The record career earnings for a woman is by Patricia Bradley (b. 24 Mar 1951) with $4 440 113 to 18 Jun 1993. The season's record is $863 578 by Elizabeth Ann 'Beth' Daniel (b. 14 Oct 1956) in 1990.

European circuit Nick Faldo (GB) won a season's record £708 522 in European Order of Merit tournaments in 1992 (worldwide, he won a record £1 558 978). He also holds the tour career earnings record with £3 457 337 (26 tour victories), 1976–92.

Most tournament wins John Byron Nelson (USA) (b. 4 Feb 1912) won a record 18 tournaments (plus one unofficial) in a year, including a record 11 consecutively from 8 Mar to 4 Aug 1945.

Sam Snead from turning professional in 1934 won 84 official US PGA tour events, 1936–65. The ladies' PGA record is 88 by Kathy Whitworth (b. 27 Sep 1939) from 1962 to 1985. The most career victories in European Order of Merit tournaments is

51 by Severiano Ballesteros (Spain) (b. 9 Apr 1957), 1974–92.

Biggest winning margin The greatest margin of victory in a major tournament is 21 strokes by Jerry Pate (USA) (b. 16 Sep 1953), who won the Colombian Open with 262 from 10–13 Dec 1981.

Cecilia Leitch won the Canadian Ladies' Open Championship in 1921 by the biggest margin for a major title, 17 up and 15 to play.

Youngest and oldest champions The youngest winner of The Open was Tom Morris Jr (1851–75) at Prestwick, Strathclyde in 1868 aged 17 yr 249 days.

The oldest Open champion was 'Old Tom' Morris (1821–1908), aged 46 yr 99 days when he won at Prestwick in 1867. Oldest this century has been the 1967 champion, Roberto de Vincenzo, at 44 yr 93 days.

The oldest US Open champion was Hale S. Irwin (USA) (b. 3 Jun 1945) at 45 yr 15 days on 18 Jun 1990.

Youngest and oldest national champions Thuashni Selvaratnam (b. 9 Jun 1976) won the 1989 Sri Lankan Ladies Amateur Open Golf Championship, aged 12 yr 324 days, at Nuwara Eliya GC on 29 Apr 1989. Maria Teresa 'Isa' Goldschmid (*née* Bevione) (b. 15 Oct 1925) won the Italian Women's Championship, aged 50 yr 200 days, at Oligata, Rome on 2 May 1976.

Most club championships Helen Gray has been ladies champion at Todmorden GC, Lancs 37 times between 1952 and 1991. The men's record is 36 (consecutive) by Richard John Fewster at Bandee Golf Club, Merredin, Australia, 1956–92.

Patricia Shepherd (b. 7 Jan 1940) won 30 consecutive championships at Turriff GC, Grampian, 1959–88.

Largest tournament The Volkswagen Grand Prix Open Amateur Championship in the United Kingdom attracted a record 321 778 (206 820 men and 114 958 women) competitors in 1984.

Holes In One

Longest The longest straight hole ever holed in one shot was, appropriately, the tenth (408 m *447 yd*) at Miracle Hills

GC, Omaha, Nebraska, USA by Robert Mitera (b. 1944) on 7 Oct 1965. Mitera stood 1·68 m *5 ft 6 in* tall and weighed 75 kg *165 lb* (11 st 11 lb). He was a two handicap player who normally drove 224 m *245 yd*. A 80 km/h *50 mph* gust carried his shot over a 265 m *290 yd* drop-off.

The longest 'dog-leg' hole achieved in one is the 439 m *480 yd* fifth at Hope Country Club, Arkansas, USA by L. Bruce on 15 Nov 1962.

The women's record is 359 m *393 yd* by Marie Robie on the first hole of the Furnace Brook GC, Wollaston, Massachusetts, USA on 4 Sep 1949.

The longest hole in one performed in the British Isles is the seventh (par-4, 359 m *393 yd*) at West Lancashire GC by Peter Richard Parkinson (b. 26 Aug 1947) on 6 Jun 1972.

Consecutive There are at least 19 cases of 'aces' being achieved in two consecutive holes, of which the greatest was Norman L. Manley's unique double 'albatross' on the par-4 301 m *330 yd* seventh and par-4 265 m *290 yd* eighth holes on the Del Valle Country Club course, Saugus, California, USA on 2 Sep 1964.

The first woman to record consecutive 'aces' was Sue Prell, on the 13th and 14th holes at Chatswood GC, Sydney, Australia on 29 May 1977.

The closest to achieving three consecutive holes in one were Dr Joseph Boydstone on the 3rd, 4th and 9th at Bakersfield GC, California, USA, on 10 Oct 1962 and Rev. Harold Snider (b. 4 Jul 1900) who aced the 8th, 13th and 14th holes of the par-3 Ironwood course, Arizona, USA on 9 Jun 1976.

Greyhound Racing

Derby Two greyhounds have won the English Greyhound Derby (instituted 1927 at White City, London over 525 yd, now over 480 m at Wimbledon) twice: *Mick the Miller* on 25 Jul 1929, when owned by Albert H. Williams, and on 28 Jun 1930 when owned by Mrs Arundel H. Kempton, and *Patricia's Hope* on 24

Derby 'triple'

The only greyhounds to win the English, Scottish and Welsh Derby 'triple' are *Trev's Perfection*, owned by Fred Trevillion, in 1947, *Mile Bush Pride*, owned by Noel W. Purvis, in 1959, and *Patricia's Hope* in 1972.

Longest odds

Apollo Prince won at odds of 250–1 at Sandown GRC, Springvale, Victoria, Australia on 14 Nov 1968

Jun 1972 when owned by Gordon and Basil Marks and Brian Stanley and 23 Jun 1973 when owned by G. & B. Marks and J. O'Connor.

The highest prize was £40 000 to *Slippy Blue* for the Derby on 23 Jun 1990.

Grand National The only greyhound to have won the Grand National (instituted 1927 over 525 yd then 500 m at White City, now 474 m at Hall Green, Birmingham) three times is *Sherry's Prince* (1967–78) owned by Mrs Joyce Mathews of Sanderstead, Surrey, in 1970–72.

Fastest greyhound The highest speed at which any greyhound has been timed is 67·14 km/h *41·72 mph* (375 m *410 yd* in 20·1 sec) by *The Shoe* on the then straightaway track at Richmond, New South Wales, Australia on 25 Apr 1968. It is estimated that he covered the last 100 yd *91·44 m* in 4·5 sec or at 73·14 km/h *45·45 mph*. The highest speed recorded for a greyhound in Great Britain is 62·97 km/h *39·13 mph* by *Beef Cutlet*, when covering a straight course of 457 m *500 yd* in 26·13 sec at Blackpool, Lancs, on 13 May 1933.

The fastest automatically timed speed recorded for a full four-bend race is 62·59 km/h *38·89 mph* at Brighton, E Sussex by *Glen Miner* on 4 May 1982 with a time of 29·62 sec for 515 m *563 yd*.

The fastest over hurdles is 60·58 km/h *37·64 mph* at Brighton by *Wotchit Buster* on 22 Aug 1978.

Most wins The most career wins is 143 by the American greyhound, *JR's Ripper* in 1982–6.

The most consecutive victories is 32 by *Ballyregan Bob*, owned by Cliff Kevern and trained by George Curtis from 25 Aug 1984 to 9 Dec 1986, including 16 track record times. His race wins were by an average of more than nine lengths.

Highest earnings The career earnings record is held by *Homespun Rowdy* with $297 000 in the USA, 1984–7.

The richest first prize for a greyhound race is $125 000 won by *Ben G Speedboat* in the Great Greyhound Race of Champions at Seabrook, New Hampshire, USA on 23 Aug 1986.

Gymnastics

World Championships *Women* The greatest number of titles won in the World Championships (including Olympic Games) is 12 individual wins and six team titles by Larisa Semyonovna Latynina (née Diriy) (b. 27 Dec 1934) of the USSR, between 1954 and 1964. The USSR won the team title on 21 occasions (11 world and 10 Olympics).

Men Boris Anfiyanovich Shakhlin (USSR) (b. 27 Jan 1932) won ten individual titles between 1954 and 1964. He also had three team wins.

The USSR won the team title a record 13 times (eight World Championships, five Olympics) between 1952 and 1992.

Youngest champions Aurelia Dobre (Romania) (b. 6 Nov 1972) won the women's overall world title at 14 yr 352 days at Rotterdam, Netherlands on 23 Oct 1987. Daniela Silivas (Romania) revealed in 1990 that she was born on 9 May 1971, a year later than previously claimed, so that she was 14 yr 185 days when she won the gold medal for balance beam on 10 Nov 1985.

The youngest male world champion was Dmitriy Bilozerchev (USSR) (b. 17 Dec 1966) at 16 yr 315 days at Budapest, Hungary on 28 Oct 1983.

Olympics The men's team title has been won a record five times by Japan (1960, 1964, 1968, 1972 and 1976) and the USSR (1952, 1956, 1980, 1988 and 1992).

The USSR won the women's title ten times (1952–80, 1988 and 1992). Note the successes in 1992 were by the Unified Team from the republics of the former USSR.

The most men's individual gold medals is six by: Boris Shakhlin (USSR) one in 1956, four (two shared) in 1960 and one in 1964; and Nikolay Yefimovich Andrianov (USSR) (b. 14 Oct 1952), one in 1972, four in 1976 and one in 1980.

Vera Cáslavská-Odlozil (b. 3 May 1942) (Czechoslovakia) has won most individual gold medals with seven, three in 1964 and four (one shared) in 1968.

Larisa Latynina won six individual gold medals and was in three winning teams from 1956–64, making nine gold medals. She also won five silver and four bronze making 18 in all—an Olympic record.

The most medals for a male gymnast is 15 by Nikolay Andrianov (USSR), seven gold, five silver and three bronze from 1972–80.

Aleksandr Nikolayevich Dityatin (USSR) (b. 7 Aug 1957) is the only man to win a medal in all eight categories in the same Games, with three gold, four silver and one bronze at Moscow in 1980. Vitaliy Scherbo (Belarus) (b. 13 Jan 1972) won a record six golds at one Games in 1992, adding four individual titles to the all-around and team gold that he won with the Unified Team.

Highest score Hans Eugster (Switzerland) (b. 27 Mar 1929) scored a perfect 10·00 in the compulsory parallel bars at the 1950 World Championships. Nadia Comaneci (Romania) (b. 12 Nov 1961) was the first to achieve a perfect score (10·00) in the Olympics, and achieved seven in all at Montreal, Canada in July 1976.

British Championships The British Gymnastic Championship was won ten times by Arthur John Whitford (b. 2 Jul 1908) in 1928–36 and 1939. He was also in four winning teams. Wray 'Nik' Stuart (b. 20 Jul 1927) equalled the record of nine successive wins, 1956–64.

Exercises Speed & Stamina

Records are accepted for the most repetitions of the following activities within the given time span.

Parallel Bar Dips—1 Hour
3726 Kim Yang-ki at the Rivera Hotel, Seoul, South Korea on 28 Nov 1991.

Press-Ups (Push-Ups)—24 Hours
46 001 Charles Servizio at Fontana City Hall, Fontana, California, USA on 24–25 Apr 1993.

Press-Ups (One Arm)—5 Hours
7683, John Decker at Congleton Cricket Club, Cheshire on 16 Jun 1991.

Press-Ups (Finger Tip)—5 Hours
7011 Kim Yang-ki at the Swiss Grand Hotel, Seoul, South Korea on 30 Aug 1990.

Press-Ups (One Finger)—Consecutive
124 Paul Lynch at the Hippodrome, Leicester Square, London on 21 Apr 1992.

Sit-Ups—24 Hours
70 715 Lou Scripa Jr at Beale Airforce Base, Marysville, California, USA on 1–2 Dec 1992.

Squats—1 Hour
4289 Paul Wai Man Chung at the Yee Gin Kung Fu of Chung Sze Health (HK) Association, Kowloon, Hong Kong on 5 Apr 1992.

Squat Thrusts—1 Hour
3552 Paul Wai Man Chung at the Yee Gin Kung Fu of Chung Sze Health (HK) Association, Kowloon, Hong Kong on 21 Aug 1992.

Burpees—1 Hour
1822 Paddy Doyle at The Irish Centre, Digbeth, Birmingham on 6 Feb 1993.

The women's record is eight by Mary Patricia Hirst (b. 18 Nov 1918) (1947, 1949–50 and 1952–6).

The most overall titles in Modern Rhythmic Gymnastics is by Sharon Taylor with five successive, 1977–81.

World Cup Gymnasts who have won two World Cup (instituted 1975) overall

---

Gymnastics/ Aerobics display
The largest number of participants is 15 017 for the 1993 Boots Aerobathon at the Earls Court Exhibition Centre, London on 9 May 1993.

Youngest international gymnast
Pasakevi 'Voula' Kouna (b. 6 Dec 1971) was aged 9yr 299days at the start of the Balkan Games at Serres, Greece on 1 Oct 1981, when she represented Greece.

Club swinging
Albert Rayner set a world record of 17 512 revolutions (4·9 per sec) in 60min at Wakefield, W Yorks on 27 Jul 1981.

---

titles are three men: Nikolay Andrianov (USSR), Aleksandr Dityatin (USSR) and Li Ning (China) (b. 8 Sep 1963), and one woman: Maria Yevgenyevna Filatova (USSR) (b. 19 Jul 1961).

Modern Rhythmic Gymnastics The most overall individual world titles in Modern Rhythmic Gymnastics is three by Maria Gigova (Bulgaria) in 1969, 1971 and 1973 (shared).

Bulgaria has a record seven team titles 1969, 1971, 1981, 1983, 1985, 1987 and 1989 (shared). Bianka Panova (Bulgaria) (b. 27 May 1960) won all four apparatus gold medals all with maximum scores, and won a team gold in 1987.

Lilia Ignatova (Bulgaria) has won both the individual World Cup titles that have been held, 1983 and 1986.

At the 1988 Olympic Games Marina Lobach (USSR) (b. 26 Jun 1970) won the rhythmic gymnastic title with perfect scores in all six disciplines.

Somersaults Ashrita Furman performed 8341 forward rolls in 10hr 30min over 19·67 km *12 miles 390 yards* from Lexington to Charleston, Massachusetts, USA on 30 Apr 1986.

Shigeru Iwasaki (b. 1960) backwards somersaulted 50m *54·68yd* in 10·8sec at Tokyo, Japan on 30 Mar 1980.

Static wall 'sit' (or Samson's Chair)
Ramesh Khachi (India) stayed in an unsupported sitting position against a wall for 11 hr 2 min at Jawahar Navodaya Vidyalaya, Theog, India on 22 Sep 1992.

Handball

Most championships *Olympic* The USSR won five titles—men 1976, 1988 and 1992 (by the Unified Team from the republics of the ex-USSR), women 1976 and 1980. South Korea has also won two women's titles, in 1988 and 1992.

World Championships (instituted 1938) For the now predominant version of the game, indoors, the most men's titles is three by: Romania, 1961, 1964 and 1970; and Sweden, 1954, 1958 and 1990. However, Germany/West Germany won the outdoor title five times, 1938–66 and have won the indoor title twice, 1938 and 1978. Three women's titles have been won by (indoor unless stated): Romania, 1956, 1960 (both outdoor) and 1962; the GDR 1971, 1975 and 1978; and the USSR 1982, 1986 and 1990.

Oh Sung-ok of South Korea, helped her team to win the Olympic handball title for a record second time in 1992.

(Photo: Allsport/Michael Hewitt)

European Champions' Cup Spartak of Kiev, USSR won 13 women's titles between 1970 and 1988.

Vfl Gummersbach, West Germany have won a record five men's titles, 1967, 1970–71, 1974, 1983. They are also the only club team to win all three European trophies; European Champions' Cup, European Cup Winners' Cup and IHF Cup.

Highest score The highest score in an international match was recorded when the USSR beat Afghanistan 86–2 in the 'Friendly Army Tournament' at Miskolc, Hungary in August 1981.

Britain *Most titles* The most men's national championship titles is seven by Brentwood '72 (British Championship, 1974; English National League, 1979–83; British League, 1985).

The most women's titles is eight by Wakefield Metros (English National League, 1982–87; British League, 1988, 1990).

Highest score The highest score in a men's league match is by Glasgow University, who beat Claremont, 69–5 at Glasgow, Strathclyde in March 1984.

The women's record is Wakefield Metros 47–13 defeat of Ruslip Eagles at Featherstone, W Yorks on 25 Feb 1990.

Highest score by an individual Graham Hammond scored 29 for Wakefield (39) against Hull Universty (13) at Eccles Recreation Centre in November 1990.

The women's record is 15 by Donna Hankinson (b. 24 Mar 1972) for Manchester United SSS (26) against Arcton (9) at Kirkby on 12 Nov 1989, Julie Wells (b. 9 Jan 1963) for Wakefield Metros (47) against Ruislip Eagles (13) at Featherstone, W Yorks on 25 Feb 1990, and by Catherine Densmore for Halewood Town (23) against Ruislip Eagles (17) at Bristol, Avon on 25 May 1991.

Harness Racing

Most successful driver In North American harness racing history has been Hervé Filion (b. 1 Feb 1940) of

Québec, Canada, who had achieved 13876 wins to 21 Jun 1993 including a then record 814 wins in a year (1989). The most wins in a year is 843 by Walter Case (USA) in 1992.

John D. Campbell (USA) (b. 8 Apr 1955) has the highest career earnings of $111731928 to 21 Jun 1993. This includes a year record of $11620878 in 1990 when he won 543 races.

Highest price The most expensive pacer is *Nihilator* who was syndicated by Wall Street Stable and Almahurst Stud Farm for $19·2million in 1984.

The highest for a trotter is $6 million for *Mack Lobell* by John Erik Magnusson of Vislanda, Sweden in 1988.

Greatest winnings For any harness horse is $4907307 by the trotter *Peace Corps*, 1988–92. The greatest amount won by a pacer is $3225653 by *Nihilator*, who won 35 of 38 races in 1984–5.

The single season records are $2217222 by pacer *Precious Bunny* in 1991 and $1878798 by trotter *Mack Lobell* in 1987.

The largest ever purse was $2161000 for the Woodrow Wilson two-year-old race over 1 mile at the Meadowlands, New Jersey, USA on 16 Aug 1984. Of this sum a record $1080500 went to the winner *Nihilator*, driven by William O'Donnell (b. 4 May 1948).

Hockey

Most Olympic medals India was Olympic champion from the re-introduction of Olympic hockey in 1928 until 1960, when Pakistan beat them 1–0 at Rome. They had their eighth win in 1980. Of the six Indians who have won three Olympic team gold medals, two have also won a silver medal — Leslie Walter Claudius (b. 25 Mar 1927), in 1948, 1952, 1956 and 1960 (silver), and Udham Singh (b. 4 Aug 1928), in 1952, 1956, 1964 and 1960 (silver).

A women's tournament was added in 1980, and there have been four seperate winners.

World Cup The World Cup for men was first held in 1971, and for women in

594

Hockey umpire
Graham Dennis Nash (b. 15 Mar 1943) umpired in five successive Olympics, 1976–92, and retired after Barcelona having officiated in a record 144 international matches.

Fastest goal in an international
John French scored 7 sec after the bully-off for England *v.* West Germany at Nottingham on 25 Apr 1971.

Champions' Trophy
First held in 1978 and contested annually since 1980 by the top six men's hockey teams in the world; the most wins is five, by Australia, 1983–5, 1989– 90. The first women's Champions' Trophy was won by the Netherlands in 1987. South Korea won in 1989 and Australia in 1991.

1974. The most wins are, (men) three by Pakistan, 1971, 1978 and 1982; (women) five by the Netherlands, 1974, 1978, 1983, 1986 and 1990.

Men

Highest international score The highest score was when India defeated the USA 24–1 at Los Angeles, California, USA in the 1932 Olympic Games.

The greatest number of goals in an international in Britain was when England defeated France 16–0 at Beckenham, Kent on 25 Mar 1922.

Most international appearances Heiner Dopp (b. 27 Jun 1956) represented West Germany 286 times between 1975 and 1990, indoors and out.

The most by a player from the British Isles is 228 by Richard Leman (b. 13 Jul 1959), 158 (106 outdoor, 52 indoor) for England and 70 for Great Britain, 1980–90. Harold David Judge (b. 19 Jan 1936) played a record 124 times for Ireland, 1957–78. The first player to achieve 100 international appearances for England was Norman Hughes (b. 30 Sep 1952) on 21 Sep 1986. The most indoor caps for England is 85 by Richard Clarke (b. 3 Apr 1952), 1976–87.

Greatest scoring feats The greatest number of goals scored in international hockey is 267 by Paul Litjens (Netherlands) (b. 9 Nov 1947) in 177 games.

M. C. Marckx (Bowden 2nd XI) scored 19 goals against Brooklands 2nd XI (score 23–0) on 31 Dec 1910. He was selected for England in March 1912 but declined due to business priorities. David Ashman has scored a record 2048 goals having played for Hampshire, Southampton, Southampton Kestrals and Hamble Old Boys (for whom he has scored 1889 goals, a record for one club), 1958–93.

Greatest goalkeeping Richard James Allen (India) (b. 4 Jun 1902) did not concede a goal during the 1928 Olympic tournament and a total of only three in 1936.

Women

Most international appearances Valerie Robinson made a record 149 appearances for England, 1963–84.

Highest scores The highest score in an international match was when England beat France 23–0 at Merton, Greater London on 3 Feb 1923.

In club hockey, Ross Ladies beat Wyeside, at Ross-on-Wye, Herefordshire 40–0 on 24 Jan 1929, when Edna Mary Blakelock (1904–89) scored a record 21 goals.

Highest attendance The highest attendance was 65 165 for the match between England and the USA at Wembley, London on 11 Mar 1978.

Horse Racing

Largest prizes The highest prize money for a day's racing is $10 million for the Breeders' Cup series of seven races staged annually in the USA since 1984. Included each year is a record $3 million for the Breeders' Cup Classic.

Most runners The most horses in a race has been 66 in the Grand National on 22 Mar 1929. The record for the Flat is 58 in the Lincolnshire Handicap at Lincoln on 13 Mar 1948.

Horses

Most successful The horse with the best win-loss record was *Kincsem*, a Hungarian mare foaled in 1874, who was unbeaten in 54 races (1876–79) throughout Europe, including the Goodwood Cup of 1878.

Longest winning sequence Camarero, foaled in 1951, was undefeated in 56 races in Puerto Rico from 19 Apr 1953 to his first defeat on 17 Aug 1955 (in his career to 1956, he won 73 of 77 races).

Career Chorisbar (foaled 1935) won 197 of his 325 races in Puerto Rico, 1937–47. *Lenoxbar* (foaled 1935) won 46 races in one year, 1940, in Puerto Rico from 56 starts.

Same race Doctor Syntax (foaled 1811) won the Preston Gold Cup on seven successive occasions, 1815–21.

Triple Crown winners The English Triple Crown (2000 Guineas, Derby, St Leger) has been won 15 times, most recently by *Nijinsky* in 1970. The fillies' equivalent (1000 Guineas, Oaks, St Leger) has been won nine times, most recently by *Oh So Sharp* in 1985. Two of these fillies also won the 2000 Guineas: *Formosa* (in a dead-heat) in 1868 and *Sceptre* in 1902. The American Triple Crown (Kentucky Derby, Preakness Stakes, Belmont Stakes) has been achieved 11 times, most recently by *Affirmed* in 1978.

Highest price Enormous valuations placed on potential stallions may be determined from sales of a minority holding, but such valuations would, perhaps, not be reached on the open market. The most paid for a yearling is $13·1 m on 23 Jul 1985 at Keeneland, Kentucky, USA by Robert Sangster and partners for *Seattle Dancer*.

Greatest winnings The career earnings record is $6 679 242 by the 1987 Kentucky Derby winner *Alysheba* (foaled 1984) from 1986–8. The most prize money earned in a year is $4 578 454 by *Sunday Silence* (foaled 1986) in the USA in 1989. His total included $1 350 000 from the Breeders' Cup Classic and a

Major Race Records

FLAT Race (Instituted)	Record Time	Most Wins Jockey	Trainer	Owner	Largest Field
Derby (1780) 1 m 4f 10yd *2423m* Epsom, Surrey	2 min 33·8sec *Mahmoud* 1936 2 min 33·84sec *Kahyasi* 1988*	9–Lester Piggott 1954, 57, 60, 68, 70, 72, 76, 77, 83	7–Robert Robson 1793, 1802, 09, 10, 15, 17, 23 7–John Porter 1868, 82, 83, 86, 90, 91, 99 7–Fred Darling 1922, 25, 26, 31, 38, 40, 41	5–3rd Earl of Egremont 1782, 1804, 05, 07, 26 5–HH Aga Khan III 1930, 35, 36, 48, 52	34 (1862)
2000 Guineas (1809) 1 mile *1609m* Newmarket, Suffolk	1 min 35·52sec *Zafonic* 1993	9–Jem Robinson 1825, 28, 31, 33, 34, 35, 36, 47, 48	7–John Scott 1842, 43, 49, 53, 56, 60, 62	5–4th Duke of Grafton 1820, 21, 22, 26, 27 5–5th Earl of Jersey 1831, 34, 35, 36, 37	28 (1930)
1000 Guineas (1814) 1 mile *1609m* Newmarket	1 min 36·85sec *Oh So Sharp* 1985	7–George Fordham 1859, 61, 65, 68, 69, 81, 83	9–Robert Robson 1818, 19, 20, 21, 22, 23, 25, 26, 27	8–4th Duke of Grafton 1819, 20, 21, 22, 23, 25, 26, 27	29 (1926)
Oaks (1779) 1 m 4f 10yd *2423m* Epsom	2 min 34·19sec *Intrepidity* 1993	9–Frank Buckle 1797, 98, 99, 1802, 03, 05, 17, 18, 23	12–Robert Robson 1802, 04, 05, 07, 08, 09, 13, 15, 18, 22, 23, 25	6–4th Duke of Grafton 1813, 15, 22, 23, 28, 31	26 (1848)
St Leger (1776) 1 m 6f 132yd *2937m* Doncaster, South Yorkshire	3 min 01·6sec *Coronach* 1926 *Windsor Lad* 1934	9–Bill Scott 1821, 25, 28, 29, 38, 39, 40, 41, 46	16–John Scott 1827, 28, 29, 32, 34, 38, 39, 40, 41, 45, 51, 53, 56, 57, 59, 62	7–9th Duke of Hamilton 1786, 87, 88, 92, 1808, 09, 14	30 (1825)
King George VI and Queen Elizabeth Diamond Stakes (1951) 1½ miles *2414m* Ascot, Berkshire	2 min 26·98sec *Grundy* 1975	7–Lester Piggott 1965, 66, 69, 70, 74, 77, 84	5–Dick Hern 1972, 79, 80, 85, 89	2–Nelson Bunker Hunt 1973, 74	19 (1951)

Race	Time	Jockey	Trainer	Owner	Age (year)
Prix de l'Arc de Triomphe (1920) 2400 metres *1 mile 864 yd* Longchamp, Paris, France	2 min 26·3 sec *Trampolino 1987*	4–Jacques Doyasbère 1942, 44, 50, 51 4–Frédéric 'Freddy' Head 1966, 72, 76, 79 4–Yves Saint-Martin 1970, 74, 82, 84 4–Pat Eddery 1980, 85, 86, 87	4–Charles Semblat 1942, 44, 46, 49 4–Alec Head 1952, 59, 76, 81 4–François Mathet 1950, 51, 70, 82	6–Marcel Boussac 1936, 37, 42, 44, 46, 49	30 (1967)
VRC Melbourne Cup (1861) 3200 metres *1 mile 1739 yd* Flemington, Victoria, Australia	3 min 16·3 sec *Kingston Rule 1990*	4–Bobby Lewis 1902, 15, 19, 27 4–Harry White 1974, 75, 78, 79	9–Bart Cummings 1965, 66, 67, 74, 75, 77, 79, 90, 91	4–Etienne de Mestre 1861, 62, 67, 78	39 (1890)
Kentucky Derby (1875) 1¼ miles *2012m* Churchill Downs, Louisville, USA	1 min 59·4 sec *Secretariat 1973*	5–Eddie Arcaro 1938, 41, 45, 48, 52 5–Bill Hartack 1957, 60, 62, 64, 69	6–Ben Jones 1938, 41, 44, 48, 49, 52	8–Calumet Farm 1941, 44, 48, 49, 52, 57, 58, 68	23 (1974)
Irish Derby (1866) 1½ miles *2414m* The Curragh, Co. Kildare	2 min 25·60 sec *St Jovite 1992*	6–Morny Wing 1921, 23, 30, 38, 42, 46	6–Vincent O'Brien 1953, 57, 70, 77, 84, 85	5–HH Aga Khan III 1925, 32, 40, 48, 49	24 (1962)
JUMPING **Grand National (1839)** 4½ miles *7242m* Aintree, Liverpool, Merseyside	8 min 47·8 sec *Mr Frisk 1990*	5–George Stevens 1856, 63, 64, 69, 70	4–Fred Rimell 1956, 61, 70, 76	3–James Machell 1873, 74, 76 3–Sir Charles Assheton-Smith 1893, 1912, 13 3–Noel Le Mare 1973, 74, 77	66 (1929)
Cheltenham Gold Cup (1924) 3¼ miles *5230m* Cheltenham, Gloucestershire	6 min 23·4 sec *Silver Fame 1951*	4–Pat Taaffe 1964, 65, 66, 68	5–Tom Dreaper 1946, 64, 65, 66, 68	7–Dorothy Paget 1932, 33, 34, 35, 36, 40, 52	22 (1982)
Champion Hurdle (1927) 2 miles *3218 m* Cheltenham *Electronically timed	3 min 50·7 sec *Kribensis 1990*	4–Tim Molony 1951, 52, 53, 54	5–Peter Easterby 1967, 76, 77, 80, 81	4–Dorothy Paget 1932, 33, 40, 46	24 (1964) 24 (1991)

Zafonic, ridden by Pat Eddery, won the 1993 2000 Guineas in record time.

(Photo: Allsport/Mike Hewitt)

$1 million bonus for the best record in the Triple Crown races: he won the Kentucky Derby and Preakness Stakes and was second in the Belmont Stakes. The leading money-winning filly or mare is *Dance Smartly* (foaled 1988) with $3 118 346 in North America, 1990–92. The one race record is $2·6 million by *Spend A Buck* (foaled 1982) for the Jersey Derby, Garden State Park, New Jersey, USA on 27 May 1985, of which $2 million was a bonus for having previously won the Kentucky Derby and two preparatory races at Garden State Park.

World speed records The highest race speed recorded is 69·62km/h *43·26 mph* by *Big Racket*, 20·8sec for ¼ mile *402 m*, at Mexico City, Mexico on 5 Feb 1945. The 4-year-old carried 51·7kg *114 lb*. The record for 1½ miles *2414 m* is 60·86km/h *37·82 mph* by 3-year-old *Hawkster* (carrying 54·9kg *121 lb*) at Santa Anita Park, Arcadia, California, USA on 14 Oct 1989 with a time of 2 min 22·8 sec.

Jockeys

Most successful Billie Lee 'Bill' Shoemaker (USA) (b. weighing 1·1 kg *2½ lb*, 19 Aug 1931), whose racing weight was 44 kg *97 lb* at 1·50m *4 ft 11 in*, rode a record 8833 winners from 40 350 mounts from his first ride on 19 Mar 1949 and first winner on 20 Apr 1949 to his retirement on 3 Feb 1990. Laffit Pincay (b. 29 Dec 1946, Panama City) has earned a career record $170 235 931 from 1964 to end of 1992.

Oldest winners

The oldest horses to win on the Flat have been the 18-year-olds *Revenge* at Shrewsbury on 23 Sep 1790, *Marksman* at Ashford, Kent on 4 Sep 1826 and *Jorrocks* at Bathurst, Australia on 28 Feb 1851. At the same age *Wild Aster* won three hurdle races in six days in March 1919 and *Sonny Somers* won two steeplechases in February 1980.

Owners

The most lifetime wins by an owner is 4775 by Marion H. Van Berg (1895–1971) in North America in 35 years. The most wins in a year is 494 by Dan R. Lasater (USA) in 1974. The greatest amount won in a year is $6 881 902 by Sam-Son Farm in North America in 1991.

The most races won by a jockey in a year is 598 from 2312 rides by Kent Jason Desormeaux (b. 27 Feb 1970) in 1989. The greatest amount won in a year is 2 356 280 400 yen (*c.* $16 250 000 or a little less than £10 million) by Yutaka Take (b. 1969) in Japan in 1990.

Wins The most winners ridden in one day is nine by Chris Wiley Antley (USA) (b. 6 Jan 1966) on 31 Oct 1987. They consisted of four in the afternoon at Aqueduct, New York, USA and five in the evening at The Meadowlands, New Jersey, USA.

One card The most winners ridden on one card is eight by six riders, most recently (and from fewest rides) by Pat Day from nine rides at Arlington International, Illinois, USA on 13 Sep 1989.

Consecutive The longest winning streak is 12 by: Sir Gordon Richards (1904–86) (one race at Nottingham on 3 Oct, six out of six at Chepstow on 4 Oct and the first five races next day at Chepstow) in 1933; and by Pieter Stroebel at Bulawayo, Southern Rhodesia (now Zimbabwe), 7 Jun–7 Jul 1958.

Jack Charles Van Berg (USA) (b. 7 Jun 1936) has the greatest number of wins in a year, 496 in 1976. The career record is 6000 by Dale Baird (USA) (b. 17 Apr 1935) from 1962 to August 1992. The greatest amount won in a year is $17 842 358 by Darrell Wayne Lukas (USA) (b. 2 Sep 1935) in 1988.

The only trainer to saddle the first five finishers in a championship race is Michael William Dickinson (b. 3 Feb 1950) of Dunkeswick, W Yorks, in the Cheltenham Gold Cup on 17 Mar 1983; he won a record 12 races in one day, 27 Dec 1982.

British Turf Records: Flat Racing

Most successful horses *Eclipse* (foaled 1764) still has the best win-loss record, being unbeaten in a career of 18 races between May 1769 and October 1770. The longest winning sequence is 21 races by *Meteor* (foaled 1783) between 1786 and 1788. The most races won in a season is 23 (from 34 starts) by three-year-old *Fisherman* in 1856. *Catherina* (foaled 1830) won a career record 79 out of 176 races, 1832–41. The most successful sire was *Stockwell* (foaled 1849) whose progeny won 1153 races (1858–76) and who in 1866 set a record of 132 races won.

The greatest amount ever won by an British-trained horse is £1 182 140 by the filly *Pebbles* (foaled 1981) in 1983–5. In 1985 she won a record £1 012 611 in one season, including the Breeders' Cup Turf in New York, USA.

The biggest winning margin in a Classic is 20 lengths by *Mayonaise* in the 1000 Guineas on 12 May 1859.

Since the introduction of the Pattern-race system in 1971, the most prolific British-trained winner of such races has been *Brigadier Gerard* (foaled 1968) with 13 wins, 1971–2.

Since the introduction in 1977 of official ratings in the International Classifications, the highest-rated horse has been *Dancing Brave* (foaled 1983) on 141 in 1986.

The only horse to win two Horse of the Year awards (instituted 1959) is the filly *Dahlia* (foaled 1970) in 1973–4.

Most successful jockeys Sir Gordon Richards won 4870 races from 21 815 mounts from his first mount at Lingfield Park, Surrey on 16 Oct 1920 to his last at Sandown Park, Surrey on 10 Jul 1954. His first win was on 31 Mar 1921. In 1953, at his 28th and final attempt, he won the Derby, six days after his knighthood. He was champion jockey 26 times between 1925 and 1953 and won a record 269 races (from 835 rides) in 1947. Lester Keith Piggott (b. 5 Nov 1935) won 4450 races in Great Britain, 1948 to May 1993, but his global total exceeds 5300. The most prize-money won in a year is £2 903 976 by William Fisher Hunter Carson (b. 16 Nov 1942) in 1990. The most wins in a day is seven by Patrick John Eddery (b. 18 Mar 1952) at Newmarket and Newcastle on 26 Jun 1992

The most Classic races won by a jockey is 30 by Lester Piggott from his first on *Never Say Die* in the 1954 Derby to the 1992 2000 Guineas on *Rodrigo di Triano*. (Derby—9, St Leger—8, Oaks—6, 2000 Guineas—5, 1000 Guineas—2.)

Most successful trainers The most wins in a season is 180 (from 446 starts) by Henry Richard Amherst Cecil (b. 11 Jan 1943) of Newmarket in 1987. The record prize money earned in a season is £2 000 330 by Michael Ronald Stoute (b. 22 Oct 1945) of Newmarket in 1989; he set a record for world-wide earnings of £2 778 405 in 1986. The most Classics won is 40 by John Scott (1794–1871) of Malton, Yorkshire between 1827 and 1863. James Croft (1787–1828) of Middleham, Yorkshire trained the first four horses in the St Leger on 16 Sep 1822. Alexander Taylor (1862–1943) of Manton, Wiltshire, was champion trainer in money won a record 12 times between 1907 and 1925. Henry Cecil has been champion in races won a record nine times since 1978.

Most successful owners HH Aga Khan III (1877–1957) was leading owner a record 13 times between 1924 and 1952. The record prize money won in a season is £2 243 755 by Sheikh Mohammed bin Rashid al Maktoum of Dubai (b. 1945) in

1990. His horses won a record 185 races in 1992. The most Classics won is 20 by George Fitzroy, 4th Duke of Grafton (1760–1844) between 1813 and 1831 and by Edward Stanley, 17th Earl of Derby (1865–1948) between 1910 and 1945.

The Derby The greatest of England's five Classics is the Derby Stakes, inaugurated on 4 May 1780, and named after Edward Stanley, 12th Earl of Derby (1752–1834). The distance was increased in 1784 from a mile to 1½ miles *2·414 km* (now officially described as 1 mile 4 furlongs 10 yd). The race has been run at Epsom Downs, Surrey, except for the two war periods,

when it was run at Newmarket, Cambs, and is for three-year-olds only. Since 1884 the weights have been: colts 57·2 kg *9 st*, fillies 54·9 kg *8 st 9 lb*. Geldings were eligible until 1906.

Largest and smallest winning margins *Shergar* won the Derby by a record 10 lengths in 1981. There have been two dead-heats: in 1828 when *Cadland* beat *The Colonel* in the run-off, and in 1884 between *St Gatien* and *Harvester* (stakes divided).

Largest prize The richest prize on the British Turf is £447 580 for the Derby won by *Commander in Chief* on 2 Jun 1993.

Jumping

Most successful horses *Sir Ken* (foaled 1947), who won the Champion Hurdle in 1952–4, won a record 16 hurdle races in succession, April 1951 to

Longest and shortest odds in the Derby

Three winners have been returned at odds of 100–1: *Jeddah* (1898), *Signorinetta* (1908) and *Aboyeur* (1913). The shortest-priced winner was *Ladas* (1894) at 2–9 and the hottest losing favourite was *Surefoot*, fourth at 40–95 in 1890.

Longest odds

The longest winning odds recorded in British horse racing is 250–1 when *Equinoctal* won at Kelso on 21 Nov 1990. Owner-trainer Norman Miller was not surprised by his horse's success despite being beaten in his previous race by 62 lengths.

Heaviest weight

The highest weight ever carried to victory in the Grand National is 79·4kg *12st 7lb* by *Cloister* (1893), *Manifesto* (1899), *Jerry M.* (1912) and *Poethlyn* (1919).

March 1953. Three other horses have also won a record three Champion Hurdles; *Hatton's Grace* (foaled 1940) 1949–51; *Persian War* (foaled 1963) 1968–70; *See You Then* (foaled 1980) 1985–7. The greatest number of Cheltenham Gold Cup wins is five by *Golden Miller* (foaled 1927), 1932–6. The mare *Dawn Run* (foaled 1978), uniquely won both the Champion Hurdle (1984) and Cheltenham Gold Cup (1986).

The greatest number of Horse of the Year awards (instituted 1959) is four by *Desert Orchid* (foaled 1979), 1987–90. The greatest amount earned by a British jumper is £652802 by *Desert Orchid*, 1983–91.

Most successful jockeys Peter Michael Scudamore (b. 13 Jun 1958) won a career record 1678 races over jumps (from 7521 mounts) from 1978 to 7 Apr 1993, when he retired.

The most wins in a season is 221 (from 663 rides) by Peter Scudamore in 1988/9. The greatest prize money won in a season is £1088320 by Thomas Richard Dunwoody (b. 18 Jan 1964) in 1992/3. The most wins in a day is six by amateur Charles James Cunningham (1849–1906) at Rugby, Warks on 29 Mar 1881. The record number of successive wins is ten by: John Alnham Gilbert (b. 26 Jul 1920), 8–30 Sep 1959; and by Philip Charles Tuck (b. 10 Jul 1956), 23 Aug–3 Sep 1986. The record number of championships is eight (one shared) by Peter Scudamore in 1982, 1986–92.

Most successful trainers Martin Charles Pipe (b. 29 May 1945) won £1203014 in prize money in 1990/91, when his horses won a record 230 races from 782 starts. Frederick Thomas Winter (b. 20 Sep 1926) of Lambourn, Berks, was champion trainer in money won a record eight times between 1971 and 1985. William Arthur Stephenson (b. 7 Apr 1920) of Leasingthorne, Co. Durham, was champion trainer in races won a record ten times between 1966 and 1977.

Grand National The first Grand National Steeple Chase may be regarded as the Grand Liverpool Steeple Chase of 26 Feb 1839 though the race was not given its present name until 1847. It became a handicap in 1843. Except for 1916–18 and 1941–5, the race has been run at Aintree, near Liverpool, over 30 fences.

Most wins The only horse to win three times is *Red Rum* (foaled 1965) in 1973, 1974 and 1977, from five runs. He came second in 1975 and 1976. *Manifesto*(foaled 1888) ran a record eight times (1895–1904). He won in 1897 and 1899, came third three times and fourth once.

Highest prize The highest prize and the richest ever over jumps in Great Britain was £99943 won by *Party Politics* on 4 Apr 1992.

Hurling

Most titles *All-Ireland* The greatest number of All-Ireland Championships won by one team is 27 by Cork between

1890 and 1990. The greatest number of successive wins is four by Cork (1941–44).

Most appearances The most appearances in All-Ireland finals is ten shared by Christy Ring (Cork and Munster) and John Doyle (Tipperary). They also share the record of All-Ireland medals won with eight each. Ring's appearances on the winning side were in 1941–4, 1946 and 1952–4, while Doyle's were in 1949–51, 1958, 1961–2 and 1964–5. Ring also played in a record 22 interprovincial finals (1942–63) and was on the winning side 18 times.

Highest and lowest scores The highest score in an All-Ireland final (60min) was in 1989 when Tipperary 41 (4 goals, 29 points) beat Antrim (3 goals, 9 points). The record aggregate score was when Cork 39 (6 goals, 21 points) defeated Wexford 25 (5 goals, 10 points) in the 80-minute final of 1970. A goal equals three points. The highest recorded individual score was by Nick Rackard (Wexford), who scored 7 goals and 7 points against Antrim in the 1954 All-Ireland semi-final. The lowest score in an All-Ireland final was when Tipperary (1 goal, 1 point) beat Galway (nil) in the first championship at Birr in 1887.

Largest crowd The largest crowd was 84 865 for the All-Ireland final between Cork and Wexford at Croke Park, Dublin in 1954.

Ice Hockey

World Championships and Olympic Games World Championships were first held for amateurs in 1920 in conjunction with the Olympic Games, which were also considered as world championships up to 1968. From 1976 World Championships have been open to professionals. The USSR won 22 world titles between 1954 and 1990, including the Olympic titles of 1956, 1964 and 1968. They have a record eight Olympic titles with a further five, 1972, 1976, 1984, 1988 and 1992 (as the CIS, with all players Russians). After the break-up of the USSR, Russia won in 1993. The longest Olympic career is that of Richard Torriani (Switzerland) (1911–88) from 1928 to 1948. The most gold medals won by any player is three, achieved by Soviet players Vitaliy Semyenovich Davydov, Anatoliy Vasilyevich Firsov, Viktor Grigoryevich Kuzkin and Aleksandr Pavlovich Ragulin in 1964, 1968 and 1972, and by Vladislav Aleksandrovich Tretyak in 1972, 1976 and 1984.

Women The first two world championships for women were won by Canada in 1990 and 1992.

Stanley Cup The Stanley Cup was first presented in 1893 (original cost $48.67) by Lord Stanley of Preston, then Governor-General of Canada. From 1894 it was contested by amateur teams for the Canadian Championship. From 1910 it became the award for the winners of the professional league play-offs. It has been won most often by the Montreal Canadiens with 24 wins in 1916, 1924, 1930–31, 1944, 1946, 1953, 1956–60, 1965–6, 1968–9, 1971, 1973, 1976–9, 1986, 1993, from a record 32 finals. Henri Richard played on a record 11

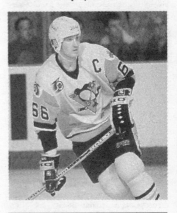

Mario Lemieux of the Pittsburgh Penguins has been leading point scorer in the NHL in 1988 and 1993. His career average is 2·03 points per game, second only to Wayne Gretzky.
(Photo: Allsport/D. Strothmeyer)

Fastest goal

From the opening whistle, the fastest is 5 sec by Doug Smail (b. 2 Sep 1957) (Winnipeg Jets) *v.* St Louis Blues at Winnipeg on 20 Dec 1981, and by Bryan John Trottier (b. 17 Jul 1956) (New York Islanders) *v.* Boston Bruins at Boston on 22 Mar 1984. Bill Mosienko (b. 2 Nov 1921) (Chicago Black Hawks) scored three goals in 21 sec *v.* New York Rangers on 23 Mar 1952.

---

winning teams for the Canadiens between 1956 and 1973.

Scoring records Wayne Gretzky (Edmonton and Los Angeles) has scored 346 points in Stanley Cup games, 110 goals and 236 assists, all are records. Gretzky scored a season's record 47 points (16 goals and a record 31 assists) in 1985. The most goals in a season is 19 by Reginald Joseph Leach (b. 23 Apr 1950) for Philadelphia in 1976 and Jari Kurri (Finland) (b. 18 May 1960) for Edmonton in 1985.

Five goals in a Stanley Cup game were scored by Maurice Richard (b. 4 Aug 1921) in Montreal's 5–1 win over Toronto on 23 Mar 1944, by Darryl Glen Sittler for Toronto (8) *v.* Philadelphia (5) on 22 Apr 1976, by Reggie Leach for Philadelphia (6) *v.* Boston (3) on 6 May 1976, and by Mario Lemieux (b. 5 Oct 1965) for Pittsburgh (10) *v.* Philadelphia (7) on 25 Apr 1989. A record six assists in a game were achieved by Mikko Leinonen (b. 15 Jul 1955) for New York Rangers (7) *v.* Philadelphia (3) on 8 Apr 1982 and by Wayne Gretzky for Edmonton (13) *v.* Los Angeles (3) on 9 Apr 1987, when his team set a Stanley Cup game record of 13 goals. The most points in a game is eight by Patrik Sundström (Sweden) (b. 14 Dec 1961), three goals and five assists, for New Jersey (10) *v.* Washington (4) on 22 Apr 1988 and by Mario Lemieux, five goals and three assists, for Pittsburgh *v.* Philadelphia.

Most games played Gordon 'Gordie' Howe (Canada) (b. 31 Mar 1928) played in a record 1767 regular season games (and 157 play-off games) over a record 26 seasons, from 1946 to 1971 for the Detroit Red Wings and in 1979/80 for the Hartford Whalers. He also played 419 games (and 78 play-off games) for the Houston Aeros and for the New England Whalers in the World Hockey Association (WHA) from 1973 to 1979, and a grand total of 2421 major league games.

Most goals and points Career The most goals scored in a season is 92 in the 1981/2 season by Wayne Gretzky for the Edmonton Oilers. He scored a record 215 points, including a record 163 assists in 1985/6. In 1981/2 in all games, adding Stanley Cup play-offs and for Canada in the World Championship, he scored 238 points (103 goals, 135 assists). The North American career record for goals is 1071 (including a record 801 in the NHL) by Gordie Howe in 32 seasons, 1946–80. He took 2204 games to achieve the 1000th goal, but Robert Marvin 'Bobby' Hull (b. 3 Jan 1939) (Chicago Black Hawks and Winnipeg Jets) scored his 1000th in his 1600th game on 12 Mar 1978.

Wayne Gretzky has the record for assists of 1563 and overall records for regular season and play-off games for assists, 1799 and total points, 2674 (2328 NHL, 346 Stanley Cup). His 875 goals (765 + 110) have come from 1223 games.

Game The North American major league record for most points scored in one game is ten by Jim Harrison (b. 9 Jul 1947) (three goals, seven assists) for Alberta, later Edmonton Oilers in a WHA match at Edmonton on 30 Jan 1973, and by Darryl Sittler (b. 18 Sep 1950) (six goals, four assists) for Toronto Maple Leafs *v.* Boston Bruins in an NHL match at Toronto on 7 Feb 1976.

The most goals in a game is seven by Joe Malone in Québec's 10–6 win over Toronto St. Patricks at Québec City on 31 Jan 1920. The most assists is seven by Billy Taylor for Detroit *v.* Chicago on 16 Mar 1947 and three times by Wayne Gretzky for Edmonton, *v.* Washington on 15 Feb 1980, *v.* Chicago on 11 Dec 1985, and *v.* Québec on 14 Feb 1986.

Goaltending Terry Sawchuk (1929–70) played a record 971 games as a goaltender, for Detroit, Boston, Toronto, Los Angeles and New York Rangers from

1950 to 1970. He achieved a record 435 wins (to 337 losses, and 188 ties) and had a record 103 career shutouts. Jacques Plante (1929–86), with 434 NHL wins surpassed Sawchuk's figure by adding 15 wins in his one season in the WHA for a senior league total of 449 from 868 games. Bernie Parent (b. 3 Apr 1945) achieved a record 47 wins in a season, with 13 losses and 12 ties, for Philadelphia in 1973/4.

Gerry Cheevers (b. 2 Dec 1940) (Boston Bruins) went a record 32 successive games without a defeat in 1971–2.

Team records Montreal Canadiens won a record 60 games and 132 points (with 12 ties) from 80 games played in 1976/7; their eight losses was also the least ever in a season of 70 or more games. The highest percentage of wins in a season was ·875% achieved by the Boston Bruins with 30 wins in 44 games in 1929/30. The longest undefeated run during a season, 35 games (25 wins and ten ties), was established by the Philadelphia Flyers from 14 Oct 1979 to 6 Jan 1980. The most goals scored in a season is 446 by the Edmonton Oilers in 1983/4, when they also achieved a record 1182 scoring points.

Game The highest aggregate score is 21 when Montreal Canadiens beat Toronto St Patrick's, 14–7, at Montreal on 10 Jan 1920, and Edmonton Oilers beat Chicago Black Hawks, 12–9, at Chicago on 11 Dec 1985. The single team record is 16 by Montreal Canadiens *v.* Québec Bulldogs (3), at Québec City on 3 Nov 1920.

The longest match was 2hr 56min 30sec (playing time) when Detroit Red Wings beat Montreal Maroons 1–0 in the sixth period of overtime at the Forum, Montreal, at 2:25 a.m. on 25 Mar 1936. Norm Smith, the Red Wings goaltender, turned aside 92 shots for the NHL's longest single shutout.

Other Records

British competitions The English National (later British) League Championship (instituted 1935) has been won by the Wembley Lions four times, in 1936–7, 1952 and 1957 and by Streatham (later Redskins) in 1950, 1953, 1960 and 1982. Murrayfield Racers have won the Northern League (instituted 1966) seven times, 1970–72, 1976, 1979–80 and 1985. The Icy Smith Cup (first held 1966), the premier British club competition until 1981, was won by Murrayfield Racers nine times, 1966, 1969–72, 1975 and 1979–81. The British Championship (instituted 1982) (Heineken Championship until 1993) has been won a record four times by Durham Wasps, 1987–8 and 1991–2. The Heineken League title has been won five times by Durham Wasps, 1985, 1988–9 and 1991–2. The 'Grand Slam' of Autumn Cup (now Benson & Hedges Cup), Heineken League and Heineken Championships has been won by Dundee Rockets (1983/4), Durham Wasps (1990/91) and Cardiff Devils (1992/3).

Most goals *Team* The greatest number of goals recorded in a world championship match was when Australia beat New Zealand 58–0 at Perth on 15 Mar 1987.

British The highest score and aggregate in a British League match was set when Medway Bears beat Richmond Raiders 48–1 at Gillingham in a Second Division fixture on 1 Dec 1985, when Kevin MacNaught (Canada) (b. 23 Jul 1960) scored a record 25 points from seven goals and 18 assists.

The most individual goals scored in a senior game is 18 by Rick Smith (Canada) (b. 28 Aug 1964) in a 27–2 win for Chelmsford Chieftains against Sheffield Sabres in an English League match on 3 Mar 1991. Steve Moria (Canada) (b. 1960) achieved the highest number of assists, 13, for Fife Flyers at Cleveland on 28 Mar 1987. Rick Fera (Canada) (b. 1964) set British season's records of 165 goals and 318 points for Murrayfield Racers in 48 games in 1986/7. Tim Salmon (Canada) (b. 27 Nov 1964) achieved a season's record 183 assists in 47 games for Ayr Bruins in 1985/6. The highest career points for the Heineken League is 1668 (714 goals, 954 assists) by Tony Hand (GB) (b. 15 Aug 1967) in 341 games to end of the 1992/3 season.

Fastest scoring In minor leagues, Per Olsen scored 2 seconds after the start of the match for Rungsted against Odense in the Danish First Division at Hørsholm, Denmark on 14 Jan 1990. Three goals in

10 seconds was achieved by Jørgen Palmgren Erichsen for Frisk v. Holmen in a junior league match in Norway on 17 Mar 1991. The Vernon Cougars scored five goals in 56 seconds against Salmon Arm Aces at Vernon, BC, Canada on 6 Aug 1982. The Kamloops Knights of Columbus scored seven goals in 2 min 22 sec v. Prince George Vikings on 25 Jan 1980.

Great Britain The fastest goal in the Heineken League was scored by Stephen Johnson for Durham Wasps after four seconds v. Ayr Bruins at Ayr, Strathclyde on 6 Nov 1983. Mark Salisbury (GB) (b. 4 Dec 1970) scored a hat-trick in 19 seconds for Basingstoke Beavers v. Telford Tigers on 26 Jan 1991.

In an English Junior League (under-16) game Jonathan Lumbis scored a hat-trick in 13 seconds for Nottingham Cougars v. Peterborough Jets on 4 Nov 1984.

Ice Skating

Figure Skating

Most titles *Olympic* The most Olympic gold medals won by a figure skater is three by: Gillis Grafström (Sweden) (1893–1938) in 1920, 1924 and 1928 (also silver medal in 1932); Sonja Henie (Norway) (1912–69) in 1928, 1932 and 1936; and Irina Konstantinovna Rodnina (USSR) (b. 12 Sep 1949) with two different partners in the Pairs in 1972, 1976 and 1980.

World The greatest number of men's individual world figure skating titles (instituted 1896) is ten by Ulrich Salchow (Sweden) (1877–1949) in 1901–5 and 1907–11. The women's record (instituted 1906) is also ten individual titles by Sonja Henie between 1927 and 1936. Irina Rodnina won ten pairs titles (instituted 1908), four with Aleksey Nikolayevich Ulanov (b. 4 Nov 1947), 1969–72, and six with her husband Aleksandr Gennadyevich Zaitsev (b. 16 Jun 1952), 1973–8. The most ice dance titles (instituted 1952) won is six by Lyudmila Alekseyevna Pakhomova (1946–86) and her husband Aleksandr Georgiyevich Gorshkov (USSR) (b. 8 Oct 1946), 1970–74 and 1976. They also won the first ever Olympic ice dance title in 1976.

British The most individual British titles are: (men) 11 by Jack Ferguson Page (1900–47) (Manchester SC) in 1922–31 and 1933; and (women) six by Magdalena Cecilia Colledge (b. 28 Nov 1920) (Park Lane FSC, London) in 1935–6, 1937 (two), 1938 and 1946, and by Joanne Conway (b. 11 Mar 1971) between 1985 and 1991. Page and Ethel Muckelt (1885–1953) won nine pairs titles, 1923–31. The most by an ice dance couple is six by Jayne Torvill (b. 7 Oct 1957) and Christopher Colin Dean (b. 27 Jul 1958), 1978–83.

Triple Crown Karl Schäfer (Austria) (1909–76) and Sonja Henie achieved double 'Grand Slams', both in the years 1932 and 1936. This feat was repeated by Katarina Witt (GDR) (b. 3 Dec 1965)

Most mid-air rotations

Kurt Browning (Canada) (b. 18 Jun 1966) was the first to achieve a quadruple jump in competition, a toe loop in the World Championships at Budapest, Hungary on 25 Mar 1988. The first woman to do so was Suruya Bonaly (France) (b. 15 Dec 1973) in the World Championships at Munich, Germany on 16 Mar 1991.

Barrel jumping on ice skates

The official distance record is 8·97 m *29 ft 5 in* over 18 barrels, by Yvon Jolin at Terrebonne, Quebec, Canada on 25 Jan 1981. The women's record is 6·20 m *20 ft 4¼ in* over 11 barrels, by Janet Hainstock at Wyandotte, Michigan, USA on 15 Mar 1980.

Distance

Robin John Cousins (GB) (b. 17 Aug 1957) achieved 5·81 m *19 ft 1 in* in an axel jump and 5·48 m *18 ft* with a back flip at Richmond Ice Rink, Surrey on 16 Nov 1983.

Speed Skating

WORLD RECORDS

MEN

Distance (m)	min:sec	Name (Country)	Venue	Date
500	36·02	Dan Jansen (USA)	Calgary, Canada	21 Mar 1993
1000	1:12·58A	Pavel Pegov (USSR)	Medeo, USSR	25 Mar 1983
	1:12·58	Igor Zhelezovskiy (USSR)	Heerenveen, Netherlands	25 Feb 1989
	1:12·05Au	Nick Thometz (USA)	Medeo, USSR	26 Mar 1987
1500	1:52·06	André Hoffmann (GDR)	Calgary, Canada	20 Feb 1988
3000	3:56·16	Thomas Bos (Netherlands)	Calgary, Canada	3 Mar 1992
5000	6:36·57	Johann Olav Koss (Norway)	Heerenveen, Netherlands	14 Mar 1991
10000	13:43·54	Johann Olav Koss (Norway)	Heerenveen, Netherlands	10 Feb 1991

u unofficial. A set at high altitude.

WOMEN

Distance (m)	min:sec	Name (Country)	Venue	Date
500	39·10	Bonnie Blair (USA)	Calgary, Canada	22 Feb 1988
1000	1:17·65	Christa Rothenburger (now Luding) (GDR)	Calgary, Canada	26 Feb 1988
1500	1:59·30A	Karin Kania (née Enke) (GDR)	Medeo, USSR	22 Mar 1986
3000	4:10·80	Gunda Kleeman (Germany)	Calgary, Canada	9 Dec 1990
5000*	7:14·13	Yvonne van Gennip (Netherlands)	Calgary, Canada	28 Feb 1988
10000*	15:25·25	Yvonne van Gennip (Netherlands)	Heerenveen, Netherlands	19 Mar 1988

* Record not officially recognized for this distance.

WORLD RECORDS - SHORT TRACK

MEN

Distance	min:sec	Name (Country)	Venue	Date
500	43·10	Mirko Vuillermin (Italy)	Beijing, China	27 Mar 1993
1000	1:28·47	Mike McMillen (New Zealand)	Denver, Colorado, USA	4 Apr 1992
1500	2:22·77	Andrew Nicholson (New Zealand)	Nobeyama, Japan	7 Mar 1992
3000	5:04·24	Tatsuyoshi Ishihara (Japan)	Amsterdam, Netherlands	17 Mar 1985
5000 relay	7:10·95	New Zealand	Beijing, China	28 Mar 1993

WOMEN

Distance	min:sec	Name (Country)	Venue	Date
500	46·72	Sylvie Daigle (Canada)	Albertville, France	16 Nov 1991
	46·72	Kim So-hee (South Korea)	Denver, Colorado, USA	3 Apr 1992
1000	1:38·93	Kim Yan-hee (South Korea)	Albertville, France	17 Nov 1991
	1:38·93	Yulia Vlasova (CIS)	Denver, Colorado, USA	4 Apr 1992
1500	2:28·26	Eden Donatelli (Canada)	Seoul, South Korea	31 Mar 1991
3000	5:18·33	Maria Rosa Candido (Italy)	Budapest, Hungary	17 Jan 1988
3000 relay	4:26·56	Canada	Beijing, China	28 Mar 1993

BRITISH RECORDS - SHORT TRACK

MEN

Distance	min:sec	Name	Venue	Date
500	44·07	Wilfred O'Reilly	Denver, Colorado, USA	3 Apr 1992
1000	1:31·65	Wilfred O'Reilly	Denver, Colorado, USA	4 Apr 1992
1500	2:22·67	Wilfred O'Reilly	Beijing, China	26 Mar 1993
3000	5:13·32	Wilfred O'Reilly	Denver, Colorado, USA	4 Apr 1992
5000 relay	7:23·01	Great Britain	Denver, Colorado, USA	4 Apr 1992

WOMEN

Distance	min:sec	Name	Venue	Date
500	50·09	Debbie Palmer	Beijing, China	21 Mar 1993
1000	1:45·00	Debbie Palmer	Denver, Colorado, USA	3 Apr 1992
1500	2:46·48	Debbie Palmer	Humberside	15 Mar 1992
3000	5:59·08	Amanda Worth	Richmond, London	1 Mar 1985
3000 relay	5:05·04	Great Britain	Budapest, Hungary	17 Jan 1988

in 1984 and 1988. The only British skaters to win the 'Grand Slam' of World, Olympic and European titles in the same year are John Anthony Curry (b. 9 Sep 1949) in 1976 and the ice dancers Jayne Torvill and Christopher Dean in 1984.

Highest marks The highest tally of maximum six marks awarded in an inter-national championship was 29 to Jayne Torvill and Christopher Dean (GB) in the World Ice Dance Championships at Ottawa, Canada on 22–24 Mar 1984. This comprised seven in the compulsory dances, a perfect set of nine for presen-tation in the set pattern dance and 13 in the free dance, including another perfect set from all nine judges for artistic presentation. They previously gained a perfect set of nine sixes for artistic presentation in the free dance at the 1983 World Championships in Helsinki, Finland in the 1984 Winter Olympic Games in Sarajevo, Yugoslavia. In their career Torvill and Dean received a record total of 136 sixes.

The most by a soloist is seven: by Donald George Jackson (Canada) (b. 2 Apr 1940) in the World Men's Championship at Prague, Czechoslovakia in 1962; and by Midori Ito (Japan) (b. 13 Aug 1969) in the World Women's Championships at Paris, France in 1989.

Largest rink The world's largest indoor ice rink is in the Moscow Olympic arena which has an ice area of 8064m² *86 800ft²*. The five rinks at Fujikyu Highland Skating Centre, Japan total 26500m² *285 243 ft²*.

Speed Skating

Most titles *Olympic* The most Olympic gold medals won in speed skating is six by Lidiya Pavlovna Skoblikova (USSR) (b. 8 Mar 1939) in 1960 (two) and 1964 (four). The male record is five by: Clas Thunberg (Finland) (1893–1973) (including one tied) in 1924 and 1928; and Eric Arthur Heiden (USA) (b. 14 Jun 1958), uniquely at one Games at Lake Placid, New York, USA in 1980. The most medals is seven by: Clas Thunberg, who additionally won one silver and one tied bronze; and Ivar Ballangrud (1904–69) (Norway), four gold, two silver and a bronze, 1928–36.

Dan Jansen (USA), current holder of the 500 m speed skating world record.

(Photo: Allsport/Pascal Rondeau)

World The greatest number of world overall titles (instituted 1893) won by any skater is five; by Oscar Mathisen (Norway) (1888–1954) in 1908–9 and 1912–14; and by Clas Thunberg in 1923, 1925, 1928–9 and 1931. The most titles won in the women's events (instituted 1936) is five by Karin Kania (*née* Enke) (GDR) (b. 20 Jun 1961) in 1982, 1984, 1986–8. Kania also won a record six overall titles at the World Sprint Championships 1980–81, 1983–4, 1986–7. A record six men's sprint overall titles have been won by Igor Zhelezovskiy (USSR/Belarus), 1985–6, 1989 and 1991–3.

The record score achieved for the world overall title is 157·396 points by Johann-Olav Koss (Norway) at Heerenveen, Netherlands on 9–10 Feb 1991. The record low women's score is 171·630 points by Jacqueline Börner (GDR) at Calgary, Canada on 10–11 Feb 1990.

World Short-track Championships The most successful skater in these championships (instituted 1978) has been Sylvia Daigle (Canada) (b. 1 Dec 1962) women's overall champion in 1979, 1983 and 1989–90.

The first British skater to win the world overall title was Wilfred O'Reilly (b. 22 Aug 1964) at Sydney, Australia on 24 Mar 1991.

Longest race The 'Elfstedentocht' ('Tour of the Eleven Towns'), which originated in the 17th century, was held in the Netherlands from 1909–63, and again in 1985 and 1986, covering 200 km *124 miles 483 yd*. As the weather does not permit an annual race in the Netherlands, alternative 'Elfstedentocht' take place at suitable venues. These venues have included Lake Vesijärvi, near Lahti, Finland; Ottawa River, Canada and Lake Weissensee, Austria. The record time for 200 km is: men, 5 hr 40 min 37 sec by Dries van Wijhe (Netherlands); and women, 5 hr 48 min 8 sec by Alida Pasveer (Netherlands), both at Lake Weissensee (altitude 1100m *3609ft*), Austria on 11 Feb 1989. Jan-Roelof Kruithof (Netherlands) won the race nine times, 1974, 1976–7, 1979–84. An estimated 16 000 skaters took part in 1986.

607

24 hours Martinus Kuiper (Netherlands) skated 546·65 km *339·67miles* at Alkmaar, Netherlands on 12–13 Dec 1988.

Ice and Sand Yachting

Highest speeds The highest speed officially recorded is 230 km/h *143 mph* by John D. Buckstaff in a Class A stern-steerer on Lake Winnebago, Wisconsin, USA in 1938. Such a speed is possible in a wind of 115 km/h *72 mph*.

Sand The official world record for a sand yacht is 107 km/h *66·48 mph* set by Christian-Yves Nau (France) (b. 1944) in *Mobil* at Le Touquet, France on 22 Mar 1981, when the wind speed reached 120 km/h *75mph*. A speed of 142·26 km/h *88·4 mph* was attained by Nord Embroden (USA) in *Midnight at the Oasis* at Superior Dry Lake, California, USA on 15 Apr 1976.

Largest yacht

The largest ice yacht was *Icicle*, built for Commodore John E. Roosevelt for racing on the Hudson River, New York in 1869. It was 21 m *68ft 11in* long and carried 99 m² *1070ft²* of canvas.

Judo

Most titles *World and Olympic* World Championships were inaugurated in Tokyo, Japan in 1956. Women's championships were first held in 1980 in New York, USA. Yasuhiro Yamashita (b. 1 Jun 1957), who won nine consecutive Japanese titles 1977–85, won five world and Olympic titles; Over 95kg 1979, 1981 and 1983, Open 1981, and the Olympic Open category in 1984. He retired undefeated after 203 successive wins, 1977–85. Two other men have won four world titles, Shozo Fujii (Japan) (b. 12 May 1950), Under 80kg 1971, 1973 and 1975, Under 78kg 1979, and Naoya Ogawa (Japan), Open 1987, 1989, 1991 and Over 95kg 1989. The only men to have won two Olympic gold medals are Wilhelm Ruska (Netherlands) (b. 29 Aug 1940), Over 93kg and Open in 1972; Peter Seisenbacher (Austria) (b. 25 Mar 1960), 86kg 1984 and 1988; Hitoshi Saito (Japan) (b. 2 Jan 1961), Over 95kg 1984 and 1988; and Waldemar Legien (Poland), 78kg 1988 and 86kg 1992. Ingrid Berghmans (Belgium) (b. 24 Aug 1961) has won a record six women's world titles (first held 1980): Open 1980, 1982, 1984 and 1986 and Under 72kg in 1984 and 1989. She has also won four silver medals and a bronze. She won the Olympic 72kg title in 1988, when women's judo was introduced as a demonstration sport.

Karen Briggs (b. 11 Apr 1963) is the most successful British player, with four women's world titles, Under 48kg in 1982, 1984, 1986 and 1989.

British The greatest number of titles (instituted 1966) won is nine by David Colin Starbrook (b. 9 Aug 1945) (6th dan): Middleweight 1969–70, Light-heavyweight 1971–5 and the Open division 1970–71. A record six titles in the women's events (instituted 1971) were won by Christine Gallie (*née* Child) (b. 1946) (6th dan): Heavyweight in 1971–5 and the Open division in 1973. Adrian Neil Adams (b. 27 Sep 1958) has the most successful international record of any British male player. He won two junior (1974 and 1977) and five senior (1979–80, 1983–5) European titles; four World Championships medals (one gold, one silver, two bronze) and two

10 hours

Gary Foster and Lee Finney completed 20052 judo throwing techniques in a ten-hour period at the Forest Judo Club, Leicester on 22 Aug 1992.

Action from the 1992 men's up-to-86kg Olympic judo final. Waldemar Legien (Poland) defeated Pascal Tayot (France) and won gold for a record second time.

(Photo: Allsport/Vandystadt/Yann Guichaoua)

Olympic silver medals. He also won eight British senior titles.

Highest grades The efficiency grades in judo are divided into pupil (*kyu*) and master (*dan*) grades. The highest awarded is the extremely rare red belt *Judan* (10th dan), given to only 13 men so far. The Judo protocol provides for an 11th dan (*Juichidan*) who also would wear a red belt, a 12th dan (*Junidan*) who would wear a white belt twice as wide as an ordinary belt, and the highest of all, *Shihan* (ductor), but these have never been bestowed, save for the 12th dan to the founder of the sport Dr Jigoro Kano.

The highest British native Judo grade is 9th dan by Charles Stuart William Palmer (b. 15 Apr 1930) in 1989. Christine Gallie was awarded her 6th dan in 1983.

Karate

World Championships Great Britain have won a record six world titles (instituted 1970) at the Kumite team event, 1975, 1982, 1984, 1986, 1988 and 1990. Two men's individual kumite titles have been won by: Pat McKay (GB) at Under 80kg, 1982 and 1984; Emmanuel Pinda (France) (b. 7 Jun 1961) at Open, 1984 and Over 80kg, 1988; Theirry Masci (France) (b. 22 Jul 1966) at Under 70kg, 1986 and 1988 and José Manuel Egea

(Spain) (b. 1964) at Under 80kg, 1990 and 1992. Four women's kumite titles have been won by Guus van Mourik (Netherlands) at Over 60kg, 1982, 1984, 1986 and 1988. Three individual kata titles have been won by men: Tsuguo Sakumoto (Japan) 1984, 1986 and 1988; women: Mie Nakayama (Japan) 1982, 1984 and 1986.

Top exponents The leading exponents among karateka are a number of 10th dans in Japan. The leading exponents in the United Kingdom are 8th dans: Tatsuo Suzuki (*Wado-ryu*) (b. 27 Apr 1928), Steve Arneil (*Kyokushinkai*), Keinosuke Enoeda and Shiro Asano (both *Shotokan*).

Lacrosse

Men

Most titles *World* The USA has won five of the six World Championships, in 1967, 1974, 1982, 1986 and 1990. Canada won the other world title in 1978 beating the USA 17–16 after extra time.

English The English Club Championship (Iroquois Cup instituted 1890), has been won most often by Stockport with 17 wins between 1897 and 1989. The record score in a final is 33 by Stockport *v.* London University (4) on 9 May 1987.

Most international appearances The record number of international representations is 42 by Peter Daniel Roden (Mellor) (b. 8 Nov 1954) from 1976–90.

Highest scores The highest score in an international match is the USA's 32–8 win over England at Toronto, Canada in 1986.

England's highest score was their 19–11 win over Canada at Melbourne, Australia in August 1974.

Women

World Championships/World Cup The first World Cup was held in 1982, replacing the World Championships which had been held three times since 1969. The USA have won three times, 1974, 1982 and 1989.

609

Most international appearances
Vivien Jones played in 64 internationals (52 for Wales, 9 for the Celts and 3 for Great Britain), 1977–90. Caro Macintosh (b. 18 Feb 1932) played in 56 internationals (52 for Scotland and four for Great Britain).

Highest score The highest score by an international team was by Great Britain and Ireland with their 40–0 defeat of Long Island during their 1967 tour of the USA.

Microlighting

The *Fédération Aéronautique Internationale* has established two classes of aircraft for which records are accepted, C1 a/o and R 1-2-3, and the following are the overall best of the two classes (all in the C1 a/o class).

World records Distance in a straight line: 1627·78km *1011·45 miles* Wilhelm Lischak (Austria), Volsau, Austria to Brest, France, 8 Jun 1988.

Distance in a closed circuit: 2702·16km *1679·04 miles* Wilhelm Lischak (Austria), Wels, Austria, 18 Jun 1988.

Marbles
Most championships

The British Championship (established 1926) has been won most often by the Toucan Terribles with 20 consecutive titles (1956–75). Three founder members, Len Smith, Jack and Charlie Dempsey, played in every title win. They were finally beaten in 1976 by the Pernod Rams, captained by Len Smith's son, Paul. Len Smith (1917–90) won the individual title 15 times (1957–64, 1966, 1968–73) but lost in 1974 to his son Alan.

The record for clearing the ring (between 1·75 and 1·9m *5¾–6¼ ft* in diameter) of 49 marbles is 2 min 56 sec by the Black Dog Boozers of Crawley, W Sussex at BBC Television Centre, London for *Record Breakers* on 14 Sep 1987.

Altitude: 9189m *30 147 ft*: Eric S. Winton (Australia), Tyagarah Aerodrome, NSW, Australia, 8 Apr 1989.

Speed over a 500km closed circuit: 293·04km/h *182 mph*: C. T. Andrews (USA), 3 Aug 1982.

David Cook set a British altitude record of 8249m *27 064 ft* on 28 Apr 1990 at Aldeburgh, Suffolk.

Endurance Eve Jackson flew from Biggin Hill, Kent to Sydney, Australia from 26 Apr 1986 to 1 Aug 1987. The flight took 279hr 55min and covered 21 950km *13 639 miles*. From 1 Dec 1987 to 29 Jan 1988, Brian Milton (GB) flew from London to Sydney with a flying time of 241hr 20min and covered 21 968km *13 650 miles*. Vijaypat Singhania (India) flew from Biggin Hill to Delhi, India, a distance of 8724km *5420 miles* in 87hr 55min, from 18 Aug to 10 Sep 1988.

Modern Pentathlon & Biathlon

Most titles *World* András Balczó (Hungary) (b. 16 Aug 1938) won a record number of world titles (instituted 1949), six individual and seven team. He won the world individual title in 1963, 1965–7 and 1969 and the Olympic title in 1972. His seven team titles (1960–70) comprised five world and two Olympic. The USSR has won a record 14 world and four Olympic team titles. Hungary has also won a record four Olympic team titles (and ten world titles).

Women's World Championships were first held in 1981, replacing the World Cup which began in 1978. Poland have won a record five women's world team titles: 1985, 1988–91; Great Britain won three world titles, 1981–3, and three World Cups, 1978–80. The only double individual champions have been Wendy Norman (GB), 1980 and 1982, Irina Kiselyeva (USSR), 1986–7 and Eva Fjellerup (Denmark), 1990–91.

Olympic (first held 1912) The greatest number of Olympic gold medals won is three, by András Balczó, a member of the winning team in 1960 and 1968 and the 1972 individual champion. Lars Hall (Sweden) (b. 30 Apr 1927) has uniquely won two individual championships (1952 and 1956). Pavel Serafimovich Lednyev (USSR) (b. 25 Mar 1943) won a record seven medals (two team gold, one team silver, one individual silver, three individual bronze), 1968–80.

The best British performance is the team gold medal in 1976 by Jim Fox, Adrian Philip Parker and Daniel Nightingale. The best individual placing is fourth by Jeremy Robert 'Jim' Fox (b. 19 Sep 1941) in 1972 and Richard Lawson Phelps (b. 19 Apr 1961) in 1984.

Probably the greatest margin of victory was by William Oscar Guernsey Grut (Sweden) (b. 17 Sep 1914) in the 1948 Games, when he won three events and was placed fifth and eighth in the other two.

British Two pentathletes have won ten British titles, Jim Fox, 1963, 1965–8, 1970–74 and Richard Phelps, 1979, 1981–4, 1986, 1988, 1990–91 and 1993. Wendy Norman won a record seven women's titles, 1978–80, 1982, 1986–8.

Biathlon

Most titles *Olympic (first held 1960)* Two Olympic individual titles have been won by: Magnar Solberg (Norway) (b. 4 Feb 1937), in 1968 and 1972; and by Franz-Peter Rötsch (GDR) (b. 19 Apr 1964) at both 10km and 20km in 1988. Aleksandr Ivanovich Tikhonov (b. 2 Jan 1947) won four relay golds, 1968–80 and also won a silver in the 1968 20km.

World (instituted 1958) Frank Ullrich (GDR) (b. 24 Jan 1958) has won a record six individual world titles, four at 10km, 1978–81, including the 1980 Olympics, and two at 20km, 1982–3. Aleksandr Tikhonov was in ten winning Soviet relay teams, 1968–80 and won four individual titles.

The Biathlon World Cup (instituted 1979) was won four times by Frank Ullrich, 1978 and 1980–82; and Franz Peter Rötsch (GDR), 1984–5 and 1987–8.

Women The first World Championships were held in 1984. The most individual titles is three by Anne-Elinor Elvebakk (Norway), 10km 1988, 7·5km 1989–90. Kaya Parve (USSR) has won six titles, two individual and four relay, 1984–6, 1988. A women's World Cup began in 1988 and women's biathlon was included at the 1992 Olympics. Anfisa Restzova (Russia) is the only double World Cup winner 1992–3, and won the Olympic 7·5 km gold medal.

Motorcycle Racing

Oldest race The oldest annually contested motorcycle races in the world are the Auto-Cycle Union Tourist Trophy (TT) series, first held on the 25·44km *15·81 mile* 'Peel' (St John's) course in the Isle of Man on 28 May 1907, and still run in the island on the 'Mountain' circuit.

Fastest circuits The highest average lap speed attained on any closed circuit is 257·958km/h *160·288mph* by Yvon du Hamel (Canada) (b. 1941) on a modified 903cc four-cylinder Kawasaki Z1 at the 31-degree banked 4·02km *2·5 mile* Daytona International Speedway, Florida, USA in March 1973. His lap time was 56·149sec.

The fastest road circuit used to be Francorchamps circuit near Spa, Belgium, then 14·12km *8·77 miles* in length. It was lapped in 3min 50·3sec (average speed 220·721km/h *137·150mph*) by Barry Stephen Frank Sheene (GB) (b. 11 Sep 1950) on a 495cc 4-cylinder Suzuki during the Belgian Grand Prix on 3 Jul 1977. On that occasion he set a record time for this ten-lap (141·20km *87·74 mile*) race

Longest circuit

The 60·72km *37·73 miles* 'Mountain' circuit on the Isle of Man, over which the principal TT races have been run since 1911 (with minor amendments in 1920), has 264 curves and corners and is the longest used for any motorcycle race.

of 38min 58·5sec (average speed 217·370km/h *135·068mph*).

United Kingdom The lap record for the outer circuit (4·453km *2·767miles*) at the Brooklands Motor Course, near Weybridge, Surrey (open between 1907 and 1939) was 80sec (average speed 200·37km/h *124·51mph*) by Noel Baddow 'Bill' Pope (later Major) (GB) (1909–71) on a Brough Superior powered by a supercharged 996cc V-twin '8-80' JAP engine developing 110bhp, on 4 Jul 1939.

Most successful riders World Championships The most World Championship titles (instituted by the *Fédération Internationale Motocycliste* in 1949) won is 15 by Giacomo Agostini (Italy) (b. 16 Jun 1942), seven at 350cc, 1968–74, and eight at 500cc in 1966–72, 1975. He is the only man to win two World Championships in five consecutive years (350cc and 500cc titles 1968–72).

Angel Roldan Nieto (Spain) (b. 25 Jan 1947) won a record seven 125cc titles, 1971–2, 1979, 1981–4 and he also won a record six titles at 50cc, 1969–70, 1972, 1975–7. Philip William Read (GB) (b. 1 Jan 1939) won a record four 250cc titles, 1964–5, 1968, 1971. Klaus Enders (West Germany) (b. 2 May 1937) won six world side-car titles, 1967, 1969–70, 1972–4.

Agostini won 122 races (68 at 500cc, 54 at 350cc) in the World Championship series between 24 Apr 1965 and 25 Sep 1977, including a record 19 in 1970, a season's total also achieved by Mike Hailwood in 1966.

Tourist Trophy The record number of victories in the Isle of Man TT races is 15 by William Joseph Dunlop (GB) (b. 25 Feb 1952), 1977–93. The first man to win three consecutive TT titles in two events was James A. Redman (Rhodesia) (b. 8 Nov 1931). He won the 250cc and 350cc events in 1963–5. Stanley Michael Bailey Hailwood (1940–81) won three events in one year, in 1961 and 1967, and this feat was repeated by Joey Dunlop in 1985 and 1988; and by Steve Hislop in 1989 and 1991.

The Isle of Man TT circuit speed record is 198·92km/h *123·61mph* by Carl George Fogarty (b. 1 Jul 1965) on 12 Jun

Loris Capirossi (Italy) (b. 4 Apr 1973) is the youngest to win a World Championship. He was 17yr 165 days when he won the 125cc title on 16 Sep 1990. The oldest was Hermann-Peter Müller (1909–76) of West Germany, who won the 250cc title in 1955 aged 46.

Most successful machines
Japanese Yamaha machines won 45 World Championships between 1964 and 1992.

1992. On the same occasion Steve Hislop set the race speed record, 1hr 51min 59·6sec for an average speed of 195·17km/h *121·28mph* to win the 1992 Senior TT on a Norton. The fastest woman around the 'Mountain' circuit is Kate Parkinson, 24, who achieved a speed of 168·31km/h *104·91mph* in the 1993 Junior TT.

Trials A record four World Trials Championships have been won by Jordi Tarrés (Spain) (b. 10 Sep 1966), 1987, 1989–91.

Moto-cross Joël Robert (Belgium) (b. 11 Nov 1943) won six 250cc Moto-cross World Championships (1964, 1968–72). Between 25 Apr 1964 and 18 Jun 1972 he won a record fifty 250cc Grand Prix. The youngest moto-cross world champion was Dave Strijbos (Netherlands) (b. 9 Nov 1968), who won the 125cc title aged 18yr 296days on 31 Aug 1986. Eric Geboers (Belgium) has uniquely won all three categories of the Moto-Cross World Championships, at 125cc in 1982 and 1983, 250cc in 1987 and 500cc in 1988 and 1990.

Motor Racing

Oldest races The oldest race in the world still regularly run, is the RAC Tourist Trophy, first staged on 14 Sep 1905, in the Isle of Man. The oldest continental race is the French Grand Prix, first held on 26–27 Jun 1906. The Coppa Florio, in Sicily, has been held irregularly since 1906.

Wayne Rainey (USA) (b. 23 Oct 1960) winner of the 500cc world championship for three successive years, 1990–92, all riding a Yamaha.

(Photo: Allsport/Chris Cole)

Fastest circuits The highest average lap speed attained on any closed circuit is 403·878km/h *250·958mph* in a trial by Dr Hans Liebold (Germany) (b. 12 Oct 1926) who lapped the 12·64km *7·85 mile* high-speed track at Nardo, Italy in 1min 52·67sec in a Mercedes-Benz C111-IV experimental coupé on 5 May 1979. It was powered by a V8 engine with two KKK turbochargers, with an output of 500hp at 6200rpm.

The fastest road circuit was the Francorchamps circuit near Spa, Belgium, then 14·10km *8·76 miles* in length which was lapped in 3min 13·4sec (average speed 262·461km/h *163·086mph*) on 6 May 1973, by Henri Pescarolo (France) (b. 25 Sep 1942) driving a 2993-cc V12 Matra-Simca MS670 Group 5 sports car.

Fastest pit stop Robert William 'Bobby' Unser (USA) (b. 20 Feb 1934) took 4seconds to take on fuel on lap 10 of the Indianapolis 500 on 30 May 1976.

Fastest race The fastest race is the Busch Clash at Daytona, Florida, USA over 50miles *80·5km* on a 2½mile *4km* 31-degree banked track. In 1987 Bill Elliott (b. 8 Oct 1955) averaged 197·802mph *318·331km/h* in a Ford Thunderbird. Al Unser Jr set the world record for a 500mile *805km* race on 9

Aug 1990 when he won the Michigan 500A at an average speed of 189·7mph *305·2km/h.*

World Championship Grand Prix Motor Racing

Most successful drivers The World Drivers' Championship, inaugurated in 1950, has been won a record five times by Juan-Manuel Fangio (Argentina) (b. 24 Jun 1911) in 1951 and 1954–7. He retired in 1958, after having won 24 Grand Prix races (two shared) from 51 starts.

Alain Prost (France) (b. 24 Feb 1955) holds the records for both the most Grand Prix points in a career, 756·5 and the most Grand Prix victories, 49 from 192 races, 1980–93. The most Grand Prix victories in a year is nine by Nigel Mansell (GB) (b. 8 Aug 1953) in 1992. The most Grand Prix starts is 247 by Ricardo Patrese (Italy) (b. 17 Apr 1954) from 1977–93. The greatest number of pole positions is 61 by Ayrton Senna (Brazil) (b. 21 Mar 1960) from 150 races (39 wins), 1985–93.

Oldest and youngest The youngest world champion was Emerson Fittipaldi (Brazil) (b. 12 Dec 1946) who won his first World Championship on 10 Sep 1972 aged 25 yr 273days. The oldest world champion was Juan-Manuel Fangio who won his last World Championship on 4 Aug 1957 aged 46 yr 41 days.

The youngest Grand Prix winner was Bruce Leslie McLaren (1937–70) of New Zealand, who won the United States Grand Prix at Sebring, Florida on 12 Dec 1959, aged 22 yr 104 days. Troy Ruttman (USA) was 22 yr 80 days when he won the Indianapolis 500 on 30 May 1952, which was part of the World Championships at the time. The oldest Grand Prix winner (in pre-World Championship days) was Tazio Giorgio Nuvolari (Italy) (1892–1953), who won the Albi Grand Prix at Albi, France on 14 Jul 1946, aged 53 yr 240 days. The oldest Grand Prix driver was Louis Alexandre Chiron (Monaco) (1899–1979), who finished sixth in the Monaco Grand Prix on 22 May 1955, aged 55 yr 292 days. The youngest driver to qualify for a Grand Prix was Michael Christopher Thackwell (New Zealand) (b. 30 Mar 1961) at the Canadian GP on 28 Sep 1980, aged 19 yr 182 days.

Manufacturers Ferrari have won a record eight manufacturers' World Championships, 1961, 1964, 1975–77, 1979, 1982–83 and have won 103 races.

The greatest dominance by one team since the Constructor's Championship was instituted in 1958 was by McLaren in 1988 when they won 15 of the 16 Grands Prix. Ayrton Senna had eight wins and three seconds, Alain Prost had seven wins and seven seconds. The McLarens, powered by Honda engines, amassed over three times the points of their nearest rivals, Ferrari. Excluding the Indianapolis 500 race, then included in the World Drivers' Championship, Ferrari won all seven races in 1952 and the first eight (of nine) in 1953.

Fastest race The fastest overall average speed for a Grand Prix race on a circuit in current use is 235·421 km/h *146·284 mph* by Nigel Mansell in a Williams-Honda at Zeltweg in the Austrian Grand Prix on 16 Aug 1987. The qualifying lap record was set by Keijó 'Keke' Rosberg (Finland) at 1 min 05·59 sec, an average speed of 258·802 km/h *160·817 mph*, in a Williams-Honda at Silverstone in the British Grand Prix on 20 Jul 1985.

Closest finish The closest finish to a World Championship race was when Ayrton Senna in a Lotus beat Nigel

Most wins

The race has been won by Porsche cars twelve times, in 1970–71, 1976–7, 1979, 1981–7. The most wins by one man is six by Jacques Bernard 'Jacky' Ickx (Belgium) (b. 1 Jan 1945), 1969, 1975–7 and 1981–2.

After a year's absence, Alain Prost returned to Formula 1 in 1993 and continued to add to his record-breaking achievements. Here he is seen winning the San Marino Grand Prix at Imola.

(Photo: Allsport/Pascal Rondeau)

Mansell in a Williams by 0·014sec in the Spanish Grand Prix at Jerez de la Frontera on 13 Apr 1986. In the Italian Grand Prix at Monza on 5 Sep 1971, 0·61sec separated winner Peter Gethin (GB) from the fifth placed driver.

British Grand Prix

First held in 1926 as the RAC Grand Prix, and held annually with the above name since 1949. The venues have been Aintree, Merseyside; Brands Hatch, Kent; Brooklands, Surrey; Donington, Leics and Silverstone, Northants.

Fastest speed The fastest race time is 1hr 18min 10·436sec, average speed 235·405km/h *146·274 mph*, when Alain Prost won in a McLaren at Silverstone on 21 Jul 1985.

Most wins The most wins by a driver is five by Jim Clark, 1962–5 and 1967, all in Lotus cars. Jim Clark and Jack Brabham (Australia) (b. 2 Apr 1926) have both won the race on three different circuits; Brands Hatch, Silverstone and Aintree. The most wins by a manufacturer is ten by Ferrari, 1951–4, 1956, 1958, 1961, 1976, 1978 and 1990.

Le Mans

The greatest distance ever covered in the 24-hour *Grand Prix d'Endurance* (first held on 26–27 May 1923) on the old Sarthe circuit at Le Mans, France is 5335·302 km *3315·203 miles* by Dr Helmut Marko (Austria) (b. 27 Apr 1943) and Gijs van Lennep (Netherlands) (b. 16 Mar 1942) in a 4907-cc flat-12 Porsche 917K Group 5 sports car, on 12–13 Jun 1971. The record for the greatest distance ever covered for the current circuit is 5331·998 km *3313·150 miles* (average speed 222·166 km/h *138·047mph*) by Jan Lammers (Holland), Johnny Dumfries and Andy Wallace (both GB) in a Jaguar XJR9 on 11–12 Jun 1988.

The race lap record (now 13·536 km *8·411 mile* lap) is 3 min 21·27 sec (average speed 242·093 km/h *150·429 mph*) by Alain Ferté (France) in a Jaguar XRJ-9 on 10 Jun 1989. Hans Stück (West Germany) set the practice lap speed record of 251·664 km/h *156·377 mph*) on 14 Jun 1985.

Indianapolis 500

The Indianapolis 500 mile *804 km* race (200 laps) was inaugurated in the USA on 30 May 1911. Three drivers have four wins: Anthony Joseph 'A.J.' Foyt Jr (USA) (b. 16 Jan 1935) in 1961, 1964, 1967 and 1977; Al Unser Sr (USA) (b. 29 May 1939) in 1970–71, 1978 and 1987; and Rick Ravon Mears (USA) (b. 3 Dec 1951) in 1979, 1984, 1988 and 1991. The record time is 2hr 41min 18·404sec (299·307 km/h *185·981mph*) by Arie Luyendyk (Netherlands) driving a Lola-Chevrolet on 27 May 1990. The record average speed for four-laps qualifying is 374·143 km/h *232·482mph* by Roberto Guerrero (Colombia) in a Lola-Buick (including a one-lap record of 374·362 km/h *232·618 mph*) on 9 May 1992. The track record is 375·673 km/h *233·433 mph* by Jim Crawford (GB) on 4 May 1992. A. J. Foyt Jr has started a record 35 races, 1958–92 and Rick Mears has started from pole position a record six times, 1979, 1982, 1986, 1988–89 and 1991. The record prize fund is $7 681 300 in 1993, and the individual prize record is $1 244 184 by Al Unser Jr in 1992.

Rallying

The earliest long rally was promoted by the Parisian daily *Le Matin* in 1907 from Peking (now Beijing), China to Paris over about 12000km *7500 miles*, on 10 June. The winner, Prince Scipione Borghese (1872–1927) of Italy, arrived in Paris on 10 Aug 1907, in his 40-hp Itala accompanied by his chauffeur, Ettore, and Luigi Barzini.

Longest The longest ever rally was the *Singapore Airlines* London–Sydney Rally over 31 107km *19 329miles* from Covent Garden, London on 14 Aug 1977 to Sydney Opera House, won on 28 Sep 1977 by Andrew Cowan, Colin Malkin and Michael Broad in a Mercedes 280E. The longest held annually is the Safari Rally (first run in 1953 as the Coronation Rally, through Kenya, Tanzania and Uganda, but now restricted to Kenya). The race has covered up to 6234km *3874 miles*, as in the 17th Safari held from 8–12 Apr 1971. It has been won a record five times by Shekhar Mehta (b. Kenya, 20 Jun 1945) in 1973, 1979–82.

Björn Waldergård won a record 19 World Rallying Championship races in his career. Here he is seen driving a Toyota during the 1980 RAC rally.

(Photo: Allsport/Don Morley)

Monte Carlo The Monte Carlo Rally (first run 1911) has been won a record four times by: Sandro Munari (Italy) (b. 27 Mar 1940) in 1972, 1975, 1976 and 1977; and Walter Röhrl (West Germany) (b. 7 Mar 1947) (with co-driver Christian Geistdorfer) in 1980, 1982–4, each time in a different car. The smallest car to win was an 851cc Saab driven by Erik Carlsson (Sweden) (b. 5 Mar 1929) and Gunnar Häggbom (Sweden) (b. 7 Dec 1935) on 25 Jan 1962, and by Carlsson and Gunnar Palm on 24 Jan 1963.

Britain The RAC Rally (first held 1932) has been recognized by the FIA since 1957. Hannu Mikkola (Finland) (b. 24 May 1942) (with co-driver Arne Hertz) has a record four wins, in a Ford Escort, 1978–9 and an Audi Quattro, 1981–2.

World Championship The World Drivers' Championships (instituted 1979) has been won by Juha Kankkunen (Finland) (b. 2 Apr 1959) on a record three occasions, 1986–7 and 1991. The most wins in World Championship races is 19 by Hannu Mikkola (b. 24 May 1942) (Finland), Markku Alén (Finland) and Björn Waldergård (Sweden) (b. 12 Nov 1958). The most wins in a season is six by Didier Auriol (France) in 1992. Lancia have won a record eleven manufacturers' World Championships between 1972 and 1992.

Piston engined The official lowest elapsed time recorded by a piston-engined dragster from a standing start for 440yd *402m* is 4·779 sec by Eddie Hill (USA) at Pomona, California on 29 Oct 1992. The highest terminal velocity at the end of a 440yd run is 488·66 km/h *303·64 mph* by Pat Austin (USA) at Atlanta, Georgia on 4 Apr 1993. For a petrol-driven piston-engined car the lowest elapsed time and terminal velocity is 7·027 sec and 313·90 km/h *195·05 mph* respectively, by Warren Johnson (USA), driving an Oldsmobile Cutlass at Houston, Texas on 5 Mar 1993. The lowest elapsed time for a petrol-driven piston-engined motorcycle is 7·615 sec by John Myers (USA) (b. 1958) at Dallas, Texas, USA on 11 Oct 1991 and the highest terminal velocity is 287·01 km/h *178·35 mph* by David Schultz (USA) at Pomona on 1 Nov 1992.

Mountaineering

Mt Everest Everest was first climbed at 11:30a.m. on 29 May 1953, when the summit was reached by Edmund Percival Hillary (b. 20 Jul 1919), of New Zealand, and Sherpa Tenzing Norgay (1914–86, formerly called Tenzing Khumjung Bhutia). The successful expedition was led by Col. (later Hon. Brigadier) Henry Cecil John Hunt (b. 22 Jun 1910).

Most conquests Ang Rita Sherpa (b. 1947), with ascents in 1983, 1984, 1985, 1987, 1988, 1990 and 1992, has scaled Everest seven times and all without the use of bottled oxygen.

Solo Reinhold Messner (Italy) (b. 17 Sep 1944) was the first to make the entire climb solo on 20 Aug 1980. Also Messner, with Peter Habeler (Austria) (b. 22 Jul 1942), made the first entirely oxygen-less ascent on 8 May 1978.

First Britons Douglas Scott (b. 29 May 1941) and Dougal Haston (1940–77) successfully completed the climb on 24 Sep 1975. The first British woman was Rebecca Stephens on 17 May 1993.

First woman Junko Tabei (Japan) (b. 22 Sep 1939) reached the summit on 16 May 1975.

Oldest Richard Daniel Bass (USA) (b. 21 Dec 1929) was aged 55 yr 130 days

Timothy John Macartney-Snape (Australia) (b. 1956) traversed Mount Everest's entire altitude from sea level to summit. He set off on foot from the Bay of Bengal near Calcutta, India on 5 Feb 1990 and reached the summit on 11 May having walked approximately 1200 km *745 miles*.
(Photo: Australian Geographic)

when he reached the summit on 30 Apr 1985.

Most successful expedition The Mount Everest International Peace Climb, a team of American, Soviet and Chinese climbers, led by James W. Whittaker (USA), in 1990 succeeded in putting the greatest number of people on the summit, 20, from 7–10 May 1990.

Most in a day On 12 May 1992, 32 climbers (30 men and 2 women) from the USA, Russia, New Zealand, India, the Netherlands, Belgium, Israel, Hong Kong and Nepal, and from five separate expeditions, reached the summit.

Mountaineer Reinhold Messner was the first person to successfully scale all 14 of the world's mountains of over 8000 m *26 250 ft*, all without oxygen. With his ascent of Kanchenjunga in 1982, he was the first to climb the world's three highest mountains, having earlier reached the summits of Everest and K2.

Greatest walls The highest final stage in any wall climb is that on the south face of Annapurna I (8091m *26 545 ft*). It was climbed by the British expedition led by Christian John Storey Bonington (b. 6 Aug 1934) when from 2 Apr to 27 May 1970, using 5500 m *18 000 ft* of rope,

Human fly
The longest climb achieved on the vertical face of a building occurred on 25 May 1981 when Daniel Goodwin, 25, of California, USA climbed a record 443·2m *1454 ft* up the outside of the Sears Tower in Chicago, USA, using suction cups and metal clips for support.

Abseiling (or Rappelling)
Wilmer Pérez and Luis Aulestia set an abseiling or rappelling record of 1029m *3376 ft* by descending from above the Angel Falls in Venezuela to its base on 24 Aug 1989. The descent took 1¼hr.

The longest descent down the side of a building is one of 446·5m *1465 ft*, by two teams of twelve, representing the Royal Marines from Great Britain and the Canadian School of Rescue Training. All twenty-four people abseiled from the Space Deck of the CN Tower in Toronto, Canada to the ground on 1 Jul 1992. Two ropes were used, the first member of each team reaching the ground at exactly the same time.

The greatest distance abseiled by a team of ten in an eight-hour period is 72·42km *45·00 miles*, by Royal Marines from the Commando Training Centre at Lympstone, Devon. They achieved the record by abseiling 1382 times down the side of the Civic Centre at Plymouth, Devon on 22 May 1993.

Donald Whillans (1933–85) and Dougal Haston scaled to the summit. The longest wall climb is on the Rupal-Flank from the base camp at 3560m *11 680 ft* to the South Point 8042m *26 384 ft* of Nanga Parbat, a vertical ascent of 4482m *14 704 ft*. This was scaled by the Austro-German-Italian expedition led by Dr Karl

617

Maria Herrligkoffer (b. 13 Jun 1916) in April 1970.

Europe's greatest wall is the 2000m *6600ft* north face of the Eigerwand (Ogre wall) first climbed by Heinrich Harrer and Fritz Kasparek of Austria and Andreas Heckmair and Wiggerl Vörg of Germany from 21–24 Jul 1938. The north-east face of the Eiger had been climbed on 20 Aug 1932 by Hans Lauper, Alfred Zurcher, Alexander Graven and Josef Knubel. The greatest alpine solo climb was that of Walter Bonatti (Italy) (b. 22 Jun 1930) of the south west pillar of the Dru, Montenvers, now called the Bonatti Pillar, with five bivouacs in 126 hr 7 min from 17–22 Aug 1955.

The most demanding free climbs in the world are those rated at 5·13, the premier location for these being in the Yosemite Valley, California, USA.

The top routes in Britain are graded E7·7b, which relates closely to 5·13.

Highest bivouac Four Nepalese bivouacked at more than 8800 m *28 870ft* in their descent from the summit of Everest on the night of 23 Apr 1990. They were Ang Rita Sherpa, on his record breaking sixth ascent of Everest, Ang Kami Sherpa (b. 1952), Pasang Norbu Sherpa (b. 1963) and Top Bahadur Khatri (b. 1960).

Oldest Teiichi Igarashi (Japan) (b. 21 Sep 1886) climbed Mount Fuji (Fujiyama) (3776 m *12 388ft*) at the age of 99 yr 302 days on 20 Jul 1986.

Mount Cameroon Reginald Esuke (Cameroon) descended from the summit 4095 m *13 435ft* to Buea at 915m *3002ft* in 1hr 2min 15sec on 24 Jan 1988, achieving a vertical rate of 51m *167·5ft* per min. Timothy Leku Lekunze (Cameroon) set the record for the race to the summit and back of 3hr 46min 34 sec on 25 Jan 1987, when the temperature varied from 35°C at the start to 0°C at the summit. The record time for the ascent is 2 hr 25 min 20 sec by Jack Maitland (GB) in 1988. The women's record for the race is 4 hr 42 min 31 sec by Luz Fabiola Rueda (Colombia) (b. 26 Mar 1963) in 1989.

24-hour records The Lakeland record is 76 peaks (approximately 11 900 m *39 000ft* of ascents and descents) from Braithwaite achieved by Mark McDermott (Macclesfield Harriers) on 19–20 Jun 1988.

The Scottish record is 28 Munro (mountains over 3000ft *914m*) summits achieved by Jon Broxap on 30–31 Jul 1988. He covered 80 miles *128 km*, with 35 000 ft *10 668 m* of ascents and descents in 23 hr 20 min from Cluanie Inn.

Bob Graham The record for the round of 42 lakeland peaks covering a total distance of 62 miles *99 km* and 26 000 ft *7900 m* of ascent and descent, is 13hr 54min by William Bland, 34, on 19 Jun 1982. Ernest Roger Baumeister (b. 17 Dec 1941) (Dark Peak Fell Runners Club) ran the double Bob Graham Round in 46hr 34½min on 30 Jun–1 Jul 1979. The women's single round record is 18 hr 49 min by Anne Stentiford (Macclesfield Harriers) on 21 Sep 1991.

Scottish 4000ft peaks The record for traversing all eight 4000 ft *1219 m* peaks, a 85 mile *136 km* cross-country route from Glen Nevis to Glen More is 21 hr 39 min by Martin Stone on 4 Jul 1987.

Scottish 3000ft peaks The Munros record for climbing and linking the 277 peaks (over 3000 ft *914 m*) entirely on foot is 66 days 22 hr by Hugh Symonds (b. 1 Feb 1953). He covered 1374 miles *2211 km* and climbed 422 000 ft *128 600m* between Ben Hope and Ben Lomond, 19 Apr–25 Jun 1990. He rowed to Skye, sailed to Mull and ran between all the other peaks. He continued on foot through England, Wales and Ireland, climbing the remaining 26 3000 ft peaks in a total of 97 days.

Welsh 3000ft peaks The record for traversing the 15 Welsh peaks is 4 hr 19 min 56 sec, from Snowdon Summit to Foel Fras by Colin Donnelly on 11 Jun 1988. The women's record is 5 hr 28 min 41 sec by Angela Carson on 5 Aug 1989.

British Three Peaks The Three Peaks route from sea level at Fort William, Highland, to sea level at Caernarvon, via the summits of Ben Nevis, Scafell Pike and Snowdon, was walked by Arthur

Eddleston (1939–84) (Cambridge H) in 5 days 23hr 37min from 11–17 May 1980. Peter and David Ford, David Robinson, Kevin Duggan and John O'Callaghan, of Luton and Dunstable, ran the distance in relay in 54hr 39min 14sec from 7–9 Aug 1981.

On 24 Oct 1990 a team of three from the Royal Electrical and Mechanical Engineers covered the distance in 7hr 59min, being transported between the peaks by helicopter. Their running time was 5hr 25min.

Stephen Poulton cycled and ran from sea level at Caernarvon, Gwynedd, via the peaks of Snowdon, Scafell Pike and Ben Nevis, to sea level Fort William, Highland in 41hr 51min, from 1–2 Jul 1980.

Multiple peaks Three members of the 'Climathon' team, Mick Cottam, Matthew Beresford and Andrew Curson, completed a climb of all 349 peaks in England over 2000ft *610 m* (walking a distance of 402½ miles *647 km*) from 21 Jul–11 Aug 1985.

Craig Caldwell took 377 days to cycle, walk and climb to the top of the 277 Munros and the 222 Corbetts (2500–3000ft *762–914 m*) in Scotland, from February 1985–March 1986. In all he cycled 4152miles *6682 km*, walked 3030 miles *4876 km* and climbed 828 491ft *252 524 m*.

Top to bottom Clive Johnson and Les Heaton of 'Mountain Adventure' climbed the highest peaks and descended the deepest caves in each of England, Scotland and Wales in 16hr 14min from 16–18 Sep 1986.

Netball

Most titles *World* Australia has won the World Championships (instituted 1963) a record six times, 1963, 1971, 1975, 1979, 1983 and 1991.

English The National Club's Championships (instituted 1966) have been won six times by Sudbury Netball Club (1968–69, 1970 (shared), 1971, 1984–5). Surrey has won the County Championships (instituted 1932) a record 22 times (1949–64, 1966, 1981, 1991, 1992: 1969 and 1986 (both shared)).

Highest netball scores
On 9 Jul 1991, during the World Championships at Sydney, Australia, the Cook Islands beat Vanuatu 120–38. The record number of goals in the World Championship by an individual is 402 by Judith Heath (England) (b. 1942) in 1971.

Most international appearances The record number of internationals is 100 by Jillean Hipsey of England, 1978–87.

Olympic Games

The earliest celebration of the ancient Olympic Games of which there is a certain record is that of July 776 BC, when Coroibos, a cook from Elis, won the foot race, though their origin dates from perhaps as early as *c.* 1370 BC. The ancient Games were terminated by an order issued in Milan in AD 393 by Theodosius I, 'the Great' (*c.* 346–95), Emperor of Rome. At the instigation of Pierre de Fredi, Baron de Coubertin (1863–1937), the Olympic Games of the modern era were inaugurated in Athens on 6 Apr 1896.

Ever present Five countries have never failed to be represented at the 23 Summer Games that have been held (1896–1992): Australia, France, Greece, Great Britain and Switzerland (only contested the Equestrian events, held in Stockholm, Sweden, in 1956 and did not attend the Games in Melbourne). Of these only France, Great Britain and Switzerland have been present at all Winter celebrations (1924–92) as well.

Most participants The greatest number of competitors at a Summer Games celebration is 9369 (6659 men, 2710 women), who represented a record 169 nations, at Barcelona, Spain in 1992. The greatest number at the Winter Games is 1719 (1269 men, 460 women) representing 64 countries, at Albertville, France in 1992.

Largest crowd The largest crowd at any Olympic site was 104 102 at the 1952

Most Medals

The total medals, for leading nations, for all Olympic events (including those now discontinued).

SUMMER GAMES (1896–92)

	Gold	Silver	Bronze	Total
USA	789	603	518	1910
USSR[1]	442	361	333	1136
Germany[2]	186	227	236	649
Great Britain	177	224	218	619
France	161	175	191	527
Sweden	133	149	171	453
GDR[3]	154	131	126	411
Italy	153	126	131	410
Hungary	136	124	144	404
Finland	98	77	112	287
Japan	90	83	93	266
Australia	78	76	98	252
Romania	59	70	90	219
Poland	43	62	105	210
Canada	45	67	80	192
Netherlands	45	52	72	169
Switzerland	42	63	58	163
Bulgaria	38	69	55	162
Czechoslovakia[4]	49	50	50	149
Denmark	26	51	53	130

Excludes medals won in Official Art competitions in 1912–48.

WINTER GAMES (1924–92)

	Gold	Silver	Bronze	Total
USSR[1]	88	63	67	218
Norway	63	66	59	188
USA	47	50	37	134
Austria	34	45	40	119
Finland	36	44	37	117
GDR3	39	36	35	110
Germany[2]	36	36	29	101
Sweden	37	25	34	96
Switzerland	24	25	27	76
Canada	16	15	20	51
France	16	15	17	48
Italy	18	16	13	47
Netherlands	14	18	14	45
Czechoslovakia[4]	2	8	16	26
Great Britain	7	4	10	21

[1] *Includes Czarist Russia to 1912, CIS 1992*
[2] *Germany 1896–1964 and 1992, West Germany 1968–88*
[3] *GDR (East Germany) 1968–88*
[4] *Includes Bohemia*

ski-jumping at the Holmenkøllen, outside Oslo, Norway. Estimates of the number of spectators of the marathon race through Tokyo, Japan on 21 Oct 1964 ranged from 500 000 to 1 500 000.

The total spectator attendance at Los Angeles in 1984 was given as 5 797 923 (⇨ General Records).

Olympic Torch relay The longest journey of the torch within one country, was for the XV Olympic Winter Games in Canada in 1988. The torch arrived from Greece at St John's, Newfoundland on 17 Nov 1987 and was transported 18 060 km *11 222 miles* (8188 km *5088 miles* by foot, 7111 km *4419 miles* by aircraft/ferry, 2756 km *1712 miles* by snowmobile and 5 km *3 miles* by dogsled) until its arrival at Calgary on 13 Feb 1988.

Most gold medals In ancient Olympic Games victors were given a chaplet of wild olive leaves. Leonidas of Rhodos won 12 running titles 164–152 BC.

The most individual gold medals won by a male competitor in the modern Games is ten by Raymond Clarence Ewry (USA) (1873–1937) (⇨ Athletics). The female record is seven by Vera Cáslavská-Odlozil (Czechoslovakia) (⇨ Gymnastics).

The most gold medals won by a British competitor is four by: Paul Radmilovic (1886–1968) in water polo, 1908, 1912 and 1920 and 4 × 200m freestyle relay in 1908; and swimmer Henry Taylor (1885–1951) in 1906 and 1908. The Australian swimmer Iain Murray Rose, who won four gold medals, was born in Birmingham, W Mids on 6 Jan 1939.

The only Olympian to win four consecutive individual titles in the same event has been Alfred Adolph Oerter (USA) (b. 19 Sep 1936), who won the discus, in 1956–68.

However, Raymond Clarence Ewry (USA) won both the standing long jump and the standing high jump at four games in succession, 1900, 1904, 1906 and 1908. This is if the Intercalated Games of 1906, which were staged officially by the International Olympic Committee, are included. Also Paul B. Elvström (Denmark) (b. 25 Feb 1928) won four successive gold medals at monotype yachting events, 1948–60, but there was a class change (1948 Firefly class, 1952–60 Finn class).

One of the most successful participants in the 1992 Paralympics in
Barcelona was Tanni Grey (GB), who
won four golds. The year 1992 was a
very successful one for Tanni as she
set wheelchair world records for
100 m, 200 m, 400 m and 800 m and
British records for 1500 m, 5000 m
half and full marathon distances.

(Photo: Allsport/Gray Mortimore)

Swimmer Mark Andrew Spitz (USA) (b.
10 Feb 1950) won a record seven golds
at one celebration, at Munich in 1972,
including three in relays. The most won
in individual events at one celebration is
five by speed skater, Eric Arthur Heiden
(USA) (b. 14 Jun 1958) at Lake Placid,
New York, USA in 1980.

Most medals Gymnast Larisa Latynina
(USSR) (b. 27 Dec 1934) won a record
18 medals and the men's record is 15 by

Nikolay Andrianov (⬦ Gymnastics). The
record at one celebration is eight by
gymnast Aleksandr Dityatin (USSR) (b. 7
Aug 1957) in 1980.

Summer and winter The only man to
win a gold medal in both the Games is
Edward Patrick Francis Eagan (USA)
(1898–1967) who won the 1920 light-
heavyweight boxing title and was a
member of the winning four-man bob
in 1932.

Christa Luding (*née* Rothenburger)
(GDR) (b. 4 Dec 1959) became the first
woman to win a medal at both Games
when she won a silver in the cycling
sprint event in 1988. She had previously
won medals for speed skating, 500m
gold in 1984, and 1000m gold and 500m
silver in 1988.

Youngest and oldest gold medallist
The youngest ever winner was a French
boy (whose name is not recorded) who
coxed the Netherlands pair in 1900. He
was 7–10 years old and he substituted
for Dr Hermanus Brockmann, who

coxed in the heats but proved too heavy. The youngest ever female champion was Marjorie Gestring (USA) (b. 18 Nov 1922, now Mrs Bowman), aged 13 yr 268 days, in the 1936 women's springboard event.

Oscar Swahn was in the winning Running Deer shooting team in 1912 aged 64 yr 258 days and in this event was the oldest medallist, silver, at 72 yr 280 days in 1920.

Youngest and oldest British competitor The youngest competitor to represent Britain in the Olympic Games was Magdalena Cecilia Colledge (b. 28 Nov 1920), aged 11 yr 73 days when she skated in the 1932 Games.

The oldest was Hilda Lorna Johnstone (1902–90), aged 70 yr 5 days, in the equestrian dressage in the 1972 Games.

Longest span The longest span of an Olympic competitor is 40 years by: Dr Ivan Osiier (Denmark) (1888–1965) in fencing, 1908–32 and 1948; Magnus Konow (Norway) (1887–1972) in yachting, 1908–20, 1928 and 1936–48; Paul Elvström (Denmark) in yachting, 1948–60, 1968–72 and 1984–88; and Durward Randolph Knowles (Great Britain 1948, then Bahamas) (b. 2 Nov 1917) in yachting, 1948–72 and 1988. Raimondo d'Inzeo (b. 8 Feb 1925) competed for Italy in equestrian events at a record eight celebrations from 1948–76, gaining one gold, two silver and three bronze medals. This was equalled by Paul Elvström and Durward Knowles in 1988 and yachtsman Hubert Raudaschl (Austria) (b. 26 Aug 1942), 1964–92 (went to Rome, 1960 but did not compete).

The longest feminine span is 28 years by Anne Jessica Ransehousen (*née* Newberry) (USA) (b. 14 Oct 1938) in dressage, 1960, 1964 and 1988. Fencer Kerstin Palm (Sweden) (b. 5 Feb 1946) competed in a women's record seven celebrations, 1964–88.

The longest span of any British competitor is 32 years by Enoch Jenkins (1892–1984) who competed in clay pigeon shooting in 1920, 1924 and 1952. The record number of appearances is six by swimmer and water polo player Paul Radmilovic, 1906–28 and fencer Bill Hoskyns, 1956–76. David Broome, who

competed in show jumping in 1960, 1964, 1968, 1972 and 1988, was a member of the British team that travelled to Barcelona in 1992. He was, however, not selected to compete.

The greatest number of appearances for Great Britain by a woman is five by javelin thrower Tessa Ione Sanderson (b. 14 Mar 1956), 1976–92. The longest feminine span is 20 years by Dorothy Jennifer Beatrice Tyler (*née* Odam) (b. 14 Mar 1920) who high-jumped from 1936–56. However, Davina Mary Galicia (b. 13 Aug 1944) who competed in alpine skiing, 1964–72, took part in speed skiing which was a demonstration sport in 1992, therefore completing a span of 28 years.

Orienteering

Most titles *World* The men's relay has been won a record seven times by

Terry Dooris (b. 22 Sep 1926) of Southern Navigators has competed in all 27 British individual championships 1967–93, whilst Lorna Collett (b. 2 Sep 1922) of South Ribble OC competed in the 24 from 1967–90.

Norway, 1970, 1978, 1981, 1983, 1985, 1987 and 1989. Sweden have won the women's relay nine times, 1966, 1970, 1974, 1976, 1981, 1983, 1985, 1989 and 1991. Three women's individual titles have been won by Annichen Kringstad (Sweden) (b. 15 Jul 1960), 1981, 1983 and 1985. The men's title has been won twice by: Åge Hadler (Norway) (b. 14 Aug 1944), in 1966 and 1972; Egil Johansen (Norway) (b. 18 Aug 1954), 1976 and 1978; and Øyvin Thon (Norway) (b. 25 Mar 1958), in 1979 and 1981.

Ski (instituted 1975) Sweden have won the men's relay title five times, 1977, 1980, 1982, 1984 and 1990. Finland have won the women's relay five times, 1975, 1977, 1980, 1988 and 1990.

The most individual titles is four by Ragnhild Bratberg (Norway), Classic 1986, 1990, Sprint 1988, 1990. The men's record is three by Anssi Juutilainen (Finland) Classic 1984, 1988, Sprint 1992.

British Geoffrey Peck (b. 27 Sep 1949) won the men's individual title a record five times, 1971, 1973, 1976–7 and 1979 as well as the over-35s title in 1985–6 and over-40s in 1989. Carol McNeill (b. 20 Feb 1944) won the women's title six times, 1967, 1969, 1972–6. She also won the over-35s title in 1984, 1985 and 1991, and the over-45s title in 1990.

Most competitors The most competitors at an event in one day is 38 000 for the Ruf des Herbstes at Sibiu, Romania in 1982. The largest event is the five-day Swedish O-Ringen at Småland, which attracted 120 000 in July 1983.

Parachuting

Most titles *World* The USSR won the men's team title in 1954, 1958, 1960, 1966, 1972, 1976 and 1980, and the women's team title in 1956, 1958, 1966, 1968, 1972 and 1976. Nikolay Ushamyev (USSR) has won the individual title twice, 1974 and 1980.

Greatest accuracy At Yuma, Arizona, USA, in March 1978, Dwight Reynolds scored a record 105 daytime dead centres, and Bill Wenger and Phil Munden tied with 43 night time DCs, competing as members of the US Army team, the Golden Knights. With electronic measuring the official FAI record is 50 DCs by Linger Abdurakhmanov (USSR) at Fergana, USSR on 18 Oct 1988, when the women's record was set at 41 by Natalya Filinkova (USSR).

The Men's Night Accuracy Landing record is 31 DCs by Vladmir Buchenev (USSR) on 30 Oct 1986. The women's record is 21 by Inessa Stepanova (USSR) at Fergana on 18 Oct 1988.

Paragliding *World* The greatest distance flown is 281·5km *174·9miles* by Alex Lowe (South Africa) from Kuruman, South Africa on 31 Dec 1992. The women's record is 124km *77miles* by Judy Leden (GB) on 9 Dec 1992. The height gain record is 4470m *14665ft* by Robby Whittal (GB) also at Kuruman on 22 Jan 1993. All these records were tow launched.

British The greatest distance flown is 253km *157miles* by Robby Whittal at Kuruman on 22 Jan 1993. The greatest distance flown within Britain is 98·56km *61·2miles* from Wetherfell to Stamford Bridge, Humberside by Ross Somerville on 30 Jul 1992 (footlaunched).

Nigel Horder scored four successive dead centres at the Dutch Open, Flevhof, Netherlands on 22 May 1983.

Pelota Vasca (Jaï Alaï)

World Championships The *Federación Internacional de Pelota Vasca* stage World Championships every four years (first in 1952). The most successful pair have been Roberto Elias (Argentina) (b. 15 Dec 1918) and Juan Labat (Argentina) (b. 10 Jan 1912), who won the *Trinquete Share* four times, 1952, 1958, 1962 and 1966. Labat won a record seven world titles in all between 1952 and 1966. Riccardo Bizzozero (Argentina) (b. 25 Nov 1948) also won seven world titles in various *Trinquete* and *Frontón corto* events, 1970–82. The most wins in the long court game *Cesta Punta* is three by José Hamuy (Mexico) (1934–83), with two different partners, 1958, 1962 and 1966.

Pelota

An electronically-measured ball velocity of 302 km/h *188 mph* was recorded by José Ramón Areitio (Spain) (b. 6 Jul 1947) at the Newport Jaï Alaï, Rhode Island, USA on 3 Aug 1979.

Pétanque

The highest score in 24 hours is by Chris Walker (b. 16 Jan 1942) and his son Richard (b. 26 Dec 1966) who scored a record 2109 points in 24 hours (172 games) at the Gin Trap, Ringstead, Norfolk on 24–25 Jun 1988.

Longest domination The longest domination as the world's No. 1 player was enjoyed by Chiquito de Cambo (*né* Joseph Apesteguy) (France) (1881–1955) from the beginning of the century until succeeded in 1938 by Jean Urruty (France) (b. 19 Oct 1913).

Largest frontón The world's largest *frontón* (enclosed stadium) is the World Jaï Alaï at Miami, Florida, USA, which had a record attendance of 15052 on 27 Dec 1975.

Pétanque

World Championships Winner of the most World Championships (instituted 1959) has been France with 12 titles to 1992. The women's World Championships (instituted 1988) have been won twice by Thailand, 1988 and 1990.

Pigeon Racing

Longest flights The official British duration record (into Great Britain) is 1887 km *1173 miles* in 15 days by *C.S.O.*, owned by Rosie and Bruce of Wick, in the 1976 Palamos Race. In the 1975 Palamos Race, *The Conqueror*, owned by Alan Raeside, homed to Irvine, Strathclyde, 1625 km *1010 miles*, in 43 hr 56 min. The greatest number of flights over 1000 miles flown by one pigeon is that of *Dunning Independence*, owned by D. Smith, which annually flew from Palamos to Dunning, Perthshire, 1672 km *1039 miles*, between 1978 and 1981.

The longest confirmed distances, flown in opposite directions, by a single pigeon were north from Rome, Italy, 1474·41 km *916·16 miles*, and south from The Faroes, 1178·82 km *732·5 miles*, by a dark cock, *GB83X 03693*, to the loft of Marley Westrop of Hitchin, Herts.

The greatest claimed homing flight by a pigeon was for one owned by the 1st Duke of Wellington (1769–1852). Released from a sailing ship off the Ichabo Islands, West Africa on 8 April, it dropped dead a mile from its loft at Nine Elms, Wandsworth, Greater London on 1 Jun 1845, 55 days later, having apparently flown an airline route of 8700 km *5400 miles*, but possibly a distance of 11 250 km *7000 miles* to avoid the Sahara Desert. In 1990 it was reported that a pigeon, owned by David Lloyd and George Workman of Nantyffyllon, Mid Glam, had completed a flight of 10 860 km *6750 miles* from its release at Lerwick, Shetland to Shanghai, China, possibly the longest non-homing flight ever. In both cases, however, the lack of constant surveillance makes it difficult to confirm that the pigeons completed the distances unaided.

Highest speeds In level flight in windless conditions it is very doubtful if any pigeon can exceed 96 km/h *60 mph*. The highest race speed recorded is one of 2952 m *3229 yd* per min (177·14 km/h *110·07 mph*) in the East Anglian Federation race from East Croydon,

Surrey on 8 May 1965 when the 1428 birds were backed by a powerful south-south-west wind. The winner was owned by A. Vigeon & Son, Wickford, Essex.

The highest race speed recorded over a distance of more than 1000km *621·37 miles* is 2224·5m *2432·7yd* per min (133·46km/h *82·93mph*) by a hen in the Central Cumberland Combine race over 1099·316km *683 miles 147yd* from Murray Bridge, South Australia to North Ryde, Sydney on 2 Oct 1971.

24-hour records The world's longest reputed distance in 24 hours is 1292km *803 miles* (velocity 1394m *1525yd* per min) by E. S. Petersen's winner of the 1941 San Antonio R.C. event in Texas, USA.

The best 24-hour performance into the United Kingdom is 1165·3km *724 miles 219yd* by E. Cardno's *Mormond Lad*, on 2 Jul 1977, from Nantes, France to Fraserburgh, Grampian. The average speed was 90·41km/h *56·18mph*.

Career records Owned by R. Green, of Walsall Wood, W Mids, *Champion Breakaway* won 59 first prizes from 1972 to May 1979.

The greatest competitive distance flown is 32318km *20 082 miles* by *Nunnies*, a chequer cock owned by Terry Haley of Abbot's Langley, Herts.

Mass release The largest ever simultaneous release of pigeons was at Orleans, France in August 1988 when over 215 000 pigeons were released for a Dutch National race. In Great Britain the largest liberation was at Beachy Head near Eastbourne, E Sussex on 11 May 1991 when 42 500 birds were released for the Save The Children Fund Eastbourne Classic.

Polo

Most titles The British Open Championship for the Cowdray Park Gold Cup (instituted 1956) has been won five times by, Stowell Park, 1973–4, 1976, 1978 and 1980, and Tramontana, 1986–9, 1991.

Highest handicap The highest handicap based on six 7½ min 'chukkas' is ten

Most chukkas
The greatest number of chukkas played on one ground in a day is 43. This was achieved by the Pony Club on the Number 3 Ground at Kirtlington Park, Oxon on 31 Jul 1991.

goals introduced in the USA in 1891 and in the UK and in Argentina in 1910. A total of 56 players have received ten-goal handicaps and there are ten currently playing in Britain, two Mexican and eight Argentinians. The last (of six) ten-goal handicap players from the UK was Gerald Balding in 1939.

The highest handicap of current UK players is eight by Howard Hipwood (b. 24 Mar 1950) although he acheived a handicap of nine in 1992. Claire J. Tomlinson of Gloucestershire attained a handicap of five, the highest ever by a woman, in 1986.

A match of two 40-goal teams has been staged on three occasions at Palermo, Buenos Aires, Argentina in 1975, in the USA in 1990 and Australia in 1991.

Highest score The highest aggregate number of goals scored in an international match is 30, when Argentina beat the USA 21–9 at Meadowbrook, Long Island, New York, USA in September 1936.

Pool

Pool or championship pocket billiards with numbered balls began to become standardized *c.* 1890. The greatest exponents were Ralph Greenleaf (USA) (1899–1950), who won the 'world' professional title 19 times (1919–37), and William Mosconi (USA) (b. 27 Jun 1913), who dominated the game from 1941 to 1956.

The longest consecutive run in an American straight pool match is 625 balls by Michael Eufemia at Logan's Billiard Academy, Brooklyn, New York, USA on 2 Feb 1960, although this was not officially recognized. The official best is 526 by Willie Mosconi at Springfield, Ohio, USA in March 1954. The greatest number of balls pocketed in 24 hours is

16497 by Paul Sullivan at the Abbey Leisure Centre, Selby N Yorks on 16–17 Apr 1993.

The record times for potting all 15 balls in a speed competition are: (men) 37·9 sec by Rob McKenna at Blackpool, Lancs on 7 Nov 1987 and (women) 44·5 sec by Susan Thompson at Shrublands Community Centre, Gorleston, Norfolk on 20 Apr 1990.

Powerboat Racing

APBA Gold Cup The American Power Boat Association (APBA) was formed in 1903 and held its first Gold Cup on the Hudson River, New York, USA in 1904. The most wins is nine by Chip Hanauer (USA), 1982–8, 1992–3. The highest average speed for the race is 143·176 mph *230·413 km/h* by Tom D'Eath (USA), piloting *Miss Budweiser* in 1990.

Cowes to Torquay This race was instituted in 1961 and at first was run from Cowes to Torquay, but from 1968 included the return journey, for a distance of 320·4 km *199 miles*. The most wins is four by Renato della Valle (Italy), 1982–5. The highest average speed is 138·24 km/h *85·89 mph* by Fabio Fuzzi (Italy), piloting *Cesa* in 1988.

Longest races The longest offshore race has been the Port Richborough London to Monte Carlo Marathon Offshore international event. The race extended over 4742 km *2947 miles* in 14 stages from 10–25 Jun 1972. It was won by *H.T.S.* (GB) driven by Mike Bellamy, Eddie Chater and Jim Brooker in 71 hr 35 min 56 sec for an average of 66·24 km/h *41·15 mph*. The longest circuit race is the 24-hour race held annually since 1962 on the River Seine at Rouen, France.

Projectiles

Throwing The greatest distance that any object has been propelled by human power is 1871·84 m *6141 ft 2 in*, in the case of an arrow shot by Harry Drake (USA) (b. 7 May 1915), using a crossbow at the 'Smith Creek' Flight Range near Austin, Nevada, USA on 30 Jul 1988.

The longest independently authenticated throw of any inert object heavier than air is 383·13 m *1257 ft*, for a flying ring, by Scott Zimmerman on 8 Jul 1986 at Fort Funston, California, USA.

Boomerang throwing The earliest mention of a word similar to 'boomerang' is wo-murrang in Collins' Acct. N. S. Wales Vocab., 1798. The earliest reliable Australian account of a returning boomerang (a term established in 1827) was by Maj. (later Sir Thomas) Mitchell in 1831.

The greatest number of consecutive two-handed catches is 801, by Stéphane Marguerite (France) on 26 Nov 1989 at Lyon, France.

The longest out-and-return distance is one of 134·2 m *440 ft 3 in* by Jim Youngblood (USA) on 12 Jun 1989 at Gaithersburg, Maryland, USA.

The longest flight duration (with self-catch) is one of 2 min 59·94 sec by Dennis Joyce (USA) at Bethlehem, Pennsylvania, USA on 25 Jun 1987.

Matthieu Weber (Switzerland) caught 73 boomerang throws in 5 min at Lyon, France on 2 Nov 1991.

The juggling record—the number of consecutive catches with two boomerangs, keeping at least one boomerang aloft at all times—is 207, by Michael Girvin (USA) at Elkton, Maryland, USA on 6 Jul 1991.

Flying disc throwing (formerly Frisbee) The World Flying Disc Federation distance records are: (men) 190·07 m *623 ft 7 in*, by Sam Ferrans (US) on 2 Jul 1988 at La Habra, California, USA; (women) 130·09 m *426 ft 10 in*, by Amy Bekken (US) on 25 Jun 1990 at La Habra, California, USA.

The throw, run and catch records are: (men) 92·64 m *303 ft 11 in*, by Hiroshi Oshima (Japan) on 20 Jul 1988 at San Francisco, California, USA; (women) 60·02 m *196 ft 11 in*, by Judy Horowitz (US) on 29 Jun 1985 at La Mirada, California, USA.

The 24-hour distance records for a pair are: (men) 583·20 km *362·40 miles*, by

David hurled stones from a sling to kill Goliath, and the latest slinging record was also set by a David— David Engvall. The equipment may be different but the principle remains the same.

(Photos: David Engvall and Beverly Hargrove)

Leonard Muise and Gabe Ontiveros (US) on 21–22 Sep 1988 at Carson, California, USA; (women) 186·12 km *115·65 miles*, by Jo Cahow and Amy Berard (US) on 30–31 Dec 1979 at Pasadena, California, USA.

The records for maximum time aloft are: (men) 16·72 sec, by Don Cain (US) on 26 May 1984 at Philadelphia, Pennsylvania, USA; (women) 11·81 sec, by Amy Bekken (US) on 1 Aug 1991 at Santa Cruz, California, USA.

Greatest distances achieved with other miscellaneous objects:

Brick..............................44·54m *146 ft 1 in* (standard 2·27 kg *5 lb* building brick) Geoff Capes at Braybrook School, Orton Goldhay, Cambs on 19 Jul 1978.

Egg (fresh hen's)......96·90m *317 ft 10 in* (without breaking it) Risto Antikainen to Jyrki Korhonen at Siilinjarvi, Finland on 6 Sep 1981.

Gumboot ('Wellie wanging', using a size 8 Challenger Dunlop boot) *Men*.......................................52·73m *173 ft* Tony Rodgers of Warminster, Wilts on 9 Sep 1978. *Women*...........................39·60m *129 ft 11 in* Rosemary Payne at Cannon Hill Park, Birmingham on 21 Jun 1975.

Haggis................55·11m *180 ft 10 in* (minimum weight 680 g *1 lb 8 oz*) Alan Pettigrew at Inchmurrin, Loch Lomond, Strathclyde on 24 May 1984.

Rolling pin...............53·47m *175 ft 5 in* (907 g *2 lb*)

Wayne Brian with his spear and atlatl. He beat the old record on two occasions in 1992.

(Photo: Richard Jamison)

Lori La Deane Adams, 21, at Iowa State Fair, Iowa, USA on 21 Aug 1979.

Slinging.................477·10 m *1565 ft 4 in* (using a 127 cm *50 in* long sling and a 62 g *2¼ oz* dart)

David P. Engvall at Baldwin Lake, California, USA on 13 Sep 1992.

Spear throwing.......194·67 m *638 ft 8 in* (using an atlatl or hand-held device which fits onto a short spear)

Cow pat tossing

The record distances in the country sport of throwing dried cow pats or 'chips' depend on whether or not the projectile may be 'moulded into a spherical shape'. The greatest distance achieved under the 'non-sphericalisation and 100 per cent organic' rule (established in 1970) is 81·1 m *266 ft*, by Steve Urner at the Mountain Festival, Tehachapi, California, USA on 14 Aug 1981.

Racketball

World Championships Instituted in 1981, held biennially since 1984 and based on the US version of the game (racquetball), the USA has won all six team titles, 1981, 1984, 1986 (tie with Canada), 1988, 1990 and 1992. The most singles titles won is two by: (men) Egan Inoue (USA), 1986 and 1990, and; (women) Cindy Baxter (USA), 1981 and 1986, and Heather Stupp (Canada), 1988 and 1990.

Britain The British Racketball Association was formed and staged inaugural British National Championships in 1984. Five titles have been won at the women's event by Elizabeth 'Bett' Dryhurst (b. 26 Nov 1945), 1985–7, 1989 and 1991.

Rackets

World Championships Of the 22 world champions since 1820, the longest reign is by Geoffrey Willoughby Thomas Atkins (b. 20 Jan 1927) who gained the title by beating the professional James Dear (1910–81) in 1954, and held it until retiring, after defending it four times, in April 1972.

Most Amateur titles Since the Amateur Singles Championship was instituted in 1888 the most titles won by an individual is nine by Edgar Maximilian Baerlein (1879–1971) between 1903 and 1923. Since the institution of the Amateur Doubles Championship in 1890 the most shares in titles has been eleven by: David Sumner Milford (1905–84), between 1938 and 1959; and John Ross Thompson (b. 10 May 1918), between 1948 and 1966; they won ten titles together. Milford also won seven Amateur Singles titles (1930–51), an Open title (1936) and held the World title from 1937 to 1946. Thompson additionally won an Open Singles title and five Amateur Singles titles.

Real/Royal Tennis

Most titles *World* The first recorded world tennis champion was Clergé (France) *c.*1740. Jacques Edmond Barre (France) (1802–73) held the title for a record 33 years from 1829 to 1862. Pierre Etchebaster (1893–1980), a Basque, holds the record for the greatest number of successful defences of the title with eight between 1928 and 1952.

The Women's World Championships (instituted 1985) has been won twice by: Judith Anne Clarke (Australia) (b. 28 Dec 1954), 1985 and 1987; and Penny Lumley (*née* Fellows) (GB), 1989 and 1991.

British The Amateur Championship of the British Isles (instituted 1888) has been won 16 times by Howard Rea Angus (b. 25 Jun 1944) 1966–80 and 1982. He also won eight Amateur Doubles Championships with David Warburg (1923–87), 1967–70, 1972–4 and 1976, and was world champion 1976–81.

Oldest court The oldest of the surviving active courts in Great Britain is that at Falkland Palace, Fife built by King James V of Scotland in 1539.

Rodeo

The largest rodeo in the world is the National Finals Rodeo, organized by the Professional Rodeo Cowboys Association (PRCA) and the Women's Professional Rodeo Association (WPRA). The top 15 money-earning cowboys in each of the six PRCA events and the top 15 WPRA barrel racers compete at the Finals. It was first held at Dallas, Texas, USA in 1959 and was held at Oklahoma City for 20 years before moving to Las Vegas, Nevada in 1985. The 1991 Finals had a paid attendance of 171 414 for ten performances. In 1992 a record $2·6 million in prize money was offered for the event, staged in Las Vegas.

Most world titles The record number of all-around titles (awarded to the leading money winner in a single season in two or more events) in the PRCA World Championships is six by Larry Mahan (USA) (b. 21 Nov 1943) in 1966–70 and 1973 and, consecutively, 1974–9 by Tom Ferguson (b. 20 Dec 1950). Roy Cooper (b. 13 Nov 1955) has record career earnings of $1 374 953, 1975–92. Jim Shoulders (b. 13 May 1928) of Henrietta, Texas won a record 16 World Championships at four events between 1949 and 1959.

The record figure for prize money in a single season is $258 750 by Ty Murray (b. 11 Oct 1969) in 1991. The record for a single rodeo is $101 531 for saddle bronc riding by Billy Etbauer at the 1991 National Finals Rodeo.

Youngest champions The youngest winner of a world title is Anne Lewis (b. 1 Sep 1958), who won the WPRA barrel racing title in 1968, at 10 years old. Ty Murray is the youngest cowboy to win the PRCA All-Around Champion title, aged 20, in 1989.

Time records Records for PRCA timed events, such as calf-roping and steer-wrestling, are not always comparable, because of the widely varying conditions due to the sizes of arenas and amount of start given the stock. The fastest time recorded for calf roping under the current PRCA rules is 6·7 sec by Joe Beaver (b. 13 Oct 1965) at West Jordan, Utah in 1986, and the fastest time for steer wrestling is 2·4 sec by: James Bynum, at Marietta, Oklahoma, USA in 1955; Carl Deaton at Tulsa, Oklahoma in 1976; and Gene Melton at Pecatonica, Illinois in 1976. The fastest team roping time is 3·7 sec, by Bob Harris and Tee Woolman at Spanish Fork, Utah in 1986.

Bull riding Jim Sharp (b. 6 Oct 1965) of Kermit, Texas became the first rider to ride all ten bulls at a National Finals Rodeo at Las Vegas in December 1988. This feat was repeated by Norm Curry of Deberry, Texas at the 1990 National Finals.

The highest score in bull riding was 100 points out of a possible 100 by Wade Leslie on Wolfman Skoal at Central Point, Oregon, USA in 1991.

The top bucking bull *Red Rock* dislodged 312 riders, 1980–88, and was finally ridden to the eight-second bell by Lane

16th March, 1990

SKATEBOARD SPEED RECORD SMASHED

HICKEY EXCEEDS THE SPEED LIMIT

American skateboard fanatic Roger Hickey, of Westminster, California, yesterday recorded the highest speed ever achieved on a skateboard, clocking 78·37 mph (126·12 km/h) on a 3 mile (5·5 kilometre) course near Los Angeles.

He set the record lying in a prone position on his skateboard, and hopes to set a speed record for a stand-up position later this year. However, skateboarding at great speed does have its dangers — Hickey has suffered 44 fractures over the years. Fortunately, the attempt was not made when members of the public were using the road, as the police would surely not have liked the fact that Hickey ignored the normal permitted speed limit in beating the record.

Frost (1963–89) (world champion bull rider 1987) on 20 May 1988. *Red Rock* had retired at the end of the 1987 season but still continued to make guest appearances.

Saddle bronc riding The highest scored saddle bronc ride is 95 out of a possible 100 by Doug Vold on *Transport* at Meadow Lake, Saskatchewan, Canada in 1979. *Descent*, a saddle bronc owned by Beutler Brothers and Cervi Rodeo Company, received a record six PRCA saddle bronc of the year awards, 1966–9, 1971–2.

Bareback riding Joe Alexander of Cora, Wyoming, scored 93 out of a possible 100 on *Marlboro* at Cheyenne, Wyoming in 1974. *Sippin' Velvet*, owned by Bernis Johnson, has been awarded a record five PRCA bareback horse of the year titles between 1978 and 1987.

Roller Skating

Most titles *Speed* The most world speed titles won is 18 by two women: Alberta Vianello (Italy), eight track and ten road 1953–65; and Annie Lambrechts (Belgium), one track and 17

Portugal are the most successful nation in the history of roller hockey, winning a record number of World and European titles. Here they are in action against Holland at the 1992 Olympic Games where roller hockey was one of the demonstration sports.

(Photo: Allsport/Bernard Asset)

road 1964–81, at distances from 500m to 10 000m.

The most British national individual men's titles have been won by Michael Colin McGeogh (b. 30 Mar 1946) with 19 in 1966–85. Chloe Ronaldson (b. 30 Nov 1939) won 40 individual and 14 team women's senior titles from 1958 to 1985.

Figure The records for figure titles are: five by Karl Heinz Losch (West Germany), 1958–9, 1961–2 and 1966; and four by Astrid Bader (West Germany), 1965–8 and Rafaella del Vinaccio (Italy), 1988–91. The most world pair titles is six by Tammy Jeru (USA), 1983–6 (with John Arishita), 1990–91 (with Larry McGrew).

Speed skating The fastest speed put up in an official world record is 43·21 km/h *26·85 mph* when Luca Antoniel (Italy) (b. 12 Feb 1968) recorded 24·99 sec for 300m on a road at Gujan-Mestras, France

on 31 Jul 1987. The women's record is 40·30 km/h *25·04 mph* by Marisa Canofogilia (Italy) (b. 30 Sep 1965) for 300m on the road at Grenoble, France on 27 Aug 1987. The world records for 10 000 m on a road or track are: (men) 14 min 55·64 sec, Giuseppe de Persio (Italy) (b. 3 Jun 1959) at Gujan-Mestras, France on 1 Aug 1988; (women) 15 min 58·022 sec, Marisa Canofogilia (Italy) at Grenoble, France on 30 Aug 1987.

Largest rink The greatest indoor rink ever to operate was located in the Grand Hall, Olympia, London. Opened in 1890 and closed in 1912, it had an actual skating area of 6300 m² *68 000 ft²*. The current largest is the main arena of 3250 m² *34 981 ft²* at Guptill Roll-Arena, Boght Corner, New York, USA. The total rink area is 3844 m² *41 380 ft²*.

Land's End to John o' Groats Damian Magee roller skated the distance in 9

631

Skateboarding

World championships have been staged intermittently since 1966. David Frank, 25, covered 435·3km *270·5 miles* in 36hr 43min 40sec in Toronto, Canada on 11–12 Aug 1985.

The highest speed recorded on a skateboard in a stand-up position is 89·20km/h *55·43mph*, achieved by Roger Hickey at San Demas, California, USA on 3 Jul 1990.

The high-jump record is 1·67m *5ft 5¾in* by Trevor Baxter (b. 1 Oct 1962) of Burgess Hill, E Sussex at Grenoble, France on 14 Sep 1982.

At the 4th US Skateboard Association Championship, at Signal Hill on 25 Sep 1977, Tony Alva, 19, jumped 17 barrels (5·18m *17ft*).

---

days 5hr 23min from 19–28 Jun 1992. The fastest time by a woman was 12 days 4hr 15min by Cheryl Fisher, 17, from 19 Sep–1 Oct 1987.

Roller Hockey

England won the first World Championships, 1936–9, since when Portugal has won most titles with 13 between 1947 and 1991. Portugal also won a record 17 European (instituted 1926) titles between 1947 and 1992.

Rowing

The earliest established sculling race is the Doggett's Coat and Badge, which was first rowed on 1 Aug 1716 from London Bridge to Chelsea as a race for apprentices, and is still contested annually.

Most Olympic medals Seven oarsmen have won three gold medals: John Brenden Kelly (USA) (1889–1960), father of the late HSH Princess Grace of Monaco, single sculls (1920) and double sculls (1920 and 1924); his cousin Paul Vincent Costello (USA) (1894–1986), double sculls (1920, 1924 and 1928); Jack Beresford Jr (GB) (1899–1977), single sculls (1924), coxless fours (1932) and

double sculls (1936), Vyacheslav Nikolayevich Ivanov (USSR) (b. 30 Jul 1938), single sculls (1956, 1960 and 1964); Siegfried Brietzke (GDR) (b. 12 Jun 1952), coxless pairs (1972) and coxless fours (1976, 1980); Pertti Karppinen (Finland) (b. 17 Feb 1953), single sculls (1976, 1980 and 1984); and Steven Geoffrey Redgrave (GB) (b. 23 Mar 1962), coxed fours (1984), coxless pairs (1988 and 1992).

World Championships World rowing championships distinct from the Olympic Games were first held in 1962, at first four yearly, but from 1974 annually, except in Olympic years.

The most gold medals won at World Championships and Olympic Games is nine at coxed pairs by the Italian brothers Giuseppe (b. 24 Jul 1959) and Carmine (b. 5 Jan 1962) Abbagnale, World 1981–2, 1985, 1987, 1989–91, Olympics 1984 and 1988. At women's events Yelena Terekhina has won a record seven golds, all at eights for the USSR, 1978–9, 1981–3 and 1985–6.

The most wins at single sculls is five by: Peter-Michael Kolbe (West Germany) (b. 2 Aug 1953), 1975, 1978, 1981, 1983 and 1986; Pertti Karppinen, 1979 and 1985 with his three Olympic wins (above); Thomas Lange (GDR/Germany) (b. 27 Feb 1964), 1987, 1989 and 1991 and two Olympics 1988 and 1992; and in the women's events by Christine Hahn (*née* Scheiblich) (GDR) (b. 31 Dec 1954), 1974–5, 1977–8 and the 1976 Olympic title.

Boat Race The earliest University Boat Race, which Oxford won, was from Hambledon Lock to Henley Bridge on 10 Jun 1829. Outrigged eights were first used in 1846. In the 139 races to 1993, Cambridge won 70 times, Oxford 68 times and there was a dead heat on 24 Mar 1877.

The race record time for the course of 6·779km *4 miles 374yd* (Putney to Mortlake) is 16min 45sec by Oxford on 18 Mar 1984. This represents an average speed of 24·28km/h *15·09mph*. The smallest winning margin has been by a canvas by Oxford in 1952 and 1980. The greatest margin (apart from sinking) was Cambridge's win by 20 lengths in 1900.

Walking on water

Rémy Bricka of Paris, France 'walked' across the Atlantic Ocean on skis 4·2m *13ft 9in* long in 1988. Leaving Tenerife, Canary Islands on 2 Apr 1988, he covered 5636km *3502miles*, arriving at Trinidad on 31 May 1988.

He also set a speed record of 7min 7·41sec for 1km *1094yd* on the Olympic pool in Montréal, Canada on 2 Aug 1989. He 'walks on water' by having ski-floats attached to his feet and by moving in the same way as in cross-country skiing, using a double-headed paddle instead of ski-poles.

Longest race

The longest annual rowing race is the annual Tour du Lac Leman, Geneva, Switzerland for coxed fours (the five-man crew taking turns as cox) over 160km *99miles*. The record winning time is 12hr 52min by LAGA Delft, Netherlands on 3 Oct 1982.

24 hours

The greatest distance rowed in 24 hours (upstream and downstream) is 217·61km *135·22miles* by a coxed quad scull (Peter Halliday, Paul Turnbull, Mike Skerry, Belinda Goglia and Margaret Munneke) on the Yarra River, Melbourne, Australia on 26–27 Jan 1992.

Boris Rankov (Oxford, 1978–83) rowed in a record six winning boats. Susan Brown (b. 29 Jun 1958), the first woman to take part, coxed the winning Oxford boats in 1981 and 1982. Daniel Topolski coached Oxford to ten successive victories, 1976–85.

The tallest man ever to row in a University boat has been Gavin Stewart (Wadham, Oxford) (b. 25 Feb 1963) at 2·04m *6ft 8½in* in 1987–8. The heaviest was Christopher Heathcote (b. March 1963), the Oxford No. 6, who weighed 110kg *243lb* in 1990. The lightest oarsman was the 1882 Oxford Stroke, Alfred Herbert Higgins, at 60kg *9st 6½lb*. The lightest coxes, Francis Henry Archer (Cambridge) (1843–89) in 1862 and Hart Parker Vincent Massey (Oxford) (b. Canada, 30 Mar 1918) in 1939, were both 32·6kg *5st 2lb*.

The youngest 'blue' ever was Matthew John Brittin (Cambridge) (b. 1 Sep 1968) at 18yr 208days, in 1986.

Head of the River A processional race for eights instituted in 1926, the Head has an entry limit of 420 crews (3780 competitors). The record for the course Mortlake–Putney (the reverse of the Boat Race) is 16min 37sec by the ARA National Squad in 1987.

Henley Royal Regatta The annual regatta at Henley-on-Thames, Oxon was inaugurated on 26 Mar 1839. Since then the course, except in 1923, has been about 2112m *1mile 550yd*, varying slightly according to the length of boat. In 1967 the shorter craft were 'drawn up' so all bows start level.

The most wins in the Diamond Challenge Sculls (instituted 1844) is six by Guy Nickalls (GB) (1866–1935), 1888–91, 1893–4 and consecutively by Stuart A. Mackenzie (Australia and GB) (b. 5 Apr 1937), 1957–62. The record time is 7min 23sec by Vaclav Chalupa (Czechoslovakia) (b. 7 Dec 1967) on 2 Jul 1989. The record time for the Grand Challenge Cup (instituted 1839) event is 5min 58sec by Hansa Dortmund, West Germany on 2 Jul 1989.

Highest speed The highest recorded speed on non-tidal water for 2000m *2187yd* is by an American eight in 5min 27·14sec (22·01km/h *13·68mph*) at Lucerne, Switzerland on 17 Jun 1984. A crew from Penn AC, USA, was timed in 5min 18·8sec (22·58km/h *14·03mph*) in the FISA Championships on the River Meuse, Liège, Belgium on 17 Aug 1930.

Cross-Channel Ivor Lloyd sculled across the English Channel in a record 3hr 35min 1sec on 4 May 1983

River Thames Malcom Knight, Simon Leifer and Kevin Thomas rowed the navigable length of the Thames, 299·14km *185·88 miles*, from Lechlade Bridge, Glos to Southend Pier, Essex in 39hr 27min 12sec in a skiff from 10–11 May 1988. The fastest time from Folly Bridge, Oxford to Westminster Bridge, London (180km *112 miles*) is 14hr 25min 15sec by an eight from Kingston Rowing Club on 1 Feb 1986.

International Dragon Boat Races Instituted in 1975 and held annually in Hong Kong, the fastest time achieved for the 640metres *700yd* course is 2min 27·45sec by the Chinese Shun De team on 30 Jun 1985. The best time for a British team was 2min 36·40sec by the Kingston Royals crew on 3 Jun 1990. Teams have 28 members: 26 rowers, one steersman and one drummer.

Rugby League

There have been four different scoring systems in Rugby League football. For the purpose of these records all points totals remain as they were under the system in operation at the time they were made.

World Cup There have been nine World Cup Competitions. Australia have most wins, with six, 1957, 1968, 1970, 1977, 1988 and 1992 as well as a win in the International Championship of 1975.

Most titles The Northern Rugby League was formed in 1901. The word 'Northern' was dropped in 1980. Wigan have won the League Championship a record 14 times (1909, 1922, 1926, 1934, 1946, 1947, 1950, 1952, 1960, 1987, 1990, 1991, 1992 and 1993).

The Rugby League Challenge Cup (inaugurated 1896/7 season) has been won a record 14 times by Wigan, 1924, 1929, 1948, 1951, 1958–9, 1965, 1985, 1988–93.

Since 1974 there have been five major competitions for RL clubs: Challenge Cup, League Championship, Premiership, Regal Trophy (formerly John Player Special Trophy) and County Cups. In 1990 these were officially called the 'Grand Slam' and as yet no club has achieved this. Wigan have won four of these in one season twice, winning all

but the Challenge Cup in 1986/7 and all but the Premiership in 1992/3. In all major competitions since 1895 Wigan have a record 78 wins.

Three clubs have won all possible major Rugby League trophies in one season: Hunslet, 1907/8 season, Huddersfield, 1914/15 and Swinton, 1927/8, all won the Challenge Cup, League Championship, County Cup and County League (now defunct).

Senior match The highest aggregate score in a game where a senior club has been concerned is 121 points, when Huddersfield beat Swinton Park Rangers by 119 (19 goals, 27 tries) to 2 (one goal) in the first round of the Northern Union Cup on 28 Feb 1914. The highest score in League football is 102 points by Leeds *v.* Coventry (nil) on 12 Apr 1913. St Helens beat Carlisle 112–0 in the Lancashire Cup on 14 Sep 1986. In the Yorkshire Cup Hull Kingston Rovers beat Nottingham City 100–6 on 19 Aug 1990. The highest score in the First Division is 90 points by Leeds *v.* Barrow (nil) on 11 Feb 1990.

Challenge Cup Final The highest score in a Challenge Cup final is 38 points (8 tries, 7 goals) by Wakefield Trinity *v.* Hull (5) at Wembley, London on 14 May 1960. The record aggregate is 52 points when Wigan beat Hull 28–24 at Wembley on 4 May 1985. The greatest winning margin was 34 points when Huddersfield beat St Helens 37–3 at Oldham, Greater Manchester on 1 May 1915.

International match The highest score in an international match is Great Britain's 72–6 defeat of France in a Test match at Headingley, Leeds, W Yorks on 2 Apr 1993.

Touring teams The record score for a British team touring Australasia is 101 points by England *v.* South Australia (nil) at Adelaide in May 1914. The record for a touring team in Britain is 92 (10 goals, 24 tries) by Australia against Bramley 7 (2 goals and 1 try) at the Barley Mow Ground, Bramley, near Leeds on 9 Nov 1921.

Most points Leigh scored a record 1436 points (258 tries, 199 goals, 6 drop goals) in the 1985/6 season, playing in 43 Cup and League games.

Most points, goals and tries in a game   George Henry 'Tich' West (1882–1927) scored 53 points (10 goals and a record 11 tries) for Hull Kingston Rovers (73) in a Challenge Cup tie v. Brookland Rovers (5) on 4 Mar 1905.

The record for a League match is 42 (4 tries, 13 goals) by Dean John Marwood (b. 22 Feb 1970) in Workington Town's 78–0 win over Highfield on 1 Nov 1992.

The most goals in a Cup match is 22 kicked by James 'Jim' Sullivan (1903–77) for Wigan v. Flimby and Fothergill on 14 Feb 1925. The most goals in a League match is 15 by Michael Stacey (b. 9 Feb 1953) for Leigh v. Doncaster on 28 Mar 1976. The most tries in a League match is ten by Lionel Cooper (b. Australia, 1922–87) for Huddersfield v. Keighley on 17 Nov 1951.

Most points   *Season and career* The record number of points in a season was 496 by Benjamin Lewis Jones (Leeds) (b. 11 Apr 1931), 194 goals, 36 tries, in 1956/7.

Neil Fox (b. 4 May 1939) scored 6220 points (2575 goals including 4 drop goals, 358 tries) in a senior Rugby League career from 10 Apr 1956 to 19 Aug 1979, consisting of 4488 for Wakefield Trinity, 1089 for five other clubs, 228 for Great Britain, 147 for Yorkshire and 268 in other representative games.

Most tries   *Season and career* Albert Aaron Rosenfeld (1885–1970) (Huddersfield), an Australian-born wing-threequarter, scored 80 tries in 42 matches in the 1913/14 season.

Brian Bevan (Australia) (1924–91), a wing-threequarter, scored 796 tries in 18 seasons (16 with Warrington, two with Blackpool Borough) from 1945 to 1964. He scored 740 for Warrington, 17 for Blackpool and 39 in representative matches.

Most goals   *Season and career* The record number of goals in a season is 221, in 47 matches, by David Watkins

Longest kicks

Arthur Atkinson (1908–63) (Castleford) kicked a penalty from his own 25-yard line, a distance of 75 yd *68 m* in a League game at St Helens on 26 Oct 1929.

The longest drop goal is 61 yd *56 m* by Joseph Paul 'Joe' Lydon (b. 22 Nov 1963) for Wigan against Warrington in a Challenge Cup semi-final at Maine Road, Manchester on 25 Mar 1989.

(b. 5 Mar 1942) (Salford) in the 1972/3 season.

Jim Sullivan (Wigan) kicked 2867 goals in his club and representative career, 1921–46.

Most consecutive scores   David Watkins (Salford) played and scored in every club game during seasons 1972/3 and 1973/4, contributing 41 tries and 403 goals, a total of 929 points, in 92 games.

Individual international records   Jim Sullivan (Wigan) played in most internationals (60 for Wales and Great Britain, 1921–39), kicked most goals (160) and scored most points (329).

Michael Sullivan (no kin) (b. 12 Jan 1934) of Huddersfield, Wigan, St Helens, York and Dewsbury played in 51 international games for England and Great Britain and scored a record 45 tries, 1954–63.

Michael O'Connor (b. 30 Nov 1960) scored a record 30 points (4 tries, 7 goals) for Australia v. Papua New Guinea at Wagga Wagga, Australia on 20 Jul 1988.

Most Challenge Cup finals   The most appearances is eight by: Andrew 'Andy' Gregory (b. 10 Aug 1961) Widnes, 1981–2, 1984, Wigan 1988–92; and Shaun Edwards (b. 17 Oct 1966), Wigan, 1984–5, 1988–93. Both were on the winning side on seven occasions. Eric Batten (b. 13 Jun 1914) (Leeds, Bradford Northern and Featherstone Rovers) also played in a record eight Challenge Cup finals, including wartime guest appearances, between 1941 and 1952 and was on four winning sides.

635

Youngest and oldest players Harold Spencer Edmondson (1903–82) played his first League game for Bramley at 15 yr 81 days. The youngest representative player was Harold Wagstaff (1891–1939) who played for Yorkshire at 17 yr 141 days, and for England at 17 yr 228 days.

The youngest player in a Cup final was Shaun Edwards at 17 yr 201 days for Wigan when they lost 6–19 to Widnes at Wembley on 5 May 1984.

The youngest Great Britain international is Paul Newlove (b. 10 Aug 1971) who played in the first Test v. New Zealand on 21 Oct 1989 at Old Trafford, Greater Manchester, aged 18 yr 72 days. The oldest player for Great Britain was Jeffrey Grayshon (b. 4 Mar 1949) at 36 yr 250 days v. New Zealand at Elland Road, Leeds on 9 Nov 1985.

Most durable player The most appearances for one club is 774 by Jim Sullivan for Wigan, 1921–46. He played a record 928 first-class games in all. The longest continuous playing career is that of Augustus John 'Gus' Risman (b. 21 Mar 1911), who played his first game for Salford on 31 Aug 1929 and his last for Batley on 27 Dec 1954.

Keith Elwell (b. 12 Feb 1950) played in 239 consecutive games for Widnes from 5 May 1977 to 5 Sep 1982. In his career, 1972–85, he received a record 28 winners' or runners-up medals in major competitions.

Most and least successful teams Wigan won 31 consecutive league games from February 1970 to February 1971.

Australia won the World Cup for a record sixth time in 1992. They beat Great Britain in the final at Wembley in front of the largest crowd for an international. Below Bob Lindner shrugs off the challenge of Ellery Hanley and Kevin Ward, and left Australia celebrate.

(Photos: Allsport/Shaun Botterill)

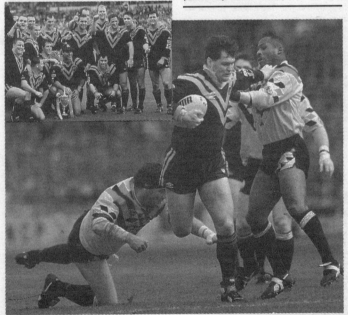

Despite winning the first four trophies of rugby league's Grand Slam—County Cup, Regal Trophy, Challenge Cup and League (seen here celebrating their success)—Wigan failed at the final hurdle in 1992/3, losing the Premiership to St Helens.

(Photo: Allsport/Steve Morton)

Huddersfield were undefeated for 40 league and cup games in 1913/14. Hull is the only club to win all League games in a season, 26 in Division II 1978/9. Runcorn Highfield holds the record of losing 55 consecutive League games from 29 Jan 1989 to 27 Jan 1991. The run was ended with a 12–12 draw with Carlisle on 3 Feb 1991.

Greatest crowds The greatest attendance at any Rugby League match is 102 569 for the Warrington *v.* Halifax Challenge Cup final replay at Odsal Stadium, Bradford on 5 May 1954.

The record attendance for any international match is 73 631 for the World Cup Final between Australia and Great Britain at Wembley Stadium, London on 24 Oct 1992.

National Cup Pilkington Recreation (St Helens, Merseyside) have won the National Cup four times (1975, 1979, 1980, 1982). John McCabe (b. 26 Jan 1952) has played in a record five National Cup finals, winning on each occasion. He played for Pilkington Recreation in each of their four successes and captained Thatto Heath (St Helens, Merseyside) to victory in 1987.

Record transfer fee
Martin Offiah (b. 29 Dec 1966) became the costliest transferred player on 3 Jan 1992 when Wigan paid Widnes a fee of £440 000.

Highest score Major competitions Humberside beat Carlisle by 138 points to nil in the second round of the National Inter-league Competition on 20 Oct 1984.

Most tries Simon Haughton (b. 10 Nov 1975) scored 130 tries, including nine in one game, from the prop-forward position for the Bingley under-14 side, W Yorks in the 1989/90 season.

Rugby Union

Records are based on the scoring system in force at the time.

World Cup

The World Cup has been held on two occasions, 1987 and 1991, with the winners being New Zealand and Australia respectively. The highest team score is New Zealand's 74–13 victory over Fiji at Christchurch on 27 May 1987 when they scored ten goals, two tries and two penalty goals. The individual match record is 30 (3 tries, 9 conversions) by Didier Camberabero (France) (b. 9 Jan 1961) *v.* Zimbabwe at Auckland on 2 Jun 1987. The leading scorer in the tournament is Grant James Fox (New Zealand) (b. 6 Jun 1962), with 170 points (including a record 126 in 1987).

International Championship

The International Championship was first contested by England, Ireland, Scotland and Wales in 1884. France first played in 1910.

Wales has won a record 21 times outright and tied for first a further 11 times to 1988. The most Grand Slams, winning all four matches, is ten by England 1913–14, 1921, 1923–4, 1928, 1957, 1980 and 1991–2.

Highest team score The highest score in an International Championship match

637

Most International Appearances

FRANCE	93	Serge Blanco (b. 31 Aug 1958)	1980–92
AUSTRALIA	73	David Ian Campese (b. 21 Oct 1962)	1982–93
IRELAND	69	Cameron Michael Henderson Gibson (b. 3 Dec 1942)	1964–79
ENGLAND	60	Rory Underwood (b. 19 Jun 1963)	1984–93
NEW ZEALAND	58	Gary William Whetton (b. 15 Dec 1959)	1981–91
WALES	55*	John Peter Rhys 'JPR' Williams (b. 2 Mar 1949)	1969–81
SCOTLAND	52	James Menzies 'Jim' Renwick (b. 12 Feb 1952)	1972–84
	52	Colin Thomas Deans (b. 3 May 1955)	1978–87
SOUTH AFRICA	38	Frederick Christoffel Hendrick Du Preez (b. 28 Nov 1935)	1960–71
	38	Jan Hendrik Ellis (b. 5 Jan 1943)	1965–76

* Gareth Owen Edwards (b. 12 Jul 1947) made a record 53 consecutive international appearances, never missing a match throughout his career for Wales, 1967–78. Willie John McBride (b. 6 Jun 1960) also had 53 consecutive appearances during his 63 games for Ireland.

was set at Swansea on 1 Jan 1910 when Wales beat France 49–14 (8 goals, 1 penalty goal, 2 tries, to 1 goal, 2 penalty goals, 1 try).

Season's scoring Jonathon Webb scored a record 67 points (3 tries, 11 penalty goals, 11 conversions) in the four games of an International Championship series in 1992. During this series, England scored a record 118 points in their four games.

Individual match records John 'Jack' Bancroft (1879–1942) kicked a record nine goals (8 conversions and 1 penalty goal) for Wales *v.* France at Swansea on 1 Jan 1910. Simon Hodgkinson kicked a Championship record seven penalty goals for England *v.* Wales at Cardiff on 19 Jan 1991.

Highest Team Scores

Internationals The highest score in any full international was when New Zealand beat Japan by 106–4 at Tokyo, Japan on 1 Nov 1987, although New Zealand did not award caps. France beat Paraguay 106–12 at Asunción, Paraguay on 28 Jun 1988.

The highest aggregate score for any international match between the Four Home Unions is 82 when England beat Wales by 82 points (7 goals, 1 drop goal and 6 tries) to nil at Blackheath, London on 19 Feb 1881. (Note: there was no point scoring in 1881.) The highest aggregate score in recent times between IRFB members is 79, when Australia beat

France 48–31 at Ballymore, Brisbane, Australia on 24 Jun 1990.

The highest score by any overseas side in an international in the British Isles is 44 points (7 goals, 1 drop goal and 2 tries) to nil when South Africa beat Scotland at Murrayfield, Edinburgh on 24 Nov 1951.

Tour match The record score for any international tour match is 117–6 for New Zealand's defeat of South Australia on 1 May 1974.

Match In Denmark, Comet beat Lindo by 194–0 on 17 Nov 1973. The highest British score is 174–0 by 7th Signal Regiment *v.* 4th Armoured Workshop, REME, on 5 Nov 1980 at Herford, Germany. Scores of over 200 points have been recorded in school matches, for example Radford School beat Hills Court 200 points (31 goals and 7 tries) to nil on 20 Nov 1886. The highest score in the Courage Clubs Championship is 146–0 by Billingham against Hartlepool Athletic in a Durham/Northumberland Division 3 match at Billingham, Co. Durham on 3 Oct 1987.

Season The highest number of points accumulated in a season by a club is 1917 points (including a record 345 tries) in 47 games by Neath, West Glamorgan in 1988/9.

Highest Individual Scores

Internationals Phil Bennett (Wales) (b. 24 Oct 1948) scored 34 points (2 tries, 10 conversions, 2 penalty goals) for

638

The most appearances in rugby union's International Championship is 42 by Serge Blanco and Philippe Sella, both of France. Sella (b. 14 Feb 1962), the world's most capped centre, is seen here in action against Scotland.

(Photo: Allsport)

Wales v. Japan at Tokyo on 24 Sep 1975, when Wales won 82–6. The highest individual points score in any match between members of the International Board is 26 by Allan Roy Hewson (b. 6 Jun 1954) (1 try, 2 conversions, 5 penalty goals and a drop goal) for New Zealand against Australia at Auckland on 11 Sep 1982.

Patrice Lagisquet (b. 4 Sep 1962) scored seven tries for France v. Paraguay on 28 Jun 1988. The most tries in an international match between IRFB members is five by George Campbell Lindsay (1863–1905) for Scotland v. Wales on 26 Feb 1887, and by Douglas 'Daniel' Lambert (1883–1915) for England v. France on 5 Jan 1907. Ian Scott Smith (Scotland) (1903–72) scored a record six consecutive international tries in 1925, comprising the last three v. France and two weeks later, the first three v. Wales. A record eight penalty goals were kicked by Mark Andrew Wyatt (b. 12 Apr 1961) when he scored all Canada's points in their 24–19 defeat of Scotland at St John, New Brunswick, Canada on 25 May 1991.

Career In all internationals Michael Patrick Lynagh (b. 25 Oct 1963) scored a record 762 points in 61 matches for Australia, 1984–93. The most by a British player is 490 by Andrew Gavin

Hastings (b. 3 Jan 1962), 424 for Scotland and 66 for the British Lions, 1986–93. The most tries is 54 by David Campese (b. 21 Oct 1962) in 73 internationals for Australia, 1982–93.

Season The first-class season scoring record is 581 points by Samuel Arthur Doble (1944–77) of Moseley, in 52 matches in 1971/2. He also scored 47 points for England in South Africa out of season.

Andy Higgin (b. 4 Mar 1963) scored a record 28 drop goals in a season in first-class rugby, for the Vale of Lune in 1986/7.

Career William Henry 'Dusty' Hare (b. 29 Nov 1952) scored 7337 points in first-class games from 1971–89, comprising 1800 for Nottingham, 4427 for Leicester, 240 for England, 88 for the British Lions and 782 in other representative matches.

Most tries Alan John Morley (b. 25 Jun 1950) scored 473 tries in senior rugby in 1968–86 including 378 for Bristol, a record for one club. John Huins scored 85 tries in 1953/4, 73 for St Luke's College, Exeter and 12 more for Neath and in trial games.

Match Jannie van der Westhuizen scored 80 points (14 tries, 9 conversions, 1 dropped goal, 1 penalty goal) for Carnarvon (88) v. Williston (12) at North West Cape, South Africa on 11 March 1972.

Most international appearances
Cameron Michael Henderson Gibson (b. 3 Dec 1942) played in 69 internationals for Ireland, 1964–79, a record for matches between the seven member countries of the International Rugby Football Board and France. Including 12 appearances for the British Lions, he played in a total of 81 international matches. William James 'Willie John' McBride (b. 6 Jun 1940) made a record 17 appearances for the British Lions, as well as 63 for Ireland.

Youngest international Edinburgh Academy pupils Ninian Jamieson Finlay (1858–1936) and Charles Reid (1864–1909) were both 17 yr 36 days old when they played for Scotland v. England in 1875 and 1881 respectively. However, as Finlay had one less leap

Highest posts

The world's highest rugby union goal posts are 33·54m *110ft ½in* high at the Roan Antelope Rugby Union Club, Luanshya, Zambia. The posts at Old Halesonines RFC, Stourbridge, W Mids are 22·16m *72ft 8½in*.

All-rounder

Canadian international Barrie Burnham scored all possible ways; try, conversion, penalty goal, drop goal, goal from mark, for Meralomas *v.* Georgians (20–11) at Vancouver, BC on 26 Feb 1966.

Most appearances

Roy Evans of Banbury played a record 1193 games of rugby union all of which were played in the front row at tight head prop. His total includes 1007 played for Osterley from 12 Sep 1950–29 Apr 1989, a record for one club.

Fastest try

The fastest try in an international game was when Herbert Leo 'Bart' Price (1899–1943) scored for England v. Wales at Twickenham on 20 Jan 1923 less than 10sec after kick-off. The fastest try in any game was scored in 8sec by Andrew Brown for Widden Old Boys v. Old Ashtonians at Gloucester on 22 Nov 1990.

year in his lifetime up to his first cap, the outright record must be credited to him. Semi Hekasilau Spec Taupeaafe played in a Test for Tonga against Western Samoa in 1989, aged 16.

County Championships The County Championships (instituted 1889) have been won a record 16 times by Lancashire (between 1891 and 1993). The most individual appearances is 104

by Richard Trickey (Sale) (b. 6 Mar 1945) for Lancashire between 1964 and 1978.

Club Championships The most outright wins in the RFU Club Competition (John Player Cup, 1971–87, now Pilkington Cup) is seven by Bath, 1984–7, 1989–90, 1992. The highest team score (and aggregate) in the final is for Bath's 48–6 win over Gloucester in 1990. In the 1989 season Bath completed the double having won the English league title, the Courage Clubs Championship, which was founded in the 1987/8 season. Bath repeated this feat in the 1992 season. The most wins in the Welsh Rugby Union Challenge Cup (Schweppes Welsh Cup, instituted 1971/2) is nine by Llanelli, 1973–6, 1985, 1988 and 1991–3. The highest team score in the final is 30 by Llanelli against Cardiff (7) in 1973. The highest aggregate is when Cardiff beat Newport 28–21 in 1986. Llanelli achieved the first league and cup double in Wales in 1993. The most wins in the Scottish League Division One (instituted 1973/4) is ten by Hawick between 1973 and 1986.

Seven-a-sides Seven-a-side rugby dates from 28 Apr 1883 when Melrose RFC Borders, in order to alleviate the poverty of a club in such a small town, staged a seven-a-side tournament. The idea was that of Ned Haig, the town's butcher.

Hong Kong Sevens This, the world's most prestigious international tournament for seven-a-side teams, was first held in 1976. The record of seven wins is held by Fiji, 1977–8, 1980, 1984, 1990–92.

Middlesex Seven-a-sides The Middlesex Seven-a-sides were inaugurated in 1926 and have been won a record 12 times by Harlequins, 1926–9, 1933, 1935, 1967, 1978, 1986–90.

Greatest crowd The record paying attendance is 104 000 for Scotland's 12–10 win over Wales at Murrayfield, Edinburgh on 1 Mar 1975.

Longest kicks The longest recorded successful drop goal is 82m *90yd* by Gerald Hamilton 'Gerry' Brand (b. 8 Oct 1906) for South Africa *v.* England at Twickenham, Greater London, on 2 Jan 1932. This was taken 6m *7yd* inside the

England 'half', 50 m *55 yd* from the posts, and dropped over the dead ball line. The place kick record is reputed to be 91m *100 yd* at Richmond Athletic Ground, London, by Douglas Francis Theodore Morkel (1886–1950) in an unsuccessful penalty for South Africa *v.* Surrey on 19 Dec 1906. This was not measured until 1932. In the match Bridlington School 1st XV *v.* an Army XV at Bridlington, Humberside on 29 Jan 1944, Ernie Cooper (b. 21 May 1926), captaining the school, landed a penalty from a measured 74m *81 yd* from the post with a kick which carried over the dead ball line. The record in an international was set at 64·22m *70 yd 8½ in* by Paul Huw Thorburn (b. 24 Nov 1962) for Wales *v.* Scotland on 1 Feb 1986.

Most successful team The Feilding senior 4ths of New Zealand played 108 successive games without defeat from 1984–9. The Chiltern mini rugby side, from their formation as an Under-8 side, played 213 games without defeat, 29 Sep 1985–8 Apr 1990.

Women's Rugby

The first women's World Cup was contested by 12 teams in 1991, with the USA beating England 19–6 in the final at Cardiff, S Glam on 14 Apr 1991.

Shinty

Most titles Newtonmore, Highland has won the Camanachd Association Challenge Cup (instituted 1896) a record 28 times, 1907–86. David Ritchie (b. 9 Jun 1944) and Hugh Chisholm (b. 14 Oct 1949) of Newtonmore, have won a record 12 winners' medals. In 1923 the Furnace Club, Argyll won the cup without conceding a goal throughout the competition.

In 1984 Kingussie Camanachd Club won all five senior competitions, including the Camanachd Cup final. This feat was equalled by Newtonmore in 1985.

Highest scores The highest Scottish Cup final score was in 1909 when Newtonmore beat Furnace 11–3 at Glasgow, Dr Johnnie Cattanach scoring eight hails or goals. In 1938 John Macmillan Mactaggart scored ten hails for Mid-Argyll in a Camanachd Cup match.

Shooting

Most Olympic medals Carl Townsend Osburn (USA) (1884–1966), in 1912, 1920 and 1924, won a record 11, five gold, four silver and two bronze. Six other marksmen have won five gold medals. The only marksman to win three individual gold medals has been Gudbrand Gudbrandsönn Skattebœ (Norway) (1875–1965) in 1906. Separate events for women were first held in 1984.

Bisley The National Rifle Association was instituted in 1859. The Queen's (King's) Prize has been shot since 1860 and has only once been won by a woman, Marjorie Elaine Foster (1894–1974) (score 280) on 19 Jul 1930. Arthur George Fulton (1887–1972) won three times (1912, 1926, 1931). Both his father and his son also won the Prize.

The highest score (possible 300) for the final of the Queen's Prize is 295 by Lindsay Peden (Scotland) on 24 Jul 1982. The record for the Silver Medals is 150 (possible 150) by Martin John Brister (City Rifle Club) (b. 1951) and (Lord) John Swansea (b. 1 Jan 1925) on 24 Jul 1971. This was equalled by John Henry Carmichael (WRA Bromsgrove RC) on 28 Jul 1979 and Robert Stafford on 26 Jul 1980, with the size of the bullseyes reduced.

Small-bore The National Small-Bore Rifle Association of Britain was formed in 1901. The British team record (1989 target) is 1976/2000 by Middlesex in 1990–91.

The British individual small-bore rifle record for 60 shots prone is 597/600, held jointly by Philip Scanlon (b. 4 Feb 1951), Alister Allan (b. 28 Jan 1944) and John Booker (b. 19 Jul 1940).

Clay pigeon Most world titles have been won by Susan Nattrass (Canada) (b. 5 Nov 1950) with six, 1974–9, 1977–9, 1981. The maximum 200/200 was achieved by Ricardo Ruiz Rumoroso at the Spanish Clay Pigeon Championships at Zaragossa on 12 Jun

641

Shooting–Individual World Records

In 1986, the International Shooting Union (UIT) introduced new regulations for determining major championships and world records. Now the leading competitors undertake an additional round with a target sub-divided to tenths of a point for rifle and pistol shooting, and an extra 25 shots for trap and skeet. Harder targets have since been introduced and the table below shows the world records, as recognised by the UIT on 1 Jan 1993, for the 13 Olympic shooting disciplines, giving in brackets the score for the number of shots specified plus the score in the additional round.

MEN

EVENT	Score		Name and Country	Venue	Date
FREE RIFLE 50m 3×40 shots	1287·9	(1186+101·9)	Rajmond Debevec (Slovenia)	Munich, Germany	29 Aug 1992
FREE RIFLE 50m 60 Shots Prone	703·5	(599+104·5)	Jens Harskov (Denmark)	Zürich, Switzerland	6 Jun 1991
AIR RIFLE 10m 60 shots	699·4	(596+103·4)	Rajmond Debevec (Yugoslavia)	Zürich, Switzerland	7 Jun 1990
FREE PISTOL 50m 60 shots	671	(579+92)	Sergey Pyzhyanov (USSR)	Munich, Germany	30 May 1990
	671	(577+94)	Spas Koprinkov (Bulgaria)	Moscow, USSR	9 Aug 1990
RAPID-FIRE PISTOL 25m 60 shots	891	(594+297)	Ralf Schumann (West Germany)	Munich, Germany	3 Jun 1989
AIR PISTOL 10m 60 shots	695·1	(593+102·1)	Sergey Pyzhyanov (USSR)	Munich, Germany	13 Oct 1989
RUNNING TARGET 10m 30+30 shots	679	(582+97)	Lubos Racansky (Czechoslovakia)	Munich, Germany	30 May 1991

WOMEN

EVENT	Score		Name and Country	Venue	Date
STANDARD RIFLE 50m 3×20 shots	689·3	(590+99·3)	Vessela Letcheva (Bulgaria)	Munich, Germany	28 Aug 1992
AIR RIFLE 10m 40 shots	500·8	(399+101·8)	Valentina Cherkasova (USSR)	Los Angeles, USA	23 Mar 1991
SPORT PISTOL 25m 60 shots	693	(593+100)	Nino Salukvadze (USSR)	Zagreb, Yugoslavia	13 Jul 1989
AIR PISTOL 10m 40 shots	492·4	(392+100·4)	Lieselotte Breker (West Germany)	Zagreb, Yugoslavia	18 May 1989

OPEN

EVENT	Score		Name and Country	Venue	Date
TRAP 200 targets	224	(200+24)	Jörg Damme (West Germany)	Moscow, USSR	18 Aug 1990
	224	(200+24)	Giovanni Pellielo (Italy)	Munich, Germany	30 Aug 1992
SKEET 200 targets	225	(200+25)	Axel Wegner (Germany)	Munich, Germany	31 Aug 1991
	225	(200+25)	Hennie Dompeling (Netherlands)	Munich, Germany	31 Aug 1991

Highest score in 24 hours

The Easingwold Rifle and Pistol Club team of John Smith, Edward Kendall, Phillip Kendall and Paul Duffield scored 120 242 points (averaging 95·66 per card) on 6–7 Aug 1983.

Championships at Zaragossa on 12 Jun 1983.

Noel D. Townend achieved the maximum 200 consecutive down-the-line targets at Nottingham and District Gun Club, Nottingham on 21 Aug 1983.

Bench rest shooting The smallest group on record at 914 m *1000 yd* is 11·112 cm *4·375 in* by Earl Chronister (USA) with a ·30-378 Weatherby Mag at Williamsport, Pennsylvania, USA on 12 Jul 1987. The smallest at 500 m *546 yd* is 5·834 cm *2·297 in* by Dennis Tobler (Australia) using a ·30-06 rifle of his own design at Canberra, Australia on 28 Mar 1992.

Skiing

Most titles *World/Olympic Championships (Alpine)* The World Alpine Championships were inaugurated at Mürren, Switzerland, in 1931. The greatest number of titles won has been by Christl Cranz (b. 1 Jul 1914) of Germany, with seven individual: four slalom (1934, 1937–9) and three downhill (1935, 1937, 1939), and five combined (1934–5, 1937–9). She also won the gold medal for the Combined in the 1936 Olympics. The most won by a man is seven by Anton 'Toni' Sailer (Austria) (b. 17 Nov 1935), who won all four in 1956 (giant slalom, slalom, downhill and the non-Olympic Alpine combination) and the downhill, giant slalom and combined in 1958.

World/Olympic Championships (Nordic) The first World Nordic Championships were those of the 1924 Winter Olympics in Chamonix, France. The greatest number of titles won is 11 by Gunde Svan (Sweden) (b. 12 Jan 1962), seven individual; 15km 1989, 30km 1985 and 1991, 50km 1985 and 1989, and Olympics, 15km 1984, 50km 1988: and

four relays; 4×10km, 1987 and 1989, and Olympics, 1984 and 1988. The most titles won by a woman is nine by Galina Alekseyevna Kulakova (USSR) (b. 29 Apr 1942), five individual and four relay in 1970–78. The most medals is 23 by Raisa Petrovna Smetanina (USSR) (b. 29 Feb 1952) including seven gold, 1974–92. Ulrich Wehling (GDR) (b. 8 Jul 1952) with the Nordic combined in 1972, 1976 and 1980, is the only skier to win the same event at three successive Olympics. The most titles won by a jumper is five by Birger Ruud (b. 23 Aug 1911) of Norway, in 1931–2 and 1935–7. Ruud is the only person to win Olympic events in each of the dissimilar Alpine and Nordic disciplines. In 1936 he won the Ski-jumping and the Alpine downhill (which was not then a separate event, but only a segment of the Combined event).

World Cup The World Cup was introduced for Alpine events in 1967. The most individual event wins is 86 (46 giant slalom, 40 slalom from a total of 287 races) by Ingemar Stenmark (Sweden) (b. 18 Mar 1956) in 1974–89, including a men's record 13 in one season in 1978/9, of which 10 were part of a record 14 successive giant slalom wins from 18 Mar 1978, his 22nd birthday, to 21 Jan 1980. Franz Klammer (Austria) (b. 3 Dec 1953) won a record 25 downhill races, 1974–84. Annemarie Moser (*née* Pröll) (Austria) (b. 27 Mar 1953) had a women's record 62 individual event wins, 1970–79. She had a

Snow shoeing

The IASSRF (International Amateur SnowShoe Racing Federation) record for covering 1 mile *1·6 km* is 5 min 56·7 sec by Nick Akers of Edmonton, Alberta, Canada on 3 Feb 1991. The 100m record is 14·07 sec by Jeremy Badeau at Canaseraga, New York, USA on 31 May 1991.

Longest run

The longest all-downhill ski run in the world is the Weissfluhjoch-Küblis Parsenn course, near Davos, Switzerland, which measures 12·23km *7·6 miles*.

Most Olympic Skiing Titles

MEN

ALPINE	3	Anton 'Toni' Sailer (Austria) (b. 17 Nov 1935)	Downhill, slalom, giant slalom, 1956
	3	Jean-Claude Killy (France) (b. 30 Aug 1943)	Downhill, slalom, giant slalom 1968
	3	Alberto Tomba (Italy) (b. 19 Dec 1966) *	Slalom, giant slalom, 1988; giant slalom, 1992
NORDIC	...4	Sixten Jernberg (Sweden) (b. 6 Feb 1929) *	50km 1956; 30km 1960; 50km and 4×10km 1964
	4	Gunde Svan (Sweden) (b. 12 Mar 1962)	15km and 4×10km 1984; 50km and 4×10km 1988
	4	Thomas Wassberg (Sweden) (b. 27 Mar 1956)	15km 1980; 50km 1984; 4×10km 1984, 1988
Jumping	...4	Matti Nykänen (Finland) (b. 17 Jul 1963)	70m hill 1988; 90m hill 1984, 1988; Team 1988

WOMEN

ALPINE	2	Andrea Mead-Lawrence (USA) (b. 19 Apr 1932)	Slalom, giant slalom 1952
	2	Marielle Goitschel (France) (b. 28 Sep 1945)	Giant slalom 1964; slalom 1968
	2	Marie-Thérèse Nadig (Switzerland) (b. 8 Mar 1954)	Downhill, giant slalom 1972
	2	Rosi Mittermaier (now Neureuther) (West Germany) (b. 5 Aug 1950)	Downhill, slalom 1976
	2	Hanni Wenzel (Liechtenstein) (b. 14 Dec 1956) *	Giant slalom, slalom 1980
	2	Vreni Schneider (Switzerland) (b. 26 Nov 1964)	Giant slalom, slalom 1988
	2	Petra Kronberger (Austria) (b. 21 Feb 1969)	Slalom, combined, 1992
NORDIC	...4	Galina Kulakova (USSR) (b. 29 Apr 1942)	5km, 10km and 3×5km relay 1972; 4×5km relay 1976
	4	Raisa Smetanina (USSR/CIS) (b. 29 Feb 1952) *	10km, 4×5km, 1976; 5km, 1980; 4×5km, 1992
(individual)	.3	Marja-Liisa Hämäläinen (Finland) (b. 10 Aug 1955)	5km, 10km and 20km 1984

Most medals (women) 10, Raisa Smetanina, four gold, five silver and one bronze.

(men) 9, Sixten Jernberg, four golds, three silver and two bronze.

In Alpine skiing, the record is four; Hanni Wenzel won a silver in the 1980 downhill and a bronze in the 1976 slalom, and Alberto Tomba won a silver in the 1992 slalom.

record 11 consecutive downhill wins from Dec 1972 to Jan 1974. Vreni Schneider (Switzerland) (b. 26 Nov 1964) won a record 13 events (and a combined) including all seven slalom events in the 1988/9 season.

The Nations' Cup, awarded on the combined results of the men and women in the World Cup, has been won a record 14 times by Austria 1969, 1973–80, 1982, 1990–93.

Ski-jumping The longest ski-jump ever recorded is one of 194 m *636 ft* by Piotr Fijas (Poland) at Planica, Yugoslavia on 14 Mar 1987. The women's record is 110 m *361 ft* by Tiina Lehtola (Finland) (b. 3 Aug 1962) at Ruka, Finland on 29 Mar 1981. The longest dry ski-jump is 92 m *302 ft* by Hubert Schwarz (West Germany) at Berchtesgarten, Germany on 30 Jun 1981.

Highest speed The official world record, as recognized by the International Ski Federation for a skier, is 233·615 km/h *145·161 mph* by Philippe Goitschel (France) on 21 Apr 1993 and the fastest by a woman is 219·245 km/h *136·232 mph* by Tarja Mulari (Finland) on 22 Feb 1992, both at Les Arcs, France. On 16 Apr 1988 Graham Wilkie (GB) (b. 21 Sep 1959) set a British men's record of 219·914 km/h *136·648 mph* and Patrick Knaff (France) set a one-legged record of 185·567 km/h *115·306 mph*. On 21 Apr 1993, a British women's record was set by Divina Galica (b. 13 Aug 1944) at 200·667 km/h *124·689 mph*, also at Les Arcs, France.

The highest average speed in the Olympic downhill race was 104·53 km/h *64·95 mph* by William D. Johnson (USA) (b. 30 Mar 1960) at Sarajevo,

Marc Girardelli won a record fifth World Cup overall title in 1993.

(Photo: Allsport/Vandystadt/Zoom)

Yugoslavia on 16 Feb 1984. The fastest in a World Cup downhill is 107·82 km/h *67·00 mph* by Harti Weirather (Austria) (b. 25 Jan 1958) at Kitzbühel, Austria on 15 Jan 1982.

Cross-country Bill Koch (USA) (b. 13 Apr 1943) on 26 Mar 1981 skied ten times round a 5 km *3·11 mile* loop on Marlborough Pond, near Putney, Vermont, USA. He completed the 50 km in 1 hr 59 min 47 sec, an average speed of 25·045 km/h *15·57 mph*. A race includes uphill and downhill sections; the record time for a 50 km race in World Championships or Olympic Games is 2 hr 3 min 31·6 sec by Torgny Mogren (Sweden) in 1991, an average speed of 24·28 km/h *15·09 mph*.

Yelena Välbe, winner of bronze in all four individual events at the 1992 Olympics, won the women's World Cup Nordic overall title for a record equalling third time in 1993.

(Photo: Allsport/Pascal Rondeau)

Most World Cup Titles

ALPINE SKIING (instituted 1967)

MEN

OVERALL	5	Marc Girardelli (Luxembourg)	1985–6, 1989, 1991, 1993
DOWNHILL	5	Franz Klammer (Austria)	1975–8, 1983
SLALOM	8	Ingemar Stenmark (Sweden)	1975–81, 1983
GIANT SLALOM	7	Ingemar Stenmark	1975–6, 1978–81, 1984
SUPER GIANT SLALOM	4	Pirmin Zurbriggen (Switzerland)	1987–90

Two men have won four titles in one year: Jean-Claude Killy (France) (b. 30 Aug 1943) won all four possible disciplines (downhill, slalom, giant slalom and overall) in 1967; and Pirmin Zurbriggen (Switzerland) (b. 4 Feb 1963) won four of the five possible disciplines (downhill, giant slalom, super giant slalom (added 1986) and overall) in 1987.

WOMEN

OVERALL	6	Annemarie Moser-Pröll (Austria)	1971–5, 1979
DOWNHILL	7	Annemarie Moser-Pröll	1971–5, 1978–9
SLALOM	4	Erika Hess (Switzerland)	1981–3, 1985
	4	Vreni Schneider (Switzerland)	1989–90, 1992–3
GIANT SLALOM	4	Vreni Schneider (Switzerland)	1986–7, 1989, 1991
SUPER GIANT SLALOM	4	Carole Merle (France)	1989–92

NORDIC SKIING (instituted 1981)

MEN

JUMPING	4	Matti Nykänen (Finland)	1983, 1985–6, 1988
CROSS-COUNTRY	5	Gunde Svan (Sweden)	1984–6, 1988–9

WOMEN

CROSS-COUNTRY	3	Marjo Matikainen (Finland)	1986–8
	3	Yelena Välbe (USSR/Russia)	1989, 1991–2

Longest races The world's greatest Nordic ski race is the Vasaloppet, which commemorates an event of 1521 when Gustav Vasa (1496–1560), later King Gustavus Eriksson, fled 85·8 km *53·3 miles* from Mora to Sälen, Sweden. He was overtaken by loyal, speedy scouts on skis, who persuaded him to return eastwards to Mora to lead a rebellion and become the king of Sweden. The re-enactment of this return journey is now an annual event at 89 km *55·3 miles*. There were a record 10 934 starters on 6 Mar 1977 and a record 10 650 finishers on 4 Mar 1979. The fastest time is 3 hr 48 min 55 sec, by Bengt Hassis (Sweden) on 2 Mar 1986.

The Finlandia Ski Race, 75 km *46·6 miles* from Hämeenlinna to Lahti, on 26 Feb 1984 had a record 13 226 starters and 12 909 finishers.

The longest downhill race is the *Inferno* in Switzerland, 15·8 km *9·8 miles* from the top of the Schilthorn to Lauterbrunnen. The record entry was 1401 in 1981 and the record time 13 min 53.40 sec by Urs von Allmen (Switzerland) in 1991.

Long-distance *Nordic* In 24 hours Seppo-Juhani Savolainen covered 415·5 km *258·2 miles* at Saariselkä, Finland on 8–9 Apr 1988. The women's record is 330 km *205·05 miles* by Sisko Kainulaisen at Jyväskylä, Finland on 23–24 Mar 1985.

Freestyle The first World Championships were held at Tignes, France in 1986, titles being awarded in ballet, moguls, aerials and combined. A record two titles have been won by a number of skiers. Of these, Edgar Grospiron (France), who won moguls in 1989 and 1991, has also won an Olympic title,

1992. The most Overall titles in the World Cup (instituted 1980) is ten by Connie Kissling (Switzerland) (b. 18 Jul 1961), 1983–92. The men's record is five by Eric Laboureix (France) (b. 12 Apr 1962), 1986–7, 1989–91.

Longest lift The longest gondola ski lift is 6239 m *3·88 miles* long at Grindelwald-Männlichen, Switzerland (in two sections, but one gondola). The longest chair lift in the world was the Alpine Way to Kosciusko Chalet lift above

Philippe Goitschel (France) failed to win gold in speed skiing at the 1992 Olympics by the narrow margin of ½ km/h, but a year later set the official world speed record.
(Photo: Allsport/Nathan Bilow)

Thredbo, near the Snowy Mountains, New South Wales, Australia. It took from

45 to 75 min to ascend the 5·6 km *3·5 miles*, according to the weather. It has now collapsed. The highest is at Chacaltaya, Bolivia, rising to 5029 m *16 500ft*.

Ski-bob *Origins* The ski-bob was the invention of J. C. Stevenson of Hartford, Connecticut, USA in 1891, and patented (No. 47334) on 19 Apr 1892 as a 'bicycle with ski-runners'. The *Fédération Internationale de Skibob* was founded on 14 Jan 1961 in Innsbruck, Austria and the first World Championships were held at Bad Hofgastein, Austria in 1967.

The highest speed attained is 166 km/h *103·1 mph* by Erich Brenter (Austria) (b. 1940) at Cervinia, Italy in 1964.

World Championships The only ski-bobbers to retain a world championship are: men Alois Fischbauer (Austria) (b. 6 Oct 1951), 1973 and 1975, Robert Mühlberger (West Germany), 1979 and 1981; women Gerhilde Schiffkorn (Austria) (b. 22 Mar 1950), 1967 and 1969, Gertrude Geberth (Austria) (b. 18 Oct 1951), 1971 and 1973.

Grass Skiing

World Championships (now awarded for Super-G, giant slalom, slalom and combined) were first held in 1979. The most titles won is ten by Ingrid Hirschhofer (Austria) 1979–89. The most by a man is seven by Erwin Gansner (Switzerland) 1981–7.

The speed record is 86·88 km/h *53·99 mph* by Erwin Gansner at Owen, Germany on 5 Sep 1982. At the same venue Laurence Beck set a British record of 79·49 km/h *49·39 mph* on 8 Sep 1985.

Skipping

10 Mile skip-run Vadivelu Karunakaren (India) skipped 10 miles *16 km* in 58 min at Madras, India, 1 Feb 1990.

Most turns *One hour* 14 628 by Park Bong-tae (South Korea) at Pusan, South Korea, 2 Jul 1989.

On a single rope, team of 90 160 by students from the Nishigoshi Higashi

Elementary School, Kumamoto, Japan, 27 Feb 1987.

On a tightrope 358 (consecutive) by Julian Albulet (USA) at Las Vegas, Nevada, USA, 2 Jul 1990.

Most on a rope (minimum 12 turns obligatory) 220 by a team at the International Rope Skipping Competition, Greeley, Colorado, USA, 28 Jun 1990.

Snooker

Most world titles The World Professional Championship (instituted 1927) was won a record 15 times by Joe Davis, on the first 15 occasions it was contested, 1927–40 and 1946. The most wins in the Amateur Championships (instituted 1963) have been two by: Gary Owen (England) in 1963 and 1966; Ray Edmonds (England) 1972 and 1974; and Paul Mifsud (Malta) 1985–6.

Maureen Baynton (*née* Barrett) won a record eight Women's Amateur Championships between 1954 and 1968, as well as seven at billiards.

World Championships *Youngest* The youngest man to win a world title is Stephen O'Connor (Ireland) (b. 16 Oct 1972), who was 18 yr 40 days when he won the World Amateur Snooker Championship in Colombo, Sri Lanka on 25 Nov 1990. Stephen Hendry (Scotland) (b. 13 Jan 1969) became the youngest World Professional champion, at 21 yr 106 days on 29 Apr 1990. He had been the youngest winner of a major professional title, at 18 yr 285 days, when he won the Rothmans Grand Prix on 25 Oct 1987.

Stacey Hillyard (GB) (b. 5 Sep 1969) won the Women's World Amateur Championship in October 1984 at the age of 15.

Highest breaks Over 200 players have achieved the 'maximum' break of 147. The first to do so was E. J. 'Murt' O'Donoghue (b. New Zealand 1901) at Griffiths, New South Wales, Australia on 26 Sep 1934. The first officially ratified 147 was by Joe Davis against Willie Smith at Leicester Square Hall, London on 22 Jan 1955. The first achieved in a

Skittles 24 hours

The highest score at West Country skittles by a team of eight is 99 051 by the 'Alkies' Skittles team at Courtlands Holiday Inn, Torquay, Devon on 4–5 Apr 1987; they reset the skittles after every ball. The highest hood skittle score in 24 hours is 136 080 pins by 12 players from the Yardley Gobion Sport and Social Club at the Yardley Gobion Recreation Centre, Northants on 15–16 May 1992. The highest long alley score is 82 767 by a team from the White Hart, Headless Cross, Worcs on 25–26 Apr 1992. The highest table skittle score in 24 hours is 116 047 skittles by 12 players at the Castle Mona, Newcastle, Staffs on 15–16 Apr 1990.

Century snooker breaks

Three consecutive century breaks were first compiled in a major tournament by Steve Davis: 108, 101 and 104 at Stoke-on-Trent, Staffs on 10 Sep 1988. Doug Mountjoy (b. 8 Jun 1942) equalled the feat: 131, 106 and 124 at Preston, Lancs on 27 Nov 1988. Jim Meadowcroft (b. 15 Dec 1946) made consecutive frame clearances of 105, 115, 117 and 125 in witnessed practice at Connaught Leisure Centre, Worthing, W Sussex on 27 Jan 1982.

major tournament were by John Spencer (b. 18 Sep 1935) at Slough, Berks on 13 Jan 1979, but the table had oversized pockets, and by Steve Davis (b. 22 Aug 1957), who had a ratified break of 147 against John Spencer in the Lada Classic at Oldham, Greater Manchester on 11 Jan 1982. The youngest to score a competitive maximum was Ronnie O'Sullivan (b. 5 Dec 1975) at 15 yr 98 days during the English Amateur Championship (Southern Area) at Aldershot, Hants on 13 Mar 1991. Cliff Thorburn (Canada) (b. 16 Jan 1948) was first to make two tournament 147 breaks on 23 Apr 1983 (the first in the World Professional Championships) and 8 Mar 1989. Paul Ebdon (b. 27 Aug 1970) and James Wattana (Thailand) (b. 17 Jan 1970) have also achieved this feat.

Steve Duggan (b. 10 Apr 1958) made a break of 148 in a witnessed practice frame in Doncaster, S Yorks on 27 Apr 1988. The break involved a free ball, which therefore created an 'extra' red, when all 15 reds were still on the table. In these very exceptional circumstances, the maximum break is 155. The only '16 red' clearance ever completed in a tournament was by Steve James (b. 2 May 1961) who made 135 against Alex Higgins (b. 18 Mar 1949) in the World Professional Championships at Sheffield, S Yorks on 14 Apr 1990.

The world amateur record break is 147 by Geet Sethi (India) in the Indian Amateur Championships on 21 Feb 1988.

The first century break by a woman in competitive play was 114 by Stacey Hillyard in a league match at Bournemouth, Dorset on 15 Jan 1985. The highest break by a woman in a professional competition is 133 by Allison Fisher in the Dubai Duty Free Classic at Blackpool, Lancs on 1 Sep 1992.

Allison Fisher, who has won the women's World Snooker Championship six times, holds the women's record for the highest break with 133.

(Photo: Allsport/Howard Boylan)

Stephen Hendry celebrates winning the World Professional Championship. In this tournament he has compiled a record 35 breaks of 100 or more, while in all competitions his career total is 206, also a record.

(Photo: Allsport/Howard Boylan)

Longest unbeaten run From 17 Mar 1990 to his defeat by Jimmy White (b. 2 May 1962) on 13 Jan 1991, Stephen Hendry won five successive titles and 36 consecutive matches in ranking tournaments. During the summer of 1992, Ronnie O'Sullivan won 38 consecutive matches but these were in qualifying competitions.

Softball

Most titles The USA has won the men's world championship (instituted 1966) five times, 1966, 1968, 1976 (shared), 1980 and 1988, and the women's title

(instituted 1965) four times in 1974, 1978, 1986 and 1990. The world's first slow-pitch championships for men's teams was held in Oklahoma City, USA in 1987, when the winners were the USA.

Speedway

World Championships The World Speedway Championship was inaugurated at Wembley, London on 10 Sep 1936. The most wins has been six by Ivan Gerald Mauger (New Zealand) (b. 4 Oct 1939) in 1968–70, 1972, 1977 and 1979. Barry Briggs (New Zealand) (b. 30 Dec 1934) made a record 18 appearances in the finals (1954–70, 1972), won the world title in 1957–8, 1964 and 1966 and scored a record 201 points from 87 races.

Ivan Mauger also won four World Team Cups (three for GB), two World Pairs (including one unofficial) and three world long track titles. Ove Fundin (Sweden) (b. 23 May 1933) won 12 world titles: five individual, one Pairs, and six World Team Cup medals in 1956–70. In 1985 Erik Gundersen (Denmark) (b. 8 Oct 1959) became the first man to hold world titles at individual, pairs, team and long-track events simultaneously.

The World Pairs Championships (instituted unofficially 1968, officially 1970) have been won a record eight times by Denmark, 1979, 1985–91. The most suc-

Speedway

Leicester are the only team to have used the same seven riders in a complete League programme. This was in 1969 when the same riders rode in all of the 36 matches.

Unbeaten sequences at squash

Heather McKay was unbeaten from 1962 to 1980. Jahangir Khan was unbeaten from his loss to Geoff Hunt at the British Open on 10 Apr 1981 until Ross Norman (New Zealand) ended his sequence in the World Open final on 11 Nov 1986.

cessful individual in the World Pairs has been Hans Hollen Nielsen (b. 26 Dec 1959) with seven wins for Denmark. His partners were Ole Olsen, 1979, Erik Gundersen, 1986–9, and Jan O. Pedersen, 1990–91. Maximum points (then 30) were scored in the World Pairs Championship by: Jerzy Szczakiel (b. 28 Jan 1949) and Andrzej Wyglenda (Poland) at Rybnik, Poland in 1971; and Arthur Dennis Sigalos (b. 16 Aug 1959) and Robert Benjamin 'Bobby' Schwartz (USA) (b. 10 Aug 1956) at Liverpool, New South Wales, Australia on 11 Dec 1982. The World Team Cup (instituted 1960) has been won a record nine times by: England/Great Britain (Great Britain 1968, 1971–3; England 1974–5, 1977, 1980, 1989); and Denmark 1978, 1981, 1983–8, 1991. Hans Nielsen (Denmark) has ridden in a record eight Team wins.

British championships League racing was introduced to British speedway in 1929 and consisted of a Southern League and Northern Dirt Track League, the National League was formulated in 1932 and continued to 1964. The Wembley Lions who won in 1932, 1946–7, 1949–53, had a record eight victories. In 1965 it was replaced by the British League which Belle Vue (who had six National League wins, 1933–6, 1939 and 1963) have won four times, including three times in succession (1970–72).

In league racing the highest score recorded was when Berwick beat Exeter 78–18 in the 16-heat formula for the National League on 27 May 1989. A maximum possible score was achieved by Bristol when they defeated Glasgow (White City) 70–14 on 7 Oct 1949 in the National League Division Two. Oxford set a record of 28 successive wins in the British League in 1986. The highest number of League points scored by an individual in a season was 563 by Hans Nielsen for Oxford in the British League in 1988. The League career record is 6471 points by Nigel Boocock (b. 17 Sep 1937), 1955–80.

Belle Vue (Manchester) had a record nine victories (1933–7, 1946–7, 1949 and 1958) in the National Trophy Knock-out Competition (held 1931–64). This was replaced in 1965 by the Knock-Out Cup, which has been won eight

times (one shared) by Cradley Heath. The highest recorded score in this competition is 81–25, when Hull beat Sheffield in 1979.

The British League Riders' Championship was instituted in 1965 and is an annual event contested by the top scorers from each team. Ivan Mauger holds the records for appearances, 15 and points scored, 146, 1965–79. The most wins is six by Barry Briggs, 1965–70.

Tests The only rider to have scored maximum points in every match of a Test series was Arthur 'Bluey' Wilkinson (1911–40) in five matches for Australia *v.* England in Sydney in 1937/8.

Squash Rackets

World Championships Jahangir Khan (Pakistan) (b. 10 Dec 1963) won six World Open (instituted 1976) titles, 1981–5 and 1988, and the International Squash Rackets Federation world individual title (formerly World Amateur, instituted 1967) in 1979, 1983 and 1985. Geoffrey B. Hunt (Australia) (b. 11 Mar 1947) won four World Open titles, 1976–7 and 1979–80 and three World Amateur, 1967, 1969 and 1971. The most women's World Open titles is five by Susan Devoy (New Zealand) (b. 4 Jan 1964), 1985, 1987, 1990–92.

Australia (1967, 1969, 1971, 1973, 1989 and 1991) has won six men's world titles. England won the women's title in 1985, 1987, 1989 and 1990, following Great Britain's win in 1979.

Most titles Open Championship The most wins in the Open Championship held annually in Britain, is ten by Jahangir Khan, in successive years, 1982–91. Hashim Khan (Pakistan) (b. 1915) won seven times, 1950–55 and 1957, and also won the Vintage title six times in 1978–83.

The most British Open women's titles is 16 by Heather Pamela McKay (*née* Blundell) (Australia) (b. 31 Jul 1941) from 1961 to 1977. She also won the World Open title in 1976 and 1979.

Longest sea wave ride

About four to six times each year ride-able surfing waves break in Matanchen Bay near San Blas, Nayarit, Mexico which makes rides of *c.*1700m *5700ft* possible.

Sponsored swimming

The greatest amount of money collected in a charity swim was £122 983·19 in 'Splash '92' organized by the Royal Bank of Scotland Swimming Club and was held at the Royal Commonwealth Pool, Edinburgh, Lothian on 25–26 Jan 1992 with 3218 participants. The record for an event staged at several pools was £548 006·14 by 'Penguin Swimathon '88', when 5482 swimmers participated at 43 pools throughout London on 26–28 Feb 1988.

Amateur Championship The most wins in the Amateur Championship is six by Abdelfattah Amr Bey (Egypt) (b. 14 Feb 1910), who won in 1931–3 and 1935–7. Norman Francis Borrett (b. 1 Oct 1917) of England won in 1946–50.

Longest and shortest championship matches The longest recorded competitive match was one of 2 hr 45 min when Jahangir Khan beat Gamal Awad (Egypt) (b. 8 Sep 1955) 9–10, 9–5, 9–7, 9–2, the first game lasting a record 1 hr 11 min, in the final of the Patrick International Festival at Chichester, W Sussex on 30 Mar 1983. Philip Kenyon (England) (b. 9 May 1956) beat Salah Nadi (Egypt) (b. 11 Jan 1956) in just 6 min 37 sec (9–0, 9–0, 9–0) in the British Open at Lamb's Squash Club, London on 9 Apr 1992.

Most international appearances The men's record is 122 by David Gotto (b. 25 Dec 1948) for Ireland. The women's record is 108 by Marjorie Croke (née Burke) (b. 31 May 1961) for Ireland, 1981–93.

Highest speed In tests at Wimbledon Squash and Badminton Club in January 1988, Roy Buckland hit a squash ball by an overhead service at a measured speed of 232·7 km/h *144·6 mph* over the distance to the front wall. This is equivalent to an initial speed at the racket of 242·6 km/h *150·8 mph.*

Largest crowd and tournament The finals of the ICI World Team Championships at the Royal Albert Hall, London had a record attendance for squash of 3526 on 30 Oct 1987. The InterCity National Squash Challenge was contested by 9588 players in 1988, a knock-out tournament record.

Surfing

Most titles World Amateur Championships were inaugurated in May 1964 at Sydney, Australia. The most titles is three by Michael Novakov (Australia) who won the Kneeboard event in 1982, 1984 and 1986. A World Professional series was started in 1975. The men's title has been won five times by Mark Richards (Australia), 1975 and 1979–82 and the women's title (instituted 1979) four times by: Frieda Zamba (USA), 1984–6, 1988; and Wendy Botha (Australia, formerly South Africa), 1987, 1989, 1991–2.

Highest waves ridden Waimea Bay, Hawaii reputedly provides the most consistently high waves, often reaching the ridable limit of 9–11m *30–35ft.* The highest wave ever ridden was the *tsunami* of 'perhaps 50 ft', which struck Minole, Hawaii on 3 Apr 1868, and was ridden to save his life by a Hawaiian named Holua.

Longest ride River bore The longest recorded rides on a river bore have been set on the Severn bore, England. The official British Surfing Association record for riding a surfboard in a standing position is 4 km *2·5 mile* by David Lawson from Lower Rea to Lower Parting on 27 Sep 1988. The longest ride on a surfboard standing or lying down is 4·73 km *2·94 miles* by Colin Kerr Wilson (b. 23 Jun 1954) on 23 May 1982.

Swimming

Largest pools The largest swimming pool in the world is the seawater

Tom Jager, the world's fastest swimmer.

(Photo: Allsport/Simon Bruty)

Matt Biondi equalled Mark Spitz's record of 11 Olympic medals, winning three at the 1992 Games at Barcelona. Here he can be seen with the other members of the successful US 4 × 100 m freestyle team (second right).

(Photos: Allsport/Simon Bruty)

Orthlieb Pool in Casablanca, Morocco. It is 480 m *1574 ft* long and 75 m *246 ft* wide, and has an area of 3·6 ha *8·9 acres*. The largest land-locked swimming pool with heated water was the Fleishhacker Pool on Sloat Boulevard, near Great Highway, San Francisco, California, USA. It measured 305×46 m *1000×150 ft* and up to 4·26 m *14 ft* deep and contained 28 390 hectolitres *6 245 050 US gal* of heated water. It was opened on 2 May 1925 but has now been abandoned. The largest land-locked pool in current use is Willow Lake at Warren, Ohio, USA. It measures 183×46 m *600×150 ft*. The greatest spectator accommodation is 13 614 at Osaka, Japan. The largest in use in the United Kingdom is the Royal Commonwealth Pool, Edinburgh, completed in 1970 with 2000 permanent seats, but the covered over and unused pool at Earls Court, London (opened 1937) could seat some 12 000 spectators.

Fastest swimmer In a 25-yd pool, Tom Jager (USA) (b. 6 Oct 1964) achieved an average speed of 8·64 km/h *5·3 mph* for 50 yards in 19·05 sec at Nashville, Tennessee, USA on 23 Mar 1990. The women's fastest is 7·21 km/h *4·48 mph* by Yang Wenyi (China) in her 50 m world record (⊳ World Record table).

Most world records Men: 32, Arne Borg (Sweden) (1901–87), 1921–9.

Swimming World Records (set in 50m pools)

MEN

Event	min:sec	Name and Country	Venue	Date
FREESTYLE				
50 metres	21-81	Tom Jager (USA) (b. 6 Oct 1964)	Nashville, Tennessee, USA	24 Mar 1990
100 metres	48-42	Matthew Nicholas Biondi (USA) (b. 8 Oct 1955)	Austin, Texas, USA	10 Aug 1988
200 metres	1:46-69	Giorgio Lamberti (Italy) (b. 28 Jan 1969)	Bonn, Germany	15 Aug 1989
400 metres	3:45-00	Yevgeniy Sadovyi (Russia)	Barcelona, Spain	29 Jul 1992
800 metres	7:46-60	Kieren John Perkins (Australia) (b. 14 Aug 1973)	Sydney, Australia	15 Feb 1992
1500 metres	14:43-48	Kieren John Perkins (Australia)	Barcelona, Spain	31 Jul 1992
4×100 metres	3:16-53	USA (Christopher Jacobs, Troy Dalbey, Tom Jager, Matthew Nicholas Biondi)	Seoul, South Korea	23 Sep 1988
4×200 metres	7:11-95	CIS (Dmitry Lepikov, Vladimir Pyechenko, Venyamin Tayanovich, Yevgeniy Sadovyi)	Barcelona, Spain	27 Jul 1992
BREASTSTROKE				
100 metres	1:01-29	Norbert Rozsa (Hungary) (b. 9 Feb 1972)	Athens, Greece	20 Aug 1991
200 metres	2:10-16	Michael Ray Barrowman (USA) (b. 4 Dec 1968)	Barcelona, Spain	29 Jul 1992
BUTTERFLY				
100 metres	52-84	Pedro Pablo Morales (USA) (b. 5 Dec 1964)	Orlando, Florida, USA	23 Jun 1986
200 metres	1:55-69	Melvin Stewart (USA) (b. 18 Nov 1968)	Perth, Australia	12 Jan 1991
BACKSTROKE				
100 metres	53-86	Jeff Rouse (USA) (b. 6 Feb 1970) (relay leg)	Barcelona, Spain	31 Jul 1992
200 metres	1:56-57	Martin López-Zubero (Spain) (b. 23 Apr 1964)	Tuscaloosa, Alabama, USA	23 Nov 1991
MEDLEY				
200 metres	1:59-36	Tamás Darnyi (Hungary) (b. 3 Jun 1967)	Perth, Australia	13 Jan 1991
400 metres	4:12-36	Tamás Darnyi (Hungary)	Perth, Australia	8 Jan 1991
4×100 metres	3:36-93	USA (David Berkoff, Richard Schroeder, Matthew Nicholas Biondi, Christopher Jacobs)	Seoul, South Korea	25 Sep 1988

3:36:93	USA (Jeff Rouse, Nelson Diebel, Pablo Morales, Jon Olsen)	Barcelona, Spain	31 Jul 1992

WOMEN

FREESTYLE

50 metres	24.79	Yang Wenyi (China) (b. 11 Jan 1972)	Barcelona, Spain	31 Jul 1992
100 metres	54.48	Jenny Thompson (USA) (b. 26 Feb 1973)	Indianapolis, Indiana, USA	1 Mar 1992
200 metres	1:57.55	Heike Friedrich (GDR) (b. 18 Apr 1970)	East Berlin, Germany	18 Jun 1986
400 metres	4:03.85	Janet B Evans (USA) (b. 28 Aug 1971)	Seoul, South Korea	22 Sep 1988
800 metres	8:16.22	Janet Evans (USA)	Tokyo, Japan	20 Aug 1989
1500 metres	15:52.10	Janet Evans (USA)	Orlando, Florida, USA	26 Mar 1988
4×100 metres	3:39.46	USA (Nicole Haislett, Dara Torres, Angel Martino, Jenny Thompson)	Barcelona, Spain	28 Jul 1992
4×200 metres	7:55.47	GDR (Manuela Stellmach, Astrid Strauss, Anke Möhring, Heike Friedrich)	Strasbourg, France	18 Aug 1987

BREASTSTROKE

100 metres	1:07.91	Silke Hörner (GDR) (b. 12 Sep 1965)	Strasbourg, France	21 Aug 1987
200 metres	2:25.35	Anita Nall (USA) (b. 21 Jul 1976)	Indianapolis, Indiana, USA	2 Mar 1992

BUTTERFLY

100 metres	57.93	Mary Terstegge Meagher (USA) (b. 27 Oct 1964)	Brown Deer, Wisconsin, USA	16 Aug 1981
200 metres	2:05.96	Mary Terstegge Meagher (USA)	Brown Deer, Wisconsin, USA	13 Aug 1981

BACKSTROKE

100 metres	1:00.31	Krizstina Egerszegi (Hungary) (b. 16 Aug 1974)	Athens, Greece	22 Aug 1991
200 metres	2:06.62	Krizstina Egerszegi (Hungary)	Athens, Greece	25 Aug 1991

MEDLEY

200 metres	2:11.65	Li Lin (China) (b. 9 Oct 1976)	Barcelona, Spain	30 Jul 1992
400 metres	4:36.10	Petra Schneider (GDR) (b. 11 Jan 1963)	Guayaquil, Ecuador	1 Aug 1982
4×100 metres	4:02.54	USA (Lea Loveless, Anita Nall, Chrissy Ahmann-Leighton, Jenny Thompson)	Barcelona, Spain	30 Jul 1992

Short-Course Swimming World Bests (set in 25m pools)

MEN

Event	min:sec	Name and country	Venue	Date
FREESTYLE				
50 metres	21·60	Mark Foster (GB) (b. 12 May 1970)	Sheffield, S Yorks	18 Feb 1993
100 metres	48·2*	Michael Gross (West Germany) (b. 17 Jun 1964)	Offenbach, Germany	11 Feb 1988
	48·33	Tommy Werner (Sweden) (b. 31 Mar 1966)	Malmö, Sweden	19 Mar 1989
200 metres	1:43·64	Giorgio Lamberti (Italy) (b. 28 Jan 1969)	Bonn, Germany	11 Feb 1990
400 metres	3:40·81	Anders Holmertz (Sweden) (b. 1 Dec 1968)	Paris, France	4 Feb 1990
800 metres	7:38·75	Michael Gross (West Germany)	Bonn, Germany	8 Feb 1985
1500 metres	14:32·40	Kieren Perkins (Australia) (b. 14 Aug 1973)	Canberra, Australia	2 Feb 1992
4×50 metres	1:27·94	Sweden	Espoo, Finland	21 Nov 1992
4×100 metres	3:14·00	Sweden	Malmö, Sweden	19 Mar 1989
4×200 metres	7:05·17	West Germany	Bonn, Germany	9 Feb 1986
BACKSTROKE				
50 metres	25·06	Mark Tewksbury (Canada) (b. 2 Jul 1968)	Saskatoon, Canada	2 Mar 1990
100 metres	51·43	Jeff Rouse (USA) (b. 6 Feb 1970)	Sheffield, S Yorks	12 Apr 1993
200 metres	1:56·60	Tamás Darnyi (Hungary) (b. 3 Jun 1967)	Bonn, Germany	8 Feb 1987
BREASTSTROKE				
50 metres	27·15	Dmitry Volkov (USSR) (b. 3 Mar 1966)	Saint-Paul de la Réunion	30 Dec 1989
100 metres	59·30	Dmitriy Volkov (USSR)	Bonn, Germany	11 Feb 1990
200 metres	2:07·93	Nicholas Gillingham (GB) (b. 22 Jan 1967)	Birmingham	20 Oct 1991
BUTTERFLY				
50 metres	23·72	Mark Foster (GB)	Gelsenkirchen, Germany	13 Feb 1993
100 metres	52·07	Marcel Gery (Canada) (b. 15 Mar 1965)	Leicester	23 Feb 1990
200 metres	1:54·21	Danyon Loader (New Zealand) (b. 26 Apr 1975)	Gelsenkirchen, Germany	13 Feb 1993
MEDLEY				
100 metres	53·78	Jani Nikanor Sievinen (Finland) (b. 31 Nov 1974)	Espoo, Finland	21 Nov 1992
200 metres	1:55·59	Jani Sievinen (Finland)	Malmö, Sweden	10 Feb 1993
400 metres	4:07·10	Jani Sievinen (Finland)	Malmö, Sweden	9 Feb 1993

4×50 metres	1:38-10	Finland	Espoo, Finland	22	Nov 1992
4×100 metres	3:34-86	University of Calgary (Canada)	Winnipeg, Canada	23	Feb 1992

WOMEN

FREESTYLE

50 metres	24.75	Franziska van Almsick (Germany) (b. 5 Apr 1978)	Schäbisch Gmünd, Germany	4	Nov 1992
100 metres	53-33	Franziska van Almsick (Germany)	Beijing, China	10	Jan 1993
200 metres	1:55-84	Franziska van Almsick (Germany)	Beijing, China	9	Jan 1993
400 metres	4:02-05	Astrid Strauss (GDR) (b. 24 Dec 1968)	Bonn, Germany	8	Feb 1987
800 metres	8:15-34	Astrid Strauss (GDR)	Bonn, Germany	6	Feb 1987
1500 metres	15:43-31	Petra Schneider (GDR) (b. 11 Jan 1963)	Gainesville, Florida, USA	10	Jan 1982
4×100 metres	1:40-63	Germany	Espoo, Finland	22	Nov 1992
4×100 metres	3:38-77	GDR	Monte Carlo, Monaco	12	Dec 1987

BACKSTROKE

50 metres	28-33	Sandra Völker (Germany) (b. 1 Apr 1974)	Sheffield, S Yorks	16	Feb 1993
100 metres	59-89	Betsy Mitchell (USA) (b. 15 Jan 1966)	Los Angeles, California, USA	26	Apr 1987
200 metres	2:06-78	Nicole Stevenson (Australia) (b. 24 Jun 1971)	Melbourne, Australia	7	Mar 1992

BREASTSTROKE

50 metres	31-19	Louise Karlsson (Sweden)	Espoo, Finland	21	Nov 1992
100 metres	1:07-05	Silke Hörner (GDR) (b. 12 Sep 1965)	Bonn, Germany	8	Feb 1986
200 metres	2:22-92	Susanne Börnike (GDR) (b. 13 Aug 1968)	Bonn, Germany	4	Feb 1989

BUTTERFLY

50 metres	27-30	Qian Hong (China) (b. 1971)	Perth, Australia	6	Jan 1991
100 metres**	58-91	Mary Terstegge Meagher (USA) (b. 27 Aug 1964)	Gainesville, Florida, USA	3	Jan 1981
200 metres	2:05-65	Mary Meagher (USA)	Gainesville, Florida, USA	2	Jan 1981

MEDLEY

100 metres	1:01-03	Louise Karlsson (Sweden) (b. 26 Apr 1974)	Espoo, Finland	22	Nov 1992
200 metres	2:10-60	Petra Schneider (GDR)	Gainesville, Florida, USA	8	Jan 1982
400 metres	4:31-36	Noemi Lung (Romania) (b. 16 May 1968)	Paris, France	31	Jan 1987
4×50 metres	1:52-44	Germany	Espoo, Finland	21	Nov 1992
4×100 metres	4:02-85	GDR	Indianapolis, Indiana, USA	8	Jan 1983

*hand timed for first leg. ** slower than long-course best.*

Swimming (British National Records)

MEN

Event	min:sec	Name	Venue	Date
FREESTYLE				
50 metres	22·43	Mark Andrew Foster (b. 12 May 1970)	Sheffield, S Yorks	24 May 1992
100 metres	50·24	Michael Wenham Fibbens (b. 31 May 1968)	Sheffield, S Yorks	22 May 1992
200 metres	1:48·92	Paul Rory Palmer (b. 18 Oct 1974)	Barcelona, Spain	26 Jul 1992
400 metres	3:50·01	Kevin Thomas Boyd (b. 23 Jun 1966)	Seoul, South Korea	23 Sep 1988
800 metres	8:00·63	Ian Wilson (b. 19 Dec 1970)	Athens, Greece	25 Aug 1991
1500 metres	15:03·72	Ian Wilson	Athens, Greece	25 Aug 1991
4×100 metres	3:21·41	GB (Michael Wenham Fibbens, Mark Andrew Foster, Paul Howe, Roland Lee)	Barcelona, Spain	29 Jul 1992
4×200 metres	7:22·57	GB (Paul Palmer, Steven Mellor, Stephen Akers, Paul Howe)	Barcelona, Spain	27 Jul 1992
BREASTSTROKE				
100 metres	1:01·33	Nicholas Gillingham (b. 22 Jan 1967)	Sheffield, S Yorks	21 May 1992
200 metres	2:11·29	Nicholas Gillingham	Barcelona, Spain	29 Jul 1992
BUTTERFLY				
100 metres	53·30	Andrew David Jameson (b. 19 Feb 1965)	Seoul, South Korea	21 Sep 1988
200 metres	2:00·21	Philip Hubble (b. 19 Jul 1960)	Split, Yugoslavia	11 Sep 1981
BACKSTROKE				
100 metres	55·92	Martin Clifford Harris (b. 21 May 1969)	Sheffield, S Yorks	13 Jun 1993
200 metres	2:01·90	Adam Ruckwood (b. 13 Sep 1974)	Sheffield, S Yorks	11 Jun 1993
MEDLEY				
200 metres	2:03·20	Neil Cochran (b. 12 Apr 1965)	Orlando, Florida, USA	25 Mar 1988
400 metres	4:24·20	John Philip Davey (b. 29 Dec 1964)	Crystal Palace, London	1 Aug 1987

4 × 100 metres ...3:42-01 GB (Neil Cochran, Adrian David Moorhouse, Andrew David Jameson, Roland Lee) ...Strasbourg, France ...23 Aug 1987

WOMEN

FREESTYLE

Event	Time	Name	Location	Date
50 metres	26-01	Caroline Woodcock (b. 23 Aug 1972)	Bonn, Germany	20 Aug 1989
100 metres	56-11	Karen Pickering (b. 19 Dec 1971)	Sheffield, S Yorks	14 Jun 1992
200 metres	1:59-74	June Alexandra Croft (b. 17 Jun 1963)	Brisbane, Australia	4 Oct 1982
400 metres	4:07-68	Sarah Hardcastle (b. 9 April 1969)	Edinburgh, Lothian	27 Jul 1986
800 metres	8:24-77	Sarah Hardcastle	Edinburgh, Lothian	29 Jul 1986
1500 metres	16:43-95	Sarah Hardcastle	Montreal, Canada	18 Apr 1985
4 × 100 metres	3:48-87	GB (Karen Pickering, Sharron Davies, Caroline Woodcock, Joanne Coull)	Bonn, Germany	17 Aug 1989
4 × 200 metres	8:13-70	England (Annabelle Cripps, Sarah Hardcastle, Karen Marie Mellor, Zara Letitia Long)	Edinburgh, Lothian	25 Jul 1986

BREASTSTROKE

Event	Time	Name	Location	Date
100 metres	1:10-39	Susannah 'Suki' Brownsdon (b. 16 Oct 1965)	Strasbourg, France	21 Aug 1987
200 metres	2:31-51	Jean Cameron Hill (b. 15 Jul 1964)	Strasbourg, France	19 Aug 1987

BUTTERFLY

Event	Time	Name	Location	Date
100 metres	1:01-33	Madeleine Scarborough (b. 18 Aug 1964)	Auckland, New Zealand	28 Jan 1990
200 metres	2:11-97	Samantha Paula Purvis (b. 24 Jun 1967)	Los Angeles, California, USA	4 Aug 1984

BACKSTROKE

Event	Time	Name	Location	Date
100 metres	1:03-49	Katharine Read (b. 30 Jun 1969)	Sheffield, S Yorks	14 Jun 1992
200 metres	2:13-91	Joanne Deakins (b. 20 Nov 1972)	Barcelona, Spain	31 Jul 1992

MEDLEY

Event	Time	Name	Location	Date
200 metres	2:17-21	Jean Cameron Hill	Edinburgh, Lothian	21 Jul 1986
400 metres	4:46-83	Sharron Davies (b. 1 Nov 1962)	Moscow, USSR	26 Jul 1980
4 × 100 metres	4:11-88	England (Joanne Deakins, Susannah 'Suki' Brownsdon, Madeleine Scarborough, Karen Pickering)	Auckland, New Zealand	29 Jan 1990

Women: 42, Ragnhild Hveger (Denmark) (b. 10 Dec 1920), 1936–42. For currently recognized events (only metric distances in 50 m pools) the most is 26 by Mark Andrew Spitz (USA) (b. 10 Feb 1950), 1967–72, and 23 by Kornelia Ender (GDR) (b. 25 Oct 1958), 1973–6.

The most world records set in a single pool is 86 in the North Sydney pool, Australia between 1955 and 1978. This total includes 48 imperial distance records which ceased to be recognized in 1969. The pool, which was built in 1936, was originally 55 yards long but was shortened to 50 metres in 1964.

Most world titles In the World Championships (instituted 1973) the most medals won is 13 by Michael Gross (West Germany) (b. 17 Jun 1964), five gold, five silver and three bronze, 1982–90.

The most by a woman is ten by Kornelia Ender with eight gold and two silver in 1973 and 1975. The most gold medals is six (two individual and four relay) by James Paul Montgomery (USA) (b. 24 Jan 1955) in 1973 and 1975.

The most medals at a single championship is seven by Matthew Nicholas Biondi (USA) (b. 8 Oct 1965), three gold, one silver, three bronze, in 1986.

Olympic Records

Most medals Men The greatest number of Olympic gold medals won is nine by Mark Spitz (USA): 100 m and 200 m freestyle 1972; 100 m and 200 m butterfly 1972; 4 × 100 m freestyle 1968 and 1972; 4 × 200 m freestyle 1968 and 1972; 4 × 100 m medley 1972. *All but one of these performances (the 4 × 200 m freestyle of 1968) were also new world records.* He also won a silver (100 m butterfly) and a bronze (100 m freestyle) in 1968 for a record 11 medals. His record seven medals at one Games in 1972 was equalled by Matt Biondi (USA) who took five gold, one silver and one bronze in 1988. Biondi has also won a record 11 medals in total, winning a gold in 1984, and two golds and a silver in 1992.

Women The record number of gold medals won by a woman is six by

Kristin Otto (GDR) (b. 7 Feb 1966) at Seoul in 1988: 100 m freestyle, backstroke and butterfly, 50 m freestyle, 4 × 100 m freestyle and 4 × 100 m medley. Dawn Fraser (Australia) (b. 4 Sep 1937) is the only swimmer to win the same event, the 100 m freestyle, on three successive occasions (1956, 1960 and 1964).

The most medals won by a woman is eight by: Dawn Fraser, four golds and four silvers 1956–64; Kornelia Ender, four golds and four silvers 1972–6; and Shirley Babashoff (USA) (b. 3 Jan 1957), two golds and six silvers 1972–6.

Most individual gold medals The record number of individual gold medals won is four by: Charles Meldrum Daniels (USA) (1884–1973) (100 m freestyle 1906 and 1908, 220 yd freestyle 1904, 440 yd freestyle 1904); Roland Matthes (GDR) (b. 17 Nov 1950) with 100 m and 200 m backstroke 1968 and 1972; Mark Spitz and Kristin Otto, and the divers Pat McCormick and Greg Louganis (⟷ Diving).

Most medals British The record number of gold medals won by a British swimmer (excluding water polo, *q.v.*) is four by Henry Taylor (1885–1951) in the mile freestyle (1906), 400 m freestyle (1908), 1500 m freestyle (1908) and 4 × 200 m freestyle (1908).

Henry Taylor won a record eight medals in all, with a further silver and three bronzes, 1906–20. The most medals by a British woman is four by Margaret Joyce Cooper (now Badcock) (b. 18 Apr 1909) with one silver and three bronze, 1928–32.

Diving

Most Olympic medals The most medals won by a diver is five by: Klaus Dibiasi (b. Austria, 6 Oct 1947) (Italy) (three gold, two silver), 1964–76; and Gregory Efthimios Louganis (USA) (b. 29 Jan 1960) (four golds, one silver), 1976, 1984, 1988. Dibiasi is the only diver to win the same event (highboard) at three successive Games (1968, 1972 and 1976). Two divers have won the highboard and springboard doubles at two Games: Patricia Joan McCormick (*née* Keller) (USA) (b. 12 May 1930), 1952 and 1956 and Louganis, 1984 and 1988.

British The highest placing by a Briton has been the silver medal by Beatrice Eileen Armstrong (later Purdy) (1894–1981) in the 1920 highboard event. The best placings by male divers are the bronze medals by Harold Clarke (b. 1888) (plain high diving, 1924) and Brian Eric Phelps (b. 21 Apr 1944) (highboard, 1960).

Most world titles Greg Louganis (USA) won a record five world titles, highboard in 1978, and both highboard and springboard in 1982 and 1986, as well as four Olympic gold medals in 1984 and 1988. Three gold medals at one event have also been won by Philip George Boggs (USA) (1949–90), springboard 1973, 1975 and 1978.

Highest scores Greg Louganis achieved record scores at the 1984 Olympic Games in Los Angeles, California, USA with 754·41 points for the 11-dive springboard event and 710·91 for the highboard. At the world championships in Guayaquil, Ecuador in 1984 he was awarded a perfect score of 10·0 by all seven judges for his highboard inward 1½ somersault in the pike position.

The first diver to be awarded a score of 10·0 by all seven judges was Michael Holman Finneran (b. 21 Sep 1948) in the 1972 US Olympic Trials, in Chicago, Illinois, for a backward 1½ somersault, 2½ twist, from the 10m board.

Channel Swimming

The first to swim the English Channel from shore to shore (without a life jacket) was the Merchant Navy captain Matthew Webb (1848–83) who swam an estimated 61 km *38 miles* to make the 33 km *21 mile* crossing from Dover, England to Calais Sands, France, in 21 hr 45 min from 12:56p.m. to 10:41a.m., 24–25 Aug 1875. Paul Boyton (USA) had swum from Cap Gris-Nez to the South Foreland in his patent life-saving suit in 23 hr 30 min on 28–29 May 1875. There is good evidence that Jean-Marie Saletti, a French soldier, escaped from a British prison hulk off Dover by swimming to Boulogne in July or August 1815.

The first crossing from France to England was made by Enrico Tiraboschi, a wealthy Italian living in Argentina, in 16 hr 33 min on 12 Aug 1923, to win the Daily Sketch prize of £1000.

The first woman to succeed was Gertrude Caroline Ederle (USA) (b. 23 Oct 1906) who swam from Cap Gris-Nez, France to Deal, England on 6 Aug 1926, in the then overall record time of 14 hr 39 min.

The first woman to swim from England to France was Florence Chadwick (USA) (b. 1918) in 16 hr 19 min on 11 Sep 1951. The first Englishwoman to succeed was Mercedes Gleitze (later Carey) (1900–81) who swam from France to England in 15 hr 15 min on 7 Oct 1927. The first twins to complete the crossing were Carole and Sarah Hunt (b. 23 Aug 1962) who swam from England and landed together in France after 9 hr 29 min on 6 Aug 1988.

Fastest The official Channel Swimming Association (founded 1927) record is 7 hr 40 min by Penny Dean (b. 21 Mar 1955) of California, USA, from Shakespeare Beach, Dover to Cap Gris-Nez, France on 29 Jul 1978.

The fastest France–England time is 8 hr 5 min by Richard Davey (b. 23 Jun 1965) in 1988.

The fastest crossing by a relay team is 6 hr 52 min (England to France) by the US National Swim Team on 1 Aug 1990. They went on to complete the fastest two-way relay in 14 hr 18 min.

Earliest and latest The earliest date in the year on which the Channel has been swum is 30 May by Kevin Murphy (GB) (b. 1949) in 1990 in a time of 13 hr 16 min and with the water at a temperature of 12°C *54°F*. The latest is 28 October by Michael Peter Read (GB) (b. 9 Jun 1941) in 1979 in 17 hr 55 min.

Double crossing The first double crossing was by Antonio Abertondo (Argentina) (b. 1919), in 43 hr 10 min on 20–22 Sep 1961. Kevin Murphy completed the first double crossing by a Briton in 35 hr 10 min on 6 Aug 1970. The first swimmer to achieve a crossing both ways was Edward Harry Temme (1904–78) on 5 Aug 1927 and 19 Aug 1934.

Franziska van Almsick set the world short course swimming records for 50m, 100m and 200m freestyle in the winter season 1992/3.
(Photo: Allsport/Simon Bruty)

The fastest double crossing was in 16 hr 10 min by Philip Rush (New Zealand) (b. 6 Nov 1963) on 17 Aug 1987. In setting this record, he completed the fastest ever crossing by a man, 7 hr 55 min (England to France), and went on to complete the fastest ever triple crossing in 28 hr 21 min on 17–18 Aug 1987. The women's double crossing record is 17 hr 14 min by Susie Maroney (Australia) (b. 15 Nov 1974) on 23 Jul 1991. The first British woman to achieve the double crossing was Alison Streeter (b. 29 Aug 1964) in 21 hr 16 min on 4 Aug 1983.

Triple crossing The first triple crossing was by Jon Erikson (USA) (b. 6 Sep 1954) in 38 hr 27 min on 11–12 Aug 1981. The first by a woman was by Alison Streeter in 34 hr 40 min on 2–3 Aug 1990. For the fastest by an individual, ⇨ Double crossing.

Most conquests The greatest number of Channel conquests is 31 by Michael Read (GB) from 24 Aug 1969 to 19 Aug 1984.

English Channel

As of May 1993, there had been 6255 attempts to swim the Channel by 4318 people. Of these, 423 individuals (283 men and 140 women) from 46 countries have made 669 successful crossings; 624 solo, 18 double and 3 triple.

Oldest Channel swimmer

The oldest conqueror has been Bertram Clifford Batt (b. 22 Dec 1919), of Australia at 67 years 241 days when he swam from Cap Gris-Nez to Dover in 18 hr 37 min from 19–20 Aug 1987. The oldest woman was Stella Ada Rosina Taylor (b. 20 Dec 1929) aged 45 years 250 days when she did the swim in 18 hr 15 min on 26 Aug 1975.

High diving

The highest regularly performed head-first dives are those of professional divers from La Quebrada ('the break in the rocks') at Acapulco, Mexico, a height of 26·7 m *87½ ft*. The base rocks, 6·4 m *21 ft* out from the take-off, necessitate a leap of 8·22 m *27 ft* out. The water is 3·65 m *12 ft* deep.

The world record high dive from a diving board is 53·9 m *176 ft 10 in*, by Olivier Favre (Switzerland) at Villers-le-Lac, France on 30 Aug 1987. The women's record is 36·80 m *120 ft 9 in*, by Lucy Wardle (US) at Ocean Park, Hong Kong on 6 Apr 1985. The highest witnessed in Britain is one of 32·9 m *108 ft* into 2·43 m *8 ft* of water at the Aqua Show at Earl's Court, London on 22 Feb 1948 by Roy Fransen (1915–85).

The most by a woman is 20 by Alison Streeter from 1982 to 22 Sep 1992 (including a record seven in one year, 1992).

Long-distance Swimming

Longest swims The greatest recorded distance ever swum is 2938 km *1826 miles* down the Mississippi River, USA between Ford Dam near Minneapolis, Minnesota and Carrollton Ave, New Orleans, Louisiana, by Fred P. Newton, (b. 1903) of Clinton, Oklahoma from 6 Jul to 29 Dec 1930. He was 742 hr in the water.

Irish Channel The swimming of the 37 km *23 mile* wide North Channel from Donaghadee, Northern Ireland to Portpatrick, Scotland was first accomplished by Tom Blower of Nottingham in 15 hr 26 min in 1947. A record time of 9 hr 53 min 42 sec was set by Alison Streeter on 22 Aug 1988. She was also the first person to complete the crossing from Scotland to Northern Ireland, in 10 hr 4 min on 25 Aug 1989. The first Irish-born swimmer to achieve the crossing was Ted Keenan on 11 Aug 1973 in 11–13°C *52–56°F* water in 18 hr 27 min. The first Scottish-born was Margaret Kidd, 22, in 15 hr 25 min 3 sec on 23 Aug 1988.

Lake swims The fastest time for swimming the 36.5 km *22.7 mile* long Loch Ness is 9 hr 57 min by David Trevor Morgan (b. 25 Sep 1963) on 31 Jul 1983. The first successful swim was by Brenda Sherratt (b. 1948) of West Bollington, Cheshire on 26–27 Jul 1966. David Morgan achieved a double crossing of Loch Ness in 23 hr 4 min on 1 Aug 1983. In 1988 he also uniquely swam Loch Ness in 11 hr 9 min on 16 Jul, Loch Lomond 34.6 km *21.5 miles* in 11 hr 48 min on 18 Jul and the English Channel in 11 hr 35 min on 20–21 Jul. The fastest time for swimming Lake Windermere, 16.9 km *10.5 miles* from Fellfoot to Waterhead, is 3 hr 49 min 12 sec by Justin Palfrey (b. 16 Jul 1971) on 7 Sep 1991.

24 hours Anders Forvass (Sweden) swam 101.9 km *63.3 miles* at the 25-metre Linköping public swimming pool, Sweden on 28–29 Oct 1989. In a 50 metre pool, Evan Barry (Australia) swam 96.7 km *60.08 miles*, at the Valley Pool, Brisbane, Australia on 19–20 Dec 1987.

The women's record is 82.1 km *51.01 miles* by Irene van der Laan (Netherlands) at Amersfoort, Netherlands on 20–21 Sep 1985.

Long-distance relays The New Zealand national relay team of 20 swimmers swam a record 182.807 km *113.59 miles* in Lower Hutt, New Zealand in 24 hours, passing 160 km *100 miles* in 20 hr 47 min 13 sec on 9–10 Dec 1983. The 24 hours club record by a team of five is 162.52 km *100.99 miles* by the Portsmouth Northsea SC at the Victoria Swimming Centre, Portsmouth,

Hants on 4–5 Mar 1993. The women's record is 143.11 km *88.93 miles* by the City of Newcastle ASC on 16–17 Dec 1986. The most participants in a one-day swim relay is 2145, each swimming a length, organized by Jeff VanBuren and David Thompson at Hamilton College at Clinton, New York, USA on 8 Apr 1989.

Underwater swimming Paul Cryne (GB) and Samir Sawan al Awami of Qatar swam 78.92 km *49.04 miles* in a 24 hour period from Doha, Qatar to Umm Said and back on 21–22 Feb 1985 using sub-aqua equipment. They were swimming underwater for 95.5 per cent of the time. A relay team of six swam 151.987 km *94.44 miles* in a swimming pool at Olomouc, Czechoslovakia on 17–18 Oct 1987.

Table Tennis

Most titles World (instituted 1926) G. Viktor Barna (1911–72) (b. Hungary, Gyözö Braun) won a record five singles, 1930, 1932–5 and eight men's doubles, 1929–35, 1939. Angelica Rozeanu (Romania) (b. 15 Oct 1921) won a record six women's singles, 1950–55, and Mária Mednyánszky (Hungary) (1901–79) won seven women's doubles, 1928, 1930–35. With two more at mixed doubles and seven team, Viktor Barna had 22 world titles in all, while 18 were won by Mária Mednyánszky. With the staging of the championships now biennially, the breaking of the above records would be very difficult.

The most men's team titles (Swaythling Cup) is 12 by Hungary, 1927–31, 1933–5, 1938, 1949, 1952 and 1979. The women's record (Marcel Corbillon Cup) is ten by China, 1965, eight successive 1975–89 (biennially) and 1993.

English Open (instituted 1921) Richard Bergmann (Austria, then GB) (1920–70) won a record six singles, 1939–40, 1948, 1950, 1952, 1954 and Viktor Barna won seven men's doubles, 1931, 1933–5, 1938–9, 1949. The women's singles record is six by Maria Alexandru (Romania) (b. 1941), 1963–4, 1970–72, 1974 and Diane Rowe (now Scholer) (b. 14 Apr 1933), won 12 women's doubles titles, 1950–56, 1960, 1962–5. Viktor

Barna won 20 titles in all, and Diane Rowe 17.

English Closed The most titles won is 26 by Desmond Hugh Douglas (b. 20 Jul 1955), a record 11 men's singles, 1976, 1979–87 and 1990, 11 men's doubles and 4 mixed doubles. A record seven women's singles were won by Jill Patricia Hammersley (now Parker, *née* Shirley) (b. 6 Dec 1951) in 1973–6, 1978–9, 1981.

Internationals Joy Foster was aged 8 when she represented Jamaica in the West Indies Championships at Port of Spain, Trinidad in August 1958. The youngest ever to play for England was Nicola Deaton (b. 29 Oct 1976), aged 13 yr 336 days, against Sweden at Burton on Trent, Staffs on 30 Sep 1990.

Jill Parker played for England on a record 413 occasions, 1967–83.

Counter hitting The record number of hits in 60 sec is 173 by Jackie Bellinger (b. 9 Sep 1964) and Lisa Lomas (*née* Bellinger) (b. 9 Mar 1967) at the Northgate Sports Centre, Ipswich, Suffolk on 7 Feb 1993. With a bat in each hand, Gary D. Fisher of Olympia, Washington, USA completed 5000 consecutive volleys over the net in 44 min 28 sec on 25 Jun 1975.

Taekwondo

The first World Taekwondo Championships were organized by the Korean Taekwondo Association and were held at Seoul in 1973. The World Taekwondo Federation was then formed and has organized biennial championships and women's events were first contested in 1987.

Most titles The most world titles won is four by Chung Kook-hyun (South Korea), light-middleweight 1982–3, welterweight 1985, 1987. Taekwondo was included as a demonstration sport at the 1988 Olympic Games.

Tennis (Lawn)

Grand Slam The grand slam is to hold at the same time all four of the world's major championship singles:

Olympic Games

Tennis was re-introduced to the Olympic Games in 1988, having originally been included at the Games from 1896 to 1924. It was also a demonstration sport in 1968 and 1984.

A record four gold medals as well as a silver and a bronze, were won by Max Decugis (France) (1882–1978), 1900–20. A women's record five medals (one gold, two silver, two bronze) were won by Kitty McKane (later Mrs Godfree) (GB) (1897–1992) in 1920 and 1924.

Greatest crowd at Wimbledon

The record crowd for one day was 39 813 on 26 Jun 1986. The record for the whole championship was 403 706 in 1989.

Wimbledon, US, Australian and French Open championships. The first man to have won all four was Frederick John Perry (GB) (b. 18 May 1909) when he won the French title in 1935. The first man to hold all four championships simultaneously was John Donald Budge (USA) (b. 13 Jun 1915) in 1938, and with Wimbledon and US in 1937, he won six successive grand slam tournaments. The first man to achieve the grand slam twice was Rodney George Laver (Australia) (b. 9 Aug 1938) as an amateur in 1962 and again in 1969 when the titles were open to professionals.

Four women have achieved the grand slam and the first three won six successive grand slam tournaments: Maureen Catherine Connolly (USA) (1934–69), in 1953; Margaret Jean Court (*née* Smith) (Australia) (b. 16 Jul 1942) in 1970; and Martina Navrátilová (USA) (b. 18 Oct 1956) in 1983–4. The fourth was Stefanie Maria 'Steffi' Graf (West Germany) (b. 14 Jun 1969) in 1988, when she also won the women's singles Olympic gold medal. Pamela Howard Shriver (USA) (b. 4 Jul 1962) with Navrátilová won a record eight successive grand slam tournament women's

The USA won the Davis Cup for a record 30th time in 1992. Here in action against Switzerland in the 1992 final is John McEnroe who has played for five winning teams, 1978–9, 1981–2 and 1992. In finals he has won nine of ten singles and three of four doubles matches.

(Photo: Allsport/Mike Powell)

doubles titles and 109 successive matches in all events from April 1983 to July 1985.

The first doubles pair to win the grand slam were the Australians Frank Allan Sedgeman (b. 29 Oct 1927) and Kenneth Bruce McGregor (b. 2 Jun 1929) in 1951.

The most singles championships won in grand slam tournaments is 24 by Margaret Court (11 Australian, 5 USA, 5 French, 3 Wimbledon), 1960–73. She

Fastest tennis service

The fastest service timed with modern equipment is 222km/h *138mph* by Steve Denton (USA) (b. 5 Sep 1956) at Beaver Creek, Colorado, USA on 29 Jul 1984.

'Golden set'

The only known example of a 'Golden set' (to win a set 6–0 without dropping a single point i.e. winning 24 consecutive points) in professional tennis was achieved by Bill Scanlon (USA) (b. 13 Nov 1956) against Marcos Hocevar (Brazil) in the first round of the WCT Gold Coast Classic at Del Ray, Florida, USA on 22 Feb 1983. Scanlon won the match, 6–2, 6–0.

Tiddlywinks

The record for potting 24 winks from 18in *45cm* is 21·8sec by Stephen Williams (Altrincham Grammar School) in May 1966. Allen R. Astles (University of Wales) potted 10 000 winks in 3hr 51min 46sec at Aberystwyth, Dyfed in February 1966.

On 21 Oct 1989 several records were set by members of the Cambridge University Tiddlywinks Club at Queens' College, Cambridge and these included: 41 winks potted in relay in three minutes by Patrick Barrie, Nick Inglis, Geoff Myers and Andy Purvis, a long jump of 9·17m *30ft 1in* by Andy Purvis and a high jump 3·49m *11ft 5in* by Adrian Jones, David Smith and Ed Wynn.

also won the US Amateur in 1969 and 1970 when this was held as well as the US Open. The men's record is 12 by Roy Stanley Emerson (Australia) (b. 3 Nov 1936) (6 Australian, 2 each French, USA, Wimbledon), 1961–7.

The most grand slam tournament wins by a doubles partnership is 20 by Althea

666

Louise Brough (USA) (b. 11 Mar 1923) and Margaret Evelyn Du Pont (*née* Osborne) (USA) (b. 4 Mar 1918), (12 US, 5 Wimbledon, 3 French), 1942–57; and by Martina Navrátilová and Pam Shriver, (7 Australian, 5 Wimbledon, 4 French, 4 USA), 1981–9.

Most wins *Women* Billie-Jean King (USA) (*née* Moffitt) (b. 22 Nov 1943) won a record 20 titles between 1961 and 1979, six singles, ten women's doubles and four mixed doubles. Elizabeth Montague Ryan (USA) (1892–1979) won a record 19 doubles (12 women's, 7 mixed) titles from 1914 to 1934.

Men The greatest number of titles by a man has been 13 by Hugh Laurence Doherty (GB) (1875–1919) with five singles titles (1902–6) and a record eight men's doubles (1897–1901, 1903–5) partnered by his brother Reginald Frank (1872–1910).

Singles Martina Navrátilová has won a record nine titles, 1978–9, 1982–7 and 1990. The most men's singles wins since the Challenge Round was abolished in 1922 is five consecutively, by Björn Rune Borg (Sweden) (b. 6 Jun 1956) in 1976–80. William Charles Renshaw (GB) (1861–1904) won seven singles in 1881–6 and 1889.

Mixed doubles The male record is four titles shared by: Elias Victor Seixas (USA) (b. 30 Aug 1923) in 1953–6; Kenneth Norman Fletcher (Australia) (b. 15 Jun 1940) in 1963, 1965–6, 1968; and Owen Keir Davidson (Australia) (b. 4 Oct 1943) in 1967, 1971, 1973–4. The female record is seven by Elizabeth Ryan (USA) from 1919 to 1932.

Most appearances Arthur William Charles 'Wentworth' Gore (1868–1928) (GB) made a record 36 appearances at Wimbledon between 1888 and 1927. In 1964, Jean Borotra (b. 13 Aug 1898) of France made his 35th appearance since 1922. In 1977 he appeared in the Veterans' Doubles aged 78.

Youngest champions The youngest champion was Charlotte 'Lottie' Dod (1871–1960), who was 15yr 285days when she won in 1887. The youngest male champion was Boris Becker (West

Germany) (b. 22 Nov 1967) who won the men's singles title in 1985 at 17 yr 227 days. The youngest ever player at Wimbledon was reputedly Mita Klima (Austria) who was 13 years old in the 1907 singles competition. The youngest seed was Jennifer Capriati (USA) (b. 29 Mar 1976) at 14 yr 89 days for her first match on 26 Jun 1990. She won this match, making her the youngest ever winner at Wimbledon.

Oldest champions The oldest champion was Margaret Evelyn du Pont (*née* Osborne) at 44 yr 125 days when she won the mixed doubles in 1962 with Neale Fraser (Australia). The oldest singles champion was Arthur Gore (GB) in 1909 at 41 yr 182 days.

United States Championships

Most wins Margaret Evelyn du Pont (*née* Osborne) won a record 25 titles between 1941 and 1960. She won a record 13 women's doubles (12 with Althea Louise Brough), nine mixed doubles and three singles. The men's record is 16 by William Tatem Tilden, including seven men's singles, 1920–25, 1929, a record for singles shared with: Richard Dudley Sears (1861–1943), 1881–7; William A. Larned (1872–1926), 1901–2, 1907–11, and at women's singles by: Molla Mallory (*née* Bjurstedt) (1884–1959), 1915–16, 1918, 1920–22, 1926; and Helen Newington Moody (*née* Wills) (USA) (b. 6 Oct 1905), 1923–5, 1927–9, 1931.

Youngest and oldest The youngest champion was Vincent Richards (1903–59), who was 15 yr 139 days when he won the men's doubles in 1918 with Bill Tilden. The youngest singles champion was Tracy Ann Austin (b. 12 Dec 1962) who was 16 yr 271 days when she won the women's singles in 1979. The youngest men's champion was Pete Sampras (b. 12 Aug 1971) who was 19 yr 28 days when he won in 1990. The oldest champion was Margaret du Pont who won the mixed doubles at 42 yr 166 days in 1960. The oldest singles champion was William Larned at 38 yr 242 days in 1911.

Most wins (from international status 1925) Margaret Court won a record 13 titles, five singles, four women's doubles and four mixed doubles, 1962–73. The men's record is nine by Henri Cochet (France) (1901–87), four singles, three men's doubles and two mixed doubles, 1926–30. The singles record is seven by Chris Evert, 1974–5, 1979–80, 1983, 1985–6. Björn Borg won a record six men's singles, 1974–5, 1978–81.

Youngest and oldest The youngest doubles champions were the 1981 mixed doubles winners, Andrea Jaeger (b. 4 Jun 1965) at 15 yr 339 days and Jimmy Arias (b. 16 Aug 1964) at 16 yr 296 days. The youngest singles winners have been: Monica Seles (Yugoslavia) (b. 2 Dec 1973) who won the 1990 women's title at 16 yr 169 days and Michael Chang (USA) (b. 22 Feb 1972) the men's at 17 yr 109 days in 1989. The oldest champion was Elizabeth Ryan who won the 1934 women's doubles with Simone Mathieu (France) at 42 yr 88 days. The oldest singles champion was Andrés Gimeno (Spain) (b. 3 Aug 1937) in 1972 at 34 yr 301 days.

Australian Championships

Most wins Margaret Jean Court (*née* Smith) (b. 16 Jul 1942) won the women's singles 11 times (1960–66, 1969–71 and 1973) as well as eight women's doubles and two mixed doubles, for a record total of 21 titles. A record six men's singles were won by Roy Stanley Emerson (Qld) (b. 3 Nov 1936), 1961 and 1963–7. Thelma Dorothy Long (*née* Coyne) (b. 30 May 1918) won a record 12 women's doubles and four mixed doubles for a record total of 16 doubles titles. Adrian Karl Quist (b. 4 Aug 1913) won ten consecutive men's doubles from 1936 to 1950 (the last eight with John Bromwich) and three men's singles.

Longest span, oldest and youngest Thelma Long won her first (1936) and last (1958) titles 22 years apart. Kenneth Robert Rosewall (b. 2 Nov 1934) won the singles in 1953 and in 1972 was, 19 years later, at 37 yr 62 days, the oldest singles winner. The oldest champion was (Sir) Norman Everard Brookes (1877–1968),

667

who was 46 yr 2 months when he won the 1924 men's doubles. The youngest champions were Rodney W. Heath, aged 17, when he won the men's singles in 1905, and Monica Seles, who won the women's singles at 17 yr 55 days in 1991.

Grand Prix Masters

The first Grand Prix Masters Championships were staged in Tokyo, Japan in 1970. They were held in New York, USA annually from 1977 to 1989 with qualification by relative success in the preceding year's Grand Prix tournaments. The event was replaced from 1990 by the ATP Tour Championship, held in Frankfurt, Germany. A record five titles have been won by Ivan Lendl, 1982–3, two in 1986 (January and December) and 1987. He appeared in nine successive finals, 1980–88. James Scott Connors (USA) (b. 2 Sep 1952) uniquely qualified for 14 consecutive years, 1972–85. He chose not to play in 1975, 1976 and 1985, and won in 1977. He qualified again in 1987 and 1988, but did not play in 1988.

A record seven doubles titles were won by John Patrick McEnroe (b. 16 Feb 1959) and Peter Fleming (b. 21 Jan 1955) (both USA), 1978–84.

Virginia Slims Championship The women's tour finishes with the Virginia Slims Championship, first contested in 1971. The Virginia Slims final is the one women's match played over the best of five sets (since 1983). Martina Navrátilová has a record six singles wins, between 1978 and 1986. She also has a record nine doubles wins, one with Billie-Jean King in 1980, and eight with Pam Shriver to 1991.

International Team

Davis Cup (instituted 1900) The most wins in the Davis Cup, the men's international team championship, has been 30 by the USA between 1900 and 1992. The most appearances for Cup winners is eight by Roy Emerson (Australia), 1959–62, 1964–7. Bill Tilden (USA) played in a record 28 matches in the final, winning a record 21, 17 out of 22 singles and 4 out of 6 doubles. He was in seven winning sides, 1920–26 and then four losing sides, 1927–30.

The British Isles/Great Britain have won nine times, in 1903–6, 1912, 1933–6.

Nicola Pietrangeli (Italy) (b. 11 Sep 1933) played a record 163 rubbers (66 ties), 1954 to 1972, winning 120. He played 109 singles (winning 78) and 54 doubles (winning 42).

The record number of rubbers by a British player is 65 (winning 43) by Michael J. Sangster (b. 9 Sep 1940), 1960–68; the most wins is 45 from 52 rubbers by Fred Perry, including 34 of 38 singles, 1931–6.

Wightman Cup (instituted 1923) The annual women's match was won 51 times by the United States and 10 times by Great Britain. The contest was suspended from 1990 after a series of whitewashes by the US team. Virginia Wade (GB) (b. 10 Jul 1945) played in a record 21 ties and 56 rubbers, 1965–85, with a British record 19 wins. Christine Marie Evert (USA) (b. 21 Dec 1954) won all 26 of her singles matches, 1971 to 1985 and including doubles achieved a record 34 wins from 38 rubbers played. Jennifer Capriati became, at 13 yr 168 days, the youngest ever Wightman Cup player when she beat Clare Wood (GB) 6–0, 6–0 at Williamsburg, Virginia, USA on 14 Sep 1989.

Federation Cup (instituted 1963) The most wins in the Federation Cup, the women's international team championship, is 14 by the USA between 1963 and 1990. Virginia Wade (GB) played each year from 1967 to 1983, in a record 57 ties, playing 100 rubbers, including 56 singles (winning 36) and 44 doubles (winning 30). Chris Evert won her first 29 singles matches, 1977–86. Her overall record, 1977–89 was 40 wins in 42 singles and 16 wins in 18 doubles matches.

Longest span as national champion Keith Gledhill (b. 17 Feb 1911) won the US National Boys' Doubles Championship with Sidney Wood in August 1926. Sixty-one years later he won the US National 75 and Men's Doubles Championship with Elbert Lewis at Goleta, California, USA in August 1987.

Dorothy May Bundy-Cheney (USA) (b. September 1916) won 180 US titles at various age groups from 1941 to March 1988.

International contest *Longest span* Jean Borotra (France) (b. 13 Aug 1898) played in every one of the twice yearly contests between the International Club of France and the I.C. of Great Britain from the first in 1929 to his 100th match at Wimbledon on 1–3 Nov 1985. On that occasion he played a mixed doubles against Kitty Godfree (GB). Both were former Wimbledon singles champions, and aged 87 and 88 respectively.

Highest earnings Monica Seles (Yugoslavia) won a women's season's record of $2 622 352 in 1992. Stefan Edberg (Sweden) (b. 19 Jan 1966) set a men's record of $2 363 575 in 1991. The career earnings records are: (men) $19 172 627 by Ivan Lendl (Czechoslovakia, now USA) (b. 7 Mar 1960); (women) $18 396 526 by Martina Navrátilová, both to the end of 1992. Earnings from special restricted events and team tennis are not included.

The greatest first-place prize money ever won is $2 million by Pete Sampras when he won the Grand Slam Cup at Munich, Germany on 16 Dec 1990. In the final he beat Brad Gilbert (USA) (b. 9 Aug 1961) 6–3, 6–4, 6–2. Gilbert received $1 million, also well in excess of the previous record figure. The highest total prize money was $6 349 250 for the 1990 US Open Championships.

Greatest crowd A record 30 472 people were at the Astrodome, Houston, Texas, USA on 20 Sep 1973, when Billie-Jean King beat Robert Larimore Riggs (USA) (b. 25 Feb 1918). The record for an orthodox tennis match is 25 578 at Sydney, New South Wales, Australia on 27 Dec 1954 in the Davis Cup Challenge Round (first day) Australia *v.* USA.

Longest game The longest known singles game was one of 37 deuces (80 points) between Anthony Fawcett (Rhodesia) and Keith Glass (GB) in the first round of the Surrey Championships at Surbiton on 26 May 1975. It lasted 31 min. Noëlle van Lottum and Sandra Begijn played a game lasting 52 min in the semi-finals of the Dutch Indoor Championships at Ede, Gelderland on 12 Feb 1984.

The longest tiebreak was 26–24 for the fourth and decisive set of a first round

men's doubles at the Wimbledon Championships on 1 Jul 1985. Jan Gunnarsson (Sweden) and Michael Mortensen (Denmark) defeated John Frawley (Australia) and Victor Pecci (Paraguay) 6–3, 6–4, 3–6, 7–6.

Tiddlywinks

World Championships Larry Kahn (USA) (b. 6 Dec 1953) has won the singles title 12 times, 1983–91 and the pairs title a record five times between 1978 and 1989.

National Championships Alan Dean (b. 22 Jul 1949) won the singles title six times, 1971–3, 1976, 1978 and 1986, and the pairs title six times. Jonathan Mapley (b. 1947) won the pairs title seven times, 1972, 1975, 1977, 1980, 1983–4 and 1987.

Trampolining

Most titles World Championships were instituted in 1964 and held biennially since 1968. The most titles won is nine by Judy Wills (USA) (b. 1948), a record five individual 1964–8, two pairs 1966–7 and two tumbling 1965–6. The men's record is four by: Yevgeniy Yanes (USSR), two individual 1976 (shared), 1978 and two pairs 1976–8; and Vadim Krasnochapaka (USSR), three pairs 1984–8 and individual 1988. Brett Austine (Australia) won three individual titles at double mini, 1982–6.

A record seven United Kingdom titles have been won by Wendy Wright (1969–70, 1972–5, 1977). The most by a man has been five by Stewart Matthews (b. 19 Feb 1962) (1976–80).

Youngest international *British* Andrea Holmes (b. 2 Jan 1970) competed for Britain at 12 yr 131 days in the World Championships at Montana, USA on 13 May 1982.

Somersaults Christopher Gibson performed 3025 consecutive somersaults at Shipley Park, Derbys on 17 Nov 1989.

The most complete somersaults in one minute is 75 by Richard Cobbing of Lightwater, Surrey, at BBC Television

Centre, London for *Record Breakers* on 8 Nov 1989. The most baranis in a minute is 78 by Zoe Finn of Chatham, Kent at BBC Television Centre, London for *Blue Peter* on 25 Jan 1988.

Triathlon

The triathlon combines long-distance swimming, cycling and running. Distances for each of the phases can vary, but for the best established event, the Hawaii Ironman (instituted 1978), competitors first swim 3·8km *2·4 miles*, then cycle 180km *112 miles*, and finally run a full marathon of 42·195km *26 miles 385 yards*. Record times for the Hawaii Ironman are: (men) 8hr 9min 8sec Mark Allen (USA) (b. 12 Jan 1958); (women) 8hr 55min 28sec Paula Newby-Fraser (Zimbabwe), both on 10 Oct 1992. Dave Scott has won a record six races, 1980, 1982–4 and 1986–7. Paula Newby-Fraser has won the women's race five times, 1986, 1988–9 and 1991–2.

The fastest time recorded over the Ironman distances is 8hr 1min 32sec by Dave Scott at Lake Biwa, Japan on 30 Jul 1989. The women's record is 8hr 55min by Paula Newby-Fraser at Roth, Germany on 12 Jul 1992.

The fastest time recorded by a Briton for the Hawaii Ironman is 9hr 7min 8sec by Chris Ray on 11 Oct 1992. The women's best is 9hr 33min 21sec by Sarah Coope (b. 31 Oct 1964) on 19 Oct 1991. However, Glenn Cook completed the Ironman distances in 8hr 37min 19sec at Roth, Germany on 11 Jul 1992.

World Championships After earlier abortive efforts a world governing body *L'Union Internationale de Triathlon* (UIT) was founded at Avignon, France on 1 Apr 1989, staging the first official World Championships in August 1989.

A 'World Championship' race has been held annually in Nice, France from 1982; the distances 3200m, 120km and 32km respectively, with the swim increased to 4000m from 1988. Mark Allen (USA) has won ten times, 1982–6, 1989–93. Paula Newby-Fraser has a record four women's wins, 1989–92. Record times: men, Mark Allen 5hr 46min 10sec in

1986; women, Erin Margaret Baker (New Zealand) (b. 23 May 1961) 6hr 27min 6sec in 1988.

Tug of War

Most titles World Championships have been held annually from 1975–86 and biennially since, with a women's event introduced in 1986. The most successful team at the World Championships has been England, who have won 15 titles in all categories, 1975–90. Sweden have won the 520kg category twice and the 560kg three times at the women's World Championships (held biennially since 1986).

The Wood Treatment team (formerly the Bosley Farmers) of Cheshire won 20 consecutive AAA Catchweight Championships 1959–78, two world titles (1975–6) and ten European titles at 720kg. Hilary Brown (b. 13 Apr 1934) was in every team. Trevor Brian Thomas (b. 1943) of British Aircraft Corporation Club is the only holder of three winners' medals in the European Open club competitions and added a world gold medal in 1988.

Volleyball

Most world titles World Championships were instituted in 1949 for men and 1952 for women. The USSR has won six men's titles (1949, 1952, 1960, 1962, 1978 and 1982) and five women's (1952, 1956, 1960, 1970 and 1990)

Most Olympic titles The sport was introduced to the Olympic Games for both men and women in 1964. The USSR has won a record three men's (1964, 1968 and 1980) and four women's (1968, 1972, 1980 and 1988) titles. The only player to win four medals is Inna Valeryevna Ryskal (USSR) (b. 15 Jun 1944), who won women's silver medals in 1964 and 1976 and golds in 1968 and 1972. The record for men is held by Yuriy Mikhailovich Poyarkov (USSR) (b. 10 Feb 1937) who won gold medals in 1964 and 1968 and a bronze in 1972, and by Katsutoshi Nekoda (Japan) (b. 1 Feb 1944) who won gold in 1972, silver in 1968 and bronze in 1964.

Tug of war (longest pulls)

The longest recorded pull (prior to the introduction of AAA rules) is one of 2hr 41min when 'H' Company beat 'E' Company of the 2nd Battalion of the Sherwood Foresters (Derbyshire Regiment) at Jubbulpore, India on 12 Aug 1889. The longest recorded pull under AAA rules (in which lying on the ground or entrenching the feet is not permitted) is one of 24min 45sec for the first pull between the Republic of Ireland and England during the world championships (640kg class) at Malmö, Sweden on 18 Sep 1988.

The longest tug of war (in distance) is the 2·6km *1·616 miles* Supertug across the Little Traverse Bay, Lake Michigan, USA. It has been contested annually since 1980 between two teams of 20 from Bay View Inn and Harbor Inn.

Most water skiers towed by one boat

A record 100 skiers were towed on double skis over a nautical mile by the cruiser *Reef Cat* at Cairns, Queensland, Australia on 18 Oct 1986. This feat, organized by the Cairns and District Powerboat and Ski Club, was then replicated by 100 skiers on single skis.

Most internationals

Great Britain Ucal Ashman (b. 10 Nov 1957) made a record 153 men's international appearances for England, 1976–86. The women's record is 171 by Ann Jarvis (b. 3 Jun 1955) for England, 1974–87.

Water Polo

Most Olympic titles Hungary has won the Olympic tournament most often with six wins in 1932, 1936, 1952, 1956, 1964 and 1976. Great Britain won in 1900, 1908, 1912 and 1920.

Five players share the record of three gold medals; Britons George Wilkinson (1879–1946) in 1900, 1908, 1912; Paulo 'Paul' Radmilovic (1886–1968), and Charles Sidney Smith (1879–1951) in 1908, 1912, 1920; and Hungarians Deszö Gyarmati (b. 23 Oct 1927) and György Kárpáti (b. 23 Jun 1935) in 1952, 1956, 1964. Paul Radmilovic also won a gold medal for the 4×200m freestyle swimming in 1908.

World Championships First held at the World Swimming Championships in 1973. The most wins is two by the USSR, 1975 and 1982, and Yugoslavia, 1986 and 1991. A women's competition was introduced in 1986, when it was won by Australia. The Netherlands won the second women's world title in 1991.

Most goals The greatest number of goals scored by an individual in an international is 13 by Debbie Handley for Australia (16) *v.* Canada (10) at the World Championship in Guayaquil, Ecuador in 1982.

Most international appearances The greatest number of international appearances is 412 by Aleksey Stepanovich Barkalov (USSR) (b. 18 Feb 1946), 1965–80. The British record is 126 by Martyn Thomas, of Cheltenham, Glos, 1964–78.

Water Skiing

Most titles World Overall Championships (instituted 1949) have been won four times by Sammy Duvall (USA) (b. 9 Aug 1962) in 1981, 1983, 1985 and 1987 and three times by two women, Willa McGuire (*née* Worthington) (b. 1928) of the USA in 1949–50 and 1955 and Elizabeth 'Liz' Allan-Shetter (USA) (b. 1951) in 1965, 1969 and 1975. Liz Allan-Shetter has won a record eight individual championship events and is the only person to win all four titles: slalom, jumping, tricks and overall in one year, at Copenhagen, Denmark in 1969. The USA have won the team championship on 17 successive occasions, 1957–89.

The most British Overall titles (instituted 1953) won by a man is seven by Michael Hazelwood (b. 14 Apr 1958) in 1974, 1976–9, 1981, 1983; the most by a

woman is ten by Philippa Mary Elizabeth Roberts (b. 11 Apr 1960), 1977, 1982, 1985–92.

Highest speed The fastest water skiing speed recorded is 230·26 km/h *143·08 mph* by Christopher Michael Massey (Australia) on the Hawkesbury River, Windsor, New South Wales, Australia on 6 Mar 1983. His drag boat driver was Stanley Charles Sainty. Donna Patterson Brice (b. 1953) set a feminine record of 178·8 km/h *111·11 mph* at Long Beach, California, USA on 21 Aug 1977.

The fastest recorded speed by a British skier over a measured kilometre is 154·38 km/h *95·93 mph* (average) on

Lake Windermere, Cumbria on 16 Oct 1989 by Darren Kirkland. The fastest speed recorded by a British woman is 141·050 km/h *87·647 mph* by Nikki Carpenter on Lake Windermere, Cumbria on 18 Oct 1988.

Barefoot

World Championships (instituted 1978) The most Overall titles is four by Kim Lampard (Australia) 1980, 1982, 1985, 1986 and the men's record is three by Brett Wing (Australia) 1978, 1980, 1982. The team title has been won five times by Australia, 1978, 1980, 1982, 1985 and 1986.

Highest speed The official barefoot speed record is 218·44 km/h *135·74 mph* by Scott Michael Pellaton (b. 8 Oct 1956) over a quarter-mile course at Chandler, Arizona, California, USA in November 1989. The fastest by a woman is 118·56 km/h *73·67 mph* by Karen Toms (Australia) on the Hawkesbury River, Windsor, New South Wales on 31 Mar 1984.

Strandpulling

The International Steel Strandpullers' Association was founded by Gavin Pearson (Scotland) in 1940. The greatest ratified poundage to date is a super-heavyweight right-arm push of 815 lb *369·5 kg* by Malcolm Bartlett (b. 9 Jun 1955) of Oldham, Greater Manchester. The record for the back press anyhow is 650 lb *295 kg* by Paul Anderson, at Hull, Humberside on 29 Mar 1992. A record 22 British Open titles have been won by Ian Storton (b. 2 Feb 1951) of Morecambe, Lancs, 1974–88.

Water Skiing Records

WORLD

Slalom

MEN: 3·5 buoys on a 10·25m line, Andrew Mapple (GB) (b. 3 Nov 1958) at Miami, Florida, USA on 6 Oct 1991.

WOMEN: 1 buoy on a 10·75m line, Susi Graham (Canada) and Deena Mapple (née Brush) (USA) at West Palm Beach, Florida, USA on 13 Oct 1990, and Kristi Overton (USA) at Shreveport, Louisiana, USA on 25 Jul 1992.

Tricks

MEN: 11150 points, Cory Pickos (USA) at Mulberry, Florida, USA on 27 Sep 1992.

WOMEN: 8580 points, Tawn Larsen (USA) at Groveland, Florida, USA on 4 Jul 1992.

Jumping

MEN: 63·4m *208ft* Sammy Duvall (USA) at Shreveport on 24 Jul 1992.

WOMEN: 47·5m *156ft*, Deena Mapple (USA) (b. 2 Mar 1960) at Charlotte, North Carolina, USA on 9 Jul 1988.

BRITISH

Slalom

MEN: (see World Listing)

WOMEN: 2 buoys at 11·25m, Philippa Roberts, Cirencester, Glos, 1990.

Tricks

MEN: 8650 points, John Battleday (b. 1 Feb 1957) at Lyon, France on 5 Aug 1984.

WOMEN: 6820 points, Nicola Rasey (b. 6 Jun 1966) at Martigues, France on 27 Oct 1984.

Jumping

MEN: 61·9m *203ft* Michael Hazelwood at Birmingham, Alabama, USA on 30 Jun 1986.

WOMEN: 44·9m *147ft*, Kathy Hulme (b. 11 Feb 1959) at Kirtons Farm, Reading, Berkshire on 1 Aug 1982.

The British records are: (men) 114·86km/h *71·37mph* by Richard Mainwaring (b. 4 Jun 1953) at Holme Pierrepont, Notts on 2 Dec 1978; (women) 80·25km/h *49·86mph* by Michele Doherty (b. 28 May 1964) (also 71·54km/h *44·45mph* backwards), both at Witney, Oxon on 18 Oct 1986.

Jumping The records are: men 26·3m *86ft 3in* by John Kretchman (USA); women 16·6m *54ft 5in* by Sharon Stekelenberg (Australia), both in 1991.

The British records are: men 19·70m *64ft 7in* by Benjamin Goggin in Belgium on 18 Aug 1991 and women 12·3m *40ft 4in* by Beverley Collins at La Mede, France om 23 Jul 1989.

Weightlifting

The first championships entitled 'world' were staged at the Café Monico, Piccadilly, London on 28 Mar 1891 and then in Vienna, Austria on 19–20 Jul 1898, subsequently recognized by the IWF. The *Fédération Internationale Haltérophile et Culturiste*, now the International Weightlifting Federation (IWF), was established in 1905, and its first official championships were held in Tallinn, Estonia on 29–30 Apr 1922.

Most titles World The most world title wins, including Olympic Games, is eight by: John Henry Davis (USA) (1921–84) in 1938, 1946–52; Tommy Kono (USA) (b. 27 Jun 1930) in 1952–9; and by Vasiliy Alekseyev (USSR) (b. 7 Jan 1942), 1970–77.

Most Olympic medals Norbert Schemansky (USA) (b. 30 May 1924) won a record four Olympic medals: gold, middle-heavyweight 1952; silver, heavyweight 1948; bronze, heavyweight 1960 and 1964.

Youngest and oldest world record holder Naim Suleimanov (later Neum Shalamanov) (Bulgaria) (b. 23 Jan 1967) (now Naim Suleymanoğlü of Turkey) set 56-kg world records for clean and jerk (160kg) and total (285kg) at 16yr 62days at Allentown, New Jersey, USA on 26 Mar 1983. The oldest is Norbert Schemansky (USA) who snatched 362lb *164·2kg* in the then unlimited Heavyweight class, aged 37yr 333days, at Detroit, Michigan, USA on 28 Apr 1962.

Most successful British lifter The only British lifter to win an Olympic title has been Launceston Elliot (1874–1930), the open one-handed lift champion in 1896 at Athens. Louis George Martin (b.

World Weightlifting Records

From 1 Jan 1993, the International Weightlifting Federation (IWF) introduced modified weight categories thereby making the then world records redundant. In February they announced that 'the results of major IWF-controlled competitions and championships will be collected until 30 Sep 1993 and the best results be declared as basic performances, with world records to be broken for the first time at the Melbourne World Championships (12–21 November)'. Therefore listed for the last time are the records for the weight categories which ended on 31 Dec 1992.

Bodyweight Class	Lift	kg	lb	Name and Country	Place	Date
52 kg *114½ lb*	Snatch	121	*266¾*	He Zhuoqiang (China)	Cardiff, South Glamorgan	29 May 1992
	Jerk	155·5	*342¾*	Ivan Ivanov (Bulgaria)	Donaueschingen, Germany	27 Sep 1991
	Total	272·5	*600¾*	Ivan Ivanov (Bulgaria)	Athens, Greece	16 Sep 1989
56 kg *123¼ lb*	Snatch	135	*297½*	Liu Shoubin (China)	Donaueschingen, Germany	28 Sep 1991
	Jerk	171	*377*	Neno Terziiski (Bulgaria)	Ostrava, Czechoslovakia	6 Sep 1987
	Total	300	*661¼*	Naim Suleimanov (Bulgaria)	Varna, Bulgaria	11 May 1984
60 kg *132¼ lb*	Snatch	152·5	*336*	Naim Suleymanoğlü (Turkey)*	Seoul, South Korea	20 Sep 1988
	Jerk	190	*418¾*	Naim Suleymanoğlü (Turkey)*	Seoul, South Korea	20 Sep 1988
	Total	342·5	*755*	Naim Suleymanoğlü (Turkey)*	Seoul, South Korea	20 Sep 1988
67·5 kg *148¾ lb***	Snatch	160	*352¾*	Israil Militosyan (USSR)	Athens, Greece	18 Sep 1989
	Jerk	200·5	*442*	Mikhail Petrov (Bulgaria)	Ostrava, Czechoslovakia	8 Sep 1987
	Total	355	*782½*	Mikhail Petrov (Bulgaria)	Seoul, South Korea	5 Dec 1987
75 kg *165¼ lb*	Snatch	170	*374¾*	Angel Guenchev (Bulgaria)	Miskolc, Hungary	11 Dec 1987
	Jerk	215·5	*475*	Aleksandr Varbanov (Bulgaria)	Seoul, South Korea	5 Dec 1987
	Total	382·5	*843¼*	Aleksandr Varbanov (Bulgaria)	Plovdiv, Bulgaria	20 Feb 1988
82·5kg *181¾lb*	Snatch	183	*403¼*	Asen Zlatev (Bulgaria)	Melbourne, Australia	7 Dec 1986
	Jerk	225	*496*	Asen Zlatev (Bulgaria)	Sofia, Bulgaria	12 Nov 1986
	Total	405	*892¾*	Yurik Vardanyan (USSR)	Varna, Bulgaria	14 Sep 1984
90 kg *198¼ lb*	Snatch	195·5	*431*	Blagoi Blagoyev (Bulgaria)	Varna, Bulgaria	1 May 1983
	Jerk	235	*518*	Anatoliy Khrapatiy (USSR)	Cardiff, South Glamorgan	29 Apr 1988
	Total	422·5	*931¼*	Viktor Solodov (USSR)	Varna, Bulgaria	15 Sep 1984
100 kg *220¼ lb*	Snatch	200·5	*442*	Nicu Vlad (Romania)	Sofia, Bulgaria	14 Nov 1986
	Jerk	242·5	*534½*	Aleksandr Popov (USSR)	Tallinn, USSR	5 Mar 1988
	Total	440	*970*	Yuriy Zakharevich (USSR)	Odessa, USSR	4 Mar 1983

110 kg *242½ lb*	Snatch	210	*462¾*	Yuriy Zakharevich (USSR)	Seoul, South Korea	27 Sep 1988
	Jerk	250·5	*552¼*	Yuriy Zakharevich (USSR)	Cardiff, South Glamorgan	30 Apr 1988
	Total	455	*1003*	Yuriy Zakharevich (USSR)	Seoul, South Korea	27 Sep 1988
Over 110 kg	Snatch	216	*476*	Antonio Krastev (Bulgaria)	Ostrava, Czechoslovakia	13 Sep 1987
	Jerk	266	*586¼*	Leonid Taranenko (USSR)	Canberra, Australia	26 Nov 1988
	Total	475	*1047*	Leonid Taranenko (USSR)	Canberra, Australia	26 Nov 1988

** Formerly Naim Suleimanov or Neum Shalamanov of Bulgaria*

*** Angel Guenchev (Bulgaria) achieved 160kg snatch, 202·5kg jerk for a 362·5kg total at Seoul, South Korea on 21 Sep 1988 but was subsequently disqualified on a positive drugs test.*

Women's Weightlifting Records

Bodyweight	Lift	kg	lb	Name and Country	Place	Date
44 kg *97 lb*	Snatch	77·5	*165¼*	Xing Fen (China)	Chiangmai, China	21 Dec 1992
	Jerk	102·5	*226*	Xing Fen (China)	Chiangmai, China	21 Dec 1992
	Total	180	*396¾*	Xing Fen (China)	Chiangmai, China	21 Dec 1992
48 kg *105¾ lb*	Snatch	83	*183*	Liao Suping (China)	Chiangmai, China	21 Dec 1992
	Jerk	105·5	*232½*	Liao Suping (China)	Chiangmai, China	21 Dec 1992
	Total	187·5	*413¼*	Liu Xiuhia (China)	Varna, Bulgaria	17 May 1992
52 kg *114½ lb*	Snatch	87·5	*192¾*	Peng Liping (China)	Varna, Bulgaria	18 May 1992
	Jerk	115	*253½*	Peng Liping (China)	Varna, Bulgaria	18 May 1992
	Total	202·5	*446¼*	Peng Liping (China)	Varna, Bulgaria	18 May 1992
56 kg *123¼ lb*	Snatch	95	*209¼*	Zhang Juhua (China)	Chiangmai, China	22 Dec 1992
	Jerk	120	*264½*	Zhang Juhua (China)	Chiangmai, China	22 Dec 1992
	Total	215	*473¾*	Zhang Juhua (China)	Chiangmai, China	22 Dec 1992
60 kg *132¼ lb*	Snatch	100	*220¼*	Su Yuanghong (China)	Chiangmai, China	22 Dec 1992
	Jerk	125	*275½*	Li Hongyun (China)	Varna, Bulgaria	20 May 1992
	Total	222·5	*490½*	Li Hongyun (China)	Varna, Bulgaria	20 May 1992
67·5 kg *148¾ lb*	Snatch	105	*231½*	Lei Li (China)	Chiangmai, China	22 Dec 1992
	Jerk	132·5	*292*	Lei Li (China)	Chiangmai, China	22 Dec 1992
	Total	237·5	*523½*	Lei Li (China)	Chiangmai, China	22 Dec 1992

<table>
		kg	lb			
continued						
67·5 kg 148¾ lb	Snatch	105	231½	Lei Li (China)	Chiangmai, China	22 Dec 1992
	Jerk	132·5	292	Lei Li (China)	Chiangmai, China	22 Dec 1992
	Total	237·5	523½	Lei Li (China)	Chiangmai, China	22 Dec 1992
75 kg 165¼ lb	Snatch	107·5	236¾	Hua Ju (China)	Varna, Bulgaria	22 May 1992
	Jerk	140	308½	Xing Shuwen (China)	Chiangmai, China	23 Dec 1992
	Total	242·5	534½	Zhang Xiaoli (China)	Donaueschingen, Germany	3 Oct 1991
82·5 kg 181¾ lb	Snatch	110·5	243½	Zang Lina (China)	Chiangmai, China	23 Dec 1992
	Jerk	145	319½	Zang Lina (China)	Chiangmai, China	23 Dec 1992
	Total	255	562	Zang Lina (China)	Chiangmai, China	23 Dec 1992
+82·5 kg	Snatch	115	253½	Li Yajuan (China)	Varna, Bulgaria	24 May 1992
	Jerk	150	330½	Li Yajuan (China)	Varna, Bulgaria	24 May 1992
	Total	265	584	Li Yajuan (China)	Varna, Bulgaria	24 May 1992
</table>

Jamaica, 11 Nov 1936) won four world and European mid-heavyweight titles in 1959, 1962–3, 1965. He won an Olympic silver medal in 1964 and a bronze in 1960 and three Commonwealth gold medals in 1962, 1966, 1970. His total of British titles was 12.

Heaviest lift to bodyweight The first man to clean and jerk more than three times his bodyweight was Stefan Topurov (Bulgaria) (b. 11 Aug 1964), who lifted 180kg *396¾lb* at Moscow, USSR on 24 Oct 1983. The first man to snatch two-and-a-half times his own bodyweight was Naim Suleymanoğlü (Turkey), who lifted 150kg *330½lb* at Cardiff, S Glam on 27 Apr 1988. The first woman to clean and jerk more than two times her own bodyweight was Cheng Jinling (China), who lifted 90kg *198lb* in the 44kg class of the World Championships at Jakarta, Indonesia in December 1988.

Women's World Championships These are held annually, first at Daytona Beach, Florida in October 1987. Women's world records have been ratified for the best marks at these championships. Peng Liping (China) won a record 12 gold medals with snatch, jerk and total in the 52kg class each year, 1988–9 and 1991–2.

Powerlifting

The sport of powerlifting was first contested at national level in Great Britain in 1958. The first US Championships were held in 1964. The International Powerlifting Federation was founded in 1972, a year after the first, unofficial world championships were held. Official championships have been held annually for men from 1973 and for women from 1980. The three standard lifts are squat, bench press and dead lift, the totals from the three lifts determining results.

Most titles *World* The winner of the most world titles is Hideaki Inaba (Japan) with 16, at 52kg 1974–83, 1985–90. The most by a women is six by Beverley Francis (Australia) (b. 15 Feb 1955) at 75kg 1980, 1982; 82·5kg 1981, 1983–5; and Sisi Dolman (Netherlands) at 52kg 1985–6, 1988–91. The most by a British lifter is seven by Ron Collins; 75kg 1972–4, 82kg 1975–7

Powerlifting Records (All weights in kilograms)

WORLD MEN

Class	Squat	Bench Press	Deadlift	Total
52 kg	247.5 Andrzej Stanashek (Pol) 1992	162.5 Andrzej Stanashek 1992	255 E S Bhaskaran (Ind) 1992	587.5 Hideaki Inaba (Jap) 1987
56 kg	250 Magnus Karlsson (Swe) 1992	166.5 Magnus Karlsson 1991	289.5 Lamar Gant (USA) 1982	625 Lamar Gant (USA) 1982
60 kg	295 Joe Bradley (USA) 1980	180.5 Magnus Karlsson 1993	310 Lamar Gant 1988	707.5 Joe Bradley 1982
67.5 kg	300 Jessie Jackson (USA) 1987	200 Kristoffer Hulecki (Swe) 1985	316 Daniel Austin (USA) 1991	762.5 Daniel Austin 1989
75 kg	328 Ausby Alexander (USA) 1989	217.5 James Rouse (USA) 1980	333 Jarmo Virtanen (Finland) 1988	850 Rick Gaugler (USA) 1982
82.5 kg	379.5 Mike Bridges (USA) 1982	240 Mike Bridges 1981	357.5 Veli Kumpuniemi (Fin) 1980	952.5 Mike Bridges 1982
90 kg	375 Fred Hatfield (USA) 1980	255 Mike MacDonald (USA) 1980	372.5 Walter Thomas (USA) 1982	937.5 Mike Bridges 1980
100 kg	422.5 Ed Coan (USA) 1989	261.5 Mike MacDonald 1977	378 Ed Coan 1989	1032.5 Ed Coan 1989
110 kg	393.5 Dan Wohleber (USA) 1981	270 Jeffrey Magruder (USA) 1982	395 John Kuc 1980	1000 John Kuc 1980
125 kg	428.5 Kirk Karwoski (USA) 1991	278.5 Tom Hardman (USA) 1982	387.5 Lars Norén (Swe) 1987	1005 Ernie Hackett (USA) 1982
125+kg	445 Dwayne Fely (USA) 1982	300 Bill Kazmaier (USA) 1981	406 Lars Norén 1988	1100 Bill Kazmaier 1981

WORLD WOMEN

Class	Squat	Bench Press	Deadlift	Total
44 kg	155 Raija Koskinen (Fin) 1992	81 Ann Leverett (USA) 1991	165 Nancy Belliveau (USA) 1985	352.5 Marie-France Vassart (Bel) 1985
48 kg	150 Claudine Cognac (France) 1990	82.5 Michelle Evris (USA) 1981	182.5 Majik Jones (USA) 1984	390 Majik Jones 1984
52 kg	175.5 Mary Jeffrey (USA) (née Ryan) 1991	105 Mary Jeffrey 1991	197.5 Diana Rowell (USA) 1984	452.5 Mary Jeffrey 1991
56 kg	191 Mary Jeffrey 1989	115 Mary Jeffrey 1988	207.5 Joy Burt (Canada) 1992	485 Mary Jeffrey 1988
60 kg	200.5 Ruthi Shafer (USA) 1983	105.5 Judith Auerbach (USA) 1989	213 Ruthi Shafer 1983	502.5 Vicki Steenrod (USA) 1985
67.5 kg	230 Ruthi Shafer 1984	120 Vicki Steenrod 1990	244 Ruthi Shafer 1984	565 Ruthi Shafer 1984
75 kg	235 Cathy Millen (NZ) 1991	142.5 Liz Odendaal (Neth) 1989	240 Cathy Millen 1991	602.5 Cathy Millen 1991
82.5 kg	240 Cathy Millen 1991	150 Beverley Francis (Aus) 1981	247.5 Cathy Millen 1991	612.5 Cathy Millen 1991
90 kg	252.5 Lorraine Constanzo (USA) 1988	132.5 Cathy Millen 1992	250 Cathy Millen 1992	622.5 Cathy Millen 1991
90+kg	262.5 Lorraine Constanzo 1987	137.5 Myrtle Augee (GB) 1989	237.5 Lorraine Constanzo 1987	622.5 Lorraine Constanzo 1987

BRITISH MEN

Class	Squat	Bench Press	Deadlift	Total
52 kg	217.5 Phil Stringer 1980	130 John Maxwell 1988	225 John Maxwell 1988	530 Phil Stringer 1982
56 kg	235 Phil Stringer 1982	137.5 Phil Stringer 1983	229 Precious McKenzie 1973	577.5 Gary Simes 1991
60 kg	247.5 Tony Galvez 1981	142.5 Clint Lewis 1985	275 Eddy Pengelly 1977	645 Eddy Pengelly 1979
67.5 kg	275 Eddy Pengelly 1981	165 Hassan Salih 1979	295 Eddy Pengelly 1982	710 Eddy Pengelly 1982
75 kg	302.5 John Howells 1979	185 Peter Fiore 1981	310 Robert Limerick 1984	760 Steve Alexander 1983
82.5 kg	337.5 Mike Duffy 1984	210 Mike Duffy 1981	355 Ron Collins 1980	855 Ron Collins 1980
90 kg	347.5 David Caldwell 1985	227.5 Jeff Chandler 1985	350.5 Ron Collins 1980	870 David Caldwell 1985

Class								
100 kg	380	Tony Stevens 1984	225.5	Brian Reynolds 1992	362.5	Tony Stevens 1984	955	Tony Stevens 1984
110 kg	372.5	Tony Stevens 1984	250	John Neighbour 1990	380	Arthur White 1982	940	John Neighbour 1987
125 kg	390	John Neighbour 1990	250	John Neighbour 1990	373	David Cullen 1992	957.5	Steven Zetolofsky 1984
125+kg	380	Steven Zetolofsky 1979	258	Terry Purdue 1971	377.5	Andy Kerr 1982	982.5	Andy Kerr 1983
BRITISH WOMEN								
44 kg	130	Helen Wolsey 1991	68	Helen Wolsey 1991	152.5	Helen Wolsey 1990	350	Helen Wolsey 1991
48 kg	132.5	Helen Wolsey 1990	75	Suzanne Smith 1985	155	Helen Wolsey 1990	355	Helen Wolsey 1990
52 kg	143	Jenny Hunter 1988	82	Jenny Hunter 1988	173.5	Jenny Hunter 1988	395	Jenny Hunter 1988
56 kg	158	Jenny Hunter 1988	88	Jenny Hunter 1988	182.5	Jenny Hunter 1988	420	Jenny Hunter 1988
60 kg	163	Rita Bass 1988	92.5	Mandy Wadsworth 1992	185	Rita Bass 1990	422.5	Rita Bass 1989
67.5 kg	175	Debbie Thomas 1988	102.5	Sandra Berry 1992	198	Sandra Berry 1992	460	Sandra Berry 1992
75 kg	202.5	Judith Oakes 1989	115	Judith Oakes 1989	215	Judith Oakes 1989	532.5	Judith Oakes 1989
82.5 kg	215	Judith Oakes 1988	122.5	Joanne Williams 1990	217.5	Judith Oakes 1989	542.5	Judith Oakes 1988
90 kg	200	Beverley Martin 1989	115	Joanne Williams 1989	215	Beverley Martin 1990	495	Beverley Martin 1989
90+kg	220.5	Myrtle Augee 1991	137.5	Myrtle Augee 1989	230	Myrtle Augee 1989	587.5	Myrtle Augee 1989

Ron Collins; 75kg 1972–4, 82kg 1975–7 and 1979.

British Edward John Pengelly (b. 8 Dec 1949) has won a record 14 consecutive national titles, 60kg 1976–9, 67½kg 1980–89. He has also won four world titles, 60kg 1976–7, 1979, 67½kg 1985, and a record ten European titles, 60kg 1978–9, 67½kg 1981, 1983–9.

Powerlifting feats Lamar Gant (USA) was the first man to deadlift five times his own bodyweight, lifting 299·5kg *661lb* when 59·5kg *131lb* in 1985. Cammie Lynn Lusko (USA) (b. 5 Apr 1958) became the first woman to lift more than her bodyweight with one arm, with 59·5kg *131lb* at a bodyweight of 58·3kg *128·5lb*, at Milwaukee, Wisconsin, USA on 21 May 1983.

Timed lifts *24 hours* A deadlifting record of 2703700kg *5960631lb* was set by a team of ten from HM Prison Wayland, Thetford, Norfolk on 10–11 May 1993. The deadlift record by an individual is 371094kg *818121lb* by Anthony Wright at HM Prison Featherstone, Wolverhampton, W Mids on 31 Aug–1 Sep 1990. A bench press record of 3869011kg *8529699lb* was set by a nine-man team from the Hogarth Barbell Club, Chiswick, London on 18–19 Jul 1987. A squat record of 2168625kg *4780994lb* was set by a ten-man team from St Albans Weightlifting Club and Ware Boys Club, Herts on 20–21 Jul 1986. A record 133380 arm-curling repetitions using three 22kg *48½lb* weightlifting bars and dumb-bells was achieved by a team of nine from Intrim Health and Fitness Club at Gosport, Hants on 4–5 Aug 1989.

12 hours An individual bench press record of 514750kg *1134828lb* was set by John 'Jack' Atherton at HM Prison Featherstone, W Mids on 27 May 1990.

Wrestling

Most titles *Olympic* Three Olympic titles have been won by: Carl Westergren (Sweden) (1895–1958) in 1920, 1924 and 1932; Ivar Johansson (Sweden) (1903–79) in 1932 (two) and 1936; and Aleksandr Vasilyevieh Medved (USSR) (b. 16 Sep 1937) in 1964, 1968 and

1972. Four Olympic medals were won by: Eino Leino (Finland) (1891–1986) at freestyle 1920–32; and by Imre Polyák (Hungary) (b. 16 Apr 1932) at Greco-Roman in 1952–64.

World The freestyler Aleksandr Medved (USSR) won a record ten World Championships, 1962–4, 1966–72 at three weight categories. The only wrestler to win the same title in seven successive years has been Valeriy Grigoryevich Rezantsev (USSR) (b. 2 Feb 1947) in the Greco-Roman 90kg class in 1970–76, including the Olympic Games of 1972 and 1976.

Most titles and longest span *British* The most British titles won in one weight class is 14 by welterweight Fitzllloyd Walker (b. 7 Mar 1957), 1979–92. The longest span for BAWA titles is 24 years by George Mackenzie (1890–1957) between 1909 and 1933. He represented Great Britain in five successive Olympiads, 1908 to 1928.

Most wins In international competition, Osamu Watanabe (b. 21 Oct 1940), of Japan, the 1964 Olympic freestyle 63kg champion, was unbeaten and did not concede a score in 189 consecutive matches. Outside of FILA sanctioned competition, Wade Schalles (USA) won 821 bouts from 1964 to 1984, with 530 of these victories by pin.

Heaviest heavyweight The heaviest wrestler in Olympic history is Chris Taylor (1950–79), bronze medallist in the super-heavyweight class in 1972, who stood 1·96m *6ft 5in* tall and weighed over 190kg *420lb*. FILA introduced an upper weight limit of 130kg *286lb* for international competition in 1985.

Sumo Wrestling

The sport's origins in Japan date from *c.* 23 BC. The most successful wrestlers have been *yokozuna* Koki Naya (b. 1940), alias Taiho ('Great Bird'), who won the Emperor's Cup 32 times up to his retirement in 1971 and the *ozeki* Tameemon Torokichi, alias Raiden (1767–1825), who in 21 years (1789–1810) won 254

The heaviest ever *rikishi* is Samoan-American Salevaa Fuali Atisanoe alias Konishiki, of Hawaii, who weighed in at 263kg *580lb* at Tokyo's Ryogoku Kokugikan on 4 Jan 1993. Weight is amassed by over-alimentation with a high-protein stew called *chankonabe*.

(Photo: Allsport/Chris Cole)

Longest bout

The longest recorded bout was one of 11hr 40min when Martin Klein (Estonia representing Russia) (1885–1947) beat Alfred Asikáinen (Finland) (1888–1942) for the Greco-Roman 75kg 'A' event silver medal in the 1912 Olympic Games in Stockholm, Sweden.

---

bouts and lost only ten for the highest ever winning percentage of 96·2.

Yokozuna Mitsugu Akimoto (b. 1 Jun 1955), alias Chiyonofuji, set a record for domination of one of the six annual tournaments by winning the Kyushu Basho for eight successive years, 1981–8. He also holds the record for the most career wins, 1045 and *Makunouchi* (top division) wins, 807. Toshimitsu Ogata (b. 16 May 1953), alias Kitanoumi, set a record in 1978 winning 82 of the 90 bouts that top *rikishi* fight annually. He is youngest of the 64 men to have attained the rank of *yokozuna* (grand champion), aged 21 years and two months in July 1974.

Hawaiian-born Jesse Kuhaulua (b. 16 Jun 1944), alias Takamiyama, was the first non-Japanese to win an official top-division tournament, in July 1972 and in September 1981 he set a record of 1231 consecutive top-division bouts. In all six divisions, the most consecutive bouts is 1631 by Yukio Shoji (b. 14 Nov 1948), alias Aobajo, 1964–86. The most bouts in a career is 1891 by Kenji Hatano (b. 4 Jan 1948), alias Oshio, 1962–88.

Hawaiian-born Chad Rowan (b. 8 May 1969), alias Akebono, became the first foreign *rikishi* to be promoted to the top rank of *yokozuna* in January 1993. He is the tallest (204cm *6ft 8in*) and heaviest (212kg *467¼ lb*) *yokozuna* in sumo history.

Yachting

Olympic titles The first sportsman ever to win individual gold medals in four successive Olympic Games was Paul B. Elvström (Denmark) (b. 25 Feb 1928) in the Firefly class in 1948 and the Finn

class in 1952, 1956 and 1960. He also won eight other world titles in a total of six classes. The lowest number of penalty points by the winner of any class in an Olympic regatta is three points (five wins, one disqualified and one second in seven starts) by *Superdocious* of the Flying Dutchman class (Lt Rodney Stuart Pattisson, RN (b. 5 Aug 1943) and Iain Somerled Macdonald-Smith (b. 3 Jul 1945)) at Acapulco Bay, Mexico in October 1968.

British The only British yachtsman to win in two Olympic regattas is Rodney Pattisson in 1968 and again with *Superdoso* crewed by Christopher Davies (b. 29 Jun 1946) at Kiel, Germany in 1972. He gained a silver medal in 1976 with Julian Brooke Houghton (b. 16 Dec 1946).

Admiral's Cup and ocean racing The ocean racing team series which has had the most participating nations (three boats allowed to each nation) is the Admiral's Cup organized by the Royal Ocean Racing Club. A record 19 nations competed in 1975, 1977 and 1979. Britain has a record nine wins.

Modern ocean racing (in moderate or small sailing yachts, rather than professionally manned sailing ships) began with a race from Brooklyn, New York, USA to Bermuda, 630 nautical miles *1166km* organized by Thomas Fleming Day, editor of the magazine *The Rudder* in June 1906. The race is still held today in every even numbered year, though the course is now Newport, Rhode Island, USA to Bermuda.

The race still regularly run with the earliest foundation, for any type of craft and either kind of water (fresh or salt), is the Chicago to Mackinac race on Lakes Michigan and Huron, first sailed in 1898. It was held again in 1904, then annually until the present day, except for 1917–20. The record for the course (333nautical miles *616km*) is 1day 1hr 50min (average speed 12·89knots *23·84km/h*) by the sloop *Pied Piper*, owned by Dick Jennings (USA) in 1987.

The current record holder of the elapsed time records for both the premier American and British ocean races (the Newport, Rhode Island, to Bermuda race

and the Fastnet race) is the sloop *Nirvana*, owned by Marvin Green (USA).

The record for the Bermuda race, 635 nautical miles *1176 km*, is 2 days 14 hr 29 min in 1982 and for the Fastnet race, 605 nautical miles *1120 km*, is 2 days 12 hr 41 min in 1985, an average speed of 10·16 knots *18·81 km/h* and 9·97 knots *18·45 km/h* respectively.

Longest race The world's longest sailing race is the Vendée Globe Challenge, the first of which started from Les Sables d'Olonne, France on 26 Nov 1989. The distance circumnavigated without stopping was 22 500 nautical miles *41 652 km*. The race is for boats between 50 and 60 ft, sailed single-handed. The record time on the course is 109 days 8 hr 48 min 50 sec by Titouan Lamazou (France) (b. 1955) in the sloop *Ecureuil d'Aquitaine* which finished at Les Sables on 19 Mar 1990.

The oldest regular sailing race around the world is the quadrennial Whitbread Round the World race (instituted August 1973) organized by the Royal Naval Sailing Association. It starts in England and the course around the world and the number of legs with stops at specified ports is varied from race to race. The distance for 1993–4 race has been set at 32 000 nautical miles *59 239 km* from Southampton and return, with stops and re-starts at Punta del Este, Uruguay; Fremantle, Australia; Auckland, New Zealand; Punta del Este, Uruguay and Fort Lauderdale, Florida, USA.

The most consistently sailed regatta is that at Cowes, where the first race for a gold cup took place on 10 Aug 1826. Since then there has been a regatta with one or more races in early August every year except for 1915–18 and 1940–45. The greatest number of boats to take part in Cowes 'Week' was in 1990 when there were 661 in 19 classes.

(Photo: Allsport/Russell Cheyne)

America's Cup The Cup was originally won as an outright prize (with no special name) by the schooner *America* from 14 British yachts at Cowes on 22 Aug 1851. It was offered in 1857 by the winners, John C. Stevens, commodore of the New York Yacht Club and syndicate, as a perpetual challenge trophy 'for friendly competiton between countries'.

There have been 28 challenges since 8 Aug 1870, with the USA winning on every occasion except 1983. In that year at Newport, Rhode Island *Australia II*, skippered by John Bertrand and owned by a Perth syndicate headed by Alan Bond, beat *Liberty* of the New York Yacht Club 4–3, the narrowest ever series victory. In individual races sailed, American boats have won 81 races and foreign challengers have won just nine.

Since 1983, the only race won by a non-American was on 10 May 1992 when, in the first series to be sailed in the specially devised IACC (International America's Cup Class), *Il Moro di Venezia* (Italy), owned by Raul Gardini, crossed the line 3 seconds ahead of *America³*, owned by Bill Koch. This is the closest result ever recorded in a race for the Cup, but not the closest finish. On 4 Oct 1901 *Shamrock II* finished 2 seconds ahead of the American *Columbia*, though the American boat won by 41 seconds on the then handicapping system.

Jules Verne Trophy winner
Commodore Explorer (⬦ p. 119 for full details)
(Photo: Allsport/Vandystadt/Thierry Martinez)

Dennis Walter Conner (USA) has been helmsman of American boats four times in succession: in 1980, when he successfully defended; in 1983, when he steered the defender, but lost; in 1987 when the American challenger regained the trophy, and in 1988, when he again successfully defended. He was also starting helmsman in 1974 with Ted Hood as skipper. Charlie Barr (USA) (1864–1911) who defended in 1899, 1901 and 1903 and Harold S. Vanderbilt (USA) (1884–1970) in 1930, 1934 and 1937, each steered the successful cup defender three times in succession.

The largest yacht to have competed in the America's Cup was the 1903 defender, the gaff rigged cutter *Reliance*, with an overall length of 43·89m *144ft*, a record sail area of 1501m² *16 160ft²* and a rig 53·3m *175ft* high.

Yacht and dinghy classes The oldest racing class still sailing is the Water Wag class of Dublin, formed in 1887. The design of the boat was changed in 1900 to that which is still used today. The oldest classes in Britain, both established in 1898 and both still racing in the same design of boat are the Seabird Half Rater, centreboard sailing dinghy of Abersoch and other north-west ports, and the Yorkshire One-design keel boat which race from the Royal Yorkshire Yacht Club at Bridlington, Humberside.

The first international class for racing dinghies was the 14-foot International, whose principal trophy in Britain is the Prince of Wales Cup which has been contested annually since 1927 (except 1940–45). The most wins is 12 by Stewart Harold Morris between 1932 and 1965.

Highest speeds The highest speed reached under sail on water by any craft over a 500-metre timed run is 45·34 knots *83·95km/h* by boardsailer Thierry Bielak (France) at Saintes Maries de-la-Mer canal, Camargue, France on 24 Apr 1993.

The women's record is by boardsailer Babethe Coquelle (France) who achieved 39·70 knots *73·57km/h* at Tarifa, Spain in July 1991.

The record for a boat is 43·55 knots *80·71km/h* by *Longshot* steered by Russell Long (USA) at Tarifa, Spain in July 1992.

British The boardsail records are (men) 41·22 knots *76·33km/h* by Nick Luget and (women) 34·61 knots *64·09km/h* by Samantha Harrison, both at Saintes Maries de-la-Mer on 22 Mar 1991.

Most competitors The most boats ever to start in a single race was 2072 in the Round Zeeland (Denmark) race on 21 Jun 1984, over a course of 235 nautical miles *435km*.

The greatest number to start in a race in Britain was 1781 keeled yachts and multihulls on 17 Jun 1989 from Cowes in the Annual Round-the-Island Race. The fastest time achieved in this annual event is 3hr 55min 28sec by the trimaran *Paragon*, owned and sailed by Michael Whipp on 31 May 1986.

The largest trans-oceanic race was the ARC (Atlantic Rally for Cruisers), when 204 boats of the 209 starters from 24 nations completed the race from Las Palmas de Gran Canaria (Canary Islands) to Barbados in 1989.

Oldest club The oldest club in the world is the Royal Cork Yacht Club which claims descent from the Cork Harbour Water Club, established in Ireland by 1720.

The oldest active club in Britain is the Starcross Yacht Club at Powderham Point, Devon. Its first regatta was held in 1772. The oldest existing club to have been truly formed as a yacht club is the Royal Yacht Squadron, Cowes, Isle of Wight, instituted as 'The Yacht Club' at a meeting at the Thatched House Tavern, St James's Street, London on 1 Jun 1815.

Boardsailing

World Championships were first held in 1973 and the sport was added to the Olympic Games in 1984 when the winner was Stephan van den Berg (Netherlands) (b. 20 Feb 1962), who also won five world titles 1979–83.

Longest sailboard

The longest 'snake' of boardsails was set by 70 windsurfers in tandem at the 'Sailboard Show '89' event at Narrabeen Lakes, Manly, Australia on 21 Oct 1989.

The world's longest sail board, 50·2m *165ft*, was constructed at Fredrikstad, Norway, and first sailed on 28 Jun 1986.

683

Stop Press

Asteroids — number and distance extremes The closest known approach to the Earth by an asteroid was to within 150000 km *93 000 miles* on 20 May 1993 by 1993KA₂, just a few hours before its discovery.

Asteroids — largest and smallest The smallest asteroid is 1993KA₂ (⟨◦ above), with a diameter of 6 m *20 ft.*

Living World

Tallest chrysanthemum A chrysanthemum measuring 2·7 m *8 ft 10 in* has been grown by Mary Comer of Desford, Leics.

Human Being

Oldest mother Information has been received casting doubt on the record of Ruth Kistler and investigations are continuing.

Longevity The estimated number of centenarians at mid-1991 in England and Wales was 513 men and 3984 women, respectively 11·6 per cent and 88·6 per cent of the total.

Oldest living person, UK The oldest living man is William Proctor (b. 29 Jun 1885), who lives in the Wirral, Merseyside.

Oldest living triplets Pamela Laybourne died in July.

Shaving Tom Rodden of Chatham, Kent shaved 262 volunteers in 60 minutes with a cut-throat razor on 4 May 1993, averaging 13·8 sec per face. He drew blood only once.

Longest moustache The moustache of Kalyan Ramji Sain of Sundargarth, India had reached a span of 339 cm *133½ in* (right side 172 cm *67¾ in* and left side 167 cm *65¾ in*) by the end of June 1993.

Brains, heaviest The heaviest brain ever recorded was that of a 30-year-old male, which weighed 2300 g *5 lb 1·1 oz* and was reported by Dr T. Mandybur of the Department of Pathology and Laboratory Medicine at the University of Cincinnati, Ohio in December 1992.

Card memorizing Mamoon Tariq (Pakistan) memorized a single pack of shuffled cards in 44·62 sec at the School of Business, Florida Institute of Technology, Melbourne, Florida, USA on 14 Jun 1993.

Heart transplants, longest surviving Arthur F. Gay died of an unrelated illness (cancer of the oesophagus) on 31 May 1993.

Transmission lines The longest power line between pylons spans 5376 m *17638 ft* across the Ameralik Fjord near Nuuk, Greenland and was constructed by A.S. Betonmast of Oslo, Norway in 1991–2.

Lifts The world's fastest domestic passenger lifts are in the 70-storey, 296 m *971 ft* tall Yokohama Landmark Tower in Yokohama, Japan, opened to the public on 16 Jul 1993. Designed and built by Mitsubishi Electric Corporation of Tokyo, the lifts operate at 45 km/h *28 mph*, taking passengers from the second floor to the 69th floor observatory in 40 seconds.

Ice-core drilling The deepest borehole in ice was reported in July 1993 to have reached the bottom of the Greenland ice sheet at a depth of 3053·51 m *10018 ft* after five years' drilling by American researchers.

Buildings & Structures

Lego tower The world's tallest Lego tower was 21·36 m *70 ft* high and built by Lego Belgium n.v./s.a. in Brussels on 26–27 Jun 1993. The tallest Lego tower in Britain measured 20·86 m *68 ft 5 in* and was built by Lego UK Ltd at Earl's Court, London in March 1993.

Advertising signs, neon The largest was erected between November 1992 and April 1993 on Hong Kong Island and measures 111·4 × 19·05 m *365 ft 6 in × 62 ft 6 in*. Its 13·14 km *8·16 miles* of neon tubing promote 999, a traditional Chinese medicine from the Nanfang Pharmaceutical Factory in China.

Snow and ice constructions, snowman The tallest stood 26·21 m *86 ft 2 in* high and was named Thiro. It was built by Pierre Lacombe and helpers at St Cyrille de Wendover in Québec, Canada and was completed on 6 Mar 1993.

Transport

Round Britain and Ireland yachting Richard Tolkein and Peter Foot set a monohull record of 10 days 3 hr 46 min in the 18·3 m *60 ft* vessel *Enif* starting and finishing at Plymouth, Devon between 4 and 22 Jul 1993.

Parade of Rolls-Royce car An uninterrupted parade of 147 Rolls-Royces, organized by the Rolls-Royce Owners' Club of Australia, drove around Lake Wendouree, Ballarat, Victoria on 19 Sep 1992.

Highest mileage Albert Klein's Volkswagen 'Beetle' had travelled 1 483 938 miles *2 388 166 km* by 5 Jul 1993.

Six continents Navin Kapila, Man Bahadur and Vijay Raman completed the drive in 39 days 7 hr, driving a Contessa Classic. They left

New Delhi, India on 22 Nov 1991 and returned to the same place on 31 Dec 1991.

Four points of the compass Tony Davies of Stafford visited the northernmost, southernmost, westernmost and easternmost stations in Great Britain in a time of 37 hr 34 min from 14–15 Apr 1993. These are Thurso, Lowestoft, Penzance and Arisaig.

Round the world — antipodal points Brother Michael Bartlett of Balham, London travelled round the world on scheduled flights, taking in exact antipodal points, in a time of 67 hr 4 min from 10–13 Jun 1993. Leaving from London he flew to New Zealand and went by car to Ti Tree Point. He later changed planes at Madrid airport, Spain (the point exactly opposite Ti Tree Point on the other side of the world). His journey took him a total distance of 41 619 km 25 861 miles.

Heaviest commercial cargo movement The heaviest single piece of cargo carried by air was by the British charter company Air Foyle, which flew a 120-tonne crane measuring 19×3m 62×10ft from Krivoy Rog, Ukraine to Berlin, Germany on 8 Sep 1992. The aircraft used was a Russian An-124 *Ruslan*.

Longest scheduled flights The longest non-stop scheduled flight currently operating is with South African Airways for their flight from New York, USA to Johannesburg, South Africa. The return flight has one stop.

The longest non-stop flight by a commercial airliner was one of 19 258 km 11 951 miles from Auckland, New Zealand to Le Bourget, Paris, France in 21 hr 46 min on 17–18 Jun 1993 by the Airbus Industrie A340-200. It was the return leg of a flight which had started at Le Bourget the previous day during the Paris Air Show.

Most flying hours — passenger Fred Finn made his 704th Concorde flight on 4 Jun 1993, increasing his total distance flown to 17 138 000 km 10 649 000 miles.

Jumble sale The 61st one-day rummage sale at the Winnetka Congregational Church, Illinois, USA on 13 May 1993 raised a record $203 247.12.

FT-SE 100 index The index passed 3000 for the first time on 11 Aug 1993, and reached an all-time intraday high of 3022·4 and a record closing figure of 3009·1 on 12 Aug 1993.

New York Stock Exchange The highest closing figure on the Dow Jones Industrial index was 3583·35 on 11 Aug 1993.

Column of coins The most valuable column of coins was worth $Can 50358 (£25191) and was 1·98m 6ft 6in high. It was built by the Rotary Club for the Kidney Foundation of Canada at Brockville, Ontario, Canada on 8 May 1993.

Trade unions The largest union in the UK is Unison, with 1·5 million members, formed on 1 Jul 1993 by the merger of Nalgo, Nupe and Cohse.

Goats 'Cynthia-Jean' ('Baba'), owned by Carolyn Freund-Nelson of Northport, New York, USA, has given milk continuously since June 1980.

Sheep shearing The UK solo record is 625 by Nicky Beynon of Gower, W Glam on 10 Jul 1993 at Canon Farm, near Carno, Powys.

Furniture The highest price paid for an item of English furniture is £1·76 million at Christie's, London on 8 Jul 1993 for the 'Anglesey' regency mahogany desk made *c.* 1812 for Lt-Gen. Lord Paget, 1st Marquis of Anglesey (1768–1854), second in command at the Battle of Waterloo.

Most rejections Steve Canton of Port Richey, Florida, USA received a record 314 rejections (and several non-acknowledgements) of his manuscript *Dusty Roads* between December 1991 and its publication in June 1993 by the Charles B. McFadden Co. Inc.

Largest marching band A record 5034 players performed under the baton of Takeo Suzuki in Kobe, Japan on 20 Jun 1993.

Highest box office gross Steven Spielberg's *Jurassic Park* (UIP) grossed a record $50 159 460 from 2404 screens in North America, and a single day record of $18 million on 12 June, during its opening weekend on 11–13 Jun 1993. It also set a UK opening record of £4 875 137 from 434 screens on 16–18 Jul 1993, and became the highest-ever grossing film in the UK, with box office takings of £27 761 741 to 8 Aug 1993.

Most judges Judgment was given in the European Court of Human Rights in Strasbourg, France by 26 judges in *Brannigan and McBride* v. *United Kingdom* on 26 May 1993. The court rejected the applicants' challenge to their detention in Northern Ireland under the Prevention of Terrorism Act.

Most prolific murderers Dominic McGlinchey was released from prison on 5 Mar 1993 having served just under seven years.

Crime prevention A team of ten, consisting of representatives from the South Aberdeen Crime Prevention Panel and Halfords employees, postcoded 594 bicycles in four hours at Halfords Superstore, Aberdeen, Grampian on 25 Apr 1993.

Robbery—jewels Jewels valued at an estimated $7 million were reported to have been stolen from the workshops of Graff jewellers in central London on 15 Jul 1993.

Human Achievements

Wedding ceremonies, attendance An estimated 30000 guests from the Belz Hassidic community attended the wedding of Aharon Mordechai Rokeah and Sara Lea Lemberger in Jerusalem, Israel on 4 Aug 1993.

Beer stein carrying Duane Osborn covered a distance of 15m *49ft 2½in* in 3·65sec with five full steins in each hand at Cadillac, Michigan, USA on 10 Jul 1992.

Blanket A hand-knitted, machine-knitted and crocheted blanket measuring 17289m² *186107·8ft²* was made by the Knitting and Crochet Guild, co-ordinated by Gloria Buckley of Bradford, W Yorks, and assembled at Dishforth Airfield, Thirsk, N Yorks on 30 May 1993.

Brick carrying The record for carrying a 9lb *4·08kg* brick in a nominated ungloved hand in an uncradled downward pincher grip is 103km *64 miles*, by Ashrita Furman of Jamaica, New York, USA on 13–14 Jun 1993.

Stretcher bearing The longest distance a stretcher with a 63·5kg *10st* 'body' has been carried is 270·15km *167·86 miles*, in 49hr 2min from 29 Apr–1 May 1993. This was achieved by two teams of four from CFB (Canadian Forces Base) Trenton in and around Trenton, Ontario, Canada.

Tightrope walking The tightrope endurance record is 205 days, by Jorge Ojeda-Guzman of Orlando, Florida, USA, on a wire 11m *36ft* long, 10·5m *35ft* above the ground. He was there from 1 Jan–25 Jul 1993.

Can construction A 1:4 scale-model of the Basilica di Sant'Antonio di Padova was built from 3245000 empty beverage cans in Padova (Padua), Italy by the charities AMNIUP, AIDO, AVIS and GPDS. The model, measuring 29·15 × 23 × 17·05m *96 × 75 × 56ft*, was completed on 20 Dec 1992 after 20000 hours.

Fabrics The oldest surviving fabric, radio-carbon-dated to *c.* 7000 BC was reported in July 1993 to have been discovered in southeastern Turkey. The semi-fossilized cloth, measuring roughly 76 × 38mm *3 × 1½in* was believed to be linen.

Flags The world's largest flag, measuring 154 × 78m *505 × 255ft* and weighing 1·36tonnes, is the American 'Superflag' owned by 'Ski' Demski of Long Beach, California, USA. It was made by Humphrey's Flag Co. of Pottstown, Pennsylvania and unfurled on 14 Jun 1993.

Sports & Games

Athletics World records: 10000m, 26min 58·38sec by Yobes Ondieki (Kenya) (b. 21 Feb 1961) at Oslo, Norway on 10 Jul 1993.

High jump, 2·45m *8ft ½in* by Javier Sotomayor (Cuba) at Salamanca, Spain on 27 Jul 1993.

British record: 110m hurdles, 12·97A sec by Colin Jackson at Sestriere, Italy on 28 Jul 1993.

Walking, world best: 10km, 41min 30sec by Ileana Salvador (Italy) (b. 16 Jan 1962) at Livorno, Italy on 10 Jul 1993.

Domino stacking Ralf Laue successfully stacked 296 dominoes on a single supporting domino on 11 Jul 1993 in Leipzig, Germany.

Boxing, shortest fights The shortest world title fight was 20seconds, when Gerald McClellan (USA) beat Jay Bell (USA) in a WBC middleweight bout at Bayamon, Puerto Rico on 7 Aug 1993.

Canoeing At the 1993 World Championships, Richard Fox (GB) won a fifth individual and a fifth team K1 slalom title.

Card throwing Jim Karol of North Catasauqua, Pennsylvania, USA threw a standard playing card 61·26m *201ft 0in* at Mount Ida College, Newton Centre, Massachusetts, USA on 18 Oct 1992.

Cricket, fastest 100 Glen Chapple completed a century in an estimated 21min off 27 balls for Lancashire *v.* Glamorgan at Old Trafford on 19 Jul 1993, when 'joke' bowlers were used to encourage a declaration.

Cricket, Test records Allan Border has played in 146 Tests, scoring 10630 runs (average 51·35) and taking 147 catches to 18 Aug 1993.

Cricket, World Cup The fifth women's World Cup was held in England in July 1993. England won the title for a second time defeating New Zealand in the final. Janette Ann Brittin (b. 4 Jul 1959), England's most capped cricketer (19 Tests and 44 one-day internationals), has a record 1696 runs in one-day internationals, including a record 1007 in World Cup matches.

Curling At the 1993 World Championships, Canada won both the men's and women's title, for the twenty-first and seventh time respectively.

Cycling World record: 1hour, 52·270km by Christopher Boardman (GB) (b. 26 Aug 1968) at Bordeaux, France on 23 Jul 1993.

Football, most durable player Peter Shilton has made a record 1374 senior appearances, including 991 League appearances.

Football, transfer fees The record fee between two British clubs is a reported

£3·75 million paid by Manchester United to Nottingham Forest for Roy Keane (b. 10 Aug 1971) on 21 Jul 1993. However, this may be surpassed by that paid by Rangers to Dundee United for Duncan Ferguson (b. 27 Dec 1971). The fee of £3·7 million for his transfer on 15 Jul 1993 could be augmented up to a total of £4·1 million, depending on Ferguson's international appearances for Scotland.

Gambling, lottery win The biggest individual gambling win is $111 240 463.10 by Leslie Robins and Colleen DeVries of Fond du Lac, Wisconsin for the Powerball lottery drawn on 7 Jul 1993.

Golf At the 1993 Open at Royal St George's, Sandwich, Kent, Nick Faldo (GB) and William Payne Stewart (USA) (b. 30 Jan 1957) both equalled the lowest round score of 63. Greg Norman (Australia) won with a record total aggregate of 267 (66, 68, 69, 64).

Hockey Australia won a sixth men's Champions' Trophy in 1993.

Speed skating Short track world records, men: 1500 metres, 2 min 22·36 sec by Eric Flaim (USA) at Beijing, China on 21 Mar 1993. 3000 metres, 5 min 00·83 sec by Chae Ji-hoon (South Korea) at Lake Placid, USA on 16 Jan 1993.
Women: 500 metres, 45·60 sec by Zhang Yanmei (China) at Beijing, China on 27 Mar 1993.
1000 metres, 1 min 37·19 sec by Chun Lee-kyung (South Korea) at Beijing, China on 26 Mar 1993.

Judo, most throws Phil Crosby and Frank Lord completed 25 526 throws at The Leys Sports Centre, Redditch, Worcs on 20 Jun 1993.

Motor racing, World Championship Alain Prost has won 51 Grand Prix races and scored 776·5 points. Ricardo Patrese has started 249 races.

Boomerang throwing The longest out-and-return distance is 149·12 m *489 ft 3 in* by Michel Dufayard (France) on 5 Jul 1992 at Shrewsbury, Shrops.

Robert Parkins (USA) caught 75 boomerang throws in 5 min at Amherst, Massachusetts, USA on 9 Aug 1992.

The juggling record—the number of consecutive catches with two boomerangs, keeping at least one boomerang aloft at all times—is 502, by Chet Snouffer (USA) at Geneva, Switzerland on 22 Aug 1992.

Flying disc throwing (formerly Frisbee) The 24-hour distance record for a pair is 592·15 km *367·94 miles*, by Conrad Damon and Pete Fust (US) on 24–25 Apr 1993 at San Marino, California, USA.

Roller skating, figure Sandro Guerra (Italy) won a record-equalling fifth men's world title in 1992, having previously won in 1987–9 and 1991. Also in 1992 Rafaella del Vinaccio (Italy) won a record fifth women's world title.

Rugby union The highest score in any full international is when Japan beat Singapore by 120–3 in the Asian Championships at Seoul, South Korea on 20 Sep 1992.

The record score for any international tour match is 128–0 when Western Samoa beat Marlborough at Blenheim on 8 Jul 1993.

Swimming World record: Men's 100 metres breaststroke, 1 min 0·95 sec by Karoly Guttler (Hungary) at Sheffield, S Yorks on 3 Aug 1993.

Short-course world bests: Men's 800 metres freestyle, 7 min 34·90 sec by Kieren Perkins (Australia) at Sydney, Australia on 25 Jul 1993. 1500 metres freestyle, 14 min 26·52 sec by Kieren Perkins at Auckland, New Zealand on 15 Jul 1993.

British records (all at Sheffield, S Yorks): Men's 200 metres freestyle, 1 min 48·84 sec by Paul Palmer on 3 Aug 1993.
400 metres freestyle, 3 min 48·14 sec by Paul Palmer on 6 Aug 1993.
100 metres backstroke, 55·75 sec by Martin Harris on 8 Aug 1993.
4 × 100 metres medley, 3 min 41·66 sec by GB (Martin Harris, Nick Gillingham, Mike Fibbens, Mark Foster) on 8 Aug 1993.
Women's 4 × 200 metres freestyle, 8 min 11·11 sec by Great Britain (Sarah Hardcastle, Debbie Armitage, Claire Huddart, Karen Pickering) on 3 Aug 1993.

Women's 24 hour distance record, 93 km *57·78 miles* by Melissa Cunningham (Australia) at Chandler Aquatic Centre, Brisbane, Australia on 2–3 July 1993.

The most participants in a one-day swim relay is 2305, each swimming a length, organized by Auburn YMCA-WEIU at Auburn, New York, USA on 5–6 Mar 1993.

Tennis, highest earnings The total prize money for the 1993 US Open Championships (30 August–12 September) is $9 022 000.

Trampolining Sue Challis (*née* Shotton) (b. 18 Oct 1965) won a record ninth United Kingdom title in 1993, having previously won in 1980–82, 1984–5, 1987 (shared), 1990 and 1992.

Index

E

onions 110
opals 49
opera 374–5
opera houses 375
operations 155–7
opossums 55, 57
optical: fibres 188;
    prisms 167
optics 146; active 192
orang-utans 59
orchestras 371–2
orchids 98, 109
Order of Merit 443
orders 440
ore/oil carriers 249–50
organs: human* 148–9,
    151, 154, 157–8;
    musical 369–70
orienteering 622–3
origins of Man 124–5
Oscars 392
ostriches 68, 70, 74
otters 56
overdue books 363
owls 71
oysters 91

P

Pacific crossings 257, 261,
    292, 307
pacing 593–4
paddle boats 246, 260
paddles 246
paella 486
pagodas 461
paint brushes 342
painters 342–3
painting 342–3, 344
palaces 204
palindromes 350
palms 98, 109
pan pipes 370
pancakes 486; tossing 486
pandemic 408, 410
panic 408, 410
papacy 463
paper: aircraft 308;
    chains 478; companies
    315; money 322–4;
    news 363–5
parachuting 305, 306, 307,
    623
paragliding 623
parallel bar dips 592
parasites 53, 87, 89, 105, 106
parent-teacher
    associations 457

parish: priests 463;
    registers 464
parking meters 278
parks 121
parliamentary divisions
    416, 420
parliaments 414–23
parrots 70, 96
parsnips 110
particle accelerators 167
particles 160–1
parties: political 416–23;
    social 473
party giving 473
pass the parcel 478
pastry 486
patents 393, 424, 428
patients 156
payouts 580
peach 111
peacocks 473
peals 369
pearls 49–50
pedal cars 277
pedigree 352
peerage 444–5
peers 420, 444–5
pelicans 69
pelota vasca 523–4
pen pals 356
pendulums 185
penguins 71
peninsulas 25
penknives 494
penny-farthings 263
pens 494
pensions 138
pentathlon 516, 610–11
perfect numbers 168
periodicals 365–6
permafrost 36
pétanque 624
petitions 415
petrol: consumption 273;
    filling stations 278–80
pets 64–8, 70, 82
petunias 107
pharmaceuticals 164, 311
pheasants 71
philately 329
philodendrons 107
phone-ins 394–5
photographs 386–7
photography 386–7
physical extremes 163–5
physicians 405
physics 160–7
pi 149, 168

pianists 370, 374
pianos 369
picnics (teddy bears) 473
piers 214–15, 239–40
pies 482, 486
pigeons: clay shooting
    641–3; racing 624–5
piggy banks 319
pigs 337–8
pillar boxes 328–9
pills 154
pilots 301–2
pine 114
pineapples 110
pinnacles 27
pinnipeds 60, 96
pipelines 178
piranhas 82
pistols 347; shooting 642
piston-engines 271, 297
pit stops 613
pizzas 486
place-names 353–4
plague 152, 408, 410
plane pulling 300
planes 289–308
planetaria 192
planets 13–14
plants* 98, 104–18
plateaux 31
plates: juggling 481;
    spinning 385
platforms: oil 181, 315, 409,
    410; railway 288
platinum 50, 180
playing cards: antique 347;
    games 547; holding 547;
    memorizing* 148;
    throwing* 547
ploughing 335
plucking: chicken 333;
    turkey 333
Pluto 13, 14
poetry 360
pogo stick jumping 478
poisons 162; animals 53, 70,
    78–9, 83, 86, 87, 91, 92,
    93; fungi 119
polar bears 57, 386
polar conquests 466–9
polders 228
pole sitting 206
pole to pole circum-
    navigation 292, 468
pole vault 508, 511, 515,
    519, 520
policies (insurance) 315
political divisions 416, 420

701

T

Acknowledgments

The Editor of *The Guinness Book of Records* wishes to thank: Lynette Bettinelli, Amanda Brooks, Debbie Collings, Ann Collins, Sheila Goldsmith, Nicholas Heath-Brown, Muriel Ling, Sarah Llewellyn-Jones, Michelle D. McCarthy, Maria Morgan, Stewart Newport, Alex Reid, David Roberts, Sarah Silvé, Amanda Ward.

PICTURE RESEARCH James Clift, Alex Goldberg

PHOTOGRAPHIC AND DUPING SERVICES Avart Design Consultants

ARTWORK, MAPS AND DIAGRAMS Ad Vantage Studios, Kathy Aldridge, Rob and Rhoda Burns/Drawing Attention, Pat Gibbon, Peter Harper, Matthew Hillier, David McCarthy, Dick Millington, Pinpoint, Jon Preston/Maltings Partnership, Mandy Sedge

PRESS AND PUBLIC RELATIONS Cathy Brooks

CONTRIBUTORS Andrew Adams, John Arblaster, Hutton Archer, Brian Bailey, Howard Bass, Michael Benton, Dennis Bird, Gerald Blake, David Boyd, Richard Braddish, Peter Brierley, Robert Brooke, Ian Buchanan, Bob Burton, Henry Button, Clive Carpenter, Roger Cass, Chris Cavey, Roberto Chiarotti, Graham Coombs, Alan Dawson, Ciaran Deane, Fabrizio Di Giorgio, Andrew Duncan, Graham Dymott, Colin Dyson, Keith Escott, Clive Everton, John Flynn, Brian Ford, Paulette Foyle, Peter Francis, Andrew Frankel, Bill Frindall, Tim Furniss, Steven Goldberg, Ian Goold, Stan Greenberg, Mark Ham, Michael Hambrey, Liz Hawley, Robert Headland, Ron Hildebrant, Rick Hogben, Jeff Howell, Sir Peter Johnson, Ove Karlsson, Bernard Lavery, Peter Lunn, John McVey, Tessa McWhirter, John Marshall, Carol Michaelson, Andy Milroy, Michael Minges, Alan Mitchell, Ray Mitchell, David Mondey, John Moody, Patrick Moore, Bill Morris, Ron Moulton, Barry Norman, Susann Palmer, Greg Parkinson, John Randall, Chris Rhys, Patrick Robertson, Dan Roddick, Jack Rollin, Adrian Room, Peter Rowan, Joshua Rozenberg, Irvin Saxton, Colin Smith, Ian Smith, Graham Snowdon, Martin Stone, Richard Underwood, Juhani Virola, Tony Waltham, David Wells, Rick Wilson, Tony Wood, Mark Young.

Grateful acknowledgment is also made to the governing bodies and organizations who have helped in our researches.